Exceptional Learners

Seventh Edition

Exceptional Learners

Introduction to Special Education

Daniel P. Hallahan
James M. Kauffman
University of Virginia

Allyn and Bacon
Boston London Toronto Sydney Tokyo Singapore

Senior Vice President and Editor-in-Chief, Education: Nancy Forsyth
Senior Editor: Ray Short
Editorial Assistant: Christine Svitila
Developmental Editor: Alicia R. Reilly
Executive Marketing Manager: Kris Farnsworth
Production Administrator: Deborah Brown
Editorial-Production Service: Susan McNally
Formatting/Page Layout Artist: DeNee Reiton Skipper
Copyeditor: Susan Freese, Communicáto, Ltd.
Text Designer: Glenna Collett
Composition/Prepress Buyer: Linda Cox
Manufacturing Buyer: Megan Cochran
Cover Administrator: Linda Knowles
Cover Designer: Studio Nine

A Viacom Company
160 Gould Street
Needham Heights, Mass. 02194-2130

Library of Congress Cataloging-in-Publication Data

Hallahan, Daniel P.
Exceptional learners: introduction to special education / Daniel P. Hallahan, James M. Kauffman. -- 7th ed.
p. cm.
Rev. ed. of : Exceptional children. 6th ed. 1994.
Includes bibliographical references (p.) and index.
ISBN 0-205-19886-4 (alk. paper)
1. Special education -- United States. I. Kauffman, James M. II. Hallahan, Daniel P. III. Title.
LC3981.H34 1997
371.9'073--dc20
96-18082
CIP

Cover Credit: Carmella Salvucci is a 45-year-old woman with multiple disabilities who loves to paint in bright colors. She lives in a group residence in Brookline (MA) and attends Gateway Crafts, an art-based vocational center where she does her painting. She was the Massachusetts representative in the Once Around America Exhibition at the Very Special Arts Gallery. She has received numerous national and international awards from all over the world and has had one-person shows in Boston, New York, and London.

Chapter-Opening Quotes:

pp. 3 and 119 from Richard H. Hungerford, 1950, "On Locusts," *American Journal of Mental Deficiency, 54,* pp. 415–418.

p. 45 from Bob Dylan, "The Times They Are A-Changin'," 1963 Warner Bros., Inc. (Renewed). All rights reserved. Used by permission. International copyright secured.

p. 85 from *The Measure of Our Success* by Marian Wright Edelman. Copyright © 1992 by Marian Wright Edelman. Reprinted by permission of Beacon Press.

p. 161 from Eileen Simpson, *Reversals: A Personal Account of Victory over Dyslexia* (Boston: Houghton Mifflin, 1979), pp. 19–20.

p. 209 from Anonymous, 1994, "First-Person Account: Schizophrenia with Childhood Onset," *Schizophrenia Bulletin, 20,* 587–588.

p. 257 from David Shields, *Dead Languages* (New York: Alfred A. Knopf, Inc., 1989).

p. 309 from Helen Keller, *The Story of My Life* (New York: Doubleday, 1954).

p. 353 from Laura Gershe, "Butterflies Are Free." Copyright by Leonard Gershe.

p. 395 from Lucy Grealy, *Autobiography of a Face* (Boston: Houghton Mifflin, 1994).

p. 451 from *The Autobiography of Mark Twain,* edited by Charles Neider. Copyright 1927, 1940, 1958, 1959 by the Mark Twain Company, copyright 1924, 1952, 1955 by Clara Clemens Somossoud, copyright 1959 by Charles Neider. Reprinted by permission of HarperCollins Publishers, Inc.

p. 497 from Christopher Nolan. (1987). *Under the Eye of the Clock: The Life Story of Christopher Nolan.* London: Weidenfeld & Nicholson, Ltd., pp. 37–38. Reprinted with permission.

The photo credits are continued on page 536 and represent an extension of the copyright page.

Printed in the United States of America
10 9 8 7 6 5 4 3 2 01 00 99 98 97

Contents

9 Visual Impairment 352

10 Physical Disabilities 394

11 Giftedness 450

Preface

This book is a general introduction to the characteristics of exceptional learners and their education. (*Exceptional* is the term that traditionally has been used to refer to persons with disabilities as well as to those who are gifted.) We emphasize classroom practices, as well as the psychological, sociological, and medical aspects of disabilities and giftedness.

We have written this text with two primary audiences in mind: those individuals who are preparing to be special educators as well as those who are preparing to be general educators. Given the current movement toward including students with disabilities in general education classrooms, general educators must be prepared to understand this special student population and be ready to work with special educators to provide appropriate educational programming for these students. This book also is appropriate for professionals in a wide variety of other fields who work with exceptional learners (e.g., speech-language pathologists, audiologists, physical therapists, occupational therapists, adapted physical educators, and school psychologists).

In Chapter 1, we begin with an overview of exceptionality and special education, including definitions, basic legal requirements, and the history and development of the field. In Chapter 2, we discuss major current issues and trends, such as inclusion, early childhood programming and the transition to adulthood programming. In Chapter 3, we address multicultural and bilingual aspects of special education. And in the following eight chapters (4 through 11), we examine each of the major categories of exceptionality (respectively): mental retardation, learning disabilities, emotional or behavioral disorders, communication disorders, hearing impairment, visual impairment, physical disabilities, and giftedness. Finally, in Chapter 12, we consider the significant issues pertaining to parents and families of persons with disabilities.

We believe that we have written a text that reaches the *heart* as well as the *mind.* It is our conviction that professionals working with exceptional learners need to develop not only a solid base of knowledge but also a healthy attitude toward their work and the people whom they serve. Further, we contend that such knowledge and attitudes must *both* evolve to remain relevant and focused. Professionals must constantly challenge themselves to learn more theory, research, and practice in special education and to develop an ever more sensitive understanding of exceptional learners and their families.

MAJOR CHANGES FOR THIS EDITION

Title Change

The first change that the many previous users of this text will probably notice is in the title, which we have changed from *Exceptional Children* to *Exceptional Learners.* This reflects the fact that over the past several editions, we have included more and more material covering the total lifespans of persons with disabilities. With this seventh edition, we thought it was time to change the title to depict more accurately our concern for adolescents and adults as well as children.

Expanded Coverage of Inclusion

Although previous editions contained much material on integrating students with disabilities in general education classrooms, this edition provides even more information on this important topic. Students who are preparing to be special educators or general educators will find this coverage particularly useful. We have added material pertinent to integration in each chapter and also present an extended and updated section on integration, including full inclusion in Chapter 2, Current Trends and Issues.

Expanded Coverage of Multicultural and Bilingual Aspects of Special Education

In the last edition, we added a new chapter on multicultural and bilingual aspects of special education. In this edition, we have expanded that chapter (Chapter 3) in order to address more fully the many multicultural issues relative to the assessment, instruction, and socialization of students with disabilities.

Expanded Coverage of Early Childhood and the Transition to Adulthood

Researchers and practitioners in the field of special education continue to expand their concerns for individuals at both ends of the age spectrum. To reflect this activity, we also have continued to increase our attention to issues related to early childhood as well those relevant to the transition to adulthood. Two major sections in Chapter 2 focus on intervention in early childhood and the transition from secondary school to adulthood, respectively. In addition, new information has been added about these two topics in each of the categorical chapters (4 through 11) as well as in Chapter 12, Parents and Families.

Expanded Coverage of Traumatic Brain Injury

As the population of persons with traumatic brain injury (TBI) has continued to grow, special educators and other professionals have expanded programming for this population. We have increased coverage of this important area in Chapter 10, Physical Disabilities. In addition, we cover the emotional aspects of traumatic brain injury in Chapter 6, Emotional or Behavioral Disorders, and the implications for communication in Chapter 7, Communication Disorders.

Expanded Coverage of Autism

Educational and psychological programming for people with autism has also continued to expand and develop. To keep pace with this growth, we have expanded our coverage of autism in Chapter 6, Emotional or Behavioral Disorders; Chapter 7, Communication Disorders; and Chapter 10, Physical Disabilities.

Success Stories: Special Educators at Work

Special educators work in a variety of settings, ranging from general education classrooms to residential institutions. Although their main function involves teaching, these professionals also engage in a variety of roles, such as counseling, collaborating, consulting, and so forth. To illustrate this variety, each of the eight categorical chapters includes an example of a special educator at work. Authored by Jean B. Crockett, an experienced special education administrator, each story focuses on a special educator's work with an individual student. These boxes are intended to show readers the wide range of challenges faced by special educators, the dynamic nature of their positions, and the competent, hopeful practice of special education.

MAJOR FEATURES RETAINED FOR THIS EDITION

Based on responses from students and instructors, we have preserved some of the popular features from previous editions.

Suggestions for Teaching Students in General Education Classrooms

Written specifically for general education teachers and updated thoroughly for the seventh edition, this feature provides a variety of teaching ideas and strategies. Placed at the end of each categorical chapter, this feature serves as an excellent starting place for general education teachers faced with teaching special education students in their classrooms. In addition to many practical, how-to-do-it suggestions, this feature provides lists of additional resources, books, and software. Joining Dr. Jane E. Nowacek, of Appalachian State University, in writing this feature is Dr. Peggy Tarpley, of Longwood College. Both are experienced resource teachers currently involved in teacher education.

Collaboration: A Key to Success

Each categorical chapter also contains a feature in which two teachers—one from general education and one from special education—talk about how they collaborate to effectively integrate exceptional learners into the mainstream. These sections serve as models of best practices for integration.

Myths and Facts Boxes

We start each chapter with a box that juxtaposes several myths and facts about the content of the chapter. This popular feature serves as an excellent advance organizer for the material to be covered. Although some of the myths and facts have changed, long-time users will recognize this feature because it dates back to our first edition in 1978.

Chapter-Opening Quotes

Also going back to our first edition is the practice of opening each chapter with an excerpt from literature or music. We draw this quote in the opening paragraphs to begin discussing the topics covered in the chapter. Some of these quotes have been replaced over the years; even so, students continue to tell us that they find the use of quotes to be an effective method of grabbing their attention and leading them into some of the issues contained in the chapter.

Special Topics Boxes

Sprinkled throughout the text are boxes of three types: some highlight research findings and their applicability to educational practice; some discuss issues facing educators in the field; and some present the human side of having a disability.

Photography

Over half of the photographs for this edition were supplied by Allyn and Bacon's photo library. The photo library is the compilation of photo shoots which were set up at school systems around the country, including California, Connecticut, Florida, Maryland, Massachusetts, Missouri, New Mexico, Utah, and Canada. The photos for our seventh edition represent the most recent photo shoots and to that extent represent a fair assessment of a school's environment related to exceptional learners and special needs within the past couple of years.

Allyn and Bacon solicited our guidance for the shoots. Only photographs are used for which we have permission from the subjects in the photographs. Allyn and Bacon's photo department is aware of the rapid changes that are occurring in special education and is committed to bringing those changes to its library.

SUPPLEMENTS

Written by Paula Crowley, the study guide includes key points, learning objectives, exercises, practice tests, and enrichment activities to reinforce key concepts.

ACKNOWLEDGMENTS

We are thankful to those individuals who reviewed of the sixth and seventh editions and readers of drafts of our revised chapters:

William N. Bender, The University of Georgia
Patricia Mulhearn Blasco, University of North Carolina
Ruth Buehler, Millersville University
Kay Butler, Syracuse University
Carolyn Callahan, University of Virginia
Ann C. Candler, Texas Tech University
Hilda R. Caton, University of Louisville
Rhoda Cummings, University of Nevada
Gary A. Davis, University of Wisconsin-Madison
Mary K. Dykes, University of Florida at Gainsville,
Steward Ehly, University of Iowa
June H. Elliot, Lyndon State College
Rebecca R. Fewell, Tulane University
Richard M. Gargiulo, University of Alabama at Birmingham

Deborah Gartland, Towson State University
Laura Gaudet, University of Wisconsin at Platteville,
Herbert Grossman, San Jose State University,
Antoinette Heppler, Nova University
Timothy E. Heron, The Ohio State University
T. Hisama, Southern Illinois University
Rebecca Dailey Kneedler, University of Virginia
Linda C. Knicker, College of DuPage
Jean Kueker, Northwestern State University
John Lagone, The University of Georgia
Jeanne E. Legan, Joliet Junior College
Ann L. Lee, Bloomsburg University
Charlene Lingo, Pittsburgh State University
Bruce L. Mallory, University of New Hampshire
B. C. Moore, Arizona State University
Donald F. Moores, Gallaudet University—Research Institute
Gayle L. Nash, Eastern Michigan University
Louise Pitt, Florida Southern College
Agnes Rainwater, Eastern Michigan University
Linda Reese, Northeastern State University
Joseph S. Renzulli, University of Connecticut
Michael S. Rosenberg, Johns Hopkins University
Robert Rueda, University of Southern California
Mara Sapon-Sevin, University of North Dakota
Jerome J. Schultz, Lesley College
Ann Turnbull, University of Kansas
Carol Jo Yanek, Howard Community College
Steven F. Warren, George Peabody College for Teachers, Vanderbilt University

We also thank Elizabeth Cottoné for her assistance on various phases of the project. At Allyn and Bacon, we are grateful to our editor, Ray Short, for his help during the project, and we are especially grateful to Alicia Reilly, our developmental editor, who contributed to various aspects of the text.

Allyn and Bacon is once again privileged to include original artwork from Very Special Arts for the seventh edition of *Exceptional Learners*. Allyn and Bacon is also pleased that Gateway Crafts' artists are represented in this text. These works, which include painting and sculpture, appear in the chapter openers. A brief biography of each artist appears below the art. The artists chosen for this edition have shown their work around the country and abroad.

Very Special Arts

Very Special Arts is an international nonprofit organization that provides learning opportunities through the arts for persons with disabilities, especially children and youth. Founded in 1974 by Jean Kennedy Smith as an affiliate of The John F. Kennedy Center for the Arts, Very Special Arts provides programs in creative writing, dance, drama, music, and the visual arts in 15,000 communities in all 50 states and in more than 85 countries worldwide. Allyn and Bacon has featured original artworks from VSA's artists with disabilities on its covers and as part of interior illustration for over ten years.

Gateway Crafts

Gateway Crafts in Brookline, Massachusetts is an arts-based vocational program operated by Vinfen Corporation that services adults with developmental and other disabilities, and that receives primary funding from the Massachusetts Department of Mental Retardation. Gateway professionally exhibits the art and crafts of Gateway artists in an on-site store and gallery which features bimonthly solo or group exhibitions.

Exceptional Learners

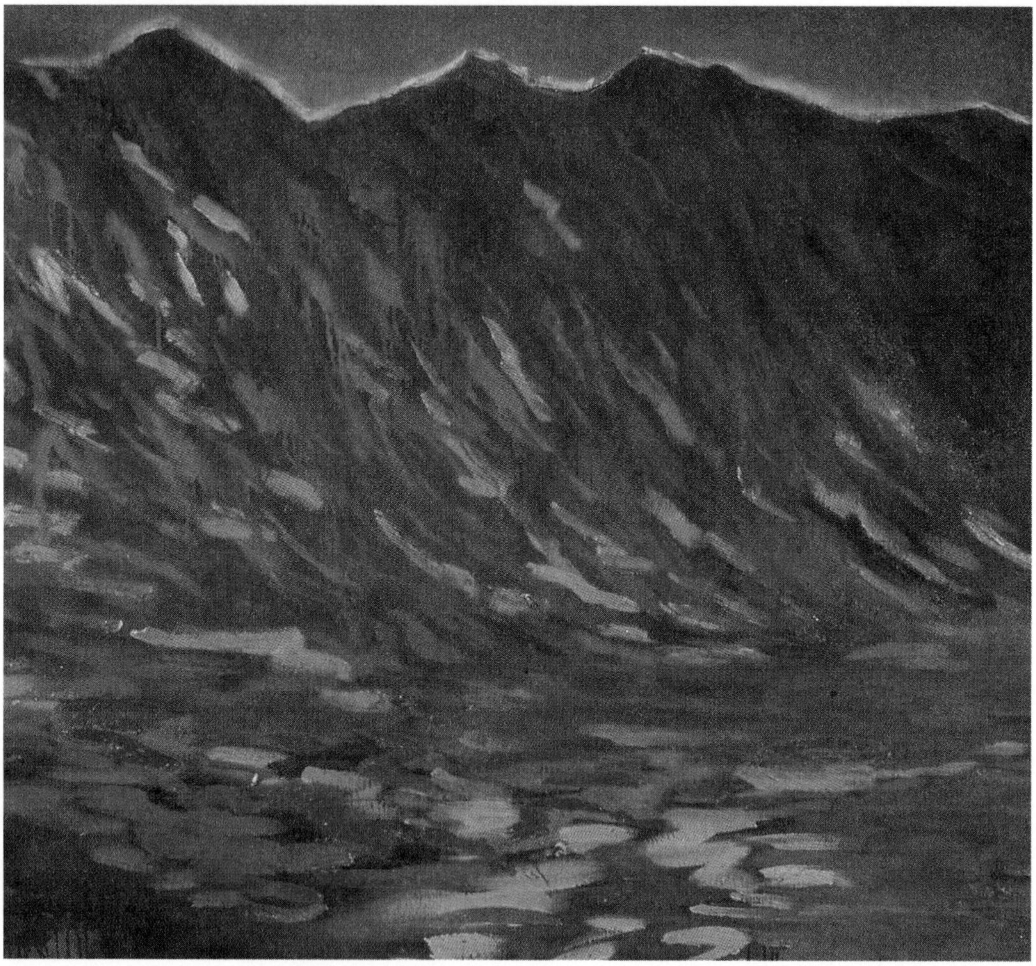

Gordon Sasaki
Gordon Sasaki, who has paraplegia, has shown his paintings and mixed media artworks throughout Hawaii and California. Mr. Sasaki has earned his living as a full-time painter for the last 13 years.

1

Exceptionality and Special Education

Only the brave dare look
upon the gray—
upon the things which
cannot be explained easily,
upon the things which often
engender mistakes,
upon the things whose cause
cannot be understood, upon
the things we must
accept and live with.
And therefore only the brave
dare look upon difference
without flinching.

Richard H. Hungerford
"On Locusts"

The study of exceptional children is the study of *differences*. The exceptional child is different in some way from the average child. In very simple terms, such a child may have problems or special talents in thinking, seeing, hearing, speaking, socializing, or moving. More often than not, he or she has a combination of special abilities or disabilities. Today, over 5 million such different children have been identified in public schools throughout the United States. About one out of every ten children in U.S. schools is considered exceptional. The fact that even many so-called normal children also have school-related problems makes the study of exceptionality very demanding.

The study of exceptional children is also the study of *similarities*. Exceptional children are not different from the average in every way. In fact, most exceptional children are average in more ways than they are not. Until recently, professionals and laypeople as well, tended to focus on the differences between exceptional and nonexceptional children, almost to the exclusion of the ways in which all children are alike. Today, we give more attention to what exceptional and nonexceptional children have in common—to similarities in their characteristics, needs, and ways of learning. As a result, the study of exceptional children has become more complex, and many so-called facts about children with disabilities and those who have special gifts or talents have been challenged.

Students of one of the "hard" sciences may boast of the difficulty of the subject matter because of the many facts they must remember and piece together. The plight of students of special education is quite different. To be sure, they study facts, but the facts are relatively few compared to the unanswered questions. Any study of human beings must take into account inherent ambiguities, inconsistencies, and unknowns. In the case of the child who deviates from the norm, we must multiply all the mysteries of normal human behavior and development by those pertaining to the child's exceptionalities. Because there is no single accepted theory of normal child development, it is not at all surprising that relatively few definite statements can be made about exceptional children.

The goal of special education is to prepare individuals with disabilities for success and a high quality of life in mainstream society.

Misconceptions about Exceptional Children

Myth Public schools may choose not to provide education for some students with disabilities.

Fact Federal legislation specifies that to receive federal funds, every school system must provide a free, appropriate education for every student regardless of any disabling condition.

Myth By law, the student with a disability must be placed in the least restrictive environment (LRE). The LRE is always the regular classroom.

Fact The law does require the student with a disability to be placed in the LRE. However, the LRE is *not* always the regular classroom. What the LRE does mean is that the student shall be separated as little as possible from home, family, community, and the regular class setting while appropriate education is provided. In many but not all instances, this will mean placement in the regular classroom.

Myth The causes of most disabilities are known, but little is known about how to help individuals overcome or compensate for their disabilities.

Fact In most cases, the causes of disabilities are not known, although progress is being made in pinpointing why many disabilities occur. More is known about the treatment of most disabilities than about their causes.

Myth People with disabilities are just like everyone else.

Fact First, no two people are exactly alike. People with disabilities, just like everyone else, are unique individuals. Most of their abilities are much like those of the average person who is not considered to have a disability. Nevertheless, a disability is a characteristic not shared by most people. It is important that disabilities be recognized for what they are, but individuals with disabilities must be seen as having many abilities—other characteristics that they share with the majority of people.

Myth A disability is a handicap.

Fact A *disability* is an inability to do something, the lack of a specific capacity. A *handicap,* on the other hand, is a disadvantage that is imposed on an individual. A disability may or may not be a handicap, depending on the circumstances. For example, the inability to walk is not a handicap in learning to read, but it can be a handicap in getting into the stands at a ball game. Sometimes handicaps are needlessly imposed on people with disabilities. For example, a student who cannot write with a pen but can use a typewriter or word processor would be needlessly handicapped without such equipment.

One major challenge to special education is to teach individuals with disabilities—as well as those around them—to focus on abilities: *what they* can *do as opposed to what they* cannot.

There are, however, patches of sunshine in the bleak gray painted by Hungerford (see p. 3). It is true that in the vast majority of cases, we are unable to identify the exact reason why a child is exceptional, but progress is being made in determining the causes of some disabilities. In a later chapter, for example, we discuss the detection of causal factors in Down syndrome—a condition resulting in the largest number of children classified as having moderate mental retardation. Likewise, the incidence of **retinopathy of prematurity (ROP)**—at one time, a leading cause of blindness—has been greatly reduced since the discovery of its cause. The cause of mental retardation associated with a metabolic disorder—**phenylketonuria (PKU)**—has been discovered. Soon after birth, infants are now routinely tested for PKU so that mental retardation can be prevented if they should have the disorder. More recently, the gene responsible for cystic fibrosis, an inherited disease characterized by chronic respiratory and digestive problems, has been identified. And in the future, the specific genes governing many other diseases and disorders will also likely be located. The locations of such genes raises the possibility of gene therapy to prevent or correct many disabling conditions.

Besides these and other medical breakthroughs, research is bringing us a more complete understanding of the ways in which the child's psychological, social, and educational environments are related to learning. For example, special educators, psychologists, and pediatricians are increasingly able to identify environmental conditions that increase the likelihood that a child will have learning or behavior problems (Hart & Risley, 1995; Patterson, Reid, & Dishion, 1992; Werner, 1986).

Educational methodology has also made strides. In fact, compared to what we know about causes, we know a lot about how exceptional children can be taught and managed effectively in the classroom. Although special educators constantly lament that all the questions have not been answered, we do know considerably more today about how to educate exceptional children than we did ten or fifteen years ago.

Before moving to the specific subject of exceptional children, we must point out that we vehemently disagree with Hungerford on an important point: We must certainly learn to live with disabling exceptionalities, but we must never accept them.

retinopathy of prematurity (ROP). Formerly referred to as *retrolental fibroplasia*; a condition resulting from administration of an excessive concentration of oxygen at birth; causes scar tissue to form behind the lens of the eye.

phenylketonuria (PKU). A metabolic genetic disorder caused by the inability of the body to convert phenylalanine to tyrosine; an accumulation of phenylalanine results in abnormal brain development.

We prefer to think there is hope for the eventual eradication of many of the disabling forms of exceptionality. In addition, we believe it is of paramount importance to realize that even children whose exceptionalities are extreme can be helped to lead fuller lives than they would without appropriate education.

We must not let people's *disabilities* keep us from recognizing their *abilities*. Many children and youths with disabilities have abilities that go unrecognized because their disabilities become the focus of our concern and we do not give enough attention to what they *can* do. We must study the disabilities of exceptional children and youths if we are to learn how to help them make maximum use of their abilities. Some students with disabilities that are not obvious to the casual observer need special programs of education and related services to help them live full, happy, productive lives. However, we must not lose sight of the fact that *the most important characteristics of exceptional children are their abilities.*

Most exceptional individuals have disabilities, and they have often been referred to as "handicapped" in laws, regulations, and everyday conversations. In this book, we make an important distinction between *disability* and *handicap*. A disability is an inability to do something, a diminished capacity to perform in a specific way. A handicap, on the other hand, is a disadvantage imposed on an individual. Thus, a disability may or may not be a handicap, depending on the circumstances. Likewise, a handicap may or may not be caused by a disability.

For example, blindness is a disability that can be anything but a handicap in the dark. In fact, in the dark, the person who has sight is the one who is handicapped. Needing to use a wheelchair may be a handicap in certain circumstances, but the disadvantage may be a result of architectural barriers or other people's reactions, not the inability to walk. Others can handicap people who are different from them (in color, size, appearance, language, and so on) by stereotyping them or not giving them opportunities to do the things they are able to do. When working and living with exceptional individuals who have disabilities, we must constantly strive to separate their disabilities from the handicaps. That is, our goal should be to confine their handicaps to those characteristics and circumstances that cannot be changed, and to make sure that we impose no further handicaps by our attitudes or our unwillingness to accommodate their disabilities.

EDUCATIONAL DEFINITION OF EXCEPTIONAL CHILDREN AND YOUTHS

For purposes of their education, *exceptional children and youths are those who require special education and related services if they are to realize their full human potential.* They require special education because they are markedly different from most children in one or more of the following ways: They may have mental retardation, learning disabilities, emotional or behavioral disorders, physical disabilities, disorders of communication, autism, traumatic brain injury, impaired hearing, impaired sight, or special gifts or talents. In the chapters that follow, we define as exactly as possible what it means to have an exceptionality.

Two concepts are important to our educational definition of exceptional children and youths: (1) diversity of characteristics and (2) need for special education. The concept of diversity is inherent in the definition of exceptionality; the need for special education is inherent in an educational definition.

Children and youths with exceptionalities are an extraordinarily diverse group compared to the general population, and relatively few generalizations apply to all

County Graduates Defy Odds to Realize Goals

Since graduating from high school, Tony Hensley has earned a bachelor's degree in business and is now working on his master's in accounting.

YOUNG PHOTOGRAPHER FOCUSES ON ATTENDING A MORE ACCESSIBLE UVA

The University of Virginia should be more accessible to Tony Hensley in a couple of years.

The problem is not academic. Right now, parts of UVa's campus are not physically accessible for the Western Albemarle High School senior.

Hensley was born with a muscular condition that left him weak, and he started using a wheelchair after he was injured in an automobile wreck.

"I plan to attend Piedmont Virginia Community College for two years and transfer to UVa," he said. "With the Americans with Disabilities Act, it should be more accessible in a couple of years."

In 1986, nine months after having two metal rods placed in his back to help correct curvature of the spine, Hensley was injured in a car accident.

He was trapped in the vehicle for 45 minutes, and his leg was broken in three places.

Being the only senior at WAHS in a wheelchair has not hindered his progress in any way, Hensley said.

The school is accessible for people with disabilities, he said. And his disability is no big deal to his classmates. He said he gets treated the same as everyone else.

He and his 215 classmates graduate tonight at 8 P.M. in Warrior Stadium at the High School.

With a 3.8 grade-point average, Hensley is in the top 10 percent of his class. He is a member of the National Honor Society and the French Honor Society and has won various academic awards. Hensley loves photography and stays busy photographing weddings and other events. He also was hired to photograph several senior portraits this year.

He became interested in photography while on the yearbook staff at Heritage Christian School.

Hensley drives a van and often goes on the Blue Ridge Parkway to take photographs that he mats and sells.

He is not sure whether photography would be profitable enough to make a living. "I'm interested in business administration," he said. "Eventually I'd like to be a business owner of some sort."

Hensley lives in North Garden with his parents, John M. and Betty Jo Hensley.

exceptional individuals. Their exceptionalities may involve sensory, physical, cognitive, emotional, or communication abilities or any combination of these. Furthermore, exceptionalities may vary greatly in cause, degree, and effect on educational progress, and the effects may vary greatly depending on the individual's age, sex, and life circumstances. Any individual we might present as an example of our definition is likely to be representative of exceptional children and youths in some respects but unrepresentative in others. Consider the two students, Tony Hensley and Matt Radcliffe, who are described in the box on pp. 8 and 9. How are these students typical and how are they atypical of the general population? How are they typical and atypical of students with disabilities? In what ways do they fit our educational definition of exceptionality? We do not provide answers to these questions here; they are intended as food for thought, and we hope you will reflect on them as you continue reading and studying.

FOR CANCER SURVIVOR AT AHS,
COLLEGE HURDLE REMAINS A CHALLENGE

Matthew Radcliffe is a fighter.

In 1985, doctors discovered a malignant tumor at the stem of his brain. At the tender age of 10, he was given a 40 to 60 percent chance of surviving.

"Before that, I was a perfect kid who had everything," he said. "I could run really well and I played soccer."

The operation was successful, but Matthew had to wear an eye patch and suffered from double vision. He temporarily lost the use of some of his motor skills. His head was shaved, and he had a huge scar from the surgery.

He went back to school almost immediately. Some of his classmates were afraid of him. They thought he was going to die.

"For some reason, I never thought I would die," he said. "I had a lot to live for—my family and my future. I wanted to graduate from school, go to college, and have a family some day."

Tonight, Matthew accomplishes one of those goals as he graduates form Albemarle High School.

But the fight isn't over.

With a 3.89 grade-point average, Matthew is in the top 10 percent of his 362-member class, is a member of the National Honor Society, is in the Beta Club, and was named to Who's Who Among American High School Students.

But he said his low SAT scores kept him from getting into the colleges he wanted to attend.

"I applied to James Madison University, the University of Virginia and William and Mary, but I wasn't accepted."

His dream was to go to JMU in Harrisonburg.

"This is my greatest disappointment," he said. "I don't think SAT scores show my ability to succeed in college."

He said he can't help but feel bitter about the rejection, but he will not give up. . . .

Matthew Radcliffe now has graduated from college, majoring in biology. He hopes to enter a graduate program in pharmacy.

He received the George and Ruth Huff Scholarship for $1,000. He does not know what kind of a career he wants but said he would probably end up working with children.

"I feel like I missed my childhood," he said. "While the other kids were playing, I was fighting for my life."

In middle school, some kids teased him because of his scar and called him nicknames like "hammerhead."

The scar has faded but the teasing he suffered still bothers him.

"Anybody can get cancer—kids or adults." "You can't catch it. People who have cancer are just like everybody else."

Source: By Tammy Poole, in *The Daily Progress,* June 12, 1992, pp. C1, C2. Copyright © 1992. Reprinted with permission.

The *typical* student who receives special education has no immediately obvious disability. He (more than half of the students served by special education are males) is in elementary or middle school and has persistent problems in learning and behaving appropriately in school. His problems are primarily academic and social or behavioral. These difficulties are not apparent to many teachers until they have worked with the student for a period of weeks or months. His problems persist despite teachers' efforts to meet his needs in the regular school program in which most students succeed. He is most likely to be described as having a learning disability or to be designated by an even broader label indicating that his academic and social progress in school are unsatisfactory due to a disability.

By federal law, an exceptional student is not to be identified as eligible for special education until careful assessment indicates that he or she is unable to make satisfactory progress in the regular school program without special services designed to meet his or her extraordinary needs. Federal special education laws and regulations include definitions of several conditions (categories such as *learning disability, mental retardation, hearing impairment*, and so on) that *might* create a need for special education. These laws and regulations require that special services be provided to meet whatever special needs are created by a disabling condition and cannot be met in the regular educational program. They do *not* require that special education be provided simply because a student has a disability.

When you read the article about Tony Hensley and Matt Radcliffe, you may have wondered whether these young men, both of whom obviously acquired disabilities at some point in their school careers, received special education. Remember that having a disability does not necessarily mean special education is required. Tony did not receive special education; his regular classroom teachers made minor adjustments to meet his needs related to his physical condition. His progress in elementary and high school was not affected by his physical problems. Upon graduating from high school, he decided to attend a community college for two reasons: (1) It was readily accessible, and (2) he wanted to explore various academic and career options before entering the University of Virginia or another four-year college or university. By the time he entered the University of Virginia in 1994, it was more readily accessible to someone in a wheelchair than it had been just a few years earlier. This increased accessibility was due in part to the Americans with Disabilities Act, a federal law we will discuss later. Tony graduated from the university's McIntire School of Commerce in 1996 and was admitted to that school's master's program in accounting. Provisions such as reserved parking for people with disabilities and modifications to make the McIntire School accessible to people with wheelchairs helped Tony explore these educational opportunities.

Like Tony, Matt did not receive special education. His regular classroom teachers helped him keep up with his work during his illness. Obviously, he had the cognitive capacity and emotional strength to deal successfully with the disabilities caused by his illness and attain an outstanding academic record without special education services. The primary school-related problems he experienced were the fear and insensitivity of some of his classmates (see his essay in Chapter 10, p. 439). When he graduated from high school, his educational goals were thwarted temporarily by college and university admissions officers' emphasis on his SAT scores, rather than his academic record. By 1995, Matt had gone eleven years without his cancer recurring but continued to experience some of the residual effects that surgery had on his vision and fine motor control. He was a member of the class of 1996 at Campbell University, majoring in biology, and hoped to enter a graduate program in pharmacy.

Tony and Matt illustrate the fact that special education may not be necessary for all students with disabilities. They also illustrate another point we made earlier: Educators must focus on exceptional students' abilities, not just accommodate their disabilities. Students with disabilities typically have ordinary or extraordinary abilities as well. We discriminate against students with disabilities when we do not foster the full development of their abilities.

Now consider another exceptional student, one with a severe disability who, nevertheless, achieved a high level of academic and athletic success. Aaron Farley (see box on p. 11) needed and received special education because of the extraordinary difficulty a student's profound deafness imposes on teaching and learning in a classroom in which all the other students can hear. The extraordinary difficulty we refer to is that of communication. Individuals with severely impaired hearing often need to learn to communicate in the language of signs—a manual language with its own grammar. Others use a combination of speech and cues called *cued speech*. Few hearing people are fluent in sign language or cued speech; in fact, most know virtually no signs or

Up to the Challenge

PITCHER DOESN'T LET HEARING IMPAIRMENT STAND IN WAY OF SUCCESS

Hitters and pitchers look for them. Catchers and coaches give them. Everyone tries to steal them. Signs are as much a part of the game of baseball as the bat and ball.

And in a society that does not always accommodate the hearing impaired, baseball—with its endless parade of signs and gestures—is an oasis where the hearing and deaf alike attend on equal footing.

Aaron Farley is deaf. He also happens to have been raised on baseball. The name given at birth—Aaron (as in Hank) Matthew (as in Eddie, only without the "s") Farley (as in Aaron's father Bob, big Braves' fan)—left little doubt that baseball would constitute a huge part of his life.

Make no mistake about it, when Farley takes the mound in this weekend's 17–18-year-old Babe Ruth state tournament in Purcellville, the 18-year-old C. B. Baker all-star will be just another baseball player.

"Baseball is one of those beautiful sports that rely so much on symbols," said Bob Farley, who also serves as all-star coach. "When the game starts we all speak a different language, anyway."

If baseball is unique in that sense, then it owes a good deal to deaf individuals such as William Hoy. An act so central to the national pastime—the umpire's animated strike call—was prompted by Hoy, a turn-of-the-century National League outfielder, who required hand signals to know if the pitch was a ball or a strike.

The symbolic code that has developed in the years since is a language Farley probably understands better than most.

Born profoundly deaf—the most severe degree of hearing impairment—Farley is capable of hearing high-decibel sounds like thunder, but little else. So he compensates with eyes. Farley confidently states that no one on the playing field sees as much as he does. His father doesn't remember him ever missing a sign.

His own safety, in fact, requires that Farley rigidly adhere to the proverbial command—keep your eye on the ball.

"He has to focus and concentrate on the entire game," said the elder Farley. "I don't know if it makes him better, but it sure makes him tired."

Moreover, it makes him intensely competitive. As one not distracted on the field, he expects nothing less from his teammates. "I don't want to make a mistake, I don't want my teammates to make a mistake," Aaron said. "I want to win."

Win he has. During the C. B. Baker regular season, Farley posted a perfect 4–0 record for champion Ruritan, the best mark in the league. He was equally successful at the plate with a .360 batting average.

Aaron Farley, of the C.B. Baker League All-Star team, did not let being deaf keep him from enjoying success as a pitcher. The 18-year-old was 6-0 during the summer of 1992 in regular season and tournament play.

In last weekend's District 5 tournament, Farley added two more wins—including Sunday's 12–6 championship victory—to help put the Charlottesville squad in today's first-round game against the District 7 champions.

On the subject of stats, try this one: 3.60. Not ERA, but GPA. In June, Farley graduated with honors from Charlottesville High School . . . .

A message blackboard in Farley's bedroom frequently carries this admonition from his father: "Most limitations are self-imposed." The son has taken the saying to heart. Consequently, Aaron Farley has not allowed his disability to get in the way of on- or off-field achievement.

He rejects the notion, however, that he is any sort of role model, but the message is clear: Being deaf is no excuse not to participate, or succeed.

Source: By Steve Lewis, in *The Daily Progress,* July, 17, 1992, pp. C1, C3.

cues. Teachers without extensive training are not able to help most students with severely impaired hearing become fluent in any language. Thus, it is imperative that students with severe hearing impairments receive specialized instruction so they can learn to communicate fluently, typically through a combination of signing, speech, and speech reading or cued speech (see Chapter 8 for further discussion).

Aaron Farley's hearing impairment was diagnosed when he was two years old. He attended a special preschool program at the University of Virginia from ages three to five years old. There, he began learning cued speech, which combines manual cues with speech (see Chapter 8). From kindergarten through elementary school, Aaron attended a special class for children with impaired hearing and also received special instruction from a speech-language therapist. The speech-language therapist helped Aaron with speech reading, articulation, and vocabulary. Beginning in middle school, he attended a special class for several hours each day and received speech-language therapy. Both these services continued through grade 12. In high school, Aaron attended the special class for two hours per day and spent a half hour each day with a speech-language therapist. The rest of the day he attended regular classes with a cued speech transliterator—a person with special training in translating spoken English into the combination of speech and cues known as cued speech. The transliterator made sure that Aaron could understand the speech of others, interpreted nonspeech sounds for Aaron, and expressed Aaron's ideas to others.

Aaron and his father list the following aids as especially helpful aspects of his education: his cued speech transliterator; note takers (hearing classmates who took notes for him in regular classes); his speech-language therapy; and in grades 10, 11, and 12, having a high school special education teacher who was deaf. This teacher became Aaron's confidant and provided a good role model for him.

Without the special education he received, Aaron likely would not have learned the academic and social skills necessary to graduate with honors and continue his academic career. His high intelligence and athletic skills may have gone undeveloped, and a handicap would have been imposed on him by not providing the means to nurture his potential. He has continued his education at Piedmont Community College near Charlottesville, Virginia.

PREVALENCE OF EXCEPTIONAL CHILDREN AND YOUTHS

Prevalence refers to the percentage of a population or number of individuals having a particular exceptionality. The prevalence of mental retardation, for example, might be estimated at 2.3 percent, which means that 2.3 percent of the population, or twenty-three people in every thousand, are assumed to have mental retardation. If the prevalence of giftedness is assumed to be between 3 percent and 5 percent, we would expect somewhere between thirty and fifty people in a sample of a thousand to have special gifts of some kind. Obviously, accurate estimates of prevalence depend on our ability to count the number of people in a given population who have a certain exceptionality.

At first thought, the task of determining the number of children and youths who have exceptionalities seems simple enough, yet the prevalence of most exceptionalities is uncertain and a matter of considerable controversy. A number of factors make it hard to say with great accuracy and confidence just how many exceptional individuals there are including vagueness in definitions, frequent changes in definitions, and the role of schools in determining exceptionality—matters we discuss in later chapters.

Government figures show that about 10 students out of every 100 are receiving special education (U.S. Department of Education, 1995). The total number of

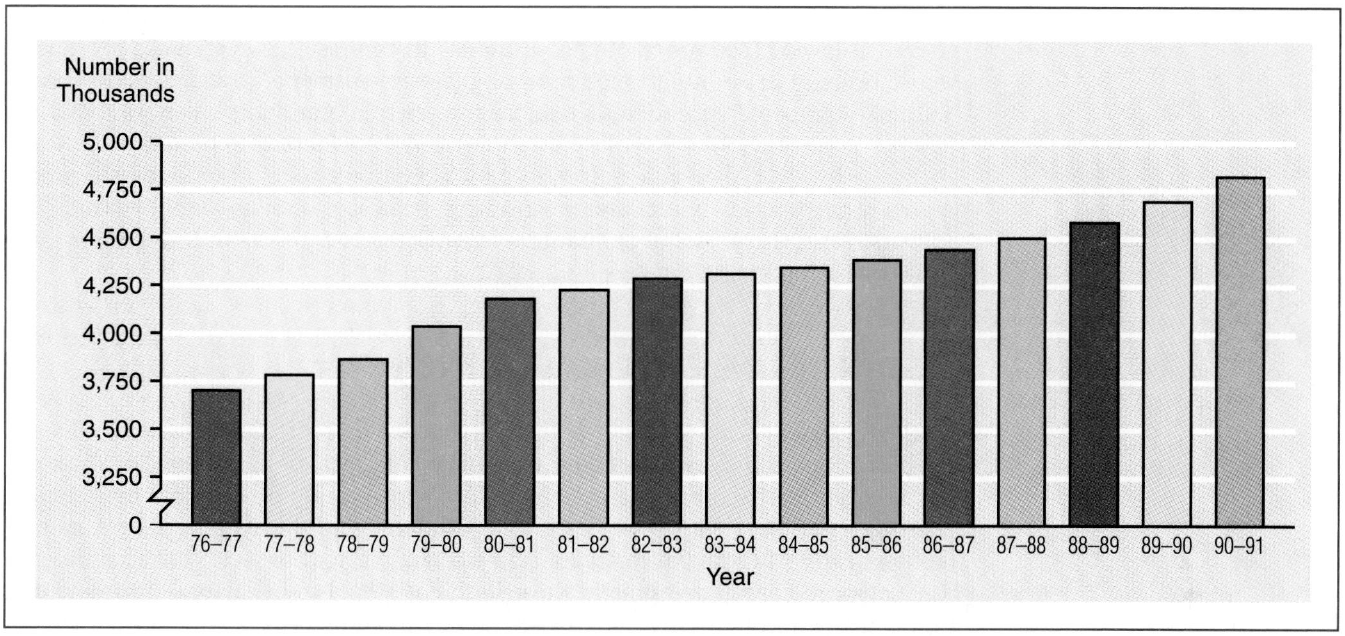

Figure 1–1 Number of students served for schoolyears 1976–77 through 1990–91. (*Source:* U.S. Department of Education. 1992. p. 4.)

students served by special education is over 5 million. Increases from 1976 to 1991 in the number of students served by special education are shown in Figure 1–1. Most of these children and youths are between the ages of six and seventeen. Although preschoolers and youths eighteen to twenty-one are being identified with increasing frequency as having disabilities, school-age children and youths in their early teens make up the bulk of the identified population. The distribution of certain disabilities has changed considerably in the past two decades. As shown in Figure 1–2, the percentage of students with disabilities in the "specific learning disabilities" category has

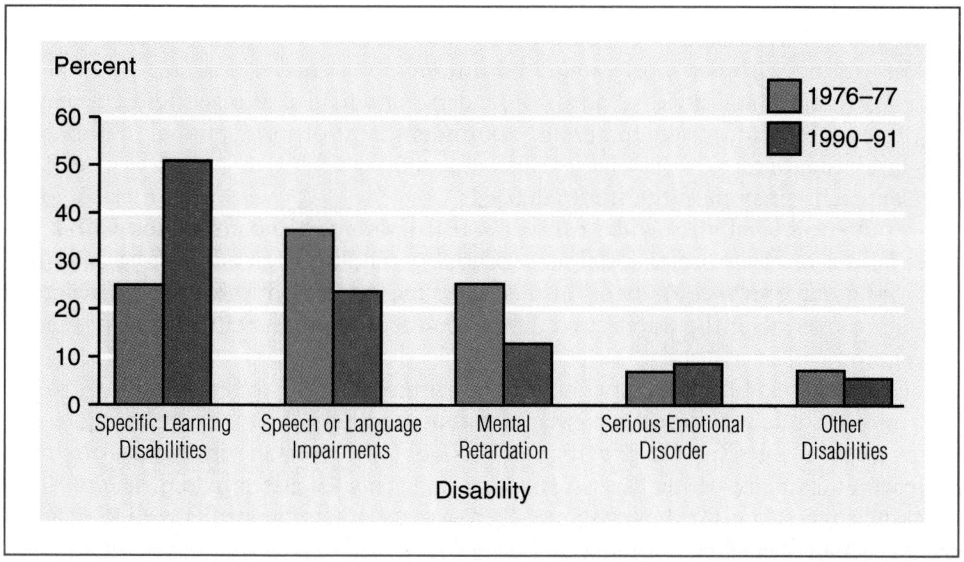

Figure 1–2

Changes in the distribution of specific disabilities for children ages 6–21 served under IDEA: Schoolyears 1976–77 and 1990–91. (*Source:* U.S. Department of Education, 1992, p. 9)

doubled since the mid-1970s. There has been a slight increase in the percentage categorized as having "serious emotional disorder." In contrast, the percentage of students whose primary disability is "speech or language impairments" has declined substantially, and the percentage identified as having "mental retardation" is now about half of what it was in 1976. No one has an entirely satisfactory explanation of these changes. However, they may reflect, in part, alterations in definitions and diagnostic criteria for certain disabilities and the growing social acceptability of the "learning disabilities" label. In subsequent chapters, we discuss the prevalence of specific categories of exceptionality.

DEFINITION OF SPECIAL EDUCATION

Special education means specially designed instruction that meets the unusual needs of an exceptional student. Special materials, teaching techniques, or equipment and/or facilities may be required. For example, students with visual impairments may require reading materials in large print or Braille; students with hearing impairments may require hearing aids and/or instruction in sign language; those with physical disabilities may need special equipment; those with emotional or behavioral disorders may need smaller and more highly structured classes; and students with special gifts or talents may require access to working professionals. Related services—special transportation, psychological assessment, physical and occupational therapy, medical treatment, and counseling—may be necessary if special education is to be effective. The single most important goal of special education is finding and capitalizing on exceptional students' *abilities*.

Providing Special Education

Several administrative plans are available for the education of exceptional children and youths, from a few special provisions made by the student's regular teacher to twenty-four-hour residential care in a special facility. Who educates exceptional students and where they receive their education depends on two factors: (1) how and how much the child or youth differs from average students and (2) what resources are available in the school and community. We describe various administrative plans for education according to the degree of physical integration—the extent to which exceptional and nonexceptional students are taught in the same place by the same teachers.

Beginning with the most integrated intervention, the *regular classroom teacher* who is aware of the individual needs of students and skilled at meeting them may be able to acquire appropriate materials, equipment, and/or instructional methods. At this level, the direct services of specialists may not be required—the expertise of the regular teacher may meet the student's needs.

At the next level, the regular classroom teacher may need consultation with a *special educator* or other professional (e.g., school psychologist) in addition to acquiring the special materials, equipment, or methods. The special educator may instruct the regular teacher, refer the teacher to other resources, or demonstrate the use of materials, equipment, or methods.

Going a step further, a special educator may provide *itinerant services* to the exceptional student and/or the regular classroom teacher. The itinerant teacher establishes a consistent schedule, moving from school to school and visiting classrooms to instruct students individually or in small groups. This teacher provides materials and teaching suggestions for the regular teacher to carry out and consults with the regular teacher about special problems.

At the next level, a *resource teacher* provides services for the students and teachers in only one school. The students being served are enrolled in the regular classroom and are seen by the specially trained teacher for a length of time and at a frequency determined by the nature and severity of their particular problems. The resource teacher continually assesses the needs of the students and their teachers and usually works with students individually or in small groups in a special classroom, where special materials and equipment are available. Typically, the resource teacher serves as a consultant to the regular classroom teacher, advising on the instruction and management of the child or youth in the classroom and perhaps demonstrating instructional techniques. The flexibility of the plan and the fact that the student remains with nondisabled peers most of the time make this a particularly attractive and popular alternative.

Diagnostic-prescriptive centers go beyond the level of intervention represented by resource teachers and rooms. In this plan, students are placed for a short time in a special class in a school or other facility so their needs can be assessed and a plan of action can be determined on the basis of diagnostic findings. After an educational prescription has been written for the pupil, the recommendations for placement may include anything from institutional care to placement in a regular classroom with a particularly competent teacher who can carry out the plan.

Hospital or homebound instruction is most often required by students who have physical disabilities, although it is sometimes employed for those with emotional or behavioral disorders or other disabilities when no alternative is readily available. Typically, the youngster is confined to the hospital or the home for a relatively short time, and the hospital or homebound teacher maintains contact with the regular teacher.

One of the most visible—and in recent years, controversial—service alternatives is the *special self-contained class*. Such a class typically enrolls 15 or fewer exceptional children or youths with particular characteristics or needs. The teacher ordinarily has

Individuals with disabilities are as diverse a group as any other; thus, a major emphasis of special education is to tailor services to meet individual needs.

Table 1–1
Examples of Service Alternatives for Special Education

Most Physically Integrated ←

Type of Placement	*Regular Class Only*	*Special Educator Consultation*	*Itinerant Teacher*	*Resource Teacher*
Major features of placement alternative	Regular teacher meets all needs of student; student may not be officially identified or labeled; student totally integrated	Regular teacher meets all needs of student with only occasional help from special education consultant(s); student may not be officially identified or labeled; student totally integrated	Regular teacher provides most or all instruction; special teacher provides intermittent instruction of student and/or consultation with regular teacher; student integrated except for brief instructional sessions	Regular teacher provides most instruction; special teacher provides instruction part of school day and advises regular teacher; student integrated most of school day
Types of students typically served	Student with mild learning disability, emotional/behavioral disorder, or mild mental retardation; student with physical disability	Student with mild learning disability, emotional/behavioral disorder, or mild mental retardation	Student with visual impairment or physical disability; student with communication disorder	Student with mild to moderate emotional/behavioral, learning, or communication disorder or hearing impairment
Primary role of special education teacher	None	To offer demonstration and instruction and to assist regular class teacher as requested	To visit classroom regularly and see that appropriate instruction, materials, and other services are provided; to offer consultation, demonstration, and referral for regular teacher and assessment and instruction of student as needed; to work toward total integration of student	To assess student's needs for instruction and management; to provide individual or small-group instruction on set schedule in regular class or resource room; to offer advice and demonstration for regular teacher; to handle referral to other agencies for additional services; to work toward total integration of student

been trained as a special educator and provides all or most of the instruction. Those assigned to such classes usually spend most or all of the school day separated from their nondisabled peers. Often students with disabilities are integrated with nondisabled students during part of the day (perhaps for physical education, music, or some other activity in which they can participate well).

Special day schools provide an all-day special placement for exceptional children and youths. The day school is usually organized for a specific category of exceptional students and may contain special equipment necessary for their care and education. These students return to their homes during nonschool hours.

→ **Least Physically Integrated**

Diagnostic-Prescriptive Center	*Hospital or Homebound Instruction*	*Self-Contained Class*	*Special Day School*	*Residential School*
Special teacher in center provides most or all instruction for several days or weeks and develops plan or prescription for regular or special education teacher; following diagnosis and prescription, student may be partially or totally integrated into regular school or class	Special teacher provides all instruction in hospital or home until student is able to return to usual school classes (regular or special) from which he or she has been temporarily withdrawn; student totally separated from regular school for short period	Special teacher provides most or all instruction in special class of students; regular teacher may provide instruction in regular class for part of school day; student mostly or totally separated from regular class	Special teacher provides instruction in separate school; also may work with teachers in regular or special classes of regular school; student totally or mostly separated from regular school	Same as special day school; special teacher also works with other staff to provide a total therapeutic environment or milieu; student totally or mostly in special setting
Student with mild disability who has been receiving no services or inadequate services	Student with physical disability; student undergoing treatment or medical tests	Student with moderate to severe mental retardation or emotional/behavioral disorder	Student with severe or profound physical or mental disability	Student with severe or profound mental retardation or emotional/behavioral disorder
To make comprehensive assessment of student's educational strengths and weaknesses; to develop written prescription for instruction and behavior management for receiving teacher; to interpret prescription for receiving teacher and assess and revise prescription as needed	To obtain records from student's school of attendance; to maintain contact with teachers (regular or special) and offer instruction consistent with student's school program; to prepare student for return to school (special or regular)	To manage and teach special class; to offer instruction in most areas of curriculum; to work toward integration of students in regular classes	To manage and teach individuals and/or small groups of students with disabilities; to work toward integration of students in regular school	Same as special day school; also to work with residential staff to make certain school program is integrated appropriately with nonschool activities

The final level of intervention is the *residential school*. Here, exceptional students receive twenty-four-hour care away from home, often at a distance from their communities. These children and youths may make periodic visits home or return each weekend, but during the week, they are residents of the institution, where they receive academic instruction in addition to management of their daily living environment.

The major features of each type of placement or service alternative, examples of the types of students most likely to be served in each, and the primary roles of the special educators who work there are shown in Table 1–1. Note that although these are the major administrative plans for delivery of special education, variations are possible. For example, special day schools and residential schools may help students make the transition to regular schools as they are able to return. Many school systems, in the process of trying to find more effective and economical ways of serving exceptional students, combine or alter these alternatives and the roles special educators and other professionals play in service delivery. Furthermore, the types of students listed under each service alternative are *examples only*; there are wide variations among school systems in the kinds of placements made for particular kinds of students. Note also that what any special education teacher may be expected to do includes a variety of items not specified in Table 1–1. We discuss these expectations for teachers in the following section.

As noted earlier, special education law requires placement of the student in the **least restrictive environment (LRE)**. What is usually meant is that the student should be separated from nondisabled classmates and from home, family, and community as little as possible. That is, his or her life should be as normal as possible, and the intervention should be consistent with individual needs and not interfere with individual freedom any more than is absolutely necessary. For example, students should not be placed in special classes if they can be served adequately by resource teachers, and they should not be placed in institutions if a special class will serve their needs just as well.

Although this movement toward placement of exceptional students in the least restrictive environment is laudable, the definition of *least restrictive* is not as simple as it seems. Cruickshank (1977) has pointed out that greater restriction of the physical environment does not necessarily mean greater restriction of psychological freedom or human potential. In fact, it is conceivable that some students could be more restricted in the long run in a regular class where they are rejected by others and fail to learn necessary skills than in a special class or day school where they learn happily and well. It is important to keep the ultimate goals for the students in mind and to avoid letting "least restrictive" become a hollow slogan that results in shortchanging them in their education (Kauffman, 1995). As Morse has noted, "The goal should be to find the most productive setting to provide the maximum assistance for the child" (1984, p. 120).

Although considerable variation in the placement of students with disabilities is found from state to state and among school systems within a given state, most

Figure 1–3

Percentage of all students with disabilities ages 3–21 served in six educational placements: Schoolyear 1992–93. (*Source:* U.S. Department of Education, 1995, p. A-40.)

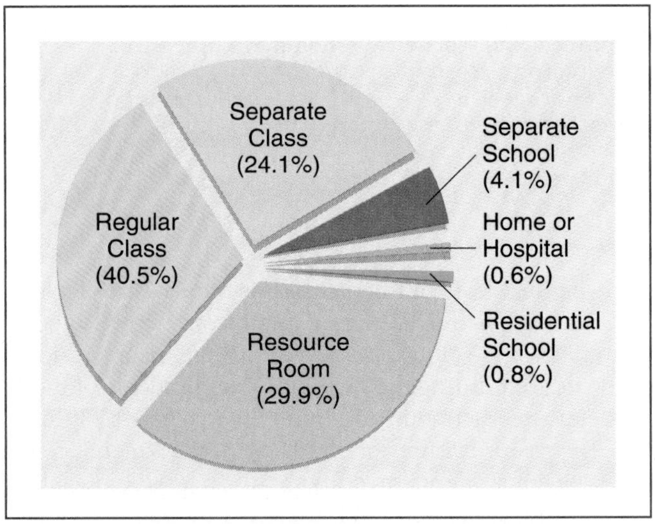

least restrictive environment (LRE). A legal term referring to the fact that exceptional children must be educated in as normal an environment as possible.

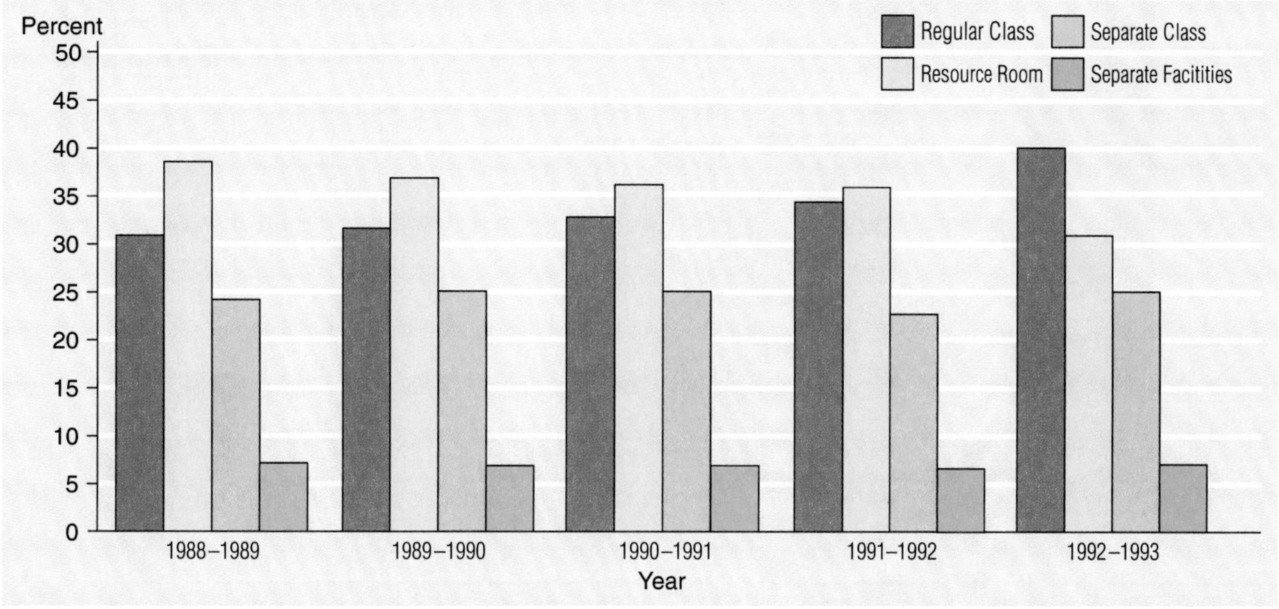

Figure 1–4 Percentage of students with disabilities ages 6–21 served in different educational environments: Schoolyears 1988–89 through 1992–93.
(*Source:* U.S. Department of Education, 1995, p. 15.)

exceptional students are educated in regular classes. Nationwide, over 40 percent of exceptional children and youths are served primarily in regular classes. Most of these students receive special instruction for part of the school day from special education resource teachers. In the United States, about one-fourth of all children and youths with disabilities are placed in separate special classes, and only about 6 percent are placed in separate schools or other special environments (e.g., residential facilities, hospital schools, and homebound instruction; see Figure 1–3). Since the late 1980s, there has been a steady trend toward placing more students with disabilities in regular classes and a corresponding trend toward placing fewer students with disabilities in resource rooms, separate classes, and separate facilities (see Figure 1–4). Placing more students in regular classes and schools reflects educational reform in the 1990s, a topic to which we return later in this chapter and in Chapter 2.

Children under the age of six less often receive education in regular classes, and more often attend separate schools than do children who have reached the usual school age. Special classes, separate schools, and other environments such as homebound instruction are used more often for older teenagers and young adults than for students of elementary and high school age as shown by Figure 1–5. We can explain these differences by several facts:

1. Preschoolers and young adults who are identified for special education tend to have more severe disabilities than students in kindergarten through grade 12.

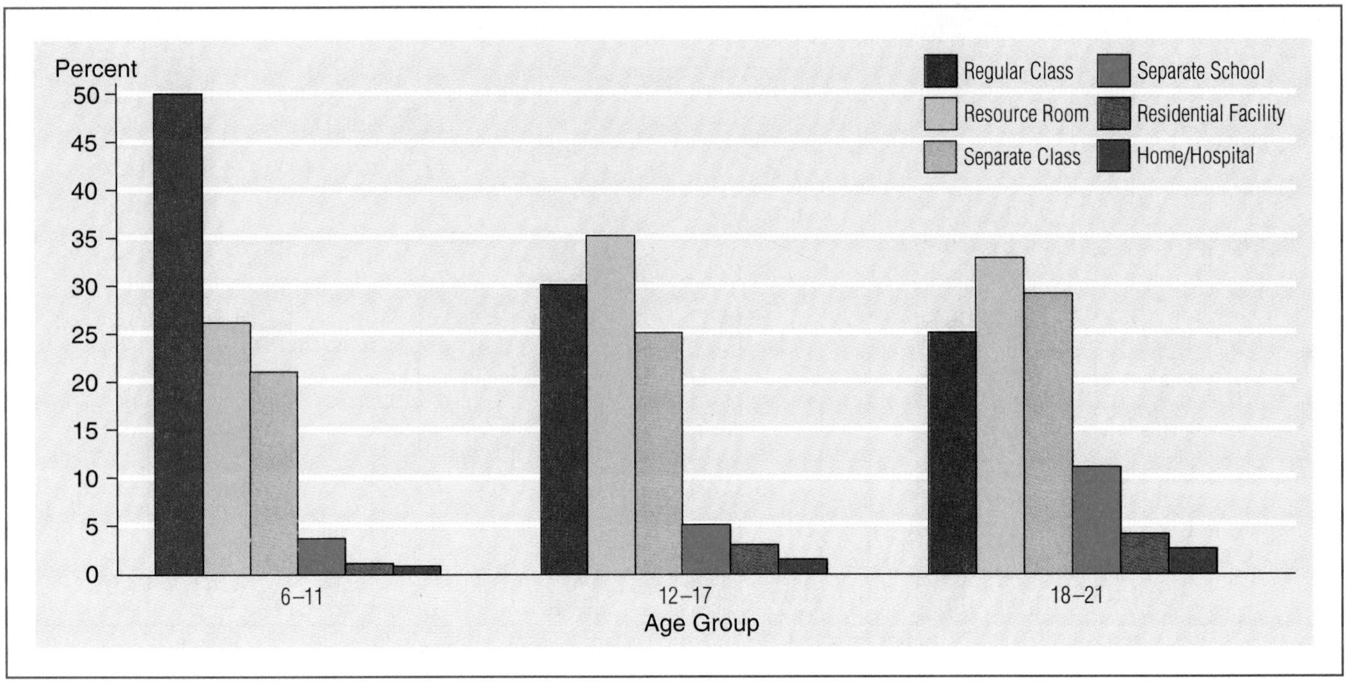

Figure 1–5 Percentage of students with disabilities by age group, served in different educational environments: Schoolyears 1992–93. (*Source:* U.S. Department of Education, 1995, p. 16.)

2. Some school systems do not have regular classes for preschoolers and young adults, and thus placements in other than regular classes are typically more available and more appropriate.
3. Curriculum and work-related educational programs for older teens and young adults with disabilities are frequently offered off the campuses of regular high schools.

The environment that is least restrictive depends, in part, on the individual's exceptionality. There is almost never a need to place in a separate class or separate school a student whose primary disability is a speech impairment. Likewise, most students with learning disabilities can be appropriately educated primarily in regular classes. On the other hand, the resources needed to teach students with severe impairments of hearing and vision may require that they attend separate schools or classes for at least part of their school careers.

TEACHERS' ROLES

We have noted that most students in public schools who have been identified as exceptional are placed in regular classrooms for at least part of the school day. Furthermore, there is good reason to believe that a large number of public school students not identified as disabled or gifted share many of the characteristics of those who are exceptional. Thus, all teachers must obviously be prepared to deal with exceptional students.

The roles of general and special education teachers are not always clear in a given case. Sometimes uncertainty about the division of responsibility can be extremely stressful; for example, teachers may feel uneasy because it is not clear whose job it is to make special adaptations for a pupil or just what they are expected to do in cooperating with other teachers.

Relationship between General and Special Education

During the 1980s, the relationship between general and special education became a matter of great concern to policymakers, researchers, and advocates for exceptional children. Proposals for changing the relationship between general and special education, including radical calls to restructure or merge the two, came to be known in the 1980s as the **regular education initiative (REI)**. In the 1990s, reform proposals have been called the **inclusive schools movement.** Moderate proponents of reform suggest that general educators take more responsibility for many students with mild or moderate disabilities, with special educators serving more as consultants or resources to regular classroom teachers and less as special teachers. More radical reformers recommend that special education be eliminated as a separate, identifiable part of education. They call for a single, unified educational system in which all students are viewed as unique and special and entitled to the same quality of education. Although many of the suggested reforms have great appeal and some could produce benefits for exceptional students, the basis for the integration of special and general education and the ultimate consequences they might bring have been questioned (Fuchs & Fuchs, 1994; Kauffman, 1995; Lloyd, Singh, & Repp, 1991; Martin, 1995).

One reason behind reform proposals is concern for pupils who are considered at risk. *At risk* is often not clearly defined, but it generally refers to students who perform or behave poorly in school and appear likely to fail or fall far short of their potential. Some advocates of reform suggest that at-risk students cannot be or should not be distinguished from those with mild disabilities. Others argue that the problems of at-risk students tend to be ignored because special education siphons resources from general education. Should special education and general education merge for the purpose of making general education better able to respond to students at risk? Or should special education maintain its separate identity and be expanded to include these students? Should general education be expected to develop new programs for at-risk students without merging with special education? There are no ready answers to these and other questions about the education of students at risk.

We discuss REI, inclusion, and their implications further in Chapter 2. Regardless of one's views, the controversy about the relationship between special and general education has made teachers more aware of the problems of deciding just which students should be taught specific curricula, which students should receive special attention or services, and where and by whom these should be provided (Kauffman & Hallahan, 1995; Ysseldyke, Algozzine, & Thurlow, 1992). There are no pat answers to the questions about how special and general education should work together to see that every student receives an appropriate education. Yet it is clear that the relationship between them must be one of cooperation and collaboration. They must not become independent or mutually exclusive educational tracks. Neither can we deny that general and special educators have somewhat different roles to play. With this in mind, we summarize some of the major expectations for all teachers, and for special education teachers, in particular.

Expectations for All Educators

Regardless of whether a teacher is specifically trained in special education, he or she may be expected to participate in educating exceptional students in any one of the following ways:

regular education initiative (REI). A philosophy that maintains that general education, rather than special education, should be primarily responsible for the education of students with disabilities.

inclusive schools movement. A reform movement designed to restructure general education schools and classrooms so they better accommodate all students, including those with disabilities.

1. *Make maximum effort to accommodate individual students' needs.* Teaching in public schools requires dealing with diverse students in every class. All teachers must make an effort to meet the needs of individuals who may differ in some way from the average or typical student. Flexibility, adaptation, accommodation, and special attention are to be expected of every teacher. Special education should be considered necessary only when a teacher's best efforts to meet a student's individual needs are not successful.
2. *Evaluate academic abilities and disabilities.* Although a psychologist or other special school personnel may give a student formal standardized tests in academic areas, adequate evaluation requires the teacher's assessment of the student's performance in the classroom. Teachers must be able to report specifically and precisely how students can and cannot perform in all academic areas for which they are responsible.
3. *Refer for evaluation.* By law, all public school systems must make extensive efforts to screen and identify all children and youths of school age who have disabilities. Teachers must observe students' behavior and refer those they suspect of having disabilities for evaluation by a multidisciplinary team. *We stress here that a student should not be referred for special education unless extensive and unsuccessful efforts have been made to accommodate his or her needs in regular classes. Before referral, school personnel must document the strategies that have been used to teach and manage the student in general education. Referral is justified only if these strategies have failed.* (See the box on p. 23.)
4. *Participate in eligibility conferences.* Before a student is provided special education, his or her eligibility must be determined by an interdisciplinary team. Therefore, teachers must be ready to work with other teachers and with professionals from other disciplines (psychology, medicine, or social work, for example) in determining a student's eligibility for special education.
5. *Participate in writing individualized education programs.* A written individualized education program (IEP) must be on file in the records of every student with a disability. Teachers must be ready to participate in a conference (possibly including the student and/or parents, as well as other professionals) in which the program is formulated.
6. *Communicate with parents or guardians.* Parents (sometimes surrogate parents) or guardians must be consulted during the evaluation of their child's eligibility for special education, formulation of the individualized education program, and reassessment of any special program that may be designed for their child. Teachers must contribute to the school's communication with parents about their child's problems, placement, and progress.
7. *Participate in due process hearings and negotiations.* When parents, guardians, or students with disabilities themselves are dissatisfied with the school's response to educational needs, they may request a due process hearing or negotiations regarding appropriate services. Teachers may be called on to offer observations, opinions, or suggestions in such hearings or negotiations.
8. *Collaborate with other professionals in identifying and making maximum use of exceptional students' abilities.* Finding and implementing solutions to the challenges of educating exceptional students is not the exclusive responsibility of any one professional group. General and special education teachers are expected to share responsibility for educating students with special needs. In addition, teachers may need to collaborate with other professionals, depending on the given student's exceptionality. Psychologists, counselors, physicians, physical therapists, and a variety of other specialists may need teachers' perspectives on students' abilities and disabilities, and they may rely on teachers to implement critical aspects of evaluation or treatment.

What Should I Do Before I Make a Referral?

If you are thinking about referring a student, probably the most important thing you should do is contact his or her parents. If you cannot reach them by phone, try a home visit or ask the visiting teacher (or school social worker, psychologist, or other support personnel) to help you set up a conference. It is very important that you discuss the student's problems with the parents *before* you refer. Parents should never be surprised to find that their child has been referred; they should know well in advance that their child's teachers have noticed problems. One of the most important things you can do to prevent conflict with parents is to establish and maintain communication with them regarding their child's progress.

Before making a referral, check *all* the student's school records. Look for information that could help you understand the student's behavioral or academic problems.

Has the student ever:

- had a psychological evaluation?
- qualified for special services?
- been included in other special programs (e.g., programs for disadvantaged children or speech or language therapy)?
- scored far below average on standardized tests?
- been retained?

Do the records indicate:

- good progress in some areas, poor progress in others?
- any physical or medical problem?
- that the student is taking medication?

Talk to the student's other teachers and professional support personnel about your concern for him or her.

Have other teachers:

- also had difficulty with the student?
- found ways of dealing successfully with the student?

The analysis of information obtained in these ways may help you teach and manage the student successfully, or help you justify to the parents why you believe their child may need special education.

Before making a referral, you will be expected to document the strategies that you have used in your class to meet the student's educational needs. Regardless of whether the student is later found to have a disabling condition, your documentation will be useful in the following ways:

1. You will have evidence that will be helpful to or required by the committee of professionals who will evaluate the student.
2. You will be better able to help the student's parents understand that methods used for other students in the class are not adequate for their child.
3. You will have records of successful and/or unsuccessful methods of working with the student that will be useful to you and any other teacher who works with the student in the future.

Your documentation of what you have done may appear to require a lot of paperwork, but careful record keeping will pay off. If the student is causing you serious concern, then you will be wise to demonstrate your concern by keeping written records. Your notes should include items such as the following:

- exactly what you are concerned about
- why you are concerned about it
- dates, places, and times you have observed the problem
- precisely what you have done to try to resolve the problem
- who, if anyone, helped you devise the plans or strategies you have used
- evidence that the strategies have been successful or unsuccessful

In summary, make certain that you have accomplished the following before you make a referral:

1. held at least one conference to discuss your concerns with the parents (or made extensive and documented efforts to communicate with the parents).
2. checked all available school records and interviewed other professionals involved with the child.
3. documented the academic and behavioral management strategies that you have tried.

Remember that you should refer a student only if you can make a convincing case that the student may have a disability and probably cannot be served appropriately without special education. Referral for special education begins a time-consuming, costly, and stressful process that is potentially damaging to the student and has many legal ramifications.

A high level of professional competence and ethical judgment is required to conform to these expectations. Teaching demands a thorough knowledge of child development and expertise in instruction. Furthermore, teachers are sometimes faced with serious professional and ethical dilemmas in trying to serve the needs of students and their parents, on the one hand, and in attempting to conform to legal or administrative pressures, on the other (Howe & Miramontes, 1992). For example, when there

Special education referrals very often begin with the recommendations of general education teachers.

are indications that a child may have a disability, should the teacher refer that child for evaluation and possible placement in special education, knowing that only inadequate or inappropriate services will be provided? Should a teacher who believes strongly that teenage students with mild retardation need sex education refrain from giving students any information because sex education is not part of the prescribed curriculum and is frowned on by the school board?

Expectations for Special Educators

In addition to being competent enough to meet the preceding expectations, special education teachers must attain special expertise in the following areas:

1. *Academic instruction of students with learning problems.* The majority of students with disabilities have more difficulty learning academic skills than do those without disabilities. This is true for all categories of disabling conditions because sensory impairments, physical disabilities, and mental or emotional disabilities all tend to make academic learning more difficult. Often, the difficulty is slight; sometimes it is extreme. Special education teachers must have more than patience and hope, though they do need these qualities; they must also have the technical skill to present academic tasks so that students with disabilities will understand and respond appropriately.
2. *Management of serious behavior problems.* Many students with disabilities have behavior problems in addition to their other exceptionalities. Some, in fact, require special education primarily because of their inappropriate or disruptive behavior. Special education teachers must have the ability to deal effectively with more than the usual troublesome behavior of students. Besides understanding and empathy, special education teachers must master the techniques that will allow them to draw out particularly withdrawn students, control those who are hyperaggressive and persistently disruptive, and teach critical social skills.
3. *Use of technological advances.* Technology is increasingly being applied to the problems of teaching exceptional students and improving their daily lives. New devices and methods are rapidly being developed, particularly for stu-

Special educators must possess and use both general and highly specialized teaching skills.

dents with sensory and physical disabilities. Special education teachers need more than mere awareness of the technology available; they must also be able to evaluate its advantages and disadvantages for teaching the exceptional children and youths with whom they work.

4. *Knowledge of special education law.* For good or ill, special education today involves many details of law. The rights of students with disabilities are spelled out in considerable detail in federal and state legislation. The laws, as well as the rules and regulations that accompany them, are constantly being interpreted by new court decisions, some of which have widespread implications for the practice of special education. Special education teachers do not need to be lawyers, but they do need to be aware of the law's requirements and prohibitions if they are to be adequate advocates for students with disabilities.

We caution here that the specific day-to-day expectations for special education teachers vary from school system to school system and from state to state. What are listed here are the general expectations and areas of competence with which every special educator will necessarily be concerned. Nevertheless, we emphasize that *special educators have the responsibility to offer not just good instruction but instruction that is highly individualized, intensive, relentless, urgent, and goal directed* (Zigmond & Baker, 1995).

ORIGINS OF SPECIAL EDUCATION

There have always been exceptional children, but there have not always been special educational services to address their needs. During the closing years of the eighteenth century, following the American and French Revolutions, effective procedures were devised for teaching children with sensory impairments—those who were blind or deaf (Winzer, 1986, 1993). Early in the nineteenth century, the first systematic attempts were made to educate "idiotic" and "insane" children—those who today are said to have mental retardation and emotional or behavioral disorders.

In the prerevolutionary era, the most society had offered children with disabilities was protection—asylum from a cruel world into which they did not fit and in which

Jean-Marc-Gaspard Itard (1775–1838)

they could not survive with dignity, if they could survive at all. But as the ideas of democracy, individual freedom, and egalitarianism swept America and France, there was a change in attitude. Political reformers and leaders in medicine and education began to champion the cause of children and adults with disabilities, urging that these "imperfect" or "incomplete" individuals be taught skills that would allow them to become independent, productive citizens. These humanitarian sentiments went beyond a desire to protect and defend people with disabilities. The early leaders sought to normalize exceptional people to the greatest extent possible and confer on them the human dignity they presumably lacked.

The historical roots of special education are found primarily in the early 1800s. Contemporary educational methods for exceptional children can be traced directly to techniques pioneered during that era. And many (perhaps most) of today's vital, controversial issues have been issues ever since the dawn of special education. In our discussion of some of the major historical events and trends since 1800, we comment briefly on the history of people and ideas, the growth of the discipline, professional and parent organizations, and legislation.

People and Ideas

Most of the originators of special education were European physicians. They were primarily young, ambitious people who challenged the wisdom of the established authorities, including their own friends and mentors (Kanner, 1964).

Jean-Marc-Gaspard Itard (1775–1838), a French physician who was an authority on diseases of the ear and on the education of students who were deaf, is the person to whom most historians trace the beginning of special education as we know it today. In the early years of the nineteenth century, this young doctor began to educate a boy of about twelve who had been found roaming naked and wild in the forests of France. Itard's mentor, Philippe Pinel (1745–1826), a prominent French physician who was an early advocate of humane treatment of insane persons, advised him that his efforts would be unsuccessful because the boy, Victor, was a "hopeless idiot." But Itard persevered. He did not eliminate Victor's disabilities, but he did dramatically improve the wild child's behavior through patient, systematic educative procedures (Itard, 1962).

Itard's student, Édouard Séguin (1812–1880), emigrated to the United States in 1848. Before that, Séguin had become famous as an educator of so-called idiotic children, even though most thinkers of the day were convinced that such children could not be taught anything of significance.

The ideas of the first special educators were truly revolutionary for their times. These are a few of the revolutionary ideas of Itard, Séguin, and their successors that form the foundation for present-day special education:

- *individualized instruction*, in which the child's characteristics, rather than prescribed academic content, provide the basis for teaching techniques
- *a carefully sequenced series of educational tasks,* beginning with tasks the child can perform and gradually leading to more complex learning
- *emphasis on stimulation* and awakening of the child's senses, the aim being to make the child more aware of and responsive to educational stimuli
- *meticulous arrangement of the child's environment*, so that the structure of the environment and the child's experience of it lead naturally to learning
- *immediate reward for correct performance*, providing reinforcement for desirable behavior

- *tutoring in functional skills*, the desire being to make the child as self-sufficient and productive as possible in everyday life
- *belief that every child should be educated to the greatest extent possible*, the assumption being that every child can improve to some degree

So far, we have mentioned only European physicians who figured prominently in the rise of special education. Although it is true that much of the initial work took place in Europe, many U.S. researchers contributed greatly during those early years. They stayed informed of European developments as best they could, some of them traveling to Europe for the specific purpose of obtaining firsthand information about the education of children with disabilities.

Thomas Hopkins Gallaudet (1787–1851)

Among the young U.S. thinkers concerned with the education of students with disabilities was Samuel Gridley Howe (1801–1876), an 1824 graduate of Harvard Medical School. Besides being a physician and an educator, Howe was a political and social reformer, a champion of humanitarian causes and emancipation. He was instrumental in founding the Perkins School for the Blind in Watertown, Massachusetts, and was also a teacher of students who were deaf and blind. His success in teaching Laura Bridgman, who was deaf and blind, greatly influenced the education of Helen Keller. In the 1840s, Howe was also a force behind the organization of an experimental school for children with mental retardation and was personally acquainted with Séguin.

When Thomas Hopkins Gallaudet (1787–1851), a minister, was a student at Andover Theological Seminary, he tried to teach a girl who was deaf. He visited Europe to learn about educating the deaf and in 1817 established the first American residential school, in Hartford, Connecticut, for students who were deaf (now known as the American School of the Deaf). Gallaudet University in Washington, D.C., the only liberal arts college for students who are deaf, was named in his honor.

The early years of special education were vibrant with the pulse of new ideas. It is not possible to read the words of Itard, Séguin, Howe, and their contemporaries without being captivated by the romance, idealism, and excitement of their exploits. The results they achieved were truly remarkable for their era. Today, special education remains a vibrant field in which innovations, excitement, idealism, and controversies are the norm. Teachers of exceptional children—and that includes, as discussed earlier, all teachers—must understand how and why special education emerged as a discipline.

Growth of the Discipline

Special education did not suddenly spring up as a new discipline, nor did it develop in isolation from other disciplines. The emergence of psychology and sociology, and especially the beginning of the widespread use of mental tests in the early years of the twentieth century, had enormous implications for the growth of special education. Psychologists' study of learning and their prediction of school failure or success by means of tests helped focus attention on children with special needs. Sociologists, social workers, and anthropologists drew attention to the ways in which exceptional children's families and communities responded to them and affected their learning and adjustment.

As the education profession itself matured and as compulsory school attendance laws became a reality, there was a growing realization among teachers and school administrators that a large number of students must be given something beyond the ordinary classroom experience. Elizabeth Farrell, a teacher in New York City in the early part of the century, was highly instrumental in the development of special education as a profession. She and the New York City superintendent of schools attempted to use information about child development, social work, mental testing, and instruction to address the needs of children and youths who were being ill served in or excluded from regular classes and schools. Farrell was a great advocate for services for students with special needs. Her motives and those of the teachers and administrators who worked with her were to see that every student—including every exceptional child or youth—had an appropriate education and received the related health and social services necessary for optimum learning in school (Hendrick & MacMillan, 1989; MacMillan & Hendrick, 1993). In 1922, Farrell and a group of other special educators from across the United States and Canada founded the Council for Exceptional Children, today still the primary professional organization of special educators.

Contemporary special education is a professional field with roots in several academic disciplines—especially medicine, psychology, sociology, and social work—in addition to professional education. It is a discipline sufficiently different from the mainstream of professional education to require special training programs but sufficiently like the mainstream to maintain a primary concern for schools and teaching.

Professional and Parent Organizations

Individuals and ideas have played crucial roles in the history of special education, but it is accurate to say that much of the progress made over the years has been achieved primarily by the collective efforts of professionals and parents. Professional groups were organized first, beginning in the nineteenth century. Effective national parent organizations have existed in the United States only since 1950.

The earliest professional organizations having some bearing on the education of children with disabilities were medical associations founded in the 1800s. With the organization of the Council for Exceptional Children (CEC) and its many divisions, educators have a professional association devoted to special education. Today, the CEC has a national membership of over 50,000, including about 10,000 students. There are state CEC organizations and hundreds of local chapters. Divisions of the CEC have been organized to meet the interests and needs of members who specialize in a particular area.

Although parent organizations offer membership to individuals who do not have exceptional children of their own, they are made up primarily of parents who do have such children and concentrate on issues of special concern to them. Parent organizations have typically served three essential functions: (1) providing an informal group for parents who understand one another's problems and needs and help one another deal with anxieties and frustrations; (2) providing information regarding services and potential resources; and (3) providing the structure for obtaining needed services for their children. Some of the organizations that came about primarily as the result of parents' efforts include the ARC (formerly the Association for Retarded Citizens), the National Association for Gifted Children, the Learning Disabilities Association, the Autism Society of America, and the Federation of Families for Children's Mental Health.

Legislation

Laws have played a major role in the history of special education. In fact, much of the progress in meeting the educational needs of children and youths with disabilities is attributable to laws requiring states and localities to include students with special needs in the public education system. We focus here on recent legislation that represents a culmination of decades of legislative history.

Two landmark federal laws were passed in 1990: the **Individuals with Disabilities Education Act (IDEA)** and the **Americans with Disabilities Act (ADA)**. IDEA amended a federal law passed in 1975, the Education for All Handicapped Children Act, also commonly known as **PL 94–142**.* IDEA ensures that all children and youths with disabilities have the right to a free, appropriate public education. ADA ensures the right of individuals with disabilities to nondiscriminatory treatment in other aspects of their lives; it provides protections of civil rights in the specific areas of employment, transportation, public accommodations, state and local government, and telecommunications.

IDEA (sometimes cited as PL 101–476) and another federal law focusing on intervention in early childhood (PL 99–457) now mandate a free, appropriate public education for every child or youth between the ages of three and twenty-one regardless of the nature or severity of the disability he or she may have. PL 99–457 also provides incentives for states to develop early intervention programs for infants with known disabilities and those considered at risk. Together, these laws require public school systems to identify all children and youths with disabilities and to provide the special education and related services they may need.

As mentioned earlier, IDEA amended an earlier law, commonly known as PL 94–142 (the Education for All Handicapped Children Act). PL 94–142 was revolutionary. It was the first federal law mandating free, appropriate public education for all children with disabilities. Its basic provisions, which are now incorporated in IDEA, are described in the box on p. 31. IDEA altered PL 94–142 in several significant ways, three of which are particularly important for our discussion here.

1. The language of the law was altered. *Children* became *individuals,* reflecting the fact that some of the students involved are young adults, not children. The term *handicapped* was changed to *with disabilities*, acknowledging the difference between limitations imposed by society (handicaps) and inability to do certain things (disabilities; recall our earlier discussion, pp. 6–7). Use of the phrase *with disabilities* also signifies that we think of the person first; the disabling condition is only one characteristic of an individual, who has many other characteristics as well.
2. Special emphasis was placed on transition. PL 94–142 required an individualized education program for every child with a disability; IDEA requires that every older student with a disability (usually beginning at age fourteen or sixteen) have an individualized plan for making the transition to work or further education following high school.
3. Two additional categories of disability were recognized as distinct entities—**autism** and **traumatic brain injury (TBI).** These categories had previously been subsumed under other categories.

In special education, as in other areas of professional practice, laws and lawsuits are numerous and technical. We do not try to lead you through the thicket of legislation and litigation. Our purpose is to describe general trends and leave you with a sense of the direction legislation and litigation have taken.

* Legislation is often designated PL (for public law), followed by a hyphenated numeral, the first set of digits representing the number of the Congress that passed the bill and the second set representing the number of that bill. Thus, PL 94–142 was the 142nd public law passed by the 94th Congress.

Individuals with Disabilities Education Act (IDEA). The Individuals with Disabilities Education Act of 1990; replaced PL 94–142.

Americans with Disabilities Act (ADA). Civil rights legislation for persons with disabilities ensuring nondiscrimination in a broad range of activities.

PL 94–142. The Education for All Handicapped Children Act, which contains a mandatory provision stating that to receive funds under the act, every school system in the nation must provide a free, appropriate public education for every child between the ages of three and eighteen (now extended to ages three to twenty-one), regardless of how or how seriously he or she may be disabled.

autism. A disorder characterized by extreme withdrawal, self-stimulation, cognitive deficits, language disorders, and onset before the age of thirty months.

traumatic brain injury (TBI). Injury to the brain (not including conditions present at birth, birth trauma, or degenerative diseases or conditions) resulting in total or partial disability or psychosocial maladjustment that affects educational performance; may affect cognition, language, memory, attention, reasoning, abstract thinking, judgment, problem solving, sensory or perceptual and motor disabilities, psychosocial behavior, physical functions, information processing, or speech.

TRENDS IN LEGISLATION AND LITIGATION

Trends in Legislation

Legislation historically has been increasingly specific and mandatory. In the 1980s, however, the renewed emphasis on states' rights and local autonomy, plus a political strategy of federal deregulation, led to attempts to repeal some of the provisions of IDEA (then still known as PL 94–142) and loosen federal rules and regulations. Federal disinvestment in education and deregulation of education programs were hallmarks of the Reagan administration (Clark & Astuto, 1988; Verstegen & Clark, 1988), so it is not surprising that federal mandates for special education came under fire during that time. Dissatisfaction with federal mandates is due in part to the fact that the federal government contributes relatively little to the funding of special education. Although the demands of IDEA are detailed, state and local governments must pay most of the cost of special education programs.

Special education laws survived the deregulation of the 1980s, and since then, the trend in legislation has been increasingly to extend civil rights to citizens with disabilities. The enactment of IDEA (the Individuals with Disabilities Education Act) and ADA (the Americans with Disabilities Act) in 1990 represents a continuing commitment to require schools, employers, and government agencies to recognize the abilities of people with disabilities. These laws require reasonable accommodations that will allow those who have disabilities to participate to the fullest extent possible in all the activities of daily living that individuals without disabilities take for granted. The requirements of ADA are intended to grant equal opportunities to people with disabilities in employment, transportation, public accommodations, state and local government, and telecommunications.

ADA has been as revolutionary for business in the 1990s as PL 94–142 was for education when it was enacted in the 1970s. You may recall that in the article about his plans for higher education, Tony Hensley mentioned how ADA would make a difference for him (see p. 8). Clearly, ADA has had great implications for many young adults with disabilities, as they have left high school for work or higher education, and for the everyday lives of all individuals with disabilities who live in our communities. Yet ADA has not been without controversy. In fact, the controversy was reflected in a special issue forum in the *Washington Post* on July 18, 1995, called "Year Five of the ADA" (Taylor, 1995). Some critics of ADA have claimed that it has not lived up to its promise of more employment for people with disabilities, whereas others have described it as too expensive and its regulations as too oppressive to business. To some, support for ADA may seem to come primarily from legislators and people with disabilities. However, a 1995 survey by Louis Harris and the National Organization on Disability (NOD) found overwhelming support for ADA among business owners (Taylor, 1995; see the box on p. 33).

Relationship of Litigation to Legislation

Legislation requires or gives permission to provide special education, but it does not necessarily result in what legislators intended. Whether the laws are administered properly is a legal question for the courts. That is, laws may have little or no effect on the lives of individuals with disabilities until courts interpret the mean—exactly what the laws require in practice. Exceptional children, primarily through the actions of parent and professional organizations, have been getting their day in court more frequently since IDEA and related federal and state laws were passed. Thus, we must examine trends in litigation to complete the picture of how the U.S. legal system may safeguard or undermine appropriate education for exceptional children.

Major Provisions of IDEA

Each state and locality must have a plan to ensure:

IDENTIFICATION	Extensive efforts must be made to screen and identify all children and youths with disabilities.
FULL SERVICE, AT NO COST	Every student with a disability must be assured an appropriate public education at no cost to the parents or guardian.
DUE PROCESS	The student's and parents' rights to information and informed consent must be assured before the student is evaluated, labeled, or placed, and they have a right to an impartial due process hearing if they disagree with the school's decisions.
PARENT/GUARDIAN SURROGATE CONSULTATION	The student's parents or guardian must be consulted about the student's evaluation and placement and the educational plan; if the parents or guardian are unknown or unavailable, a surrogate parent must be found to act for the student.
LEAST RESTRICTIVE ENVIRONMENT (LRE)	The student must be educated in the least restrictive environment that is consistent with his or her educational needs and, insofar as possible, with students without disabilities.
INDIVIDUALIZED EDUCATION PROGRAM (IEP)	A written individualized education program must be prepared for each student with a disability. The program must state present levels of functioning, long- and short-term goals, services to be provided, plans for initiating and evaluating the services, and needed transition services (from school to work or continued education) for students at an appropriate age (usually by age fourteen or sixteen).
NONDISCRIMINATORY EVALUATION	The student must be evaluated in all areas of suspected disability and in a way that is not biased by his or her language or cultural characteristics or disabilities. Evaluation must be by a multidisciplinary team, and no single evaluation procedure may be used as the sole criterion for placement or planning.
CONFIDENTIALITY	The results of evaluation and placement must be kept confidential, though the student's parents or guardian may have access to the records.
PERSONNEL DEVELOPMENT, INSERVICE	Training must be provided for teachers and other professional personnel, including inservice training for regular teachers, in meeting the needs of students with disabilities.

Detailed federal rules and regulations govern the implementation of each of these major provisions. The definitions of some of these provisions—LRE and nondiscriminatory evaluation, for example—are still being clarified by federal officials and court decisions.

Trends in Litigation

Zelder (1953) noted that in the early days of public education, school attendance was seen as a *privilege* that could be awarded or withheld from an individual child at the discretion of local school officials. During the late-nineteenth and early-twentieth centuries, the courts typically found that disruptive children or those with mental retardation could be excluded from school for the sake of preserving order, protecting

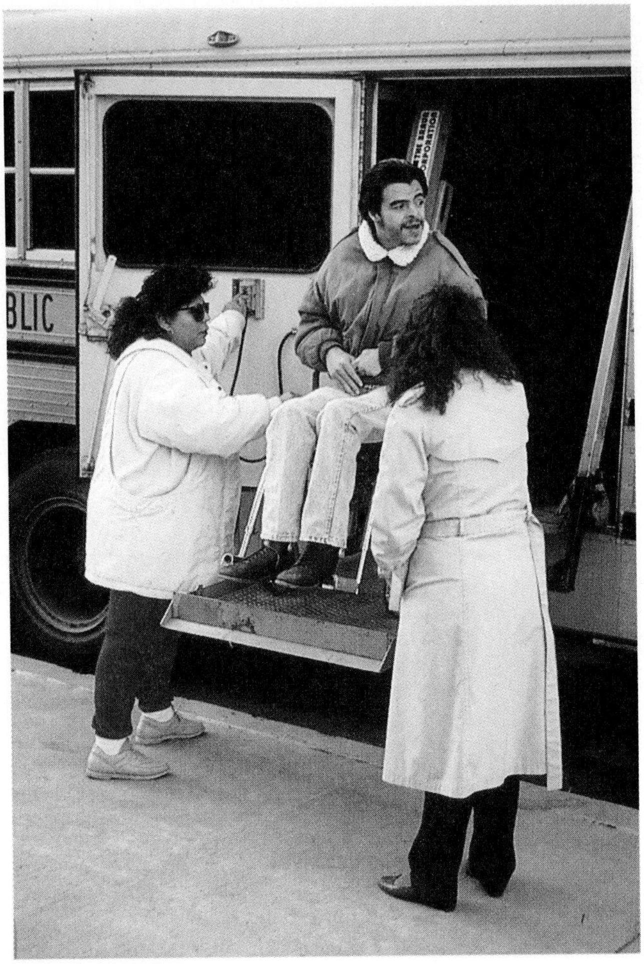

The Individuals with Disabilities Education Act (IDEA), passed in 1990, requires public schools to provide equal education opportunities for all students with disabilities.

the teacher's time from excessive demands, and sparing children the "pain" of seeing others who are disabled. In the first half of the twentieth century, the courts tended to defend the majority of school children from a disabled minority. But now, the old excuses for excluding students with disabilities from school are no longer thought to be valid. Today, the courts must interpret laws that define school attendance as the *right* of every child, regardless of his or her disability. Litigation is now focused on ensuring that every child receives an education *appropriate for his or her individual needs*.

Litigation may involve legal suits filed for either of two reasons: (1) because special education services are not being provided for students whose parents want them or (2) because students are being assigned to special education when their parents believe they should not be. Suits filed *for special education* have been brought primarily by parents whose children are unquestionably disabled and are being denied any education at all or being given very meager special services. The parents who file these suits believe that the advantages of their children's identification for special education services clearly outweigh the disadvantages. Suits *against special education* have been brought primarily by parents of students who have mild or questionable disabilities and who are already attending school. These parents believe that their children are being stigmatized and discriminated against rather than helped by special education. Thus, the courts today are asked to make decisions in which individual students' characteristics are weighed against specific educational programs.

Findings of Louis Harris/NOD Survey Employers Overwhelmingly Support the ADA—and Jobs

BUSINESS OWNERS WERE ASKED:
SHOULD THE ADA BE CHANGED?

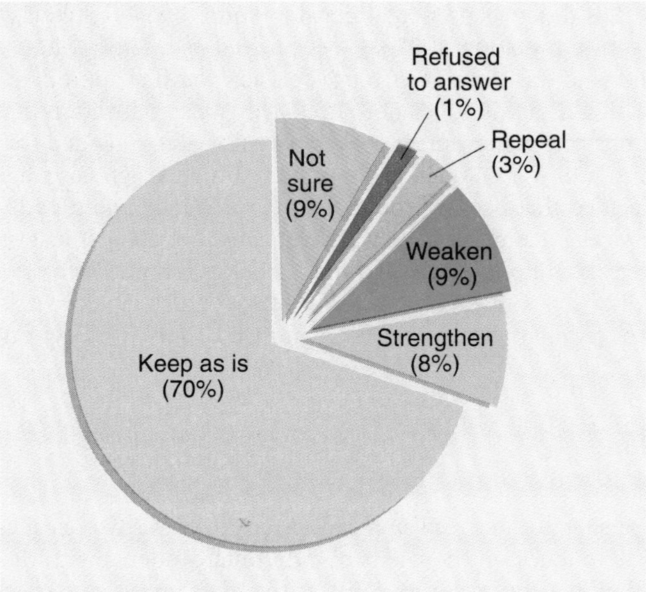

The number of corporate employers with policies and programs for hiring people with disabilities has increased substantially, from 46 percent to a current 57 percent.

- One of the most dramatic findings of this survey is that the number of companies that say accommodations have been made in the workplace has almost doubled since 1986. More than eight out of ten (81%) managers now say changes have been made as compared to 51 percent in 1986.
- However, the number of companies who have hired people with disabilities has scarcely changed. The number is up only very slightly to 64 percent in 1995 from 62 percent in 1986. While this overall increase is insignificant, among the larger and medium sized companies the change has been more pronounced. On the other hand smaller companies show a decrease from 54 percent to a current 48 percent.
- Corporate managers' attitudes toward the job performance of employees with disabilities are generally very positive. Very few (3% say only fair) give these employees negative marks. Furthermore, bringing more people with disabilities into the workforce is seen as being a real boost to the nation.
- The survey confirms the findings of earlier research that people with disabilities represent an untapped potential; fully 73 percent of employers see it that way. Comparably large numbers of employers also say that their employees would support policies to increase the number of people with disabilities.
- Three-quarters (75%) of the managers say they are likely to make greater efforts to hire people with disabilities in the next three years. Almost all corporate managers say that there will be at least the same amount of opportunity for people with disabilities. No one said that these opportunities would lessen.

The picture painted by this survey is not all positive towards employment of people with disabilities. The most important negative result involves costs.

- Twice as many managers today as compared to 1986 (27% vs. 14%) say that the average cost of employing a person with a disability is greater than employing a person without a disability. However, by an 82 percent to 5 percent margin, the top managers and EEO managers also say that these costs will be worth it.
- It is important to note that the costs of accommodation seem to be fairly modest. Among those executives who could provide figures, the median figure per accommodation is $223 per employee.

The direct impact of the ADA is difficult to gauge. However, the overwhelming majority of corporate employers are strongly supportive of the ADA. Knowledge and awareness of the law are nearly unanimous, as is support for its basic provisions. However, most managers also say that it has had no direct impact on their companies as yet.

- A large majority thinks that the ADA should not be changed. Only 12 percent think that the law should be weakened or even repealed. Eight percent say it should be strengthened.
- Those surveyed say that because of the ADA their costs to accommodate people with disabilities have increased. However, most say that the costs have increased only a little. This echoes the other results in the survey.

Generally, the corporate managers are strongly supportive of the basic ideas of the ADA even if they also say that the law has had little direct impact. Contrary to some reports in the media, there is no sign of a corporate backlash against the ADA. Change has occurred and seems likely to continue to do so in the future.

Source: From "Louis Harris/N.O.D. survey finds employers overwhelmingly support the ADA—and jobs," by H. Taylor, 1995, July 18, *The Washington Post,* p. A10.

Note: Humphrey Taylor is president of Louis Harris Associates, Inc. To obtain a copy of the NOD/Harris 1995 survey of Employment of People with Disabilities, write to: National Organization on Disability, 910 16th St. NW, Washington, DC 20006.

Parents want their children with disabilities to have a free public education that meets their needs but does not stigmatize them unnecessarily and that permits them to be taught in the regular school and classroom as much as possible. The laws governing education recognize parents' and students' rights to such an education. In the courts today, the burden of proof is ultimately on local and state education specialists, who must show in every instance that the student's abilities and disabilities have been completely and accurately assessed and that appropriate educational procedures are being employed.

One court case of the 1980s deserves particular consideration. In 1982, the U.S. Supreme Court made its first interpretation of PL 94–142 in *Hudson v. Rowley*, a case involving Amy Rowley, a child who was deaf. The Court's decision was that appropriate education for a deaf child with a disability does not necessarily mean education that will produce the maximum possible achievement. Amy's parents had contended that she might be able to learn more in school if she were provided with a sign language interpreter. But the Court decided that because the school had designed an individualized program of special services for Amy and she was achieving at or above the level of her nondisabled classmates, the school system had met its obligation under the law to provide an appropriate education. Court cases in the 1990s will undoubtedly help to clarify what the law means by *appropriate* education and *least restrictive* environment (Huefner, 1994).

The Intent of Legislation: An Individualized Education Program

The primary intent of the special education laws passed during the past two decades has been to require educators to focus on the needs of individual students with disabilities. The **individualized education program (IEP)** is the most important aspect of this focus; it spells out just what teachers plan to do to meet an exceptional student's needs, and the plan must be approved by the student's parents or guardian. IEPs vary greatly in format and detail and from one school district to another. Some school districts use computerized IEP systems to help teachers determine goals and instructional objectives and to save time and effort in writing the documents. Many school systems, however, still rely on teachers' knowledge of students and curriculum to complete handwritten IEPs on the district's forms. Federal and state regulations do not specify exactly how much detail must be included in an IEP, only that it must be a *written* statement developed in a meeting of a representative of the local school district, the teacher, the parents or guardian, and, whenever appropriate, the child, and that it must include certain elements (see the box on p. 35).

The IEPs written in most schools contain much information related to the technical requirements of IDEA in addition to the heart of the plans—their instructional components. According to Bateman (1996), five components of the IEP are central to legally correct and educationally useful plans:

1. unique characteristics or needs
2. present levels of performance
3. special education, related services, and modifications
4. instructional objectives
5. annual goals

Other components of IEPs may be necessary and useful, but these central components focus most clearly on what makes special education special: instruction that is individualized, intensive, relentless, urgent, and goal directed (see Zigmond & Baker, 1995).

individualized education program (IEP). PL 94–142 requires an IEP to be drawn up by the educational team for each exceptional child; the IEP must include a statement of present educational performance, instructional goals, educational services to be provided, and criteria and procedures for determining that the instructional objectives are being met.

Figures 1–6 and 1–7 contain excerpts from two IEPs written as suggested by Bateman (1996). Figure 1–6 shows the program for one behavior problem (noncompliance) and one curriculum area (reading) for Amy, an elementary student with mild mental retardation. Amy received special instruction in reading and math in a special self-contained class but was included in most other school activities with her nondisabled peers. (Remember that this IEP excerpt shows only the elements related to reading. An entire IEP may be a document of ten pages or more, depending on the format and the extent and complexity of the student's disabilities.) Figure 1–7, the second IEP, is for Curt, a ninth-grader who was low achieving and poorly motivated and posed a disciplinary problem. He was described by school personnel as having a "bad attitude" and by his parents as being "discouraged" and "frustrated." Curt had learning disabilities that were especially evident in the language arts.

Note that the two IEP excerpts contain the same types of information but presented in different formats. As mentioned earlier, there is no standard IEP format used by all schools. The emphasis should be on writing IEPs that are clear, useful, and legally defensible, not on the IEP format (Bateman, 1996). In both excerpts shown in Figures 1–6 and 1–7, the components are keyed to each other. These clear and explicit relationships among IEP components are required to make sure that the focus of the individualized program—special, individually tailored instruction to meet unique needs—is not lost. In Amy's IEP (Figure 1–6), each unique characteristic or need is numbered, and the subsequent descriptions of present levels of performance, special services, objectives, and goals are keyed back to the characteristic or need to which it is related. For instance, all the items labeled "2a" correspond to "Unique Characteristic or Need" number 2a: "Very slow reading rate." In Curt's IEP (Figure 1–7), the relationships among the components are maintained by the alignment of

Individualized Education Program (IEP)

WHAT IS AN IEP?

An IEP is a written agreement between the parents and the school about what the child needs and what will be done to address those needs. It is, in effect, a contract about services to be provided for the student. By law, an IEP must include the following:

1. the student's present levels of academic performance
2. annual goals for the student
3. short-term instructional objectives related to the annual goals
4. the special education and related services that will be provided and the extent to which the child will participate in regular education programs
5. plans for starting the services and the anticipated duration of the services
6. appropriate plans for evaluating, at least annually, whether the goals and objectives are being achieved.
7. for older students, plans for transition to work or further schooling.

ARE TEACHERS LEGALLY LIABLE FOR REACHING IEP GOALS?

No. Federal law does not require that the stated goals be met. However, teachers and other school personnel are responsible for seeing that the IEP is written to include the components listed, that the parents have an opportunity to review and participate in developing the IEP, that the IEP is approved by the parents before placement, and that the services called for in the IEP are actually provided. Teachers and other school personnel are responsible for making a good-faith effort to achieve the goals and objectives of the IEP.

information across columns. Reading across the form, we first read a description of the unique characteristic or need, then the special services and modifications needed to address that need, and then the present levels, instructional objectives, and goals related to the need. Note that one unique need is stated as a "present level" of performance (see upper-left corner, "Lashes out . . .") and that modifications to the regular program are written at the end of the IEP across the first two columns.

The process of writing an IEP and the document itself are perhaps the most important features of compliance with the spirit and letter of IDEA. When the IEP is prepared as intended by the law, it means that:

- The student's needs have been carefully assessed.
- A team of professionals and the parents have worked together to design a program of education to best meet the student's needs.
- Goals and objectives are clearly stated so that progress in reaching them can be evaluated.

Government regulation of the IEP process has always been controversial. Some of the people who were influential in formulating the basic law (IDEA) have expressed great disappointment in the results of requiring IEPs (Goodman & Bond, 1993, p. 413). Others question whether the requirement of long-term and short-term objectives is appropriate:

> The IEP assumes that instructors know in advance what a child should and can learn, and the speed at which he or she will learn. . . . This is a difficult projection to make with nondisabled children of school age—for preschool children with cognitive, emotional, and social disabilities, it is near impossible. (Goodman & Bond, 1993, p. 415)

A major problem is that the IEP—the educational *program*—is too often written at the wrong time and for the wrong reason (Bateman, 1996). As illustrated in Figure 1–8, the legal IEP is written following evaluation and identification of the student's disabilities and *before* a placement decision is made; what the student needs is determined first, and then a decision is made about placement in the least restrictive environment in which the needed services can be provided. Too often, we see the educationally wrong (and illegal) practice of basing the IEP on an available placement; that is, the student's IEP is written *after* available placements and services are considered.

Writing IEPs that meet all the requirements of the law and that are also educationally useful is no small task. Computerized IEPs and those based only on standardized testing or developmental inventories are likely to violate the requirements of the law or be of little educational value or both (Bateman, 1996; Goodman & Bond, 1993). However, much of the controversy about IEPs and the disappointment in them appear to result from misunderstanding of the law or lack of instructional expertise or both. Within the framework of IDEA and other regulations, it is possible to write IEPs that are both legally correct and educationally useful (Bateman, 1996).

Legislation and litigation were initially used in the 1960s and 1970s to include exceptional children in public education with relatively little regard for quality. In the 1980s and 1990s, laws and lawsuits have been used to try to ensure individualized education, cooperation, and collaboration among professionals; parental participation; and accountability of educators for providing high-quality, effective programs.

PL 99–457 and IDEA, for example, are noteworthy for their expansion of the idea of individualized planning and collaboration among disciplines. PL 99–457 mandated an **individualized family service plan (IFSP)** for infants and toddlers

individualized family service plan (IFSP). A plan for services for young children with disabilities (under 3 years of age) and their families drawn up by professionals and parents; similar to an IEP for older children, mandated by PL 99-457.

INDIVIDUALIZED EDUCATION PROGRAM

Student: *Amy North* **Age:** *9* **Grade:** *1* **Date:** *Oct. 17.1995*

1. Unique Characteristics or Needs: Noncompliance

Frequently noncompliant with teacher's instructions

1. Present Levels of Performance
   Complies with about 50% of teacher requests/commands
2. Special Education, Related Services, and Modifications
   Implemented immediately, strong reinforcement for compliance with teacher's instructions (Example: "Sure I will!" plan including precision requests and reinforcer menu for points earned for compliance, as described in The Tough Kid Book, by Rhode, Jenson, & Reavis, 1992); within 3 weeks, training of parents by school psychologist to use precision requests and reinforcement at home.
3. Objectives (Including Procedures, Criteria, and Schedule)
   Within one month, will comply with teacher requests/commands 90% of the time; compliance monitored weekly by teacher
4. Annual Goals
   Will become compliant with teacher's requests/commands

2. Unique Characteristics or Needs: Reading

2a. Very slow reading rate
2b. Poor comprehension
2c. Limited phonics skills
2d. Limited sight-word vocabulary

1. Present Levels of Performance
   2a. Reads stories of approximately 100 words on first-grade level at approximately 40 words per min.
   2b. Seldom can recall factual information about stories immediately after reading them
   2c. Consistently confuses vowel sounds, often misidentifies consonants, and does not blend sounds
   2d. Has sight-word vocabulary of approximately 150 words
2. Special Education, Related Services, and Modifications
   2a–2c. Direct instruction 30 minutes daily in vowel discrimination, consonant identification, and sound blending; begin immediately, continue throughout schoolyear
   2a & 2d. Sight word drill 10 minutes daily in addition to phonics instruction and daily practice; 10 minutes practice in using phonics and sight-word skills in reading story at her level; begin immediately, continue for schoolyear
3. Objectives (Including Procedures, Criteria, and Schedule)
   2a. Within 3 months, will read stories on her level at 60 words per minute with 2 or fewer errors per story; within six months, 80 words with 2 or fewer errors; performance monitored daily by teacher or aide
   2b. Within 3 months will answer oral and written comprehension questions requiring recall of information from stories she has just read with 90% accuracy (e.g., Who is in the story? What happened? When? Why?) and be able to predict probable outcomes with 80% accuracy; performance monitored daily by teacher or aide
   2c. Within 3 months, will increase sight-word vocabulary to 200 words, within 6 months to 250 words, assessed by flashcard presentation
4. Annual Goals
   2a–2c. Will read fluently and with comprehension at beginning-second-grade level.

Figure 1–6
Sample Excerpt of the IEP for Amy.

INDIVIDUALIZED EDUCATION PROGRAM

Student: Curt **Age:** 15 **Grade:** 9 **Date:** 10/12/94

Unique Characteristics/Needs	Special Education, Related Services, Modifications	(begin duration)	Present Levels, Objectives, Annual Goals (Objectives to include procedure, criteria, schedule)
Social Needs: — To learn anger management skills, especially regarding swearing — To learn to comply with requests	1. Teacher and/or counselor consult with behavior specialist regarding techniques and programs for teaching social skills especially anger management.		Goal: During the last quarter of the academic year, Curt will have 2 or fewer detentions for any reason.
	2. Provide anger management training for Curt.	30 min., 3 X week	Objective 1: At the end of the 1st quarter, Curt will have had 10 or fewer detentions.
Present Level: Lashes out violently when not able to complete work, uses profane language, and refuses to follow further directions from adults	3. Establish a peer group which involves role playing, etc. so Curt can see positive role models and practice newly learned anger management skills.	30 min., 2 X week	Objective 2: At the end of 2nd quarter, Curt will have had 7 or fewer detentions. Objective 3: At the end of 3rd quarter, Curt will have had 4 or fewer detentions.
	4. Develop a behavior plan for Curt which gives him responsibility for charting his own behavior.		Goal: Curt will manage his behavior and language in a reasonably acceptable manner as reported by faculty/peers.
	5. Provide a teacher or some other adult mentor to spend time with Curt (could be talking, game play, physical activity).	30 min., 2 X week	Objective 1: At 2 weeks, asked at end of class if Curt's behavior language was acceptable or not, 3 out of 5 teachers will say "acceptable."
	6. Provide training for the mentor regarding Curt's needs/goals.		Objective 2: At 6 weeks, asked same question, 4 out of 6 teachers will say "acceptable." Objective 3: At 12 weeks, 6 out of 6 will say "acceptable."

Adaptations to regular program:
— In all classes, Curt should be seated near front of class
— Curt should be called on often to keep him involved and on task
— All teachers should help Curt with study skills as trained by spelling/language specialist and resource room teacher
— Teachers should monitor Curt's work closely in the beginning weeks/months of his program

Figure 1–7 Sample Excerpt of the IEP for Curt. (*Source:* From *Better IEPs* [2nd ed.], by B. D. Bateman, 1996, Longmont, Co: Sopris West. Copyright © 1996 by Barbara D. Bateman. Used with permission.)

Unique Characteristics/Needs:	Special Education, Related Services, Modifications	(begin duration)	Present Levels, Objectives, Annual Goals (Objectives to include procedure, criteria, schedule)
Study skills/organization — How to read text — Note taking — How to study — Memory work — Be prepared for class with materials — Lengthen and improve attention span and on-task behavior	1. Speech/lang. therapist. Resource room teacher and contact area teachers will provide Curt with direct and specific teaching of study skills. i.e. — note taking from lectures — note taking while reading text — how to study notes for a test — remorization hints — strategies for reading text to retain information 2. Assign a "study buddy" for Curt in each content area class. 3. Prepare a motivation system for Curt to be prepared for class with all necessary materials. Curt should be responsible for making and keeping checklist and being accountable to one teacher at end of each day. 4. Develop a motivational plan to encourage Curt to lengthen his attention span and time on task.		Goal: At end of academic year, Curt will have better grades and by his own report: will have learned new study skills. Objective 1: Given a 20–30 min. lecture/oral lesson, Curt will take appropriate notes as judged by that teacher. Objective 2: Given 10–15 pgs. of text to read, Curt will employ an appropriate strategy for retaining info.—i.e., mapping, webbing, outlining, notes, etc—as judged by the teacher. Objective 3: Given notes to study for a test, Curt will do so successfully as evidenced by his test score. Present Level: See Characteristics
Academic Needs/Written Language			
— Needs strong remedial help in spelling, punctuation, capitalization, and usage	1. Provide aide to monitor on-task behaviors in first month or so of plan and teach Curt self-monitoring techniques. 2. Provide motivational system and self-recording form for completion of academic tasks in each class. — Provide direct instruction in written language skills (punctuation, capitalization, usage, spelling) by using a highly structured, well-sequenced program. — 50 minutes daily in res. rm. in small group of no more than 4. — Build in continuous and cumulative review to help with short-term rote memory difficulty. — Develop a list of commonly used words in student writing (or use one of many published lists) for Curt's spelling program.		Goal: Curt will improve his on-task behavior from 37% to 80% as measured by a qualified observer at year's end. Objective 1: By 1 month, Curt's on-task behavior will increase to 45%. Objective 2: By 3 months, Curt's on-task behavior will increase to 60%. Objective 3: By 6 months, Curt's on-task behavior will increase to 80% and maintain or improve until end of year. Present Level: See Characteristics.

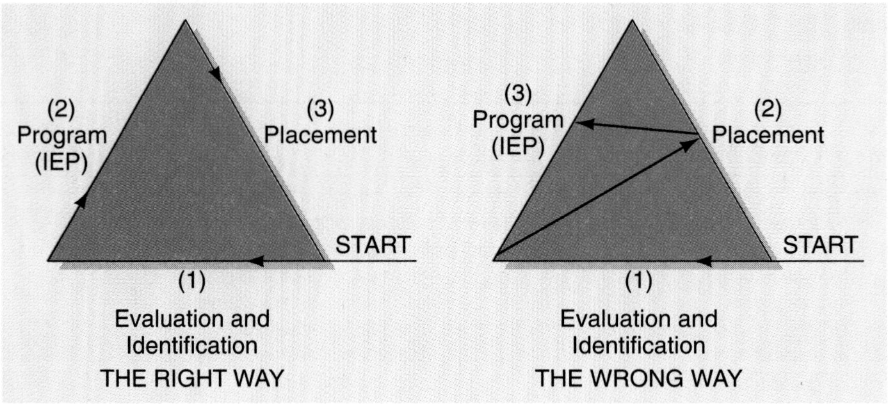

Figure 1–8

The right way and the wrong way to determine placement.

(*Source:* From *Better IEPs* [2nd ed.], by B. D. Bateman, 1996, Longmont, Co: Sopris West. Copyright © 1996 by Barbara D. Bateman. Used with permission.)

with disabilities. An IFSP is similar to an IEP for older children in that it requires assessment and statement of goals, needed services, and plans for implementation. As we discuss in Chapter 2, an IFSP also requires more involvement of the family, coordination of services, and plans for making the transition into preschool. IDEA mandated the inclusion of plans for transition from school to work for older students as part of their IEPs. Other provisions of IDEA are intended to improve the quality of services received by children and youths with disabilities.

A PERSPECTIVE ON THE PROGRESS OF SPECIAL EDUCATION

Special education has come a long way since it was introduced into American public education over a century ago. It has become an expected part of the U.S. public education system, a given rather than an exception or an experiment. Much progress has been made since PL 94–142 (now IDEA) was enacted about two decades ago. Now parents and their children have legal rights to free, appropriate education; they are not powerless in the face of school administrators who do not want to provide appropriate education and related services. The enactment of PL 94–142 (IDEA) was one of very few events in the twentieth century that altered the power relationship between schools and parents (Sarason, 1990).

We can best illustrate some of the progress special education has made by returning to an example used in discussing the educational definition of exceptional children and youths. Recall our earlier discussion of the accomplishments of Aaron Farley and the special education he received (see p.11). Aaron's special education was important in helping him achieve what he has. Nevertheless, his education was not all that it might have been. Had Aaron been born a decade later, his education might have allowed him to achieve even more. Aaron's father, a special education teacher of students with emotional and behavioral disorders, notes the positive changes that have occurred since Aaron was an infant. Aaron's brother John, who is eleven years younger than Aaron and also deaf, is receiving better educational services. His hearing impairment was diagnosed at the age of two weeks (recall that Aaron's was not diagnosed until he was two years old). John's special training, therefore, began much earlier than Aaron's. John was fitted with an auditory trainer (a type of hearing aid; see Chapter 8) at a very early age, and he uses this device constantly in school, an advantage Aaron did not have. He goes to a resource room for an hour each day and receives speech-language therapy in addition; the rest of the time, he is in regular classes and uses his auditory trainer. John is also accompanied by a cued speech transliterator, who allows him to have equal access to all speech communication and environmental sounds at all times. Compared to Aaron, he is included much more of the school day in activities with hearing children. Now in middle school, John is reading on grade level. Aaron never attained grade-level reading skills, although clearly he has high intellectual ability; his reading level is more typical of students with profound deafness who were not diagnosed early and have not had early, intensive language instruction.

The differences between Aaron's and John's educations, their academic and social progress, and their opportunities for socialization might be explained in several ways. We must be aware that their parents learned from their experience with Aaron and were thus better prepared to nurture and advocate for John. Yet their parents' greater preparedness for John's education does not tell the whole story. The public schools, too, learned from their experience with Aaron and other students with disabilities and were encouraged by legislation and parent advocacy to provide better programs. Aaron was born before PL 94–142 was enacted. The law, passed in 1975, went into effect in 1978, four years after Aaron's birth. By the time John was born in 1981, schools had already been implementing the law for several years. By then, school administrators and teachers knew more about accommodating students with disabilities and working with parents to provide the services that these students' parents agree are appropriate. Whereas Aaron was provided a full-time cued speech transliterator only after his parents secured a court order through a lawsuit, John was provided this service without court action.

In spite of the fact that IDEA and related laws and court cases have not resulted in flawless programs for exceptional children, they have done much to move American public schools toward providing better educational opportunities for those with disabilities. Laws like PL 99–457 (see p. 29) help ensure that, like John Farley, all infants and toddlers with disabilities will receive early intervention. Laws like ADA (see p. 29) help ensure that young adults like Aaron Farley will not be discriminated against in U.S. society. Laws and court cases cannot eliminate all problems in our society, but they can certainly be of enormous help in our efforts to equalize opportunities and minimize handicaps for people with disabilities.

We have made much progress in special education, but making it all that we hope for is—and always will be—a continuing struggle. In Chapter 2, we discuss current trends and issues that highlight dissatisfaction with the way things are and represent hope for what special education and related services might become.

SUMMARY

The study of exceptional children is the study of similarities and differences among individuals. Exceptional children differ from most others in specific ways, but they are also similar to most others in most respects. Children's exceptionalities—their differences—must not be allowed to obscure the ways in which they are like others. We distinguish between an exceptionality that is a disability and one that is a handicap. A *disability* is an inability to do something. A *handicap* is a disadvantage that may be imposed on an individual. A disability may or may not be a handicap.

For purposes of education, *exceptional children and youths* are defined as those who require special education and related services if they are to realize their full human potential. Special education strives to make certain that students' handicaps are confined to those characteristics that cannot be changed.

Current government figures show that approximately one student in ten is identified as exceptional and receiving special education services. Most children and youths identified as exceptional are between the ages of six and seventeen, although identification of infants and young adults with disabilities is increasing.

Special education refers to specially designed instruction that meets the unusual needs of exceptional children and youths. The single most important goal of special education is finding and capitalizing on exceptional students' abilities. Special education may be provided under a variety of administrative plans. Some exceptional students are served in the regular classroom by their regular classroom teacher, sometimes in consultation with other professionals, such as psychologists or teachers with more experience or training. Some are served by an itinerant teacher who moves from school to school or by a resource teacher. Itinerant and resource teachers may teach students individually or in small groups for certain periods of the school day and provide assistance to regular classroom teachers. Sometimes children are placed in a diagnostic-prescriptive center so their special needs can be determined. The special self-contained class is used for a small group of students, who are usually taught in the special class all or most of the day. Special day schools are sometimes provided for students whose disabilities necessitate special equipment and methods for care and education. Hospital and homebound instruction are provided when the student is unable to go to regular classes. Finally, the residential school provides educational services and management of the daily living environment for students with disabilities who must receive full-time care.

Present law requires that every exceptional child and youth be placed in the least restrictive environment (LRE) so that educational intervention will be consistent with individual needs and not interfere with individual freedom and the development of potential. Today, therefore, most students with exceptionalities are educated primarily in regular classes.

All teachers need to be prepared to some extent to deal with exceptional students because many of these students are placed for part of the day in regular classrooms. Furthermore, many students not identified as exceptional share some of the characteristics of disability or giftedness. Although the relationship between general and special education must be one of collaboration and shared responsibility for exceptional students, the roles of special and general educators are not always clear. Both may be involved in educating exceptional students by making maximum efforts to accommodate individual students' needs, evaluating academic abilities and disabilities, referring students for further evaluation, participating in eligibility conferences, writing individualized education programs, (IEPs)—communicating with parents, participating in due process hearings, and collaborating with other professionals. In addition, special educators must have particular expertise in instructing students with learning problems, managing serious behavioral problems, using technological aids, and interpreting special education law.

Systematic attempts to educate children with disabilities, especially those with mental retardation and emotional and behavioral disorders, began in the early 1800s. European physicians like Itard, Pinel, and Séguin pioneered in these educational efforts. Their revolutionary ideas included individualized instruction, carefully sequenced series of educational tasks, emphasis on stimulation and the awakening of the child's senses, meticulous arrangement of the child's environment, immediate reward for correct performance, tutoring in functional skills, and the belief that every child should be educated to the greatest extent possible. Howe and Gallaudet brought special education techniques and ideas to the United States.

Many other disciplines, especially psychology and sociology, were involved in the emergence of special education as a profession. Much of the progress in special education has resulted from the efforts of professional and parent organizations. The Council for Exceptional Children (CEC) is an influential group with many divisions devoted to such things as the study of specific exceptionalities; the administration, supervision, and implementation of special programs; teacher training and placement; and research. Organizations such as the ARC provide parents, schools, and the public with information about exceptionalities and the structure for obtaining needed services.

The legal basis of special education has evolved over the years from permissive legislation, allowing public funding of special programs for exceptional children, to mandatory legislation, requiring such expenditures. The contemporary commitment to the principle that every individual has the right to as normal a life and education as possible prompted much legislation and litigation in the 1970s and 1980s. Special education legislation has historically been increasingly specific and mandatory. The Individuals with Disabilities Education Act (IDEA) mandated that in order to receive funds under the act, *every school system in the country must make provision for a free, appropriate education for every child with a disability.*

Laws and regulations may have little effect until their meanings are interpreted by the courts through litigation. Litigation today focuses on ensuring that every exceptional child and youth receives an education that is appropriate for his or her individual needs. Lawsuits *for* special education tend to be filed on behalf of students who are unquestionably disabled but are receiving no education at all or only meager services. Lawsuits *against* special education tend to be filed on behalf of students whose disabilities are mild or questionable and for whom special education is thought to be more stigmatizing and discriminatory than helpful. Future court cases will undoubtedly result in clarification of the term *appropriate* with reference to education for exceptional students.

The primary intent of special education legislation has been to require educators to focus on the needs of individual students. Thus, a central feature of IDEA is the requirement that every student receiving special education under the law must have an individualized education program (IEP). An IEP is a written plan, which must be approved by the child's parents or guardian, that specifies the following: (1) the student's current level of performance; (2) annual goals; (3) instructional objectives; (4) special services to be provided and the extent to which the student will participate in regular education; (5) plans for starting services and their expected duration; (6) plans for evaluation; and (7) for older students, the services needed to ensure a successful transition from school to work or higher education. These goals are based on the view that special education must be *individualized, intensive, relentless, urgent, and goal directed.*

Special education has made much progress during the past century. It is now an expected part of American public education, not an exception or experiment. Parents of students with disabilities now have more involvement in their children's education. In part, this progress has occurred because of laws requiring appropriate education and other services for individuals with disabilities.

Louise Bego
Louise Bego, a resident of Michigan, has overcome the effects of a closed-head injury and the trauma and memory loss caused by an automobile accident in 1973. She now paints full-time, working mostly in abstract acrylics. Ms. Bego competes in local and statewide competitions and has been a member of the Very Special Arts Gallery registry since 1993.

2

Current Trends and Issues

Come writers and critics
Who prophesy with your pen
And keep your eyes wide,
The chance won't come again.
And don't speak too soon
For the wheel's still in spin
And there's no tellin' who
That it's namin'
For the loser now
Will be later to win
For the times they are
a-changin'.

Bob Dylan
"The Times They Are A-Changin'"

Bob Dylan could have written his song "The Times They Are A-Changin' " (see excerpt on p. 45) for the field of special education, which has a rich history of controversy and change. In fact, controversy and change are what make the teaching and study of people with disabilities so challenging and exciting. The 1980s and 1990s have seen especially dramatic changes in the education of people with disabilities, and current thinking indicates that the field is poised for still more changes.

In this chapter, we explore three major trends in the field and issues related to them. The first trend is for people with disabilities to be more integrated with the larger, nondisabled society. The second is for greater emphasis to be placed on early intervention. And the third is for a greater emphasis to be placed on programming for transition from secondary school to adulthood.

INTEGRATION

The trend of integrating people with disabilities into the larger society began in the 1960s and continues stronger than ever today. Champions of integration are proud of the fact that they have reduced the number of people with disabilities who reside in institutions and the number of special education students who attend special schools and special self-contained classes. Some of today's more radical proponents of integration, however, will not be satisfied until virtually all institutions, special schools, and special classes are eliminated. These proponents recommend that all students with disabilities be educated in regular classes. And even today's more conservative advocates of integration recommend a much greater degree of interaction between students with and without disabilities than was ever dreamed of by most special educators in the 1960s and 1970s.

This movement toward more integration has led to some of the bloodiest professional battles ever waged in the field of special education. The disputes between radical integrationists and those of a more conservative persuasion have threatened to rip apart the field of special education. No matter whose point of view ultimately prevails, it is fair to say that there will be dramatic changes over the next few years in how and especially where we educate students with disabilities.

Philosophical Roots: The Principle of Normalization

A key principle behind the trend toward more integration of people with disabilities into society is normalization. First espoused in Scandinavia (Bank-Mikkelsen, 1969) before being popularized in the United States, **normalization** is the philosophical belief that we should use "means which are as culturally normative as possible, in order to establish and/or maintain personal behaviors and characteristics which are as culturally normative as possible" (Wolfensberger, 1972, p. 28). In other words, under the principle of normalization, both the means and the ends of education for students with disabilities should be as much like those for nondisabled students as possible. Regarding the means, for example, we should place students with disabilities in educational settings as similar to those of nondisabled students as possible. And we should use treatment approaches that are as close as possible to the ones we use with the rest of the student population. Regarding the ends, we should strive to help students with disabilities weave into the larger fabric of society.

normalization. A philosophical belief in special education that every individual, even the most disabled, should have an educational and living environment as close to normal as possible.

Misconceptions about Persons with Disabilities

Myth Normalization, the philosophical principle that dictates that the means and ends of education for students with disabilities should be as culturally normative as possible, is a straightforward concept with little room for interpretation.

Fact There are many disagreements pertaining to the interpretation of the normalization principle. As just one example, some educators have interpreted it to mean that all people with disabilities must be educated in regular classes, whereas others maintain that a continuum of placements (residential schools, special schools, special classes, resource rooms, regular classes) should remain available as options.

Myth All professionals agree that technology should be used to its fullest to aid people with disabilities.

Fact Some believe that technology should be used cautiously because it can lead people with disabilities to become too dependent on it. Some professionals believe that people with disabilities can be tempted to rely on technology, rather than develop their own abilities.

Myth Research has established beyond a doubt that special classes are ineffective and that mainstreaming is effective.

Fact Research comparing special versus mainstream placement has been inconclusive because most of these studies have been methodologically flawed. Researchers are now focusing on finding ways of making mainstreaming work more effectively.

Myth Professionals agree that labeling people with disabilities (e.g., "retarded," "blind," "behavior disordered") is more harmful than helpful.

Fact Some professionals maintain that labels help them communicate, explain the atypical behavior of some people with disabilities to the public, and spotlight the special needs of people with disabilities for the general public.

Myth People with disabilities are pleased with the way the media portrays them, especially in stories about the extraordinary achievements of such persons.

Fact Some disability rights advocates are disturbed with what they believe are too frequent overly negative *and* overly positive portrayals in the media.

Myth Everyone agrees that teachers in early intervention programs need to assess parents as well as their children.

Fact Some authorities now believe that, although families are an important part of intervention programming and should be involved in some way, special educators should center their assessment efforts primarily on the child, not the parents.

Myth Everyone agrees that good early childhood programming for students with disabilities should follow the same guidelines as that for nondisabled preschoolers.

Fact There is considerable disagreement about whether early intervention programming for children with disabilities should be child directed, as is typical of regular preschool programs, or more teacher directed.

Myth Professionals agree that all students with disabilities in secondary school should be given a curriculum focused on vocational preparation.

Fact Professionals are in conflict over how much vocational versus academic instruction students with mild disabilities should receive.

Although on the face of it, the principle of normalization seems simple enough, numerous controversies have swirled around the implementation of this important concept. We shall mention three of the more hotly contested issues:

1. The phrase *as culturally normative as possible* is open to interpretation. Even though the originators of the normalization principle saw the need for a variety of service delivery options—including residential institutions, special schools, and special classes—more recently, some have interpreted normalization to mean the abolishment of such separate settings.
2. Some groups of people with disabilities are leery about being too closely integrated with nondisabled society. For example, some people who are deaf, because of their difficulty in communicating with the hearing world, prefer associating with other people who are deaf. For them, normalization does not translate into integration with the larger society (Lord, 1991; Padden & Humphries, 1988).
3. Some have questioned whether the rapidly expanding use of technology to assist people with disabilities actually works against the goal of normalization. Certainly, there is little doubt that technology has made it possible for more and more people with disabilities to take part in activities that previously were inaccessible to them. Thus, in many instances, technology serves as a means for achieving normalization. Some people with disabilities, however, have expressed concern that individuals might be too quick to rely on technology instead of working to improve their own abilities. Reliance on artificial means of interacting with the environment when more natural means are possible could jeopardize a person's quest for normalization.

Just how sensitive some people with disabilities are to the issue of technology and independence is captured in the following incident. The National Federation of the Blind of New Mexico was upset about an electronic guidance system being used at the University of New Mexico. In this system, wires under the floor transmit a signal to an electronic cane. The cane acts as a receiver, beeping whenever it is near a wire. Fred Schroeder, president of the federation, wrote a letter to the developer of the electronic system in which he listed his complaints:

> The guidance system which you have installed . . . poses a limitation to independent travel rather than an opening of new freedom of movement for the blind.
>
> The fundamental problem with an electronic guidance system is the philosophical premise upon which it is based. The underlying attitude behind its creation stems from an image of the hopeless, helpless blind groping their way timidly through the world fraught with danger and uncertainty.
>
> By installing an electronic guidance system the public is reinforced in its belief that the blind are unable to travel without elaborate accommodation. . . . Our success in improving social and economic conditions for the blind has come from our ability to adapt ourselves to the world rather than relying on the benevolence of the world to adapt to us.

As technology becomes ever more sophisticated, the issue of independence will become ever more important. One general guideline might be that if the technology allows people with disabilities to do something they could not do without it, then the technology is in their best interest. If, however, it allows them to do something new or better but at the same time imposes new limitations, then one might need to rethink the technology's benefits.

Protests by disability rights activists are reminiscent of and perhaps direct descendants of the Civil Rights protests of the 1960s.

Historical Roots: Deinstitutionalization and the Regular Education Initiative

The idea of integrating people with disabilities into society is hardly new. Professionals have been advocating for and implementing programs of integration for 30 or 40 years. Although the amount of interaction between people with and without disabilities has increased relatively steadily over this time, two movements have helped speed up integration: deinstitutionalization and the regular education initiative.

Deinstitutionalization. At one time it was common to place children and adults with retardation and/or mental illness in residential institutions, especially if they had relatively severe problems. The 1960s and 1970s, however, witnessed a systematic drive to move people out of institutions and back into closer contact with the community. Referred to as **deinstitutionalization**, this movement caused more and more children with disabilities to be raised by their families. Today, smaller facilities, located within local neighborhoods, are now common. Halfway houses exist as placements for individuals with emotional difficulties who no longer need the more isolated environment of a large institution. For people with mental retardation, group homes house small numbers of individuals whose retardation may range from mild to severe. More and more people with disabilities are now working, with assistance from "job coaches," in competitive employment situations.

A major impetus for deinstitutionalization was the recognition by both the general public and the special education profession that many large institutions of the 1960s were offering grossly inadequate care. The publication of the classic *Christmas in Purgatory* (Blatt & Kaplan, 1966), a pictorial essay on the squalid conditions of institutional life, did much to raise the sentiment against institutions. This book and others like it have shown how bad residential living *can be* for persons with disabilities.

deinstitutionalization. A social movement of the 1960s and 1970s whereby large numbers of persons with mental retardation and/or mental illness were moved from large mental institutions into smaller community homes or into the homes of their families; recognized as a major catalyst for integrating persons with disabilities into society.

We emphasize *can be* because some professionals maintain that residential institutions, even large ones, need not be sordid (Crissey & Rosen, 1986; Landesman & Butterfield, 1987; Zigler, Hodapp, & Edison, 1990). They point out that not all institutions are alike. Smallness and proximity to the community do not guarantee high quality. Very small homes, located in community settings, can be every bit as dehumanizing as large institutions. and large institutions can provide very humane treatment for their residents.

Some professionals assert that deinstitutionalization has been implemented, in certain cases, without much forethought. They maintain that although deinstitutionalization has the potential to improve the quality of life for most people who, in previous generations, would have been lifelong residents of institutions, it has failed other people because of poor planning. Some individuals, for instance, have been turned out of institutions onto the streets without making adequate living arrangements for them. Research in this area has made it evident that much still needs to be done to improve the quality of life for some persons with disabilities who have been released from institutions (Kauffman & Hallahan, 1992).

The Regular Education Initiative. The **regular education initiative (REI)**, was first formally introduced by former Assistant Secretary of Education Madeleine C. Will. Through speeches and articles, Will (1986) called for general educators to become more responsible for the education of students who have special needs in school, including those who are economically disadvantaged and those who are bilingual, as well as those with disabilities.

For several years before Will's directive, special educators had advocated **mainstreaming,** which is the practice of placing students with disabilities in classes and schools with their nondisabled peers. These placements can be for all or part of the day and for all or only a few subjects. For example, a student might be mainstreamed for physical education, art, and math but served in a special education resource room for language arts. An important assumption of mainstreaming is that students with disabilities are primarily the responsibility of the special education system, *not* the general education system. In other words, students are identified as special education students, and special educators assume primary responsibility for their overall educational programming.

Advocates of REI saw mainstreaming as only a half-hearted attempt to integrate students with disabilities into general education. Will (1986) questioned the legitimacy of special education as a system of education distinct from general education. And as a high-ranking government official, she lent official sanction to the notion that general education should take over many of the functions traditionally thought the province of special education.

regular education initiative (REI). A philosophy that maintains that general education, rather than special education, should be primarily responsible for educating students with disabilities.

mainstreaming. The placement of students with disabilities in general education classes for all or part of the day and for all or only a few classes; special education teachers maintain the primary responsibility for students with disabilities.

full inclusion. All students with disabilities are placed in their neighborhood schools in general education classrooms for the entire day; general education teachers have the primary responsibility for students with disabilities.

Full Inclusion

Questions raised by REI advocates soon led to calls for **full inclusion.** Although there are different conceptualizations of what this term means (Laski, 1991; Sailor, 1991; Stainback & Stainback, 1992), most definitions contain the following elements:

1. *All* students with disabilities—no matter the types or severities of disabilities—attend all classes in general education. In other words, there are *no* separate special education classes.
2. All students with disabilities attend their neighborhood schools (i.e., the one they would normally go to if they had no disabilities).

3. General education, not special education, assumes primary responsibility for students with disabilities.

With regard to this last point, some full-inclusionists propose the total elimination of special education. Others hold that professionals such as special educators and speech therapists are still needed but that their main duties should be carried out in general education classrooms along with general education teachers.

Full Inclusion versus a Continuum of Placements

Educational programming for students with disabilities has traditionally been built on the assumption that a variety of service delivery options need to be available. As mentioned in Chapter 1, special education law stipulates that schools place students with disabilities in the least restrictive environment (LRE). The notion of LRE assumes that there are alternatives along a continuum of restrictiveness, with residential institutions on one end and regular classes on the other. For the most part, special educators have been proud of this continuum of placements. They have viewed the LRE concept as the lifeblood of special education, something they fought hard to get enacted into law. Before LRE was enacted into law, school personnel were free to claim that they did not have services for children with disabilities and to deny these children access to regular classes.

Advocates of full inclusion, however, favor eliminating a continuum of placements:

> Three generations of children subject to LRE are enough. Just as some institution managers and their organizations—both overt and covert—seek refuge in the continuum and LRE, regional, intermediate unit, and special school administrators and their organizations will continue to defend the traditional and professionally pliable notion of LRE. The continuum is real and represents the status quo. However, the morass created by it can be avoided in the design and implementation of reformed

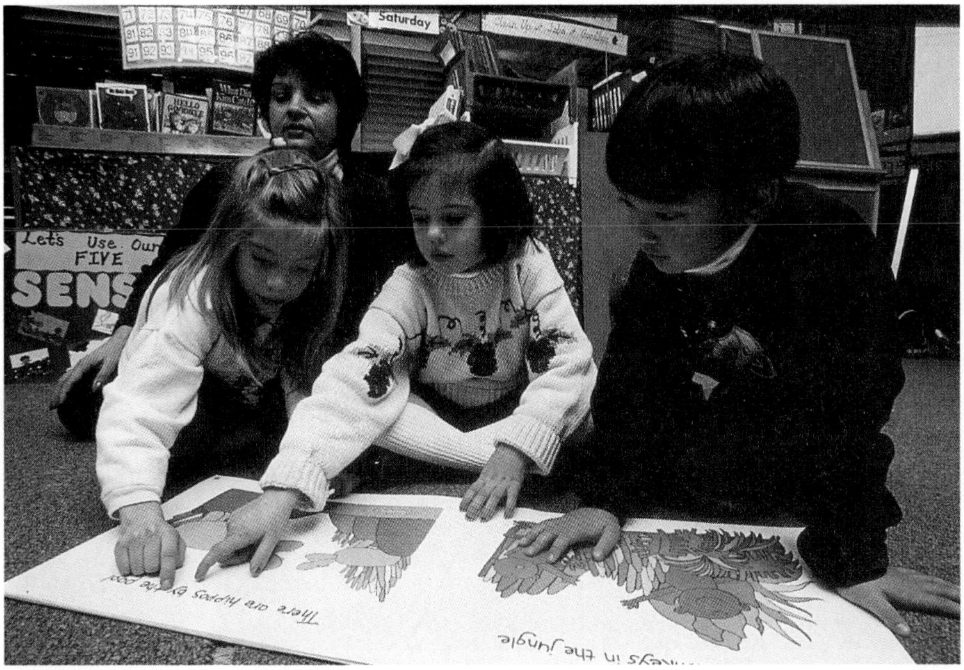

Some advocates of full inclusion feel that all students, regardless of the severity of their disabilities, should be mainstreamed in regular classroom settings.

> systems by focusing all placement questions on the local school and routinely insisting on the home school as an absolute and universal requirement. In terms of placement, the home-school focus renders LRE irrelevant and the continuum moot. (Laski, 1991, p. 413)

Premises of Full Inclusion Those who advocate full inclusion base their position on at least the following four premises:

1. Labeling people is harmful.
2. Special education pull-out programs have been ineffective.
3. People with disabilities should be viewed as a minority group.
4. Ethics should take precedence over empiricism.

We consider each of these premises in the sections that follow.

Labeling Is Harmful. Some people fear that a "special education" label can cause a child to feel unworthy or to be viewed by the rest of society as a deviant and hence grow to feel unworthy. This fear is not entirely unfounded. Most of the labels used to designate students for special education carry negative connotations (see the box on p. 53). Being so described may lower a person's self-esteem or cause others to behave differently toward him or her. Consequently, advocates for people with disabilities have suggested using different labels or, to the extent possible, avoiding the use of labels altogether.

Antilabeling sentiment is based, in part, on the theory that disabilities are a matter of social perceptions and values, not inherent characteristics. Bogdan (1986) suggests that *disability* is a socially created construct. Its existence depends on social interaction. Only in a very narrow sense, according to Bogdan, does a person *have* a disability. For example, the fact that a person cannot see only sets the stage for his or her being labeled "blind."

When the use of labels takes precedence over recognizing individual characteristics, labels themselves can become disabling. For instance, if we view this young man only in terms of his blindness, we might overlook things about him that don't fit our stereotype of blind people.

Cutting through Prejudicial Barriers with Humor

Most special education professionals and people with disabilities would agree that there are many ways to break down attitudinal barriers toward those who have disabilities. Humor may be one of the most effective weapons against such prejudices, especially if humor and disability are merely coincidental. In her syndicated cartoon feature "For Better or For Worse," Lynn Johnston occasionally includes a teacher who uses a wheelchair. This teacher experiences the frustrations and successes of any other in managing and teaching students, and her use of a wheelchair is typical of humor in this vein.

Others make frontal attacks on attitudinal barriers through humor in which disability is central, not incidental. One of the best-known cartoonists taking this approach is John Callahan, who is quadriplegic (as a result of an auto accident) and a recovering alcoholic. His cartoons, which often feature so-called black humor about disability, have appeared in *The New Yorker, Penthouse, National Lampoon, American Health,* and a variety of other magazines, newspapers, and books. Callahan's autobiography, *Don't Worry, He Won't Get Far on Foot,* is a book that some may find offensive but others find liberating in its irreverence and ability to make people laugh at disability.

For Better or For Worse® **by Lynn Johnston**

Source: *For Better or Worse.* Copyright © 1992 Lynn Johnston Prod., Inc. Reprinted with permission of *Universal Press Syndicate.* All rights reserved.

Once we call a person "blind," a variety of undesirable consequences occur. Our interactions are different because of the label. That is, we view the person primarily in terms of the blindness. We tend to interpret everything he or she can or cannot do in terms of the blindness, and the label takes precedence over other things we may know about the individual. This labeling opens the door for viewing the person in a stereotypical and prejudicial manner because, once labeled, we tend to think of all people with blindness as being similar to one another but different from the rest of society.

Research on the effects of labeling has been inconclusive (Brantlinger & Guskin, 1987). On the one hand, studies indicate that people tend to view labeled individuals differently from nonlabeled ones. People are more likely both to expect deviant behavior from labeled individuals and to see abnormality in nondisabled individuals if told (incorrectly) that nondisabled persons are deviant. On the other hand, labels may also make nondisabled people more tolerant of those with disabilities. That is, labels may provide explanations or justifications for differences in appearance or behavior for which the person with a disability otherwise might be blamed or stigmatized even more (Fiedler & Simpson, 1987). For example, it is probably fairly common for the nondisabled adult to tolerate a certain degree of socially immature behavior in a child with mental retardation while finding the same behavior unacceptable in a nondisabled child.

In addition to serving as an explanation for unusual behavior, some special educators defend the use of labels on other grounds. First, they argue that the elimination of one set of labels would only prompt development of another set. In other words, they believe that individuals with special problems will always be perceived as different. Second, these special educators contend that labels help professionals communicate with one another. In talking about a research study, for example, it helps to know with what type of population the study was conducted. Third, they assert that labels help spotlight the special needs of people with disabilities for the general public: "Like it or not, it is a fine mixture of compassion, guilt, and social consequence that has been established over these many years as a conditioned response to the label 'mental retardation' that brings forth . . . resources [monies for specialized services]" (Gallagher, 1972, p. 531). The taxpayer is more likely to react sympathetically to something that can be labeled.

Special Education Pull-Out Programs Have Been Ineffective. Some special educators assert that research shows **pull-out programs** to be ineffective. These educators maintain that students with disabilities have better, or at least no worse, scores on cognitive and social measures if they stay in regular classes than if they are pulled out for all (self-contained classes) or part (resource rooms) of the school day.

Many research studies have compared students with disabilities in more and less segregated settings; over the past 30 years, there have been more than 50 such studies. Results, when taken at face value, have not been very supportive of pull-out programs. Critics of this research, however, argue that taking these investigations at face value is highly questionable (Kauffman & Hallahan, 1992). The biggest problem with this line of research is that most of the studies are methodologically flawed. For example, in only two studies did the researchers randomly assign students to the different treatment groups. For ethical reasons, school personnel are hesitant to leave placement decisions to chance. It is difficult, however, to compare students who have been assigned to a self-contained class to those left in a general education class because the former, if appropriately placed, are probably more severely disabled and have poorer prognoses for improvement. Critics maintain that unless students are randomly assigned, students from the less restrictive setting will invariably have an advantage over students from more restrictive settings.

People with Disabilities as a Minority. Advocates of full inclusion tend to see people with disabilities as members of a minority group, rather than as individuals who have difficulties as an inherent result of their disabilities. In other words, the problems that people with disabilities face are seen as the result of society's discrimination and prejudice. The Stainbacks typify this point of view:

> In the past, educators have assumed a "functional limitations" approach to services. This paradigm locates the difficulty within students with disabilities when they experience problems in learning or adapting in general education classrooms. From this perspective, the primary task of educators is to remediate these students' functional deficits to the maximum extent possible. That is, educators attempt to fix, improve, or make ready the students who are being unsuccessful by providing them with the skills to be able to succeed in a mainstreamed educational environment that is *not* adapted to meet their particular needs, interests, or capabilities. And if this is not

pull-out programs. Special education programs in which students with disabilities leave the general education classroom for part or all of the school day (e.g., to go to special classes or resource room).

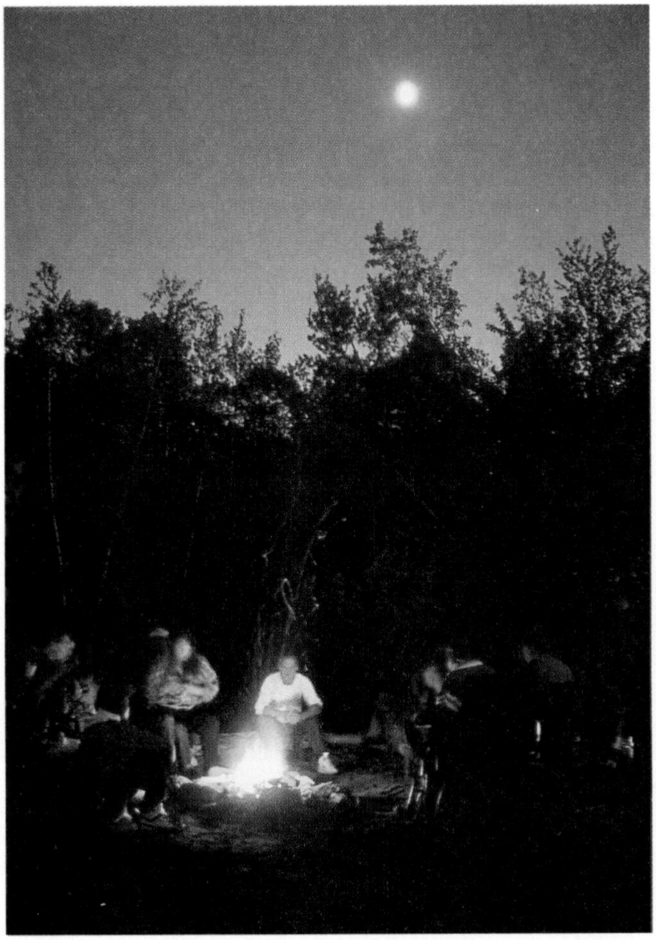

Children with disabilities would become further disabled if they were restricted from exploring their environments and participating in active pursuits.

possible, they must be relegated to special, separate learning settings. In the "functional limitations" paradigm the student is expected to fit into the existing or educational environment.

> This paradigm is gradually being replaced by a minority group paradigm. The minority group paradigm of school operation locates the principle [sic] difficulties of students with disabilities as not residing in the student, but rather in the organization of the general education environment. That is, school failure is the result of such things as educational programs, settings, and criteria for performance that do not meet the diverse needs of students. From this perspective, the problem is with the educational organization or environment that needs to be fixed, improved, or made ready to address the diverse needs of all students. (Stainback & Stainback, 1992, p. 32)

The notion of people with disabilities as a minority is consistent with the views of disability rights activists. These activists are a part of the **disability rights movement**, which is patterned after the civil rights movement of the 1960s. Disability activists claim that they, like African Americans and other ethnic minority groups, are an oppressed minority. They have coined the term *handicapism*, a parallel of *racism*. **Handicapism** is a "set of assumptions and practices that promotes the differential and unequal treatment of people because of apparent or assumed physical, mental, or behavioral differences" (Bogdan & Biklen, 1977, p. 14).

disability rights movement. Patterned after the civil rights movement of the 1960s, this is a loosely organized effort to advocate for the rights of people with disabilities through lobbying legislators and other activities. Members view people with disabilities as an oppressed minority.

handicapism. A term used by activists who fault the unequal treatment of individuals with disabilities. This term is parallel to the term *racism,* coined by those who fault unequal treatment based on race.

Although more and more people with disabilities—and nondisabled professionals too—are supporting the disability rights movement, there are several impediments to its achieving the same degree of impact as the civil rights movement. Some believe that the political climate in the United States has not been conducive to fostering yet another rights movement. Whereas the civil rights movement of the 1960s was spawned in an era of liberal ideology, the disability rights movement has coincided with a more conservative climate (Gartner & Joe, 1986). Activists themselves have been unable to agree on the best ways to meet the movement's general goals. For example, some believe that individuals with disabilities should receive special treatment in such things as tax exemptions or reduced public transportation fares. Others maintain that such preferential treatment fosters the image that people with disabilities are dependent on the nondisabled for charity (Gartner & Joe, 1986).

People with disabilities are an incredibly heterogeneous population. Although general goals can be the same for all people with disabilities, specific needs vary greatly, depending to a large extent on the particular type and severity of disability the person has. Clearly, the *particular* problems an adolescent with severe retardation and blindness faces are considerably different from those of a Vietnam veteran who has lost the use of his or her legs. Although activists admit it would not be good for the public to believe that all people with disabilities are alike—any more than they already do (Gartner & Joe, 1986)—the heterogeneity does make it more difficult for people with disabilities to join forces on specific issues.

But perhaps what has been missing most and what is hardest to achieve is a sense of pride. The civil rights movement for African Americans and the women's movement fostered pride in their supporters. For example, there has been no equivalent of the "Black is beautiful" slogan within the disability rights movement, although the movement is attempting to develop a sense of identity and community. One of the vehicles for accomplishing this is a publication, *The Disability Rag*, which highlights disability as a civil rights issue. (See the box on pp. 58–59.)

In fact, the following article from *The Disability Rag* targets pride as a major problem for people with disabilities:

> Ten women sat around a conference table on a Saturday afternoon, engrossed in the faces and voices on the videotape. They watched and listened as, one after another, women on the screen talked about their lives, their loves, their work and themselves. In the meeting room, the expressions on the faces of those watching showed recognition and relief, as the women saw and heard their own lives mirrored and validated.
>
> The women on the video, like the women at the conference table, had a variety of disabilities. The video, produced by Access Oregon, Portland's independent living center, was called "Don't Go To Your Room, and Other Affirmations for Disabled Women." I had been asked to co-present a session on feminism and disability issues for a group of women being trained as peer counselors at the Center for People with Disabilities in Boulder, Colo. We used the video as part of our presentation, and once again saw how powerful it could be in opening women to the truth and strength of their own lives.
>
> When it finished, silence filled the room for a few minutes.
>
> Then a middle-aged woman with multiple sclerosis, who had been disabled for several years, said, "This is the first time I have felt proud since I became disabled."
>
> Her comment struck me deeply at the time, and has stayed with me ever since. At first I was tempted to read it as typical of a "new crip," someone who hadn't yet

turned to disability cool, or come to terms with her own life as a woman with a disability. But I soon acknowledged her words as an expression of a sentiment that is pretty common among my friends and colleagues who have disabilities, and that I saw even in myself.

More and more I have realized how familiar it is within the disability community, that feeling of no pride. Those of us in the movement don't talk about it much—either to each other, for fear of being politically incorrect, perhaps compromising our leadership status; or to others, for what we say might somehow be used against us, to confirm the assumptions of the nondisabled that our shame is an inevitable, and therefore permanent, outgrowth of our disabilities.

But don't we all, like the woman in the training, struggle for a sense of pride? How many of us truly live in that place, where everyone has the right to live: a place of power, effectiveness, validation, connection, beauty—in other words, in pride?

It's a feeling that is not easy to come by in this segregated, inaccessible, often discriminatory world. Even the coolest of us do our share of internalizing the oppression all around us. . . .

Here's how I've started to resolve the issue for myself: Maybe it is important to differentiate between a feeling of pride, or no pride, and the deeper reality of existential pride. I might go through periods of self-doubt, but on a deeper level I know I'm worthy and powerful. The emotional experience of shame is strong, difficult to endure, and quite real, but it doesn't define my whole life. There's a more lasting knowledge available to me that transcends those painful moments. (Hershey, 1991, pp. 1, 4–5)*

People in the disability rights movement have been active on a variety of fronts, ranging from lobbying legislators and employers to criticizing the media for being guilty of representing people with disabilities in stereotypical and inaccurate ways. Disability activists have been particularly critical of television and movies (Klobas, 1985; Longmore, 1985). They argue that the depictions are typically overly negative or overly positive. On the negative side, electronic media often treat people with disabilities as criminals, monsters, potential suicides, maladjusted people, or sexual deviants. These portrayals offer the viewer absolution for any difficulties faced by persons with disabilities and allow the nondisabled to "blame the victims" for their own problems. Rarely do movie themes acknowledge society's role in creating attitudinal barriers for people with disabilities.

When television attempts to portray people with disabilities in a positive light, it often ends up highlighting phenomenal accomplishments—a one-legged skier, a wheelchair marathoner, and so forth. The superhero image, according to some disability activists, is a mixed blessing. It does promote the notion that being disabled does not automatically limit achievement. Such human interest stories, however, may make other more ordinary people with disabilities somehow feel inferior because they have not achieved such superhuman goals. These stories also imply that people with disabilities can prove their worth only by achieving superhuman goals and reinforce "the view that disability is a problem of individual emotional coping and physical overcoming, rather than an issue of social discrimination against a stigmatized minority" (Longmore, 1985, p. 35).

*This article appeared in the July/August 1991 issue of *The Disability Rag*. Copyright © 1991 by The Advocado Press. Reprinted by permission. Subscription information may be obtained from The Advocado Press, PO Box 145, Louisville, KY 40201.

From Rags to Rages

A DAVID AMONG MAGAZINES RAISES
A MIGHTY VOICE FOR PEOPLE WITH DISABILITIES

A Hollywood writer scripting a movie that will star William Hurt needs some quick, authoritative insight into the world of the disabled. She calls *The Disability Rag.*

The Easter Seal Society of Canada wants to know which terms disabled people find acceptable and objectionable. They query *The Disability Rag.*

The British Broadcasting Corp. is gathering material for a documentary on a movement in Berkeley, Calif., in the 1970s and '80s to make independent living possible for the disabled. The phone rings at *The Disability Rag.*

"It's really funny when these people contact us," says managing editor Sharon Kutz-Mellem. "They think we're this whole big staff."

By which she means that it is not really funny at all. Ironic, maybe.

Begun in Louisville on an impulse 12 years ago, the *Rag* has come to the attention of a selective but international audience for its coverage of disability issues. Universities—Harvard, Yale and Vienna among them—subscribe to it. So do social workers in Greece and Sweden. Requests for information have come from China and India.

And yet, as its reputation grows, one thing about the *Rag* stays the same.

It struggles to survive.

Although its readership has been estimated at 28,000, its paid following hovers at a very modest—if devoted—4,000 to 5,000 subscribers. Its present staff is at an all-time high of two full-timers and two part-timers, which seems hardly enough. Its financial condition cycles with almost annual regularity between leanness and desperation.

"It ekes by," says Cass Irvin, one of the magazine's founders. "One of my biggest regrets is that the community has not supported it the way I'd like to see." The *Rag* is, she sighs, "Louisville's best-kept secret."

If you sought out the *Rag* on a local newsstand—and you could look far before locating it—you would find it at first blush unprepossessing.

It's bimonthly and these days runs to 30- or 40-odd pages. It has clean but unremarkable layout, no color, few pictures and virtually no ads. It is printed on inexpensive newsprint. It looks like nothing so much as one of those cheeky counterculture publications common in the 1960s and early '70s.

The resemblance is not coincidence. To read the *Rag* is to take a bracing plunge into '60s-style advocacy.

The magazine has a clear, unwavering premise: The disabled are America's last, great, unacknowledged, oppressed minority, and it's time they banded together and asserted themselves.

In pushing this message, the *Rag* has been vigorous, iconoclastic and unabashed. A few years ago exercise guru Richard Simmons, in a moment of raised consciousness, wrote a book on exercise programs for the disabled and promoted it on national television. He said proceeds from the book would go to build special fitness centers for the disabled.

A wonderful idea? Not to the *Rag,* which believes the disabled should be able to go to the same fitness centers as everybody else. "Simmons doesn't understand what it is he's promoting," wrote *Rag* staffer Lauri Klobas. "He's allowing the non-disabled public to avoid making way for their friends, neighbors and relatives who have disabilities. Even worse . . . he's becoming a spokesman on this special form of 'apartheid.'"

There was more. Simmons had, in his enlightenment, begun picking up phrases like "physically challenged" and "handi-capable." Writer Mary Jane Owen found these terms "particularly odious" for their glossing over of the real problems faced by disabled people and concluded, with table-pounding fervor, "Move over, Richard! You're irrelevant—and you're in our way!"

All of which was, for the *Rag,* mere batting practice. "We've gone after some pretty big boys," notes Kutz-Mellem.

The *Rag* has taken on telethons that raise money for people with disabilities, in particular the Jerry Lewis Labor Day Telethon, for presenting the disabled in what it considers a pitiable, demeaning fashion. It reports tenaciously,

Although disability activists, for the most part, have been extremely displeased with television's handling of disabilities, they have been more complimentary of TV advertising that uses characters with disabilities. Beginning in the mid-1980s, advertisers began to experiment with the use of persons with disabilities. The last few years have seen a dramatic increase in actors with disabilities in TV advertising, whether out of corporate America's desire to be more socially responsive or their recognition of the large market of buyers with disabilities. (See the box on pp. 62–63.)

and with discernible relish, on protests against Lewis and the Muscular Dystrophy Association, and on the association's "whining" and "crybaby" responses.

It has also curled a lip at Mother Teresa's Missionaries of Charity order, because the order's New York shelter was not accessible to the disabled; at the National Organization on Disability, which has taken, in the *Rag's* opinion, a Milquetoast approach to disability issues; and at the mass media for various sins, including portrayals of the disabled as brave conquerors of adversity—the "supercrip" syndrome. . . .

Julie Shaw Cole, a contributing editor and longtime *Rag* supporter, says a key function is to provide a forum in which the disabled can speak their minds. "The *Rag* gives them that opportunity."

And they seize it. Debate buzzes through the *Rag's* letters pages. Readers write in to approve, suggest, cheer, dispute.

"By golly, the March/April *Rag* has a right-on article," writes Kandy Penner of Gainesville, Fla.

But Geeta Dardick of North San Juan, Calif., thinks the *Rag* may be getting too soft on questions of terminology: "Get the point, *Rag.* Give us a break! Keep supporting all of the language rules the leaders of the disability movement have agreed upon."

But Damian Anthony Rheaume, of Greendale, Wis., has had enough. "I received a renewal form for your magazine. Renew? Are you kidding? . . . Good luck. May your lives be as bitter as your outlook on life."

Then there is another letter, a short one posted on a wall in the *Rag's* offices. The writing is an uneven scrawl that struggles across the page, but the message is clear and strong: "Please continue to fight oppression and tyranny towards the disabled. It's stuff like that that feeds your sanity. . . . I need a lot of fuel to fight this uphill battle."

It is signed, "Monica."

Throughout its existence the *Rag* has heard quietly and often from the Monicas of the world, says Mary Johnson. "We get almost a standard letter all the time from people saying, 'We've been so isolated, I never knew other people felt this way.'"

Those letters, for Johnson, validate what she has done. She is the mother of the *Rag,* and to this day she sounds slightly bemused by how she came to do it.

Johnson is not disabled. But a number of years ago she became involved in disability issues through an activist friend who was disabled, and she came to see how hard it was to organize the disabled and get them to envision their problems as a civil-rights issue.

And then one day in 1980, Johnson says, "I was just sitting in my house, and I thought, 'Well, I'm going to put this thing out.' There was no planning. It was totally spur of the moment."

"This thing" was a four-page newsletter called *The Disability Rag*—the name, like the idea, just came to her, Johnson says. The first issue, she recalls, printed a long article that had been circulating among disability activists.

"It was sort of like a call to arms," Johnson remembers, "It was a florid piece of writing."

She sent the newsletter out to perhaps 30 or 40 people she knew in the local disabled community. Anonymously. "I was very keen on being anonymous at the time," she says. Why? "Paranoia, I guess."

She was not sure how some of the radical notions in the newsletter would be received. The *Rag* was, in a sense, a way of finding out. She kept putting it out, and things happened. She attached her name to it. She joined forces with Irvin, a quadriplegic and disability activist.

The *Rag* grew; Johnson credits Irvin with putting it on a business-like footing. They incorporated, began to sell subscriptions nationwide and discovered an audience for what they were saying.

Under the auspices of its publisher, The Advocado Press, the *Rag* now prints a variety of disability-related educational materials, including a newsletter explaining the Americans with Disabilities Act and cards that can be slapped on the windshields of cars improperly parked in handicapped-only parking spaces. The cards are a popular item.

Source: By David McGinty, *The Courier Journal,* Louisville, KY, June 14, 1992, pp. 1, 3. Features Section.

Ethics over Empiricism. Full-inclusion proponents emphasize that people with disabilities are a minority group who have undergone discrimination. Thus, these proponents tend to approach issues of integration from an ethical, rather than an empirical, perspective. Many proponents of full inclusion are not interested in pursuing the question of whether full inclusion is effective. For them, empirical data on the comparative effectiveness of full inclusion versus pull-out programs are irrelevant. Apparently, even if one were to find, through well-controlled research, that pull-out programs lead to better academic and social outcomes than do full-inclusion programs, these advocates would still favor full inclusion on ethical grounds. For them,

> by far the most important reason for including all students into the mainstream is that it is the fair, ethical, and equitable thing to do. It deals with the value of EQUALITY. As was decided in the *Brown versus Board of Education* decision, SEPARATE IS NOT EQUAL. All children should be part of the educational and community mainstream.
>
> It is discriminatory that some students, such as those labeled disabled, must earn the right or be prepared to be in the general education mainstream or wait for educational researchers to prove that students with disabilities can profit from the mainstream, when other students are allowed unrestricted access simply because they have no label. No one should have to pass anyone's test or prove anything in a research study to live and learn in the mainstream of school and community life. It is a basic right, not something one has to earn. (Stainback & Stainback, 1992, p. 31)

Arguments against Full Inclusion. The notion of full inclusion has met with considerable resistance. At least six arguments against full inclusion have been offered:

1. General educators, special educators, and parents are largely satisfied with the current continuum of placements.
2. General educators are unwilling and/or unable to cope with all students with disabilities.
3. Justifying full inclusion by asserting that people with disabilities are a minority is flawed.
4. Full-inclusion proponents' unwillingness to consider empirical evidence is professionally irresponsible.
5. The available empirical evidence does not support full inclusion.
6. In the absence of data to support one service delivery model, special educators must preserve the continuum of placements.

Satisfaction with the Current Continuum of Placements. Defenders of the full continuum point out that, for the most part, teachers, parents, and students are satisfied with the degree of integration into general education now experienced by children with disabilities. In a poll conducted by Louis Harris and Associates, Inc. (ICD Survey III, 1989), 77 percent of parents of students with disabilities were satisfied with the special education system. On the question of mainstreaming, most parents were satisfied with the current level of integration. In a survey of teachers, both general and special education teachers indicated their satisfaction with the current continuum of placements (Semmel, Abernathy, Butera, & Lesar, 1991). Interviews with secondary students with learning disabilities who had been identified for special education since elementary school also did not support the full-inclusion position (Guterman, 1995). Although students were unhappy with having been identified as learning disabled because of the stigma it brought, the majority did not regret that they had not been educated in general education classes. As one student summed up:

> [Full-inclusion] would make it worse. Basically it would be embarrassing for that person (a student with learning disabilities). It (an inclusive classroom) would be egging it more. People would be getting into a lot more fights because somebody is always going to joke around and say something like, "He's a retard." (Guterman, 1995, p. 120)

Critics of full inclusion claim that the idea of full inclusion is being championed by only a few radical special educators.

General Educators Are Unwilling and/or Unable to Cope. The attitudes of many general educators toward including students with disabilities in regular classes have been less than enthusiastic. In a synthesis of over two dozen surveys of general educators' views on integrating students with disabilities into their classes, only about half thought that integration could provide some benefits (Scruggs & Mastropieri, in press). Furthermore, only about one-fourth to one-third thought they had sufficient time, skills, training, and resources needed for working with students with disabilities.

Many critics of full inclusion maintain that the reason special education came into being in the first place was that general educators were unable to handle students with disabilities. And these critics further maintain that general educators are in no better position today to accommodate the needs of these students than they were in the past (Fuchs & Fuchs, 1991; Walker & Bullis, 1991). They point out that most classroom teachers are already overburdened and that the current emphasis on students achieving higher academic levels is at odds with accepting more students with disabilities into general education classes. As one critic of full inclusion asked:

> Can [advocates of full inclusion]. . . possibly believe that children in regular classrooms are taught and educated in accordance with their individuality? Individualization in regular classrooms is quite a dead issue and has been for years. The barrage of curriculum materials, syllabi, grade-level expectations for performance, standardized tests, competency tests, and so on continue to overwhelm even the most flexible teachers. Individualization calls for child centeredness, and child centeredness has been on the run since the 1960s. . . .

Positive media portrayals of individuals with disabilities have helped change attitudes toward them, but in some cases, such portrayals also may have set unrealistic expectations for these individuals as well.

Regular classroom teachers attempt to meet physical-motor, cognitive-intellectual, and social-emotional needs just as special educators do. Yet, their focus tends to be different. Regular class teachers are given an agenda called the curriculum. They are provided with it prior to seeing any student. They are told that this is what they have to teach, and sometimes what book to use and even how to use it. This more standardized approach to education for the masses generally succeeds . . . for the masses. It misses some individual children by a mile, who may be normal and a little bit different, or who may be disabled and a lot different. The greater the difference, the greater the chance that the student will fall through the cracks of any standard way of doing something. (Lieberman, 1992, pp. 15, 21–22)

Ad Ventures for the Disabled

NEW VISIBILITY MARKS A CHANGE IN ATTITUDES

The Sears commercial is a fast-paced kaleidoscope of beaming customers showing off their new clothes, reaching for tools, painting their houses, videotaping their kids' Easter egg hunts—all while a singer croons about "the many sides of Sears." In one scene, a fisherman relaxes on a dock at sunset with his pals and his dog; the fisherman is in a wheelchair.

Then there's the double-page magazine ad for Saturn that, like all Saturn's advertising, features a real-life car buyer or dealer. The photo shows satisfied customer June Rooks, a 44-year-old Navy research analyst, wearing a broad grin and a bright dress, and balanced on a pair of crutches. "When you've tackled everything else life has thrown your way," the headline says, "a little traffic won't stop you."

And a TV spot for Nike, in which an athletic young man runs picturesquely through the forest and foothills of Malibu Canyon, presents his story in stark white-on-black titles: "Ric Munoz, Los Angeles. 80 miles every week, 10 marathons every year. HIV-positive." Followed by Nike's familiar hortatory slogan: "Just Do It."

After years of lobbying for inclusion in the imagery that penetrates virtually every American home, people with disabilities are becoming far more visible in mainstream advertising. Kellogg's corn flakes commercials, for instance, have starred a deaf teenager (who signs enthusiastically about crunchiness) and a woman in a wheelchair. A Home Depot spot scheduled to air in 20 cities (including Washington) next month feature an employee with a prosthetic arm—70-year-old Henry Gibson of Houston, to be precise—touting hardware. This list of big-budget advertisers whose TV commercials and print spreads incorporate actors and models with disabilities also included AT&T, Toys R Us, McDonald's, Mitsubishi, Target, Nordstrom, Chrysler and Toyota. "This has been a real breakthrough," says Barrett Shaw, editor of the Louisville-based magazine the *Disability Rag.*

Advertising historically has been the domain of the perfect, off-limits not only to the disabled but to almost everyone who isn't young, lithe and gorgeous. Sandra Gordon, a former Easter Seal executive who now consults with major corporations on disability issues, remembers in the '70s urging advertisers to include a single wheelchair-user in ads with group photographs. "I was told that I was crazy, that it was a disgusting idea," Gordon recalls. "It would turn consumers off; they might think using the product would make *them* disabled."

It's now more common for executives to talk like Sears marketing chief John Costello: "We are really committed to reflecting the full diversity of our consumer group in our advertising." Sears has one of the largest marketing budgets of any U.S. company. Its "many sides" ad, produced by Young & Rubicam and expected to air nationally in both 30- and 60-second versions throughout the year, marks first time the company has used a disabled person in an ad. But Costello says, "you can expect to see more."

The ads themselves have also evolved since the first few appeared, with long intervals between them, in the '80s. Probably the most-remembered of the early entries was the spot that introduced Bill Demby, a Vietnam vet and double amputee who was shown vigorously playing basketball on artificial feet developed by DuPont. The ad and Demby were inspiring. But, Gordon notes, "it's very hard, if you're a person who's deaf or blind or uses a wheelchair, to live up to those 'Supergimp' stereotypes."

Current ads are less apt to emphasize heroic conquests, more likely to show people with disabilities in ordinary situations. Editor Shaw, for instance, was particularly impressed with the Saturn ad, which was created by Hal Riney and Partners and has run in the *Atlantic Monthly, Gourmet, Essence, Newsweek* and *Scientific American,* among other magazines. June Rooks, Shaw notes, "was treated the same way other people in Saturn ads are."

Not all may share such a jaundiced view of general education, but most critics of full inclusion sympathize with the classroom teacher's already arduous job. Although some critics blame teachers for their unwillingness to accommodate more students with disabilities, many agree that their hesitation to do so is justified.

Justifying Full Inclusion by Asserting That People with Disabilities Are a Minority Is Flawed. Many critics of full inclusion do not deny that, in many ways, people with disabilities have been treated similarly to oppressed minority groups, such as

As with other corporate attempts at "diversity," the inclusion of people with disabilities in marketing efforts serves several purposes at once. It shows sensitivity and creates goodwill, and some business executives think it may actually help effect social change. "We believe advertising changes America's attitudes on a lot of fronts," says Ron Hatley, consumer affairs manager at AT&T, which has run several print and TV ads featuring disabled actors. "When we see people of color in ads, we relate to them as individuals, we have a less segregated society. Including people with disabilities in ads will help change attitudes, too." . . .

Beyond the public relations factors, however, companies also have designs on a large and potentially lucrative market. The Census Bureau estimates that a startling 49 million Americans have some degree of disability, meaning that they have "difficulty" performing certain functions or activities; this group, which is disproportionately elderly, could include everyone from the blind or deaf to someone with learning disabilities like dyslexia. Of this group, 24 million describe disabilities that the Census Bureau classifies as "severe." The larger group of 49 million controls $188 billion in discretionary income; the smaller, severely disabled group has a spare $55 billion to spend.

Far from feeling exploited by such wooing, advocates for disabled people say, the market is happy to be courted. "It helps to see people with disabilities as a contributing force in this society—tax-paying citizens who also buy Charmin or Colgate—not just people who are asking for things," says Sandra Gordon.

Source: From "Ad Ventures for the Disabled," by P. Span, March 7, 1995, pp. D-1, D-8. Copyright © 1995 by *The Washington Post*. Reprinted with permission.

ANGELFISH ROCKER
Ride the waves while rocking the bright yellow fish. The

Advertisers in recent years have sought to demonstrate their sensitivity, and to activate potentially lucrative markets, by including diverse societal groups in their print and television advertising, and this trent has not overlooked individuals with disabilities, whose presence in the glossy world of advertising may be at once a reflection and an agent of changing attitudes toward disabilities.

African Americans, Hispanics, and women. They have experienced discrimination on the basis of their disability and, thus, can be considered an oppressed minority group.

These critics, however, do not see that this minority group status translates into the same educational placement decisions as it does for African Americans, Hispanics, and women (Kauffman, 1989; Kauffman & Hallahan, 1993). They argue that for the latter groups, separation from the mainstream cannot be defended on educational grounds, but for students with disabilities, separation can. Students with disabilities are sometimes placed in special classes or resource rooms to accommodate their educational needs better. Placement in separate educational environments is inherently unequal, these critics maintain, when it is done for factors irrelevant to learning (e.g., skin color), but such placements may result in equality when done for instructionally relevant reasons (e.g., student's ability to learn, difficulty of material being presented, preparation of the teacher).

Finally, critics of full inclusion argue that the most important civil right of the minority in question—students with disabilities and their parents—is the right to choose. That is, the Individuals with Disabilities Education Act (IDEA) (discussed in Chapter 1) gives parents and students themselves when appropriate, the right to choose the environment *they*, not advocates of total inclusion, consider most appropriate and least restrictive.

Unwillingness to Consider Empirical Evidence Is Professionally Irresponsible. Some professionals see as folly the disregard of empirical evidence espoused by some proponents of full inclusion (Fuchs & Fuchs, 1991). These professionals believe that ethical actions are always of the utmost importance. They assert, however, that decisions of what is ethical should be informed by research. In the case of mainstreaming, they think it is important to have as much data as possible on its advantages and disadvantages and how best to implement it before deciding if and how it should be put into practice. Some critics maintain that full-inclusion proponents have gone too far in championing their cause, that they have resorted to rhetoric rather than reason. These critics assert that backers of full inclusion have traded in their credentials as scientific researchers in favor of becoming advocates and lobbyists.

Available Empirical Evidence Does Not Support Full Inclusion. There are few rigorous studies of full inclusion, but those available suggest that full inclusion has not led to social or academic benefits, according to critics. For example, one study found that students with disabilities in full-inclusion classrooms were not very well liked by their general education peers (Sale & Carey, 1995). The authors concluded that their results were similar to those of previous studies of students with disabilities who were served in resource rooms. With respect to academics, the combined results of three longitudinal studies indicate that, even after investing tremendous amounts of financial and professional resources, 40 percent of fully included students with learning disabilities "were slipping behind at what many would consider a disturbing rate" (Zigmond et al., 1995, p. 539).

In perhaps the most extensive study of full inclusion, researchers interviewed school personnel and students and observed in classrooms in five full-inclusion sites around the United States (Baker & Zigmond, 1995; Zigmond, 1995; Zigmond & Baker, 1995). Based on their data, the researchers claimed that teachers did not individualize instruction or plan ahead for how to accommodate the needs of students with disabilities. In fact, the individualization that did occur was most often carried

Critics of full inclusion assert that it is unrealistic to expect the general education system—with its fast, competitive pace and whole-group focus—to provide the individualized attention often required by learners with disabilities.

out by peers (using peer tutoring—see pp. 69–70) or paraprofessionals (teacher aides). The researchers concluded:

> Regardless of how well prepared a general educator is, the focus of general education practice is on *the group:* managing instruction for a large group of students, managing behavior within a large group of students, designing assessments suitable for a large group, and so forth. The special educator's focus has always been, and should continue to be, on *the individual,* providing unique and response-contingent instruction, teaching socially appropriate behavior, designing tailored assessments that are both diagnostic and summative, and so forth. (Zigmond & Baker, 1995, pp. 249–250)

Preserving the Continuum of Placements. Critics of full inclusion argue that, given that empirical evidence is scant and that what is available does not support any one service delivery option, it is wise to be cautious about changing the current configuration too quickly or drastically. They admit that there are problems with the current special education system and that there may even be a need for more integration of students with disabilities, including the use of full inclusion. They are leery, however, about eliminating the range of service delivery options currently available to school personnel and parents. Fuchs and Fuchs (1991), for example, have stated:

> [Proponents of full inclusion] . . . seem fond of battle metaphors. We'll piggyback on their favored imagery by suggesting that, for many . . . [defenders of a continuum of services] regular education remains a foreign and hostile territory, neglecting many children with disabilities. PL 94–142, with its declaration of a free and appropriate education and its cascade of services and the LRE principle, represented in 1975 the capturing of a beachhead for children with disabilities. It is time to gather our energies and courage; validate comprehensive integration strategies; pressure mainstream administrators and teachers for greater accommodations; move inland! But as we mount this new offensive, we, like any general worthy of his rank, must make certain

> that the beachhead remains secure. It's the beachhead, after all, that provides supplies and, in a worst-case scenario, guarantees a safe retreat. The cascade of services is a source of strength and a safety net for the children we serve. Let's not lose it. (pp. 253–254)

Mainstreaming Practices

Whether or not one supports the concept of full inclusion, the fact is that most special educators are in favor of some degree of mainstreaming—integrating students with disabilities with nondisabled students. Educators have devised a number of strategies for implementing mainstreaming. Most of these practices are still in the experimental stages; that is, we do not have a wealth of evidence indicating their effectiveness. However, various authorities have recommended the following eight strategies:

1. prereferral teams
2. peer collaboration
3. collaborative consultation
4. cooperative teaching
5. cooperative learning
6. peer tutoring
7. partial participation
8. curriculum materials designed to change attitudes

In the following sections, we briefly describe each of these approaches.

Prereferral Teams. Groups of professionals called **prereferral teams (PRTs)** work with general education teachers to recommend different strategies for working with children who exhibit academic and/or behavioral problems. One of the primary goals is to establish "ownership" of these children by general and not special educators. In other words, PRTs try to keep down the number of referrals to special education by stressing that general educators try as many alternative strategies as possible before deciding that difficult-to-teach students need to become the primary responsibility of special educators.

The makeup of PRTs varies from one place to another, sometimes including the school principal or a school psychologist but almost always including a special educator and a general educator. In fact, because of the emphasis on general education's ownership, some have maintained that general educators are the most important team members (Chalfant, Pysh, & Moultrie, 1979; Gerber & Semmel, 1985). A major justification for using classroom teachers to make decisions regarding referral to special education is that they may have information on individual children that is even more important than results of the usual standardized tests: "Teachers observe tens of thousands of discrete behavioral events during each school day. Formal tests of ability and achievement are based on analysis of only small samples of student behavior. Clearly teachers have available to them, if they choose to use it, a far richer and varied sample of student behavior than the typical 'test'" (Gerber & Semmel, 1984, p. 141).

There is very little research on the effectiveness of PRTs (Lloyd, Crowley, Kohler, & Strain, 1988). The few evaluations that have been done indicate two things: (1) They do cut down on the number of referrals to special education; and (2) team members and administrators report that they are effective (Schram et al., 1984).

prereferral teams (PRTs). Teams made up of a variety of professionals, especially regular and special educators who work with regular class teachers to come up with strategies for teaching difficult-to-teach children. Designed to influence regular educators to take ownership of difficult-to-teach students and to minimize inappropriate referrals to special education.

Peer Collaboration. The use of **peer collaboration** is similar to that of PRTs in that both are methods that general educators can employ for dealing with students' problems before turning to special education for help. Peer collaboration differs, however, in that it typically involves only two professionals, both general educators. These two teachers engage in a structured dialogue designed to generate interventions for a student who is having problems (Johnson & Pugach, 1991). The process starts with the student's teacher writing a brief description of the problem. The other teacher serves as a kind of "sounding board" for the student's teacher, who then develops at least three possible interventions and proposes ways of collecting data to determine whether the intervention was successful.

Researchers found that teachers who used peer collaboration reduced their number of referrals to special education and became more confident in dealing with students' problems (Pugach & Johnson, 1995). In addition, teachers reported that over 86 percent of the strategies they developed were successful (Johnson & Pugach, 1991). One limitation of this research, however, is that it relied on teacher opinions and did not include measures of student outcomes.

Collaborative Consultation. In the late 1970s and early 1980s, the notion that teachers or school psychologists should provide consultation to general education teachers became quite popular. In this model, the special education room teacher or psychologist acts as an expert in providing advice to the classroom teacher. The special education teacher may see the child with disabilities in a resource room, or the student may receive all of his or her instruction in the general education class.

More recently, authorities have begun to advocate a variation of this approach that differs in two important ways. Referred to as **collaborative consultation**, this approach stresses mutuality and reciprocity: "Mutuality means shared ownership of a common issue or problem by professionals. Reciprocity means allowing these parties to have equal access to information and the opportunity to participate in problem identification, discussion, decision making, and all final outcomes" (West & Idol, 1990, p. 23). In collaborative consultation, then, the special educator and the general educator assume equal responsibility for the student with disabilities, and neither assumes more authority in making recommendations about how to teach the child. Like PRTs and peer collaboration, collaborative consultation can be used to keep teachers from referring difficult-to-teach students to special education or after the child has been identified for special education.

Research suggests that collaborative consultation is a promising approach to meeting the needs of many students with disabilities in general education settings. Nevertheless, much remains unknown about what makes consultation effective or ineffective in meeting students' needs.

Cooperative Teaching. Sometimes referred to as *collaborative teaching*, cooperative teaching takes the notions of mutuality and reciprocity in collaborative consultation one step further. In **cooperative teaching** general educators and special educators jointly teach in the same general education classroom composed of students with and without disabilities. In other words, the special educator comes out of his or her separate classroom (sometimes permanently) to teach in the regular class setting. In addition to promoting the notions of mutuality and reciprocity, one of the advantages that proponents of this model point out is that it helps the special educator know the everyday curricular

peer collaboration. A process in which two general educators engage in structured dialogue to generate ideas for working with a student having problems in the general education class, rather than referring him or her to special education; the student's classroom teacher proposes interventions and how to measure their success, while the other teacher guides the process.

collaborative consultation. An approach in which a special educator and a general educator collaborate to come up with teaching strategies for a student with disabilities. The relationship between the two professionals is based on the premises of shared responsibility and equal authority.

cooperative teaching. An approach in which general educators and special educators teach together in the general classroom; it helps the special educator know the context of the regular classroom better.

demands faced by the student with disabilities. The special educator sees the context within which the student must function to succeed in the mainstream. As one teacher, when interviewed, put it:

> I have learned so much about the content itself which has helped me to teach English and math to students in my resource class. . . . I certainly have gained insights into the students themselves. For instance, when I do observation for [re-evaluations]. . . . I am able to go into a class on one day and that's what I see, how that particular child performed on that particular day. But to be able to see kids on a day-in and day-out basis, I really feel I have a much better sense of who tunes outs [sic] when and why and who plugs away every minute of the day and still has difficulty because he hasn't understood. I can see their interactions with their peers. I can see their interest in the subject matter. I have a much more complete view of each child. (Nowacek, 1992, p. 275)

Cooperative teaching can vary with regard to who has the primary instructional responsibility in the classroom: the general educator, the special educator, or both. In some arrangements, the general educator assumes primary responsibility for instruction of academic content, while the special educator teaches academic survival skills, such as note taking and organizing homework assignments. This form of cooperative teaching is popular at the secondary level because it is difficult for special educators to have expertise in all content areas (e.g., history, biology, chemistry, Spanish, French, and so forth). In another arrangement, which is more popular at the elementary level, the special educator and general educator practice team teaching. They jointly plan and teach all content to all students, taking turns being responsible for different aspects of the curriculum. Under this model, a person walking into the classroom would have a difficult time telling which of the two teachers is the special educator.

Research on cooperative teaching is in its infancy. Researchers are consistently finding, however, that its success is dependent on at least two factors (Nowacek, 1992; Trent, 1992; Reeve & Hallahan, 1994). First, enough time needs to be built into the general and special educators' schedules for cooperative planning. Second, the two teachers' personalities and working styles need to be compatible. As one teacher said:

> The biggest drawback I could see to using the collaborative model would be for the school system to say, "We're going to do this. We're going to train you teachers and you two are going to work together." That would not work at all. Carol and I have a relationship where it works. I'm sure there are other teachers that I couldn't work with. I think it's very person-specific. . . . It does take a lot of adjustment for the classroom teacher because we're used to being in control—in charge—and all of a sudden, there's this other person in your room. (Nowacek, 1992, p. 274)

Because of the importance of interpersonal skills in making cooperative teaching and collaborative consultation successful, some researchers have cautioned teachers against neglecting the actual teaching of the *students* (Fuchs & Fuchs, 1992). In other words, teachers engaged in cooperative teaching or collaborative consultation need to work on getting along together, but not to the neglect of the students they are teaching.

cooperative learning. A teaching approach in which the teacher places students with heterogeneous abilities (for example, some might have disabilities) together to work on assignments.

Cooperative Learning. Much emphasis is placed on competition in the traditional regular class. This focus, some believe, is detrimental to the success of all students, especially those with disabilities or of lower ability (Johnson & Johnson, 1986; Slavin, 1988, 1991). The Johnsons have found that **cooperative learning**—involving students with disabilities and nondisabled peers in situations in which they must cooperate with one another—leads to better attitudes on the part of the nondisabled toward their peers with disabilities as well as to better attitudes of students with disabilities toward themselves.

The Johnsons believe that cooperative situations foster differentiated, dynamic, and realistic views of group members, especially when students with disabilities take part in the cooperative venture. By *differentiated*, the authors mean that a child is viewed as possessing more attributes than just the stereotypic ones that accompany his or her label. And by *dynamic*, they mean that a child's attributes may not be viewed by other group members as relevant to all aspects of the task at hand. Once the teacher places students in small, heterogeneous groups for the purpose of working toward a common goal, Johnson and Johnson believe that a number of positive events will occur.

Although the Johnsons' use of cooperative learning has led to positive changes in *attitudes,* they have been less successful in affecting *achievement.* They have looked at achievement in only a few of their studies, and the results have been mixed. However, investigator Robert Slavin (1988, 1991) has designed cooperative learning situations that have led to achievement gains.

Although only a few of Slavin's studies have included formally identified students with disabilities, he has used cooperative learning with low-ability students. To have positive effects on achievement, he concludes that cooperative learning must involve two elements: (1) There must be group incentives, and (2) there must be individual accountability. What should be avoided are situations in which the group's solution to a problem can be found by just one or two members. One way of avoiding this is to base rewards on the group's average so each individual's score contributes to the total score of the group.

peer tutoring. A method that can be used to integrate students with disabilities in general education classrooms, based on the notion that students can effectively tutor one another. The role of learner or teacher may be assigned to either the student with a disability or the nondisabled student.

Peer Tutoring. Yet another recommended method of integrating students with disabilities into the mainstream is **peer tutoring** (Jenkins & Jenkins, 1987), defined as one student tutoring another. Professionals have advocated using children with disabilities as tutors as well as tutees. When a child with a disability assumes the role of tutor, the tutee is usually a younger peer.

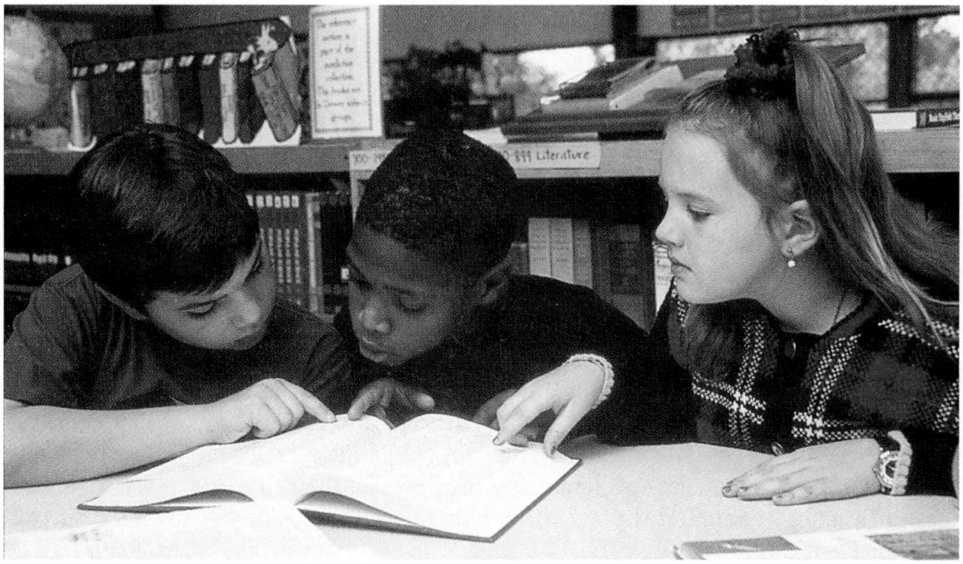

Cooperative learning situations can enhance mutual understanding and improve relationships between students with disabilities and nondisabled learners.

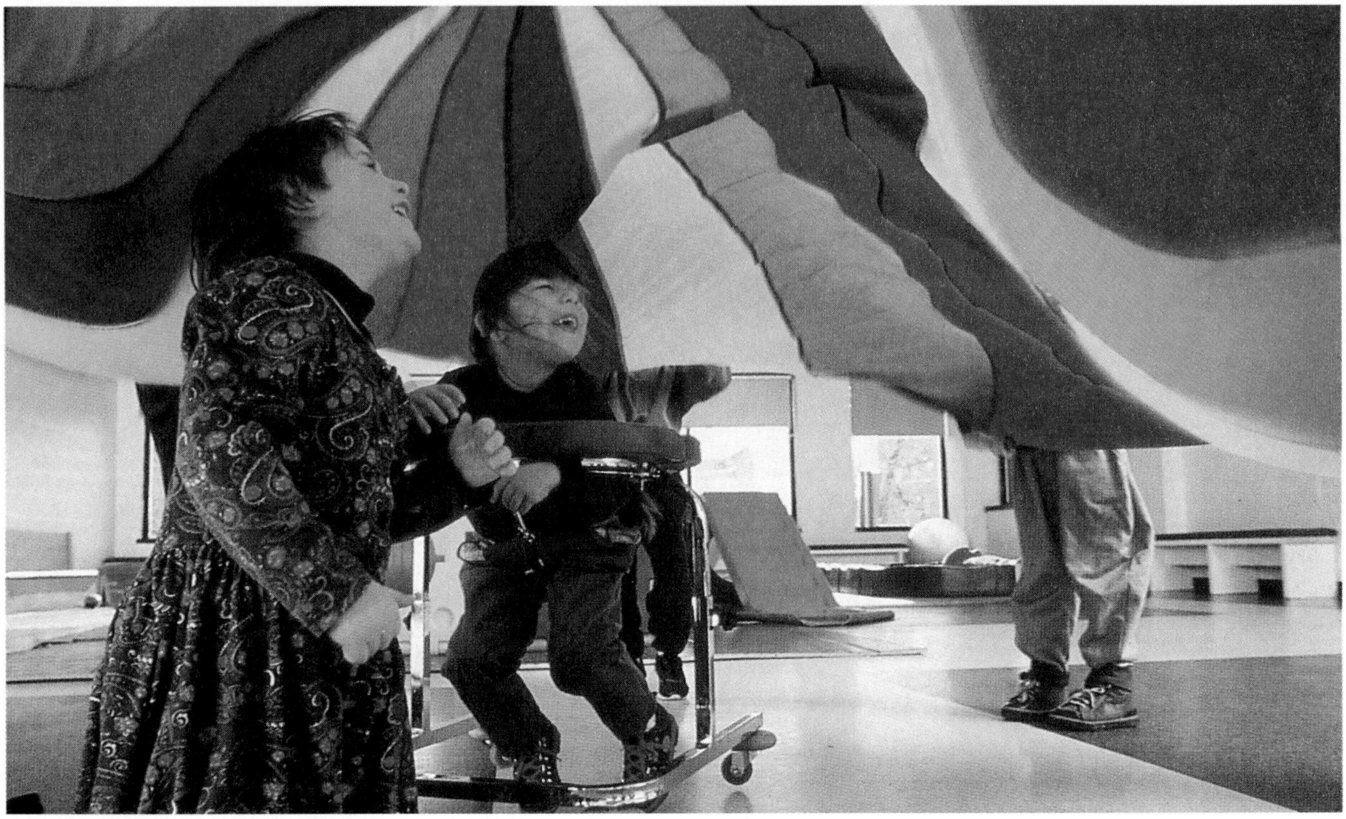

Public Law 99–457, passed in 1986, stipulates that states must provide preschool services to all children between the ages of three and five who have disabilities. This law also provides incentives for establishing special education programs for infants and toddlers.

Research results on the effectiveness of peer tutoring are mixed (Scruggs & Richter, 1986). Evidence suggests that students with mild disabilities can benefit academically when serving as tutor or tutee. There are few empirical data, however, to show that peer tutoring improves self-concept.

It is important to remember that, contrary to what some educators believe, peer tutoring does not save time (Gerber & Kauffman, 1981). A good peer-tutoring situation requires continuous organization and monitoring by the teacher.

partial participation. An approach in which students with disabilities, while in the general education classroom, engage in the same activities as nondisabled students but on a reduced basis; the teacher adapts the activity to allow each student to participate as much as possible.

Partial Participation. Professionals concerned with mainstreaming students with relatively severe disabilities advocate the concept of partial participation (Giangreco & Putnam, 1991; Raynes, Snell, & Sailor, 1991). **Partial participation** means having students with disabilities participate, on a reduced basis, in virtually all activities experienced by all students in the general education classroom. Partial participation questions the assumption that it is a waste of time to include students with severe mental and physical limitations in certain activities because they cannot benefit from them in the same way that nondisabled students can. Instead of excluding anyone from these activities, advocates of partial participation recommend that the teacher accommodate the student with disabilities by such strategies as "providing assistance for more difficult parts of a task, changing the 'rules' of the game or activity to make it less difficult, or changing the way in which a task or activity is organized or presented" (Raynes et al., 1991, p. 329).

The objectives of partial participation are twofold. First, proponents maintain that it provides exposure to academic content that the student with disabilities might otherwise miss. Second, it helps students with disabilities achieve a greater degree of social interaction with nondisabled peers.

Curriculum Materials Designed to Change Attitudes. Authors have developed curriculum materials to enlighten nondisabled students about students with disabilities. These materials often involve activities constructed to teach children about different aspects of disabilities, such as causes and characteristics, as well as to let students explore their feelings about children with disabilities. These materials range from full-blown curricula, such as *Accepting Individual Differences* (Cohen, 1977) and *What If You Couldn't? An Elementary School Program about Handicaps* (Children's Museum of Boston, 1978), to individual books, such as *Don't Feel Sorry for Paul* (Wolf, 1974). Many of these approaches involve a variety of media and activities. One especially creative approach is "Kids on the Block" (The Kids on the Block, Inc. Alexandria, VA), a puppet show with Muppet-like characters that have different kinds of disabilities (e.g., mental retardation, cerebral palsy, visual impairment, behavior disorders). The show comes with scripts designed to explain basic concepts about children with disabilities and has a variety of curriculum suggestions.

Another curricular approach to improving pupils' attitudes toward their peers who have disabilities is the use of simulations. Some professionals believe that teachers can promote understanding of disabilities by having nondisabled students simulate disabilities in and out of school (Wesson & Mandell, 1989). Walking through the school while blindfolded, wearing glasses smeared with petroleum jelly, or trying to button clothing with hands covered with thick socks, for example, may help students understand and appreciate the disabilities of their peers who have limited vision or mobility.

Although more and more schools are using materials designed to teach children in regular education about students with disabilities, very few efforts have been mounted to evaluate these curricular modifications systematically.

EARLY INTERVENTION

Many educators and social scientists believe that the earlier in life a disability is recognized and a program of education or treatment is started, the better the outcome for the child. Bricker (1986) states three basic arguments for early intervention:

1. A child's early learning provides the foundation for later learning, so the sooner a special program of intervention is begun, the further the child is likely to go in learning more complex skills.
2. Early intervention is likely to provide support for the child and family that will help prevent the child from developing additional problems or disabilities.
3. Early intervention can help families adjust to having a child with disabilities; give parents the skills they need to handle the child effectively at home; and help families find the additional support services they may need, such as counseling, medical assistance, or financial aid.

Children whose disabilities are diagnosed at a very young age tend to be those with specific syndromes (Down syndrome, for example) or obvious physical disabilities.

Many have severe and multiple disabilities. Typically, such a child's needs cannot be met by a single agency or intervention, so many professionals must work together closely if the child is to be served effectively. If the child's disabilities are recognized at an early age and intervention by all necessary professionals is well coordinated, the child's learning and development can often be greatly enhanced.

Legislative History

A major reason to be encouraged about educational programming for infants and preschoolers with disabilities is that the federal government has been and continues to be committed to supporting research and educational efforts in this area. More and more early intervention programs are springing up around the country. The federal government has made substantial inroads in providing monies and leadership in this most important area. Two crucial pieces of federal legislation for early intervention with children and families with disabilities are PL 90–538 and PL 99–457.

PL 90–538. In 1968 Congress passed **PL 90–538**, establishing the **Handicapped Children's Early Education Program (HCEEP)**, the first federal special education program aimed specifically at young children with disabilities and their families. HCEEP has funded model demonstration projects for delivering experimental educational programming for young children with disabilities. In addition, outreach projects have taken some of the best practices from the demonstration projects and transferred them to other sites. By 1981, HCEEP had funded 280 demonstration projects (at a cost of over $85 million) and 140 outreach projects (costing over $35 million) (Hebbeler, Smith, & Black, 1991).

Independent evaluations of HCEEP projects have designated them as highly successful. These projects have not only provided direct services to young children and their families, but they have also produced curriculum materials, assessment devices, and parent training materials.

PL 99–457. Passed in 1986, **PL 99–457** stipulates that states must provide preschool services to all children with disabilities, ages three to five years. In addition, it provides incentives to states to establish programs for infants and toddlers with disabilities, ages birth to three years, and their families. All states have elected to provide services for infants and toddlers (Turnbull & Turnbull, 1990). Today, we have many more early childhood programs for students with disabilities than were available 20 years ago.

Infants and toddlers ages birth to three years are eligible for services if they (1) are experiencing a developmental delay in cognitive, physical, language and speech, psychosocial, or self-help development or (2) have a physical or mental condition with a high probability of resulting in a developmental delay.

Under PL 99–457, a variety of early intervention services, such as special education instruction, physical therapy, speech and language therapy, and medical diagnostic services, are available to help remediate the developmental delays of these infants and toddlers. In addition, this legislation involves the development of an **individualized family service plan (IFSP)**. As discussed in Chapter 1, an IFSP is similar to an individualized education program (IEP) for older children, but it broadens the focus to include the family as well as the child. In fact, federal regulations stipulate that the family be involved in the development of the IFSP. Other important requirements are that the IFSP must contain statements of the:

PL 90–538. Federal legislation passed in 1968 that created the Handicapped Children's Early Education Program (HCEEP).

Handicapped Children's Early Education Program (HCEEP). The first federal special education program aimed at young children with disabilities and their families. It has funded numerous demonstration and outreach projects.

PL 99–457. Federal legislation that extended the requirements of PL 94–142 to children ages three to five, with special incentives to states for instituting programs for ages birth to three years.

individualized family service plan (IFSP). A plan mandated by PL 99–457 to provide services for young children with disabilities (under three years of age) and their families; drawn up by professionals and parents; similar to an IEP for older children.

- child's present levels of functioning in cognitive, physical, language and speech, psycho-social, and self-help development
- family's resources, priorities, and concerns relating to the child's development
- major expected outcomes for the child and family, including criteria, procedures, and time lines for assessing progress
- specific early intervention services necessary to meet the child's and the family's needs, including frequency, intensity, location, and method of delivery
- projected dates for initiating and ending the services
- name of the case manager
- steps needed to ensure a smooth transition from the early intervention program into a preschool program

Types of Programs

One common way of categorizing the variety of early intervention programs is to consider whether the primary location of the services is in a center, a home, or a combination of the two. The earliest early intervention programs for children with disabilities were center based. In center-based programs, the child and the family come to the center for training and/or counseling. One advantage to center-based programs is that center staff can see more children. Furthermore, some professionals believe that this program allows center staff to have more influence over what goes on in the interaction between parent and child.

In more recent years, authorities have advocated home-based programs or a combination of center- and home-based approaches. There are several advantages to approaches that take place in the home. A couple of the most important are that (1) with the increase in mothers working outside the home and single-parent families, home-based programs are more convenient for more family members and (2) skills and techniques learned by children and adults at the center need to be transferred to the home, but when these skills are learned in the natural environment—that is, the home—this transfer is not necessary.

Issues

Compared to special education, in general, special education for infants, toddlers, and preschoolers has had few controversial issues. This is probably because so many professionals have fought for so long to get the needs of very young children recognized that they have not had time to engage in many debates about specific details concerning early intervention. In a sense, early childhood special educators have been bound together by the common goal of securing legislation and programming for young children with disabilities. Nevertheless, there have been and continue to be some areas of disagreement among early childhood special education professionals. Two of the most compelling issues relate to (1) the appropriate role of the family in early intervention and (2) whether it is better to have a child- or a teacher-directed curriculum.

Appropriate Role of the Family. Shaping up as a significant issue is how the family should be involved in early intervention programming. One characteristic of recent early intervention programming (Guralnick, 1991), and indeed, one of the hallmarks of the IFSP, has been the involvement of parents. Federal regulations, however, have not specifically directed *how* parents should be included in early intervention programming.

For example, some special educators hold that parents should be trained to use intervention techniques with their preschoolers. Research on the effectiveness of this approach is scant, but one team of researchers found that preschoolers with language disorders made comparable progress whether they received intervention from professionals or from their parents who had been trained to deliver the intervention (Eiserman, Weber, & McCoun, 1995). Other educators are concerned that the notion of including parents may be being misinterpreted to mean that professionals should focus more on changing the family than the child. Slentz and Bricker (1992), for example, have pointed out that federal regulations stipulate that any services provided for the family are for the purpose of meeting the needs of the child.

In particular, Slentz and Bricker are opposed to early childhood special educators becoming heavily involved in assessment of family members. If they do, "parents may legitimately question why providing such information is necessary when they thought the purpose of the early intervention program was to help their child. Many families perceive this process as an invasion of privacy" (Slentz & Bricker, 1992, p. 14). Instead, they believe that professionals should take a low-key approach to assessing families. Slentz and Bricker recommend that professionals briefly interview parents to find out the needs of the family and the child, rather than administer a lengthy battery of tests. If parents indicate a need for it, they can be referred for further evaluation.

Closely related to the issue of assessment is the larger issue of who should be in control over decision making for the family. Slentz and Bricker (1992) believe that "in large measure, families should decide on their goals and priorities with the early intervention staff assisting in the attainment of those goals" (pp. 17–18). As one expert summed up:

> Family decision making and control is clearly the approach policy makers wished to endorse in the current legislation. . . . The law intends to leave the final decision about children in the hands of their parents. The family is encouraged to seek professional advice on complex issues beyond its own expertise. Indeed, family members would not be performing their responsibilities if they did not do so. But the family is expected to maintain executive control over the important decisions and not cede that control to professionals, no matter how distinguished their credentials. (Gallagher, 1992, p. 8)

Child-Directed versus Teacher-Directed Programs. For some time, tension has existed between early childhood educators concerned with nondisabled populations and those focused on children with disabilities over the degree of teacher direction that is most appropriate. Heavily influenced by the theories of Piaget, most early childhood teachers are oriented toward a curriculum that allows children to explore their environment relatively freely. These teachers advocate a developmental approach that assumes that children's development will unfold naturally with encouragement, guidance, and support from the teacher (Position Statement of National Association for the Education of Young Children and National Association of Early Childhood Specialists in State Departments of Education, 1991).

Many early interventionists, on the other hand, come from a tradition that assumes children with disabilities need a heavy dose of direction from adults if they are to learn the skills they lack. Furthermore, early childhood special educators have generally had a greater focus on individualizing instruction for preschoolers through task analysis, adaptation of materials and activities, and systematic assessment (Carta,

1995). As more and more children with disabilities have been integrated with nondisabled preschoolers, the issues of teacher direction and individualization have come to the fore.

A major task facing early childhood special educators is to reach agreement with mainstream early childhood educators regarding programming for preschoolers with disabilities. Both sides can undoubtedly learn from each other. On the one hand, researchers have known for a long time that that preschoolers with disabilities do better in highly structured, teacher-directed, individualized programs (Abt Associates, 1976–1977). On the other hand, authorities have noted that moving from a highly structured preschool intervention program to a traditional kindergarten can present problems:

> The ecology of special education preschool classrooms may preclude opportunities for students to practice skills that foster independence. Students in special education preschools spend more time in small groups of individual instruction, and receive much more teacher prompting than do peers in typical preschool classes. Although these instructional arrangements may facilitate skill acquisition, they may inhibit the acquisition of the very academic support skills that facilitate a successful transition to the academic mainstream. Children in these special education classrooms have few opportunities to acquire or practice the independent skills that are important for success in kindergarten. (Fowler, Schwartz, & Atwater, 1991, p. 138)

Moving toward the Twenty-First Century

As we move toward the twenty-first century, we are hopeful that early childhood education will continue to play an important role in eliminating and lessening the impact of disability on children and their families. We caution, however, not to assume that early intervention alone will mean fewer children with disabilities. Although educators are devising more effective programs of early intervention, the number of children with disabilities is increasing. The reasons for this increase are many and complex and are related to changes in economic and social conditions in the United States. Today, compared to a decade or two ago:

- More young children and their mothers live in poverty, have poor nutrition, and are exposed to environmental conditions likely to cause disease and disability.
- More babies are born to teenage mothers.
- More babies are born to mothers who receive inadequate prenatal care, have poor nutrition during pregnancy, and abuse substances that can harm the fetus.
- More babies are born with a low birthweight.
- Environmental hazards, both chemical and social, have increased.
- More children are subjected to abuse and an environment in which violence and substance abuse are pervasive.
- Cuts in social programs have widened the gap between needs and the availability of social services.

These facts prompted the President's Committee on Mental Retardation and the National Coalition on Prevention of Mental Retardation to speak of a *new morbidity*—a new set of disabilities (Baumeister, Kupstas, & Klindworth, 1990). The new morbidity includes a variety of behavioral, health, and school problems that affect a growing number of U.S. children and are caused by many of the preceding factors.

Implementing and expanding the services provided under PL 99–457 and training the early childhood specialists necessary to provide effective early intervention are major challenges as we head toward the twenty-first century.

TRANSITION FROM SECONDARY SCHOOL TO ADULTHOOD

Preparing students for continued education, adult responsibilities, independence, and employment have always been goals of public secondary education. Most students complete high school and find jobs, enter a vocational training program, or go to college without experiencing major adjustment difficulties. We know that dropout and unemployment rates are far too high for all youths, especially in economically depressed communities, but the outlook for students with disabilities may be even worse (Hendrick, MacMillan, & Balow, 1989; Wolman, Bruininks, & Thurlow, 1989).

Published figures on dropout rates must be viewed with caution because there are many different ways of defining *dropout* and computing the statistics (MacMillan et al., 1992). Studies of what happens to students with disabilities during and after their high school years strongly suggest, however, that a higher percentage of them, compared to students without disabilities, have difficulty in making the transition from adolescence to adulthood and from school to work. Many students with disabilities drop out of school, experience great difficulty in finding and holding jobs, do not find work suited to their capabilities, do not receive further training or education, or become dependent on their families or public assistance programs (Heal & Rusch, 1995; Rusch, Szymanski, & Chadsey-Rusch, 1992; Sitlington, Frank, & Carson, 1992).

Good transition programming should address more than just employment; a person's quality of life, well-being, and personal fulfillment also should be considered.

Federal Initiatives

As was the case with early childhood programs, much of the impetus for programming for transition to adulthood came from the federal government. In 1990, Congress enacted **PL 101–476** mandating that schools must provide transition services for all students with disabilities. The federal government defines *transition services* as:

> a coordinated set of activities for a student, designed within an outcome-oriented process, which promotes movement from school to post-school activities, including post-secondary education, vocational training, integrated employment (including supported employment), continuing and adult education, adult services, independent living, or community participation.

To ensure proper planning for transition services, the federal government also requires that students with disabilities have transition plans integrated into their individualized education programs (IEPs). Each student's IEP must contain a statement of needed transition services for him or her, beginning no later than sixteen years of age and annually thereafter. (For students for whom it is appropriate, the statement is to be included in the IEP at a younger age.) In addition, the IEP must include a statement of the linkages and/or responsibilities of each participating agency before the student leaves the school setting.

An important aspect of this legislation is that it recognizes that transition involves more than just employment. This broad emphasis on independent living, community adjustment, and so forth has been applauded by many authorities. For example, some have championed the idea that transition programming should be aimed at increasing the quality of life for people with disabilities (Chadsey-Rusch & Heal, 1995; Halpern, 1993; Sands & Kozleski, 1994; Szymanski, 1994). Although *quality of life* is difficult to define, Halpern (1993) points to personal choice as its underlying principle. He also identifies three important quality of life domains: (1) physical and material well-being; (2) performance of adult roles (e.g., employment, leisure, personal relationships, social responsibility); and (3) personal fulfillment (e.g., happiness).

Supported Employment. With the federal mandate for transition services has come an increase in the use of supported employment. In fact, it is cited in the federal definition of transition services as an example of integrated employment (see above). **Supported employment**, designed to assist persons with disabilities who cannot function independently in competitive employment, is a method of ensuring that they are able to work in integrated work settings. *Competitive employment* is defined as working at least twenty hours per week. *Integrated work settings* are defined as:

> settings where (a) most workers are not handicapped and (b) individuals with handicaps are not part of a work group consisting only of others with handicaps, or are part of a small work group of not more than eight individuals with handicaps. Additionally, if there are no co-workers or the only co-workers are members of a small group of not more than eight individuals with handicaps, individuals with handicaps must have regular contact with nonhandicapped individuals, other than personnel who provide support services. Finally, these regulations require that supported employees be provided follow-up services at least twice monthly at the job site, except in the case of chronic mental illness. (Rusch & Hughes, 1990, p. 9)

In a typical supported employment situation, an employment specialist, or **job coach**, places the individual in a job with a business. The job coach then provides onsite training that is gradually reduced as the worker is able to function more independently on the job.

PL 101–476. Enacted in 1990, this federal legislation stipulates that schools provide transition services from secondary school to adulthood for all students with disabilities; scope includes postsecondary education, vocational training, integrated employment, continuing and adult education, independent living, and community living; stipulates that a transition plan must be included in the IEP no later than sixteen years of age.

supported employment. A method of integrating people with disabilities who cannot work independently into competitive employment; includes use of an employment specialist, or job coach, who helps the person with a disability function on the job.

job coach. A person who assists adult workers with disabilities (especially those with mental retardation), providing vocational assessment, instruction, overall planning, and interaction assistance with employers, family, and related government and service agencies.

Issues

Like early intervention programming, little controversy surrounds the basic premise of transition programming for students as they move from school to work. All special educators agree that transition programming is critical for the successful adjustment of adults with disabilities. However, there is some controversy regarding the specifics of transition. Much of this has to do with trying to meet the diverse requirements of the federal mandate. Some professionals are debating how best to build a curriculum that covers education, employment, independent living, and community participation. This concern for meeting the diverse needs of students is manifested somewhat differently for students with more severe disabilities than for those with milder disabilities.

Students with Severe Disabilities. For students with severe disabilities, much of the concern focuses on the coordination and linkage of the many agencies outside the school setting (DeStefano & Wermuth, 1992). Many special education personnel are unaccustomed to working with nonschool agencies. For example, the relationship between vocational and special education has traditionally been ambiguous. Federal regulations, however, now require that special education work with vocational education as well as with other agencies in the community.

For a number of years, special educators at the secondary level have been moving toward more involvement in the community, but the federal transition mandate has hastened the need for these outreach efforts. Approaches such as supported employment, for example, require that special educators work with local employers in setting up and instituting training and working environments for students with disabilities. Not all special educators have been trained for this expanded role, however. We are still in the infancy stage of knowing how best to accomplish this interface between the school and community environments. There is a need for experimentation with approaches to educating special educators for this broader role.

Students with Mild Disabilities. For students with mild disabilities, much of the concern centers on attempting to meet their academic as well as their vocational needs. Teachers of secondary students are constantly faced with the decision of how much to stress academics versus vocational preparation. Because their disabilities are milder, many children with learning disabilities, for example, may be able to go on to postsecondary educational institutions, such as community colleges or universities. It is often difficult to tell as early as tenth grade (when such decisions need to be made) whether to steer students with learning disabilities toward college preparatory or more vocationally oriented curricula.

Some authorities believe that too many students with learning disabilities have been "sold short" on how much they can achieve academically. These authorities believe that such students are written off as academic failures who can never achieve at the college level. This diminished expectation for academic success translates into a curriculum that makes few academic demands on students. For example, one study of students in learning disabilities classrooms at the secondary level found an "environmental press against academic content" (Zigmond & Miller, 1992, p. 25).

Other authorities maintain that an overemphasis on academics leaves many students with learning disabilities unprepared to enter the world of work upon leaving school. They believe that the learning problems of students with learning disabilities tend to be minimized. These authorities assert that just because students with learn-

Case Study: Tom

Tom is average in height and slightly immature physically. He is relatively low-functioning with an attained IQ of 70, second-grade reading skills, and third-grade math skills. His behavior is noticeably inappropriate at times; he is very excitable and difficult to get along with. His speech tends to be disjointed, and he often uses clichés (which he generally misstates) to appear more knowledgeable and on top of things. He has only one friend, a slightly higher-functioning special education peer, whom he tries to dominate during social interactions. He drives and has his own car. He lives at home with his family and has no plans to move out.

He was adopted at birth; his parents were unaware of his disability until he was referred for testing in kindergarten. As he was growing up, they made every effort to provide a supportive and protective environment for him, although Tom thought they babied him too much.

Throughout high school, Tom saw himself as competent and intelligent. He never admitted to having a learning disability and dismissed any conversation suggesting such an idea. He felt he had been incorrectly placed in special classes that were below his ability and was anxious to graduate. He thought a lot about what he should do after graduation, and on one self-description survey indicated "need advice on what to do after high school." He talked about becoming an electrician, a contractor, a welder, and a forest ranger, but mostly he aspired to be a contractor (he had worked part time for a contractor, a family friend since ninth grade). Tom finally decided to enroll in a training program at the junior college to prepare him for a contractor's license. The summer after graduation, he began attending classes but again felt they were below his ability and he had been incorrectly placed (a college counselor had enrolled him in an Independent Living Skills class for disabled students). Tom dropped the course and took a leave of absence from school for a year so he could work full time with the contractor. Shortly afterward, the contractor's company went out of business and Tom lost his job. Tom's family arranged for him to work with an uncle who was also a contractor and welder (two of his cousins worked for Tom's uncle as well). After a few months, Tom lost that job, too.

At this point, no school, no job, Tom confided in the field researcher (whom he had known for over a year) of his fear that he might not have a "normal" future (he had confided in few people before about his learning problem). He acknowledged the extent of his learning disability and his concern about its impact on his plans for contractor's work. He seemed hopeless and his self-confidence had dropped markedly. He felt tremendous pressure "to decide about something" and asked the field researcher for help. Tom had one last hope, that perhaps he could enroll in a vocationally oriented junior college (i.e., trade technical college), and that maybe his uncle (the contractor) and the field researcher could help him check out the school. Tom seemed to be identifying with his uncle—Tom described him as "also learning disabled"—as though his uncle more than anyone could understand Tom's problem. It also seemed to reassure Tom to know he was not alone in the world with his learning disability.

Tom pursued admission to the contractor's program at the trade tech junior college and began attending classes during the spring semester. Within a few weeks of his starting the program, Tom's self-confidence and hopes for the future were restored. He boasted that going to trade tech is the best thing he has ever done.

Source: From A. G. Zetlin and A. Hosseini, Six postschool case studies of mildly learning handicapped young adults, *Exceptional Children, 55*(5) (1989), 405–411.

ing disabilities are characterized as having mild disabilities, they do not necessarily have insignificant learning impairments.

Along these same lines, some professionals think that far too few support services are available to students with mild disabilities. Whereas transition services such as supported employment are available to persons with severe disabilities, individuals with milder disabilities are often left to fend for themselves once they graduate from secondary school. (See the box above.)

Goals 2000 and Transition Programming for Students with Mild Disabilities. Adding to the confusion over the debate about academics versus vocational preparation is the current federal emphasis on academics. Beginning in the late 1980s and continuing into the 1990s, a number of national reports have criticized the general educational system in the United States. Pointing to the low achievement levels of American youths, compared with those of other industrialized countries, these reports have resulted in a call for higher standards in the nation's schools.

Goals 2000: Educate America Act. Legislation passed in 1994, aimed at increasing the academic standards in U.S. schools; some educators fear that the focus on high standards may harm students with disabilities.

In 1994, Congress passed the **Goals 2000: Educate America Act**, which set eight national goals for the year 2000 (see Table 2–1). Critics assert that these goals largely ignore the educational needs of students with disabilities. What's more, they fear that the emphasis on higher standards has taken away the focus from the needs of students with disabilities who are unable to meet such high standards. As one example, critics point to the fact that several states now require students to pass minimum competency tests to receive their high school diplomas. Some special educators have expressed concern that these requirements might be unfair to students with disabilities (Halpern, 1992).

Table 2-1
Eight Goals Established by Goals 2000: Educate America Act

1	*Readiness for school*	By the year 2000, all children in the United States will start school ready to learn.
2	*High school completion*	By the year 2000, the high school graduation rate will have increased to at least 90 percent.
3	*Student achievement and citizenship*	By the year 2000, all students will leave grades 4, 8, and 12 having demonstrated competency over challenging subject matter (including English, mathematics, science, history, foreign languages, civics and government, economics, arts, and geography), and every school in the U.S. will ensure that all students learn to use their minds well, so they may be prepared for responsible citizenship, further learning, and productive employment in modern economy.
4	*Teacher education and professional development*	By the year 2000, the nation's teaching force will have access to programs for the continued improvement of their professional skills and the opportunity to acquire the knowledge and skills needed to instruct and prepare all U.S. students for the next century.
5	*Science and mathematics*	By the year 2000, U.S. students will be first in the world in science and mathematics achievement.
6	*Adult literacy and lifelong learning*	By the year 2000, every adult American will be literate and will possess the knowledge and skills necessary to compete in a global economy and exercise the rights and responsibilities of citizenship.
7	*Safe, disciplined, and alcohol- and drug-free schools*	By the year 2000, every school in the U.S. will be free of drugs and violence, and the unauthorized presence of firearms and alcohol and will offer a disciplined environment conducive to learning.
8	*Parental participation*	By the year 2000, every school will promote partnerships that increase parental involvement and participation in promoting the social, emotional, and academic growth of children.

Source: U. S. Senate-House Conference, 1994

Moving toward the Twenty-First Century

It is still too early to tell how much impact Goals 2000 will have on students with disabilities. But as we move toward the twenty-first century, despite some of the unresolved issues, we can be encouraged by all the attention that special educators have given to the area of transition. A variety of transition opportunities are available now that were unavailable just a few years ago.

In considering transition issues, it is helpful to keep in mind that a smooth and successful transition to adult life is difficult for any adolescent. Individuals find many different routes to adulthood, and we would be foolish to prescribe a single pattern of transition. Our goal must be to provide the special assistance needed by adolescents and young adults with disabilities that will help them achieve the most rewarding, productive, independent, and integrated adult lives possible. This goal cannot be achieved by assuming that all adolescents and young adults with disabilities, or even all individuals falling into a given special education category, will need the same special transition services or that all will achieve the same level of independence and productivity. One of education's great challenges is to devise an effective array of programs that will meet the individual needs of students on their paths to adulthood.

SOME CONCLUDING THOUGHTS REGARDING TRENDS AND ISSUES

If you are feeling a bit overwhelmed at the controversial nature of special education, then we have achieved our objective. We, too, are constantly amazed at the number of unanswered questions our field faces. It seems that just as we find what we think are the right answers to a certain set of questions about how to educate students with disabilities, another set of questions emerges. And each new collection of questions is as complex and challenging as the last.

It would be easy to view this inability to reach definitive conclusions with which everyone agrees as indicative of a field in chaos. We disagree. We prefer to view this constant state of questioning as a sign of health and vigor. The controversial nature of special education is what makes it exciting and challenging. We would be worried (and we believe people with disabilities and their families would be worried, too) if the field were suddenly to decide that it had reached complete agreement on most of the important issues. We should constantly be striving to find better ways to provide education and related services for persons with disabilities. In doing this, it is inevitable that there will be differences of opinion.

SUMMARY

Special education has changed dramatically during its history, and the field appears poised for more changes. Three major trends are integration, early intervention programming, and programming for transition from secondary school to adulthood. With an increase in these three areas have come a number of issues.

The trend toward integration of people with disabilities into the larger society began in the 1960s and continues stronger than ever today. Much of the philosophical rationale for integration comes from the principle of normalization. Normalization dictates that both the means and ends of education for people with disabilities should be as normal as possible. Controversies have surrounded implementation of the normalization principle. There is disagreement about whether it means the abolition of residential programs and special classes. Members of some groups, such as those who are deaf, have questioned whether normalization should mean integration for them. And some have cautioned that the overuse of technology may go against the concept of normalization.

Two important movements in the drive toward more integration have been deinstitutionalization and the regular education initiative. Started in the 1960s, deinstitutionalization is a trend to move people with disabilities into closer contact with the community and home. More and more people with disabilities are living in smaller group homes, rather than large institutions. Some professionals believe there is no need for large residential institutions of any kind, whereas others believe they need to be a part of a continuum of educational placements.

In the 1980s, the federal government began the regular education initiative (REI), a loosely defined movement to have general education teachers assume more responsibility for children with special needs, such as those who are bilingual, economically disadvantaged, and/or those who have disabilities. Special educators have long advocated the practice of mainstreaming students with disabilities in general education classrooms for all or part of the day yet still identifying them as special education students. Advocates of full inclusion contend that there should be no separate special education classes, that students should attend their neighborhood schools, and that the general education system should have the primary responsibility for all students. Others believe that although mainstreaming should be employed more than is currently the case, what's needed is a continuum of placements (e.g., residential institutions, special schools, special classes, resource rooms, general classes) from which parents and professionals can choose.

Full inclusion is based on four premises: (1) Labeling of people is harmful; (2) special education pull-out programs have been ineffective; (3) people with disabilities should be viewed as a minority group; and (4) ethics should take precedence over empiricism.

Sentiment against labeling arose out of the fear that labeling students for special education stigmatizes them and makes them feel unworthy. Research on the effects of labeling is inconclusive. People do tend to view labeled individuals differently than they do those without labels. Some educators maintain, however, that labels may provide an explanation for atypical behavior.

Over the past thirty years, more than fifty studies have compared outcomes for students with disabilities placed in special education versus regular classes, or resource rooms versus general education classes. The results have not been very supportive of special education. Critics of this research, however, point out that virtually all these studies have been methodologically flawed.

Advocates of full inclusion tend to believe that the problems people with disabilities face are due to their being members of a minority group, rather than the result of their disability. This view is consistent with that of the disability rights movement, whose members have advocated for a variety of civil rights for persons with disabilities and have been influential in lobbying legislators and promoting more appropriate media portrayals of people with disabilities.

Some full-inclusion advocates do not care if full inclusion is more or less effective than pull-out special education programs; they believe in full inclusion because they think it is the ethical thing to do.

Opponents of full inclusion argue that (1) professionals and parents are largely satisfied with the current level of integration, (2) general educators are unwilling and/or unable to cope with all students with disabilities, (3) although equating disabilities with minority group status is, in many ways, legitimate, it has limitations when it comes to translation into educational programming recommendations, (4) an unwillingness to consider empirical evidence is professionally irresponsible, (5) available empirical evidence does not support full inclusion, and (6) in the absence of data to support one service delivery model, special educators must preserve the continuum of placements.

Even those special educators who do not believe in full inclusion believe there needs to be more integration of students into general classes and more research on better ways to implement mainstreaming. Some of the most popular mainstreaming practices are prereferral teams, peer collaboration, collaborative consultation, cooperative teaching, cooperative learning, peer tutoring, partial participation, and curriculum materials designed to change attitudes.

Early intervention programs for children with disabilities and their families are now mandated by law. PL 99–457 stipulates that states must provide preschool services for all children with disabilities ages three to five years and provides incentives for programming from birth to three years. A cornerstone of PL 99–457 is the individualized family service plan (IFSP). The IFSP is like an IEP, but it broadens the focus to include the family.

There are several types of early intervention programs. A common way of categorizing them is according to whether they are center-based, home-based, or a combination of the two.

Three issues pertaining to early childhood intervention are (1) the appropriate role of the family, (2) whether the curriculum should be teacher or child centered, and (3) the best way to ensure a smooth transition from early intervention programs to preschools and from preschools to schools.

Federal law now also stipulates programming for transition from secondary school to adulthood. *Transition* is defined as including a variety of postschool activities, including postsecondary education, vocational training, integrated employment, continuing and adult education, adult services, independent living, or community participation. The law mandates that transition plans must be incorporated into the IEPs of students with disabilities. The law emphasizes both employment and issues pertaining to the quality of life of people with disabilities.

Supported employment is one way to integrate persons with disabilities into the workplace. In a typical supported employment situation, a job coach provides onsite training, which gradually tapers off as the worker learns to perform the job independently.

Issues pertaining to implementing transition from secondary school to adulthood for people with severe disabilities focus largely on coordinating and linking the many agencies outside the school setting. For people with mild disabilities, many of the issues center on providing programming that balances their vocational and academic needs. Some educators are concerned that the recent press for more rigorous academic standards—articulated by the Goals 2000: Educate America Act passed in 1994—in the schools generally will result in the disregard of the needs of students with disabilities.

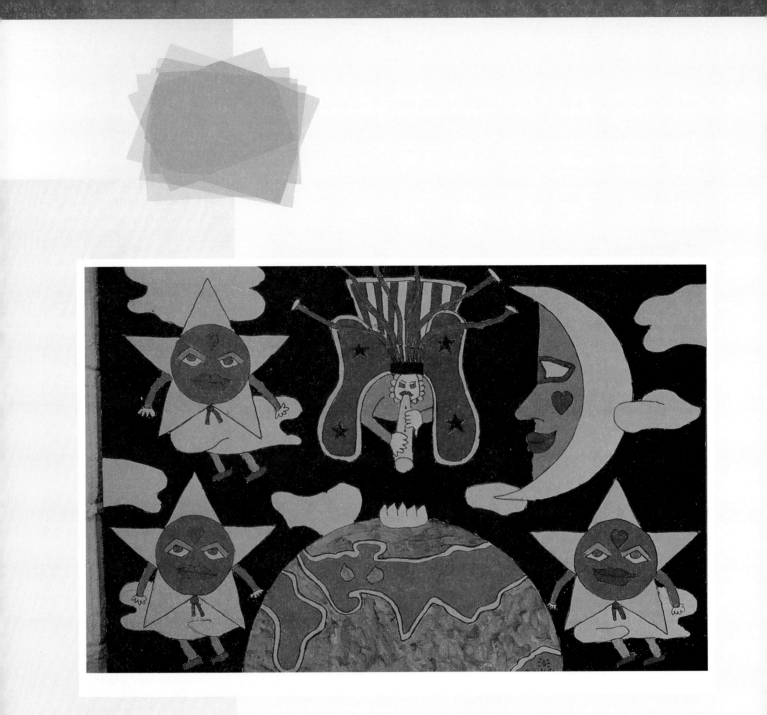

Daniel Napier
Daniel Napier is a disabled Native American veteran who finds many ideas for paintings outside the back window of his trailer on Collington Island in North Carolina's outer banks. His star people paintings were discovered by an art collector visiting a Carolina surf shop who convinced Napier to have a one-man show at the Galaxy Hut in Arlington, Virginia.

3

Multicultural and Bilingual Aspects of Special Education

Remember and help America remember that the fellowship of human beings is more important than the fellowship of race and class and gender in a democratic society. . . . All children need [a] pride of heritage and sense of history of their own people and of all the people who make up the mosaic of this great nation. African American and Latino and Asian American and Native American children should know about European history and cultures, and white children should know about the histories and cultures of diverse peoples of color with whom they share a city, a nation, and a world. I believe in integration. But that does not mean I become someone else or ignore or deny who I am. I learned the Negro National anthem, "Lift Every Voice and Sing," at the same time I learned "The Star Spangled Banner" and "America the Beautiful" and I love them all. I have raised you, my children, to respect other people's children, not to become their children but to become yourselves at your best. I hope others will raise their children to respect you.

Marian Wright Edelman
The Measure of Our Success: A Letter to My Children and Yours

In the last decade of the twentieth century, many nations and regions have splintered into factions, clans, tribes, and gangs. In some cases, this splintering has been accompanied by extreme cruelty of individuals or groups toward others. Differences—especially those of religion, ethnic origin, color, custom, and social class—are too often the basis for viciousness toward other people. This has been the case throughout human history, and it remains a central problem of humankind. All cultures and ethnic groups of the world can take pride in much of their heritage, but most, if not all, also bear a burden of shame because at some time in their history, they have engaged in the ruthless treatment or literal enslavement of others. Sometimes this treatment has extended to certain members of their own group whose differences have been viewed as undesirable or intolerable.

In virtually every nation, society, religion, ethnic group, tribe, or clan, discrimination exists against those who are different in some dimension of human identity. The discrimination that we practice or experience stems from and perpetuates fear, hatred, and abusive relationships. If a group feels discriminated against or subjugated and sees no hope of becoming valued and being treated fairly, it inevitably will seek to become separate and autonomous, sometimes threatening or subjugating others in the process.

It is critically important, therefore, that we learn and help others learn *tolerance*. Furthermore, it is necessary for special educators, as well as general educators, to understand the purpose of **multicultural education.** Namely, multicultural education aims to change educational institutions and curricula so that they will provide equal educational opportunities to students regardless of their gender, social class, ethnicity, race, disability, or other cultural identity.

Our desire as Americans is to build a diverse but just society in which the personal freedom and pride of all cultural groups and respect for others' cultural heritage are the norm, a society in which fear, hate, and abuse are eliminated. Working toward this ideal demands a multicultural perspective, one from which we can simultaneously accomplish two tasks. First, as a nation of increasing cultural diversity, we must renew our efforts to achieve social justice and take specific steps to understand and appreciate one anothers' cultures. Second, in doing so we must pledge our first loyalty to common cultural values that make diversity a strength rather than a fatal flaw. We seek a commitment to our common humanity and to democratic ideals that bind people together for the common good and give all the freedom to revel in a pride of heritage. These two tasks of multicultural education in a multicultural nation are expressed in the words of Marian Wright Edelman in her letter to her children and others (see p. 85).

Since the civil rights movement of the 1960s, educators have become increasingly aware of the extent to which differences among cultural and ethnic groups affect children's schooling. Gradually, educators and others are coming to understand that the cultural diversity of the United States and the world demands multicultural education. Progress in constructing multicultural education has been slow, however, in part because of the way all cultural groups tend to view themselves as the standard against which others should be judged. Rogoff and Morelli (1989) note that in the United States, this view has led to a focus on minority cultures:

> The United States, like many modern nations, is an aggregate of peoples of many cultural backgrounds. However, the role of culture is most noticeable when any of us views the practices of some other group than our own, and so the study of culture has generally focused on minorities in the United States and on people of other

multicultural education. Aims to change educational institutions and curricula so they will provide equal educational opportunities to students regardless of their gender, social class, ethnicity, race, disability, or other cultural identity.

Misconceptions about
Multicultural and Bilingual Aspects of Special Education

Myth Multicultural education addresses the concerns of ethnic minorities who want their children to learn more about their history and the intellectual, social, and artistic contributions of their ancestors.

Fact This is a partial truth. In fact, multicultural education seeks to help the children of all ethnic groups appreciate their own and others' cultural heritages—plus our common American culture that sustains multiculturalism.

Myth Everyone agrees that multicultural education is critical to our nation's future.

Fact Some people, including some who are members of ethnic minorities, believe that multicultural education is misguided and diverts attention from our integration in a distinctive, cohesive American culture.

Myth Implementing multicultural education is a relatively simple matter of including information about all cultures in the curriculum and teaching respect for them.

Fact Educators and others are struggling with how to construct a satisfactory multicultural curriculum and multicultural instructional methods. Nearly every aspect of the task is controversial—which cultures to include, how much attention to give to each, and what and how to teach about them.

Myth Multiculturalism includes only the special features and contributions of clearly defined ethnic groups.

Fact Ethnicity is typically the focal point of discussions of multiculturalism, but ethnicity is sometimes a point of controversy if it is defined too broadly (for example, by lumping all Asians together). Besides ethnic groups, other groups and individuals—such as people identified by gender, sexual orientation, religion, and disability—need consideration in a multicultural curriculum.

Myth Disproportionate representation of ethnic minorities in special education is no longer a problem.

Fact Some ethnic minorities are still underrepresented or overrepresented in certain special education categories. For example, African American students, especially males, are overrepresented in programs for students with emotional or behavioral disorders and underrepresented in programs for gifted and talented students.

Myth Disability is never related to ethnicity.

Fact Some disabilities are genetically linked and therefore more prevalent in some ethnic groups. For example, sickle cell disease (a severe, chronic, hereditary blood disease) occurs disproportionately in children with ancestry from Africa, Mediterranean and Caribbean regions, Saudi Arabia, and India.

Myth If students speak English, there is no need to be concerned about bilingual education.

Fact Conversational English is not the same as the more formal and sometimes technical language used in academic curriculum and classroom instruction. Educators must make sure that students understand the language used in teaching, not just informal conversation.

> nations. It is easy for dominant cultural groups to consider themselves as standard and other groups as variations. (Think of the number of people who comment on other people's accents and insist that they themselves do not have one.) (p. 341)

Education that takes full advantage of the cultural diversity in our schools and the larger world requires much critical analysis and planning. The box below illustrates how difficult it may be for all cultural or ethnic groups to find common satisfaction in a curriculum, even if they are all seeking what they consider the multicultural ideal. Moreover, some argue that the multicultural ideal is misguided, that the more important goal is finding the common American culture and ensuring that our children have a common cultural literacy (Hirsch, 1987). Consider the perspective represented in the box on page 90 (see also Rodriguez, 1982, 1992). Even the metaphors we use for dealing with cultural diversity and cultural unity are points of controversy. The United States has often been called a "cultural melting pot," but some now reject the notion of total melding or amalgamation—they reject the metaphor of an alloy in which metals are dissolved in each other and fused into a new substance (Price, 1992). For example, one teacher in a videotaped case study of multicultural education comments about the American melting pot, "I have no desire to melt, but I would love to enrich. But I *do* not want to melt! . . . Back to my stew, if I'm going in as a carrot, I want to be tasted as a carrot and then still add to the flavor of the entire" (McNergney, 1992). To continue with the "stew" metaphor, there is controversy regarding how "chunky" our American culture should be.

That racism and discrimination remain serious problems in the United States and most other societies is obvious. These problems have no simple resolution, and they are found among virtually all ethnic groups. People of every cultural description struggle with the meaning of differences that may seem trivial or superficial to some

Diversity Tests Schools

AREA EDUCATORS STRUGGLE
TO BALANCE CURRICULUM

While pouring over the new, "multicultural" version of history the Prince George's County school system adopted for its students . . . , a group of white parents detected a "slant" in some of the lessons.

In their view, the social studies curriculum on display at the local library favored black scholars whose theories that ancient Egypt was a purely black African civilization contradicted the work of classically trained historians.

The new lessons presented as "incontrovertible" the theory that Egyptians were black, said Claire Matte, a Bowie resident with two children in county schools who says the theory is much more open to debate.

No sooner had the guides received further editing, however, when a group of black parents offered its own 18-page critique.

The reworked material's writers, they said, displayed an "alarming" tendency to put qualifying language around the claims of Afrocentric researchers, but to present as "undisputed fact" traditional views such as whether Columbus was the first explorer to reach North America.

Such earnest disagreements—about whether history is an objective truth or a matter of interpretation—have been one by-product of the county's move toward a multicultural curriculum, an effort to give blacks, Hispanics, women, the elderly and other minority groups a more prominent place in increasingly diverse public school classrooms.

Although few have quarreled with the school system's goal, the word-for-word changes have kindled debate over whether they succeed in balancing previously lopsided lessons or fall into the realm of bias. Today, with another school year underway, the long-awaited curriculum has yet to find its way into the hands of teachers, and the initiative that put Prince George's at the forefront of the national multicultural movement has instead come to represent how difficult and politically charged such changes can be.

Source: By Lisa Leff, *The Washington Post*, November 28, 1992, pp. A1, A12.

but elicit powerful emotional responses and discrimination from others. Russell (1992), for example, describes color discrimination that is practiced not only between whites and African Americans but also among African Americans of varied hues. Consider the hostilities and suffering associated with differences in color as well as in gender, religion, sexual orientation, abilities and disabilities, and political beliefs.

The solution is not as simple as becoming sensitized to differences. Too often, Eurocentrism is met with Europhobia, Afrocentrism with Afrophobia, homocentrism with homophobia, sensitivity to difference with hypersensitivity about being different. Perhaps the solution must include both engendering sensitivity to differences and building confidence that one's own differences will not be threatened by others'. The solution may also require transforming the curriculum in ways that help students understand how knowledge is constructed and how to view themselves and others from different perspectives (Banks, 1995; Dean, Salend, & Taylor, 1993).

Perhaps we *can* find a uniquely American culture, one that celebrates valued diversities within a framework of clearly defined common values. This perspective recognizes that not all diversity is valued, that tolerance has its limits, and that American culture is dynamic and continuously evolving:

> There are limits to cultural tolerance, a lesson the 20th century has repeatedly taught us. There are, among some cultures, deeply held convictions—about women and their bodies; about races; about children; about authority; about lawbreakers, the sick, the weak, the poor and the rich—that we absolutely deplore. The fact is, we need absolutes. Where a plurality of cultures exists, we need an overarching set of values cherished by all. Otherwise what begins as multicultural harmony inevitably descends into balkanization or chaos. . . .
>
> The simple truth, which is either denied or distorted by the prevailing orthodoxies, is that a thriving national culture does exist. It is neither a salad bowl nor static, received tradition, but an ever-evolving national process which selects, unrepresentatively, from the marketplace of raw, particular identities, those that everyone finds it useful and gratifying to embrace and transform into their own. (Patterson, 1993, p. C2)

We are optimistic about multicultural education because it is an opportunity to face our shared problems squarely and to extract the best human qualities from each cultural heritage. Without denying any culture's inhumanity to others or to its own members, we have the opportunity to develop an appreciation of our individual and shared cultural treasures and to engender tolerance, if not love, of all differences that are not destructive of the human spirit. We concur with Price (1992):

> The appropriate antidote for cultural insularity is a culture of inclusiveness that infuses every facet of our society. . . . Were those who ardently preach American values truly to practice them, then perhaps our collective anxiety about the growing intolerance and insularity in America would, shall we say, melt away. (p. 213)

Multiculturalism is now a specialized field of study and research in education and its full exploration is far beyond the scope of this chapter (see, for example, Banks & Banks, 1993; Lynch, Modgil, & Modgil, 1992a, 1992b, 1992c, 1992d; Spring 1994). Of particular concern to special educators is how exceptionalities are related to cultural diversity and the way in which special education fits within the broader general education context in a multicultural society (Garcia & Malkin, 1993). Cultural diversity presents particular challenges for special educators in three areas: (1) assessment of abilities and disabilities, (2) instruction, and (3) socialization. Before discussing each of these challenges, we summarize some of the major concepts about education and cultural diversity that set the context for multicultural and bilingual special education.

A Surprising Argument for American Culture

Richard Rodriguez makes the astonishing claim that America exists. "There is an America here. There is a culture here," he almost pleads.

This, of course, is not an original thought. What is original is its provenance—Rodriguez is a Mexican American, an intellectual, a prose poet—and its stinging repudiation of the prevailing ethnic ethos. Rodriguez calls it "that multiculturalism crap," or "Hispanic pseudo-nationalism."

He scoffs: "The notion that you can hold on to your culture—or lose it, for that matter—is an impossibility. Walt Disney is my culture! Howdy Doody is my culture!"

This resolute Americanism in the face of diversity worship may be why his celebrated first book, "Hunger of Memory" (1982), struck such a chord—a dulcet one to Americans fed up with ethnic special pleading, and a dissonant one to Americans passionately embracing their group identities. This onetime "poster child of affirmative action"—he sneers at the phrase—has become that creed's professional apostate.

Which may be why, among other honors that regularly come Rodriguez's way, . . . he received one of the Charles Frankel humanities awards from President Bush. Had he lived to attend, academic scourge Allan Bloom would have been among the other recipients (along with Shelby Foote, Eudora Welty, and Harold K. Skramstad Jr., director of the Henry Ford Museum).

The award comes as Rodriguez, who lives in San Francisco, is touring the country to promote his latest, and only other, book, "Days of Obligation: An Argument with my Mexican Father." Like the autobiographical "Hunger of Memory," "Days" harvests the fruits of research Rodriguez conducted mainly in the vineyard of the self.

Source: By Charles Truehard, *The Washington Post* November 28, 1992, p. F1. © 1992, The Washington Post. Reprinted with permission.

EDUCATION AND CULTURAL DIVERSITY: CONCEPTS FOR SPECIAL EDUCATION

Culture has many definitions. As Banks (1994) points out, however, "Most contemporary social scientists view culture as consisting primarily of the symbolic, ideational, and intangible aspects of human societies" (p. 83). Banks suggests six major components or elements of culture:

1. values and behavioral styles
2. languages and dialects
3. nonverbal communication
4. awareness (of one's cultural distinctiveness)
5. frames of reference (normative world views or perspectives)
6. identification (feeling part of the cultural group)

These elements may together make up a national or shared culture, sometimes referred to as a **macroculture.** Within the larger macroculture are **microcultures**—smaller cultures that share the common characteristics of the macroculture but have their unique values, styles, languages and dialects, nonverbal communication, awareness, frames of reference, and identities. An individual may identify with the macroculture and also belong to many different microcultures, as shown in Figure 3–1. The variety of microcultures to which a person belongs affects his or her behavior.

macroculture. A nation or other large social entity with a shared culture.

microculture. A smaller group existing within a larger cultural group and having unique values, style, language, dialect, ways of communicating nonverbally, awareness, frame of reference, and identification.

Macroculture in the United States consists of certain overarching values, symbols, and ideas, such as justice, equality, and human dignity. Microcultures within the U.S. macroculture may share these common values but differ in many additional ways. The number of microcultures represented in U.S. schools has increased in recent decades because of the variety of immigrants from other countries, particularly Southeast Asia. Duke (1990) notes that "these newcomers contribute to a diversity of cultures and languages that probably has not characterized American society since the

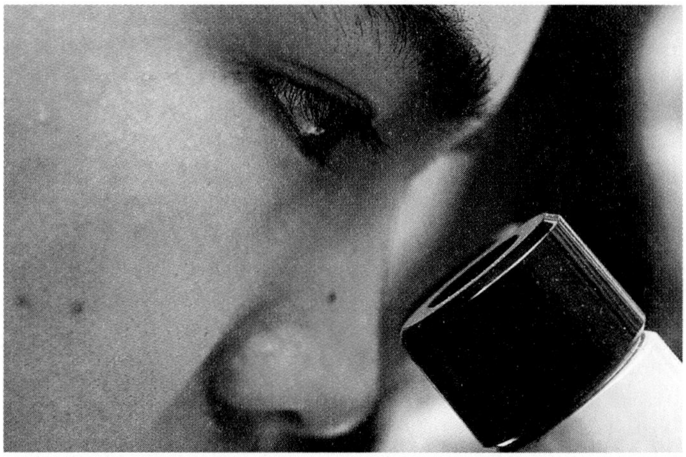

An individual's membership in any cultural, ethnic, racial, regional, gender, social class, or disability group should not affect what educational opportunities are available to him or her.

turn of the century" (pp. 69–70). Students from some microcultures in U.S. society do extremely well in school, but others do not. The factors accounting for the school performance of microcultural minorities are complex, and social scientists are still searching for the attitudes, beliefs, behavioral styles, and opportunities that foster the success of specific microcultural groups (Jacob & Jordan, 1987).

Researchers have reported that Southeast Asian (Indochinese) refugee families adopting an orientation to certain American values—acquiring material possessions and seeking fun and excitement—have children whose academic performance is lower than that of children from families maintaining traditional Southeast Asian values—persistence, achievement, and family support (Caplan, Choy, & Whitmore, 1992). This finding suggests that schools and teachers may face an impossible task unless

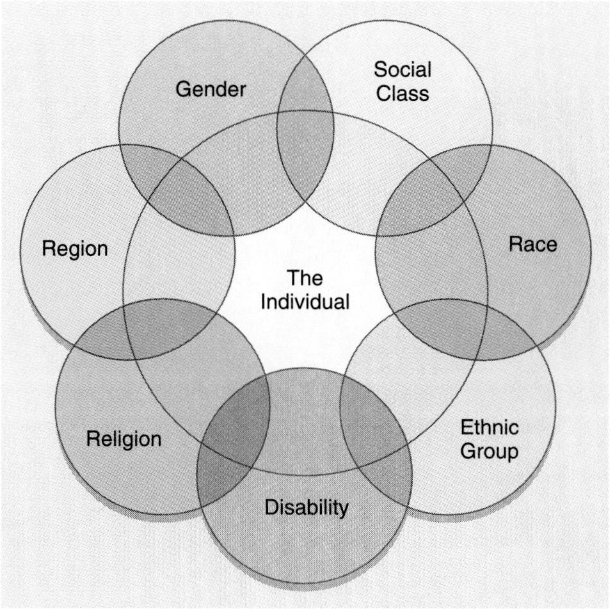

Figure 3–1

Individuals belong to many different microcultural groups.
(*Source:* From J. A. Banks, *Multiethnic Education: Theory and Practice,* [3rd ed.]. p. 89. Copyright © 1994 by Allyn & Bacon. Reprinted with permission.)

changes occur in students' home cultures. "It is clear that the U.S. educational system can work—if the requisite familial and social supports are provided for the students outside school" (Caplan et al., 1992, p. 36).

Ogbu (1992) also notes the critical role played by different minority communities in encouraging academic success among their children and youth. He differentiates between immigrant, or *voluntary,* minorities who have come to the United States primarily for their own economic and social benefit and castelike, or *involuntary,* minorities who were originally brought to the United States against their will. Most Chinese and Punjabi Indians, for example, are voluntary minorities; African American children and youths are, for the most part, members of an involuntary minority. Ogbu (1992) concludes that "minority children do not succeed or fail only because of what schools do or do not do, but also because of what the community does" (p. 12). He continues:

> At this point in my research I suggest four ways in which the involuntary minority community can encourage academic striving and success among its children. One is to teach the children to separate attitudes and behaviors that lead to academic success from attitudes and behaviors that lead to a loss of ethnic identity and culture or language. . . . Second, the involuntary minority community should provide the children with concrete evidence that its members appreciate and value academic success as much as they appreciate and value achievements in sports, athletics, and entertainment.
>
> Third, the involuntary minority community must teach the children to recognize and accept the responsibility for their school adjustment and academic performance. . . .
>
> Finally, the involuntary minority middle class needs to reevaluate and change its role vis-à-vis the community. (p. 12)

Ogbu (1992) goes on to describe two ways in which minority individuals who have achieved middle-class status might interact with the minority community. For example, successful, educated, professional people might provide highly visible role

Family support (or the lack thereof) is recognized as a key factor in children's academic success.

models for youths, demonstrating how they can achieve success in the wider society and retain their collective identity and bona fide membership in the minority community. This is the example typically provided by voluntary minorities. Ogbu also notes that:

> in contrast, involuntary minorities seem to have a model that probably does not have much positive influence on schooling. Members of involuntary minorities seem to view professional success as "a ticket" to leave their community both physically and socially, to get away from those who have not "made it." People seek education and professional success, as it were, in order to leave their minority community. (Ogbu, 1992, p. 13)

Although there is considerable evidence that various ethnic minority communities have a strong influence on students' achievement and school behavior, we offer three cautions:

1. We need to guard against stereotypes—assumptions that one's cultural identity is sufficient to explain academic achievement or economic success. The Doonesbury cartoon above makes the point rather well, we feel.
2. The fact that minority communities may have a strong influence on school success does not relieve schools of the obligation to provide a multicultural education. All students need to feel that they and their cultural heritage are included in the mainstream of American culture and schooling.
3. Unless teachers and other school personnel value minority students—see value and promise in them and act accordingly by setting demanding but not unreachable expectations—the support of families and the minority community may be insufficient to improve the academic success of minority students (Steele, 1992). Too often, minority students are devalued in school, regardless of their achievements and behaviors (Boutte, 1992; Steele, 1992).

The general purposes of multicultural education are (1) to promote pride in one's own cultural heritage and understanding of microcultures different from one's own, (2) to foster positive attitudes toward cultural diversity, and (3) to ensure equal educational opportunities for all students. These purposes cannot be accomplished unless students develop an understanding and appreciation of their own cultural heritage, as well as an awareness and acceptance of cultures different from their own. Understanding and appreciation are not likely to develop automatically through

Educators will be more successful in addressing individual needs if they are sensitive to the possibility that attitudes toward disabilities vary among different cultural groups.

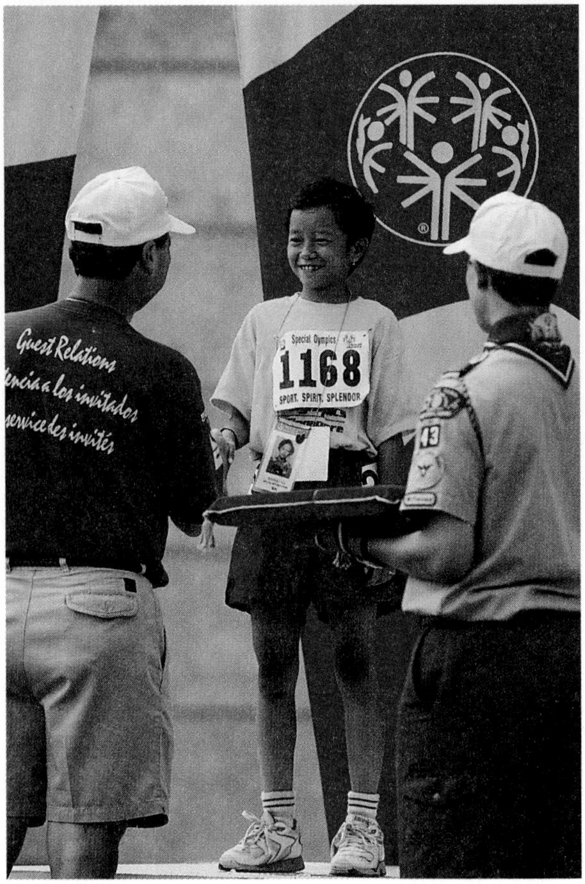

unplanned contact with members of other microcultures. Rather, teachers must plan experiences that teach about culture and provide models of cultural awareness and acceptance and the appreciation of cultural diversity.

On the surface, teaching about cultures and engendering an acceptance and appreciation of cultural diversity appear to be simple tasks. However, two questions immediately complicate the matter when we get below the surface and address the actual practice of multiculturalism in education: (1) Which cultures shall we include? (2) What and how shall we teach about them?

The first question demands that we consider all the microcultures that might be represented in the school and the difficulties inherent in including them all. The United States has more than 100 distinct microcultures based on national origin alone. In some urban school districts with large numbers of immigrant children, more than twenty different languages may be spoken in students' homes. But ethnic or national origin is only one dimension of cultural diversity, one branch of many in the multicultural program. Many advocates of multiculturalism consider gender, sexual orientation, religion, disability, and so on to be additional dimensions of cultural diversity that require explicit attention. Moreover, some microcultural groups find the traditions, ceremonies, values, holidays, and other characteristics of other microcultures unacceptable or even offensive. That is, when it comes to what and how to teach about other cultures, the stage may be set for conflict. Treating all cultures with equal attention and respect may present substantial or seemingly insurmountable logistical and interpersonal problems.

One of the most controversial aspects of multicultural education is the use of language. For instance, is it appropriate to refer to a *minority* or *minorities* when the group or aggregates to which we refer constitute half or more of the population in a given school, district, region, or state? What labels and terms are acceptable for designating various groups? What languages or dialects should be used for instruction? With the arrival of many immigrants to the United States, the issue of bilingual education and its relationship to multiculturalism has become increasingly important. The box on page 96 illustrates how controversial the issue of language can be. As we discuss later, bilingual education is of even greater concern when children with disabilities are considered (Gersten, Brengelman, & Jimenez, 1994).

Given the multiplicity of microcultures, each wanting—if not demanding—its precise and fair inclusion in the curriculum, it is not surprising that educators sometimes feel caught in a spiral of factionalism and feuding. Furthermore, additional questions about cultural values inevitably must be addressed: Which cultural values and characteristics should we embrace? Which, if any, should we shun? Would we, if we could, fully sustain some cultures, alter some significantly, and eliminate others? Consider, for example, cultures in which women are treated as chattel, as well as the drug culture, the culture of street gangs, the culture of poverty. To what extent does every culture have a right to perpetuate itself? How should we respond to some members of the Deaf culture, for example, who reject the prevention of deafness or procedures and devices that enable deaf children to hear, preferring deafness to hearing and wishing to sustain the deaf culture deliberately? Depending on how we define culture, the values of our own cultural heritage, and our role in multicultural education, we may find ourselves embroiled in serious cultural conflicts. No wonder that some describe the 1980s and 1990s as an era of "culture wars" (Hunter, 1991; Shor, 1986). To deal effectively with the multicultural challenge, we must focus on the challenges most pertinent to special education.

IMPLEMENTING MULTICULTURAL AND BILINGUAL SPECIAL EDUCATION

The microcultures of particular importance for special education are ethnic groups and exceptionality groups. Banks (1988) defines an *ethnic group* as "a group that shares a common ancestry, culture, history, tradition, and sense of peoplehood" (p. 91). An ethnic group may be a majority or a minority of people in a given country or region. We define an *exceptionality group* as a group sharing a set of specific abilities or disabilities that are especially valued or that require special accommodation within a given microculture. Thus, a person may be identified as exceptional in one ethnic group (or other microculture defined by gender, social class, religion, etc.) but not in another. Being unable to read or speak standard English, for example, may identify a student as having a disability in an Anglo-dominated microculture, although the same student would not be considered disabled in a microculture in which English-language skills are unimportant. In certain cultures, children avoid direct eye contact with adults in positions of authority. Given this, a child who does not look directly at the teacher may mistakenly be assumed to be inattentive or oppositional by adults from cultures in which eye contact between the teacher and pupil is expected. This child could be inappropriately identified as having a disability requiring special education.

Plan to Meld Cultures Divides D.C. School

BILINGUAL TEACHING FOCUS OF DISPUTE

From the "Welcome/Bienvenidos" sign by the front door to the hand-drawn maps of Nicaragua and Mexico lining the halls to the dual-language lunch announcements over the loudspeaker, H. D. Cooke Elementary School has tried to nurture the Latino children who make up about half of its student body.

When the D.C. school system won a $1 million federal grant last month to make the school in Adams-Morgan formally bilingual, giving students the chance to learn in Spanish and English, officials were proud of the prize. They hoped teachers and parents would share their excitement over the doors it could open to all Cooke students.

Instead, the plan has split the school into two hostile camps. Although the school already offers some bilingual classes, many black teachers and parents oppose a sweeping transformation, and the once-harmonious corridors are now filled with charges of racial prejudice, immigrant bashing and deception. Teachers have stalked out of a meeting with school officials, and angry parent have confronted the principal.

As a result, school officials have discussed switching the grant—which also would provide more teachers and equipment for the aging Cooke, at 17th and Euclid streets NW—to a more receptive school in the same working-class neighborhood. The only other bilingual school in the District, Oyster School at 29th and Calvert streets NW, draws middle-class children from across the city.

"We were a little H. D. Cooke family, but this has really divided us. I never thought we had racism in this school, but now I know it exists, and it hurts," said Isabel Martinez, who teaches English as a Second Language. "This would be such a great opportunity, and the English-only students would benefit most, but some people are just against change."

"Many black parents are struggling as it is to teach their kids good English. Why are they suddenly going to start teaching them 80 percent in Spanish?" asked Katherine Warner, a black mathematics teacher. "Why did they come into a peaceful, racially diverse school and drop this document with the potential to incite such emotions?"

The bilingual program would begin next fall in kindergarten and gradually expand through all grades. No student would be forced to participate, but those who do would study in both Spanish and English, with two teachers in each classroom. Through third grade, 80 percent of teaching would be in Spanish; after that, the balance would even out gradually.

The goals of the program are ambitious. Through sharing language, Latino and non-Latino children are expected to develop more empathy for one another and their cultures, which coexist but often fail to blend in urban neighborhood life. At Cooke, 269 of the 434 students are immigrants, and most of these are from Central America.

So far, however, the proposal has had the opposite effect on the adults at Cooke. Although teachers are the most

Ethnicity and exceptionality are distinctly different concepts. In fact, multicultural special education must focus on two primary objectives that go beyond the general purposes of multicultural education:

1. ensuring that ethnicity is not mistaken for educational exceptionality
2. increasing understanding of the microculture of exceptionality and its relationship to other microcultures

Ethnicity may be mistaken for exceptionality when one's own ethnic group is viewed as setting the standard for all others. For example, patterns of eye contact, physical contact, use of language, and ways of responding to persons in positions of authority may vary greatly from one ethnic group to another. Members of each ethnic group must realize that what they see as deviant or unacceptable in their own group may be normal and adaptive in another ethnic group. That is, we must not mistakenly conclude that a student has a disability or is gifted just because he or she is different.

Members of minority ethnic groups are more apt to be identified as disabled because their differences are not well understood or valued by others. In part, this higher risk may be a result of prejudice—unreasonable or irrational negative attitudes, feelings, judgments, or behaviors based on ignorance or misunderstanding. Prejudice may cause individuals to be judged as deviant or disabled on the basis of characteristics that are typical for their ethnic group or from stereotyping. That is, an individual's bitterly divided, black parents also have organized to fight the proposal. Many come from families that have sent their children to Cooke for years, and they resent seeing the school radically altered to accommodate an influx of newcomers from other countries.

"This is my neighborhood. My brothers and sisters and cousins went to Cooke, my kids go to Cooke, and don't want to see the nature of the school changed," said Nancy Bryant, who lives half a block away. "We have nothing against Hispanics, they are all God's children, but we do not want our children to be knocked out. I will do everything in my power to stop this."

Latino parents, interviewed as they brought their children to school, seemed less informed about the proposal, and they have not organized to support it. Some said they would welcome an opportunity for their children to learn two languages at once, while others were more eager to have their children learn perfect English than preserve their native tongue.

"I've only heard a little about it, but it seems to me a fantastic idea," says Maribel Ventura, a Salvadoran refugee who arrived in the United States nine years ago. "I have learned a few words of English here and there to survive, but it would be wonderful for my children to grow up really bilingual. What a shame that other people don't think the same way," Ventura said, in Spanish.

Most opponents say they do not object to children learning Spanish, and many agree it would be beneficial. But they fear that the plan would weaken younger students' English skills by teaching them to read only in Spanish until third grade. They also worry that the plan would displace neighborhood children who do not choose to participate with others from outside the area who volunteer.

Black teachers at Cooke are upset that they were not consulted in preparing the grant proposal, and they charge that officials deceived them about its purpose. Some say they fear they would be transferred because they do not speak Spanish. And they resent the fact that the proposal describes them as having "low expectations" for immigrant children and tending to "marginalize" them in class.

School officials say opponents fears are exaggerated. They say there is no danger of job loss and no intent to squeeze out neighborhood students in favor of those elsewhere whose parents want bilingual education. They also stress that most details of the plan can be altered before the program begins, including reducing from 80 to 50 percent the proportion of teaching done in Spanish.

"We have an entire year to make any adjustments so this plan fits the needs of this school community," said Elena Izquierdo, director of the Office of Language Minority Affairs for the District schools. "Change always brings anxiety and uneasiness, but this is a wonderful grant that can add new dimensions to every single child."

Source: By Pamela Constable, *The Washington Post,* October 26, 1994, pp. A1, A24. © 1994, The Washington Post. Reprinted with permission.

One of the most controversial aspects of multicultural education are whether English and non-English languages should be combined in classrooms and, if so, how.

identity as a member of an ethnic group may result in the automatic assumption that he or she will behave in certain ways (see Davidson & Davidson, 1994).

People with certain exceptionalities can develop their own microcultures (Gollnick & Chin, 1994). Those with severe hearing impairments, for example, are described by some as belonging to a Deaf culture that is not well understood by most normally hearing people and that results in feelings of isolation or separation from people with normal hearing (Martin, 1987; Padden & Humphries, 1988). An important aspect of multicultural special education is developing an increased awareness, understanding, and appreciation of cultural differences involving disabilities. Multicultural special education is not merely a matter of overcoming students' prejudice and stereotyping. We must also educate ourselves as teachers to improve methods of assessment, provide effective instruction, and foster appropriate socialization.

We now turn to specific problems in assessment, instruction, and socialization involving microcultural groups, including students with exceptionalities.

Assessment

Assessment is a process of collecting information about individuals or groups for the purpose of making decisions. In education, assessment ordinarily refers to testing, interviewing, and observing students. The results of assessment should help us decide whether problems exist in a student's education and, if problems are identified, what to do about them (Wallace, Larsen, & Elksnin, 1992). Ysseldyke and Marston (1988) have discussed several characteristics of assessment that are important in the U.S. macroculture: "Assessment is a practice integral to making decisions about people. In our society there is a fundamental concern for accuracy, justice, and fairness in making decisions about individuals" (p. 21).

Unfortunately, the accuracy, justice, and fairness of many educational assessments, especially those involving special education, are open to question. Particularly when ethnic microcultures are involved, traditional assessment practices have frequently violated the U.S. ideals of fairness and equal opportunity, regardless of ethnic origin, gender, or disability. That is, the assessment practices of educators and psychologists have frequently come under attack as being (1) biased, resulting in misrepresentation of the abilities and disabilities of ethnic minorities and exceptional students, and (2) useless, resulting only in

One of the purposes of multicultural education is to ensure that children with disabilities are not further disabled by their unique cultural backgrounds.

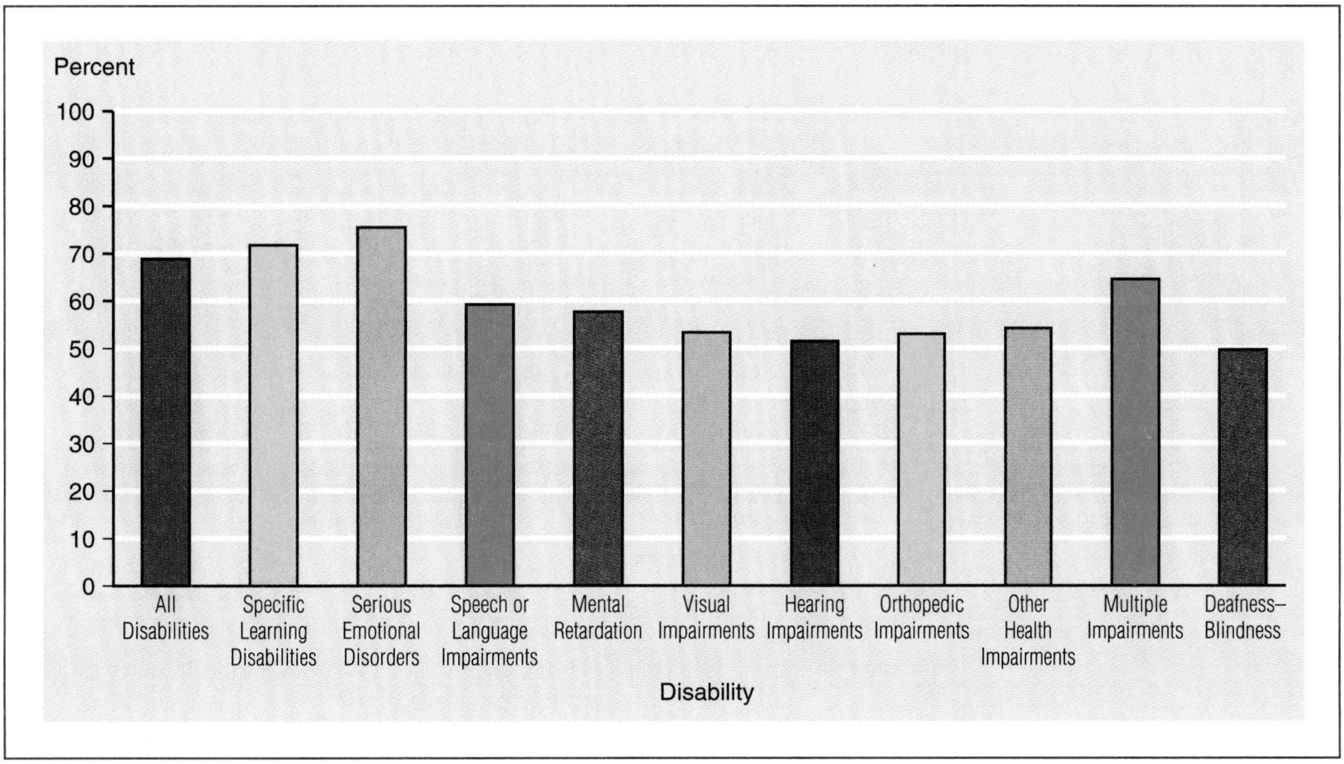

Figure 3–2 Percentage of youths ages 13–21 with disabilities who are male.
(*Source:* U.S. Department of Education, 1992, p. 12.)

labeling or classification rather than improved educational programming (Council for Children with Behavioral Disorders, 1989; Reschly, 1987; Wallace et al., 1992).

The problems of assessing students to qualify for special education are numerous and complex, and there are no simple solutions. Many of the problems are centered on traditional standardized testing approaches to assessment that have serious limitations: (1) They do not take cultural diversity into account, (2) they focus on deficits in the individual alone, and (3) they do not provide information useful in teaching. Although these problems have not been entirely overcome, awareness of them and the use of alternative assessment strategies are increasing.

Standardized tests may be biased because most of the test items draw on specific experiences that students from different microcultures may not have had. Tests may, for example, be biased toward the likely experiences of white, middle-class students; be couched in language unfamiliar to members of a certain microculture; or be administered in ways that penalize students with impaired vision, hearing, or ability to answer in a standard way. Because test scores are often the basis for deciding that a student qualifies for special education, many scholars suspect that test bias accounts for the disproportionate representation of certain groups in special education, especially males and children of color (Chinn & Hughes, 1987).

Disproportional representation of male and black and Hispanic youths in special education is shown in Figures 3–2 and 3–3. These figures demonstrate that disproportional representation is much greater among students in some disability categories than in others in the 13–21 age range. Figure 3–2 above shows that males are especially

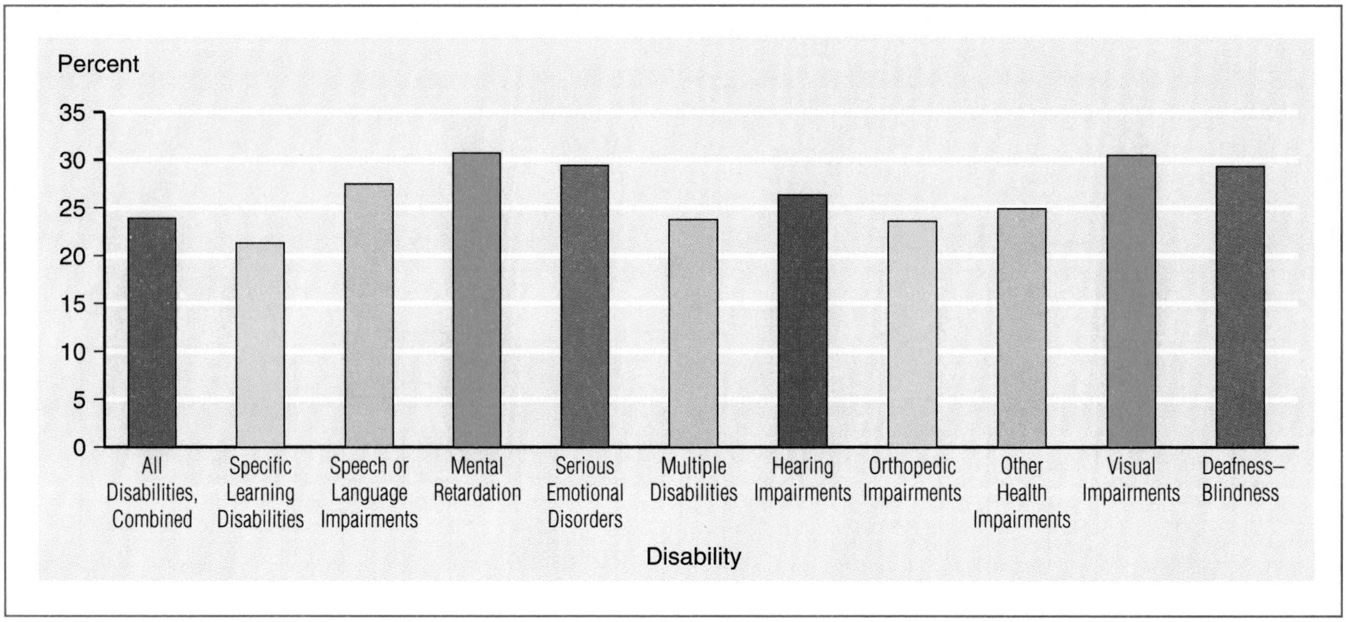

Figure 3–3a Percentage of black youths ages 13–21 by specific disability category. (*Source:* U.S. Department of Education, 1992, p. 17.)

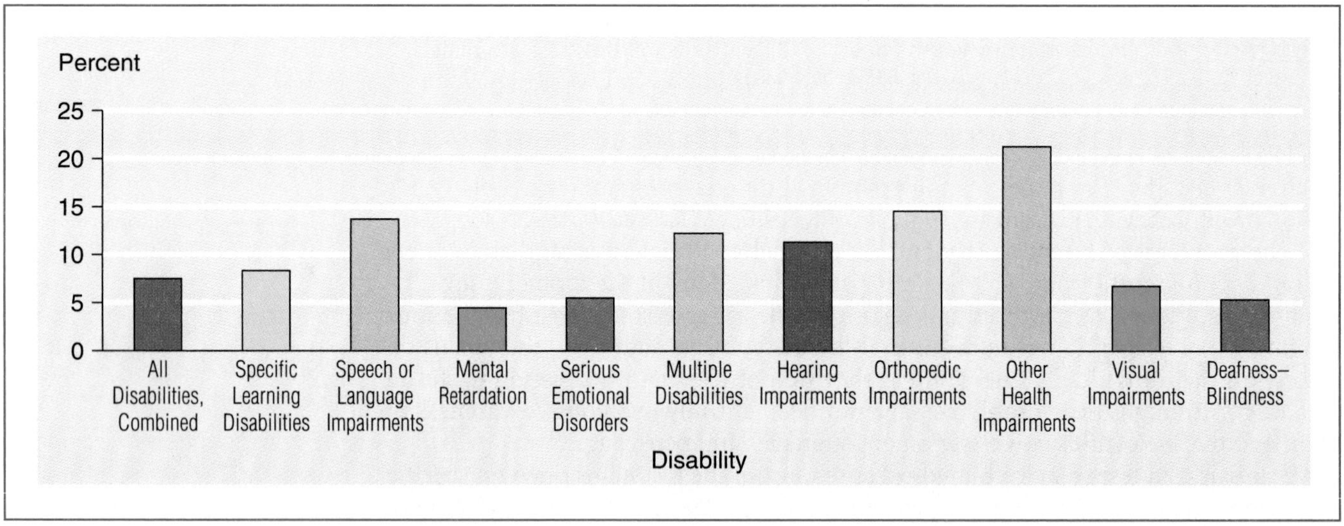

Figure 3–3b Percentage of Hispanic youths ages 13–21 by specific disability category. (*Source:* U.S. Department of Education, 1992, p. 17.)

overrepresented in the categories of serious emotional disturbance and specific learning disabilities. Females are not overrepresented in any category. Figure 3–3 above shows that for all categories combined, nearly 25 percent of youths age 13–21 who are receiving special education are black and about 8 percent are Hispanic. It is important to know that the percentage of high school students who are white is approximately 65 percent; approximately 12 percent are black and about 8 percent are Hispanic. In commenting on the disproportionately high representation of black students in all categories, the U.S. Department of Education commented, "It is possible that black youth were more likely than their white counterparts to have experienced poor prenatal, perinatal, or postnatal health care and early childhood nutrition which may have resulted in actual disabilities" (1992, p. 15). Hispanic students are underrepresented in some disability categories (e.g., mental retardation and serious emotional disturbance) and overrepresented in others, especially orthopedic and other health impairments. The reasons for this overrepresentation are not clear. In any case, nonbiased assessment is a critical issue. The disproportionality should not be the result of biased testing or bias in other forms of assessment.

At best, test scores represent a sample of an individual's ability to respond to a standard set of questions or tasks; they do not tell us *all* the important things an individual has learned or how much he or she *can* learn. Controversy over the biases inherent in standardized tests and the search for so-called culture-free and culture-fair tests continue (McLoughlin & Lewis, 1990; Ysseldyke & Marston, 1988; Wallace et al., 1992). Three cautions are in order:

1. Tests give only clues about what a student has learned.
2. Test scores must be interpreted with recognition of the possible biases the test contains.
3. Testing alone is an insufficient basis for classifying a student or planning an instructional program.

Traditional assessment procedures focus on the student, not on the environment in which he or she is being taught. Critics of traditional assessment have decried the assumption that any deficit identified will be a deficit of the student. So in addition to assessing the student's behavior or performance, many educators now suggest assessing the instructional environment (Bender, 1988; Ysseldyke & Christenson, 1987). Doing so may involve classroom observation and interviews with the student and teacher. It focuses on such items as whether instruction is presented clearly and effectively, the classroom is effectively controlled, the teacher's expectations are appropriate, appropriate curriculum modifications are made, thinking skills are being taught, effective motivational strategies are used, the student is actively engaged in academic responding and given adequate practice and feedback on performance, and progress is directly and frequently evaluated. The purpose of assessing the instructional environment is to make sure that the student is not mistakenly identified as the source of the learning problem. An underlying assumption is that this approach will decrease the likelihood that cultural differences will be mistaken for disabilities.

Traditional assessment procedures result in test scores that *may* be useful in helping to determine a student's eligibility for special education or other special services. These testing procedures do not, however, typically provide information that is useful in planning for instruction. A variety of alternative assessment procedures were devised in the late 1980s and early 1990s, focusing on students' performance in the curriculum or on tasks in everyday contexts, as opposed to how well they did on standardized tests (Poteet, Choate, & Stewart, 1993). The intent of these procedures is to avoid the artificiality and biased nature of traditional testing and obtain a more fair and instructionally useful assessment of students' abilities.

One such alternative approach that emerged in the 1980s is *curriculum-based assessment* (Deno, 1985; Howell & Morehead, 1987). This method of assessment contrasts sharply with traditional testing, in which students are tested infrequently and may never before have seen the specific items on the test. Curriculum-based assessment involves students' responses to their usual instructional materials; it entails direct and frequent samples of performance from the curriculum in which students are being instructed. (We discuss curriculum-based assessment in more detail in Chapter 5.) This form of assessment is thought to be more useful for teachers than traditional testing and to decrease the likelihood of cultural bias.

Finally, we note that fair and accurate assessment is an issue in identifying special gifts and talents as well as disabilities. Too often, the extraordinary abilities of students of color or other ethnic difference and those with disabilities are overlooked because of bias or ignorance on the part of those responsible for assessment. In Chapter 1, we emphasized the importance of identifying the abilities as well as the disabilities of students. To that we want to add the importance of being aware of culturally relevant gifts and talents and recognizing and valuing the abilities of minority students (Patton, 1992; Pattern & Baytops, 1995; Steele, 1992).

Instruction

A major objective of multicultural education is ensuring that all students are instructed in ways that do not penalize them because of their cultural differences and that, in fact, capitalize on their cultural heritage. The methods used to achieve this objective are among the most controversial topics in education today. All advocates of multicultural education are concerned with the problem of finding instructional methods that help equalize educational opportunity and achievement for all microcultural groups—that is, methods that break down the inequities and discrimination that have been part of the U.S. public education system. Yet there is considerable debate over the question: What instructional methods are most effective in achieving this goal?

The controversy regarding instruction is generated by what Minow (1985) calls "the dilemma of difference." The dilemma is that either ignoring or recognizing students' linguistic or cultural differences can perpetuate them and maintain inequality of social power and opportunity among ethnic or other microcultural groups. If students' differences are ignored, the students will probably be given instruction that is not suited to their cultural styles or needs. They will then likely fail to learn many skills, which will in turn deny them power and opportunity in the dominant culture. For example, if we ignore non-English-speaking students' language and cultural heritage and force them to speak English, they may have great difficulty in school. "This story [of the harm children experience when their language and cultural differences are not recognized] manifests one half of the difference dilemma: nonacknowledgment of difference reiterates difference" (p. 838).

However, the answer to this problem is not necessarily recognition of students' differences, for instruction geared to individual students' cultural styles may teach only skills valued by their own microcultures. Because the dominant culture does not value these skills, the students' difference will be perpetuated. For example, if non-English-speaking students are taught in their native language and are not required to learn English, their progress in the English-speaking society will be slowed:

> Here . . . is the other side of the dilemma; acknowledgment of difference can create barriers to important aspects of the school experience and delay or derail successful entry into the society that continues to make that difference matter. Both sides of the dilemma appear and reappear in the history of education for students who are not native English speakers. (Minow, 1985, p. 384)

Should a student who speaks no English be forced to give up his or her native language in school and learn to use only English (ignoring the cultural–linguistic difference)? Or should the student's native language be used as the primary vehicle of

Teachers must recognize and confront their own attitudes about people from various cultural groups, or they may inadvertently discriminate against their own students. Achieving this awareness is a key factor in the success or failure of multicultural education.

instruction, while English is taught as a second language (acknowledging the cultural–linguistic difference) (Gersten & Woodward, 1994)? We could pose similar questions for students with severe hearing impairments: Should we teach them by using primarily sign language or spoken language? And the same dilemma of difference appears in providing instruction for students with other disabilities: To what extent should they be treated as different and provided with special accommodations, and to what extent should they be treated just like everyone else?

To a great extent, the controversy over the dilemma of difference has to do with how students fare in society after their school years, not just how they are treated in school. Delpit (1988, 1995) examines a variety of perspectives on the problem of multicultural education, including the following position:

> Children have the right to their own language, their own culture. We must fight cultural hegemony and fight the system by insisting that children be allowed to express themselves in their own language and style. It is not they, the children, who must change, but the schools. (Delpit, 1988, p. 291)

Delpit's response to this perspective acknowledges both the benefit of recognizing and valuing different cultural styles and the necessity of accepting the realities of the society in which we live:

> I believe in diversity of style, and I believe the world will be diminished if cultural diversity is ever obliterated. Further, I believe strongly. . . that each cultural group should have the right to maintain its own language style. When I speak, therefore, of the culture of power, I don't speak of how I wish things to be but of how they are.
>
> I further believe that to act as if power does not exist is to ensure that the power status quo remains the same. To imply to children or adults. . . that it doesn't matter how you talk or how you write is to ensure their ultimate failure. I prefer to be honest with my students. Tell them that their language and cultural style is unique and wonderful but that there is a political power game that is also being played, and if they want to be in on that game there are certain games that they too must play. . . . They [my

> colleagues] seem to believe that if we accept and encourage diversity within classrooms of children, then diversity will automatically be accepted at gatekeeping points. . . .
>
> I believe that will never happen. What will happen is that the students who reach the gatekeeping points . . . will understand that they have been lied to and react accordingly. (1988, p. 292)

The gatekeeping points to which Delpit refers are admission to higher education and employment.

Hilliard (1989) also notes the necessity of taking students' cultural styles into account in teaching and the equal necessity of good teaching that prepares students of all cultural groups for the demands of the larger society:

> There is something we can call style—a central tendency that is characteristic of both individuals and groups. This style is cultural—learned. It is meaningful in the teaching and learning interaction. Students' style is not, however, to be used as an excuse for poor teaching or as an index of low capacity. (p. 69)

Clearly, the problem of instruction in multicultural education is not easily resolved, especially for bilingual students in special education (Gersten et al., 1994). Most authorities now agree, however, that accepting and fostering cultural diversity must not be used as an excuse for not teaching students the skills they need to survive and prosper in the larger context of American macroculture (Delpit, 1988; Hilliard, 1989; Ogbu, 1990, 1992).

Among the multicultural controversies of the 1990s are Afrocentric instruction and special African-American programs and schools. Afrocentric instruction is an alternative to the Eurocentrism of the prevailing curriculum and methods of instruction; it highlights African culture and seeks distinctively African modes of teaching and learning. Some suggest that Afrocentrism is a regressive practice that detaches students from the realities of their American social environment (Wortham, 1992). Others call for instructional practices that are culturally sensitive—attuned to the particular cultural characteristics of African-American learners (Ford, Obiakor, & Patton, 1995; Franklin, 1992). The assumption underlying culturally sensitive instruction is that students with different cultural backgrounds need to be taught differently, that certain aspects of a student's cultural heritage determine to a significant extent how he or she learns best. For example, Franklin (1992) suggests that African-American students differ from others in the cultural values of their homes and families, their language and patterns of movement, their responses to variety and multiplicity of stimulation, and their preference for divergent thinking.

Perhaps it is understandable that when emphasis is placed on differences in the ways students learn, there is also emphasis on devising special programs and schools that cater to these differences. Furthermore, the greater the diversity of cultural backgrounds of students in one class, the greater the difficulty in teaching all students effectively—if we assume that cultural background determines how students are best taught. Of course, we might hypothesize that certain methods of instruction are equally effective for all students in a culturally diverse group. That is, some instructional approaches (e.g., cooperative learning, peer tutoring, and cross-age grouping) allow teachers to provide culturally sensitive instruction to all members of a diverse group at once.

Nevertheless, the notion that certain curricula and instructional practices are more appropriate for students of one ethnic origin than another may be used to justify distinctive programs, including African-American immersion schools, in which all instruction is geared to the presumed particular learning characteristics of a single ethnic group (see Ascher, 1992; Leake & Leake, 1992). Such schools are often said to be segregationist in practice and intent, but Leake and Leake (1992) suggest that their philosophy opposes the concept of segregation:

> True integration occurs naturally when the differences between peers are minimal. Therefore, the bane of segregation is a culturally and ethnically diverse population of academically competent and self-confident individuals. The African-American immersion schools were designed to provide academically challenging and culturally appropriate experiences for their students. It was hoped that the anticipated increase in student achievement would work to vitiate the African-American students' feelings of inadequacy and impotence. (p. 784)

Do special programs designed with specific learning characteristics in mind help students learn more than they otherwise would and increase their self-esteem? This is a central controversy for both special education and multicultural general education, and research has not provided a clear answer for special programs of either type. Given that ethnicity and disability are two separate dimensions of human difference, however, special programming might be much more appropriate and effective for one dimension of difference than the other.

Hilliard (1992) poses the question of differential programming for students with disabilities as follows: "Can learning impediments be overcome or eliminated, allowing the formerly impaired student to perform significantly better than he or she would have without the services, or allowing the student to perform well in the mainstream academic program?" (p. 171). Research does not answer this question resoundingly—either affirmatively or negatively—for any model of delivering special education services. The question remains open as to whether making special education multicultural in its best sense will add to the weight of evidence regarding special education's effectiveness in improving disabled students' academic performance and success in the mainstream.

What is not an open question, however, is this: Must both special and general education adopt instructional programs that value all students and help all to be as successful as possible in American society, regardless of their specific cultural heritage? This question has been answered resoundingly in the affirmative, not by research but by our common commitment to the American values of equality of opportunity and fairness for all. The pursuit of equality and fairness has led educational reformers toward four instructional goals:

1. teaching tolerance and appreciation of difference
2. working cooperatively with families
3. improving instruction for language-minority students
4. adopting effective teaching practices

Teaching Tolerance and Appreciation. Noted historian Ronald Takaki (1994), whose grandparents were Japanese immigrant plantation laborers in Hawaii, suggests that the American promise of equality and fairness can become a reality only if we free ourselves from a legacy of racism and prejudice. We can do so by acknowledging the reality of our past and learning more about ourselves and our heritage. Takaki believes that schools have a special responsibility in achieving this:

> I think schools are a crucial—probably the most crucial—site for inviting us to view ourselves in a different mirror. I think schools have the responsibility to teach Americans about who we are and who we have been. This is where it's important for schools to offer a more accurate, a more inclusive multicultural curriculum.

Schools should be a place where students from different cultural and ethnic groups can learn about themselves and one another in natural, nonintimidating ways.

> The classroom is the place where students who come from different ethnic or cultural communities can learn not only about themselves but about one another in an informed, systematic and non-intimidating way. I think the schools offer us our best hope for working it out. I would be very reluctant to depend upon the news media or the entertainment media, which do not have a responsibility to educate. (Takaki, 1994, p. 15)

Overcoming prejudice and teaching students to appreciate those who are different from themselves will be by no means easy. Moreover, this is not an area in which research can provide definitive guidelines (Lynch et al., 1992b). Yet proposed methods for how teachers can help students learn both self-esteem and tolerance of difference (e.g., Davidson & Davidson, 1994; Siccone, 1995) seem promising. For example, pupils might study the contributions of other languages and cultures to the development of English in order to understand its multicultural roots (Carnes, 1994), or they might analyze dialects to understand their rules and origins (Adger, Wolfram, & Detwyler, 1993). Students might also correspond with pen pals to dispel regional or other stereotypes (Williams, 1994) or collaborate in small groups or teams to learn social responsibility and conflict resolution (Siccone, 1995).

Teaching tolerance is not, of course, limited to ethnic, regional, or language differences but includes differences of all types, including disabilities. By teaching tolerance, we hope to overcome the kind of prejudice Angie Erickson describes in the box on pages 108–109. In addition, we hope to teach the self-acceptance and pride in identity Angie articulates.

Working with Families. Schools have always depended, in part, on family involvement and support for their success. The ability of teachers to understand and communicate with their students' parents has been particularly important. The increasing separation of economic and social classes, along with the increasing diversity of racial and ethnic groups in public schools, have created greater demands on teachers' understanding of their students' parents and families. "As the experiential gap between teachers and their students increases, so does teachers' fear of crossing what they perceive as barriers to communication with poor families, and, in particular, families from racial groups other than their own" (Harry, Torguson, Katkavich & Guerrero, 1993, p. 48).

Teachers should realize that the parents of low-income and minority children may feel alienated from schools, especially if their children have disabilities or histories of school problems. In fact, any parent who associates schools with failure, anxiety, or rejection is likely to shy away from involvement with teachers and avoid participation in school activities. Given this avoidance, teachers may perceive that parents have low expectations for their children. Even in cases in which parents seem unconcerned and do not participate in parent–teacher conferences or other school activities, it is important for teachers to maintain high expectations for students (Sleeter & Grant, 1994). Teachers must reach out to parents—visiting parents' homes, if possible—even if they are skeptical or fearful of what they will encounter (Harry et al., 1993). Building two-way communication, sharing concern for the child's welfare, and focusing on the student's strengths, particularly in initial meetings with parents, are critically important (Sleeter & Grant, 1994).

Improving Instruction for Language-Minority Students. Students for whom English is a second language face the simultaneous demands of learning a new language and mastering traditional subject matter. Those who have disabilities encounter the third demand of coping with the additional hurdles imposed by their exceptionalities. Bilingual special education is therefore particularly controversial, presenting difficult dilemmas and paradoxes.

We have already discussed the dilemma of difference—the fact that both recognizing and ignoring linguistic or other differences can put children at a disadvantage (Minow, 1985). In addition, language-minority students with disabilities face the paradox of simultaneous overrepresentation and underrepresentation. Ethnic- and language-minority students may be overrepresented in special education if they are referred and misidentified for problems that are not disabilities. At the same time, students from language-minority groups may be underreferred. They may "truly need specialized assistance, but . . . languish in general education classrooms, benefiting little from conventional instruction" (Gersten & Woodward, 1994, p. 312). Addressing these issues effectively demands that we examine different approaches to second-language instruction.

One approach to teaching language-minority students is to emphasize use of their native languages. In this approach, all academic instruction is initially provided in each student's native language, and English is taught as a separate subject. Later, when the student has demonstrated adequate fluency in English, he or she makes the

It's OK to Be Different

STOP MAKING FUN OF MY DISABILITY

Why me? I often ask myself. Why did I have to be the one? Why did I get picked to be different? Why are people mean to me and always treating me differently? These are the kinds of questions that I used to ask myself. It took more than 10 years for me to find answers and realize that I'm not *more* different than anyone else.

I was born on June 29, 1978. Along with me came my twin sister, Stephanie. She was born with no birth defects, but I was born with cerebral palsy. For me, CP made it so I shake a little; when my sister began to walk, I couldn't. The doctors knew it was a minor case of cerebral palsy. But they didn't know if I'd ever walk straight or do things that other kids my age could do.

At first my disability did not bother me, because when you're a toddler, you do things that are really easy. When it took me a little longer to play yard games, because I couldn't run that well, my friends just thought I was slow. My disability was noticed when other children were learning how to write and I couldn't. Kids I thought were my friends started to stay away from me because they said I was different. Classmates began commenting on my speech. They said I talked really weird. Every time someone was mean to me, I would start to cry and I would always blame myself for being different.

People thought I was stupid because it was hard for me to write my own name. So when I was the only one in the class to use a typewriter, I began to feel I was different. It got worse when the third graders moved on to fourth grade and I had to to stay behind. I got held back because the teachers thought I'd be unable to type fast enough to keep up. Kids told me that was a lie and the reason I got held back was because I was a retard. It really hurt to be teased by those I thought were my friends.

After putting up with everyone making fun of me and me crying about it, I started sticking up for myself when I was 10, in fourth grade. I realized if I wanted them to stop, I would have to be the person who made them stop. I finally found out who my real friends were, and I tried to ignore the ones who were mean. Instead of constantly thinking about the things I couldn't do, I tried to think about the things I *could* do, and it helped others, and myself, understand who I really was. When there was something I couldn't do such as play Pictionary, I sat and I watched or I would go find something else to do. A few people still called me names and made fun of me, but after a while, when they saw they didn't get a reaction, they quit, because it wasn't fun anymore. What they didn't know was that it did still hurt me. It hurt me a lot more than they could ever imagine.

When I was 12, my family moved. I kept this fairy tale in my head that, at my next school, no one would be mean to me or would see that I had a disability. I'd always wished I could be someone other than myself. I found out the hard way that I wasn't going to change, that I'd never be able to write and run with no problems. When kids in my new school found out that I couldn't write and my talking and walking were out of the ordinary, they started making fun of me. They never took time to know me.

transition to instruction in English in all academic subjects. A different approach is to offer content-area instruction in English from the beginning of the student's schooling but at a level that is "sheltered," or constantly modified to make sure the student understands it. The goal of this approach is to help the student learn English while learning academic subjects as well.

In the first approach—**native-language emphasis**—students are taught for most of the day in their native languages and later make a transition to English. In the second, **sheltered-English approach**, students receive instruction in English for most of the school day from the beginning of their schooling. The question as to which approach is better for students with disabilities has not been answered, although it is clear that changing from one approach to the other when students change schools creates particular difficulties (Gersten & Woodward, 1994).

Another issue for language-minority instruction is whether an emphasis on the natural uses of language or, alternatively, on skills such as vocabulary and pronunciation is most effective. However, this controversy may be based on a false dichotomy. What students need is an effective balance between skill building and language that is meaningful and relevant to their lives and interests (Gersten et al., 1994). Instructional materials must make sense to students and provide explicit links to their own experi-

native-language emphasis. An approach to teaching language-minority pupils in which the student's native language is used for most of the day and English is taught as a separate subject.

sheltered-English approach. A method in which language-minority students are taught all their subjects in English at a level that is modified constantly according to individuals' needs.

Everything went back to the way it was before. I went back to blaming myself and thinking that, since I was different, I'd never fit in. I would cry all the time, because it was so hard for me to make friends again. I didn't know whether I should trust anyone—I thought that if people knew that I had a disability they would not like me anymore. It took me a long time to understand that I had to return to not caring about what other people say.

People make fun of others because of insecurity. They have to show off to feel better about themselves. When a person made fun of me everyone thought it was just a big joke. After a while I just started laughing along with them or walking away. It really made some kids mad that they weren't getting any reaction out of me. Yeah, it still hurt a lot. I wanted to break down and start crying right then and there, but I knew I didn't want them to get their pleasure out of my hurt feelings. I couldn't cry.

I still get really frustrated when I can't do certain things, and I probably always will. I thought I should give people a better chance to get to know me, but I knew that I would probably get hurt. I never thought that anyone would want to be friends with somebody who had cerebral palsy. At times I have trouble dealing with kids making fun of me, but these are people who need help figuring out things in life and need to be treated better themselves. Maybe then they'll treat others the same. They look disappointed when I walk away or laugh when they try to make fun of me. Perhaps they're hurting more than I am.

It took a lot of willpower on my part and a lot of love from family and friends to get where I am today. I learned that no one was to blame for my disability. I realize that I can do things and I can do them very well. Some things I can't do, like taking my own notes in class or running in a race, but I will have to live with that. At 16, I believe I've learned more than many people will learn in their whole lives. I have worked out that some people are just mean because they're afraid of being nice. They try to prove to themselves and others that they are cool, but, sooner or later, they're going to wish they hadn't said some of those hurtful things. A lot of people will go through life being mean to those with disabilities because they don't know how to act or what to say to them—they feel awkward with someone who's different.

Parents need to teach their children that it's all right to be different and it's all right to be friends with those who are. Some think that the disabled should be treated like little kids for the rest of their lives. They presume we don't need love and friends, but our needs are the same as every other human being's.

There are times when I wish I hadn't been born with cerebral palsy, but crying about it isn't going to do me any good. I can only live once, so I want to live the best I can. I am glad I learned who I am and what I am capable of doing. I am happy with who I am. Nobody else could be the Angela Marie Erickson who is writing this. I could never be, or ever want to be, anyone else.

Erickson, now a sophomore at Wayzata High School in Plymouth, Minn., wrote this essay as a ninth grader at junior high.
Source: By Angie Erickson, "It's OK to Be Different," from *Newsweek*, October 24, 1994.

ences. While teaching specific language skills, teachers must use language and create language variations that students understand. And students must be encouraged to learn to express complex ideas and feelings using increasingly complex sentences as they acquire fluency in English (Gersten & Woodward, 1994). In short, language-minority instruction needs to be constructed in the context of what we know about effective teaching.

Adopting Effective Teaching Practices. In a sense, effective multicultural education requires only that we implement what we know about effective instruction. Namely, effective teaching practices are sensitive to each student's cultural heritage, sense of self, view of the world, and acquired knowledge and skills. Teaching about various cultures, individual differences, and the construction of knowledge should permeate and transform the curriculum (Banks, 1993, 1994, 1995). Nonetheless, for language-minority students—indeed, for all students—we can articulate more specific components of effective teaching. We offer the following description of six components of effective teaching outlined by Gersten et al. (1994, p. 9):

1. *Scaffolding and strategies.* Students learn more efficiently when they are provided a "scaffold," or structure, for ideas and strategies for problem solving. In

scaffolded instruction, the teacher assists the student in learning a task and then phases out the help as the student learns to use the strategy independently. (See Chapter 5 for further discussion). Means of helping students learn more easily include stories, visual organizers (e.g., pictures, diagrams, outlines), **mnemonics** (tactics that aid memory, such as rhymes or images), and **reciprocal teaching** (in which the student sees the teacher use a learning strategy and then tries it out).

2. *Challenge.* Too much of education, even special education, is not appropriately challenging for students. All students—including those who are from cultural minorities, who are at high risk for failure, and who have disabilities—need to be given challenging tasks. *Appropriately challenging tasks* are those that a given student finds just manageable. While these tasks are not impossible, they do require serious effort and stretch the student's capabilities. Too often, teachers underestimate the capabilities of minority and exceptional students and underteach them (Delpit, 1995).
3. *Involvement.* Students must be engaged in extended conversations, in which they use complex linguistic structures. Verbal exchanges between teachers and pupils must not always be short, simple, and direct (although such exchanges have their place). Rather, teachers must probe with questions, share experiences, and elicit from pupils the kind of language that demonstrates their active involvement in learning.
4. *Success.* Students at the highest risk of failure and dropping out are those who have low rates of success in daily school activities. *All* students need to experience frequent success, and teachers must present challenging tasks at which *all* students can be successful. Failure should not be perpetuated.
5. *Mediation and feedback.* Too often, students work for long periods without receiving feedback, or are given feedback that is not comprehensible, or are asked for rote responses to which they attach little or no meaning. Providing frequent, comprehensible feedback on performance is vital to effective teaching, as is focusing on the meanings of responses—how evidence and logic are used to construct questions and their answers.
6. *Responsiveness to cultural and individual diversity.* The content of instruction must be related to students' experiences, including those as individuals and as members of various cultural groups. The issues of cultural and individual diversity cannot be adequately considered in a few special lessons; rather, they must be included routinely in all curriculum areas.

As Banks (1993) points out, a viable multicultural curriculum cannot be created and handed out to teachers. Teachers must be invested in the endeavor, as their values, perspectives, and teaching styles will affect what is taught and how. The effective implementation of a multicultural curriculum requires teaching strategies that are involvement oriented, interactive, personalized, and cooperative.

This perspective applies to our own teaching and writing as well. In any textbook, the adequate treatment of multicultural issues cannot be confined to a single chapter. A chapter like this one—devoted specifically to multicultural education—may be necessary to ensure that the topic is given sufficient focused attention. Our intention in this book, however, is to prompt consideration of multicultural issues in every chapter.

Socialization

Academic instruction is one of two primary purposes of education. The other, socialization, involves helping students develop appropriate social perceptions and interactions with others and learn how to work for desirable social change.

scaffolded instruction. A cognitive approach to instruction in which the teacher provides temporary structure or support while students are learning a task; the support is gradually removed as the students are able to perform the task independently.

mnemonics. Techniques that aid memory, such as using rhymes, songs, or visual images to remember information.

reciprocal teaching. A method in which students and teachers are involved in a dialogue to facilitate learning.

Destructive and stereotypic social perceptions and interactions among differing microcultural groups are long-standing problems in schools and communities in the United States. The most obvious examples involve racial discrimination, although sex discrimination and discrimination against people of differing religions and disabilities are also common in our society. Teachers must become keenly aware of their own cultural heritages, identities, and biases before they can help their students deal with cultural diversity in ways that enhance democratic ideals, such as human dignity, justice, and equality (Banks, 1994). Becoming comfortable with one's own identity as a member of microcultural groups is an important objective for both teachers and students. Depending on the cultural context, accepting and valuing one's identity can be quite difficult. In the box on page 112, Ved Mehta (1989) describes his feelings of discomfort with his identity as a member of two microcultural groups—India, an Eastern culture, and persons who are blind.

Teaching about different cultures and their value may be important in reducing racial and ethnic conflict and promoting respect for human differences. Equally important, however, is structuring classroom interactions to promote the understanding and appreciation of others. One of the most effective ways of breaking down prejudice and encouraging appropriate interaction among students with different characteristics is *cooperative learning* (Johnson & Johnson, 1986; Slavin, 1988). In cooperative learning, students of different abilities and cultural characteristics work together as a team, fostering interdependence. In *Among Schoolchildren*, Tracy Kidder describes this approach to socialization as it was used by a fifth-grade teacher, Chris Zajac:

> Then came fifteen minutes of study, during which teams of two children quizzed each other. Chris paired up good spellers with poor ones. She also made spelling an exercise in socialization, by putting together children who did not seem predisposed

Educational programming for all *learners must challenge them to stretch their abilities. History warns teachers not to "underteach" minority learners.*

> to like each other. She hoped that some would learn to get along with classmates they didn't think they liked. At least they'd be more apt to do some work than if she paired them up with friends. Her guesses were good. Alice raised her eyes to the florescent-lit ceiling at the news that she had Claude for a spelling partner. Later she wrote, "Today is the worst day of my life." Clarence scowled at the news that he had Ashley, who was shy and chubby and who didn't look happy either. A little smile collected in one corner of Chris's mouth as she observed the reactions. "Now, you're not permanently attached to that person for the rest of your life," she said to the class. (1989, pp. 28–29)

Teachers of exceptional children and youths must be aware of the variety of microcultural identities their students may be developing and struggling with. Review the multiple aspects of cultural identity suggested by Figure 3–1 (page 91) and reflect on the combinations of these and other subcultures that a given student might adopt. One of the microcultural identities not included in Figure 3–1 is sexual orientation. Yet many children and adolescents, including many with educational exceptionalities, experience serious difficulties with what some have called the "invisible culture" of gay and lesbian youth (McIntyre, 1992a). Students who are "straight" may struggle with their own prejudices against homosexuals, prejudices all too often fostered by both their peers and adults and sometimes given justification by identification with a religious or political microculture. Gay and lesbian students are often harassed and abused verbally and physically in school and may suffer from serious depression or other psychological disorders as a result (McIntyre, 1992a; Uribe & Harbeck, 1992). Consider also that a student might be both gay or lesbian and gifted, physically disabled, mentally retarded, or have any other educational exceptionality.

Difference in Identity: The Struggle for Acceptance

In the following passage from one of his autobiographical books, Ved Mehta describes his feelings—during his college years—of social isolation and contempt for his identity as a person who is blind and from an Eastern culture. How might his college classmates and instructors have enhanced his feelings of self-worth as a member of these two microcultural groups?

> Mandy went home most weekends. At first, I worried that she never invited me to go with her and meet her family. She never even offered to give me her home address or telephone number. But here, again, far from condemning her behavior, I came to condone it, thinking I should be grateful to her for protecting me from her family's ire. Putting myself in her father's place, I reflected that if I had a daughter who had got herself involved with a handicapped person I would vigorously oppose the romance and try to persuade her not to consider throwing away her life on a handicapped person out of some misguided notion that she could make up for the magnitude of his problems. (Coming from a country with practically no tradition of romantic love, I assumed that dating was tantamount to marriage.) Moreover, I told myself that I was not only handicapped but also a foreigner, who, no matter how superficially Westernized, could never have the same grasp of the English language and American customs that an American had. Just as living in a sighted society was making me contemptuous of everything to do with being blind, studying in America was making me contemptuous of everything to do with being Indian. As a freshman in college, I had taken courses in the history of Western civilization, the philosophy of Western civilization, and the classical music of Western civilization. In Berkeley, I was studying Western economics and American history. (Similar courses in Indian civilization were unheard of.) In the light of this Western education, everything Indian seemed backward and primitive. I remember once listening to a record of Mozart and being awed by the dozens of instruments magically playing in harmony, and then listening to a record of a sitar and being filled with scorn for the twang-twang of the gut.

Source: From © Ved Mehta, *The Stolen Light,* p. 260, first published by HarperCollins UK 1989 and W.W. Norton & Co 1989. Reprinted with permission.

Multicultural education may teach us to understand and embrace individual differences, rather than try to erase them.

Our point is that the task of socialization in a multicultural society demands attention to the multitude of identities that students may assume. It also demands an awareness that any of these identities may carry the consequence of social rejection, isolation, and alienation. Our task as educators is to promote understanding of cultural differences and acceptance of individuals whose identities are different from one's own.

Building pride in one's cultural identity is a particular concern in teaching exceptional students. As we have noted elsewhere (Hallahan & Kauffman, 1994), many people in the Deaf community prefer to be called "the Deaf," which runs contrary to the current use of terms such as *hearing impaired.* Deaf people and blind people have begun to express pride in their identities and microcultures. In fact, for increasing numbers of people with disabilities, labels are to be embraced, not hidden. For example, one adult with learning disabilities said in an interview, "I need to be proud of myself. As long as I was ashamed of being LD [learning disabled], it was difficult to proceed" (Gerber, Ginsberg, & Reiff, 1992, p. 481).

Cultural Differences in Discipline

The lack of knowledge that most educators possess regarding both child abuse (McIntyre, 1987) and culturally different childrearing (Garcia, 1978; McIntyre, 1992c) creates fertile ground for misjudging the appropriateness of parental practices. Teachers who adhere to the disciplinary practices of the majority culture may find themselves viewing culturally different practices as being abusive. This would mean that use of culturally diverse childrearing practices places parents at greater risk for being reported to agencies in charge of handling abuse and neglect reports. A few of these practices and the reporting dilemmas they cause for concerned educators are addressed below:

A novice teacher in a poor urban school district is distressed when, upon seeking advice from colleagues regarding discipline, he is told by them to use physical punishment. This coincides with the advice of the students in his class who tell him to "Hit 'em upside the head." In fact, physical punishment is more accepted in the low socio-economic classes (Gollnick & Chinn, 1990; Horton & Hunt, 1968; Persky, 1974; Spinetta & Rigler, 1972; Hanna, 1988), and educators who teach these students are more likely to approve of corporal punishment (McDowell & Friedman, 1979; Bauer, Dubanoski, Yamauchi, & Honbo, 1990), perhaps believing that one must "use what they know."

A teacher phones a student's parents to inquire as to how that pupil came to have welts on his body. She is given a religious defense based on the biblical Book of Proverbs that promotes the use of "the rod." Indeed, Fundamentalists, Evangelists, and Baptists respond more punitively in disciplinary situations than people who are affiliated with other major religious orientations (Hyman, 1988). . . .

In the faculty lounge, a teacher hears that a student of hers has been locked out of his house. An Asian-American colleague mentions that this is a common disciplinary practice among Southeast Asian families. It is meant to shame "Americanized" children who have not met traditional familial expectations and obligations (Bempechat & Omori, 1990).

A newly certified teacher accepts a position at a school near an Indian reservation. She is appalled by the lack of guidance provided by a number of parents of her Native American students. Like many teachers from the mainstream culture (Swisher, 1990), she believes that the parents are neglectful and letting their children "run wild." She is unaware that among many tribes, non-interference, except in times of danger, is the guardians' policy (Devore & Schlesinger, 1987). . . . Additionally, many clans and tribes assign a great deal of the childraising responsibility to relatives, especially the grandparents (Devore & Schlesinger, 1987).

A teacher wrestles with the issue of whether to report a poor student's parents who are, in her mind, neglectful. She is aware that in low-income areas, early independence with limited guidance or training is the norm (Horton & Hunt, 1968; Miller, 1959), as is the use of inconsistent and harsh physical punishment whereby children are taught to obey rather than reason (Farrington, 1986; Hanna, 1988; Stack, 1974). However, these practices violate her beliefs regarding proper childrearing.

A teacher is told by the parents of a poor, urban black youth to "whup" (paddle) him if he misbehaves in class. The use of controlling and punitive child treatment is more likely to occur in the low-income black culture (Hanna, 1988; Stack, 1974) and may even be viewed by the child as a sign of caring and affection (Rosenfeld, 1971; Silverstein & Krate, 1975). The middle-class oriented behavior management techniques that avoid the expected swift physical punishment may actually cause anxiety for the youth (Hanna, 1988; Harrison-Ross & Wyden, 1973).

Source: From T. McIntyre & P. Silva (1992), Culturally diverse childrearing practices: Abusive or just different? *Beyond Behavior, 4*(1), 8–9. Reprinted with permission.

People from many segments of society, or microcultures—such as parents of children with disabilities, senior citizens, religious groups, recovering alcoholics, and so on—find that congregating for mutual support and understanding enhances their feelings of self-worth. Educators need to consider the possible value of having students with disabilities congregate for specific purposes. As Edgar and Siegel (1995) have noted:

> In a naive and overzealous rush to implement fully inclusive school environments, we risk overlooking and discarding the discovery of identity, common will, and support that comes from the opportunity to congregate with those engaged in struggles that share characteristics of ability, culture, status, or environment. (p. 274)

By trying to avoid labels and insisting that students with disabilities always be placed with those who do not have disabilities, perhaps we risk giving the message that those with have disabilities are less desirable or even not fit to associate with as peers. Bateman (1994) suggests that "something is terribly and not very subtly insulting about saying a bright learning disabled student ought not attend a special school with other students who have learning disabilities because he needs to be with nondisabled students" (p. 516). In striving for true multicultural awareness, we may learn that it is more productive in the long run to embrace identities associated with exceptionalities, while working to increase tolerance and understanding of differences, than it is to avoid labels or refrain from congregating students with specific characteristics.

One of the most difficult tasks of teaching is socializing students through classroom discipline—that is, through the management of classroom behavior. Managing classroom behavior presents a serious challenge for nearly all teachers and a particularly difficult challenge for most special education teachers (Kauffman, Mostert, Nuttycombe, Trent, & Hallahan, 1993). Two considerations are critical: (1) the relationship between the teacher's approach to classroom discipline and the parents' childrearing practices and (2) the sensitivity of the teacher to cultural differences in responses to discipline.

Middle-class American teachers may have an approach to classroom discipline that they consider effective and humane but that differs radically from some cultures' accepted childrearing practices. As McIntyre and Silva (1992) point out, educators, like everyone else, are often ethnocentric, believing that their views are correct and those of others are inferior. In the case of discipline involving students of culturally diverse backgrounds, the teacher may face difficult ethical decisions about child abuse or neglect. When do one's own beliefs about the treatment of children demand that a culturally condoned disciplinary practice be confronted as abuse? Answering this question is not easy, and you may want to reflect on the problems posed by McIntyre and Silva in the box on page 114.

McIntyre (1992b) summarizes some of the cultural differences we might find in expectations regarding classroom behavior. He also describes the cultural sensitivity demanded in managing behavior effectively and humanely. For example, students from different cultures may differ markedly in their pattern of eye contact with the teacher or another authority (especially when being corrected), interpretation of peer assistance on academic work, response to praise or external rewards, touching or being touched, response to deadlines, physical activity level during learning, response to explanations and questions, response to peer pressure, attitude toward corporal punishment, and so on. In selecting classroom management strategies, the teacher must be sensitive to such cultural differences but, at the same time, use an approach that is effective, fair, just, and ethically and legally defensible. This is, to say the least, a highly demanding task.

Finally, we note that education should not merely socialize students to fit into the existing social order. The goals of multicultural education include teaching students to work for social change (Banks, 1994), which entails helping students who are members of oppressed minorities become advocates for themselves and other members of their microcultures.

SUMMARY

Education for cultural diversity involves managing tension between microcultural diversity, on the one hand, and common macrocultural values, on the other. Many microcultures are found in the U. S. macroculture, which values justice, equality, and human dignity. Progress in multicultural education is difficult because each microculture tends to see many of its own values as the standards against which others should be judged. Special educators and general educators alike must understand how to provide an education that gives equal opportunity to students regardless of gender, socioeconomic status, ethnic group, disability, or other cultural identity. Doing so may require that educators change students' knowledge construction of their own and others' cultural identities. Devising a multicultural curriculum that is satisfactory to all groups is difficult, and not everyone agrees that understanding cultural diversity is as important as building the common culture. Although multiculturalism is fraught with conflicts, it offers an opportunity to practice American values of tolerance, justice, equality, and individualism.

Communities and families contribute much to students' attitudes toward education and academic achievement. Minority communities can encourage academic success among students by highlighting values consistent with school achievement. However, we must guard against ethnic stereotypes of achievement or failure and understand that community and family attitudes toward schooling do not excuse educators from their responsibility to provide an effective and multicultural education for all students.

Multicultural education may at first seem a relatively simple matter, but it is complicated by questions about what cultures to include and what and how to teach about them. Many distinct microcultures exist, and some have values or customs that others find unacceptable or offensive. Microcultural groups may be distinguished not only by gender and ethnicity but also by religious or political affiliation and sexual orientation. Finding a balance among cultural values and traditions that satisfies all groups is often quite difficult. Moreover, this balance may vary from school to school. Controversy often exists in communities where so-called minorities constitute well over half the school population. Issues such as language differences and bilingual education have become divisive within many such communities.

The types of cultural diversity most relevant to special education are ethnicity and disability or giftedness. We must remember, however, that students may be members of a variety of microcultural groups besides those designating educational exceptionality. Multicultural special education must give special attention to ensuring that ethnicity is not mistaken for educational exceptionality and to increasing the understanding of educational exceptionality and its relationship to other microcultures. Members of ethnic minority groups may be mistakenly identified as disabled or overlooked in attempts to identify special gifts and talents if their cultural practices and languages are not understood by teachers. Individuals with certain exceptionalities (deafness, for example) may develop their own microcultures, and it is important to help others understand and appreciate these cultures.

Three specific problems in multicultural special education are assessment, instruction, and socialization. Assessment is a particularly critical issue because it forms the basis for decisions about instruction and placement; therefore, it is imperative that assessment be accurate, fair, and directly related to designing effective instruction. Traditional testing procedures, such as standardized tests, are problematic for members of many ethnic minorities. Curriculum-based assessment and performance assessment are gaining wide acceptance as alternatives. Assessment of the learning environment may be as important as assessment of students' skills.

Instruction presents many points of controversy for multicultural and bilingual special education. One of the great and pervasive problems of special education is the dilemma of difference. Recognizing students' differences and providing special services of any kind may be helpful, but identification and special programming may also carry stigmas and perpetuate the differences. Some leading scholars in multicultural education suggest that instruction should help students understand and preserve their own microcultures while at the same time help students learn to function successfully in the American macroculture. The pursuit of equality and fairness has led educators to four instructional goals: (1) teaching tolerance and appreciation of differences; (2) working cooperatively with families; (3) improving the instruction of language-minority students; and (4) adopting effective teaching practices.

Socialization is an aspect of education that some believe is as important as academic instruction. Multicultural special education must seek to improve students' understanding and acceptance of others' differences and to help students develop pride in their own cultural identities. Teachers may encounter particular multicultural problems in managing classroom behavior because of differences between their own views of discipline and childrearing and those of their students and students' parents.

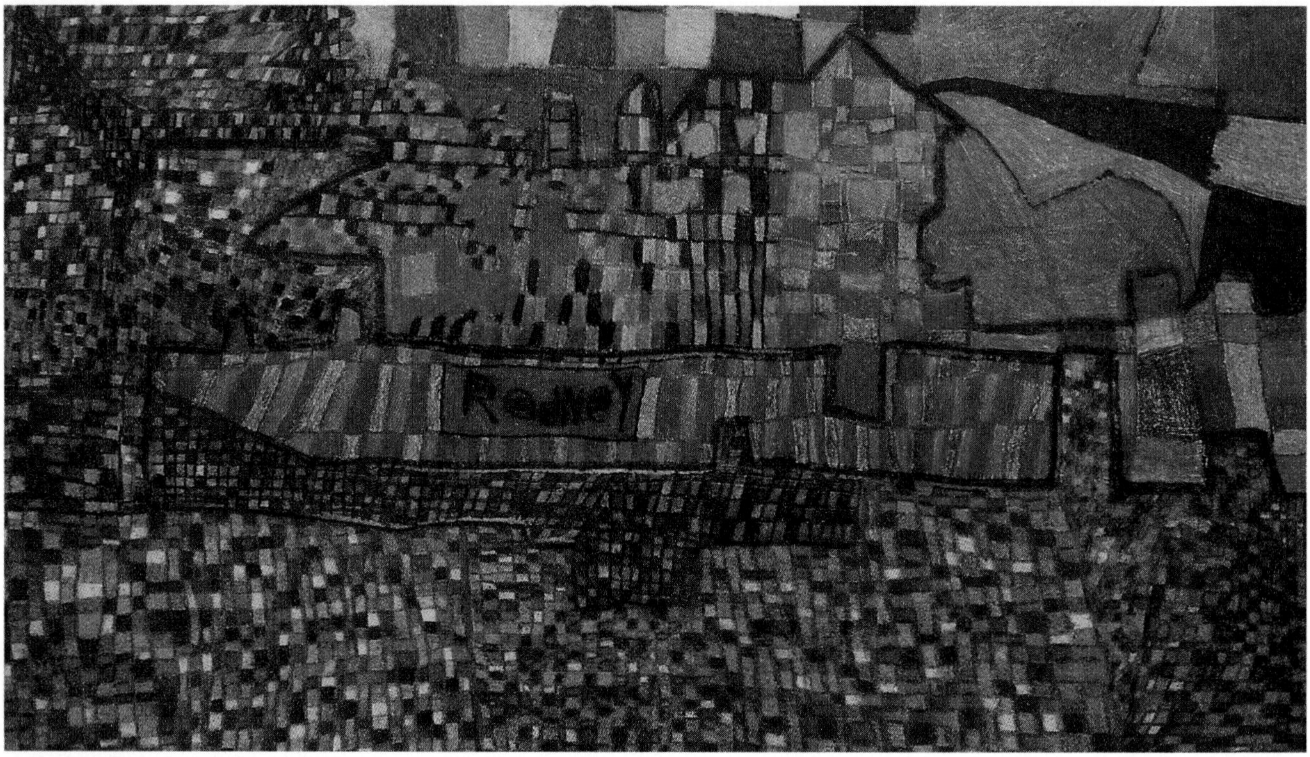

Rodney Sullivan

For the past three years, Rodney Sullivan has been involved in an art and design group as part of his treatment for a mental disability. During this time he has grown tremendously as an artist. He has exhibited widely including the office of Congresswoman Eleanor Holmes Norton and the Washington, D.C. Chamber of Commerce.

4

Mental Retardation

Everywhere, however, we hear talk of sameness. "All men are created equal" it is declared. And at the ballot box and the subway rush, in Hiroshima and Coney Island it almost seems that way. Moreover, coming back from Staten Island on the ferry, as you see an unkempt bootblack lift his head to gaze at the Manhattan skyline—you know these words of Jefferson are not mere snares for votes and popularity. But standing on the same boat with the hand of your idiot son in one of yours—with mingled love and distaste placing a handkerchief against his drooling mouth—you know that Jefferson's words are not easy to understand.

There is a difference in sameness. Perhaps the days of our years are for the bootblack. But assuredly the nights are for our idiot son.

Richard H. Hungerford
"On Locusts"

There is considerable danger in relying on Hungerford's portrayal (p. 119) for our only view of what it is like to have a child who is retarded. Such children may be heartbreakingly different from the children next door in some ways but also like them in others. More and more research evidence indicates that retardation is quantitative rather than qualitative. In many areas, it seems, the retarded child functions like a nondisabled child—but a nondisabled child at a younger chronological age. Even the differences that do exist need not cause parents a lifetime of constant heartache. Hungerford's statement is valuable, however, because it presents honest feelings. Unlike the romanticized portraits found in many TV dramas, movies, and books, children with retardation can evoke agony, hatred, sorrow, and frustration, as well as love, in their parents.

The Hungerford quote, published in 1950, points out something else, as well. It reflects the once-popular stereotype of the person with retardation as a clumsy, drooling, helpless creature. Today, we know this is simply not true. First, most children classified as mentally retarded are *mildly* retarded and look like the hypothetical average child living next door. Second, it can be misleading to characterize even the more severely retarded as helpless. With advanced methods of providing educational and vocational training, we are finding that people with retardation are capable of leading more independent lives than was previously thought possible. Given appropriate preparation, many are able to live and work with relatively little help from others.

The field of mental retardation has undergone a number of other exciting changes since the time Hungerford wrote. No longer is institutionalization the norm for persons who are severely retarded. More and more students with retardation are spending greater portions of their time in regular classrooms in their neighborhood schools. Terminology, too, is changing. Whereas the term *idiot,* which Hungerford uses, was once acceptable, today professionals try to use terms that are less stigmatizing.

Perhaps the most significant change since Hungerford wrote "On Locusts" is the fact that designating someone as mentally retarded has become much more difficult. Today, professionals are more reluctant to apply the label of mental retardation than they once were. At least three reasons account for this more cautious attitude toward identification of students as retarded:

1. Professionals became concerned about the misdiagnosis of children from ethnic minority groups as retarded. Twenty to thirty years ago, it was much more common for children from ethnic minorities, especially African-American and Hispanic students, to be labeled "mentally retarded" because they did not achieve well in school and they scored poorly on intelligence tests.
2. Another reason for using more stringent criteria for determining retardation is related to the fear that the stigma of such a diagnosis can have harmful consequences for the individual. Some believe that the label of mental retardation causes children to have poor self-concepts and to be viewed negatively by others.
3. Some professionals now believe that, to a certain extent, mental retardation is a socially constructed condition. For example, sociologist Jane Mercer (1973) holds that a person's social system determines whether he or she is retarded. She notes that most students labeled "retarded," particularly those who are higher functioning, do not officially become retarded until they enter school. The school, as a social system, has a certain set of expectations some children do not meet.

Misconceptions about
Persons with Mental Retardation

Myth	Fact
Myth Mental retardation is defined by how a person scores on an IQ test.	**Fact** The most commonly used definition specifies that in order for a person to be considered mentally retarded, he or she must meet two criteria: (1) low intellectual functioning *and* (2) low adaptive skills.
Myth Once diagnosed as mentally retarded, a person remains within this classification for life.	**Fact** A person's level of mental functioning does not necessarily remain stable; this is particularly true for those individuals who are mildly retarded. With intensive educational programming, some persons can improve to the point that they are no longer retarded.
Myth In most cases, we can identify the cause of retardation.	**Fact** In most cases, especially those of people who are mildly retarded or who require less intensive support, we cannot specify the cause. For many children who are mildly retarded, poor environment may be a causal factor, but it is extremely difficult to document.
Myth Most mentally retarded children look different from nondisabled children.	**Fact** The majority of children with mental retardation are mildly retarded (or require less intensive support), and most of these look like nondisabled children.
Myth We can identify most cases of mental retardation in infancy.	**Fact** Most children with retardation are not identified as such until they go to school, for several reasons: (1) Because most children with retardation are mildly retarded; (2) because infant intelligence tests are not very reliable and valid; and (3) because intellectual demands on the child increase greatly upon entrance to school.
Myth Persons with mental retardation tend to be gentle people who have an easy time making friends.	**Fact** Because of a variety of behavioral characteristics and because they sometimes live and work in relatively isolated situations, some persons with mental retardation have difficulty making and holding friends.
Myth The teaching of vocational skills to students with retardation is best reserved for secondary school and beyond.	**Fact** Many authorities now believe it appropriate to introduce vocational content in elementary school to students with mental retardation.
Myth When workers with mental retardation fail on the job, it is usually because they do not have adequate job skills.	**Fact** When they fail on the job, it is more often because of poor job responsibility (poor attendance and lack of initiative) and social incompetence (interacting inappropriately with co-workers) than because of incompetence in task production.
Myth Persons with mental retardation should not be expected to work in the competitive job market.	**Fact** More and more persons who are mentally retarded hold jobs in competitive employment. Many are helped through supportive employment situations, in which a job coach helps them and their employer adapt to the work place.

DEFINITION

A more conservative approach to identifying students as mentally retarded is reflected in changes in definition that have occurred over the years. Since 1950, seven official definitions of *mental retardation* have been endorsed by the American Association on Mental Retardation (AAMR) (formerly the American Association on Mental Deficiency), the major professional organization dealing with persons with mental retardation. The current AAMR definition reads:

> *Mental retardation* refers to substantial limitations in present functioning. It is characterized by significantly subaverage intellectual functioning, existing concurrently with related limitations in two or more of the following applicable adaptive skill areas: communication, self-care, home living, social skills, community use, self-direction, health and safety, functional academics, leisure, and work. Mental retardation manifests before age 18. (AAMR Ad Hoc Committee on Terminology and Classification, 1992, p. 5)

intellectual functioning. The ability to solve problems related to academics; usually estimated by an IQ test; one of two major components (the other is adaptive skills) of the AAMR definition.

adaptive skills. Skills needed to adapt to one's living environment (e.g., communication, self-care, home living, social skills, community use, self-direction, health and safety, functional academics, leisure, and work); usually estimated by an adaptive behavior survey; one of two major components (the other is intellectual functioning) of the AAMR definition.

In making this definition operational, the professional is to rely on assessment of two areas: intellectual functioning and adaptive skills. **Intellectual functioning**, usually estimated by an IQ test, refers primarily to ability related to academic performance. **Adaptive skills**, usually estimated by adaptive behavior surveys, refers to abilities related to coping with one's environment.

This definition, like each of its predecessors, continues three trends consistent with a more cautious approach to diagnosing students as mentally retarded:

1. a broadening of the definition beyond the single criterion of an IQ score
2. a lowering of the IQ score used as a cutoff for qualification as retarded
3. a conceptualization of retardation as a condition that can be improved and that is not necessarily permanent

The term adaptive behavior *refers to self-help skills, such as the ability to execute everyday tasks, use a telephone, or operate a computer.*

Broadening the Definition

At one time, it was common practice to diagnose individuals as retarded solely on the basis of an IQ score. Today, we recognize that IQ tests are far from perfect and that they are but one indication of a person's ability to function. Professionals came to consider adaptive skills in addition to IQ in defining retardation because they began to recognize that some students might score poorly on IQ tests but still be "street-wise"—able to cope, for example, with the subway system, with an afterschool job, with peers. Much of the current emphasis on adaptive skills can be traced to the 1970 report of the President's Committee on Mental Retardation, entitled "The Six-Hour Retarded Child." It held that some students may function in the retarded range while they are in school for six hours of the day but behave just fine—adjust and adapt competently—once they return to their neighborhoods for the other eighteen hours.

Crafters of the current AAMR definition have been very specific in pointing to a broadening of the definition of mental retardation. They view intelligence as multifaceted. In their rationale for the revised definition, they identify three types of intelligence: conceptual, practical, and social (AAMR Ad Hoc Committee on Terminology and Classification, 1992). **Conceptual intelligence** is primarily assessed in IQ tests. Practical and social intelligence are the bases for the adaptive skills aspect of the definition. **Practical intelligence** is defined as the "ability to maintain and sustain oneself as an independent person managing the ordinary activities of daily living" (p. 15). **Social intelligence** "refers to the ability to understand social expectations and the behavior of other persons and to judge appropriately how to conduct oneself in social situations" (p. 15).

Lowering the IQ Score Cutoff

It was also common at one time for practitioners to use a cutoff score of 85 on an IQ test as an indicator of mental retardation. This cutoff score was endorsed by the AAMR until the mid-1970s, when they made it more difficult for people to be identified as retarded by establishing a cutoff score of 70 to 75. The current AAMR definition also sanctions this cutoff of 70 to 75. A 5-point spread of 70 to 75 has been established to reinforce the notion that IQ scores should not be regarded as precise measurements, that professionals should use some clinical judgment in interpreting IQ scores.

conceptual intelligence. The traditional conceptualization of intelligence emphasizing problem solving related to academic material; what IQ tests primarily assess.

practical intelligence. The ability to solve problems related to activities of daily living; an aspect of the adaptive skills component of the AAMR definition.

social intelligence. The ability to understand social expectations and to cope in social situations; an aspect of the adaptive skills component of the AAMR definition.

Retardation as Improvable and Possibly Nonpermanent

At the time of the Hungerford quote (see p. 119), many authorities held little hope for significantly enhancing the functioning of people with retardation and essentially believed retardation to be incurable. Over the years, however, professionals have become more optimistic about the beneficial effects of educational programming. Not only do they believe that the functioning of virtually all persons with retardation can be improved, but they have forwarded the notion that some persons with retardation, especially those with mild retardation, can eventually improve to the point that they are no longer classified as retarded.

In agreement with the notion that mental retardation is improvable and not necessarily permanent, the developers of the latest AAMR definition hold that mental retardation is not a condition that resides solely in the individual. Instead, they believe that mental retardation results from an interaction between the individual's intellectual and adaptive behavior skills and the environment (Schalock et al., 1994). Thus, how well a person with mental retardation functions is directly related to the amount of support he or she receives from the environment. With enough support, he or she can improve and possibly overcome the retardation.

The importance of support, in fact, is underscored in the AAMR's classification scheme, to which we now turn.

CLASSIFICATION

Professionals have typically classified persons with mental retardation according to the severity of their problems. For many years, the AAMR promoted the use of the terms **mild**, **moderate**, **severe**, and **profound retardation**, with each of these levels keyed to approximate IQ levels. For example, mild mental retardation is from 50–55 to approximately 70, and severe retardation is from 20–25 to 35–40. Most school systems now classify their students with mental retardation using these terms or a close approximation of them.

In 1992, however, the AAMR recommended a radical departure from this system of classification (AAMR Ad Hoc Committee on Terminology and Classification, 1992). Rather than categorize students based on their IQ scores, the AAMR recommended that professionals classify them according to how much support they need to function as competently as possible. Table 4–1 depicts these **levels of support.**

The authors of the AAMR's most recent classification scheme believe it is better than categorization based on IQ for at least three reasons:

1. As we stated earlier, the newer scheme implies that persons with retardation can achieve positive outcomes with appropriate support services.
2. The new classification scheme avoids reliance on a single IQ score.

mild retardation. A classification used to specify an individual whose IQ is approximately 55–70.

moderate retardation. A classification used to specify an individual whose IQ is approximately 40–55.

severe retardation. A classification used to specify an individual whose IQ is between approximately 25–40.

profound retardation. A classification used to specify an individual whose IQ is below approximately 25.

levels of support. The basis of the AAMR classification scheme; characterizes the amount of support needed for someone with mental retardation to function as competently as possible as (1) intermittent, (2) limited, (3) extensive, or (4) pervasive.

Table 4–1
AAMR Classification Scheme for Mental Retardation Based on Levels of Support

Intermittent	Supports on an "as needed basis." Characterized by episodic nature, person not always needing the support(s), or short-term supports needed during life-span transitions (e.g., job loss or an acute medical crisis). Intermittent supports may be high or low intensity when provided.
Limited	An intensity of supports characterized by consistency over time and time-limited but not of an intermittent nature, may require fewer staff members and less cost than more intense levels of support (e.g., time-limited employment training or transitional supports during the school-to-adult period).
Extensive	Supports characterized by regular involvement (e.g., daily) in at least some environments (such as work or home) and not time-limited (e.g., long-term home living support).
Pervasive	Supports characterized by their constancy, high intensity, provided across environments; potential life-sustaining nature. Pervasive supports typically involve more staff members and intrusiveness than do extensive or time-limited supports.

Source: From AAMR Ad Hoc Committee on Terminology and Classification. (1992). *Mental retardation: Definition, classification, and systems of support*. Copyright © 1992 by American Association on Mental Retardation. Reprinted with permission.

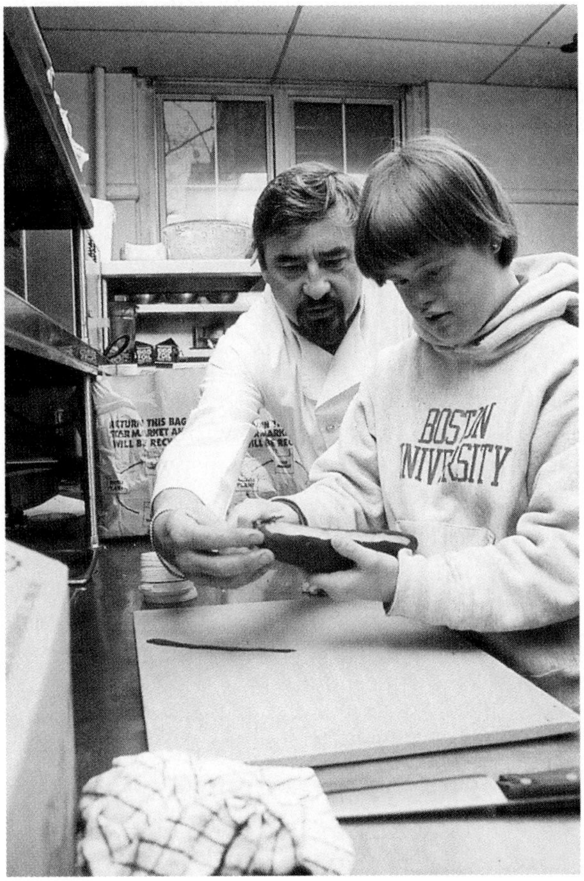

Critical to how well some individuals with mental retardation function is the amount of support they receive from the people around them.

3. When considered in combination with adaptive skills, the new classification can result in descriptions that are more meaningful. Rather than saying, for example, that a person has "severe retardation," one might say the person has retardation that requires "extensive supports in self-care, home living, and work."

CRITICISMS OF THE AAMR DEFINITION AND CLASSIFICATION

Not all professionals support the AAMR definition and classification system; citing at least two major objections:

1. Some believe that the notion that mental retardation does not reside in the individual may be too radical. They suggest that believing that retardation is a condition that a person has does not necessarily mean that it is permanent and immutable.
2. Critics have questioned the usefulness and purpose of the new classification system based on levels of support (MacMillan, Gresham, & Siperstein, 1993; Smith, 1994). They point to the long tradition of classifying individuals on the basis of severity and argue that it will be difficult to develop ways of reliably

measuring the levels of support different people need. Furthermore, critics of the AAMR classification wonder if, in practice, the four levels of support will simply replace the four levels of severity (e.g., the category *intermittent* will replace *mild, limited* will replace *moderate,* and so forth). If this substitution would occur, what would be gained by changing the classification?

It is still too early to tell whether the new AAMR definition and classification scheme will replace the old one in practice.

PREVALENCE

The average (mean) score on an IQ test is 100. Theoretically, we expect 2.27 percent of the population to fall two standard deviations (IQ = 70 on the Wechsler Intelligence Scale for Children–Revised, or WISC–III) or more below this average. This expectation is based on the assumption that intelligence, like so many other human traits, is distributed along a *normal curve.* Figure 4–1 below shows the hypothetical normal curve of intelligence. This curve is split into eight areas by means of standard deviations. On the latest edition of the Wechsler, the WISC–III, where one standard deviation equals 15 IQ points, 2.14 percent of the population scores between 55–70 and 0.13 percent scores below 55. Thus, it would seem that 2.27 percent should fall between 0–70. (See pp. 134–135 for more on intelligence tests.)

Since the federal government started requiring public schools to report actual counts of how many students they were officially identifying as mentally retarded, the prevalence figures have been much lower—somewhere around 1 to 1.5 percent. Authorities have pointed to three possible sources for the discrepancy.

1. The fact that students who are mentally retarded must now meet the dual criteria of low IQ *and* low adaptive skills may have resulted in fewer identified children.

Figure 4–1

Theoretical distribution of IQ scores based on normal curve.
(*Source:* U.S. Department of Education, 1992)

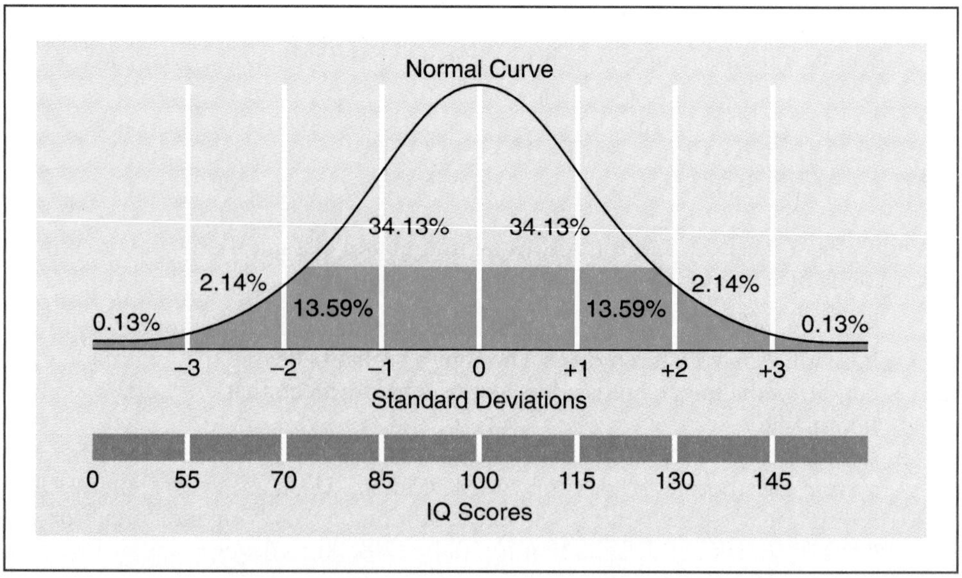

2. Litigation focusing on the improper labeling of minority students as "mentally retarded" may have made school personnel more cautious about identifying these children as retarded.
3. In cases in which the IQ score is in the 70s, thus making identification as retarded a close call, parents and school officials may be more likely to identify children as "learning disabled" than mentally retarded because learning disabled is perceived as a less stigmatizing label.

CAUSES

Many experts estimate that we are able to pinpoint the cause of mental retardation in only about 10 to 15 percent of the cases. Although some overlap is evident, for the most part, causal factors for persons with mild retardation (requiring less intensive support services), differ from those for persons with more severe retardation (requiring more intensive support services).

Persons with Mild Retardation, or Those Requiring Less Intensive Support

Most individuals identified as retarded are classified as mildly retarded and need less intensive support to function. They typically do not differ in appearance from their nondisabled peers, and they are usually not diagnosed as retarded until they enter school and begin to fall behind in schoolwork. In the majority of these cases, the exact cause of the retardation cannot be specified. Although there are no definitive data, the estimate of 10 to 15 percent of identifiable causes of all retardation is undoubtedly even lower when considering only persons who are mildly retarded.

Professionals often refer to individuals with mild retardation as having **cultural-familial retardation**. Some use this term to refer to a person with a mild degree of retardation who has (1) no evidence of brain damage, (2) at least one parent who is retarded, and (3) at least one sibling who is retarded (if he or she has siblings) (Heber, 1959). The term was originally intended to indicate retardation that was caused by poor parenting (poor intellectual stimulation) from parents who were retarded (Garber, Hodge, Rynders, Dever, & Velu, 1991). Today professionals use the term more broadly to indicate mild retardation that may be due to an unstimulating environment (possibly but not necessarily specifically caused by poor parenting) and/or genetic factors. Just which factor is most influential—environment or heredity—has been the subject of debate for years.

The Nature versus Nurture Controversy. In the early part of this century, the predominant viewpoint among educators was that genetics determines intellectual development. The classic study of Skeels and Dye (1939), however, did much to strengthen the position of the environmentalists. Skeels and Dye investigated the effects of stimulation on the development of infants and young children in an orphanage, many of whom were classified as mentally retarded. One group of children remained in the typical orphanage environment, while the other group was given stimulation. For the latter group, nurturance was provided by teenage girls who were retarded. The effects were clearcut: Average IQs for members of the group given stimulation increased, whereas the other children's IQs decreased. Even more dramatic were the results of Skeels's follow-up study, done twenty-one years later.

cultural-familial retardation. Today, a term used to refer to mild retardation due to an unstimulating environment and/or genetic factors.

Controversy surrounds the issues of whether and to what extent poor social–environmental conditions contribute to retardation.

In the adult follow-up study, all cases were located and information obtained on them, after a lapse of 21 years. . . .

All 13 children in the experimental group were self-supporting, and none was a ward of any institution. . . . In the contrast group of 12 children, one had died in adolescence following continued residence in a state institution for the mentally retarded, and four were still wards of institutions, one in a mental hospital, and the other three in institutions for the mentally retarded.

In education, disparity between the two groups was striking. The contrast group completed a median of less than the third grade. The experimental group completed a median of the 12th grade. Four of the subjects had one or more years of college work, one received a B.A. degree and took some graduate training.

Marked differences in occupational levels were seen in the two groups. In the experimental group all were self-supporting or married and functioning as housewives. The range was from professional and business occupations to domestic service, the latter the occupations of two girls who had never been placed in adoptive homes. In the contrast group, four (36 percent) of the subjects were institutionalized and unemployed. Those who were employed, with one exception, were characterized as "hewers of wood and drawers of water.". . .

Eleven of the 13 children in the experimental group were married: nine of the 11 had a total of 28 children, an average of three per family. On intelligence tests, these second generation children had IQs ranging from 86 to 125, with a mean of 104. In no instance was there any indication of mental retardation or demonstrable abnormality. . . .

In the contrast group, only two subjects had married. One had one child and subsequently was divorced. Psychological examination of the child revealed marked mental retardation. . . . Another male subject had a nice home and a family of four children, all of average intelligence. (Skeels, 1966, pp. 54–55)*

* From "Adult Status of Children with Contrasting Early Life Experiences," by H. M. Skeels, 1966, *Monographs of the Society for Research in Child Development, 31*(Ser. No. 105), Chicago: University of Chicago Press. Reprinted with permission.

By the 1960s, many educators supported the environmental (nurture) position. During this time, for example, the federal government established the Head Start program, which was based on the premise that the negative effects of poverty could be reduced through educational and medical services during the preschool years.

For many years, theoreticians tended to view the nature-nurture issue from an either/or perspective—either you believed that heredity held the key to determining intellectual development or you held that the environment was the all-important factor. Today, however, most authorities hold that both genetics and the environment are critical determinants of intelligence. Some scientists have tried to discover *how much* of intelligence is determined by genetics versus the environment, but many view this quest as futile. They assert that genetics and the environment do not combine in an additive fashion to produce intelligence. Instead, the *interaction* between genetics and the environment results in intelligence.

The following exchange between a professor of biopsychology and his student points out the importance of viewing intelligence in this way: that is, as the result of an interaction between genetics and experience and not a simple addition of the two:

> Recently, one of my students told me that she had read that intelligence was one-third genetic and two-thirds experience, and she wondered whether this was true. She must have been puzzled when I began my response by describing an alpine experience. "I was lazily wandering up a summit ridge when I heard an unexpected sound. Ahead, with his back to me, was a young man sitting on the edge of a precipice, blowing into a peculiar musical instrument. I sat down behind him on a large sun-soaked rock, and shared his experience with him. Then, I got up and wandered back down the ridge, leaving him undisturbed. I have frequently wondered about the musician, his music, and the powerful effect that it had on me. Then I put the following question to my student: "If I wanted to get a better understanding of the musician, would it be reasonable for me to begin by asking how much of it came from the musician and how much of it came from the instrument?"
>
> "That would be dumb," she said, "The music comes from both; it makes no sense to ask how much comes from the musician and how much comes from the instrument. Somehow the music results from the interaction of the two, and you would have to ask about the interaction."
>
> That's exactly right," I said. "Now, do you see why. . ."
>
> "Don't say any more," she interrupted. "I see what you're getting at. Intelligence is the product of the interaction of genes and experience, and it is dumb to try to find how much comes from genes and how much comes from experience."
>
> "And the same is true of any other behavioral trait," I added.
>
> Several months later the same student strode into my office, reached into her pack and pulled out a familiar object. It was an instrument like the one that had intrigued me. "I believe that this is your mystery instrument," she said. "It's a Peruvian panpipe." She was right . . . again. (Pinel, 1993, p. 32)*

Persons with More Severe Retardation, or Those Requiring More Intensive Support

Determining causes of retardation is easier in persons whose retardation is more severe than in those who are mildly retarded. Unlike persons with mild retardation, individuals with more severe retardation often do look different from their nondisabled

* From *Biopsychology* (2nd ed.), by P. J. Pinel, 1993, Boston: Allyn and Bacon. Reprinted with permission.

peers and they are often diagnosed in infancy or before entering school. We can divide causes of retardation in persons with more severe retardation into two general categories—genetic factors and brain damage (MacMillan, 1982).

Genetic Factors. Mental retardation has a number of genetically related causes. These are, generally, of two types: those resulting from some damage to genetic material, such as chromosomal abnormalities, and those due to hereditary transmission. We discuss four conditions: (1) Down syndrome, which results from chromosomal abnormality, and (2) Fragile X syndrome, (3) PKU (phenylketonuria), and (4) Tay-Sachs disease, which are all inherited.

Estimated to account for about 5 to 6 percent of all cases of retardation (Patton, Payne, & Beirne-Smith, 1990), **Down syndrome** is associated with a range of distinctive physical characteristics that vary considerably in number from one individual to another. Persons with Down syndrome may have thick epicanthal folds in the corners of the eyes, making them appear to slant upward slightly. Other common characteristics include small stature, decreased muscle tone (hypotonia), hyperflexibility of the joints, speckling of the iris in the eye, a small oral cavity that can result in a protruding tongue, short and broad hands with a single palmar crease, and a wide gap between the first and second toes (Batshaw & Perret, 1986; Blackman, 1984a). In addition, persons with Down syndrome are at risk for congenital heart defects and visual impairments, upper-respiratory infections, and leukemia. Some researchers are also considering a possible link between Down syndrome and Alzheimer's disease. (See the box below.)

Down syndrome. A condition resulting from a chromosomal abnormality; characterized by mental retardation and such physical signs as slanted-appearing eyes, flattened features, shortness and a tendency toward obesity; the type of Down syndrome is trisomy 21 most common.

The degree of retardation varies widely among people with Down syndrome; most individuals fall in the moderate range. In recent years, more children with Down syndrome have achieved IQ scores in the mildly retarded range, presumably because of intensive preschool programming.

Down Syndrome and Alzheimer's Disease

It has been well over a century since researchers first noted a high prevalence of senility in persons with Down syndrome (Fraser & Mitchell, 1876, cited in Evenhuis, 1990). And it was in the early-twentieth century that postmortem studies of the brains of people with Down syndrome revealed neuropathological signs similar to those of people with Alzheimer's disease (Carr, 1994). It was not until the 1980s and 1990s, however, that scientists started to address this correlation seriously.

Part of the reason for this shift in priority was the observation that the life expectancy for people with Down syndrome had increased dramatically over the twentieth century. In the first half of this century, very few people with Down syndrome lived until adulthood. But today, due to medical advances, it is not unusual for people with Down syndrome to live into their fifties and sixties. Even so, the life expectancy of people with Down syndrome is still well below that of the nondisabled population.

Postmortem studies of the brains of people with Down syndrome indicate that virtually all who reach the age of thirty-five have brain abnormalities very similar to those of persons with Alzheimer's disease (Wisniewski, Silverman, & Wegiel, 1994; Hof, Bouras, Perl, Sparks, Mehta, & Morrison, 1995). Behavioral symptoms, such as memory and speech problems, also seem evident, although they are more difficult to document because of the low cognitive ability of persons with Down syndrome (Evenhuis, 1990; Rasmussen & Sobsey, 1994).

Findings that link Down syndrome to Alzheimer's disease have made researchers optimistic about uncovering the genetic underpinnings of both conditions. For example, researchers have found that some types of Alzheimer's are related to mutations of the twenty-first pair of chromosomes (Pinel, 1993).

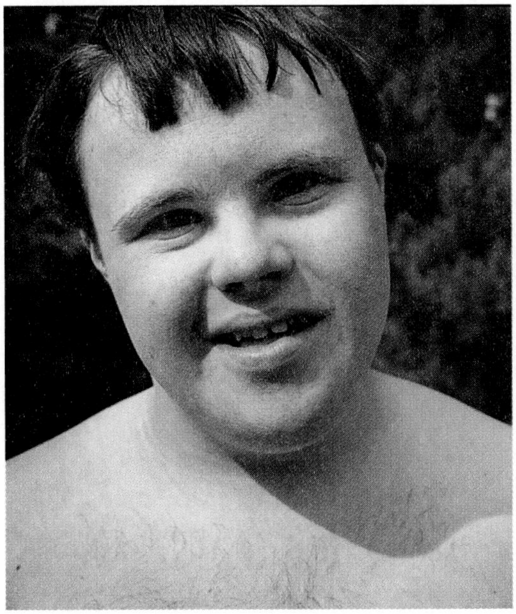

Down syndrome is usually characterized by physical traits such as upwardly slanted eyes.

trisomy 21. A type of Down syndrome in which the twenty-first chromosome is a triplet, making forty-seven, rather than the normal forty-six, chromosomes in all.

chromosome. A rod-shaped entity in the nucleus of the cell; contains genes, which convey hereditary characteristics.

amniocentesis. A medical procedure that allows examination of the amniotic fluid around the fetus; sometimes recommended to determine the presence of abnormality.

chorionic villus sampling (CVS). A method of testing the unborn fetus for a variety of chromosomal abnormalities, such as Down syndrome; a small amount of tissue from the chorion (a membrane that eventually helps form the placenta) is extracted and tested; can be done earlier than amniocentesis but the risk of miscarriage is slightly higher.

sonography. A medical procedure in which high-frequency sound waves are converted into a visual picture; used to detect major physical malformations in the unborn fetus.

Fragile X syndrome. A condition in which the bottom of the X chromosome in the twenty-third pair of chromosomes is pinched off; can result in a number of physical anomalies as well as mental retardation; occurs more often in males than females; thought to be the most common hereditary cause of mental retardation.

There are several different types of Down syndrome, but the most common, by far, is **trisomy 21**. In someone with this condition, the twenty-first set of **chromosomes** is a triplet, rather than a pair. (The normal human cell contains twenty-three pairs of chromosomes.)

The likelihood of having a child with Down syndrome increases with the age of the mother. For example, for mothers between the ages of forty and forty-four, there is a 1 in 80 chance of giving birth to a child with Down syndrome (Hansen, 1978). In addition to the age of the mother, researchers are pointing to other variables as possible causes, such as age of the father, exposure to radiation, and exposure to some viruses (Patton et al., 1990). Research on these factors is still preliminary, however.

Tests are available for diagnosing Down syndrome and some other birth defects during pregnancy. Three such tests are **amniocentesis, chorionic villus sampling (CVS)**, and **sonography:**

- In amniocentesis, the physician takes a sample of amniotic fluid from the sac around the fetus and analyzes the fetal cells for chromosomal abnormalities. In addition, the amniotic fluid can be tested for the presence of proteins that may have leaked out of the fetus's spinal column, indicating the presence of spina bifida (a condition in which the spinal column fails to close properly).
- In CVS, the physician takes a sample of villi (structures that later become the placenta), and tests them for chromosomal abnormalities. One advantage of CVS is that it can be done earlier than amniocentesis.
- In sonography, high-frequency sound waves are converted into pictures of the fetus, allowing the physician to detect physical malformations, such as spina bifida.

Fragile X syndrome is thought to be the most common hereditary cause of mental retardation (Finucane, 1988). It is associated with the X chromosome in the twenty-third pair of sex chromosomes. In males, the twenty-third pair consists of an X and a Y chromosome; in females, it consists of two X chromosomes. This disorder

phenylketonuria (PKU). A metabolic genetic disorder caused by the inability of the body to convert phenylalanine to tyrosine; an accumulation of phenylalanine results in abnormal brain development.

Tay-Sachs disease. An inherited condition that can appear when both mother and father are carriers; results in death; it can be detected before birth through amniocentesis.

rubella (German measles). A serious viral disease, which, if it occurs during the first trimester of pregnancy, is likely to cause a deformity in the fetus.

syphilis. A venereal disease that can cause mental subnormality in a child, especially if it is contracted by the mother-to-be during the latter stages of fetal development.

herpes simplex. A type of venereal disease that can cause cold sores or fever blisters; if it affects the genitals and is contracted by the mother-to-be in the later stages of fetal development, it can cause mental subnormality in the child.

meningitis. A bacterial or viral infection of the linings of the brain or spinal cord.

encephalitis. An inflammation of the brain; can affect the child's mental development adversely.

pediatric AIDS. Acquired immune deficiency syndrome that occurs in infants or young children; can be contracted by unborn fetuses from the blood of the mother through the placenta or through blood transfusions; an incurable virus that can result in a variety of physical and mental disorders.

is called *Fragile* X syndrome because in affected individuals, the bottom of the X chromosome is pinched off in some of the blood cells. Fragile X occurs less often in females because they have an extra X chromosome, giving them better protection if one of their X chromosomes is damaged. Persons with Fragile X syndrome may have a number of physical features, such as a large head; large, flat ears; long, narrow face; prominent forehead; broad nose; prominent, square chin; large testicles; and large hands, with nontapering fingers. In addition, people with Fragile X are more subject to having heart murmurs and repeated ear infections in childhood (Finucane, 1988).

Phenylketonuria (PKU) involves the inability of the body to convert a common dietary substance—phenylalanine—to tyrosine; the accumulation of phenylalanine results in abnormal brain development. Babies can undergo a screening test for PKU in the first few days after birth, and many states require that this test be performed before an infant leaves the hospital. Unless a baby with PKU starts a special diet controlling the intake of phenylalanine in infancy and continues it into middle childhood, the child will usually develop severe retardation (Guthrie, 1984). Because some studies have shown that a decrease in IQ occurs if the diet is stopped at middle childhood, many authorities believe the diet should be maintained indefinitely (Batshaw & Perret, 1986). In addition to treating PKU once it has been detected, more and more emphasis is being placed on screening parents to determine if they are possible carriers of the PKU gene. Even though the chance of two carriers marrying is slim (about 1 in 3,600) if this does occur, genetic counseling is highly advised.

Tay-Sachs disease, like PKU, can appear when both the mother and father are carriers. It results in progressive brain damage and eventual death. This condition occurs almost exclusively among Ashkenazi Jews—that is, those of East European extraction. Public health personnel have used genetic screening programs to identify carriers. The disease can also be detected *in utero*.

Brain Damage. Brain damage can result from a host of factors that fall into two general categories—infections and environmental hazards.

Infections. Infections that may lead to mental retardation can occur in the mother-to-be or the infant or young child after birth. **Rubella (German measles), syphilis,** and **herpes simplex** in the mother can all cause retardation in the child. Rubella is most dangerous during the first trimester (three months) of pregnancy. The venereal diseases, syphilis and herpes simplex, present a greater risk at later stages of fetal development (Hetherington & Parke, 1986). (Herpes simplex, which shows as cold sores or fever blisters, is not usually classified as a venereal disease unless it affects the genitals.)

Three examples of infections in the child that can affect mental development are meningitis, encephalitis, and pediatric AIDS. **Meningitis** is an infection of the covering of the brain that may be caused by a variety of bacterial or viral agents. **Encephalitis,** an inflammation of the brain, results more often in retardation and usually affects intelligence more severely. **Pediatric AIDS** is the fastest-growing infectious cause of mental retardation. The majority of children with this disease obtained their infection during birth from their mothers, who used intravenous drugs or were sexually active with infected men (Baumeister, Kupstas, & Klindworth, 1990).

Infections, as well as other causative factors, can also result in microcephalus or hydrocephalus. **Microcephalus** is a condition characterized by a small head with a sloping forehead. It can be caused by infections such as rubella or AIDS (Rubinstein, 1989) or by a genetic disorder. The retardation that results usually ranges from severe to profound. **Hydrocephalus** results from an accumulation of cerebrospinal fluid inside or outside the brain. Blockage of the circulation of the fluid, which results in a buildup of excessive pressure on the brain and enlargement of the skull, can occur for a variety of reasons—encephalitis, meningitis, malformation of the spine, or tumors. The degree of retardation depends on how early the condition is diagnosed and treated. Treatment consists of surgical implacement of a shunt (tube) that drains the excess fluid away from the brain and into a vein behind the ear or in the neck.

Environmental Hazards. Examples of environmental hazards that can result in mental retardation are blows to the head, poisons, radiation, malnutrition, prematurity or postmaturity, and birth injury. Although we are discussing these potential causal agents in this section, which deals with the causes of more severe forms of retardation, there is considerable evidence that in their milder forms, each of these factors can result in mild retardation.

It should be obvious that a blow to a child's head can result in mental retardation. The obviousness of this connection, in fact, has served as an impetus for many of the mandatory laws pertaining to the use of child restraints in automobiles. Besides the usual accidents that can lead to brain damage, more and more authorities are citing child abuse as a cause of brain damage that results in mental retardation and other disabilities (see Chapter 10).

Poisoning resulting in mental retardation can occur in the expectant mother or in the child. We are now much more aware of the harmful effects of a variety of substances, from obvious toxic agents, such as cocaine and heroin, to more subtle potential poisons, such as tobacco, alcohol, caffeine, and even food additives. In particular, research has shown that pregnant women who smoke and/or consume alcohol have a greater risk of having babies with behavioral and physical problems. For example, women who are heavy smokers are more likely than nonsmokers to have premature babies (Hetherington & Parke, 1986). And premature babies are at risk for a variety of developmental disabilities.

Researchers have exposed **fetal alcohol syndrome (FAS)** as a significant health problem for expectant mothers who consume large quantities of alcohol and for their unborn children (Hetherington & Parke, 1986; F. R. Schultz, 1984; see also Chapter 10). In fact, FAS occurs in about one-third of the babies of pregnant alcoholic women. Children with FAS are characterized by a variety of physical deformities as well as mental retardation.

Although pregnant women who drink moderately may not risk having children with FAS, evidence shows that even their infants will differ behaviorally from those born to women who do not drink during pregnancy. Among expectant mothers who drink moderately, there is evidence that the amount of alcohol they consume is related to their infants' arousal levels and central nervous system functioning (Streissguth, Barr, & Martin, 1983).

Some prescription drugs must also be avoided or used with caution by pregnant women. Research has linked some antibiotic, anticonvulsant, and anticancer medications to fetal malformations (Batshaw & Perret, 1986). Medication given to women during labor and delivery has also come under close scrutiny.

Although its use is now prohibited, infants still become poisoned by eating lead-based paint chips, particularly in impoverished areas. Lead poisoning varies in its effect on children; high levels can result in death. The federal government now requires that automobile manufacturers produce cars that use only lead-free gasoline to lower the risk of inhaling lead particles from auto exhaust.

microcephalus. A condition causing development of a small head with a sloping forehead; proper development of the brain is prevented, resulting in mental retardation.

hydrocephalus. A condition characterized by enlargement of the head because of excessive pressure of the cerebrospinal fluid.

fetal alcohol syndrome (FAS). Abnormalities associated with the mother's drinking alcohol during pregnancy; defects range from mild to severe.

We have recognized the hazards of radiation to the unborn fetus for some time. Physicians, for example, are cautious not to expose pregnant women to X-rays unless absolutely necessary. Since the mid- to late-1970s, however, the public has become even more concerned over the potential dangers of radiation from improperly designed or supervised nuclear power plants.

Retardation caused by improper nutrition can occur because the expectant mother is malnourished or because the child, once born, does not have a proper diet (Cravioto & DeLicardie, 1975; Hallahan & Cruickshank, 1973).

Disorders due to an abnormal length of pregnancy—either too short (prematurity) or too long (postmaturity)—can also result in retardation. The latter is not as likely to cause retardation, although it is possible that the fetus will suffer from poor nutrition if it is long overdue (Robinson & Robinson, 1976). Prematurity is sometimes defined by the length of the pregnancy and sometimes by the weight of the infant at birth (5.5 pounds or lower is often used as an index of prematurity). Both premature and small infants are candidates for a variety of physical and behavioral abnormalities, including retardation (Blackman, 1984b). Prematurity itself is associated with a number of factors—poor nutrition, teenage pregnancy, drug abuse, and excessive cigarette smoking.

Brain injury can also occur during delivery if the child is not positioned properly in the uterus. One problem that sometimes occurs because of difficulty during delivery is **anoxia** (complete deprivation of oxygen).

ASSESSMENT

Two major areas are assessed to determine whether a person is mentally retarded: intelligence and adaptive skills. To assess intelligence, a professional administers an intelligence test to the person. To assess adaptive skills, a parent or professional who is familiar with the person responds to a survey about different adaptive skills.

Intelligence Tests

There are many types of IQ tests. Because of their accuracy and predictive capabilities, practitioners prefer individually administered tests over group tests. Two of the most common individual IQ tests for children are the Stanford-Binet (4th ed.; Thorndike, Hagen, & Sattler, 1986) and the Wechsler Intelligence Scale for Children–Third Edition (WISC–III) (Wechsler, 1991). Both of these tests are verbal, although the WISC–III is intended to assess both verbal and performance aspects of intelligence. It has a verbal and a performance scale with a number of subtests. The *full-scale IQ*, a statistical composite of the verbal and performance IQ measures, is used when a single overall score for a child is desired.

Another relatively common IQ test is the Kaufman Assessment Battery for Children (K–ABC) (Kaufman & Kaufman, 1983). Some psychologists recommend using the K–ABC with African-American students because they believe it is less culturally biased (Kamphaus & Reynolds, 1987).

Although not all IQ tests call for this method of calculation, we can get a rough approximation of a person's IQ by dividing **mental age** (the age level at which a person is functioning) by **chronological age** and multiplying by 100. For example, a ten-year-old student who performs on an IQ test as well as the *average* eight-year-old (and thus has a mental age of eight years) would have an IQ of 80.

Compared to most psychological tests, IQ tests such as the Stanford-Binet, WISC–III, and K–ABC are among the most reliable and valid. By *reliability*, we mean

anoxia. The loss of oxygen; can cause brain injury.

mental age. Refers to the IQ test score that specifies the age level at which an individual is functioning.

chronological age. Refers to how old a person is; used in comparison with mental age to determine IQ:

$$IQ = \frac{\text{mental age}}{\text{chronological age}} \times 100$$

that a person will obtain relatively similar scores if given the test on two separate occasions that are not too close or far apart in time. *Validity* generally answers the question of whether the instrument measures what it is supposed to measure. A good indicator of the validity of an IQ test is the fact that it is generally considered the best single index of how well a student will do in school. It is wise to be wary, however, of placing too much faith in a single score from any IQ test. There are at least four reasons for caution:

1. Even on very reliable tests, an individual's IQ can change from one testing to another, and sometimes the change can be dramatic (McCall, Applebaum, & Hogarty, 1973).
2. All IQ tests are culturally biased to a certain extent. Largely because of differences in language and experience, children from minority groups are sometimes at a disadvantage in taking such tests.
3. The younger the child, the less validity and reliability the test has. Infant intelligence tests are particularly questionable.
4. IQ tests are not the absolute determinant when it comes to assessing a person's ability to function in society. A superior IQ does not guarantee a successful and happy life, nor does a low IQ doom a person to a miserable existence. Other variables are also important determinants of a person's coping skills in society. That is why, for example, professionals also assess adaptive skills, to which we now turn. (See also the box below.)

Keeping Tests in Perspective

Most professionals agree that tests, such as IQ tests and adaptive behavior instruments, are necessary. Tests can be helpful in making placement decisions and in evaluating program effectiveness. It is important to keep in mind, however, that they are far from perfect predictors about how a particular individual will function in the real world. The following excerpt from the case study of a woman with mental retardation makes this point nicely:

> When I first saw her—clumsy, uncouth, all-of-a-fumble—I saw her merely, or wholly, as a casualty, a broken creature, whose neurological impairments I could pick out and dissect with precision. . . .
>
> The next time I saw her, it was all very different. I didn't have her in a test situation, "evaluating" her in a clinic. I wandered outside, it was a lovely spring day, with a few minutes in hand before the clinic started, and there I saw Rebecca sitting on a bench, gazing at the April foliage quietly, with obvious delight. Her posture had none of the clumsiness which had so impressed me before. Sitting there, in a light dress, her face calm and slightly smiling, she suddenly brought to mind one of Chekov's young women—Irene, Anya, Sonya, Nina—seen against the backdrop of a Chekovian cherry orchard. She could have been any young woman enjoying a beautiful spring day. This was my human, as opposed to my neurological, vision . . . .
>
> Why was she so de-composed before, how could she be so re-composed now? I had the strongest feeling of two wholly different modes of thought, or of organization, or of being. The first schematic—pattern-seeing, problem-solving—this is what had been tested, and where she had been found so defective, so disastrously wanting. But the tests had given no inkling of anything *but* the deficits, anything, so to speak, *beyond* her deficits.
>
> They had given me no hint of her positive powers, her ability to perceive the real world—the world of nature, and perhaps of the imagination—as a coherent, intelligible, poetic whole: her ability to see this, think this, and (when she could) live this; they had given me no intimation of her inner world, which clearly *was* composed and coherent, and approached as something other than a set of problems or tasks. . . .
>
> It was perhaps fortunate that I chanced to see Rebecca in her so-different modes—so damaged and incorrigible in the one, so full of promise and potential in the other—and that she was one of the first patients I saw in our clinic. For what I saw in her, what she showed me, I now saw in them all.

Source: From O. Sacks, *The Man Who Mistook His Wife for a Hat And Other Clinical Tales,* pp. 170–173.

Adaptive Skills

Many adaptive skills measures are available. Three of the most commonly used are probably the Vineland Adaptive Behavior Scales (Sparrow, Balla, & Cicchetti, 1984), the AAMD Adaptive Behavior Scale–School Edition (Lambert & Windmiller, 1981), and the Adaptive Behavior Inventory for Children (Mercer & Lewis, 1977). The basic format of these instruments requires that a parent, teacher, or other professional answer questions related to the subject's ability to perform adaptive skills. The particular skills assessed differ slightly from one measure to another, but they generally cover the adaptive skills stated in the AAMR definition: communication, self-care, home living, social skills, community use, self-direction, health and safety, functional academics, leisure, and work.

PSYCHOLOGICAL AND BEHAVIORAL CHARACTERISTICS

In considering the psychological and behavioral characteristics of persons with mental retardation, we hasten to point out that *individual* persons with mental retardation may not display all the characteristics. There is great variability in the behavior of persons who are retarded, and we must consider each person as unique. In this section, we discuss the following characteristics: attention, memory, self-regulation, language development, academic achievement, social development, and motivation.

Attention

The importance of attention for learning is critical. A person must be able to attend to the task at hand before he or she can learn it. For years, researchers have posited that we can attribute many of the learning problems of persons with retardation to attention problems (e.g., Brooks & McCauley, 1984; Zeaman & House, 1963). Often attending to the wrong things, many people who are retarded have difficulty allocating their attention properly.

Memory

One of the most consistent research findings is that persons with mental retardation have difficulty remembering information. Many authorities have conceptualized these memory problems within a theoretical framework that stresses the depth of processing that an individual must perform to remember certain material (Craik & Lockhart, 1972; Craik & Tulving, 1975). Researchers have found that memory tasks requiring deeper levels of processing—those that are more complicated—are even more likely to show disparities between persons with retardation and their nondisabled peers than are memory tasks requiring shallow levels of processing—those that are less complicated (E. E. Schultz, 1983).

Self-Regulation

One of the primary reasons that persons with mental retardation have problems with memory is that they have difficulties in self-regulation (Whitman, 1990). **Self-regulation** is a broad term referring to an individual's ability to regulate his or her

self-regulation. Refers generally to a person's ability to regulate his or her own behavior (e.g., to employ strategies to help in a problem-solving situation); an area of difficulty for persons who are mentally retarded.

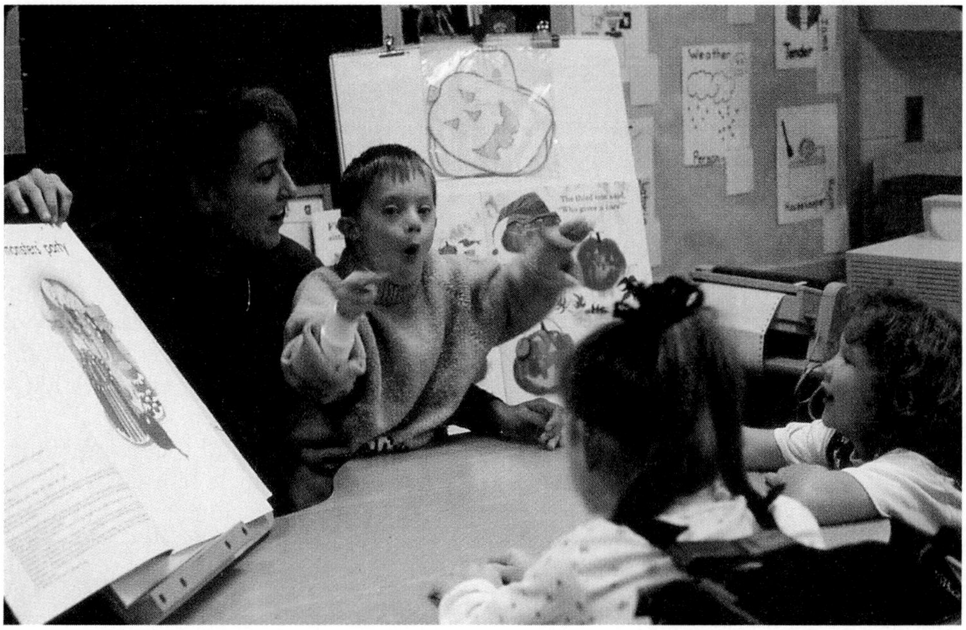

The self-concepts of children with retardation are influenced by their relationships with their peers. Positive personal interactions are as important to these individuals as to anyone.

own behavior. For example, when given a list of words to remember, most people rehearse the list aloud or to themselves in an attempt to keep the words in memory. In other words, they actively regulate their behavior by employing a strategy that will help them remember. People who are retarded are less likely than their nondisabled peers to use self-regulatory strategies such as rehearsal.

Closely connected to the ability to self-regulate is the concept of metacognition. **Metacognition** refers to a person's awareness of what strategies are needed to perform a task and "the ability to use self-regulatory mechanisms . . . such as planning one's moves, evaluating the effectiveness of one's ongoing activities, checking the outcomes of one's efforts" (Baker, 1982, pp. 27–28). Self-regulation is, thus, a component of metacognition. Persons with mental retardation have difficulties in metacognition. (We discuss metacognition again in Chapter 5.)

Researchers are working on developing techniques to improve the metacognitive abilities of individuals with mental retardation (Whitman, 1990). More and more, teachers are emphasizing that students who are retarded should be taught metacognitive skills, including self-regulation.

Language Development

Delayed or deviant language development is evident in virtually all persons with mental retardation (Warren & Abbeduto, 1992). Speech problems—for example, articulation errors—also frequently accompany mental retardation. In general, the language of persons who are retarded, especially those who are less severely retarded, follows the same developmental course as that of nonretarded persons, but their language development progresses at a slower rate.

Poor language development and problems in self-regulation are connected (Whitman, 1990). Because many self-regulation strategies are linguistically based, individuals who have poor language skills are at a disadvantage in using self-regulation tactics.

metacognition. A person's (1) awareness of what strategies are necessary to perform a task and (2) ability to use self-regulation strategies.

Academic Achievement

Because of the strong relationship between intelligence and achievement, it is not surprising that students who are mentally retarded lag well behind their nonretarded peers in all areas of achievement. Students who are retarded also tend to be underachievers in relation to expectations based on their intellectual levels (MacMillan, 1982).

Social Development

Some authorities have argued that retardation should be determined primarily by whether a person is able "to perform certain crucial social roles (e.g., worker, friend, neighbor) more than by the ability to master academic tasks" (Greenspan & Granfield, 1992, p. 443). What is important, ultimately, is the individual's ability to function in society.

People with mental retardation are candidates for a variety of social problems. They often have problems making friends (Luftig, 1988; Zetlin & Murtaugh, 1988) and have poor self-concepts for at least two reasons. First, many do not seem to know how to strike up social interactions with others, and this difference is evident as early as preschool (Kopp, Baker, & Brown, 1992). Second, even when not attempting to interact with others, people who are retarded may exhibit behaviors that "turn off" their peers. For example, they engage in higher rates of inattention and disruptive behavior than their nonretarded classmates. (See the box on p. 139 for a discussion of the importance of friendship.)

Motivation

Many of the problems pertaining to attention, memory, self-regulation, language development, academic achievement, and social development place persons who are retarded at risk to develop problems of motivation. If these individuals have experienced a long history of failure, they can be at risk to develop **learned helplessness**—the feeling that no matter how hard they try, they will still fail. Believing they have little control over what happens to them and that they are primarily controlled by other people and events, some persons with retardation tend to give up easily when faced with challenging tasks.

Professionals recognize the need to provide people with mental retardation with as much success as possible. (See, for example, the Collaboration Box on pp. 140–141, in which two teachers, Bruce Wojick and Theone Hug, work hard at making sure that the student, Cindy, achieves success.) In addition, they recognize that a good educational or vocational program for persons with mental retardation needs to contain a component focused on motivational problems.

EDUCATIONAL CONSIDERATIONS

Although there is some overlap, in general, the focus of educational programs varies according to the degree of the student's retardation, or how much he or she requires support services. For example, the lesser the degree of retardation, the more the teacher emphasizes academic skills, and the greater the degree of retardation, the more stress there is on self-help, community living, and vocational skills. Keep in mind, however, that this distinction is largely a matter of emphasis; in practice, all students who are retarded, no matter the severity level, need academic, self-help, community living, and vocational skills.

learned helplessness. A motivational term referring to a condition wherein a person believes that no matter how hard he or she tries, failure will result.

The Importance of Friendship

Professionals often overlook the fundamental importance of friendship. The following extract highlights the critical role friendship can play in the lives of people who are mentally retarded:

> A sense of belonging, of feeling accepted and of having personal worth are qualities that friendship brings to a person. Friendship creates an alliance and a sense of security. It is a vital human connection.
>
> People who are mentally retarded want and need friendship like everyone else. Yet they typically have few opportunities to form relationships or to develop the skills necessary to interact socially with others. Their exposure to peers may be limited because they live and work in sheltered or isolated environments. They usually lack a history of socializing events like school clubs, parties, or sleepovers that help to develop or refine personal skills. They may not know how to give of themselves to other people and may be stuck in an egocentric perspective. Persons who are retarded may also respond inappropriately in social situations. Many people shun adults with retardation who freely hug or kiss strangers when greeting them. . . .
>
> Because of their few contacts and opportunities, persons with retardation may attempt to befriend strangers or unwitting individuals. Many attempt to become social acquaintances with their professional contacts. In their effort to maintain the contacts and relationships they have developed, some individuals will overcompensate: calling their friend too many times, talking too long on the phone, demanding attention, and not being able to let up. . . .
>
> Friends can play a vital role in the adjustment to community living of adults who are retarded by providing the emotional support and guidance through the exigencies of daily life. Certain organizations have begun to address the need for friendship by initiating social opportunities. . . [There are] social club[s] for adults with retardation in which members plan their own parties and projects. Some programs offer supervised dating; others establish one-to-one relationships between volunteers and clients for the purpose of aiding adjustment. (Patton, Payne, & Beirne-Smith, 1990)

With the increase in mainstreaming, many hope the problems that numerous persons with mental retardation have in obtaining and holding friendships will decrease. In the future, it will be interesting to see to what degree professionals will organize social clubs exclusively for persons with mental retardation versus having them socialize with nondisabled persons.

Source: From *Mental Retardation,* 3rd ed., by James R. Patton, Mary Beirne-Smith, and James S. Payne. Copyright © 1990 by Merrill Publishing Company (pp. 408–409).

We now discuss some of the major features of educational programs for students with mental retardation. We focus on the elementary school level here; we discuss preschool and secondary programming in later sections. Although the lines are sometimes blurred, we have divided our coverage into programming for students with mild retardation, or those requiring less intensive support, and students with more severe retardation, or those requiring more intensive support.

Students with Mild Retardation, or Those Requiring Less Intensive Support

Early elementary education is heavily oriented toward providing children who are retarded with **readiness skills:** abilities that are prerequisites for later learning. They include such things as the ability to:

1. sit still and attend to the teacher
2. discriminate auditory and visual stimuli
3. follow directions
4. develop language
5. increase gross and fine motor coordination (e.g., hold a pencil or cut with a pair of scissors)
6. develop self-help skills (e.g., tie shoes, button and unbutton, zip and unzip, use the toilet)
7. interact with peers in a group situation

collaboration

a key to success

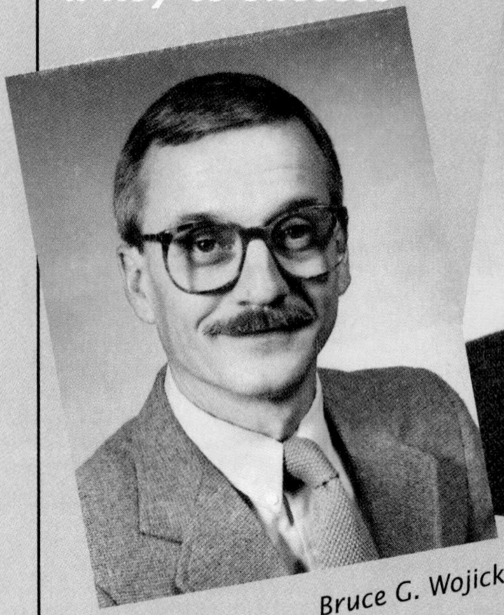

Bruce G. Wojick

Theone Thomas Hug

Bruce I see about seventy students daily, a few more boys than girls. They range in age from thirteen to sixteen; forty are white, twenty-eight are black, and two are Native American. Their disabling conditions include mental retardation, learning disabilities, and emotional disturbance. Their reading grade equivalents range from 1.5 to 3.8; math from 3.0 to 5.2.

Theone I teach different groups of seventh- and eighth-grade students for ten weeks at a time. I see approximately 100 students daily and have four separate preparations per day just for the regular classes. My students range in age from twelve to sixteen. Classes include basic, average, and merited (gifted) abilities. I usually have one to three mainstreamed students per class who have mental retardation, learning disabilities, or behavioral disorders. For one ten-week period per year, I teach a self-contained class of no more than twelve students who have mental retardation and behavioral disorders. My classes have about the same ethnic composition as Bruce's. As a teacher with very little background in exceptional education, most of my learning has come from actual experience and trial and error. I find it extremely important that special education teachers give me a background on each student. I'm eager for their suggestions and find good communication and mutual backup and support a necessity for the student's success.

Bruce We've decided to describe our work with a student we'll call Cindy. Cindy was fourteen, an eighth-grader who was tall, was overweight, and had poor hygiene. She had poor gross motor coordination but adequate fine motor skills. Her reading and math were lower than second-grade level. She had very poor social skills and was basically nonverbal. She started the school year with only one close friend, also nonverbal. She had a very limited attention span and a negative self-image, and she tended to daydream a lot. Her large stature, battle with adolescent skin problems, and unkempt hair contributed to the little effort her classmates made to befriend her. It was obvious she came from a background where dress and neatness were unimportant.

Theone Cindy was introverted in her speech and social skills. She wouldn't volunteer, and she'd never bring any attention to herself. She always sat alone in the cafeteria. But she was cooperative with adults. She really tried her best to complete assignments. She always tried to contribute when we called on her, even though she wasn't always correct. She was very helpful and seemed to like being in school. Her attendance was good. In terms of learning, she was very slow and required extremely clear and repetitive instructions. Her total lack of self-esteem and extremely quiet nature made it necessary for her teachers to recognize when she needed help, as she wouldn't solicit any.

Bruce We immediately recognized that Cindy needed as much positive reinforcement as we could give her. She also needed to fit in with her peers in both our classes. So, as a team we decided that we would praise every effort she made, every response she gave. We made sure that we communicated about her work and efforts so that we could really just about double the positive reinforcement she would get.

Theone As a regular classroom teacher I make a special effort with every mainstreamed child to make him or her feel comfortable—an important part of my class. I start out by carefully planning an assignment that I'm almost certain the student can complete successfully, and I give this assignment the first few days the special student is in my class. When Cindy came to my class, I gave the entire class

Bruce G. Wojick is a middle school special education teacher, Niagara Falls (New York) Public Schools; B.S.Ed., Exceptional Education (Mental Retardation), State University College of New York at Buffalo; M.S. Ed., Niagara University. **Theone Thomas Hug** is a middle school home/career skills teacher; B.S.Ed., Home Economics Education, State University College of New York at Buffalo; M.S.Ed., Home Economics Education, State University College of New York at Buffalo.

instructions about a project. Then, while they were working, I went around the room and repeated the instructions to several students, spending extra time with Cindy. Once I got her started and she seemed comfortable, I reminded her frequently to keep working and keep up the good effort. Then, after she completed the project, I used hers as an example for the rest of the class of what we were trying to achieve. This encouraged other kids in the class to accept her—they recognized her personal success. Of course, this raised her self-esteem, too. And I told Bruce about her success so that he could give her additional praise. I felt it was really important to build up Cindy's confidence. Once she got some confidence, I felt we'd see improvement in her academic work.

Bruce This kind of teamwork doesn't just happen. You see, once a student's schedule is completed by the special education department, I wait for at least a week to let the student get acquainted with each regular classroom teacher. Then I ask the student how he or she feels about each class and each teacher. It's really important that the student feel comfortable with the teacher I choose to team up with. The teachers who seem to show more interest in the students are the ones I always tend to work with on a closer basis. I want lots of positive reinforcement—praise, recognition for good behavior and achievement—to always be available from the regular teacher as well as from me. I believe that from the beginning Cindy felt fairly comfortable in both of our classes because of the positive reinforcement we agreed to give her. She got praise and encouragement from both of us, repeated over and over in and out of our classrooms.

Theone Yes, we felt we could work well together as teachers. But we were really frustrated by the lack of concern on the part of Cindy's parents. They did come to parent conferences, but it seemed to us that otherwise they didn't seem to care very much how Cindy was doing.

Bruce Any assignments or projects we gave Cindy to take home were always completed in school with our help. We're not saying that Cindy's parents never helped her, but on the other hand there wasn't much evidence that they did. Cindy was the type of student who needed constant praise and attention to overcome her difficulties. And as far as we could tell the only place she got this was in school. Our working with Cindy during the school day just wasn't enough. Every new week with Cindy was a fresh start on building up her self-esteem—it seemed like it just disappeared every weekend and holiday.

Theone Even so, we saw some really fantastic progress in Cindy in school. At the end of eight weeks in my class I gave an assignment to write a paper about a chosen career. Cindy chose babysitting. Students were supposed to find two pages worth of information, set it up in outline form, and eventually share it with the class as an oral report. This was a really, really big challenge for Cindy. Bruce and I both felt that our work had paid off when Cindy—well prepared, without hesitation—stood in front of the class and presented her report. She even looked at the class while she spoke! She had good information, and even showed pictures of babies and babysitters she had cut and mounted from magazines. Along with the pictures, she shared a photograph of herself as a baby with the rest of the class.

Bruce The most rewarding aspect of working together as colleagues is being able to share the simple smiles and accomplishments of the student. Actually to see the results of our efforts is reward in itself. Sharing always makes the reward doubly nice.

Theone I agree. And aside from the student-generated personal rewards is the professional reward. We both agree that being able to work with a colleague who is flexible, interested, and willing to communicate new ideas makes the work atmosphere more productive and enjoyable. Being able to work with a colleague who takes the time to listen, make suggestions, and honestly evaluate joint efforts promotes personal gratification through student successes. After years of teaching, this kind of cooperative experience renews your eagerness to be more effective.

Bruce Right. But it isn't easy to make this happen. Finding time during the school day for teachers to get together is next to impossible The time the special student spends with the regular teacher is often the only break the special teacher has during the day. Theone and I agree that this problem of time or scheduling is the greatest barrier to working together.

I want lots of positive reinforcement . . . to always be available from the regular teacher as well as from me.

Theone As a regular classroom teacher, I find I am often forgotten when it comes to giving me information about a mainstreamed student. Unfortunately, in the past the lack of communication has set up situations in which I didn't even know that students were being mainstreamed until several weeks after they came into my class! The way a special education teacher can help me most is to take the time to identify and give me a quick background on each student he or she is mainstreaming into my class.

Bruce I believe that it is my responsibility as the special education teacher to inform each receiving teacher of the student's potential, capabilities, idiosyncrasies, and so on. It's also my responsibility to acquaint myself with the mainstreamed class so that I can more realistically prepare an intelligent and rational IEP for the student.

Theone Sometimes there is an unfortunate tendency for the special education teacher to claim "sole ownership" of students. This can impair effective, cooperative working relationships and build impenetrable barriers.

The teacher provides instruction in language and concept development. In addition, the teacher needs to help children who are retarded in the rudiments of socialization. Programs are available for training socially adaptive behaviors. An example is ACCEPTS (A Curriculum for Children's Effective Peer and Teacher Skills) (Walker et al., 1983), a tightly structured and sequenced set of activities designed to teach children to get along with their peers.

In the later elementary years, emphasis is greater on academics, usually on what are known as **functional academics**. Whereas the nonretarded child is taught academics, such as reading, in order to learn other academic content, such as history, the child with mental retardation is often taught reading in order to learn to function independently. In functional academics, the child learns academics in order to do such things as read a newspaper, read the telephone book, read labels on goods at the store, make change, and fill out job applications.

Although the rudiments of community and vocational living skills are emphasized much more in high school, some children with mild retardation are taught these skills in later elementary school (Hasazi & Clark, 1988). Many professionals believe that because some students who are retarded take a relatively long time to learn particular skills, it is best to acquaint them with these skills as early as elementary school.

Students with More Severe Retardation, or Those Requiring More Intensive Support

Most authorities agree that the following features should characterize educational programs for students who are more severely retarded:

1. age-appropriate curriculum and materials
2. functional activities
3. community-based instruction
4. integrated therapy
5. interaction with nondisabled students
6. family involvement

Age-Appropriate Curricula and Materials. The tendency in the past was to "baby" even older persons with severe retardation because of their intellectual limitations. Authorities now agree that this is not only demeaning but also educationally harmful (Bates, Renzaglia, & Wehman, 1981). Using infantile materials works against the goal of fostering as much independent behavior as possible.

Functional Activities. Because so much of educational programming for students with severe retardation is focused on preparing them to live as independently as possible, activities need to be practical (Wehman, Moon, Everson, Wood, & Barcus, 1988). Learning to dress oneself by practicing on a doll, for example, is not as effective as practice with one's own clothes. Some students with severe retardation can learn some academic skills. Because teaching them basic reading and math is very time consuming, however, it is important to teach only what they will need and can learn (Snell, 1988).

Community-Based Instruction. In keeping with the notion of functional skills, educational programming for people with severe retardation needs to take place in the community as much as possible. Because many of the skills they learn are for use in settings outside the classroom, such as on public transportation or in the grocery

functional academics. Practical skills (e.g., reading a newspaper or telephone book), rather than academic learning skills.

Community-based instruction focuses on everyday living skills, such as grocery shopping, learned in their actual settings.

store, instruction in such activities has proved more effective when done in those settings (Sailor et al., 1986). The teacher may want to use simulated experiences in the classroom—by creating a mini-grocery store with a couple of aisles of products and a cash register, for example—to prepare students before they go to a real store. But such simulations by themselves are not enough. Students need the experience of going into the actual settings in which they will need to use the skills they are learning.

Integrated Therapy. Many persons with severe retardation have multiple disabilities, necessitating the services of a variety of professionals, such as speech, physical, and occupational therapists. In keeping with the notion of functional activities, many authorities believe it better that these professionals integrate what they do with students into the overall educational program, rather than meet with them alone in a therapy room. For example, professionals point out that it is better to teach students how to walk up and down the actual stairs in the school they attend than to use the specially made stairs that are traditionally placed in therapy rooms for this purpose (Snell, 1988).

Interaction with Nondisabled Students. Professionals agree that students who are severely retarded and their nondisabled peers benefit from interaction. As we noted in Chapter 2, however, professionals do not always agree about how or how much interaction there should be. Some believe it is best to include students with severe retardation in regular classes alongside their nondisabled peers for the entire school day. Others believe the interaction should be on a more limited basis. For example, one method some schools use involves having nondisabled students act as tutors or classroom helpers in classes for students with severe retardation.

Family Involvement. As we discuss in Chapter 12, family involvement is important for the success of educational programming for students with disabilities of all types and severity levels. Family involvement is particularly important for students

SUCCESS STORIES

Orono, ME: Thirteen-year-old, **Molly Berry** *is helpful and energetic, much like her parents, Karen and Dave. As a fifth-grader, Molly is a student council representative at her school. Because of her drive (and despite her limitations), the Berrys have advocated for Molly to be included in general education classes since preschool. Special educator Lisa Douville and general educator Mike Morcom are collaborating to maximize Molly's learning before she leaves elementary school.*

Mike Morcom readied his class for the totem pole project and rehearsed positive behaviors for cooperative learning groups. As Molly listened to reminders about sound levels and cleaning up, she seemed eager to start. "I'm going to make a unicorn for my totem pole," she said, and started to paint an ice-cream container white. She never sat still for long, as she repeatedly left her project to inspect others. She told a friend, "When you finish painting, you'll need some glue."

Karen and Dave Berry agree that Molly is distractible, but they feel she has made significant social gains in the mainstream classroom. Special educator Lisa Douville also sees improvement in Molly's ability to focus. "She has a good attitude and responds without much grumbling! She hasn't needed sticker reinforcement so far this year."

The Berrys have what they call a "healthy adversarial relationship" with Molly's school district. They are strong advocates for parents being closely involved in the educational decisions affecting their children. According to Dave Berry, "When parents and professionals are both well informed, then they're on even ground." The Berrys have received training in individualized education program (IEP) development and how to exercise their rights. Karen Berry says, "I always ask that IEPs be available to all Molly's teachers. Then, I check to see if they are being used."

For the Berrys, the key issue in Molly's education is effective communication and teamwork from year to year. This means that teachers exchange information and that parents and educators listen carefully to each other. "Everyone needs to know it's okay to speak up for the real needs of the child, despite the costs or inconveniences," says Dave Berry. "We've all worked hard to help Molly make progress."

In June, Molly will graduate from the pine-paneled elementary school where she has attended general education classes since grade 1. Triennial testing has been completed and a meeting will soon be held to determine how Molly can best make the transition to middle school for grade 6.

When the Pupil Evaluation Team meets, Lisa Douville and Mike Morcom will attend, along with Dave and Karen Berry. Molly's social goals will be reviewed to determine her progress toward independence in beginning work, attention to task, and use of appropriate behaviors in managing stress. New academic goals will be set and supports will be updated to reflect any changes in modifications, such as shortened written assignments or notes copied from a sheet on her desk, rather than from the board.

Karen and Dave Berry are committed advocates for Molly and have worked closely with a psychologist to obtain an objective assessment of her abilities and potential for

applied behavior analysis. The application and evaluation of principles of learning theory in teaching situations; used with all types of students with disabilities but particularly appropriate for persons with severe and profound disabilities; consists of six steps: identifying overall goals, accumulating further information through baseline measurement, specifying

who are severely retarded because many of the skills they are taught will be used in their homes (Bates et al., 1981). The involvement can range from simply informing parents about the progress of their children to having parents act as classroom aides.

Using Applied Behavior Analysis to Teach Students with Mental Retardation

Although teachers use applied behavior analysis with all types of students with disabilities, it is particularly applicable with students who are mentally retarded, especially those with more severe learning problems. **Applied behavior analysis** is the application and evaluation of principles of learning theory in teaching situations. According to Wolery, Bailey, and Sugai (1988), it consists of six steps.

Special Educators at Work

successful inclusion. Together with the team, they have crafted an IEP that describes areas that interfere with Molly's learning:

> Molly exhibits delays in the development of perceptual-motor skills, a mild to moderate phonological disorder, a moderate to severe expressive language delay, and difficulties comprehending complex verbal material. When compared to her peers, Molly has difficulties in the following areas: working independently and initiating and completing tasks. Off-task behaviors consist of unpredictable episodes of physical and visual wandering and ignoring teacher requests. This behavior is compounded in situations when Molly perceives tasks as being difficult. Her levels of performance are consistent with test results and classroom observations.

This year, Molly; her best friend, Jenny; and two other special needs students are among the twenty-two members of Mike Morcom's fifth-grade class. "I don't want the kids to patronize Molly, and they don't seem to," says Mike. "We work on building sensitivity to differences and modeling ways of interacting."

Mike acknowledges that it would be hard to manage instructionally without a classroom aide, and he sees this as a key to Molly's success. Janet Metcalf, a certified teacher, has worked as the educational technician with Molly's class for two years. So has special educator Lisa Douville, who supervises Janet, works directly with Molly on reading and math skills in the resource room, and manages her educational plan. Lisa and Mike jointly track Molly's progress.

Molly's math program is carried out by the educational technician in the classroom and guided by individualized packets of materials assembled by Lisa Douville. If the class is working as a group or taking a test, Janet Metcalf will often adapt the activity, pull the next item from Molly's packet, or develop a criterion-referenced test, based on Molly's third-grade-level goals. For social studies and science, Janet adapts Mike Morcom's materials and activities for the special needs students in the class. Janet also keeps a daily school/home journal with the Berrys.

Like her math program, Molly's reading and spelling programs are directed by Lisa Douville and similarly carried out in the classroom. However, these are areas in which Molly has less confidence and fears failure. She is stronger at receiving information orally but has difficulty decoding words when reading. Says Lisa, "Molly is embarrassed to be seen with the second–third-grade-level books she is able to read. She is aware of her social environment and needs help with handling sensitive issues appropriately."

In reflecting on his daughter's progress, Dave Berry recalls that once Molly was provided with a well-trained aide and resource support, the role of her general educators changed. "We started to work as a team when the second grade teacher wisely identified the supports Molly needed in the classroom. Her fourth- and fifth-grade teachers have been terrific at working closely with special educators. We don't expect the classroom teachers to do it all, but we do expect them to have help."

As they plan for Molly's future, this team of parents and professionals hope that she will be able to remain in classes with her nondisabled peers as much as is appropriate for her. Says Dave Berry, "I work with students everyday, and I think it must be said that while this approach works for my child, inclusion in a regular class might not be appropriate for someone else's child. Karen Berry agrees. "I don't want Molly just to be *included*. It's what is *done* for her in the classroom that counts."

—By Jean Crockett

1. The teacher identifies the overall goal. This usually consists of a skill area the student needs more work in or an inappropriate behavior that he or she needs to decrease.
2. Further information is obtained on the identified skill area or behavior by taking a baseline measurement. The **baseline** measurement tells at what level the student is currently functioning; the teacher can later compare the student's performance after instruction with the original baseline performance.
3. The teacher decides on a specific learning objective; that is, he or she breaks down the overall goal into specific skills the child is to learn.
4. The teacher implements an intervention designed to increase needed skills or decrease inappropriate behavior—for example, a drill and practice routine for math problems or a reward system for good behavior.

learning objectives, implementing the intervention, monitoring student performance, and evaluating the intervention.

baseline. A measure of current functioning used to assess the effects of an intervention; the therapist or teacher measures the client's or student's skill or behavior before instruction.

5. The child's progress is monitored by measuring performance frequently, usually daily.
6. The teacher evaluates the effects of the intervention, usually by charting the student's performance during intervention and comparing it with the baseline performance. Based on this evaluation, the teacher decides whether to continue, modify, or end the intervention.

Service Delivery Models

Administrative placements for students with mental retardation range from general education classes to residential facilities. Although special classes for these students tend to be the norm, more and more students with retardation are being placed in more integrated settings. The degree of integration tends to be determined by the level of severity, with students who are less severely retarded being the most integrated. However, as we discussed in Chapter 2, some professionals believe that the degree of severity is relatively unimportant in decisions regarding placement. Some believe all students with retardation should be educated in the general education classroom and that schools should provide the necessary support services (e.g., a special aide or special education teacher) in the class.

It is too early to tell how successful the movement to place all students with retardation in general education classes will be. But the prevailing philosophy dictates that students with retardation should enjoy more integration with nondisabled students than is often the case. Virtually all special educators agree that placement in a self-contained class with *no* opportunity for interaction with nondisabled students is inappropriate. At the same time, even parents who favor integrated settings often believe that it is good for their children to interact *with* other children with disabilities, too (Guralnick, Connor, & Hammond, 1995). In other words, these parents do not want their children to be the only ones with disabilities in their classes. The issue of how much interaction is appropriate among nondisabled persons has also surfaced in the highly popular Special Olympics. (See the box on pp. 147.)

Although large residential facilities for persons with mental retardation still exist, they now tend to house a much higher percentage of residents who are more severely retarded and who have multiple disabilities than they once did (Cunningham & Mueller, 1991). As we discussed in Chapter 2, there is a distinct trend toward smaller, community-based facilities, referred to as community residential facilities. The **community residential facility (CRF)**, or group home, accommodates small groups (three to ten people) in houses under the direction of "house parents." The level of retardation in people living in CRFs ranges from mild to severe. CRFs have been established for children, adolescents, and adults, with each home focused on a specific age range. Placement can be permanent or, with higher-functioning individuals, it can serve as a temporary arrangement to prepare them for independent living. In either case, the purpose of the CRF is to teach independent living skills in a more normal setting than a large institution offers.

community residential facility (CRF). A place, usually a group home, in an urban or residential neighborhood where about three to ten adults with retardation live under supervision.

EARLY INTERVENTION

We can categorize preschool programs for children with mental retardation as (1) those whose purpose is to prevent retardation and (2) those designed to further the development of children already identified as retarded. In general, the former address children who are at risk for mild retardation, and the latter are for children who are more severely retarded.

The Special Olympics: A Good or Bad Idea?

Founded in 1968 by the Joseph P. Kennedy, Jr., Foundation, the Special Olympics was designed as a way of promoting physical fitness, sportsmanship, and feelings of self-worth in persons with mental retardation. If participation and publicity are used as yardsticks, the Special Olympics has achieved great success. Thousands of athletes and nondisabled volunteers from around the world take part in these games, and there is now extensive television coverage of the ceremonies and the competition.

Not everyone is happy with the specialness of the Special Olympics, however. Criticisms have revolved around the segregated nature of the games (Orelove, Wehman, & Wood, 1982) and the possibility that people who are not disabled will focus on the *differentness* of the athletes (Polloway & Smith, 1978). To alleviate these concerns, the Unified Games were introduced in 1989. This competition mixes nondisabled athletes and those with mental retardation on the same teams.

Unfortunately, little research is available to guide the organizers of these games. In one study, participant's parents were overwhelmingly satisfied with the traditional Special Olympics, and very few were concerned about including nondisabled athletes (Klein, Gilman, & Zigler, 1995). But this sample is somewhat biased, since it comprised the parents of athletes who were already participants. In another study, volunteers in the Special Olympics showed improved attitudes about people with retardation compared to those who did not volunteer. But those who had volunteered for several years actually had more stereotypical attitudes than those who were novices (Roper, 1990). And a comparison between the athletes with mental retardation competing in the Special Olympics versus those in the Unified Games found little difference in their self-concepts or perceived social acceptance (Riggen & Ulrich, 1993).

More research is needed to determine the benefits and drawbacks of both the Special Olympics and the Unified Games.

Early Childhood Programs Designed for Prevention

The 1960s witnessed the birth of infant and preschool programs for at-risk children and their families. Since the late 1970s, when many of the young children placed in these programs were reaching their teenage years, we have been able to assess the effects of some of these programs. In 1993, for example, a follow-up study was done on the Perry Preschool Project (Schweinhart & Weikart, 1993). Begun in the early 1960s, the Perry Preschool Project was designed to answer the question: Can high-quality early childhood education help improve the lives of low-income children and their families and the quality of life of the community as a whole? A sample of 123 three- and four-year-old African-American children from impoverished backgrounds and having IQs between 60–90 was randomly assigned either to an experimental group that received two years of a cognitively oriented curriculum or to a control group that received no preschool program. When these students were studied again at 27 years of age, a number of differences favored those who had received the preschool program over those who had not:

- More had completed the twelfth grade.
- Fewer had been arrested.
- More owned their own homes.
- Fewer had ever been on welfare.
- They had a lower teenage pregnancy rate.
- They earned a better than average income.
- They were less likely to have been classified as disabled, especially as mentally retarded.

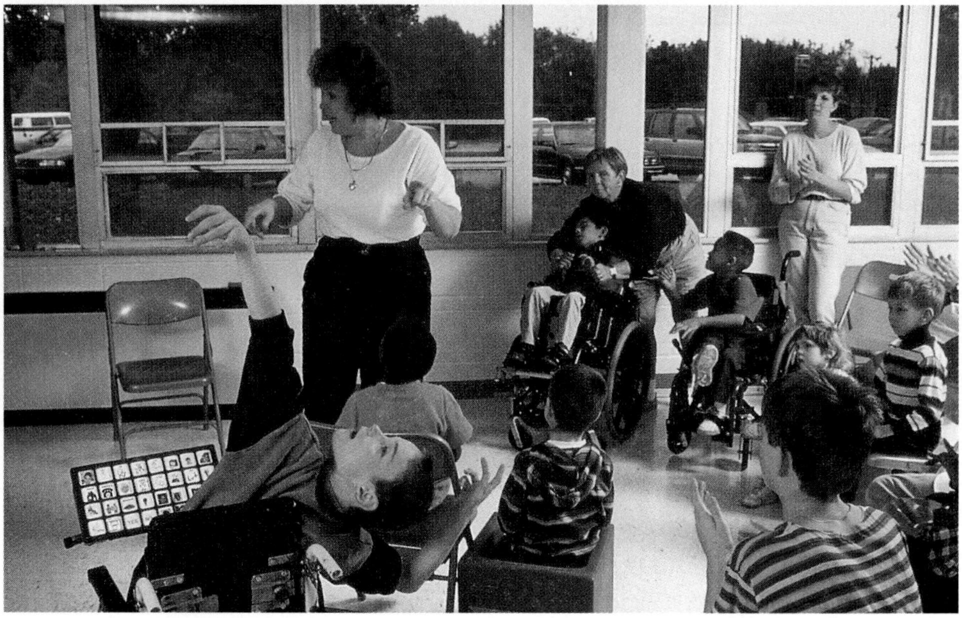

Educators still disagree over which approach most benefits learners with mental retardation: integrating them with nondisabled peers or keeping them primarily with others with mental retardation.

Furthermore, a cost-benefit analysis—taking into account such things as costs in welfare and the criminal justice system and benefits on taxes on earnings—showed a return of $7.16 for every dollar invested in the Perry Preschool Project.

One of the best-known infant stimulation programs among those started more recently is the Abecedarian Project (Ramey & Campbell, 1984, 1987). Participants were identified before birth by selecting children from a pool of pregnant women living in poverty. After birth, the infants were randomly assigned to one of two groups: half to a day-care group, which received special services, and half to a control group, which received no such services. The day-care group participated in a program that provided experiences to promote perceptual-motor, intellectual, language, and social development. The families of these children also received a number of social and medical services. Results of the Abecedarian Project, reported through the end of third grade, indicated that the students from the day-care group had achieved higher IQ scores and academic achievement than those from the control group (Campbell & Ramey, 1994).

Early Childhood Programs Designed to Further Development

Unlike preschool programs for children at risk, in which the goal is to prevent retardation from developing, programs for infants and preschoolers who are already identified as retarded are designed to help them achieve as high a cognitive level as possible. These programs place a great deal of emphasis on language and conceptual development. Because these children often have multiple disabilities, other professionals—for example, speech therapists and physical therapists—are frequently involved in their education. Also, many of the better programs include opportunities for parent involvement. Through practice with their children, parents can reinforce some of the skills that teachers work on. For example, parents of infants with physical disabilities, such as cerebral palsy, can learn from physical therapists the appropriate ways of handling their children to further their physical development. Similarly, parents can learn appropriate feeding techniques from speech therapists.

TRANSITION

Transition programming for individuals with mental retardation involves two related areas—community adjustment and employment. Most authorities agree that although the degree of emphasis on transition programming should be greater for older than for younger students, such programming should begin in the elementary years. Table 4–2 (see p. 150) depicts some examples of curriculum activities across the school years pertaining to domestic, community living, leisure, and vocational skills.

Community Adjustment

For persons with mental retardation to adjust to living in the community, they need to acquire a number of skills, many of which are in the area of self-help. Researchers have found, for example, that successful living in the community depends on such things as the ability to manage money, prepare meals, maintain a clean house, and keep one's clothing and self groomed (Schalock & Harper, 1978; Schalock, Harper & Carver, 1981). In general, research has shown that attempts to train community survival skills can be successful, especially when the training occurs within the actual setting in which the individuals live.

One of the keys to being able to live in the community is ensuring that the citizenry is prepared to accept persons with retardation. Even those individuals who are able to live independently (i.e., not in a community residential facility) may require some special accommodations. Although not many data are available, one survey of landlords renting to individuals with mental retardation indicated that a substantial number of landlords have some problems (Salend & Giek, 1988). Examples of these problems are independent living difficulties, such as failing in the upkeep of the property and overdependence on the landlord, and deviant behavior, such as playing the television too loudly. Fortunately, most of these kinds of problems can be avoided by providing landlords with a modest degree of information and assistance before they rent to tenants who are retarded.

Employment

Traditionally, employment figures for adults with mental retardation have been appalling (Chadsey-Rusch, Rusch & O'Reilly, 1991; Hasazi, Collins & Cobb, 1988; Hasazi et al., 1985; Wehman et al., 1988). One statewide survey, for example, found that of students with mental retardation who had graduated from high school, only 41 percent were employed full or part time in the competitive job market (Hasazi et al., 1985).

Even though employment statistics for workers who are retarded have been pessimistic, most professionals working in this area are optimistic about the potential for providing training programs that will lead to meaningful employment for these adults. Research indicates that with appropriate training, persons with retardation can hold down jobs with a good deal of success measured by such things as attendance, employer satisfaction, and length of employment (Brown et al., 1986; Martin, Rusch, Tines, Brulle, & White, 1985; Rusch, Martin, & White, 1985; Stodden & Browder, 1986).

When persons with retardation are not successful on the job, the cause is more often related to behaviors related to job responsibility and social skills than to job performance per se (Butterworth & Strauch, 1994; Heal, Gonzalez, Rusch, Copher, & DeStefano, 1990; Salzberg, Lignugaris/Kraft, & McCuller, 1988). In other words, the problem is not so much that people with retardation cannot perform the job as it is

Table 4–2

Examples of Curriculum Activities across the School Years for Domestic, Community Living, Leisure, and Vocational Skills

Skill Area			
Domestic	*Community Living*	*Leisure*	*Vocational*
Elementary School Student: Tim			
Picking up toys Washing dishes Making bed Dressing Grooming Eating skills Toileting skills Sorting clothes Vacuuming	Eating meals in a restaurant Using restroom in a local restaurant Putting trash into container Choosing correct change to ride city bus Giving the clerk money for an item he wants to purchase	Climbing on swing set Playing board games Playing tag with neighbors Tumbling activities Running Playing kickball	Picking up plate, silverware, and glass after a meal Returning toys to appropriate storage space Cleaning the room at the end of the day Working on a task for a designated period (15–20 minutes)
Junior High School Student: Mary			
Washing clothes Cooking a simple hot meal (soup, salad, and sandwich) Keeping bedroom clean Making snacks Mowing lawn Raking leaves Making a grocery list Purchasing items from a list Vacuuming and dusting living room	Crossing streets safely Purchasing an item from a department store Purchasing a meal at a restaurant Using local transportation system to get to and from recreational facilities Participating in local scout troop Going to neighbor's house for lunch on Saturday	Playing volleyball Taking aerobics classes Playing checkers with a friend Playing miniature golf Cycling Attending high school or local college basketball games Playing softball Swimming	Waxing floors Cleaning windows Filling lawn mower with gas Hanging and bagging clothes Bussing tables Working for 1-2 hours Operating machinery (such as dishwasher, buffer, etc.) Cleaning sinks, bathtubs, and fixtures Following a job sequence
High School Student: Sandy			
Cleaning all rooms in place of residence Developing a weekly budget Cooking meals Operating thermostat to regulate heat or air conditioning Doing yard maintenance Maintaining personal needs Caring for and maintaining clothing	Utilizing bus system to move about the community Depositing checks into bank account Using community department stores Using community grocery stores Using community health facilities (physician, pharmacist)	Jogging Archery Boating Watching college basketball Video games Card games (UNO) Athletic club swimming class Gardening Going on a vacation trip	Performing required janitorial duties at J.C. Penney Performing housekeeping duties at Days Inn Performing grounds keeping duties at VCU campus Performing food service at K St. Cafeteria Performing laundry duties at Moon's Laundromat Performing photography at Virginia National Bank Headquarters

Source: Adapted from P. Wehman, M. S. Moon, J. M. Everson, W. Wood, & J. M. Barcus, *Transition from School to Work: New Challenges for Youth with Severe Disabilities* (Baltimore: Paul H. Brookes, 1988), pp. 140–142. Reprinted with permission.

Transition programming, using supported competitive employment and job coaches, has become more common due to its proven successes.

that they have difficulty with such issues as attendance, initiative, responding to criticism, and interacting socially with co-workers and supervisors. This latter problem—social interaction—most consistently distinguishes workers who are retarded from those who are not.

A variety of vocational training and employment approaches for individuals with mental retardation are available. Most of these are subsumed under two very different kinds of arrangements—the sheltered workshop and supported competitive employment.

Sheltered Workshops. The traditional job-training environment for adults with mental retardation, especially those classified as more severely retarded, has been the sheltered workshop. A **sheltered workshop** is a structured environment where a person receives training and works with other workers with disabilities on jobs requiring relatively low skills. This can be either a permanent placement or a transitional placement before a person obtains a job in the competitive job market.

sheltered workshop. A facility that provides a structured environment for persons with disabilities in which they can learn skills; can be either a transitional placement or a permanent arrangement.

Although sheltered workshops remain a relatively popular placement, more and more authorities are voicing dissatisfaction with them (Wehman et al., 1988). Among the criticisms are the following:

1. Workers make only between one and five dollars per day. Sheltered workshops rarely turn a profit. Usually managed by personnel with limited business management expertise, they rely heavily on charitable contributions.

2. There is no integration of workers who are disabled with those who are nondisabled. This restricted setting makes it difficult to prepare workers who are mentally retarded for working side by side with nondisabled workers in the competitive work force.
3. Sheltered workshops offer only limited job-training experiences. A good workshop should provide opportunities for trainees to learn a variety of new skills. All too often, however, the work is repetitive and does not make use of current industrial technology.

Supported Competitive Employment. In contrast to sheltered employment, **competitive employment** is an approach that provides jobs for at least the minimum wage in integrated work settings in which most of the workers are not disabled. Although the ultimate goal for some adults with mental retardation may be competitive employment, many will need supported employment for a period of time or even permanently. In **supported competitive employment**, the person with retardation has a competitive employment position but receives ongoing assistance, often from a job coach. The major responsibilities of the **job coach**

> may include job identification and development, vocational assessment and instruction, transportation planning, and interactions with parents, employers, Social Security, and other related service agencies. Job coaches provide on-site training to clients which addresses not only actual job tasks, but also social skill development and independent living skills. They monitor employee progress through performance observation and communication with employers and coworkers. (Berkell, 1988, pp. 164–165)

The use of supported competitive employment has grown dramatically. Since its inception in the late 1980s, the number of workers in supported employment has doubled to around 75,000 (Revell, Wehman, Kregel, West, & Rayfield, 1994). Researchers have found that movement from sheltered work environments to supported employment has proved cost effective for society; moreover, this approach has resulted in a 500 percent increase in salaries for workers with mental retardation (McCaughrin, Ellis, Rusch, & Heal, 1993; Revell et al., 1994).

One potential problem with the supported competitive employment model is that clients can become too dependent on the support provided by their job coaches (Lagomarcino, Hughes, & Rusch, 1989). If they are to move into competitive employment settings, workers must learn to function independently. Even if they stay in supported situations, it is important that they develop as much independence as possible.

To combat overdependence on job coaches, authorities have recommended that professionals teach employees who are retarded to use self-management techniques (Lagomarcino et al., 1989; Rusch & Hughes, 1988; Rusch, et al., 1985; Wheeler, Bates, Marshall, & Miller, 1988). For example, some authorities recommend the use of **self-monitoring,** which involves workers observing their own performance and then recording it. For example, an individual might observe and record the number of times he or she is late for work per week. (We talk more about the use of self-monitoring in the classroom for students with learning disabilities in Chapter 5.)

Job coaches also have the potential to interfere with opportunities for workers with mental retardation to interact socially with nondisabled workers (Ferguson, McDonnell, & Drew, 1993). Researchers have noted that when job coaches are present, workers may tend to interact with them rather than with co-workers or supervisors. Because workers who are retarded already have difficulties managing appropriate social interactions at work, job coaches should avoid serving as social buffers for them.

competitive employment. A workplace that provides employment that pays at least minimum wage and one in which most workers are nondisabled.

supported competitive employment. A workplace where adults who are disabled or retarded earn at least minimum wage and receive ongoing assistance from a specialist or job coach; the majority of workers in the workplace are nondisabled.

job coach. A person who assists adult workers with disabilities (especially those with mental retardation), providing vocational assessment, instruction, overall planning, and interaction assistance with employers, family, and related government and service agencies.

self-monitoring. A type of cognitive behavior modification technique that requires individuals to keep track of their own behavior.

Importance of the Family

More and more authorities point to the family as a critical factor in whether persons with mental retardation will be successful in community adjustment and employment (Blacher & Baker, 1992). The majority of adults with mental retardation live with their families (Krauss et al., 1992). And even for those who live away from home, the family can still be a significant source of support for living in the community and finding and holding jobs.

Prospects for the Future

Current employment figures and living arrangements for adults with mental retardation may look bleak, but there is reason to be optimistic about the future. Surveys indicate that although the sheltered workshop remains the most common work environment for adults who are retarded, placement in competitive employment is increasing (Schalock, McGaughey, & Kiernan, 1989). Evidence also shows that employers are taking a more favorable attitude toward hiring workers who are mentally retarded (Levy, Jessop, Rimmerman, & Levy, 1992). With the development of innovative transition programs, many persons with mental retardation are achieving levels of independence in community living and employment that were never thought possible.

Suggestions for Teaching
Students with Mental Retardation in General Education Classrooms

By Peggy L. Tarpley

WHAT TO LOOK FOR IN SCHOOL

Although children with more severe mental retardation are identified before entering school, students who are mildly retarded typically are identified during their first years of school. A primary indicator of mild mental retardation is the delayed development of motor, language, social, and independent skills. Students with mild retardation are able to learn these skills, but their rate of learning is slow, and as a result, their level of development resembles that of younger children (Lewis & Doorlag, 1991). In addition, many students with mild mental retardation have short-term memory problems and do not know how to use learning strategies that nondisabled students seem to use spontaneously. Given these problems, it is not surprising that students with mild retardation have difficulty learning in all academic areas.

HOW TO GATHER INFORMATION

If you think one of your students may be mentally retarded, collect several examples of his or her work in arithmetic, reading, and writing. Share these samples—along with your observations of the student's motor, language, and social behaviors—with the special educator, counselor, or administrator in your building who manages the child-study committee. This committee considers persistent problems individual students experience in school and suggests modifications that may promote their learning and/or appropriate school behavior. If these modifications do not result in improvement, the committee may recommend that the student receive a full educational, medical, sociological, and psychological evaluation to determine eligibility for special education. Student work samples, your records, and your observations will provide necessary information to the child-study committee.

TEACHING TECHNIQUES TO TRY

To meet the needs of students with retardation, teachers emphasize instruction in functional academics and in daily living, social, and vocational skills (Polloway & Patton, 1993). To teach these skills, they use a variety of teacher-directed, student-directed, and peer-mediated approaches.

Teacher-Directed Methods

As you know from reading this chapter, we often use applied behavior analysis to teach students with mental retardation. Other approaches directed by teachers include task analysis, modeling, and scaffolding.

In the first method, teachers analyze a given task to determine what skills are needed before the student can be taught that skill (prerequisite skills) and what individual skills are needed to complete the task (component skills). To develop a task analysis, teachers often observe someone who is performing the task and record each step. Then, teachers perform the task using the steps they have noted to check for accuracy and completeness. Before beginning instruction, they teach any prerequisite skills students do not have. For a detailed description of how to construct a task analysis, see Moyer and Dardig's (1978) article "Practical task analysis for special educators."

A second teacher-directed approach is *modeling,* a method in which the teacher demonstrates the behavior or uses another individual who actively performs the behavior to be learned. After repeated demonstration, students imitate the model. To facilitate students' imitation and mastery of the modeled skill, teachers provide much practice, reinforcement, and feedback. Modeling plays an important role in a student's acquisition of language skills, which is often an area of delayed development for children with mental retardation.

Teachers model both observable and nonobservable behavior. By expressing their thoughts or thinking aloud as they complete tasks, teachers model their thinking for students. Olson and Platt (1992) provide the following example of a think-aloud used by Mr. Clarke as he taught reading:

> Today, I'd like to share with you a strategy I use when I come to a word that I don't know. . . . [Mr. Clarke reads the first sentence, "The weatherman said there will be snow flurries."] I know I've heard the word "flurries" before, but I don't know what it means. The word before "flurries" is "snow," so it has something to do with snow . . . I'll read on. The next sentence says, "When the little boy heard the weather report, he became angry, because he wanted to build a snowman." I think that can help me, because I know that you have to have a lot of snow to build a snowman. . . . Now, I may know what the word means. I'll bet it means light snow. Let me go back and check. (p. 212)

Frequently, teachers supplement think-alouds by giving students a list of the steps involved in solving the problem. For example, in the think-aloud described above, Mr. Clarke provided students with the following procedural steps (or strategy):

1. Read the unknown word in the sentence.
2. See if any other words in the sentence can help you figure out the unknown word.
3. Use any background information you have to help you.
4. Read more of the sentences.
5. Repeat steps 2 and 3.
6. Substitute the new meaning.
7. Reread the sentences to see if the new meaning makes sense (Olson & Platt, 1992).

Like modelling, *scaffolding* is a teacher-directed approach that encourages increased student participation as teacher support is decreased. Bos and Vaughn (1994) suggest that scaffolding provides "an adjustable and temporary support that can be removed when no longer necessary" (p. 50). Teachers can use scaffolded instruction in many situations with various techniques.

Hendrickson and Frank (1993) give an example using a teacher-questioning sequence known as *response-dependent questioning.* Moving from full support to no support:

1. The teacher begins with a complete model question, such as: "Lynn bought a new car. Now you tell me what did Lynn do?"
2. Decreasing the support of the complete model in subsequent discussions, the teacher asks yes or no questions, such as: "Did Lynn buy a new car?"
3. Next, the teacher asks a restricted alternative question, such as: "Lynn did not watch television or go to the park. What did Lynn do?"
4. The teacher then moves the student toward less support by asking a multiple-choice question, such as: "Did Lynn watch television, go to the park, or buy a car?"
5. Finally, the teacher asks an open question, such as: "What did Lynn do on Saturday?"

The teacher might choose to start the sequence with the open question, building the scaffold as the student's needs dictate toward the full support of the complete model question and then removing the support as the student responds with less prompting or cueing.

Cognitive modeling and scaffolding help move students from teacher-directed to student-directed learning.

Student-Directed Procedures

Increasingly, educators are facilitating students' use of self-regulation procedures, such as self-monitoring, self-administering consequences, and self-instruction. These procedures are student directed and promote student independence. Self-monitoring involves teaching students to record their own behaviors so they become aware of their behaviors and regulate them. Self-administering requires students, not teachers, to give themselves predetermined consequences contingent on their own behaviors.

A recent review of self-management procedures used to teach persons with mental retardation reported that these two procedures typically are used to increase the occurrence of behaviors students already know how to perform, such as work and daily living skills (Harchik, Sherman, & Sheldon, 1992). Self-instruction, which involves students making directive verbal statements about their own behaviors, is used to teach skills students have not yet mastered, such as academic skills (Harchik et al., 1992). (See Chapter 5 for additional information about these procedures.)

Peer-Mediated Procedures

Given the context of large, heterogeneous classes, teachers often use peer-mediated procedures to provide the additional practice and individual help students with mental retardation need. One such arrangement is *peer tutoring,* a technique that under certain conditions has been shown to benefit both tutor and tutee academically, behaviorally, and socially. In student tutoring programs, teachers typically provide instruction to all class members. Then students in the class (peer tutors) or older students (cross-age tutors) who have mastered the learning assist those individuals who require additional instruction and practice.

Tutors can take on a variety of responsibilities, such as reviewing lessons, directing and monitoring the performance of newly learned skills, and providing feedback and reinforcement. Planning, supervising, and evaluating a peer-tutoring program requires careful planning and on-going supervision by the teacher. Several studies and reviews (Gerber & Kauffman, 1981; Jenkins & Jenkins, 1985; Knapczyk, 1989) indicate that several conditions are necessary for effective peer tutoring. They include:

1. Tutors are trained to understand instructional objectives, discriminate between correct and incorrect responses, deliver feedback and reinforcement, and monitor progress and record keeping.
2. Instructional steps are carefully sequenced and clearly outlined in a lesson format that tutors can follow easily.
3. Teachers actively monitor tutor and tutee performance frequently.
4. Teachers provide reinforcement frequently and consistently to the tutor and tutee contingent on their appropriate performances.
5. Tutorial sessions are scheduled for approximately 15 to 30 minutes at least two or three times each week.

Specific training information is available from Joseph Jenkins, Director of the Experimental Education Unit, Child Development and Mental Retardation Center, University of Washington, Seattle, WA.

A specific example of peer tutoring in the area of reading is given by Mathes, Fuchs, Fuchs, Henley, and Sanders (1994). Along with others on their research team, they have formulated what they call Peabody Classwide Peer Tutoring (CWPT) to assist teachers in accommodating the diversity of reading abilities in their classrooms and to increase students' opportunities to practice reading skills. In general, all students in the class are paired, with each pair consisting of a higher- and a lower-performing student. The teacher assigns pairs to one of two teams for which they earn points. Typically, CWPT is implemented for three 35-minute sessions each week for 15 weeks.

During a session, the tutor and tutee engage in three specific activities:

1. In *partner reading,* the stronger reader reads the text first, providing a model for the weaker reader, who then reads the same text.
2. In *paragraph shrinking,* comprehension is emphasized through reading one paragraph at a time and stopping after each to identify its main idea.
3. Finally, the *prediction-relay portion* of the session encourages reading for a purpose. The reader makes a prediction about what will happen in a portion of text, reads the text, confirms or disconfirms the prediction, summarizes the text read, and then makes a prediction about the next portion of text.

Throughout the session, the tutor gives corrective feedback and reinforcement and also awards points for each activity. Each pair works cooperatively to earn points for their team, thereby involving both cooperative and competitive motivation.

The inclusion of students with severe retardation in general education classrooms has resulted in increased interest among educators in procedures that promote improvement in skills and enhance the social acceptance of these students. Recent reviews of methods for individualizing curriculum and instruction reported by Thousand and Villa (1990) suggest three approaches in addition to peer tutoring: mastery learning, computer-assisted instruction, and cooperative learning.

To implement *mastery learning,* teachers conduct frequent, brief assessments of each student (e.g., curriculum-based assessment); develop individual objectives and establish specific preset mastery criteria; provide frequent feedback to students regarding their performance and progress toward mastery; and adjust or supplement instruction or practice of students who do not meet their mastery criteria. Individual goals include daily living, social, and vocational skills.

Teachers also use *computer-assisted instruction (CAI)* in several areas of instruction. For students with severe retardation, CAI may be used to introduce new information and to supplement teacher instruction (i.e., tutorials). CAI may also be used to provide the additional drill and practice these students require. Consult with a special educator in your school regarding appropriate software programs that meet the specific needs of your students.

Cooperative learning, an arrangement in which diverse students work in small groups to meet common goals, is a third approach teachers use to enhance learning in social and other skill areas. In Vermont, for example, specialists worked with classroom teachers to form cooperative learning groups that included intensively challenged students. To illustrate how these students were integrated into cooperative group activities, Thousand and Villa (1990) reported a seventh-grade biology lesson in which Bob, a thirteen-year-old with multiple disabilities was a participant. This lesson focused on dissecting a frog. Although Bob did not participate directly in the dissection, during this process he worked on his individual goals, which centered on structured communication. Group members helped Bob achieve his lesson objectives as they dissected the frog.

In preparing to integrate special students into general education classes and to promote the social acceptance of these students, Lewis and Doorlag (1991) recommend informing classmates about disabilities. Teachers often introduce this topic by discussing the concept of *individual differences.* Asking students to think about their own strengths and weaknesses promotes awareness of the fact that each person is unique and possesses different abilities and disabilities. Depending on the grade, teachers frequently follow-up this discussion with information about disabilities directly or with structured assignments and projects in which students conduct their own research. In addition, teachers provide experiences with people who have disabilities (Lewis & Doorlag, 1990). They invite adults with disabilities into the classroom, arrange visits to special education classes in the school, or use commercially developed materials, such as Kids on the Block, which includes puppets portraying children with disabilities. Once students with disabilities are mainstreamed, it is important that teachers provide structured interactions between nondisabled students and students with disabilities, using arrangements such as peer tutoring and cooperative learning.

HELPFUL RESOURCES

School Personnel

The special educator who also teaches students who are mentally retarded may provide additional instructional suggestions that have been successful in improving performance. This teacher also can recommend and perhaps obtain learning materials designed for special education students and suggest ways in which regular class materials can be adapted to students with retardation. In addition, he or she can recommend books on a variety of subjects that are of high interest to older students and written at lower reading levels.

Finally, this teacher and the school psychologist are good resources for specific cognitive and behavioral information about your student.

Instructional Methods

Bos, C. S., & Vaughn, S. (1994). *Strategies for teaching students with learning and behavior problems.* Boston: Allyn & Bacon.

Fowler, G. L., & Davis, M. (1985). The storyframe approach: A tool for improving reading comprehension. *Teaching Exceptional Children, 17,* 296–298.

Hamre-Nietupski, S., McDonald, J., & Nietupski, J. (1992). Integrating elementary students with multiple disabilities into supported regular classes. *Teaching Exceptional Children, 24,* 6–9.

Horton, S. (1983). Delivering industrial arts instruction to mildly handicapped learners. *Career Development for Exceptional Individuals, 6,* 85–92.

Isaacson, S. (1988). Teaching written expression; directed reading and writing; self-instructional strategy training; and computers and writing instruction, *Teaching Exceptional Children, 20,* 32–39.

Jenson, W. R., Sloane, H. N., & Young, K. R. (1988). *Applied behavior analysis in education: A structured teaching approach.* Englewood Cliffs, NJ: Prentice Hall.

Maheady, L., Harper, G.F., & Sacca, M. K. (1988). Peer-mediated instruction: A promising approach to meeting the diverse needs of LD adolescents. *Learning Disability Quarterly, 11,* 108–113.

Matson, J. L. (Ed.) (1990). *Handbook of behavior modification with the mentally retarded* (2nd ed.). New York: Plenum.

McDonnell, J., Wilcox, B., & Hardman, M. L. (1991). *Secondary programs for students with developmental disabilities.* Boston: Allyn & Bacon.

Olson, J., & Platt, J. (1992). *Teaching children and adolescents with special needs.* New York: Merrill/Macmillan.

O'Shea, L., & O'Shea, D. (1988). Using repeated readings. *Teaching Exceptional Children, 20,* 26–29.

Polloway, E., & Patton, J. (1993). *Strategies for teaching learners with special needs* (5th ed.). New York: Merrill/Macmillan.

Robinson, G. A., & Polloway, E. A. (Eds.). (1987). *Best practices in mental disabilities (Vol. 1).* Des Moines, IA: Iowa State Department of Education Bureau of Special Education.

Schloss, P. J., & Sedlak, R. A. (1982). Behavioral features of the mentally retarded adolescent: Implications for mainstreamed educators. *Psychology in the Schools, 19,* 98–105.

Schultz, J. B., Carpenter, C. D., & Turnbull, A. C. (1991). *Mainstreaming exceptional students: A guide for classroom teachers* (3rd ed.). Boston: Allyn & Bacon.

Curricula

Agran, M., & Moore, S. C. (1994). *How to teach self-instruction of job skills.* Washington, DC: American Association on Mental Retardation.

Bender, M., & Valletutti, P. C. (1990). *Teaching function academics.* Austin, TX: Pro-Ed.

Carnine, D., Silbert, J., & Kameenui, E. J. (1990). *Direct instruction reading.* Columbus, OH: Merrill/Macmillan.

Dixon, B., & Engelmann, S. (1979). *Corrective spelling through morographs.* Chicago, IL: Science Research Associates.

Engelmann, S., & Bruner, E. C. (1974). *DISTAR reading.* Chicago, IL: Science Research Associates.

Engelmann, S., & Bruner, E. C. (1983). *Reading mastery.* Chicago, IL: Science Research Associates.

Engelmann, S., Carnine, D., Johnson, G., & Meyers, L. (1988). *Corrective reading: Decoding.* Chicago, IL: Science Research Associates.

Engelmann, S., Carnine, D., Johnson, G., & Meyers, L. (1989). *Corrective reading: Comprehension.* Chicago, IL: Science Research Associates.

Silbert, J., & Carnine, D. (1981). *Direct instruction mathematics.* Columbus, OH: Merrill.

Wehman, P., & McLoughlin, P. J. (1990). *Vocational curriculum for developmentally disabled persons.* Austin, TX: Pro-Ed.

LITERATURE ABOUT INDIVIDUALS WITH MENTAL RETARDATION

Elementary

Anderson, R. (1989). *The bus people.* New York: Henry Holt. (Grades 5–8) (Fiction = F)

Carrick, C. (1985). *Stay away from Simon!* New York: Carion. (Ages 8–11) (F)

Clifton, L. (1980). *My friend Jacob.* New York: E. P. Dutton. (Ages 6–10) (F)

Gillham, B. (1981). *My brother Barry.* London: A. Deutsch. (Ages 9–12) (F)

Hasler, E. (1981). *Martin is our friend.* Nashville, TN: Abingdon. (Ages 9–12) (F)

Rabe, B. (1988). *Where's Chimpy?* Berkeley, CA: Gray's Book Company. (Ages 4–7) (F)

Shyer, M. F. (1988). *Welcome home, Jellybean.* New York: Aladdin. (F)

Wright, B. R. (1981). *My sister is different.* Milwaukee, WI: Raintree. (Ages 4–7) (F)

Secondary

Bates, B. (1980). *Love is like peanuts.* New York: Holiday House. (Ages 13–15) (F)

Dougan, T., Isbell, L., & Vyas, P. (1983). *We have been there: A guidebook for families of people with mental retardation.* Nashville, TN: Abingdon. (Nonfiction = NF)

Hill, D. (1985). *First your penny.* New York: Atheneum. (F)

Hull, E. (1981). *Alice with golden hair.* New York: Atheneum. (F)

Kaufman, S. Z. (1988). *Retarded isn't stupid, Mom!* Baltimore, MD: Brookes. (NF)

Miner, J. C. (1982). *She's my sister.* Mankato, MN: Crestwood House. (Reading levels: Grade 3–4; Interest level: Grades 7–12) (F)

Rodowsky, C. F. (1996). *What about me?* New York: Viking. (Grades 7–12) (F)

Slepian, J. (1980). *The Alfred summer.* New York: Macmillan. (F)

Slepian, J. (1981). *Lester's turn.* New York: Macmillan. (F) (A sequel to *The Alfred Summer*)

Software

Alphabet Circus, DLM Teaching Resources, One DLM Park, Allen, TX 75002, (880) 527–5030 (Activities focus on letter recognition, alphabetical order, problem solving).

Animal Photo Farm, DLM Teaching Resources, One DLM Park, Allen, TX 75002, (880) 527–5030.

Bake and Take, Mindplay, 160 W. Ft. Lowell, Tucson, AZ 85705, (800) 221–7911 (Life skills).

Bobo's Park, Academic Technologies, Inc., (609) 778–4435 (Life skills).

Calendar Skills, Hartley Courseware, Inc., 3451 Dunkle Drive, Suite 200, Lansing, MI 48911-4216, (800) 247–1380.

Clock Works, MECC, 6160 Summit Drive N., Minneapolis, MN 55430–4003, (800) 685–6322 (Time telling on digital and analog clocks).

Coins 'n Keys, Castle Special Computer Services, Inc., 9801 San Gabriel N.E., Albuquerque, NM 87111, (505) 293–8379 (Coin recognition and counting).

Comparative Buying Series, MCE, 157 S. Kalamazoo Mall, Suite 250, Kalamazoo, MI 49007.

Computer CUP, Amidon Publication, 1966 Benson Avenue, St. Paul, MN 55116, (800) 328–6502 (Nine discs teach basic concepts such as right-left, as many, beginning).

Counting Critters, MECC, 6160 Summit Drive N., Minneapolis, MN 55430, (800) 685–6322 (Basic number skills 1–20).

Daily Living Skills, Looking Glass Learning Products, 276 Howare Avenue, Des Plaines, IL 60018–1906, (800) 545–5457 (Reading prescriptions, medical product labels, classified ads, telephone directory, job applications, and paychecks).

Dinosaurs, Advanced Ideas, 680 Hawthorne Drive, Tiburon, CA 94920, (415) 425–5086 (Game format teaches matching, sorting, and counting).

Easy as ABE, Springboard/Spinnaker, Spinnaker Software, 201 Broadway, Sixth Floor, Cambridge, MA 02139, (800) 826–0706 (Games help young children identify and sequence alphabet letters and match upper- and lower-case letters).

Job Success Series, MCE, 157 S. Kalamazoo Mall, Suite 250, Kalamazoo, MI 49007.

Language L.A.B., Specialsoft, P.O. Box 1983, Santa Monica, CA 90406, (800) 421–6534.

Library and Media Skills, Educational Activities, P.O. Box 392, Freeport, Long Island, NY 11520, (800) 645–3777.

Library Skills, Micro Power & Light Company, 12820 Hillcrest Road, Suite 219, Dallas, TX 75230.

Reader Rabbit, Learning Company, 6493 Kaiser Drive, Fremont, CA 94555, (800) 852–2255.

Spell It!, Davidson & Associates, 19840 Pioneer Avenue, Torrance, CA 90503, (800) 545–7677.

Stickybear Town Builder, Optimum Resource, Inc., 5 Hitech Lane, Hilton Head, SC 29926, (800) 327–1473 (Map reading, planning, hypothesizing, problem solving).

Telling Time, Random House, 400 Hahn Road, Westminister, MD 21157.

Vocabulary Challenge, Learning Well, 2200 Marcus Avenue, New Hyde Park, NY 11040, (800) 646–6564.

Vocabulary Game, J & S Software, 140 Reid Avenue, Port Washington, NY 11050.

Ways to Read Words, Intellectual Software, 798 North Avenue, Bridgeport, CT 06606.

Whole Brain Spelling, SubLogic, 713 Edgebrook Drive, Champaign, IL 61820.

World of Work, Computer Age Education, 1442A Walnut Street, Suite 341, Berkeley, CA 94709.

Work Habits for Job Success, MEC, 1800 South 35th Street, Galesburg, MI 49078, (800) 421–4157.

Organizations

American Association on Mental Retardation, 1719 Kalorama Road, N.W., Washington, DC 20009, (202) 387–1968.

ARC, The, 500 E. Border Street, Suite 300, Arlington, TX 76010, (817) 261–6003, Fax (817) 277–3491.

Mental Retardation Association of America, 211 E. 300 Street, Suite 212, Salt Lake, UT 84111, (801) 328–1575.

Mental Retardation Division of the Council for Exceptional Children, 1920 Association Drive, Reston, VA 22091, (703) 620–3660.

National Association for Down Syndrome, P.O. Box 4542, Oak Brook, IL 60522, (708) 325–9112.

BIBLIOGRAPHY FOR TEACHING SUGGESTIONS

Bos, C. S., & Vaughn, S. (1994). *Strategies for teaching students with learning and behavior problems.* Boston: Allyn & Bacon.

Gerber, M., & Kauffman, J. M. (1981). Peer tutoring in academic settings. In P.S. Strain (Ed.). *The utilization of classroom peers as behavior change agents* (pp. 155–187). New York: Plenum Press.

Harchik, A. E., Sherman, J. A., & Sheldon, A. B. (1992). The use of self-management procedures by people with developmental disabilities: A brief review. *Research in Developmental Disabilities, 13,* 211–227.

Hendrickson, J. M., & Frank, A. R. (1993). Engagement and performance feedback: Enhancing the classroom achievement of students with mild mental disabilities. In R. A. Gable & S. F. Warren (Eds.), *Strategies for teaching students with mild to severe mental retardation.* Baltimore: Paul H. Brookes.

Jenkins, J., & Jenkins, L. (1985). Peer tutoring in elementary and secondary programs. *Focus on Exceptional Children, 17,* 1–12.

Knapczyk, D. R. (1989). Peer-mediated training of cooperative play between special and regular class students in integrated play settings. *Education and Training in Mental Retardation, 24,* 255–264.

Lewis, R. B., & Doorlag, D. H. (1995). *Teaching special students in the mainstream* (4th ed.). New York: Merrill/Macmillan.

Mathes, P. G., Fuchs, D., Fuchs, L. S., Henley, A. M., & Sanders, A. (1994). Increasing strategic reading practice with Peabody Classwide Peer Tutoring. *Learning Disabilities Research and Practice., 9*(1), 44–48.

McCann, S. K., Semmel, M. I., & Nevin, A. (1985). Reverse mainstreaming: Nonhandicapped students in special education classrooms. *Remedial and Special Education, 6,* 13–19.

Moyer, B., & Dardig, M. (1978). Practical task analysis for special educators. *Teaching Exceptional Children, 10,* 16–18.

Odom, S. L., Deklyen, M., & Jenkins, J. R. (1984). Integrating handicapped and nonhandicapped preschoolers: Developmental impact on nonhandicapped children. *Exceptional Children, 51,* 41–48.

Olson, J., & Platt, J. (1992). *Teaching children and adolescents with special needs.* New York: Merrill/Macmillan.

Polloway, E., & Patton, J. (1993). *Strategies for teaching learners with special needs* (5th ed.). New York: Merrill/Macmillan.

Poorman, C. (1980). Mainstreaming in reverse with a special friend. *Teaching Exceptional Children, 12,* 136–142.

Thousand, J. S., & Villa, R. A. (1990). Strategies for educating learners with severe disabilities within their local home schools and communities. *Focus on Exceptional Children, 23*(3), 1–24.

SUMMARY

Professionals are generally more cautious about identifying students as retarded than they once were because (1) there has been a history of misidentifying students from minority groups, (2) the label "mental retardation" may have harmful consequences for students, and (3) some believe that, to a certain extent, mental retardation is socially constructed. Changes in the definition of the American Association on Mental Retardation over the years reflect this cautious attitude toward identification. The current AAMR definition continues three trends: (1) a broadening of the definition beyond the single criterion of an IQ score (adaptive skills as well as conceptual intelligence are measured), (2) a lowering of the IQ score used as a cutoff, and (3) a view of retardation as a condition that can be improved.

The AAMR has traditionally classified persons as having *mild, moderate, severe,* or *profound* retardation based on their IQ scores. Currently, however, the AAMR is recommending classification according to the level of support needed: *intermittent, limited, extensive,* or *pervasive.**

From a purely statistical-theoretical perspective, 2.27 percent of the population should score low enough on an IQ test (below about 70) to qualify as retarded. Figures indicate, however, that about 1 to 1.5 percent of the population is identified as mentally retarded. The discrepancy may be due to three factors: (1) Both low adaptive skills and low conceptual intelligence are needed to consider a person retarded; (2) school personnel tend to be cautious about labeling minority children; and (3) parents and professionals may prefer to have students labeled "learning disabled" rather than "mentally retarded" because they perceive it as less stigmatizing.

There are a variety of causes of mental retardation. We can actually specify the cause, only in a few cases, especially among those with more mild retardation or those requiring less intensive support. Most people with mild retardation are considered culturally-familially retarded, a term used to include causes related to poor environmental and/or hereditary factors. Although the nature-nurture debate has raged for years, most authorities now believe that the interaction between heredity and the environment is important in determining intelligence.

We can categorize causes of more severe retardation, or that requiring more intensive support, as due to genetic factors or brain damage. Down syndrome, Fragile X syndrome, PKU, and Tay-Sachs disease are all examples of genetic causes. Down syndrome results from a chromosomal abnormality but is not inherited as such. Fragile X syndrome, PKU, and Tay-Sachs are inherited. Authorities believe that Fragile X syndrome is the most common hereditary cause of retardation. Brain damage can result from infectious diseases—for example, meningitis, encephalitis, rubella, and pediatric AIDS—or environmental hazards, such as poisons (e.g., cocaine and alcohol) and excessive radiation. Premature birth can also result in mental retardation. Using amniocentesis, chorionic villus sampling, and sonography, physicians are now able to detect a variety of defects in the unborn fetus.

Two of the most common IQ tests are the Stanford-Binet and the Wechsler Intelligence Scale for Children—Third Edition (WISC–III). The latter has verbal and performance subscales. Some professionals recommend using the Kaufman Assessment Battery for Children (K–ABC) with African-American students because they believe it less culturally biased.

There are several cautions in using and interpreting IQ tests: (1) An individual's IQ score can change; (2) all IQ tests are culturally biased to some extent; (3) the younger the child, the less reliable the results; and (4) a person's ability to live a successful and fulfilling life does not depend solely on his or her IQ. In addition to IQ tests, several adaptive behavior scales are available.

*Critics of the new classification scheme suggest that it will be too difficult to implement.

Persons with mental retardation have learning problems related to attention, memory, self-regulation, language development, academic achievement, social development, and motivation. An important concept related to self-regulation is *metacognition*—the awareness of what strategies are needed to perform a task and the ability to use self-regulatory mechanisms before, during, and after performing a task.

Educational goals for students with mild retardation emphasize readiness skills at younger ages and functional academics and vocational training at older ages. Functional academics are for the purpose of enabling the person to function independently. Educational programs for students with more severe retardation are characterized by (1) age-appropriate curricula and materials, (2) functional activities, (3) community-based instruction, (4) integrated therapy, (5) interaction with nondisabled students, and (6) family involvement.

Depending to a large extent on the degree of retardation or the need for support, schools may place students in learning environments ranging from regular classrooms to residential institutions. Although residential institutions still exist and special classes in public schools are common, the trend is to include students who are mentally retarded in more integrated settings.

Preschool programs differ in their goals according to whether they are aimed at preventing retardation or furthering the development of children already identified as retarded. For the most part, the former types of programs are aimed at children at risk of developing mild retardation, whereas the latter are for children with more severe retardation. Research supports the clear link between such interventions and success later in life.

Transition programming for individuals with retardation includes goals related to domestic living, community living, leisure, and vocational skills. Although the emphasis on transition programming increases with age, authorities recommend that such efforts begin in elementary school.

The employment picture for workers with retardation is changing. Although sheltered work environments remain popular, authorities have pointed out their weaknesses: (1) Wages are very low; (2) there is no integration with nondisabled workers; and (3) they offer only limited job-training experiences. Placement of workers who are retarded in supported competitive employment has increased dramatically since its inception in the early 1980s. In supported competitive employment, the worker (1) receives at least minimum wage, (2) works in a setting with mostly nondisabled workers, and (3) receives assistance from a job coach. Many authorities advocate the use of self-management techniques (e.g., picture cues, self-instruction, self-monitoring, and self-reinforcement) to help workers with retardation function more independently. Although employment figures are still discouraging, the growth in innovative programs gives reason to be hopeful about the future of community living and employment for adults with mental retardation.

Robin Chappell
Robin Chappell is a prolific painter who shows in galleries around Washington, D.C. Early in his career, Mr. Chappell painted with a china marker and with only primary colors. He has been diagnosed with a learning disability and attention deficit hyperactivity disorder. He has developed groups of paintings that use light and shadow, such as "Night Series" and "Cloud Series," as a metaphor for the role of perception in consciousness.

5

Learning Disabilities

Miss Henderson and now Auntie: There seemed to be nothing I could do to please either of them. How, in the past, had it been so easy, so effortless to be a favorite? With a feeling of impending doom I would begin. I might get halfway through the first sentence before Auntie would say in a dry, controlled voice, "In the context the word cannot possibly be 'saw.' 'The man saw going home.' Does that make sense to you? It must be 'was.'"

I'd repeat, "The man was going home." In the next sentence, or the one after, meeting the word again, I'd hesitate. Had I said 'was' before and had Auntie corrected it to 'saw,' or vice versa? My brain ached.

"Don't tell me you don't recognize that word. *I just told it to you.* You're *not trying.*"

Both my teachers accused me of not trying. They had no idea what an effort I was making. Was, saw, was, saw. How were they so sure which it was? Rattled by Auntie's foot tapping, I decided for "saw."

"No, no, NO. How *can* you be so stupid? The word is 'was.' WASWASWAS. And for heaven's sake *stop snivelling.* If those nuns hadn't fallen for your tears, you'd be able to read by now and we wouldn't be going through this."

Eileen Simpson
Reversals: A Personal Account of Victory over Dyslexia

Certainly, not all students with learning disabilities have reading problems and those who do may not ordinarily have problems in reversing letters (e.g., reading *saw* for *was*). Nonetheless the struggle Eileen Simpson experienced (see p. 161) illustrates the frustration felt by virtually all students with learning disabilities, no matter what their particular problems. Even though they may be no less intelligent than their nondisabled classmates, such students have learning difficulties in school. As was the case with Simpson, reading often poses a major block, but difficulties in other academic areas (e.g., math, spelling, written expression) are also common. Students with learning disabilities are also apt to be inattentive and/or hyperactive. In the early school years, their parents may see them as simply overenergetic. Later, this unconcern may turn to desperation when, unlike their playmates, these children fail to outgrow their poor school performance and ungovernable ways.

Professionals, too, have been frustrated by the problems presented by students with learning disabilities. Some of the most intense battles in all of special education have been waged over issues related to educating students with learning disabilities. We can attribute much of the reason for this professional turmoil to two factors:

1. The enigma of children who are not retarded but who have severe academic problems has often led parents of these children, as well as professionals, to seek quick-and-easy "miracle" cures. We now recognize that, in most cases, learning disability is a lifelong condition with which a person must learn to cope.
2. The field of learning disabilities is a relatively new category of special education, having been recognized by the federal government in 1969. It is also now the largest category, constituting almost half of all students identified as eligible for special education. Much professional and popular media exposure has focused on this rapidly expanding category, creating a hotbed in which controversies can ferment.

Although the field of learning disabilities has had to struggle to overcome its penchant for questionable practices and to survive the intense scrutiny of professionals and the lay public, most who work within this field are happy to be part of it. For them, controversy and ambiguity only add excitement to the already challenging task of educating students with learning disabilities.

One controversy that has nagged the field for some time is that of defining *learning disabilities*. In the next section, we look at several common definitions and what criteria they use.

DEFINITIONS

minimal brain injury. A term used to describe a child who shows behavioral but not neurological signs of brain injury; the term is not as popular as it once was, primarily because of its lack of diagnostic utility (i.e., some children who learn normally show signs indicative of minimal brain injury).

At a parents' meeting in New York City in the early 1960s, Samuel Kirk proposed the term *learning disabilities* as a compromise because of the confusing variety of labels then used to describe the child with relatively normal intelligence who was having learning problems. Such a child was likely to be referred to as *minimally brain injured*, a *slow learner*, *dyslexic*,* or *perceptually disabled*.

Many parents as well as teachers, however, believed the label "minimal brain injury" to be problematic. **Minimal brain injury** refers to individuals who show behavioral but not neurological signs of brain injury. They exhibit behaviors (e.g., distractibility,

*Dyslexia refers to a severe impairment of the ability to read.

Misconceptions about Persons with Learning Disabilities

Myth	Fact
Myth All students with learning disabilities are brain damaged.	**Fact** Although more students with learning disabilities show evidence of damage to the central nervous system (CNS) than their nondisabled peers, many do not. Many authorities now refer to students with learning disabilities as having *CNS dysfunction*, which suggests a malfunctioning of the brain rather than actual tissue damage.
Myth IQ-achievement discrepancies are easily calculated.	**Fact** A complicated formula determines a discrepancy between a student's IQ and his or her achievement.
Myth Standardized achievement tests are the most useful kind of assessment device for teachers of students with learning disabilities.	**Fact** Standardized achievement tests do not provide much information about *why* a student has achievement difficulties. Informal reading inventories and formative evaluation measures give teachers a better idea of the particular problems a student is experiencing.
Myth We need not be concerned about the social-emotional well-being of students with learning disabilities because their problems are in academics.	**Fact** Many students with learning disabilities also develop problems in the social-emotional area.
Myth The most serious problem of children who are hyperactive is their excessive motor activity.	**Fact** Although children who are hyperactive do exhibit excessive motor activity, most authorities now believe that their most fundamental problems lie in the area of inattention.
Myth Medication for children with attention deficit hyperactivity disorder (ADHD) is overprescribed and presents a danger for many children.	**Fact** Some children who receive medication do not need it, but there is little evidence that vast numbers are inappropriately medicated. Medication can be an important part of a total treatment package for persons with ADHD.
Myth Most children with learning disabilities outgrow their disabilities as adults.	**Fact** Learning disabilities tend to endure into adulthood. Most individuals with learning disabilities who are successful must learn to cope with their problems and show extraordinary perseverance.

Learning disabilities can be difficult to identify and classify; their manifestations are complex and sometimes elusive, and their causes are often mysterious.

hyperactivity, and perceptual disturbances) similar to those of people with real brain injury, but their neurological examinations are indistinguishable from those of nondisabled individuals.

Historically, the diagnosis of minimal brain injury was sometimes dubious because it was based on questionable behavioral evidence rather than on more solid neurological data. Moreover, minimal brain injury was not an educationally meaningful term because such a diagnosis offered little real help in planning and implementing treatment. The term *slow learner* described the child's performance in some areas but not in others—and besides, intelligence testing indicated that the *ability* to learn existed. *Dyslexic*, too, fell short as a definitive term because it described only reading disabilities, and many of these children had problems in other academic areas such as math. To describe a child as *perceptually disabled* just confused the issue further, for perceptual problems might be only part of a puzzling inability to learn. So, the New York parents' group finally agreed on the educationally oriented term *learning disabilities*. Accordingly, they founded the Association for Children with Learning Disabilities, now known as the Learning Disabilities Association of America. A few years later, following the lead of the parents, professionals and the federal government officially recognized the term, as well.

The interest in learning disabilities evolved as a result of a growing awareness that a large number of children were not receiving needed educational services. Because they were within the normal range of intelligence, these children did not qualify for placement in classes for children with retardation. And although many of them *did* show inappropriate behavior or personality disturbances, some of them *did not*. Thus, it was felt that placement in classes for students with emotional disturbance was inappropriate. Parents of children who were not achieving at their expected potential—children who are *learning disabled*—wanted their children's *academic achievement* problems corrected.

Factors to Consider in Definitions of Learning Disabilities

Eleven different definitions of learning disabilities have enjoyed some degree of acceptance since the field's inception in the early 1960s (Hammill, 1990). Created by individual professionals and committees of professionals and lawmakers, each definition provides a slightly different slant. Four factors—each of which is included in some definitions, but not all—have historically caused considerable controversy:

1. IQ-achievement discrepancy
2. presumption of central nervous system dysfunction
3. psychological processing disorders
4. learning problems not due to environmental disadvantage, mental retardation, or emotional disturbance

We discuss these factors briefly and then present the two most commonly used definitions.

IQ-Achievement Discrepancy. A child with an **IQ-achievement discrepancy** is not achieving up to potential as usually measured by a standardized intelligence test. Professionals have used a number of methods to determine such a discrepancy. For many years, they simply compared the mental age obtained from an intelligence test to the grade-age equivalent taken from a standardized achievement test. A difference of two years was often considered enough to indicate a learning disability. Two years below expected grade level is not equally serious at different grade levels, however. For example, a child who tests two years below grade 8 has a less severe deficit than one who tests two years below grade 4. So professionals have developed formulas that take into account the relative ages of the students.

Although some states and school districts have adopted different formulas for identifying IQ-achievement discrepancies, many authorities have advised against their use. Some of the formulas are statistically flawed and lead to inaccurate judgments (McKinney, 1987b), and those that are statistically adequate are difficult and expensive to implement. Furthermore, they give a false sense of precision. That is, they tempt school personnel to reduce to a single score the complex and important decision of identifying a learning disability.

In addition to the problem of using formulas, some authorities have objected to using an IQ-achievement discrepancy to identify learning disabilities on other conceptual grounds (Fletcher et al., 1994; Kavale, 1995; Pennington, Gilger, Olson, & deFrees, 1992; Siegel, 1989; Stanovich & Siegel, 1994). For example, some authorities have pointed out that IQ scores of students with learning disabilities are subject to underestimation because performance on IQ tests is dependent on reading ability, to some extent (Siegel, 1989). In other words, students with poor reading skills have difficulty expanding their vocabularies and learning about the world. As a result, they obtain lower than average scores on IQ tests, which lessens the discrepancy between IQ and achievement. Finally, some educators have pointed out that the idea of discrepancy is practically useless in the earliest elementary grades. In the first or second grade, a child is not expected to have achieved very much in reading or math, so it would be difficult to find a discrepancy (Mather & Roberts, 1994).

Even with all these problems, many professionals still subscribe to the notion that an IQ-achievement discrepancy is an important characteristic of students with learning disabilities. The support for this notion is probably based on the observation that there continue to be children who have normal intelligence yet do not achieve up to their expected performance. Perhaps the most reasonable position, however, is not to use

IQ-achievement discrepancy. Academic performance markedly lower than would be expected based on a student's intellectual ability.

the IQ-achievement discrepancy as the sole criterion for determining a learning disability (Kavale, 1995) and to shy away from the use of formulas to calculate discrepancies.

Central Nervous System (CNS) Dysfunction. Many of the theoretical concepts and teaching methods associated with the field of learning disabilities grew out of work done in the 1930s and 1940s with children who were mentally retarded and brain injured (Werner & Strauss, 1941). When the field of learning disabilities was emerging, professionals noted that many of these children displayed behavioral characteristics similar to those exhibited by children known to have brain damage (e.g., distractibility, hyperactivity, perceptual disturbances).

In the case of most children with learning disabilities, however, there is little neurological evidence of brain damage. Some professionals have been content to attribute brain damage to children with learning disabilities on the basis of behavioral characteristics alone. More recently, there has been a trend away from considering a child to be brain damaged unless the results from a neurological examination provide unquestionable evidence. The term *dysfunction* has come to replace *injury* or *damage*. Thus, a child with learning disabilities is now more likely to be referred to as having *central nervous system dysfunction* than *brain injury*. The change in terminology reflects the awareness of how hard it is to diagnose brain damage. Dysfunction does not necessarily mean tissue damage; instead, it signifies a malfunctioning of the brain, or central nervous system.

Psychological Processing Disorders. The field of learning disabilities was founded on the assumption that children with such disabilities have deficits in the ability to perceive and interpret visual and auditory stimuli—that is, they have *psychological processing problems*. These problems are not the same as the visual and auditory acuity problems evidenced in blindness or deafness. Rather, they are difficulties in organizing and interpreting visual and auditory stimuli.

Researchers have found that many students with learning disabilities do indeed have such information-processing problems (see Hallahan, 1975, for a review). Many of the early advocates of this viewpoint, however, also believed that training students in visual- and auditory-processing skills in isolation from academic material would help them conquer their reading problems (Frostig & Horne, 1964; Kephart, 1971, 1975; Kirk & Kirk, 1971). For instance, such training might involve finding and tracing figures embedded within other lines or connecting dots as they are drawn on a chalkboard by a teacher.

Researchers ultimately determined that these perceptual and perceptual-motor exercises did not result in benefits for students' reading achievement (see Hallahan & Cruickshank, 1973, for a review); thus, very few teachers use these practices today.

Environmental Disadvantage, Mental Retardation, or Emotional Disturbance. Most definitions of *learning disability* exclude those children whose learning problems stem from environmental disadvantage, mental retardation, or emotional disturbance. The belief that such an exclusion clause is necessary attests to how difficult sometimes it can be to differentiate between some of these conditions. There is ample evidence, for example, that children from disadvantaged backgrounds are more apt to exhibit learning problems, and students with mental retardation or emotional disabilities often display some of the same behavioral characteristics as pupils who are learning disabled (Hallahan & Kauffman, 1977). Most definitions assume that children with learning disabilities have intrinsic learning problems because of a central nervous system dysfunction, thus ruling out the environment as a causal factor. These definitions state that learning disabilities can occur along with environmen-

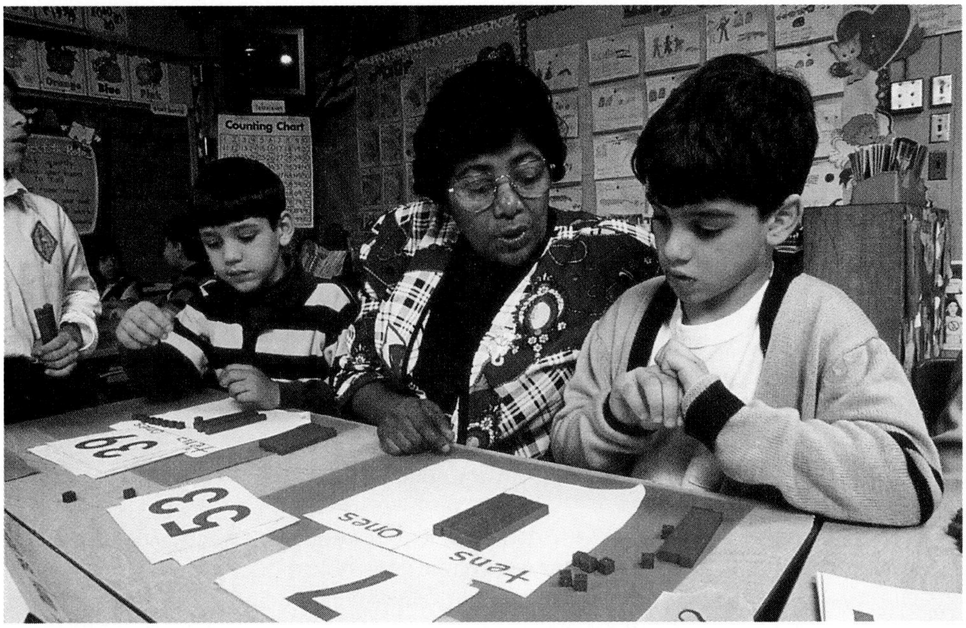

Some learning disabilities involve difficulties with perceiving and interpreting (as opposed to sensing) visual or auditory stimuli.

tal disadvantage, mental retardation, or emotional disturbance, but for children to be considered learning disabled, their learning problems must be primarily the result of their learning disabilities.

We turn now to two of the most popular definitions: The federal definition and the National Joint Committee for Learning Disabilities definition.

The Federal Definition

Probably the most commonly accepted definition is that endorsed by the federal government:

> "Specific learning disability" means a disorder in one or more of the basic psychological processes involved in understanding or in using language, spoken or written, which may manifest itself in an imperfect ability to listen, think, speak, read, write, spell, or to do mathematical calculations. The term includes such conditions as perceptual handicaps, brain injury, minimal brain dysfunction, dyslexia, and developmental aphasia. The term does not include children who have learning problems which are primarily the result of visual, hearing, or motor handicaps, of mental retardation, of emotional disturbance, or of environmental, cultural, or economic disadvantage. (*Federal Register,* 1977, p. 65083)

The National Joint Committee for Learning Disabilities (NJCLD) Definition

The National Joint Committee on Learning Disabilities (NJCLD), made up of representatives of several professional organizations, has issued an alternative definition:

> Learning disabilities is a general term that refers to a heterogeneous group of disorders manifested by significant difficulties in the acquisition and use of listening, speaking, reading, writing, reasoning, or mathematical abilities. These disorders are intrinsic to the individual, presumed to be due to central nervous system dysfunction, and may occur across the life span.

> Problems in self-regulatory behaviors, social perception and social interaction may exist with learning disabilities but do not by themselves constitute a learning disability.
>
> Although learning disabilities may occur concomitantly with other handicapping conditions (for example, sensory impairment, mental retardation, serious emotional disturbance) or with extrinsic influences (such as cultural differences, insufficient or inappropriate instruction), they are not the result of those conditions or influences. (National Joint Committee on Learning Disabilities, 1989, p. 1)

Similarities and Differences in the Federal and NJCLD Definitions

There are some important similarities between the federal and NJCLD definitions. Both view central nervous system dysfunction as a potential cause; specify that listening, speaking, reading, writing, and math can be affected; and exclude learning problems due primarily to other conditions (e.g., mental retardation, emotional disturbance, cultural differences).

There are also some important differences between the two definitions. The authors of the NJCLD definition point out that it does not use the phrase *basic psychological processes,* which has been so controversial (because such processes are not observable and hence difficult to measure), and does not mention perceptual handicaps, dyslexia, or minimal brain dysfunction, which have been so difficult to define (Hammill, Leigh, McNutt, & Larsen, 1981). Furthermore, the NJCLD definition clearly states that a learning disability may be a lifelong condition.

The federal government's conceptualization of learning disabilities also stresses the notion of an IQ-achievement discrepancy, as discussed earlier. Although such a discrepancy is not part of the definition, the federal regulations for identifying learning disabilities refer to a severe discrepancy between intellectual ability and academic achievement.

PREVALENCE

According to figures kept by the federal U.S. government, the public schools have identified as learning disabled slightly more than 5 percent of students six to seventeen years of age. Students with learning disabilities is by far the largest category of special education. About half of all students identified by the public schools as needing special education are learning disabled. The size of the learning disabilities category has more than doubled since 1976–1977, when prevalence figures first started being kept by the federal government.

Many authorities maintain that the rapid expansion of the learning disabilities category reflects poor diagnostic practices. They believe that children are being overidentified, that teachers are too quick to label students with the slightest learning problem as "learning disabled" rather than entertain the possibility that their teaching practices are at fault. Other authorities, however, argue that the claim of overidentification has been exaggerated and that there are logical explanations for the increase in students with learning disabilities (see box on p. 169).

Boys outnumber girls by about three to one in the learning disabilities category (U.S. Department of Education, 1992). Some researchers have suggested that the prevalence of learning disabilities among males is due to their greater biological

Is the Increase in Diagnosis of Learning Disabilities Justified?

In 1976–1977, about 23 percent of all students identified for special education were learning disabled. Today, that figure stands at about 50 percent. Many practitioners, researchers, and officials in the federal government have decried the expansion of the learning disabilities category. They believe that the increase represents the misidentification of many children as learning disabled.

Not all are convinced that the increase is completely unwarranted. Hallahan (1992), for example, asserts that much of the increase may represent the identification of bona fide cases of learning disabilities. He points to two factors that may have led to the doubling of the learning disabilities population. First, when figures started being kept in 1976–1977, the learning disabilities category had been in official existence for only a short time. Hallahan speculates that it may have taken professionals a few years to decide how to go about identifying children for this category of services. Indirect evidence for this comes from the fact that the increase in identification of cases of learning disabilities has slowed dramatically since the mid-1980s.

Second, Hallahan points to an abundance of social/cultural changes that he believes have raised children's vulnerability to developing learning disabilities. For example, an increase in poverty has placed children at greater risk for biomedical problems, including central nervous system dysfunction (Baumeister, Kupstas, & Klindworth, 1990). Furthermore, even families who are not in poverty are under more stress than ever before, which takes its toll on the time children have for concentrating on their schoolwork and on their parents' ability to offer social support.

In addition to being bombarded with a variety of attractive diversions—television, video games, videotape rentals—today's children spend an enormous number of hours each year being transported to and from school and numerous extracurricular activities (e.g., athletics, clubs, dance or music lessons). And parents have fewer hours in the day to devote to helping their children with schoolwork. Hallahan cites a survey (Leete-Guy & Schor, 1992) showing that since 1969, the amount of leisure time for families in the United States has declined dramatically. Those who hold jobs are working longer hours. Furthermore, in single-parent families and families in which both parents work, the time parents have to monitor their children's progress in school is reduced further.

Hallahan concludes:

> Undoubtedly, some students are misidentified as learning disabled. The business of identification depends on clinical judgment, and clinical judgment always results in errors. But misdiagnosis may not account for all of the growth in the learning disabilities population. Exactly what proportion of the increase represents bogus cases of learning disabilities is open for speculation and future research. In the meantime, we should be open to the idea that at least some of the increase represents students who are in very real need of learning disabilities services. (p. 528)

vulnerability. The infant mortality rate for males is higher than that for females, and males are at greater risk than females for a variety of biological abnormalities.

Other researchers have contended, however, that the higher prevalence of learning disabilities among males may be due to referral bias. They suggest that academic difficulties are no more prevalent among boys than among girls, but that boys are more likely to be referred for special education when they do have academic problems because of other behaviors that bother teachers, such as hyperactivity. Research on this issue is mixed (Clarizio & Phillips, 1986; Leinhardt, Seewald, & Zigmond, 1982; Shaywitz, Shaywitz, Fletcher, & Escobar, 1990). So at this point, it is probably safest to conclude that

> some bias does exist but that the biological vulnerability of males also plays a role. For example, the federal government's figures indicate that all disabilities are more prevalent in males, including conditions that are difficult to imagine resulting from referral or assessment bias, such as hearing impairment (53% are males), orthopedic impairment (54% are males), and visual impairment (56% are males). (Hallahan, Kauffman, & Lloyd, 1996, p. 51)

CAUSES

electroencephalogram (EEG). A graphic recording of the brain's electrical impulses.

computerized axial tomographic (CAT) scans. A neuroimaging technique whereby X-rays of the brain are compiled by a computer to produce a series of pictures of the brain.

magnetic resonance imaging (MRI). A neuroimaging technique whereby radio waves are used to produce cross-sectional images of the brain; used to pinpoint areas of the brain that are dysfunctional.

positron emission tomography (PET) scans. A computerized method for measuring bloodflow in the brain; during a cognitive task, a low amount of radioactive dye is injected in the brain; the dye collects in active neurons, indicating which areas of the brain are active.

In most cases, the cause of a child's learning disabilities remains a mystery. Possible causes fall into three general categories—organic and biological, genetic, and environmental.

Organic and Biological Factors

For years, many professionals suspected that neurological factors were a major cause of learning disabilities. Not all agreed, however, because the evidence for a neurological cause was based on relatively crude neurological measures. In recent years, however, researchers have begun to harness advanced technology to assess brain activity more accurately. One research team, for example, has found that many students with learning disabilities have abnormal brain waves, as measured by the digitally computerized recording and analysis of an **electroencephalogram (EEG)**. An EEG consists of electrical recordings obtained from electrodes placed at various sites on the head.

The most recent types of technology being used by researchers to document neurological dysfunction in some persons with learning disabilities include **computerized axial tomographic (CAT) scans, magnetic resonance imaging (MRI)**, and **positron emission tomography (PET) scans.**

- A CAT scan involves placing the patient's head in a large ring and then taking a series of X-rays. The X-rays are then fed into a computer that plots a series of pictures of the brain (see Figure 5–1).
- An MRI uses radio waves instead of radiation to create cross-sectional images of the brain (see Figure 5–2).
- Whereas a CAT scan or MRI is usually used when the subject is resting, a PET scan is performed while he or she is engaged in a task, such as reading. The subject is injected with a substance containing a low amount of radiation, which collects in

Figure 5–1

Procedure for doing a CAT scan.
(*Source:* From *Biopsychology* [2nd ed.], p. 131, Fig. 5.2, by P. J. Pinel, 1993. Boston: Allyn & Bacon. Copyright 1993 by Allyn & Bacon. Reprinted with permission.)

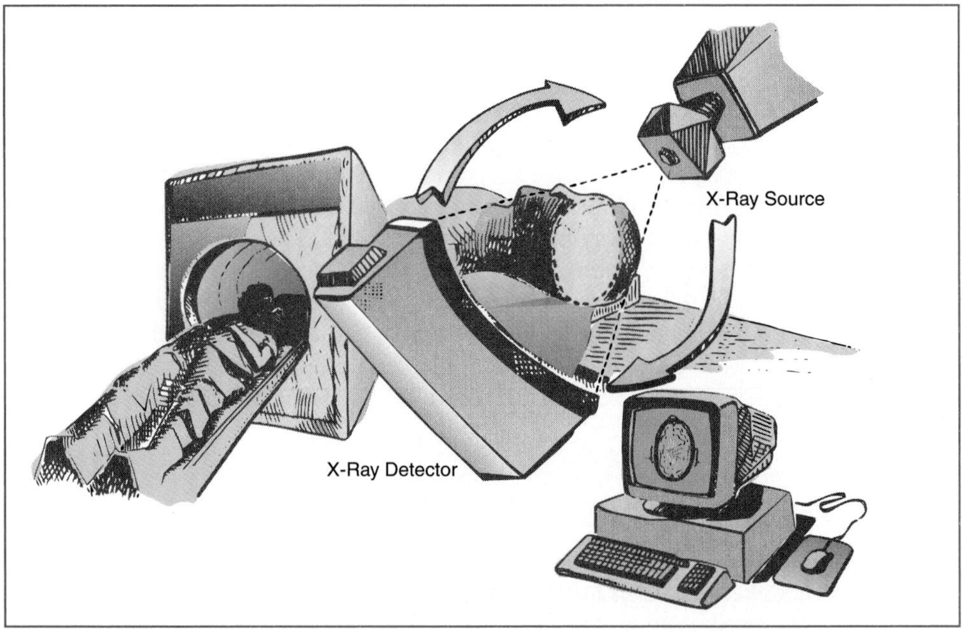

active neurons. Using a scanner to detect the radioactive substance, researchers can tell which parts of the brain are actively engaged during various tasks.

Using CAT scans and MRIs, researchers have found evidence for a neurological cause in some cases of learning disabilities (Hynd, Marshall, & Gonzalez, 1991; Willis, Hooper, & Stone, 1992). Using PET scans and similar techniques for measuring bloodflow, researchers have found differences in brain metabolism between persons with severe reading disabilities and those who are not disabled (Flowers, 1993; Flowers, Wood, & Naylor, 1991; Gross-Glenn et al., 1991; Hagman et al., 1992).

Taken as a whole, these studies are not definitive evidence of a neurological basis for all students identified as learning disabled. Some researchers have noted that, for the most part, the studies have been conducted on individuals with severe learning disabilities. The results, however, have turned many who were formerly skeptical into believers that central nervous system dysfunction may be the cause of many cases of learning disabilities.

Genetic Factors

Over the years, evidence has accumulated that learning disabilities can be inherited. The two most common types of studies used to look at the genetic basis of learning disabilities are familiality studies and heritability studies.

Familiality studies examine the degree to which a certain condition, such as a learning disability, occurs in single family. Researchers have found that the first-degree relatives of persons with reading disabilities—that is, the immediate birth family (parents and siblings)—have an increased risk of having reading disabilities (Hallgren, 1950; Olson, Wise, Conners, Rack, & Fulker, 1989; Pennington, 1990). The same increase in familiality has also been found in families of people with speech and language disorders (Beichtman, Hood, & Inglis, 1992; Lewis, 1992).

familiality studies. A method of determining the degree to which a given condition is inherited; looks at the prevalence of the condition in relatives of the person with the condition.

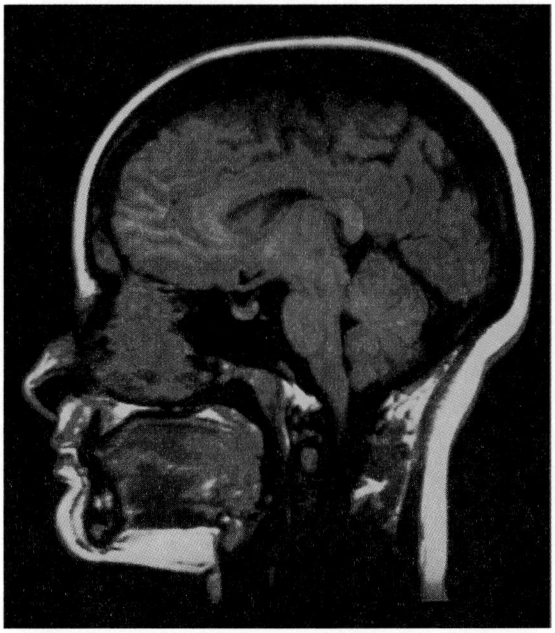

Figure 5–2

An MRI.

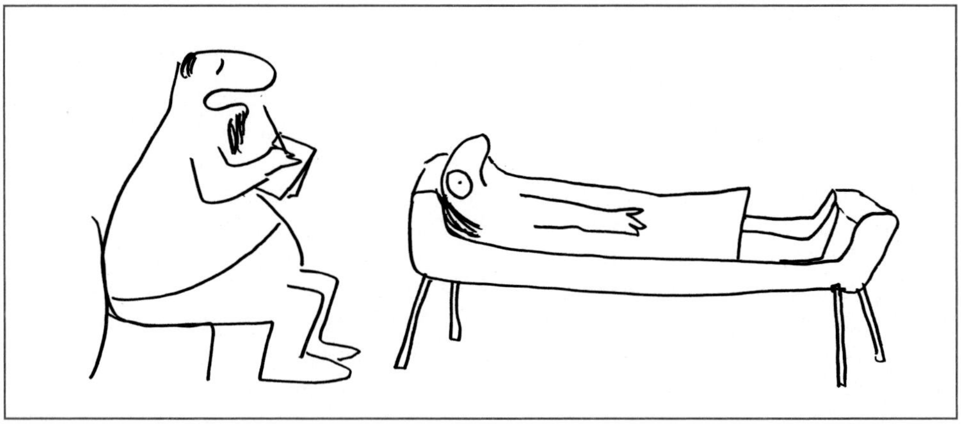

"Your feelings of insecurity seem to have started when Mary Lou Gurnblatt said, 'Maybe I don't have a learning disability—maybe you have a teaching disability.'"

Source: J. H. Crouse and P. T. McFarlane (1975), "Monopoly, myth, and convivial access to the tools of learning," *Phi Delta Kappan, 56*(9), 593. Drawn by Tony Saltzman.

The tendency for learning disabilities to run in families *may also* be due to environmental factors. For example, it is possible that parents with learning disabilities may pass on their disabilities to their children through their childrearing practices. Given this, a more convincing method of determining whether learning disabilities are inherited is **heritability studies**—comparing the prevalence of learning disabilities in identical (monozygotic, from the same egg) versus fraternal (dizygotic, from two eggs) twins. Researchers have found that identical twins are more concordant than fraternal twins for reading disabilities and speech and language disorders (DeFries, Gillis, & Wadsworth, 1993; Lewis & Thompson, 1992). In other words, if an identical twin and a fraternal twin each have a learning disability, the second identical twin is more likely to have a learning disability than the second fraternal twin.

Environmental Factors

Environmental causes of learning disabilities are difficult to document. Much evidence shows that environmentally disadvantaged children are more prone to exhibit learning problems. But it is still not clear whether this is due strictly to inadequate learning experiences or to biological factors, such as brain damage or nutritional deprivation (Cravioto & DeLicardie, 1975; Hallahan & Cruickshank, 1973).

Another possible environmental cause of learning disabilities is poor teaching (Engelmann, 1977; Lovitt, 1977). Some believe that if teachers were better prepared to handle the special learning problems of children in the early school years, some learning disabilities could be avoided.

heritability studies. A method of determining the degree to which a condition is inherited; a comparison of the prevalence of a condition in identical (i.e., monozygotic, from the same egg) twins versus fraternal (i.e., dizygotic, from two eggs) twins.

ASSESSMENT

Four types of assessment are popular in the field of learning disabilities:

1. standardized achievement tests
2. informal reading inventories
3. formative evaluation methods
4. authentic assessment

Teachers may use the results of informal reading inventories in designing instructional interventions for students.

Standardized Achievement Tests

Teachers and psychologists commonly use standardized achievement tests with students who are learning disabled because achievement deficits are the primary characteristic of these students. The fact that the test is *standardized* means that it has been administered to a large group so that any one score can be compared to the *norm*, or average. Several standardized achievement tests are currently in use. One of the most recent is the Wechsler Individual Achievement Test (WIAT), which assesses achievement in all the areas pertaining to the federal definition of learning disabilities: basic reading, reading comprehension, spelling, written expression, mathematics reasoning, numerical operations, listening comprehension, and oral expression. The developers of the WIAT designed the test so it could be used in conjunction with the Wechsler Intelligence Scale for Children (WISC) in order to look for discrepancies between achievement and ability.

One limitation to most standardized tests is that they cannot be used to gain much insight into *why* students have difficulty. Teachers and clinicians use these tests primarily to identify students with learning problems and to provide gross indicators of academic strengths and weaknesses.

The notion of using assessment data to help plan educational strategies has gained much of its popularity from professionals working in the area of learning disabilities. Two methods of assessment—informal reading inventories and formative evaluation measures—are better suited to the philosophy that test scores are more useful for teachers if they can be translated into educational recommendations. We discuss each in a following section.

Informal Reading Inventories

A common method of assessment used by teachers in the area of reading is an **informal reading inventory (IRI)** which is a series of reading passages or word lists graded in order of difficulty. The teacher has the student read from the series, beginning with a list or passage that is likely to be easy for the student. The student continues to read increasingly more difficult lists or passages while the teacher monitors his or her performance.

informal reading inventory (IRI). A method of assessing reading in which the teacher has the student read progressively more difficult series of passages or word lists; the teacher notes the difficulty level of the material read and the types of errors the student makes.

After the results of the IRI have been compiled, the teacher can use them to estimate the appropriate difficulty level of reading material for the student, as well as to determine what kinds of reading errors he or she typically makes (e.g., mispronunciations, omissions, hesitations). The teacher can then use this error analysis in designing instructional interventions for the student.

Formative Evaluation Methods

Formative evaluation methods directly measure a student's behavior to keep track of his or her progress (Deno, 1985; Fuchs, 1986; Fuchs & Fuchs, 1986; Germann & Tindal, 1985; Marston & Magnusson, 1985; White & Haring, 1980). Formative evaluation is less concerned with how the student's performance compares with that of other students and more concerned with how the student performs in light of his or her abilities. Although there are a variety of formative evaluation models, at least five features are common to all of them:

1. The assessment is usually done by the child's teacher, rather than a school psychologist or diagnostician.
2. The teacher assesses classroom behaviors directly. For instance, if the teacher is interested in measuring the child's pronunciation of the letter *l*, he or she looks at that particular behavior and records whether the child can pronounce that letter.
3. The teacher observes and records the child's behavior frequently and over a period of time. Most other kinds of tests are given once or twice a year at the most. In formative evaluation, performance is measured at least two or three times a week.
4. The teacher uses formative evaluation to assess the child's progress toward educational goals. After an initial testing, the teacher establishes goals for the child to reach in a given period of time. For example, if the child can orally read 25 words correctly in one minute out of a certain book, the teacher may set a goal, or *criterion,* of being able to read 100 words correctly per minute after one month. This aspect of formative evaluation is sometimes referred to as **criterion-referenced testing**.
5. The teacher uses formative evaluation to monitor the effectiveness of educational programming. For instance, in the preceding example, if after a few days the teacher realizes it is unlikely that the child will reach the goal of 100 words, the teacher can try a different educational intervention.

formative evaluation methods. Measurement procedures used to monitor an individual student's progress; they are used to compare how an individual performs in light of his or her abilities, in contrast to standardized tests, which are primarily used to compare an individual's performance to that of other students.

criterion-referenced testing. A procedure used to determine a child's level of achievement; when this level is established, a criterion, or goal, is set to fix a level at which the child should be achieving.

curriculum-based assessment (CBA). A formative evaluation method designed to evaluate performance in the particular curriculum to which students are exposed; usually involves giving students a small sample of items from the curriculum in use in their schools; proponents argue that CBA is preferable to comparing students with national norms or using tests that do not reflect the curriculum content learned by students.

Curriculum-Based Assessment. One particular model of formative evaluation is **curriculum-based assessment (CBA).** Although it draws heavily on earlier research, CBA was largely developed by Deno and his colleagues (Deno, 1985; Fuchs, Deno, & Mirkin, 1984).

Because it is a type of formative evaluation, CBA has the five features just listed. In addition, it has two other distinguishing characteristics:

1. It is designed to measure children's performances on the particular curriculum to which they are exposed. In spelling, for example, a typical CBA assessment strategy is to give children two-minute spelling samples, using dictation from a random selection of words from the basal spelling curriculum. The number of words or letter sequences correctly spelled serves as the performance measure. In math, the teacher may give children two minutes to compute samples of problems from the basal text and record the number of digits computed correctly. Proponents of

CBA state that this reliance on the curriculum is an advantage over commercially available standardized achievement tests, which are usually not keyed to the curriculum in any particular school.

2. CBA compares the performance of students with disabilities to that of their peers in their own school or school division. Deno and his colleagues suggest that the teacher take CBA measures on a random sample of nondisabled students so this comparison can be made. Comparison with a local reference group is seen as more relevant than comparison with the national norming groups used in commercially developed standardized tests.

Researchers have found that CBA results in positive changes for both teachers and students with learning disabilities. Teachers who use CBA have more objective information for assessing whether students are meeting their goals and are more likely to modify instruction if students are not meeting those goals (Fuchs, Fuchs, & Strecker, 1989). Students also make more academic progress when CBA is used (Fuchs, 1986).

Authentic Assessment

Some educators question the authenticity of typical test scores—especially those from standardized tests—asserting that they do not reflect what students do in situations in which they work with or receive help from, teachers, peers, parents, or supervisors. The purpose behind **authentic assessment** is to assess students' critical-thinking and problem-solving abilities in real-life situations.

Portfolios. An example of authentic assessment is **portfolios**. Portfolios are a collection of samples of a student's work done over time. Some authorities recommend that the work:

- be collected systematically at predetermined intervals
- show various stages of learning concepts or skills
- be discussed with the student in order to identify strengths and weaknesses
- be used to modify instruction (Hoy & Gregg, 1994)

authentic assessment. A method that evaluates a student's critical-thinking and problem-solving ability in real-life situations in which he or she may work with or receive help from peers, teachers, parents, or supervisors.

portfolios. A collection of samples of a student's work done over time; a type of authentic assessment.

Authentic assessment and performance assessment techniques, such as portfolios and videotapes, may be particularly well suited to students whose learning disabilities affect their performance on standardized tests.

In fact, portfolio assessment is more difficult and time consuming than many educators realize (Hallahan, Kauffman, & Lloyd, 1996). Knowing what to include and how to evaluate it can be challenging. For example, some products, such as written stories, lend themselves more readily to inclusion in portfolios than others, such as oral reading or storytelling. The latter may require videotaping or audiotaping of a student's performance.

PSYCHOLOGICAL AND BEHAVIORAL CHARACTERISTICS

Before discussing some of the most common characteristics of persons with learning disabilities, we point out two important features of this population: Persons with learning disabilities exhibit a great deal of *inter*individual and *intra*individual variation.

Interindividual Variation

In any classroom of students with learning disabilities, some will have problems in reading, some will have problems in math, some will have problems in spelling, some will be inattentive, and so on. One term for such interindividual variation is *heterogeneity*. Although heterogeneity is a trademark of children from all the categories of special education, the old adage "No two are exactly alike" is particularly appropriate for students with learning disabilities.

The broad range of disabilities has made it extremely difficult for teachers and researchers to work with and study students with learning disabilities. Teachers have found it difficult to plan educational programs for the diverse group of children they find in their classrooms. Researchers have been faced with the uncertainty of knowing whether inconsistent results from study to study are indeed real or caused by variations in children selected for one study versus another.

Teams of researchers have been tackling the problem of heterogeneity since the mid-1980s, attempting to find subgroups, or subtypes, of learning disabilities. Using sophisticated statistical techniques, these investigators have just begun to find suggestive evidence of subtypes (e.g., McKinney, 1987a, 1989; McKinney & Feagans, 1984; McKinney, Short, & Feagans, 1985; McKinney & Speece, 1986; Speece, McKinney, & Applebaum, 1985). It is still too early to tell, however, whether the search for subtypes will yield information useful for teachers and researchers.

Intraindividual Variation

In addition to differences among one another, children with learning disabilities also tend to exhibit variability within their own profiles of abilities. For example, a child may be two or three years above grade level in reading but two or three years behind grade level in math. Such uneven profiles account for references to *specific* learning disabilities in the literature on learning disabilities. Some children have specific deficits in just one or a few areas of achievement or development.

Some of the pioneers in the field of learning disabilities alerted colleagues to what is termed *intraindividual* variation. Samuel Kirk was one of the most influential in advocating the notion of individual variation in students with learning disabilities. He developed the Illinois Test of Psycholinguistic Abilities, which purportedly measured variation in processes important for reading. Researchers ultimately found that Kirk's test did not measure processes germane to reading (Hallahan & Cruickshank, 1973;

Hammill & Larsen, 1974), and the test is rarely used today. Nonetheless, most authorities still recognize intraindividual differences as a feature of many students with learning disabilities.

We now turn to a discussion of some of the most common characteristics of persons with learning disabilities.

Academic Achievement Problems

Academic deficits are the hallmark of learning disabilities. By definition, if there is no academic problem, a learning disability does not exist.

Reading. Reading poses the most difficulty for most students with learning disabilities. Most authorities believe that this problem is related to deficient language skills, especially **phonological skills**—the ability to understand the rules of how various sounds go with certain letters to make up words (Adams & Bruck, 1995; Ball & Blackman 1991; Foorman & Liberman, 1989; Liberman & Shankweiler, 1991; Stanovich, 1991b). It is easy to understand why problems with phonology would be at the heart of many reading difficulties. If a person has problems breaking words into their component sounds, he or she will have trouble learning to read.

Even though phonological problems may be the cause of many reading problems, there is mounting evidence that a small proportion of reading problems may be due to difficulty in processing the *orthographic,* or visual, information from letters (Stanovich, 1991b). It is still too early to tell how significant visual/orthographic problems are for persons with reading disabilities.

Written Language. People with learning disabilities often have problems in one or more of the following areas: handwriting, spelling, and composition (Newcomer & Barenbaum, 1991). Although even the best students can have less than perfect handwriting, the kinds of problems manifested by some students with learning disabilities are much more severe. These children are sometimes very slow writers and their written products are sometimes illegible. Spelling can be a significant problem because of the difficulty (noted in the previous section) in understanding the correspondence between sounds and letters.

In addition to the more mechanical areas of handwriting and spelling, students with learning disabilities also frequently have difficulties in the more creative aspects of composition (Englert, 1992; Englert et al., 1988; Montague & Graves, 1992; Montague, Graves, & Leavell, 1991; Thomas, Englert, & Gregg, 1987). Englert and her colleagues have identified three types of difficulties:

1. These students are not aware of the basic purpose of writing as an act of communication; instead, they approach writing as a test-taking task.
2. These students' writing lacks fluency—they write short sentences and stories. For example, they have problems elaborating about the emotional and cognitive states of the characters in their stories (Montague & Graves, 1992).
3. These students do not spontaneously use writing strategies, such as planning, organizing, drafting, and editing.

Spoken Language. Many students with learning disabilities have problems with the *mechanical* (Mann, Cowin, & Schoenheimer, 1989; Vellutino, 1987) and *social uses of language* (Bryan & Bryan, 1986; Mathinos, 1988). Mechanically, they have trouble with **syntax** (grammar), **semantics** (word meanings), and, as we have already

phonological skills. The ability to understand grapheme-phoneme correspondence—the rules by which sounds go with letters to make up words; generally thought to be the reason for the reading problems of many students with learning disabilities.

syntax. The way words are joined together to structure meaningful sentences (i.e., grammar).

semantics. The study of the meanings attached to words.

The term pragmatics *refers to the social uses of language. Individuals with learning disabilities who have problems with pragmatics may find it difficult to carry on conversations.*

noted, **phonology** (the ability to break words into their component sounds and blend individual sounds together to make words).

With regard to social uses of language—commonly referred to as **pragmatics**—students with learning disabilities are often inept in the production and reception of discourse. In short, they are not very good conversationalists. They are unable to engage in the mutual give and take that conversations between individuals require.

For instance, individuals with learning disabilities are often agreeable and cooperative but tend to be unpersuasive and deferential. Their conversations are frequently marked by long silences because they do not use the relatively subtle strategies that their nondisabled peers do to keep conversations going. They are not skilled at responding to others' statements or questions and tend to answer their own questions before their companions have a chance to respond. They tend to make task-irrelevant comments and make those with whom they talk uncomfortable. In one often-cited study, for example, children with and without learning disabilities took turns playing the role of host in a simulated television talk show (Bryan, Donahue, Pearl, & Sturm, 1981). Analysis of the verbal interactions revealed that in contrast to nondisabled children, children with learning disabilities playing the host role allowed their nondisabled guests to dominate the conversation. Also, their guests exhibited more signs of discomfort during the interview than did the guests of nondisabled hosts.

phonology. The study of how individual sounds make up words.

pragmatics. The study within psycholinguistics of how people use language in social situations; emphasizes the functional use of language, rather than mechanics.

Math. Although disorders of reading, writing, and language have traditionally received more emphasis than problems of mathematics, the latter are now gaining a great deal of attention. Authorities now recognize that math problems are second only to reading disabilities as an academic problem area for students with learning disabilities. In one large-scale study of over 1,000 students with learning disabilities, for example, the *average* math percentile score was at about the 30th percentile (Kavale & Reese, 1992).

There is abundant evidence that students with learning disabilities who exhibit problems in math can have trouble computing math facts (Mercer & Miller, 1992) and/or difficulties in math problem solving (Cawley & Parmar, 1992). In one study, the poor performance of students with learning disabilities on word problems was due to difficulties selecting and applying problem-solving strategies, rather than to computational errors (Montague & Bos, 1990).

Perceptual, Perceptual-Motor, and General Coordination Problems

Studies indicate that some children with learning disabilities exhibit visual and/or auditory perceptual disabilities (see Hallahan, 1975, for a review). A child with visual perceptual problems might, for example, have trouble solving puzzles or seeing and remembering visual shapes, or he or she might have a tendency to reverse letters (e.g., mistake a *b* for a *d*). A child with auditory perceptual problems might have difficulty discriminating between two words that sound alike (e.g., *fit* and *fib*) or following orally presented directions.

Teachers and parents have also noted that some students with learning disabilities have difficulty with physical activities involving motor skills. They describe some of these children as having "two left feet" or "ten thumbs." The problems may involve both fine-motor (small motor muscles) and gross-motor (large motor muscles) skills. Fine-motor skills often involve coordination of the visual and motor systems.

As we noted earlier, several early theorists in the learning disabilities field believed that by training visual-perceptual skills in isolation from academic material, students with learning disabilities would read better. However, researchers have shown that such training does not improve reading ability (see Hallahan & Cruickshank, 1973, for a review).

Disorders of Attention and Hyperactivity

Students with attention problems display such characteristics as distractibility, impulsivity, and hyperactivity. Teachers and parents of these children often characterize them as being unable to stick with one task for very long, failing to listen to others, talking nonstop, blurting out the first things on their minds, and being generally disorganized in planning their activities in and out of school.

A person with severe attention problems may be diagnosed by a psychiatrist or psychologist as having **attention deficit hyperactivity disorder (ADHD).** In making this diagnosis, the clinician looks at several factors related to inattention and hyperactivity/impulsivity (American Psychiatric Association, 1994). For example, one of the criteria for inattention is "often does not seem to listen when spoken to directly" (p. 83). Examples of criteria for hyperactivity and impulsivity, respectively, are "is often 'on the go' or often acts as if 'driven by a motor'" (p. 84) and "often has difficulty awaiting turn" (p. 84). Depending on the combination of criteria exhibited, a person may be diagnosed as having (1) ADHD with predominantly inattention, (2) ADHD with predominantly hyperactivity/impulsivity, or (3) ADHD with both inattention and hyperactivity/impulsivity.

Individuals with learning disabilities often have attention problems (Hallahan, Kauffman, & Lloyd, 1996), and they are often severe enough to be diagnosed as ADHD. Although estimates vary, researchers have consistently found that between one-fifth and one-third of students with learning disabilities have also been diagnosed as having ADHD (Riccio, Gonzalez, & Hynd, 1994; Shaywitz & Shaywitz, 1987).

attention deficit hyperactivity disorder (ADHD). A condition characterized by severe problems of inattention, hyperactivity, and/or impulsivity; often found in persons with learning disabilities.

In the case of those students who have ADHD but do *not* have learning disabilities, the question often arises as to whether they can be identified for special education. The Individuals with Disabilities Education Act (IDEA; Public Law 101–476), passed in 1990, does not formally recognize ADHD as a separate category of disability. However, in 1991, the U.S. Department of Education took the position that students with ADHD may be eligible for services under a category called "other health impaired" in instances in which "the ADD is a chronic or acute health problem that results in limited alertness, which adversely affects educational performance."

At one time, it was thought that ADHD diminished with adolescence but authorities now recognize that this condition often continues into adulthood (Hallowell & Ratey, 1994; Weiss & Hechtman, 1993). The research on ADHD in adulthood is still too new, however, to determine how prevalent ADHD is in adults. Some researchers have estimated that at least half of children with ADHD continue to have significant symptoms in adulthood.

Some of the same factors that cause learning disabilities have also been linked to ADHD, especially heredity and neurological dysfunction. Using PET scans, researchers have found evidence that malfunctioning of the frontal lobes of the brain may lead to ADHD in some persons (Zametkin et al., 1990).

Memory, Cognitive, and Metacognitive Problems

We discuss memory, cognitive, and metacognitive problems together because they are closely related. A person who has problems in one of these areas is likely to have problems in the other two, as well. Parents and teachers are well aware that students with learning disabilities have problems remembering such things as assignments and appointments. In fact, they often exclaim in exasperation that they can't understand how a child so smart could forget things so easily. Numerous researchers have documented that many students with learning disabilities have a real deficit in memory (Hallahan, 1975; Hallahan, Kauffman, & Ball, 1973; Swanson, 1987; Torgesen, 1988; Torgesen & Kail, 1980).

Students with learning disabilities have problems that affect at least two types of memory: short-term memory (Hallahan, 1975; Hallahan, Kauffman, & Ball, 1973; Torgesen, 1988) and working memory (Swanson, 1994). Problems with **short-term memory** involve difficulty recalling information shortly after having seen or heard it. A typical short-term memory task would require a person to repeat a list of words presented visually or aurally—something many students with learning disabilities would find hard to do. Problems with **working memory** affect a person's ability to keep information in mind while simultaneously doing another cognitive task. Trying to remember an address while listening to instructions on how to get there is an example of working memory. Again, this sort of memory task would be difficult for some people with learning disabilities.

Researchers have found that one of the major reasons that children with learning disabilities perform poorly on memory tasks is that, unlike their nondisabled peers, they do not use *strategies*. For example, when presented with a list of words to memorize, most children will rehearse the names to themselves. They will also make use of categories by rehearsing words in groups that go together. Students with learning disabilities are not likely to use these strategies spontaneously.

The deficiency in the use of strategies on memory tasks also indicates that children with learning disabilities demonstrate problems in cognition. **Cognition** is a broad term covering many different aspects of thinking and problem solving. Stu-

short-term memory. The ability to recall information after a short period of time.

working memory. The ability to remember information while also performing other cognitive operations.

cognition. The ability to solve problems and use strategies; an area of difficulty for many persons with learning disabilities.

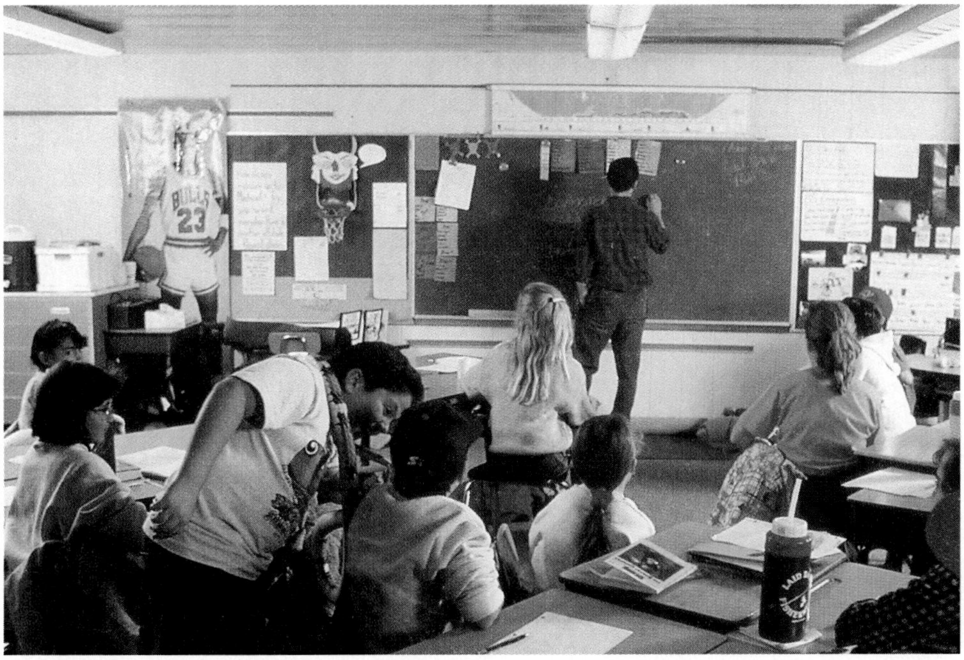

Individuals with learning disabilities often have attention problems that can lead to impulsivity and hyperactivity.

dents with learning disabilities often exhibit disorganized thinking that results in problems with planning and organizing their lives at school and at home.

Closely related to these cognitive problems are problems in metacognition (Hallahan, Kneedler, & Lloyd, 1983; Kneedler & Hallahan, 1984; Short & Weissberg-Benchell, 1989). **Metacognition** has two components:

> (1) An awareness of what skills, strategies, and resources are needed to perform a task effectively; and (2) the ability to use self-regulatory mechanisms to ensure the successful completion of the task, such as planning one's moves, evaluating the effectiveness of one's ongoing activities, checking the outcomes of one's efforts, and remediating whatever difficulties arise. (Baker, 1982, pp. 27–28)

An example of difficulties with the first component—awareness of skills, strategies, and resources—was evident in a study in which the experimenter asked children how they would go about remembering different things (Torgesen, 1977). When asked such questions as "Suppose you lost your jacket while you were at school; how would you go about finding it?" students with learning disabilities could not produce as many strategies as could their nondisabled peers.

An example of the second component of metacognition—ability to self-regulate—is comprehension monitoring. **Comprehension monitoring** refers to the abilities employed while one reads and attempts to comprehend textual material. Investigators have found that many students with reading disabilities have problems, for example, in being able to sense when they are not understanding what they are reading (Bos & Filip, 1982). Good readers are able to sense this and make necessary adjustments, such as slowing down and/or rereading difficult passages. Students with reading problems are also likely to have problems picking out the main ideas of paragraphs. Good readers spend more time and effort focusing on the major ideas contained in the text they read.

metacognition. One's understanding of the strategies available for learning a task and the regulatory mechanisms needed to complete the task.

comprehension monitoring. The ability to keep track of one's own comprehension of reading material and to make adjustments to comprehend better while reading; often deficient in students with learning disabilities.

Social-Emotional Problems

Although not all, perhaps not even a majority, of children with learning disabilities have significant social-emotional problems, they do run a greater risk than their nondisabled peers of having these types of problems (Pearl, 1992). Specifically, children with learning disabilities tend to be rejected by their peers and have poor self-concepts.

One plausible reason for the social problems of some students with learning disabilities is that they have deficits in social cognition. That is, they misread social cues and may misinterpret the feelings and emotions of others. Most children, for example, are able to tell when their behavior is bothering others. Students with learning disabilities sometimes act as if they are oblivious to the effect their behavior is having on their peers. They also have difficulty taking the perspective of others, of putting themselves in someone else's shoes.

It may also be that some of these behavioral characteristics of children with learning disabilities annoy others and/or make it difficult for others to interact with them. For example, if a child with learning disabilities has problems with conversational skills, he or she may have difficulty acquiring and maintaining friendships. Or if a child has an attention deficit hyperactivity disorder that causes him or her to intrude into other people's conversations, others may shun him or her.

Motivational Problems

Another source of problems for many persons with learning disabilities is their *motivation,* or feelings about their abilities to deal with life's many challenges and problems. People with learning disabilities may appear content to let events happen without attempting to control or influence them. These individuals have what is referred to as an *external,* rather than an *internal,* **locus of control.** In other words, they believe their lives are controlled by external factors, such as luck or fate, rather than internal factors, such as determination or ability (Hallahan, Gajar, Cohen, & Tarver, 1978; Short & Weissberg-Benchell, 1989). People with this outlook sometimes display **learned helplessness:** a tendency to give up and expect the worst because they think that no matter how hard they try, they will fail (Schunk, 1989; Seligman, 1992).

What makes these motivational problems so difficult for teachers, parents, and individuals with learning disabilities to deal with is the interrelationship between cognitive and motivational problems (Borkowski, 1992). A vicious cycle develops: To begin, the student learns to expect failure in any new situation, based on past experience. This expectancy of failure, or learned helplessness, may then cause him or her to give up too easily when faced with a difficult or complicated task. As a result, not only does the student fail to learn new skills; he or she also has another bad experience, reinforcing feelings of helplessness and even worthlessness—and so the cycle goes.

locus of control. A motivational term referring to how people explain their successes or failures; people with an internal locus of control believe they are the reason for success or failure, whereas people with an external locus of control believe outside forces influence how they perform.

learned helplessness. A motivational term referring to a condition in which a person believes that no matter how hard he or she tries, failure will result.

The Child with Learning Disabilities as an Inactive Learner with Strategy Deficits

Many of the psychological and behavioral characteristics we have described can be summed up by saying that the student who is learning disabled is an inactive learner, lacking in strategies for attacking academic problems (Hallahan & Bryan, 1981; Hallahan & Reeve, 1980; Torgesen, 1977). Specifically, research describes the student with learning disabilities as someone who does not believe in his or her own abilities (learned helplessness), has an inadequate grasp of what strategies are available for problem solving (poor metacognitive skills), and has problems producing appropriate learning strategies spontaneously.

The practical implications of this constellation of characteristics is that students with learning disabilities may have difficulties working independently. They are not likely to be "self-starters." Assignments or activities requiring them to work on their own may cause problems, unless the teacher carefully provides an appropriate amount of support. Homework, for example, may pose particular problems (see box below). (Many of the cognitive training procedures we discuss later are designed to overcome the passive learning style characterized by many students with learning disabilities.)

EDUCATIONAL CONSIDERATIONS

In the next section, we consider two major approaches to alleviating the academic problems of students with learning disabilities:

- cognitive training
- direct instruction

And later in the chapter, we review four major approaches for dealing with students who have attention deficit hyperactivity disorder:

- structure and stimulus reduction
- behavior modification
- cognitive training
- medication

Although we look at these approaches individually, in practice, they are often used in combination.

Homework and the Student with Learning Disabilities

The combination of calls for higher standards in the schools by general education reformers and for increased mainstreaming of students who are learning disabled by special education reformers has not mixed well in all respects. One of the problem areas is homework (Hallahan, 1992; Polloway, Foley, & Epstein, 1992).

In response to reformers' criticisms, teachers—especially general education teachers—are increasing the amount of homework they assign their pupils (Bryan & Donahue, 1994; U.S. Department of Education, 1990). Unfortunately, the behavioral characteristics of many students with learning disabilities make them prime candidates for having homework problems. Their generally passive approach to learning and difficulty in working independently make it hard for many students with learning disabilities to tackle homework.

Evidence of this comes from a survey of teachers and parents (Polloway et al., 1992). Both groups rated students with learning disabilities as having overwhelmingly more problems with homework than their nondisabled peers. Students' difficulties ranged from failing to bring home their homework, to being distracted while doing homework, to forgetting to bring their assignments back to class.

As one parent has put it, "Homework has dominated and ruined our lives for the past eight years" (Baumgartner, Bryan, Donahue, & Nelson, 1993, p. 182).

Many authorities on homework believe that teachers should use it primarily for having students practice proficiency in skills they already possess, rather than for learning new skills. This dictum would appear even more crucial for students with learning disabilities, who are so frequently characterized by their inability to work independently. Asking students to acquire new information during homework only puts students with learning disabilities further behind their peers and jeopardizes the goal of mainstreaming.

SUCCESS STORIES

San Francisco, CA: Like many students across the country, eleven-year-old ***Eliot Danner*** *attends a private school that does not provide any special education services. His parents had to look elsewhere for specialized training to help him learn to read. They found that help with special educators Nancy Cushen White and Mia Callahan Russell.*

Eliot met Nancy Cushen White, a clinical faculty member at the University of California at San Francisco and a learning specialist for the San Francisco City Schools, in the summer before second grade, when he first attended an intense special education program designed to address language disabilities. Up to that point, perceptually oriented therapies had been tried with Eliot, but without clear success. Everyone knew he had trouble reading, but no one was sure what to do about it.

Since kindergarten, Eliot has attended independent schools designed for high academic achievers, not for students with learning disabilities. In the early grades, he had passionate interests and easily memorized stories read to him, but for all his curiosity and interest, Eliot could not read by himself. A psychological evaluation identified problems with spatial orientation, word attack, spelling, and composition skills. After one year of tutoring in phonological awareness to complement his school's whole-language approach, Eliot was still anxious and unsure if he would ever learn to read. "We needed to respond to that, or we feared we would lose him as a reader," says his mother, Nancy Pietrefesa.

Eliot's parents considered enrolling him in another school but kept him in place following an assessment that suggested he would do best in this challenging but relaxed atmosphere. Says Nancy Cullen White, "This wasn't a question of settings but of strategies. Eliot is a child with dyslexia who needed to learn how to read."

"Teaching kids with learning disabilities is not a casual engagement," says Nancy Pietrefesa. She believes her son's success began the summer he met Nancy White and Mia Callahan Russell, both teachers trained to address language disabilities. They could accurately describe Eliot's problems, clearly articulate his strengths and weaknesses, and prescribe intense remedial instruction. Through that process, Eliot assumed greater control and self-acceptance. He began to understand himself as a reader.

It was Nancy White who specifically described his problem:

> Eliot does not have a weakness in any one modality. He has great difficulty with auditory, visual, and kinesthetic integra-

Educational Methods for Academic Problems

Cognitive Training. The approach termed **cognitive training** involves three components: (1) changing thought processes, (2) providing strategies for learning, and (3) teaching self-initiative. Whereas the behavior modification approach focuses on modifying observable behaviors (see page 190), cognitive training is concerned with modifying unobservable thought processes, prompting observable changes in behavior. Cognitive training has proven successful in resolving a variety of academic problems for many students with learning disabilities (Borkwowski, 1992; Pressley, Symons, Snyder, & Cariglia-Bull, 1989).

cognitive training. A group of training procedures designed to change thoughts or thought patterns.

Authorities give at least two reasons as to why cognitive training is particularly appropriate for students with learning disabilities. Namely, it aims at helping them overcome:

1. cognitive and metacognitive problems by providing them with specific strategies for solving problems

Special Educators at Work

tion, particularly in association with his long-term visual memory. In the summer of 1992, his phonological awareness was poor and he was not able to segment syllables into individual sounds for spelling or to blend sounds into syllables for decoding. In addition, he had difficulties with visual discrimination and both short-term and long-term visual memory for words. Unable to rely on his memory, it all became a jumble when he had to write things down.

That July, eight-year-old Eliot began an intensive regimen of language training and educational therapy that has paid off. Along with a group of ten other students from public and private schools, he attended a three-week summer program for three-and-one-half hours of daily direct instruction in language skills. Says Nancy White, "What some folks learn on their own, these kids need to be taught."

Getting students to think through the process of language is the program's goal. Skills are taught in specific sequence to foster automatic use, and students are given the rationale so they can see how the rules of the English language fit together. "There is emphasis on repetition and practice, much like in sports or in music," says Nancy Pietrefesa. "Have you ever seen how football coaches make kids practice plays over and over?"

Nancy White trains teachers to keep sessions lively. Emphasis is on the active student, self-checking and always thinking. "Nobody should just sit!" she says. "Success hinges on developing the simultaneous association of hearing, saying, seeing, and writing. Students are taught there is a system and they can use it!"

According to Eliot, it was all "fiddle faddle" until the end of the first summer, when he began to see himself improve. "He was immersed daily," says his mother, "and this intense immersion is what enabled him to see the fruits of his labors." To keep up this pace for grades 2 and 3, a creative schedule was developed with Eliot's private school. Monday through Thursday, he attended classes from 9 to 12 and was tutored at home daily for two and one half hours. He was present for a full day on Friday. Teacher Mia Russell was trained by Nancy White as an educational therapist, and her intensive tutorial work with Eliot was tailored specifically to his individual patterns and errors. After several summers of training, in the fourth-grade, Eliot worked with Mia eight hours a week in a room provided for them at his school. The sessions were reduced to three hours a week in grade 5. "The staff at the school is very cooperative," says Mia. "They see Eliot as a bright, articulate student who needs specific interventions they are not equipped to offer."

Eliot has worked hard to become an expert on how he learns, and he is eager to start sixth grade. "He has really knocked himself out," says his mom. He is an independent learner, conscious of which strategies he needs to follow to get to what he wants to know. Says Eliot, "Learning that stuff is not fun, but it works!"

—By Jean Crockett

2. motivational problems of passivity and learned helplessness by stressing self-initiative and involving them as much as possible in their own treatment

A variety of specific techniques falls under the heading of cognitive training. Here we present three techniques that are particularly useful for students with learning disabilities: self-instruction, mnemonic keyword method, and scaffolded instruction. (We discuss another cognitive training approach, the Learning Strategies Curriculum, in the section on secondary educational programming.) Keep in mind that these approaches can have a great deal of overlap.

Self-Instruction. The idea of **self-instruction** is to make students aware of the various stages of problem-solving tasks while they are performing them and to bring behavior under verbal control (Meichenbaum, 1975; Meichenbaum & Goodman, 1971). All this is usually done gradually. Typically, the teacher first models the use of the verbal routine while solving the problem. Then he or she closely supervises the stu-

self-instruction. A type of cognitive training technique that requires individuals to talk aloud and then to themselves as they solve problems.

dents using the verbal routine while doing the task, and then the students do it on their own.

One study using self-instruction as an integral feature of instruction involved fifth- and sixth-grade students with learning disabilities solving math word problems (Case, Harris, & Graham, 1992). The five-step strategy the students learned to use involved saying the problem out loud, looking for important words and circling them, drawing pictures to help explain what was happening, writing the math sentence, and writing the answer. Furthermore, students were prompted to use the following self-instructions:

1. *problem definition:* "What do I have to do?"
2. *planning:* "How can I solve this problem?"
3. *strategy use:* "The five-step strategy will help me look for important words."
4. *self-evaluation:* "How am I doing?"
5. *self-reinforcement:* "Good job. I got it right."

An example of self-instruction used for spelling involved having a boy (1) say the word out loud, (2) say the first syllable of the word, (3) name each of the letters in the syllable three times, (4) say each letter as he wrote it, and (5) repeat steps 2 through 4 for each succeeding syllable (Kosiewicz, Hallahan, Lloyd, & Graves, 1982).

Mnemonic Keyword Method. The **mnemonic keyword method** is designed to help students with memory problems remember information by presenting them with pictorial representations of abstract concepts (Mastropieri & Scruggs, 1988; Scruggs & Mastropieri, 1992). By making abstract information more concrete, students are better able to remember content in a variety of subjects, such as English, history, science, and foreign languages. For example:

> to teach that "radial symmetry" refers to structurally similar body parts that extend out from the center of organisms, such as starfish, an acoustically similar keyword, ("radio cemetery") was constructed from the unfamiliar term, radial symmetry. In the picture, radio cemetery was shown in the shape of a star, with radios as headstones, and skeletons dancing to the music from the radios. Each arm of the star is shown to be similar in appearance to each other arm, to enforce the concept. (Scruggs & Mastropieri, 1992, p. 222)

mnemonic keyword method. A cognitive training strategy used to help children with memory problems remember curriculum content; the teacher transforms abstract information into a concrete picture, which depicts the material in a more meaningful way.

scaffolded instruction. A cognitive approach to instruction in which the teacher provides temporary structure or support while students are learning a task; the support is gradually removed as the students are able to perform the task independently.

reciprocal teaching. A method in which students and teachers are involved in a dialogue to facilitate reading comprehension.

Scaffolded Instruction. In **scaffolded instruction** assistance is provided to students when they are first learning tasks and then gradually reduced, so that eventually, students do the tasks independently. This approach is supported by Russian psychologist Lev Vygotsky's theory that children learn from their elders in ways that are similar to how apprentices learn their crafts from masters. Several investigators have recommended that teachers provide this kind of temporary support to students with learning disabilities (Englert, Raphael, Anderson, Anthony, & Stevens, 1991; Palincsar, 1986).

The types of supports, or *scaffolds,* that teachers can use vary. One approach that uses scaffolded instruction is called **reciprocal teaching** because the teacher and students take turns teaching the content to one another. In this method, students (1) see cognitive strategies modeled by the teacher and (2) try out those strategies while being monitored by the teacher. The idea is for the teacher's monitoring to become less vigilant as the students become more adept at learning. Here is an example of reciprocal teaching in action:

> The adult teacher assigned a segment of the passage (usually a paragraph) to be read and either indicated that it was her turn to be the teacher or assigned one of the students to teach the segment. The adult teacher and the students then read the assigned segment silently. After reading the text, the teacher (student or adult) for that segment summarized (reviewed) the content, discussed and clarified any difficulties, asked a question that a teacher or test might ask on the segment, and finally, made a prediction about future content. All of these activities were embedded in as natural a dialogue as possible, with the teacher and other students giving feedback to one another. (Brown & Campione, 1984, p. 174)

Direct Instruction. The **Direct Instruction** method focuses specifically on the instructional process. Advocates of Direct Instruction stress a systematic analysis of the concept to be taught, rather than analysis of the characteristics of the student. A variety of Direct Instruction programs is available for reading, math, and language (Englemann, Carnine, Endlemenn, & Kelly, 1991; Englemann, Carnine, Johnson, & Meyers, 1998, 1989). These programs consist of precisely sequenced, fast-paced lessons taught to small groups of four to ten. There is a heavy emphasis on drill and practice. The teacher teaches from a well-rehearsed script, and pupils follow the lead of the teacher, who often uses hand signals to prompt participation. The teacher offers immediate corrective feedback for errors and praise for correct responses.

Direct Instruction programs are among the most well-researched commercial programs available for students with learning disabilities. Use of these programs not only results in immediate academic gains but may also bring long-term academic gains (see Lloyd, 1988, for a review of this research).

Direct Instruction. A method of teaching academics, especially reading and math; emphasizes drill and practice and immediate feedback; lessons are precisely sequenced, fast-paced, and well-rehearsed by the teacher.

Educational Methods for Attention Deficit Hyperactivity Disorders

Structure and Stimulus Reduction. William Cruickshank developed an educational program for students with learning disabilities based on earlier work with children who were mentally retarded (Strauss & Kephart, 1955; Strauss & Lehtinen,

Direct instruction programs bring both immediate and long-term academic gains in students with learning disabilities.

collaboration

a key to success

Myla Young Burgess

Laura Clark Miles

Myla Two years ago, Pat Parrot, Chesterfield County's collaborative teaching program facilitator, introduced me to collaborative teaching. She explained that collaborative teaching was an additional service delivery model that would help bridge the gap between special education and regular education.

As my students with learning disabilities experienced difficulties in mainstreaming, it became evident that I should try collaborative teaching. I began by attending a three-day workshop. My principal, Wes Hicks, attended on the day designated for administrators and teachers. After the workshop, he and I agreed we should try collaborative teaching on a small scale at the fourth-grade level.

My first step was to select a co-teacher. I learned in the workshop that co-teachers should choose to work collaboratively and should share common beliefs and goals. With my manual in hand, I excitedly called Laura to ask her to be my co-teacher. She accepted with great enthusiasm. After telling our principal that Laura and I would be co-teaching, he immediately rearranged the fourth-grade rolls so that the five students with learning disabilities we had chosen to participate in the program would all be in Laura's classroom. Having attended the workshop and believing in the philosophy of collaboration, he was more than willing to make these adjustments.

Laura Before the schoolyear started a couple of years ago, Myla called me to tell me about the collaborative teaching model. She had discussed it with our principal, and plans were underway to implement the program. I was excited by the prospect of participating in this new approach. As a classroom teacher for thirteen years, I had often felt very inadequate in meeting the needs of students with learning disabilities who were mainstreamed into my regular classroom. I was anxious to learn new strategies and techniques to meet their needs.

That September was truly a new beginning for both of us. Our class consisted of five students with learning disabilities and twenty average to above-average-ability students. We began collaborative teaching using a complementary instruction approach, which allows the general classroom teacher to maintain the primary responsibility for teaching the academic curriculum while the special educator teaches organizational and study skills that students need to master the material. As the year progressed, we moved to a team teaching approach, which is when the general educator and special educator plan and teach the academic curriculum to all students within the classroom. Under this approach, we alternated presenting segments of lessons with whomever was not teaching being responsible for monitoring student performance and/or behavior. We continued using both approaches throughout the schoolyear.

After Mr. Hicks had closely monitored our classroom the first year and reviewed the progress of all students, he was as committed to this program as we were. In planning our second year of collaborative teaching, we felt that an increase in collaboration time would better meet the needs of the upcoming fourth grade students with learning disabilities. To achieve this goal, our first priority was scheduling. Mr. Hicks played a vital role in creating the schedule and determining class size and student placement.

This class consisted of twenty-five students, including ten with learning disabilities, two with language impairment, and thirteen average to above-average-ability students. We used collaborative teaching for science/social studies, the majority of math, and 1 hour and 15 minutes of language arts. All students remained in the regular classroom all day, with the exception of four students with learning disabilities who went to a resource room during language arts. These four students were two

Myla Young Burgess is a learning disabilities specialist; B.S., Communication Disorders, Hampton University; M.E.d., University of North Carolina at Greensboro. **Laura Clark Miles** is a fourth-grade teacher; B.A., Music Education, Longwood College; Elementary certification; M.A., Educational Psychology, University of Virginia.

or more years below grade level in reading. During this year, we moved almost entirely to the team-teaching approach, with Myla stressing independent learning strategies that benefited all students in the classroom.

Myla We have found several advantages in using the collaborative teaching approach. First, there is more mastery of skills by all students. Two teachers in the classroom allow more individualized help, which enhances mastery of skills. With two teachers, we can give students more instruction, reteaching, and enrichment when needed.

It is also helpful to have two judgments on assessments, classroom objectives, and lesson presentations. For example, it is good to have two points of view regarding the appropriateness of the format and validity of written tests as well as the appropriateness of alternative assessments for students with disabilities. Sometimes our presentations are not received by students as we had expected. The second teacher can sometimes interpret from a student's point of view what went wrong with the lesson.

We gain from each other's experiences. Each of us is continually attending workshops or classes in our fields. This brings more and more ideas and resources to the classroom. We each learn from each other, and the class receives instruction based on the strengths of each of us.

Laura We also have more time to address emotional needs. Students with learning disabilities often have emotional needs that interfere with their academics. With the support of the guidance counselor, school psychologist, and teacher of students with emotional disturbance, individual needs are better met with two teachers in the classroom. For example, while one of us is teaching academics, the other is free to address emotional or attention problems that might interfere, without instruction being interrupted.

Myla Students seem to gain a sense of self-worth and confidence in their own ability by displaying strengths and improving on their weaknesses in a regular classroom environment. They also have a better sense of belonging because they are with the same students all day and have the same schedule.

Laura Collaborative teaching with flexible groups makes it possible to provide enrichment, practice, reteaching, and teaching at all levels of instruction. Flexible groups means having different groups, determined daily, based on specific instructional and social objectives for a particular day. These groups are set up for cooperative learning activities or station teaching, which is instructional content divided into two parts. Half the group is taught topics such as vocabulary expansion or comprehension. We then switch groups so that all students receive the same instruction. Because it is rare that both of us are absent on the same day, collaborative teaching allows for stability of classroom instruction. Stability of classroom instruction is also increased because there is less time wasted with students traveling to and from the resource room.

We also think that this approach facilitates modeling and the teaching of strategies. We find we draw on each other's strengths to model certain strategies. Myla, because of her training in special education, is familiar with many more strategies. For example, we teach students strategies for paragraph writing, test taking, and a variety of mnemonic strategies.

It has been our experience that this program increases the expectations for students with disabilities. Students' performances have often exceeded our initial expectations. We find it appropriate to allow students to go as far and as fast as they can. Students with learning disabilities must know that the expectations held for them are the same as those for regular students.

Collaborative teaching also lowers the pupil-teacher ratio. It is very important that the classroom size does not exceed twenty-five students. Too many students create obstacles for a successful program. We believe that students with learning disabilities should not comprise more than half the class and that at least half of the class should be average or above average in ability.

Myla I'd like to describe just one student, who is probably our greatest success story. Mary is a determined and motivated young lady who functions in the low-average range of intellectual ability with skill deficits in visual perception, nonverbal reasoning, and visual-motor integration. She has been in the learning disabilities program since kindergarten. Mary has difficulty with word recognition, word attack, reading comprehension, written language, math concepts, recalling math facts, comprehension of social studies and science concepts, and copying from the board.

Students with learning disabilities must know that the expectations held for them are the same as those for regular students.

As a fourth-grader, Mary's schedule in the morning included science/social studies, which alternated every nine weeks, and math. We taught all these collaboratively. After lunch, she went to the learning disabilities resource room for the remainder of the day for instruction in reading and written language.

We began the schoolyear with many doubts and concerns as to how and to what extent we would be able to meet Mary's needs. Most important, we did not lower our expectations for Mary's performance. Our philosophy was to improve Mary's self-esteem, increase her independence, and have her achieve the highest level of success possible.

Mary far exceeded our original expectations. We worked very closely with her parents, who were very supportive, and the combined effort contributed greatly to her success. Using all the techniques and modifications of the program allowed her to function in the regular classroom, learning the required skills and concepts.

1947). Cruickshank's approach (Cruickshank, Bentzen, Ratzeburg, & Tannhauser, 1961) included three principles:

1. structure
2. reduction of environmental stimulation
3. enhancement of intensity of teaching materials

Basically, a **structured program** is heavily teacher directed—that is, the teacher determines most of the activities for the student. The rationale for this approach is that children with attention problems cannot make their own decisions until carefully educated to do so.

Because it is assumed that children with attention problems are susceptible to distraction, irrelevant stimuli are reduced and relevant stimuli are focused upon. For instance, what the teacher wants the child to attend to is increased in intensity (often through the use of bright colors). Conversely, **stimulus reduction** is achieved by some of the following modifications:

- soundproofed walls and ceilings
- carpeting
- opaque windows
- enclosed bookcases and cupboards
- limited use of colorful bulletin boards
- use of cubicles and three-sided work areas

It is rare today to see teachers using all the components of Cruickshank's program. Most authorities now believe that a structured program may be important in the early stages of working with some students with ADHD but that these students gradually need to become more independent in their learning. Many authorities also believe that not all children with ADHD are distracted by things in their environment. For those who are distractible, however, some authorities recommend the use of such things as cubicles to reduce extraneous stimulation.

Behavior Modification. Many authorities point to behavior modification as a way of controlling inattentive behavior. The use of reinforcement (e.g., verbal praise, extra time on the computer) to increase attentive behaviors and punishment (e.g., reduced time for recess) to reduce them can have powerful effects on behavior. A good example of a behavior modification program used to increase attentive behaviors is the classic study of a disruptive first-grader named Levi (Hall, Lund, & Jackson, 1968). In this study, the teacher's attention to the student served as a reinforcer. Levi's attention increased dramatically when the teacher ignored him when he was not attending and responded to him only when he was on task.

Some teachers are hesitant to use behavior modification because they believe it is too manipulative and controlling. They also cite the difficulty of applying it in regular classrooms, where most students do not need a behavior modification program. Other teachers, especially those who work in special settings, are staunch advocates of behavior modification for students with attention problems.

Cognitive Training. Many authorities recommend cognitive training techniques as a way of getting students with attention deficit hyperactivity disorder to take control over their own behavior. These authorities believe that if students can think about their behavior more carefully, they can regulate their impulsive and inattentive behavior.

structured program. A concept largely developed by Cruickshank; emphasizes a teacher-directed approach in which activities and environment are structured for children who are distractible and hyperactive.

stimulus reduction. A concept largely developed by Cruickshank; an approach to teaching distractible and hyperactive children that emphasizes reducing extraneous (nonrelevant to learning) material.

An example of a cognitive training technique that teachers have used to help students with attention problems is self-monitoring (Hallahan, Lloyd, Kosiewicz, Kauffman, & Graves, 1979; Lloyd, Hallahan, Kosiewicz, & Kneedler, 1980). **Self-monitoring** refers to procedures that require the person to keep track of his or her behavior. In self-monitoring of attention, students monitor whether they are paying attention while engaged in academic work. The procedure is simple: The teacher places a tape recorder near the child. While the child is engaged in some kind of academic activity, a tape containing tones is played. (The time between tones varies randomly.) Whenever he or she hears a tone, the child is to stop work and ask, "Was I paying attention?" He or she then records on a separate score sheet a "yes" or "no," depending on his or her own assessment of attentional behavior.

Researchers have documented the effectiveness of self-monitoring with students ranging in age from elementary (Hallahan et al., 1979; Hallahan & Reeve, 1980; Harris, Graham, Reid, McElroy, & Hamby, 1994) to the secondary grades (Prater, Joy, Chilman, Temple, & Miller, 1991). And some investigators have shown that adding a component in which the students graph their own assessments of their on-task behavior is also effective (DiGangi, Maag, & Rutherford, 1991). One explanation for the effects of self-monitoring is that it helps students with attention problems become more aware of and in control of their own attention processes.

Medication. For years, physicians have been prescribing medication for children with attention deficit hyperactivity disorder. Although antidepressants are sometimes used, psychostimulants, such as Ritalin, are most common. In the past, the use of drugs was controversial. Critics claimed, for example, that the use of drugs represented a conspiracy of the middle class to keep the lower class docile and oppressed and that the use of these drugs in childhood led to drug abuse in the teenage years. Today, however, most authorities recognize that drugs can be a very important part of a total treatment package for many students with attention deficit hyperactivity disorder.

Research on the effectiveness of psychostimulants for helping children better attend is plentiful (see Henker & Whalen, 1989; Kauffman & Hallahan, 1979; Pelham & Murphy, 1986; Shaywitz & Shaywitz, 1987; Weiss & Hechtman, 1993 for reviews). The major organization of parents of children with attention deficit disorders, Children with Attention Deficit Disorders (Ch.A.D.D., 1992), has also endorsed the use of medication as an effective treatment approach for many persons with these disorders.

There is no doubt that medication helps many children with attention deficit hyperactivity disorder. Furthermore, now that ADHD has been recognized as occurring in adults, medication is often recommended for them, as well (Hallowell & Ratey, 1994).

Despite the effectiveness of medication in treating students with ADHD, some important cautions should be kept in mind:

- Although most children respond favorably to medication, it is not effective for a few.
- Some relatively common side effects go along with the psychostimulants (e.g., insomnia and loss of appetite).
- Parents and teachers need to monitor closely the behavior of the student while on medication. The best dosage level can sometimes be difficult to establish.
- Teachers and parents need to be careful not to give children the message that the drug is the only answer to their problems. Children should not become so dependent on the drug that they give up taking responsibility for their behavior.

self-monitoring. A type of cognitive training technique that requires individuals to keep track of their own behavior.

- These drugs are relatively powerful substances. As such, they should not be prescribed at the least hint of inattention or poor schoolwork. Physicians, parents, and teachers need to communicate effectively before making the decision to medicate a student.

With these cautions in mind, medication can be an indispensable aspect of treatment for many students with attention deficit hyperactivity disorder.

Service Delivery Models

Although students with learning disabilities sometimes attend residential programs or special classes, the resource room is the most common form of service delivery. Because students with learning disabilities, as usually defined, have at least near-average intelligence and may have deficits in only a few areas of academic achievement, they are often seen as good candidates for such placement. The amount of time an individual student spends in the resource room varies considerably, depending on his or her characteristics and the philosophy of the particular school. Some students may spend an hour or two per day in a resource room, whereas others may receive special services only an hour or two per week.

As we discussed in Chapter 2, more and more schools are moving toward some kind of cooperative teaching arrangement, in which regular and special education teachers work together in the regular classroom. Some believe this model is particularly appropriate for students with learning disabilities, since it allows them to stay in the regular classroom for all or almost all of their instruction.

Because students with learning disabilities are the largest category of special education and because their academic and behavioral problems are not as severe as those of students with mental retardation or behavior disorders, they are often candidates for full inclusion. However, all the major professional and parent organizations have developed position papers against placing all students with learning disabilities in full-inclusion settings. The following excerpt is from a position paper of the Learning Disabilities Association of America, the major organization for parents of children with learning disabilities:

> The Learning Disabilities Association of America does not support "full inclusion" or any policies that mandate the same placement, instruction, or treatment for ALL students with learning disabilities. Many students with learning disabilities benefit from being served in the regular education classroom. However, the regular education classroom is not the appropriate placement for a number of students with learning disabilities who may need alternative instructional environments, teaching strategies, and/or materials that cannot or will not be provided within the context of a regular classroom placement. (Learning Disabilities Association of America, 1993)

EARLY INTERVENTION

Very little preschool programming is available for children with learning disabilities because of the difficulties in identifying them at such a young age. When we talk about testing preschool children for learning disabilities, we are really talking about *prediction,* rather than *identification* (Keogh & Glover, 1980). In other words, because preschool children do not ordinarily engage in academics, it is not possible, strictly speaking, to say that they are "behind" academically. Unfortunately, all other things being equal, prediction is always less precise than identification.

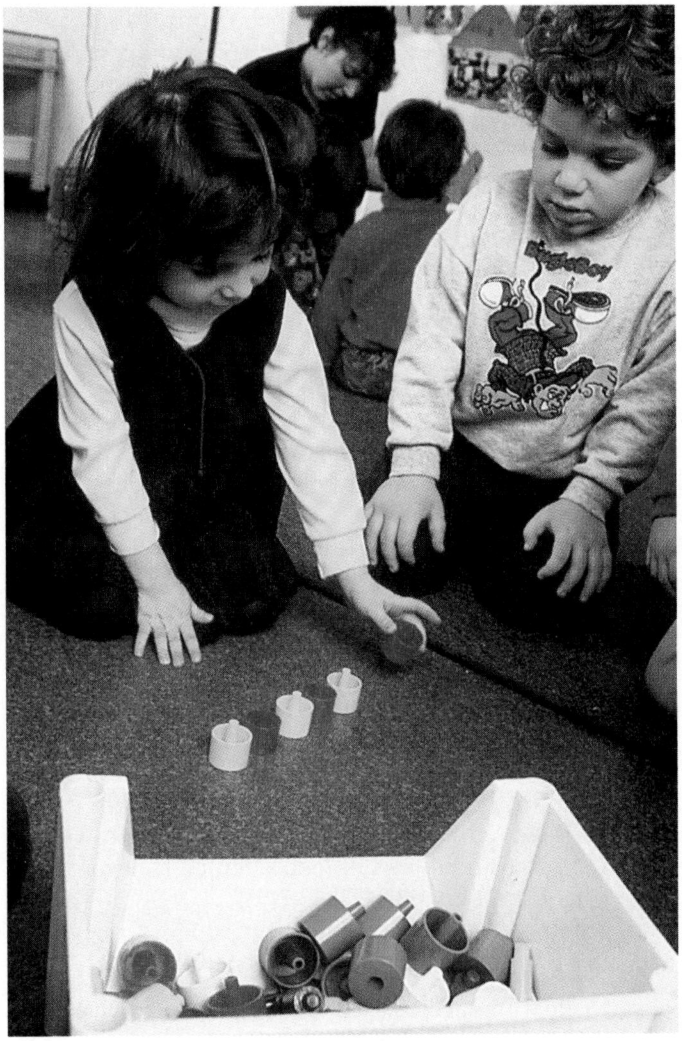

The most accurate predictors of academic problems are preacademic skills, such as counting and identifying of letters, numbers, shapes, and colors.

At least two factors make predicting later learning disabilities particularly difficult at the preschool age:

1. In many cases of learning disabilities, the problems are relatively mild. Many of these children seem bright and competent until faced with a particular academic task, such as reading or spelling. Unlike many other children with disabilities, children with learning disabilities are not so immediately identifiable.
2. It is often difficult to determine what is a true developmental delay and what is merely maturational slowness. Many nondisabled children show slow developmental progress at this young age, but they soon catch up with their peers.

There has been growing sentiment among some professionals not to use the "learning disability" label with preschoolers (Haring et al., 1992). Noting that this label implies deficits in academics, which are not ordinarily introduced until kindergarten or first grade, these professionals favor using more generic labels for preschool children such as "developmentally delayed" or "at risk." Those who favor using the "learning disability" label argue that the sooner a child's specific problems can be identified, the sooner teachers and parents can make plans for the long-term nature of the condition.

To aid parents and professionals, research is needed on developing better predictive tests at the preschool level. At present, we know that the most accurate predictors are preacademic skills (Mercer, Algozzine, & Trifiletti, 1979). **Preacademic skills** are behaviors that are needed before formal instruction can begin, such as identification of letters, numbers, shapes, and colors.

TRANSITION

Until the late 1970s and early 1980s, relatively little educational programming for students with learning disabilities extended beyond the elementary school years. This attitude of benign neglect probably emanated from the mistaken impression that children with learning disabilities would outgrow them. Although the long-term prognosis for individuals with learning disabilities is generally more positive than that for children with some other disabilities (e.g., behavior disorders), there is still the potential for difficulty. There is a danger, for example, that students with learning disabilities will drop out of school in their teenage years. Also, some run the risk of engaging in delinquent behaviors.

The majority of students with learning disabilities do not engage in delinquent behaviors and or drop out of school. Nonetheless, their futures can be uncertain. Many adults with learning disabilities have persistent problems in learning, socializing, holding jobs, and living independently (Gerber & Reiff, 1991; Gerber, Ginsberg, & Reiff, 1992; Haring, Lovett, & Smith, 1990; Kavale, 1988; Reiff & Gerber, 1992; Spekman, Goldberg, & Herman, 1992; White, 1992). And even those individuals who are relatively successful in their transition to adulthood often must devote considerable energy to coping with daily living situations.

For example, in an intensive study of adults with learning disabilities, one of the subjects (S3), an assistant dean of students at a large urban university, found it

> essential that organization and routines remain constant. For example, she recounted that her kitchen is arranged in a specific fashion. Most implements are visible rather than put away because she would not be able to remember where to find them. Once, when her roommate changed the kitchen setup, S3 had great difficulty finding anything, and when she did, she couldn't remember where to return it. She had to reorganize the kitchen to her original plan. When she moved from her home state to the New Orleans area, she kept her kitchen set up in exactly the same way as previously. "I don't know if that's just because I'm stubborn or because it's comfortable."
>
> The need for organization and structure seems to pervade her daily living. She mentioned that she imposes structure on everything from the arrangement of her medicine cabinet to her professional life. She has her work day carefully organized and keeps close track of all her appointments. She has trouble coping with unannounced appointments, meetings or activities. She said that if her work routine is interrupted in such a fashion, "I can't get it together." (Gerber & Reiff, 1991, p. 113)

preacademic skills. Behaviors that are needed before formal academic instruction can begin (e.g., ability to identify letters, numbers, shapes, and colors).

Factors Related to Successful Transition

How any particular adult with learning disabilities will fare depends on a variety of factors and is difficult to predict. Several researchers have been addressing the topic of what contributes to successful adjustment of adults with learning disabilities (Gerber

Recognition of the prevalence of learning disabilities among adults has led to reexamination of the possible reasons for dissatisfaction or difficulties with work and other areas of life.

& Reiff, 1991; Gerber et al., 1992; Kavale, 1988; Murphy, 1992; Reiff & Gerber, 1992; Spekman et al., 1992). Their results have consistently pointed to at least five factors that distinguish individuals who are successful from those who are not:

1. Perhaps most important, those who succeed have shown an extraordinary degree of perseverance. The following quotes from successful adults with learning disabilities are typical:

   "I've always had a kind of burning feeling . . . kind of like being on fire to be successful."

   "You fight until you can't fight anymore, and then you fight some more . . . you take the hurt and turn it inward and it becomes part of the burn . . . it has to burn."

   "If the fires of your drive go out, you will lose your self-respect." (Gerber et al., 1992, p. 480)

2. Successful adults with learning disabilities set goals for themselves. As one highly successful individual explained, "'Successful people have a plan. You have to have a plan, goals, strategy; otherwise you are flying through the clouds and then you hit the mountain'" (Gerber et al., 1992, p. 480).
3. Successful individuals have a realistic acceptance of their weaknesses coupled with an attitude of building on their strengths. They do not wallow in self-pity. As one team of researchers concluded, "They seemed to compartmentalize their learning disability and saw it as only one aspect of their identity rather than define themselves entirely by it" (Spekman et al., 1992, p. 167). And one way some of them build on their strengths is by selecting occupations that match their abilities and minimize their difficulties.
4. Those who succeed tend to have access to a strong informal network of social support. They have been able to draw on help from parents, husbands, friends, and so forth at various stages during and after transition to adulthood.

5. Adults with learning disabilities are more likely to succeed if they have had intensive and long-term educational intervention (Kavale, 1988). Fortunately, numerous secondary programs are now available for students with learning disabilities, and there has been a blossoming of programs at the college level.

Secondary Programming

Approaches to educating students with learning disabilities at the secondary level differ, depending on whether the goal is to prepare students for college or work. With this in mind, Zigmond (1990) has developed two models, both of which contain four components: (1) instruction in basic skills, (2) instruction in survival skills, (3) completion of courses required for graduation, and (4) planning for life after high school. The models differ according to the amount and type of instruction delivered by general education versus special education teachers. In the college-bound model, for instance, students receive instruction in content areas (e.g., math, science, foreign language) from general education teachers, and special education teachers consult with these teachers and provide instruction in English/reading courses, survival skills classes, and supervised study halls. In the work-bound model, special educators teach survival skills classes as well as virtually all the content-area courses. In addition, students attend four years of vocational education classes.

Regardless of whether the student is planning to attend college or get a job, the curriculum often needs to be modified in order to meet the learning-strategy deficits discussed earlier (see pp. 180–181). One such example is the Learning Strategies Curriculum.

Learning Strategies Curriculum. The idea behind the Learning Strategies Curriculum is that before adolescents with learning disabilities can be expected to master specific subject content, they need to be taught strategies that will help them learn how to learn (Deshler & Schumaker, 1986; Ellis, Deshler, & Schumaker, 1989).

Accordingly, the organization of the Learning Strategies Curriculum is determined by the major demands of the secondary curriculum. It therefore comprises three strands. One is devoted to helping students acquire information from written materials. A second strand helps students remember important information and facts. A third strand helps students improve written expression, complete assignments on time, and take tests.

Multipass is an example of one set of the strategies used in strand 1, designed for getting information from written materials (Schumaker, Deshler, Alley, Warner, & Denton, 1982). Based on the SQ3R reading method (Robinson, 1946), Multipass has the student make many "passes" (hence the name) through the reading material. The three major passes are the Survey, the Size-Up, and the Sort-Out. These three passes are embedded in a context of highly individualized programming and a heavy reliance on ensuring that the student achieves certain performance goals before moving on to the next stage. Here is a description of Multipass:

> The purpose of the Survey Pass was to familiarize the student with main ideas and organization of the chapter. Thus, this previewing pass required the student to: (a) read the chapter title, (b) read the introductory paragraph, (c) review the chapter's relationship to other adjacent chapters by perusing the table of contents, (d) read the major subtitles of the chapter and notice how the chapter is organized, (e) look at illustrations and read their captions, (f) read the summary paragraph, and (g) paraphrase all the information gained in the process.

The Size-Up Pass was designed to help students gain specific information and facts from a chapter without reading it from beginning to end. This pass required the student to first read each of the questions at the end of the chapter to determine what facts appeared to be the most important to learn. If the student was already able to answer a given question as a result of the Survey Pass, a check mark (√) was placed next to the question. The student now progressed through the entire chapter following these steps: (a) look for a textual cue (e.g., bold-face print, subtitle, colored print, italics); (b) make the cue into a question (e.g., if the cue was the italicized vocabulary word *conqueror,* the student asked, "What does conqueror mean?"; if the cue was the subtitle "The Election of 1848," the student might ask, "Who won the election of 1848?" or "Why was the election of 1848 important?"; (c) skim through the surrounding text to find the answer to the question; and (d) paraphrase the answer to yourself without looking in the book. When the student reached the end of the chapter using these four steps for each textual cue, he/she was required to paraphrase all the facts and ideas he/she could remember about the chapter.

The Sort-Out Pass was included to get students to test themselves over the material presented in the chapter. In this final pass, the student read and answered each question at the end of the chapter. If the student could answer a question immediately, he/she placed a checkmark next to it. If the student was unable to answer a question, however, the answer was sought by (a) thinking in which section of the chapter the answer would most likely be located, (b) skimming through that section for the answer, (c) if the answer was not located, thinking of another relevant section, and (d) skimming that section, and so on until the student could answer the question. A checkmark was then placed next to the question, and the student moved on to answer the next question. (Schumaker et al., 1982, pp. 298–299)*

Postsecondary Programming. Postsecondary programs include vocational and technical programs as well as community colleges and four-year colleges and universities. More and more individuals with learning disabilities are enrolling in colleges and universities, and more and more universities are establishing special programs and services for these students. One of the major difficulties students with learning disabilities face in the transition from high school to college is the decrease in the amount of guidance provided by adults (Siperstein, 1988). Many students find this greater emphasis on self-discipline particularly difficult. The greater demands on writing skills (Gajar, 1989) and note taking also present major problems for many college students with learning disabilities.

For many LD [learning-disabled] adults, the task of taking notes in lectures is overwhelming, nor is it any wonder. Note-taking requires simultaneous listening, comprehending, and synthesizing and/or extracting main ideas while retaining them long enough to formulate a synopsis and write it down. The writing act, in turn, requires automaticity and speed in letter formation and sufficient legibility and spelling ability to decipher what has been written at a later time. (Vogel, 1987, p. 523)

Siperstein (1988), believing in a long-range view of programming for college-bound students with learning disabilities, has conceptualized service delivery as consisting of three transitions: (1) high school to college, (2) during college, and (3) college to employment.

During the first stage, high school to college, a major goal is to foster awareness of what college options are available. Because of their frequent experiences with fail-

* From "Multipass: A Learning Strategy for Improving Reading Comprehension," by J. B. Schumaker et al., 1982, *Learning Disability Quarterly,* 5(3), 295–304. Reprinted with permission.

Table 5–1
Examples of Common Adjustments for College Students with Learning Disabilities

1	**Adjustments in Course Requirements and Evaluation** ▪ Giving extra time on exams ▪ Allowing students to take exams in distraction-free rooms ▪ Allowing students to take exams in different formats (e.g., substituting an oral exam for a written one)
2	**Modifications in Program Requirements** ▪ Waiving or substituting certain requirements (e.g., foreign language requirements) ▪ Allowing students to take a lighter academic load each semester
3	**Auxiliary Aids** ▪ Providing tape recordings of textbooks ▪ Providing access to a Kurzweil Reading Machine (a computer that scans text and converts it into auditory output) ▪ Recruiting and assigning "note takers" for lectures

Source: From *Introduction to learning disabilities,* by D. P. Hallahan, J. M. Kauffman, & J. W. Lloyd, 1996. Boston: Allyn & Bacon. Copyright © 1996 by Allyn & Bacon. Reprinted with permission.

ure, many students with learning disabilities do not aspire to education beyond high school. The emphasis should be preparing students to make the right choices of colleges as well as on delineating what accommodations they will need in their programs. Parents and students need to consider the unique characteristics of the individual as well as those of different colleges and their programs in matching him or her with the appropriate institution (McGuire & Shaw, 1987). During this stage, pupils and their families may take advantage of published guides to college programs for students with learning disabilities (Kravets & Wax, 1993; Slovak, 1995; Straughn, 1988; Thomas & Thomas, 1991). Also students can be made aware of the special accommodations available for students who are learning disabled when they take the Scholastic Aptitude Test (SAT) and the American College Test (ACT).

The second stage of service delivery, which covers the time during college, focuses on enhancing the chances of successfully earning a degree. It includes support services for both academic and social functioning. Section 504 of the Vocational Rehabilitation Act of 1973 (Public Law 93–112) requires that colleges make reasonable accommodations for students with disabilities so that they will not be discriminated against because of their disabilities. These accommodations are of three general types: (1) the ways in which specific courses are taught, (2) use of auxiliary aids, and (3) modifications in program requirements (Brinckerhoff, Shaw, & McGuire, 1992). Table 5–1 lists some relatively common adjustments made for college students with learning disabilities.

Another important programming resource at this second stage is other college students who are learning disabled. Third- and fourth-year students with learning disabilities can help establish peer-support systems. Furthermore, some have recommended helping students with learning disabilities become self-advocates. Helping these students become aware of their own strengths and weaknesses and able to explain them to instructors can prove helpful (Roffman, Herzog, & Wershba-Gershon, 1994).

The third stage, transition from college to employment, is important because even if they survive the rigors of college, many individuals with learning disabilities have difficulties obtaining appropriate employment in the competitive job market. Possible strategies for accomplishing this are workshops for career awareness, job-search strategies, and job-maintenance skills (Siperstein, 1988).

There is little doubt that much remains to be learned about programming effectively for students with learning disabilities at the postsecondary level. However, the field has made great strides in opening windows of opportunity for these young adults. Authorities have noted that many college applicants with learning disabilities attempt to hide their disabilities for fear they will not be admitted (Shaywitz & Shaw, 1988). If the burgeoning interest in postsecondary programming for individuals who are learning disabled continues, we may in the near future see the day when students and colleges routinely collaborate to use information concerning students' learning disabilities in planning their programs.

Suggestions for Teaching
Students with Learning Disabilities in General Education Classrooms

By E. Jane Nowacek

WHAT TO LOOK FOR IN SCHOOL

All persons with learning disabilities, by definition, have near-average, average, or above-average intelligence. Although they may learn some academic skills easily, they acquire other skills with difficulty. In addition to underachievement in some school subjects, these students exhibit other behaviors that may help you identify them in your classrooms.

In primary grades, they may appear to be delayed in language, motor, and readiness skills. They may experience general coordination problems or have difficulties with specific fine motor skills, such as lacing shoes, cutting with scissors, and writing. Their use of language also may lag behind that of their classmates. They may speak in an immature or "babyish" way and have difficulty expressing themselves in conversation and group discussions. Sometimes children with learning disabilities do not demonstrate reading-readiness skills, such as right-left and up-down orientations, spatial relationships, and eye-hand coordination.

In intermediate grades, students with learning disabilities may have difficulty following directions. They may have problems reading written materials and understanding abstract concepts and inferences. In addition, they may be ineffective learners who do not know how to plan their work or approach problems.

Some students with learning disabilities in middle and high school may appear to be unmotivated. They seem to need extra prodding to work independently in class and to complete homework assignments. In addition, acting before thinking may result in their turning in "careless," incomplete papers, and getting in trouble for interacting impulsively with other students. Individuals with learning disabilities also may be disorganized. They often lose or misplace books, pencils, and homework. Furthermore, they may be easily frustrated with tasks that are too difficult and mask this problem by saying they "had better things to do" or "didn't feel like it." The social problems that many of these students experience at all ages may be increasingly apparent as they mature. Frequently, they misread social situations and say and do wrong things unknowingly.

The wide range of academic and social problems persons with learning disabilities experience complicates identification. You can be instrumental in helping to identify students with learning disabilities by collecting achievement information, by recording observations of their social-emotional behaviors, and by sharing this information with the special education teacher or counselor in your school. In fact, classroom teachers usually are the first to recognize signs of learning disabilities and to refer students to child-study teams.

HOW TO GATHER INFORMATION

You can use a variety of materials and procedures to gather information about your student's achievement. Reading a student's cumulative folder provides information about past school performance that may indicate whether the problems you are observing are new or part of a pattern exhibited across several grades. This folder also contains attendance and retention data and group achievement test results that provide a comparison of your student's achievement with that of other students of the same grade. Talking with former teachers may provide additional information about your student's ability to meet regular class demands, necessary instructional modifications, and his or her social adjustment.

To gather current information, you can conduct any of several informal assessment procedures, such as informal inventories (p. 173), criterion-referenced tests (p. 174), and curriculum-based assessments (p. 174). You also may analyze samples of your student's work for error patterns and inconsistent use of skills. These practices also may help you pinpoint modifications that will promote student learning.

Once you have determined your student's learning strengths and needs through informal assessment, consider the characteristics of your classroom. Surveying the ecology of the classroom may help you determine the influence that the instructional environment has on students' learning and behavior. Wood (in press) recommends analyzing environmental characteristics such as the type of instruction presented (e.g., lecture, self-directed study, group work); class procedures used (e.g., reading aloud, lab work, student presentations); and evaluation practices employed (e.g., timed multiple-choice, fill-in-the-blank, or essay tests). When you have completed this assessment of your classroom's ecology, look for areas in which there is a mismatch between the expectations and requirements of the class and the abilities, knowledge, and skills of your students. For example, suppose one of these expectations is that students will complete assignments independently in class, and you discover that Jack, a student with learning disabilities, does not know how to plan his work, manage his time, or monitor his own progress. You will have identified an area of mismatch. For students like Jack, who are not able to meet classroom expectations, individualizing and modifying may provide the support they need to be successful. (Specific procedures for assessing the ecology of your classroom are available in Fuchs, Fernstrom, Scott, Fuchs, & Vandermeer, 1994; Welch, 1994; Wood, in press; and Ysseldyke, Christenson, & Kovaleski, 1994.)

TEACHING TECHNIQUES TO TRY

One of the most effective approaches to individualizing instruction for students with learning disabilities is to present them with the strategies they have not learned—strategies that nondisabled students seem to learn without specific instruction. Research indicates that strategic learners know many strategies as well as when to use them (Jones, Palincsar, Ogle, & Carr, 1987). For example, they use contextual and graphic clues to understand words and ideas they do not grasp immediately, or they may reread and question. Strategic learners know the purpose of their study and summarize and integrate information with that purpose in mind. In contrast, many individuals with learning disabilities do not have a repertoire of strategies and/or do not understand how to use strategies flexibly.

Learning to Learn Strategies

Two of the most common difficulties students with learning disabilities face are (1) not knowing how to plan, monitor, and check their performance and (2) being unable to remediate the problems they experience in learning. Several strategies have been created to teach these metacognitive processes. For example, TARGETS (Ellis & Lenz, 1987) is a problem-solving strategy that incorporates a first-letter mnemonic to help students recall each of the seven steps:

T = **Task** specified in a question
A = **Answer** question
R = **Review** past performance
G = **Goal** written
E = **Enter** planned behaviors
T = **Try** planned behaviors
S = **Step** evaluated

One student used this strategy to help him solve the problem of not completing his homework. He completed the following plan using TARGETS:

T = How can I finish my homework?
A = I can do it as soon as I get home, before I watch TV or go out with my friends.
R = I wait until late at night and don't have enough time to do my homework, and I don't know how to do some of it.
G = I will finish my homework.
E = I will do my homework before I watch TV or see my friends, and I will ask my study buddy if I can call him for help when I don't understand my homework.
T = I tried my plan.
S = It worked. The only problem was that when I called my study buddy, he was not home.

To help students complete independent assignments during class, Archer (cited in Salend, 1994) developed the following procedure:

Plan it.
Read the directions and circle the words that tell you what to do.
Get out the material you need.
Tell yourself what to do.

Complete it.
Do all items.
If you can't do an item, go ahead or ask for help.
Use HOW (see below).

Check it.
Did you do everything?
Did you get the right answer?
Did you proofread?

Turn it in.

This procedure assists students in monitoring their own performances by providing prompts for specific actions. In order to help students recall all the steps in this procedure, you may suggest that each student write the steps on an index card, which he or she then tapes to the inside of a notebook or individual assignment folder.

HOW is a procedure that specifies the formats of assignments that students turn in to teachers. It outlines how students' papers should look. For example, a teacher may request that students format their papers as follows:

H = Heading	O = Organized	W = Written neatly
1. Name	1. Write on the front side only.	1. Write on the lines.
2. Date	2. Leave one blank line at the top.	2. Make neat erasures.
3. Subject	3. Leave one blank line at the bottom.	3. Do not cross out anything.

Teachers can adapt this procedure to include the specific information and structures they prefer.

As discussed earlier in the chapter (p. 190), self-monitoring strategies provide students with new ways of thinking about their performance and reinforce the idea that students control their own behavior. Rankin and Reid (1995) point out that self-monitoring has focused on two primary areas with students with mild disabilities: on-task behavior and academic responding. To help teachers implement self-monitoring of academic responses, these educators describe the steps used in self-monitoring and illustrate activities within each step that Ms. M., a teacher in a mainstreamed classroom, provided for a fifth-grade student with learning disabilities known as HB:

1. *Select the behavior.* Begin by selecting a behavior that is specific, observable, and appropriate to the student's cognitive and developmental levels and to the classroom setting. Ms. M. was concerned with the high percentage of errors HB made on his math assignments because he seemed to rush through the problems. She selected accuracy of math performance as an appropriate behavior for HB to self-monitor.
2. *Collect baseline data.* To have both an objective measure of the extent of the problem and a point of comparison from which to assess the effectiveness of this strategy, Ms. M. gathered information about the accuracy of HB's math computation. Five days prior to introducing self-monitoring, she collected and scored HB's math assignments. The average for this period was 12.6 problems correct of the 20 problems assigned each day.
3. *Obtain willing cooperation from the student.* Because the student will be responsible for monitoring, he or she must "buy into" the procedure. To "sell" self-monitoring, Ms. M. emphasized outcomes that would be meaningful to HB: reducing the number of problems he would have to correct, thereby increasing the time he would have to spend playing the sports he enjoyed.
4. *Instruct the student in the procedure.* Training involves defining precisely the selected behavior for the student, teaching the specific steps in the procedure, and teaching the student how to record his or her behavior. HB was taught these steps:
   (1) Work the problem.
   (2) Ask myself, Do I think my answer is correct?
   (3) Check for accuracy.
   (4) Mark the square on the tally sheet with an X.
   (5) Make corrections, if necessary.
   (6) Continue until all the problems have been worked.
   (7) Count the number of Xs and write the number by the day's total.
   (8) Graph the number.

   Ms. M. taught HB to record his behavior on a self-monitoring form. He was instructed to record an X each time he checked a math problem for accuracy; to count the Xs at the end of math period and write the number in the box labeled "Total"; and then to graph the daily total on a separate form entitled "Problems Checked for Accuracy."
5. *Have the student independently perform the self-monitoring procedure.* Ms. M. placed the strategy steps and a self-monitoring form inside HB's math folder, and for the first few days, she monitored his accuracy closely. She also put the answer key for the day's math problems in a folder on the work table near her desk, so that HB would have access to it to check the accuracy of his problems. As Ms. M. circulated around the classroom, monitoring students' progress in math, she also checked to see that HB was using the self-monitoring form and graphing the results. She provided prompts as needed. With these supports, HB was able to self-monitor and to improve his percentage of correct responses.
6. *Evaluate the effectiveness of the intervention.* After HB began to self-monitor independently, Ms. M. collected samples of his math assignments, as she had done during baseline collection. She compared the average number correct after self monitoring with that before self-monitoring. She found that HB had completed 17.4, 14.9, and 18.1 problems correct during the three weeks he had used self-monitoring, which represented an improvement over the 12.6 problems correct during baseline.

In HB's case Ms. M. used self-monitoring to improve the quality of his performance. Self-monitoring also has been used to increase the quantity of work completed.

Academic Strategies

Students with learning disabilities also need to learn strategies in academic areas. Note that most of the following strategies include components designed to teach specific skills and the metacognitive procedures students need to use them successfully.

Reading Comprehension

To facilitate students' understanding of text, educators have developed several strategies that promote learning by activating students' prior knowledge, establishing a purpose for reading, directing attention to important features of the text and vocabulary, and checking for problems in comprehension. One such strategy, Think-Aloud (Davey, 1983), teaches students to think of questions that help them monitor their understanding while they read by observing a good reader (e.g., teacher) verbalize the strategies he or she uses. The process a teacher models in Think-Aloud sessions includes the following self-questioning strategies (Wisconsin Department of Public Instruction, 1989):

Before Reading

"Before I read I ask myself several questions": Why am I reading this selection (purposes)? What will I do with this information? What do I know already about this topic? What do I think I'll learn about this topic?" (predictions)

During Reading

"As I read I ask myself: Am I understanding? Does this make sense to me? Is this what I expected? What parts are similar to and different from my predictions?"

After Reading

"When I finish reading, I wonder: What were the most important points? Which part of the text support them? How do I feel about this information?" What new information did I learn and how does it fit with what I already know? Do I need to go back and reread part so I can understand better?" (p. 158)

After every self-question the teacher poses he or she talks through his or her answers aloud. Consequently, Think-Alouds model not only the strategy of self-questioning but also the thought processes used to monitor and regulate comprehension. (For specific explanations of other strategies and sample lesson plans, see *Strategic Learning in the Content Areas,* available from the Wisconsin Department of Public Instruction, 125 South Webster Street, P.O. Box 7841, Madison, WI 53707-7841.)

Composition

Many students with learning disabilities do not know how to approach the process of writing, and many experience difficulties completing the work required at various stages in the process. The POWER strategy assists them in using the steps in the writing process (Englert, Raphael, Anderson, Anthony, & Stevens, 1991):

P = **Plan**
O = **Organize**
W = **Write**
E = **Edit/Editor**
R = **Revise**

Bos and Vaughn (1994) point out techniques teachers can use during each step in this strategy. For example, these authors suggest that during the planning or prewriting stage, teachers should encourage students to select the topics they will write about by asking them to brainstorm topics they know and would like to share with others. In addition, teachers may present various types of writing, including stories, factual accounts, personal observations, and so on.

Once each student has decided on a topic, the teacher models by Thinking-Aloud, the processes he or she used to organize the ideas he or she wants to present. In Thinking-Aloud, the teacher might use a brainstorming sheet that provides prompts that help organize ideas (i.e., Name; Date; Working Title; Setting: Where, When, Who, Action, and Ending). The brainstorming sheet can be formatted as an outline or web, and students can select the form they prefer. As students write, the teacher should encourage them to share their work with him or her, with individual peers, and with small groups.

Some teachers establish an Author's Chair as a formal means of sharing writing. When a student sits in the Author's Chair, he or she reads the writing and then other students comment or ask questions about the work. To structure the feedback students give to the "author," teachers often establish guidelines, such as:

Raise your hand so the author can call on students one at a time.
Comment on what you like about the work.
Tell what you would like more information about.
Ask questions about what you do not understand.

Following feedback, students begin to edit and revise, which are especially difficult processes for many students with learning disabilities. Bos and Vaughn (1994) remind teachers that it is important to focus on the *content* during revision and to work on *mechanics* during editing. Once students are satisfied with the content of the writing, teachers often pair them with another student who serves as "editor." Students may be expected to circle words they do not know how to spell, put boxes in spots where they think some punctuation mark should be, and underline sentences in which the language may not be correct. Writers are expected to correct known errors, (i.e, those they have identified), but not all errors.

Arithmetic

Research indicates that many students with learning disabilities not only experience problems in reading and written expression but also in mathematics. These difficulties begin early in school and continue throughout high school (Mercer & Miller, 1992). In Table 5–2, Rivera and Bryant (1992) outline several techniques teachers can use to assist students at each stage of learning.

HELPFUL RESOURCES

School Personnel

Several people in your school system can help you identify and manage the special education students in your classroom. The resource teacher or consultant has information about learning and behavior problems that you may find helpful. This teacher also may be able to suggest specific materials, additional learning strategies, and methods that will help your students learn. If the resource teacher also teaches your mainstreamed students, arrange regularly scheduled meetings with him or her. These meetings may facilitate planning, coordination of the instructional programs you both are implementing, and the exchange of information about your students' progress

Instructional Methods

Bender, W. N. (Ed.). (1993). *Learning disabilities: Best practices for professionals.* Boston: Andover Medical.

Bley, N. S., & Thornton, C. A. (1994). *Teaching mathematics to students with learning disabilities.* Austin, TX: Pro-Ed.

Block, C. C. (1993). Strategy instruction in a literature-based reading program. *Elementary School Journal, 94,* 139–151.

Bos, C. S., & Vaughn, S. (1994). *Strategies for teaching students with learning and behavior problems* (3rd ed.). Boston: Allyn and Bacon.

Bulgren, J. A., & Carta, J. J. (1992). Examining the instructional contexts of students with learning disabilities. *Exceptional Children, 59,* 182–191.

Cook, R. E., Tessier, A., & Klein, M. P. (1992). *Adapting early childhood curricula for children with special needs* (3rd ed.). New York: Macmillan.

Decker, K., Spector, S., & Shaw, S. (1992). Teaching study skills to students with mild handicaps: The role of the classroom teacher. *Clearinghouse, 65,* 280–284.

Deschler, D., Ellis, E., & Lenz, K. (1995). *Teaching adolescents with learning disabilities: Strategies and methods* (2nd ed.). Denver: Love.

Dowdy, C., Patton, J. R., Smith, T. E. C., & Polloway, E. A. (1995). *Attention deficit hyperactivity disorder in the classroom.* Austin, TX: Pro-Ed.

Ellett, L. (1993). Instructional practices in mainstreamed secondary classrooms. *Journal of Learning disabilities, 26,* 57–64.

Fister, S., & Kemp, K. (1993). Translating research: Classroom application of validated instructional strategies. In R. C. Eaves & P. J. McLaughlin, (Eds.), *Recent advances in special education and rehabilitation* (pp.107–126). Boston: Andover Medical.

Gajar, A., Goodman, L., & McAfee, J. (1993). *Secondary schools and beyond: Transition of individuals with mild disabilities.* New York: Merrill.

Hammill, D. D., & Bartel, N. R. (1995). *Teaching students with learning and behavior problems* (6th ed.). Boston: Allyn and Bacon.

Hoover, J. J., & Patton, J. R. (1995). *Teaching students with learning problems to use study skills.* Austin, TX: Pro-Ed.

Howell, K. W., Fox, S. L., & Morehead, M. K. (1993). *Curriculum-based evaluation* (2nd ed.). Pacific Grove, CA: Brooks/Cole.

Hubbard, J. J. (1990). *Using study skills and learning strategies in the classroom: A teacher's handbook.* Boulder, CO: Hamilton.

Keefe, C. H., & Keefe, D. R. (1993). Instruction for students with learning disabilities: A whole language model. *Intervention in School and Clinic, 28,* 172–177.

Lerner, J. W., Lowenthal, B., & Lerner, S. R. (1995). *Attention deficit disorders: Assessment and teaching.* Pacific Grove, CA: Brooks/Cole.

Lewis, M. E. H. (1995). *Thematic methods and strategies in learning disabilities.* San Antonio, TX: Psychological Corporation.

Lovitt, T. C. (1995). *Tactics for teaching* (2nd ed.) Englewood Cliffs, NJ: Merrill.

Masters, L. F., Mori, B. A., & Mori, A. A. (1993). *Teaching secondary students with mild disabilities and behavior problems: Methods, materials, and strategies.* Austin, TX: Pro-Ed.

Mastropieri, M. A., & Scruggs, T.E. (1994). *Effective instruction for special education* (2nd ed.). Austin, TX: Pro-Ed.

Meese, R. L. (1992). Adapting textbooks for children with learning disabilities in mainstreamed classes. *Teaching Exceptional Children, 24,* 49–51.

Mercer, C. D., & Mercer, A. R. (1993). *Teaching students with learning problems* (4th ed.). New York: Merrill.

Meltzer, L. J. (Ed.). (1993). *Strategy assessment and instruction: From theory to practice.* Austin, TX: Pro-Ed.

Miles, D. D., & Forcht, J. P. (1995). Mathematics strategies for secondary students with learning disabilities or mathematics deficiencies: A cognitive approach. *Intervention in School and Clinic, 31,* 91–96.

Miller, S. P., & Mercer, C.D. (1993). Mnemonics: Enhancing the math performance of students with learning disabilities. *Intervention in School and Clinic, 29,* 78–82.

Table 5–2
Examples of Instructional Techniques for the Stages of Learning

Acquisition	▪ Modeling ▪ "Thinking aloud" ▪ Practice opportunities ▪ Manipulatives	▪ Peer tutoring ▪ Corrective feedback ▪ Reinforcement
Proficiency	▪ Novel practice opportunities ▪ Peer tutoring ▪ Timings	▪ Error drill ▪ Reinforcement
Maintenance	▪ Practice opportunities ▪ Learning centers	▪ Seat work ▪ Cooperative learning
Generalization	▪ Instructional games ▪ Learning centers ▪ Cue cards	▪ Reinforcement ▪ Self-monitoring checklist
Adaptation	▪ Problem-solving situations ▪ Cooperative learning ▪ Thematic units	▪ Daily living skills ▪ Learning centers

Source: From "Mathematics Instruction for Students with Special Needs," by D. M. Rivera & B. R. Bryant, 1992. *Interviews in Schools and Clinics, 28,* 71–86. Reprinted with permission of Pro-Ed.

Olson, J., & Platt, J. (1992). *Teaching children and adolescents with special needs.* New York: Merrill.

Polloway, E. A., & Patton, J. R. (in press). *Strategies for teaching learners with special needs* (6th ed.) Englewood Cliffs, NJ: Merrill.

Polloway, E. A., & Smith, T. E. C. (1992). *Language instruction for students with disabilities* (2nd ed.). Denver: Love.

Prater, M. A. (1994). Improving academic and behavior skills through self-management procedures. *Preventing School Failure, 38,* 5–9.

Pressley, M., & Associates. (1995). *Cognitive strategy instruction that really improves children's academic performance.* Cambridge, MA: Brookline Books.

Rogan, J., & Havir, C. L. (1993). Using accommodations with students with learning disabilities. *Preventing School Failure, 38,* 12–15.

Salend, S. J. (1994). *Effective mainstreaming: Creating inclusive classrooms* (2nd ed.). New York: Macmillan.

Scheid, K. (1993). *Helping students become strategic learners: Guidelines for teaching.* Cambridge, MA: Brookline Books.

Schloss, P. J., Smith, M. A., & Schloss, C.N. (1995). *Instructional methods for adolescents with learning and behavior problems.* Boston: Allyn and Bacon.

Smith, T. E. C., Polloway, E. A., Patton, J. R., & Dowdy, C. A. (1995). *Teaching children with special needs in inclusive settings.* Boston: Allyn and Bacon.

Strichart, S. S., & Mangrum, C.T. (1993). *Teaching study strategies to students with learning disabilities.* Boston: Allyn and Bacon.

Wood, J. W. (in press) *Adapting instruction for mainstreamed and at-risk students* (3rd ed.). Englewood Cliffs, NJ: Merrill.

Wood, J. W. (1993). *Mainstreaming: A practical approach for teachers* (2nd ed.). New York: Macmillan.

Curricula and Instructional Materials

Aune, E. P., & Ness, J. E. (1991). *Tools for transition: Preparing students with learning disabilities for postsecondary education.* Circle Pines, MN: American Guidance Services.

Brigance, A. H. (1991). *Victory!* East Moline, IL: LinguiSystem.

Carnine, D., & Kameenui, E. J. (1992). *Higher-order thinking: Designing curriculum for mainstreamed students.* Austin, TX: Pro-Ed.

Carnine, D., Silbert, J., & Kameenui, E. J. (1990). *Direct instruction reading.* (2nd ed.). Columbus, OH: Merrill.

Cawley, J. F., Fitzmaurice-Hayes, A., & Shaw, R. (1988). *Mathematics for the mildly handicapped: Guide to curriculum and instruction.* Boston: Allyn and Bacon.

Cronin, M. E., & Patton, J. R. (1993). *Life skills for students with special needs.* Austin, TX: Pro-Ed.

Deiner, P. L. (1993). *Resources for teaching children with diverse abilities.* Fort Worth, TX: Harcourt Brace Jovanovich.

Dixon, R., & Engelmann, S. (1979). *Corrective spelling through morographs.* Chicago: Science Research Associates.

Dixon, R., Engelmann, S., Meier, M., Steely, D., & Wells, T. (1989) *Spelling mastery.* Chicago. Science Research Associates.

Englemann, S., & Bruner, E. C. (1983). *Reading mastery.* Chicago: Science Research Associates.

Englemann, S., & Carnine, D. (1982). *Corrective mathematics program.* Chicago: Science Research Associates.

Englemann, S., Carnine, D., Johnson, G., & Meyers, L. (1988). *Corrective reading: Decoding.* Chicago: Science Research Associates.

Englemann, S., Carnine, D., Johnson, G., & Meyers, L. (1989). *Corrective reading: Comprehension.* Chicago: Science Research Associates.

Mercer, C. D., & Miller, S. P. (1991). *Strategic math series.* Lawrence, KS: Edge Enterprises.

Schumaker, J. B., Hazel, J. S., & Pederson, C. S. (1989). *Social skills for daily living.* Circle Pines, MN: American Guidance Service.

Silbert, J., Carnine, D., & Stein, D. (1990). *Direct instructional mathematics* (2nd. Ed.) Columbus, OH: Merrill.

Software

Ace Detective, Mindplay, 160 W. Ft. Lowell, Tucson, AZ 85705, (800) 221-7911.

Access to Math, Don Johnson, Inc., 1000 N. Rand Road, Bldg. 115, Wauconda, IL 60084, (800) 999-4660. (Apple IIe, Apple IIGS) (can be used to create addition, subtraction, multiplication, and division problems).

Arthur's Birthday, Life Science Associates, 1 Fenimore Road, Bayport, NY 11705–2115, (516) 472–2111. (Macintosh).

Beamer, Data Command, Inc., P.O. Box 548, Kankakee, IL 60901, (800) 528–7390. (Apple IIe; Apple IIGS).

Blueprint for Decision Making, Lawrence Productions (Apple IIe; Apple IIGS).

Bubblegum Machine, Heartsoft, Inc., P.O. Box 691381, Tulsa, OK 74169–1381, (800) 285–3475. (Apple IIe; Apple IIGS; DOS) (language development, language arts).

Calendar Skills, Hartley Courseware, Inc., 3451 Dunkle Drive, Suite 200, Lansing, MI 48911–4216, (800) 247–1380. (Apple IIe; Apple IIGS; DOS).

Capitalization, Hartley Courseware, Inc., 3451 Dunkle Drive, Suite 200, Lansing, MI 48911–4216, (800) 247–1380. (Apple IIe; Apple IIGS).

Cause and Effect, Hartley Courseware, Inc., 3451 Dunkle Drive, Suite 200, Lansing, MI 48911–4216, (800) 247–1380. (Apple IIe; Apple IIGS).

Clock, Hartley Courseware, Inc., 3451 Dunkle Drive, Suite 200, Lansing, MI 48911–4216, (800) 247–1380. (Apple IIe; Apple IIGS; DOS).

Coin Changer, Heartsoft, Inc., P.O. Box 691381, Tulsa, OK 74169–1381, (800) 285–3475. (Apple IIe, Apple IIGS; DOS).

Collaborative Writer, Research Design Associates, Inc. (Macintosh) (memos, proposals, reports).

Conquering Fractions, MECC, 6160 Summit Drive, N., Minneapolis, MN 55430–4003, (800) 685–6322. (Apple IIe, Apple IIGS).

Essay Ease, MindPlay, 160 W. Ft. Lowell, Tucson, AZ 85705, (800) 221–7911. (Apple IIe, Apple IIGS).

Explore-a-Story, William K. Bradford Publishing, Co., 310 School Street, Acton, MA 01720, (800) 421–2009. (Apple IIe; Apple IIGS; Macintosh; DOS).

Explore-a-Science, William K. Bradford Publishing, Co., 310 School Street, Acton, MA 01720, (800) 421–2009. (Apple IIe; Apple IIGS; Macintosh; DOS).

Fact or Opinion, Hartley Courseware, Inc., 3451 Dunkle Drive, Suite 200, Lansing, MI 48911–4216, (800) 247–1380. (Apple IIe; Apple IIGS; DOS).

Fast-Track Fractions, SRA/DLM, 250 Old Wilson Bridge Road, Worthington, OH 43085. (800) 468–5850. (Apple IIe; Apple IIGS) (compare, add, subtract, multiply, divide fractions).

Fraction Fuel-Up, SRA/DLM, 250 Old Wilson Bridge Road, Worthington, OH 43085. (800) 468–5850. (Apple IIe; Apple IIGS).

Grammar Study Center, Teach Yourself by Computer Software, 340–0 Monroe Avenue, Rochester, NY 14618, (800) 724–4691. (Apple IIe; Apple IIGS).

How to Read for Everyday Living, Educational Activities, Inc., P.O. Box 392, Freeport, NY 11520, (800) 645–3739. (Apple IIe; DOS).

How to Write for Everyday Living, Educational Activities, Inc., P.O. Box 392, Freeport, NY 11520, (800) 645–3739. (Apple IIe; DOS).

Integer/Equations, Hartley Courseware, Inc., 3451 Dunkle Drive, Suite 200, Lansing, MI 48911–4216, (800) 247–1380.

Map Skills, Optimum Resources, Inc., 5 Hiltech Lane, Hilton Head, SC 29926, (800) 327–1473.

Math Concepts, Hartley Courseware, Inc., 3451 Dunkle Drive, Suite 200, Lansing, MI 48911–4216, (800) 247–1380. (Apple IIe; Apple IIGS).

Money Works, MECC, 6160 Summit Drive, N., Minneapolis, MN 55430–4003, (800) 685–6322. (Apple IIe, Apple IIGS).

Multiply with Balancing Bear, Sunburst Communications, 101 Castleton Street, Pleasantville, NY 10570, (800) 628–8897. (Apple IIe; Apple IIGS; DOS).

Outliner, MECC, 6160 Summit Drive, N., Minneapolis, MN 55430–4003, (800) 685–6322.

Presidents—It All Started with George, IBM: Eduquest, 2929 North Central Avenue, Phoenix, AZ 85012 (800) 426–4EDU. (DOS).

Read, Write, and Publish Series, William K. Bradford Publishing, Co., 310 School Street, Acton, MA 01720, (800) 421–2009. (Apple IIe; Apple IIGS, DOS).

Reader Rabbit, Learning Company, 6493 Kaiser Drive, Fremont, CA 94555, (800) 852-2255. (Apple IIe; Apple IIGS; Macintosh; DOS) (basic reading and spelling skills).

Spelling Machine, SWEPS Educational Software, Inc., 9 Barker Drive, P.O. Box 1510, Pine. AZ 85544–1510, (800) 880–8814. (Apple IIe; Apple IIGS; DOS).

Spelling Mastery, SRA/DLM, 250 Old Wilson Bridge Road, Worthington, OH 43085. (800) 468–5850. (Apple IIe; Apple IIGS).

Special Writer Coach, Tom Snyder Productions, 80 Coolidge Hill Road, Watertown, MA 02172–2817, (800) 342–0236. (Macintosh)

Stickeybear's Math Town, Optimum Resources, Inc., 5 Hiltech Lane, Hilton Head, SC 29926, (800) 327–1473. (Macintosh)

Stickeybear Reading, Optimum Resources, Inc., 5 Hiltech Lane, Hilton Head, SC 29926, (800) 327–1473. (Apple IIe; Apple IIGS; DOS).

Survival Math, Sunburst Communications, 101 Castleton Street, Pleasantville, NY 10570, (800) 628–8897. (Apple IIe, Apple IIGS, DOS).

Type to Learn, Sunburst Communications, 101 Castleton Street, Pleasantville, NY 10570, (800) 628–8897. (Apple IIe; Apple IIGS; Macintosh; DOS).

What's First? What's Next? Hartley Courseware, Inc., 3451 Dunkle Drive, Suite 200, Lansing, MI 48911–4216, (800) 247–1380. (Apple IIe; Apple IIGS) (sequencing).

Word-Processing Programs: No Graphics

Bank Street Writer Plus, Brøderbund Software, Inc., 500 Redwood Blvd., P.O. Box 6121, Novato, CA 94948–6121, (800) 521–6263.

Children's Writing and Publishing Center, Learning Company, 6493 Kaiser Drive, Fremont, CA 94555, (800) 852–2255.

Dr. Peet's Talking Text Writer, Hartley Courseware, Inc., 3451 Dunkle Drive, Suite 200, Lansing, MI 48911–4216, (800) 247–1380.

Magic Slate II, Sunburst Communications, 101 Castleton Street, Pleasantville, NY 10570, (800) 628–8897.

Writing Center, Learning Company, 6493 Kaiser Drive, Fremont, CA 94555, (800) 852–2255. (Macintosh).

Word-Processing Programs: Graphics

Bank Street Story Book, Mindscape, 1345 West Diversey Parkway, Chicago, IL 60614, (312) 525-1500.

Story Board, Data Command, Inc., P.O. Box 548, Kankakee, IL 60901, (800) 528–7390.

Videodiscs

Earth Science, Systems Impact, Inc., 200 Girard Street, Suite 214, Gaithersburg, MD 20877, (301) 869–0400.

Interactive Mathematics, Ferranti Educational Systems.

Mastering Decimals and Percents, Systems Impact, Inc.

Mastering Equations, Roots, and Exponents, Systems Impact, Inc.

Mastering Fractions, Systems Impact, Inc.

Mastering Ratios and Word Problem Strategies, Systems Impact, Inc.

Principles of Alphabet Learning Systems (PALS), IBM.

Understanding Chemistry and Energy, Systems Impact, Inc.

Videodisc Compendium for education and training. (1989). St. Paul, MN: Emerging Technology Consultants, Inc. (Lists describe more than 400 instructional videodiscs.)

Organizations

Council for Exceptional Children, Division of Learning Disabilities, 1920 Associate Drive, Reston, VA 22091, (703) 620–3660.

Council for Learning Disabilities, P.O. Box 40303, Overland Park, KS 66204, (913) 492–8755.

Learning Disabilities Association of America, 4156 Library Road, Pittsburgh, PA 15234, (412) 341–1515.

National Center for Learning Disabilities, 99 Park Avenue, Sixth Floor, New York, NY 10016, (212) 687–7211.

Orton Dyslexia Society, 724 York Road, Baltimore, MD 21204, (301) 296–0232.

BIBLIOGRAPHY FOR TEACHING SUGGESTIONS

Bos, C. S., & Vaughn, S. (1994). *Strategies for teaching students with learning and behavior problems* (3rd ed.). Boston: Allyn and Bacon.

Davey, B. (1983). Think Aloud—Modeling the cognitive processes of reading comprehension. *Journal of Reading, 27,* 44–47.

Ellis, E. S., & Lenz, B. L. (1987). A component analysis of effective learning strategies for LD students. *Learning Disabilities Focus, 2,* 94–107.

Englert, C. S., Raphael, T. W., Anderson, L. M., Anthony, H. M., & Stevens, D. D. (1991). Making strategies and self-talk visible: Writing instruction in regular and special education classrooms. *American Educational Research Journal, 23,* 337–372.

Fuchs, D., Fernstrom, P., Scott, S., Fuchs, L., & Vandermeer, L. (1994). Classroom ecological inventory. *Teaching Exceptional Children, 26,* 11–15.

Jones, B. F., Palincsar, A., Ogle, D. S., & Carr, E. G. (Eds.). (1987). *Strategic teaching and learning: Cognitive instruction in the content areas.* Alexandria, VA: Association for Supervision and Curriculum Development.

Mercer, C. D., & Miller, S. P. (1992). Teaching students with learning problems in math to acquire, understand, and apply basic math facts. *Remedial and Special Education, 13,* 19–35, 61.

Rankin, J. L., & Reid, R. (1995). The SM Rap—Or, here's the rap on self-monitoring. *Intervention in School and Clinic, 30,* 181–188.

Rivera, D. M., & Bryant, B. R. (1992). Mathematics instruction for students with special needs. *Intervention in School and Clinic, 28,* 71–86.

Salend, S. J. (1994). *Effective mainstreaming: Creating inclusive classrooms* (2nd ed.). New York: Macmillan.

Welch, M. (1994). Ecological assessment: A collaborative approach to planning instructional interventions. *Intervention in School and Clinic, 29,* 160–164, 183.

Wisconsin Department of Public Instruction (1989). *Strategic reading in the content areas.* Madison: Wisconsin Department of Public Instruction.

Wood, J. W. (in press). *Adapting instruction for mainstreamed and at-risk students* (3rd ed.). Englewood Cliffs, NJ: Merrill.

Ysseldyke, J. E., Christensen, S., & Kovaleski, J. F. (1994). Identifying students' instructional needs in the context of classroom and home environments. *Teaching Exceptional Children, 26,* 37–41.

SUMMARY

In the early 1960s, parents and professionals advocated a new category of special education—learning disabilities—to describe individuals who, in spite of normal or near-normal intelligence, have a puzzling array of learning problems. What prompted the creation of this area was the realization that many children with learning problems were not receiving needed educational services.

The four most common factors in definitions of learning disabilities are (1) IQ-achievement discrepancy, (2) presumption of central nervous system (CNS) dysfunction, (3) psychological processing problems, and (4) learning problems not due to environmental disadvantage, mental retardation, or emotional disturbance. The most commonly used definition is that of the federal government's, which includes all four factors. Another popular definition, that of the National Joint Committee for Learning Disabilities, does not include psychological processing problems and includes the assertion that learning disabilities may continue into adulthood.

The prevalence of students identified as learning disabled has increased dramatically, more than doubling since 1976–1977. Some believe this growth indicates that teachers are too quick to label students as learning disabled; others argue that social–cultural factors (e.g., increased poverty, increased stress on families) have contributed to the growth of learning disabilities. Boys outnumber girls in the learning disabilities category by three to one; researchers do not agree on the reasons for this prevalence, however.

Causal factors for learning disabilities fall into organic and biological, genetic, and environmental categories. More and more evidence is accumulating that many persons with learning disabilities have CNS dysfunction. Also, evidence is accruing that some cases of learning disabilities are attributable to genetic factors. Environmental causes have been more difficult to pinpoint, although some professionals believe that poor teaching can lead to learning disabilities.

Practitioners use tests of four general types to assess students with learning disabilities: standardized achievement tests, informal reading inventories, formative evaluation measures, and authentic assessment. Formative evaluation methods, have five features: (1) the teacher usually does the assessment; (2) the teacher assesses classroom behaviors directly; (3) the measures are taken frequently and over a period of time; (4) the assessment is done in conjunction with the setting of educational goals; and (5) the teacher uses the assessment information to decide whether the educational program for an individual student is effective. Curriculum-based assessment is a type of formative evaluation. Authentic assessment methods, such as portfolios, evaluate students' critical-thinking and problem-solving abilities in real-life situations.

Persons with learning disabilities exhibit a great deal of inter- and intraindividual variation in their psychological and behavioral characteristics. The inter-individual variation is reflected in the heterogeneity of this population. Intraindividual variation means that persons with learning disabilities often have uneven profiles of abilities.

Academic deficits are the hallmarks of learning disabilities. Reading disabilities are often related to poor phonological skills. Students with learning disabilities can also have problems in written or spoken language and math.

Some persons with learning disabilities have problems in perceptual, perceptual-motor, or general coordination. Research has not documented the claim of early theorists that training in these skills would help resolve reading problems.

Between one-third and one-fifth children with learning disabilities have a higher prevalence of attention deficit hyperactivity disorder (ADHD). There has been considerable controversy over whether the federal government should recognize ADHD as a separate category or whether the needs of students with attention deficits who have educational problems are met by existing categories such as learning disabilities. It is now recognized that ADHD can continue into adulthood.

Many individuals with learning disabilities demonstrate memory deficits. They have cognitive problems that lead to disorganization and metacognitive problems that interfere with their awareness of learning strategies and the ability to regulate their use.

Persons with learning disabilities tend to be rejected by their peers and to have poor self-concepts. In addition, they can have motivational problems as demonstrated by an external locus of control and learned helplessness.

Some authorities believe that a composite of many of the preceding characteristics indicates that many students with learning disabilities are passive rather than active learners. Many of their problems, such as a propensity to have problems with homework, may be due to this inactive approach to learning.

Educational methods for alleviating the academic problems of students with learning disabilities include cognitive training and direct instruction.

Cognitive training focuses on (1) changing thought processes, (2) providing strategies for learning, and (3) teaching self-initiative. Self-instruction, mnemonic keyword method, and scaffolded instruction are all examples of cognitive training.

Direct instruction focuses even more directly on academics than does cognitive training. It concentrates on instructional processes and a systematic analysis of the concept to be taught, rather than on characteristics of the student.

Methods for the attention problems of students with learning disabilities are structure and stimulus reduction, behavior modification, cognitive training, and medication. A structured and stimulus reduction approach emphasizes a highly teacher-directed approach combined with a reduction in extraneous simulation. In behavior modification, the student's attention is rewarded and his or her inattention is ignored or punished.

Cognitive training for attention problems assumes that students can regulate their impulsive and inattentive behavior by thinking about their behavior more carefully. An example of a cognitive training technique for attention problems is self-monitoring, the self-evaluation and self-recording of on- and off-task behavior.

Medication can be highly effective for increasing the concentration of persons with ADHD, including adults. Because the medication is powerful, with some possible side effects, teachers, parents, and physicians need to work together to monitor its effects.

The resource room is the most common placement for students with learning disabilities. Cooperative teaching, in which regular and special education teachers work together in the regular classroom, is gaining in popularity. Students with learning disabilities are often seen as the most likely candidates for full-inclusion programs, although many professional and parent organizations have resisted overuse of this approach.

Most professionals are cautious about establishing programs for children with learning disabilities at the preschool level because it is so hard to predict at that age which children will develop later academic problems. Some prefer to label preschoolers as "at risk" or "developmentally delayed." We do know that certain preacademic skills—such as letter, shape, and color recognition—are the best predictors of later academic learning.

The importance of educational programming at the secondary level and beyond is underscored by evidence that persons with learning disabilities do not automatically outgrow their problems as adults. Students with learning disabilities are at risk to drop out of school, and evidence suggests a higher prevalence of learning disabilities among juvenile delinquents. The majority who stay in school and do not engage in delinquent behaviors are still at risk of having problems in learning, socializing, holding jobs, and performing daily living skills. Factors related to successful transition to adulthood are (1) perseverance, (2) goal setting, (3) realistic acceptance of weaknesses coupled with building on strengths, (4) a supportive social network, and (5) intensive and long-term educational intervention.

Educational programming at the secondary level varies according to whether the goal is preparation for college or work. Service delivery models also differ, depending on the amount and type of instruction delivered by general educators versus special educators.

Geraldine Mlynek
"It is fortunate," says Geraldine Mlynek, "that my disability does not affect my work, and leaves me time to study, work, and grow." Ms. Mlynek, who has an emotional disability, has worked in several artistic styles and for the past several years has worked in monoprints and mixed media. She has studied at the Cleveland Institute of Art and the University of New Mexico in Albuquerque, where she now lives.

6

Emotional or Behavioral Disorders

It has always been hard for me to have friends. I want friends, but I don't know how to make them. I always think people are being serious when they are just joking around, but I don't figure that out until a lot later. I just don't know how to adapt.

I get into fights with people all the time. I take their teasing seriously and get into trouble. I don't remember having as much trouble getting along with kids when I was little. They seemed to feel sorry for me or thought I was weird. I used to run away from kids and hide in the bathroom at school or under my desk.

After I got back from the hospital, I really couldn't get along with anyone. That was when kids first began calling me "retard." I am not retarded, but I get confused and can't figure out what is going on. At first I couldn't figure out what they were saying to me. Finally one girl in my special education class became my friend. She kind of took care of me. I had another friend in junior high who was also nice and kind to me. But my best friend is my dog Cindie. Even though I give her a hard time, she is always ready to love me.

I like to play by myself best. I make up stories and fantasies. My mother says it is too bad I have such a hard time writing, because with my imagination and all the stories I have created in my mind I could write a book.

Anonymous

Children and youths who have emotional or behavioral disorders are not typically good at making friends. In fact, their most obvious problem is failure to establish close and satisfying emotional ties with other people. As the youth in the excerpt on page 209 describes, it may be easier for these individuals to hide, both physically and emotionally. Typically, their peers are not attracted to them, and few adults find them pleasant to be around, either.

Some of these children are withdrawn. Other children or adults may try to reach them, but these efforts are usually met with fear or disinterest. In many cases, this kind of quiet rejection continues until those who are trying to make friends give up. Because close emotional ties are built around reciprocal social responses, people naturally lose interest in individuals who do not respond to social overtures.

Many other children with emotional or behavioral disorders are isolated from others not because they withdraw from friendly advances but because they strike out with hostility and aggression. They are abusive, destructive, unpredictable, irresponsible, bossy, quarrelsome, irritable, jealous, defiant—anything but pleasant. Naturally, other children and adults choose not to spend time with children like this unless they have to, and others tend to strike back at youngsters who show these characteristics. It is no wonder, then, that these children and youths seem to be embroiled in a continuous battle with everyone.

Where does the problem start? Does it begin with behavior that frustrates, angers, or irritates other people? Or does it begin with a social environment so uncomfortable or inappropriate that the only reasonable response of the child is to withdraw or attack? These questions cannot be answered fully on the basis of current research. The best thinking today is that the problem is not just in the child's behavior or just in the environment. The problem arises because *the social interactions and transactions between the child and the social environment are inappropriate*. This is an *ecological* perspective—an interpretation of the problem as a negative aspect of the child *and* the environment in which he or she lives.

Special education for these students is, in many ways, both confused and confusing. The terminology of the field is inconsistent, and there is much misunderstanding of definitions. Reliable classifications of children's behavior problems have only recently emerged from research. The large number of theories regarding the causes and the best treatments of emotional and behavioral disorders makes it difficult to sort out the most useful concepts. Thus, study of this area of special education demands more than the usual amount of perseverance and critical thinking.

TERMINOLOGY

Many different terms have been used to designate children who have extreme social-interpersonal and/or intrapersonal problems, including *emotionally handicapped, emotionally impaired, behaviorally impaired, socially/emotionally handicapped, emotionally conflicted, having personal and social adjustment problems,* and *seriously behaviorally disabled.* These terms do not designate distinctly different types of disorders; that is, they do not refer to clearly different types of children and youths. Rather, the different labels appear to represent personal preferences for terms and perhaps slightly different theoretical orientations. The terminology of the field is so variable and confusing that it is possible to pick a label of choice simply by matching words from

Misconceptions about
Persons with Emotional or Behavioral Disorders

Myth Most children and youths with emotional or behavioral disorders are not noticed by people around them.

Fact Although it is difficult to identify the types and causes of problems, most children and youths with emotional or behavioral disorders, whether aggressive or withdrawn, are quite easy to spot.

Myth Students with emotional or behavioral disorders are usually very bright.

Fact Relatively few students with emotional or behavioral disorders have high intelligence; in fact, most have below-average IQs.

Myth Youngsters who exhibit shy, anxious behavior are more seriously impaired than those whose behavior is hyperaggressive.

Fact Youngsters with aggressive, acting-out behavior patterns have less chance for social adjustment and mental health in adulthood. Neurotic, shy, anxious children and youths have a better chance of getting and holding jobs, overcoming their problems, and staying out of jails and mental hospitals, unless their withdrawal is extreme. This is especially true for boys.

Myth Most students with emotional or behavioral disorders need a permissive environment, in which they feel accepted and can accept themselves for who they are.

Fact Research shows that a firmly structured and highly predictable environment is of greatest benefit for most students.

Myth Only psychiatrists, psychologists, and social workers are able to help children and youths with emotional or behavioral disorders overcome their problems.

Fact Most teachers and parents can learn to be highly effective in helping youngsters with emotional or behavioral disorders, often without extensive training or professional certification. Many of these children and youths do require services of highly trained professionals, as well.

Myth Undesirable behaviors are only symptoms; the real problems are hidden deep in the individual's psyche.

Fact There is no sound scientific basis for belief in hidden causes; the behavior and its social context are the problems. Causes may involve thoughts, feelings, and perceptions.

Column A with words from Column B below (and, if it seems appropriate, adding other qualifiers, such as *serious* or *severe*):

Column A	***Column B***
Emotional	Disturbance
Social	Disorder
Behavioral	Maladjusment
Personal	Handicap
	Impairment

Seriously emotionally disturbed was the term used in 1975, when the Education for All Handicapped Children Act (PL 94–142)—the legislation that led to IDEA—was enacted; today, that term is criticized as inappropriate. *Behaviorally disordered* is consistent with the name of the Council for Children with Behavioral Disorders (CCBD, a division of the Council for Exceptional Children) and has the advantage of focusing attention on the clearly observable aspect of these children's problems—disordered behavior. Many authorities favor terminology indicating that these children may have emotional *or* behavioral problems *or both* (Forness & Knitzer, 1992; Kauffman, 1997).

In 1990, the National Mental Health and Special Education Coalition, representing over thirty professional and advocacy groups, proposed the new terminology *emotional or behavioral disorder* to replace *serious emotional disturbance* in federal laws and regulations (Forness & Knitzer, 1992). It now appears that *emotional or behavioral disorder* may become the generally accepted terminology of the field, although changes in federal and state laws and regulations may be slow in coming.

DEFINITION

Defining emotional and behavioral disorders has always been problematic. Professional groups and experts have felt free to construct individual working definitions to fit their own professional purposes. For practical reasons, we might say that someone has had an emotional or behavioral disorder whenever an adult authority said so. Until very recently, no one has come up with a definition that is understandable and acceptable to a majority of professionals.

Definitional Problems

There are valid reasons for the lack of consensus regarding definition (Kauffman, 1997). Defining emotional and behavioral disorders is somewhat like defining a familiar experience—anger, loneliness, or happiness, for example. We all have an intuitive grasp of what these experiences are, but forming objective definitions is far from simple. The factors that make it particularly difficult to arrive at a good definition of emotional and behavioral disorders are:

- lack of precise definitions of mental health and normal behavior
- differences among conceptual models
- difficulties in measuring emotions and behavior
- relationships between emotional or behavioral disorder and other disabilities
- differences in the professionals who diagnose and serve children and youths

Consider each of these problems in turn. Mental health and normal behavior have been hard to define precisely. It is no wonder, then, that the definition of emotional or behavioral disorder presents a special challenge. Professionals who work with youngsters who have emotional or behavioral disorders have been guided by a variety of conceptual models, as we will discuss further. These conceptual models—assumptions or theories about why people behave as they do and what we should do about it—may offer conflicting ideas about just what the problem is. Thus, people who adopt different conceptual models may define emotional or behavioral disorders in very different terms.

Measurement is basic to any definition, and emotions and behavior—the disorders, in this case—are notoriously difficult to measure in ways that make a precise definition possible. Ultimately, subjective judgment is called for, even with the best measurements of emotions and behavior available. Emotional or behavioral disorders tend to overlap a great deal with other disabilities, especially learning disabilities and mental retardation. It is therefore hard to define emotional or behavioral disorders as disabilities clearly distinct from all others.

Finally, each professional group has its own reasons for serving individuals with emotional or behavioral disorders. For example, clinical psychologists, school psychologists, social workers, teachers, and juvenile justice authorities all have their particular concerns and language. Differences in the focuses of different professions tend to produce differences in definition, as well.

Children with emotional and behavioral disorders frequently behave in ways that frustrate adults and others around them.

Current Definitions

Although the terminology used and the relative emphasis given to certain points vary considerably from one definition to another, it is possible to extract several common features of current definitions. There is general agreement that emotional or behavioral disorder refers to:

- behavior that goes to an extreme—that is not just slightly different from the usual
- a problem that is chronic—one that does not quickly disappear
- behavior that is unacceptable because of social or cultural expectations

One definition that must be considered is included in the federal rules and regulations governing the implementation of IDEA. In federal laws and regulations, *seriously emotionally disturbed* has been defined as follows:

> (i) The term means a condition exhibiting one or more of the following characteristics over a long period of time and to a marked extent, which adversely affects educational performance:
> (A) An inability to learn that cannot be explained by intellectual, sensory, or health factors;
> (B) An inability to build or maintain satisfactory relationships with peers and teachers;
> (C) Inappropriate types of behavior or feelings under normal circumstances;
> (D) A general pervasive mood of unhappiness or depression; or
> (E) A tendency to develop physical symptoms or fears associated with personal or school problems.
> (ii) The term includes children who are schizophrenic or autistic.* The term does not include children who are socially maladjusted unless it is determined that they are seriously emotionally disturbed. (45 CFR 121a.5[b][8] [1978])

*The U.S. Department of Education later decided that autism will no longer be included under the category of seriously emotionally disturbed. See Bower (1982) for comment on this change. In 1990, autism became a separate category under IDEA.

Individuals with traumatic brain injury (TBI) may experience emotional difficulties as they attempt to adjust to new life circumstances. Problems may also be directly related to physiological causes stemming from the injury.

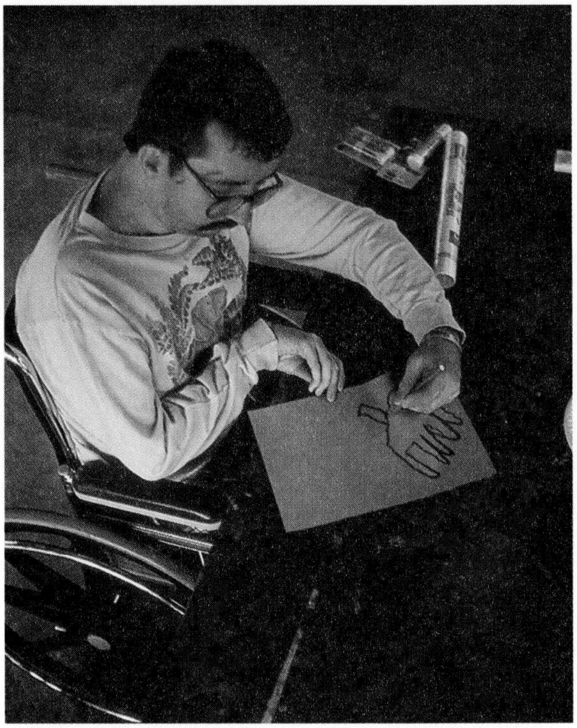

The federal definition is modeled after one proposed by Bower (1981). Bower's definition, however, does not include the statements found in part (ii) of the federal definition. These inclusions and exclusions are, as Bower (1982) and Kauffman (1986, 1997) point out, unnecessary. Common sense tells us that Bower's five criteria for emotional disturbance indicate that autistic and schizophrenic children *must be included* and that socially maladjusted children *cannot be excluded*. Furthermore, the clause *which adversely affects educational performance* makes interpretation of the definition impossible, unless the meaning of *educational performance* is clarified. Does *educational performance* refer only to academic achievement? If so, then children with other characteristics who achieve on grade level are excluded.

In recent years the federal definition has been widely criticized, and the federal government has more than once mandated study of it. One of the most widely criticized and controversial aspects of the definition is its exclusion of children who are socially maladjusted but not emotionally disturbed. Strong moves have been made in some states and localities to interpret *social maladjustment* as **conduct disorder**—aggressive, disruptive, antisocial behavior. This is the most common type of problem exhibited by students who have been identified as having emotional or behavioral disorders. Cline (1990) notes that excluding students with conduct disorder is inconsistent with the history of IDEA. Moreover, the American Psychological Association and the CCBD have condemned this practice. Lawyers have defended the exclusion. The controversy may be timeless (e.g., Forness, 1992; Nelson, Rutherford, Center, & Walker, 1991; Skiba & Grizzle, 1992; Slenkovich, 1992a, 1992b).

conduct disorder. A disorder characterized by overt, aggressive, disruptive behavior or covert antisocial acts such as stealing, lying, and fire setting; may include both overt and covert acts.

A second definition that must be considered is the one proposed in 1990 by the National Mental Health and Special Education Coalition. The coalition's proposed definition is:

(i) The term emotional or behavioral disorder means a disability characterized by behavioral or emotional responses in school so different from appropriate age, cultural, or ethnic norms that they adversely affect educational performance. Educational performance includes academic, social, vocational, and personal skills. Such a disability:
  (A) is more than a temporary, expected response to stressful events in the environment;
  (B) is consistently exhibited in two different settings, at least one of which is school-related; and
  (C) is unresponsive to direct intervention in general education, or the child's condition is such that general education interventions would be insufficient.

(ii) Emotional and behavioral disorders can co-exist with other disabilities.

(iii) This category may include children or youths with schizophrenic disorders, **affective disorders, anxiety disorder,** or other sustained disorders of conduct or adjustment when they adversely affect educational performance in accordance with section (i). (Forness & Knitzer, 1992, p. 13)

The coalition is working to have the proposed definition and terminology adopted in federal laws and regulations, with the hope that states will adopt them, as well. Advantages of the proposed definition over the federal definition include the following:

- It uses terminology reflecting current professional preferences and concern for minimizing stigma.
- It includes both disorders of emotions and disorders of behavior and recognizes that they may occur either separately or in combination.
- It is school-centered but acknowledges that disorders exhibited outside the school setting are also important.
- It is sensitive to ethnic and cultural differences.
- It does not include minor or transient problems or ordinary responses to stress.
- It acknowledges the importance of prereferral interventions but does not require slavish implementation of them in extreme cases.
- It acknowledges that children and youths can have multiple disabilities.
- It includes the full range of emotional or behavioral disorders of concern to mental health and special education professionals without arbitrary exclusions.

CLASSIFICATION

Since emotional or behavioral disorders are evidenced in many ways, it seems reasonable to expect that individuals could be grouped into subcategories according to the types of problems they have. Still, there is no universally accepted system for classifying emotional or behavioral disorders for special education.

Psychiatric classification systems have been widely criticized. Hobbs (1975) commented, "It is important to note that competent clinicians would seldom use for treatment purposes the categories provided by diagnostic manuals; their judgment would be more finely modulated than the classification schemes, and more sensitive than any formal system can be to temporal, situational, and developmental changes" (pp. 58–59). Clearly, the usual diagnostic categories—for example, those found in publications of the American Psychiatric Association—have little meaning for teachers. Many psychologists and educators have recommended relying more on individual

affective disorder. A disorder of mood or emotional tone characterized by depression or elation.

anxiety disorder. A disorder characterized by anxiety, fearfulness, and avoidance of ordinary activities because of anxiety or fear.

assessment of the child's behavior and situational factors than on traditional diagnostic classification.

An alternative to traditional psychiatric classifications is the use of statistical analyses of behavioral characteristics to establish clusters, or *dimensions,* of disordered behavior. Using sophisticated statistical procedures, researchers look for patterns of behavior that characterize children who have emotional or behavioral disorders. By using these methods, researchers have been able to derive descriptive categories that are less susceptible to bias and unreliability than the traditional psychiatric classifications (Achenbach, 1985; Richardson, McGauhey, & Day, 1995).

Achenbach and others (Achenbach, Howell, Quay, & Conners, 1991; Quay, 1986; Walker & Severson, 1990) have identified two broad, pervasive dimensions of disordered behavior: **externalizing** and **internalizing**. Externalizing behavior involves striking out against others. Internalizing behavior involves mental or emotional conflicts, such as depression and anxiety. A variety of more specific dimensions has been found by several researchers. Quay and Peterson (1987), for example, describe six dimensions characterized by the following kinds of behavior:

1. *conduct disorder*—seeks attention, shows off, is disruptive, annoys others, fights, has temper tantrums
2. *socialized aggression*—steals in company with others, is loyal to delinquent friends, is truant from school with others, has "bad" companions, freely admits disrespect for moral values and laws
3. *attention problems-immaturity*—has short attention span and poor concentration; is distractible and easily diverted from task at hand; answers without thinking; is sluggish, slow-moving, and lethargic
4. *anxiety-withdrawal*—is self-conscious, easily embarrassed, and hypersensitive; feelings are easily hurt; is generally fearful, anxious, depressed, and always sad
5. *psychotic behavior*—expresses far-fetched ideas, has repetitive speech, shows bizarre behavior
6. *motor excess*—is restless, unable to sit still, tense, unable to relax, and overtalkative

externalizing. Acting-out behavior; aggressive or disruptive behavior that is observable as behavior directed toward others.

internalizing. Acting-in behavior; anxiety, fearfulness, withdrawal, and other indications of an individual's mood or internal state.

pervasive developmental disorder. A severe disorder characterized by abnormal social relations, including bizarre mannerisms, inappropriate social behavior, and unusual or delayed speech and language.

autism. A disorder characterized by extreme withdrawal, self-stimulation, cognitive deficits, language disorders, and onset before the age of thirty months.

schizophrenia. A disorder characterized by psychotic behavior manifested by loss of contact with reality, distorted thought processes, and abnormal perceptions.

Individuals may show behaviors characteristic of more than one dimension; that is, the dimensions are not mutually exclusive. For instance, a child or youth might exhibit several of the behaviors associated with the attention problems-immaturity dimension (short attention span, poor concentration) and perhaps several of those defining conduct disorder, as well (fighting, disruptive behavior, annoying others).

Furthermore, children may exhibit characteristic types of behavior with varying degrees of intensity or severity. That is, all dimensions of behavior may be exhibited to a greater or lesser extent; the range may be from normal to severely disordered. For example, an individual might have a severe conduct disorder. The classification of the severe disorders typically called **pervasive developmental disorders** presents particular problems. Children with these disorders exhibit behavior that is qualitatively as well as quantitatively different from that of others (for examples, see Sacks, 1995; Schopler & Mesibov, 1994, 1995; Wenar, Ruttenberg, Kalish-Weiss, & Wolf, 1986). They are often described as inaccessible to others, unreachable, out of touch with reality, or mentally retarded. Prior and Werry (1986) have said of such children that "[their] interpretation of [themselves], of the world, and of [their] place in it is so seriously at variance with the actual facts of the matter as to interfere with everyday adaptation and to strike the impartial observer as incomprehensible" (p. 156).

Two types of severe childhood disorders are distinguished by most researchers: **autism** and **schizophrenia.** Children with autism are characterized by a lack of

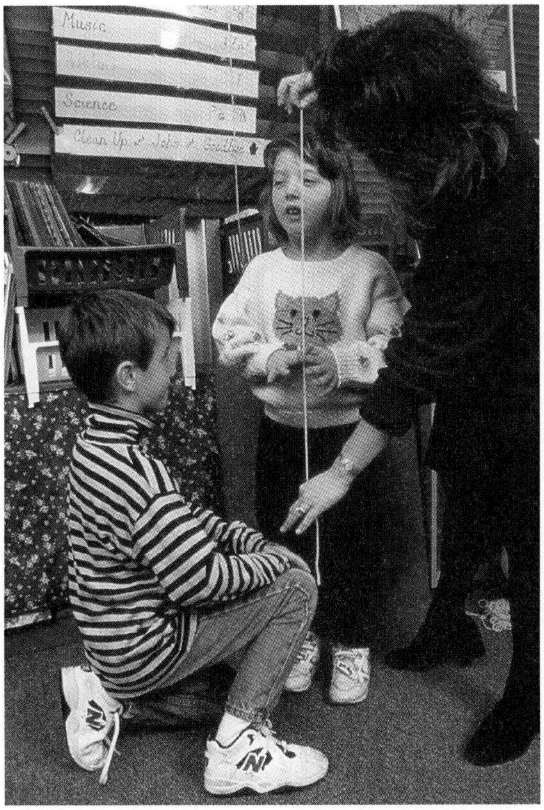

The causes of autism—one of the more severe behavioral disorders—are only recently beginning to be understood.

responsiveness to other people, major problems in communication (many do not have any useful language), peculiar speech patterns (e.g., parroting what they hear), and bizarre responses (e.g., peculiar interests in or attachments to objects). They often engage in repetitive, stereotyped behavior. Children with schizophrenia have a severe disorder of thinking. They may believe they are controlled by alien forces or have other delusions or hallucinations. Typically, their emotions are inappropriate for the actual circumstances, and they tend to withdraw into their own private worlds.

One major difference between autism and schizophrenia is that a child with autism is typically recognized as having a disorder before the age of three years. Childhood schizophrenia is a disorder that typically begins after a normal period of development during early childhood. Autism and schizophrenia in children, then, are differentiated partly on the basis of the child's age at the first appearance of symptoms. There are also other differences between the two conditions, especially these:

1. Children with schizophrenia usually have delusions (bizarre ideas) and hallucinations (seeing or hearing imaginary things), whereas children with autism usually do not.
2. Children with schizophrenia tend to have psychotic episodes interspersed with periods of near normal behavior, whereas children with autism tend to have persistent symptoms.
3. About 25 percent of children with autism have epileptic seizures, whereas children with schizophrenia seldom have seizures (Rutter & Schopler, 1987).

As mentioned in the discussion of the definition of emotional or behavioral disorders, autism is no longer considered by the U.S. Department of Education under the category "seriously emotionally disturbed" (described in this chapter as emotional or behavioral disorders). There are likely several reasons for this reclassification. First, the parents of children with autism objected—and with good reason—to the blame implied by the term *emotional disturbance,* particularly the explicit blame heaped upon them by prominent psychoanalytical thinking (e.g., Bettelheim, 1950, 1967). And second, autism seems clearly to be caused by a neurological or biochemical dysfunction. Autism is discussed in this chapter and Chapter 7 because of the implications of having autism. For instance, (1) the child exhibits highly problematic emotional and behavioral responses to everyday circumstances; and (2) the child's problems are often centered on difficulty in communicating. Autism is discussed briefly in Chapter 10 also because it involves a brain disorder.

In summary, the most useful classifications of emotional or behavioral disorders describe behavioral dimensions. The dimensions described in the literature involve a wide range of problems, including conduct disorder, socialized aggression, attention problems and immaturity, anxiety and withdrawal, excessive movement, and pervasive developmental disorders. These dimensions include a variety of antisocial conduct, delinquent behavior, substance abuse, depression, and autism and schizophrenia. Nevertheless, because of ambiguity in the federal definition of *serious emotional disturbance,* controversy persists regarding the classifications that should be included for special education purposes.

PREVALENCE

Estimates of the prevalence of emotional or behavioral disorders in children and youths have varied tremendously because there has been no standard and reliable definition or screening instrument. For decades, the federal government estimated that 2 percent of the school-age population was seriously emotionally disturbed. The government's estimate was *extremely* conservative, however. Rather consistently, credible studies in the United States and many other countries have indicated that at least 6 to 10 percent of children and youths of school age exhibit serious and persistent emotional/behavioral problems (Brandenburg, Friedman, & Silver, 1990; Kauffman, 1997; Kazdin, 1989). Data published by the U.S. Department of Education (1995), however, show that only about 1 percent of schoolchildren in the United States are identified as seriously emotionally disturbed. The Department of Education now recognizes that this is an underserved category of special education students whose needs are particularly complex.

The most common types of problems exhibited by students placed in special education for emotional or behavioral disorders are externalizing—that is, aggressive, acting-out disruptive behavior. Boys outnumber girls in displaying these behaviors by a ratio of 5 to 1 or more. Overall, boys tend to exhibit more aggression and conduct disorder than girls do (Achenbach et al., 1991; Anderson & Werry, 1994).

Juvenile delinquency and the antisocial behavior known as conduct disorder present particular problems in estimating prevalence. Delinquent youths constitute a considerable percentage of the population. About 3 percent of U.S. youths are referred to a juvenile court in any given year. Many others engage in serious antisocial behavior but are not referred to the courts (see Siegel & Senna, 1994). One point of view is that *all* delinquent and antisocial youths should be thought of as having emotional or behavioral disorders. Some argue, however, that most delinquents and others who commit frequent antisocial acts are socially maladjusted, not seriously emotionally disturbed, for special education purposes.

Clearly, disabling conditions of various kinds are much more common among juvenile delinquents than among the general population (Henggeler, 1989). Just as clearly, the social and economic costs of delinquency and antisocial behavior are enormous. Adolescent males account for a disproportionately high percentage of serious and violent crime in U.S. society. Those who exhibit serious antisocial behavior are at high risk for school failure as well as other negative outcomes (Kazdin, 1995; Patterson, DeBaryshe, & Ramsey, 1989; Walker, Calvin, & Ramsey, 1995). If schools are to address the educational problems of delinquent and antisocial children and youths, the number served by special education will increase dramatically.

CAUSES

The causes of emotional or behavioral disorders have been attributed to four major factors:

1. biological disorders and diseases
2. pathological family relationships
3. undesirable experiences at school
4. negative cultural influences

Although in the majority of cases there is no conclusive empirical evidence that any of these factors is directly responsible for the disorder, some factors may give a child a predisposition to exhibit problem behavior and others may precipitate or trigger it. That is, some factors, such as genetics, influence behavior over a long time and increase the likelihood that a given set of circumstances will trigger maladaptive responses. Other factors (such as observing one parent beating the other), may have a more immediate effect and may trigger maladaptive responses in an individual who is already predisposed to problem behavior.

Another concept important in all theories is the idea of *contributing factors*. It is extremely unusual to find a *single* cause that has led directly to a disorder. Usually, several factors together contribute to the development of a problem. In almost all cases, the question of what specifically has caused the disorder cannot be answered because no one really knows.

Some studies have found rates of juvenile delinquency higher among youths with emotional and behavioral disorders.

Biological Factors

Behaviors and emotions may be influenced by genetic, neurological, or biochemical factors or by combinations of these. Certainly, there is a relationship between body and behavior, and it would therefore seem reasonable to look for a biological causal factor of some kind for certain emotional or behavioral disorders. But only rarely is it possible to demonstrate a relationship between a specific biological factor and an emotional or behavioral disorder. Many children with emotional or behavioral disorders have no detectable biological flaws that account for their actions, and many behaviorally normal children have serious biological defects. For most children with emotional or behavioral disorders, there simply is no real evidence that biological factors alone are at the root of their problems. For those with severe and profound disorders, however, there is evidence to suggest that biological factors may contribute to their conditions (Asarnow et at., 1994; Harris, 1995).

All children are born with a biologically determined behavioral style, or **temperament.** Although children's inborn temperaments may be changed by the way they are reared, some believe that children with so-called difficult temperaments are predisposed to develop emotional or behavioral disorders (Thomas & Chess, 1984). There is no one-to-one relationship between temperament and disorders, however. A difficult child may be handled so well or a child with an easy temperament so poorly that the outcome will be quite different from what one might predict on the basis of initial behavioral style. Other biological factors besides temperament—disease, malnutrition, and brain trauma, for example—may predispose children to develop emotional or behavioral problems (Baumeister, Kupstas, & Klindworth, 1990; Lozoff, 1989). Substance abuse also may contribute to serious emotional and behavioral problems (Gottesman, 1991; Newcomb & Bentler, 1989). Except in rare instances, it is not possible to determine that these factors are direct causes of problem behavior.

As is the case in mental retardation, there is more often evidence of a biological cause among children with severe or profound disabilities. Children with autism or schizophrenia frequently (but not always) show signs of neurological defects (Prior & Werry, 1986). There is convincing evidence that genetic factors contribute to schizophrenia (Gottesman, 1991; Plomin, 1989), although the role of specific biological factors often remains a mystery, even when there is severe and profound disorder (Kauffman, 1997; Prior & Werry, 1986). It is now generally accepted that autism is a neurological disorder, but the nature and causes of the neurological defect are unknown.

As biological and psychological research have become more sophisticated, it has become apparent that biological factors cause or set the stage for many disorders that formerly were widely assumed to be caused mostly or entirely by social interactions. Schizophrenia and autism are the foremost examples. Another example is **Tourette's syndrome**, which is characterized by multiple motor tics (i.e., repetitive, stereotyped movements) and verbal tics (i.e., the individual makes strange noises or says inappropriate words or phrases). Although we now understand that autism, schizophrenia, Tourette's disorder, attention deficit hyperactivity disorder (ADHD), some forms of depression, and many other disorders are caused wholly or partly by brain or biochemical dysfunctions, these biological causal factors remain poorly understood. That is, we do not know exactly *how* genetic, neurological, and other biochemical factors contribute to these disorders, nor do we know how to correct the biological problems involved in these disorders.

It is clear that traumatic brain injury, now a separate category of disability under IDEA, may cause psychosocial problems. Depending on what part of the brain is injured and when the injury occurs during development, the individual may experience serious difficulty in psychosocial behavior—responding appropriately to social

temperament. One's inborn behavioral style, including general level of activity, regularity or predictability, approach or withdrawal, adaptability, intensity of reaction, responsiveness, mood, distractibility, and persistence; is present at birth but may be modified by parental management.

Tourette's syndrome. A neurological disorder beginning in childhood (about three times more prevalent in boys than in girls) in which stereotyped motor movements (tics) are accompanied by multiple vocal outbursts (e.g., grunting or barking noises) or socially inappropriate words or statements.

circumstances, controlling rage reactions or aggression, showing appropriate affect, and so on.

Four points are important to remember about biological causes:

1. The fact that disorders have biological causes does not mean that they are not emotional or behavioral disorders. An emotional or behavioral disorder can have a physical cause; the biological malfunction is a problem because of the disorder it creates in the individual's emotions or behavior.
2. Causes are seldom exclusively biological or psychological. Once a biological disorder occurs, it nearly always creates psychosocial problems that then also contribute to the emotional or behavioral disorder, as well.
3. Biological or medical treatment of the disorder is seldom sufficient to resolve the problem. Medication may be of great benefit, but it is seldom the only intervention that is needed. The psychological and social aspects of the disorder must also be addressed
4. Medical or biological approaches are sometimes of little or no benefit and the primary interventions are psychological or behavioral, even though the disorder is known to have primarily a biological cause. Medications do not work equally well for all cases, and for some disorders, no generally effective medications are known.

Family Factors

Mental health specialists have been tempted to blame behavioral difficulties primarily on parent-child relationships because the nuclear family—father, mother, and children—has a profound influence on early development. In fact, some advocates of psychoanalysis believe that almost all severe problems of children stem from early negative interactions between mother and child.

However, empirical research on family relationships indicates that the influence of parents on their children is no simple matter and that children with emotional or behavioral disorders may influence their parents as much as their parents influence them. It is increasingly clear that family influences are interactional and transactional and that the effects parents and children have on one another are reciprocal (Patterson, DeBaryshe, & Ramsey, 1989; Patterson, Reid, & Dishion, 1992). Even in cases of severe and profound emotional or behavioral disorders, it is not possible to find consistent and valid research findings that allow the blame for the children's problem behavior to be placed primarily on their parents (Gottesman, 1991).

The outcome of parental discipline depends not only on the particular techniques used but also on the characteristics of the child (Rutter, 1985). Generalizations about the effects of parental discipline are difficult to make, for as Becker (1964) commented long ago, "There are probably many routes to becoming a 'good parent' which vary with the personality of both the parents and children and with the pressure in the environment with which one must learn to cope" (p. 202). Nevertheless, sensitivity to children's needs, love-oriented methods of dealing with misbehavior, and positive reinforcement (attention and praise) for appropriate behavior unquestionably tend to promote desirable behavior in children. Parents who are generally lax in disciplining their children but are hostile, rejecting, cruel, and inconsistent in dealing with misbehavior are likely to have aggressive, delinquent children. Broken, disorganized homes, in which the parents themselves have arrest records or are violent are particularly likely to foster delinquency and lack of social competence (see Reitman & Gross, 1995).

In discussing the combined effects of genetics and environment on behavioral development, Plomin (1989) warns against assuming that the family environment will make siblings similar. "Environmental influences do not operate on a family-by-family basis but rather on an individual-by-individual basis. They are specific to each child rather than general for an entire family" (p. 109). Thus, although we know that some types of family environments (abusive, neglectful, rejecting, and inconsistent, for example) are destructive, we must also remember that each child will experience and react to family relationships in his or her unique way.

Educators must be aware that most parents of youngsters with emotional or behavioral disorders want their children to behave more appropriately and will do anything they can to help them. These parents need support resources—not blame or criticism—for dealing with very difficult family circumstances. The Federation of Families for Children's Mental Health was organized in 1989 to help provide such support and resources, and parents are organizing in many localities to assist each other in finding additional resources (Jordan, Goldberg, & Goldberg, 1991). In the box on page 224, one of the founding members shares her perspective on why parents are so often blamed for their children's emotional or behavioral disorders.

School Factors

Some children already have emotional or behavioral disorders when they begin school; others develop such disorders during their school years, perhaps in part because of damaging experiences in the classroom itself. Children who exhibit disorders when they enter school may become better or worse according to how they are managed in the classroom (Walker, Colvin, & Ramsey, 1995). School experiences are no doubt of great importance to children, but like biological and family factors, we cannot justify many statements regarding how such experiences contribute to the child's behavioral difficulties. A child's temperament and social competence may interact with the behaviors of classmates and teachers in contributing to emotional or behavioral problems. When a child with an already difficult temperament enters school lacking the skills for academic and social success, he or she is likely to get negative responses from peers and teachers (Martin, 1992).

There is a very real danger that such a child will become trapped in a spiral of negative interactions, in which he or she becomes increasingly irritating to and irritated by teachers and peers. The school can contribute to the development of emotional problems in several rather specific ways. For instance, teachers may be insensitive to children's individuality, perhaps requiring a mindless conformity to rules and routines. Educators and parents alike may hold too high or too low expectations for the child's achievement or conduct, and they may communicate to the child who disappoints them that he or she is inadequate or undesirable.

Discipline in the school may be too lax, too rigid, or inconsistent. Instruction may be offered in skills for which the child has no real or imagined use. The school environment may be such that the misbehaving child is rewarded with recognition and special attention (even if that attention is criticism or punishment), whereas the child who behaves is ignored. Finally, teachers and peers may be models of misconduct—the child may misbehave by imitating them (Kauffman, 1997).

In considering how they may be contributing to disordered behavior, teachers must ask themselves questions about their expectations, instructions, and approaches to behavior management (Kauffman, Mostert, Nuttycombe, Trent, & Hallahan, 1993). Teachers must not assume blame for disordered behavior to which they are not contributing, yet it is equally important that teachers eliminate whatever contributions they may be making to their students' misconduct.

Poor parenting may be a factor in causing many behavioral problems in children, but by itself, it is not an adequate or correct explanation. Even so, the parents of children with emotional and behavioral disorders are often made to feel responsible for their children's problems.

Cultural Factors

Children, their families, and schools are embedded in cultures that influence them (Rogoff & Morelli, 1989; Walker et al., 1995). Aside from family and school, many environmental conditions affect adults' expectations of children and children's expectations of themselves and their peers. Values and behavioral standards are communicated to children through a variety of cultural conditions, demands, prohibitions, and models. Several specific cultural influences come to mind: the level of violence in the media (especially television and motion pictures), the use of terror as a means of coercion, the availability of recreational drugs and the level of drug abuse, changing standards for sexual conduct, religious demands and restrictions on behavior, and the threat of nuclear accidents or war.

Undoubtedly, the culture in which a child is reared influences his or her emotional, social, and behavioral development. Case studies of rapidly changing cultures bear this out. Other studies suggest cultural influences on anxiety, depression, and aggression. The level of violence depicted on television and in movies is almost certainly a contributing factor in the increasing level of violence in U.S. society (see Walker et al., 1995).

Garmezy (1987) and Baumeister, Kupstas, and Klindworth (1990) also note the changing cultural conditions in the United States during the 1980s that predisposed children to develop emotional or behavioral disorders and a variety of other disabling conditions. Among these are dramatic increases in the number of children living in poverty. There have also been substantial increases in the number of children born to teenage mothers and to mothers who have abused "crack" cocaine and other substances. At the same time, medical and social services available to poor children and their families have been cut substantially. In short, we are living in an era of enormous affluence for some Americans but also a period in which poverty and related problems continue to grow rapidly. Neglect of the problems of poor children and their families have led some to question the importance of the health and welfare of children in U.S. culture (Hodgkinson, 1995; see also Freedman, 1993; Kozol, 1995; Moynihan, 1995).

Personal Reflections: Family Factors

Dixie Jordan is the parent of a nineteen-year-old son with an emotional and behavioral disorder, coordinator of the EBD Project at the PACER Center in Minneapolis (a resource center for parents of children with disabilities), and a founding member of the Federation of Families for Children's Mental Health.

Why do you think there is such a strong tendency to hold parents responsible for their children's emotional or behavioral disorders?

I am the parent of two children, the younger of which has emotional and behavioral problems. When my firstborn and I were out in public, strangers often commented on what a "good" mother I was, to have such an obedient, well-behaved, and compliant child. Frankly, I enjoyed the comments, and really believed that those parents whose children were throwing tantrums and generally demolishing their environments were simply not very skilled in child-rearing. I recall casting my share of reproachful glances in those days, and thinking with some arrogance that raising children should be left to those of us who knew how to do it well. Several years later, my second child and I were on the business end of such disdain, and it was a lesson in humility that I shall never forget. Very little that I had learned in the previous 3 years as a parent worked with this child; he was neurologically different, hyperactive, inattentive, and noncompliant even when discipline was consistently applied. His doctors, his neurologist, and finally his teachers referred me to "parenting classes," as though the experiences I had had with my older child were nonexistent; his elementary principal even said that there was nothing wrong that a good spanking wouldn't cure. I expected understanding that this was a very difficult child to raise, but the unspoken message was that I lacked competence in basic parenting skills, the same message that I sent to similarly situated parents just a few years earlier.

Most of us in the world today are parents. The majority of us have children who do not have emotional or behavioral problems. Everything in our experience suggests that when our children are successful and obedient, it is because of our parenting. We are reinforced socially for having a well-behaved child from friends, grandparents, even strangers. It makes sense, then, to attribute less desirable behaviors in children to the failure of their parents to provide appropriate guidance or to set firm limits. Many parents have internalized that sense of responsibility or blame for causing their child's emotional problems, even when they are not able to identify what they might have done wrong. It is a very difficult attitude to shake, especially when experts themselves cannot seem to agree on causation. With most children, the "cause" of an emotional or behavioral disorder is more likely a complex interplay of multiple factors than "parenting styles," "biology," or "environmental influences" as discrete entities, but it is human nature to latch onto a simple explanation—and inadequate parenting is, indeed, a simple explanation. When systems blame parents for causing their child's emotional or behavioral disorders, the focus is no longer on services to help the child learn better adaptive skills or appropriate behaviors, but on rationalizing why such services may not work. When parents feel blamed, their energies shift from focusing on the needs of their child to defending themselves. In either instance, the child is less well served.

Another reason that people hold parents responsible for their children's emotional or behavioral disorders is that parents may be under such unrelenting stress from trying to manage their child's behavior that they may resort to inappropriate techniques because of the failure of more conventional methods. A parent whose 8-year-old hyperactive child smashes out his bedroom window while being timed out for another problem may know that tying the child to a chair is not a good way to handle the crisis, but may be out of alternatives. It may not have been the "right" thing for the parent to do, but [he or she] is hardly responsible for causing the child's problems in the first place. It would be a mistake to attribute the incidence of abuse or neglect as "causing" most emotional or behavioral disorders without consideration that difficult children are perhaps more likely to be abused due to their noncompliant or otherwise difficult behaviors.

Source: Reprinted with the permission of Macmillan Publishing Company from *Characteristics of emotional and behavioral disorders of children and youth* (6th ed), by James M. Kauffman. Copyright © 1997 By Macmillan Publishing Company.

Clearly, cultural influences affect how children behave in school. But even when culture is considered as a cause, we must be aware of interactive effects. Schools and families *influence* culture; they are not simply products of it. Finally, refer back to Chapter 3 and the importance of a multicultural perspective. Consideration of cultural factors in causing emotional or behavioral disorders requires that culturally normative behavior not be construed as disordered.

IDENTIFICATION

It is much easier to identify disordered *behaviors* than it is to define and classify types and causes of emotional or behavioral disorders. Most students with emotional or behavioral disorders do not escape the notice of their teachers. Occasionally, such students will not bother anyone and thus be invisible, but it is usually easy for experienced teachers to tell when students need help.

The most common type of emotional or behavioral disorder—conduct disorder—attracts immediate attention, so there is seldom any real problem in identification. Immature students and those with personality problems may be less obvious, but they are not difficult to recognize. Students with emotional or behavioral disorders are so readily identified by school personnel, in fact, that few schools bother to use systematic screening procedures. Also, the availability of special services for those with emotional or behavioral disorders lags far behind the need—and there is not much point in screening for problems when there are no services available to treat them.

Children with pervasive developmental disorders are also easily recognized. In fact, the parents of children with autism frequently report that soon after their child's birth, they noticed that he or she was strange or different from most children—unresponsive, rigid, or emotionally detached, for example. Likewise, children with schizophrenia are seldom mistaken for those who are developing normally. Their unusual language, mannerisms, and ways of relating to others soon become matters of concern to parents, teachers, and even many casual observers. But children with these disorders are a small percentage of those with emotional or behavioral disorders, and problems in their identification are not usually encountered.

Even so, do not conclude that there is never any question about whether a student has an emotional or behavioral disorder. The younger the child, the more difficult it is to judge whether his or her behavior signifies a serious problem. And some children with emotional or behavioral disorders are undetected because teachers are not sensitive to their problems or because they do not stand out sharply from other children in the environment who may have even more serious problems. Furthermore, even sensitive teachers sometimes make errors of judgment. Also keep in mind that some students with emotional or behavioral disorders do not exhibit problems at school.

Formal screening and accurate early identification for the purpose of planning educational intervention are complicated by the problems of definition already discussed. In general, however, teachers' informal judgments have served as a fairly valid and reliable means of screening students for emotional or behavioral problems (as compared with judgments of psychologists and psychiatrists). When more formal procedures are used, teachers' ratings of behavior have turned out to be quite accurate.

Walker and his colleagues have devised a screening system for use in elementary schools based on the assumption that a teacher's judgment is a valid and cost-effective though greatly underused method of identifying children with emotional or behavioral disorders (Walker & Severson, 1990; Walker, Severson, & Feil, 1994). Although teachers tend to overrefer students who exhibit externalizing behavior problems (i.e., those with conduct disorders), they tend to underrefer students with internalizing problems (i.e., those characterized by anxiety-withdrawal). To make certain that children are not overlooked in screening but that time and effort are not wasted, a three-step process is used:

1. The teacher lists and ranks students with externalizing and internalizing problems. Those who best fit descriptions of students with externalizing problems and those who best fit descriptions of those with internalizing problems are listed. Then they are ordered from most like to least like the descriptions.

2. The teacher completes two checklists for the three highest-ranked pupils on each list. One checklist asks the teacher to indicate whether each pupil exhibited specific behaviors during the past month (such as "steals," "has tantrums," "uses obscene language or swears"). The other checklist requires the teacher to judge how often (never, sometimes, frequently) each pupil shows certain characteristics (e.g., "follows established classroom rules," or "cooperates with peers in group activities or situations").
3. Pupils whose scores on these checklists exceed established norms are observed in the classroom and on the playground by a school professional other than the classroom teacher (a school psychologist, counselor, or resource teacher).

Classroom observations indicate the extent to which the pupil meets academic expectations; playground observations assess the quality and nature of social behavior. These direct observations of behavior, in addition to teachers' ratings, are then used to decide whether the child has problems that warrant classification for special education. Such carefully researched screening systems may lead to improved services for children with emotional or behavioral disorders. Systematic efforts to base identification on teachers' judgments *and* careful observation should result in services being directed to those students most clearly in need (Walker et al., 1995).

PSYCHOLOGICAL AND BEHAVIORAL CHARACTERISTICS

Describing the characteristics of children and youths with emotional or behavioral disorders is an extraordinary challenge because disorders of emotions and behaviors are extremely varied. We provide a general picture of these children; however, individuals may vary markedly in intelligence, achievement, life circumstances, and emotional and behavioral characteristics.

Intelligence and Achievement

The idea that children and youths with emotional or behavioral disorders tend to be particularly bright is a myth. Research clearly shows that the average student with an emotional or behavioral disorder has an IQ in the dull–normal range (around 90) and that relatively few score above the bright–normal range. Compared to the normal distribution of intelligence, more children with emotional or behavioral disorders fall into the ranges of slow-learner and mild mental retardation. On the basis of a review of the research on the intelligence of students with emotional or behavioral disorders, Kauffman (1997) hypothesized distributions of intelligence as shown in Figure 6–1.

Of course, we have been referring to children with emotional or behavioral disorders as a group. Some children who have emotional or behavioral disorders are extremely bright and score very high on intelligence tests. We caution, too, that intensive early behavioral intervention may reveal cognitive abilities that have not been apparent. That is, some individuals may have cognitive deficits that early intensive intervention can largely overcome; these individuals may be mistakenly assumed to have permanent cognitive deficits.

There are pitfalls in assessing the intellectual characteristics of a group of children by examining the distribution of their IQs. Intelligence tests are not perfect instruments for measuring what we mean by *intelligence,* and it can be argued that emotional or behavioral difficulties may prevent children from scoring as high as they are capable of scoring. That is, it might be argued that intelligence tests are biased

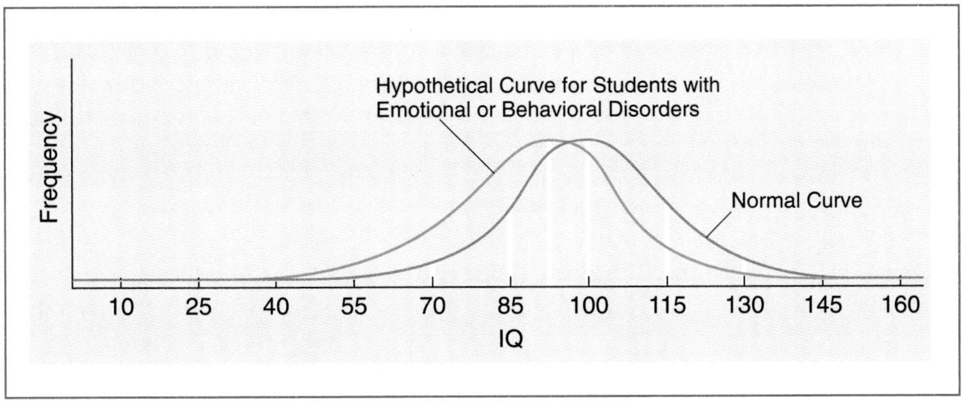

Figure 6–1

Hypothetical frequency distributions of IQ for students with emotional or behavioral disorders as compared to a normal frequency distribution.
(*Source:* Reprinted with the permission of Macmillan Publishing Company from *Characteristics of emotional and behavioral disorders of children and youth* [6th ed.] by James M. Kauffman. Copyright © 1997 by Macmillan Publishing Company.)

against children with emotional or behavioral disorders and that their true IQs are higher than test scores indicate. Still, the lower-than-normal IQs for these students do indicate lower ability to perform tasks other students perform successfully, and the lower scores are consistent with impairment in other areas of functioning (academic achievement and social skills, for example). IQ is a relatively good predictor of how far a student will progress academically and socially, even in cases of severe disorders.

Most students with emotional or behavioral disorders are also underachievers at school, as measured by standardized tests (Kauffman, 1997). A student with an emotional or behavioral disorder does not usually achieve at the level expected for his or her mental age; seldom are such students academically advanced. In fact, many students with severe disorders lack even the most basic reading and arithmetic skills, and the few who seem to be competent in reading or math are often unable to apply their skills to everyday problems. Some children with severe disorders do not even possess basic self-care or daily living skills, such as using the toilet, grooming, dressing, and feeding.

Social and Emotional Characteristics

Previously, we described two major dimensions of disordered behavior based on analyses of behavior ratings: externalizing and internalizing. The externalizing dimension is characterized by aggressive, acting-out behavior; the internalizing dimension is characterized by anxious, withdrawn behavior. Our discussion here focuses on the aggressive and withdrawn types of behavior typically exhibited by students with emotional or behavioral disorders.

Although both aggressive and withdrawn behaviors are commonly seen in most children with emotional or behavioral disorders, we discuss the characteristics of severe disorders in a separate section (see pp. 216–218). These children may be qualitatively as well as quantitatively different from others, for certain behavioral features set them apart. Remember, too, that a given student might, at different times, show both aggressive and withdrawn behaviors. Many students with emotional or behavioral disorders have multiple problems (Walker et al., 1995).

At the beginning of this chapter, we said that most students with emotional or behavioral disorders are not well liked by their peers. Studies of the social status of students in regular elementary and secondary classrooms indicate that those who are identified as having emotional or behavioral disorders are seldom socially accepted.

Given what we know about the behavioral characteristics of these students and the behavioral characteristics that support social acceptance, this should come as no surprise: "The research indicates that children—whether normal or exceptional—who are in frequent conflict with authority, who fight or bother others a great deal, and who demonstrate verbal aggression are rarely the objects of social acceptance" (Drabman & Patterson, 1981, p. 53). Students who show these characteristics are actively rejected, not just neglected, by their peers.

Aggressive, Acting-Out Behavior (Externalizing). As noted earlier, conduct disorder is the most common problem exhibited by students with emotional or behavioral disorders. Hitting, fighting, teasing, yelling, refusing to comply with requests, crying, destructiveness, vandalism, extortion—these behaviors, if exhibited often, are very likely to earn a child or youth the label "disturbed." Normal children cry, scream, hit, fight, become negative, and do almost everything else children with emotional or behavioral disorders do, only not so impulsively and often. Youngsters of the type we are discussing here drive adults to distraction. These youths are not popular with their peers either, unless they are socialized delinquents who do not offend their delinquent friends. They typically do not respond quickly and positively to well-meaning adults who care about them and try to be helpful.

Some of these students are considered to have attention deficit hyperactivity disorder or brain injury; some are called **sociopathic** because they appear to hurt others deliberately and without any sense of wrongdoing. Their behavior is not only extremely troublesome but also appears to be resistant to change through typical discipline. Often, they are so frequently scolded and disciplined that punishment means little or nothing to them. Because of adult exasperation and their own deviousness, these youths get away with misbehavior a lot of the time. These are children who behave horribly not once in a while but so often that the people they must live with

sociopathic. Describes behavior characteristic of a sociopath; someone whose behavior is aggressively antisocial and who shows no remorse or guilt for misdeeds.

Aggressive children, who have frequent negative confrontations with others, may develop debilitating problems with social interaction.

or be with cannot stand them. Of course, aggressive, acting-out children typically cannot stand the people they have to live and be with either, and often for good reason. Such children are screamed at, criticized, and punished a lot. The problem, then, is not just the individual children's behavior. What must be examined if the child or anyone else is to be helped is the *interaction between the child's behavior and the behavior of other people in his or her environment.*

Aggression has been analyzed from many viewpoints. The analyses that have the strongest support in empirical research are those of social learning theorists, such as Bandura (1973, 1986), and behavioral psychologists, such as Patterson (Patterson, Reid, & Dishion, 1992). Their studies take into account the child's experience and his or her motivation, based on the anticipated consequences of aggression. In brief, they view aggression as *learned* behavior, and assume that it is possible to identify the conditions under which it will be learned.

Children learn many aggressive behaviors by observing parents, siblings, playmates, and people portrayed on television and in movies. Individuals who model aggression are more likely to be imitated if they are high in social status and are observed to receive rewards and escape punishment for their aggression, especially if they experience no unpleasant consequences or obtain rewards by overcoming their victims. If children are placed in unpleasant situations and they cannot escape from the unpleasantness or obtain rewards except by aggression, they are more likely to be aggressive, especially if this behavior is tolerated or encouraged by others.

Aggression is encouraged by external rewards (social status, power, suffering of the victim, obtaining desired items), vicarious rewards (seeing others obtain desirable consequences for their aggression), and self-reinforcement (self-congratulation or enhancement of self-image). If children can justify aggression in their own minds (by comparison to the behaviors of others or by dehumanizing their victims), they are more likely to be aggressive. Punishment may actually increase aggression under some circumstances: when it is inconsistent or delayed, when there is no positive alternative to the punished behavior, when it provides an example of aggression, or when counterattack against the punisher seems likely to be successful.

Teaching aggressive children to be less so is no simple matter, but social learning theory and behavioral research do provide some general guidelines. In general, research does not support the notion that it is wise to let children act out their aggression freely. The most helpful techniques include providing examples (models) of nonaggressive responses to aggression-provoking circumstances, helping the child rehearse or role-play nonaggressive behavior, providing reinforcement for nonaggressive behavior, preventing the child from obtaining positive consequences for aggression, and punishing aggression in ways that involve as little counteraggression as possible (e.g., using "time-out" or brief social isolation rather than spanking or yelling) (Walker et al., 1995).

The seriousness of children's aggressive, acting-out behavior should not be underestimated. It was believed for decades that although these children cause a lot of trouble, they are not as seriously disabled as children who are shy, anxious, or neurotic. Research has exploded this myth. When combined with school failure, aggressive, antisocial behavior in childhood generally means a gloomy future in terms of social adjustment and mental health, especially for boys. Neurotic, shy, anxious children are much more likely to be able to get and hold jobs, overcome their emotional problems, and stay out of jails and mental hospitals than are adults who had conduct problems and were delinquent as children (see Kazdin, 1995).

Of course, there are exceptions to the rule. Nonetheless, there is a high probability that the aggressive child who is a failure in school will become more of a social

aggression. Behavior that intentionally causes others harm or that elicits escape or avoidance responses from others.

misfit as an adult than will the withdrawn child. When we consider that conduct disorders and delinquency are highly correlated with school failure, the importance of meeting the needs of acting-out and underachieving children is obvious (Kauffman, 1997; Walker et al., 1995).

Immature, Withdrawn Behavior (Internalizing). In noting the seriousness of aggressive, acting-out behavior, we do not intend to downplay the disabling nature of immaturity and withdrawal. In their extreme forms, withdrawal and immaturity may be characteristics of schizophrenia and autism. Such disorders not only have serious consequences for individuals in their childhood years but also carry a very poor prognosis for adult mental health. The child whose behavior fits a pattern of extreme immaturity and withdrawal cannot develop the close and satisfying human relationships that characterize normal development. Such a child will find it difficult to meet the pressures and demands of everyday life.

All children exhibit immature behavior and act withdrawn once in a while. Children who fit the withdrawn, immature description, however, are typically infantile in their ways or reluctant to interact with other people. They are social isolates who have few friends, seldom play with children their own age, and lack the social skills necessary to have fun. Some retreat into fantasy or daydreaming; some develop fears that are completely out of proportion to the circumstances; some complain constantly of little aches and pains and let their supposed illnesses keep them from participating in normal activities; some regress to earlier stages of development and demand constant help and attention; and some become depressed for no apparent reason (see Rabian & Silverman, 1995; Stark, Ostrander, Kurowski, Swearer, & Bowen, 1995).

As in the case of aggressive, acting-out behavior, withdrawal and immaturity may be interpreted in many different ways. Proponents of the psychoanalytic approach are likely to see internal conflicts and unconscious motivations as the underlying causes. Behavioral psychologists tend to interpret such problems in terms of failures in social learning; this view is supported by more empirical research data than other views (Kauffman, 1997). A social learning analysis attributes withdrawal and immaturity to an inadequate environment. Causal factors may include overrestrictive parental discipline, punishment for appropriate social responses, reward for isolated behavior, lack of opportunity to learn and practice social skills, and models (examples) of inappropriate behavior. Immature or withdrawn children can be taught the skills they lack by arranging opportunities for them to learn and practice appropriate responses, showing models engaging in appropriate behavior, and providing rewards for improved behavior.

A particularly important aspect of immature, withdrawn behavior is depression. Only recently have mental health workers and special educators begun to realize that depression is a widespread and serious problem among children and adolescents (Forness, 1988; Guetzloe, 1991; Klass & Koplewica, 1993). Today, the consensus of psychologists is that the nature of depression in children and youths is quite similar in many respects to that of depression in adults. The indications of depression include disturbances of mood or feelings, inability to think or concentrate, lack of motivation, and decreased physical well-being. A depressed child or youth may act sad, lonely, and apathetic; exhibit low self-esteem, excessive guilt, and pervasive pessimism; avoid tasks and social experiences; and/or have physical complaints or problems in sleeping, eating, or eliminating. Sometimes depression is accompanied by such problems as bed-wetting (nocturnal enuresis), fecal soiling (encopresis), extreme fear of or refusal to go to school, failure in school, or talk of suicide or suicide attempts. Depression also frequently occurs in combination with conduct disorder (McCracken, Cantwell, & Hanna, 1993).

Suicide has increased dramatically during the past decade among those between the ages of fifteen and twenty-four; it is now among the leading causes of death in this age group (Guetzloe, 1991; Hawton, 1986). Depression, especially when severe and accompanied by a sense of hopelessness, is linked to suicide and suicide attempts. Therefore, it is important for all those who work with young people to be able to recognize the signs. Substance abuse is also a major problem among children and teenagers and may be related to depression (Newcomb & Bentler, 1989).

Depression sometimes has a biological cause, and antidepressant medications have, at times, been successful in helping depressed children and youths overcome their problems. In many cases, however, no biological cause can be found. Depression can also be caused by environmental or psychological factors, such as the death of a loved one, separation of one's parents, school failure, rejection by one's peers, or a chaotic and punitive home environment. Interventions based on social learning theory—instructing children and youths in social interaction skills and self-control techniques and teaching them to view themselves more positively, for example—have often been successful in such cases.

Characteristics Associated with Traumatic Brain Injury (TBI)

As mentioned earlier, *traumatic brain injury (TBI)* is a separate category under IDEA, but it may be accompanied by a variety of serious emotional and behavioral effects. Many disturbing behavior patterns, such as violence or other extreme examples of social maladjustment, cannot be connected to brain damage. However, we know that TBI can cause violent aggression, hyperactivity, impulsivity, inattention, and a wide range of other emotional or behavioral problems, depending on just what parts of the brain are damaged (Allison, 1993).

The possible effects of TBI includes a long list of other psychosocial problems, some of which include (see Deaton & Waaland, 1994):

- displaying inappropriate manners or mannerisms
- failing to understand humor or "read" social situations
- becoming easily tired, frustrated, or angered
- feeling unreasonable fear or anxiety
- being irritable
- experiencing sudden, exaggerated swings of mood
- having depression
- perseveration (persistent repetition of one thought or behavior)

The emotional and behavioral effects of TBI also depend on the person's age at the time of injury and the social environment he or she lived in before and after the injury occurred (Deaton & Waaland, 1994). For instance, home, community, or school environments that are conducive to the misbehavior of any child or youth are extremely likely to exacerbate the emotional or behavioral problems of someone with TBI. In fact, arranging an environment for someone with TBI that is conducive to and supportive of appropriate behavior is one of the greatest challenges of dealing effectively with the effects of brain injury (Bergland & Hoffbauer, 1996; Deaton, 1994). The physical effects of TBI cannot often be undone through medical treatment. Although it may be known that the resulting emotional or behavioral problems are caused by the brain injury, these problems must be addressed primarily through environmental modifications—changing other people's demands, expectations, responses to behavior and adapting the physical surroundings or equipment available for accomplishing various tasks.

TBI often results in a shattered sense of self, and recovery or rehabilitation of identity and behavior may be a slow, painstaking process, requiring multidisciplinary efforts. For students with TBI, effective education and treatment often require not only classroom behavior management but family therapy, medication, and communication training, as well (Feeney & Urbanczyk, 1994; see also the discussion of TBI in Chapters 7 and 10). If the student with TBI is to regain an acceptable sense of self and be prepared for transition into the next higher level of education or the work force, then intensive personal counseling, behavior modification programs, physical modifications of the classroom, vocational training, and academic and personal support systems may be required (Bergland & Hoffbauer, 1996; Pollack, 1994).

Characteristics Associated with Schizophrenia, Autism, and Other Pervasive Developmental Disorders

The characteristics of schizophrenia, autism, and other pervasive developmental disorders are not entirely distinct. Differentiating among these conditions is often difficult, especially in young children. Although autism and schizophrenia are typically distinguished by certain characteristics, particularly age of onset (see page 217), some types of behavior are common among children with a variety of severe disorders. If exhibited to a marked extent and over a long period of time, these behaviors typically carry a poor prognosis; even with early, intensive intervention, a significant percentage of children are unlikely to recover completely (Asarnow, Tompson, & Goldstein, 1994; Lovaas, 1987; Werry, McClellan, Andrews, & Ham, 1994).

The following behaviors are typical of individuals with autism and other pervasive developmental disorders (although not all such individuals exhibit all these characteristics):

- *absent or distorted relationships with people*—inability to relate to people except as objects, inability to express affection, or ability to build and maintain only distant, suspicious, or bizarre relationships
- *extreme or peculiar problems in communication*—absence of verbal language or language that is not functional, such as **echolalia** (i.e., parroting what one hears), misuse of pronouns (e.g., *he* for *you* or *I* for *her*), **neologisms** (i.e., made-up, meaningless words or sentences), talk that bears little or no resemblance to reality
- *self-stimulation*—repetitive, stereotyped behavior that seems to have no purpose other than providing sensory stimulation; this may take a wide variety of forms, such as swishing saliva, twirling objects, patting one's cheeks, flapping one's hands, staring, and the like
- *self-injury*—repeated physical self-abuse, such as biting, scratching, or poking oneself, head banging, and so on
- *perceptual anomalies*—unusual responses or absence of responses to stimuli that seems to indicate sensory impairment or unusual sensitivity
- *apparent cognitive deficits*—inability to respond adequately to intelligence and achievement tests or inability to apply apparent intelligence to everyday tasks
- *aggression toward others*—severe tantrums or calculated physical attacks that threaten or injure others
- *lack of daily living skills*—absence or significant impairment of ability to take care of one's basic needs, such as dressing, feeding, or toileting

echolalia. The meaningless repetition (echoing) of what has been heard.

neologism. A coined word that is meaningless to others; meaningless words used in the speech of a person with a mental disorder.

EDUCATIONAL CONSIDERATIONS

Students with emotional or behavioral disorders typically have low grades and other unsatisfactory academic outcomes, have higher dropout and lower graduation rates than other student groups, and are often placed in highly restrictive settings. Moreover, these students are disproportionately from poor and ethnic-minority families and frequently encounter the juvenile justice system (Chesapeake Institute, 1994; U.S. Department of Education, 1994).

In response to these and other findings, the federal government launched an effort in the early 1990s to establish a national agenda for educating students with serious emotional disturbance. (Note that this terminology is that of federal legislation—*serious emotional disturbance*—rather than the proposed terminology, *emotional or behavioral disorders*.) By 1992, the national agenda consisted of seven interdependent, strategic targets:

- *Target 1: Expand positive learning opportunities and results*. To foster the provision of engaging, useful, and positive learning opportunities. These opportunities should be result-driven and should acknowledge as well as respond to the experiences and needs of children and youth with serious emotional disturbance.
- *Target 2: Strengthen school and community capacity*. To foster initiatives that strengthen the capacity of schools and communities to serve students with serious emotional disturbance in the least restrictive environments appropriate.
- *Target 3: Value and address diversity*. To encourage culturally competent and linguistically appropriate exchanges and collaborations among families, professionals, students, and communities. These collaborations should foster equitable outcomes for all students and result in the identification and provision of services that are responsive to issues of race, culture, gender, and social and economic status.
- *Target 4: Collaborate with families*. To foster collaborations that fully include family members on the team of service providers that implements family-focused services to improve educational outcomes. Services should be open, helpful, culturally competent, accessible to families, and school-based as well as community-based.

Current federal guidelines for addressing emotional and behavioral disorders emphasize collaboration with family members.

SUCCESS STORIES

Herndon, VA: Fourteen-year-old **Christina Isaacs** *attends a special program for students with emotional and behavioral disorders that is attached to a large, public middle school. Special educator Teresa Zutter, principal of this co-facility for seventh- and eighth-graders, knows her sixty students and their families well. She and Christina's mother, Brenda Isaacs, agree that this close community provides Chrissy with the individual support she needs to merge slowly into the mainstream.*

Eighth-grader Chrissy Isaacs stood wide-eyed at the principal's door. "I've called you to my office, Chrissy, because you are a star!" said Teresa Zutter. "In the past year, you have made real progress toward your goals."

At Teresa's invitation, a relieved Chrissy sat down at a dark wooden table and talked about all she had accomplished. "I worked hard last year, and by January, my teachers thought I could join a mainstream drama class. I loved it!" "And she was good!" added Zutter.

Chrissy's goals included increasing academic achievement, reducing reliance on adults, and developing friendships as well as confidence in her abilities and performance. This year, Chrissy was included daily in general classes for PE and teen life and sang with the middle school chorus five days a week. She says with pride, her eyes glancing down at her reflection in the glass-topped table, "I want to do well in the mainstream because I want to be a cheerleader and get a regular high school diploma."

According to Teresa Zutter, Chrissy started seventh grade as a girl in distress, but she took advantage of all the resources available to her. Remembers Zutter, "When I first met Chrissy, she gave the impression of being physically frail and frightened. As we walked around her new school, she grabbed my arm and asked, 'Will I like it here?'" Chrissy admits, "I was nervous last year. The school was so big and beautiful!"

The Herndon Center, a co-facility with Herndon Middle School, is two years old and serves sixty students in grades 7 and 8 who have emotional or behavioral disorders and need individual support to prepare for experiences in the mainstream. Each classroom is equipped with a "hot-line" telephone connected to the main office and a carpeted quiet room that serves as a "time-out" area for angry students. There is also frequent communication between Teresa Zutter and parents who are alerted of misbehaviors, and, in some instances, called to take their sons or daughters home. Rules and policies are clear for students, teachers, and families. "There is an absolute need for structure and for individualization to get the trust factor going," says Teresa. "We have so many people here to help and to talk to students, no one has to hit to communicate."

The thrust of the program is to offer a low student–teacher ratio to students who need close attention. In addition to Principal Zutter, there are thirteen teachers and

- *Target 5: Promote appropriate assessment.* To promote practices ensuring that assessment is integral to identification, design, and delivery of services for children and youth with SED [serious emotional disturbance]. These practices should be culturally appropriate, ethical, and functional.
- *Target 6: Provide ongoing skill development and support.* To foster the enhancement of knowledge, understanding, and sensitivity among all who work with children and youth who have or who are at risk of developing SED. Support and development should be ongoing and should aim at strengthening the capacity of families, teachers, service providers, and other stakeholders to collaborate, persevere, and improve outcomes for children and youth with SED.
- *Target 7: Create comprehensive and collaborative systems.* To promote systems change resulting in the development of coherent services built around the individual needs of children and youth who have or who are at risk of developing SED. These services should be family-centered, community-based, and appropriately funded. (U.S. Department of Education, 1994, pp. 119–120)

Special Educators at Work

a support staff that includes a psychologist, social worker, guidance counselor, health awareness monitor, and conflict resolution teacher. Weekly clinical staff meetings address the needs of individual students and provide a regular forum for educators and support staff to address problems. As described by Teresa, "This is such a spirited staff. We laugh a lot and take care of each other."

The center assumes a treatment model based on the belief that students thrive on positive reinforcement. Nonphysical punishment is employed briefly and only to the degree necessary, while instruction is geared toward remediation and cultivation of coping mechanisms. "Girls and boys who are stressed can be made to feel better," maintains Teresa. "They [do not just have emotional or behavioral disorders] for a while but have entrenched behaviors; it's a life struggle. They won't be okay without interventions and without being taught how to cope with stress."

Most of the students at the Herndon Center are male, a fact Chrissy Isaacs was quick to note. "I'm at that age where I like boys," she says. When she started grade 7, Chrissy had little sense of her own reality, she often gazed at her reflection and slipped into the protection of fantasy. She was also limited in her awareness of social interactions and needed to learn how to respond to various situations. Lost in her own thoughts, she would have tantrums or provoke other students, not understanding the impact these behaviors had on her relationships. She was also becoming oppositional. Academically, Chrissy was below grade level in most areas. Although she could easily decode words, she had problems comprehending what she read and organizing her thoughts.

With frequent reassurance and a great deal of help to stay on task, Chrissy made gains and was performing at grade level in all classes by the end of seventh grade. Speech therapy helped her vocabulary development, particularly in using words with multiple meanings, as used in jokes and riddles. Academic supports included receiving extra adult attention, additional time to complete classwork and tests, shortened assignments, and peer/work helpers and having directions stated several times. Although she daydreamed frequently, Chrissy demonstrated two real strengths: a willingness to work hard and an ability to focus when provided with support. She is now described as a conscientious student who worries about the quality of her work.

As long as she is confronted gently and not embarrassed in front of other students, Chrissy is responsive to correction. She takes great pride in her appearance and talents and is still attracted to anything that captures her image. Socially, she tries to be everybody's friend, but peers are still leery of her erratic behavior which quickly turns antagonistic. "Chrissy tends to be overly sensitive to what others are saying, whether it relates to her or not," says her mother, Brenda Isaacs. And when she is angry, Chrissy resorts to profanity, inappropriate comments, and even physical threats. This year, to her credit, she has managed to develop some stable friendships with a few girls, which she cherishes.

"With all this support, I see my daughter proud and happy and becoming more mature," says Brenda Isaacs. Teresa Zutter agrees: "Chrissy will always have some difficulties, but with help she can be eased from her world of fantasy. Hopefully, she'll value herself and stay in reality."

—By Jean Crockett

This national agenda is clearly ambitious. Substantial resources will need to be allocated to make achieving these targets possible (cf. Smith & Couthino, in press).

Contrasting Conceptual Models

The statement of a national agenda should not be taken to mean that there is consensus among special educators about how students with emotional or behavioral disorders should be taught. In fact, several different conceptual models may guide educators, as shown in Table 6-1. As Kauffman (1997) points out, few practitioners are guided strictly and exclusively by a single model. Nevertheless, a teacher must have a solid grounding in one conceptual orientation to guide competent practice.

Of the five models included in Table 6-1, two guide most educational programs today: the psychoeducational and behavioral models. We illustrate these models in action with actual case descriptions. (See Kauffman, 1997, for description and case illustrations of other models.)

Table 6–1

Approaches to Educating Students with Emotional or Behavioral Disorders

	Psychoanalytic Approach	*Psychoeducational Approach*	*Humanistic Approach*	*Ecological Approach*	*Behavioral Approach*
The Problem	A pathological imbalance among the dynamic parts of the mind (id, superego, ego)	Involves both underlying psychiatric disorders and readily observable misbehaviors and underachievement	The student is out of touch with his or her own feelings and can't find fulfillment in traditional educational settings	The student interacts poorly with the environment; the student and environment affect each other reciprocally and negatively	The student has learned inappropriate responses and failed to learn appropriate ones
Purpose of Educational Practices	Use of psychoanalytic principles to help uncover underlying mental pathology	Concern for unconscious motivation/underlying conflicts and academic achievement/positive surface behavior	Emphasis on enhancing self-direction, self-evaluation, and emotional involvement in learning	Attempts to alter the entire social system so it will support desirable behavior when intervention is withdrawn	Manipulates the student's immediate environment and the consequences of behavior
Characteristics of Teaching Methods	Reliance on individual psychotherapy for the student and parents; little emphasis on academic achievement; a highly permissive atmosphere	Emphasis on meeting individual needs of students; reliance on projects and creative arts	Use of nontraditional educational settings in which the teacher serves as a resource and catalyst rather than a director of activities; a nonauthoritarian, open, affective, personal atmosphere	Involves all aspects of a student's life—including classroom, family, neighborhood, and community—in teaching useful life and educational skills	Involves measurement of responses and subsequent analyses of behaviors to change them; emphasis on reward for appropriate behavior

Psychoeducational Model. The psychoeducational model addresses unconscious motivations and underlying conflicts (hallmarks of psychodynamic models), yet also stresses the realistic demands of everyday functioning in school, home, and community. One basic assumption of the psychoeducational model is that teachers must understand unconscious motivations if they are to deal most effectively with students' academic failures and misbehaviors. To do so, teachers are not expected to focus on resolving unconscious conflicts, as psychotherapists might. Rather, teachers must focus on how to help students acquire self-control through reflection and planning. Intervention may include therapeutic discussions or *life space interviews* (*LSIs*), which are designed to help the youth:

1. understand that what he or she doing is a problem
2. recognize his or her motivations
3. observe the consequences of his or her actions
4. plan alternative ways of responding to similar circumstances in the future

The emphasis is on the youngster gaining insight that will result in behavioral change, not on changing behavior directly (see Wood, 1990; Wood & Long, 1991). The following case of Andy, drawn from James and Long (1992), illustrates the psychoeducational model in action:

Andy

Andy, 14, was referred for special education due to his oppositional and sometimes verbally threatening behavior. In addition to disobeying adults in other ways, he frequently left the classroom without permission and roamed the hallways. He appeared to enjoy confronting his teachers and taunting his peers, especially a deaf peer, Drew, who also had few social skills.

One morning, Drew came to school very agitated, which required that the teacher spend most of her time before lunch calming him down. At lunch, Andy persistently aggravated Drew. When the teacher told Andy to stop and go back to his desk, Andy began yelling that Drew had called him a "fag" and that he (Drew) was the one who should return to his desk. The teacher repeated her instruction. Andy then shoved a desk across the room and left the classroom without permission. In the hall, Andy began pacing and disturbing other students. So the teacher and another staff member then escorted Andy to a quiet room, where he went without resistance. In the quiet room, the teacher used LSI techniques to help Andy think through the reasons for his behavior and how he might behave in more adaptive ways.

Through skillful interviewing about the incident with Drew, the teacher was able to help Andy see that he was jealous and resentful of the time she spent with Drew. Andy lived with his mother and an older sister. His sister had multiple disabilities, was very low functioning, and demanded a lot of his mother's attention. His father had left home when Andy was eight and his mother was not in good health. This meant that Andy had to take on some adult responsibilities at an early age.

The goals of the teacher's LSI about this particular incident were to get Andy to understand that she cared about him and wanted to prevent him from disrupting the group. Most importantly, she wanted Andy to understand that there were similarities in his situation at home and at school that gave rise to similar feelings and behavior.

Andy's teacher used what James and Long (1992) call a "red flag interview," a discussion that addresses the transfer of problems from home to school. A red flag interview follows a predictable sequence in which a student like Andy is helped to understand that:

1. He experiences a stressful situation at home (e.g., a beating, overstimulation, etc.).
2. His experience triggers intense feelings of anger, helplessness, and the like.
3. These feelings are not expressed to the abusive person at home because he is fearful of retaliation.
4. He contains his feelings until he gets on the bus, enters school, or responds to a demand.
5. He acts out his feelings in an environment that is safer and directs his behavior toward someone else.

The LSI may be based on the psychoanalytic notion of *defense mechanisms*—tactics that people use to avoid dealing with issues, events, or people that may be unpleasant or hurtful. Nonetheless, the LSI also must end with a return to the reality of the situation. In Andy's case, this meant his return to the class and anticipation of future problems. His teacher ended the LSI as follows:

Interviewer: What do you think Drew might do when we walk into the room?
Andy: He will probably point at me and laugh.
Interviewer: That might happen. How can you deal with that?
Andy: I can ignore him.

Interviewer: That will not be easy for you. It will take a lot of emotional strength to control your urge to tease him back. And if you do that and Drew teases you, who is going to get into trouble?

Andy: Drew.

Interviewer: That's right. You are now beginning to think more clearly about your actions. Also, I will set up a behavior contract for you. If you are able to ignore Drew's teasing, you will earn positive one-on-one time with me.

Andy: Agreed. (James & Long, 1992, p. 37)

Behavioral Model. Two major assumptions underlie the behavioral model: (1) The essence of the problem is the behavior itself, and (2) behavior is a function of environmental events. Maladaptive behavior is viewed as inappropriate learned responses to particular demands or circumstances. Therefore, intervention should consist of rearranging antecedent events and consequences to teach more adaptive behavior.

Actually, the behavioral model is a natural science approach to behavior, emphasizing precise definition, reliable measurement, careful control of the variables thought to maintain or change behavior, and establishment of replicable cause–effect relationships. Interventions consist of choosing target responses, measuring their current levels, analyzing probable controlling environmental events, and changing antecedent or consequent events until reliable changes are produced in the target behaviors (see Alberto & Troutman, 1995; Kerr & Nelson, 1989; Walker et al., 1995). The following case of Sven, based on a study by Dunlap et al. (1994), illustrates how a behavioral model might guide teaching:

Sven

Sven—an 11-year-old attending a special self-contained class for students with emotional or behavioral disorders—showed inadequate attention to tasks, inappropriate and aggressive talk, and physically aggressive behavior. An observer recorded Sven's behavior during brief (15 second) intervals for 15–30 minutes of his English lesson each day. These observations showed that Sven was engaged in academic tasks less than 60 percent of the time on average and that his behavior was disruptive about 40 percent of the time.

The professionals working with Sven assumed that students who exhibit maladaptive behaviors do so for a variety of reasons, including not only the consequences the behaviors bring but the settings in which they occur and the demands for performance—the antecedents. In this case, the antecedents related to Sven's maladaptive behavior were changed. The antecedents of his off-task, disruptive behavior—what he was assigned to do, especially if it was an assignment he did not like—seemed to be at least as much a problem as the consequences of his behavior. Therefore, the primary strategy used to modify Sven's behavior was to give him his choice of six to eight task options in his English class. The task options were constructed as variations on the work he normally would do, any one of which was acceptable and would lead to the same instructional objective. Under these conditions, Sven engaged in academic tasks about 95 percent of the time, and his disruptive behavior dropped to an average of less than 10 percent.

Clearly, giving Sven assignments about which he had choices—all of them acceptable variations—improved his attention to his tasks and markedly decreased his disruptive behavior. Use of behavioral methods such as rewarding consequences for appropriate behavior and academic performance are critically important. In addition, teachers may also use knowledge of behavior principles to alter the conditions of instruction in ways that defuse task *resistance* and encourage task *attention*.

Balancing Behavioral Control with Academic and Social Learning

Some writers have observed that the quality of educational programs for students with emotional or behavioral disorders is often dismal, regardless of the conceptual model underlying practice. The focus is often on rigid external control of students' behavior, and academic instruction and social learning are often secondary or almost entirely neglected (Knitzer, Steinberg, & Fleisch, 1990). Although the quality of instruction is undoubtedly low in too many programs, examples can be found of effective academic and social instruction for students at all levels (Peacock Hill Working Group, 1991)

Behavioral control strategies are an essential part of educational programs for students with externalizing problems. Without effective means of controlling disruptive behavior, it's extremely unlikely that academic and social learning will occur. Excellent academic instruction will certainly reduce many behavior problems (Kauffman et al., 1993). Nevertheless, even the best instructional programs will not eliminate the disruptive behaviors of all students. Teachers of students with emotional or behavioral disorders must have effective control strategies, preferably those involving students as much as possible in self-control. In addition, teachers must offer effective instruction in academic and social skills that will allow their students to live, learn, and work with others (Walker et al., 1995).

Importance of Integrated Services

Children and youths with emotional or behavioral disorders tend to have multiple and complex needs. For most, life is coming apart in more ways than one. In addition to their problems in school, they typically have family problems and a variety of difficulties in the community (e.g., engaging in illegal activities, an absence of desirable relationships with peers and adults, substance abuse, difficulty finding and maintaining employment). Thus, children or youths with emotional or behavioral disorders may need, in addition to special education, a variety of family-oriented services, psychotherapy or counseling, community supervision, training related to employment, and so on. No single service agency can meet the needs of most of these children and youths. Integrating these needed services into a more coordinated and effective effort is now seen as essential. (Edgar & Siegel, 1995; Nelson & Pearson, 1991).

Strategies That Work

Regardless of the conceptual model that guides education, we can point to several effective strategies. Most are incorporated in the behavioral model, but other models may include them, as well. Successful strategies at all levels, from early intervention through transition, balance concern for academic and social skills and provide integrated services. These strategies include the following elements (Peacock Hill Working Group, 1991):

- *systematic, data-based interventions*—interventions that are applied systematically and consistently and that are based on reliable research data, not unsubstantiated theory
- *continuous assessment and monitoring of progress*—direct, daily assessment of performance, with planning based on this monitoring;

- *provision for practice of new skills*—skills are not taught in isolation but are applied directly in everyday situations through modeling, rehearsal, and guided practice
- *treatment matched to the problem*—interventions that are designed to meet the needs of individual students and their particular life circumstances, not general "formulas" that ignore the nature, complexity, and severity of the problem
- *multicomponent treatment*—as many different interventions as are necessary to meet the multiple needs of students (e.g., social skills training, academic remediation, medication, counseling or psychotherapy, family treatment or parent training, etc.)
- *programming for transfer and maintenance*—interventions designed to promote transfer of learning to new situations, recognizing that "quick fixes" nearly always fail to produce generalized change
- *commitment to sustained intervention*—interventions designed with the realization that many emotional or behavioral disorders are developmental disabilities and will not be eliminated entirely or cured.

Service Delivery Models

Only a relatively small percentage of children and youths with emotional or behavioral disorders are officially identified and receive any special education or mental health services. Consequently, those individuals who *do* receive special education tend to have very serious problems, although most (along with those who have mild mental retardation or learning disabilities) have typically been assumed to have only mild disabilities. That is, the problems of the typical student with an emotional or behavioral disorder who is identified for special education may be more serious than many people have assumed. Severe does not apply only to the disorders of autism and schizophrenia; a child can have a severe conduct disorder, for example, and its disabling effects can be extremely serious and persistent (Kauffman, 1997; Kazdin, 1995; Patterson et al., 1992; Wolf, Braukmann, & Ramp, 1987).

Compared to students with most other disabilities, a higher percentage of students with emotional or behavioral disorders are educated outside regular classrooms and schools, probably in part because students with these disorders tend to have more serious problems before they are identified. Emotional or behavioral disorders include many different types of behavioral and emotional problems, which makes it hard to make generalizations about how programs are administered.

Even so, the trend in programs for students with emotional or behavioral disorders is toward integration into regular schools and classrooms. Even when students are placed in separate schools and classes, educators hope for reintegration into the mainstream. Integration of these students is typically difficult and requires intensive work on a case-by-case basis (Fuchs, Fuchs, Fernstrom, & Hohn, 1991; Kauffman, Lloyd, Baker, & Riedel, 1995; Walker & Bullis, 1991).

Placement decisions for students with emotional or behavioral disorders are particularly problematic (Kauffman, Lloyd, Hallahan, & Astuto, 1995). Educators who serve students with the most severe emotional or behavioral disorders provide ample justification for specialized environments for these children and youths. That is, it is impossible to replicate in the context of a regular classroom in a neighborhood school the intensive, individualized, highly structured environments with very high adult–student ratios offered in special classes and facilities (see Kauffman & Hallenbeck, in press).

Hence, it is extremely important that the full continuum of placement options be maintained for students with emotional or behavioral disorders and that placement decisions be made on an individual basis, after an appropriate program of education and related services has been designed. Students must not be placed outside regular classrooms and schools unless their needs require it. The IDEA mandate of placement in the least restrictive environment (LRE) applies to students with behavioral disorders as well as those in all other categories. In other words, they are to be taught in regular schools and classes and with their nondisabled peers to the extent that doing so is consistent with their appropriate education. However, students' needs for appropriate education and safety take priority over placement in a less restrictive environment (Bateman & Chard, 1995).

Prior to being identified for special education, many students with emotional or behavioral disorders have been in regular classrooms, where they could observe and learn from appropriate peer models. In reality, though, these students usually fail to imitate these models. They are unlikely to benefit merely from being with other students who have not been identified as disabled, as incidental social learning is insufficient to address their difficulties (Hallenbeck & Kauffman, 1995; Kauffman & Pullen, 1996; Rhode, Jensen, & Reavis, 1992). In order for students with emotional or behavioral disorders to learn from peer models of appropriate behavior, most will require explicit, focused instruction about whom and what to imitate. In addition, they may need explicit and intensive instruction in social skills, including when, where, and how to exhibit specific types of behavior (Walker et al., 1995).

The academic curriculum for most students with emotional or behavioral disorders parallels that for most students. The basic academic skills have a great deal of survival value for any individual in society who is capable of learning them; failure to teach a student to read, write, and perform basic arithmetic deprives him or her of any reasonable chance for successful adjustment to the everyday demands of life. Students who do not acquire academic skills that allow them to compete with their peers are likely to be socially rejected (Kauffman, 1997).

Students with emotional or behavioral disorders may need specific instruction in social skills, as well. We emphasize two points: (1) Effective methods are needed to teach basic academic skills, and (2) social skills and affective experiences are as crucial as academic skills. How to manage one's feelings and behavior and how to get along with other people are essential features of the curriculum for many students with emotional or behavioral disorders. These children cannot be expected to learn such skills without instruction, for the ordinary processes of socialization obviously have failed (Walker et al., 1995).

Students with schizophrenia and other major psychiatric disorders vary widely in the behaviors they exhibit and the learning problems they have. Some may need hospitalization and intensive treatment; others may remain at home and attend regular public schools. Again, the trend today is away from placement in institutions or special schools and toward inclusion in regular public schools. In some cases, students with major psychiatric disorders who attend regular schools are enrolled in special classes.

Educational arrangements for juvenile delinquents are hard to describe in general terms because *delinquency* is a legal term, not an educational distinction, and because programs for extremely troubled youths vary so much among states and localities. Special classes or schools are sometimes provided for youths who have histories of threatening, violent, or disruptive behavior. Some of these classes and schools are administered under special education law, but others are not because the pupils

collaboration

a key to success

Jay Shipman

Bob Raboin

Jay We'll describe our work with Todd, a fifth-grader. Todd was small but strong, and a good runner. He had dark hair, somewhat protruding blue eyes, and enough braces on his teeth to rechrome a '58 Buick. He rarely spoke to anyone, and when he did, it was almost impossible to hear him. He typically did not respond to adults or children who talked to him, and he didn't look at them either. Todd was capable of above-average academic work in all areas, but he did so little that it took a long time to figure out what he knew. If I asked him to correct a mistake, no matter how gently I phrased it, he would deny he had made a mistake and call me a liar. Then he might sneer and swear, turn over his desk, throw his books, and make loud noises or bark like a dog for two or three hours. This scenario was repeated three or four days a week. Todd acted this way anytime he was asked to do something he didn't care to do at the moment. His tantrums could take place anytime I asked him to sit down or use a pencil instead of a pen. He would hit me or punch other students and teachers when things didn't go his way. For example, once he got his book bag tangled up with another boy's as they were getting on the bus. Todd was instantly furious, thrashing like a wild animal caught in a net. When he was free, he slugged a boy—who just happened to be standing in front of him—in the back of the head. He threw his tray at the woman who served the school lunches and called her a "fucking bitch" because she wouldn't give him a second helping. He seemed to have missed the fact that there wasn't any food left. The first three months of the year, Todd rarely left my room. He had no friends and was still trying to see if we would let him be the person in charge. I saw him as fearful, withdrawn, and furious.

Bob You get the idea we weren't dealing with a typical fifth-grader here!

Jay My first job as the special education teacher was to reduce Todd's aggression and increase his compliance. I talked with Todd's parents and concluded that the major factors contributing to Todd's behavior were manipulative behaviors he had learned in the family. His mother seemed concerned but helpless. Todd could manipulate her easily. His father appeared unconcerned and condescending, as though I had a problem. It wasn't hard to see why Todd was used to getting his own way and felt that others should do his bidding or there was something wrong with them. I started very early to make sure that he knew I was in charge. I set up a program with his parents: We would make rules and stick to them. Todd could throw tantrums all he wanted—we really couldn't stop him—but that wouldn't change the consequences. We wanted to show him that he had the power to choose how he reacted to the rules, but he did not have the power to change or make the rules. Home and school tried to accentuate the positive and withhold what he liked when he made poor choices. We tried to keep the consequences logical: You don't go out for recess when you don't work; you don't go to the movies when you swear at your mother. The point with Todd wasn't to punish him—that only would have made things worse. He simply needed to know that eleven-year-olds don't tell adults what to do. My job was to ride out his tantrums calmly so he would be left with the consequences of his choices. If I got upset, then he would get more reinforcement for being manipulative and aggressive.

Bob My first contact with Todd was when Jay introduced me to him in the hall. I tried to make casual conversation. This wasn't easy because Todd didn't talk to me, but I kept it up. I ran into Todd on the playground, usually to pry his hands off some other kid's throat. I don't think this made him a big fan of mine, but I'm not sure it did much damage either. Todd

Jay Shipman teaches students with behavioral disorders, grades K-6, Coolidge School, Neenah, Wisconsin; B.A. History, St. Norbert College; M.Ed., Special Education, University of Wisconsin-Oshkosh. **Bob Raboin** is a fifth-grade teacher; B.S.E., University of Wisconsin-Superior.

was so turned in on himself that I don't think he even remembered me when he came to my class in December. He came to my special project class at first. We do string art and woodworking and macramé, among other things. Todd came as a reward for doing well in the special education class. By December, Todd would have done anything to get away from Jay, and he liked the stuff we did. My job was to be as aware as possible of what Jay and Todd had gone through so far. Jay and I do not teach the same way; we don't need to be alike. I did need to make sure that the consequences were the same for Todd, even if our rules and personal styles were different. Jay sends me a rating slip for every class. I teach the way I normally do, and Todd takes the rating slip back to Jay after every class. Todd gets the same consistent consequences; I don't have to design an individual reward system, and the changes are kept to a minimum for Todd. My part of the bargain is to teach fifth grade, and I need to provide the best possible environment for Todd to see and practice appropriate social behavior. I talk a lot with my students about the individual needs of various students. We learn to tolerate differences and eventually respect them. Jay and I talk when we need to, sometimes three times a day and sometimes not for a week. Todd gradually participated in more and more classes. We had minor problems but nothing major. Jay's job is to get the kid to the point of being able to handle a class in my room. He should show up in my room with the right materials and follow the rules. I make individual adjustments for most of my students when I can. If the students cannot meet my minimum standards over a period of time, they go back to Jay's room for awhile. Jay's never questioned that. Good teachers do what's best for a student, but we all have limits. Knowing your limits isn't a sign of weakness; it shows insight and respect for others.

Jay The most challenging aspect of teamwork is the communication. This is hard when you have a violent student in your room that you cannot leave alone. Talking confidentially about a mainstreamed student is hard when you're holding onto one of them. The major challenge I faced with Todd was a private issue for me. I had to find reasons to want to work with and for Todd. He insulted me verbally, lashed out at me physically, and was the most rude and cruel student I had worked with in years. I wasn't sure Todd would last five days in Bob's class. I told Bob I had this boy who was usually extremely withdrawn but could, without apparent provocation, jump on some kid and start crushing his windpipe. Bob said that Todd sounded fine, and he anticipated no major problems. I knew that meant that Todd was welcome and we would take it one day at a time, one class at a time. I think Todd saved most of his major acting out for times when he wasn't in Bob's room. He couldn't break the habits of ten years in three months, but he had lots of respect for Bob and worked very hard to do well and not "let him down." We wanted not to shield Todd from consequences and gradually to transfer the responsibility for applying those consequences to Bob.

Bob My challenges as a fifth-grade teacher were different. I had to get to know Todd. I had to get accurate information from Jay on what I could reasonably expect academically and behaviorally. I also had to try to predict how Todd was going to affect and be affected by the other students in my class. I had to make sure I filled out the rating slips after every class so Jay could apply the proper consequences and help Todd get any late work done. This seems like a small thing, but with about thirty students, it isn't always easy to remember to do it. I had one more person to teach, one more batch of papers to correct, and one more child to show that I cared about him and respected him. These are things I think any student should take for granted. My point is that they take time.

Jay Any of the students we work with have been badly damaged through the malice or ignorance of others. It is extremely gratifying to see a student who was chronically depressed or angry finally become happy much of the time. Most people have given up on our students. We get a chance to experience the joy of watching a boy discover that life can be a gift as well as a burden. This is what makes teaching a wonderful profession.

Bob I think collaboration is primarily a product of the desire to work together and the amount of time and resources available.

Jay I think my primary responsibility is to make sure that the situation is productive and successful for the student and the regular teacher. A big part of my time is devoted to establishing and maintaining good working relationships with other teachers. I have to earn the respect of secretaries, custodians, teachers, bus drivers, and the principal. If you do not find it easy to get along with a wide variety of people, being a teacher of children with emotional and behavioral disorders will be very difficult. You have to be aware of personal and classroom stress and plan accordingly. You think about who has the time and the personality that will work for a given child. The most common mistake in mainstreaming is placing a student who isn't ready or picking a poor placement.

> ***We would take it one day at a time, one class at a time.***

Bob My teaching doesn't change much when I have a student with an emotional/behavioral disorder. I've been told what to expect, but I've never been told to change what I do. Jay has asked me to make adjustments for a given child, and we've always at least worked out a compromise. I have the hardest time when I don't think I have the resources that a student needs. There are times when the numbers or group chemistry just make it impossible to give a student the attention he or she may need.

assigned to them are not considered seriously emotionally disturbed. In jails, reform schools, and other detention facilities housing children and adolescents, wide variation is found in educational practices (Nelson, Rutherford, & Wolford, 1987). Education of incarcerated children and youths with learning disabilities is governed by the same laws that apply to those who are not incarcerated, but the laws are not always carefully implemented. Many incarcerated children do not receive assessment and education appropriate for their needs because of lack of resources, poor cooperation among agencies, and the attitude that delinquents and criminals are not entitled to the same educational opportunities as law-abiding citizens (Leone, 1990; Leone, Rutherford & Nelson, 1991).

Given all this, it is clear that teachers of students with emotional or behavioral disorders must be able to tolerate a great deal of unpleasantness and rejection without becoming counteraggressive or withdrawn. Most of the students they teach are rejected by others. If kindness and concern were the only things required to help these students, they probably would not be considered to have disabilities. Teachers cannot expect caring and decency always to be returned. They must be sure of their own values and confident of their teaching and living skills. They must be able and willing to make wise choices for students who choose to behave unwisely (Kauffman, 1997; Kauffman et al., 1993).

EARLY INTERVENTION

Early identification and prevention are basic goals of intervention programs for any category of disability. For students with emotional or behavioral disorders, these goals present particular difficulties—yet they hold particular promise. The difficulties are related to definition and measurement of emotional or behavioral disorders, especially in young children; the particular promise is that young children's social-emotional behavior is quite flexible, so preventive efforts seem to have a good chance of success.

As mentioned previously, defining emotional or behavioral disorders in such a way that children can be reliably identified is a difficult task. Definition and identification involving preschool children are complicated by several additional factors:

1. The developmental tasks that young children are expected to achieve are much simpler than those expected of older children, so the range of normal behaviors to be used for comparison is quite restricted. Infants and toddlers are expected to eat, sleep, perform relatively simple motor skills, and respond socially to their parents. School-age children, however, must learn much more varied and complex motor and cognitive skills and develop social relations with a variety of peers and adults.
2. There is wide variation in the childrearing practices of good parents and in family expectations for preschool children's behavior in different cultures, so we must guard against inappropriate norms used for comparison. What is described as *immature, withdrawn,* or *aggressive* behavior in one family may not be perceived as such in another.
3. In the preschool years children's development is rapid and often uneven, making it difficult to judge what spontaneous improvements might occur.
4. The most severe types of emotional or behavioral disorders often are first observed in the preschool years. But it is frequently difficult to tell the difference between emotional or behavioral disorders and other conditions, like

mental retardation or deafness. Often the first signs are difficulty with basic biological functions (e.g., eating, sleeping, eliminating) or social responses (e.g., responding positively to a parent's attempts to offer comfort or "molding" to the parent's body when being held). Difficulty with these basic areas or in achieving developmental milestones like walking and talking indicate that the child may have an emotional or behavioral disability. But these difficulties may also be indicators of other conditions, such as mental retardation, sensory impairment, or physical disability.

The patterns of behavior that signal problems for the preschool child are those that bring them into frequent conflict with or keep them aloof from their parents or caretakers and their siblings or peers. Many children who are referred to clinics for disruptive behavior when they are seven to twelve years of age showed clear signs of behavior problems by the time they were three or four—or even younger (Loeber, Green, Lahey, Christ, & Frick, 1992). Infants or toddlers who exhibit a very "difficult temperament"—who are irritable; have irregular patterns of sleeping, eating, and eliminating; have highly intense responses to many stimuli and negative reactions toward new situations—are at risk for developing serious behavior problems unless their parents are particularly skillful at handling them. Children of preschool age are likely to elicit negative responses from adults and playmates if they are much more aggressive or much more withdrawn than most children their age. (Remember the critical importance of same-age comparisons. Toddlers frequently grab what they want, push other children down and throw things and kick and scream when they don't get their way; toddlers normally do not have much finesse at social interaction and often hide from strangers.)

Because children's behavior is quite responsive to conditions in the social environment and can be shaped by adults, the potential for *primary prevention*—preventing

Including students with emotional and behavioral disorders in regular classrooms may be particularly problematic given that social interactions are a primary area of concern.

Preschool intervention for children with emotional and behavioral disorders has been shown quite effective in preventing or reducing subsequent problems. However, identifying these disorders at such an early age can be difficult, particularly for parents who have limited knowledge and experience regarding such disorders.

serious behavior problems from occurring in the first place—would seem to be great. If parents and teachers could be taught effective child management skills, perhaps many or most cases could be prevented (Walker et al., 1995). Furthermore, one could imagine that if parents and teachers had such skills, children who already have emotional or behavioral disorders could be prevented from getting worse (*secondary prevention*). But as Bower (1981) notes, the task of primary prevention is not that simple. For one thing, the tremendous amount of money and personnel needed for training in child management are not available. For another, even if the money and personnel could be found, professionals would not always agree on what patterns of behavior should be prevented or on how undesirable behavior could be prevented from developing (Kazdin, 1995).

If overly aggressive or withdrawn behavior has been identified in a preschooler, what kind of intervention program is most desirable? Behavioral interventions are highly effective (see also Peacock Hill Working Group, 1991; Strain et al., 1992; Walker et al., 1995). A behavioral approach implies defining and measuring the child's behaviors and rearranging the environment (especially adults' and other children's responses to the problem child) to teach and support more appropriate conduct. In the case of aggressive children, social rewards for aggression should be prevented. For example, hitting another child or throwing a temper tantrum might result in brief social isolation or "time-out" instead of adult attention or getting one's own way.

Researchers are constantly seeking less punitive ways of dealing with problem behavior, including aggression. The best way of handling violent or aggressive play or play themes, for example, would be one that effectively reduces the frequency of aggressive play yet requires minimum punishment. In one study with children between the ages of three and five, violent or aggressive theme play (talk or imitation of weapons, destruction, injury, etc.) was restricted to a small area of the classroom defined by a carpet sample (Sherburne, Utley, McConnell, & Gannon, 1988). Children engaging

Creative expression can help children with emotional and behavioral disorders communicate their feelings and channel their energy.

in imaginative play involving guns, for example, were merely told by the teacher, using a pleasant tone of voice, "If you want to play guns, go over on the rug" (p. 169). If violent theme play continued for more than ten seconds after the teacher's warning, the child or children were physically assisted to the rug. They were not required to stay on the rug for a specific length of time; rather, they merely had to go there if they wanted to engage in aggressive play. This simple procedure was quite effective in reducing violent and aggressive themes in the children's play.

In summary, it *is* possible to identify preschool children who are at high risk for having emotional or behavioral disorders (Loeber et al., 1992; Walker et al., 1994; Wehby, Dodge, & Valente, 1993). These children exhibit extreme aggression or social withdrawal compared to their agemates. They should be identified as early as possible, and their parents and teachers should learn how to teach them essential skills and management of their problem behavior using positive, nonviolent procedures (see Timm, 1993; Walker et al., 1995). If children with serious emotional or behavioral disorders are identified very early and intervention is sufficiently comprehensive, intense, and sustained, then there is a good chance that they can recover and exhibit developmentally normal patterns of behavior (cf. Lovaas, 1987; Timm, 1993; Walker et al., 1995).

Nevertheless, research suggests that in practice, early intervention typically does not occur. In fact, intervention does usually not begin until the child has exhibited an extremely disabling pattern of behavior for several years (Duncan, Forness, & Hartsough, 1995). The primary reasons given as to why early, comprehensive, intense, and sustained intervention is so rare include worry about labeling and stigma, optimism regarding the child's development (i.e., the assumption that he or she will "grow out of it"), lack of resources required to address the needs of any but the most severely problematic children, and ignorance about the early signs of emotional or behavioral problems (Kauffman, 1997).

TRANSITION

The programs designed for adolescents with emotional or behavioral disorders have varied widely in aims and structure. Nelson and Kauffman (1977) describe the following types, which remain the basic options today:

- regular public high school classes
- consultant teachers who work with regular teachers to provide individualized academic work and behavior management
- resource rooms and special self-contained classes to which students may be assigned for part or all of the school day
- work-study programs in which vocational education and job experience are combined with academic study
- special private or public schools that offer the regular high school curriculum in a different setting
- alternative schools that offer highly individualized programs that are nontraditional in both setting and content
- private or public residential schools

Incarcerated youths with emotional or behavioral disorders are an especially neglected group in special education (McIntyre, 1993; Nelson, Rutherford, & Wolford, 1987). One suspects that the special educational needs of many (or most) of these teenagers who are in prison are neglected because incarcerated youths are defined as *socially maladjusted* rather than *seriously emotionally disturbed.* The current federal definition appears to allow denial of special education services to a large number of young people who exhibit extremely serious misbehaviors and have long histories of school failure.

One of the reasons it is difficult to design special education programs at the secondary level for students with emotional or behavioral disorders is that this category of youths is so varied. Adolescents categorized for special education purposes as seriously emotionally disturbed may have behavioral characteristics ranging from autistically withdrawn to aggressively delinquent, intelligence ranging from severely retarded to highly gifted, and academic skills ranging from preschool to college level. Therefore, it is hardly realistic to suggest that any single type of program or model will be appropriate for all such youths. In fact, youths with emotional or behavioral disorders, perhaps more than any other category of exceptionality, need a highly individualized, creative, and flexible education. Programs may range from teaching daily living skills in a sheltered environment to advanced placement in college, from regular class placement to hospitalization, and from the traditional curriculum to unusual and specialized vocational training.

Transition from school to work and adult life is particularly difficult for adolescents with emotional or behavioral disorders. Many of them lack the basic academic skills necessary for successful employment. In addition, they often behave in ways that prevent them from being accepted, liked, and helped by employers, co-workers, and neighbors. It is not surprising that students with emotional or behavioral disorders are among the most likely to drop out of school and among the most difficult to train in transition programs (Carson, Sitlington, & Frank, 1995; Edgar & Siegel, 1995).

Many children and youths with emotional or behavioral disorders grow up to be adults who have real difficulties leading independent, productive lives. The outlook is especially grim for children and adolescents who have conduct disorder. Contrary to popular opinion, the child or youth who is shy, anxious, or neurotic is not the most likely to have psychiatric problems as an adult. Rather, it is the conduct-disordered (hyperaggressive) child or youth whose adulthood is most likely to be characterized by socially intolerable behavior (Kazdin, 1995). About half the children who are hyperaggressive will have problems that require legal intervention or psychiatric care when they are adults.

Successful transition to adult life is often complicated by neglectful, abusive, or inadequate family relationships. A high percentage of adolescents with conduct disorder have family relationships of this nature.

Examples of relatively successful high school and transition programs are available, most of which employ a behavioral approach (Edgar & Siegel, 1995; Peacock Hill Working Group, 1991). However, it is important to stress *relatively* because many adolescents and young adults with severe conduct disorder appear to have a true developmental disability that requires intervention throughout their life span (Wolf, Braukmann, & Ramp, 1987). By the time these antisocial youths reach high school, the aim of even the most effective program is to help them accommodate their disabilities. Rather than focusing on remediation of academic and social skills, these programs attempt to teach youths the skills they will need to survive and cope in school and community, to make a transition to work, and to develop vocations (Walker et al., 1995).

Suggestions for Teaching
Students with Emotional or Behavioral Disorders in General Education Classrooms

By Peggy L. Tarpley

WHAT TO LOOK FOR IN SCHOOL

Recognizing students with emotional or behavioral disorders is sometimes easy and sometimes complex. Some children and adolescents with these disorders are aggressive. They act out in ways that are obviously inappropriate for school. For example, they may physically provoke others to frequent fights, or they may verbally annoy others by constantly criticizing or teasing. Their aggressive, overt behavior quickly suggests potentially serious behavior problems.

On the other hand, some students with emotional or behavioral disorders are withdrawn. They exhibit more subtle behaviors, which, in the context of a busy classroom, may be difficult to identify. In the early elementary grades, they may whine or cry in situations that usually don't cause such responses. They also may be dependent, asking others for help to complete work they can do on their own. They may be alone, without friends, or sad or depressed much of the time.

The key to identifying both the aggressive and withdrawn types of emotional or behavioral disorders is the persistence and severity of the behaviors. To be considered serious, students must show these behaviors to a marked degree over a long period of time in a variety of settings.

HOW TO GATHER INFORMATION

If you suspect any of your students may have serious emotional or behavioral problems, you can help identify them in several ways. Record each specific behavior you observe, including the approximate time of the day and the date, the context in which the behavior occurred, and the consequences. For example, you might note, "Alan slapped and kicked Sam after a softball game during recess on Monday, November 2" and describe the circumstances provoking the incident as well as the consequences for Alan.

Noting the exact times for more subtle behavior problems may be difficult. Recording your observations at the end of the day or during a planning period is helpful. For example, you might report that "Laura was alone while other students talked together before school in class, during lunch in the cafeteria, and at recess outdoors on Tuesday, October 30." This log will provide an important record of the frequency, severity, and circumstances surrounding the behaviors, which may help you and the school psychologist, counselor, or special education teacher identify the exact nature of the problem.

Describing particularly serious events in greater detail is also helpful. The student's comments regarding these events and the consequences of the behavior provide valuable information. For example, one teacher reported:

> David started a fire in the art storage area adjacent to the art room after school on Friday, December 11. He said he did it to get back at the art teacher, who sent him to the principal's office during class that day for splattering paint on another student's holiday project for parents. His parents were called and came to school immediately. Following a discussion of the seriousness of his behavior and the potential legal ramifications, David was suspended for 10 days. No charges were filed.

It is also important to note relevant information from parents, such as descriptions of the student's behavior at home, effective techniques used by the parents, or treatment he or she is receiving outside of school.

TEACHING TECHNIQUES TO TRY

Although there are several approaches to the treatment of children and adolescents with emotional or behavioral disorders, one that teachers often use identifies the factors in school that contribute to a given student's inappropriate behaviors and the factors in school that can be altered to change those behaviors. Interventions include helping the student to increase appropriate behaviors, decrease inappropriate ones, and learn behaviors he or she does not know already.

To manage students' behaviors Lewis and Doorlag (1990) suggest teachers follow a step-by-step process:

1. State the behavioral expectations for all students in the class.
2. Determine whether students who meet these expectations are receiving reinforcement so they will continue to meet the expectations.
3. If there are students who do not meet the expectations, determine whether they understand the expectations and whether they have the needed skills to perform the behaviors.
4. For students who use inappropriate behaviors, identify a behavior to change.
5. Decide how you will observe and gather information on this behavior.
6. After reviewing the information you have collected, determine whether the behavior needs to be increased, decreased, or learned.
7. Choose a strategy that is positive, rather than punishing.
8. While using the strategy, collect information on the student's behavior.
9. Review this information to decide whether this strategy should be continued, modified, or stopped.
10. When the student performs the behavior at the desired level, continue to monitor and return to Step 4 if the student has other behaviors that require intervention.

Selecting Approaches

An important consideration in choosing a behavior management approach is the degree of intrusiveness and restrictiveness it involves. *Intrusiveness* refers to the extent to which interventions impinge on students' rights and/or bodies and the degree to which they interrupt educational activities (Kerr & Nelson, 1989). Less intrusive procedures, for example, do not restrict students' movements or interrupt typical, ongoing educational activities. "Restrictiveness refers to the extent to which an intervention inhibits students' freedom to be treated like all other pupils" (Kerr & Nelson, 1989, p.107).

Although most experts agree it is preferable to begin managing behavior by selecting the least intrusive and restrictive procedure appropriate to the behavior you want to change, they do not agree on the order of these procedures. Kerr and Nelson (1989, p. 107) suggest the following hierarchy, listing from less to more restrictive or intrusive:

Enhancement Procedures:	***Reductive Procedures:***
Self-regulation	Differential reinforcement
Social reinforcement	Extinction
Modeling	Verbal aversives
Contracting	Response cost
Activity reinforcement	"Time-out"
Token reinforcement	Overcorrection
Tangible reinforcement	Physical aversives
Edible reinforcement	
Tactile and sensory reinforcement	

It is important to note that some of the procedures listed under "Enhancement Procedures" may be used both to increase and decrease behaviors. For example, teachers may use models to strengthen, weaken, or maintain behavior (Bandura, 1969). However, those listed under "Reductive Procedures" are used only to decrease behaviors. The remainder of the section will discuss the less intrusive and restrictive procedures listed above.

Increasing Appropriate School Behaviors

Reinforcement

One strategy teachers use to increase a student's appropriate behavior involves rewarding, or *reinforcing*, that behavior each time the student exhibits it. The reward can take many forms. For instance, it may be a point or token exchangeable at a later time for a special privilege. Because *social reinforcement* is less intrusive and restrictive than other types of reinforcement, teachers typically select it first. Verbal praise, such as "Good work, Tony. I liked the way you worked by yourself on the math problems," is an example of social reinforcement. Smiles, handshakes, nods, gentle pats on the back are other examples. However, not all students like the same rewards. You will want to find the one that works with a particular student or groups of students.

Activity reinforcement follows the application of the Premack Principle, which also is called "Grandma's law" because it is based on the same idea that prompted Grandma to say, "If you eat your vegetables, then you can have your dessert" (Polloway & Patton, 1993.). The Premack principle makes high frequency behaviors, such as talking with a friend or playing computer games, contingent on the performance of low-frequency behaviors, such as completing assignments or responding appropriately to adults (cf. Premack, 1959). Some activities that teachers are reinforcing for their students include being a team leader, receiving extra story time, listening to music, and looking at magazines.

Like social and activity reinforcement, *token reinforcement* is contingent upon the performance of a specific desired behavior. In a token system, or token economy, students receive tokens, such as points or chips, which they can trade at a later time for activity reinforcers, tangible reinforcers (e.g., stickers, certificates, magnets, markers), or edible reinforcers (e.g., pretzels, popcorn). Polloway and Patton (1993) point out that in token reinforcement systems, students earn tokens for appropriate behavior just as adults receive money for their job performance.

Several variables are important in making reinforcers most effective. In *The Tough Kid Book,* Rhode, Jensen, and Reavis (1993) state these as the IFEED-AV rules:

- *I* stands for *immediately.* Timing is very important. The longer the teacher waits to reinforce appropriate behavior, the less effective the reinforcer will be.
- *F* stands for *frequently.* This is especially true when a student is learning a new behavior or skill. A good guidline is to grant three or four positive reinforcers for every one negative consequence (including verbal reprimands).
- *Es* stands for how the teacher gives reinforcement. The first *E* stands for *enthusiasm.* The teacher should respond in a manner that shows the student he or she has done something important. The next *E* stands for *eye contact.* By making eye contact, the teacher demonstrates that the student is special and has the teacher's undivided attention.
- *D* stands for *describe* the behavior. Be explicit about what behavior is being reinforced.
- *A* stands for *anticipation.* Building anticipation for the reward (reinforcement) can motivate students to do their best.
- Finally, *V* stands for *variety.* Reinforcers may need to be changed often to keep their potency.

Once the student exhibits the desirable behavior regularly, then you can begin gradually to decrease the frequency of the reward until he or she continues to use the behavior at the specified level with less frequent rewards. The following example illustrates how one teacher used positive reinforcement to increase her student's assignment completion:

> Sara is a thirteen-year-old student of average intelligence with behavior disorders who rarely turns in her class assignments. Her teacher, Mrs. Ellenon, wanted to increase to 80 percent the percentage of class assignments Sara handed in daily, after noting that Sara completed only one out of five assignments (20 percent) each day for a week. Mrs. Ellenon also observed that during seatwork, Sara often became very upset and then cried. When this happened, Mrs. Ellenon immediately comforted her by talking individually with her until the crying stopped. In reviewing these observations, Mrs. Ellenon suspected her individual attention to Sara was reinforcing the crying, and she decided to use that attention to reward Sara each time she turned in an assignment. The first day she used the reward strategy, Sara completed three out of five assignments (60 percent), and Mrs. Ellenon talked privately with her after she handed in each paper. Sara did so well that on the third day, with Sara's consent, Mrs. Ellenon reduced the reward to one individual talk after Sara completed two assignments and then only after she finished three assignments. By the eleventh day, Sara had reached the 80 percent criterion level Mrs. Ellenon established.

Contracting

In addition to reinforcement and modeling procedures, teachers can increase appropriate behaviors by using a behavioral contract, which systematizes the use of reinforcement. This written agreement between adult(s) and the student specifies what rewards and consequences will be contingent on the student's performance of a specific behavior. Like any contract, its contents are negotiated and all participants must agree to its terms. A contract states:

- the behavior to be performed
- the conditions under which the behavior will be performed
- the criterion for successful performance of the behavior
- the reward for performing the behavior
- the consequences for failing to perform the behavior
- the signatures of the contract participants
- the date

(Teachers who plan to use several contracts to improve a student's behaviors also often include the number of the contract.)

The following is an example of a contract negotiated by Mrs. Randolph, Bill, and Bill's parents to decrease his arguing and fighting.

> BEHAVIORAL CONTRACT
>
> Mrs. Randolph will check a Good Play card for Bill each time he plays during recess without fighting or arguing with any student. When Bill has earned 10 checks from Mrs. Randolph and has had his card signed by his parents, he may use the computer for 15 minutes.
>
> Signed: ______________________ (Student)
>
> ______________________ (Teacher)
>
> ______________________ (Parents)
>
> Written on (date) ________

Modeling

To increase specific behaviors, teachers also may provide a *model* of the behavior for students to imitate. Students imitate more readily the behavior of models who are similar to themselves in some way, who have high status, and who have been reinforced (Kerr & Nelson, 1989). Both live and vicarious models, such as those shown in videotapes or films, have been effective in altering behavior in public school classrooms. Kerr and Nelson point out that although behavioral procedures, such as reinforcement and modeling, are often discussed separately in textbooks, in practice, they often are used in combination. For example, teachers may model a behavior, such as expressing anger appropriately, and then have students practice this skill in role-plays and reinforce their performance.

Teaching Social Skills

The purpose of social skills training is to provide the student who behaves antisocially with the skills needed to avoid interpersonal rejection by peers and adults. Several social skills programs have been developed to address these needs. All follow a similar format, using modeling, role-play, behavioral and metacognitive strategy training (e.g., self-monitoring, self-evaluation, self-reinforcement, etc.), and feedback and reinforcement. Rutherford and Nelson (1995) state that through social skills training, "The student is provided with the tools to evaluate the environment, consider the alternatives, choose prosocial behaviors or strategies, monitor the effects of those behaviors, and adjust his or her behavior accordingly" (p. 10).

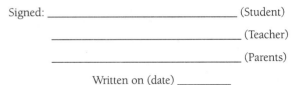

Similar to social skills programs are programs for managing anger or replacing aggression. One such program, developed by Goldstein and Glick (1987), teaches students to answer provocations that in the past ended in anger with a chain of self-awareness/self-control responses that include the following:

1. *triggers*—noting internal and external events that arouse anger
2. *cues*—identifying physiological factors that indicate anger has been aroused
3. *reminders*—making self-statements to reduce anger
4. *reducers*—using strategies such as counting backward, deep breathing, and reflecting on consequences of behavior
5. generating and selecting alternatives to anger and aggression
6. evaluating the use and results of the anger control sequence

Decreasing Inappropriate School Behaviors

Just as some students need help increasing appropriate behaviors, others require help in reducing behaviors that are not appropriate for school. Frequently, teachers select *differential reinforcement of incompatible behaviors* (*DRI*) which involves reinforcing a behavior that is incompatible with the one the teacher wants to decrease. A related positive approach teachers frequently use is *differential reinforcement of alternate behaviors* (*DRA*). During this procedure, teachers reinforce alternatives to the specific behavior targeted for change. For example, if you want to promote a student raising his or her hand instead of talking out in class, you would reinforce handraising.

Although several techniques are effective in decreasing behaviors, many involve using types of punishment. *Punishment* is defined as consequences that reduce the future probability of a behavior (Kauffman, 1997). When using any form of punishment, teachers should:

1. Combine punishment with positive reinforcement of alternative behaviors.
2. Manage punishment procedures carefully and use them consistently and immediately, as suggested by the 10-step process discussed previously (see p. 250).
3. Use punishment only after positive procedures have been unsuccessful.

The more restrictive procedures, such as "time-out," overcorrection, and physical aversives, should only be used by trained professionals.

Less intrusive punishment procedures include purposeful ignoring of a student's behavior, withholding other rewards, and public postings. Teachers, for example, have used public postings to improve behaviors such as disruptions in the halls (Staub, 1987, cited in Kerr & Nelson, 1989) by recording the daily performance of the class and "best record to date" on a large poster displayed at both ends of a school corridor. One of the most frequently used forms of punishment is reprimands. When using reprimands, make them privately, not publicly; stand near the student while reprimanding; and give his or her direct eye contact before scolding (Kerr & Nelson, 1989).

Preventing of Inappropriate School Behaviors

Because using even mild forms of punishment is less desirable than using positive strategies, teachers may reduce the need to use punishing techniques by preventing many behavior problems. Kerr and Nelson (1989) suggest that the notion of *structuring* is helpful in prevention. They recommend that teachers carefully consider the antecedents of inappropriate behavior to include the use of physical space, daily scheduling, and rules and routines to influence or structure student behavior. As you think about using classroom rules and routines, reflect on the following suggestions made by Lewis and Doorlag (1987):

1. Make rules and routines positive, concrete, and functional, relating them to the accomplishments of learning and order in the classroom (e.g., "Work quietly at the learning centers" rather than "Don't talk when working").
2. Design rules and routines to anticipate potential classroom problems and to manage these situations. For example, teachers may want students to raise their hands when they need help rather than calling out or leaving their seats to locate the teacher.
3. Establish classroom rules and routines at the beginning of the schoolyear by introducing them the first day.
4. Demonstrate or model rules and routines, and continue to provide opportunities for students to practice them until they have mastered them.
5. Associate rules and routines with simple signals that tell students when they are to carry out or stop specific activities and behaviors.
6. Monitor how students follow rules and routines, rewarding students for appropriate behaviors.

HELPFUL RESOURCES

School Personnel

In addition to the school personnel listed in previous chapters, school psychologists may be helpful in understanding and managing students with serious emotional or behavioral disorders. These professionals can provide specific information about students' problems based on their individual evaluations, recommend procedures teachers can use in their classrooms, and offer individual or group counseling for students with emotional or behavioral disorders.

School counselors are valuable in-building resources. They may help when students have behavioral crises. In addition, they are an important link between the classroom teacher and parents. They can provide frequent reports of student's progress and coordinate home-school plans to improve students' behavior and performance.

Instructional Methods

Cartledge, G., & Milburn, J. F. (1986). *Teaching social skills to children.* New York: Pergamon Press.

Center, D. B. (1989). *Curriculum and teaching strategies for students with behavioral disorders*. Englewood Cliffs, NJ: Prentice Hall.

Erickson, M. T. (1992). *Behavior disorders of children and adolescents: Assessment, etiology, and intervention*. Englewood Cliffs, NJ: Prentice Hall.

Grossman, H. (1990) *Trouble-free teaching: Solutions to behavior problems in the classroom*. Mountain View, CA: Mayfield.

Kauffman, J. J., Hallahan, D. P., Mostert, M. P., Trent, S. C., & Nuttycombe, D. G. (1993). *Managing classroom behavior: A reflective case-based approach.* Boston: Allyn & Bacon.

Kaplan, J. S., & Drainville, B. (1991). *Beyond behavior modification* (2nd ed.). Austin, TX: Pro-Ed.

Kerr, M. M., & Nelson, C. M. (1989). *Strategies for managing behavior problems in the classroom* (2nd ed.). Columbus, OH: Merrill.

Knowlton, D. (1995). Managing children with oppositional behavior. *Beyond Behavior, 6*(3), 5–10.

Macht, J. (1990). *Managing classroom behavior*. New York: Longman.

Morgan, D. P., & Jenson, W. R. (1988). *Teaching behaviorally disordered students: Preferred practices*. New York: Merrill/ Macmillan.

Morgan, S. R., & Reinhart, J. A. (1991). *Interventions with students with emotional disorders*. Austin, TX: Pro-Ed.

Nelson, C. M., & Pearson, C. (1991). *Integrating services for children and youth with emotional and behavioral disorders*. Reston, VA: Council for Exceptional Children.

Rhone, G., Jensen, W. R., & Reavis, H. K. (1993). *The tough kid book*. Longmont, CO: Sopris West.

Rockwell, S. (1995). *Back off, cool down, try again: Teaching students how to control aggressive behavior.* Reston, VA: Council for Exceptional Children.

Rosenberg, M. S., Wilson, R., Maheady, L., & Sindelar, P. (1992). *Educating students with behavior disorders*. Boston: Allyn & Bacon.

Schroeder, C. S., & Gordon, B. N., (1991). *Assessment and treatment of childhood problems*. New York: Guilford Press.

Smith, D. D. (1984). *Effective discipline*. Austin, TX: Pro-Ed.

Walker, H. M. (1995). *The acting out child: Coping with classroom disruption*. Longmont, CO: Sopris West.

Walker, H. M., Colvin, G., & Ramsey, E. (1995). *Antisocial behavior in schools: Strategies and best practices*. Pacific Grove, CA: Brooks/Cole.

Curricula and Instructional Materials

Dowd, T., & Tierney, J. (1992). *Teaching social skills to youth: A curriculum for child-care providers*. Boys Town, NE: Boys Town Press.

Goldstein, A. P., & Glick, B. (1987). *Aggression replacement training*. Champaign, IL: Research Press.

Goldstein, A. P., Sprafkin, R. P., Greshaw, N. J., & Klein, P. (1980). *Skillstreaming the adolescent: A structural learning approach to teaching prosocial skills*. Champaign, IL: Research Press.

Hazel, J. S., Shumaker, J. B., Sherman, J. A., & Sheldon-Wildgen, J. (1981). *ASSET: A social program for adolescents*. Champaign, IL: Research Press.

Jackson, N. F., Jackson, D. A., & Monroe, C. (1983). *Getting along with others*. Champaign, IL: Research Press.

Mannix, D. (1990). *I can behave*. Austin, TX: Pro-Ed.

McGinnis, E., Goldstein, A. P., Sprafkin, R. P., & Gershaw, N. J. (1984). *Skillstreaming the elementary school child: A guide for teaching prosocial skills*. Champaign, IL: Research Press.

Rutherford, R. B., Chipman, J., DiGangi, S. A., & Anderson, K. (1992). *Teaching social skills: A practical instructional approach*. Ann Arbor, MI: Exceptional Innovations.

Stokes, T. F., & Baer, D. M. (1988). *The social skills curriculum*. Circle Pines, MN: American Guidance Service.

Walker, H., McConnell, S., Holms, D., Todis, B., Walker, J., & Golden, N. (1983). *The Walker social skills curriculum: The ACCEPTS program*. Austin, TX: Pro-Ed.

Weisgerber, R., Appleby, J., & Fong, S. (1984). *Social solution curriculum* (developed at American Institute for Research, Palo Alto, CA). Burlingame, CA: Professional Associated Resources.

Literature about Individuals with Behavioral Disorders

Elementary

Berger, T. (1979). *I have feelings, too*. New York: Human Sciences Press. (Fiction = F)

Sheehan, C. (1981). *The colors that I am*. New York: Human Science Press. (F)

Simon, N. (1974). *I was so mad!* Chicago: A. Whitman. (Middle School) (F)

Hamilton, V. (1971). *The planet of Junior Brown*. New York: Macmillan. (F)

Patternson, K. (1978). *The great Gilly Hopkins*. New York: Cromwell. (F)

Platt, K. (1968). *The boy who could make himself disappear*. Dell. (F)

Secondary/Adult

Berger, G. (1981). *Mental illness*. New York: Franklin Watts. (Nonfiction = NF)

Greenfeld, J. (1978). *A place for Noah*. New York: Washington Square Press. (NF)

Greenfeld, J. (1986). *A client called Noah*. San Diego: Harcourt Brace Jovanovich. (NF)

Hayden, T. L. (1980). *One child*. New York: Putnam. (NF)

Heide, F. P. (1976). *Growing anyway up*. Philadelphia: Lippincott.

Hyde, M. O. (1983). *Is this kid "crazy"? Understanding unusual behavior*. Philadelphia: Westminister. (NF)

Software

Little Computer People, Triton Products Company, P.O. Box 8123, San Francisco, CA 94128, (800)227–6900.

Videodisc

Interactive Videodisc Social Skills (IVSS) Program, Ron Thorkildsen, Department of Special Education, Utah State University, Logan, UT, 84322–6500, (801)750–1999.

Organizations

Council for Children with Behavioral Disorders, 1920 Association Dr., Reston, VA 22091.

National Consortium for Child Mental Health Services, 3615 Wisconsin Avenue NW, Washington, DC 20016, (202) 966–7300.

BIBLIOGRAPHY FOR TEACHING SUGGESTIONS

Bandura, A. (1969). *Principles of behavior modification*. New York: Holt, Rinehart, & Winston.

Dowd, T., & Tierney, J. (1992). *Teaching social skills to youth: A curriculum for child-care providers*. Boys Town, NE: Boys Town Press.

Goldstein, A. P., & Glick, B. (1987). *Aggression replacement training*. Champaign, IL: Research Press.

Kauffman, J. M. (1997). *Characteristics of emotional and behavioral disorders of children and youth* (6th ed.). Columbus, OH: Merrill/Macmillan.

Kerr, M. M., & Nelson, C. M. (1989). *Strategies for managing behavior problems in the classroom* (2nd ed.). Columbus, OH: Merrill.

Lewis, R. B., & Doorlag, D. H. (1990). *Teaching special students in the mainstream* (3rd ed.). New York: Merrill/Macmillan.

Polloway, E. A., & Patton, J. S. (1993). *Strategies for teaching learners with special needs* (5th ed.). New York: Merrill/Macmillan.

Premack, D., (1959). Toward empirical behavior laws: I. Positive reinforcement. *Psychological Review, 66*, 219–233.

Rhode, G., Jensen, W. R., & Reavis, H. K. (1993). *The tough kid book.* Longmont, CO: Sopris West.

Rutherford, R. B., & Nelson, C. M. (1995). Management of aggressive and violent behavior in the schools. *Fouus on Exceptional Children, 27,* 1–15.

SUMMARY

Emotional or behavioral disorders are not simply a matter of undesirable or inappropriate behaviors. They involve inappropriate social interactions and transactions between the child or youth and the social environment.

Many different terms have been used for children's emotional or behavioral disorders. In the language of federal laws and regulations, they are *seriously emotionally disturbed*. The term *emotional or behavioral disorder* is becoming widely accepted, due primarily to the work of the National Mental Health and Special Education Coalition, which proposed a new definition and terminology in 1990.

The proposed definition defines *emotional or behavioral disorders* as a disability characterized by behavioral or emotional responses to school so different from appropriate age, cultural, or ethnic norms that they adversely affect educational performance. *Educational performance* is defined as more than academic performance; it includes academic, social, vocational, and personal skills. An emotional or behavioral disorder is more than a temporary or expected response to stressful events. It is exhibited in more than one setting, and it is unresponsive to direct intervention in general education. Finally, the proposed definition notes that the term *emotional or behavioral disorders* covers a wide variety of diagnostic groups, including sustained disorders of conduct or adjustment that adversely affect educational performance and can coexist with other disabilities.

Estimates of the prevalence of emotional or behavioral disorders vary greatly, in part because the definition is not precise. Most researchers estimate that 6 to 10 percent of the child population is affected, but only about 1 percent of the school-age population is currently identified as having emotional or behavioral disorders and is receiving special education services. Most children and youths who are identified for special education purposes are boys, and most exhibit externalizing behavior. About 3 percent of U.S. youths are referred to juvenile court in any given year. Relatively few of these receive special education services for emotional or behavioral disorders.

A single, specific cause of an emotional or behavioral disorder can seldom be identified. In most cases, it is possible only to identify causal factors that contribute to the likelihood that a child will develop a disorder or that predispose him or her to developing a disorder. Major contributing factors are found in biological conditions, family relationships, school experiences, and cultural influences. Possible biological factors include genetics, temperament (i.e., an inborn behavioral style), malnutrition, brain trauma, and substance abuse. Most biological causes are poorly understood, and social as well as medical intervention is almost always necessary.

Family disorganization, parental abuse, and inconsistent discipline are among the most important family factors contributing to emotional or behavioral disorders. However, poor parenting is not always or solely the cause. Furthermore, family factors appear to affect each family member in a different way. School factors that may contribute to emotional or behavioral disorders are insensitivity to students' individuality, inappropriate expectations, inconsistent or inappropriate discipline, unintentional rewards for misbehavior, and undesirable models of conduct. Cultural factors include the influences of the media, values and standards of the community and peer group, and social services available to children and their families. Family, school, and the wider culture create a complex web of cultural causal factors.

Most children and youths with emotional or behavioral disorders—especially those with serious conduct disorder or autism—are easily recognized. Few schools use systematic screening procedures, partly because services would be unavailable for the many students likely to be identified. The most effective identification procedures use a combination of teachers' rankings and ratings and direct observation of students' behavior. Peer rankings or ratings are often used, as well.

The typical student with an emotional or behavioral disorder has an IQ in the dull-normal range. The range of intelligence is enormous: A few are brilliant, and more than in the general population have mental retardation. Most children and youths with emotional or behavioral disorders lack, in varying degrees, the ability to apply their knowledge and skills to the demands of everyday living.

Students who express their problems in aggressive, acting-out behavior are involved in a vicious cycle. Their behavior alienates others so that positive interactions with adults and peers become less likely. Children and youths whose behavior is consistently antisocial have less chance of learning to make social adjustments and of achieving mental health in adulthood than do those who are shy, anxious, or neurotic.

Students with traumatic brain injury (TBI) may have problems related both to the actual brain damage and, depending on the age of onset, to personal adjustment issues. Students with autism or other pervasive developmental disorders often lack basic self-care skills, may appear to be perceptually disabled, and appear to have serious cognitive limitations. Especially evident and important is their inability to relate to other people. In addition, deviations in speech and language abilities, self-stimulation or self-injury, and the tendency to injure others deliberately combine to give these students a poor prognosis. Some of them function permanently at a level of mental retardation and require sustained supervision and care. Recent research brings hope that many may make remarkable progress with early intensive intervention. Some may learn an alternative means of communication.

Alarming findings concerning poor academic outcomes, high dropout rates, and frequent juvenile delinquency problems among students with emotional or behavioral disorders has led the U.S. Department of Education to establish an ambitious national agenda for these students, identifying seven targets: (1) expand positive learning opportunities/results; (2) strengthen school and community capacity; (3) value and address diversity; (4) collaborate with families; (5) promote appropriate assessment; (6) provide ongoing skill development and support; and (7) create comprehensive and collaborative systems.

Aside from the national agenda, special education is guided by one or a combination of conceptual models. The most commonly used are the psychoeducational model, which focuses on conscious and unconscious motivations, and the behavioral model, which stresses behaviors as functions of environmental events.

Regardless of the conceptual model guiding intervention or the characteristics of the students involved, the following strategies work: using systematic, data-based interventions; assessing and monitoring progress continuously; providing opportunities to practice new skills; providing treatment matched to the student's problem; offering multicomponent treatment to meet all the student's needs; programming for transfer and maintenance of learning; and sustaining intervention as long as it is needed.

A relatively small percentage of children and youths with emotional or behavioral disorders receive special education and related services. Only those with the most severe problems are likely to be identified, one consequence of which is that many are educated outside regular classrooms and schools. The trend, however, is toward greater integration in regular schools and classes. Because difficulty with social interactions is a hallmark of emotional and behavioral disorders, such placements can be particularly problematic.

Early identification and prevention are goals of early intervention programs. The problem behavior of many children later referred to clinics for emotional or behavioral disorders is evident early in life. Early intervention has been shown to be highly successful; however, it often does not occur due to worry about labeling and stigma, optimism that the child will "grow out of it," lack of resources, and ignorance about the early signs of problems. With early, intensive intervention, great improvements can be seen in nearly all cases.

Programs of special education for adolescents and young adults with emotional or behavioral disorders are extremely varied and must be highly individualized because of the wide differences in students' intelligence, behavioral characteristics, achievements, and circumstances. Transition from school to work and adult life is particularly difficult for students with emotional or behavioral disorders, and they are among those most likely to drop out of school. The outlook for adulthood is particularly poor for youths with severe conduct disorder; many require intervention throughout their lives.

John A. Haas
John Haas, diagnosed with schizophrenia, began painting at 19 and often collaborates with his brother. The brothers Haas founded The Happy JAH (John and Henry) Company, which makes enlightening and entertaining artifacts such as the "schizobarometer." Both brothers consider painting to be therapy and a positive expression of a mental disorder that gets a "bad rap from the media."

7

Communication Disorders

I said goodbye and turned to go, but she wrapped her purple-green arms around my neck, kissed my cheek, and said, "I love you, Jeremy."

"I'll miss you so much."

"I really, truly love you with all my soul," she said.

"My Dad's waiting. I better go."

She took her arms off me and stepped back, straightened her smock. Then she said, "I've already told you I love you, Jeremy. Can't you say, 'I love you, Faith'?"

"I love you," I said.

"I love you, *Faith*," she insisted.

This little scene in the garage occurred only a few months after my futile attempt to say *Philadelphia* in the living room. Stutterers have a tendency to generalize their fear of one word that begins with a particular sound to a fear of all words that begin with the same sound. In the space of the summer I'd effectively eliminated every *F* from my vocabulary, with the exception of the preposition, "for," which for the time being was too small to incite terror. A few weeks later, my fear of *F* ended when another letter—I think it was *L*—suddenly loomed large. But at the moment, early October 1962, in Faith's garage, I was terrified of *F*s. I simply wasn't saying them. I hadn't called Faith by her first name for nearly a month and had, instead, taken to calling her Carlisle, as if her patronymic had become a term of jocular endearment.

"I can't," I said. "I can't say that."

David Shields
Dead Languages

Communication is such a natural part of our everyday lives that we seldom stop to think about it. Social conversation with families, friends, and casual acquaintances is normally so effortless and pleasant that it is hard to imagine having difficulty with it. Most of us have feelings of uncertainty about the adequacy of our speech or language only in stressful or unusual social situations, such as talking to a large audience or being interviewed for a job. If we always had to worry about communicating, we would worry about every social interaction we had.

Not all communication disorders involve disorders of speech. Not all speech disorders are as handicapping in social interactions as **stuttering,** nor is stuttering the most common disorder of speech. The problem Shields describes (see p. 257) affects only about one person in a hundred, and then usually just during childhood. But stuttering is a mystery, a phenomenon about which theories continue to surface (Bloodstein, 1993; Bobrick, 1995; Culatta & Goldberg, 1995). Its causes and cures remain largely unknown, although for many years, it captured a large share of speech-language pathologists' attention.

In one sense, then, stuttering is a poor example to use in introducing a chapter on communication disorders. It is not the most representative disorder, it is difficult to define precisely, its causes are not fully understood, and few suggestions about how to overcome it can be made with confidence. But in another sense, stuttering is the best example. When people think of speech and language disorders, they tend to think first of stuttering (Owens, 1986). It is a disorder we all have heard and recognized (if not experienced) at one time or another, its social consequences are obvious, and although it *appears* to be a simple problem with obvious logical solutions ("Just slow down"; "Relax, don't worry"; "Think about how to say it"), these seemingly common-sense approaches do not work.

Today, difficulty such as that described by Shields (p. 257) is viewed within the broad context of **communication disorders** because of the obstacle it presents to social interaction, a major purpose of language (Zebrowski, 1995). Jeremy's stuttering was an inability to convey his thoughts and feelings to Faith, not just a problem of being fearful and unable to say certain words. In thinking about communication disorders, the context in which communication occurs must be considered in addition to people's reasons for communicating, and the rules that govern the "games" of discourse and dialogue (Nelson, 1993; Owens, 1995).

Our points here are simply these: First, all communication disorders carry social penalties. And second, communication is among the most complex human functions, so disorders of this function do not always yield to intuitive or common-sense solutions.

stuttering. Speech characterized by abnormal hesitations, prolongations, and repetitions; may be accompanied by grimaces, gestures, or other bodily movements indicative of a struggle to speak, anxiety, blocking of speech, or avoidance of speech.

communication disorders. Impairments in the ability to use speech or language to communicate.

language. An arbitrary code or system of symbols to communicate meaning.

speech. The formation and sequencing of oral language sounds during communication.

DEFINITIONS

Speech and language are tools used for communication. Communication requires *encoding* (sending in understandable form) and *decoding* (receiving and understanding) messages. It always involves a sender and a receiver of messages, but it does not always involve language. Animals communicate through movements and noises, for example, but their communication does not qualify as true language. We are concerned here only with communication through language.

Language is the communication of ideas through an arbitrary system of symbols used according to certain rules that determine meaning. When people think of language, they typically think of the oral language most of us use. **Speech**—the behavior

Misconceptions about Persons with Communications Disorders

Myth Children with language disorders always have speech difficulties, as well.

Fact It is possible for a child to have good speech yet not make any sense when he or she talks; however, most children with language disorders have speech disorders, as well.

Myth Individuals with communication disorders always have emotional or behavioral disorders or mental retardation.

Fact Some children with communication disorders are normal in cognitive, social, and emotional development.

Myth How children learn language is now well understood.

Fact Although recent research has revealed quite a lot about the sequence of language acquisition and has led to theories of language development, exactly *how* children learn language is still unknown.

Myth Stuttering is primarily a disorder of people with extremely high IQs. Children who stutter become stuttering adults.

Fact Stuttering can affect individuals at all levels of intellectual ability. Some children who stutter continue stuttering as adults; most, however, stop stuttering before or during adolescence with help from a speech-language pathologist. Stuttering is primarily a childhood disorder, found much more often in boys than in girls.

Myth Disorders of phonology (or articulation) are never very serious and are always easy to correct.

Fact Disorders of phonology can make speech unintelligible; it is sometimes very difficult to correct phonological or articulation problems, especially if the individual has cerebral palsy, mental retardation, or emotional or behavioral disorders.

Myth There is no relationship between intelligence and communication disorders.

Fact Communication disorders tend to occur more frequently among individuals of lower intellectual ability, although they may occur in individuals who are extremely intelligent.

Myth There is not much overlap between language disorders and learning disabilities.

Fact Problems with verbal skills—listening, reading, writing, speaking—are often central features of learning disabilities. The definitions of language disorders and several other disabilities are overlapping.

Myth Children who learn few language skills before entering kindergarten can easily pick up all the skills they need, if they have good peer models in typical classrooms.

Fact Early language learning is critical for later language development; a child whose language is delayed in kindergarten is unlikely to learn to use language effectively merely by observing peer models. More explicit intervention is typically required.

Definitions of the American Speech-Language-Hearing Association

I. A COMMUNICATION DISORDER is an impairment in the ability to receive, send, process, and comprehend concepts or verbal, nonverbal and graphic symbol systems. A communication disorder may be evident in the processes of hearing, language, and/or speech. A communication disorder may range in severity from mild to profound. It may be developmental or acquired. Individuals may demonstrate one or any combination of communication disorders. A communication disorder may result in a primary disability or it may be secondary to other disabilities.

A. A SPEECH DISORDER is an impairment of the articulation of speech sounds, fluency, and/or voice.

1. AN ARTICULATION DISORDER is the atypical production of speech sounds characterized by substitutions, omissions, additions, or distortions that may interfere with intelligibility.
2. A FLUENCY DISORDER is an interruption in the flow of speaking characterized by atypical rate, rhythm, and repetitions in sounds, syllables, words, and phrases. This may be accompanied by excessive tension, struggle behavior, and secondary mannerisms.
3. A VOICE DISORDER is characterized by the abnormal production and/or absences of vocal quality, pitch, loudness, resonance, and/or duration, which is inappropriate for an individual's age and/or sex.

B. A LANGUAGE DISORDER is impaired comprehension and/or use of spoken, written, and/or other symbol systems. The disorder may involve (1) the form of language (phonology, morphology, syntax), (2) the content of language (semantics), and/or (3) the function of language in communication (pragmatics) in any combination.

1. Form of Language
   a. PHONOLOGY is the sound system of a language and the rules that govern the sound combinations.
   b. MORPHOLOGY is the system that governs the structure of words and the construction of word forms.
   c. SYNTAX is the system governing the order and combination of words to form sentences, and the relationships among the elements within a sentence.
2. Content of Language
   a. SEMANTICS is the system that governs the meanings of words and sentences.
3. Function of Language
   a. PRAGMATICS is the system that combines the above language components in functional and socially appropriate communication.

II. COMMUNICATION VARIATIONS

A. COMMUNICATION DIFFERENCE/DIALECT is a variation of a symbol system used by a group of individuals that reflects and is determined by shared regional, social, or cultural/ethnic factors. A regional, social, or cultural/ethnic variation of a symbol system should not be considered a disorder of speech or language.

B. AUGMENTATIVE/ALTERNATIVE COMMUNICATION systems attempt to compensate and facilitate, temporarily or permanently, for the impairment and disability patterns of individuals with severe expressive and/or language comprehension disorders. Augmentative/alternative communication may be required for individuals demonstrating impairments in gestural, spoken, and/or written modalities.

Source: American Speech-Language-Hearing Association. (1993). "Definitions of communication disorders and variations." *ASHA, 35* (Suppl. 10), pp. 40–41. Reprinted with permission.

augmentative communication. Alternative forms of communication that do not use the oral sounds of speech.

speech disorders. Oral communication that involves abnormal use of the vocal apparatus, is unintelligible, or so inferior that it draws attention to itself and causes anxiety, feelings of inadequacy, or inappropriate behavior in the speaker.

of forming and sequencing the sounds of oral language—is the most common symbol system used in communication between humans. Some languages, however, are not based on speech. For example, American Sign Language (ASL) does not involve speech sounds; it is a manual language used by many people who cannot hear speech. **Augmentative communication** for people with disabilities involving the physical movements of speech may consist of alternatives to the speech sounds of oral language.

The American Speech-Language-Hearing Association (ASHA, 1993) provides definitions of disorders of communication, including speech disorders, language disorders, and variations in communication (differences or dialects and augmentative systems) that are not disorders (see the box above). **Speech disorders** are impairments in the production and use of oral language. They include disabilities in making speech sounds **(articulation)**, producing speech with a normal flow **(fluency)**, and producing voice.

Language disorders include problems in comprehending and using language for communication, regardless of the symbol system used (spoken, written, or other). The *form, content,* and/or *function* of language may be involved:

- The form of language includes sound combinations **(phonology)**, construction of word forms such as plurals and verb tenses **(morphology)**, and construction of sentences **(syntax)**.
- The content of language refers to the intentions and meanings people attach to words and sentences **(semantics)**.
- Language function is the use to which language is put in communication, and it includes nonverbal behavior as well as vocalizations that form the pattern of language use **(pragmatics)**.

Differences in speech or language that are shared by people in a given region, social group, or cultural/ethnic group should not be considered disorders. For example, African American English (Ebonics or Black English Vernacular), Appalachian English, and the New York dialect are varieties of English, not disorders of speech or language. Similarly, the use of augmentative communication systems does not imply that a person has a language disorder. Rather, such systems are used by those who have temporary or permanent inabilities to use speech satisfactorily for communication. Those who use augmentative communication systems may or may not have language disorders in addition to their inability to use speech.

articulation. The movements the vocal tract makes during production of speech sounds; enunciation of words and vocal sounds.

fluency. The flow with which oral language is produced.

language disorders. Oral communication that involves a lag in the ability to understand and express ideas, putting linguistic skill behind an individual's development in other areas, such as motor, cognitive, or social development.

phonology. The study of how individual sounds make up words.

morphology. The study within psycholinguistics of word formation; how adding or deleting parts of words changes their meaning.

syntax. How words are joined together to structure meaningful sentences; grammar.

semantics. The study of the meanings attached to words and sentences.

pragmatics. The study within psycholinguistics of how one uses language in social situations; emphasizes the functional use of language, rather than its mechanics.

PREVALENCE

Establishing the prevalence of communication disorders is difficult because they are extremely varied, sometimes difficult to identify, and often occur as part of other disabilities (e.g., mental retardation, traumatic brain injury, learning disability, or autism, see Shames, Wiig, & Secord, 1994). Federal data indicate that about a million children—about one-fifth of all children identified for special education—receive services primarily for language or speech disorders (U.S. Department of Education, 1995). Moreover, speech-language therapy is one of the most frequently provided related services for children with other primary disabilities (e.g., mental retardation or learning disability).

Estimates are that about 10 to 15 percent of preschool children and about 6 percent of elementary and secondary school students have some sort of speech disorder.

Categorical Factors Associated with Childhood Language Disorders

I. Central factors
   A. Specific language disability
   B. Mental retardation
   C. Autism
   D. Attention deficit hyperactivity disorder
   E. Acquired brain injury
   F. Others

II. Peripheral factors
   A. Hearing impairment
   B. Visual impairment
   C. Physical impairment

III. Environmental and emotional factors
   A. Neglect and abuse
   B. Behavioral and emotional development problems

IV. Mixed factors

Source: From N. W. Nelson, *Childhood language disorders in context: Infancy through adolescence.* Copyright © 1993 by Allyn and Bacon. Reprinted by permission.

The box above outlines the other categories associated with language disorders of children and youths. The outline suggests the multiple, interrelated causes of language disorders and other disabilities:

- *Central factors* refer to causes associated with central nervous system (i.e., brain) damage or dysfunction.
- *Peripheral factors* refer to sensory or physical impairments that are not caused by brain injury or dysfunction but that, nevertheless, contribute to language disorders.
- *Environmental and emotional factors* refer to language disorders that have their primary origin in the child's physical or psychological environment.
- *Mixed factors* are included because language disorders often have multiple causes—combinations of central, peripheral, and environmental or emotional factors.

Estimates are that about 10 to 15 percent of preschool children and about 6 percent of students in elementary and secondary grades have speech disorders; about 2 to 3 percent of preschoolers and about 1 percent of the school-age population have language disorders (Matthews & Frattali, 1994). Communication disorders of all kinds are predicted to increase during the coming decades, as medical advances preserve the lives of more children and youths with severe disabilities that affect communication. Thus, there is a need for more speech-language pathologists in the schools as well as for greater knowledge of communication disorders by special and general education teachers and greater involvement of teachers in helping students learn to communicate effectively (Matthews & Frattali, 1994).

Communication disorders cannot be understood and corrected without knowledge of normal language development. So before discussing the disorders of language and speech, we provide a brief description of normal language development. Language disorders are discussed first and more extensively than speech disorders because the primary focus of speech-language pathologists and other specialists in communicative disorders has shifted from speech to language during the evolution of special education and related services.

LANGUAGE DEVELOPMENT

The newborn makes few sounds other than cries. The fact that within a few years, the human child can form the many complex sounds of speech, understand spoken and written language, and express meaning verbally is one of nature's great miracles. The major milestones in this miraculous ability to use language are fairly well known by child development specialists. The underlying mechanisms that control the development of language are still not well understood, however. What parts of the process of learning language are innate, and what parts are controlled by the environment? What is the relationship between cognitive development and language development? These and many other questions about the origins and uses of language cannot yet be answered definitively.

Sequence of Development

Research has demonstrated that infants are much more adept at communication than was previously thought. They receive and give messages to their caretakers in ways that were not formerly understood. Mothers and other caretakers approach babies as if they can communicate. This is significant in understanding early language learning because it highlights the social nature of the process. Interaction of infants and caregivers includes joint reference to objects (e.g., "Oh, look!"), joint action (e.g., games such as peek-a-boo), turn taking (often during joint action), and situational variations (e.g., games played during bathing or diaper changing but not when the infant is being put to sleep in the crib). It is the need to communicate—to exchange meanings involving social interactions—that sets the stage for the development of language. Recognition of this principle has led to intense interest in the social contexts and uses of language. As you read the description of the emergence of oral language, keep in mind the social uses of language for children at various stages of development.

At about two to three months of age, babies begin "gooing," and by four to six months, they are babbling. That is, they make some of the vowel and consonant sounds and other noises over and over, often apparently just to explore their vocal apparatus and to entertain themselves. Sometimes, they babble when they are alone and will stop abruptly if an adult attends to them, and at other times, babbling occurs when they are being cared for or played with. These vocalizations may be social—used to communicate with their caretakers.

Babbling soon turns into vocal play. The sounds children are able to make gradually increase in variety. They begin to string sounds together (*da-da-da*) and, toward the end of the first year, to put different syllables together (*duh-buh*). They make vocal sounds more frequently and seem to take delight in their own performance. But they also begin to take interest in listening to the speech of adults and attempt to carry on conversations by answering when spoken to. Now they begin to use intonations, changing the pitch and intensity of their vocal productions to make them sound like adults' commands, questions, or exclamations. At this stage, children experiment with rhythm and intonation patterns.

What they are saying is still meaningless gibberish, if taken out of its social context—but it sounds as if they are talking. Their vocalizations, facial expressions, and gestures may be a form of effective communication with adults who know them well. Mother and child may make their desires and intentions mutually understood, even though other adults may be unable to interpret the child's speech. Children play delightedly (and delightfully) with vocalizations and may continue this kind of vocal play for a few years, even though by that age, they have acquired a vocabulary of several hundred words and may be putting two and three words together in simple sentences. It is important to note here that at more advanced stages of normal language development, there is greater variation in the age at which milestones are reached. For example, there is greater variation in the age at which children usually speak their first words than there is in the age at which children normally begin to babble.

At about the same time children learn to walk and feed themselves—roughly between ten and eighteen months—they normally say their first words. Actually, it is not at all easy to pinpoint when a child starts to use words because approximations of words often occur in an infant's vocalizations, and it is often impossible to judge their communicative intent. Even before they have started to say what everyone would agree are words, babies have begun to exhibit an understanding of simple questions and commands. During the second year, vocal play continues. Children may utter unintelligible strings of syllables, with occasional understandable words mixed in. They may sometimes be *echolalic* (i.e., repeating what they have heard without understanding it or being able to use it appropriately in conversation). Many of their words are idiosyncratic or poorly articulated. They may use single words in place of entire phrases or sentences (e.g., *sue* to indicate *Put on my shoe*). The listener has to rely on intonations, facial expressions, gestures, and the social contexts to interpret the meaning of these single-word expressions. Children may also use one word to indicate a single, undifferentiated class of objects (*doggie* to indicate all animals).

After age two, children's language develops rapidly (Bloom, 1991). Their single-word utterances are replaced by speech more closely approximating the syntax used by adults when they speak to each other. At the age of two years, children ordinarily use expressions that average about two words in length; by the time they are five years old, their average sentence is up to about six words in length. At age two, they may have a vocabulary of several hundred words; by age five, they know many more, and their vocabularies continue to increase at a rapid rate. By the time children are about five, their speech is readily understandable by anyone. And by the time they begin school, they are fluent speakers and have mastered most of the basic *morphological* characteristics of language—that is, they can construct word forms such as plurals, verb tenses, and compound words correctly. By the time they are eight or nine years old, they have mastered all the *phonemic* components of language, which means that their articulation of the speech sounds is correct.

Again, *there is a great variability in the age at which children demonstrate particular levels of speech or language performance* (Owens, 1994, 1995; Stoel-Gammon, 1991). The discussion here is intended to provide guidelines for judging the adequacy of an individual's language development but only very general guidelines. For example, one should not jump to the conclusion that an eight-year-old who still makes a few errors in articulation and constructs a few incorrect plurals is significantly slow in speech or language development (see Nelson, 1993).

Theories of Development

Although no one knows exactly how or why children learn language, we do know that language development is related in a general way to physical maturation, cognitive development, and socialization. But the details of the process—the particulars of what happens physiologically, cognitively, and socially in the learning of language—are still being debated.

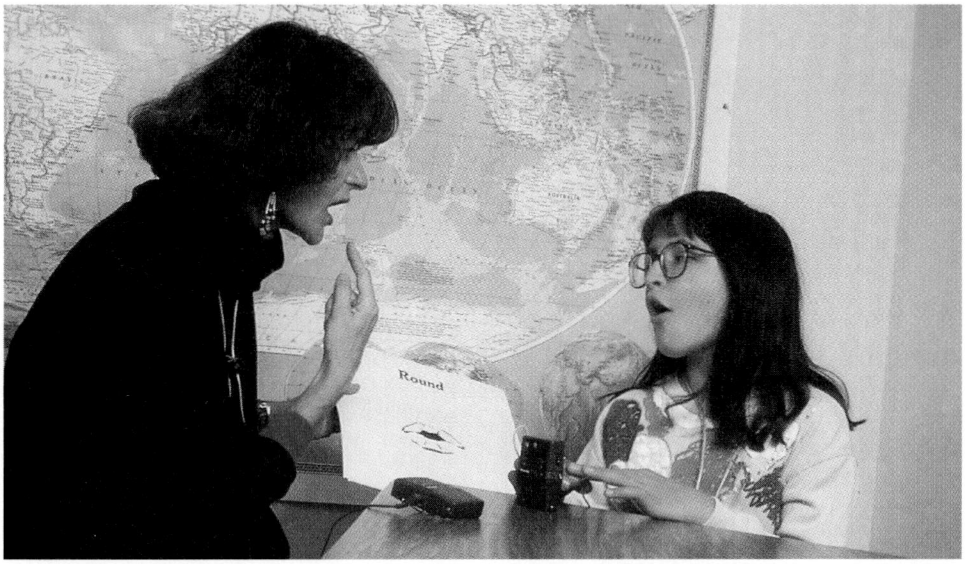

Children with speech disorders often need explicit instruction to learn and produce intelligible speech.

Carrow-Woolfolk (1988) and Nelson (1993) discuss six theories of language that have dominated the study of human communication at various times. Although all six theories have made significant contributions to our understanding of language and its disorders, not all are now equally popular among communication scientists. Neuropsychological theories were dominant in the 1950s, behavioral and information-processing theories were popular in the 1960s, and linguistic and cognitive organization theories were widely held in the 1970s. In the 1980s and 1990s, pragmatic, social interactional theories have received the most attention.

Pragmatic theories emphasize that language is taught and learned through social interactions and that comprehending and producing language are equally important. The social and cultural contexts of language determine what language will be learned, how it will be learned, and how it will be used for communication (Duchan, Hewitt, & Sonnenmeier, 1994). The pragmatic view of language makes it extremely difficult, if not impossible, to separate language development from cognitive and social development (Nelson, 1993). Indeed, one of the limitations or criticisms of pragmatic theories is that "pragmatics is so broad that it moves into boundaries of all learning" (Carrow-Woolfolk, 1988, p. 83).

Theories of language development and research based on them have established the following:

- Language learning depends on brain development and proper brain functioning; language disorders are sometimes a result of brain dysfunction, and ways to compensate for the dysfunction can sometimes be taught.
- Language learning is affected by the consequences of language behavior; language disorders can be a result of inappropriate learning, and consequences can sometimes be arranged to correct disordered language.
- Language can be analyzed as inputs and outputs related to the way information is processed; faulty processing may account for some language disorders, and more effective processing skills can sometimes be taught.
- Language is based on linguistic rules; language disorders can be described as failures to employ appropriate rules for encoding and decoding messages, and

sometimes these disorders can be overcome by teaching the use of linguistic rules.

- Language is one of many cognitive skills; language disorders reflect basic problems in thinking and learning, and sometimes these disorders can be addressed effectively by teaching specific cognitive skills.
- Language arises from the need to communicate in social interactions; language disorders are a breakdown in ability to relate effectively to one's environment, and the natural environment can sometimes be arranged to teach and support more effective interaction.

All these theories contain elements of scientific truth, but none is able to explain the development and disorders of language completely. All six theories have advantages and disadvantages for assessing language disorders and devising effective interventions. Pragmatic or social interactional theory is widely viewed as having the most direct implications for speech-language pathologists and teachers. We now turn to the disorders of language and speech.

LANGUAGE DISORDERS

As discussed earlier, speech-language pathologists have shifted their concern away from speech disorders. Much more interest is now shown in the disorders of language. The primary reason for this shift in focus is the recognition that disorders of language are much more debilitating—they are much more at the center of difficulties in communication. The distinction between speech and language disorders is significant. It is possible for a child to have normal speech—to have acceptable voice, articulation, and fluency—yet not make sense when talking or misinterpret the meaning of what is heard or read. *Speech* has to do with intelligible vocal encoding of messages; *language* has to do with the formulation and interpretation of meaning. Language involves listening and speaking, reading and writing, technical discourse, and social interaction. Language problems are basic to many of the disabilities discussed in this text, especially hearing impairment, mental retardation, learning disability, traumatic brain injury, and autism.

Classification

Language disorders can be classified according to several criteria. The ASHA (1993) definitions on page 260 provide a classification scheme involving five subsystems of language: *phonology* (sounds), *morphology* (word forms), *syntax* (word order and sentence structure), *semantics* (word and sentence meanings), and *pragmatics* (social use of language). Difficulty with one of these dimensions of language is virtually certain to be accompanied by difficulty with one or more of the others. However, children with language disorders often have particular difficulty with one dimension. Language disorders involving these subsystems are illustrated in the box on pages 268–269.

Another way of classifying language disorders is based on the presumed cause or related conditions. The literature on language disorders frequently includes chapters and articles on the particular communication disorders of individuals with other specific disabling conditions, such as autism, traumatic brain injury, mental retardation, and cerebral palsy (e.g., Owens, 1995; Shames et al., 1994; Szekeres & Meserve, 1995). Owens (1995) discusses seven diagnostic categories of language impairments, each of which tends to present difficulties in particular areas (as shown in Table 7–1):

Table 7–1

Language Learning Requirements and the Difficulties of Children with Language Impairment*

		LANGUAGE IMPAIRMENT						
	Requirements	*Mental Retardation*	*Language Learning Disability*	*Specific Language Impairment*	*Autism*	*Traumatic Brain Injury*	*Expressive Language Delay*	*Neglect/ Abuse*
1	**Perception**	X	X	X	X	X		
2	**Attention**		X		X	X		
3	**Use of symbols**	X	X	X	X	X	X	X
4	**Use of language rules**	X	X	X	X		X	
5	**Overall mental ability**	X		X		X		X
6	**Social interaction related to communication**				X			X

*Xs represent problem areas in language learning and use.

Source: From R. E. Owens, *Language disorders: A functional approach to assessment and intervention*, (2nd ed.). Copyright © 1995 by Allyn and Bacon. Adapted by permission.

perception, attention, use of symbols, use of language rules, overall mental ability, and social interaction related to communication. In addition, each diagnostic category is characterized by particular problems in the five language subsystems—phonology, morphology, syntax, semantics, and pragmatics—and problems in language comprehension.

Several of the seven conditions included in Table 7–1 are defined in other chapters: mental retardation is the topic of Chapter 4; learning disability (of which **language learning disability** is a subset focused on disabilities in understanding and using language) is the topic of Chapter 5; autism and traumatic brain injury (TBI) are first defined in Chapter 6 and, along with abuse and neglect, are discussed further in Chapter 10.

Specific language impairment (SLI) refers to language disorders that have no identifiable causes. These disorders are not due to mental retardation or to the perceptual problems that characterize language learning disability. Rather, SLI is defined more by the exclusion of other plausible causes than by a clearly defined set of characteristics, and for this reason it is controversial. **Early expressive language delay** (**EELD**) refers to a significant lag in expressive language that the child will not outgrow (i.e., the child does not have a fifty-word vocabulary or use two-word utterances by age two). About half the children whose language development is delayed at age two *will* gradually

language learning disability. A learning disability in the specific area of language.

specific language impairment (SLI). A language disorder with no identifiable cause; language disorder not attributable to hearing impairment, mental retardation, brain dysfunction, or other plausible cause; also called specific language disability.

early expressive language delay (EELD). A significant lag in the development of expressive language that is apparent by age two.

Disorders of the Five Subsystems of Language

Oral language involves communication through a system of sound symbols. Disorders may occur in one or more of the five subsystems of oral language: *phonology* (sounds and sound combinations), *morphology* (words and meaningful word parts), *syntax* (sequences and combinations of words), *semantics* (meanings or content), and *pragmatics* (use for communication). The following interactions illustrate disorders in each of these subsystems. Note that a given illustration may involve more than a single subsystem.

PHONOLOGY

Alvin has just turned 6. He is in kindergarten, but has been receiving speech therapy for 2 years. At 4, his parents sought assistance when his speech and language remained unintelligible and he did not appear to be "growing out" of his problem. He has two older siblings whose speech and language are well within the normal range. Alvin substitutes and omits a number of speech sounds, and in addition, he has difficulty with other subsystems of language as shown in the example below:

Clinician: I'd like you to tell me about some words. Here's something that you may have for breakfast: orange juice. What's orange juice?
Alvin: I doh noh. [I don't know.]
Clinician: See if you can guess. What color is orange juice?
Alvin: Ahnge. N you dink i. [Orange. And you drink it.]
Clinician: That's good. Tell me some more about orange juice.
Alvin: Doh noh.
Clinician: Let's try another. What's sugar? Tell me what sugar is.
Alvin: Yukky.
Clinician: Yukky? Why?
Alvin: Cah i wahtuns yer tee. ['Cause it rottens your teeth.]

MORPHOLOGY

Children with language disorders in the morphological realm will exhibit difficulty in either understanding or producing morphological inflections. These include the ability to add *-s* to change a word from singular to plural; to include *'s* to make a word a possessive; *-ed* to change the tense of a word from present to past; or to use other inflectional endings to differentiate comparatives and superlatives, among others.

Children with morphological difficulties will use inappropriate suffixes. . . . Here are a few . . . examples, taken from the test protocols of school-age children:

Examiner: Anna, say this after me: *cow.*
Anna: (*age 6*) Cow.
Examiner: Good. Now say *boy.*
Anna: Boy.
Examiner: Now put them together. Say *cowboy.*
Anna: Boy.

Examiner: Frank, find two little words in this big word: *outside.*
Frank: (*age 7*) Outside.
Examiner: Not quite right. We need *two* words.
Frank: (*Shrugs and looks around the room*)
Examiner: Well, if one word is *side,* the other would be . . . ?
Frank: Be?

Examiner: Jamie, can you tell me a story?
Jamie: (*age 8*) I can't think of none.
Examiner: What if the story began, "One night I walked into a dark haunted house . . . and . . .
Jamie: I met a ghost. He wanted to kill me. But he couldn't. I ran very, very fastest. And all of a sudden I saw a coffin. I hides in there. And all of a sudden there a ghostes inside there. And I sent out of the coffin. And then there weres a guy named Count. And then he tried to suck my blood. And then he couldn't find me because I hided. And then I met a mummy. And then he wanted to tie me up . . . and . . . that's all.

SYNTAX

Marie is 8 years old and in a special first-grade class. Her syntactical difficulties are demonstrated in the following story-telling event:

Clinician: Marie, I want you to listen carefully. I am going to tell you a story; listen, and when I'm done, I want you to tell me the story.

catch up developmentally with their age peers; however the other half will not catch up and will continue to have language problems throughout their school years.

A scientific approach to problems demands classification, but human beings and their language are very difficult to categorize. Thus, all classification systems contain ambiguities, and none can account for all cases. Owens (1995) notes:

Marie: (*interrupting*) I don't know.
Clinician: I haven't told you the story yet. Remember, listen carefully to my story. When I'm done, you are to tell me everything you can remember about the story. One day Mr. Mouse went for a walk. As he was walking, he saw a cat lying in the road. The cat had a stone in his paw so he couldn't walk. Mr. Mouse pulled the stone out of the cat's paw. The cat thanked Mr. Mouse for helping him. They shook hands and walked down the road together.
Marie: Uh, uh, uh . . . Cat was on the road and Mr. Mouse taken out the stone his paw, and then they walked down together the hill and they said thanks, and they walk on the hill, and the mouse chase him.

This task of retelling a story reveals that Marie has difficulty not only in syntax but in the ordering of events and in accurate recall. Indeed, Marie seems unaware that she has modified the story considerably, including giving the story a new ending.

SEMANTICS

Clinician: Burt, tell me about birthday parties.
Burt: (*age 6*) Sing "Happy Birthday," blow away candles, eat a birthday cake, open your presents.
Clinician: All right. Now listen to this story and then say it back to me . . . tell me the whole story: "One day, a little boy went to school. He went up the steps of the school and opened the door. The boy went into his classroom and started playing with his friends. The teacher said, 'Time to come to circle.' The boy put away his toys and sat down on the rug."
Burt: A teacher . . . a boy played with a teacher's toys . . . time for us to come to circle . . . and it's the end.

You will note that Burt does not "blow out" candles; rather, his retrieval of information from semantic memory provides the response "blow away." In addition, it is clear that even the immediate retelling of a story, which in reality represents a string of events well within Burt's everyday experience, is very difficult for Burt. The pauses noted reflect the period of time during which Burt attempted to recall the necessary information.

PRAGMATICS

Greg, age 7, interacts with his special education teacher. Greg is in a self-contained classroom for mentally retarded children and is one of the more verbal children in the class. Assessment by the speech-language pathologist indicates difficulties in phonology, syntax, morphology, and semantics. He has been identified as suffering from a significant language delay. On most language tests, he functions between 2:7* and 3:6 years of age. His teacher, who has visited his home many times, notes that there are no toys, no books, no playthings, and that there appears to be little communication between Greg and his mother, a single parent. The teacher is eager to draw Greg into conversation and story-telling, and has arranged a "talking and telling time" as part of the daily activities with the seven children who comprise her class.

Teacher: Greg, I'd like you to tell me a story. It can be about anything you like.
Greg: No me.
Teacher: Go ahead, it's your turn.
Greg: (*having had previous instruction on "taking turns"*) No, s'yer turn.
Teacher: You do it. It's your turn.
Greg: I can't. I forget.
Teacher: I bet you can tell me a story about school.
Greg: You eat snack. What we have for snack?

Greg's teacher praises his contribution to the conversation and moves on to another student. She grins to herself; she and Greg have had a running joke about "turns." She feels that Greg tends to use "it's your turn" (when it is inappropriate) to delay the necessity to respond. This time she has enticed him into contributing to the conversation by requesting that he recall something that happens frequently within the school context. Greg attempts to comply, recalling from memory a favored episodic event—a small victory for both Greg and his teacher.

*The age designation 2:7 means "2 years, 7 months" old.

Source: By K. G. Butler, *Language disorders in children* (Austin, TX: Pro-Ed, 1986), pp. 13–14, 16–17, 19, 23, 28–29. Reprinted with permission.

Most [college and university] students are in need of a 1-sentence summary statement that once and for all distinguishes each language impairment from the others. Unfortunately, I do not have one forthcoming. We are discussing real human beings who do not like to be placed in boxes and asked to perform in certain ways. (p. 56)

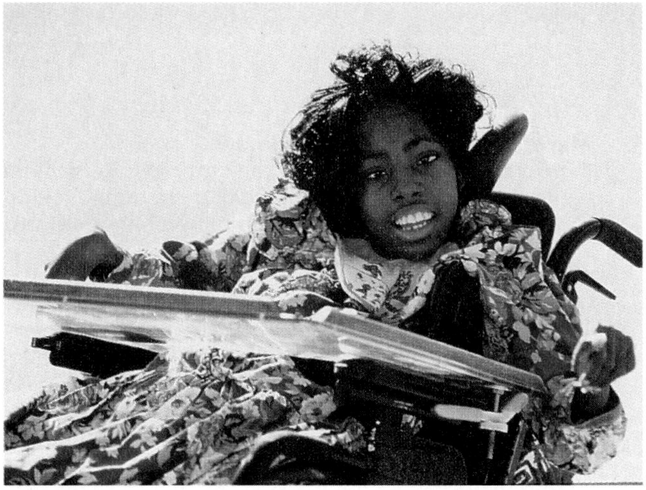

The causes of communication disorders may be linked to other disabilities; however, many cannot be attributed to specific causes, and must simply be dealt with according to presenting symptoms.

Strategies for Assessment and Intervention

Two general strategies of language assessment are (1) to determine, in as much detail as possible, what the child's current language abilities are and (2) to observe the ease and speed with which the child learns new language skills. The first strategy typically involves use of standardized testing, nonstandardized testing, developmental scales, and behavioral observations (Wallace, Larsen, & Elksnin, 1992). Standardized testing has many dangers and is not always useful in planning an intervention program, but it can sometimes be helpful in making crude comparisons of the child's abilities in certain areas. Development scales are ratings or observations that may be completed by direct observation or based on memory or records of developmental milestones. Nonstandardized tests and behavioral observations are nonnormative in nature, but they may yield the most important assessment information. The subjective judgment of an experienced clinician based on observation of the child's language in a variety of environments and circumstances may provide the most useful basis for intervention. Because language disorders vary widely in nature and are seen in individuals ranging from early childhood through old age, assessment and intervention are never simple and always idiosyncratic (Nelson, 1993; Owens, 1995).

An intervention plan must consider the content, form, and use of language. That is, it must consider:

1. what the child talks about and should be taught to talk about,
2. how the child talks about things and how he or she could be taught to speak of those things more intelligibly,
3. how the child uses language and how his or her use of it could be made to serve the purposes of communication and socialization more effectively.

In arranging a training sequence, one might base instruction on the normal sequence of language development. Other sequences of instruction might be more effective, however, since children with language disorders obviously have not learned in the normal way and research suggests that different sequences of learning may be more effective. It is more and more apparent that effective language intervention must occur in the child's natural environment and involve parents and classroom teachers, not just speech-language pathologists (Nelson, 1993; Owens, 1995).

The increasing inclusion of children with all types of disabilities in general education means that all teachers must become aware of how they can address language

Natural language paradigm approaches focus on teaching children language skills according to practical needs in natural settings—for example, having them relate what they want for breakfast, as opposed to memorizing lists of vocabulary not directly relevant to everyday use.

problems in the classroom. Before discussing the classroom teacher's role in helping students learn to use language more effectively (see pp. 277–282), we consider several special cases: the special communication problems of students with autism, delayed language development, and traumatic brain injury. Other disabilities may present special communication problems, as well, and they are discussed in other chapters. For example, the language problems of children with learning disabilities are discussed in Chapter 5, and those of children with hearing impairments are discussed in Chapter 8.

Language Disorders Associated with Autism

Recall from our discussion in Chapter 6 that autism is a pervasive developmental disability that is typically diagnosed between the ages of eighteen and thirty months. Autism is a poorly understood neurological problem of unknown origin, and the developmental problems associated with it may range from mild to severe. The primary features of autism include impairments of social interaction and communication and restricted interests or activities (Schopler, Misibov, & Hearsey, 1995). The cognitive abilities of children with autism may range from giftedness to severe mental retardation; a high proportion of such children appear to have mental retardation. Children with autism may exhibit repetitive or stereotypic behavior and peculiar patterns of speech as well as problems in learning or using language. Because the inability to communicate effectively is perhaps the single most disabling feature of autism, we focus here exclusively on disorders of speech and language.

A substantial proportion of children with autism—perhaps 50 percent—learn little or no oral language at all, unless they receive intensive language intervention. Some go through periods of apparently normal language development and then regress (Brown & Prelock, 1995). Even many of those who do learn oral language have difficulty learning to use speech to communicate effectively, as their language is qualitatively different from the norm. For example, their speech often has a wooden, robotlike quality or fails to convey appropriate affect. They may exhibit echolalia (as mentioned earlier), a parrotlike repetition of words or phrases, and some use jargon or nonsense words that fail to communicate meaning to someone not intimately familiar with the individual's speech. Some children with autism also confuse the use of pronouns, for example, substituting *you* for *I* or *me*) (Lee, Hobson, & Chiat, 1994).

In the 1960s and 1970s, systematic efforts to teach language to nonverbal children with autism consisted of using *operant conditioning* methods. That is, a step-by-step sequence of behaviors approximating functional language was established, and the child's responses at each step in the sequence were rewarded. The rewards typically consisted of praise, hugs, and food given by the teacher immediately following the child's performance of the desired behavior. At the earliest step in the sequence, a child might be reinforced for establishing eye contact with the teacher. The next step might be making any vocalization while looking at the teacher, then making a vocalization approximating a sound made by the teacher, then imitating words spoken by the teacher, and finally replying to the teacher's questions. Of course, this description is a great simplification of the procedures that were employed; nonetheless nonverbal children were taught basic oral language skills through such methods (Koegel, Rincover, & Egel, 1982).

A major problem of early research on operant conditioning methods was that few of the children studied acquired truly functional language, even after intensive and prolonged training. Their speech tended to maintain a stereotyped, mechanical quality, and they often could use their language for only very restricted social purposes.

A current trend in language training for nonverbal children—indeed, for all children with language disorders—is to emphasize *pragmatics,* making language more functional in social interactions and to motivate children to communicate (Koegel & Koegel, 1995). So, instead of training children to imitate words in isolation or to use syntactically and grammatically correct forms, instruction might involve training them to use language to obtain a desired result. For example, the child might be taught to say "I want juice" (or a simplified form: "Juice" or "Want juice") in order to get a drink of juice.

This emphasis on learning and fostering more natural acts of communication is contrasted with the older analogue approach in Table 7–2. Note that under the "Natural Language Paradigm (NLP) condition," the emphasis is on pragmatics—using language in social interactions.

Increasingly, language intervention for people with autism involves structuring opportunities to use language in natural settings (Sigafoos, Kerr, Roberts, & Couzens, 1994). For example, the teacher may set up opportunities for children to make requests by using a missing-item strategy (e.g., giving the child a coloring book but not crayons, prompting a request for crayons), interrupting a chain of behavior (e.g., stopping the child on his or her way out to play, prompting a request to go out), or delaying assistance with tasks (e.g., waiting to help the child put on his or her coat until he or she asks for assistance). This structuring opportunities approach is much like the milieu teaching described by Kaiser et al. (1995) (see p. 276) and is compatible with today's emphasis on including children with autism in regular preschool and elementary school programs (Harris, 1995).

Current research suggests that people with autism have special difficulty understanding the communication of social and emotional meanings (Happe, 1994; Happe & Frith, 1995; Sigman, 1994). Namely, they may be unable to get a coherent picture of social contexts, use social imagination, accurately attribute mental states or feelings to others, or understand jokes, pretense, lies, or figures of speech. In fact, some believe that the core disability in autism is an absence of a "theory of mind," or the inability to understand the existence of subjective mental states (e.g., beliefs, desires, intentions) and how they help people explain and make sense of behavior (Happe, 1994; Happe & Frith, 1995). Language intervention, then, might focus on helping

Table 7–2
Differences between the Analogue and Natural Language Paradigm (NLP) Conditions

	Analogue Condition	*Natural Language Paradigm (NLP) Condition*
Stimulus items	a. Chosen by clinician b. Repeated until criterion is met c. Phonologically easy to produce irrespective of whether they were functional in the natural environment	a. Chosen by child b. Varied every few trials c. Age-appropriate items that can be found in child's natural environment
Prompts	a. Manual (e.g., touch tip of tongue, or hold lips together)	a. Clinician repeats item
Interaction	a. Clinician holds up stimulus item (i.e., stimulus item not functional within interaction)	a. Clinician and child play with stimulus item (i.e., stimulus item functional within interaction)
Response	a. Correct responses or successive approximations reinforced	a. Looser shaping contingency so that attempts to respond verbally (except self-stimulation) also reinforced
Consequences	a. Edible reinforcers paired with social reinforcers	a. Natural reinforcer (e.g., opportunity to play with the item) paired with social reinforcers

Source: From R. L. Koegel, M. C. O'Dell, and K. K. Koegel, "A natural language teaching paradigm for nonverbal autistic children," *Journal of Autism and Developmental Disorders, 17* (1987), p. 191. Copyright © 1987 by Plenum. Reprinted with permission of the publisher and the authors.

children with autism understand more about how language is used to communicate about subjective mental states as well as more object-centered social interactions.

Autism is a developmental puzzle that many people would like to solve, for obvious reasons. Perhaps that explains the frequent and often misleading claims of so-called breakthrough interventions. For example, in the early 1990s, claims that normal or extraordinary intelligence and communicative competence in children and adults with autism using a procedure called *facilitated communication* (discussed further in the section on augmentative and alternative communication; see p. 287) attracted much attention (Biklen, 1990; Biklen & Schubert, 1991). However, by the mid-1990s, researchers had accumulated overwhelming evidence that facilitated communication is not a reliable means of communication, except perhaps in very rare cases (e.g., Crews et al., 1995; Montee, Miltenberger, & Wittrock, 1995; Shane, 1994; Siegel, 1995).

The language training procedures, based on operant conditioning applied to natural language contexts, have not led to dramatic breakthroughs or a cure for autism. Nonetheless, reliable research, done over a period of decades now, supports their use as a highly effective means of helping children with autism learn to communicate more effectively (e.g., Koegel & Koegel, 1995; Koegel, O'Dell, & Koegel, 1987; Koegel et al., 1982; Lovaas, 1987). To be sure, progress depends on careful, programatic research.

Table 7–3
Pattern of Development Shown by a Child with a Language Disorder and a Child with Normal Language Development

LANGUAGE-DISORDERED CHILD			*NORMALLY DEVELOPING CHILD*		
Age	*Attainment*	*Example*	*Age*	*Attainment*	*Example*
27 months	First words	*this, mama, bye bye, doggie*	13 months	First words	*here, mama, bye bye, kitty*
38 months	50-word vocabulary		17 months	50-word vocabulary	
40 months	First two-word combinations	*this doggie, more apple, this mama, more play*	18 months	First two-word combinations	*more juice, here ball, more T.V. here kitty*
48 months	Later two-word combinations	*Mimi purse, Daddy coat, block chair, dolly table*	22 months	Later two-word combinations	*Andy shoe Mommy ring cup floor, keys chair*
52 months	Mean sentence length of 2.00 words		24 months	Mean sentence length of 2.00 words First appearance of *-ing*	*Andy sleeping*
55 months	First appearance of *-ing*	*Mommy eating*			
63 months	Mean sentence length of 3.10 words		30 months	Mean sentence length of 3.10 words First appearance of *is*	*My car's gone.*
66 months	First appearance of *is*	*The doggie's mad.*			
73 months	Mean sentence length of 4.10 words		37 months	Mean sentence length of 4.10 words First appearance of indirect requests	*Can I have some cookies?*
79 months	Mean sentence length of 4.50 words First appearance of indirect requests	*Can I get the ball?*	40 months	Mean sentence length of 4.50 words	

Source: From L. Leonard, "Language disorders in preschool children," in *Human communication disorders: An introduction* (4th ed.), edited by G. H. Shames, E. H. Wiig, and W. A. Secord, Copyright © 1994 by Allyn and Bacon. Reprinted by permission.

Delayed Language Development

A child may progress through the normal stages of language development with one principal exception: He or she may do so at a significantly later age than most children. Children with language disorders may follow the same sequence of development as most children but achieve each skill or milestone at a later-than-average age. Some children with language disorders reach final levels of development significantly below that of their peers who do not have disabilities. Still other children may be generally delayed in language development but show great discrepancies in the rate at which they acquire certain features of language. Differences between the development of a child with a language disorder and a normal child are outlined in Table 7–3. Note that, in general, the sequence of development is similar for the two children, but the child with the language disorder reaches milestones at later ages.

Some children are "late bloomers," who, in time, will catch up with their age peers (Owens, 1995). Yet many children whose language development is delayed show a developmental lag that they will not outgrow. They are frequently diagnosed as having mental retardation or another developmental disability. Sometimes, these children come from environments where they have been deprived of many experiences, including the language stimulation from adults that is required for normal language development, or they have been severely abused or neglected. Regardless of the reasons for a child's delayed language, however, it is important to understand the nature of the delay and to intervene to give him or her the optimal chance of learning to use language effectively.

Some children three years of age or older show no signs that they understand language and do not use language spontaneously. They may make noises, but they use them to communicate in ways that may characterize the communication of infants and toddlers before they have learned speech. In other words, they may use **prelinguistic communication**. For example, they may use gestures or vocal noises to request objects or actions from others, to protest, to request a social routine (e.g., reading), or to greet someone (Ogletree, Wetherby, & Westling, 1992; Yoder, Warren, Kim, & Gazdag, 1994; Warren, Yoder, Gazdag, Kim, & Jones, 1993). (We return to the importance of prelinguistic communication later in our discussion of early intervention; see pp. 295–298.)

When assessing and planning intervention for children with delayed language, it is important to consider what language and nonlanguage behaviors they imitate, what they comprehend, what communication skills they use spontaneously, and what part

prelinguistic communication. Communication through gestures and noises before the child has learned oral language.

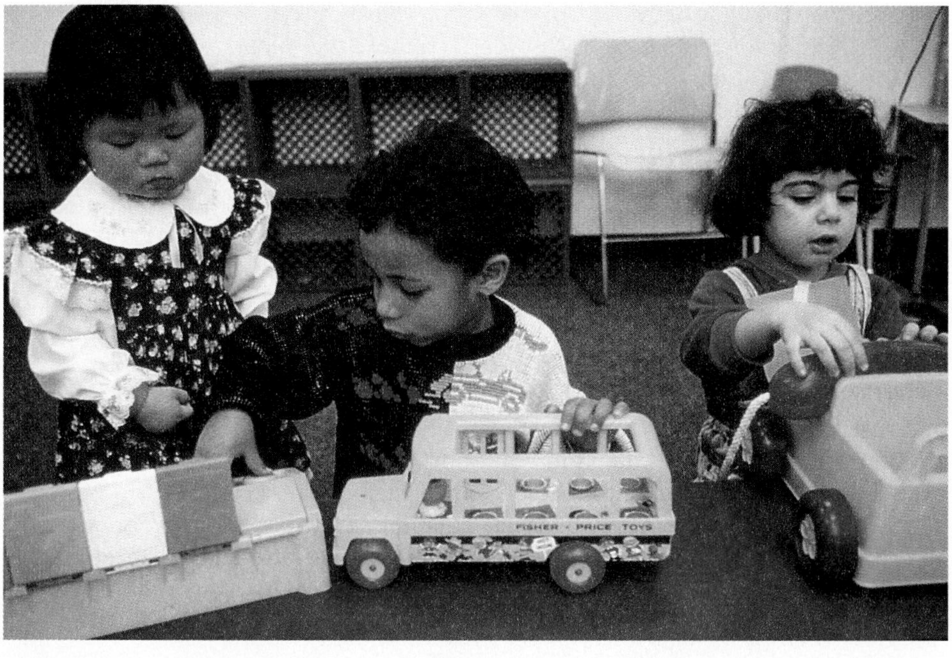

The term early expressive delay *refers to a significant lag in expressive language that a child will not outgrow.*

communication plays in their lives. It is also important, particularly with young children, to provide intervention in contexts in which language is used for normal social interaction. For example, parents or teachers may use a **milieu teaching** approach, "a naturalistic language intervention designed to teach functional language skills" (Kaiser et al., 1995, p. 40). In this approach, teaching is built around the child's interests. When the child requests some action, object, or activity from the adult, the adult prompts the child's language and makes access to what is requested contingent on an attempt to communicate. Milieu teaching is a naturalistic approach, in that it encourages designing interventions that are similar to the conversational interactions that parents and children ordinarily have.

Early intervention with children who have delayed language is critically important for two primary reasons:

1. The older the child is before intervention is begun, the smaller the chance that he or she will acquire effective language skills (other things being equal).
2. Without having functional language, the child cannot become a truly social being (Warren & Abbaduto, 1992). Of all the skills in which a child may be lagging, language—communication—is the most important, as it is the foundation of academic and social learning.

Language Disorders Associated with Traumatic Brain Injury (TBI)

Most disabling conditions associated with language disorders are developmental in nature. That is, the communication problems are part of a developmental disorder such as cerebral palsy, mental retardation, or autism, and the child's language does not emerge normally. In traumatic brain injury (TBI), the individual may acquire a language disorder after a period of normal development, or he or she may acquire a more severe language disorder than existed prior to the injury. It is important to remember that individuals with TBI are a very diverse population, although "a disproportionate number of students with TBI have a pretrauma history of learning problems or delayed speech and language" (Ylvisaker, Szekeres, Haarbauer-Krupa, Urbanczyk, & Feeney, 1994).

The acquisition of a language disorder or a more severe one can be an extremely frustrating, even devastating, disability. In fact, language disorders may be the greatest complicating factor in most students' return to school following TBI (Blosser & DePompei, 1989). The brain injury may affect the student's speech (as described later in our discussion of speech disorders; see pp. 291–294) or language ability. A loss of ability to understand and formulate language due to brain injury is sometimes referred to as **acquired aphasia** (Swindell, Holland, & Reinmuth, 1994). The student with aphasia may have problems ranging from finding or saying words to being able to construct sentences but not ones that are appropriate for the topic of conversation or social context. Problems like these are a source of frustration, anger, and confusion for some students with TBI (Feenick & Judd, 1994).

The language problems acquired with TBI are primarily related to the cognitive and social demands of communication (Ylvisaker et al., 1994). The student may have problems with tasks that demand responding quickly, organizing, dealing with abstractions, sustaining attention (especially if there are distractions), learning new skills, responding appropriately in social situations, and showing appropriate affect. In fact, TBI can potentially disrupt all aspects of the give-and-take of social interaction that are required for effective communication.

milieu teaching. A naturalistic approach to language intervention in which the goal is to teach functional language skills in a natural environment.

acquired aphasia. Loss or impairment of the ability to understand or formulate language because of accident or illness.

The outcomes of TBI are extremely variable, and careful assessment of the given individual's abilities and disabilities is critically important. Interventions may range from making special accommodations—such as allowing more response time or keeping distractions to a minimum—to focusing on instruction in social skills.

Depending on the site and degree of brain damage, a person with TBI may have motor control problems that interfere with communication, with or without the cognitive and social aspects of communication disorders already discussed. Some students with TBI are not able to communicate orally using the muscles of speech and must rely on alternative or augmentative communication systems, described later (see pp. 282–288).

EDUCATIONAL CONSIDERATIONS

Helping children overcome speech and language disorders is not the responsibility of any single profession. Rather, identification is the joint responsibility of the classroom teacher, the speech-language pathologist, and the parents. The teacher can carry out specific suggestions for individual cases. By listening attentively and empathetically when children speak, providing appropriate models of speech and language for children to imitate, and encouraging children to use their communication skills appropriately, the classroom teacher can help not only to improve speech and language but also to prevent disorders from developing in the first place.

The primary role of the classroom teacher is to facilitate the *social use of language*. Phonology, morphology, syntax, and semantics are certainly important. Yet the fact that a student has a language disorder does not necessarily mean the teacher or clinician must intensify efforts to teach the student about the form, structure, or content of language. Rather, language must be taught as a way of solving problems by making oneself understood and making sense of what other people say.

The classroom offers many possibilities for language learning. It should be a place in which there are almost continuous opportunities for students and teachers to employ language and obtain feedback in constructive relationships. Language is the basic medium through which most academic and social learning takes place in school. Nevertheless, the language of school, in both classrooms and textbooks, is often a problem for students and teachers (Nelson, 1993; Owens, 1995).

School language is more formal than the language many children use at home and with playmates. It is structured discourse, in which listeners and speakers or readers and writers must learn to be clear and expressive, to convey and interpret essential information quickly and easily. Without skill in using the language of school, a child is certain to fail academically and virtually certain to be socially unsuccessful, as well.

Teachers need the assistance of speech-language specialists in assessing their students' language disabilities and in devising interventions. Part of the assessment and intervention strategy must also examine the language of the teacher. Problems in classroom discourse involve how teachers talk to students as well as how students use language. Learning how to be clear, relevant, and informative and how to hold listeners' attention are not only problems for students with language disorders but also problems for their teachers. Table 7–4 lists some general guidelines for how parents and teachers should interact with students to facilitate language development.

One example of the role of the teacher's language in classroom discourse is asking questions. Blank and White (1986) note that teachers often ask students questions in

Table 7–4
Guidelines for Parents' and Teachers' Interactive Styles

1	Talk about things in which the child is interested.
2	Follow the child's lead. Reply to the child's initiations and comments. Share his excitement.
3	Don't ask too many questions. If you must, use questions such as *how did/do . . .*, *why did/do . . .*, and *what happened . . .* that result in longer explanatory answers.
4	Encourage the child to ask questions. Respond openly and honestly. If you don't want to answer a question, say so and explain why. (*I don't think I want to answer that question; it's very personal.*)
5	Use a pleasant tone of voice. You need not be a comedian, but you can be light and humorous. Children love it when adults are a little silly.
6	Don't be judgmental or make fun of a child's language. If you are overly critical of the child's language or try to "shotgun" all errors, he will stop talking to you.
7	Allow enough time for the child to respond.
8	Treat the child with courtesy by not interrupting when he is talking.
9	Include the child in family and classroom discussions. Encourage participation and listen to his ideas.
10	Be accepting of the child and of the child's language. Hugs and acceptance can go a long way.
11	Provide opportunities for the child to use language and to have that language work for him to accomplish his goals.

Source: From R. E. Owens, *Language disorders: A functional approach to assessment and intervention* (2nd ed.). Copyright © 1995 by Allyn and Bacon. Adapted by permission.

areas of their identified weaknesses. For example, a teacher might ask a preschooler who does not know colors to identify colors repeatedly. Unfortunately, teachers may not know how to modify their questions to teach concepts effectively, so their questions merely add to children's confusion.

The following exchange between a teacher and a child diagnosed as having difficulties with problem solving and causal reasoning illustrates this point:

Teacher: How could grass in a jungle get on fire?
Child: 'Cause they (*referring to animals*) have to stay in the jungle.
Teacher: (*in an incredulous tone*) You mean the grass gets on fire because the animals stay in the jungle?

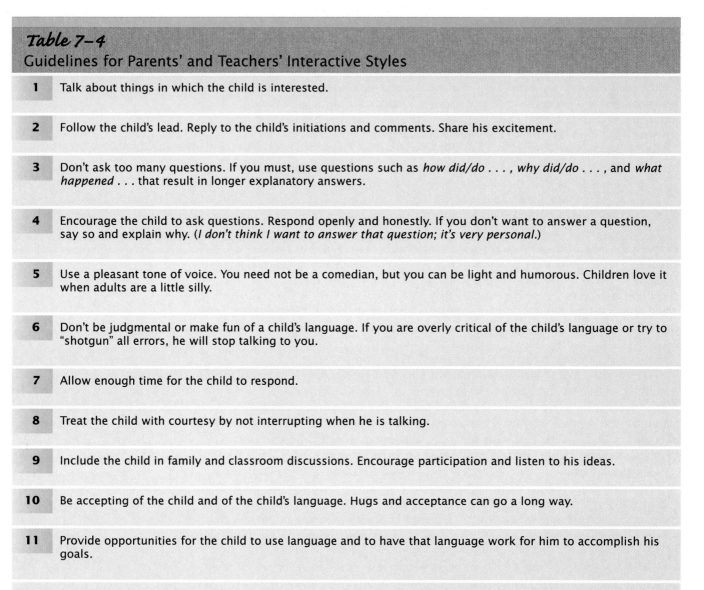

Child: Yeah.
Teacher: I don't think so. What if there was a fire in somebody's house—
Child: (*interrupting*) Then they're dead, or hurt.
Teacher: Yeah, they'd be hurt. But how would a fire start in somebody's house?
Child: By starting something with matches.
Teacher: A match, okay. Now do you think this could have started with a match?
Child: Yeah.
Teacher: This fire in the jungle? Who would have a match in the jungle? The animals?
Child: A monkey.
Teacher: A monkey would have a match in the jungle?
Child: (*nodding*) I saw that on TV. (Blank & White, 1986, p. 4.)

After seventeen more exchanges, the teacher gave up.

Alternative question-asking strategies can be used to help students think through problems successfully. When a student fails to answer a higher-order question because it is beyond his or her level of information or skill, the teacher should reformulate the problem at a simpler level. After the intermediate steps are solved, the teacher can return to the question that was too difficult at first, as illustrated by the following dialogue:

Adult: Why do we use tape for hanging pictures?
Child: 'Cause it's shiny.
Adult: Here's a shiny piece of paper and here's a shiny piece of tape. Let's try them both. Try hanging the picture with the shiny paper.
Child: (*does it*)
Adult: Does it work?
Child: No, it's falling.

An attitude of acceptance and openness to a child's language can go a long way in encouraging improvement.

SUCCESS STORIES

Garden City, NY: College student **Ryan McGarr** *has overcome difficulties in speech and language processing as well as problems with memory and organization since being severely injured in a car accident on Thanksgiving Day, 1992. Ryan remained comatose for three days, with a traumatic brain injury and fractures to his hip and legs. "I know it happened," says Ryan, "but I still find it hard to believe." His mother, Kathy McGarr, finds it hard to forget. Although Ryan's physical injuries healed quickly, his residual difficulties in language and cognitive processing presented an academic challenge. Fortunately, an innovative special education project came to his assistance, providing a bridge between rehabilitation services and school re-entry.*

Special educator Nancy Maher-Maxwell coordinates the New York State Education Department's TBI Project for the Board of Cooperative Educational Services of Nassau County. Hospitals, rehabilitation centers, and school districts know to give her name to families who face the maze of issues following their children's head injuries. Since 1991, the project has coordinated services to support families and train teachers to meet the individual needs of students re-entering their classrooms.

Kathy McGarr is grateful that someone at the hospital told her about the project: "Just the trauma and trying to take care of your other children— the whole family tends to fall apart. I didn't have the concentration or anything to deal with this." Nancy Maher-Maxwell understands this: "Research is showing that kids who have this connection between rehabilitation and school re-entry, as well as the ongoing staff support once they've returned, have a greater success rate than those who don't. The gulf between rehabilitation and school re-entry is too big for families to have to negotiate on their own."

In Ryan's case, several factors combined to make a successful outcome possible, including coordinated services, compensatory instructional strategies, strong support from family and friends, spontaneous neurological recovery, and his own spirit and desire to achieve.

Others were aware of this determination, too. His mother recalls, "The psychologist at the hospital, who evaluated Ryan nine weeks after the accident, told me he would probably never finish school and that I was overwhelming him with academics. But it was what he wanted and I had to let him try to do it." Nancy Maher-Maxwell met Ryan six weeks after the accident and remembers his using crutches and speaking in a slow monotone voice. He said he was determined to graduate with his class and wanted tutoring.

To start the process Nancy contacted Ryan's school district. His former English teacher, Maria Webster, agreed to be his home tutor. Despite Ryan's memory problems and slowness in learning, Maria was optimistic; she remembered Ryan as an expressive writer. With Nancy's help, Maria's

Adult: Now, try the tape.
Child: (*does it*)
Adult: Does it work?
Child: Yeah, it's not falling.
Adult: So, why do we use the tape for hanging pictures?
Child: It won't fall. (Blank & White, 1986, p. 5)

Teachers sometimes do not clearly express their intent in questioning students or fail explicitly to delimit the topic of their questions. Consequently, students become confused. Teachers must learn to clarify the problems under such circumstances. As Blank and White (1986) note, "Teachers do not establish psychological comfort and eagerness to learn by making students spend as much, if not more, energy deciphering the intent than the content of their questions" (p. 8). Teachers must also give unambiguous feedback to students' responses to their questions. Too often, teachers

Special Educators at Work

lessons were individualized, concentrating on vocabulary and word meanings. She used flashcards and, together with Ryan, made up funny sentences using mnemonics to help him remember information. Instead of giving him a chapter to read in history, Maria "chunked" the material to be learned, breaking it into smaller units. Ryan remembers that being helpful: "It used to be that I even had to reread novels two or three times just to get the meaning."

Kathy McGarr recalls that it was hard to tell if Ryan would regain his language abilities. "In speech therapy, he had a terrible time with categorization skills. His therapist asked him to name five green vegetables, and he couldn't do it! What was even more surprising was that he couldn't imagine that anyone could!"

Ryan returned to school parttime in April 1993. He went to an outpatient rehab for therapies in the morning and then to his local public high school in the afternoon for English, social studies, art, and resource room. He returned fulltime for his senior year, carrying a full program of academic courses, with resource room support for forty-five minutes daily.

The TBI project coordinated Ryan's re-entry into the regular educational environment by providing inservice workshops as well as personal and continual support for his teachers. They were alerted to changes in Ryan's cognitive processing, such as his memory for sequences used in multistep problem solving. Training emphasized Ryan's need to take in new information in a variety of ways, so teachers were shown techniques to reinforce study skills, like taking notes on lectures, outlining chapters, and organizing projects. As Nancy Maher-Maxwell explains, "Often, the typical high school teacher will lecture on the subject, expect the kids to take good notes, and evaluate them on a test. Because of the disruptions in the learning systems of students with TBI, there may be a slower rate in processing, so extended time is often necessary both in teaching and in testing."

TBI is an acquired injury that demands new adjustments. "If I hadn't spoken with Nancy," says Kathy McGarr, "I wouldn't have known to put Ryan in a resource room, since he never needed special education before." Head injuries can also make the future hard to predict. Nancy recalls, "That early neuropsychological evaluation that said he could forget about his academic aspirations never took into account Ryan's determination and the compensatory strategies that special education could provide. It was devastating to everybody—and look how wrong such a prediction can be with TBI!"

Ryan has been fortunate. He spontaneously regained much of his academic strength, and now, having just completed his first year of college, he can see how far he has come: "When I look back, I realize how slow I was as a result of the head injury." Ryan still finds that he is more easily distracted than he used to be, and he continues to need extended time on some college exams. Nevertheless, he has emerged confident: " I'll succeed in the world doing whatever I want to do. I have no doubts about that."

—By Jean Crockett

do not tell students explicitly that their answers are wrong, for fear of showing nonacceptance. Lack of accurate, explicit feedback, however, prevents students from learning the concepts involved in instruction.

Our points here are these:

1. The teacher's role is not merely to instruct students *about* language but also to teach them *how to use it.* More specifically, the teacher must help students learn *how to use language in the context of the classroom.*
2. The teacher's own use of language is a key factor in helping students learn effectively, especially if students have language disorders.

Written language is a special problem for many students with language disorders. In fact, as students progress through the grades, written language takes on increasing importance. Students are expected to read increasingly complex and difficult material and understand its meaning. In addition, they are expected to express themselves more clearly in writing. The interactions teachers have with students about their writing—the questions they ask to help students understand how to write for their readers—are critical to overcoming disabilities in written language (Wong, Wong, Darlington, & Jones, 1991).

Finally, we note that intervention in language disorders employs many of the same strategies used in intervention in learning disabilities. As discussed earlier, the definitions of *specific language disability* and *specific learning disability* are parallel, if not nearly synonymous. Metacognitive training, strategy training, and other approaches that we discuss in Chapter 5 are typically appropriate for use with students who have language disorders (see also Hallahan, Kauffman, & Lloyd, 1996; Wallach & Butler, 1994).

AUGMENTATIVE AND ALTERNATIVE COMMUNICATION

For some individuals, oral language is out of the question; they have physical or cognitive disabilities that preclude their learning to communicate through normal speech. A system of augmentative or alternative communication (AAC) must be designed for them. Franklin and Beukelman (1991) define *augmentative communication* as follows:

> Augmentative communication refers to the variety of communication approaches that are used to assist persons who are limited in their ability to communicate messages through natural modes of communication. These approaches may be unaided, as in manual sign and adapted gestures, or aided, with utilization of communication boards or electronic devices. Regardless of the communication mode employed, the goals of augmented communicators are similar to those of natural speakers, that is, to express wants and needs, to share information, to engage in social closeness, and to manage social etiquette. (p. 321)

Individuals whose motor disabilities prevent them from communicating orally may benefit from augmentative and alternative communication systems.

Students for whom AAC must be designed range in intelligence from highly gifted to profoundly retarded, but they all have one characteristic in common—the inability to communicate effectively through speech because of a physical impairment. Some of these individuals may be unable to make any speech sounds at all; others need a system to augment their speech when they cannot make themselves understood because of environmental noise, difficulty in producing certain words or sounds, or unfamiliarity with the person with whom they want to communicate.

As Franklin and Beukelman (1991) note, manual signs or gestures may be useful for some individuals. But many individuals with severe physical limitations are unable to use their hands to communicate through gestures or signs; they must use another means of communication, usually involving special equipment. The problems to be solved in helping these individuals communicate include selecting a vocabulary and giving them an effective, efficient means of indicating elements in their vocabularies. Although the basic ideas behind AAC are quite simple, selecting the best vocabulary and devising an efficient means of indication for many individuals with severe disabilities are extraordinarily challenging. Since its founding in 1983, the International Society for Augmentative and Alternative Communication (ISAAC) has challenged experts from a variety of disciplines to devise better AAC systems (Schlosser & Lloyd, 1991).

A variety of approaches to AAC have been developed, some involving relatively simple or so-called low-technology solutions and some requiring complex or high-technology solutions:

> There are many different ways to provide an individual with a means to indicate the elements of his message, all of which are elaborations on combinations of two fundamental approaches: direct selection and scanning. With direct selection, the individual points directly to his selection in some fashion. With scanning, someone or something points to the items for the individual one at a time. When the item the individual desires is indicated, he or she gives some type of signal. The game "Twenty Questions" is an example of the scanning approach. Another example is a rotating arrow that the individual could stop. A person pointing to items one at a time until signaled by the handicapped individual would be another example of scanning. (Vanderheiden, 1984, p. 41)

An extremely wide variety of direct-selection and scanning methods have been devised for AAC, depending on individual capabilities. The system used may involve pointing with the hand or a headstick, eye movements, or operation of a microswitch by foot, tongue, head movement, or breath control. Sometimes, the individual can use a typewriter or computer terminal fitted with a key guard, so that keys are not likely to be pressed accidentally, or use an alternative means for selecting keystrokes. Often, communication boards are used. A *communication board* is an array of pictures, words, or other symbols that can be operated with either a direct-selection or scanning strategy. The content and arrangement of the board will vary, depending on the person's capabilities, preferences, and communication needs.

Speed, reliability, portability, cost, and overall effectiveness in helping a person communicate independently are factors to be considered in designing and evaluating AAC (Beukelman, 1991; Nelson, 1992). Some AAC systems are very slow, unreliable (either because of the equipment or a poor match with the abilities of the user), cumbersome, or useful only in very restricted settings. Beukelman (1991) notes that people typically think of the equipment and material costs involved in AAC but that the real costs must include instruction and learning. A communication board will not necessarily be useful just because it is available. And the most sophisticated technological solution to communication is not always the one that will be most useful in the long run.

collaboration

a key to success

Ardell Fitzgerald

Ellen Bruno

Ardell My caseload includes twenty-nine children from kindergarten to fifth grade, both in regular education and a special education classroom. The speech and language disorders I work with include articulation, stuttering, voice, language/learning disabilities, developmental apraxia, and hearing impairment. I'm responsible for evaluation, diagnosis, and remediation. I also team teach four days a week in a special education kindergarten class (eight children with a teacher and an aide) and pull out children in small groups who have been identified as having communication disorders from fifteen regular classrooms. I also meet with the school support team weekly to discuss interventions for children who are having problems in regular classrooms. I screen children referred by teachers, parents, and the support team and help make decisions about the necessity for diagnostic testing.

Ellen Before assuming my present position as a special education kindergarten teacher, I taught children with hearing impairments for seven years, kids with behavior disorders for four years, and students with communication disorders for five years. Now I'm teaching five- to seven-year-olds who are more than two years below age level in at least one of the following developmental areas: cognitive, psychomotor, speech/language, or social/emotional. The SEED classroom has a maximum of eight children with special needs who are integrated with a group of sixteen normal children in a morning kindergarten program. An early childhood educator, two educational aids, and I team teach all twenty-four children.

Ardell We'll describe our work with Sara, a seven-year-old.

Ellen I met Sara at the very beginning of the schoolyear. I was pleased to have a second-grade girl in my all-boy class and excitedly asked about her summer. She beamed and rambled on and on. I had no idea what she was saying but politely nodded and commented, "Gee, that sounds like fun!"

Ardell Sara's severely disordered articulation and language interfered with communication. Because of her developmental apraxia (difficulty planning and sequencing motor movements), she was almost 90 percent unintelligible to the unfamiliar listener. She produced many of her sounds in the back of her mouth, substituting /k/ and /g/ for the tongue-tip sounds. Not only her speech sounds but also her sentence structure was disordered.

Ellen In the classroom, Sara was especially slow to tune into instructions. She needed to be alerted before she could take in information. Because of her low muscle tone and trunk support, she was unable to sit at her desk or on the floor for an activity longer than ten minutes. She was weak in understanding basic concepts. She had difficulty sequencing, retelling a simple story, following directions, predicting, and telling why. These problems were common to many of my communication-disordered students. Academically, Sara was on a readiness level in reading and on a first-grade level in math.

Ardell Sara had many strengths. Her intelligence was normal. Her ability to understand language was better than her expressive ability. She was pleasant, cooperative, and willing to try a task several times. In spite of her communication problems, she readily initiated conversation with peers and teachers. At the beginning of the schoolyear, Ellen and I discussed what we had learned about Sara from reports, individual assessments, and classroom observation. I shared information about Sara's speech patterns and disordered language structures. We decided that

Ardell Fitzgerald is a speech-language pathologist, Montezuma Elementary School, Albuquerque Public Schools; B.A., Speech Pathology, University of Colorado; M.A., Speech Pathology, University of Colorado; Certificate of Clinical Competence in Speech-Language Pathology, American Speech-Language-Hearing Association.
Ellen Bruno is a special education early development (SEED) kindergarten teacher, Rio Rancho Elementary School, Albuquerque Public Schools; B.S., Speech and Hearing, Indiana State University; M.Ed., Deaf Education, University of Miami.

I could best address these areas in individual sessions in my room but that I would keep Ellen and others informed about Sara's progress so they could reinforce phonological skills in the classroom. For example, during reading sessions Ellen would know which words Sara could pronounce correctly. We also involved Sara's parents. I set up a weekly time for her mother to join our therapy session; she was very conscientious about participating in the sessions. Sara's father had severe cerebral palsy and was unable to model correct speech, but he often lent emotional support for Sara just by his presence.

Ellen My job was to address many of the language concerns within the classroom. Ardell and I have similar philosophies about language intervention. We believe it doesn't stop when the speech-language pathologist (SLP) leaves the classroom or the child leaves the SLP's room. It goes on during math, art, and science, and throughout the day. One of our goals was to present information on a level that Sara could understand and respond to successfully. It was our job to make sure our "teacher talk" matched Sara's level. We were able to help one another analyze our own language and its effect on the children by giving one another feedback. Occasionally, we videotaped lessons. Many times, we had to adapt reading questions or directions on commercially made materials so Sara would understand the materials.

Ardell Ellen and I wrote individualized instructional plans for all our students, including Sara. Ellen was responsible for the academic goals, and I developed speech goals. We collaborated on the language goals because both of us would be implementing them. Many of the students in Ellen's classroom had communication disorders, so we set up a weekly forty-five-minute period when we would team teach a language lesson. Because we worked so closely together, we held parent conferences together.

Ellen At the beginning of the semester, Ardell and I set aside a long planning time to map out the units we wanted to team teach during the next few months. We used curriculum guides to help us choose themes in science, social studies, and literature. We also met weekly to write objectives for each unit. During our meetings, we would decide who was to make or bring the necessary materials to do the lesson. Sometimes, we would take turns writing a script for the lesson.

Ardell Another member of our team was the occupational therapist (OT). She was able to answer our "what-to-do" questions about Sara's sensory-motor integration problems. The OT worked with us during the weekly classroom language lesson and came to our weekly planning sessions.

Ellen One of the most challenging aspects of teaming was keeping communication going when both of us had busy schedules. Many times we had planning sessions over a brown-bag lunch. We often didn't have enough time to plan our classroom activities and talk about needs of specific children like Sara. We sometimes talked during recess and sent quick notes back and forth about Sara, but we needed to develop a better system.

Ardell We juggled our schedules, and toward the middle of the year we began meeting for team planning when Ellen's class was having PE. We started a "traveling notebook" for Sara, in which parents, teachers, and specialists wrote daily or almost daily progress notes, questions, comments, and home and school activity suggestions for carryover of skills. The notebook gave us a way to communicate that included the parents. One of the most rewarding aspects of working as a team was seeing positive changes in Sara and her classmates. We saw less fragmenting of learning and more generalization of skills. Sara's end-of-the-year evaluation showed substantial gains. Her receptive language skills were on her age level. Although Sara's speech was still difficult to understand at times, she began to generalize new articulation skills to her reading and spontaneous speech. Her reading level increased to first grade, and her math increased to second-grade level. Ellen and I shared Sara's triumphs—they made it worth giving up our lunch times! As a result of teaming, we became friends as well as colleagues.

Ellen Students benefited from our teaming, and so did I. My positive experience made it very comfortable to step into a different teaming program this year at a new school. I'm now teaching a special kindergarten class with eight children and teaming with a regular kindergarten teacher with sixteen children. We have two aides.

> ***. . . Teaming requires a commitment . . . to set aside sufficient time to communicate about students.***

Our children are in the same classroom all morning. After the half-day morning session ends, my special education children remain in school and receive an additional hour of instruction from the special education team, including the SLP, OT, and me. Planning time and home visits are built into the program after 1:30 P.M. dismissal.

Ardell One barrier to teaming is time. Especially in the beginning, teaming requires a commitment by the team to set aside sufficient time to talk about students. Another barrier is lack of clarity in sharing assignments and responsibilities. One team member can feel she or he is carrying most of the responsibility for planning and be resentful. Expectations have to be clearly defined.

Ellen Another barrier is differences in philosophies and teaching styles. This can be overcome if there is a willingness to listen and learn from one another. The specialist may be uncomfortable in a classroom and prefer to do therapy in a private setting. Or the classroom teacher may feel threatened by the expertise of the specialist.

Today, increasingly innovative and creative technological solutions to the problem of nonvocal communication are being found. At the same time, the importance of making decisions on a highly individual basis has been recognized (Calculator & Jorgensen, 1991). Until rather recently, AAC was seen primarily as a means of allowing users to demonstrate the language skills they have already acquired. But now, there is increasing emphasis on how AAC is used as a tool for teaching language—for helping AAC users not only to give voice to what they feel and know about specific tasks but also to acquire increasingly sophisticated language skills (Nelson, 1992).

Researchers are attempting to make it possible for young AAC users to talk about the same kinds of things that other youngsters do (Marvin, Beukelman, Brockhaus, & Kast, 1994). Other efforts are directed at training AAC users to tell those with whom they communicate how to interact with them more effectively—that is, to train AAC users in pragmatics. The box on page 287 summarizes how Vivian, a twelve-year-old sixth grader with quadriplegia due to cerebral palsy, was taught to understand and resolve her friends' problematic styles of interacting with her (Buzolich & Lunger, 1995). Vivian used an AAC device called a Light Talker, which allowed her to select letters and programmed phrases (represented by icons) for output from a computerized display by pointing an infrared light sensor attached to her glasses. Notice how Vivian was taught to recognize communicative problems, such as her friends being positioned where she could not see them, and use explicit language strategies to overcome them.

Users of AAC encounter three particular challenges not faced by natural communicators:

1. AAC is much slower than natural communication—perhaps one-twentieth the typical rate of speech. This can result in great frustration for both the AAC users and natural communicators.
2. Users of AAC who are not literate must rely on a vocabulary and symbols that are selected by others. If the vocabulary and symbols, as well as other features of the system, are not well chosen, AAC will be quite limited in the learning and personal relationships it allows.
3. AAC must be constructed to be useful in a variety of social contexts, allow accurate and efficient communication without undue fatigue, and support the individual's learning of language and academic skills (Franklin & Beukelman, 1991).

Progress in the field of AAC requires that all of these challenges be addressed simultaneously.

The need for AAC is increasing as more people with severe disabilities are surviving and taking their places in the community. As Franklin and Beukelman (1991) observe:

> A relatively large number of individuals communicate entirely or in part using an augmentative mode as they attempt to participate in their homes, schools, recreational activities, and employment settings. The number of augmented communicators is growing rapidly. (p. 334)

As more students with severe disabilities are integrated into regular educational programs at all levels, the availability and appropriate use of AAC in such classrooms become more critical issues (Calculator & Jorgensen, 1991). Although relatively few AAC users were found in higher education in the late 1980s, Huer (1991) notes that "access to technology for improved communication (both spoken and written) is a service that will become increasingly important to disabled university students" (p. 236).

AAC Pragmatics Training

WHAT ABLE-BODIED KIDS ARE LIKELY TO DO WHEN THEY TALK TO YOU AND WHAT YOU CAN DO ABOUT IT

Friend's Style	*System User's Strategy (Vivian)*
Friend stands/sits in a position that is uncomfortable for you.	Let your friend know in a nice way that you'd rather have them be somewhere else when you're talking. For example, "Can you sit next to me here?" or "Can you come over here where I can see you?"
Friend asks lots of yes/no questions.	Answer yes/no then program additional information on your Talker; e.g., "Yes, I saw *Wayne's World* and I loved it," or answer yes/no then ask partner a question, "No, I didn't. What did you do?"
Friend brings up all the topics.	Switch to a related topic when you finish talking about your friend's topic. Use a phrase such as "Do you know what?" to prepare your friend for a new topic.
Friend does all the talking.	Use a phrase such as "It'll take me a minute to spell what I want to say," "Just a minute," "Wait a second," "I need more time" to alert your friend to use some waiting strategies and give you enough time to talk.
Friend doesn't understand you but acts like he/she does.	Check in with your friend to be sure he/she is understanding you if you suspect he/she isn't. E.g., if your friend doesn't say anything or has a confused look on his/her face, ask him/her, "Did you understand that?" or "Do you know what I mean?" Tell your friend exactly what you are going to do: e.g., "I'll say it again," "Wait, let me say it differently."
Friend watches as you prepare a message but doesn't say anything.	Let your partner know what you want him or her to do as you spell. "Say each letter as I point to it." "Please predict as I spell."

Source: From "Empowering system users in peer training," by M. J. Buzolich & J. Lunger, 1995, *Augmentative and Alternative Communication, 11,* p. 41. Reprinted with permission of Decker Periodicals, Inc.

The remarkable increase in the power and availability of microcomputers is radically changing our ability to provide AAC. New applications of microcomputers may lead to breakthroughs that will allow people with severe disabilities to communicate more effectively, even if they have extremely limited muscle control. Furthermore, existing microcomputer software suggests ways of encouraging children to use their existing language skills. Technological developments will no doubt revolutionize AAC by the time we enter the twenty-first century.

One type of AAC that burst upon the scene in the early 1990s is called *facilitated communication* (*FC*). In it, a facilitator physically assists the user in typing out messages on a keyboard or in pointing to items on a communication board. FC has been used with people with a variety of severe disabilities but especially those with autism and mental retardation.

Proponents of FC have reported that it reveals unexpected intelligence and literacy in many individuals with severe developmental disabilities, including autism and mental retardation (e.g., Biklen, 1990, 1992a, 1992b; Biklen & Schubert, 1991). However, these reports quickly led to controversy because of the seemingly miraculous results obtained and doubts about the authenticity of the messages constructed by FC users. A large number of well-controlled studies have now demonstrated that in very nearly all cases, the messages attributed to FC users were actually created (often unknowingly), by the facilitators. In fact, careful analyses have shown no unexpected literacy in people with disabilities (cf. Mesibov, 1995; Montee et al., 1995; Shane, 1994; Simpson & Myles, 1995).

In sum, new methods should be developed to allow people with severe disabilities to communicate (Montee et al., 1995). However, any AAC procedure must represent the communication of the *user,* not someone else. If FC or any other AAC device misrepresents the user's communication, then it demeans them through pretense. This is not acceptable, as all people with disabilities should be treated with dignity and respect.

COMMUNICATION VARIATIONS

As defined earlier in this chapter (see the box on p. 260), *communication variations* include language that is unique to a particular region, ethnic group, or other cultural group. Thus, the fact that a student does not use the language expected in school does not necessarily mean that he or she has a language disorder. Of course, an individual may both have a language disorder *and* exhibit a variation that is not a disorder; such an individual will be unable to communicate effectively even with others who use the same language variation (see Battle, 1993).

Encouraging the communication of children whose cultural heritage or language patterns are not those of the professionals' microculture is of increasing concern to classroom teachers and speech-language clinicians. (See Chapter 3 for a discussion of microculture.) On the one hand, care must be taken not to mistake a cultural or ethnic difference with a disorder; on the other hand, disorders existing in the context of a language difference must not be overlooked (Nelson, 1993; Seymour, Champion, & Jackson, 1995). When assessing children's language, the professional must be aware of the limitations of normative tests and other sources of potential bias.

A child may not have a language disorder yet have a communicative difference that demands special teaching. Delpit (1995) and Foster (1986) discuss the need for

Patterns of communication within different families are a significant factor in language development.

teaching children of nondominant cultures the rules for effective communication in the dominant culture while understanding and accepting the effectiveness of the children's home languages in their cultural contexts. Failure to teach children the skills they need to communicate effectively according to the rules of the dominant culture will deny them many opportunities. In effect, children of minority language groups may need to learn to live in two worlds—one in which their home language is used and one in which school language is used (Westby & Roman, 1995).

Nelson (1993) notes that many students for whom language difference is an issue do not speak entirely different languages, but variations peculiar to certain groups of speakers—that is, *dialects*. For example, one dialect that is different from standard English but is not a language disorder is African American English (AAE) or Black English Vernacular (BEV). AAE has certain features not shared by other English dialects because it originated from features of West African languages. Teachers must understand—and help their students understand—that other dialects are not inferior or limited language systems (Seymour et al., 1995).

As we have already noted, however, students must also understand the value of learning and using the language rules of the dominant culture (Delpit, 1995). Furthermore, it is critical that communication specialists and teachers keep recognition of language difference and language disorder in perspective:

> Difficult questions arise for language disorders specialists when they attempt to differentiate language disorder from language difference. Professionals may either "undercompensate" for language difference—and run the risk of identifying children as disabled when they are merely using language skills different from those tapped by most testing methods—or they may "overcompensate" for language difference, and assume that any child from a sociolinguist community that differs from the mainstream must not have a language disorder. . . . Both practices are discriminatory and must be avoided. (Nelson, 1993, p. 34)

Recently, researchers have turned their attention to how the language of different cultural groups is related to school learning. Anderson and Battle (1993) and Westby (1994) note that different cultural groups provide very different language environments for infants and young children. However, these differences are more often matters of social class than ethnicity. "Socioeconomic status is more critical to the development of language than race or ethnicity" (Anderson & Battle, 1993, p. 180).

Families also differ greatly in the ways they talk to children and in the language they expect children to use. Conversational interactions—called **narratives**—differ widely in families. Narratives can be classified as **genres**, which are purposes or plans for discourse—for example, to recount recent events, to explain the reason for doing something, or to tell an imaginative story.

Children's experiences with language prior to coming to school are an important factor in determining how they respond to the language demands of the classroom. Although students may not have language *disorders,* their language *variations* may put them at a disadvantage in using language in an academic context. Consider the cultural variations across narrative genres described by Westby (1994) in Table 7–5. The major implication of these differences is that teachers must be able to understand linguistic variations and help students generate narratives through skillful questioning that will help them comprehend and learn to use the language of school.

A major concern today in both special and general education is teaching children who are learning English as a second language (ESL), who are non-English proficient (NEP), or who have limited English proficiency (LEP). Bilingual education is a field of concern and controversy because of the rapidly changing demographics in many

narrative. Self-controlled, self-initiated discourse; description or storytelling.

genre. A plan or map for discourse; type of narrative discourse.

Table 7–5
Cultural Variations in Narrative Genres

	CULTURE				
Genre	*Mainstream*	*Mexican American*	*Chinese American*	*White Working Class*	*Black Working Class*
Recounts (Tell Daddy about our trip to . . .)	Common with young children Open-ended scaffolding Invitations to recount decrease with age	Rare	Rare	Predominant genre Tightly scaffolded	Rare
Accounts (Did you hear what happened to . . . ?)	Begun before two years Adults request further explanation Adults suggest alternative outcomes Adults assess attitudes and actions of actor	Frequent Occur especially in family gathering	At home; asked about events of day Not outside the home or with strangers	Not until school Must be accurate Privilege of older adults	Frequent in response to teasing Exaggeration values May be produced cooperatively
Eventcasts (I'm putting the soda in the chest, and then I'll load the car.)	Begun with preverbal Continue throughout the preschool	Almost never in daily events Family may cooperatively plan future events	Occur during ongoing activities More frequent for girls than boys	In play with young children In planning family projects with older children	Rare
Stories (Once upon a time . . .)	Frequent story reading Story comprehension negotiated Produce own imaginative stories	Bruja tales Stories about real events embellished with new details and about historical figures and events Children's literature absent	Tales about historical people and events Prefer informational rather than fictional books	Listen to stories read Comprehension not negotiated	No children's story books

Source: From C. E. Westby, "The effects of culture and genre, structure, and style of oral and written texts," in ***Language learning disabilities in school-age children and adolescents: Some principles and applications***, edited by G. P. Wallach & K. G. Butler. Copyright © 1994 by Allyn and Bacon. Reprinted with permission.

American communities (see Crawford, 1992). Spanish-speaking children comprise a rapidly growing percentage of the students in many school districts (Fradd, Figueroa, & Correa, 1989). Moreover, a large number of Asian/Pacific children have immigrated to the United States during the past decade (Cheng, 1989). Many of these children have no proficiency or limited proficiency in English, and some have disabilities, as well. Bilingual special education is "an emerging discipline with a brief history" (Baca & Amato, 1989, p. 168). As we discussed in Chapter 3, finding the best way to teach children to become proficient in English, particularly when they have disabilities as well as language differences, is a special challenge for the 1990s (Gersten, Brengelman, & Jimenez, 1994; Gersten & Woodward, 1994; Ortiz, Yates, & Garcia, 1990).

SPEECH DISORDERS

As we noted at the beginning of the chapter, speech disorders include disorders of voice, articulation, and fluency. Remember that an individual may have more than one speech disorder and that speech and language disorders sometimes occur together.

We provide only brief descriptions of the major speech disorders for two reasons:

1. Compared to language disorders, speech disorders pose a much smaller problem for classroom teachers.
2. Most speech disorders will be treated primarily by speech-language pathologists, not classroom teachers. Teachers are expected to be aware of possible speech disorders and to refer students they suspect of having such disorders for evaluation by speech-language pathologists. Furthermore, teachers are expected to work with speech-language pathologists to help students correct speech as well as language disorders in the classroom (see the box page 292).

Voice Disorders

People's voices are perceived as having pitch, loudness, and quality. Changes in pitch and loudness are part of the stress patterns of speech. Vocal quality is related not only to production of speech sounds but also to the nonlinguistic aspects of speech.

Voice disorders, though difficult to define precisely, are characteristics of pitch, loudness, and/or quality that are abusive of the **larynx;** hamper communication; or are perceived as markedly different from what is customary for someone of a given age, sex, and cultural background. Voice disorders can result from a variety of biological and nonbiological causes, including growths in the larynx (e.g., nodules, polyps, or cancerous tissue), infections of the larynx (laryngitis), damage to the nerves supplying the larynx, or accidental bruises or scratches on the larynx (Love, 1992). Misuse or abuse of the voice also can lead to a quality that is temporarily abnormal. High school cheerleaders, for example, frequently develop temporary voice disorders (Campbell, Reich, Klockars, & McHenry, 1988). Disorders resulting from misuse or abuse can damage the tissues of the larynx. Sometimes a person has psychological problems that lead to a complete loss of voice (aphonia) or to severe voice abnormalities.

Voice disorders having to do with **resonance**—vocal quality—may be caused by physical abnormalities of the oral cavity (such as **cleft palate**) or damage to the brain or nerves controlling the oral cavity. Infections of the tonsils, adenoids, or sinuses can also influence how the voice is resonated. Most people who have severe hearing loss typically have problems in achieving a normal or pleasingly resonant voice. Finally, sometimes a person simply has not learned to speak with an appropriately resonant voice. There are no biological or deep-seated psychological reasons for the problem; rather, it appears that he or she has learned faulty habits of positioning the organs of speech (Moore & Hicks, 1994).

When children are screened for speech and language disorders, the speech-language pathologist is looking for problems in voice quality, resonance, pitch, loudness, and

larynx. The structure in the throat containing the vocal apparatus (vocal cords); laryngitis is a temporary loss of voice caused by inflammation of the larynx.

resonance. The quality of the sound imparted by the size, shape, and texture of the organs in the vocal tract.

cleft palate. A condition in which there is a rift or split in the upper part of the oral cavity; may include the upper lip (cleft lip).

The Speech-Language Pathologist

A speech-language pathologist is a highly trained professional capable of assuming a variety of roles in assisting persons who have speech and language disorders. Entering the profession requires rigorous training and demonstration of clinical skills under close supervision. Certification requires completion of a master's degree in a program approved by the American Speech-Language-Hearing Association (ASHA). You may want to write to ASHA, 10801 Rockville Pike, Rockville, MD 20852 for a free booklet, *Careers in Speech-Language Pathology and Audiology*.

Because of the emphasis on *least restrictive environment,* or mainstreaming (see Chapters 1 and 2), speech-language pathologists are doing more of their work in regular classrooms and are spending more time consulting with classroom teachers than they have in the past. Speech-language pathologists of the future will need more knowledge of classroom procedures and the academic curriculum—especially in reading, writing, and spelling—and will be more involved in the overall education of children with communication disorders. More emphasis will be placed on working as a team member in the schools to see that children with disabilities obtain appropriate educations. Because of legislation and changing population demographics, speech-language pathologists of the future will also probably be more involved with preschool children and those with learning disabilities and severe, multiple disabilities. There will be broader concern for the entire range of communication disorders, including both oral and written communication.

duration. If a problem is found, referral to a physician is indicated. A medical report may indicate that surgery or other treatment is needed because of a growth or infection. Aside from the medical evaluation, the speech-language pathologist will evaluate when the problem began and how the individual uses his or her voice in everyday situations and under stressful circumstances. Besides looking for how voice is produced and structural or functional problems, the pathologist also looks for signs of infection or disease that may be contributing to the disorder as well as for signs of serious illness.

Articulation Disorders

Articulation disorders involve errors in producing words. Word sounds may be omitted, substituted, distorted, or added. Lisping, for example, involves a substitution or distortion of the [s] sound (e.g., *thunthine* or *shunshine* for *sunshine*). Missing, substituted, added, or poorly produced word sounds may make a speaker difficult to understand or even unintelligible. Such errors in speech production may also carry heavy social penalties, subjecting the speaker to teasing or ridicule.

When are articulation errors considered a disorder? That depends on a clinician's subjective judgment, which will be influenced by his or her experience, the number and types of errors, the consistency of these errors, the age and developmental characteristics of the speaker, and the intelligibility of the person's speech.

Young children make frequent errors in speech sounds when they are learning to talk. Many children do not master all the phonological rules of the language and learn to produce all the speech sounds correctly until they are eight or nine years old. Furthermore, most children make frequent errors until after they enter school. The age of the child is thus a major consideration in judging the adequacy of articulation. Another major consideration is the phonological characteristics of the child's community because children learn speech largely through imitation. For instance, a child reared in the deep South may have speech that sounds peculiar to residents of Long Island, but that does not mean that the child has a speech disorder.

The number of children having difficulty producing word sounds decreases markedly during the first three or four years of elementary school. Among children with other disabilities, especially mental retardation and neurological disorders like cerebral palsy, the prevalence of articulation disorders is higher than in the general population (Schwartz, 1994).

Lack of ability to articulate speech sounds correctly can be caused by biological factors. For example, brain damage or damage to the nerves controlling the muscles used in speech may make it difficult or impossible to articulate sounds (Love, 1992). Furthermore, abnormalities of the oral structures, such as a cleft palate, may make normal speech difficult or impossible. Relatively minor structural changes, such as loss of teeth, may produce temporary errors. Delayed phonological development may also result from a hearing loss.

The parents of a preschool child may refer him or her for assessment if he or she has speech that is really difficult to understand. Most schools screen all new pupils for speech and language problems, and in most cases, a child who still makes many articulation errors in the third or fourth grade will be referred for evaluation. Older children and adults sometimes seek help on their own when their speech draws negative attention. A speech-language pathologist will assess not only phonological characteristics but also social and developmental history, hearing, general language ability, and speech mechanism.

Although speech-language pathologists' interest in articulation disorders has appeared to decrease in recent years, with more attention being given to language, persistent articulation disorders may have serious long-term consequences. A follow-up study found that children with moderate articulation disorders persisting through at least first grade were different—twenty-eight years later—from a comparison group. Specifically, compared to those without articulation disorders, the children with disorders tested lower in articulation, expressive language ability, and receptive language; however, they did not appear to have lower nonverbal reasoning ability or to have more personality problems than the comparison group (Felsenfeld, Broen, & McGue, 1992).

The decision about whether to include a child in an intervention program will depend on his or her age, other developmental characteristics, and the type and consistency of the articulatory errors. Articulation disorders are often accompanied by other disorders of speech or language; thus, the child may need intervention in multiple aspects of communication (Ruscello, St. Louis, & Mason, 1991). The decision will also depend on the pathologist's assessment of the likelihood that the child will self-correct the errors and of the social penalties, such as teasing and shyness, the child is experiencing. If he or she misarticulates only a few sounds but does so consistently and suffers social embarrassment or rejection as a consequence, an intervention program is usually called for.

Fluency Disorders

Normal speech is characterized by some interruptions in speech flow. We occasionally get speech sounds in the wrong order (*revalent* for *relevant*), speak too quickly to be understood, pause at the wrong place in a sentence, use an inappropriate pattern of stress, or become *disfluent*—that is, stumble and backtrack, repeating syllables or words, and fill in pauses with *uh* while trying to think of how to finish what we have to say. It is only when the speaker's efforts are so intense or the interruptions in the flow of speech are so frequent or pervasive that they keep him or her from being understood or draw extraordinary attention that they are considered disorders. Besides, listeners have a greater tolerance for some types of disfluencies than others. Most of us will more readily accept speech-flow disruptions we perceive as necessary corrections of what the speaker has said or is planning to say than disruptions that appear to reflect the speaker's inability to proceed with the articulation of what he or she has decided to say.

The most frequent type of fluency disorder is stuttering. About 1 percent of children and adults are considered stutterers. More boys than girls stutter. Many children quickly outgrow their childhood disfluencies. These children generally use regular and effortless disfluencies, appear to be unaware of their hesitancies, and have parents and teachers who are unconcerned about their speech patterns (Shames & Ramig, 1994). Those who stutter for more than a year and a half or two appear to be at risk for becoming chronic stutterers (Yairi & Ambrose, 1992).

A child who is thought to stutter should be evaluated by a speech-language pathologist. Early diagnosis is important if the development of chronic stuttering is to be avoided. Unfortunately, many educators and physicians do not refer potential stutterers for in-depth assessment because they are aware that disfluencies are a normal part of speech-language development. But nonreferral is extremely detrimental to children who are at risk for stuttering. If their persistent stuttering goes untreated, it may result in a lifelong disorder that affects their ability to communicate, develop positive feelings about self, and pursue certain educational and employment opportunities (Benson, 1995; Bloodstein, 1993; Culatta & Goldberg, 1995). "It is now recognized that early intervention is a crucial component of adequate health care provision for stuttering" (Onslow, 1992, p. 983).

Speech Disorders Associated with Neurological Damage

The muscles that make speech possible are under voluntary control. When there is damage to the areas of the brain controlling these muscles or to the nerves leading to them, there is a disturbance in the ability to speak normally. These disorders may involve articulation of speech sounds **(dysarthria)** or selecting and sequencing speech **(apraxia).** Difficulties in speaking happen because the muscles controlling breathing, the larynx, the throat, the tongue, the jaw, and/or the lips cannot be controlled precisely. Depending on the nature of the injury to the brain, perceptual and cognitive functions may also be affected; the individual may have a language disorder in addition to a speech disorder (Hardy, 1994; LaPointe & Katz, 1994; Love, 1992).

In Chapter 10, we discuss the many possible causes of brain injury. Among them are physical trauma, oxygen deprivation, poisoning, diseases, and strokes. Any of these can cause dysarthria or apraxia. Probably the condition that most frequently accounts for these disorders in children is *cerebral palsy*—brain injury before, during, or after birth that results in muscular weakness or paralysis. Vehicular accidents are a frequent cause of traumatic brain injury in adolescence and young adulthood.

The speech-language pathologist will assess the ability of the person with neurological impairment to control breathing, phonation, resonation, and articulatory movements by listening to the person's speech and inspecting his or her speech mechanism (Love, 1992). Medical, surgical, and rehabilitative specialists in the treatment of neurological disorders also must evaluate the person's problem and plan a management strategy. In cases in which the neurological impairment makes the person's speech unintelligible, augmentative or alternative communication systems may be required.

dysarthria. A condition in which brain damage causes impaired control of the muscles used in articulation.

apraxia. The inability to move the muscles involved in speech or other voluntary acts.

EARLY INTERVENTION

The study of children's early development has shown that the first several years of life are a truly critical period for language learning. Much of children's language and social development depends on the nature and quantity of the language interactions they have with parents or other caregivers. In the homes of children who come to school ready to learn, the language interactions between parents and children have typically been frequent, focused on encouragement and affirmation of the children's behavior, emphasized the symbolic nature of language, provided gentle guidance in exploring things and relationships, and demonstrated the responsiveness of adults to children. By contrast, children who enter school at a disadvantage tend to have experienced much lower rates of language interaction; heard primarily negative, discouraging feedback on their behavior; and heard language that is harsh, literal, and emotionally detached.

Based on extensive observations in homes, Hart and Risley (1995) compared the language experiences of children of professional parents, working-class parents, and parents on welfare. The contrasts in language experiences and the effects observed in children's academic achievement and behavior are stark, but the differences are unrelated to income or ethnicity. Rather, the differences are related to *how* and *how much the* parents talked to their children. As summed up by the authors:

> Our data showed that the magnitude of children's accomplishments depends less on the material and educational advantages available in the home and more on the amount of experience children accumulate with parenting that provides language diversity, affirmative feedback, symbolic emphasis, gentle guidance, and responsiveness. By the time children are 3 years old, even intensive intervention cannot make up for the differences in the amount of such experience children have received from their parents. If children could be given better parenting, intervention might be unnecessary. (Hart & Risley, 1995, p. 210)

Thus, it appears that the key to preventing many disabilities related to language development is to help parents improve how they relate to their children when they are infants and toddlers. Nevertheless, for many young children, intervention in the preschool and primary grades will be necessary.

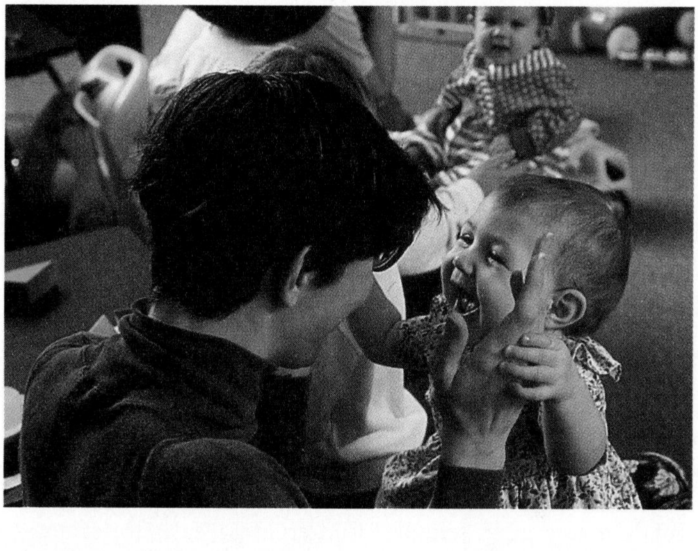

The first several years of life are truly critical for language learning.

Preschoolers who require intervention for a speech or language disorder occasionally have multiple disabilities that are sometimes severe or profound. Language is closely tied to cognitive development, so impairment of general intellectual ability is likely to have a retarding influence on language development. Conversely, lack of language may hamper cognitive development. Because speech is dependent on neurological and motor development, any neurological or motor problem might impair ability to speak. Normal social development in the preschool years depends on the emergence of language, so a child with language impairment is at a disadvantage in social learning. Therefore, the preschool child's language is seldom the only target of intervention (Nelson, 1993).

Researchers have become increasingly aware that language development has its beginning in the earliest mother–child interactions. Concern for the child's development of the ability to communicate cannot be separated from concern for development in other areas. Therefore, speech-language pathologists are a vital part of the multidisciplinary team that evaluates an infant or young child with disabilities and develops an individualized family service plan (IFSP) (see Chapter 2). Early intervention programs involve extending the role of the parent. This means a lot of simple play with accompanying verbalizations. It means talking to the child about objects and activities in the way most mothers talk to their babies. But it also means choosing objects, activities, words, and consequences for the child's vocalizations with great care so the chances that the child will learn functional language are enhanced (Fey, Catts, & Larrivee, 1995; McKnight-Taylor, 1989).

Early childhood specialists now realize that *prelinguistic* intervention is critical for language development—that is, intervention should begin *before* the child's language emerges. The foundations for language are laid in the first few months of life through the nonverbal dialogues infants have with their mothers and other caretakers (Nelson, 1993).

In the early years of implementing IFSPs, emphasis was placed on assessing families' strengths and needs and training parents how to teach and manage their children. More recently, professionals have come to understand that assessing families in the belief that professionals know best is often misguided (Crais, 1991; Slentz & Bricker, 1992). Parents can, indeed, be helped by professionals to play an important role in their children's language development (Alpert & Kaiser, 1992). But the emphasis today is on working with parents as knowledgeable and competent partners whose preferences and decisions are respected (see also discussion in Chapter 12).

Intervention in early childhood is likely to be based on assessment of the child's behavior related to the content, form, and especially the use of language in social interaction. For the child who has not yet learned language, assessment and intervention will focus on imitation, ritualized and make-believe play, play with objects, and functional use of objects. At the earliest stages in which the content and form of language are interactive, it is important to evaluate the extent to which the child looks at or picks up an object when it is referred to, does something with an object when directed by an adult, and uses sounds to request or refuse things and call attention to objects. When the child's use of language is considered, the earliest objectives involve him or her looking at the adult during interactions; taking turns in and trying to prolong pleasurable activities and games; following the gaze of an adult and directing the behavior of adults; and persisting in or modifying gestures, sounds, or words when an adult does not respond.

discourse. Conversation; the skills used in conversation, such as turn taking and staying on the topic.

In the preschool, teaching **discourse** (conversation skills) is a critical focus of language intervention. In particular, emphasis is placed on teaching children to use the discourse that is essential for success in school. Children must learn, for example, to report their experiences in detail and to explain why things happen, not just add to their vocabularies. They must learn not only word forms and meanings but also how to take turns in conversations and maintain the topic of a conversation or change it in an appropriate way (Johnston, Weinrich, & Glaser, 1991). Preschool programs in which such language teaching is the focus may include teachers' daily individualized conversations with children, daily reading to individual children or small groups, and frequent classroom discussions. A plan for a lesson in sticking to the topic, appropriate for children in kindergarten or primary grades, is shown in the box below.

Current trends are directed toward providing speech and language interventions in the typical environments of young children (Cirrin & Penner, 1995). This means that classroom teachers and speech-language pathologists must develop a close working relationship. The speech-language pathologist may work directly with children in the classroom and advise the teacher about the intervention that he or she can carry out as part of the regular classroom activities (Wilcox, Kouri, & Caswell, 1991). The child's peers may also be involved in intervention strategies. Because language is essentially a social activity, its facilitation requires involvement of others in the child's social environment—peers as well as adults (Fey et al., 1995). Normally developing peers have been taught to assist in the language development of children with disabilities by doing the following during playtimes: establishing eye contact; describing their own or others' play; and repeating, expanding, or requesting clarification of what the child with disabilities says (Goldstein & Strain, 1989). Another intervention

Pragmatic Lesson Plan: *Primary (K–3) Topicalization*

ACTIVITY: Describing objects

MATERIALS: Large bag containing several objects of different textures (such as a spoon, washcloth, sandpaper, hairbrush and cotton ball)

PRAGMATIC GOALS: The student will

1. establish a topic and make comments
2. stay on topic for appropriate number of utterances
3. signal change of topic
4. terminate a topic appropriately

INSTRUCTIONS: The students take turns putting a hand inside the bag and feeling the objects. As a student describes one of the objects in detail (shape, texture, size, use), the other students try to identify the object.

Example
Mickey: It has a long handle. It is bigger at one end.
Instructor: How does it feel?
Mickey: The handle is hard. The big end feels soft.
Kathy: Is it a sponge? My mommy has six sponges.
Instructor: Let's describe the object some more.
Mickey: You use it for your hair.
Kathy: Is it a brush?
Samantha: Since Kathy guessed the brush, it is my turn to describe the next object.

Source: From *A sourcebook of pragmatic activities: Theory and intervention for language therapy (PK–6)* (rev. ed.), by E. B. Johnston, B. D. Weinrich, & A. J. Glaser, 1991, p. 32. Tucson, AZ: Communication Skill Builders. Reprinted with permission.

strategy involving peers is *sociodramatic play*. Children are taught in groups of three, including a child with disabilities, to act out social roles, such as those people might take in various settings (e.g., a restaurant or shoe store). The training includes scripts that specify what each child is to do and say, which may be modified by the children in creative ways. Goldstein and Strain (1989) reviewed research showing that such interventions result in significant improvements in the quality of normally developing children's playtime interactions as well as in advances in language development of children with disabilities.

TRANSITION

In the past, adolescents and adults in speech and language intervention programs generally fell into three categories: (1) the self-referred, (2) those with other health problems, and (3) those with severe disabilities. Adolescents or adults may refer themselves to speech-language pathologists because their phonology, voice, or stuttering is causing them social embarrassment and/or interfering with occupational pursuits. These are generally persons with long-standing problems who are highly motivated to change their speech and obtain relief from the social penalties their differences impose.

Adolescents and adults with other health problems may have experienced damage to speech or language capacities as a result of disease or injury, or they may have lost part of their speech mechanism through injury or surgical removal. Treatment of these individuals always demands an interdisciplinary effort. In some cases of progressive disease, severe neurological damage, or loss of tissues of the speech mechanism, the outlook for functional speech is not good. However, surgical procedures, medication, and prosthetic devices are making it possible for more people to speak normally. Loss of ability to use language is typically more disabling than loss of the

The classroom environment can provide students with many opportunities to sharpen their communication skills.

Identifying Possible Language-Related Problems

REASONS TO CONSULT WITH A COMMUNICATIVE SPECIALIST ABOUT OLDER CHILDREN AND ADOLESCENTS WITH MULTIPLE DISABILITIES

- **Failure to understand instructions.** When a person has difficulty performing essential job or daily living tasks, consider the possibility that the person may not understand the language of instructions and may not have sufficient communicative skill to ask for repetition or clarification.
- **Inability to use language to meet daily living needs.** When individuals can produce enough words to formulate a variety of utterances, including questions, then they can travel independently, shop independently, use the telephone when they need to, and ask for assistance in getting out of problem situations when they arise. If persons cannot function in a variety of working, shopping, and social contexts, consider that communicative impairments may be limiting their independence.
- **Violation of rules of politeness and other rules of social transaction.** The ability to function well in a variety of contexts with friends, acquaintances, and one-time contacts depends on sensitivity to the unspoken rules of social interaction. One of the most frequently cited reasons for failure of workers with disabilities to "fit in" with fellow workers is their inability to engage in small-talk during work breaks. Examples that might cause difficulty are failure to take communicative turns when offered, or conversely, interrupting the turns of others; saying things that are irrelevant to the topic; not using politeness markers or showing interest in what the other person says; making blunt requests owing to lack of linguistic skill for softening them; failing to shift style of communication for different audiences (e.g., talking the same way to the boss as to co-workers); and any other communicative behavior that is perceived as odd or bizarre. If people seem to avoid interacting with the target person, referral may be justified.
- **Lack of functional ability to read signs and other symbols and to perform functional writing tasks.** The ability to recognize the communicative symbols of the culture enables people to know how to use public transportation, to find their way around buildings, to comply with legal and safety expectations, and to fill out forms or use bank accounts. Communicative specialists may be able to assist in identifying the best strategies for teaching functional reading and writing skills and encouraging the development of other symbol-recognition and -use skills.
- **Problems articulating speech clearly enough to be understood, stuttering, or using an inaudible or inappropriate voice.** Other speech and voice disorders may interfere with the person's ability to communicate. When such problems are noted, refer the individual to a speech-language pathologist.

Source: From N. W. Nelson, *Childhood language disorders in context: Infancy through adolescence.* Copyright © 1993 by Allyn and Bacon. Reprinted by permission.

ability to speak. Traumatic brain injury may leave the individual with a seriously diminished capacity for self-awareness, goal setting, planning, self-directing or initiating actions, inhibiting impulses, monitoring or evaluating one's own performance, or problem solving (Ylvisaker et al., 1994). Recovering these vital language-based skills is a critical aspect of transition of the adolescent or young adult from hospital to school and from school to independent living.

Individuals with severe disabilities may need the services of speech-language pathologists to help them achieve more intelligible speech. They may also need to be taught an alternative to oral language or given a system of augmented communication. One of the major problems in working with adolescents and adults who have severe disabilities is setting realistic goals for speech and language learning. Teaching simple, functional language—such as social greetings, naming objects, and making simple requests—may be realistic goals for some adolescents and adults.

A major concern of transition programming is ensuring that the training and support provided during the school years are carried over into adult life (Falvey, McLean, & Rosenberg, 1988). To be successful, the transition must include speech-language services that are part of the natural environment. That is, the services must be community based and integrated into vocational, domestic, recreational, consumer, and mobility training activities. Speech-language interventions for adolescents and young adults with severe disabilities must emphasize functional communication—understanding and making oneself understood in the social circumstances most likely to be encountered in everyday life. For example, Lord (1988) identified two primary goals for the communication of adolescents with autism: participating in age-appropriate social relationships outside the family and developing the ability to use language to pursue one's interests. Developing appropriate conversation skills (e.g., establishing eye contact, using greetings, taking turns, and identifying and staying on the topic), reading, writing, following instructions related to recreational activities, using public transportation, and performing a job are examples of the kinds of functional speech-language activities that may be emphasized.

Today, much more emphasis is being placed on the language disorders of adolescents and young adults who do not fit into any of the categories just described. Many of these individuals were formerly seen as having primarily academic and social problems that were not language related. But now it is understood that underlying many or most of the school and social difficulties of adolescents and adults are basic disorders of language (Wallach & Butler, 1994). These language disorders are a continuation of difficulties experienced earlier in the person's development.

Classroom teachers are in a particularly good position to identify possible language-related problems and request help from a communication specialist. The box on p. 299 describes for teachers several characteristics exhibited by older children and adolescents that may indicate a need for intervention. Addressing problems like these as early and effectively as possible is important in helping youngsters make successful transitions to more complex and socially demanding environments.

Some adolescents and adults with language disorders are excellent candidates for *strategy training*, which teaches them how to select, store, retrieve, and process information (see Hallahan et al., 1996, and Chapter 5). Others, however, do not have the required reading skills, symbolic abilities, or intelligence to benefit from the usual training in cognitive strategies. Whatever techniques are chosen for adolescents and older students, the teacher should be aware of the principles that apply to intervention with these individuals.

Suggestions for Teaching
Students with Communications Disorders in General Education Classrooms

By E. Jane Nowacek

WHAT TO LOOK FOR IN SCHOOL

As you know from reading the chapter, the term *communication disorders* encompasses a wide variety of speech and language disabilities. This section will focus on the communication problems experienced by students of near-average or above-average intelligence who do not have sensory or orthopedic disabilities. For information about modifications for students with sensory impairments and physical disabilities, see Chapters 8, 9, and 10. Mild and moderate speech disorders may be easy to identify because they affect voice quality, speech fluency, and articulation. A general question to ask yourself is: "Is the listener so intrigued with *how* the message is being communicated that attention is drawn away from *what* is being communicated?" (Oyer, Hall, & Haas, 1994, p. 7). Consider the following indicators (Lewis & Doorlag, 1995):

Voice Quality: The student's voice is:
- unpleasant
- hoarse or husky
- like a whisper
- nasal
- monotone
- very high pitched or low pitched
- very loud or soft

Speech Fluency: The student's speech is:
- generally fluent with occasional hesitations, repetitions, and/or prolongations of sounds and syllables
- frequently dysfluent and characterized by hesitations, repetitions, and/or prolongations of sounds and syllables

Articulation: The student (Cantwell & Baker, 1987):
- omits certain sounds from speech (e.g., *ca* for *cat*)
- substitutes certain sounds for other sounds (e.g., *wabbit* for *rabbit*)
- reverses the order of the sounds within words (e.g., *aminal* for *animal*)
- has difficulty saying certain speech sounds (e.g., s/l/th)

In contrast to speech disorders, many language disorders remain unidentified until children are in school. Language disorders are generally indicated by an inability to use the symbols of language through:

1. proper use of words and their meanings
2. appropriate grammatical patterns
3. proper use of speech sounds

Teachers should listen for indicators of language problems such as (Shore, 1986;Wiig & Semel, 1984):

- *primary grades:* difficulty following verbal directions; problems with preacademic skills (e.g., recognizing sound differences), phonics, word attack, and structural analysis; limited vocabulary
- *intermediate grades:* word substitutions; frequent confusion of language concepts such as *on* and *in;* confusion with verb tenses; inappropriate use of pronouns; difficulty recalling the names of familiar objects and people
- *middle and high school:* inability to understand abstract concepts and multiple word meanings; difficulty using grammatically correct and complex sentences; difficulty communicating information to others and varying communication to accommodate listener differences

TEACHING TECHNIQUES TO TRY

It is clear that language problems, such as those listed above, can adversely affect students academically and socially. Teachers play an important role in assisting their students with communication disorders by providing appropriate language models and opportunities for communication and by making modifications to accommodate individual students' needs.

Providing Appropriate Models

Because students imitate the language they hear, it is important that classroom teachers model correct language usage, grammar, and articulation in their own communication. Teachers also can provide appropriate language models by reading fiction and nonfiction to students; making audiotapes of content-area material available; and showing selected television programs on videotapes (Gearheart, Weishahn, & Gearheart, 1992).

When reading to students, teachers can help them recognize and interpret figurative language (i.e., nonliteral words and phrases), which is difficult for many students to comprehend. To assist students in understanding metaphors and similes, Wiig and Semel (1984) suggest first explaining that both devices compare an object or person and a descriptive image; however, words such as *like* and *as* indicate similes, whereas metaphors state direct comparisons. Next, present illustrations of literal and nonliteral meanings of words and phrases, such as *It's raining cats and dogs.* After comparing the illustrations, ask students to identify the correct interpretation from the two alternatives. For example, inquire whether *It's raining cats and dogs* means *"Cats and dogs are dropping from the sky"* or *"It is raining very hard."*

Providing Communication Opportunities

Facilitating Conversations

Most students with disabilities need specific instruction in foundational language skills; however, even after having received such instruction, many students are unable to transfer these skills to new settings and situations. To promote generalization, many educators integrate language instruction into the conversational interactions that occur naturally in the classroom. Hoskins (1994) offers the following guidelines for facilitating conversations:

1. Base the content of conversations on the student's interests and concerns.
2. Once a topic of conversation has been selected, assist the student or group of students in exploring different aspects of it (e.g., by brainstorming, sequencing events).
3. During the conversation, help the student communicate what he or she has to say, not by direct correction but by following the student's message with a correct version and by using prompts and cues.
4. Structure opportunities for the student to practice specific foundation skills (e.g., by guiding students to ask each other questions or to give directions and explanations), and highlight the regularities in language.

Facilitating Language Structures

Teachers may also use several child-centered techniques to facilitate language (Nowacek, in press):

- *Expansion* involves the teacher restating and elaborating a student's utterance so that it approximates more mature, grammatically correct speech. However, this does not mean expanding the meaning beyond that which the student intended. For example, if a student reported, "Pen broke," the teacher might reply, "The pen is broken." Lowenthal (1995) points out that this technique is useful for children who can talk but not in complete sentences.
- *Extension,* as the name suggests, demonstrates how a specific language behavior might be used in a slightly different context by providing additional information (Reed, 1994). For instance, a teacher might extend a student's statement "Joe go game" by replying, "Oh, Joe went to see the Bulldogs play at the stadium."
- *Self-talk* models how competent people speak. Teachers typically use this technique as a general language stimulation approach or to emphasize specific aspects of language the students need to acquire (Reed, 1994). If, for example, a student has not mastered the form *"am" + verb + "-ing,"* the teacher might use the ongoing classroom context of looking at a book to engage in self-talk that features this form:

  > I am opening the book. I am looking at the picture. I am pointing to the dog. I am turning the page. Oh, there is a new picture. I am pointing to the ball. [Now] I am looking at the cat. (p. 461)

  When using self-talk, Lowenthal (1995) recommends that teachers (1) speak in simple, short phrases and sentences; (2) describe their actions and thoughts; and (3) not expect children to imitate them.
- *Parallel-talk* serves the same instructional purposes as self-talk, but focuses on what the student is currently doing or what is presently occurring in the environment. For instance, if a student has not yet learned the *subject "are" + verb + "-ing"* structure, the teacher may use the ongoing classroom activity of a writing a first draft to engage in parallel-talk:

  > What are you writing about today? You are thinking about an idea. Oh, you are listing some points you want to include in the draft. Now you are getting ready to write your topic sentence. Good work.
- *Responsive interaction* is intended to increase a student's social communication by enhancing the quality of his or her interaction with an adult. As in the other facilitation techniques, interaction typically is initiated and controlled by the student. The teacher avoids direct instruction; instead, he or she responds to the student's behavior in ways appropriate for the student's current interests and developmental abilities. (Warren & Yoder, 1994).

In addition to these child-centered techniques, teachers can use the language intervention techniques discussed earlier in the chapter for students with autism and delayed language development (e.g., missing item, interruption, and delay strategies), and milieu teaching can be used with students who have language disorders resulting from other causes.

Embedding Interventions in Instructional Activities

Besides using the conversational interactions that occur in classrooms, teachers should also plan opportunities for students to use language in ongoing instructional activities. One way to do so is through *cooperative learning,* an arrangement in which students work together in small, heterogeneous groups to reach a common goal. To prepare for cooperative learning and to facilitate positive interactions among group members, educators often discuss the concept of cooperation and other social skills, such as expressing opposition and managing conflict. This instruction is particularly useful for students who have difficulties with the use of socially appropriate language. In addition, to encourage all members to participate in the group, teachers may assign students specific roles, such as summarizer, elaborator, or encourager (Johnson, Johnson, & Holubec, 1994). Role specification helps integrate students with disabilities who might not otherwise be active participants in the group.

To further ensure that students use their listening and speaking skills, teachers also may select cooperative learning activities that maximize communication among all members of the group, such as:

- *The three-step interview,* which includes the following steps (Kagan, 1990):
  1. Within each four-person cooperative group, teachers form pairs and students conduct one-way interviews regarding the topic being discussed.
  2. Next, students reverse roles and the interviewers become the interviewees.
  3. Finally, all students take turns sharing the information they learned during the interview in a roundrobin fashion.
- *Group retellings* involve giving members different assignments to read. All materials are related to the same topic, but they may come from a wide variety of sources and reflect different reading levels (e.g., an excerpt from a textbook and an encyclopedia, a newspaper article, a pictorial magazine account). Teachers ask students to read the information silently and then retell it in their own words. At any point, group members may interject or elaborate on similar information from their own readings and background knowledge (Wood & Algozzine, 1994).

- *Dyadic learning* is built on the notion that creating images and analogies (elaboration) and monitoring our own comprehension (metacognition) promotes understanding of text. It also provides a rich context for language use. In this approach, students are paired to read and learn information in any content area. The teacher asks them to read a specific number of paragraphs or pages silently. Initially, one student assumes the role of recaller and orally summarizes the reading, and the other student acts as the listener/facilitator and corrects mistakes and adds information. When the next reading assignment is given the students switch roles. They may draw pictures, create graphs, or develop outlines or webs to depict the major ideas in the selection (Wood & Algozzine, 1994).

It is important to note that although teachers may integrate language use into ongoing instructional activities, in order to facilitate communicative competence, they must develop goals in language as well as academics for students with communication disorders. In addition, teachers must monitor and provide feedback on students' communications.

Modifying the Instructional Environment

We have discussed ways in which teachers can provide models of communicative competence, and we have outlined techniques that educators may use to facilitate and promote that competence. In this final section, we suggest several modifications that teachers can make to the instructional environment.

Norris and Hoffman (1993) suggest providing an *integrated curriculum,* in which instruction in all subject areas is based on a single theme (e.g., the weather). For students with less flexible language systems, this approach reduces the demand to address numerous topics in separate subject areas. Furthermore, integrating the curriculum may provide the teacher with an increased opportunity to select materials at various levels of difficulty, which students can use to explore themes without being stigmatized.

A second modification involves integrating oral-to written and written-to oral activities. For example, teachers may use oral-based activities in composition instruction. Doing so provides a transition between these two forms of communication, which students with disabilities may find difficult to make. Rubin (1994) offers the following suggestions for oral-to-written activities:

- Conduct discussions before students begin writing (e.g., brainstorming, interviews).
- Encourage students to taperecord notes and ideas as a prewriting step (e.g., before doing a first draft).
- Provide time for students to critique each others' writing in peer conferences.
- Allow group revising, in which students interested in the same topic talk together and craft a final draft.
- Provide opportunities for students to read their writing aloud to various audiences.

In addition to modifying the curriculum and instruction, teachers should be aware of the complexity of their own discourse. By simplifying their vocabulary and sentence structure and monitoring the rate at which they speak, teachers can help all students better comprehend directions and explanations. Paul (1995) suggests the following methods to assist students with language and learning disabilities in understanding classroom presentations, regardless of the content:

- Provide contextual cues—for instance, distribute outlines of oral presentations or written text and use visuals such as charts, pictures, and diagrams.
- Use redundancy—for instance, review key points throughout the lesson and paraphrase information.
- Relate new information to prior knowledge—for instance, ask students to discuss what they already know about a topic and encourage them to talk about relevant past experiences.

HELPFUL RESOURCES

School Personnel

Speech-language pathologists are responsible for assessing and providing therapy to students with communication disorders. For a discussion of the roles they play in educating students, see page 292.

Technological Resources

The ERIC (Educational Resources Information Center) system provides several ways of accessing the ERIC database and publications (see *Teaching Exceptional Children,* 27(13), p. 80). If you have a computer, a modem, and access to the Internet (an electronic network), you can obtain journals and ERIC documents from libraries and also locate additional information and resources provided on AskERIC, an online question-answering service for teachers, administrators, parents, and students. To use AskERIC, send your e-mail (electronic) inquiry on the Internet (the worldwide electronic mail network) to the following address: "askeric@ericir.syr.edu" (exactly as shown except for quotes).

To "gopher" to AskERIC on the Internet (i.e., to proceed through various online menus), gopher to "ericir.syr.edu" or access the National Gopher System through "gopher.micro.umn.edu" and move through the following directories:

- Other Gopher and Information Servers/
- North America/
- USA/
- General/
- AskERIC

To telnet to the AskERIC site:

1. Telnet to "ericir.syr.edu".
2. Log in as directed (typical login is "gopher").
3. Access the National Gopher System.
4. Move through the directories to file transfer protocol (FTP) to the AskERIC site.
5. Log in to your local host and invoke FTP.
6. Type "ericir.syr.edu" as the remote host computer.
7. For "user name," type "anonymous".
8. For "password," type your e-mail user name.

You also can access ERIC through commercial online services (e.g., CompuServe, America Online). Contact a customer service representative for further information regarding subscribing to these services, which charge monthly and/or hourly fees.

Instructional Methods

Adler, S., & King, D. A. (1994). *Oral communication problems in children and adolescents* (2nd ed.). Boston: Allyn and Bacon.

Bernstein, D. K., & Tigerman, E. (1993). *Language and communications disorders in children* (3rd ed.). New York: Merrill/Macmillan.

Butler, K. G. (1994). *Best practices II: The classroom as an intervention context.* Gaithersburg, MD: Aspen.

Butler, K. G. (Ed.). (1991). *Communicating for learning.* Gaithersburg, MD: Aspen.

Christensen, S. S., & Luckett, C. H. (1990). Getting into the classroom and making it work. *Language, Speech, and Hearing Services in Schools, 21,* 110–113.

Fey, M. E. (1986). *Language intervention with young children.* San Diego: College-Hill Press.

Fey, M. E. Windsor, J., & Warren, S. F. (Eds.). (1995). *Language intervention: Preschool through the elementary years.* Baltimore: Paul H. Brookes.

Gruenewalk, L. J., & Pollak, S. A. (1990). *Language interaction in curriculum and instruction* (2nd ed.). Austin, TX: Pro-Ed.

Haynes, W. O., Moral, M. J., & Pindzola, R. H. (1991). *Communication disorders in the classroom.* Dubuque, IA: Kendall/Hunt.

LaBlance, G. R., Steckol, K. F., & Smith, V. L. (1994). Stuttering: The role of the classroom teacher. *Teaching Exceptional Children, 27,* 10–12.

Larson, V. L., & McKinley, N. L. (1995). *Communication assessment and intervention strategies for adolescents.* Eau Claire, WI: Thinking Publications.

Lowenthal, B. (1995). Naturalistic language intervention in inclusive environments. *Intervention in School and Clinic, 31,* 114–118.

Merritt, D. D., & Culatta, B. (1996). *Collaborative language intervention in the classroom.* San Diego: Singular Publishing.

Nelson, C. D. (1991). *Practical procedures for children with language disorders: Preschool-adolescence.* Austin, TX: Pro-Ed.

Nelson, N. W. (1993). *Childhood language disorders in context: Infancy through adolescence.* New York: Merrill/Macmillan.

Norris, J. A., & Hoffman, P. R. (1993). *Whole language intervention for school-aged children.* San Diego: Singular Publishing.

Nowacek, E. J. (in press). Spoken language. In E. Polloway and J. Patton (Eds.), *Strategies for teaching learners with special needs* (6th ed.). Englewood Cliffs: Merrill/Prentice Hall.

Owens, R. E. (1995). *Language disorders: A Functional approach to assessment and intervention,* (2nd ed). Boston: Allyn and Bacon.

Oyer, H. J., Hall, B. J., & Haas, W. H. (1994). Introduction to speech, language, and hearing problems in the schools. In *Speech, language, and hearing disorders: A guide for teachers* (2nd ed.). Boston: Allyn and Bacon.

Polloway, E. A., & Smith, T. E. C. (1992). *Language instruction for students with disabilities* (2nd ed.). Denver: Love.

Paul, R. (1995). *Language disorders from infancy through adolescents.* St. Louis, MO: Mosby.

Reed, V. A. (1994). *An introduction to children with language disorders* (2nd ed.). New York: Merrill/Macmillan.

Wallach, G. P., & Butler, K. G. (Eds.). (1994). *Language learning disabilities in school-age children and adolescents: Some principles and application.* New York: Merrill/Macmillan.

Wiig, E. H., & Semel, E. (1984). *Language assessment and intervention for the learning disabled.* (2nd ed.). Columbus, OH: Merrill.

Curricular and Instructional Materials

Auslin, M. S. (1989). *Idiom workbook series.* Austin, TX: Pro-Ed.

Bloomin' Series (provides activities to improve pragmatics by focusing on such areas as holidays, recipes, experiments, and language arts). LinguiSystems, 3100 Fourth Avenue, P.O. Box 747, East Moline, IL.

Flowers, A. M. (1986). *The big book of language through sounds* (3rd ed.). Austin, TX: Pro-Ed.

Frimmer, B. (1986). *Sounds and language: A work/play approach.* Danville, IL: Interstate Printers and Publishers.

Help Series (includes exercises in areas such as language processing, concepts, paraphrasing, problem solving, and pragmatics). LinguiSystems, 3100 Fourth Avenue, P.O. Box 747, East Moline, IL.

Holloway, J. A. (1987). *Aunt Amanda: On cloud nine and other idioms and expressions.* Danville, IL: Interstate Printers and Publishers.

Johnston, E. B., Weinrich, B. D., & Johnson, A. R. (1991). *A sourcebook of pragmatic activities: Theory and intervention for language therapy (PK–6) (Rev).* Tucson, AZ: Communication Skill Builders.

Mannix, D. (1995). *Social skills activities.* Tucson, AZ: Communication Skill Builders.

Nelson, N. W., & Gillespie, L. L. (1992). *Analogies for thinking and talking.* Tucson, AZ: Communication Skill Builders.

Paul, R. (1992). *Pragmatic activities for language intervention.* Tucson, AZ: Communication Skill Builders.

Strategies for instruction: A handbook of performance activities. (1992). San Antonio, TX: The Psychological Corporation (Levels K; Grades 1 & 2; Grades 3 & 4; Grades 5 & 6; Reading Grades 7–12; Mathematics Grades 7–12; Language Grades 7–12; Science/Social Studies Grades 7–12).

Weinrich, B. D., Glaser, A. J., & Johnston, E. B. (1995). *A sourcebook of adolescent pragmatic activities: Theory and intervention for language therapy (Grades 7–12 and ESL) (Rev.).* Tucson, AZ: Communication Skill Builders.

Wiig, E. H., & Bray, C. W. (1983). *Let's talk for children.* San Antonio, TX: The Psychological Corporation.

Wiig, E. H. (1985). *Words, expression and contexts: A figurative language program.* San Antonio, TX: The Psychological Corporation.

Literature about Individuals with Communication Disorders

Elementary

Arthur, R. (1985). *The three investigators in the mystery of the stuttering parrot.* New York: Random House. (Ages 9–12) (Fiction = F)

Brown, A., & Forsberg, G. (1989). *Lost boys never say die.* New York: Delacorte Press. (Ages 9–12) (F)

communication disorders

Bunting, E. (1980). *Blackbird singing.* New York: Macmillan. (Ages 9–12) (F)

Corrigan, K. (1984). *Emily, Emily.* Toronto: Annick Press. (Elementary) (Stuttering) (F)

Cosgrove, S. (1983). *Creole.* Los Angeles: Price Stern Sloan. (Elementary) (Stuttering) (F)

Hague, K. (1985). *The Legend of the veery bird.* New York: Harcourt, Brace, Jovanivich. (Elementary) (Stuttering) (F)

Knopp, P. (1980). *Wilted.* New York: Coward, McCann & Geoghegan. (Ages 9–12) (F)

Secondary

Berger, G. (1981). *Speech and language disorders.* New York: Franklin-Watts. (Ages 13–18) (Nonfiction = NF).

Evans, J. (1983). *An uncommon gift.* Philadelphia, PA: Westminster. (Ages 13–18) (NF).

SOFTWARE

Alphabet Sounds, Data Command, Inc., P.O. Box 548, Kankakee, IL 60901, (800) 528–7390. (Apple IIe; Apple IIGS).

Conceptual Skills, Psychological Software Services, Inc., 6555 Carrollton Avenue, Indianapolis, IN 46220, (312) 257–9672. (Apple IIe, Atari) (math problem solving).

Confusing Words, Bill & Richard's Software, P.O. Box 1075, Litchfield, CT 06759, (203) 567–4307. (Macintosh).

Conversations, Educational Activities, Inc., P.O. Box 392, Freeport, NY 11520, (800) 645–3739. (DOS).

Dr. Peet's Talkwriter, Hartley Courseware, Inc., 3451 Dunkle Drive, Suite 200, Lansing, MI 48911–4216, (800) 247–1380. (Apple IIe; Apple IIGS).

Elephant Ears, Ballard and Tighe, Inc. (Apple IIe; Apple IIGS) (language, prereading).

Exploring Vocabulary Series, Laureate Learning Systems, Inc., 110 E. Spring Street, Winooski, VT 05404, (800) 562–6801. (Apple IIe; Apple IIGS; Macintosh; DOS).

Fay's Word Rally, Didatech Software, Inc., 4250 Dawsen Street, Suite 200, Bernaby, BC, Canada V5C 4B1, (800) 665–0667. (Apple IIe; DOS) (language arts).

Fish Scales, SRA/DLM, 250 Old Wilson Bridge Road, Worthington, OH 43085, (800) 468–5850. (Apple IIe; Apple IIGS) (weights, length, and distance measurement).

Functional Vocabulary Plus for Windows, Parrot Software, 6506 Pleasant Lake Court, West Bloomfield, MI 48322, (800) 727–7681. (Windows).

Grammar Study Center, Teach Yourself By Computer Software, 340–0 Monroe Avenue, Rochester, NY 14618, (800) 724–4691. (Apple IIe; Apple IIGS).

Kid Works 2, Davidson and Associates, Inc., 19840 Pioneer Avenue, Torrance, CA 90503, (800) 545–7677. ((Macintosh; DOS; Windows).

Kid Works 2, Bilingual, Davidson and Associates, Inc., 19840 Pioneer Avenue, Torrance, CA 90503, (800) 545–7677. (Macintosh) (read stories in English and Spanish).

Mi Escuela, Laureate Learning Systems, Inc., 110 E. Spring Street, Winooski, VT 05404, (800) 562–6801. (Macintosh; DOS) (functional language stimulation program in Spanish).

Muppet Word Book, Sunburst Communications, 101 Castleton Street, Pleasantville, NY 10570, (800) 628–8897. (Apple IIe; Apple IIGS) (language development).

New Talking Stickeybear Opposites, Optimum Resources, Inc., 5 Hiltech Lane, Hilton Head, SC 29926, (800) 327–1473. (Apple IIGS).

Opposites, Hartley Courseware, Inc., 3451 Dunkle Drive, Suite 200, Lansing, MI 48911–4216, (800) 247–1380. (Apple IIe; Apple IIGS; DOS).

Paint with Words, MECC, 6160 Summit Drive, N., Minneapolis, MN 55430–4003, (800) 685–6322. (Apple IIe; Apple IIGS).

Reading Around Word Program, Taylor Associates, 200–2 East 22nd Street, Huntington Station, NY 11746, (800) 732–3758. (Apple IIe; Apple IIGS; DOS).

Stickeybear Opposites, Optimum Resources, Inc., 5 Hiltech Lane, Hilton Head, SC 29926, (800) 327–1473. (Apple IIe; Apple IIGS; DOS).

Sight Word Spelling, Exceptional Children's Software, P.O. Box 487, Hays, KS 67601, (913) 625–9281. (Apple IIe).

Soft Text: Word Study, Continental Press, Inc., 520 E. Bainbridge Street, Elizabethtown, PA 17022, (800) 233–0759. (Apple IIe; Apple IIGS)

Talking Textwriter, Scholastic Software, 730 Broadway, Dept. JS, New York, NY, 10003, (800) 541–5513. (Apple IIe; Apple IIGS, DOS).

Turn-Taking, R. J. Cooper and Associates, 24843 Del Prado, Suite 283, Dana Point, CA 92629, (800) RJ–COOPER (714–240–1912). (Macintosh, Windows).

Understanding Questions I and II, Sunset Software, 9277 E. Corrine Drive, Scottsdale, AZ 85260, (602) 451–0753. (Apple IIe; Apple IIGS).

Understanding Sentences II: Abstract Meanings, Sunset Software, 9277 E. Corrine Drive, Scottsdale, AZ 85260, (602) 451–0753. (Apple IIe; Apple IIGS).

Vocabulary Detective, SWEPS Educational Software, Inc., 9 Barker Drive, P.O. Box 1510, Pine. AZ 85544–1510, (800) 880–8814. (Apple IIe; Apple IIGS; DOS).

Vocabulary Machine, SWEPS Educational Software, Inc., 9 Barker Drive, P.O. Box 1510, Pine. AZ 85544–1510, (800) 880–8814. (Apple IIe; Apple IIGS; DOS).

Organizations

American Speech-Language-Hearing Association, 10801 Rockville Pike, Rockville, MD 20852, (301) 897–5700.

Division for Children with Communication Disorders, Council for Exceptional Children, 1920 Association Drive, Reston, VA 22091.

BIBLIOGRAPHY FOR TEACHING SUGGESTIONS

American Speech-Language-Hearing Association (ASHA). (n.d.). *Speech and language disorders and the speech-language pathologist.* Rockville, MD: Author.

Cantwell, D. P., & Baker, L. (1987). *Developmental speech and language disorders.* New York: Guilford Press.

Gearheart, B. R., Weishahn, M. W., & Gearheart, C. J. (1992). *The exceptional student in the regular classroom* (5th ed.). New York: Merrill/Macmillan.

Hoskins, B. (1994). Language and literacy: Participating in the conversation. In K. G. Butler (Ed.). *Best practices II: The classroom as an intervention context.* Gaithersburg, MD: Aspen.

Johnson, D. W., Johnson, R. T., & Holubec, E. J. (1994). *The new circles of learning.* Alexandria, VA: Association for Supervision and Curriculum Development.

Kagan, S. (1990). The structured approach to cooperative learning. *Educational Leadership. 47,* 12–15.

Lewis, R., & Doorlag, D. H. (1995). *Teaching special students in the mainstream* (4th ed.). Englewood Cliffs, NJ: Merrill/Prentice Hall.

Lowenthal, B. (1995). Naturalistic language intervention in inclusive environments. *Intervention in School and Clinic, 31,* 114–118.

Norris, J. A., & Hoffman, P. R. (1993). *Whole language intervention for school-aged children.* San Diego: Singular Publishing.

Nowacek, E. J. (in press). Spoken language. In E. Polloway and J. Patton (eds.), *Strategies for teaching learners with special needs* (6th ed.). Englewood Cliffs, NJ: Merrill/Prentice Hall.

Oyer, H. J., Hall, B. J., & Haas, W. H. (1994). Introduction to speech, language, and hearing problems in the schools. In *Speech, language, and hearing disorders: A guide for teachers* (2nd ed.). Boston: Allyn and Bacon.

Paul, R. (1995). *Language disorders from infancy through adolescence.* St. Louis, MO: Mosby.

Reed, V. A. (1994). *An introduction to children with language disorders* (2nd ed). New York: Merrill/Macmillan.

Rubin, D. L. (1994). Divergence and convergence between oral and written communication. In K. G. Butler (Ed.), *Best practices I: The classroom as an assessment arena.* Gaithersburg, MD: Aspen.

Shore, K. (1986). *The special education handbook.* New York: Teachers College Press.

Warren, S. F., & Yoder, P. J. (1994). Communication and language intervention: Why a constructivist approach is insufficient. *Journal of Special Education, 28,* 248–258.

Wiig, E. H., & Semel, E. (1984). *Language assessment and intervention for the learning disabled* (2nd ed.). Columbus, OH: Merrill.

Wood, K. D., & Algozzine, B. (1994). *Teaching reading to high-risk learners: A unified perspective.* Boston: Allyn and Bacon.

SUMMARY

Communication requires sending and receiving meaningful messages. *Language* is the communication of ideas through an arbitrary system of symbols that are used according to specified and accepted rules. *Speech* is the behavior of forming and sequencing the sounds of oral language. Communication disorders may involve language or speech or both. The prevalence of communication disorders is difficult to determine, but disorders of speech and language are among the most common disabilities of children.

Language development begins with the first mother–child interactions. The sequence of language development is fairly well understood, but relatively little is known about how and why children learn language. Some theories of language development include the following major ideas: (1) Language learning depends on brain development and proper brain functioning; (2) language learning is affected by the consequences of language behavior; (3) language is learned from inputs and outputs related to information processing; (4) language learning is based on linguistic rules; (5) language is one of many cognitive (thinking) skills; (6) language arises from the need to communicate in social interactions. Research supports some aspects of all theories, but social interactional or pragmatic theory is now accepted as having the most important implications for speech-language pathologists and teachers.

Language disorders may be classified according to the five subsystems of language: phonology, morphology, syntax, semantics, and pragmatics. They may also be categorized according to the presumed causes of disorders or related conditions. For example, conditions such as mental retardation, traumatic brain injury, and autism are associated with their own respective communication problems.

Assessment and intervention in language disorders require standardized testing and more informal clinical judgments. An intervention plan must consider what the child talks about and should talk about, how the child talks and should speak to become more intelligible, and how the child uses language for communication and socialization. Helping children learn to use language effectively is not the task of any single professional group. Speech-language pathologists now regularly work with classroom teachers to make language learning an integral part of classroom teaching. Recent approaches to addressing communication problems associated with autism, delayed language, and traumatic brain injury have stressed a functional approach, emphasizing social and pragmatic skills that students use frequently.

Augmentative or alternative communication systems are needed for those whose physical or cognitive disabilities preclude oral language. These systems create a way to select or scan an array of pictures, words, or other symbols. Microcomputers have radically changed augmentative communication. Facilitated communication, a recent and controversial approach to augmented communication, has been largely discredited.

Dialect or native language differences must not be mistaken for language disorders. However, the language disorders of children with communicative differences must not be overlooked. Bilingual special education is an emerging discipline, as more children have little or no proficiency in English. Research has also begun to focus on differences in socioeconomic status and language development.

Children may have more than one type of speech disorder, and disorders of speech may occur along with language disorders. Voice disorders may involve pitch, loudness, and quality of phonation, which may be unpleasant to the listener, interfere with communication, or abuse the larynx. Articulation or phonological disorders involve omission, substitution, distortion, or addition of word sounds, making speech difficult to understand. The most common fluency disorder is stuttering. Neurological damage can affect people's speech by making it difficult for them to make the voluntary movements required.

Children requiring early intervention for speech and language disorders typically have severe or multiple disabilities. A young child's ability to communicate cannot be separated from other areas of development. Children's language and social interactions with parents and caregivers are being looked at as key factors. Consequently, early language intervention involves all social interactions between a child and his or her caretakers and peers and emphasizes functional communication in the child's natural environment.

Adolescents and young adults with speech and language disorders may be self-referred, have health problems, or have multiple and severe disabilities. Transition programming has provided for the carryover of training and support during the school years into adult life. Emphasis today is on functional communication skills taught in naturalistic settings. Language disorders among young children are the basis for academic and social learning problems in later years.

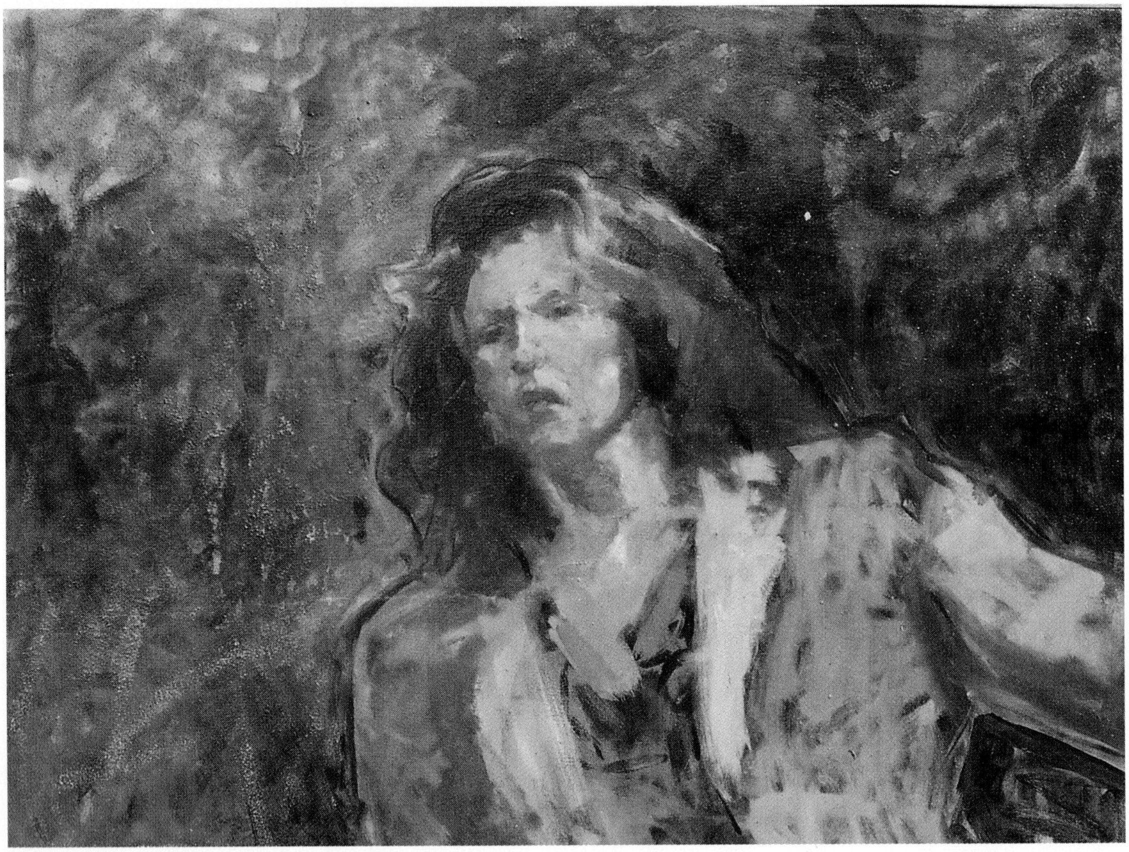

Mary Thornley
Mary Thornley is a nationally recognized painter who is deaf. She describes her work as "art about life, about being a deaf person, about being different." Her work often incorporates images, themes, and characterizations related to hearing impairment.

8

Hearing Impairment

No deaf child who has earnestly tried to speak the words which he has never heard—to come out of the prison of silence, where no tone of love, no song of bird, no strain of music ever pierces the stillness—can forget the thrill of surprise, the joy of discovery which came over him when he uttered his first word. Only such a one can appreciate the eagerness with which I talked to my toys, to stones, trees, birds and dumb animals, or the delight I felt when at my call Mildred ran to me or my dogs obeyed my commands. It is an unspeakable boon to me to be able to speak in winged words that need no interpretation.

Helen Keller
The Story of My Life

Although Helen Keller's achievements were unique in the truest sense of the word, the emotions she conveys here are not (see page 309). The child who is deaf who does acquire the ability to speak must certainly experience a "joy of discovery" similar to Keller's. Hearing impairment is a great barrier to the normal development of the English language. As we will see, even if the impairment is not severe enough for the child to be classified as "deaf" but rather as "hard of hearing," the child with a hearing impairment is at a distinct disadvantage in virtually all aspects of English language development. The importance of the English language in U.S. society, particularly in school-related activities, is obvious. A significantly large group of educators believe that many of the problems of people with hearing impairment related to social and intellectual development are primarily due to their deficiencies in English. We explore this issue in some depth in this chapter.

Another related controversy inherent in Keller's words is the debate concerning whether the child who is deaf should be educated to communicate orally or through manual **sign language.** Keller's opinion is that the ability to speak offers a richer means of communication. But she was extraordinary; extremely few individuals who are deaf attain her level of fluency. Furthermore, because for many years educators exclusively emphasized teaching children who are deaf to speak and actively discouraged their use of sign language, they unwittingly denied these children access to communication. Equal to the poignancy of Keller's breakthrough with verbal language was Lynn Spradley's discovery of communication through sign language after years of frustration with trying to speak:

> "Tom! Bruce! Come quick!" . . .
>
> I jumped up. In an instant we were in Lynn's room.
>
> "Watch!" Louise said, tears streaming down her face. "She said it two times!" Lynn, legs crossed in front of her, sat at the head of her bed. Louise, sitting on the edge, turned back to Lynn.
>
> "I—love—you," her voice came through the tears as she signed. She hugged Lynn, then sat back and waited.
>
> Lynn, beaming, held up two tiny fists, crossed them tightly against her heart, then pointed knowingly at Louise. Without hesitating, she reached out and hugged Louise tightly. The room was blurred; fighting back tears, I picked up Lynn, pulled her close in a long embrace, then sat back on the edge of her bed.
>
> "I—love—you," I signed slowly, my voice quivering as I spoke. I dropped my hands and waited.
>
> "Love you," Lynn signed clearly, confidently, then reached out to hug me. I looked at Louise. There were tears in our eyes.
>
> Bruce hugged his little sister. "I love you," he signed perfectly, a broad smile on his face.
>
> "Love you," Lynn signed back, this time in a more definite exaggerated rhythm.
>
> She had found her voice! (Spradley & Spradley, 1978, pp. 245–246)

The oral versus manual debate has raged for centuries. For many years there was no middle ground. Although some educators still debate the merits of each, many now have begun to use a method of *total communication,* which involves a combination of both orientations.

sign language. A manual language used by people who are deaf to communicate; a true language with its own grammar.

DEFINITION AND CLASSIFICATION

There are many definitions and classification systems of *hearing impairment.* By far the most common division is between *deaf* and *hard of hearing.* This would seem simple enough, except that the two categories are defined differently by different professionals.

Misconceptions about Persons with Hearing Impairment

Myth	Fact
Myth Deafness is not as severe a disability as blindness.	**Fact** Although it is impossible to predict the exact consequences of a disability on a person's functioning, in general, deafness poses more difficulties in adjustment than does blindness. This is largely due to the effects hearing loss can have on the ability to understand and speak oral language.
Myth It is unhealthy for people who are deaf to socialize almost exclusively with others who are deaf.	**Fact** Many authorities now recognize that the phenomenon of a Deaf culture is natural and should be encouraged. In fact, some are worried that too much mainstreaming will diminish the influence of the Deaf culture.
Myth In learning to understand what is being said to them, people with hearing impairment concentrate on reading lips.	**Fact** *Lipreading* refers only to visual cues arising from movement of the lips. Some people who are hearing impaired not only read lips but also take advantage of a number of other visual cues, such as facial expressions and movements of the jaw and tongue. They are engaging in what is referred to as *speechreading*.
Myth Speechreading is relatively easy to learn and is used by the majority of people with hearing impairment.	**Fact** Speechreading is extremely difficult to learn, and very few people who are hearing impaired actually become proficient speechreaders.
Myth American Sign Language (ASL) is a loosely structured group of gestures.	**Fact** ASL is a true language in its own right with its own set of grammatical rules.
Myth ASL can convey only concrete ideas.	**Fact** ASL can convey any level of abstraction.
Myth People within the Deaf community are in favor of mainstreaming students who are deaf into regular classes.	**Fact** Some within the Deaf community have voiced the opinion that regular classes are not appropriate for many students who are deaf. They point to the need for a critical mass of students who are deaf in order to have effective educational programs for these individuals. They see separate placements as a way of fostering the Deaf culture.
Myth Families in which both the child and the parents are deaf are at a distinct disadvantage compared to families in which the parents are hearing.	**Fact** Research has demonstrated that children who are deaf who have parents who are also deaf fare better in a number of academic and social areas. Authorities point to the parents' ability to communicate with their children in ASL as a major reason for this advantage.

The extreme points of view are represented by those with a physiological orientation versus those with an educational orientation.

Those maintaining a strictly physiological viewpoint are interested primarily in the *measurable degree* of hearing loss. Children who cannot hear sounds at or above a certain intensity (loudness) level are classified as "deaf;" others with a hearing loss are considered "hard of hearing." Hearing sensitivity is measured in **decibels** (units of relative loudness of sounds). Zero decibels (0 dB) designates the point at which the average person with normal hearing can detect the faintest sound. Each succeeding number of decibels indicates a certain degree of hearing loss. Those who maintain a physiological viewpoint generally consider people with hearing losses of about 90 dB or greater to be deaf and people with less to be hard of hearing.

People with an educational viewpoint are concerned with how much the hearing loss is likely to affect the child's ability to speak and develop language. Because of the close causal link between hearing loss and delay in language development, these professionals categorize primarily on the basis of spoken language abilities. Following is the most commonly accepted set of definitions reflecting this educational orientation:

- *Hearing impairment*: is generic term indicating a hearing disability that may range in severity from mild to profound; it includes the subsets of *deaf* and *hard of hearing*.
- A *deaf* person is one whose hearing disability precludes successful processing of linguistic information through audition, with or without a hearing aid.
- A person who is *hard of hearing* generally, with the use of a hearing aid, has residual hearing sufficient to enable successful processing of linguistic information through audition (Brill, MacNeil, & Newman, 1986, p. 67)

decibels. Units of relative loudness of sounds; zero decibels (0 dB) designates the point at which people with normal hearing can just detect sound.

Educators are extremely concerned about the *age of onset* of the hearing impairment. Again, the close relationship between hearing loss and language delay is the

A current issue in defining deafness *is that many people in the Deaf community do not want to be considered as having a disability; instead, they would like to be thought of as members of a cultural group that has its own language: American Sign Language (ASL).*

key here. The earlier the hearing loss occurs in a child's life, the more difficulty he or she will have developing the language of the hearing society (e.g., English). For this reason, professionals frequently use the terms **congenitally deaf** (those who were born deaf) and **adventitiously deaf** (those who acquire deafness at some time after birth).

Two other frequently used terms are even more specific in pinpointing language acquisition as critical: **Prelingual deafness** is "deafness present at birth, or occurring early in life at an age prior to the development of speech or language"; **postlingual deafness** is "deafness occurring at any age following the development of speech and language" (Brill et al., 1986, p. 67). Experts differ regarding the dividing point between prelingual and postlingual deafness. Some believe it should be at about eighteen months, whereas others think it should be lower, at about twelve months or even six months (Meadow-Orlans, 1987).

The following hearing threshold classifications are common: mild (26–54 dB), moderate (55–69 dB), severe (70–89 dB), and profound (90 dB and above). These levels of severity according to loss of hearing sensitivity cut across the broad classifications of "deaf" and "hard of hearing." The broader classifications are not directly dependent on hearing sensitivity. Instead, they stress the degree to which speech and language are affected.

Some authorities object to following any of the various classification systems too strictly. Because these definitions deal with events that are difficult to measure and that occur in variable organisms, they are not precise. Thus, it is best not to form any hard-and-fast opinions about an individual's ability to hear and speak solely on the basis of a classification of his or her hearing disability.

In considering issues of definition, it is important to point out that there is growing sentiment among people who are deaf that deafness should not even be considered a disability (Lane, 1992; Padden & Humphries, 1988). They argue that deafness only renders a person disabled with respect to acquiring the language of the dominant culture (i.e., English in the United States). Supporters of this view note that deafness does not prohibit a person from learning sign language. Furthermore, they object to labels such as "prelingual" and "postlingual" deafness because such distinctions are keyed to spoken language (Andersson, 1994). Proponents argue that instead of being considered disabled, people who are deaf should be considered a cultural minority with a language of their own—sign language.

Later in the chapter, we discuss more thoroughly the issues of sign language as a true language and the nature and purpose of the Deaf culture. But for now it is enough to be aware of the challenges that have been raised to the very notion of considering deafness a disability.

congenitally deaf. Deafness that is present at birth; can be caused by genetic factors, by injuries during fetal development, or by injuries occurring at birth.

adventitiously deaf. Deafness that occurs through illness or accident in an individual who was born with normal hearing.

prelingual deafness. Deafness that occurs before the development of spoken language, usually at birth.

postlingual deafness. Deafness occurring after the development of speech and language.

PREVALENCE

Estimates of the number of children with hearing impairment vary considerably. Such factors as differences in definition, populations studied, and accuracy of testing contribute to the varying figures. The U.S. Department of Education's statistics indicate that about 0.14 percent of the population from six to seventeen years of age is identified as deaf or hard of hearing by the public schools. Although the U.S. Department of Education does not report separate figures for the categories of "deaf" and "hard of hearing," some authorities believe that many children who are hard of hearing who could benefit from special education are not being served.

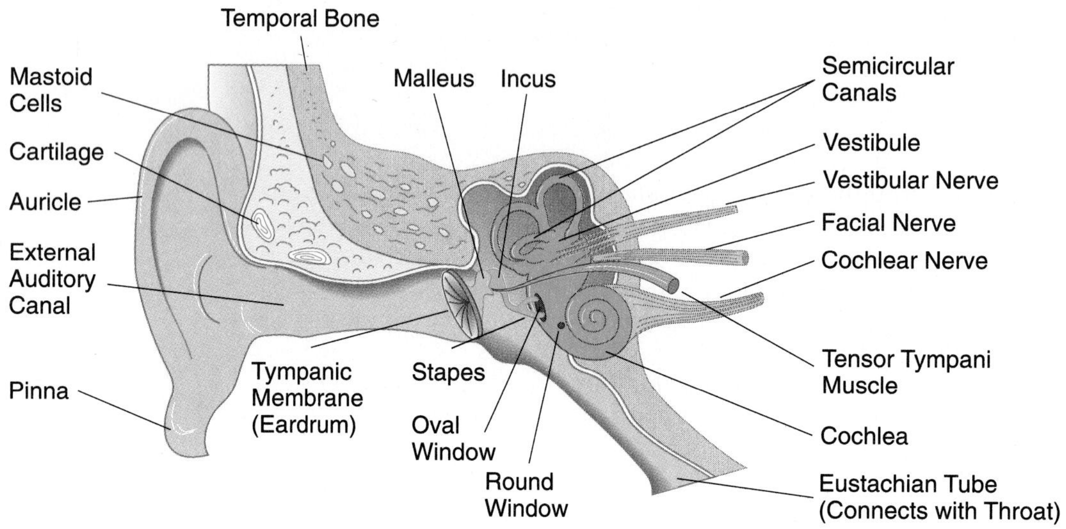

Figure 8–1 Illustration of the outer, middle, and inner ear. (*Source:* Adapted from H. L. Davis and S. R. Silverman [Eds.], *Hearing and deafness,* 4th ed. Copyright © 1978 by Holt, Rinehart & Winston, Inc. Reprinted by permission.)

tympanic membrane (eardrum). The anatomical boundary between the outer and middle ears; the sound gathered in the outer ear vibrates here.

auricle. The visible part of the ear, composed of cartilage; collects the sounds and funnels them via the external auditory canal to the eardrum.

ossicles. Three tiny bones (malleus, incus, and stapes) that together make possible an efficient transfer of sound waves from the eardrum to the oval window, which connects the middle ear to the inner ear.

malleus. The hammer-shaped bone in the ossicular chain of the middle ear.

incus. The anvil-shaped bone in the ossicular chain of the middle ear.

stapes. The stirrup-shaped bone in the ossicular chain of the middle ear.

oval window. The link between the middle and inner ears.

ANATOMY AND PHYSIOLOGY OF THE EAR

The ear is one of the most complex organs of the body. The many elements that make up the hearing mechanism are divided into three major sections: the outer, middle, and inner ear. The outer ear is the least complex and least important for hearing; the inner ear is the most complex and most important for hearing. Figure 8–1 shows these major parts of the ear.

The Outer Ear

The outer ear consists of the auricle and the external auditory canal. The canal ends with the **tympanic membrane (eardrum)**, which is the boundary between the outer and middle ears. The **auricle** is the part of the ear that protrudes from the side of the head. Although the auricle is the one part of the ear visible to all, it is the least important in terms of hearing (Martin, 1986). The part that the outer ear plays in the transmission of sound is relatively minor. Sound is collected by the auricle and is funneled through the external auditory canal on to the eardrum, which vibrates, sending the sound waves on to the middle ear.

The Middle Ear

The middle ear comprises the eardrum and three very tiny bones (**ossicles**) called the **malleus** (hammer), **incus** (anvil), and **stapes** (stirrup) contained within an air-filled space. The chain of the malleus, incus, and stapes conducts the vibrations of the eardrum along to the **oval window,** which is the link between the middle and inner ears. To prevent a significant loss of energy between the vibration of the eardrum and the vibration of the oval window, the chain of bones is constructed in a way that takes advantage of the physical laws of leverage. Because of this, there is an efficient transfer of energy from the air-filled cavity of the middle ear to the dense, fluid-filled inner ear (Davis, 1978a; Martin, 1986).

The Inner Ear

About the size of a pea, the inner ear is an intricate mechanism of thousands of moving parts. Because it looks like a maze of passageways and is highly complex, this part of the ear is often called a *labyrinth.* The inner ear is divided into two sections according to function: the vestibular mechanism and the cochlea. These sections, however, do not function totally independently of each other.

The **vestibular mechanism,** located in the upper portion of the inner ear, is responsible for the sense of balance. It is extremely sensitive to such things as acceleration, head movement, and head position. Information regarding movement is fed to the brain through the vestibular nerve.

By far the most important organ for hearing is the **cochlea.** Lying below the vestibular mechanism, this snail-shaped organ contains the parts necessary to convert the mechanical action of the middle ear into an electrical signal in the inner ear that is transmitted to the brain. In the normally functioning ear, sound causes the malleus, incus, and stapes of the middle ear to move. When the stapes moves, it pushes the oval window in and out, causing the fluid in the cochlea of the inner ear to flow. The movement of the fluid in turn causes a complex chain of events in the cochlea, ultimately resulting in excitation of the cochlear nerve. With stimulation of the cochlear nerve, an electrical impulse is sent to the brain, and the sound is heard.

MEASUREMENT OF HEARING ABILITY

There are three general types of hearing tests: pure-tone audiometry, speech audiometry, and specialized tests for very young children. Depending on the characteristics of the examinee and the use to which the results will be put, the **audiologist** may choose to give any number of tests from any one or a combination of these three categories.

Pure-Tone Audiometry

Pure-tone audiometry is designed to establish the individual's threshold for hearing at a variety of different frequencies. (Frequency, measured in **hertz (Hz)** units has to do with the number of vibrations per unit of time of a sound wave; the pitch is higher with *more* vibrations, lower with *fewer*.) A person's threshold for hearing is simply the level at which he or she can first detect a sound; it refers to how *intense* a sound must be before the person can detect it. As mentioned earlier, hearing sensitivity, or intensity, is measured in decibels (dB).

Pure-tone audiometers present tones of various intensities (dB levels) at various frequencies (Hz). Audiologists are usually concerned with measuring sensitivity to sounds ranging from 0 to about 110 dB. A person with average-normal hearing is barely able to hear sounds at a sound-pressure level of 0 dB. The zero decibel level is frequently called the *zero hearing-threshold level (HTL),* or **audiometric zero.**

Hertz are usually measured from 125 Hz (low sounds) to 8,000 Hz (high sounds). Sounds below 125 Hz or above 8,000 Hz are not measured because most speech does not fall outside this range. (The whistle designed to call dogs, for example,

vestibular mechanism. Located in the upper portion of the inner ear; consists of three soft, semicircular canals filled with a fluid; sensitive to head movement, acceleration, and other movements related to balance.

cochlea. A snail-shaped organ that lies below the vestibular mechanism; its parts convert the sound coming from the middle ear into an electrical signal in the inner ear, which is transmitted to the brain.

audiologist. An individual trained in audiology, the science dealing with hearing impairments, their detection, and remediation.

pure-tone audiometry. A test whereby tones of various intensities and frequencies are presented to determine a person's hearing loss.

hertz (Hz). A unit of measurement of the frequency of sound; refers to the highness or lowness of a sound.

audiometric zero. The lowest level at which people with normal hearing can hear.

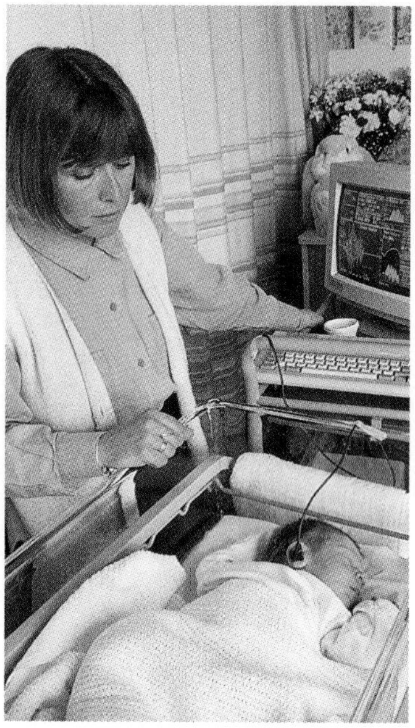

Hearing ability can now be assessed in infancy by measuring babies' autonomic responses to auditory stimuli.

has a frequency too high to be heard by human beings.) Frequencies contained in speech range from 80 to 8,000 Hz, but most speech sounds have energy in the 500 to 2,000 Hz range.

The procedure for testing a person's sensitivity to pure tones is relatively simple. Each ear is tested separately. The audiologist presents a variety of tones within the range of 0 to about 110 dB and 125 to 8,000 Hz until he or she establishes at what level of intensity (dB) the individual can detect the tone at a number of frequencies—125 Hz, 250 Hz, 500 Hz, 1,000 Hz, 2,000 Hz, 4,000 Hz, and 8,000 Hz. For each frequency, there is a measure of degree of hearing impairment. A 50 dB hearing loss at 500 Hz, for example, means the individual is able to detect the 500 Hz sound when it is given at an intensity level of 50 dB, whereas the average person would have heard it at 0 dB.

Speech Audiometry

Because the ability to detect and understand speech is of prime importance, a technique called **speech audiometry** has been developed to test a person's detection and understanding of speech. Speech detection is defined as the lowest level (in dB) at which the individual can detect speech without understanding. More important is the determination of the dB level at which one is able to *understand* speech. This is known as the **speech reception threshold (SRT).** One way to measure the SRT is to present the person with a list of two-syllable words, testing each ear separately. The dB level at which he or she can understand half the words is often used as an estimate of SRT level.

Tests for Young and Hard-to-Test Children

A basic assumption for pure-tone and speech audiometry is that the individuals who are being tested understand what is expected of them. They must be able to comprehend the instructions and show with a head nod or raised hand that they have heard the tone or word. They must also be cooperative. Obviously, none of this may be possible for very young children (under about four years of age) or for children with other disabilities.

Play Audiometry. This technique establishes rapport with the child and motivates him or her to respond. The examiner sets up the testing situation as a game. Using pure tones or speech, the examiner teaches the child to do various activities whenever he or she hears a signal. The activities are designed to be attractive to the young child. For example, the child may be required to pick up a block, squeeze a toy, or open a book.

Infant Responses to Sound and Reflex Audiometry. It is now possible to test the hearing ability of an infant within the first three months of life (Robinshaw, 1994). This can be done by measuring changes in the infant's heartrate or sucking when presented with auditory stimuli. In addition, infants normally possess some reflexive behaviors to loud sounds, which are useful for the testing of hearing by **reflex audiometry.** Reflex action can be observed through the *Moro reflex*, present from birth, which is defined as a movement of the face, body, arms, and legs and a blinking of the eyes. Another response that may be used to determine hearing ability is the *orienting response*. This response is evident when the infant turns his or her head and body toward the source of a sound.

speech audiometry. A technique that tests a person's detection and understanding of speech, rather than using pure tones to detect hearing loss.

speech reception threshold (SRT). The decibel level at which a person can understand speech.

reflex audiometry. The testing of responses to sounds by observation of such reflex actions as the orienting response and the Moro reflex speech.

Evoked-Response Audiometry. Another method of measuring hearing in a person unable to make voluntary responses is **evoked-response audiometry.** This technique involves measuring changes in brain-wave activity by using an electroencephalograph (EEG). All sounds heard by an individual result in electrical signals within the brain, so this method has become more popular with the development of sophisticated computers. Although very expensive and difficult to interpret, evoked-response audiometry has certain advantages. It can be used during sleep, and the child can be sedated and thus not be aware that he or she is being tested.

School Screening

Virtually all children who have severe hearing losses are identified before they reach school, but this is not always the case for children with mild hearing impairments. Many schools, therefore, have routine programs for screening. Hearing screening tests are administered either individually or in groups. These tests, especially those that are group administered, are less accurate than those administered in an audiologist's office. Children detected through screening as having possible problems are referred for more extensive evaluation.

CAUSES

Conductive, Sensorineural, and Mixed Impairments

Professionals classify causes of hearing loss on the basis of the location of the problem within the hearing mechanism. There are three major classifications: conductive, sensorineural, and mixed hearing losses. A **conductive hearing impairment** refers to an impairment that interferes with the transfer of sound along the conductive pathway of the middle or outer ear. A **sensorineural hearing impairment** involves problems in the inner ear. A **mixed hearing impairment** is a combination of the two.

Audiologists attempt to determine the location of malfunctioning. The first clue may be the severity of the loss. A general rule is that hearing losses greater than 60 or 70 dB involve some inner-ear problem. Audiologists use the results of pure-tone testing to help determine the location of a hearing impairment, converting the results to an *audiogram*—a graphic representation of the weakest (lowest dB) sound the individual can hear at each of several frequency levels. The profile of the audiogram helps determine whether the loss is conductive, sensorineural, or mixed.

Impairments of the Outer Ear

Although impairments of the outer ear are not as serious as those of the middle or inner ear, several conditions of the outer ear can cause a person to be hard of hearing. In some children, for example, the external auditory canal does not form, resulting in a condition known as atresia. Children may also develop **external otitis**, or "swimmer's ear" an infection of the skin of the external auditory canal. Tumors of the external auditory canal are another source of impairment.

Impairments of the Middle Ear

Although abnormalities of the middle ear are generally more serious than problems of the outer ear, they, too, usually result in a person's being classified as "hard of hearing" rather than "deaf." Most middle-ear hearing losses occur because the mechanical

evoked-response audiometry. A technique involving electroencephalograph measurement of changes in brain wave activity in response to sounds.

conductive hearing impairment. A hearing loss, usually mild, resulting from malfunctioning along the conductive pathway of the ear (i.e., the outer or middle ear).

sensorineural hearing impairment. A hearing loss, usually severe, resulting from malfunctioning of the inner ear.

mixed hearing impairment. A hearing loss resulting from a combination of conductive and sensorineural hearing impairments.

external otitis. An infection of the skin of the external auditory canal; also called "swimmer's ear."

Routine hearing examinations, conducted in schools, often provide the first identification of mild hearing problems.

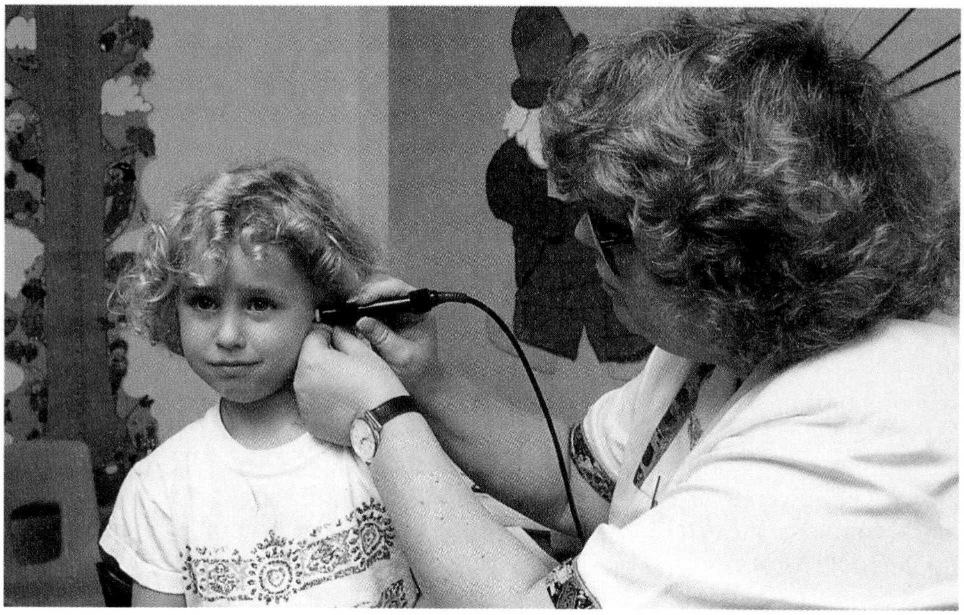

action of the ossicles is interfered with in some way. Unlike inner-ear impairments, most middle-ear impairments are correctable with medical or surgical treatment.

The most common problem of the middle ear is **otitis media**—an infection of the middle-ear space caused by viral and bacterial factors, among others. It is primarily a disease of childhood and is not easy to detect, especially in infancy when it often occurs with no symptoms (Giebink, 1990). Otitis media is linked to abnormal functioning of the eustachian tubes. If the eustachian tube malfunctions because of a respiratory viral infection, for example, it cannot do its job of ventilating, draining, and protecting the middle ear from infection (Giebink, 1990). The prevalence of otitis media is much higher in children with Down syndrome or cleft palate because these conditions often result in malformed eustachian tubes. Otitis media can result in temporary conductive hearing loss and, if untreated, can lead to rupture of the tympanic membrane.

Nonsupperative otitis media is more subtle in its effects but still a childhood middle-ear problem of some significance. This condition, which can occur without infection, also usually results from disruption of the functioning of the eustachian tube. It is generally preceded by a bout with infectious otitis media. In addition, some authorities hold that allergies can cause nonsupperative otitis media by leading to eustachian tube malfunctioning (Castiglia, Aquilina, & Kemsley, 1983).

otitis media. Inflammation of the middle ear.

nonsupperative otitis media. Inflammation of the middle ear that occurs without an infection; often preceded by infectious otitis media.

Impairments of the Inner Ear

The most severe hearing impairments are associated with the inner ear. Unfortunately, inner-ear hearing losses present the greatest problems for both education and medicine. Troubles other than those related to loss of threshold sensitivity are frequent. For example, sound distortion often occurs. Disorders of the inner ear can result in problems of balance and vertigo along with hearing loss. Also, some individuals with inner-ear impairments may hear roaring or ringing noises.

Causes of inner-ear disorders can be hereditary or acquired. The most frequent cause of childhood deafness is heredity (Schildroth, Rawlings, & Allen, 1989). Acquired hearing losses of the inner ear include those due to bacterial infections (e.g., meningitis, the second most frequent cause of childhood deafness), prematurity, viral infections (e.g., mumps and measles), anoxia (i.e., deprivation of oxygen) at birth, prenatal infections of the mother (e.g., maternal rubella, congenital syphilis, and cytomegalovirus), Rh incompatibility (which can now usually be prevented with proper prenatal care of the mother), blows to the head, unwanted side effects of some antibiotics, and excessive noise levels.

Congenital cytomegalovirus (CMV) is the most frequent viral infection in newborns, occurring in 0.4 to 2.3 percent of live births (Williamson, Demmler, Percy, & Catlin, 1992). CMV can result in a variety of conditions, such as mental retardation, visual impairment, and especially hearing impairment. Approximately 10 percent of infants born with CMV show symptoms of hearing impairment at birth, and an additional 15 percent eventually develop hearing impairment. Amniocentesis can detect CMV prenatally, although authorities disagree about the accuracy of this screening method (Donner, Liesnard, Brancart, & Rodesch, 1994; Moaven, Gilbert, Cunningham, & Rawlinson, 1995).

congenital cytomegalovirus (CMV). The most frequently occurring viral infection in newborns; can result in a variety of disabilities, especially hearing impairment.

PSYCHOLOGICAL AND BEHAVIORAL CHARACTERISTICS

Hearing loss can have profound consequences for some aspects of a person's behavior and little or no effect on other characteristics. Consider the question: If you were forced to choose, which would you rather be—blind or deaf? On first impulse, most of us choose deafness, probably because we rely on sight for mobility and because many of the beauties of nature are visual. But in terms of functioning in an English language–oriented society, the person who is deaf is at a much greater disadvantage than someone who is blind.

English Language and Speech Development

By far the most severely affected areas of development in the person who is hearing impaired and living in the United States are the comprehension and production of the *English* language. We stress *English* because that is the predominant language in the United States of those who can hear. In other words, people who are hearing impaired are generally deficient in the language used by most people of the hearing society in which they live. The distinction is important because people who are hearing impaired can be expert in their own form of language. The current opinion is that individuals who use American Sign Language (ASL) also the produce and comprehend a true language. We return to this point later in this chapter (see p. 331).

Regarding English, however, it is an undeniable fact that individuals with hearing impairment are at a distinct disadvantage. This is true in terms of language comprehension, language production, and speech. With regard to speech, for example, teachers report that 23 percent of students with hearing impairment have speech that is not intelligible, 22 percent have speech that is barely intelligible, and 10 percent are unwilling to speak in public. Speech intelligibility is linked to degree of hearing loss, with 75 percent of children who are profoundly deaf having nonintelligible speech but only 14 percent of children with less than severe hearing loss having nonintelligible speech (Wolk & Schildroth, 1986).

In addition, it is much more difficult for children who are prelingually deaf to learn to speak than for those who have acquired their deafness, mainly because they do not receive auditory feedback from the sounds they make. They have not heard an adult language model. An interesting research finding is that infants born deaf enter the babbling stage at the same time as hearing infants but soon abandon it (Ling & Ling, 1978; Schow & Nerbonne, 1980; Stoel-Gammon & Otomo, 1986). By as early as eight months of age and possibly earlier, babies who are hearing impaired babble less than hearing infants, and the babbling they do is of a qualitatively different nature (Stoel-Gammon & Otomo, 1986). It is thought that these differences occur because hearing infants are reinforced by hearing their own babbling and by hearing the verbal responses of adults. Children who are unable to hear either themselves or others are not reinforced.

The lack of feedback has also been named as a primary cause of poor speech production in children who are deaf. According to Fry (1966), hearing children learn to associate the sensations they receive when they move their jaws, mouths, and tongues with the auditory sounds these movements produce. Children with hearing impairment are obviously handicapped in this process. In addition, these children have a difficult time hearing the sounds of adult speech, which nonimpaired children hear and imitate. As a result, children with hearing impairment do not have an adequate adult model of spoken English.

Table 8–1 gives general examples of the effects various degrees of hearing loss may have on English language development. This is only a general statement of these relationships, since many factors interact to influence language development in the child with hearing impairment.

Intellectual Ability

Historically, the intellectual ability of children with hearing impairment has been a subject of much controversy. For many years, professionals believed that the conceptual ability of individuals who are deaf was deficient because of their deficient spoken language. This belief was erroneous for two reasons:

1. The assumption that language can be equated with cognitive abilities, popularized by famous Russian psychologist Lev Vygotsky (1962), has been largely debunked. Vygotsky assumed that the early speech of children became interiorized as inner speech and that inner speech became the equivalent of thought. Most psychologists now believe that Vygostky's notions of the primary role of language in the development of cognition were misguided.
2. Researchers have warned that we should not assume that persons who cannot speak because they are deaf have no language. They may not have a *spoken* language, such as English, but if they use American Sign Language, they are using a true language with its own rules of grammar. (Again, we return to this point later.)

Another reason that hearing professionals may have assumed that children who are deaf are cognitively deficient is that they have had so much trouble communicating with them. Even if these children use sign language, divided attention is a problem (Wood, 1991). In any teaching situation, the child who is being signed to must attend to the signs as well as to any instructional materials. Some adults, not allowing for the extra cognitive load placed on the child who is deaf, may become frustrated with his or her seemingly slow absorption of the lesson being taught.

Table 8–1
Relationship of Degree of Impairment to Understanding of Language and Speech

	Average of the Speech Frequencies in Better Ear	*Effect of Hearing Loss on Understanding of Language and Speech*
Slight	27–40 dB	▪ May have difficulty hearing faint or distant speech. ▪ May experience some difficulty with language arts subjects.
Mild	41–55 dB	▪ Understands conversational speech at a distance of 3–5 feet (face to face). ▪ May miss as much as 50 percent of class discussions if voices are faint or not in line of vision. ▪ May exhibit limited vocabulary and speech anomalies.
Marked	56–70 dB	▪ Conversation must be loud to be understood. ▪ Will have increased difficulty in group discussions. ▪ Is likely to have defective speech. ▪ Is likely to be deficient in language usage and comprehension. ▪ Will have limited vocabulary.
Severe	71–90 dB	▪ May hear loud voices about 1 foot from the ear. ▪ May be able to identify environmental sounds. ▪ May be able to discriminate vowels but not all consonants. ▪ Speech and language defective and likely to deteriorate.
Extreme	91 dB or more	▪ May hear some loud sounds but is aware of vibrations more than tonal patterns. ▪ Relies on vision rather than hearing as primary avenue for communication. ▪ Speech and language defective and likely to deteriorate.

Note: Impairment means medically irreversible conditions and those requiring prolonged medical care.

Source: Adapted from Report of a Committee for a Comprehensive Plan for Hearing-Impaired Children, May 1968, Office of the Superintendent of Public Instruction, Title VI, Elementary and Secondary Education Act, and the University of Illinois, Division of Services for Crippled Children.

Any intelligence testing done with people who are hearing impaired must take into account their English-language deficiency. Performance tests, rather than verbal tests, especially if they are administered in sign, offer a much fairer assessment of the IQ of a person with a hearing impairment. The Wechsler performance scales are most often used with persons who are deaf (Braden, 1992).

Academic Achievement

Unfortunately, most children with hearing impairment have extreme deficits in academic achievement. Reading ability, which relies heavily on English language skills and is probably the most important area of academic achievement, is most affected. Numerous studies paint a bleak picture for the reading achievement of students with hearing impairment (Allen, 1986; Trybus & Karchmer, 1977; Wolk & Allen, 1984). Representative findings are that the growth in reading achievement of students with hearing impairment is about one-third that for hearing students. Upon graduation from high school, it is not at all unusual for students who are deaf to be able to read at no more than a fourth-grade level, barely at newspaper literacy level. Even in math, which is their best academic subject, students with hearing impairment trail their hearing peers by substantial margins.

Several studies have demonstrated that children who are deaf who have parents who are deaf have higher reading achievement than do those who have hearing parents (Kampfe & Turecheck, 1987). Authorities speculate that this is due to two factors:

1. Parents who are deaf are able to communicate better with their children through the use of ASL, providing the children with needed support.
2. Children who are deaf who have parents who are deaf are more likely to be proficient in ASL, and ASL aids these children in learning written English and reading (Lane, 1992).

Social Adjustment

Social and personality development in the hearing population depend heavily on communication—and the situation is no different for those who are deaf. The hearing person has little difficulty finding people with whom to communicate. The person who is deaf, however, may face problems in finding others with whom he or she can converse. Studies have demonstrated that many students who are deaf are at risk for loneliness (Charlson, Strong, & Gold, 1992; Loeb & Sarigiani, 1986). Two factors are important in considering the possible isolation of students who are deaf: mainstreaming and hearing status of the parents.

Researchers have shown that in mainstream settings, very little interaction typically occurs between students who are deaf and those who are not (Gaustad & Kluwin, 1992). Furthermore, in mainstream settings, students who are deaf feel more emotionally secure if they have other students who are deaf with whom they can communicate (Stinson & Whitmire, 1992). This is not always possible, however, because of the low prevalence of hearing impairment. Some authorities believe that students who attend residential schools are less likely to experience isolation because they have other students with whom they can easily communicate. At the same time, children in residential schools are prone to feel alienated from their families.

Some authorities believe that the child who is deaf who has hearing parents runs a greater risk of being unhappy than if he or she has parents who are deaf. This is because many hearing parents do not become proficient in ASL and are unable to communicate with their children easily. Given that over 90 percent of children who are deaf have hearing parents, this problem in communication may be critical.

The need for social interaction is probably most influential in leading many persons with hearing impairment to associate primarily with others with hearing impairment. If their parents are deaf, children who are deaf are usually exposed to other deaf families from an early age. Nonetheless, many persons who are deaf end up, as adults, socializing predominantly with others who are deaf, even if they had hearing parents and even if they did not come into contact as children with many other children who were deaf. This phenomenon of socializing with others who are deaf is attributable to the influence of the *Deaf culture.*

The Deaf Culture. In the past, most professionals viewed isolation from the hearing community on the part of many people who are deaf as a sign of social pathology. But now more and more professionals agree with the many people who are deaf who believe in the value of having their own Deaf culture. They view this culture as a natural condition emanating from the common bond of sign language.

The unifying influence of sign language is the first of six factors noted by Reagan (1990) as demarcating the Deaf community as a true culture:

1. linguistic differentiation
2. attitudinal deafness
3. behavioral norms
4. endogamous marital patterns
5. historical awareness
6. voluntary organizational networks

Regarding *linguistic differentiation,* Reagan (1990) states that the Deaf community can most accurately be described as bilingual, with individuals possessing varying degrees of fluency in ASL and English. *Attitudinal deafness* refers to whether a person thinks of himself or herself as deaf. It may not have anything to do with a person's hearing acuity. For example, a person with a relatively mild hearing loss may think of himself or herself as deaf more readily than does someone with a profound hearing loss. The Deaf community has its own set of *behavioral norms* with regard to such things as eye contact and physical touching. *Endogamous marriage patterns* are evident from surveys showing rates of ingroup marriage as high as 90 percent. The Deaf community has a long history that has contributed to its *historical awareness* of significant people and events pertaining to people who are deaf. Finally, there are an abundance of *voluntary organizational networks* for the Deaf community, such as the National Association of the Deaf, the World Games for the Deaf (Deaf Olympics), and the National Theatre of the Deaf.

These six factors help us understand the Deaf culture from a theoretical perspective. The following statement portrays just how strong the Deaf culture is from a practical perspective:

> Although deaf people comprise a minority group that reflects the larger society, they have devised their own codes of behavior. For example, it's all right to drop in unannounced, because many people don't have the special TTY telephone hookups. How else could they contact their friends to let them know they're coming? If a deaf person has a job that needs to be done—from electrical wiring to accounting—he's expected to go to a deaf person first. The assumption is that deaf people won't take advantage of each other and that they need to support their own kind. . . . The deaf world has its own heroes, and its own humor, some of which relies on visual puns made in sign language, and much of which is quite corny. Because deafness is a disability that cuts across all races and social backgrounds, the deaf world is incredibly heterogeneous. Still, deafness seems to take precedence over almost everything else in a person's life. A deaf person raised a Catholic will more likely attend a Baptist deaf service than a hearing mass. (Walker, 1986, p. 22)

Some social scientists debate whether the Deaf culture is equivalent to what anthropologists and sociologists typically mean when they define *culture* as the customary beliefs, norms, and practices of a certain group (Andersson, 1994; Stokoe, 1995; Street, 1994; Turner, 1994). For the most part, however, this debate hinges on subtle nuances of that definition. For example, one researcher has commented:

> For my part, I believe that the fact that signing deaf people can be thought of within a linguistic and cultural model rather than a medical one does not therefore mean that deaf culture is in all respects the equivalent of culture when commonly or technically used to refer to other human groupings. The situation of signing deaf people is quite unique. Our definitions may fail a critical test because borrowed terms may fail to name and identify that which is unique to the situation of signing deaf people in cultural, linguistic, and physical terms. We might need new names or

at least a willingness to see deaf cultures and deaf sign languages in their own terms. (Johnston, 1994, p. 138)

Such theoretical arguments not withstanding, many people who are deaf—along with a growing number of professionals—believe that the experience of being deaf unites people in a culture that is every bit as authentic as those of other groups of people sharing common languages (e.g., the French, Spanish, Italian, etc.)

Many within the Deaf community and some within professional ranks are concerned that the cultural status of children who are deaf is in peril (Gaustad & Kluwin, 1992; Janesick & Moores, 1992). They believe that the increase in mainstreaming is eroding the cultural values of the Deaf culture. In the past, much of Deaf culture was passed down from generation to generation through contacts made at residential schools, but today's children who are deaf may have little contact with other children who are deaf, if they attend local schools. Some authorities have recommended that schools provide classes in Deaf history and culture for students who are deaf who attend local schools. These authorities further recommend that such classes be taught by people who are deaf so they can serve as role models (Drasgow, 1993).

The Deaf community has become more and more active in advocating a variety of social, educational, and medical policies. For example, the Deaf Coalition—an alliance of Deaf theater organizations and other groups related to deafness—has been active in promoting the use of actors who are deaf in movies and theater. The coalition maintains that a hearing person could never pass for a native signer, even after years of practice. Moreover, for the Deaf community, seeing a hearing actor playing the role of a person who is deaf is demeaning in the same way that seeing a white actor in "blackface" would be demeaning to an African American.

Another example of Deaf activism occurred in 1988 at Gallaudet University—a liberal arts college for the deaf and hard of hearing—where students and faculty protested the board of trustees' selection of a hearing president. Since its founding in 1864, Gallaudet had never had a deaf president. After shutting down the university for several days, the school's administration acquiesced to the students' demands for a deaf president and a reconfiguration of the board to include a majority of members who are deaf.

Deaf activists have also been aggressive in attacking what they consider an oppressive medical and educational establishment. An example of just how much this segment of the Deaf community is at odds with many professionals is its opposition to the medical procedure referred to as **cochlear implantation** (see the box on p. 325.)

cochlear implantation. A surgical procedure that allows people who are deaf to hear some environmental sounds; an external coil fitted on the skin by the ear picks up sound from a microphone worn by the person and transmits it to an internal coil implanted in the bone behind the ear, which carries it to an electrode implanted in the cochlea of the inner ear.

total communication approach. An approach for teaching students with hearing impairment that blends oral and manual techniques.

EDUCATIONAL CONSIDERATIONS

The problems facing the educator working with students with hearing impairment are formidable. As we would expect, one major problem is communication. Dating back to the sixteenth century, there has been a raging debate concerning how individuals who are deaf should converse (Lane, 1984). This controversy is sometimes referred to as the *oralism–manualism debate* to represent two very different points of view—one of which advocates teaching people who are deaf to speak and the other, to use of some kind of manual communication. Manualism was the preferred method until the middle of the nineteenth century, when oralism began to gain predominance. Currently, most educators advocate the use of both oral and manual methods in what is referred to as a **total communication approach.**

We first discuss the major techniques that make up the oral approach and the oral portion of the total communication approach; then we take up total communication, and then we discuss the controversy surrounding the use of ASL in classrooms.

Controversy Surrounds Cochlear Implants

In 1990, after several years of experimentation, the U.S. Food and Drug Administration (FDA) approved the use of cochlear implants for children. A cochlear implant consists of an internal magnetic coil, with an electrode that runs into the cochlea of the inner ear, and an external coil. The surgeon implants the internal coil in the bone behind the ear and fits an external coil on the skin over the internal coil. The person with the implant wears a microphone, which picks up sound and carries it to the cochlea nerve via the external coil, internal coil, and electrode implanted in the cochlea.

Cochlear implants are generally recommended for children who have virtually no hearing (Moog & Geers, 1991). Some professionals report that implants allow such children to hear some environmental sounds that they could not hear previously (e.g., car horns and ringing telephones).

This device is far from a cure-all for deafness, however. A cochlear implant does not automatically enable the individual to understand speech; a significant amount of training is needed to help him or her make use of the sounds he or she is hearing for the first time. Nonetheless, authorities predict that in the future, more and more implants will be done and the procedure will be perfected so that someday it will lead to significant improvements in hearing.

Although hailed as a medical breakthrough by some professionals, some within the Deaf community see cochlear implants as overly zealous medical tinkering. They do not think the benefits (which, thus far, have been rather limited) warrant the invasive medical procedures:

> When societies rush to implement high cost medical interventions like the cochlear implant without educational, cultural, and social policies and services that already meet the needs of deaf people, it is little wonder that in the discourse of deaf people the cochlear implant is so negatively portrayed. (Johnston, 1994, p. 137)

And at least one authority has argued that even if the procedure is eventually perfected, it should not be used if one truly believes that children who are deaf are a cultural minority group and not disabled:

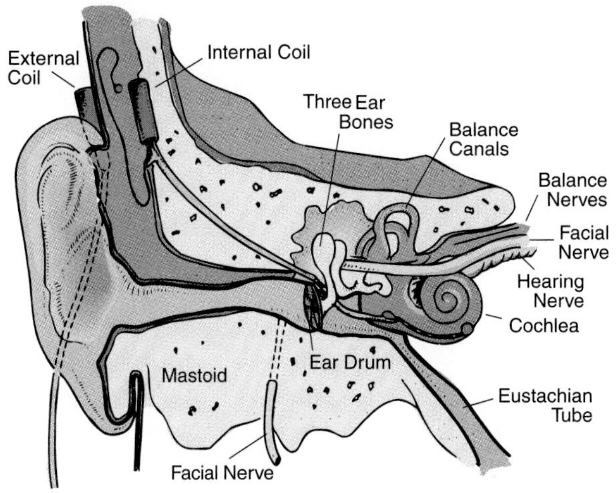

A cochlear implant. (*Source: Helix*, Winter 1983. Drawing by F. J. Kabir. Reprinted with permission.)

> I expect that most Americans would agree that our society should not seek the scientific tools or use them, if available, to change a child biologically so he or she will belong to the majority rather than the minority—even if we believe that this biological engineering might reduce the burdens the child will bear as a member of a minority. Even if we could take children destined to be members of the African American, or Hispanic American, or Native American, or Deaf American communities and convert them with bio-power into white, Caucasian, hearing males—even if we could, we should not. We should likewise refuse cochlear implants for young deaf children even if the devices were perfect. (Lane, 1992, p. 237)

Many professionals and laypeople alike consider this position too radical. However, it typifies the strong feelings some activists have about preservation of Deaf culture.

Oral Approach: Auditory-Verbal Approach and Speechreading

auditory-verbal approach. Part of the oral approach to teaching students who are hearing impaired; stresses teaching the person to use his or her remaining hearing as much as possible; heavy emphasis on use of amplification.

The Auditory-Verbal Approach. The **auditory-verbal approach** stresses using techniques designed to encourage children to make use of what hearing they possess. According to Auditory-Verbal International, Inc., a major professional organization promoting the auditory-verbal philosophy (Goldberg, 1993), some of the principles behind this approach are:

- Auditory-verbal training must begin as early as possible.
- The majority of children who are hearing impaired have some residual hearing.

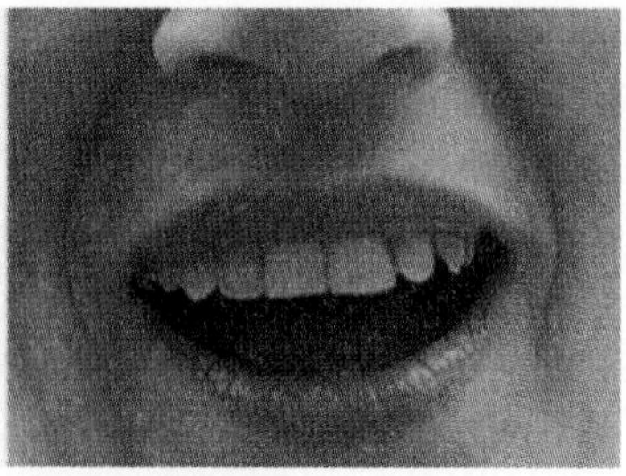
[ȧ]

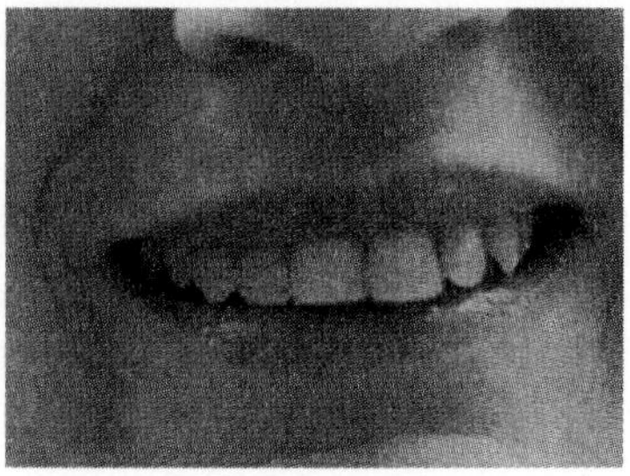
[ē]

Figure 8–2 Differentiation among vowels is made on the basis of jaw opening and lip shaping. The contrast between /ȧ/ (as in *father*) and /ē/ (as in *he*) is shown here.

- The use of amplification (e.g., hearing aids), starting at an early age, is critical.
- With proper amplification, most children with hearing impairment are able to hear sounds in the frequency range relevant to speech.
- Children should be taught to be active listeners, rather than allowed to rely only on the visual modality.
- Parents do not need to learn sign language.
- Parents, as the primary language models for their children, are a critical component in any treatment plan.

Speechreading. Sometimes inappropriately called lipreading, **speechreading** involves teaching children who are hearing impaired to use visual information to understand what is being said to them. *Speechreading* is a more accurate term than *lipreading* because the goal is to teach students to attend to a variety of stimuli in addition to specific movements of the lips. For example, proficient speechreaders read contextual stimuli so they can anticipate certain types of messages in certain types of situations. They are able to use facial expressions to help them interpret what is being said to them. Even the ability to discriminate the various speech sounds that flow from a person's mouth involves attending to visual cues from the tongue and jaw as well as the lips. For example, to learn to discriminate among vowels, the speechreader concentrates on cues related to the degree of jaw opening and lip shaping (see Figure 8–2).

Cued speech is a method of augmenting speechreading. In cued speech, the individual uses hand shapes to represent specific sounds while speaking. Although it has some devoted advocates, cued speech is not used widely in the United States.

speechreading. A method that involves teaching children to use visual information from a number of sources to understand what is being said to them; more than just lipreading, which uses only visual clues arising from the movement of the mouth in speaking.

cued speech. A method to aid speechreading in people with hearing impairment; the speaker uses hand shapes to represent sounds.

Criticisms of the Oral Approach. Several authorities have been critical of using an exclusively oral approach with students who have hearing impairment (Lane, 1992; Padden & Humprhies, 1988). In particular, they object to the de-emphasis of this approach on sign language, especially for children who are deaf. These critics assert that for many children with severe or profound degrees of hearing loss, it is unreasonable to assume that they have enough hearing to be of use. As such, denying these children access to ASL is denying them access to a language to communicate.

Critics of the oral approach also point out that speechreading is extremely difficult and good speechreaders are rare. It is easy to overlook some of the factors that make speechreading difficult. For instance, speakers produce many sounds with little obvious movement of the mouth. Another issue is that the English language has many **homophenes**—different sounds that are visually identical when spoken. For example, a speechreader cannot distinguish among the pronunciations of [p], [b], and [m]. There is also variability among speakers in how they produce sounds. Finally, such factors as poor lighting, rapid speaking, and talking with one's head turned are further examples of why good speechreading is a rare skill (Menchel, 1988).

Total Communication

As noted previously, most schools have adopted the total communication approach, a combination of oral and manual methods. The shift from exclusively oral instruction to total communication in the 1970s occurred primarily because researchers found that children who were deaf fared better academically and socially if they had parents who were deaf than if they had hearing parents (Moores & Maestas y Moores, 1981). Investigators attributed this difference to the greater likelihood of signing in families in which children and parents were both deaf.

Signing English Systems. Signing English systems are the type of manualism most often used in the total communication approach. **Signing English systems** refer to approaches that professionals have devised for teaching people who are deaf to communicate. There are several such systems, for example, Signing Exact English (Gustason, Pftezing, & Zawolkow, 1972) and Signed English (Bornstein, Hamilton, & Saulnier, 1983). The fact that teachers use signing English systems instead of ASL has sparked heated debate. **Fingerspelling**, the representation of letters of the English alphabet by finger positions, is also used occasionally to spell out certain words (see Figure 8–3 on page 330).

homophenes. Sounds that are identical in terms of revealing movements (i.e., visible articulatory patterns).

signing English systems. Used simultaneously with oral methods in the total communication approach to teaching students who are deaf; different from American Sign Language because they maintain the same word order as spoken English.

fingerspelling. Spelling the English alphabet by using various finger positions on one hand.

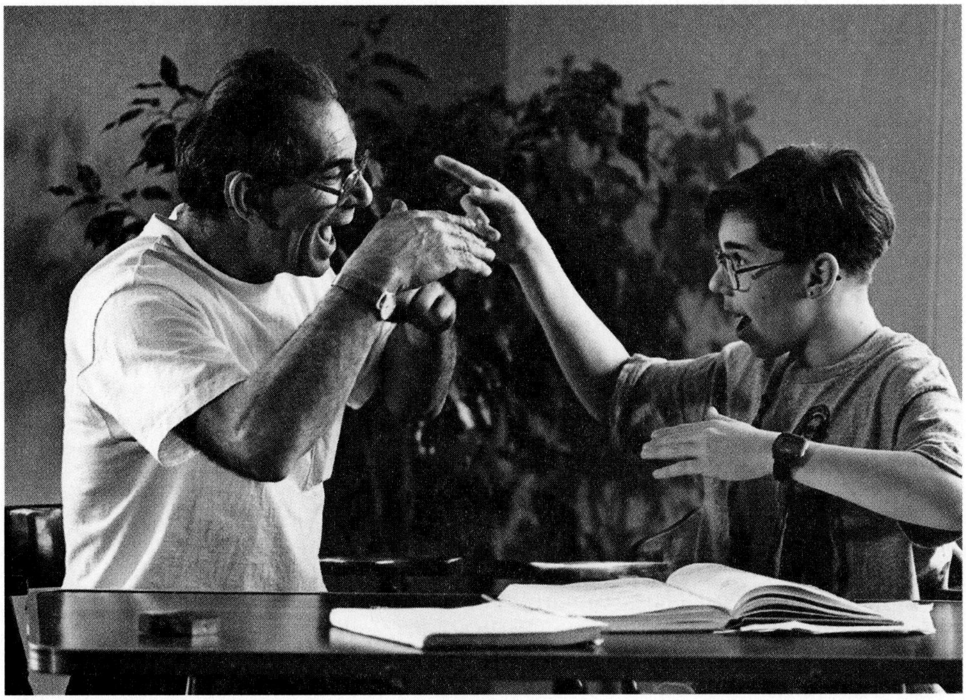

A total communication approach blends oral and manual methods.

collaboration

a key to success

Ken Alexander

Lynn Pott

Ken The eight students I currently teach range in age from eight to eleven. They have severe to profound bilateral sensorineural hearing losses and are placed in my total communication class at Bellerive Elementary. (Total communication, which utilizes the simultaneous methods of speech, lipreading, amplification, and sign language, is one of two types of programs offered by our special district; the other is auditory/oral, which emphasizes understanding and using spoken language.) Two of my students have parents who are deaf, and three have one or more siblings who are deaf. Although all the students are encouraged to use their best speech, only two of the eight have good to excellent conversational speech. The other six are generally unintelligible to those unfamiliar with the speech of persons who are deaf. Three of these students have transferred from oral programs at age eight or older. Seven of the eight have excellent signed communication skills. Five of the eight have good written English-language skills. (This means they have generally good written English for children who are deaf. For instance, the structure of the language may be correct, but they may have problems in verb conjugation.) The other three have concepts and ideas to express in writing but have great difficulty with basic English patterns.

Lynn My fifth-grade class of twenty-eight is a heterogeneous group. The average academic level is above national norms, but my students have a wide range of ability—third-grade to seventh-grade reading levels. I teach all subject areas.

Ken We'll describe our work with Beth, a twelve-year-old. Her father is a fluent signer and knowledgeable of Deaf culture. Her mother is also a skilled communicator in sign language. Picture an artistic, creative student who is continuously struggling with perfection. She is eager to learn English and its relationship to American Sign Language. She is equally enthusiastic about reading and expressing herself in written English. She is above average in intelligence, a charming student with an amiable manner, but one whose emotions are usually kept in check. She's a visual-manual learner who relies on an interpreter to facilitate communication in the mainstream. A child who is profoundly deaf, she has a good sense of communication and languages and therefore is remarkable in her communicative skills, although her speech intelligibility is only fair. She's a student who feels responsible for her own destiny. In short, you can see that she's the cat's pajamas!

Lynn Beth is an achiever. She wants to be sure her assignments are completed correctly and neatly. During her first month in my class, she didn't ask any questions, but she answered questions through the interpreter. Beth is a listener and an observer. She watches everything that goes on in the classroom. Because she is so attentive, she has become a leader among her three classmates who are hearing impaired. She knows what's going on and clarifies concepts for the other students with hearing impairments. Sometimes, she gets frustrated with them. I've learned to watch her facial expressions and the forcefulness in her signing. I can tell when she's frustrated. At first, she didn't want to call attention to herself, so she'd save her questions and ask for Ken's help when she returned to his classroom. By the second semester, she'd lost much of her shyness and would ask questions. As she grew more confident in my classroom, she began to speak as she signed. Some of her speech could be understood but with difficulty.

Ken Beth was mainstreamed for science, social studies, and language at the fifth-grade level. As the teacher for students who are deaf, I was responsible for any

Ken Alexander is a teacher of students who are deaf/hard of hearing, total communication, Special District of St. Louis County; B.A., Education and Psychology, Webster University; M.Ed., Education of the Deaf, Western Maryland College. **Lynn Pott** is a fifth-grade teacher, Bellerive Elementary School, and instructor, Washington University; B.S., Elementary Education, University of Missouri; M.Ed., Maryville College; doctoral student, St. Louis University.

preteaching, reviewing, and additional explanations to ensure success. Sometimes, specific vocabulary for science and social studies needed to be invented, based on concepts of American Sign Language and consistent with signs already in existence. I taught these in my classroom to facilitate speedy and appropriate interpreting while Beth was in hearing classes.

Lynn As a classroom teacher, I was responsible for presenting the curriculum content, giving the assignments, and testing for understanding. At the beginning of the year, I needed to understand Beth's capabilities and what I could expect of her.

Ken I recall one instance that was a particular problem—beginning note taking. Fifth grade introduces note taking as part of beginning outline skills and conceptualization of content. I had decided not to use a note taker and the usual paper. I knew that outlining skills were more important. I took the time to explain to Beth that in sixth grade, note takers would be used but that in the fifth grade, it was more important to write a simple outline. She needed to learn specialized techniques to develop memory skills. I helped her learn techniques to use at home during independent study. Her parents were also involved in the various study techniques. All this helped her learn to discriminate important information from what was less important. Another challenging aspect of our teamwork, unrelated to her academic skills, was her overall social development—as a person who is deaf with a peer group that is deaf coexisting within a larger hearing society. Another matter requiring immediate attention was parental denial. One of her parents felt that her academic successes meant that she was ready to be totally mainstreamed with the necessary support. This was a denial of her deafness. The fact is that Beth's hearing peers could never know her as a person, although they could admire her for her abilities or academic skills. She didn't seek out deep, meaningful communication with hearing peers; therefore, they had virtually no sense of her as a person. Through discussion in our classroom, as well as guided discussion groups led by a counselor for students who are deaf, we were able to help Beth come to grips with this issue. She came to accept these realities as she saw them: She was deaf; she enjoyed socializing primarily with her peers who are deaf or within the Deaf community; she could learn more content being mainstreamed with an interpreter and be more challenged intellectually within a larger, hearing-student classroom. In the final analysis, she had a strong self-identity as a person who is deaf existing within a larger hearing society.

Lynn I definitely needed Ken's help. I had never had students with hearing impairment in my classroom before, and I had twenty-eight other students. Ken kept me informed of any concerns or problems that Beth was having. He was similar to a private tutor to Beth. Rather than burden me with reteaching, he would clarify concepts and strategies so Beth would have confidence in the regular classroom. It worked. As the year progressed, Beth began volunteering on a regular basis. He was the link that helped connect the integrated classroom to the comfortable, but isolated, deaf/hard-of-hearing classroom.

Ken During the course of Beth's fifth-grade year, I saw attitude changes because of the way Lynn and I worked as a team. In the beginning of the year, Beth was concerned about how she would be perceived by her hearing peers. She was afraid they would reject her because of her speech skills or that they might equate her poor speech production with lower IQ. Instead, her hearing peers began to see her as a well-functioning fifth-grader. We worked within a framework that facilitated relaxed integration in academic areas as well as nonacademic areas. This allowed her hearing peers to see her during work and play, and it also helped her to develop more self-confidence about her abilities compared to those of her hearing peers. Consequently, she acquired a strong, healthy self-concept outside of her small group of peers who are deaf. A rewarding outcome of my collaboration with Lynn was that we saw Beth come to accept herself better within the larger mainstream.

Lynn There were other rewards, too. As the students in my classroom began to understand Beth's feelings, they grew to respect and admire her for her abilities. She became their classmate and friend. I also grew as a teacher. I learned from Ken and Beth to watch people so that I can understand them—all people, not just those with disabilities. I remember Ken saying how significant facial expressions and body language are to his students. As a class, we talked about this. We all became more aware of the different aspects of communication. My students began to learn sign language so they could communicate with Beth.

> *A rewarding outcome . . . was that we saw Beth come to accept herself better within the larger mainstream.*

Ken I guess the major barriers that keep special and general education teachers from working together are the intense and often acrimonious feelings associated with ethnocentric identity. These attitudes often include an "us-them" mentality, denigration of American Sign Language, the feeling that speech is all important, low expectations of people with disabilities, and a focus on disability rather than ability.

Lynn Classroom teachers need to be aware of their own feelings and the feelings that students who are deaf experience. It is so important to have a teacher of children with hearing impairment who truly understands the frustrations of the students and is patient with the classroom teacher. If that special teacher doesn't provide input, a barrier could materialize. Perhaps this is why some mainstreaming programs are not successful.

Figure 8–3

Fingerspelling alphabet.
(*Source:* Adapted from L. J. Fant, Jr., *Say it with hands.* Copyright © 1971 from National Association for the Deaf, 1971, Silver Spring, MD, pp. 1–2. Reprinted with permission.)

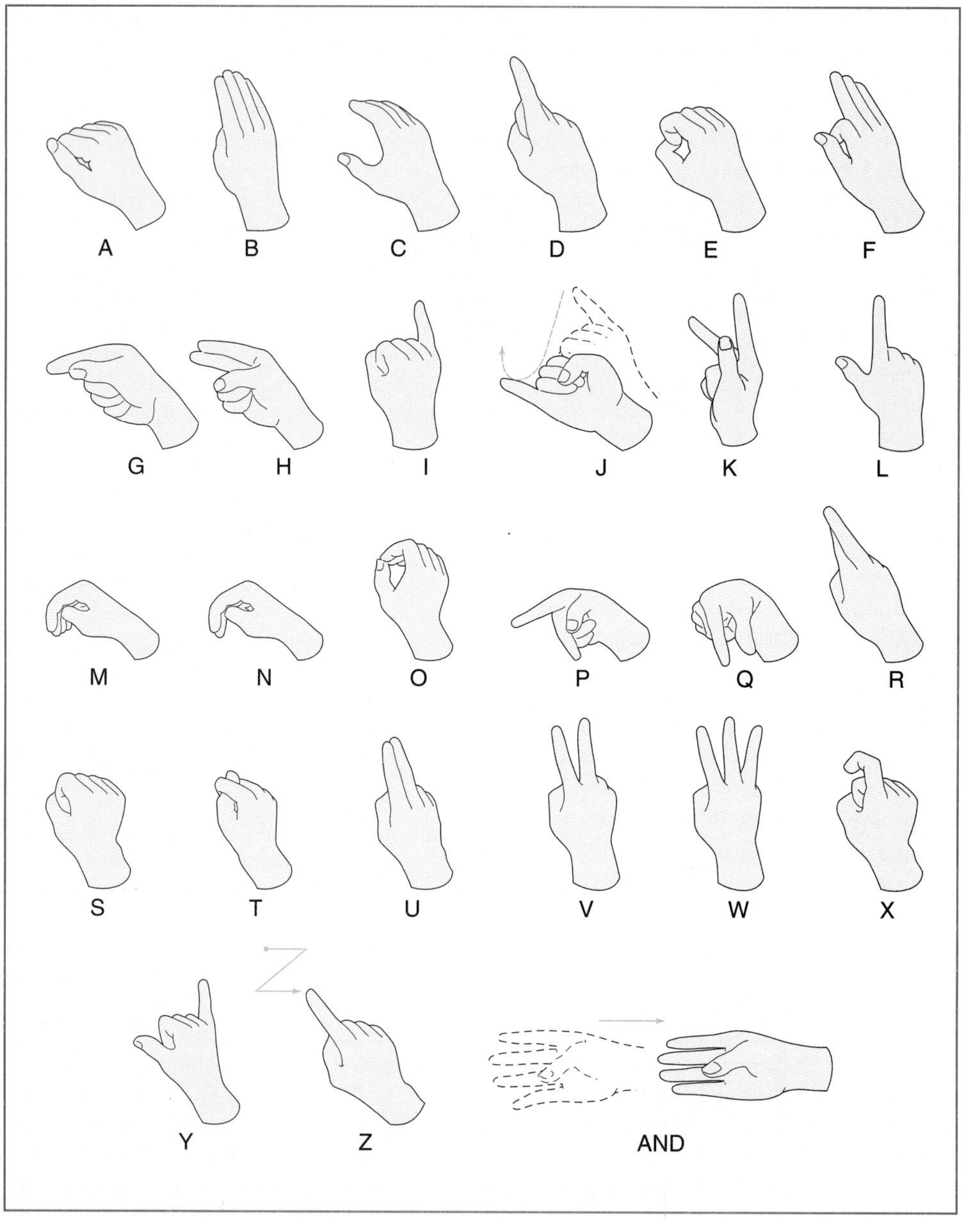

Controversy over Using ASL in the Classroom

Even though the use of ASL in public school classrooms is still rare and those people who employ a total communication approach almost always use a blend of oralism and a signing English system of some sort, there are those within the Deaf community who champion the use of ASL, rather than signed English (Drasgow, 1993; Lane, 1987, 1992; Padden & Humphries, 1988). This small but growing group of advocates asserts that ASL is the natural language of people who are deaf and that it should be fostered because it is the most natural and efficient way for students to learn about the world. To clarify, signing English systems are not true languages, such

American Sign Language Is a True Language

Many people, even some of those working in the area of deaf education, have the misconception that ASL and other sign languages are not true languages. (There is no universal sign language; ASL is only one among many. Most of them are nearly as different from each other as the spoken languages of the world.) Some people believe ASL is merely a loosely constructed system of gestures, and some believe that the signs are so highly pictorial in nature that they limit ASL to the representation of concrete, rather than abstract, concepts. Research has demonstrated that ASL's detractors are wrong on both counts.

ASL HAS ITS OWN GRAMMAR

Far from a disorganized system, ASL has its own very complicated grammar. Linguist William Stokoe first submitted that, analogous to the phonemes of spoken English, each sign in ASL consists of three parts: handshape, location, and movement (Stokoe, 1960; Stokoe, Casterline & Croneberg, 1976). He proposed that there are nineteen different handshapes, twelve locations, and twenty-four types of movements. Scoffed at by his colleagues when he first advanced his theory, Stokoe has come to be regarded as a genius for his pioneering work on the structure of ASL (Sacks, 1989; Wolkomir, 1992).

Research since the pioneering work of Stokoe has further confirmed the grammatical complexity of ASL. For example, researchers have found that young children who are deaf make errors in the early stages of learning ASL that are analogous to those made by hearing children learning English (Bellugi & Klima, 1991; Crowson, 1994). For example, children who are deaf make overgeneralization errors similar to those made by hearing children (e.g., using *-ed* to form past tenses *goed* or *eated*).

One team of researchers compared the signing of (1) individuals fluent in ASL to that of (2) a child who was deaf who had, over a period of years, developed a system of gestures for communicating to his hearing parents to that of (3) a group of previously nonsigning hearing adults and children who were asked to communicate with each other nonverbally (i.e., to invent a signing system) (Singleton, Morford, & Goldin-Meadow, 1993). These researchers found that, in contrast to the ASL group, the child and final group did not produce sets of signs that were coherent and systematic. In other words, evidence suggested that it is necessary for a signing system to evolve over time, to be passed down from one generation to another, as ASL has. This evolution is needed in order for the signing system to develop the systematic and internally consistent forms that identify it as a true language.

ASL CAN BE USED TO CONVEY ABSTRACT IDEAS

The misconception that ASL transmits primarily concrete ideas probably comes from the popular belief that signs are made up mostly of pictorial, or iconic, cues. Actually, the origin of some signs is iconic, but over time, even many of these iconic signs have lost their pictorial qualities (Klima & Bellugi, 1979). Sacks (1989) notes that it is the duality of signing—the use of the abstract and the concrete—that contributes to its vividness and aliveness. The following description captures the beauty of signing:

> The creativity can be remarkable. A person can sculpt exactly what he's saying. To sign "flower growing," you delicately place the fingertips at each side of the nose as if sniffing the flower, then you push the fingertips of one hand up through the thumb and first finger of the other. The flower can bloom fast and fade, or, with several quick bursts, it can be a whole field of daffodils. In spoken English, most people would seem silly if they talked as poetically as some supposedly illiterate deaf people sign. With one handshape—the thumb and little finger stretched out, the first finger pointing forward—you can make a plane take off, encounter engine trouble and turbulence, circle an airport, then come in for a bumpy landing. That entire signed sentence takes a fraction of the time than saying it aloud would. (Walker, 1986, p. 48)

as ASL (see box above). Signing English systems have been invented by one or a few people in a short period of time, whereas true sign languages, such as ASL, have evolved over several generations of users.

One of the most important differences between the two is that signing English systems follow the same word order as spoken English, thus making it possible to sign and speak at the same time; ASL has a different word order, making the simultaneous use of spoken English and ASL extremely difficult. Defenders of signing English systems state that the correspondence in word order between signing English systems and English helps students learn English better. Advocates of ASL assert that the use of signing English systems is too slow and awkward to be of much benefit in

SUCCESS STORIES

New York, NY: **Najia Elyoumni-Pinedo** *will turn six on Christmas Day. Her mother, Esther Pinedo, is from Peru, and her father, Ahmed Elyoumni, is from Morocco. Her parents met in an English language class in Manhattan one year before Najia's birth. When she was two, Najia was diagnosed as profoundly deaf. Since she had no extended family in the United States a special day school for students who are deaf or hearing impaired became Najia's second home.*

It was snack time, and the six kindergarten children decided to crush their cookies and eat crumbs. Their teacher, Wanda Frankel, and her assistant, Maria Diaz-Schwartz, readied chairs for the morning meeting, while Raihiem silently made a mountain. Suddenly, hands flew as another child signed, "Look! Raihiem has the most crumbs!" Warding off further comparisons, Wanda signed for the children to clean up and come to the circle. "Najia," she signed, "What is your job this week?" A dark-haired girl went to get paper towels as she signed back, "To wash the table."

Wanda Frankel is certified as a Teacher of the Deaf. She has taught at the Lexington School for the Deaf for twelve years. Effortlessly, she signs and speaks with her students, using a loud voice to facilitate what hearing some might have. "Usually, I wear a microphone, or an FM system as it's called. Then I don't need to speak so loudly, since I can set the mike to amplify my voice a little louder than other sounds coming through individual hearing aids. Today, it's broken!" Fortunately, there is an audiology repair shop on campus to assist with this and other problems, such as when students' hearing aids fail.

It is this kind of service that Najia's parents, Esther and Ahmed, have come to expect at Lexington. "We want to know everything about deafness," says Ester. "We come here for conferences and for sign language classes. We have cried with other parents and shared our experiences at meetings."

In this specialized setting, Najia has benefited from the intensity of instruction in sign language; from the small classes of six children, one teacher, and one assistant; and from the flexibility of a curriculum that focuses on her needs and interests.

Najia's progress is also linked to the school's resources for parental education and support. The school serves a large immigrant community with many parents like Najia's who must learn both English and sign language. For Najia and her parents, sign is their common language. Many mothers and fathers are also taught new skills as hearing parents of a deaf child. Says Wanda Frankel, "Counseling services addressing unique communication issues are available to help these parents learn to better communicate with their deaf child as well as to help deaf children express their feelings and anger in nonphysical ways."

learning English. They argue that word order is not the critical element in teaching a person to use and comprehend English. Furthermore, they believe that fluency in ASL provides students with a rich background of information that readies them for the learning of English:

> Sound waves, movements of lips, printed words, or signs play only a small role in leading us to understand a sentence. The meaning of each word and its grammatical class are likewise not the basis of comprehension. In interpreting a sentence, in arriving at its sense, we rely unconsciously, and thus much more than we realize, on our knowledge of life, knowledge that is not specific to the particular language in which the sentence is communicated, knowledge that comes from general acculturation. Would a person commit an action like the one I understood? Can it be done in principle? Would the subject of the sentence be likely to do it? Acculturation is also the key to composing good sentences; children who know a lot about life have a lot to talk about, and they know which words and structures tend to come together. Thus, student-

Special Educators at Work

Najia's progress cannot be separated from her parents' struggle to find her help. Najia was eighteen months old when her father finally became convinced that she was deaf. "He said, 'I clapped, I slammed a door, I made a lot of noise,'" recalls Najia's mother. Before that, other reasons seemed to explain why Najia did not answer to her name. Since Najia and her parents lived with three other Moroccan families and their seven children, Esther and Ahmed thought that she was too busy playing to respond. They also thought it was a foreign language issue. "When Najia was with me and my friends, we spoke Spanish," explains Esther. "At home, her father and the other families spoke Arabic."

Since the Elyoumni-Pinedos had no family members in the United States to provide support, they were helped by an American acquaintance to make appointments at two audiology centers in Manhattan. The first evaluation found that Najia had a severe hearing loss. "I cried, 'No, not Najia,'" remembers Esther. She hoped the second evaluation would prove the initial finding false; instead, the results indicated a profound loss. At that point, the Elyoumni-Pinedos were advised to take Najia to the nearby Lexington School for early intervention services. She was two years old.

Now in kindergarten, Najia receives an intense classroom focus on communication. She has developed a strong language base and is acquiring beginning reading skills. She knows the alphabet and can sightread the days of the week and names of favorite people. Along with her classmates, she participates in hands-on math readiness activities in basic addition and subtraction. Since there is also a schoolwide emphasis on developing independent learners, children in all grades learn to prepare and to predict through actual problem solving. "Najia comes up with some great solutions," says Wanda Frankel.

At the morning meeting, Najia and her classmates watch Wanda closely, as her lively hands draw their attention. "Listen," she says as she extend her arms and waves her hands, encouraging the children to watch each other. Raihiem is expressive in sign, and his clowning gestures make Najia laugh. She, in turn, signs that she is proud of her body tracing that hangs on the wall. It is decorated in detail and dressed with a feather belt and silver beads for earrings.

"Najia is so artistic," says Wanda. "Last year, she started to draw pictures using perspective! She's very bright." Says Najia's mother, "My husband and I like to think she will be a professional."

The resources of this special school have built a solid foundation for both Najia and her parents. When Esther and Ahmed's second child was born with a hearing loss, the Lexington School was able to provide his evaluation and referral to another program for children with less intense needs.

Esther Pinedo spoke with emotion and her eyes filled as she said, "We are so lucky to have found this school! We are so lucky to be in America!"

—By Jean Crockett

> centered education conducted in the child's most fluent language is actually fostering his literacy in English even without a single word of English spoken. Of course, English must also be taught explicitly, with the aid of the child's most fluent language. (Lane, 1992, p. 182)

Two Models of Bilingual Education for Students Who Are Deaf. Those who advocate using ASL often approach educating children who are deaf from a *bilingual perspective.* In other words, they believe that the same issues that arise, for example, in educating Hispanic American students also apply to educating students who are deaf. The rationale behind the bilingual approach to teaching students who are deaf is to give them a foundation in their natural language, ASL, so that it can serve as a basis for learning spoken English.

There are two general models of bilingual education for students who are deaf (Drasgow, 1993). One emphasizes allowing children to acquire ASL naturally from

The issue of using American Sign Language (ASL) in general education classrooms becomes even more complex when the needs of non-English-speaking students are to be considered.

teachers who are deaf or truly bilingual before formally teaching them English. This approach is based on the idea that English will be easier to learn if the child first has a solid ASL foundation. Advocates of the second model do not see an advantage to teaching one language before the other. Instead, they stress exposing the child to both ASL and English from as early an age as possible, as long as the two languages are used consistently in separate contexts or by different people. For example, ASL might be used in some subjects and English, in others, and/or ASL might be used by one teacher and English, by another.

Service Delivery Models

Students with hearing impairment can be found in settings ranging from general education classes to residential institutions. Since passage of the Education for All Handicapped Children Act (PL 94–142) in 1975, more and more of these students are attending local schools in self-contained classes, resource rooms, and regular classes (Schildroth & Hotto, 1991).

Many within the Deaf community, however, have been critical of the degree of mainstreaming that is occurring (Lane, 1987, 1992; Padden & Humphries, 1988). They argue that residential schools (and to a lesser extent, day schools) have been a major influence in fostering the concept of a Deaf culture and the use of ASL. Mainstreaming, they believe, forces students who are deaf to lose their Deaf identity and places them in a hearing and speaking environment in which it is almost impossible to succeed. In particular, critics of mainstreaming argue that when a student who is deaf is placed in a setting with nondisabled children, he or she is usually the only student with a hearing impairment in the class. This leads to a high degree of social isolation because the student who is deaf lacks peers with whom he or she can communicate (Innes, 1994).

Even professionals who advocate some sort of integration point to the need for a "critical mass" of students who are deaf in order for education to be effective (Higgins, 1992; Innes, 1994; Kluwin, 1992). As one investigator describes:

> Communication occurs not only between students and teachers. Interaction with peers is crucial to the child's overall development, as is interaction with significant others in the environment. For normal development to occur, deaf children, like all children, must have opportunities for interaction with peers who share their language and mode of communication. The presence of a sufficient number of language-mode peers is an important factor. (Innes, 1994, p. 155)

In order to achieve the critical mass necessary to provide what are considered effective programs, more school districts may move toward centralizing their programs. Some have already begun to place many of the students who are deaf in one building. Although the majority of students in the building are hearing, students who are deaf can be placed in self-contained classes, resource rooms, and/or regular classes. In addition to consolidating services and fostering a Deaf culture, such an arrangement lessens the need for frequent school changes, given the possibility that a child will need a variety of placements over several years (Moores, Cerney, & Garcia, 1990).

Research on the effects of integrating students who are deaf with hearing peers has consistently found that social and academic outcomes vary depending on the individual. For some, full integration is beneficial; for others, a separate setting is best. For example, after conducting an extensive longitudinal study of the effects of mainstreaming on academic outcomes, one researcher concluded:

> Ultimately, we can neither condemn nor support any one type of educational placement for deaf students because multiple factors enter into a complex constellation of relationships. We are, in fact, thrown back to the very basis for special education, that is, the individual consideration of each child and each situation. (Kluwin, 1993, p. 80)

This researcher has attached diodes to her fingertips to trace the graceful and complex patterns created by fluent sign language, which many feel is the superior method of communication for individuals with hearing impairment.

It is safe to conclude that although mainstreaming may be beneficial for some students who are deaf, it is more problematic for them than for students from most other categories of special education. The difficulties associated with integrating students who are deaf into classrooms of hearing peers have been noted by officials of the U.S. Department of Education; they caution that the intent of PL 94–142 was *not* to place all students who are deaf in general education classrooms (Viadero, 1992). Likewise, professional and advocacy groups for those who are deaf have voiced concerns about promoting full inclusion (i.e., integrating all students with disabilities for the entire schoolday in general education classrooms in their neighborhood schools). These professionals and advocates believe that full inclusion is harmful for many students who are deaf (see the box on p. 337).

Technological Advances

A number of technological advances have made it easier for persons with hearing impairment to communicate with and/or have access to information from the hearing world. This technological explosion has involved primarily five areas: hearing aids, television, telephones, computer-assisted instruction, and the "information highway."

Hearing Aids. The two main types of hearing aids are those that fit in the ear and those that are worn behind the ear. The behind-the-ear hearing aid is the one recommended for children because it can be used with FM systems available in some classrooms (Hawkins, 1990). In an FM system, the teacher wears a wireless lapel microphone and the student wears an FM receiver (about the size of a cigarette package). The student hears the amplified sound either through a hearing aid that comes attached to the FM receiver or by attaching a behind-the-ear hearing aid to the FM receiver. (More and more personal behind-the-ear hearing aids are being manufactured with this capability.) Whether a student will be able to benefit from a hearing aid by itself depends a great deal on the acoustic qualities of the classroom. Most classrooms have such poor acoustics that an FM system is needed to help the child (Hawkins, 1990).

Although hearing aids are an integral part of educational programming for students with hearing impairment, some children who are deaf cannot benefit from them because of the severity and/or kind of their hearing impairment. Generally, hearing aids make sounds louder, not clearer, so if a person's hearing is distorted, a hearing aid will merely amplify the distorted sound.

For those who can benefit from hearing aids, it is critical for the student, parents, and teachers to work together to ensure the maximum effectiveness of the aid. This means that the teacher should be familiar with the operation and maintenance of the instrument. Research has generally shown a high degree of malfunction in personal hearing aids and FM systems used in schools (Hawkins, 1990).

Television Captioning. Over 400 hours of television programs are now captioned for use by people with hearing impairment, and many videotapes available from rental stores are captioned, as well (Withrow, 1994). A special decoder attached to the television allows the viewer to see captions for live (e.g., sporting events and news shows) and taped television programs as well as videotapes. Special decoders are not necessary for some newer television sets. Federal law requires that a chip be placed in TVs with screens over 13" that takes the place of a decoder.

Telephone Adaptations. Persons with hearing impairment have traditionally had problems using telephones, either because their hearing loss was too great or because of acoustic feedback—noise caused by closeness of the telephone receiver to

Excerpts from "Position Statement on Full Inclusion"

PREPARED BY THE CONSUMER ACTION NETWORK (CAN) OF, BY, AND FOR DEAF AND HARD OF HEARING AMERICANS

A hearing loss can have a devastating effect on an individual's ability to participate in a regular educational environment and in society. Being deaf creates a communication difference. Deaf people, as a result of their hearing loss, are visually oriented individuals, and may have considerable difficulty participating in an environment that relies primarily on sounds to communicate and learn. Deaf people use many different approaches to communicate. No two deaf people are alike. It is incorrect to assume that all deaf people can be taught to lipread or all deaf people can be taught to speak or use hearing aids. . . .

CAN believes that, in addition to addressing the communication needs of all deaf children, the educational placement decision must consider the cultural background of the deaf student. One of these cultural features is the use of ASL for language and communication. . . .

When deaf people are among their peers there is no feeling of being left out or missing critical aspects of communication. Communication is much more easily accomplished and the cultural aspects are both understood and accepted. If a person who could hear and was not fluent in sign language and placed with a group of deaf people, that person would immediately experience isolation. The situation, not the hearing loss, creates the barrier to effective and fluent communication. . . .

CAN believes that the philosophy of full inclusion puts undue emphasis on the physical placement of deaf children with hearing children at the expense of the needs of deaf students. Placement of deaf students without consideration for their communication, cultural, academic, social, and emotional needs would result in turning a potential ability situation into a disability situation. . . .

CAN believes that the philosophy of full inclusion for all deaf students is clearly in violation of IDEA since it does not ensure the availability of a continuum of alternative placements. Many deaf and hard of hearing students cannot progress satisfactorily in a regular education environment even with the use of supplementary aids and services. . . .

It is the position of . . . CAN that all deaf children, youth and young adults are entitled to a continuum of educational placements. This includes residential and day programs . . . , center schools in public education environments, self-contained classes within a public school setting, and other educational placements that are deemed appropriate, based on thorough assessment of each child's unique abilities. The educational placement decision for deaf children, youth and young adults should take into consideration each individual's communication, academic, social, emotional and cultural needs. CAN urges that students, parents, families, and professionals recommending the educational placement option take into consideration all of the necessary factors and the desired outcomes to be pursued. Further, CAN believes that deaf adults, while having the same desired outcomes and careers as those of their hearing peers, cannot attain these goals unless their education places appropriate emphasis on the unique communication and cultural needs that deafness presents.

It is the position of CAN that education in a local public school setting will not meet the individual needs of ALL deaf children, youth and young adults. CAN believes that programming of this type will not meet the unique communication, culture, academic, social and emotional needs of all deaf children. In addition, CAN also recognizes that there is a severe shortage of trained personnel, including teachers familiar with the implications that deafness presents and qualified interpreters to facilitate communication.

CAN was founded in 1993. The founding members are the American Association of the Deaf-Blind; the American Athletic Association of the Deaf; the American Society for Deaf Children; the Association of Late Deafened Adults; the Deaf and Hard of Hearing Entrepreneurs Council; Deaf Women United, Inc.; the National Association of the Deaf; National Black Deaf Advocates; the National Congress of the Jewish Deaf; the National Fraternal Society of the Deaf; the National Hispanic Council of Deaf and Hard of Hearing People; and Telecommunications for the Deaf, Inc.

Source: "Position statement on full inclusion," January 11, 1994. Used with permission from the Consumer Action Network (CAN), 814 Thayer Avenue, Silver Spring, MD 20910.

their hearing aids. The development of the **teletypewriter (TTY)** has allowed these people access to the telephone. A person can use a TTY connected to a telephone to type a message to anyone else who has a TTY, and a special phone adaptation allows someone without a TTY to use the pushbuttons on his or her phone to "type" messages to someone with a TTY.

The federal government now requires each state to have a relay service for use by people with TTYs. A **relay service** allows a person with a TTY to communicate with anyone through an operator, who conveys the message to a person who does not have

teletypewriter (TTY). A device connected to a telephone by a special adapter; allows communication over the telephone between persons who are hearing impaired and those with hearing.

Visual displays of speech patterns on computer screens can help individuals with hearing impairment and their families learn American Sign Language (ASL).

a TTY. The TTY user can carry on a conversation with the non-TTY user, or the TTY user can leave a message. The latter is useful for carrying out everyday activities, such as scheduling appointments.

Some educators have incorporated TTY use into their classroom activities as a way of fostering friendships while providing practice in reading and writing (Jensma, 1994; Moseley & Moseley, 1994). More and more people with hearing impairments are also making use of another telephone device—the fax.

Computer-Assisted Instruction (CAI). The explosion of microcomputer and related technology (e.g., videodiscs, CD-ROMs) is expanding learning capabilities for people who are deaf and their families. For example, visual displays of speech patterns on a computer screen can help someone with hearing impairment learn speech. Videodisc programs showing people sign are also available for use in learning ASL.

The "Information Superhighway." What has come to be called the "information superhighway" is also opening up a variety of communication possibilities for people who are deaf. For example, electronic mail allows people who are deaf to communicate with one another as well as with hearing individuals. People who are deaf may also subscribe to online lists and newsgroups devoted to deafness, along with a multitude of other subjects. And, certainly, the ever-expanding World Wide Web provides access to a variety of information sources.

relay service. A system whereby a person with a teletypewriter (TTY) can communicate with a non-TTY user through an operator; now required by federal law in all states.

In addition to providing people who are deaf with a way to access information, the information superhighway can also be used by educators to help students who are deaf practice reading and writing skills. For instance, teachers can set up newsgroups through which students can communicate with others in the class, the school, or even worldwide.

EARLY INTERVENTION

Researchers and practitioners have espoused the importance of education for infants and preschoolers with hearing impairments. Because language development is such an issue with children who are hearing impaired and because early childhood is such an important time for the development of language, it is not surprising that many of the most controversial issues surrounding early intervention in the area of deafness focus on language. As indicated in the earlier discussion of oralism versus manualism, some people maintain that English language should be the focus of intervention efforts, and others hold that ASL should be used starting in infancy. Among English language advocates, some professionals recommend a total communication approach, combining spoken English and some kind of signed English system.

Research comparing children who are deaf who have parents who are deaf versus those with parents who are hearing has consistently found that the latter are at greater risk for having a variety of problems (Meadow-Orlans, 1990). For example, infants who are deaf who have parents who are deaf develop ASL at a rate similar to the rate at which hearing infants of hearing parents develop English. But infants who are deaf who have hearing parents do not develop either English or ASL at as fast a rate. And in the social arena, children who are deaf who have hearing parents tend to be more immature and dependent on the teachers. The fact that over 90 percent of children who are deaf have parents who are hearing underscores the importance of intervention for many infants who are deaf.

Authorities point to the use of ASL by parents who are deaf as a major factor in the developmental differences found between children who are deaf who have parents who are deaf and those children whose parents are not deaf. Also, parents who use sign with their children are more likely to have cohesive families, with a high degree of emotional bonding and sharing of interests (Kluwin & Gaustad, 1994).

In addition to facility with ASL, parents who are deaf also have the advantage of being better prepared to cope with their infant's deafness (Meadow-Orlans, 1990). While hearing parents are likely to be taken by surprise with their baby's so-called handicap, parents who are deaf are more likely to view the deafness as normal. Parents who are deaf

> know the educational opportunities available . . . and the vocational possibilities that lie ahead. They can anticipate rearing their deaf child as they themselves were reared, or perhaps with modifications based on experiences they want to avoid. For parents with normal hearing, all these areas provide unknown vistas. . . .
>
> For most parents with normal hearing, the diagnosis of deafness . . . comes as a profound shock. . . . The struggle to achieve a firm medical opinion about the child's condition may be debilitating for parents, and this concern and confusion interferes with early childrearing practices. (Meadow-Orlans, 1990, p. 286)

Some of this interference in childrearing practices apparently involves the day-to-day interactions between the parent and the infant. Researchers have found, for example, that interactions between mothers and infants are more facilitative and natural when both the infant and parents are deaf than when the infant is deaf and the parents are hearing. Hearing mothers of infants who are deaf tend to be more directive in their interactions with their infants—that is, they are more likely to start interactions that are unrelated to the child's activity or expressed interest (Spencer & Gutfreund, 1990). Researchers have also suggested that too much maternal directiveness leads to slower language development.

Hearing mothers, especially if they desire to teach their infants sign language, may need help in understanding the importance of the visual modality in communicating with their infants (Koester & Meadow-Orlans, 1990; MacTurk, Meadow-Orlans, Koester, & Spencer, 1993). Hearing mothers need to understand, for example, that the eye gaze of the infant who is deaf is extremely important because it is his or her way of expressing interest and motivation. These mothers also need to be aware that, just as hearing babies babble vocally, babies who are deaf engage in babbling with their hands, as they begin to acquire sign language (Wolkomir, 1992).

Hearing parents of children who are deaf face a quandary over how to provide their children with appropriate sign language models. Both signed English and ASL, especially the latter, are difficult to learn to a high degree of fluency in a relatively short period of time. And like any language, ASL is harder to acquire as an adult and can rarely be learned to the same degree of fluency as obtained by a native ASL signer.

Educators have established preschool intervention projects in order to teach the basics of sign language to the parents of children who are deaf, as well as the children themselves. Such projects are generally successful at teaching the rudiments of sign to parents and infants. Once the child is ready to progress beyond one- and two-word signed utterances, however, it is important that native signers be available as models. Authorities recommend that adults who are deaf be part of early intervention efforts because they can serve as sign language models and can help hearing parents form positive expectations about their children's potential (Spencer, 1993).

Even though hearing parents may never be able to communicate fluently in sign language, it is important that they continue to sign with their child. Not only does signing allow parents a means of communicating with their child; it also demonstrates that they value the child's language and the Deaf culture. One study found that teenagers whose hearing parents use sign are more likely to have high self-esteem (Desselle, 1994).

TRANSITION

Before the mid-1960s, the only institution established specifically for the postsecondary education of students with hearing impairment was Gallaudet College (now Gallaudet University). Except for this one institution, these students were left with no choice but to attend traditional colleges and universities. However, traditional postsecondary schools were generally not equipped to handle the special needs of students with hearing impairment. It is little wonder, then, that a study by Quigley, Jenne, and Phillips (1968) was able to identify only 224 graduates with hearing impairment of regular colleges and universities in the United States between 1910 and 1965.

Findings such as these led to the expansion of postsecondary programs. The federal government has now funded a wide variety of postsecondary programs for students with hearing impairment. In 1965, the National Technical Institute for the Deaf (NTID) (established at the Rochester Institute of Technology) was founded. The NTID program, emphasizing training in technical fields, complements the liberal arts orientation of Gallaudet University. At NTID, some students with hearing impairment also attend classes with hearing students at the Rochester Institute of Technology. Research has indicated that this mainstreaming is related to better academic achievement and future career adjustment (Saur, Coggiola, Long, & Simonson, 1986).

Following the establishment of NTID, an explosion of postsecondary programs occurred. There are now well over 100 postsecondary programs in the United States and Canada for students with hearing impairment. By law, Gallaudet and NTID are responsible for serving students from all fifty states and territories. Others serve students from several states, from one state only, or from specific districts only.

Although many people who are deaf who enroll in higher education choose to attend Gallaudet, NTID, or colleges with special programs, some go to traditional colleges and universities. These students usually take advantage of the expanding roles of university programs that have been established to facilitate the academic experiences of students with disabilities. One of the accommodations often recommended is to provide sign language interpreters in the classes of students with hearing impairment.

The role of interpreters generates a debate comparable to the one in total communication classrooms concerning ASL versus signed English (discussed earlier). The central conflict is over the use of transliteration, rather than ASL, by the majority of interpreters. **Transliteration**, which is similar to signed English, maintains the same word order as spoken English. ASL, on the other hand, requires the interpreter to digest the meaning of what is said before conveying it through signs. Although interpreters find it more difficult to use ASL, research has shown that it is more effective than transliteration (Livingston, Singer, & Abrahamson, 1994).

transliteration. A method used by sign language interpreters in which the signs maintain the same word order as that of spoken English; although used by most interpreters, found through research not to be as effective as American Sign Language (ASL).

Most college instructors have limited, if any, experience in working with sign language interpreters. Even so, it is critical that instructors and interpreters work closely together in order to provide the optimum learning experience for students who are deaf, while not disrupting other students in the class (Siple, 1993). The box below provides some tips for working with sign language interpreters.

Tips for Working with Sign Language Interpreters

In an article for the journal *College Teaching,* Linda Siple (1993) provides some practical tips for working with sign language interpreters. She notes that first, the entire class must have a trusting relationship with the interpreter. His or her job is to translate *everything* that is said in the presence of the student who is deaf, which may include irrelevant or inappropriate comments made during class breaks—even jokes or negative remarks about the student for whom the interpreter is signing.

The interpreter also is expected to maintain confidentiality with regard to sensitive information about the student who is deaf. For example, if the same individual also interprets for the student in other situations (e.g., student health services, financial aid, etc.), any information revealed must be maintained in confidence.

Siple offers the following suggestions for instructors and their classes:

- The interpreter should have copies of all handouts and, if possible, copies of textbooks.
- If a fellow student or the instructor wishes to speak to the student who is deaf, he or she should speak directly to the student, not to the interpreter.
- It is more difficult to interpret in a class in which there is a lot of discussion. Participants should try to talk one at a time, and the instructor should realize that the time-lag between what is spoken and when it is signed will put the student who is deaf at a disadvantage during discussion.
- In a lecture class, the instructor should be aware of the pace of his or her delivery, perhaps pausing more frequently than usual.
- If the instructor is comfortable, he or she may request that the interpreter stop the class if something becomes too complicated to interpret. In fact, the interpreter's need to clarify may very well be an indication that the rest of the students do not understand the information either.
- The interpreter should not be considered a participant in the class. Questions for him or her should not be addressed when he or she is not interpreting.

Source: Based on L. A. Siple, "Working with the sign language interpreter in your classroom," *College Teaching, 41,* 139–142, 1993. Reprinted with permission of the Helen Dwight Reid Educational Foundation. Published by Heldref Publications, 1319 Eighteenth St., N.W., Washington, D.C. 20036-1802.

There has also been an increase in transition programming for students who are deaf who are *not* going on to postsecondary education. Unfortunately, some of this programming is not yet very well articulated, especially in local public schools (Bull & Bullis, 1991). Because residential schools have a much longer history of dealing with transition issues, they have better transition plans than do local school districts. Transition programs in local schools for students who are hearing impaired should improve in quality as they become more accustomed to delivering such services.

Even though postsecondary programs for persons who are hearing impaired have greatly expanded, there is still considerable room for improvement. In an extensive follow-up (Bullis, Bull, Johnson, & Peters, 1995) of persons three to four years after high school, researchers found that, in comparison with hearing peers, those who were deaf demonstrated a lower rate of attendance at four-year colleges and postsecondary training programs. Individuals who were deaf were also more likely to be unemployed, to earn lower wages, and to have fewer close friends. Even though these data come from only three states in the Pacific Northwest, they generally agree with national statistics on young deaf adults (Valdes, Williamson, & Wagner, 1990).

There has been a long tradition of preparing students who are deaf for manual trades (Lane, 1992). But today, unskilled and semiskilled trades are fast disappearing from the workforce in favor of jobs requiring higher-level skills. As a result, adults who are deaf face even greater obstacles when they enter the job market.

With regard to raising a family, persons who are deaf often face some unique challenges. National statistics indicate that 95 percent of adults who are deaf choose deaf spouses, and 90 percent of the offspring of these marriages have normal hearing (Buchino, 1993). Unfortunately, this family makeup can sometimes create conflict, particularly when hearing children are called on more frequently than they would

Educational programs for students of all ages and abilities should include activities to develop creativity.

A Daughter Remembers Being the Hearing Child of Parents Who Are Deaf

Lou Ann Walker is the hearing daughter of two deaf parents. From the time she was a toddler, she served as liaison between her parents and an outside world that did not always understand or welcome people with such problems. Her unusual situation (and a deep love and respect for her parents) gives her a unique vision, enabling her to enter the sometimes impenetrable world of deafness.

Ms. Walker currently lives in New York City, and is a professional writer who contributes to several national publications. She also teaches classes in sign language in her spare time and was the recipient of a Rockefeller Foundation Humanities grant to research the subject of hearing children of deaf parents.

The following excerpts from her autobiography, *A Loss for Words: The Story of Deafness in a Family,* describe the author's memories of having to shield her parents from the callousness of others.

> Curled up in the seat, chin dug into my chest, I noticed there was a lull in the conversation. Dad was a confident driver, but Mom was smoking more than usual.
>
> "Something happened? That gas station?" Mom signed to me.
>
> "No, nothing," I lied.
>
> "Are you sure?"
>
> "Yes. Everything is fine." Dad and I had gone in to pay and get directions. The man behind the counter had looked up, seen me signing and grunted, "Huh, I didn't think mutes were allowed to have driver's licenses." Long ago I'd gotten used to hearing those kinds of comments. But I never could get used to the way they made me churn inside. . . .
>
> As I sat in the living room, I realized that if all my parents had to endure—and all my sisters and I ever had to hear—was a little name-calling, life would have been much easier. On the face of it, deafness seems to be a simple affliction. If you can't hear, people assume you can make up for that lack by writing notes, that you can pass your spare time reading books, that you can converse by talking and reading lips. Unfortunately, things are always more complicated than they seem.
>
> Until they're about the age of two, babies are tape recorders, taking in everything that is being said around them. The brain uses these recordings as the basis of language. If for any reason a baby is deprived of those years of language, he can never make up the loss. For those who become completely deaf—"profoundly" is the term audiologists apply—during infancy, using the basics of English becomes a task as difficult as building a house without benefit of drawings or experience in carpentry. Writing a grammatically correct sentence is a struggle. Reading a book is a Herculean effort. . . .

Source: By Lou Ann Walker, *A loss for words: The story of deafness in a family* (New York: Harper and Row Publishers, 1986), pp. 9, 19, 20.

like to interpret for their parents who are deaf (see the box above). Although these children can cite the benefits that this responsibility brings—including the early opportunity to develop self-confidence around adult authority figures (e.g., doctors, lawyers, insurance agents)—they also admit to frequently resenting the fact that being called on to interpret for their parents interfered with their social lives (Buchino, 1993).

Although the educational, work, and social opportunities for adults who are deaf are often limited, there are reasons to be optimistic about the future. With the continued expansion of transition programming and greater public awareness of the potential of people who are deaf should come a brighter outlook for more adults who are deaf.

h e a r i n g i m p a i r m e n t

Suggestions for Teaching

Students with Hearing Impairment in General Education Classrooms

By E. Jane Nowacek

WHAT TO LOOK FOR IN SCHOOL

Children with mild hearing losses may be identified after entering school. Although by this time, these students may have learned to compensate for their hearing difficulties in many situations, they still are at a disadvantage when compared academically to their nondisabled classmates and at risk for becoming socially isolated from other mainstreamed students. For these reasons, it is important that you be aware of the following indicators of hearing loss:

1. frequent absences due to earaches, sinus congestion, colds, sore throats, and related conditions
2. consistent turning of the head to one side when listening
3. preference for loud volume on electronic equipment
4. inappropriate responses to environmental sounds and spoken communication
5. disorientation or confusion, especially when noise levels are high
6. inattention and daydreaming or appearance of disconnectedness
7. difficulties in understanding spoken language and/or speaking
8. frequent imitation of other students' behaviors in the classroom
9. difficulties in verbal skills, including reading and writing
10. difficulties in following directions and/or frequent requests for directions to be repeated

HOW TO GATHER INFORMATION

If these signs occur consistently, contact the speech and language specialist assigned to your school who can administer tests to determine whether there is a hearing loss. If your student is found eligible for special education, support will be available. The type of assistance will depend on the student's specific needs and the services provided by your school system. It is important that you understand both the services your student will receive and the complete educational plan he or she will follow. For example, you may want to ask the special education teacher the following questions (White, 1981):

- Do I have the information I need to plan an effective educational program in all subjects I teach? Do I have appropriate materials to carry out this program?
- How should I schedule and group students to maximize educational and social opportunities?
- What amplification equipment will be used by the student? By me?
- Who is responsible for demonstrating the use of this equipment and for maintaining it?
- Whom do I contact and what procedures do I follow to request assistance if a problem arises?

If a student with hearing impairment is to be mainstreamed into your class, Jaussi (1991) recommends preparing classmates in several ways:

- Lead class discussions about hearing losses, hearing aids, and other amplification devices. Encourage students to talk about their own feelings about deafness.
- Introduce them to persons with hearing impairments by arranging classroom visits with children or adults who are deaf or who have hearing losses.
- Read accounts of persons with hearing impairment. (See *Literature* at the end of the chapter for specific references for fictional and nonfictional books on persons with hearing losses.)

In addition, if an educational interpreter will be providing services in the classroom, it is important to introduce him or her to the class and to explain his or her role. Salend and Longo (1994) recommend that the teacher explains that the interpreter is in the room to facilitate communication. If class members understand this responsibility, they may feel more comfortable with having the interpreter assist them in conversing with students with hearing impairment. It is also important that all students understand that the interpreter's role does not include assisting with assignments and tests, tutoring, or monitoring behavior.

TEACHING TECHNIQUES TO TRY

Students who are mainstreamed can be expected to follow the regular curriculum if they have the prerequisite skills (Ross, Brackett, & Maxon, 1991). Students with hearing losses, however, may require modifications of the physical, instructional, and social environments to benefit fully from education in the mainstream.

Modifying the Physical Environment

Modifications of the physical environment may involve simple changes in seating, such as moving students away from sources of background noise like open windows and doors and noisy heating and cooling systems (Ross, 1982). Adapting seating arrangements so students are located in the front of the room with their chairs or desks turned slightly so they can see the faces of all the other students, permitting free movement around the classroom to reduce the distance between themselves and the speakers, and using flexible seating arrangements that allow students to change seats as activities change promote understanding and participation in class activities (Ross, 1982). In addition, arranging desks in a staggered pattern, rather than in straight rows, enables the bodies of students to further reduce reflected sound and improves the acoustics of the classroom (Gearheart, Weishahn, & Gearheart, 1992).

Teachers and administrators should also consider school factors that influence the learning environment for students with hearing impairments. For example, students should be placed in classrooms that are not adjacent to cafeterias, gymnasiums, playgrounds, and loading docks—areas that tend to have high noise levels, which may prevent optimal learning. Similarly, if possible open classroom arrangements should be avoided, in which there are no walls between teaching groups and noise travels from one area to another (Flexer, 1994).

Modifying the Instructional Environment

Instructional modifications also can enhance the learning of students who are hearing impaired. Using teaching formats that include exhibits, demonstrations, experiments, and simulations provides hands-on experiences that tend to promote understanding and are easier to follow than lectures and whole-class discussions. Writing directions in short, simple sentences and using pictures to illustrate the procedure or process supplements the oral explanations you give during demonstrations (Waldron, Diebold, & Rose, 1985).

When you do use lecture and discussion formats, promote understanding (Kampfe, 1984; Palmer, 1988; Ross et al., 1991) by:

- positioning yourself so your face is illuminated even when the room is darkened to show slides or videotapes
- using an overhead projector to note important points, key words, directions, and assignments so you can face students while speaking
- providing lecture notes or outlines
- avoiding moving around the room and turning your back to students when speaking so they can see your face
- shortening and simplifying verbalizations
- repeating main points or paraphrasing them into a simpler forms
- repeating questions and answers given by other students
- providing summaries throughout lectures or discussions
- using nonverbal cues, such as facial expressions, body movements, and gestures
- signaling changes in topic within lectures or discussions
- calling speakers' names to reduce time spent locating sources of speech
- requiring students to raise hands to reduce the noise and confusion that results when several people are talking at once
- checking student comprehension of instruction often

In addition to modifying oral communication, educators also emphasize the importance of adapting written materials because the "best instructional format with deaf students. . . is predominately pictorial with some. . . verbal information" (Waldron, et al., 1985, p. 40). Adapting materials by using visual displays, such as diagrams, pictures, graphs, and flowcharts reduces language and reading demands.

Ross and his colleagues (1991) pinpoint specific difficulties students with hearing impairment may experience in school subjects and offer the following suggestions for modifications:*

*Adapted with permission from *Assessment and management of mainstreamed hearing-impaired children: Principles and practices,* by M. Ross, D. Brackett, and A. B. Maxon, 1991, Austin, TX: Pro-Ed.

Subject Situation	Difficulty	Modifications
Language-based subjects (e.g., social studies, English)	1. Student's daily work is poor. 2. Student's performance is poor on comprehension questions, although he or she reads well. 3. Student repeats an answer already given by another student.	1. Review or preview concepts. 2. Preview vocabulary. 3. Enhance comprehension (e.g., DRTA, see p. 346; provide study guides; use reciprocal teaching, see p. 186. 4. Aim the microphone at the student who is responding. 5. Repeat questions and answers given by other students.
Spelling	1. Student's performance on tests is poor even after studying. 2. Student has words on spelling test numbered incorrectly.	1. Encourage students to study how words sound as well as how they are spelled. 2. When testing, state the word, use it in context, and then restate the word. 3. When testing, stand near the child or use an FM system. 4. During testing, pause so that the student can look up before you state "Number 5 is . . ."
Independent classwork	1. Student asks for teacher's help frequently. 2. Student does not know what to do on his or her own. 3. Student does not complete work.	1. Establish a routine for requesting help (e.g., raise hand; circle then skip problem and continue with those that can be done; assign a "study buddy"). 2. Teach vocabulary used in written and oral directions. 3. Follow directions with an example.
Group projects/work	1. Student is not selected for groups. 2. Student does not participate.	1. Assign all students to groups. 2. Assign each group member a specific role (e.g., recorder, encourager, reporter). 3. Select activities that require all students to participate.

Subject Situation	Difficulty	Modifications
Test taking	1. Student's performance on tests is poor. 2. Student does wrong page. 3. Student asks several questions regarding what is expected.	1. Give tests outside class and provide extended time. 2. Write questions that are short and succinct and expressed in simple vocabulary. 3. Ask student to demonstrate that he or she understands the assignment and directions (e.g., ask to repeat, ask to complete a sample item).

You can also make general instruction modifications that will enhance the learning of students who are hearing impaired. Regardless of the teaching format you use, you should follow a preview, teach, and review cycle (Flatley & Gittinger, 1990; Ross et al., 1991). Several preview strategies are available. For example, *word maps* are graphic representations that encourage students to integrate their background knowledge as they learn new vocabulary and concepts (Wisconsin Department of Public Instruction, 1989). When the teacher completes word maps as a prereading activity with the entire class, he or she allows students to pool their prior knowledge. In addition, word maps provide students with more useful information than simple definitions because they specify attributes and provide examples.

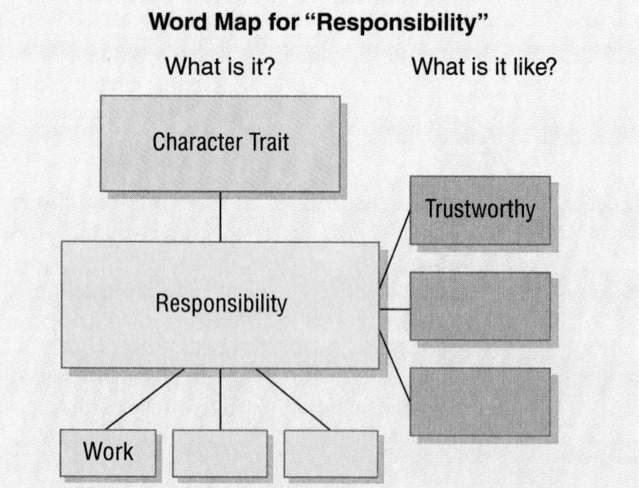

(*Source:* From *Strategic learning in the content areas,* by Wisconsin Department of Public Instruction, 1989, Madison, WI: Wisconsin Department of Public Instruction.) Used with permission.

A second strategy involves *categorizing* ideas (Flatley & Gittinger, 1990). Like word maps, this strategy activates prior knowledge—in this case, by asking students to brainstorm a list of words they associate with the concept or topic under study. Once the list has been completed, the students and teacher define the words, group them by category, and then label the categories. Like graphic organization, categorization provides a framework with which students can organize information. In fact, many teachers arrange the words on large charts to create graphic organizers of concepts or topics.

A third preview strategy, *directed reading thinking activity (DRTA),* guides students to activate their prior knowledge, predict outcomes, and establish a purpose for reading before they actually begin to read (Wisconsin Department of Public Instruction, 1989). First, the teacher asks students to look at the title of the passage or at an introductory picture, then they consider what they already know about the topic or event. Again, this sharing of ideas permits students to benefit from all class members' previous experience. Next, the teacher encourages students to predict what the selection will be about and to provide evidence to support their predictions. Finally, students are directed to read to confirm or reject their predictions.

Modifying the Social Environment

Just as previewing helps students access prior knowledge, organize new information, and integrate it with existing knowledge, so *reviewing* reinforces new vocabulary and concepts. Student tutors can assist in the review process, and pupils with hearing impairments may benefit socially as well as academically from tutoring by classmates. Tutors can provide additional examples, practice, and clarification, as needed. Also, tutors can help prepare students with hearing impairments for quizzes and coach them in test-taking strategies.

Peers also can function as note takers because students with hearing impairment cannot read signs and write simultaneously. In selecting note takers, Salend and Longo (1994) recommend that teachers consider students who demonstrate content mastery, note-taking skill, sensitivity toward students with disabilities, and independence. Teachers can facilitate the note-taking process by providing carbonless paper or by xeroxing the notes.

In addition to these classroom arrangements that promote social interactions among nonhearing and hearing students, some schools offer American Sign Language (ASL) as a foreign language alternative. The desired purpose of doing so is to increase the modes of communication that all students have in common and thus expand the social interactions that occur among students.

Recently, school systems have begun to employ educational interpreters to facilitate communication among students with hearing impairment, teachers, and others in the classroom and school. A report of the National Task Force on Educational Interpreting (Stuckless, Avery, & Harwitz, 1989) outlines the appropriate roles for these interpreters within mainstream classes:

1. The primary responsibility of educational interpreters is to facilitate communication between deaf persons and others in schools.
2. This role may include interpreting during out-of-class activities, such as field trips, club meetings, and sporting events.
3. In addition, educational interpreters can be expected to participate in planning meetings with classroom teachers. During these meetings, they coordinate plans for the student with hearing impairment by discussing course content, lesson plans, and

upcoming tests. Educational interpreters also need preparation time to preview instructional materials and to become oriented to the content and vocabulary.

4. Expanded responsibilities of tutoring, sign language instruction, and general classroom assistance may be provided by educational interpreters.

The task force report reminds teachers that "educational interpreters should not be asked to assume responsibilities for duties for which they do not have the needed training and/or background knowledge" (p. 9). With this recommendation in mind, teachers should not ask educational interpreters to provide formal instruction or classroom supervision. However, interpreters may inform teachers about students who are experiencing difficulties with content and provide information regarding students' progress to educational teams (Kluwin, Moores, & Gaustad, 1992).

Many educators strongly recommend that the specialist trained in hearing impairment, the classroom teacher, the educational interpreter, and the student meet at the beginning of the semester to discuss their roles and responsibilities in detail (LeBuffe, 1988; Salend & Longo, 1994).

HELPFUL RESOURCES

Instructional Methods

Andrews, J. E., & Mason, J. M. (1991). Strategy usage among deaf and hearing readers. *Exceptional Children, 57,* 536–545.

Berry, V. (1992). Communication priorities and strategies for the mainstreamed child with hearing loss. *Volta Review, 94*(1), 29–36.

Brackett, D. (1990). Communication management of the mainstreamed hearing impaired student. In M. Ross (Ed.), *Hearing impaired children in the mainstream* (pp. 119–130). Parkton, MD: York Press.

Christensen, K. M (1993). A multicultural approach to education of children who are deaf. In K. M. Christensen & G. L. Delgado (Eds.), *Multicultural issues in deafness* (pp. 17–27). New York: Longman.

Church, G., Glennen, S. (Eds.). (1993). *The handbook of assistive technology.* San Diego: Singular.

Conway, L. (1990). Issues relating to classroom management. In M. Ross (Ed.), *Hearing impaired children in the mainstream* (pp. 131–157). Parkton, MD: York Press.

Flexer, C. (1994). *Facilitating hearing and listening in young children.* San Diego: Singular.

French, M. (1992). Grammar and meaning in a whole language framework. *Perspectives in Education and Deafness, 10,* 19–24.

French, M. (1994). Spelling in the real world. *Perspectives in Education and Deafness, 12,* 18–22.

Gjerdingen, D., & Manning, F. D. (1991). Adolescents with profound hearing impairments in mainstreamed education: The Clarke Model. *Volta Review, 93,* 139–148.

Hammond, L. B. (1991). *FM auditory trainers: A winning choice for students, teachers, and parents.* Hopkins, MN: Hearing Resources.

Lindsay, J. D. (Ed.). (1993). *Computers and exceptional individuals* (2nd ed.). Austin, TX: Pro-Ed.

Loera, P. A., & Meichenbaum, D. (1993). The potential contribution of cognitive behavior modification for literacy training for deaf students. *American Annals of the Deaf, 138, 87–95.*

Luckner, J. (1994). Developing independent and responsible behaviors in students who are deaf and hard of hearing. *Teaching Exceptional Children, 26,* 13–17.

Luetke-Stahlman, B. (1994). Research-based language intervention strategies adapted for deaf and hard of hearing children. *American Annals of the Deaf, 138,* 404–410.

Luetke-Stahlman, B., & Luckner, J. (1991). *Effectively educating students with hearing impairments.* White Plains, NY: Longman.

Mangiardi, A. (1993). *A child with a hearing loss in your classroom? Don't panic: A guide for teachers.* Washington, DC: Alexander Graham Bell Association.

Maxon, A., & Brackett, D. (1992). *The hearing impaired child: Infancy through high school years.* Boston: Andover Medical Publishers.

Moore, M. S., & Levitan, L. (Eds.). (1993). *For hearing people ONLY: Answers to some of the most commonly asked questions about the deaf community, its culture, and the "deaf reality."* Rochester, NY: Deaf Life Press.

Moseley, K. A., & Moseley, P. L. (1994). The TTY: A tool for inclusion. *Perspective in Education and Deafness, 13,* 10–11, 18.

Nussbaum, D. (1988). *There's a hearing impaired child in my class.* Washington, DC: Gallaudet University Press.

Paul, P. V., & Quigley, S. P. (1994). *Language and deafness* (2nd ed.). San Diego: Singular.

Rees, T. (1992). Students with hearing impairments. In L. G. Cohen (Ed.), *Children with exceptional needs in regular classrooms* (pp. 98–117). Washington, DC: National Education Association.

Reynolds, K. E. (1994). Dialog journals. *Perspectives for teachers of the hearing impaired, 12,* 8–25.

Rittenhouse, R. K., & Freeman, S. (1991). Building vocabulary: Tools for reading. *Perspective in Education and Deafness, 10,* 16–19.

Ross, M. (1992). *FM auditory training systems, characteristics, selection, and use.* Parkston, MD: York Press.

Ross, M. (Ed.). (1990). *Hearing-impaired children in the mainstream.* Parkston, MD: York Press.

Ross, M., Brackett, D., & Maxon, A. B. (1991). *Assessment and management of mainstreamed hearing-impaired children: Principles and practices.* Austin, TX: Pro-Ed.

Schleper, D. R. (1993). Whole language works—and I've got proof. *Perspectives for teachers of the hearing impaired, 11,* 10–15.

Shirmer, B. R. (1994). *Language and literacy development in children who are deaf.* New York: Merrill/Macmillan.

Curricular and Instructional Materials

Bornstein, H., & Saulnier, K. L. (1987). *Sign/word flash cards.* Washington, DC: Gallaudet University Press.

Cowen, N. (1986). *Preparing for work.* Washington, DC: Gallaudet University Press.

Fitz-Gerald, M. (1986). *Information on sexuality for young people and their families.* Washington, DC: Gallaudet College (ERIC Document Reproduction Service No. ED 294–407).

Gillespie, S. (1988). *Science curriculum guide: Kendall Demonstration Elementary School* (2nd ed.). Washington, DC: Gallaudet College (ERIC Document Reproduction Service No. ED 298–741).

Hafer, J. C., & Wilson, R. (1990). *Come sign with us.* Washington, DC: Clere Books.

Introduction to communication. (1986). Washington, DC: Outreach, Pre-College Programs, Gallaudet College (ERIC Document Reproduction Service No. ED 298–746).

Kurlychek, K. (1991). *Software to go.* Washington, DC: Gallaudet University Press (this catalog lists and describes commercial software that may be borrowed by educators of students with hearing impairments).

Lane, L. G. (1990). *Gallaudet survival guide to signing* (2nd ed.). Washington, DC: Gallaudet University Press.

Pucciarelli, C. S. (Ed.). (1987). *Curriculum for mainstreamed preschool children who are hearing impaired.* Westbury, NY: Nassau County Board of Cooperative Educational Services (ERIC Document Reproduction Service No. ED 299–778).

Simko, C. B. (1986). *Wired for sound: An advanced student workbook on hearing and hearing aids.* Washington, DC: Kendall Green Publications, Gallaudet University Press (designed for high school students; 18 lessons examine topics such as how hearing aids help and how to take care of a hearing aid).

Sunal, D. W., & Sunal, C. S. (1981). *Teachers guide for science—adapted for the hearing impaired: Introduction and Levels 3–7.* Morgantown, WV: West Virginia University (ERIC Document Reproduction Service No. ED JUNRIE).

Curricular guides and materials designed for students who are hearing impaired are available for several subject areas from the bookstore at Gallaudet University. For a free catalogue of current offerings, write or call: Gallaudet Bookstore, P.O. Box 103, Washington, DC 20002, (202) 651–5380. Lists of captioned videotapes are also available from the Gallaudet bookstore.

Captioned films that address subjects such as business, English, mathematics, and career education are available from: Modern Talking Picture Service, Captioned Films Division, 500 Park Street, St. Petersburg, FL 33709, (800) 237–6213.

Literature about Individuals with Hearing Impairment

Elementary

Andrews, J. F. *The flying fingers club mystery series.* Washington, DC: Gallaudet University Press.

Andrews, J. F. (1992). *Hasta leugo, San Diego.* Washington, DC: Gallaudet University Press. (Ages 9–12) (Fiction = F)

Aseltine, L., & Mueller, E. (1986). *I'm deaf and it's okay.* New York: Albert Whitman. (Ages 5–8) (F)

Bove, L. (1980). *Sesame street sign language fun.* New York: Random House (Nonfiction = NF)

Bornstein, H., & Saulnier, K. L. (1990). *Little Red Riding Hood.* Washington, DC: Gallaudet University Press (signed English drawings to help children with language skills).

Bridges, C. (1980). *The hero.* Northridge, CA: Joyce Media. (F)

Chaplin, S. (1986). *I can sign my ABCs.* Washington, DC: Gallaudet University Press. (Juvenile) (NF)

Crowley, J. (1981). *The silent one.* New York: Knopf. (Ages 9–12) (F)

Curtis, P. (1981). *Cindy a hearing ear dog.* New York: E. P. Dutton. (NF)

Guccione, L. D. (1989). *Tell me how the wind sounds.* New York: Scholastic. (Ages 9–12) (F)

Hess, L. (1985). *The good luck dog.* New York: Scribner's. (F)

Hlibok, B. (1981). *Silent dancer.* New York: Messner. (Ages 9–12) (NF)

King Midas with selected sentences in American Sign Language. (1990). Washington, DC: Gallaudet University Press.

Levi, D. H. (1989). *A very special friend.* Washington, DC: Kendall Green Publications. (F)

Pollock, P. (1982). *Keeping it secret.* New York: Putnam. (Ages 9–12) (F)

Riskind, M. (1981). *Apple is my sign.* Boston: Houghton Mifflin. (Ages 9–12) (F)

Starowitz, A. M. (1988). *The day we met Cindy.* Washington, DC: Gallaudet University Press. (Ages 5–8) (F)

Secondary

Albronda, M. (1980). *Douglas Tilden: Portrait of a deaf sculptor.* Silver Springs, MD: T. J. Publications. (Ages 16–18) (NF)

Batson, T., & Bergman, E. (Eds.). (1985). *Angels and outcasts: An anthology of deaf characters in literature.* Washington, DC: Gallaudet University Press. (Ages 16–Adult) (NF)

Bragg, B. (1989). *Lessons in laughter: The autobiography of a deaf actor* (as signed to E. Bergman). Washington, DC: Gallaudet University Press. (Ages 13–Adult) (NF)

Carroll, C. (1992). *Clerc: The story of his early years.* Washington, DC: Gallaudet University Press. (Ages 13–15) (NF)

Clark, M. G. (1980). *Who stole Kathy Young?* New York: Dodd, Mead. (Ages 13–15) (F)

Fletcher, L. (1987). *Ben's story: A deaf child's right to sign.* Washington, DC: Gallaudet University Press. (Ages 13–Adult) (NF)

Glick, F. P., & Pellman, D. R. (1982). *Breaking silence: A family grows with deafness.* Scottdale, PA: Harold Press. (Ages 13–18) (NF)

Hepper, C. (1992). *Seeds of disquiet: One deaf woman's experience.* Washington, DC: Gallaudet University Press. (16–Adult) (NF)

Hodge, L. L. (1987). *A season of change.* Washington, DC: Gallaudet University Press. (Ages 13–16) (F)

Holcomb, M., U Wood, S. (1989). *Deaf women: A parade through the decades.* San Diego: Dawn Sign Press. (Ages 13–Adult) (NF)

Jacobs, L. M. (1989). *A deaf adult speaks out.* Washington, DC: Gallaudet University Press. (Ages 16–Adult) (NF)

Lane, H. (1992). *The mask of benevolence: Disabling the deaf community.* New York: Knopf. (Ages 16–Adult) (NF)

Levinson, N. S. (1981). *World of her own.* New York: Harvey House. (Ages 13–15) (F)

Morganroth, B. (1981). *Will the real Renie Lake please stand up?* New York: Atheneum. (Ages 13–15) (F)

Quinn, P. (1991). *Matthew Pinkowski's special summer.* Washington, DC: Gallaudet University Press.

Ray, N. L. (1981). *There was this man running.* New York: Macmillan. (Ages 13–15) (F)

Rosen, L. (1984). *Just like everyone else.* New York: Harcourt Brace Jovanavich. (Ages 13–15) (F)

Sacks, O. (1989). *Seeing voices: A journey into the world of the deaf.* Berkeley: University of California Press. (Ages 16–Adult) (NF)

Schein, J. D. (1989). *A home among strangers: Exploring the deaf community in the United States.* Washington, DC: Gallaudet University Press. (Ages 16–Adult) (NF)

Schrader, S. L. (1995). *Silent alarm: On the edge with a deaf EMT.* (Ages 13–Adult) (NF)

Scott, V. M. (1986). *Belonging.* Washington, DC: Gallaudet University Press. (Ages 13–18) (F)

Zazove, P. (1994). *When the phone rings, my bed shakes: Memories of a deaf doctor.* Washington, DC: Gallaudet University Press.

Software

Adventures of Jimmy Jumper: Prepositions, Exceptional Children's Software, P.O. Box 487, Hays, KS 67601, (913) 625–9281. (Apple IIe).

Capitalization, Hartley Courseware, Inc., 3451 Dunkle Drive, Suite 200, Lansing, MI 48911–4216, (800) 247–1380. (Apple IIe; Apple IIGS).

Early Emerging Rules Series: Negation, Plurals, Prepositions, Laureate Learning Systems, Inc., 110 E. Spring Street, Winooski, VT 05404, (800) 562–6801. (Apple IIe; Apple IIGS; DOS).

Fingernumbers, James Stanfield, Co., P.O. Box 41058, Santa Barbara, CA 93140, (800) 421–6534. (Apple IIe; Apple IIGS).

Fingerspeller, James Stanfield, Co., P.O. Box 41058, Santa Barbara, CA 93140, (800) 421–6534. (Apple IIe; Apple IIGS).

Micro LADS, Laureate Learning Systems, Inc., 110 E. Spring Street, Winooski, VT 05404, (800) 562–6801. (Apple IIe; Apple IIGS; Macintosh; DOS).

Sign Language Quiz, Data Assist, 659 Lakeview Plaza Blvd., Suite H, Columbus, OH 43085, (614) 888–8088. (DOS).

Speech Viewer, (IBM; allows deaf or hearing impaired person to see voice on the screen, then attempt to match proper sounds).

Spell It Plus, Davidson and Associates, Inc., 19840 Pioneer Avenue, Torrance, CA 90503 (800) 545–7677. (Apple IIe; Apple IIGS; Macintosh; DOS) (Grades 3–9).

Stickeybear Reading, Optimum Resource, Inc., 5 Hiltech Lane, Hilton Head, SC 29926, (800) 327–1473. (Apple IIe; Apple IIGS; DOS).

Who, What, Where, Why? Hartley Courseware, Inc., 3451 Dunkle Drive, Suite 200, Lansing, MI 48911–4216, (800) 247–1380. (Apple IIe; Apple IIGS; DOS) (Grades 1–4).

Services

National Center for Law & Deafness, 800 Florida Avenue NE, Washington, DC 20002.

National Information Center on Deafness, Gallaudet University, 800 Florida Avenue NE, Washington, DC 20002, (202) 651–5051 (voice), (202) 651–5053 (TDD).

National Institute on Deafness and Other Communication Disorders Clearinghouse, P.O. Box 37777, Washington, DC 20013–777.

Postsecondary programs for deaf students in the United States. (1992). *American Annals of the Deaf, 137,* 182–191.

Schools and programs for deaf students in the United States. (1992). *American Annals of the Deaf, 137,* 102–167.

Supportive and rehabilitative programs for the deaf in the United States. (1992). *American Annals of the Deaf, 137,* 214–239.

Organizations

American Graham Bell Association for the Deaf, 3417 Volta Place NW, Washington, DC 20007.

American Society for Deaf Children, 814 Thayer Avenue, Silver Spring, MD 20910, (310) 587–1788 (voice/TDD).

National Association for the Deaf, 814 Thayer Avenue, Silver Spring, MD 20910, (301) 587–1788.

National Foundation for Children's Hearing Education and Research, 928 McLean Avenue, Yonkers, NY 10704, (914) 237–2676.

Self-Help for Hard of Hearing People, 7800 Wisconsin Avenue, Bethesda, MD 20814, (301) 657–2248.

BIBLIOGRAPHY FOR TEACHING SUGGESTIONS

Dilka, K. L. (1984). The professions and others who work with the hearing-impaired child in school. In R. H. Hull & K. L. Dilka (Eds.), *The hearing-impaired child in school* (pp. 69–82). Orlando, FL: Grune & Stratton.

Flatley, J. K., & Gittinger, D. J. (1990). Teaching abstract concepts: Keys to the world of ideas. *Perspectives for Teachers of the Hearing Impaired, 8,* 7–9.

Flexer, C. (1994). *Facilitating hearing and listening in young children.* San Diego: Singular.

Gearheart, B. R., Weishahn, M. W., & Gearheart, C. J. (1992). *The exceptional student in the regular classroom* (5th ed.). New York: Merrill/Macmillan.

Jaussi, K. R. (1991). Drawing the outsiders in: Deaf students in the mainstream. *Perspectives for Teachers of the Hearing Impaired, 9,* 12–15.

Kampfe, C. M. (1984). Mainstreaming: Some practical suggestions for teachers and administrators. In R. H. Hull & K. O. Dilka (Eds.), *The hearing-impaired child in school* (pp. 99–112). Orlando, FL: Grune & Stratton.

Kluwin, T. N., Moores, D. F., & Gaustad, M. G. (1992). *Toward effective public school programs for deaf students.* New York: Teachers College Press.

LeBuffe, A. R. (1988). A clarification of the roles and responsibilities of teachers, students, and interpreters in a mainstream setting. *Perspectives for Teachers of the Hearing Impaired, 6,* 5–7.

Maxon, A. B., & Brackett, D. (1992). *The hearing impaired child infancy through high-school years.* Boston: Andover Medical Publishers.

Palmer, L. (1988). Speechreading as communication. *Volta Review, 90,* 33–42.

Robinson, E. B. (1984). Hamilton P.S.: An alternative that's working. *Perspectives for Teachers of the Hearing Impaired, 3,* 11–12.

Ross, M. (1982). *Hard of hearing children in regular schools.* Englewood Cliffs, NJ: Prentice Hall.

Ross, M., Brackett, D., & Maxon, A. B. (1991). *Assessment and management of mainstreamed hearing-impaired children.* Austin, TX: Pro-Ed.

Salend, S. J., & Longo, M. (1994). The roles of the educational interpreter in mainstreaming. *Teaching Exceptional Children, 26,* 22–28.

Stuckless, E. R., Avery, J. C., & Hurwitz, T. A. (Eds.). (1989). *Educational interpreting for deaf students: Report of the National Task Force on Educational Interpreting.* Rochester, NY: National Technical Institute for the Deaf.

Waldron, M. B., Diebold, T. J., & Rose, S. (1985). Hearing impaired students in regular classrooms: A cognitive model for educational services. *Exceptional Children, 52,* 39–43.

White, N. A. (1981). The role of the regular classroom teacher. In V. J. Froehlinger (Ed.), *Today's hearing-impaired child: Into the mainstream of education* (pp. 108–127). Washington, DC: Alexander Graham Bell Association for the Deaf.

Wisconsin Department of Public Instruction. (1989). *Strategic learning in the content areas.* Madison, WI: Author.

SUMMARY

In defining *hearing impairment,* educators are concerned primarily with the extent to which the hearing loss affects the ability to speak and understand spoken language. They refer to people with hearing impairment who cannot process linguistic information as *deaf* and those who can as *hard of hearing.* In addition, those who are deaf at birth or before language develops are referred to as having *prelingual deafness,* and those who acquire their deafness after spoken language starts to develop are referred to as having *postlingual deafness.* Professionals favoring a physiological viewpoint define deaf children as those who cannot hear sounds at or above a certain intensity level; they call others with hearing impairment "hard of hearing." Many people who are deaf resent being defined as "disabled" at all; they prefer to be considered a cultural or language minority.

The three most commonly used types of tests for hearing acuity are pure-tone audiometry, speech audiometry, and specialized tests for very young and hard-to-test children. The examiner uses pure tones or speech to find the intensity of sound (measured in decibels) the person can hear at different frequency levels (measured in Hertz). Audiologists often test very young children, using play, reflex, or evoked-response audiometry. During the first three months of life, hearing can be measured by changes in heartrate and sucking reflexes in response to auditory stimuli.

Professionals often classify causes of hearing loss according to the location of the problem within the hearing mechanism. *Conductive* losses are impairments that interfere with transferral of sound along the conductive pathway of the ear. *Sensorineural* problems are confined to the complex inner ear and are apt to be more severe and harder to treat.

Impairments of the outer ear are caused by such things as infections of the external canal or tumors. Middle-ear troubles usually occur because of some malfunction of one or more of the three tiny bones called ossicles in the middle ear. Otitis media, a condition stemming from eustachian tube malfunctioning, is the most common problem of the middle ear. The most common inner-ear troubles are linked to hereditary factors. Acquired hearing losses of the inner ear include those due to bacterial infections (such as meningitis), viral infections (such as mumps and measles), prenatal infections of the mother (such as cytomegalovirus, maternal rubella, and syphilis), and deprivation of oxygen at birth.

Impairment of hearing ability can have a profound effect on people, largely because of the emphasis on spoken language in U. S. society. In the past, because they held to the notion that language is the equivalent of thought, professionals believed that deafness led to intellectual inferiority. Researchers now question the theory that thought is dependent on language. Furthermore, authorities now recognize that sign language is as true a language as spoken language. They recommend that people who are deaf be tested in sign language and/or with nonverbal tests of intelligence.

In general, the academic achievement of students with hearing impairment is very low. Even in math, their best academic area, they demonstrate severe underachievement. Several studies have shown that children who are deaf who have parents who are deaf have higher reading achievement than children who are deaf who have hearing parents. This is probably because parents who are deaf are able to communicate more easily with their children through sign language.

Because of problems finding people with whom to communicate, students who are deaf are at risk for loneliness. This problem is particularly acute in mainstream settings, in which there are few students with hearing impairment with whom to communicate. Some authorities also believe that students who are deaf who have hearing parents may experience more unhappiness because of the difficulty they have in communicating with their parents.

Because of these problems in communicating with the larger society, many people who are deaf socialize almost exclusively with others who have hearing impairment. At one time, many professionals viewed this tendency toward isolation as negative. More and more authorities are pointing out the potential benefits of a Deaf culture. The Deaf culture is built on six features: linguistic differentiation, attitudinal deafness, behavioral norms, endogamous marriage patterns, historical awareness, and voluntary organizational networks.

Some believe that the cultural status of students who are deaf is vulnerable because of the current emphasis on mainstreaming in the schools. Deaf activists have increasingly decried what they consider to be an oppressive medical educational establishment.

For many years, there were two basic approaches to teaching students with hearing impairment: oralism and manualism. Today, most educators of students who are deaf favor *total communication,* a blend of oralism and manualism. Most educators who use total communication stress the auditory—verbal approach, speechreading, and signing English systems.

Signing English systems are not true languages, in that they follow the same word order of spoken English. Proponents of American Sign Language (ASL) argue that it is a grammatically sophisticated, highly evolved language of its own. Moreover, these proponents believe that deaf children should be proficient in ASL and that their education should be based on bilingual models.

Students with hearing impairment can be found in a variety of settings, ranging from inclusion in general education classrooms to residential settings. An increase in mainstreaming has been viewed with skepticism by many in the Deaf community and other professionals.

Numerous technological advances are helping persons with hearing loss. These innovations are occurring primarily in the areas of hearing aids, television, telephones, computer-assisted instruction (CAI), and the "information superhighway."

There are now many programs for infants and preschoolers with hearing impairment. Research indicates that the families of children who are deaf who have hearing parents may be in greater need of intervention than are families of children who are deaf who have parents who are also deaf. One reason for this is that hearing parents generally are not proficient in ASL, which is difficult to learn quickly.

In addition to Gallaudet University and the National Technical Institute for the Deaf, which focus on the education of students who are hearing impaired, there are now several postsecondary programs for students with hearing impairment. Deaf students enrolled in traditional colleges can take advantage of the increasing presence of sign language interpreters and other university programs. Transition programming for students who do not intend to take part in postsecondary programs is also expanding. Unemployment and the number of persons who are overqualified for their jobs among people who are hearing impaired are still exceedingly high.

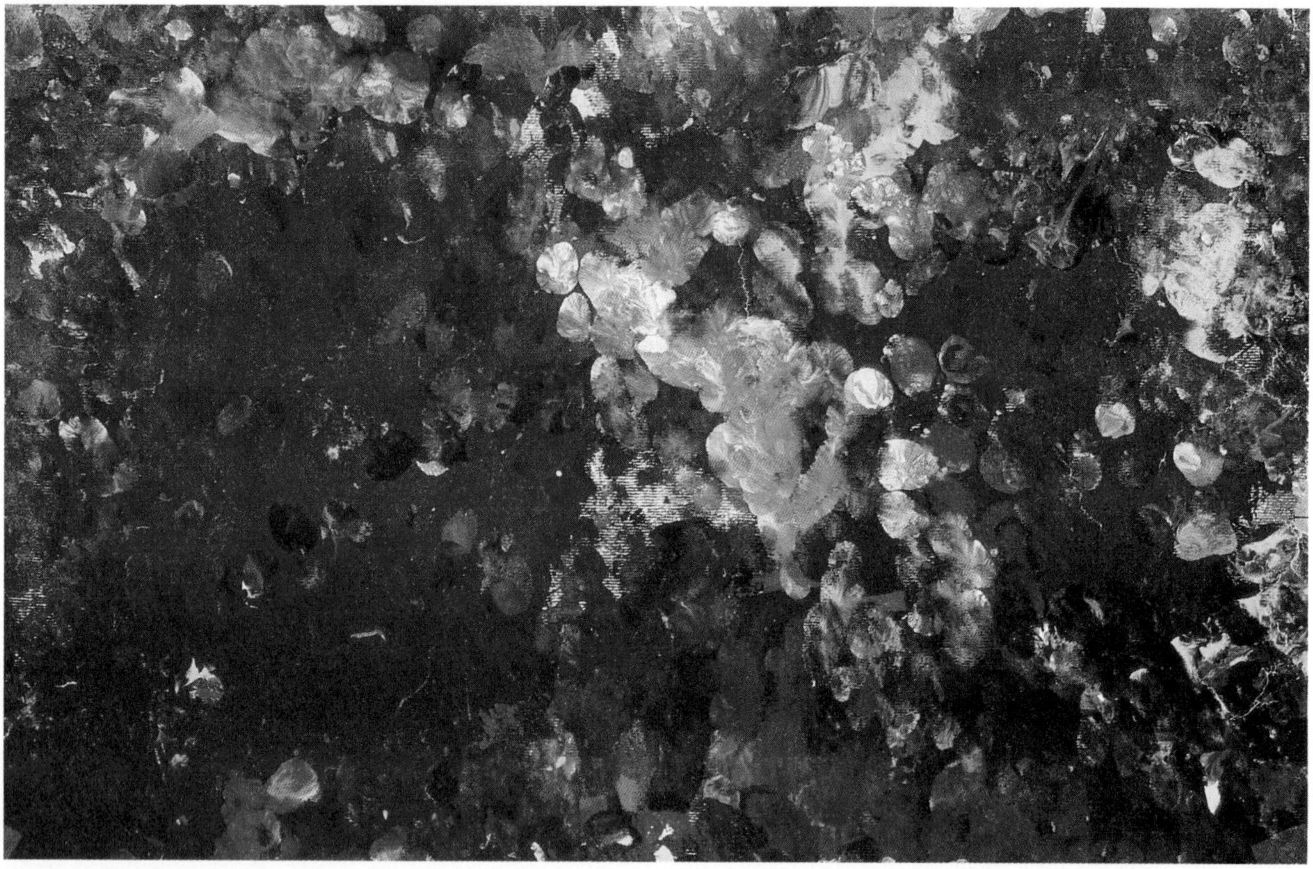

Fran Benson
Fran Benson is a 43-year-old painter with multiple disabilities who has been blind since birth. She is a talented pianist and often paints with her hands while listening to or humming music. She lives with her family in Canton, Massachusetts, and exhibits in the Boston area.

9

Visual Impairment

Jill: God, I can't find anything in my place. The ketchup usually winds up in my stocking drawer and my stockings are in the oven. If you really want to see chaos, come and look at . . . (She catches herself, self-consciously), I mean . . . I meant . . .

Don: I know what you mean. Relax. I'm no different from anyone else except that I don't see. The blindness is nothing. The thing I find hard to live with is other people's reactions to my blindness. If they'd only behave naturally. Some people want to assume guilt—which they can't because my mother has that market cornered—or they treat me as though I were living in some Greek tragedy, which I assure you I'm not. Just be yourself.

Jill: I'll try . . . but I've never met a blind person before.

Don: That's because we're a small, very select group—like Eskimos. How many Eskimos do you know?

Jill: I never thought blind people would be like you.

Don: They're not all like me. We're all different.

Jill: I mean... I always thought blind people were kind of . . . you know . . . spooky.

Don: (*In a mock-sinister voice*) But, of course. We sleep all day hanging upside-down from the shower rod. As soon as it's dark, we wake up and fly into people's windows. That's why they say, "Blind as a bat."

Leonard Gershe
Butterflies Are Free

Jill's discomfort with Don's blindness in the opening dialogue (see p. 353) is not that unusual. Visual impairments seem to evoke more awkwardness than most other disabilities. Why are we so uncomfortably aware of blindness? For one thing, blindness is *visible*. We often do not realize that a person has impaired hearing, for example, until we actually talk to him or her. The person with visual impairment, however, usually has a variety of symbols—cane, thick or darkened glasses, a guide dog.

Another possible reason for being self-conscious around people who are blind is the role that eyes play in social interaction. Poets, playwrights, and songwriters have long recognized how emotionally expressive the eyes can be for people who are sighted. We all know how uncomfortable it can be to talk with someone who does not make eye contact with us. Think how often we have heard someone say or have ourselves said that we prefer to talk "face to face" on an important matter, rather than over the telephone. We seem to rely a great deal on the expressiveness of people's eyes to judge how they are responding to what we are saying.

Also, research has shown that most of us have a special fear of blindness (Conant & Budoff, 1982). It is reportedly the third most feared condition, with only cancer and AIDS outranking it (Jernigan, 1992). One reason we may be so frightened of becoming blind is that our eyes seem so vulnerable. Our ears feel safely tucked away; eyes seem dangerously exposed. Another reason we fear loss of vision is that the sense of sight is linked so closely with the traditional concept of beauty. We derive great pleasure from our sight. Our feelings about others are often based largely on physical appearances that are visually perceived.

So, despite the fact that blindness is the least prevalent of all disabilities, people dread it. With a bit of reflection, however, it becomes obvious that our anxieties about blindness are irrational. Most of our apprehension can be attributed to our lack of experience in interacting with individuals with visual impairment. It is not until we talk to people with visual impairment or read about their appreciation of sounds, smells, and touch that we begin to realize that sight is not the only sense that enables us to enjoy beauty or interact socially with other people.

Like anyone with a disability, the person who is blind wants to be treated like everyone else. Most people who are blind do not seek pity or unnecessary help. In fact, they can be fiercely protective of their independence. As Don says in the introductory dialogue, "We're all different." In this chapter, we hope to change the idea that children with visual impairment are all alike in some odd way. We start by presenting a fact that most sighted people do not know: The majority of people who are blind can actually see.

DEFINITION AND CLASSIFICATION

The two most common ways of describing *visual impairment* are the legal and educational definitions. The former is the one laypeople and those in the medical professions use; the latter is the one educators favor.

Legal Definition

The legal definition of *visual impairment* involves assessment of visual acuity and field of vision. A person who is **legally blind** has visual acuity of 20/200 or less in the better eye even with correction (e.g., eyeglasses) or has a field of vision so narrow that its widest diameter subtends an angular distance no greater than 20 degrees. The fraction 20/200 means that the person sees at 20 feet what a person with normal vision

legally blind A person who has visual acuity of 20/200 or less in the better eye even with correction (e.g., eyeglasses) or has a field of vision so narrow that its widest diameter subtends an angular distance no greater than 20 degrees.

Misconceptions about Persons with Visual Impairment

Myth	Fact
Myth People who are legally blind have no sight at all.	**Fact** Only a small percentage of people who are legally blind have absolutely no vision. Many have a useful amount of functional vision.
Myth People who are blind have an extra sense that enables them to detect obstacles.	**Fact** People who are blind do not have an extra sense. Some can develop an "obstacle sense" by noting the change in pitch of echoes as they move toward objects.
Myth People who are blind automatically develop better acuity in their other senses.	**Fact** Through concentration and attention, individuals who are blind can learn to make very fine discriminations in the sensations they obtain. This is not automatic but rather represents a better use of received sensations.
Myth People who are blind have superior musical ability.	**Fact** The musical ability of people who are blind is not necessarily better than that of sighted people; however, many people who are blind pursue musical careers as one way in which they can achieve success.
Myth Braille is not very useful for the vast majority of people who are blind; it should only be tried as a last resort.	**Fact** Very few people who are blind have learned Braille, primarily due to fear that using it is a sign of failure and to an historical professional bias against it. Authorities acknowledge the utility of Braille for people who are blind.
Myth Braille is of no value for those who have low vision.	**Fact** Some individuals with low vision have conditions that will eventually result in blindness. More and more, authorities think that these individuals should learn Braille to be prepared for when they cannot read print effectively.
Myth If people with low vision use their eyes too much, their sight will deteriorate.	**Fact** Only rarely is this true. Visual efficiency can actually be improved through training and use. Wearing strong lenses, holding books close to the eyes, and using the eyes often cannot harm vision.
Myth Mobility instruction should be delayed until elementary or secondary school.	**Fact** Many authorities now recognize that even preschoolers can take advantage of mobility instruction, including the use of a cane.
Myth The long cane is a simply constructed, easy-to-use device.	**Fact** The National Academy of Sciences has drawn up specifications for the manufacture of the long cane and using it properly.
Myth Guide dogs take people where they want to go.	**Fact** The guide dog does not "take" the person anywhere; the person must first know where he or she is going. The dog is primarily a protection against unsafe areas or obstacles.

sees at 200 feet. (Normal visual acuity is thus 20/20.) The inclusion of a narrowed field of vision in the legal definition means that a person may have 20/20 vision in the central field but severely restricted peripheral vision. Legal blindness qualifies a person for certain legal benefits, such as tax advantages and money for special materials.

In addition to this medical classification of blindness, there is also a category referred to as *partially sighted.* According to the legal classification system, persons who are partially sighted have visual acuity falling between 20/70 and 20/200 in the better eye with correction.

Educational Definition

Many professionals, particularly educators, have found the legal classification scheme inadequate. They have observed that visual acuity is not a very accurate predictor of how people will function or use whatever remaining sight they have. Although a small percentage of individuals who are legally blind have absolutely no vision, the majority are able to see. For example, an extensive study of students who are legally blind found that only 18 percent were totally blind (Willis, 1976).

Many of those who recognize the limitations of the legal definition of blindness and partial sightedness favor the educational definition, which stresses the method of reading instruction. For educational purposes, individuals who are blind are so severely impaired they must learn to read Braille or use aural methods (audiotapes and records). (**Braille,** a system of raised dots by which blind people read with their fingertips, consists of quadrangular cells containing from one to six dots whose arrangement denotes different letters and symbols.) Educators often refer to those individuals with visual impairment who can read print, even if they need magnifying devices or large-print books, as having **low vision.**

Braille. A system in which raised dots are used to allow people who are blind to read with their fingertips; each quadrangular cell contains from one to six dots, whose arrangement denotes different letters and symbols.

low vision. A term used by educators to refer to individuals whose visual impairment is not so severe that they are unable to read print of some kind; they may read large or regular print, and they may need some kind of magnification.

cornea. A transparent cover in front of the iris and pupil in the eye; responsible for most of the refraction of light rays in focusing on an object.

aqueous humor. A watery substance between the cornea and lens of the eye.

PREVALENCE

Blindness is primarily an adult disability. Most estimates indicate that blindness is approximately one-tenth as prevalent in school-age children as in adults. Only about .05 percent of the population ranging from six to seventeen years of age is classified by the federal government as "visually impaired." This makes visual impairment one of the least prevalent disabilities in children.

ANATOMY AND PHYSIOLOGY OF THE EYE

The anatomy of the visual system is extremely complex, so our discussion here will focus just on basic characteristics. Figure 9–1 shows the functioning of the eye. The physical object being seen becomes an electrical impulse sent through the optic nerve to the visual center of the brain, the occipital lobes. Before reaching the optic nerve, light rays reflecting off the object being seen pass through several structures within the eye. The light rays:

1. pass through the **cornea** (a transparent cover in front of the iris and pupil), which performs the major part of the bending (refraction) of the light ray so that the image will be focused
2. pass through the **aqueous humor** (a watery substance between the cornea and lens of the eye)

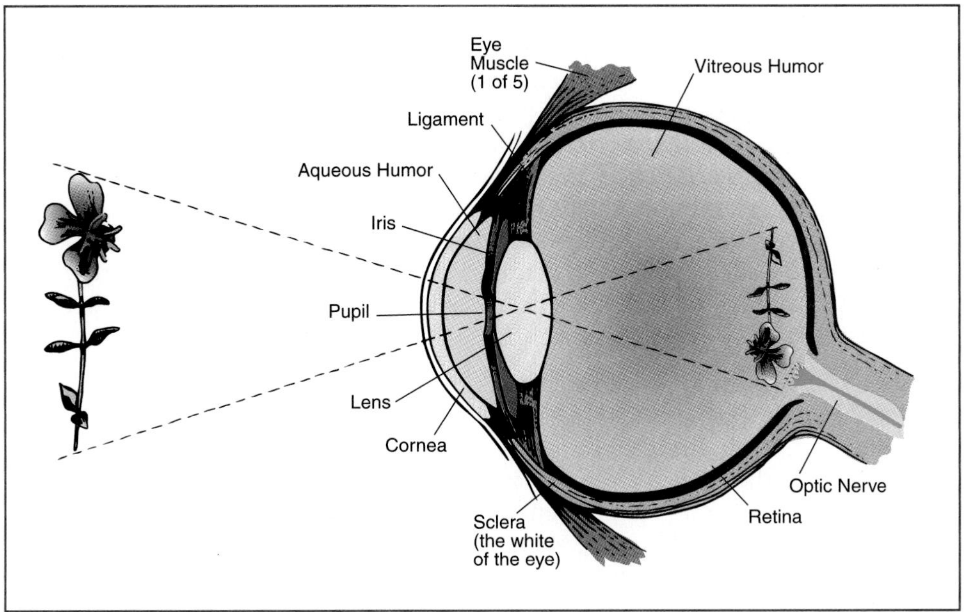

Figure 9–1

The basic anatomical features of the eye and the visual process.

3. pass through the **pupil** (the contractile opening in the middle of the **iris**, the colored portion of the eye that contracts or expands, depending on the amount of light striking it)
4. pass through the **lens**, which refines and changes the focus of the light rays before they pass through the **vitreous humor** (a transparent gelatinous substance that fills the eyeball between the retina and lens)
5. come to a focus on the **retina** (the back portion of the eye, containing nerve fibers connected to the optic nerve)

pupil. The contractile opening in the middle of the iris of the eye.

iris. The colored portion of the eye; contracts or expands, depending on the amount of light striking it.

lens. A structure that refines and changes the focus of the light rays passing through the eye.

vitreous humor. A transparent, gelatinous substance that fills the eyeball between the retina and the lens of the eye.

retina. The back portion of the eye, containing nerve fibers connected to the optic nerve.

Snellen chart. Used in determining visual acuity; consists of rows of letters or *E*s arranged in different positions; each row corresponds to the distance at which a normally sighted person can discriminate the letters; does not predict how accurately a child will be able to read print.

MEASUREMENT OF VISUAL ABILITY

Visual acuity is most often measured with the **Snellen chart**, which consists of rows of letters (for individuals who know the alphabet) or *E*s (for the very young and for those who cannot read). In the latter case, the *E*s are arranged in various positions, and the person's task is to indicate in what direction the "legs" of the *E*s are face. Each row corresponds to the distance at which a person with normal vision can discriminate the directions of the *E*s. (There are eight rows, one corresponding to each of the following distances: 15, 20, 30, 40, 50, 70, 100, and 200 feet.) People are normally tested at the 20 foot distance. If they can distinguish the direction of the letters in the 20 foot row, they are said to have 20/20 central visual acuity for far distances. If they can distinguish only the much larger letters in the 70 foot row, they are said to have 20/70 central visual acuity for far distances.

The Snellen chart is not very useful for predicting the ability to read print for at least two reasons:

1. It measures visual acuity for distant but not near objects—which is why it is necessary to report the results in terms of central visual acuity for *far* distances. Many educational activities, particularly reading, require visual acuity

at close distances, and there are a variety of methods available for measuring it. The results of some of these methods can be used to estimate what kinds of reading material the person will be able to read (e.g., store catalogs, children's books, or high school texts).

2. The Snellen chart is not very appropriate for predicting ability to read print because visual acuity does not always correspond with visual efficiency. **Visual efficiency** refers to the ability, for example, to control eye movement, discriminate objects from their background, and pay attention to important details. Barraga and colleagues have developed the Diagnostic Assessment Procedure (DAP) to assess visual efficiency (Barraga, 1983; Barraga & Collins, 1979) accompanied by a 150-lesson curriculum.

visual efficiency. A term used to refer to how well one uses his or her vision, including such things as control of eye movements, attention to visual detail, and discrimination of figure from background; believed by some to be more important than visual acuity alone in predicting a person's ability to function visually.

myopia. Nearsightedness; vision for distant objects is affected; usually results when the eyeball is too long.

hyperopia. Farsightedness; vision for near objects is affected; usually results when the eyeball is too short.

astigmatism. Blurred vision caused by an irregular cornea or lens.

There are screening procedures less time consuming than the DAP but more thorough than the Snellen (Rathgeber, 1981). Using these screening tests, teachers can identify children in need of more complete eye exams. Unfortunately, some schools use only the Snellen chart as a screening procedure. Because it does not pick up all possible types of visual problems, teachers should be alert to other signs that children might have visual impairment. The National Society for the Prevention of Blindness (1972) has listed a number of signs of possible eye problems (see the box below.).

CAUSES

The most common visual problems are the results of errors of refraction. **Myopia** (nearsightedness), **hyperopia** (farsightedness), and **astigmatism** (blurred vision) are all examples of refraction errors that affect central visual acuity. Although each can be serious enough to cause significant impairment (myopia and hyperopia are the most common impairments of low vision), wearing glasses or contact lenses usually can bring vision within normal limits.

Myopia results when the eyeball is too long. In this case, the light rays from the object in Figure 9–1 would be in focus in front of, rather than on, the retina. Myopia affects vision for distant objects, but close vision may be unaffected. When the eyeball

Signs Indicating Possible Eye Problems

BEHAVIOR

- rubs eyes excessively
- shuts or covers one eye, tilts head, or thrusts head forward
- has difficulty reading or doing other work requiring close use of the eyes
- blinks more than usual or is irritable when doing close work
- holds books close to the eyes
- is unable to see distant things clearly
- squints eyelids together or frowns

APPEARANCE

- crossed eyes
- red-rimmed, encrusted, or swollen eyelids
- inflamed or watery eyes
- recurring styes

COMPLAINTS

- eyes itch, burn, or feel scratchy
- cannot see well
- dizziness, headaches, or nausea following close eye work
- blurred or double vision

is too short, hyperopia (farsightedness) results. In this case, the light rays from the object in the diagram would be in focus behind, rather than on, the retina. Hyperopia affects vision for close objects, but far vision may be unaffected. If the cornea or lens of the eye is irregular, the person is said to have astigmatism. In this case, the light rays from the object in the figure would be blurred or distorted.

Among the most serious impairments are those caused by glaucoma, cataracts, and diabetes. These conditions occur primarily in adults, but each, particularly the latter two, can occur in children.

Glaucoma is a condition in which there is excessive pressure in the eyeball. Left untreated, the condition progresses to the point at which the blood supply to the optic nerve is cut off and blindness results. The cause of glaucoma is presently unknown (although it can be caused secondarily by other eye diseases), and its onset can be sudden or very gradual. Because its incidence increases dramatically after age thirty-five and because it can be prevented if detected early, it is often strongly recommended that *all* adults have periodic eye examinations after age thirty-five. A common complaint during the early stages of glaucoma is that lights appear to have halos around them (Thomas, 1985).

Cataracts are caused by a clouding of the lens of the eye, which results in blurred vision. In children, the condition is called *congenital cataracts*, and distance and color vision are seriously affected. Surgery can usually correct the problems caused by cataracts. Diabetes can cause **diabetic retinopathy,** a condition resulting from interference with the blood supply to the retina.

Several other visual impairments primarily affect children. Visual impairments of school-age children are often due to prenatal causes, many of which are hereditary. We have already discussed congenital (meaning present at birth) cataracts and glaucoma. Another congenital condition is **coloboma,** a degenerative disease in which the central and/or peripheral areas of the retina are not completely formed, resulting in impairment of the visual field and/or central visual acuity. Another prenatal condition is **retinitis pigmentosa,** a hereditary disease resulting in degeneration of the retina. Retinitis pigmentosa causes the person's field of vision to narrow. Also included in the "prenatal" category are infectious diseases that affect the unborn child, such as syphilis and rubella.

One of the most dramatic medical discoveries in the causes of blindness involved a condition now referred to as **retinopathy of prematurity (ROP)** (previously called *retrolental fibroplasia*). ROP, which results in scar tissue forming behind the lens of the eye, began to appear in the 1940s in premature infants. In the 1950s, researchers determined that excessive concentrations of oxygen often administered to premature infants was causing blindness. The oxygen was necessary to prevent brain damage, but it was often given at too high a level. Since then, hospitals have been careful to monitor the amount of oxygen administered to premature infants. When the cause of ROP was discovered, some authorities thought its occurrence would be drastically reduced, but this has not happened. In fact, there appears to be a resurgence of ROP (Bishop, 1991; Ferrell et al., 1990). With medical advances, many more premature babies are surviving, but they need very high levels of oxygen.

Two other conditions resulting in visual problems can be grouped because both are caused by improper muscle functioning. **Strabismus** is a condition in which one or both eyes are directed inward (crossed eyes) or outward. Left untreated, strabismus can result in permanent blindness because the brain will eventually reject signals from a deviating eye. Fortunately, most cases of strabismus are correctable with eye exercises or surgery. Eye exercises sometimes involve the person wearing a patch over

glaucoma. A condition of excessive pressure in the eyeball; the cause is unknown but if untreated, blindness results.

cataracts. A condition caused by clouding of the lens of the eye; affects color vision and distance vision.

diabetic retinopathy. A condition resulting from interference of the blood supply to the retina; the fastest-growing cause of blindness.

coloboma. A degenerative disease in which the central and/or peripheral areas of the retina are incompletely formed, resulting in impairment of the visual field and/or central visual acuity.

retinitis pigmentosa. A hereditary condition resulting in degeneration of the retina; causes a narrowing of the field of vision.

retinopathy of prematurity (ROP). A condition resulting from administration of an excessive concentration of oxygen at birth; causes scar tissue to form behind the lens of the eye; formerly referred to as retrolental fibroplasia.

strabismus. A condition in which the eyes are directed inward (crossed eyes) or outward.

Consider how people with certain visual impairments see the world: (a) Retinitis pigmentosa, a hereditary disease, causes a narrowing of the field of vision. (b) Cataracts create a haziness over the entire field of vision, causing images to appear out of focus.

(a)

(b)

the good eye for periods of time in order to force use of the eye that deviates. Surgery involves tightening or loosening the muscles that control eye movement. **Nystagmus** is a condition in which there are rapid involuntary movements of the eyes, usually resulting in dizziness and nausea. Nystagmus is sometimes a sign of brain malfunctioning and/or inner-ear problems.

PSYCHOLOGICAL AND BEHAVIORAL CHARACTERISTICS

Language Development

Most authorities believe that lack of vision does not have a very significant effect on the ability to understand and use language. They point to the many studies that show that students who are visually impaired do not differ from sighted students on verbal intelligence tests. Authorities also note that studies comparing the two groups have found no differences with regard to major aspects of language (McGinnis, 1981; Matsuda, 1984). Because auditory more than visual perception is the sensory modality through which we learn language, it is not surprising that studies have found that people who are blind are not impaired in language functioning. The child who is blind is still able to hear language and may even be more motivated than the sighted child to use language because it is the main channel through which he or she communicates with others.

However, there are a few subtle differences in the way in which language usually develops in children who are visually impaired compared to sighted children (Andersen, Dunlea, & Kekelis, 1984; Warren, 1984). The early language of children who are visually impaired tends to be somewhat restricted by lack of visual experiences. For example, whereas their language tends to be more self-centered, sighted children use language more readily to refer to activities involving other people and objects. Such differences are relatively subtle and do not indicate that children with blindness will lead a linguistically deficient existence. Nevertheless, it is a good idea to provide children who are blind with as rich an exposure to language as possible at as young an age as possible (Warren, 1984).

nystagmus. A condition in which there are rapid involuntary movements of the eyes; sometimes indicates a brain malfunction and/or inner-ear problems.

Intellectual Ability

Performance on Standardized Intelligence Tests. Samuel P. Hayes pioneered the intelligence testing of people who are blind (Hayes, 1942, 1950). He took verbal items from a commonly used IQ test of his time—the Stanford-Binet—to assess individuals with blindness. His rationale was that people without sight would not be disadvantaged by a test that relied on verbal items: therefore, this kind of test would be a more accurate measure of intelligence than tests containing items of a visual nature.

Since the work of Hayes, professionals have continued to use verbal IQ tests with individuals with visual impairment, but they have also emphasized the importance of measuring areas of intelligence related to spatial and tactual abilities. Many professionals advocate the use of intelligence tests that assess spatial and tactual skills because these abilities have a direct bearing on how well persons with visual impairment can traverse their environment and read Braille. Several intelligence tests that emphasize these nonverbal areas are now available in a few countries, such as the Blind Learning Aptitude Test (Newland, 1979) and Intelligence Test for Visually Impaired Children (Dekker, Drenth, Zaal, 1991; Dekker, Drenth, Zaal, & Koole, 1990).

At one time, it was popular for researchers to compare the intelligence of sighted persons with that of persons with blindness. Most authorities now believe that such comparisons are virtually impossible because finding comparable tests is so difficult (Warren, 1984). Using verbal tests is not entirely satisfactory because they exclude important performance areas. Some researchers have used performance tests with individuals with visual impairment and sighted individuals, while requiring the latter to wear blindfolds, but this is problematic because sighted individuals are unaccustomed to doing performance tasks without using their vision. From what is known, however, there is no reason to believe that blindness results in lower intelligence.

Conceptual Abilities. The same problems have also hindered research involving laboratory-type tasks of conceptual ability. Many researchers, using conceptual tasks originally developed by noted psychologist Jean Piaget, have concluded that children who are blind lag behind their sighted peers (e.g., Davidson, Dunn, Wiles-Kettenmann, & Appelle, 1981; Stephens & Grube, 1982). But these comparisons are questionable because, like comparisons on IQ tests, it is virtually impossible to find equivalent tasks for people with and without sight.

Nevertheless, some important differences exist between how those with and without sight perceive the world, most of which are due to the difference between tactual and visual experiences. Persons who are blind rely much more on tactual and auditory information to learn about the world than do those who are sighted, who obtain a great deal of information through sight. As one person who is blind described it, he "sees with his fingers" (Hull, 1990).

An important difference between individuals with and without sight is that the latter need to be much more vigilant in order to pick up information from their environment:

> For the sighted child, the world meets him halfway. What he sees encourages him to move further out into his environment and to explore it. He learns literally hundreds of thousands of things from observation, imitation, and identification, without any effort on his part or on the part of his parents or teachers. (Scott, 1982, p. 34)

Children with visual impairment need to take much more initiative in order to learn what they can from their environment. In addition, they apparently become adept at being able to obtain concepts through what they hear from others (Groenveld & Jan, 1992).

Little is known about the tactual sense of children who are blind and how best to develop it, but we do know that good tactual perception, like good visual perception, relies on being able to use a variety of strategies (Berlá, 1982; Griffin & Gerber, 1982). The child with blindness who compares a pencil and ruler, for example, by using such strategies as comparing the length of each to body parts and listening to differences in pitch when each is banged against a table will have an advantage in understanding the differences and similarities between these two objects. Research has shown that the earlier the child with visual impairment is trained to use such strategies, the more beneficial the training will be for his or her tactual development (Berlá, 1981).

We also know that the degree of visual impairment and the age of its onset are important determinants of how the child will explore his or her environment. Children whose blindness was present at birth will generally rely more on their tactual sense to learn about the world than will those who acquire their blindness later. Likewise, children who are totally blind will depend more on the tactual sense for concept development than will those with low vision.

Mobility

A very important ability for the successful adjustment of many people with visual impairment is their mobility—their skill in moving about in their environments. Mobility skills depend to a great extent on spatial ability.

The spatial abilities of persons who are blind continue to develop throughout childhood and adolescence; full development does not occur until well into the teenage years (Ochaita & Huertas, 1993). Authorities have identified two ways in which persons with visual impairment process spatial information—as a sequential route or as a map depicting the general relation of various points in the environment (Bigelow, 1991; Herman, Chatman, & Roth, 1983; Rieser, Guth, & Hill, 1982). The latter method, referred to as **cognitive mapping**, is preferable because it offers more flexibility in navigating. Consider three sequential points—A, B, and C. A sequential mode of processing spatial information restricts a person's movement so he or she can move from A to C only by way of B. But a person with a cognitive map of points A, B, and C can go from A to C directly without going through B.

cognitive mapping. A nonsequential way of conceptualizing the spatial environment that allows a person who is visually impaired to know where several points in the environment are simultaneously; allows for better mobility than does a strictly sequential conceptualization of the environment.

obstacle sense. A skill possessed by some people who are blind whereby they can detect the presence of obstacles in their environments; research has shown that it is not an indication of an extra sense, as popularly thought; it is the result of being able to detect subtle changes in the pitches of high-frequency echoes.

Mobility skills vary greatly among people with visual impairment. (And even the best of travelers who are blind occasionally run into problems in navigating; see the box on p. 363 for an account of how *not* to help someone who is blind when he or she is lost.) It is surprisingly difficult to predict which individuals will be the best travelers. For example, common sense seems to tell us that mobility would be better among those who have more residual vision and those who lose their vision later in life, but this is not always the case (McLinden, 1988; Warren, & Kocon, 1974). A critical variable appears to be *motivation*. Some authorities have noted that people who have more residual vision and those who become visually impaired later in life may tend to become more frustrated by their loss of vision and less motivated to acquire mobility skills.

Obstacle Sense. For some persons who are blind, the ability to detect physical obstructions in the environment is a large part of their mobility skills. Walking along the street, they often seem able to sense an object in their path. This ability has come to be known as the **obstacle sense**—an unfortunate term, in some ways, because many laypeople have taken it to mean that people who are blind somehow develop

How Not to Help a Person Who Is Blind and Lost

When people who are sighted encounter someone who is lost, their natural inclination is to ask the person where he or she is headed. As the following entry in the diary of John M. Hull (1990) indicates, this question can lead to confusion when the person lost happens to be blind.

Getting Lost **8 November**

I think it is David Scott Blackhall, in his autobiography *The Way I See Things* (London, Baker, 1971), who remarks how annoying he found it when people refused to answer his question about where he was and insisted on asking him where he was trying to get to. I share this experience.

Going home the other night I was turned out of my way by some construction work on one of the footpaths. By mistake I turned along a side street, and after a block or so, when I realized I had made a mistake somewhere, I was not sure exactly where I was. There were some chaps working on a car parked on the roadside. "Excuse me," I said. "Could you tell me please where I am? What is the name of this street?"

The chap replied, "Where are you trying to get to?"

With what I hoped was a good-humored laugh, I said, "Never mind about that, just tell me, please, what street this is?"

"This is Alton Road, You usually go up Bournbrook Road, don't you? It's just a block further along."

I thanked him, and explained that I needed now to know exactly whereabouts on Alton Road I was so that I could get to Bournbrook Road. "Which side of Alton Road am I on? If I face that way, am I looking towards Bristol Road or is it the other way?"

"You live high up Bournbrook Road, don't you? Well, if you take the next road to the left you'll be OK."

But which way is "left"? Does he mean me to cross the road or to stay on this side? At this point, the blind and sighted enter into mutual bafflement.

When a sighted person is lost, what matters to him or her is not where he is, but where he is going. When he is told that the building he is looking for lies in a certain direction, he is no longer lost. A sighted person is lost in the sense that he does not know where the building he is looking for is. He is never lost with respect to what street he is actually on; he just looks at the street sign on the corner of the block. It is his direction he has lost, rather than his position. The blind person lost has neither direction nor position. He needs position in order to discover direction. This is such a profound lostness that most sighted people find it difficult to imagine.

Source: From *Touching the rock*, by John M. Hull, pp. 144–145.

an extra sense. It is easy to see why this misconception exists. Even people who are blind have a very difficult time explaining the phenomenon (Hull, 1990). A number of experiments have shown that, with experience, people who are blind come to be able to detect subtle changes in the pitches of high-frequency echoes as they move toward objects. Actually, they are taking advantage of the **Doppler effect**, a physical principle that says the pitch of a sound rises as a person moves toward its source.

Although obstacle sense can be important for the mobility of someone without sight, by itself, it will not make its user a highly proficient traveler. It is merely an aid. Extraneous noises (traffic, speech, rain, wind) can render obstacle sense unusable. Also, it requires walking at a fairly slow speed to be able to react in time.

Doppler effect. A term used to describe the phenomenon of the pitch of a sound rising as the listener moves toward its source.

The Myth of Sensory Acuteness. Along with the myth that people with blindness have an extra sense is the general misconception that they automatically develop better acuity in their other senses. This is not true. People who are blind do not, for

American Boswell Drives into the Dark

DUDLEY DOUST ON A REMARKABLE PLAYER

After he had stooped to feel the texture of the grass, and finger the edge of the cup, Charley Boswell paced with his caddie across the green to his ball. He counted as he went . . . 48, 49, 50 feet. "It's mostly downhill," said his caddie, crouching to line up the face of Boswell's putter. "Take off about 10 feet, and putt it like a 40-footer."

Boswell stroked the ball. It sped across the green, climbed and fell, curved, slowed down and dropped with a rattle into the hole. Boswell grinned: "Did you see that one?" Yes, I had seen it. But he hadn't. Charley Boswell is blind. In fact, he is one of the most remarkable blind sportsmen in the world and playing off a handicap as low as 12, he has won the United States Blind Golfers' Association Championship 17 times.

Putting, oddly enough, is one of Boswell's strong departments. Given, of course, the fact that his caddie reads the putt, his execution is immaculate. "A tip that we blind golfers can pass on to the sighted player," he said, "I don't worry about the breaks on a green. Don't try to curb your putt because, as Bobby Jones always said, every putt is a straight putt and let the slopes do the work."

A few weeks ago I met Boswell in California, where he was playing a benefit match for the Braille Institute of America. He had come up from Alabama, where he is the State Commissioner in the Department of Revenue, a remarkable enough job, and now he was walking to the second tee on a course in the lush Coachelle Valley. A wind blew down from the mountains. "Funny thing," he said, "wind is really the only thing that bothers me. It affects my hearing, and that ruins my sense of direction."

On the second tee his caddie, who is his home professional back in Alabama, lined up the face of Boswell's driver and stepped away. Boswell, careful not to lose this alignment, did not waggle his clubhead. He paused, setting up some inner rhythm, and swung with the certainty of a sighted player. He groaned as the ball tailed off into a slice.

"There are two ways I can tell if I hit a good shot," he said, frowning. "I can feel it through the clubhead and, more important, I finish up high on my follow-through. Come on, let's walk. I can't stand golf carts—they bother my judgment of distance."

Boswell has been walking down darkened fairways since shortly after the Second World War. Blinded when a German antitank gun scored a direct hit on his vehicle in the Ruhr, he was sent back to an American hospital for rehabilitation. A former gridiron footballer and baseball player, Boswell did not take easily to pampered, supervised sport.

"I tried swimming, and it bored me. I tried horseback riding until I rode under a tree and got knocked off. I tried ten-pin bowling, and that wasn't any good either—I fell over the ball-track." He laughed, idly swinging his club as he walked. "Then one day this corporal came in and suggested we play golf. I told him to get the hell out of my room."

Boswell had never swung a golf club in his life but, a few days later, aged 28, he gave it a try: "He handed me a brassie. I took six practice swings, and then he teed one up and I hit it dead centre, right out of the sweet spot. I tell you, I was lucky. If I'd missed the ball that first time I would have quit golf." There are no false heroics about Boswell.

Some holes later he, or rather we, found his ball in a bunker. The bunker shot was clearly the most difficult shot in Boswell's bag. Playing it required him to break two Rules of Golf: he not only needed his usual help from someone to line up his club but, to avoid topping the ball, or missing it altogether, he had to ground his club in the sand. "Also, I can't get fancy and cut across the ball," he said. "I have to swing square to the line of flight. I have to play it like an ordinary pitch."

These handicaps, he later pointed out, were in part counterbalanced by the actual advantages of being blind on a golf course. Boswell, for instance, is never tempted to play a nine-iron when a seven-iron will do the job. "In a match blind players play the course, not their opponents, because we can't see what they're doing anyway," he said, on the way to a score of 91 which, for him, was neat but not gaudy. "You know, I was once playing with Bob Hope, and he said: 'Charley, if you could see all the trouble on this golf course, you wouldn't be playing it.' And I suppose he was right."

Source: By Dudley Doust, *The Sunday Times* [London], February 6, 1977. Reprinted by permission.

example, have lowered thresholds of sensation in touch or hearing. What they are able to do is make better use of the sensations they obtain. Through concentration and attention, they learn to make very fine discriminations.

Another common belief is that people who are blind automatically have superior musical talent. Some do follow musical careers, but this is because music is an area in which they can achieve success.

Academic Achievement

Most professionals agree that direct comparisons of the academic achievement of students who are blind with that of sighted students must be interpreted cautiously because the two groups must be tested under different conditions. There are, however, Braille and large-print forms of some achievement tests. The few studies that have been done suggest that both children with low vision and those who are blind are behind their sighted peers (Rapp & Rapp, 1992; Suppes, 1974). Their academic achievement, however, is not as adversely affected as that of students who are hearing impaired. Hearing is evidently more important for school learning than seeing. There is speculation that the low achievement of some students who are blind may be due to low expectations and lack of exposure to Braille, not necessarily to actual ability.

Social Adjustment

At one time, the prevailing opinion of professionals was that people with visual impairment were at risk to exhibit personality disturbances. Most authorities now agree that personality problems are not an inherent condition of blindness. What social difficulties may arise are more likely due to society's inappropriate reaction to blindness than to personality flaws of people without sight.

Much of this inappropriateness may be caused by the average person's unfamiliarity with people who are blind. Because we do not have many acquaintances who are blind, we are not used to their usual patterns of social interaction. Social skills that come naturally to the sighted may be very difficult for some people with visual impairment. One good example is smiling. Smiling is a strong *visual* cue, used by two sighted people to provide feedback to one another. For some people with visual impairment, however, smiling is not as spontaneous a social response as it is for those who are sighted. John M. Hull, whose eyesight deteriorated gradually over several years, kept a diary of his experiences. The following two entries pertain to smiling:*

[1] Nearly every time I smile, I am conscious of it. I am aware of the muscular effort; not that my smiles have become forced, as if I were pretending, but it has become a more or less conscious effort. Why is this? It must be because there is no reinforcement. There is no returning smile. . . . Most smiling is responsive. You smile spontaneously when you receive a smile. For me it is like sending dead letters. Have they been received, acknowledged? Was I even smiling in the right direction? (Hull, 1990, p. 34)

Yesterday morning I was kneeling on the floor, helping Lizzie to get dressed. When she was finished, I stood her up in front of me and said, "Now! Let's have a look at you." I held her face lightly between my hands while she stood there, and gave her a big smile.

We remained like that for a moment and then she said, "Daddy, how can you smile between you and me when I smile and when you smile because you're blind?" . . .

"You mean, how do I know when to smile at you?" . . .

"Yes," she said, "when you're blind."

"It's true, darling," I said, "that blind people often don't know when to smile at people, and I often don't know when to smile at you, do I?"

She agreed.

"But today I knew you were smiling, darling, because you were standing there, and I was smiling at you, and I thought you were probably smiling at me. Were you?"

Happily she replied, "Yes!"

*From *Touching the rock*, by John M. Hull, Copyright © 1990 by John M. Hull. Reprinted by permission of Pantheon Books, a division of Random House, Inc.

One stereotype of people who are blind is that they do not adjust well socially; in fact, though, this assumption is no more valid than others based on stereotypes.

collaboration

a key to success

Ricki Curry

Jenny Garrett

Ricki: In a regional program serving children with low-incidence disabilities in six rural localities, my students were in general education classes, using some variation of the inclusion model, and received itinerant services from one to four times a week. Dennis, one of my students with severe visual impairment, was fully included in Jenny's class.

Jenny: My fourth-grade class consisted of twenty-three nine- and ten-year-old students, including two children with learning disabilities: one student with severe behavior disorders and Dennis. They began the year reading anywhere from a first- to a sixth-grade level.

Ricki: Although he has some usable vision, Dennis can see no details from a distance of more than about two feet and uses large-print texts for reading. Dennis comes from a very highly educated family and is a very bright, verbal, curious child. Although academically he is right on or above grade level, his independent work skills are very poor.

Jenny: Dennis has some difficulty making friends because of his immaturity, his compulsive talking, and his inability to listen. On the other hand, Dennis has a good sense of humor and is quick with language. He loves to take things apart and fiddle with anything mechanical. Dennis is amazingly agile and navigates the classroom, school corridors, and playground with ease. It is often easy to forget the severity of his visual handicap, but when we venture out of the school environs, he clings to the chaperone's hand and is markedly less self-confident.

Ricki: Dennis had been included in this school since kindergarten, but the early grades are extremely developmental in approach, and this was the first year that things were going to get really academic for him. Both Jenny and I had concerns about his ability to be a functioning member of the class.

Jenny: Dennis was in my class all day long for every academic subject. Ricki worked with him at the back of the room during a large chunk of the language arts block, teaching Braille. She would come to school during the last half of my planning period, which gave us a daily opportunity to discuss assignments, homework, curricular adaptations, equipment, and the like. Homework was an enormous issue. For the first time, Dennis had challenging nightly assignments. Ricki helped him set up a notebook with a homework contract enclosed and a special highlighter, which he used to mark off completed assignments. He had to write down the assignments himself, remember to take the notebook home, complete the assignments, get a parent's signature, and get it back to school. Homework was extremely stressful for Dennis and his parents, both of whom worked full time. Ricki often played the "bad cop" when assignments were not returned and was always calm, matter of fact, but hard nosed about consequences.

Ricki: I've always felt that ownership is a very important issue in successfully including students. If I present a student with visual impairment to a classroom teacher as "mine," then that teacher has every right to abdicate responsibility for the student and expect me to create a program that somehow will fit the student into the class. The student is always seen as an "extra" and not as a real member of the class. If I can communicate to a teacher that I'm only there to help and that the student "belongs" to the classroom teacher, the inclusion process goes much more smoothly. This can be a tricky relationship to establish because I don't want to look as though I'm trying get away with doing a minimum job—presenting myself as a helper instead of the leader of our little two-person team. But

Ricki Curry is an itinerant teacher for students with visual impairment, Piedmont Regional Education Program; A.B., Experimental Psychology, Brown University; M.Ed., Special Education for the Visually Impaired, University of Virginia. **Jenny Garrett** is a fourth-grade teacher, Stone-Robinson Elementary School, Albemarle, Virginia; B.A. English, College of William and Mary; M.Ed. Curriculum and Instruction, University of Virginia.

if I come on too strong, as knowing a lot about the student and trying to influence decisions about the student's program, a teacher will often feel intimidated and defer to me about everything, giving up responsibility for the student's inclusion.

Jenny: The hardest part of working with Dennis was the start-up period. I had to get to know him, his visual capabilities, his strengths and weaknesses, his coping strategies. I began adapting my teaching style, using an easel rather than the blackboard so that he could scoot up to it. I had to decide how hard to push, what to expect from his parents, and what to demand from Dennis. Part of the start-up stress was getting to know and trust Ricki. When someone spends an hour a day in your classroom, they see it all! Thankfully, we were a good match, and there were respect and trust on both ends.

Ricki: I often found myself overwhelmed by the number of things that Jenny and/or Dennis needed help with in the short time that I was in the building. And so many things seemed to go wrong in the time between when I left one day and arrived again the next day! Dennis couldn't seem to keep track of his papers or get his homework done and back into school, or he'd hit someone on the bus or he'd come into school in tears and refuse to talk to anyone about what was going on. I knew Jenny really didn't have time to deal with the intensive care that Dennis seemed to require, but it was hard for me to come up with effective ways of dealing with his behavioral issues when I usually wasn't around when things happened or when consequences needed to be applied. I would end up getting Jenny's side of the story, trying to figure out from what Dennis said what he thought the situation was, and then trying to come up with a plan of action. I often felt that all I could really do was produce a "Band-aid" solution. All this mediation and problem solving also took up a lot of the time I had with Jenny and Dennis, so instructional issues got less time than they needed.

Jenny: The most rewarding aspect of this collaboration was being part of an inclusion model that worked beautifully! Ricki was like a fairy godmother, continually pulling out material resources to enable Dennis to participate in activities, whether it was sewing our quilt with a darning needle and lab goggles or adapting the computer with a magnification program. Her attitude was: How can I make it work? What can I do? She was creative with her solutions and ideas, energetic, and appreciative of my efforts. It was wonderful to have a colleague in the room to laugh and work with. (Teachers are often extremely isolated from other adults.) Ricki was invaluable in helping Dennis deal with organizational and homework demands. She added so much to the life of the classroom, helping me plan a New Year's party and teaching a unit on Braille. While Dennis was Brailling and was working with reading groups at the front of the room, other students would quietly go to Ricki for help with their classwork. She was our cheerleader, Dennis's advocate, and a huge plus for our room.

Ricki: Although I was frustrated by the limitations imposed by time constraints, the beauty of the inclusion model was that I was very aware of the true gestalt of Dennis's program and knew exactly what he was involved in all the time. Had I been taking him out to do an hour of Braille in isolation four times a week, I would never have been aware of all the management issues Jenny had to deal with—getting Dennis to keep track of his magnifiers and finding his large print books quickly when he needed them; getting his spelling work, which was done on the computer, printed and hole-punched and put in his notebook on time, instead of being half-finished or left under the computer cart; crying when another student accidentally bumped into him; eating snacks while everyone else was back at work; rummaging through his desk, completely out of touch, while the class was being given the daily assignments. I knew when Jenny came to me with a problem that she wasn't just imagining it or being overly picky! I was able to see for myself how difficult a time Dennis was having being a regular fourth-grader and how much support he needed to grow toward that goal. Seeing Jenny at work also made it clear to me that she truly didn't have time to deal with all Dennis's problems and that she wasn't abdicating responsibility or just whining when she asked for my direct help. Had I not had an almost daily view of Dennis's classroom performance, I might not have believed how hard it was to integrate this very bright, verbal, personable child into Jenny's class. I admired Jenny tremendously for persisting, and in spite of the stress Jenny and I went through, I think Dennis's inclusion was one of the most successful I've seen.

Ownership is a very important issue in successfully including students.

Jenny: Collaboration works best when there is match of personalities as well as energy, enthusiasm for teaching, and professionalism. Both of us genuinely like children and enjoy the learning process. During the last several weeks of school, Dennis was absent because of medical problems. Frankly, I was surprised by how much easier it was. I didn't have to be constantly remembering to enlarge assignments or pop over to his desk to check on him or to present every assignment so that he could have maximum visual advantage. In retrospect, teaching Dennis was enriching and stressful, challenging and difficult. His mother wrote at the end of the year, "You have been the turning point for Dennis. He has come a long way this year, and he still has a long way to go. You really gave him a badly needed structure and 'push.'"

> [2] So this little child, having just had her fourth birthday, is able to articulate the breakdown which blindness causes in the language of smiles. I noticed the fine distinction she made by implication between smiling at someone and the smiling which takes place between people. (Hull, 1990, pp. 202–203)

In addition to smiling, sighted people usually use a number of other subtle visual cues when communicating with one another—cues that may be missing from the normal repertoire of people who are blind. For instance, sighted people use a variety of facial expressions, hand gestures, and body movements to convey their feelings during social interaction.

An important point to keep in mind is that even though people with visual impairment differ from the sighted in how they interact socially, this does *not* mean that they are socially maladjusted. It does mean, however, that *initial* interactions between people with and without sight may be strained. We emphasize initial because once sighted individuals and those without sight become acquainted, these problems in communication largely disappear (Fichten, Judd, Tagalakis, Amsel, & Robillard, 1991).

Another important point is that it should not only be up to people who are visually impaired to change their ways of interacting socially. Sighted people should also be responsible for instances of faulty communication with people who are blind:

> For instance, a sighted professor was overheard telling a student who was blind, "OK. Just grab those (he pointed to a bunch of papers) and we can go." In another instance, while giving a lift to an acquaintance who was blind, the driver remarked, "We're at the junction you specified. Which house is it—the one with the brown or yellow balconies?" The response to this innocent, but inappropriate query was delivered with a chuckle, "I don't know about brown or yellow balconies; take me to the building on the right." (Fichten et al., 1991, p. 371)

Not only may some people with visual impairment profit from instruction in using appropriate visually based cues (e.g., facial expressions, head nods, and gestures), but sighted people also can learn to use their natural telephone skills when communicating with persons who are blind. Two sighted people talking on the telephone use a variety of auditorially based cues to help them communicate, even though they cannot see each other (e.g., assenting with "uh hum" or "yeah," asking for more information, adjusting tone of voice) (Fichten et al., 1991). If sighted individuals consciously try to use these strategies when interacting with people who are blind, communication may be smoother.

stereotypic behaviors. Any of a variety of repetitive behaviors (e.g., eye rubbing) that are sometimes found in individuals who are blind, severely retarded, or psychotic; sometimes referred to as *stereotypies* or *blindisms*.

blindisms. Repetitive, stereotyped movements (e.g., rocking or eye rubbing; also characteristic of some persons who are blind, severely retarded, or psychotic; more appropriately referred to as stereotypic behaviors.

Stereotypic Behaviors. An impediment to good social adjustment for some students with visual impairment is **stereotypic behaviors**: repetitive, stereotyped movements such as body rocking, poking or rubbing the eyes, repetitive hand or finger movements, and grimacing. For many years, the term **blindisms** was used to refer to these behaviors because it was thought that they were manifested only in people who are blind; however, they are also sometimes characteristic of children with normal sight who are severely retarded or disturbed.

Several competing theories concern the causes of stereotypic behaviors. Most involve the notion that these behaviors are physiological attempts to stabilize one's level of arousal (Baumeister, 1978). For example, one position holds that children with low levels of sensory stimulation, such as those without sight, make up for this deprivation by stimulating themselves in other ways (Thurrell & Rice, 1970). Another theory holds that, even with adequate sensory stimulation, social isolation can cause individuals to seek added stimulation through stereotypic behaviors (Warren, 1981, 1984).

Stereotypic behaviors can be manifested as early as a few months of age. Researchers have found that eye poking and body rocking are among the most prevalent types of stereotypic behaviors and the most difficult to eliminate (Bambring & Troster, 1992). Most authorities agree that it is important to eliminate stereotypic behaviors. In addition to being socially stigmatizing and possibly physically damaging, they can interfere with the child's ability to learn (Bambring & Troster, 1992). Engaging in such behaviors means less time for active learning.

The reduction of stereotypic behaviors can be very difficult. In recent years, researchers have tried cognitive and metacognitive training as ways of decreasing the frequency of such behaviors (Estevis & Koenig, 1994; McAdam, O'Cleirigh, & Cuvo, 1993; Ross & Koening, 1991; Van Reusen & Head, 1994). One team of researchers, for example, had a student clasp his hands together and tell himself that he did not want to rock whenever he began to rock. This procedure resulted in reduced rocking, presumably due to the student's exerting cognitive control over his behavior.

EDUCATIONAL CONSIDERATIONS

Lack of sight can severely limit a person's experiences because a primary means of obtaining information from the environment is not available. What makes the situation even more difficult is that educational experiences in the typical classroom are frequently visual. Nevertheless, most experts agree that students who are visually impaired should be educated in the same general way as sighted children. Teachers need to make some modifications, but they can apply the same general educational principles. The important difference is that students with visual impairment will have to rely on other sensory modalities to acquire information.

The student with little or no sight will possibly require special modifications in four major areas: (1) Braille, (2) use of remaining sight, (3) listening skills, and (4) mobility training. The first three pertain directly to academic education, particularly reading; the last refers to skills needed for everyday living.

Braille

In nineteenth-century France, Louis Braille introduced a system of writing for people who, like him, were blind. That system was based on a military method of writing messages using raised-line characters, which could be read in the dark using the sense of touch, not sight. The basic system created by Braille is still used today, although the raised-line characters have been replaced by various patterns of raised dots.

One Braille code, called *literary Braille,* is used for most everyday situations; other codes are available for more technical reading and writing. Some people support adoption of a Unified Braille Code that would combine these several codes into one. These proponents argue that, "in this modern, high-tech society, most of us must perform some activities that were once reserved for so-called technical types" (Jackson, Bogart, & Caton, 1993, p. 1110). At this point, it is not clear how accepting persons who are blind would be of a Unified Braille Code.

The basic unit of Braille is a quadrangular *cell,* containing from one to six dots (see Figure 9-2). Different patterns of dots represent letters, numbers, and even punctuation marks. Generally, the best method of reading Braille involves using both hands (Davidson, Appelle, & Haber, 1992). Doing so allows the reader to scan new text with one hand while re-reading material with the other hand.

Two basic means of writing in Braille are the Perkins Brailler and the slate and stylus. The **Perkins Brailler** has six keys, one for each of the six dots of the cell (see

Perkins Brailler. A system that makes it possible to write in Braille; has six keys, one for each of the six dots of the cell, which leave an embossed print on the paper.

Figure 9–2

Examples of symbols from Braille.

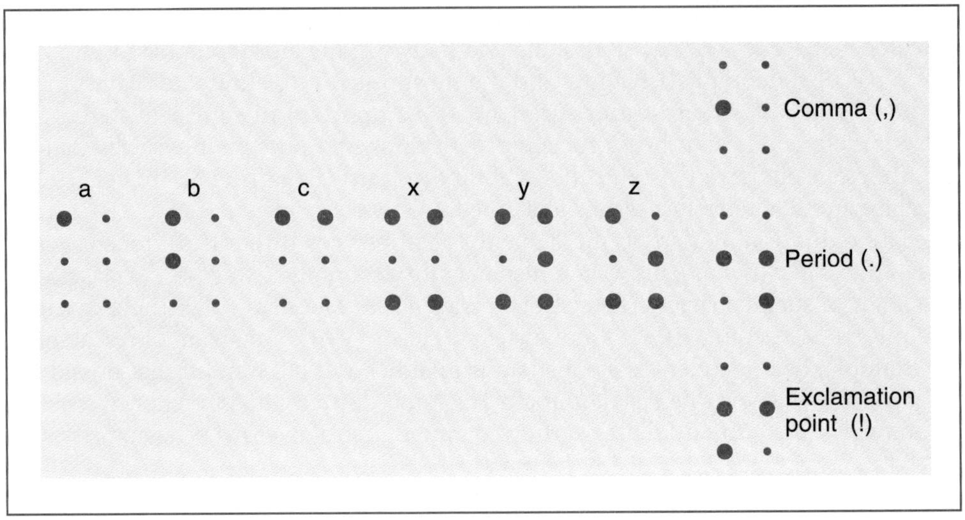

Figure 9-3). When depressed simultaneously, the keys leave an embossed print on the paper. More portable than the Perkins Brailler is the **slate and stylus** (see Figure 9-4). The stylus—a pen-shaped instrument—is pressed through the opening of the slate, which holds the paper between its two halves. Using this method, the Braille cells are written in reverse order, which makes the slate and stylus more difficult to use than the Perkins Brailler.

slate and stylus. A method of writing in Braille in which the paper is held in a slate while a stylus is pressed through openings to make indentations in the paper.

Perhaps the most hotly debated topic in the field of visual impairment concerns whether students who are blind should be taught to use Braille or one of the other methods of communication, such as a tape recorder or voice-activated computer. At one time, it was fairly common for students with blindness to use Braille, but over the past several years, its usage has declined dramatically. For example, the percentage of students who are blind who use Braille has steadily declined since the mid-1960s, when nearly half used Braille, to the most recent statistics, which indicate that only 10.1 percent use Braille (Pierce, 1991).

Many within the community of blind people are alarmed at the reduced availability of Braille and assert that it has led to a distressing rate of illiteracy (Hatlen, 1993;

Figure 9–3

A Perkins Brailler.

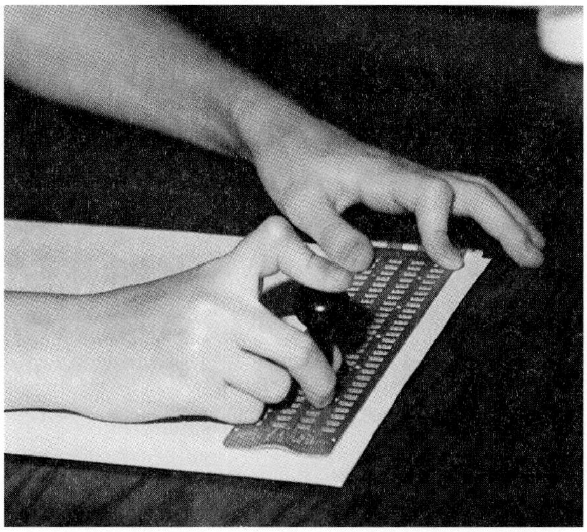

Figure 9–4

A slate and stylus in use.

Ianuzzi, 1992; Mauer, 1991; Nicely, 1991; Raeder, 1991; Schroeder, 1990, 1992). They charge that too few sighted teachers are proficient in Braille and that they do little to discourage the notion held by some children that using Braille indicates inferiority. As the Executive Director of the National Braille Press has put it:

> *There is an institutionalized prejudice against blindness and Braille.* Braille for the blind student is sometimes shunned by the teacher, administrator, or even the parent or student because it further identifies the student as being blind; and, in all too many minds, albeit oftentimes subconsciously, there is a stigma attached to blindness and a damaging attitude of unduly diminished expectations of blind students. (Raeder, 1991, p. 36)

Advocates of Braille point out that it is essential for most students who are legally blind to learn Braille in order to lead independent lives. They argue that although tape recorders, computers, and other technological devices can contribute much to reading and acquiring information, these devices cannot replace Braille. For example, finding a specific section of a text or "skimming" (using a tape recorder) are difficult, but these kinds of activities are possible when using Braille. Taking notes for class, reading a speech, or looking up words in a dictionary is easier when using Braille than when using a tape recorder (Maurer, 1991). Braille proponents are especially concerned that the slate and stylus be preserved as a viable method of taking notes (Walhof, 1993). They point out that just as computers have not replaced the pen and pencil for people who are sighted, neither can they take the place of the slate and stylus for people who are blind.

Many authorities now recommend that some students with low vision who are able to read large print or print with magnification should also be taught Braille (Holbrook & Koenig, 1992), similar to the way some Hispanic students are taught both Spanish and English. There are many students with low vision whose condition dictates that their visual acuity will worsen over the years. Learning Braille at an early age would prepare them for the time when their eyesight no longer allowed them to read print. The vignette in the box on page 375 demonstrates how important Braille instruction can be for these students and how social stigma can get in the way of learning Braille.

As a way of ensuring that Braille becomes more readily available, advocates have lobbied for **Braille bills**. Although the specific provisions of these bills vary from state

Braille bills. Legislation passed in several states to make Braille more available to students with visual impairment; specific provisions vary from state to state, but major advocates have lobbied for (1) making Braille available if parents want it and for (2) ensuring that teachers of students with visual impairment are proficient in Braille.

SUCCESS STORIES

Charlottesville, VA: Nineteen-year-old **Patrick Pugh** *has no vision in his left eye and only partial sight in his right. His speech is slurred, and he does not have functional use of his left arm or leg. Patrick's disabilities were caused by being born prematurely. For fourteen years, Patrick's mother, Audrey Pugh, and special educator Ricki Curry have been partners in Patrick's education. They know that, over time, parents and professionals must collaborate and compromise to help students meet their goals.*

Patrick Pugh likes to read Braille, and translate printed sentences with a unimanual Brailler. Now, instead of awkwardly holding a book two inches from his right eye, he reads with a relaxed posture, as his fingers scan the Brailled page of his easy reader. Ricki Curry, an itinerant teacher of students with visual impairment, taught Patrick to Braille two years ago. She is proud of his achievements. "Patrick keeps exceeding everybody's expectations. Every time we've taught him something, he's had some success in learning it. We've come to believe in him, and to set our expectations higher, as a result."

This description of her second son does not surprise Audrey Pugh. "Opportunity is the main thing," she says. "All I want anyone to do is give Patrick a fair chance. I think it would be easier if he were either blind or physically disabled, but he's both, and that makes it even harder."

Patrick's progress is the result of his own persistence, the collaboration of his family and teachers, and the continuity of specialized personnel, instruction, and equipment over many years. Ricki and Audrey also credit much of Patrick's progress to a key ingredient: time. Patrick's story is an example of special education not as a fix-it model or cure-all but as a means of providing services over time to persons whose abilities often take much longer than usual to develop.

Patrick started vision and physical therapy when he was two years old. "The physical therapist asked me why he didn't have therapy before," recalls Audrey, "but no one ever told us it was available to infants or that Patrick needed it."

Ricki remembers the youngster whose eyes would lift aimlessly to the ceiling, not using what vision he had. "Our basic goal was for Patrick to learn to use his sight by tracking objects and looking at pictures, but as a five-year-old, he was stubborn, difficult, and noncompliant." Despite his reluctance, Patrick successfully learned literal information and concrete routines. To be sure, he was highly distractible and progress was very slow. His parents hoped all he needed was extra time, so he stayed in a preschool for children with special needs until he was seven.

to state, the National Federation of the Blind, a major proponent of Braille bills, has drafted a model bill that specifies two important components:

1. Braille must be available for students if any members of the individualized education program (IEP) team, including parents, indicate that it is needed;
2. Teachers of students with visual impairment need to be proficient in Braille.

To provide a way of determining the Braille proficiency of licensed teachers of students who are blind, the Library of Congress released a National Literary Braille Competency Test in 1994. It is still too early to tell how many schools will use this test to ensure the Braille competency of these teachers.

Use of Remaining Sight

For many years, there was a great deal of resistance to having children with visual impairment use their sight in reading and some other activities. Many myths explain the controversy about this issue; among the most common are these:

Special Educators at Work

Audrey had problems with the school district when Patrick was ready for first grade. "They told me there was no place for him in the public schools, so I said, ëWell, find one!'" Patrick was placed in a self-contained class for children with learning disabilities in the nearest physically accessible elementary school. Ricki continued to provide weekly sessions and to supervise Patrick's vision services. He was also given a personal aide to assist with mobility and visual modifications. As Ricki points out, "In some ways, kids with personal aides never have any problems, so they don't learn any problem solving skills! On the other hand, there are some effective strategies that can be used with close attention." Since Patrick's hand use is limited, Ricki trained his aide to assist him as a scribe. In addition, Patrick's math was broken down into small steps, his reading was individualized, and he was taught to write using a large-print word processor.

Patrick finished elementary school, two years older than most of his classmates. Yet he was only able to do rote math and was similarly concrete in reading; he could decode text but remained literal in his understanding of the material. "He could answer factual questions, but he couldn't make that leap to the abstract," recalls Ricki. "Patrick was in a middle school science class, learning about mitochondria. That's when it really hit me: Sure, he could learn the definition of mitochondria, but was this functional for him? He'd never use this word again!"

Patrick was thirteen when his mother was told that he needed a class that emphasized functional academics, such as money skills. Audrey agreed to the placement, but it was devastating because it seemed an admission that her son was mentally retarded. "At that point, we all knew this was what he needed," says Ricki. "Patrick has multiple learning needs, and it takes him a long time to learn; it takes intensive care and a lot of specific teaching. This class gave him the right information at the right pace. We forgot about the mitochondria and were now reading for *comprehension*."

Patrick started high school when he was seventeen, and a creative program was crafted for him, blending functional academics, work experience, and independent living skills. He spent his mornings in two periods of functional English and math. He then boarded a van for the vocational center three afternoons a week, where he ate lunch with co-workers. He spent two afternoons a week at an independent living, center learning to clean, shop, and travel about the community.

Patrick works with Ricki sixty minutes a day on Braille skills that are geared toward vocational goals. Ricki is optimistic. "I think there's a job out there for Patrick. We've got two years to get those skills really sharp."

Patrick's odyssey has not been easy for his mother, Audrey. She knows Ricki respects her high expectations, yet she has come to trust that alternate routes hold promise for Patrick's future. Audrey says, "I'd like to think of him living happily in a group home someday, with friends, and, of course, with some supervision and support. I think it's only realistic to imagine he'd need that."

—By Jean Crockett

1. Holding books close to the eyes harms them.
2. Strong lenses hurt the eyes.
3. Using the eyes too much injures them (Hanninen, 1975).

At one time, classes for students with low vision were called *sight conservation* or *sight-saving* classes, reflecting the popular assumption that using the eyes too much caused them to deteriorate. It is now recognized that this is true only in very rare conditions. In fact, studies have shown that teachers can actually train students to use what visual abilities they do have to better advantage (Barraga & Collins, 1979; Collins & Barraga, 1980).

The two general methods of aiding children with visual impairment to read print are large-print books and magnifying devices. Large-print books are simply books printed in larger-size type. The text in this book, printed primarily for sighted readers, is printed in 10-point type. Figure 9–5 on page 374 shows print in 18-point type, which is one of the most popular sizes for large-print materials. Type sizes for readers with visual impairment may range up to 30-point type.

Figure 9–5

Typefaces come in various sizes. Large-print books often use 18 pt. type and 24 pt. type.

This is an example of 10-point type.

This is an example of 18-pt. type.

This is an example of 24-pt. type.

The major difficulty with large-print books is that they are bigger than usual and thus require a great deal of space to store them. In addition, they are of limited availability, although, along with the American Printing House for the Blind, a number of commercial publishers are now publishing and marketing large-print books.

Magnifying devices range from glasses and hand-held lenses to closed-circuit television scanners that present enlarged images on a TV screen. These devices can be used with normal-size type or large-print books.

Listening Skills

The importance of listening skills for children who are blind cannot be overemphasized. The less a child is able to rely on sight for gaining information from the environment, the more crucial it is that he or she become a good listener. Some professionals still assume that good listening skills will develop automatically in children who are blind. This belief is unfortunate, for it is now evident that children do not spontaneously compensate for poor vision by magically developing superior powers of concentration. In most cases, they must be taught how to listen. A variety of curriculum materials and programs are available to teach children listening skills (e.g., Bischoff, 1979; Swallow & Conner, 1982).

Listening skills are becoming more important than ever because of the increasing accessibility of recorded material. The American Printing House for the Blind and the Library of Congress are major sources for these materials. Listeners can simply play the material at normal speed or use a compressed speech device that allows them to read at about 250 to 275 words per minute. The idea behind this method is to discard very small segments of the speech. Some of the more sophisticated compressed speech devices use a computer to eliminate those speech sounds that are least necessary for comprehension.

Mobility Training

How well individuals cope with a visual disability depends to a great extent on how well they are able to move about. And whether a person withdraws from the social environment or becomes independent depends greatly on mobility skills. Four general methods are available to aid the mobility of people with visual impairment: (1) the long cane, (2) guide dogs, (3) human guides, and (4) electronic devices.

long cane. A mobility aid used by individuals with visual impairment, who sweep it in a wide arc in front of them; proper use requires considerable training; the mobility aid of choice for most travelers who are blind.

The Long Cane. Professionals most often recommend the long cane for those individuals with visual impairments in need of a mobility aid. It is called a **long cane** because it is longer than the canes typically used for support or balance. Research has

Braille Is Not Just for People Who are Blind

There are many individuals whose visual impairment is not severe enough in childhood to require learning and using Braille but whose condition will worsen in time to the point where using Braille will be a desirable option. For these students, it makes sense to start Braille instruction before they actually need to rely on it extensively. Unfortunately, as the following vignette shows, one of the barriers to beginning Braille instruction with these students is the social stigma attached to using Braille:

> When I was seven years old, I became legally blind from a condition known as Stephens-Johnson's Syndrome. This left me with visual acuity in the neighborhood of 20/400. Prior to this time I was fully sighted and had completed first, and one-half of second, grade receiving ordinary print reading instruction.
>
> Because of associated health problems, I remained at home for two and one-half years, receiving home teaching services from the local school district. At that time, there were no special education services available for low vision children, and the concept of "sight saving" was generally held by practicing opthalmologists. For this reason, all of my lessons were conducted orally—two to three times a week for an hour at a time. At the age of ten, I returned to public school, participating in a regular fifth grade class. While I was not aware that I would eventually lose the remainder of my sight, my mother must have been informed and began searching for someone to teach me braille. Since I had some sight, I did not regard myself as a blind person, and therefore, had no interest in learning braille. Additionally, my poor eyesight mostly represented a source of embarrassment for me, resulting in an aversion to learning braille. I would much rather have hidden my eye problem, rather that making it public through braille reading.
>
> While the home teacher was diligent, I never practiced between lessons, and read the braille visually rather than by touch. He was using the Illinois Series, which used single-sided braille for the first two books, allowing me to read it visually without too much problem. When I got to the third book, which was inter-point braille, I could no longer read the material with my eyes, causing frustration by me and my teacher, with the end result of braille instruction being dropped.
>
> Throughout school, I was exempt from any assignment which I could not see well enough to complete. As can be imagined, my education was limited primarily to what I could pick up from sitting in class.
>
> Toward the end of junior high school, my vision began deteriorating further. A long series of eye surgeries ensued, resulting in total blindness at the age of sixteen. At this point, I was in the Fall semester of my senior year of high school and was again receiving home instruction, since my many eye surgeries prevented me from attending school. A home teacher again provided me with the Illinois Braille Series which I used to teach myself braille. After completing the Illinois Series, I read my first novel—*Animal Farm*. When I began, I was reading a page in forty-eight minutes. One hundred fifty-five pages later, when I finished the book, I was reading a page in sixteen minutes. My slow reading rate was due to poor braille reading techniques associated with being self-taught, coupled with a lack of reading experience, overall. I read with the index finger of my right hand only-scrubbing up and down, and back-tracking frequently. My general lack of literacy was a major impediment to acquiring any reasonable proficiency in braille. I can remember puzzling over the word "neighbor," which seemed incomprehensible with my limited knowledge of phonics.
>
> I wish to stress that my experience with print and braille reading must not be viewed simply as an example of poor training. As a young child, blindness represented inferiority to me and a constant source of feelings of inadequacy. I believed that I was less capable than others, and believed it was due to my poor vision. I could not imagine that techniques used by the blind could allow me to function competitively. Some training was available to me, but my own attitudes about blindness caused me to reject braille at the cost of self-confidence and basic literacy.

Frederic K. Schroeder
Santa Fe, New Mexico

Source: Caton, H. (Ed.), (1991). *Print and Braille literacy: Selecting appropriate learning media.* Louisville, KY: American Printing House for the Blind. Reprinted with permission.

determined that the long cane should extend at least from the floor to the user's armpit (Plain-Switzer, 1993).

> The long cane is the most effective and efficient mobility aid yet devised for safe, independent travel by the majority of visually impaired people. The scanning system in which the user operates the cane supplies echo-ranging cues and force-impact data that give vital information about the immediate environment. It informs the traveler about the nature and condition of the surface underfoot, gives sufficient forewarning of downsteps or dropoffs to prevent falls or injury, and protects the lower part of the body from collision. The cane informs the user about various ground-surface textures which can be related to specific areas and destinations. It is a highly maneuverable aid that allows investigation of the environment without actual hand contact.
> (Farmer, 1980, p. 359)

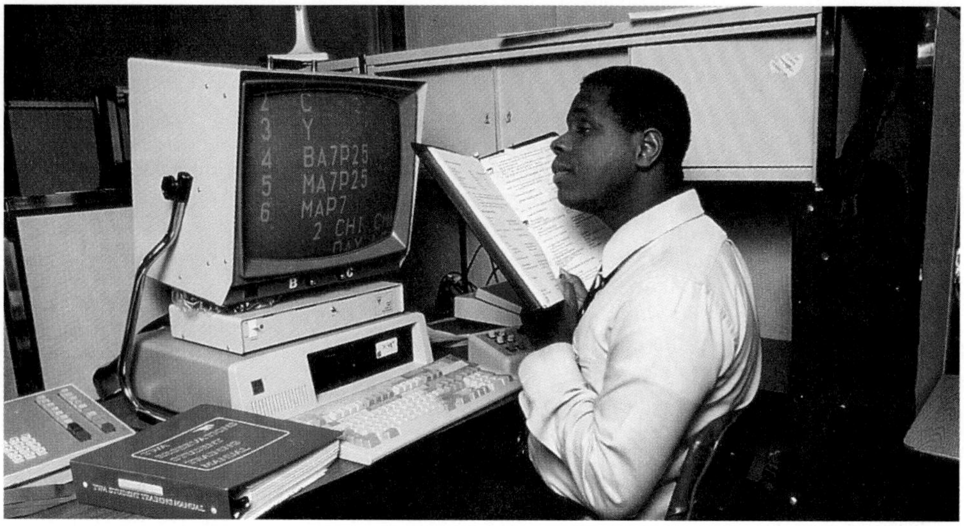

Computer monitors that provide large-print images can aid some individuals with visual impairments.

Although the long cane looks like a simple device, scientists, mobility specialists, and others working under the auspices of the National Academy of Sciences have drawn up specifications for its construction. And although watching a skilled user of the long cane may give the impression that it is easy to manipulate, extensive training in its proper use is often required.

The traveler holds the butt or crook of the long cane at about the height of the navel and sweeps it in an arc wide enough to protect the body, lightly touching the ground in front with the cane tip (Plain-Switzer, 1993). Considerable coordination between the sweeping of the cane and the movement of the feet is required for proper touch technique. Authorities also recommend that long-cane training take place in the natural environment—that is, in the places where the user of the cane will most likely travel (Bailey & Head, 1993).

At one time, orientation and mobility teachers thought that young children were not old enough to be taught mobility skills. Before 1980, it was very difficult for the parents of a preschooler with visual impairment to find him or her a cane. Parents, especially sighted parents, also may have reinforced some of this negative reaction toward the use of canes with young children. In the past, parents may have seen the use of a cane as too stigmatizing. As one person who is blind said:

> When I was growing up, you didn't get a cane when you were six or four or three years old. The cane was the thing that my parents put off for as long as they could, and they did it with the support of educators. For them the cane was the symbol. It transformed me from being their blind son—which was okay—to being somebody who might grow up to be a blind man. That wasn't okay. So I didn't see a cane until I was about eleven years old. (Wunder, 1993, p. 568)

Today, however, more and more preschoolers are learning cane techniques (Cheadle, 1991; Dykes, 1992). In fact, many professionals recommend that cane training be initiated as soon as the child is walking independently with only minor irregularities in balance and gait (Skellenger & Hill, 1991).

Instead of using long canes with preschoolers, some professionals encourage the use of other devices, such as push-toys or hula-hoops, that the child can push along the ground in front of himself or herself. Researchers have also designed canes that are generally shaped like the long cane but have a wider base or different grip (Foy, Von Scheden, & Waiculonis, 1992; Pogrund, Fazzi, & Schreier, 1993). Some authorities, however, have reservations about the value of using devices like these that differ greatly from the basic design of the long cane. They think that some of these adapted devices are actually more complex and difficult to use than the standard long cane (Cheadle & Boone, 1994). Much more research is needed to determine the efficacy of these different types of mobility aids.

Although used less commonly than the long cane, the guide dog is still used with great success by some individuals with vision impairment.

Guide Dogs. Contrary to popular notions, the use of a **guide dog** is not recommended very often for people with visual impairment. Extensive training is required to learn how to use guide dogs properly. The extended training—as well as the facts that guide dogs are large, walk relatively fast, and need to be cared for—make them particularly questionable for children. For some adults, however, guide dogs have proven to be valuable aides and companions. Also contrary to what most people think, the guide dog does not "take" the person who is blind anywhere. The person must first know where he or she is going; the dog is primarily a safeguard against walking into dangerous areas. Some users of guide dogs point out that the dogs are able to alert their owners to important things in the environment—such as stairways, entrances, exits, and elevators—sooner than can be detected by a cane (Gabias, 1992).

People who are sighted should keep a few guidelines in mind pertaining to guide dogs and their owners (Ulrey, 1994):

- Although it may be tempting to pet a guide dog, you should do so only after asking the owner's permission. Guide dogs are not just pets—they are working for their owner.
- If someone with a guide dog appears to need help, approach on his or her right side (guide dogs are almost always on the left side) and ask if he or she needs assistance.
- Do not take hold of the dog's harness, as this may confuse the dog and the owner.

Human Guides. Human guides undoubtedly enable people with visual impairment to have the greatest freedom in moving about safely, but this arrangement is not practical in most cases. Furthermore, too much reliance on another person causes a dependency that can be harmful. Even people who are blind who are highly proficient travelers have noted that a certain degree of independence is sacrificed when walking accompanied by a sighted person (Hull, 1990). In order to converse with the companion, for instance, the person without sight can be distracted from paying attention to the cues he or she needs to travel efficiently and may come to rely on the sighted companion. This also can give the sighted individual the false impression that the person who is blind does not have good mobility skills.

Most people who travel unaccompanied do not need help from those around them. However, if a person with visual impairment looks as though he or she needs assistance, you should first *ask* if help is wanted. If physical guidance is required, allow the person to hold onto your arm above the elbow and to walk a half-step behind you. Sighted people tend to grasp the arms of persons without sight and to sort of push them in the direction they are heading.

guide dog. A dog specially trained to help guide a person who is blind; not recommended for children and not used by very many adults who are blind because the user needs special training in how to use the dog properly; contrary to popular opinion, the dog does not "take" the person anywhere but serves primarily as a safeguard against walking into dangerous areas.

Electronic Devices. Researchers are working on a number of sophisticated electronic devices for sensing objects in the environment. Most are still experimental, and most are expensive. Representative examples that have been under development for some time are the Laser cane and the Sonicguide. These devices operate on the principle that human beings can learn to locate objects by means of echoes, much as bats do.

More and more professionals are recommending that cane techniques and mobility training be started at a much earlier age than has historically been the norm.

The *Laser cane* can be used in the same way as the long cane or as a sensing device that emits three beams of infrared light (one up, one down, and one straight ahead), which are converted into sound after they strike objects in the path of the traveler (Farmer, 1975). The *Sonicguide* is for use with individuals ranging in age from infancy to adulthood (Bower, 1977; Kay, 1973; Strelow & Boys, 1979). Worn on the head, the device emits ultrasound and converts reflections from objects into audible sound. Depending on the characteristics of the sound, such as its pitch, clarity, and direction, the Sonicguide wearer can learn about such things as the distances, textures, and directions of objects.

A word of caution is in order in considering the use of electronic mobility devices: Because of their amazing technology, it is easy to be too optimistic about these devices. At least five things should be kept in mind in this regard. Electronic devices are:

1. still experimental, we need to know a lot more about them;
2. still very expensive; they are not available to everyone;
3. not a substitute for more conventional techniques such as the long cane;
4. not easily used; they require extensive training;
5. not a substitute for spatial concepts, the device may aid in the perception of objects, but the person who is blind must use the perceptual information gained to form spatial concepts, or cognitive maps, of his or her environment. (Warren, 1984)

Optacon. A device used to enable persons who are blind to read; consists of a camera that converts print into images of letters, which are then produced by way of vibration onto the finger.

Technological Aids

In recent years, a technological explosion has resulted in the creation of new electronic devices for use by people with visual impairment. Among the first was the **Optacon**, a hand-held scanner that converts print to tactile letters that are felt on the index finger. There is also an Optacon II for scanning computer screens. A major advantage of the Optacon and Optacon II is portability; major disadvantages are expense and the slow rate of reading they allow.

The **Kurzweil Reading Machine** and the **PC/Kurzweil Personal Reader**, especially the former, are less portable than the Optacon but allow a reading rate as fast as human speech. They convert print with practically any typeface into synthesized speech. The user places the material on a scanner which reads the material with an electronic voice. Because of expense, Kurzweil Reading Machines are limited mainly to libraries and institutions. The much smaller Kurzweil Personal Reader can be purchased for about $10,000. In addition, there is a PC/Kurzweil Personal Reader, starting at about $4,000, that can be used with an IBM or Apple personal computer (PC) to convert print to speech.

In addition to these stand-alone reading machines, there are also PC-based reading machines that scan a page of print and convert the text to synthesized speech, Braille, or large-print output. Because they are PC based, these machines also have the advantage of being usable with other typical computer software (Andrews, 1995).

Two of the most popular electronic Braille note takers are the **Braille 'n Speak** and the **BrailleMate** (Leventhal & Uslan, 1992). These portable devices can serve the same function as the Perkins Brailler or slate and stylus but offer additional speech synthesizer and word processing capabilities. Each costs about $1,500.

Thus far, consumers who are blind have found it easier to use personal computers with text-based DOS than graphics-based interfaces such as Windows, because the latter require the user to move a mouse to a relatively precise position on the screen in order to click on the desired function. Nonetheless, graphics-based interfaces have become increasingly popular in the general PC market. Given this trend, the job prospects of many workers who are blind are now threatened. Researchers are working on the challenge of making graphics interfaces that rely on use of a mouse easier to use for people who are blind (Chong, 1994).

Similar to closed captioning for people with hearing impairment, a service is now available for making television more accessible to people with visual impairment (Cronin & King, 1990). The **Descriptive Video Service**, developed by National Public Radio Station WGBH in Boston, is available for several public television programs. A narrated description of key visual features of the program is inserted between lapses in the dialogue.

Service Delivery Models

The four major educational placements for students with visual impairment, from most to least segregated, are (1) residential school, (2) special class, (3) resource room, and (4) regular class with itinerant teacher help. Even though some professionals still argue for this continuum of placements (e.g., Erwin, 1991), in practice, most students with visual impairment are educated either in residential schools or in regular classes with itinerant teacher services (especially the latter). The fact is, there are so few students with visual impairment that most schools find it difficult to provide services through special classes or resource rooms (Hatlen, 1993). Both residential institutions and **itinerant teacher services**—wherein a special education teacher visits several different schools to work with students and their general education classroom teachers—make more efficient use of professionals than do resource rooms or special classes. Residential institutions allow for a concentration of specialized services in one place, and itinerant teacher services allow for a distribution of services over several different areas.

In the early 1900s, virtually all children who were blind were educated in residential institutions, but today, itinerant teacher services to general education classrooms is the most popular placement for students with visual impairment. Much of

Kurzweil Reading Machine. A computerized device that converts print into speech for persons with visual impairment; the user places the printed material over a scanner that then reads the material aloud by means of an electronic voice.

PC/Kurzweil Personal Reader. A version of the Kurzweil Reading Machine that can be used with an IBM or Apple personal computer.

Braille 'n Speak. A portable electronic Braille note taker with speech-synthesizing capabilities.

BrailleMate. A portable electronic Braille note taker with speech-synthesizing capabilities.

Descriptive Video Service. A service for use of people with visual impairment that provides audio narrative of key visual elements; available for several public television programs.

itinerant teacher services. Services for students who are visually impaired, in which the special education teacher visits several different schools to work with students and their general education classroom teachers; the students attend their local schools and remain in general education classrooms.

this migration out of residential institutions occurred in the years following the passage of Public Law 94–142, the Education for All Handicapped Children Act, in 1975. (Recall that this law was updated in 1990 with passage of the Individuals with Disabilities Education Act, or IDEA.) Very few children who are blind are now placed in residential schools, unless they have additional disabilities, such as mental retardation or deafness.

The prevailing philosophy of integrating children with visual impairments with the sighted is also supported by the fact that many residential facilities have established cooperative arrangements with local public schools (Cronin, 1992; Erin, 1993; Scholl, 1993). In these arrangements, students who are visually impaired may come on a regular basis (e.g., once per week) to the institution as day students. Or they may enroll in short-term (e.g., one or two weeks) intensive courses as residential students. The staff of the residential facility usually concentrates on training independent living skills, such as mobility, personal grooming, and home management, while local school personnel emphasize academics. Also, support services, such as speech and physical therapy, are sometimes better delivered by personnel from institutions because they have had more experience working with children who are blind. And as some point out, given the low prevalence of blindness, having these children come to residential sites periodically affords them an opportunity to interact with other children who have the same types of disabilities (Cronin, 1992).

EARLY INTERVENTION

For many years, psychologists and educators believed that the sighted infant was almost totally lacking in visual abilities during the first half year or so of life. We now know that the young sighted infant is able to take in a great deal of information through the visual system. This fact makes it easy to understand why professionals are usually eager to begin intensive intervention as early as possible to help the infant with visual impairment begin to explore the environment.

An area of particular importance in early intervention for children with visual impairment is *mobility* (Palazesi, 1986). Some infants who are totally blind are late to crawl, which authorities speculate is due to the fact that they have not learned that there are things in their environments worth pursuing (Fraiberg, 1977). Infants who cannot see may not be as motivated as sighted infants to explore their extended environments because they are more engaged in examining things close to their bodies. Parents can sometimes contribute to their infants' lack of exploration. Concerned for the safety of their infants who are blind, some parents are reluctant to let them investigate their surroundings. Moreover, parents sometimes have difficulty assessing the proper amount of caution. By about six months of age, the sighted child spontaneously reaches out to visually perceived objects. Without specific training, the infant who is totally blind may not reach out to things he or she hears until late in the first year.

Unfortunately, as noted earlier in the discussion of mobility training, for many years, professionals did not begin training motor development and mobility until children with visual impairment were in the elementary grades. Today, most authorities agree that mobility training should be a critical component of preschool programming. In addition to introducing cane techniques to children as soon as they are able to walk relatively well, some researchers are experimenting with methods of encouraging infants at the crawling stage to explore their environments more actively. For example, one study was successful in increasing the exploratory behaviors of infants who were

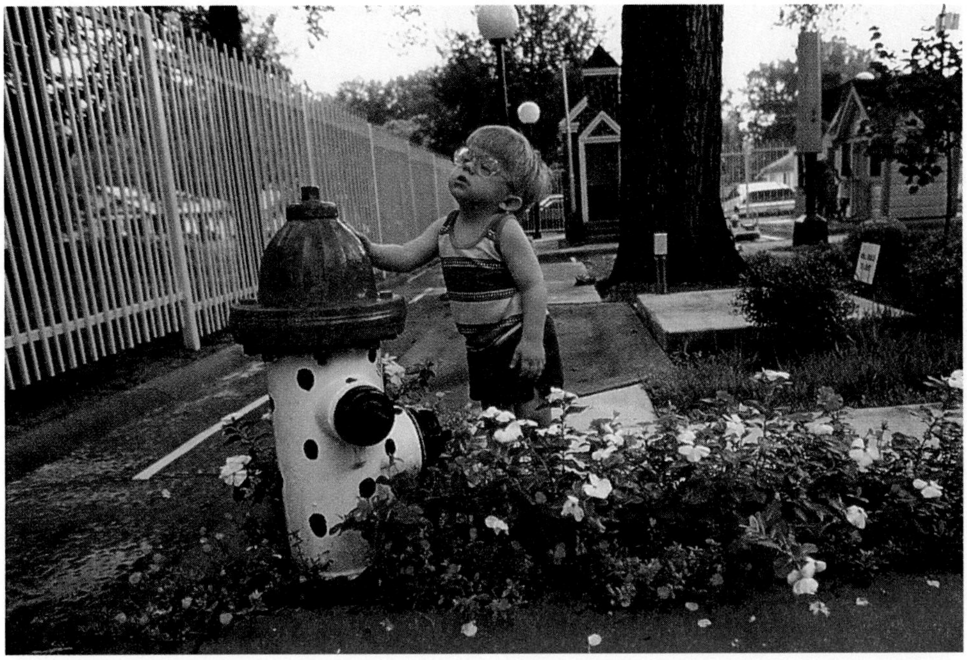

Children with visual impairment should be given many opportunities to explore and learn about their environments. Touchtown *is a program used to develop children's sense of orientation and to stimulate all their senses by providing a "palpable city."*

blind, using a specially constructed room containing a variety of tactile and auditory stimuli (Nielsen, 1991).

Most authorities agree that it is extremely important to involve parents of infants with visual impairment in early intervention efforts. Parents can become actively involved in working at home with their young children, helping them with fundamental skills, such as mobility and feeding. Parents, too, sometimes need support in coping with their reactions to having a baby with visual impairment. Sometimes, there is an overwhelming sense of grief. Professionals working in early intervention programs for infants who are blind often recommend that initial efforts should focus on helping parents cope with their own reactions to having a child who is blind (Maloney, 1981).

TRANSITION

Two closely related areas are difficult for some adolescents and adults with visual impairment—independence and employment.

Independent Living

When working with adolescents and adults with visual impairment, it is extremely important to keep in mind that achieving a sense of independence is often difficult for them. Many authorities point out that much of the problem of dependence is because of the way society treats persons without sight. A common mistake is to assume that such individuals are helpless. Many people think of blindness as a condition to be pitied.

People with visual impairment have a long history of arguing against paternalistic treatment by sighted society (see the box on p. 383). Back in the 1960s, Scott (1969) warned of the demeaning attitude of those who worked in agencies established to

Athletic activities are no longer considered off limits for people with visual impairment.

help people with visual impairment. The National Federation of the Blind has for several years argued fiercely that they want jobs, not handouts:

> What we need most is not, as the professionals would have it, medical help or psychological counseling but admission to the main channels of daily life and citizenship, not custody and care but understanding and acceptance. Above all, what we need is not more government programs or private charitable efforts. Instead, we want jobs, opportunity, and full participation in society. (Jernigan, 1985, p. 388)

Many people who are blind point to the Federal Aviation Administration's (FAA) policy toward airline travelers who are blind as an example of a paternalistic attitude. For years, the National Federation of the Blind has battled with the FAA and the airline industry over the right for people who are blind to sit by exits on airplanes. The current FAA policy stipulates that a person must be able to receive visual directions and be able to assess escape paths outside the aircraft. Individual airlines have varied in how they have interpreted these policies. Some have allowed people who are blind to take seats in exit rows while others have insisted that persons be able to see well enough, for example, to read the safety directions printed on the card in the seat pocket. The following is the reaction of a spokesperson for the National Federation of the Blind:*

> It is not enough to show that a given blind person in a given instance may block an exit or pose a safety hazard. Blind persons are just as diverse and variable in their behavior and characteristics as sighted persons are. . . . It must be shown that they are not being held to a higher standard of conduct than others. . . . and that there is something about blindness that makes the blind less capable. . . .
>
> If safety is the only consideration, no one at all will fly. But just as in using automobiles, there are tradeoffs, and we are willing to accept a certain amount of risk. . . .

* From "Equality, Disability, and Empowerment," by K. Jernigan, June 1992, in *The Braille Monitor,* pp. 292–298. Reprinted with permission

Fighting for Independence

Probably no other group of people with disabilities is more concerned about fostering and safeguarding their independence than are people who are blind. Perhaps this concern arises from the society's treatment of them. All too often, the sighted world assigns a certain degree of helplessness to people who cannot see. Whatever the reason, people who are blind tend to be unusually sensitive to being treated in a patronizing or condescending manner. This sensitivity often leads to their taking positions on issues that, at first, appear counterintuitive to the sighted. Two examples are the positions regarding Braille money and detectable warnings, taken by the National Federation of the Blind (NFB), the major U.S. organization representing people who are blind.

In 1994, Marc Maurer, president of the 50,000-member NFB learned that the U.S. Department of the Treasury was contemplating altering currency to accommodate people who are blind. Department of Treasury officials noted that Braille symbols on bills would help people who are blind distinguish among different denominations while also making it easier to detect counterfeit money. (Counterfeiters would not have easy access to the sophisticated equipment required to replicate Braille markings.) In a series of letters originally sent to *The Numismatist,* a magazine devoted to issues pertaining to currency and republished in *The Braille Monitor,* Maurer wrote:

> Part of the disadvantage of producing Braille money is the negative impression which will result. Having Braille on the money suggests that blind people are not able to manage in the world without all kinds of special adaptations. This is not the case. In fact, the question of real importance to the blind is not how to identify the money but how to get it in the first place. . . .
>
> It would serve as a constant reinforcement of the false idea that blind people cannot compete in the ordinary world with everybody else. In almost every pocket, in cash registers, in bank vaults, in dresser drawers, and under mattresses there would be this silent but ubiquitous reminder that changes are required in the world to accommodate the disadvantage caused by blindness. . . .
>
> The blind of the United States do not object to bills of different sizes or to bills with raised markings if it has been determined by the Department of the Treasury that this will be beneficial for the country as a whole. Coins are already of different sizes, and they have identifiable tactile markings. However, we do object to the creation of a currency which has been modified specifically to accommodate the blind. If it is a good idea for the country to have a currency which consists of bills of various sizes or which contains tactile markings for the purpose of preventing counterfeiting, the blind will be happy to use it. In fact, we will use whatever currency is developed. (Maurer, 1994, pp. 346–348)

Maurer's dry wit belies the seriousness with which he and the NFB take the issue of Braille currency.

The NFB has also taken a strong stand against what are referred to as **detectable warnings:** 24-inch-wide, hard-rubber strips with raised bumps, which the U.S. Department of Transportation has mandated (as part of the Americans with Disabilities Act of 1990) be installed along railway and subway platform edges. Instead of thanking the government for looking out for their welfare, the NFB has vehemently fought the use of detectable warnings, arguing that research has not proven them effective, and that they undermine independence:

> Do we as blind people want government to assert and maintain responsibility for our safety? Do we want government to require the rebuilding of the world for blind people as a result of this assertion of its responsibility? Or do we blind people wish to assert and maintain responsibility for ourselves, take the time and make the effort to learn the skills to protect ourselves as we move about our communities? . . .
>
> The time has now come in this debate as well as in other areas of the social contract to ask the painful but increasingly necessary question: how much is society willing to pay to save one or a very few lives? Presumably there would be fewer accidents at intersections, for example, if traffic engineers were to employ railroad-crossing-style barriers instead of red lights. But the cost would be staggering, and drivers would resent both the implication that they were likely to behave irresponsibly and the inconvenience of losing precious seconds as the light turned green. (Gashel, 1995, "Detectable Warnings Debate Continues," pp. 1084–1086)

It should be noted that not all individuals who are blind oppose the use of detectable warnings. In fact, the 42,000-member American Council of the Blind has come out in favor of them. Critics see the NFB position as being stubborn and endangering people's lives. The NFB, however, sees the use of detectable warnings as unnecessary and as one more demonstration of society's patronizing attitude toward people who are blind.

> The next fallback position for maximum safety in air travel would probably be to place trained, healthy airline officials in the exit rows, but the airlines say this is unacceptable because of the lost revenue. . . .
>
> If we go to the next fallback position for maximum safety, it would probably be to widen the exit row aisles and have no one sit in them at all . . . Again the airlines are not willing—and again for the same reason, economics. . . .

detectable warnings. Rubberized strips with raised bumps; designed to help people who are blind detect railway and subway platform edges; mandated by ADA.

Adjusting to Blindness and Cultural Difference

Ved Mehta was born in India in 1928 and educated in India, the United States, and England. During the first half of this century, educational opportunities for children who were blind were scarce, certainly in India. In spite of being relatively wealthy, his family hoped for little more than that Ved might avoid becoming a "blind beggar boy," holding out a tin cup on the streets of Bombay or Calcutta.

His series of autobiographical novels known as *Continents of Exile,* chronicles his experiences as a small child at boarding school in Bombay through his years at Harvard, Pomona College, and Oxford. The following excerpt is from his novel *Sound-Shadows of the New World,* which covers his adolescent years spent at the Arkansas School for the Blind, in Little Rock:

> Two birds fluttered overhead. I wondered what color they were. I wondered whether in some part of my mind I could remember the colors I had seen before I went blind, and whether, if I did, that would help me to understand Wayne's hatred of Negroes. I repeated to myself, "White, Negro, white, black." Sometimes people spoke of white as clean and black as dirty, but how could "clean" or "dirty" be applied to a whole race of people? Some people thought that the blind lived in darkness, but that was nonsense. The point was that the blind had no perception of light or darkness. Perhaps darkness was like the quiet of the night. I wondered how dark I was, how much I looked like a Negro, and what my kinship with the Negro was—where I fitted into the social puzzle. I wanted somehow or other to find out where I stood in the shading from white to black, to connect myself to the rest of the world. I ached to see, even for just a moment. (p. 74)

Source: From *Sound-shadows of the new world,* by V. Mehta, 1985, New York: W. W. Norton.

> Then perhaps the airlines could at least refuse to sell liquor to people who sit in the exit rows or ask for volunteers to sit there who do not intend to drink anyway. They decline to do the first of these things because of lost revenue and the second because of concern about frightening the passengers by reminding them of possible crashes or in-flight emergencies.
>
> Of course, none of this makes the case for permitting blind persons to sit in the exit rows, but it does demonstrate that safety is not the only (or perhaps even the prime) factor being considered. . . .
>
> Blind persons are either a greater hazard than others seated in exit rows or they aren't. If they are, they shouldn't sit there—and any blind person with any sense wouldn't want to. If they aren't a greater safety hazard than others, then prohibiting them from sitting in the exit row is discrimination. . . .
>
> So where does this leave us? Never in the history of commercial aviation has there been a single recorded instance of a blind person's blocking an exit, slowing an evacuation, or contributing to an accident. But there are recorded instances to the contrary. At night or when the cabin has been filled with smoke, blind persons have on more than one occasion found the exits and led others out. (Jernigan, 1991, pp. 51–53)

No matter which side one takes on the issue of airline seating, there is little doubt that the public has, at times, been at fault in creating an environment that fosters dependency in people with blindness. The accomplished author Ved Mehta has written several books dealing with his adjustment to blindness and going to school in the United States (Mehta, 1982, 1984, 1985, 1989). (See the box above.) In the book dealing with his adolescent years at the Arkansas School for the Blind, he talks about experiences that people who are blind typically have to face, experiences that undoubtedly can foster dependence:

> I decided that I didn't like going to coffee shops. I had generally eaten at a table, either with my family or with students and staff at a school, and eating alone at a counter filled me with sadness. Moreover, there were always incidents in the coffee

> shops that would leave me shaken. The waitresses would shout out the menu to me as if I were half deaf, and so attract the attention of everyone in the coffee shop. Even when they got to know me and treated me normally, I would have to contend with customers who didn't know me. I remember that once when I asked for my bill the waitress said, "A man already took care of it."
>
> "I insist on paying for myself."
>
> The waitress refused to accept the money. "The man done gone," she said to the coffee shop. "What does the kid want me to do—take money twice for the same ham sandwich? He should be thankful there are nice people to pay for him." I felt anything but thankful, however. I thought that I'd been an object of pity.
>
> I remember that another time Tom took me to a new coffee shop. The waitress, instead of asking me for my order, turned to him and asked, "What does he want to eat?"
>
> "A ham sandwich," I said, speaking up for myself. She brought me the ham sandwich, but throughout lunch she ignored me, talking to Tom as if I weren't there. (Mehta, 1985, pp. 198–199)

Rickelman and Blaylock (1983) conducted a survey of persons who were blind in which they were asked, among other things, to indicate how sighted individuals might respond to them to decrease their dependent behavior. The following surveyed individuals gave these main suggestions:

> 1. *Respecting and encouraging the blind person's individuality, capabilities, and independence:*
> Do not assume that because you can do something more conveniently or quickly you should automatically do it for the blind person.
> Blind people often do not need help. Ask, "Can I be of assistance?" instead of initiating help. Do not feel embarrassed or rejected if a blind person declines your offer of assistance. . . .
>
> 2. *Talking with the blind:*
> Feel free to approach and talk to a blind person. You have the right to ask any questions you wish. The blind person has the right to respond as he wishes.
> Identify yourself before beginning a conversation or offering assistance. . . .
> When you leave the presence of a blind person, always let him or her know that you are leaving.
> Talk in a normal tone of voice. Do not assume deafness or other disability.
> If your business is with a blind person, speak directly to the person rather than to sighted companions or relatives to get information.
>
> 3. *Becoming knowledgeable about guide techniques:*
> Let the blind person take your arm and walk slightly behind you. Never take his or her arm and push the blind person ahead of you. Walk at a normal pace.
> Always go through a door ahead of a blind person, telling him or her which way the door opens. (Rickelman & Blaylock, 1983, pp.10–11)

Many independent living skills that are learned incidentally by sighted people need to be taught explicitly to those who are visually impaired—for example, how to work household appliances, prepare and cook food, and even some parenting skills. Regarding the latter, the National Federation of the Blind promotes a booklet (*Parent Tips,* available from Janiece Betker, 1886 29th Ave. N.W., New Brighton, MN 55112), prepared by a parent who is blind, that provides tips on parenting. The booklet provides useful suggestions on such topics as carrying the baby safely, taking the baby's temperature, keeping the baby's clothing color-coordinated and socks matched, and giving liquid medicine and vitamins.

Obtaining gainful, fulfilling employment should not be an unrealistic goal for someone with visual impairment.

Droppers or syringes can be purchased which draw up only ½ or 1 teaspoonful of liquid. Droppers can also be saved from vitamin or liquid pain-reliever bottles, washed thoroughly and used for future medicines. When the dropper can no longer reach the medicine in the bottle, the medicine can be poured into small cups such as those that come with certain cold relief liquids. The dropper or syringe is placed into the cup and the liquid medicine drawn up. The remainder is then returned to the bottle.

In some ways, it is more important for people with visual impairment to learn to be independent than it is for those who are sighted. Adults with visual impairment often find that they need to take more initiative to achieve the same level of success as people who are sighted. As one job counselor put it when speaking to a group of college students with visual impairment: "As blind students, you will need to spend time on activities your sighted peers never think about—recruiting and organizing readers, having textbooks prepared in alternative media, getting an early start on term papers" (Rovig, 1992, p. 239).

Employment

Many working-age adults with visual impairment are unemployed, and those who do work are often overqualified for the jobs they hold (Freeman, Goetz, Richards, & Groenveld, 1991; Kirchner & Peterson, 1989). Some authorities attribute this unfortunate situation to inadequate transition programming at the secondary school level

(Hanley-Maxwell, Griffin, Szymanski, & Godley, 1990; Sacks & Pruett, 1992). Even well-educated adults with visual impairment, when surveyed, indicated that they had not received training to meet their career development needs (Wolffe, Roessler, & Schriner, 1992).

Reports of adults with visual impairment who achieve successful independent living and employment are becoming more and more common—although they are still not as common as one would hope. Innovative programs are being developed to meet the transition needs of students with visual impairment. For example, one successful program involves having adolescents and young adults with visual impairment come together with professionals for a three-week summer training session devoted to issues of transition (Sacks & Pruett, 1992). Among other things, this project used job shadowing in which each student is paired with an adult with a similar visual disability and a job that matches the student's interest. The students spend a couple of days with their partners, observing them on the job.

Visual impairment no doubt poses a real challenge for adjustment to everyday living, but remember Don's comments in the introduction to the chapter (see p. 353). People with visual impairment share many similarities with people in the rest of society. Special and general educators need to achieve the delicate balance between providing special programming for students with visual impairment and treating them in the same manner as they do the rest of their students.

Suggestions for Teaching
Students with Visual Impairment in General Education Classrooms

By E. Jane Nowacek

WHAT TO LOOK FOR IN SCHOOL

Children whose vision is severely impaired are usually diagnosed before they enter school, whereas students who have less severe visual problems are often identified during vision screenings conducted in schools. These routine examinations, however, are not foolproof. For example, they often do not measure near-point vision. Consequently, the problems of students who can read materials at a far distance but who cannot read those that are near may go undetected. In addition, some students develop visual problems after the primary grades, when schools usually stop screening. Other students may experience changes in vision as they spend more time reading and as the formats of reading materials become more dense and detailed. Teachers have many opportunities to observe students reading under a variety of conditions and to record their observations by noting signs indicating possible vision problems (see the box on p. 358).

HOW TO GATHER INFORMATION

Once you have recorded your observations, discuss them with the school nurse or the person who conducts the vision screenings in your school. He or she may want to conduct additional observations of the student. Share this information with the student's parents, who should be encouraged to arrange a professional eye examination.

TEACHING TECHNIQUES TO TRY

Adapting Educational Materials

From reading the chapter, you know that the primary educational difference between students with low vision and students who are blind is their ability to read print. Students who have low vision can read print, although they may use magnifying devices and require materials written in large print. Individuals who are blind, however, must be instructed by using materials written in Braille and by aural methods, including records, cassettes, and CDs. Therefore, one required modification for students who are mainstreamed is adaptation of instructional materials.

Although the itinerant or resource teacher will prepare or provide instructional materials written in Braille, you may find that tape recording instructional lessons, assignments, and tests saves time and reduces the need for planning far in advance. In addition, several organizations, such as the Library of Congress and the American Printing House for the Blind, provide audiotapes and records of a variety of textbooks and materials for pleasure reading. Other organizations, such as Recording for the Blind, also make a large selection of books available to students and have readers who will record especially requested materials.

In addition to adapted printed materials, there are a variety of other aids that your students may find useful in your classroom.

A. Science aids
   1. Braille thermometers
   2. insect identification kits
   3. machine kits, including working models (e.g., pulleys and levers)
B. Mathematical aids
   1. a Cranmer abacus (pocket-sized)
   2. compasses, rulers, and protractors with Braille markings
   3. hand-held models of geometric area and of volume
   4. form boards for manipulation of whole and fractional parts
   5. calculators with voice output
C. Writing aids
   1. raised-line checkbooks
   2. signature guides
D. Geography aids
   1. Braille atlases
   2. embossed relief and landform maps
   3. enlarged or textured maps
E. Physical education aids
   1. audible balls
   2. audible goal locators
   3. raised drawings and models of various sport fields or courts (Gearheart, Mullen, & Gearheart (1993), pp. 301–302)

In addition, itinerant or resource teachers who are trained to work with students who are visually impaired also can advise you about curricula specifically designed for these students, such as *Science Activities for the Visually Impaired* or *Project MAVIS,* a curriculum for social studies.

In addition to providing aids specifically designed for students with visual impairment, you can modify existing instructional materials by:

1. using real objects or tactile models in place of pictures whenever possible
2. selecting materials with clear type and pictures
3. printing or typing handouts in large print (Alumnae of the Visually Impaired Program at the University of British Columbia, 1994)

To illustrate how these modifications can be implemented, let's look into a typical primary-grade classroom. Here, the teacher often reads "big books" and stories to the class. When students with visual impairment cannot see the illustrations by sitting close to the reader, the teacher may provide them with their own copies of the book or reproduce the story, enlarging the print. To promote independent reading, the teacher may select and cut out large pictures and place them in a notebook, so the children can read these picture books. Or the teacher may transcribe students' stories and enlarge the print, so the children can read their own work. In addition, the teacher may encourage students to create books by using real objects that are placed in felt pockets and glued to the page. Finally, the teacher may create interactive story boards with real objects or with simple, enlarged pictures to use during story discussions (Rogow, 1994).

Written Materials

In discussing the use of written materials in all grades, Harley and Lawrence (1984) recommend that teachers provide materials that:

- offer high contrast, such as black lettering on nongloss white paper or white chalk on a dark chalkboard
- are uncrowded
- are printed on one side of the page only
- avoid overprinting letters on background pictures

Similarly, when selecting computer software programs, teachers should consider the clarity and size of the text and graphics. Large-size print and boldface type options are desirable features. A simple guideline to selecting print size is to be sure that students can see individual letters (Rogow, 1994).

Adapting Instructional Methods

Besides selecting and adapting materials, you can modify instruction and instructional procedures to enhance learning for students with visual impairment. For example, identify potentially difficult concepts and provide firsthand experiences, such as hands-on learning and concrete materials (Best, 1991). One teacher, for instance, created clay models to illustrate geological features and provided raised diagrams by drawing lines on construction paper with airplane glue (Travis, 1990). Encourage listening and oral communication skills through instruction with multisensory materials and in activities such as storytelling and small-group projects. Verbally describe classroom demonstrations and exhibits, and, when possible, encourage students to touch exhibits. For laboratory work, assign partners.

In order to provide time for students with visual impairment to prepare and read printed information, give them advanced lists of assignments and lecture notes. Similarly, allow them extra time to complete tests. Giving tests orally or via tape recorder are also helpful modifications, as is permitting students to respond to test items orally (Alumnae, 1994). Furthermore, consider alternating activities that require close eye work with those that are less visually demanding (Harley & Lawrence, 1984). Finally, make a notebook available that contains the information displayed in the classroom, such as bulletin board announcements and classroom rules, to ensure that all students have access to this information (MacCuspie, 1992).

Adapting the Classroom Environment

When students with visual impairment first enter your class, they will require orientation to the physical arrangement of the room that includes learning the location of materials, desks, activity areas, teacher's desk, and exits. You may orient your students more rapidly if you familiarize them with these features from one focal point, such as their desk (Ashcroft & Zambone-Ashley, 1980). For safety purposes, be sure that doors and drawers are kept consistently open or closed. Low-hanging objects, such as signs, and items that protrude from the walls should be pointed out. Rugs and mats should be taped firmly to the floor, and students should be reminded to push chairs underneath desks and tables (Alumnae, 1994).

Once students are oriented to the classroom, they should become familiar with the school and surrounding grounds, learning the locations of the gym, library, restrooms, cafeteria, water fountains, and playground. Keep students informed of changes in and additions to the classroom or school arrangements. Although you should encourage them to move about without the aid of sighted guides, you may want to assign a guide for special events and activities that occur outside the classroom, such as fire drills and assemblies (Craig & Howard, 1981).

In addition to providing an orientation to the school and classroom, Best (1991) suggests making sure that work surfaces in the class are glare free and large enough to accommodate a Brailler; that desks are positioned near the chalkboard and demonstrations; and that the lighting is appropriate. Natural light should come from behind or the side of the student, and a lamp should be available to illuminate the work surface, if needed. Modifications also may be necessary when using videotapes, filmstrips, and films. Torres and Corn (1990) recommend asking another student to read subtitles aloud to the class; using a rear-screen projector, which allows students who are visually impaired to sit right in front of the screen, when possible; and permitting students to view the material before or after the class to ensure they understood all the visual concepts presented.

As educators have pointed out, students with visual impairment deserve the same instruction in all content areas as their nondisabled classmates. However, they also deserve instruction in skill areas required to meet their specific needs, such as social, sensory-motor, independent, daily living skills, and orientation and mobility training (Curry & Hatlen, 1988, Sacks, Kekelis, & Gaylord-Ross, 1992). Although other professionals will conduct this training, you can play an important role by being aware of the times your mainstreamed students will receive instruction outside your class and by scheduling, whenever possible, new learning and special events when all students are in your room.

HELPFUL RESOURCES

Catalogues of Appliances, Aids, and Books

American Foundation for the Blind, 15 West Sixteenth Street, New York, NY 10011.

American Printing House for the Blind, Inc., 1939 Frankfort Avenue, Louisville, KY 40206.

BIT Corporation, 52 Roland Street, Boston, MA 02129.

Braille Book Review, National Library Service for the Blind and Physically Handicapped, 1291 Taylor Street N.W., Washington, DC 20542.

Carroll Center for the Blind, 770 Centre Street, Newton, MA 02649.

Hearsay, Association of Radio Reading Services, National Office, 4200 Wisconsin Avenue, Suite 106–346, Washington, DC 20016.

Independent Living Aids, 27 East Mall, Plainview, NY 11803–4404.

National Association for Visually Handicapped, 22 West 21st Street, New York, NY 10010.

Sensory Aids Foundation, Suite 12, 399 Sherman Avenue, Palo Alto, CA 94306.

Talking Book Topics, National Library Service for the Blind and Physically Handicapped, Library of Congress, 1291 Taylor Street N.W., Washington, DC 20542 (lists recorded books and magazines that are available through a national network of cooperating libraries).

Books and Records

Books on Tape, Inc., P.O. Box 7900, Newport Beach, CA 92658.

Braille Book Bank of the National Braille Associates, 422 Clinton Avenue South, Rochester, NY 14620.

Braille Institute of America, 741 North Vermont Avenue, Los Angeles, CA 00029.

Computerized books for the blind and print handicapped, University of Montana, 33 N. Corbin Hall, Missoula, MT 59812.

IBM National Support Center for Persons with Disabilities, P.O. Box 2150, Atlanta, GA 30055.

Library Reproduction Service, The Microfilm Company of California, Inc., 1977 South Los Angeles Street, Los Angeles, CA 90011.

Oakmont Visually Handicapped Workshop, Oakmont Adult Community, 6637 Oakmont Drive, Santa Rosa, CA 94505.

National Braille Press, Inc., (617) 266–6160.

Recording for the Blind, Inc., 20 Roszel Road, Princeton, NJ 08540.

Regional Libraries of the Library of Congress.

Taping for the Blind, 3935 Essex Lane, Houston, TX 77027, (713) 622-2767.

Vision Foundation, 818 Mt. Auburn Street, Watertown, MA 02172, (617) 926–4232.

Toys and Games

Touch Toys and How to Make Them:

For Information: Eleanor Timburg, 3519 Porter Street N.W., Washington, DC 20016.

To order: Touch Toys, P.O. Box 2224, Rockville, MD 20852.

Gallagher, P. (1978). *Educational games for visually handicapped children.* Denver: Love Publishing.

Services

Associated Services for the Blind, 919 Walnut Street, Philadelphia, PA 19107, (215) 627–0600.

Blind Outdoor Leisure Development, 533 East Main Street, Aspen, CO 81611.

Directory of services for blind and visually impaired persons in the United States (23rd ed.), American Foundation for the Blind, 15 West 16th Street, New York, NY 10011.

Division of Blind and Visually Impaired, 330 C. Street S.W., Washington, DC 20202.

Guide Dog Foundation for the Blind, 371 East Jericho Turnpike, Smithtown, NY 11787, (516) 265–2121.

Guiding Eyes for the Blind, 611 Granite Springs Road, Yorktown Heights, NY 10598, (914) 245–4024.

Jewish Guild for the Blind, 15 West 65th Street, New York, NY 10023.

Job Accommodation Network (JAN), West Virginia University, 809 All Hall, P.O. Box 6123, Morgantown, WV 26506–6123.

National Braille Association, 1290 University Avenue, Rochester, NY 14607.

New York Lighthouse Low Vision Service, 111 East 59th Street, New York, NY 10022.

Visions, Services for the Blind and Visually Impaired, 817 Broadway, 11th Floor, New York, NY 10003, (212) 477–3800.

Instructional Methods

Asen, S. (1994). *Teaching and learning with technology* (Teacher's Guide). Alexandria, VA: Association for Supervision and Curriculum Development.

Barraga, N. C., & Erin, J. N. (1992). *Visual handicaps and learning* (3rd ed.). Austin, TX: Pro-Ed.

Best, A. B. (1991). *Teaching children with visual impairments.* Philadelphia: Open University Press.

Chapman, E. K., & Stone, J. M. (1988). *The visually handicapped child in your classroom.* London: Cassell.

Haring, N., & Romer, L. (Eds.) (1995). *Welcoming students who are deaf-blind into typical classrooms: Facilitating school participating, learning, friendships.* Baltimore: Paul H. Brookes.

Hazekamp, J., & Huebner, K. M. (Eds). (1989). *Program planning and evaluation for blind and visually impaired students.* New York: American Foundation for the Blind.

Hill, J. L. (1990). Mainstreaming visually impaired children: The need for modifications. *Journal of Visual Impairment and Blindness, 84,* 354–360.

Koenig, A. J. (1992). A framework for understanding the literacy of individuals with visual impairments. *Journal of Visual Impairment and Blindness, 86,* 277–284.

Koenig, A. J., & Holbrook, M. C. (1991). Determining the reading medium for visually impaired students via diagnostic teaching. *Journal of Visual Impairment and Blindness, 85,* 61–68.

Lander, C. R. (1992). *Developing positive attitudes about disabilities.* Ballwin, MO: Claymont School.

Lewis, R. (1993). *Special education technology: Classroom applications.* Pacific Grove, CA: Brookes/Cole.

Lewis, R., & Doorlag, D. H. (1995). *Teaching special students in the mainstream* (4th ed., pp. 414–442). Englewood Cliffs, NJ: Merrill Prentice Hall.

Liedtke, W. W., & Stainton, L. B. (1994). Fostering the development of number sense—Selected ideas for the blind. *B.C. Journal of Special Education, 18,* 24–32.

McCoy, K. A. (1995). *Teaching special learners in the general education classroom.* Denver, CO: Love Publishing.

Rogow, S. M. (1994). Literacy and children with severe visual problems. *B.C. Journal of Special Education, 18,* 101–108.

Sacks, S. K., Kekelis, L. S., & Gaylord-Ross, R. J. (Eds.). (1992). *The development of social skills by blind and visually impaired students.* New York: American Foundation for the Blind.

Spenciner, L. J. (1992). Mainstreaming the child with a visual impairment. In L. G. Cohen (Ed.), *Children with exceptional needs in regular classrooms* (pp. 82–97). Washington, DC: National Education Association.

Torres, I. (1990). *When you have a visually handicapped child in your classroom: Suggestions for teachers* (2nd ed.). New York: American Foundation for the Blind.

Wisconsin Department of Public Instruction. (1990). *A guide to curriculum planning in education for the visually impaired.* Milwaukee: Wisconsin Department of Public Instruction.

Software

2 + 2, R. J. Cooper and Associates, 24843 Del Prado, Suite 283, Dana Point, CA 92629, (800) RJ–COOPER (714–240–1912). (Macintosh, Windows).

Arithmetic Critters, MECC, 6160 Summit Drive N., Minneapolis, MN 55430–4003, (800) 685–6322. (Apple IIe; Apple IIGS).

Beginning Reading Skills, Micro–Ed, P.O. Box 24750, Edina, MN 55424, (612) 929–2242. (Commodore) (uses speech).

Big Book Maker: Letters, Numbers, and Shapes, Pelican Software, Inc., 768 Farmington Avenue, Farmington, CT 06032, (800) 822–DISK.

Big Book Maker: Myths and Legends, Pelican Software, Inc., 768 Farmington Avenue, Farmington, CT 06032, (800) 822–DISK.

Big Book Maker: Tall Tales and American Folk Heroes, Pelican Software, Inc., 768 Farmington Avenue, Farmington, CT 06032, (800) 822–DISK.

Big Type Typing, Harbor Computing Services, P.O. Box 2181, Gig Harbor, WA 98335 (206) 858–9459. (Apple IIe; Apple IIGS) (requires ECHO speech synthesizer).

Elementary Volume 1: Mathematics, American Printing House for the Blind, P.O. Box 6085, 18339 Frankfort Avenue, Louisville, KY 40206–0085, (800) 223–1839. (Apple IIe; Apple IIGS) (requires ECHO speech synthesizer).

Food Facts, American Printing House for the Blind, P.O. Box 6085, 18339 Frankfort Avenue, Louisville, KY 40206–0085, (800) 223–1839. (Apple IIe; Apple IIGS) (requires ECHO speech synthesizer).

Illustrations Picture Disks, Access Unlimited, 3535 Briarpark Drive, Suite 102, Houston, TX 77042–5235. (Apple IIe; Apple IIGS).

Jo-Jos Reading Circus, MindPlay, 160 W. Ft. Lowell, Tucson, AZ 85705, (800) 221–7911. (Macintosh) (interactive reading).

Keys to Success: Computer Keyboard Skills for Blind Children, Life Science Associates, 1 Fenimore Road, Bayport, NY 11705–2115, (516) 472–2111. (Apple IIe) (requires ECHO II speech synthesizer).

Language Experience Recorder, Teacher Support Software, 1035 N.W. 57th Street, Gainesville, FL 32605, (800) 228–2871. (Apple IIe; Apple IIGS; Macintosh; DOS).

LetterTalk, American Printing House for the Blind, P.O. Box 6085, 18339 Frankfort Avenue, Louisville, KY 40206–0085, (800) 223–1839. (Apple IIe; Apple IIGS) (requires ECHO) (typing tutor).

Pix Cells, Raised Dot Computing, Inc., 408 S. Baldwin Street, Madison, WI 53703, (800) 347–9594.

Milt's Math Drills, Hartley Courseware, Inc., 3451 Dunkle Drive, Suite 200, Lansing, MI 48911–4216, (800) 247–1380. (Apple IIe; Apple IIGS).

Noteworthy GW Micro, Inc. (DOS) (a note-taking program).

Perfect Scribe, Arts Computer Products, Inc., 33 Richdale Avenue, P.O. Box 604, Cambridge, MA 02140, (617) 547–5320. (WordPerfect 5.1 and 6.0 tutorial).

Prefixes, American Printing House for the Blind, P.O. Box 6085, 18339 Frankfort Avenue, Louisville, KY 40206–0085, (800) 223–1839. (Apple IIe; Apple IIGS).

Story Board, Data Command, Inc., P.O. Box 548, Kankakee, IL 60901, (800) 528–7390. (Apple IIe; Apple IIGS) (interactive writing program).

Talking Checkbook, Talking Computer Products, 100 Main, Wallace, KS 67761, (913) 891–3522. (Apple IIe; Apple IIGS) (requires ECHO speech synthesizer).

Texttalker, American Printing House for the Blind, P.O. Box 6085, 18339 Frankfort Avenue, Louisville, KY 40206–0085, (800) 223–1839. (Apple IIe; Apple IIGS) (a text-to-speech program for many Apple programs—requires ECHO speech synthesizer).

Word-Processing Programs

Dr. Peet's Talkwriter, Hartley Courseware, Inc., 3451 Dunkle Drive, Suite 200, Lansing, MI 48911–4216, (800) 247–1380. (Apple IIe; Apple IIGS) (requires speech synthesizer)

Magic Slate II, Sunburst Communications, 101 Castleton Street, Pleasantville, NY 10570, (800) 628–8897. (Apple IIe; Apple IIGS).

Large-Print Programs

1-2-3 Sequence Me, Sunburst Communications, 101 Castleton Street, Pleasantville, NY 10570, (800) 628–8897. (Apple IIe; Apple IIGS; Macintosh) (beginning readers sequence pictures or words to create a story).

Big Book Maker: Favorite Fairy Tales and Nursery Rhymes, Pelican Software, Inc., 768 Farmington Avenue, Farmington, CT 06032, (800) 822–DISK. (prints strips that tape together to create "big books").

Big Book Makes: Letters, Numbers, and Shapes. Pelican Software, Inc., 768 Farmington Avenue, Farmington, CT 06032, (800) 822–DISK.

Big Book Maker: Tall Tales and American Fold Heros, Pelican Software, Inc., 768 Farmington Avenue, Farmington, CT 06032, (800) 822–DISK.

Big Book Maker: Feeling Good about Yourself, Pelican Software, Inc., 768 Farmington Avenue, Farmington, CT 06032, (800) 822–DISK.

Cotton Tales, MindPlay, 160 W. Ft. Lowell, Tucson, AZ 85705, (800) 221–7911. (Apple IIe; Apple IIGS; Macintosh; DOS).

Letter Recognition, Hartley Courseware, Inc., 3451 Dunkle Drive, Suite 200, Lansing, MI 48911–4216, (800) 247–1380. (Apple IIe; Apple IIGS).

Math Tri-Pack, Dataflo Computer Services, Inc., 531 U.S. Rt. 4, Enfield, NH 03748 (603) 448–2223. (Apple IIe; Apple IIGS; DOS).

Railroad Snoop, Sunburst Communications, 101 Castleton Street, Pleasantville, NY 10570, (800) 628–8897. (Apple IIe; Apple IIGS) (requires Magic slate 11 40-column) (story writing for fifth–seventh grades).

Schoolcraft Games I, Kidsview Software, P.O. Box 98, Warner, NH 03278, (800) 562–7501. (Apple IIe; Apple IIGS).

Schoolcraft Math 1, Kidsview Software, P.O. Box 98, Warner, NH 03278, (800) 562–7501. (Apple IIe; Apple IIGS).

Schoolcraft Word 1, Kidsview Software, P.O. Box 98, Warner, NH 03278, (800) 562–7501. (Apple IIe; Apple IIGS).

Ready-Set-Read, Continental Press, Inc., 520 E. Bainbridge Street, Elizabethtown, PA 17022, (800) 233–0759. (Apple IIe; Apple IIGS).

Organizations

American Council of the Blind, 1155 Fifteenth Street N.W., Suite, 720, Washington, DC 20005, (202) 467–5081.

American Council of the Blind Parents, c/o American Council of the Blind, 1155 Fifteenth Street N.W., Suite, 720, Washington, DC 20005, (202) 467–5081.

American Foundation for the Blind, 15 West 16th Street, New York, NY 10011, (212) 620–2000.

Association for Education and Rehabilitation of the Blind and Visually Impaired, 206 North Washington Street, Alexandria, VA 22314, (703) 548–1884.

Division for the Visually Handicapped, Council for Exceptional Children, 1920 Association Drive, Reston, VA 22091, (703) 620–3660.

National Federation of the Blind, 1800 Johnson Street, Baltimore, MD 21230, (301) 659–9314.

United States Association for Blind Athletes, 33 N. Institute Street, Brown Hall, Suite 015, Colorado Springs, CO 80903.

BIBLIOGRAPHY FOR TEACHING SUGGESTIONS

Alumnae of the Visually Impaired Program, Faculty of Education, University of British Columbia. (1994). Visually impaired children in regular classrooms: A guide for resource and classroom teachers. *B.C. Journal of Special Education, 18,* 173–180.

Ashcroft, S. C., & Zambone-Ashley, A. M. (1980). Mainstreaming children with visual impairments. *Journal of Research and Development in Education, 13,* 22–35.

Best, A. B. (1991). *Teaching children with visual impairments.* Philadelphia: Open University Press.

Craig, R., & Howard, C. (1981). Visual impairment. In M. L. Hardman, M. W. Egan, & D. Landau (Eds.), *What will we do in the morning?* (pp. 180–209). Dubuque, IA: William C. Brown.

Curry, S. A., & Hatlen, P. H. (1988). Meeting the unique educational needs of visually impaired pupils through appropriate placement. *Journal of Visual Impairment and Blindness, 82,* 417–424.

Gearheart, B., Mullen, R. C., & Gearheart, C. J. (1993). *Exceptional individuals.* Pacific Grove, CA: Brooks/Cole.

Harley, R. K., & Lawrence, G. A. (1984). *Visual impairment in the schools* (2nd ed.). Springfield, IL: Charles C. Thomas.

MacCuspie, A. (1992). Tips for teachers. *DVH Quarterly, 27,* 11.

Project MAVIS. (1979). Boulder, CO: Social Science Education Consortium.

Rogow, S. M. (1994). Literacy and children with severe visual problems. *B. C. Journal of Special Education, 18,* 101–108.

Sacks, S. Z., Kekelis, L. S., & Gaylord-Ross, R. J. (1992). *The development of social skills by blind and visually impaired students*. New York: American Foundation for the Blind.

Science activities for the visually impaired. (1977). Berkeley, CA: Lawrence Hall of Science, University of California.

Scott, E. P. (1982). *Your visually impaired student: A guide for teachers*. Baltimore: University Park Press.

Torres, I., & Corn, A. L. (1990). *When you have a visually handicapped child in your classroom: Suggestions for teachers*. New York: American Foundation for the Blind.

Travis, J. W. (1990). Geology and the visually impaired student. *Journal of Geological Education, 38*, 41–49.

SUMMARY

There are two definitions of *visual impairment*—legal and educational. The legal definition depends on the measurement of visual acuity and field of vision. A person who is legally blind has visual acuity of 20/200 or less in the better eye, even with correction, or has a very narrow (less than 20 degrees) field of vision. Individuals who are partially sighted have visual acuity between 20/70 and 20/200 in the better eye with correction.

Educators, however, prefer to define *blindness* according to how well the person functions, especially in reading. For the educator, blindness indicates the need to read Braille or use aural methods. Those who can read print, even though they may need magnification or large-print books, have low vision. The majority of those who are legally blind have some vision. Many students who are legally blind are not educationally blind because they can read print.

Blindness is one of the least prevalent disabling conditions in childhood but is much more prevalent in adults.

The Snellen chart, consisting of rows of letters or of *E*s arranged in different positions, measures visual acuity for far distances. Special charts measure visual acuity for near distances. There are also methods for measuring visual efficiency.

Most visual problems are the results of errors of refraction. That is, because of faulty structure and/or malfunction of the eye, light rays do not focus on the retina. The most common visual impairments are myopia (nearsightedness), hyperopia (farsightedness), and astigmatism (blurred vision). Eyeglasses or contact lenses can usually correct these problems. More serious impairments include glaucoma, cataracts, diabetic retinopathy, coloboma, retinitis pigmentosa, retinopathy of prematurity (ROP), strabismus, and nystagmus. Most serious visual impairments in school-age students are due to hereditary factors. When scientists first discovered that ROP was caused by high levels of oxygen administered to premature newborns, incidents of this condition decreased. Research indicates, however, that ROP is on the rise due to medicine's efforts to keep more premature babies alive.

Most authorities believe that visual impairment may result in a few subtle language differences but not in deficient language skills. Also, blindness does not result in intellectual retardation. There are some differences in conceptual development because children with visual impairment rely more on touch to learn about the world. They also need to be more vigilant to pick up information from their environment. Research has shown that early training in the use of strategies helps children who are blind use their sense of touch more efficiently.

A very important ability for the successful adjustment of people with visual impairment is mobility. There is no one-to-one relationship between the age at onset and the degree of visual loss and mobility skills. Mobility is greatly affected by motivation. Mobility skills depend largely on spatial ability. Those who are able to conceptualize their environments as cognitive maps have better mobility skills than do those who process their environments sequentially.

People who are blind do not, as is commonly thought, have an inherent obstacle sense. But some can develop the ability to detect obstacles by detecting changes in the pitches of echoes as they approach obstacles. Another myth is that people who are blind automatically develop better acuity in other senses. What they actually do is become adept at picking up other sensory cues in their surroundings, thus making better use of their intact senses.

Comparing the academic achievement of students with visual impairment to that of students who are sighted is difficult because the two are tested under different conditions. Evidence suggests, however, that students with visual impairment are behind their sighted peers in achievement.

Personality problems are not an inherent condition of visual impairment. Any social adjustment problems that students with visual impairment have are usually due to society's reaction to blindness. The stereotypic behaviors (e.g., eye poking and body rocking) exhibited by a few persons who are blind can be an impediment to social acceptance, but researchers are working on developing techniques to diminish their occurrence.

Educational experiences in regular classrooms are frequently visual. But with some modifications, teachers can usually apply the same general principles of instruction to both students with and without visual impairment. Since the mid-1960s, there has been a sharp decline in the use of Braille. Many professionals are now decrying this decrease because they believe it has led to a high rate of illiteracy. The National Federation of the Blind has lobbied for Braille bills to increase the availability of Braille and to establish Braille competency for all teachers of students with visual impairment. Braille is now also being recommended for those whose low vision might worsen over the years:

In addition to Braille, large-print books and audiotapes are available. Also, scientists are developing a number of technological devices; examples are the Optacon, the Kurzweil Reading Machine, and the PC/Kurzweil Personal Reader. Various PC-based reading machines are becoming available, as well.

Mobility training can involve the use of the long cane, guide dogs, human guides, and electronic devices. Most mobility instructors recommend the long cane for the majority of individuals who are blind. At one time, mobility instruction for children did not begin until elementary or secondary school. Now, most authorities recommend that mobility instruction should begin in preschool.

The four basic educational placements for students with visual impairment from most to least segregated, are residential school, special class, resource room, and regular class with itinerant teacher services. Residential placement, at one time the most popular alternative, is now recommended much less frequently than regular classrooms with itinerant services. The relatively low incidence of visual impairment makes the use of resource rooms and special classrooms less practical.

Without special attention, infants with visual impairment may lag behind their sighted peers, especially in mobility. Impaired vision may restrict their interaction with their environment. Early intervention often focuses on parental interaction with the child and parental reaction to the child's disability.

Education for the adolescent and adult stresses independent living and employment skills. Independence is a particularly important area because society often mistakenly treats people with visual impairment as helpless. Many adults with visual impairment are unemployed or overqualified for their jobs. Professionals are attempting to overcome the bleak employment picture by using innovative approaches.

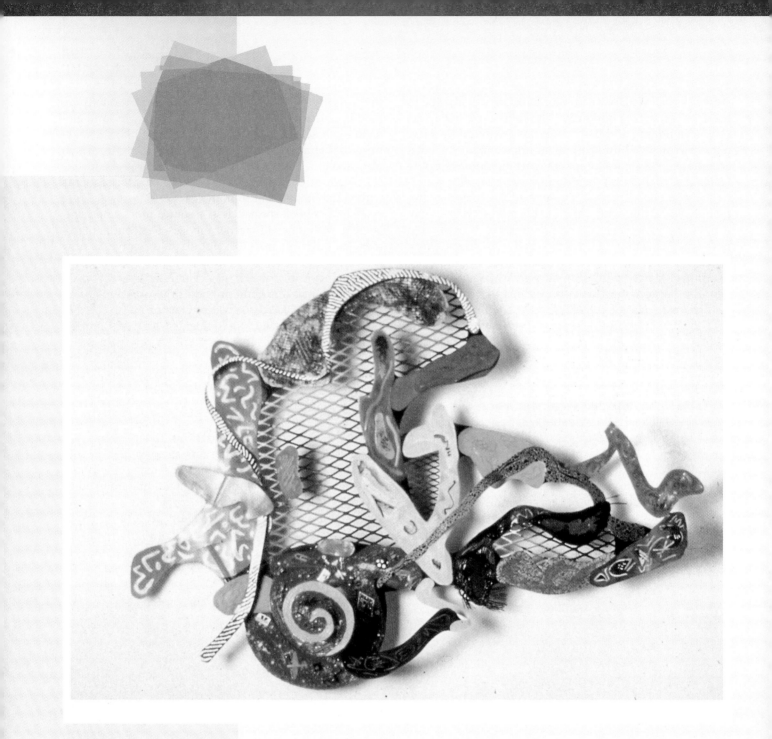

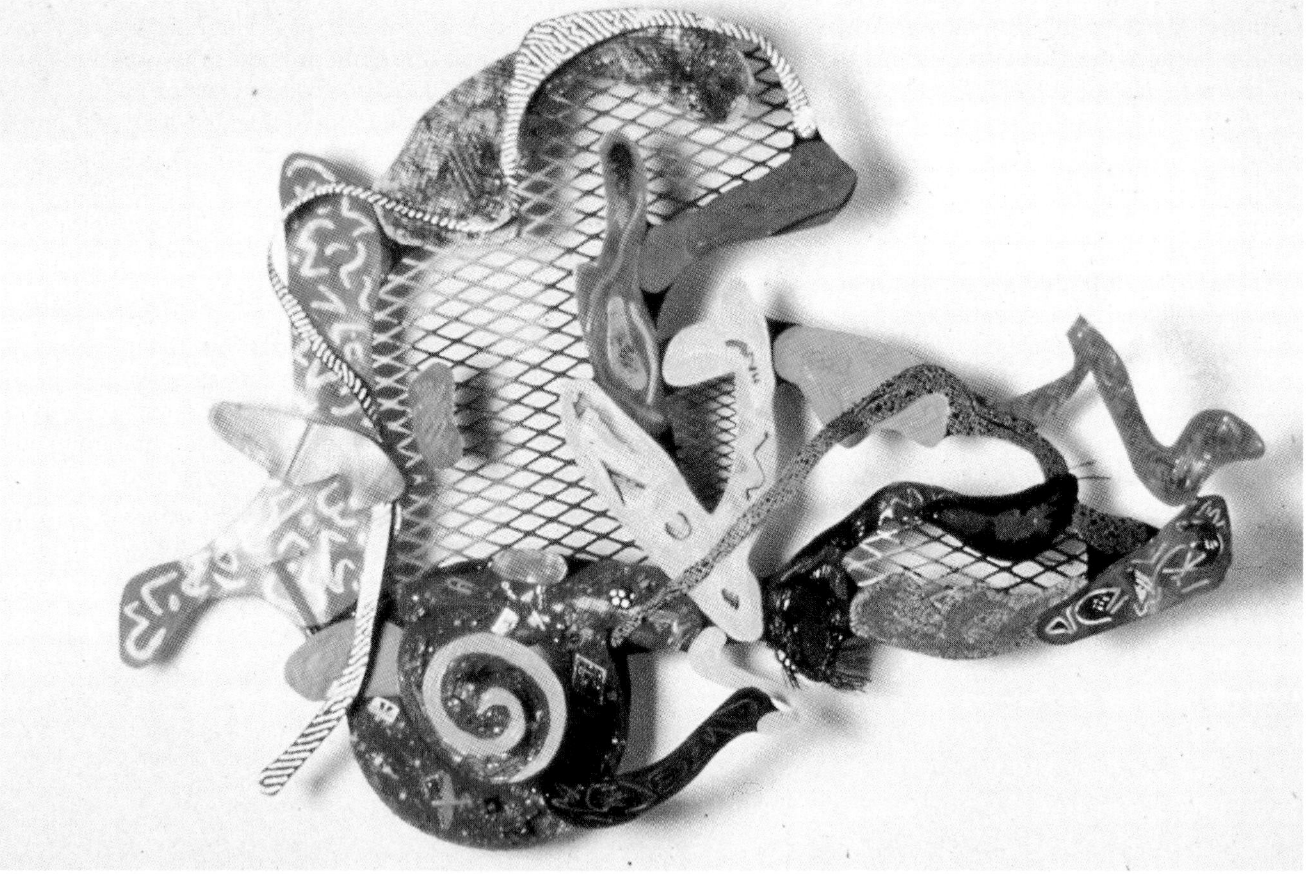

Greg DePauw
Greg DePauw, who has quadriplegia, has been a full-time exhibiting artist for fifteen years. He works in watercolor, acrylic, aluminum, and sheet metal. His assemblages are part of collections owned by AT&T, Sheraton Inns, Hilton Inns, and many others.

10

Physical Disabilities

My friend Stephen and I used to do pony parties together. . . . We were invariably late for the birthday party, a result of loading the ponies at the last minute, combined with our truly remarkable propensity for getting lost. . . .

Once we reached the party, there was a great rush of excitement. The children, realizing that the ponies had arrived, would come running from the backyard in their silly hats; their now forgotten balloons, bobbing colorfully behind them, would fly off in search of some tree or telephone wire. . . .

My pleasure at the sight of the children didn't last long, however. I knew what was coming. As soon as they got over the thrill of being near the ponies, they'd notice me. Half my jaw was missing, which gave my face a strange triangular shape, accentuated by the fact that I was unable to keep my mouth completely closed. When I first started doing pony parties, my hair was still short and wispy, still growing in from the chemo. But as it grew I made things worse by continuously bowing my head and hiding behind the curtain of hair, furtively peering out at the world like some nervous actor. Unlike the actor, though, I didn't secretly relish my audience, and if it were possible I would have stood behind that curtain forever, my head bent in an eternal act of deference. I was, however, dependent upon my audience. Their approval or disapproval defined everything for me, and I believed with every cell of my body approval wasn't written into my particular script. I was fourteen years old.

Lucy Grealy
Autobiography of a Face

In Western culture, people are almost obsessed with their bodies. They don't just want to be healthy and strong; they want to be beautiful—well-formed and attractive to others. In fact, some people seem to be more concerned about the impression their bodies make than they are about their own well-being. They may even endanger their health in an effort to become more physically alluring. It is not really surprising, then, that people with physical disabilities must fight two battles—the battle to overcome the limitations imposed by their physical conditions and the battle to be accepted by others.

Individuals with physical disabilities or differences are often stared at, teased, socially rejected, or, in other ways, treated with cruelty. In the excerpt from her autobiography (see p. 395), Lucy Grealy—who at the age of eight had cancer, necessitating disfiguring surgery and chemotherapy—describes the lack of acceptance and approval she felt from others. And later in this chapter, Matt Radcliffe—who had a brain tumor that affected his appearance and abilities in childhood and adolescence—also describes the fear, teasing, and lack of acceptance shown by his peers (see the box on pp.438–439). The reactions of others are major barriers to the social and educational development of children and youths with physical differences or disabilities.

Children with physical disabilities often face more than the problem of acceptance, however. For many, accomplishing the seemingly simple tasks of everyday living is a minor—or major—miracle.

DEFINITION AND CLASSIFICATION

In this chapter, we consider children whose primary distinguishing characteristics are health or physical problems. For the purposes of this book, *children with physical disabilities* are defined as those whose physical limitations or health problems interfere with school attendance or learning to such an extent that special services, training, equipment, materials, or facilities are required. Our definition excludes children whose *primary* characteristics are visual or auditory impairments, although some children with physical disabilities have these deficiencies as *secondary* problems. Children who have physical disabilities may also have mental retardation, learning disabilities, emotional or behavioral disorders, communication disorders, or special gifts or talents. Thus, we consider in this chapter those children whose physical condition is the first and foremost concern but whose additional characteristics may be extremely varied. The child's physical condition is, of course, the proper concern of the medical profession—but when physical problems have obvious implications for education, teaching specialists may need to enter the scene.

The fact that the primary distinguishing characteristics of children with physical disabilities are medical conditions, health problems, or physical limitations highlights the necessity of interdisciplinary cooperation. There simply *must* be communication between physicians and special educators to maintain the child's health and at the same time develop whatever capabilities he or she has (Bigge, 1991).

There is a tremendous range and variety of physical disabilities. Children may have **congenital anomalies** (defects they are born with), or they may acquire disabilities through accident or disease after birth. Some physical disabilities are comparatively mild and transitory; others are profound and progressive, ending in total incapacitation and early death. So it is difficult to discuss physical disabilities in general. Most of the remainder of the chapter is organized around specific conditions and diseases

congenital anomaly. An irregularity (anomaly) present at birth; may or may not be due to genetic factors.

Misconceptions about Persons with Physical Disabilities

Myth	Fact
Myth Cerebral palsy is a contagious disease.	**Fact** Cerebral palsy is not a disease. It is a nonprogressive neurological injury. It is a disorder of muscle control and coordination caused by injury to the brain before or during birth or in early childhood.
Myth Physical disabilities of all kinds are decreasing because of medical advances.	**Fact** Because of advances in medical technology, the number of children with severe disabilities is increasing. The number of survivors of serious medical conditions who develop normally or have mild impairments, such as hyperactivity and learning disabilities, is also increasing.
Myth The greatest educational problem involving children with physical disabilities is highly specialized instruction.	**Fact** The greatest educational problem is teaching people without disabilities about what it is like to have a disability and how disabilities can be accommodated.
Myth The more severe a person's physical disability, the lower his or her intelligence.	**Fact** A person may be severely physically disabled by cerebral palsy or another condition but have a brilliant mind.
Myth People with epilepsy are mentally ill.	**Fact** People with epilepsy (seizure disorder) are not any more or less disposed to mental illness than those who do not have epilepsy.
Myth Arthritis is found only in adults, particularly those who are elderly.	**Fact** Arthritic conditions are found in people of any age, including young children.
Myth People with physical disabilities have no need for sexual expression.	**Fact** People with physical disabilities have sexual urges and need outlets for sexual expression.
Myth The effects of traumatic brain injury are not distinguishable from those of other disabilities, such as mental retardation, learning disabilities, and emotional or behavioral disorders.	**Fact** A person who has had traumatic injury to the brain may, indeed, show cognitive, social, emotional, and behavioral characteristics much like those associated with other disabilities. However, the causes of these characteristics, their prognosis and course, and their management may be quite different from those of other disabilities.

In the past, physical disabilities kept children from engaging in many everyday activities, but today, they are encouraged to participate to the fullest extent possible.

falling under one of several categories: traumatic brain injury (TBI), other neurological impairments, musculoskeletal conditions, and other conditions affecting health or physical ability.

PREVALENCE AND NEED

Figures from the U.S. Department of Education (1994) indicate that over 200,000 students are being served under three special education categories related to physical disabilities:

1. orthopedic impairments (about 53,000)
2. other health impaired (about 66,000)
3. multiple disabilities (about 103,000)

However, the needs of many students with physical disabilities appear to be unmet for a number of reasons, including the fact that the population of children and youths with physical disabilities is growing but the availability of health and social service programs is not (Martin, 1992).

Part of the increase in the prevalence of physical disabilities may be due to improvements in the identification of and medical services to children with certain conditions. Ironically, medical advances have not only improved the chances of preventing or curing certain diseases and disorders; they have also assured the survival of more children with severe medical problems (Blum, 1992; Brown, 1993). Many children with severe and multiple disabilities and those with severe, chronic illnesses or severe injuries, who in the past would not have survived long, today can have a normal lifespan. So declining mortality rates do not necessarily mean there will be fewer individuals with disabilities. Moreover, improvements in medical care may not lower the number of individuals with disabilities unless there is also a lowering of risk factors in the environment—factors such as accidents, toxic substances, poverty, malnutrition, disease, and interpersonal violence (Baumeister, Kupstas, & Klindworth, 1990; Pless, 1994).

TRAUMATIC BRAIN INJURY (TBI)

In Chapter 1, we noted that IDEA (the Individuals with Disabilities Education Act of 1990) created a new category of disability, **traumatic brain injury (TBI),** under which students may be found eligible for special education and related services. Synonymous terms designating the same general type of neurological damage are frequently used—for example, *traumatic head injury, cerebral trauma,* and *craniocerebral trauma.* However, we will use the term traumatic brain injury, as it is the language used in IDEA.

TBI is not a new phenomenon, but it only recently was made a separate category of disability for several reasons:

- It is an increasingly frequent cause of neurological impairment in children and youths.
- It presents unique educational problems that have been poorly understood and often mismanaged.
- Recent medical advances have greatly improved its diagnosis and treatment.

traumatic brain injury (TBI). Injury to the brain (not including conditions present at birth, birth trauma, or degenerative diseases or conditions), resulting in total or partial disability or psychosocial maladjustment that affects educational performance; may affect cognition, language, memory, attention, reasoning, abstract thinking, judgment, problem solving, sensory or perceptual and motor disabilities, psychosocial behavior, physical functions, information processing, or speech.

Definition and Variety of Causes

The definition of TBI specifies that:

1. There is injury to the brain caused by an external force.
2. The injury is *not* caused by a degenerative or congenital condition.
3. There is a diminished or altered state of consciousness.
4. Neurological or neurobehavioral dysfunction results from the injury (Begali, 1992; Snow & Hooper, 1994).

TBI may involve *open* head injuries—in which there is a penetrating head wound—from such causes as a fall, gunshot, assault, vehicular accident, or surgery. TBI may involve *closed* head injuries, in which there is no open head wound, but

In many cases, traumatic brain injury, or TBI, is the result of a motor vehicle or bike accident.

brain damage is caused by internal compression, stretching, or other shearing motion of neural tissues within the head (cf. Savage & Wolcott, 1994). Closed injuries may be caused by a variety of events including a fall, accident, or abuse, such as violent shaking.

Brain injury can be acquired from a variety of nontraumatic causes, as well: hypoxia (reduced oxygen to the brain, as might occur in near drowning), infection of the brain or its linings, stroke, tumor, metabolic disorder (such as may occur with diabetes, liver disease, or kidney disease), or toxic chemicals or drugs.

The box on page 401 describes the variety of traumatic and nontraumatic causes of brain damage. Although the resulting neurological problems may be similar for traumatic and nontraumatic brain injuries, our discussion in this chapter focuses on TBI; subsequently, we discuss other neurological impairments that usually have nontraumatic causes.

The educational definition of TBI focuses on impairments in one or more areas important for learning, such as cognition, language, speech, memory, information processing, attention, reasoning, abstract thinking, judgment, problem solving, perceptual abilities, psychosocial behavior, and physical abilities (Tyler & Colson, 1994). The various **sequelae** (consequences) of TBI create a need for special education; the injury itself is a medical problem.

Prevalence and Common Causes

The exact prevalence of TBI is difficult to determine, but we do know that TBI occurs at an alarming rate among children and youths. Estimates are that *each year,* about 0.5 percent of school-age children acquire a brain injury. And by the time they graduate from high school, nearly 4 percent of students may have TBI (Begali, 1992; Savage & Wolcott, 1994). Moreover, estimates of the percentages of students receiving special education who sustained TBI at some time before they were found eligible for special education range from 8 percent to 20 percent (Begali, 1992).

Males are more prone to TBI than females, and the age range in which TBI is most likely to occur for both males and females is late adolescence and early adulthood. Under age five, falls are the dominant cause of TBI, with vehicular accidents and child abuse causing substantial injuries, as well. After age five, and increasingly through adolescence, vehicular accidents (including accidents involving pedestrians, bicycles, and motorcycles) account for the overwhelming majority of TBI; assaults and gunshot wounds are increasingly prevalent among youths at older ages (Snow & Hooper, 1994).

Savage (1988) refers to TBI as a "pervasive epidemic in our children and young adults" (p. 2), and Bigge (1991) notes that although the assessment and treatment of TBI have improved dramatically in recent years, "the sheer number of cases is depressing" (p. 13). The prevalence is all the more depressing because so many of the causes of TBI are entirely preventable or avoidable, as we discuss later in a section on prevention (see pp. 413–416).

Effects

The effects of TBI may range from very mild to profound and may be temporary or permanent (Savage & Wolcott, 1994; Snow & Hooper, 1994). In fact, effects may not be seen at all immediately after the injury; some effects may appear months or even years afterward (Allison, 1992; Mira & Tyler, 1991). About half the children and

sequelae. Consequences or secondary results.

Acquired Pediatric Brain Damage: Diverse Causes

TRAUMATIC CAUSES

Every year 200,000 children sustain traumatic brain injuries; 89 percent of those injuries are caused by falls and by bicycle, motor vehicle, and sporting accidents. Other causes of traumatic damage include child abuse, gunshot wounds, and injury from other projectiles.[1]

Age is a strong predictor of the cause of brain injury in children:

- At least 80 percent of deaths from head trauma in children under 2 years of age are the result of nonaccidental trauma.[2]
- Preschoolers are the second highest risk group for brain injury.[3]
- Children between the ages of 6 and 12 are involved in twice as many pedestrian/motor vehicle accidents as younger children.[4]
- Youths, ages 15 to 25, are the highest risk group for traumatic brain injury; 220 [out of] 100,000 youths under age 15 will sustain a head injury each year.[2] Teenagers, 14 to 19 years old, are most susceptible to sports and auto-occupant accidents.[4]
- Also, boys are two to four times as likely to sustain brain injury as girls.[3]

NONTRAUMATIC CAUSES

Infectious diseases remain a major cause of neurologic disability in children, although early recognition and treatment substantially improve outcome. In one study, evidence of cerebral herniation was found in 25 percent of 302 children with bacterial meningitis.[5]

Environmental toxicity causes damage to many young brains. In a study conducted between 1976 and 1980, 700,000 children in the United States under age 6 were found to have elevated blood lead levels.[6] The effects of lead paint poisoning include learning disabilities, mental retardation, convulsions, coma, and death.[7]

Developmental abnormalities of the brain account for 30 percent to 40 percent of deaths during the first year of life. Surviving children sometimes develop intellectual impairments.[8]

Subarachnoid hemorrhage in a child with a history of seizure disorder usually suggests arteriovenous malformation (AVM). Mortality from bleeding as a result of AVM is less than that associated with ruptured aneurysms, but morbidity is higher. Periventricular-intraventricular hemorrhage occurs in 40 percent of infants born weighing less that 1500 grams.[5]

White matter abnormalities (perinatal leukoencephalopathies) are significantly higher in preterm infants. Cerebral palsy alone is 25 to 30 times greater in infants weighing less than 1.5 kg at birth. White matter destruction can also occur in children with meningitis. Cystic white matter lesions only occur in 3 percent to 7 percent of very low birth-weight infants, but when these lesions occur, the association with cerebral palsy can be as high as 100 percent.[9]

Low birthweight infants have a high risk of developing bronchopulmonary dysplasia (BPD). In turn, these low-weight, BPD infants are twice as likely to develop respiratory illnesses that can lead to impaired neurologic and cognitive status.[10]

NOTES

1. Humphreys, R., "Patterns of Pediatric Brain Injury" in Miner, M. & Wagner, K. (Eds), *Neurotrauma 3-Treatment, Rehabilitation and Related Issues,* Butterworths, 1989: 115–26.
2. Bruce, D. et al., *Pediatric Annals,* 1989; 18, 8: 482–94.
3. Waaland, P., "Pediatric Traumatic Brain Injury" *Special Topic Report,* The Rehabilitation Research & Training Center on Severe Traumatic Brain Injury, Medical College of Virginia, Richmond, VA, 1990.
4. Dandrinos-Smith S., *Crit. Care Nurs. Clin. North Am.,* 1991; 3, 3: 387–89.
5. LeRoux, P., et al., *Childs Nerv Syst,* 1991; 7: 34–39.
6. Rabin, R., *Am J Pub Health,* 1989; 79, 12: 1668–74.
7. Centers for Disease Control, *JAMA,* 1990; 265, 16: 2050–52.
8. Weisberg, L., et al., "Neurologic Disorders of Childhood," *Essentials of Clinical Neurology,* Aspen, 1989: 219–243.
9. Leviton, A., & Paneth, N. *Early Hum Dev,* 1990; 24: 1–22.
10. Vohr, B., et al., *Dev. Med. Child Neurol,* 1991; 33, 690–97.

Source: By Paul Pipitone, *Headlines,* 1992, *3*(5), p. 5. Reprinted with permission.

youths who experience serious TBI will require special education, and those who return to regular classes will require modifications if they are to be successful (Mira & Tyler, 1991).

As mentioned previously, TBI may have many sequelae involving various aspects of cognition, memory, attention, perception, emotional states, behavior, and movement. These sequelae may be misattributed to other causes or conditions if the brain injury is not diagnosed and understood (Savage & Mishkin, 1994).

Educational Implications

The educational implications of TBI can be extremely varied, depending on the nature and severity of the injury and the age and abilities of the individual at the time of injury. The box on page 403, "The Story of My Head Injury" depicts the experience of one eight-year-old child. A significant issue in educating someone who has experienced TBI is helping family members, teachers, and peers respond appropriately to the sudden and sometimes dramatic changes that may occur in the student's academic abilities, appearance, behavior, and emotional states. Both general and special education teachers need training about TBI and its ramifications if students are to be reintegrated successfully into the schools and classrooms they attended before the injury.

Savage (1988) suggests that the following characteristics are essential features of appropriate education for students with TBI:

1. Transition from a hospital or rehabilitation center to the school requires that both institutions be involved; information must be shared to ensure a smooth transition.
2. The school must use a team approach, involving regular and special educators, other special teachers, guidance counselor, administrators, and the student's family.
3. The individualized education program (IEP) for the student must be concerned with cognitive, social/behavioral, and sensorimotor domains.
4. Most students with TBI experience problems in focusing and sustaining attention for long periods, remembering previously learned facts and skills, and learning new things. These students tend to have difficulty with organization, abstraction, and flexible thinking. They often lose basic academic skills and learning strategies and experience high levels of frustration, fatigue, and irritability. They also may have difficulty reestablishing associations with peers and controlling appropriate social behavior.
5. Programs for students with TBI must emphasize the cognitive processes through which academic skills are learned as well as curriculum content.
6. The school needs to consider the student's long-term needs in addition to his or her annual IEP goals, but initial IEP goals should be reviewed at least every six weeks because rapid changes sometimes take place early in recovery (Savage, 1988; see also Tyler & Mira, 1993).

Some types of neurological impairment occur before, during, or soon after birth and do not involve sudden changes in a person's abilities. TBI is a special case of neurological impairment, in which there is a sudden alteration in abilities; this can often cause frustration in the student and teachers who must cope with this loss. The student must undergo medical treatment to address the biophysical aspects of the injury, and it is critical that educators understand the implications of the injury for structuring the student's psychological and social environments in school (Savage & Mishkin, 1994). Teachers may obtain helpful informational materials from the National Head Injury Foundation, 1776 Massachusetts Ave., Suite 100, Washington, DC 20036.

OTHER NEUROLOGICAL IMPAIRMENTS

TBI involves brain damage with an identifiable external cause: trauma. However, in many cases of brain damage, it is impossible to identify the exact cause of the impairment. The important point is that *when a child's nervous system is damaged, no matter*

The Story of My Head Injury

I was 8 years old when I got my head injury. I was riding my bike on the sandpit road when a high school kid came around the corner and hit me. I don't remember anything about it. My brother Ian was with me and he saw the car smack me and me fly over the car into the bushes. My bike got run over cause the kid that hit me was drinking. And he didn't even stop until he saw my brother and his friends up the road. That's all stuff that Ian told me because I was unconscious.

I don't remember the hospital much. I remember my mom holding me and rubbing my head. My leg hurt the most cause it got broke in the accident. My mom says I was unconscious for 16 days and nights. She says they had to feed me with tubes and I had another tube to help me breathe. Mrs. R. had the kids in school send me cards. My mom read them to me over and over. I wanted to be back in school real bad. I missed our Halloween party.

After I got home a teacher worked with me. Then I went back to school. I only remember how happy I was to be back. I didn't remember where my desk was. I guess I cried the first day cause everything was so hard and the kids were way ahead of me. My mom says I cried all week. I had to take two medicines for my head injury. I don't know what they were.

Now I'm in the 5th grade and I am doing much better. I got 2 B's, and 3 C's on my last report card. My mom says to say that it is still hard for me to read and think for a long time. As for me, I hate spelling. But I hated it before my head injury too. It takes me a while to get things and sometimes I have to bring work to my special teacher Mr. M. He helps me every afternoon for 45 minutes. When I first went back to school I saw him all afternoon. He says cause of me he is a head injury expert—Ha, Ha.

One thing I remember in grade 3 is not being able to stay awake long. I was tired a lot. I even fell asleep in school. And I hated lunch, not the food. But I got mixed up cause everything was so loud. Mrs. R used to let me eat lunch with her. This was good except she made me practice my math as we ate lunch.

I am suppose to tell you about my friends too. Ian, my brother, is still my best friend. He helps me with my homework and he is teaching me his computer. He said to say that I also have friends like Tommy, Jason, Franky, and Mica. We are on the same baseball team. We ride our bikes almost every day. I got a new bike after a year. My dad sent it from New York. My mom wasn't too happy about it. But I told her not to worry.

Right now I feel very good. I only take one medicine for my head injury. I think I am the same but sometimes it is still hard for me to learn stuff like reading for ideas and stuff. My teacher says I have come a long ways. Next year will be better, I hope. (pp. 405–406)

Source: From "A neuroeducational model for teaching students with acquired brain injuries," by R. C. Savage and by L. Mishkin, 1994, in *Educational dimensions of acquired brain injury,* edited by R. C. Savage and G. F. Wolcott, pp. 393–411, Austin, TX: Pro-Ed. Reprinted with permission.

what the cause, muscular weakness or paralysis is almost always one of the symptoms. And because these children cannot move about like most others, their education typically requires special equipment, special procedures, or other accommodations for their disabilities. We turn now to some additional types of neurological impairments for which the causes are often unknown.

Cerebral Palsy

Cerebral palsy (CP) is not a disease. It is not contagious, it is not progressive (except that improper treatment may lead to complications), and there are no remissions. Although it is often thought of as a motor problem associated with brain damage at birth, it is actually more complicated. For practical purposes, cerebral palsy can be considered part of a syndrome that includes motor dysfunction, psychological dysfunction, seizures, or emotional or behavioral disorders due to brain damage.

cerebral palsy (CP). A condition characterized by paralysis, weakness, incoordination, and/or other motor dysfunction; caused by damage to the brain before it has matured.

Some individuals with CP show only one indication of brain damage, such as motor impairment; others may show combinations of symptoms. The usual definition of CP refers to a condition characterized by paralysis, weakness, lack of coordination, and/or other motor dysfunction because of damage to the child's brain before it has matured (Batshaw & Perret, 1986). Symptoms may be so mild that they are detected only with difficulty or so profound that the individual is almost completely incapacitated.

Although there is no cure for CP, advances in medical and rehabilitation technology offer increasing hope of overcoming the disabilities imposed by neurological damage. For example, intensive, long-term physical therapy in combination with a surgical procedure called *selective posterior rhizotomy*—in which the surgeon cuts selected nerve roots below the spinal cord that cause spasticity in the leg muscles—allow some children with spastic CP to better control certain muscles. Such treatment allows some nonambulatory children walk and helps others walk more normally (Dyar, 1988).

Causes. Anything that can cause brain damage during the brain's development can cause CP. Before birth, maternal infections, chronic diseases, physical trauma, or maternal exposure to toxic substances or X-rays, for example, may damage the brain of the fetus. During the birth process, the brain may be injured, especially if labor or birth is difficult or complicated. Premature birth, hypoxia, high fever, infections, poisoning, hemorrhaging, and related factors may cause harm following birth. In short, anything that results in oxygen deprivation, poisoning, cerebral bleeding, or direct trauma to the brain can be a possible cause of CP.

Although CP occurs at every social level, it is more often seen in children born to mothers in poor socioeconomic circumstances. Children who live in such circumstances have a greater risk of incurring brain damage because of such factors as malnutrition of the mother, poor prenatal and postnatal care, environmental hazards during infancy, and low birthweight (see Baumeister et al., 1990; Stanley & Blair, 1994).

hemiplegia. A condition in which one half (right or left side) of the body is paralyzed.

diplegia. A condition in which the legs are paralyzed to a greater extent than the arms.

quadriplegia. A condition in which all four limbs are paralyzed.

paraplegia. A condition in which both legs are paralyzed.

spasticity. Characterized by muscle stiffness and problems in voluntary movement; associated with spastic cerebral palsy.

choreoathetoid. Characterized by involuntary movements and difficulty with balance; associated with choreoathetoid cerebral palsy.

atonic. Characterized by lack of muscle tone; associated with atonic cerebral palsy.

Types. It may seem reasonable to classify CP according to the time period during which brain damage occurred (prenatal, natal, or postnatal), but ordinarily, it is impossible to pinpoint the exact time of the damage. The two means of classification that have been most widely accepted specify the limbs involved and the type of motor disability.

Classification according to the extremities involved applies not just to CP but to all types of motor disability or paralysis. The most common classifications and the approximate percentage of individuals with CP falling into each class may be summarized as follows:

- **Hemiplegia:** One-half (right or left side) of the body is involved (35 to 40 percent).
- **Diplegia:** Legs are involved to a greater extent than arms (10 to 20 percent).
- **Quadriplegia:** All four limbs are involved (15 to 20 percent).
- **Paraplegia:** Only the legs are involved (10 to 20 percent).

About half the cases of CP involve problems of voluntary movement or **spasticity**—stiffness or tenseness of muscles and inaccurate voluntary movement. Other types are characterized by abrupt, involuntary movements and difficulty maintaining balance, known as **choreoathetoid** movements, or muscles that give the appearance of floppiness, known as **atonic** muscles. Some individuals have a mixtures of various types of CP.

The important point about CP is that the brain damage affects strength and the ability to move parts of the body normally. The difficulty of movement may involve the limbs as well as the muscles used to control facial expressions and speech. As a result someone with CP may have difficulty moving or speaking or may exhibit facial contortions or drooling. But these results of brain damage do not necessarily mean that the person's intelligence or emotional sensitivity has been affected by the damage affecting muscle control.

Associated Disabilities and Educational Implications. Research during the past few decades has made it clear that CP is a developmental disability—a multidisabling condition far more complex than a motor disability alone (Batshaw & Perret, 1986). When the brain is damaged, sensory abilities, cognitive functions, and emotional responsiveness as well as motor performance are usually affected. A high proportion of children with CP are found to have hearing impairments, visual impairments, perceptual disorders, speech problems, emotional or behavioral disorders, mental retardation, or some combination of several of these disabling conditions, in addition to motor disability. They may also exhibit such characteristics as drooling or facial contortions.

Some individuals with CP have normal or above-average intellectual capacity, and a few test within the gifted range. The *average* tested intelligence of children with CP, however, is clearly lower than the average for the general population (Batshaw & Perret, 1986). However, we must be very cautious in interpreting the test results of children with CP, as many standardized tests of intelligence and achievement may be inappropriate for individuals with special difficulties in perception, movement, or response speed. Furthermore, the movement problems of a child with CP may become more apparent in a state of emotional arousal or stress; this can complicate using typical testing procedures, which tend to be demanding and stressful.

The educational problems of children who have CP are as multifaceted as their disabilities. Not only must special equipment and procedures be provided because the children have physical disabilities, but the same special educational procedures and equipment required to teach children with vision, hearing, or communication disorders, learning disabilities, emotional or behavioral disorders, or mental retardation are often needed. Careful and continuous educational assessment of the individual child's capabilities is particularly important. Teaching the child who has CP demands competence in many aspects of special education and experience in working with a variety of disabling conditions in a multidisciplinary setting (Bigge, 1991; Tyler & Colson, 1994; Zadig, 1983).

Seizure Disorder (Epilepsy)

A person has a **seizure** when there is an abnormal discharge of electrical energy in certain brain cells. The discharge spreads to nearby cells, and the effect may be loss of consciousness, involuntary movements, or abnormal sensory phenomena. The effects of the seizure will depend on the location of the cells in which the discharge starts and how far the discharge spreads.

People with *epilepsy* have recurrent seizures (Engel, 1995). About 6 percent of the population will have a seizure at some time during life, but most of them will not be diagnosed as having epilepsy because they do not have repeated seizures (Batshaw & Perret, 1986). Seizures reflect abnormal brain activity, so it is not surprising that they occur more often in children with developmental disabilities (e.g., mental retardation or cerebral palsy) than in children without disabilities (Batshaw & Perret, 1986; Coulter, 1993; Sillanpaa, 1992).

seizure (convulsion). A sudden alteration of consciousness, usually accompanied by motor activity and/or sensory phenomena; caused by an abnormal discharge of electrical energy in the brain.

Causes. Seizures apparently can be caused by almost any kind of damage to the brain. The most common causes include lack of sufficient oxygen (hypoxia), low blood sugar (hypoglycemia), infections, and physical trauma. Certain conditions, like those named, tend to increase the chances that neurochemical reactions will be set off in brain cells (Batshaw & Perret, 1986). In many cases, the causes are unknown (Engel, 1995; Wolraich, 1984). Some types of seizures may be progressive; that is, they may damage the brain or disrupt its functioning in such a way that having a seizure increases the probability of having another (Girvin, 1992). Even though the cause of seizures is not well understood, it is important to note that with proper medication most people's seizures can be controlled.

Types of Seizures. Seizures may take many forms and differ along at least the following dimensions:

- *Duration:* They may last only a few seconds or for several minutes.
- *Frequency:* They may occur as frequently as every few minutes or only about once a year.
- *Onset:* They may be set off by certain identifiable stimuli or be unrelated to the environment, and they may be totally unexpected or be preceded by certain internal sensations.
- *Movements:* They may cause major convulsive movements or only minor motor symptoms (e.g., eye blinks).
- *Causes:* They may be caused by a variety of conditions, including high fever, poisoning, trauma, and other conditions mentioned previously; but in many cases, the causes are unknown.
- *Associated disabilities:* They may be associated with other disabling conditions or be unrelated to any other medical problem or disability.
- *Control:* They may be controlled completely by drugs, so that the individual has no more seizures, or they may be only partially controlled.

Educational Implications. About half of all children with seizure disorders have average or higher intelligence. Among those without mental retardation, however, there seems to be a higher than usual incidence of learning disabilities (Besag, 1995; Westbrook, Silver, Coupey, & Shinnar, 1991). Although many children who have seizure disorders have other disabilities, some do not. Consequently, both general and special education teachers may expect to encounter children who have seizures. Besides obtaining medical advice regarding management of the child's particular seizure disorder, teachers should know first aid for epileptic seizures (see the box on page 407). Ignorance about the causes of seizures and about first aid are among the most common misconceptions about epilepsy (Gouvier, Brown, Prestholdt, Hayes, & Apostolas, 1995).

Seizures are primarily a medical problem and require primarily medical attention. Educators are called on to deal with the problem in the following ways:

1. General and special teachers need to help dispel ignorance, superstition, and prejudice toward people who have seizures and provide calm management for the occasional seizure the child may have at school.
2. Special education teachers who work with students with severe mental retardation or teach children with other severe developmental disabilities need to be prepared to manage more frequent seizures as well as to handle learning problems. The teacher should record the length of a child's seizure and the type of activity the child was engaged in before it occurred. This information

First Aid for Epileptic Seizures

A major epileptic seizure is often dramatic and frightening. It lasts only a few minutes, however, and does not require expert care. These simple procedures should be followed:

- *Remain calm.* You cannot stop a seizure once it has started. Let the seizure run its course. Do not try to revive the child.
- If the child is upright, ease him to the floor and loosen his clothing.
- Try to prevent the child from striking his head or body against any hard, sharp, or hot objects; but do not otherwise interfere with his movement.
- Turn the child's face to the side so that saliva can flow out of his mouth.
- *Do not insert anything between the child's teeth.*
- Do not be alarmed if the child seems to stop breathing momentarily.
- After the movements stop and the child is relaxed, allow him to sleep or rest if he wishes.
- It isn't generally necessary to call a doctor unless the attack is followed almost immediately by another seizure or the seizure lasts more than ten minutes.
- Notify the child's parents or guardians that a seizure has occurred.
- After a seizure, many people can carry on as before. If, after resting, the child seems groggy, confused, or weak, it may be a good idea to accompany him or her home.

Source: Courtesy of Epilepsy Foundation of America.

will help physicians in diagnosis and treatment. If a student is being treated for a seizure disorder, the teacher should know the type of medication and its possible side effects.

Some children who do not have mental retardation but have seizures exhibit learning and behavior problems (Huberty, Austin, Risinger, & McNelis, 1992; Westbrook et al., 1991). These problems may result from damage to the brain that causes other disabilities, as well, or they may be the side effects of anticonvulsant medication or the result of mismanagement by parents and teachers. Teachers must be aware that seizures of any type may interfere with the child's attention or the continuity of education (McCarthy, Richman, & Yarbrough, 1995). Brief seizures may require the teacher to repeat instructions or allow the child extra time to respond. Frequent major convulsions may prevent even a bright child from achieving at the usual rate.

Children with seizure disorders have emotional or behavioral problems more often than most children (Freeman, Jacobs, Vining, & Rabin, 1984; Hoare, 1984). We must not, however, conclude that seizure disorders *cause* emotional and behavioral problems directly. The stress of having to deal with seizures, medications, and stigma, as well as adverse environmental conditions, is more likely to cause these problems. Moreover, Freeman and his research group (1984) have shown that the school adjustment of students with seizure disorders can be improved dramatically if they are properly assessed, placed, counseled, taught about seizures, and given appropriate work assignments.

Spina Bifida

During early fetal development, the two halves of the embryo grow together or fuse at the midline. When the closure is incomplete, a congenital *midline defect* is the result. Cleft lip and cleft palate are examples of such midline defects (see Chapter 7).

spina bifida. A congenital midline defect resulting from failure of the bony spinal column to close completely during fetal development.

Spina bifida is a congenital midline defect resulting from failure of the bony spinal column to close completely during fetal development. The defect may occur anywhere from the head to the lower end of the spine. Because the spinal column is not closed, the spinal cord (nerve fibers) may protrude, resulting in damage to the nerves and paralysis and/or lack of function or sensation below the site of the defect. Spina bifida is often accompanied by paralysis of the legs and of the anal and bladder sphincters because nerve impulses are not able to travel past the defect (Batshaw & Perret, 1986).

Surgery to close the spinal opening is performed in early infancy, but this does not repair the nerve damage. The mortality rate for children with spina bifida has lowered over the years, meaning that more severely impaired children are surviving and attending school (Korabek & Cuvo, 1986). Although spina bifida is one of the most common birth defects resulting in physical disability, its causes are not known.

Educational Implications. The extent of the paralysis resulting from spina bifida depends on the location of the spinal cord defect (how high or low on the spinal column it is). Some children will walk independently, some will need braces, and others will have to use wheelchairs. Some children will have acute medical problems, which may lead to repeated hospitalizations for surgery or treatment of infections (Batshaw & Perret, 1986). Among the other considerations for teachers are the following:

- Spina bifida is often accompanied by *hydrocephalus,* a condition in which there is excessive pressure of the cerebrospinal fluid, sometimes leading to an enlarged head or to attention disorders, learning disabilities, or mental retardation (see Chapter 4). Hydrocephalus is typically treated surgically by installing a shunt to drain the cerebrospinal fluid into a vein. Another possible complication of spina bifida is *meningitis* (bacterial infection of the linings of the brain or spinal cord).
- Damage to nerves along the spine may result in complications, in which the child is likely to fracture bones in the lower extremities.
- Lack of sensation in certain areas of the skin may increase the risk of burns, abrasions, and pressure sores. The child may need to be positioned periodically during the schoolday and monitored carefully during some activities in which there is risk of injury. Because the student has deficiencies in sensation below the defect, he or she may have particular problems in spatial orientation, spatial judgment, sense of direction and distance, organization of motor skills, and body image or body awareness.
- Lack of bowel and bladder control in some children will require periodic **catheterization.** Many children can be taught to do the procedure known as *clean intermittent catheterization* themselves, but teachers should know what to do or obtain help from the school nurse.
- Spina bifida generally has no effect on a child's stamina, and most children with defects can participate in a full day of school activities.

Autism and Other Neurological Disorders Not Causing Paralysis

Autism is a relatively rare neurological disorder that does not cause muscle weakness or lack of muscle control. However, as discussed in Chapters 6 and 7, it typically does affect a child's ability to communicate, form social relationships, and perform normally on tests of intelligence and academic achievement (Gillberg, 1989; Schopler & Mesibov, 1994, 1995). Recall from the discussion in those chapters that most students with autism require intensive intervention in communication, social, and academic skills. However, some individuals with autism are highly talented, intellectually superior, and able to communicate the experience of autism with great clarity (see Grandin, 1995; Sacks, 1995).

catheterization. Insertion of a tube into the urethra to drain urine from the bladder.

The cause or causes of autism and the exact nature of the neurological problem remain mysteries. Likewise, a variety of other neurological disorders that may affect behavior but not result in muscle weakness or paralysis have causes that are known to be brain related. Yet scientists do not know exactly what happens in the brain to cause the symptoms. **Tourette's syndrome** is an example. The behavioral symptoms of Tourette's—sudden repetitive movements known as *tics,* often accompanied by vocalizations of a socially inappropriate nature—are known to be caused by neurological dysfunction, but the exact nature of that dysfunction is unknown (Kerbeshian & Burd, 1994; Sacks, 1995).

MUSCULOSKELETAL CONDITIONS

Some children are physically disabled because of defects or diseases of the muscles or bones. Even though they do not have neurological impairments, their ability to move is affected. Most of the time, muscular and skeletal problems involve the legs, arms, joints, or spine, making it difficult or impossible for the child to walk, stand, sit, or use his or her hands. The problems may be congenital or acquired after birth, and the causes may include genetic defects, infectious diseases, accidents, or developmental disorders.

Two of the most common musculoskeletal conditions affecting children and youths are muscular dystrophy and juvenile rheumatoid arthritis. **Muscular dystrophy** is a hereditary disease that is characterized by progressive weakness caused by degeneration of muscle fibers (Batshaw & Perret, 1986). The exact biological mechanism responsible for muscular dystrophy is not known nor is there any cure, at present. **Juvenile rheumatoid arthritis** is a potentially debilitating disease in which the muscles and joints are affected; the cause and cure are unknown (Bigge, 1991). It can be a very painful condition and is sometimes accompanied by complications such as fever, respiratory problems, heart problems, and eye infections. Among children with other physical disabilities, such as cerebral palsy, arthritis may be a complicating factor that affects the joints and limits movement. These and other conditions can significantly affect a student's social and academic progress at school. The box below describes how arthritis affected one child.

Tourette's syndrome. A neurological disorder beginning in childhood (about 3 times more prevalent in boys than in girls) in which stereotyped motor movements (tics) are accompanied by multiple vocal outbursts that may include grunting or barking noises or socially inappropriate words or statements.

muscular dystrophy. A hereditary disease characterized by progressive weakness caused by degeneration of muscle fibers.

juvenile rheumatoid arthritis. A systemic disease with major symptoms involving the muscles and joints.

Juvenile Rheumatoid Arthritis

"I feel more and more like a regular person these days," Amy Levendusky says. This is not the sort of thing a 9-year-old girl should have to say. But Amy has juvenile rheumatoid arthritis, which affects 71,000 children in this country. The disease gripped Amy at the age of 4 and spread from her feet to every joint in her body. "She'd be sitting there not able to move because it hurt so much," says her father, John. "I'd have to pick her up to take her from one place to another." Now a fourth grader, Amy attends a school outside her home district in Whitefish Bay, Wis., because it has an elevator. Most days she doesn't go outside for recess—even a bump might send a shock of pain through her whole body.

Still, Amy has shown signs of improvement in the last year. She has a daily regimen of joint exercises, and an anti-inflammatory drug called methotrexate seems to be helping. "There's not as much pain or stiffness most of the time," she says. "I can walk up the stairs normally now. Before, I had to pull myself up with my hands." She began piano lessons as therapy two years ago and discovered a love for the keyboard. "She just wants to be seen as a normal little girl," says her mother, Susan. But in one unexpected way the disease may have made Amy special. "I think she has developed a keener sensitivity," Susan says. "There will be times when she'll notice how beautiful things look outside and say, 'Let's take a walk.' Most kids her age wouldn't pay attention to things like that."

Source: From Melinda Beck with Mary Hager and Vern E. Smith, "Living with arthritis," *Newsweek,* March 20, 1989, p. 67.

A wide variety of other congenital conditions, acquired defects, and diseases also can affect the musculoskeletal system (see Batshaw & Perret, 1986; Bigge, 1991; Blackman, 1984). In all these conditions, as well as in cases of muscular dystrophy and arthritis, intelligence is unaffected, unless there are additional associated disabilities. Regarding the musculoskeletal problem itself, special education is necessary only to improve the student's mobility, to see that proper posture and positioning are maintained, to provide for education during periods of confinement to hospital or home, and otherwise to make the educational experience as normal as possible.

OTHER CONDITIONS AFFECTING HEALTH OR PHYSICAL ABILITY

In addition to those discussed so far, an extremely wide array of diseases, physiological disorders, congenital malformations, and injuries may affect students' health and physical abilities and create a need for special education and related services. Several of these are described in Table 10–1.

Table 10–1

Additional Physical Conditions

Condition	*Description*
Asthma	A chronic respiratory condition characterized by repeated episodes of difficulty in breathing, especially exhalation
Cystic fibrosis	An inherited disease characterized by chronic respiratory and digestive problems, including thick, sticky mucus and glandular secretions
Diabetes	A hereditary or developmental problem of sugar metabolism caused by failure of the pancreas to produce enough insulin
Nephrosis and nephritis	Disorders or diseases of the kidneys due to infection, poisoning, burns, crushing injuries, or other diseases
Sickle-cell anemia	A severe, chronic hereditary blood disease in which red blood cells are distorted in shape and do not circulate properly
Hemophilia	A rare, sex-linked disorder in which the blood does not have a sufficient clotting component and excessive bleeding occurs
Rheumatic fever	Painful swelling and inflammation of the joints (typically following strep throat or scarlet fever) that can spread to the brain or heart
Tuberculosis	Infection by the tuberculosis bacterium of an organ system, such as lungs, larynx, bones and joints, skin, gastrointestinal tract, genitourinary tract, or heart
Cancer	Abnormal growth of cells that can affect any organ system

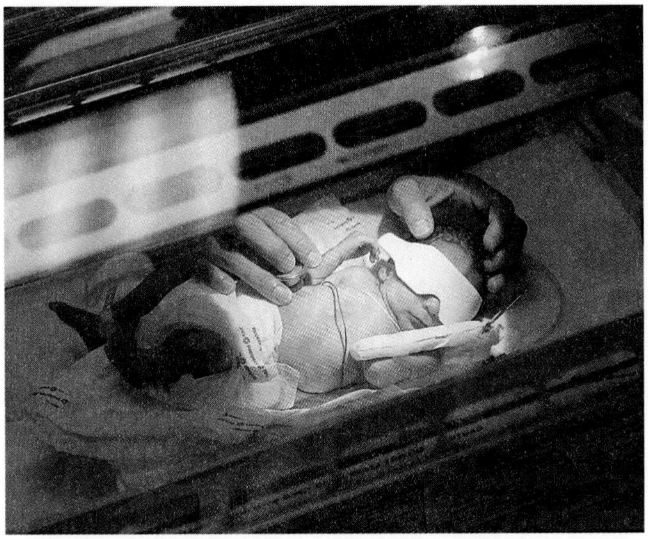

The AIDS virus can be detected in infants who have been infected in utero.

Congenital Malformations

Congenital malformations and disorders may occur in any organ system, and they may range from minor to fatal flaws in structure or function. In many cases, the cause of the malformation or disorder is not known, but in others, it is known to be hereditary or caused by maternal infection or substance use by the mother during pregnancy. For instance, **fetal alcohol syndrome (FAS),** which is now one of the most common syndromes involving malformations and mental retardation—is caused by the mother's use of alcohol during pregnancy.

Accidents

More children die in accidents each year than are killed by all childhood diseases combined. Millions of children and youths in the United States are seriously injured and disabled temporarily or permanently in accidents each year. Many of those who do not acquire TBI receive spinal cord injuries that result in partial or total paralysis below the site of the injury. Others undergo amputations or are incapacitated temporarily by broken limbs or internal injuries.

Acquired Immune Deficiency Syndrome (AIDS)

Acquired immune deficiency syndrome (AIDS) is often thought to be a disease that merely makes one susceptible to fatal infections. However, children with AIDS often acquire neurological problems, as well, including mental retardation, cerebral palsy, seizures, and emotional or behavioral disorders (Rudigier, Crocker, & Cohen, 1990).

As children and youths with AIDS live longer, due to improved medical treatments, there will be an increasing need for special education and related services. Teachers should be aware that "there is no serious concern regarding transmission of HIV [the virus that causes AIDS] infection in the setting of usual developmental services" (Rudigier et al., 1990). Most states now have policies emphasizing that children with AIDS should be educated in regular classrooms (Katsiyannis, 1992).

fetal alcohol syndrome (FAS). Abnormalities associated with the mother's using alcohol during pregnancy; defects range from mild to severe, including growth retardation, brain damage, mental retardation, hyperactivity, anomalies of the face, and heart failure; also called *alcohol embryopathy.*

acquired immune deficiency syndrome (AIDS). A fatal virus-caused illness resulting in a breakdown of the immune system; currently, no known cure exists.

Children Born to Substance-Abusing Mothers

We have already mentioned fetal alcohol syndrome, which results in disabilities acquired by children of mothers who abuse alcohol during pregnancy. The abuse of other substances by mothers also has negative implications for their children. The effects of maternal cocaine addiction involve not only multiple physiological, emotional, and cognitive problems of newborns but also a high probability of neglect and abuse by the mother after her baby is born. Many women who are intravenous drug users not only risk chemical damage to their babies but also give them venereal diseases such as syphilis, which can result in disabilities. As the number of substance-abusing mothers increases, the number of infants and young children with severe and multiple disabilities will increase, as well.

There is no question that the percentage of babies exposed to drugs before birth has increased dramatically in the 1980s and 1990s (Sautter, 1992). The consequences of this prenatal exposure to drugs are very serious and can result in severe or mild disabilities that are seen in the children when they come to school (Van Dyke & Fox, 1992). However, initial reaction to the problems of "crack" babies—the assumption that these children are uniquely, severely, and permanently damaged—was unfounded. Authorities now realize that "crack" baby is a misnomer. Many of the pregnant women who abuse crack cocaine are multiple drug users, and it is seldom known which drug was responsible for their babies' problems. Furthermore, many of the problems of babies born exposed to drugs also occur if mothers have received inadequate prenatal care and live in conditions of poverty, further complicating the causal factors involved in the child's developmental problems.

In spite of the multiple causal factors involved, the prospects of effective early intervention with children exposed prenatally to drugs are much better than previously thought. True, many such children will have developmental disabilities. Like the developmental disabilities having other causes, however, those of children exposed before birth to drugs are amenable to modification. The box on pages 414–415 provides recommendations for educators dealing with children exposed to drugs prenatally.

Children Who Are Medically Fragile and Children Dependent on Ventilators or Other Medical Technology

Children who are medically fragile have special health needs that demand immediate attention to preserve life or to prevent or retard further medical deterioration. Delicate medical conditions may arise from a variety of diseases and disorders, and it is important to make distinctions among students whose conditions are *episodic, chronic,* and *progressive:*

> These students include those with special health needs who are having a temporary medical crisis, those who are consistently fragile, and those whose diseases are progressive in nature and will eventually lead to a fragile state. The concept that must be remembered is that any student with a special health need can be fragile at times, but only a small portion of those who are fragile will remain fragile. (Bigge, 1991, p. 71)

Programs for students who are medically fragile must be particularly flexible and open to revision. Daily health care plans and emergency plans are essential, as are effective lines of communication among all who are involved with the student's treatment, care, and schooling. Decisions regarding placement of these students must be made by a team including health care providers and school personnel as well as the student and his or her parents.

An increasing number of children are returning home from hospitalization able to breathe only with the help of a ventilator (a mechanical device forcing oxygen into the lungs through a tube inserted into the trachea). Many of these children are also returning to public schools, sometimes with the assistance of a full-time nurse. It is debatable as to which conditions are appropriate for children who are dependent on ventilators or other medical technology to attend regular classrooms. Educators and parents together must make decisions in each individual case, weighing medical judgment regarding danger to the child as well as the interest of the child in being integrated into as many typical school activities as possible with his or her peers.

PREVENTION OF PHYSICAL DISABILITIES

Although some physical disabilities are not preventable by any available means, many or most are. For instance, failure to wear seatbelts and other safety devices accounts for many disabling injuries. Likewise, driving under the influence of alcohol or other drugs, careless storage of drugs and other toxic substances, use of alcohol and other drugs during pregnancy, and a host of unsafe and unhealthful practices that could be avoided cause many disabilities.

Teenage mothers are more likely than older women to give birth to premature or low-birthweight babies, and these babies are at high risk for a variety of psychological and physical problems when they reach school age (McCormick, Brooks-Gunn, Workman-Daniels, Turner, & Peckham, 1992). Thus, preventing adolescent pregnancies would keep many babies from being born with disabilities. Inadequate prenatal care also contributes to the number of babies born with disabilities. And for young children, immunizing them against preventable childhood diseases could lower the number of those who acquire disabilities.

Teenage girls are more likely than older women to give birth to premature or low-birthweight babies, who are at high risk for learning problems when they reach school age.

Child Abuse and Neglect

Child abuse is a significant contributing factor in creating physical disabilities in the United States, and its prevention is a critical problem. Many thousands of children, ranging in age from newborns to adolescents, are battered or abused each year. They are beaten, burned, sexually molested, starved, or otherwise neglected or brutalized by their parents, stepparents, or other older persons.

The consequences of child abuse may be permanent neurological damage, other internal injuries, skeletal deformity, facial disfigurement, sensory impairment, or death. Psychological problems are an inevitable outcome of abuse. Evidence indicates that the abuse of children is increasing. Abuse and neglect by adults is now a leading cause of injury—both physical and psychological—and death among children.

Child abuse and neglect constitute some of the most complex problems confronting U.S. society today and require multidisciplinary approaches to prevention (Deden, 1993). There is a need for better understanding of the nature and extent of the problems among both the general public and professionals. Education for parenting and child management, including family life education in the public schools, is an obvious need in society. In perhaps as many as 50 percent of cases of serious child

Ten Recommendations for Educators

1. Cease using the labels *crack babies* and *crack children.* "We don't know whether crack children exist," insists Jackson. "We know from research on other self-fulfilling prophecies on grouping children that when you identify children with derogatory terms, you set low expectations for them that are likely in and of themselves to be fulfilled," she explains.

   "And I've seen many cases of schools that worried hysterically about 'crack kids' and how different these children are. But they did not actually know that the children were born prenatally exposed. Lots of people don't know what they are talking about.

   "As important, the literature and researchers say that most drug-abusing mothers are polysubstance abusers. So it is not clear which drug may or may not have done damage to the child. For example, alcohol and tobacco are in many cases far more detrimental in terms of effect on the child. Additionally, many children are misdiagnosed by teachers or schools that have no medical evidence for their fears. So that's why it makes little sense to label these children."

2. Do not identify, label, and segregate children because it is believed that they have been prenatally exposed to drugs. "There appears to be no educational reason to set up an early identification system," Jackson says. "If the child has been prenatally exposed to crack cocaine, how will the teacher treat that differently from a case of prenatal exposure to alcohol or just coming from a dysfunctional environment? The manifesting behaviors are the same.

   "Children affected by psychosocial trauma and children who may be affected by prenatal exposure to drugs have the same kind of behaviors. The researchers cannot tell the difference between children exposed to drugs in utero and those with postnatal psychosocial traumatic conditions.

   "So there is no need for [teachers] to do anything differently. All they could do is label and segregate the children and start a cycle of self-fulfilling prophecies. These students for the most part will be in regular classrooms. About 40% have developmental lags, but they are the same kind of things you find among children traumatized by poverty—attention disorders, the restlessness that these children show, and some of the antisocial behaviors are similar.

   "If a child is living in an environment with the using parents, then that child is being exposed to a lot of neglect and trauma," Jackson explains. "Whether it is prenatal or postnatal, you have to deal with the behavior of that particular child.

   "Identification systems by schools could also lead to legal entanglements. If they get mothers to 'tell' of their prenatal drug use, many states have laws that punish those whom the schools help to self-incriminate. The schools may get involved in something that they do not really need."

3. Provide all teachers with staff development to prepare and encourage them to use practices that have been learned from research about the ways to successfully teach children who are experiencing psychosocial trauma. "All regular classroom teachers need to know how to teach children who are experiencing some kind of difficulty because of psychosocial trauma," Jackson says. "More and more of our schools, even in the richest school districts, are finding a lot more of their children with a lot of behaviors that in the past were associated with poor children.

   "There is a lot of destabilization going on in the society," she notes, "economic destabilization, lots of latchkey children. The schools—whether the richest or

mistreatment, the adults responsible for the child's welfare have substance abuse problems (Murphy et al., 1991). Thus, progress in preventing child abuse and neglect may be partly limited by the extent of progress in lowering the prevalence of substance abuse in the United States.

Teachers can play an extremely important role in detecting, reporting, and preventing child abuse and neglect because, next to parents, they are the people who spend the most time with children. It is therefore vital that teachers be aware of the indicators that a child is being abused or neglected at home (see the box on pp. 416–417). Teachers must also be aware of the reporting procedures that should be followed when they suspect abuse or neglect. These vary from one area and state to another, but ordinarily, the teacher is required to report suspected cases of child abuse or neglect to a school administrator, law enforcement officer, or social services official. A professional who fails to report child abuse or neglect may be held legally liable.

the poorest—are seeing a different kind of child. So teachers are going to have to learn, from some of the excellent techniques that have been developed through special education and through Head Start, ways to deal with children who have less readiness or eagerness to learn."

4. Schools should provide developmentally appropriate early childhood education programs for all children—but especially poor children. "If these kids don't receive the sound early intervention, then it is unlikely that they are going to experience success in school," Jackson asserts.
5. Plan the guidance of social and emotional development as an integral part of the curriculum. Positive social behaviors should be modeled and taught directly, not incidentally, especially for children experiencing behavioral difficulties. Such behaviors "include perseverance, industry, independence, cooperation, negotiating, solving interpersonal problems nonviolently, self-control, dealing with fears, and intrinsic motivation," explains Jackson. "Some children just don't come from environments where they have learned these things. If they come to school not knowing these things, especially in the primary grades, our job has to be the guidance of social/emotional development as an integral part of the curriculum."
6. Schools should remember that classroom limits of two adults for every 20 children are recommended for the preschool and primary years. Early childhood educators concur on this standard for developmentally appropriate programs. "In all of the programs I contacted," says Jackson, "the directors spoke emphatically to the question of class size."
7. Schools should organize multidisciplinary trans-agency teams of providers of health and social services to assist children and families in solving problems that transcend the reach of schools and teachers. "Teachers can only do so much, and we have to support them" so that they have time enough "to actually teach children as their number-one priority," Jackson argues. This requires an easy system of teacher referral to medical or counseling aid. Schools have to reach out to public health-care providers to create these networks.

   "The schools see a lot of things that need attention, but the teacher should not be responsible for solving all the problems. But so many of these problems are presenting barriers to learning that we can't ignore them anymore."
8. Establish effective home/school partnerships that help care givers become actively involved in the education of their children. "The important thing to emphasize is the real care giver," says Jackson, "whether grandmother or foster parent or other family member. We must deal with the reality of the new family."
9. Schools should plan active and intensive drug-prevention programs for all children, especially those living in communities with a widespread drug culture.
10. Schools should cooperate with others in the community to provide drug-prevention treatment or seminars for women of child-bearing age, including middle and high school students.

Source: R. C. Sautter. (1992). "Crack: Healing the children." ***Phi Delta Kappan, 74,*** K8–K9 [Kappan Special Report]. Copyright © 1992, Phi Delta Kappan. Reprinted with permission of R. C. Sautter.

Children who are already disabled physically, mentally, or emotionally are more at risk for abuse than are nondisabled children (Crosse, Kaye, & Ratnofsky, n.d.; Grayson, 1992). Because children with disabilities are more vulnerable and dependent, abusive adults find them easy targets. The poor social judgment and limited experience of many children with disabilities make them even more vulnerable to sexual abuse. Moreover, some of the characteristics of children with disabilities are sources of additional stress for their caretakers and may be contributing factors in physical abuse—they often require more time, energy, money, and patience than children without disabilities. Parenting any child is stressful; parenting a child with a disability can demand more than some parents are prepared to give. It is not surprising that children with disabilities are disproportionately represented among abused children and that the need for training is particularly great for parents of children with disabilities.

Protecting Abused Kids

Q. Is child abuse still a problem in this country?
A. Emphatically, yes. We have succeeded in making the problem visible but not in reducing it. It remains a pervasive, debilitating societal problem that affects many, many children and adults.
Q. How common is child abuse?
A. A conservative estimate is that at least 30 percent of our population will be abused at some time during childhood. Every year two or three percent of all U.S. children are reported as having been abused or neglected.
Q. What are the various forms of abuse?
A. The usual classifications are neglect, physical abuse (causing physical injury), sexual abuse, and emotional abuse.
Q. Does abuse "run" in families?
A. Persons who have abused their children very often say they themselves were abused as children.
Q. Who abuses children? Is there a specific "abusing" personality?
A. That depends on the type of abuse. Generally, people who have already abused children are quite likely to do it again. The trick is finding out who has that kind of history.

Potential child abusers don't have any obvious physical or mental features that make them stand out in a crowd. When there's no available record of abuse, you need to know a lot of personal things about someone to recognize that potential.
Q. How can child abuse be detected? What kind of physical symptoms or injuries are present?
A. Teachers can learn to recognize signs of physical abuse. They should be concerned if a child repeatedly comes to class in the morning with swellings and bruises. Teachers also should be concerned if a child habitually wears long sleeves or layers of clothing even when the weather is warm. Some kids will tell a teacher they're being abused if the teacher just comes out and asks them.

School-based child abuse education programs emphasize the importance of telling someone about the abuse. Often a sexually abused child in such a program will tell someone about his or her situation. When you give children definitions of abuse—especially sexual abuse—they'll more clearly understand that what is happening to them is wrong, and they'll be more likely to report it.

Teachers also can pick up on abuse by keeping an eye out for behavioral problems. A child who all of a sudden starts acting out or becomes violent could just be displaying something learned at home. Teachers should wonder, "Where did this child pick up this behavior? Where did he or she learn this violence?" Most likely it came from a parent.
Q. What should a teacher do who suspects a student is being abused?
A. Every state has a law requiring teachers to report cases of child abuse. So it's imperative that teachers receive training on how to deal with the issue and how to handle the situation. Unfortunately, not enough of this kind of instruction is going on.
Q. What determines how much psychological damage an abused child suffers, and when is such damage likely to show up?
A. The amount of damage depends on how severe and intense the abuse is, how long it lasts, and when it starts. The earlier in life abuse begins, the worse effects it's likely to have later in life.

Abuse causes more psychological damage to children at certain ages than at others. But even those children who are abused at particularly vulnerable points in their

PSYCHOLOGICAL AND BEHAVIORAL CHARACTERISTICS

Academic Achievement

It is impossible to make many valid generalizations about the academic achievement of children with physical disabilities because they vary so widely in the nature and severity of their conditions. Many students with physical disabilities have erratic school attendance because of hospitalization, visits to physicians, the requirement of bed rest at home, and so on. Some learn well with ordinary teaching methods; others require special methods because they have mental retardation or sensory impairments in addition to physical disabilities. Because of the frequent interruptions in their schooling, some fall considerably behind their agemates in academic achievement, even though they have normal intelligence and motivation. Some children with mild development may not show any abnormality from abuse until later in life. Sexually abused children, for example, usually don't manifest problems until they're older, when they're beginning to develop and understand their own sexuality.

Q. Do some children withstand abuse better than others?

A. It appears that they do, but the exact reasons are hard to sort out. Some children survive severe abuse and emerge as successful, healthy adults; others become virtually disabled psychologically.

Genetic factors seem to play some role, but a lot of evidence indicates that the most important factor in "surviving" child abuse may be a long-term relationship with a supportive, healthy adult, perhaps a relative or a teacher, who stays interested and available.

Q. How can child abuse be prevented or at least reduced?

A. In-home services are quite effective in combatting either neglect or physical abuse—except for sexual abuse. Someone (usually a social worker from the school or a local social service agency) comes into the home on friendly terms with the family and provides any kind of support that's possible. This person teaches parents to be parents—often they don't know how—and serves as a role model.

This kind of friendly relationship with the family takes a long time to develop. In-home service people often drop in five or six times a day. They teach abusive parents to live for the next day. All too often, abusive people live only for today because they don't know whether there will be a tomorrow.

It's important to know that abuse is compulsive, repetitive behavior. It's habitual, like an addiction.

And, again like substance abusers, child abusers can find help and support in groups of people who share their problem. One group, "Parents Anonymous," has been around for over 30 years and has a chapter in almost every city. Its program is modeled after the 12-step Alcoholics Anonymous program.

Q. Has child abuse declined with the increase in education and publicity over the years?

A. In the '70s we did fairly well in managing the situation and preventing abuse, but in the '80s services for abused children and their families deteriorated dramatically. Although reporting of cases has improved and society's consciousness has been raised, little has been done in recent years to actually improve the situation for these children.

Q. Beyond reporting the problem, what role can school employees play in helping abused children?

A. School employees can play a crucial role. First, they can teach about abuse and prevention. In California, for example, school districts must provide every child with at least three child abuse education courses between kindergarten and high school.

Second, abused children lack a sense of security. We know that comfortable relationships with adults—and school employees can be very important adults in this respect—can make a big difference in abused children's health. Beyond recognizing the problems and getting help for the victims, that's a very important contribution school employees can make.

Source: From D. Chadwick, "Protecting abused kids," *NEA Today, 8* (5) (1989), 23. Copyright © by National Education Association. Reprinted with permission.

or transitory physical problems have no academic deficiencies at all; others have severe difficulties. Some students who have serious and chronic health problems still manage to achieve at a high level. Usually these high-achieving children have high intellectual capacity, strong motivation, and teachers and parents who make every possible special provision for their education. Children with neurological impairments are, as a group, most likely to have intellectual and perceptual deficits and therefore to be behind their agemates in academic achievement (see Batshaw & Perret, 1986; Bigge, 1991).

Personality Characteristics

Research does not support the notion that there is a certain personality type associated with any physical disability. Children and youths with physical disabilities are as varied in their psychological characteristics as nondisabled children, and they are

Depending on the age of onset of traumatic brain injury (TBI), personal adjustment problems may be a major concern.

apparently responsive to the same factors that influence the psychological development of other children. How children adapt to their physical limitations and how they respond to social-interpersonal situations greatly depends on how parents, siblings, teachers, peers, and the public react to them (Bigge, 1991).

Public Reactions. Public attitudes can have a profound influence on how children with physical disabilities see themselves and on their opportunities for psychological adjustment, education, and employment. If the reaction is one of fear, rejection, or discrimination, they may spend a great deal of energy trying to hide their stigmatizing differences. If the reaction is one of pity and an expectation of helplessness, people with disabilities will tend to behave in a dependent manner. To the extent that other people can see children with physical disabilities as persons who have certain limitations but are otherwise just like everyone else, children and youths with disabilities will be encouraged to become independent and productive members of society.

Several factors seem to be causing greater public acceptance of people with physical disabilities. Professional and civic groups encourage support and decrease fear of people who are disabled through information and public education. Government insistence on the elimination of architectural barriers that prevent citizens with disabilities from using public facilities serves to decrease discrimination. Programs to encourage hiring workers with disabilities help the public see those with physical disabilities as constructive, capable people. Laws that protect *every* child's right to public education bring more individuals into contact with people who have severe or profound disabilities. But there is no doubt that many children with physical disabilities are still rejected, feared, pitied, or discriminated against. The more obvious the physical flaw, the more likely it is that the person will be perceived in negative terms by the public.

Public policy regarding children's physical disabilities has not met the needs of most such children and their families (Baumeister et al., 1990; Hobbs, Perrin, & Ireys, 1984). Particularly, as successful medical treatment prolongs the lives of more and more children with severe, chronic illnesses and other disabilities, issues of who should pay the costs of treatment and maintenance (which are often enormous) and which children and families should receive the limited available resources are becoming critical (Lyon, 1985).

Children's and Families' Reactions. As suggested earlier, children's reactions to their own physical disabilities are largely a reflection of how they have been treated by others. Shame and guilt are learned responses; children will have such negative feelings only if others respond to them by shaming or blaming them (and those like them) for their physical differences. Children will be independent and self-sufficient (within the limits of their physical disabilities) rather than dependent and demanding, only to the extent that they learn how to take care of their own needs. And they will have realistic self-perceptions and set realistic goals for themselves only to the extent that others are honest and clear in appraising their conditions.

However, certain psychological reactions are inevitable for the child with physical disabilities, no matter how he or she is treated. The wish to be nondisabled and participate in the same activities as most children and the fantasy that the disability will disappear are to be expected. With proper management and help, the child can be expected eventually to accept the disability and live a happy life, even though he or she knows the true nature of the condition. Fear and anxiety, too, can be expected. It is natural for children to be afraid when they are separated from their parents, hospitalized, and subjected to medical examinations and procedures that may be painful. In these situations, too, proper management can minimize emotional stress. Psychological trauma is not a necessary effect of hospitalization. The hospital environment may, in fact, be better than the child's home in the case of abused and neglected children.

Other important considerations regarding the psychological effects of a physical disability include the age of the child and the nature of the limitation (e.g., whether it is congenital or acquired, progressive or not). But even these factors are not uniform in their effects. A child with a relatively minor and short-term physical disability may become more maladjusted, anxious, debilitated, and disruptive than another child with a terminal illness because of the way the child's behavior and feelings are managed. Certainly, understanding the child's and the family's feelings about the disability are important. But it is also true that managing the consequences of the child's behavior is a crucial aspect of education and rehabilitation.

The box on pages 420–421 illustrates how one person with epilepsy and her family dealt with her disorder. Note in this case how family support played an important role in the child's learning to cope with the onset of the disorder at age thirteen and how, as she grew into young adulthood, she asserted her independence and sense of self in a realistic and adaptive way. The family and its cultural roots are important determinants of how and what children with physical disabilities will learn; thus, it is important to take cultural values into account in teaching children not only about the academic curriculum but about their disability as well (Walker, 1995).

I Am Not Defined by My Disorder

This is a shared story by a father and his daughter. Both tell their own side. Jennifer's remarks are in boldface.

I had just sat down to dinner with my wife, Susan, our daughter, Jennifer, nearly 13, and son, Jonathan, 8, when Jennifer said her tongue mysteriously felt as though she'd bitten it. The mystery's frightening answer unfolded a few mornings later: Jennifer's arms flew up and her body jerked and she crashed to the floor, shaken into unconsciousness in the hands of an invisible, raging giant.

I felt helpless, unable to do more than cradle my daughter's head on my knees. Hours later in a hospital emergency room, I began to learn more about the strange giant that had taken hold of Jennifer—the chronic brain disorders that are collectively termed epilepsy.

"Is that what I have?" Jennifer asked hazily after a nurse mentioned the word. "Epilepsy?" I looked down at her on the hospital bed. She was half-conscious with the pounding, sledge-hammer headache that, we would learn, sometimes follows a grand mal seizure. "I think so," I said, squeezing her hand. But I didn't know anything about epilepsy, and so I looked away to hide my fear.

I don't mind my epilepsy. If I had to pick a disorder to live with, this would probably be it. The whole thing is kind of fascinating: why some people are epileptic, how seizures are triggered, which drugs work for which seizures.

I now know that epilepsy is an ancient and mysterious malady, still misunderstood, that afflicts about one percent of the U.S. population— some 2 million people, estimates the Epilepsy Foundation of America. It's important to know that most of them lead normal lives. They attend schools, hold jobs, raise families. They make history: Alexander the Great had epilepsy. So did Socrates, Napoleon, van Gogh, and Alfred Nobel.

Epilepsy's causes are unclear. Its manifestations—seizures—result from the excessive, disorderly and unfiltered firing of neurons within the brain. Grand mal seizures are the ones in which the body thrashes and consciousness departs. Although frightful, they cause no lasting injury. If you see someone in the grip of a grand mal seizure, do no more than cushion his head for the few minutes the seizure will last. Don't try to restrain him or force anything into his mouth. Other forms of seizures include absence spells (brief losses of awareness, occasionally with rapid eye blinking) and partial seizures (jerking seizures on one side of the body, or in one leg or arm). Many children with epilepsy outgrow their seizures.

We were never sure if it was the side effects of her first anticonvulsant drugs or the still-recurring seizures, but entire days began disappearing from Jennifer's memory. Her grades plummeted. After she tumbled down a flight of stairs at school, educators held a meeting to consider Jennifer's future there but stopped short of forcing her into a special class for students with learning disabilities.

On the whole, my teachers made sincere attempts at being understanding. Some seemed afraid of epilepsy. They'd tell me not to worry about doing my homework or taking tests on time. Others were overly demanding and wouldn't accept reasons for late or poor work. After I fell down the stairs, I wasn't allowed to walk to or from classes by myself, and I had to leave classes early to avoid the rush of students. It was frustrating, but I never felt that I was being discriminated against.

"The problem for Jennifer is that, although she takes her medications regularly (many patients don't), she does have a lot of side effects," said Dr. John Kelly Sullivan, her current neurologist.

My memory stinks. There are parts of my life—things I've done, films I've seen, books I've read, people I've

PROSTHETICS, ORTHOTICS, AND ADAPTIVE DEVICES FOR DAILY LIVING

prosthesis. A device designed to replace, partially or completely, a part of the body (e.g., artificial teeth or limbs).

orthosis. A device designed to restore, partially or completely, a lost function of the body (e.g., a brace or crutch).

Many individuals with physical disabilities use prosthetics, orthotics, and other adaptive devices to help them better function on a daily basis. A **prosthesis** is an artificial replacement for a missing body part (e.g., an artificial hand or leg); an **orthosis** is a device that enhances the partial function of a part of a person's body (a brace or a device that allows a person to do something; see Figures 10–1 to 10–4). **Adaptive devices** for daily living include a variety of adaptations of ordinary items found in the home, office, or school—such as a device to aid bathing or handwashing or walk-

met—that I can't remember. One thing epilepsy did for me is that it showed me the value of the human brain.

Susan and I realized, as an Epilepsy Foundation pamphlet warns: "Severe and frequent seizures in a child inevitably put additional strains on the family, and even the most devoted and understanding parents are sometimes overwhelmed by the child's needs." Jonathan sometimes saw his older sister thrown to the floor and has disliked talking about it. "It was scary," he said.

Being epileptic means I may have a seizure anywhere, anytime. But I'm not going to worry about it or limit myself in where I go, or what I do, because of it. I am not defined by my disorder.

More tests yielded a refined diagnosis: Jennifer has what neurologists now call "juvenile myoclonic epilepsy." It is rarely outgrown, nor can the patient ever discontinue drug therapy. Jennifer takes Depakote and Diamox.

Even as Jennifer grew out of her teen years, we dared not let go too much too soon. In the spring of 1990, after earning honor grades at a prep school, Jennifer was accepted at Goucher College in Baltimore. I said goodbye at the Portland airport that fall with a hug I hoped could somehow protect her from the giant.

My parents occasionally have been overprotective: Don't swim. Don't ride bikes. Don't drive. Don't drink. Don't get stressed. Don't go sailing without a lifeline. don't stay out late. Don't go near flashing lights (they could trigger seizures). Don't spend the night at a friend's home. Allow for seizure time in the morning. Don't walk up or down stairs unattended. Don't forget your pills.

I never thought the best solution was to live a limited life. I'd rather do things and take risks than do nothing at all. Going to college far from home wasn't something I felt afraid of. I felt very capable of taking care of myself.

She had 22 seizure-free months before the giant grabbed her in a dormitory shower. Another young woman found her and called me: bumps and bruises, no serious injuries, no bleeding. The call gave me a darker sense of frustration, but I realized that the caller's calmness had come from my daughter's careful explanations of epilepsy to her dorm mates. Jennifer was taking more and more responsibility for her life. I could not forever seek to shield her from all harm, I realized, nor should I try.

I feel that most people who know me should know that I am epileptic. I tell all my professors, because I may miss classes or have to make up tests. I tell dorm mates, because they should be forewarned. What to do and what not to do is something I explain to everyone I know. I try to explain what seizures look like, why I have them, what may set them off, what I'm like afterward. (I usually forget things.) Although I've felt frustrated and occasionally angry, I've never felt embarrassed by it. I have epilepsy, but epilepsy doesn't have me.

The giant returns less often now, and Jennifer is officially an adult. When she called home during the spring semester and told me, in a voice bubbling with excited pride, how she had been rockclimbing (in the company of skilled mountaineers), I felt the strength of her self-esteem and realized, finally, that the giant may cause her to stumble once in a while but will never stop her. A good thing for a parent to know.

For more information, write: Epilepsy Foundation of America, Dept. PP, 4351 Garden City Drive, Landover, MD. 20785. Or call 1-800-332-1000.

Source: From John Lovell and Jennifer Lovell, "I am not defined by my disorder," *Parade Magazine*, August 15, 1993, p. 6.

ing—that make performing the tasks required for self-care and employment easier for the person who has a physical disability.

The most important principles to keep in mind are use of residual function, simplicity, and reliability. For example, an artificial hand is operated by the muscles of the arm, shoulder, or back. This may be too complicated or demanding for an infant or young child with a missing or deformed upper limb. Depending on the child's age, the length and function of the amputated limb, and the child's other abilities, a passive "mitt" or a variety of other prosthetic devices might be more helpful (Gover & McIvor, 1992). Choice of the most useful prosthesis will depend on careful evaluation of each individual's needs. A person without legs may be taught to use his or her arms

adaptive devices. Special tools that are adaptations of common items to make accomplishing self-care, work, or recreation activities easier for people with physical disabilities.

Figure 10–1

Examples of thermoform leg braces. The braces are molded to fit the contour of the wearer's leg and hold the knee, ankle, and/or foot in a more correct or acceptable position. The orthoses are lighter in weight, more functional, and cosmetically more acceptable than older-style braces and can be worn with a variety of footwear.

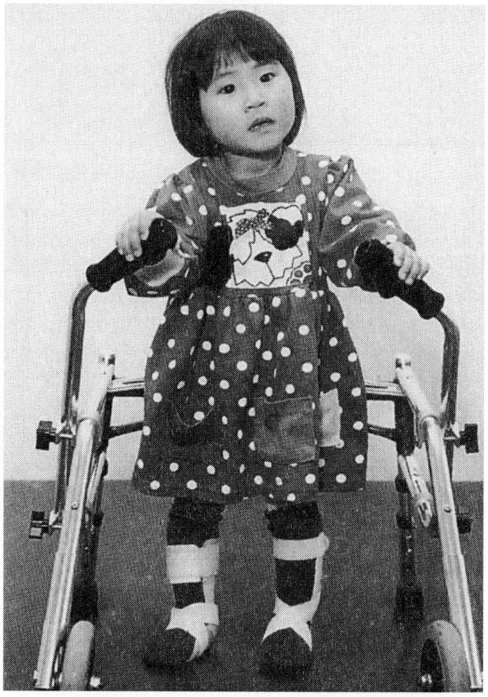

Figure 10–2

Devices to assist a person with a physical disability in eating: plate attached to table to keep it from moving; rim around plate keeps food from being accidentally pushed off and helps in getting food on utensil; cuff on wrist and hand allows someone with weak grasp to hold utensil.

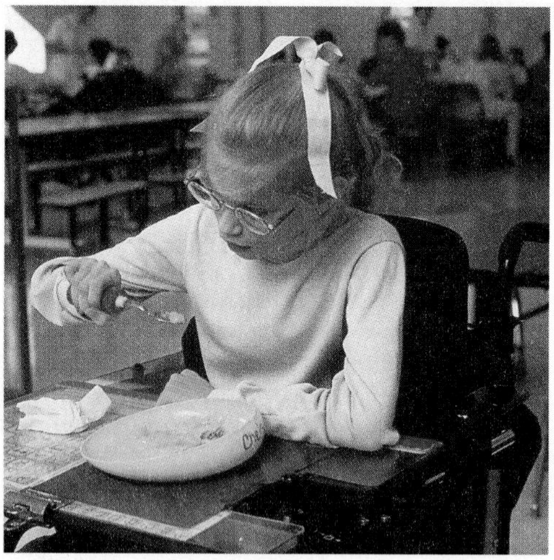

to move about in a wheelchair or to use his or her torso and arms to get about on artificial legs (perhaps using crutches or a cane in addition). Again, each individual's abilities and preferences must be evaluated in designing the prosthesis.

Two points regarding prosthetics, orthotics, and residual function must be kept in mind.

1. Residual function is often important, even when a prosthesis, orthosis, or adaptive device is not used. For example, it may be crucial for the child with cerebral palsy or muscular dystrophy to learn to use the affected limbs as well as possible without the aid of any special equipment because using residual

function alone will make the child more independent and may help prevent or retard physical deterioration. Moreover, it is often more efficient for a person to learn not to rely completely on a prosthesis or orthosis, as long as he or she can accomplish a task without it.

2. Spectacular technological developments often have very limited meaning for the immediate needs of the majority of individuals with physical disabilities. It may be years before expensive experimental equipment is tested adequately and marketed at a cost most people can afford, and a given device may be applicable only to a small group of individuals with an extremely rare condition (Moore, 1985). For example, the new technology described in Figure 10–5 costs about $35,000 per patient, and only about 14,000 of the 90,000

Figure 10–3

A device to help someone who uses a wheelchair to pick up objects on the floor or on shelves too high to reach from a sitting position.

Figure 10–4

A mouthstick or wand allows people who cannot use their hands to point, turn pages, type, paint, and so on. The wand may also be attached to head straps to allow the person to use neck and head motion (see Figure 10–11).

people with quadriplegic spinal cord injuries in the United States would be good candidates for using it, if it were perfected and readily available (Valentine, 1995). And even though the device described in the box on page 426 has given Stephanie Hergert greater ability to participate in ordinary childhood activities, the current cost of such devices clearly provides a barrier to their common use. Thus, for a long time to come, common standby prostheses, orthoses, and other equipment adapted to the needs of individuals will be the most practical devices. A few such devices that are helpful to persons with various physical disabilities are shown in Figures 10–1 through 10–4. (See Bigge, 1991; DuBose & Deni, 1980; Fraser & Hensinger, 1983; Verhaaren & Connor, 1981b, for additional illustrations of such devices.)

Figure 10–5

Help for paralyzed people.

(*Source:* Paul W. Valentine, "Every movement counts: Device gives quadriplegics a chance to grasp," *The Washington Post,* March 21, 1995, p. A8. © The Washington Post. Reprinted with permission.)

A new technology is being tested that could bring some help to paralyzed people, enabling them to use their hands to grasp and release objects. The medical device, called the *Neuroprosthetic Hand Grasp System,* is being tested on people with spinal cord injuries who are able to move their shoulders and bend their elbows but cannot move their hands and fingers.

How It Works

Some of the equipment for the system is internal; an 8- to 12-hour surgery is required to implant the components.

The paralyzed person moves a shoulder to activate the system. An external sensor, mounted on the skin over the shoulder, senses that movement and sends a signal to a computerized unit that is usually mounted on the back of a wheelchair. That control unit sends radio signals to an internal device implanted in the patient's upper chest. This internal receiver/stimulator is connected to wires that lead to electrodes in the paralyzed arm.

The electrodes, which are attached to the paralyzed forearm and hand muscles, stimulate those muscles to grasp and release objects.

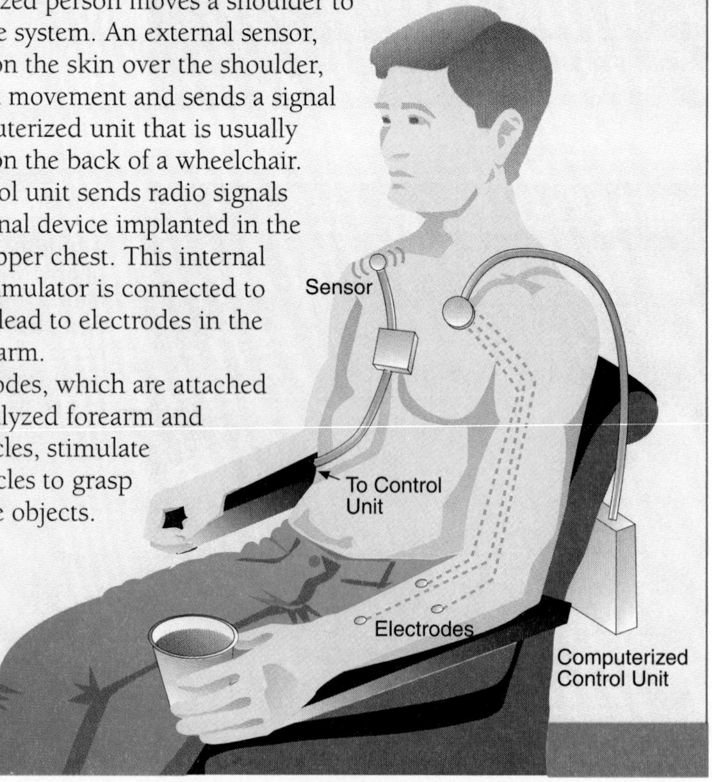

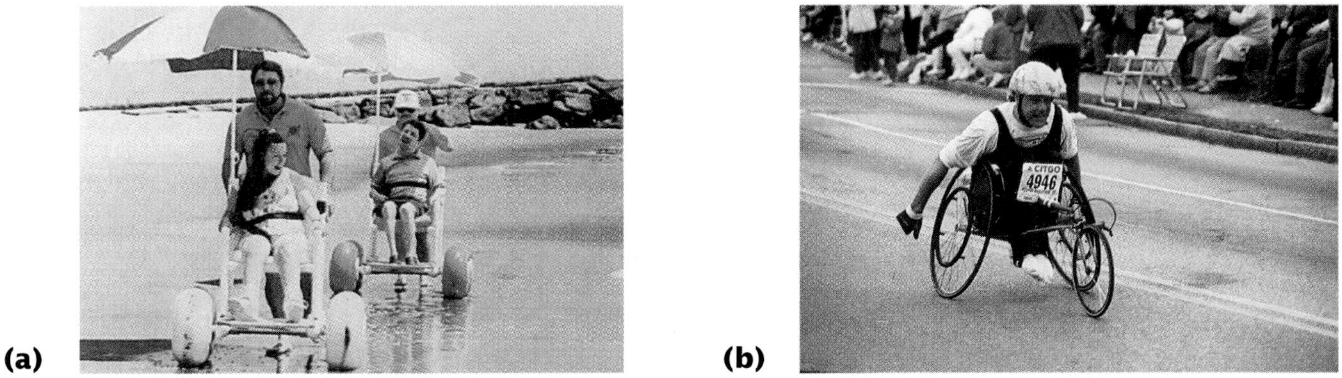

Figure 10–6 Rehabilitation engineers are redesigning wheelchairs for use in off-the-street recreational and work environments: **(a)** chairs suitable for use at the beach or in other soft terrain; **(b)** a chair specially designed for racing.

We do not mean to downplay the importance of technological advances for people with physical disabilities. Our point here is that the greatest significance of a technological advance often lies in how it changes seemingly ordinary items or problems. For example, technological advances in metallurgy and plastics have led to the designs of much more functional braces and wheelchairs. The heavy metal-and-leather leg braces formerly used by many children with cerebral palsy or other neurological disorders—which were cumbersome, difficult to apply, and not very helpful in preventing deformity or improving function—have been largely supplanted by braces constructed of thermoform plastic (see Figure 10–1). Wheelchairs are being built of lightweight metals and plastics and redesigned to allow users to go places inaccessible to the typical wheelchair (see Figure 10–6). And an increasing number of computerized devices are improving the movement and communication abilities of people with disabilities.

The greatest problem today is not devising new or more sophisticated assistive technology but rather accurately evaluating children and youths to determine what would be most useful and then making that technology available. Many children and youths who need prostheses or other assistive devices, such as computers, special vehicles, and self-help aids, are not carefully evaluated and provided with the most appropriate equipment (Parette & VanBiervliet, 1991).

EDUCATIONAL CONSIDERATIONS

Too often, we think of people who have physical disabilities as being helpless or unable to learn. It is easy to lower our expectations for them because we know that they are indeed unable to do some things. We forget, though, that many people with physical disabilities can learn to do many or all the things most nondisabled persons do, although sometimes they must perform these tasks in different ways (e.g., a person who does not have the use of the hands may have to use the feet or mouth). Accepting the limitations imposed by physical disabilities without trying to see how much people can learn or how the environment can be changed to allow them to respond more effectively is an insulting and dehumanizing way of responding to physical differences.

Taking Big Steps

Stephanie Hergert, a talkative 7-year-old, was fitted with her first orthotic device at age 18 months. Born with spina bifida, she is paralyzed from the rib cage down.

Stephanie uses a wheelchair at the Coronado elementary school she attends, but at home she uses an orthotic device designed by Saxton, an owner of Southern California Orthotics and Prosthetics (SCOPe), which has five patient-care centers in San Diego County.

Saxton said he created the device by combining an Orlau Swivel Walker and a Rochester Parapodium. The parapodium holds Stephanie upright in a rigid, stable frame, and the base of the frame is mounted on swiveling foot plates.

By leaning forward and swinging her arms, Stephanie can move forward, Saxton explained. By leaning backward and swinging her arms, she can move backward.

"Five years ago, someone like Stephanie would not have had the opportunity to stand upright," said Stephanie's mother, Robin Hergert.

Indeed, the fact that her daughter can stand, let alone move with the aid of a brace, is more than Hergert ever expected.

"When she was born, the picture was grim," Hergert said. Doctors were very discouraging.

However, she said therapists and orthotists "gave us more hope."

Though the technology is available to custom-design devices such as Stephanie's, the cost to fund such devices is quite another matter.

Stephanie's brace cost close to $7,000. And Saxton said neither the state nor most managed health organizations cover the cost of high-technology devices, only basic or prefabricated devices.

Source: From Sharon F. Griffin, "Taking big steps," *The San Diego Union-Tribune,* February 13, 1994, pp. D1, D2. Used with permission.

Educating students with physical disabilities is not so much a matter of special instruction for children with disabilities as it is of educating the nondisabled population. People with physical disabilities solve many of their own problems, but their lives are often needlessly complicated because the nondisabled give no thought to what life is like for someone with specific physical limitations. Design adaptations in buildings, furniture, household appliances, and clothing can make it possible for someone with a physical disability to function as efficiently as a nondisabled person in a home, school, or community.

Individualized Planning

Students with complex physical disabilities typically require a wide array of related services as well as special education. The IEPs (individualized education programs) for such students tend to be particularly specific and detailed. The instructional goals and objectives often include seemingly minute steps, especially for young children with severe disabilities. Many of the children under the age of three years who need special education and related services are children with physical disabilities. These children are required by law (PL 99–457) to have an **individualized family service plan (IFSP)** rather than an IEP (see Chapters 1 and 12). These plans must specify how the family will be involved in intervention as well as what other services will be provided.

individualized family service plan (IFSP). A plan for services for young children with disabilities (under three years of age) and their families, drawn up by professionals and parents, similar to an IEP for older children; mandated by PL 99–457.

Educational Placement

Children with physical disabilities may be educated in any one of several settings, depending on the type and severity of the condition, the services available in the community, and the medical prognosis for the condition. If such children ordinarily attend regular public school classes but must be hospitalized for more than a few days, they may be included in a class in the hospital itself. If they must be confined to their homes for a time, a visiting or homebound teacher may provide tutoring until they can return to regular classes. In these cases—which usually involve children who have been in accidents or who have conditions that are not permanently and severely disabling—relatively minor, common-sense adjustments are required to continue the children's education and keep them from falling behind their classmates. At the other extreme—usually involving serious or permanent disabilities—the child may be taught for a time in a hospital school or a special public school class designed specifically for children with physical disabilities. Today, most are being integrated into the public schools because of advances in medical treatment: new developments in bioengineering, allowing them greater mobility and functional movement; decreases in or removal of architectural barriers and transportation problems; and the movement toward public education for all children (Bigge, 1991).

Educational Goals and Curricula

It is not possible to prescribe educational goals and curricula for children with physical disabilities as a group because their individual limitations vary so greatly. Even among children with the same condition, goals and curricula must be determined after assessing each child's intellectual, physical, sensory, and emotional characteristics.

A physical disability, especially a severe and chronic one that limits mobility, may have two implications for education. (1) The child may be deprived of experiences that nondisabled children have, and (2) the child may find it impossible to manipulate educational materials and respond to educational tasks the way most children do. For example, a child with severe cerebral palsy cannot take part in most outdoor play activities and travel experiences and may not be able to hold and turn pages in books, write, explore objects manually, or use a typewriter without special equipment.

For children with an impairment that is only physical, curriculum and educational goals should ordinarily be the same as for nondisabled children: reading, writing, arithmetic, and experiences designed to familiarize them with the world about them. In addition, special instruction may be needed in mobility skills, daily living skills, and occupational skills. That is, because of their physical impairments, these children may need special, individualized instruction in the use of mechanical devices that will help them perform tasks that are much simpler for those without disabilities. For children with other disabilities in addition to physical limitations, curricula will need to be further adapted (Bigge, 1991; Hanson & Harris, 1986).

Educational goals for students with severe or profound disabilities must be related to their functioning in everyday community environments. Only recently have educators begun to address the problems of analyzing community tasks (e.g., crossing streets, using money, riding public transportation, greeting neighbors) and planning efficient instruction for individuals with severe disabilities (Bigge, 1991; Snell & Browder, 1986). Efficient instruction in such skills requires that teaching occur in the community environment itself.

The range of educational objectives and curricula for children with physical disabilities is often extended beyond the objectives and curricula typically provided for other students in school. For example, very young children and those with severe neuromuscular problems may need objectives and curricula focusing on the most basic self-care skills (e.g., swallowing, chewing, self-feeding). Older students may need not only to explore possible careers in the way all students should but to consider the special accommodations their physical limitations demand for successful performance, as well.

SUCCESS STORIES

Albertson, NY: Sixteen-year-old **David Womack** *is in the ninth grade at an academic day school for students with severe physical disabilities. He has been dependent on a ventilator since a spinal cord injury nine years ago. A collaborative team of teachers and therapists work closely with David and his parents, Brenda and David Womack, Sr., to maximize his independence through technology.*

On the second day of second grade, seven-year-old David Womack was hit by a car as he stepped from the school bus in front of his home. The accident injured David's spinal cord, leaving him a quadriplegic, with no movement below his neck and no ability for spontaneous respiration.

During David's two-year rehabilitation in a Baltimore hospital, his father, David Womack, Sr., traveled four hours every other weekend to be with his son and his wife, Brenda, who rented a nearby apartment. Their twelve-year-old daughter stayed behind with her grandmother in the Long Island community that rallied in support to raise funds for a home computer system for David and to help his family buy and renovate an accessible home.

Upon David's release from the hospital, his parents and educators from their school district made the decision to enroll nine-year-old David in Henry Viscardi School, a special day school for students with intense medical and physical needs. Unlike most schools, Viscardi is equipped with a large medical and therapeutic staff. Nurses as well as physical and occupational therapists team with teachers, so that students benefit from closely monitored physical and instructional management.

In 1989, David was the first student dependent on a ventilator to attend the school. He made his third-grade entrance in a large electronic "sip-and-puff" wheelchair, directed by airflow he provided through a straw-like mouthpiece. "The vent," as this life-support system is also called, was mounted on the back of his chair and detected by its rhythmic sound. Never more than several feet away was a private-duty nurse, who monitored him at all times. "It was so scary," recalls Brenda Womack. "I could tell everybody was nervous."

The school's task included helping all the Womacks adjust to a different life and stimulating David to discover his new potential. Before the first day of school, staff occupational therapist Ginette Howard worked closely with David to ready him for classroom technology, as well as with his teachers, all of whom were certified in both special and general education. Even though the staff was experienced in dealing with difficult physical issues, David presented a challenge and the presence of the ventilator, necessary equipment, and private nurse emphasized his fragility. Says Ginette, "Before long, we realized we had to raise everybody's expectations and start treating David like a student instead of a patient!"

David's progress has been built slowly but steadily on a foundation of trust, and his achievements are the result of both sophisticated instructional technology and effective collaboration among teachers, therapists, nurses, and his home community. It was the school's team approach to technology that supported David's classroom learning. Ginette Howard and computer teacher Maryann Cicchillo combined their knowledge of instructional software and sophisticated electronics to provide David with the tools to read, write, and compute. Classroom teachers followed their lead, and so did his nurse, Gail Nolan, who was committed to his academic and social growth.

"The first year, we needed to overcome fear and develop trust," recalls Ginette Howard. David was frightened to leave the hospital, so the first task was to secure his venti-

Although all students may profit from a discussion of death and dying, education about these topics may be particularly important in classrooms in which a student has a terminal illness. As Bigge notes regarding the teacher's responsibilities in dealing with students who are terminally ill, "The role of educators is complex, requiring them to deal directly with the dying child as well as with the family, classmates, and peers" (1991, p. 124). Teachers should be direct and open in their discussion of death and dying. Death should not be a taboo subject, nor should teachers deny their own feelings or squelch the feelings of others. Confronted with the task of educating a

Special Educators at Work

lator equipment for school mobility and classroom use. "We made sure there was a plastic casing over the dials since he was afraid someone might play with the settings," Ginette explains. The second year, David became more confident and was willing to try out new pieces of educational technology. Over six years, Ginette and Maryann have seen David progress from being withdrawn and fearful, to trusting, to finally developing real interest in computer applications. Providing him with computer access has been the challenge.

"David has chin supports to keep his head erect, and he can move his mouth," says Ginette. She and Maryann selected a small alternative-access keyboard, worked by an electronic mouthstick called a *wand.* With much effort, David would clench the mouthstick in his teeth and gently tap the attached wand on the miniature impulse-sensitive keyboard set on a height-adjustable table in front of him. The classroom computer would directly respond, and Maryann ensured that appropriate software was available to David's teacher through the school's network. Very gradually, David became accustomed to the awkwardness of the mouthstick and to the expectation that he was independently responsible for his schoolwork. As Ginette remembers, "David is extremely artistic, and he increased his facility by using adapted paintbrushes. By his second and third year, I was making mouthsticks like you wouldn't believe!"

Now in ninth grade, David no longer needs the adapted access of the miniature system, since he has developed greater facial mobility. Having used mouthsticks for numerous functional tasks, he has the flexibility and range of motion to use one with an angled standard keyboard. "My goal for David is for him to become an independent thinker via technology," says his science teacher, Dorothy Vann. "This direct keyboard access gives him much more freedom in class."

Since David tires easily, he uses a word-prediction and abbreviation/expansion program to reduce the number of keystrokes and increase his speed in writing assignments. He also has started to use a laptop computer with a trackball, further challenging his accuracy and increasing his speed. David's technology sessions have been used to increase his independence as a student. "I can't tell you how many times we've explored technology to support homework assignments, to take tests, or complete a paper," says Maryann. "Last year, we used the word prediction and abbreviation/expansion program to write formal letters," recalls Ginette Howard. "David learned to program the abbreviations for salutations and common phrases, such as "DS" for "Dear Sir," or "YT" for "Yours Truly." When he keyed in the abbreviations, the phrases would appear."

"Science is my favorite subject," says David, now a quiet young man who speaks in a soft, breathy voice. Dorothy Vann's science lab is fully accessible to him, with adjustable tables and low sinks; it is also equipped with instructional technology that David needs to fully participate. In biology, he views slides through a stereo microscope, which utilizes a small attached video camera to project images onto a TV monitor. "I knew David was capable of doing more than he initially showed us," says Dorothy. "Now he uses the video microscope in labs, and in the future, he will use the computerized video laser disc player for independent research on science topics."

Working with David has been an evolving process for each of the collaborators. "When some teachers see and hear that ventilator, their tendency is to pamper the child," observes Brenda Womack. "But I have a sixteen-year-old son and I want him treated like any other student."

In reflecting on their work with David, Ginette Howard and Maryann Cicchillo think there is a breaking-in period, in which teachers and the child who is newly ventilator dependent have to overcome their fears. Says Dorothy Vann, "It also takes a while for the child to accept goals for achievement and believe in his or her own success."

—By Jean Crockett

child or youth with a terminal illness, teachers should seek available resources and turn to professionals in disciplines for help (Bigge, 1991).

Links with Other Disciplines

In the opening pages of this chapter, we made two points: (1) Children with physical disabilities have medical problems, and (2) interdisciplinary cooperation is necessary in their education. It is important for the teacher to know what other disciplines are involved in the child's care and treatment and to be able to communicate with

collaboration

a key to success

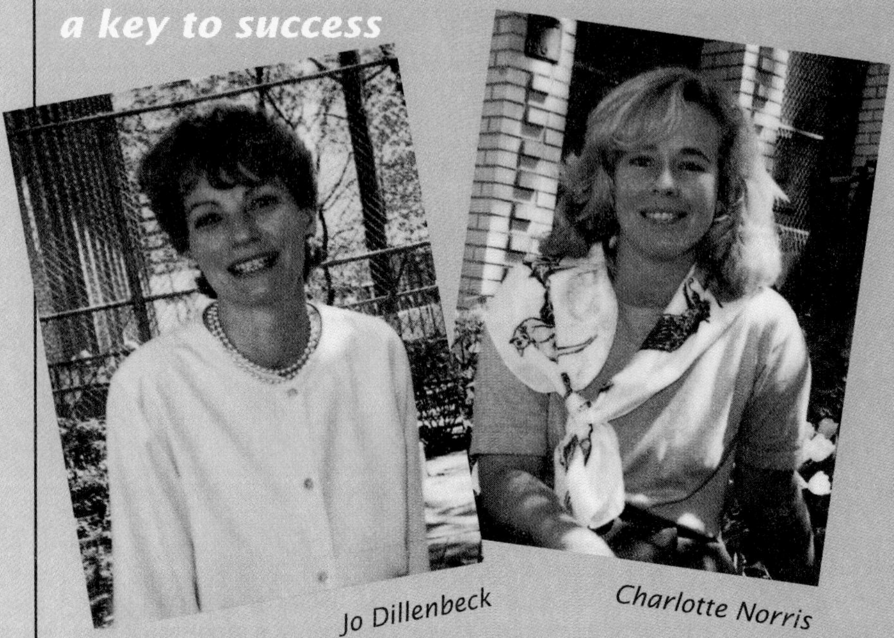

Jo The kids in my class were five and six years old. There were ten in all, four had cerebral palsy and one had spina bifida. There were language needs that emerged with their reading, and they had some emotional and learning issues as well, but they were certainly ambulatory. In terms of their gross motor development, they were all age appropriate. They really enjoyed experiential learning and were especially engaged when we used manipulatives and brought real-life experiences into the classroom, or brought them out of the classroom into their neighborhoods or environments. Basically, I didn't have a lot of behavioral problems.

Charlotte I had ten boys and eighteen girls, all roughly kindergarten age, so they matched up pretty well with Jo's group. My kids were a very mixed group in terms of their academic level. I had children who were new to school and had never been in any kind of school setting, which was certainly a challenge. This was actually a good mix because the students who were at a somewhat higher level were able to help out a lot with the students who were at lower levels, especially in group learning situations.

Jo One very successful collaboration experience that Charlotte and I have had was with a student named Sunita. She's a good example because she was a real median, right there in the middle as far as capability goes. She had spina bifida, so she wasn't ambulatory, but she could scamper around the floor like you wouldn't believe. She was a very high-spirited kid. Whenever it was her turn to be calendar monitor, I would ask if she wanted to do it from the chair or if she wanted to sit on my lap, and she wanted no part of that: She just really wanted me to get away from the calendar so she could run the show! We would have parents come and observe the class, and I'd bet that some of the kids that are in that class this year are there because the parents just fell in love with Sunita.

Charlotte Sunita was so alive, so bright, so friendly, so vivacious—you couldn't help but want know her. I think it was very easy for my students to relate to her because she so easily related to them. Sunita could talk, she could say what she was thinking, and she could write or draw what she was thinking with ease. I think that my children could see that, even though she may not have been able to walk or run like them, she could do so much *like* them.

Jo Sunita's verbal skills were really superior, even to those of the other children. I think that the hands-on kinds of activities we were doing, especially in science and music, were good for Sunita and all the children in that setting. The differences were not so apparent. We combined the children into two groups, A and B. Each group was made up of half my children and half of Jo's children. We'd occasionally put the two groups together—for instance, when we went to the fish store or on an exploration out in the schoolyard. I became an expert in a certain content area. I taught it to two groups and Charlotte did the same.

Charlotte Our classes are scheduled for music together because of our collaboration. We had a music teacher come in who taught music to both classes as a large group; however, Jo and I did stay in the classroom to facilitate management needs because it was such a large group for one teacher to handle. In fact, we had to teach the music teacher some management ideas. It was a little overwhelming for someone to come in here with a new teacher and to be faced with thirty-eight children with such a diverse range of

Jo Dillenbeck is a special education teacher in New York City; B.S. Special Education/ Elementary, Long Island University, C. W. Post Campus, Long Island, New York; M.S. Special Education, Adelphi University, Long Island, New York. **Charlotte Norris** is a regular education teacher in New York City; B.A. Journalism, New York University, New York, New York; M.S. Early Childhood Education, Queens College, Queens, New York.

skills and abilities and actual needs. The music teacher selected a song and said, "Okay, now we're going to interpret it by wiggling our bodies on the floor." Jo and I looked at each other as if to say, "Oh, no!" She didn't think about the special needs, so it really pointed out that you need to consider how *everyone* can share and participate in particular activities.

Jo The music teacher wasn't used to David, for instance, who has spastic quadriplegia. Her affect was a little inappropriate; when he was participating in the song, she over-praised him. Singing is one of his strengths, and I wasn't surprised at all that he could stay on key and that he could get involved. We wanted to be delicate and kind with her, yet let her know that David is one of us. He's one of the guys!

Charlotte It was a good experience for her; she was able to see how you can work with a range and variety of children. It's important to find someone who has a similar philosophy and treats children the way you do, but it also must be someone you can get along with, who has the same tolerance that you do. Had we not been friendly, liked each other, and respected the way each other did things, we would not have been successful. We have seen collaborations that were not as successful as ours because they did not develop out of commonalities.

Jo One of the most demanding things about our collaboration was keeping up with the kids, keeping them on pace, and trying to make it valuable for them educationally. As much as I want this very worthwhile social experience for my special needs kids, am I giving them the multisensory nuts-and-bolts special education that they need? I constantly have to try and strike a balance between the social needs of the children, and the intense requirements of their special needs.

Charlotte The most demanding thing about our collaboration was not working together ourselves, but effectively meeting the needs of the children. That's really the most demanding thing: living up to them. When you're in your own classroom, working in isolation, if something doesn't happen, only you really know about it. But when you work with someone else in collaboration, that forces you to keep your end of the bargain at all times. That's demanding but wonderful.

Jo The rewarding part of our collaboration is that our kids, disabled or not, see one another as comrades, as peers. They know one another on the playground. They seek each other out on the playground. I really feel good about my teaching. I feel as though I am this superb professional. I feel that I can learn something new every day right in the classroom, that I really have my own hands-on laboratory with a very, very fine teacher. It keeps me engaged. Yes, it's hard work, but the personal and professional rewards are really there constantly, and they're immeasureable.

Charlotte I'm going to sound like Jo, but it's true: The most rewarding thing about our work together is hearing my children call those children by name in the lunchroom and seeing them wave to one another at the tables.

Jo I have to talk about what Erica's mother said! (Erica's one of Charlotte's kids.) She was just so thrilled with this collaboration process, and she said, "I'm so happy that Charlotte's her teacher because I really think she has gotten the best in a teacher in a teaching situation. But what's *most* important to me is I overheard her talking to her two-year-old sister the other day. Erica was writing her name and playing with sentences and her sister was trying to do the very same thing. So Erica went over to her sister and said, 'Oh, I see you're making your very best zero. I'm so proud of you.'" Erica's mother continued, "That didn't come from me. That didn't sound like me. I know that came from the school. And to me, that's is as important as how she's going to succeed in math and writing and academics. Erica's really a good person. I really have to give credit to the program, to what you two did." It made my heart stop. I was really just so thrilled.

Charlotte I see what we've learned about people carry over in our classroom from year to year. The sensitivity to others, that people are different, and that we do all learn to read differently, to write differently. What's easy for one is hard for another and vice versa. In fact, I had that conversation with them today. Somebody said the math group was just too easy, and you know, we really had to talk about that—that at the same time it was hard for others and that although we're so similar, in some things we're not.

> ***You need to consider how everyone can share and participate in special activities.***

Jo I remember when they weren't understanding the directions, for instance. When Charlotte's kids were off and about and involved in the project, they needed a little bit of coaching. We worked in groups of four so children would be partners or would have to work with three other kids. The demands were to keep children's behaviors appropriate to what the group was doing, not to splash the water around, for instance. We had some younger kids—not in age so much as developmentally. They sometimes acted inappropriately with the materials, and we had to kind of teach them what to do. The kids in Charlotte's class have learned to use the right words—instead of saying, "Don't do this," they say, "Well, let's try this." "How about if we do this?" When you remember how little these kids are—five and six years old—that is really remarkable.

Advances in the designs of prosthetic devices have broadened the range of activities possible for individuals who have lost limbs.

professionals in these areas about the child's physical, emotional, and educational development.

It goes almost without saying that knowing the child's medical status is crucial. Many children with physical disabilities will need the services of a physical therapist and/or occupational therapist. Both can give valuable suggestions about helping the child use his or her physical abilities to the greatest possible extent, continuing therapeutic management in the classroom, and encouraging independence and good work habits. The teacher should be particularly concerned about how to handle and position the child so that the risk of further physical disability will be minimized and independent movement and manipulation of educational materials can be most efficiently learned.

Specialists in prosthetics and orthotics design and build artificial limbs, braces, and other devices that help individuals who are physically disabled function more conventionally. By conferring with such specialists, the teacher will get a better grasp of the function and operation of a child's prosthesis or orthosis and understand what the child can and cannot be expected to do.

Social workers and psychologists are the professionals with whom most teachers are quite familiar. Cooperation with them may be particularly important in the case of a child with a physical disability. Work with the child's family and community agencies is often necessary to prevent lapses in treatment. The child may also be particularly susceptible to psychological stress, so the school psychologist may need to be consulted to obtain an accurate assessment of intellectual potential.

Speech-language therapists are often called on to work with children with physical disabilities, especially those with cerebral palsy. The teacher will want advice from the speech-language therapist on how to maximize the child's learning of speech and language.

EARLY INTERVENTION

All who work with young children with physical disabilities have two concerns: (1) early identification and intervention and (2) development of communication. Identifying signs of developmental delay so intervention can begin as early as possible is important in preventing further disabilities that can result from lack of teaching and proper care. Early intervention is also important for maximizing the outcome of therapy. Communication skills are difficult for some children with physical disabilities to learn, and they are one of the critical objectives of any preschool program (see Chapter 7). For young children with TBI, the ultimate level of functioning they are able to attain is very difficult to predict, and appropriate early intervention is critical (Savage & Mishkin, 1994; Walker, 1993).

Probably the first and most pervasive concerns of teachers of young children with physical disabilities should be handling and positioning. *Handling* refers to how the child is picked up, carried, held, and assisted; *positioning* refers to providing support for the child's body and arranging instructional or play materials in certain ways. Proper handling makes the child more comfortable and receptive to education. Proper positioning maximizes physical efficiency and ability to manipulate materials; it also inhibits undesirable motor responses while promoting desired growth and motor patterns (Bigge, 1991; Fraser & Hensinger, 1983).

What constitutes proper positioning for one child may not be appropriate for another. It is important that teachers of children who are physically disabled be aware of some general principles of positioning and handling; in addition, they must work closely with physical therapists and physicians so that each child's particular needs are met.

The physical problems that most often require special handling and positioning involve muscle tone. Some children have **spastic** muscles—that is, chronic increased muscle tone. As a result, their limbs may be either flexed or extended all the time. If nothing is done to counteract the effects of the chronic imbalance of muscle tone, the child develops **contractures**, permanent shortening of muscles and connective tissues that result in deformity and further disability. Other children have athetosis, or fluctuating muscle tone, that results in almost constant uncontrolled movement. If these movements are not somehow restrained, the child cannot accomplish many motor tasks successfully. Still other children have muscles that are **hypotonic.** These children appear floppy, as their muscles are flaccid and weak. The hypotonia may prevent them from learning to hold up their heads or to sit or stand. All these muscle tone problems can occur together in the same child, they can occur with varying degrees of severity, and they can affect various parts of the body differently.

Another major problem that involves handling and positioning is the presence of abnormal reflexes that most children exhibit during certain developmental periods but not after a given age. An example is the **asymmetrical tonic neck reflex (ATNR),** which babies normally show from birth to about four months but which is definitely abnormal or pathological if exhibited by a child who is one year old. The stimulus that elicits ATNR is turning the head to either side while lying on the back. The reflex is characterized by extension of the arm and leg on the side toward which the head is turned and flexion of the other arm and leg (see Figure 10–7). Four major problems are caused by a pathological ATNR:

1. Rolling over is difficult or impossible.
2. The child who is on all fours will collapse if the face is turned to either side.
3. The child may not be able to get both hands to the midline for manual activities.
4. Self-feeding and walking are difficult.

spastic. A term describing a sudden, involuntary contraction of muscles that makes accurate, voluntary movement difficult.

contractures. Permanent shortenings of muscles and connective tissues and consequent distortion of bones and/or posture because of neurological damage.

hypotonic. A term describing low muscle tone; sometimes occurs as a result of cerebral palsy.

asymmetrical tonic neck reflex (ATNR). A normal reflex in babies up to about four months of age, in which turning the head to one side results in extension of the arm and leg on the side toward which the head is turned and flexion of the opposite arm and leg; an abnormal reflex, indicative of brain injury in infants older than about four months.

Handling and positioning the child who is physically disabled demands attention to supporting the child's body at various points and to how various postures influence muscle tone and ability to move. There are several key points—neck and spine, shoulder girdle, and pelvic area—where support should be given because pressure on these points controls muscle tone in the extremities and influences voluntary movement. Picking up, carrying, or handling children without attention to support at these key points may only make the child's voluntary movements more difficult (Hanson & Harris, 1986). Simple adaptive equipment is frequently required to keep the child positioned properly for movement and learning. Often such equipment can easily be made (Bigge, 1991; DuBose & Deni, 1980; Fraser & Hensinger, 1983; Hanson & Harris, 1986). Examples of such positioning equipment are shown in Figures 10–8, 10–9, and 10–10. Some adaptive equipment for positioning can be purchased, but it often needs to be tailored to the needs of the individual child.

The teacher of young children with physical disabilities must know how to teach gross motor responses, such as head control, rolling over, sitting, standing, and walking. If the child has severe neurological and motor impairments, the teacher may need to begin by focusing on teaching the child to eat (e.g., how to chew and swallow) and to make the oral movements required for speech (Bigge, 1991). Fine motor skills, such as pointing, reaching, grasping, and releasing, may be critically important. These motor skills are best taught in the context of daily lessons that involve self-help and communication. That is, motor skills should not be taught in isolation but as part of daily living and learning activities that will increase the child's communication, independence, creativity, motivation, and future learning.

Figure 10–7

The asymmetrical tonic neck reflex. As shown in this illustration, the ATNR causes a student to assume a "fencing" position every time his head is turned.

(*Source:* Adapted from B. A. Fraser and R. N. Hensinger, *Managing physical handicaps: A practical guide for parents, care providers, and educators.* Copyright © by Paul H. Brookes, p. 167. Used with permission.)

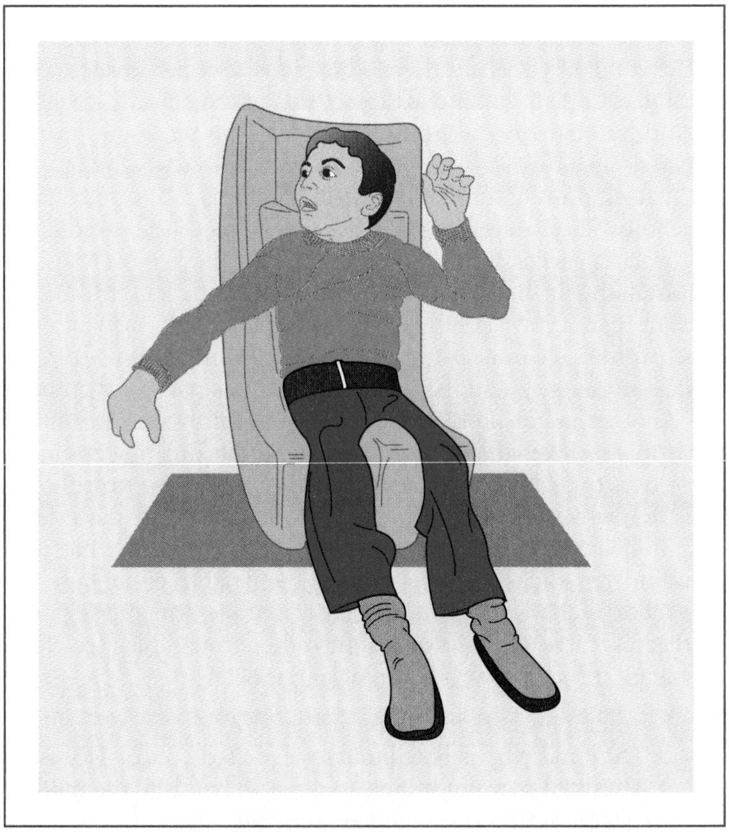

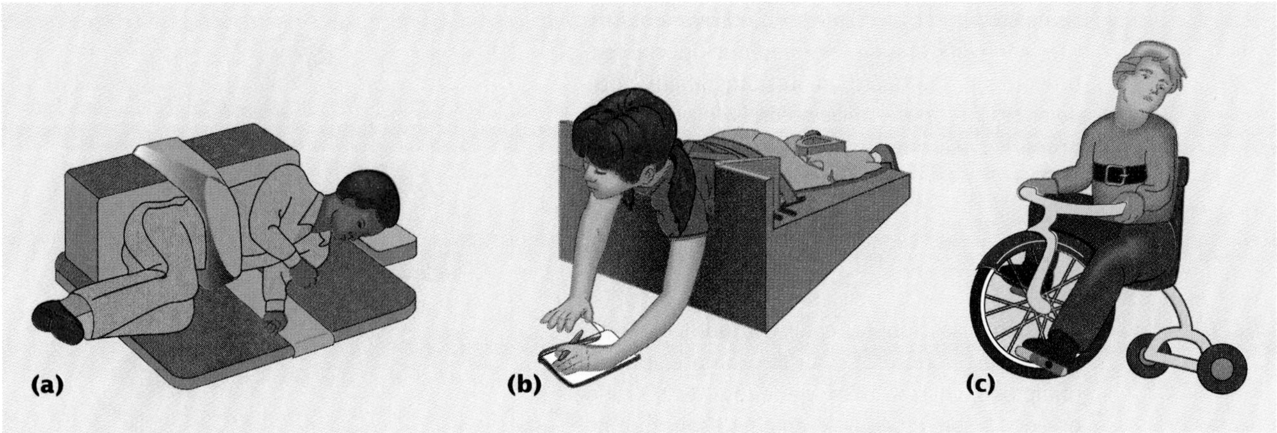

Figure 10–8 Alternatives to allow change of position throughout the day: **(a)** sidelyer, **(b)** wedge, **(c)** tricycle with built up back and pedals. Adult three-wheeled bikes are available for larger children. (*Source:* Bigge, June L., *Teaching individuals with physical and multiple disabilities,* 3rd ed., Copyright © 1991, p. 137. Reprinted by permission of Prentice Hall, Upper Saddle River, New Jersey.)

Motor and communication skills necessary for daily living are not the only areas in which the teacher must provide instruction. Learning social responsiveness, appropriate social initiation, how to play with others, and problem solving, for example, are important goals for which the teacher must develop instructional strategies. Some children who are well beyond the typical preschooler's age may still be functioning at a very early developmental level. Consequently, the muscle tone, posture, and movement problems discussed here (as well as the approach to teaching just described), apply to some older students, too.

TRANSITION

Transition involves a turning point, a change from one situation or environment to another. When special educators speak of *transition,* they typically refer to change from school to work or from adolescence to adulthood. For children with physical disabilities, however, transition is perhaps a more pervasive concern than it is for children with other disabilities. It may involve discharge from intensive care or transition from hospital to home at any age. Neisworth and Fewell (1989) note that "in an era of increasingly sophisticated medical technology, transition begins for some families at or shortly after the birth of a child" (p. xi). Nevertheless, we focus here on the transition concerns of adolescents and young adults with physical disabilities.

You may recall from Chapter 1 our discussion of Matt Radcliffe (see page 9). The box on pages 438–439 is Matt's story as he wrote it, as a high school sophomore for the school newspaper. Note the social and psychological as well as physical transitions that Matt was required to make due to his illness and its aftermath.

Two areas of concern for transition stand out clearly for adolescents and young adults with physical disabilities: careers and sociosexuality. Adolescents begin

Figure 10–9 Some children need to be supported in a tilted semistanding or kneeling position by a board so they can work at a table or counter. Special features of a prone board are its adjustability and devices to keep the child securely in place and properly positioned. (*Source:* Bigge, June L., *Teaching individuals with physical and multiple disabilities,* 3rd ed., Copyright © 1991, p. 190. Reprinted by permission of Prentice Hall, Upper Saddle River, New Jersey.)

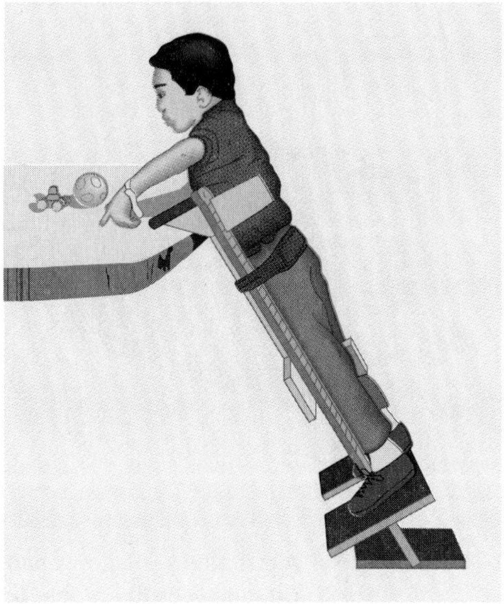

Figure 10–10 Alternative seating: **(a)** chair without legs and added post in front of chair to promote abduction of hips, **(b)** chair with arms and foot rests—runners or skis can be added to keep chair from tipping, **(c)** sandbags as supports, **(d)** and **(e)** corner seats (with lap straps, leg positioners, and perhaps a tray, **(f)** partial recliner. (*Source:* Bigge, June L., *Teaching individuals with physical and multiple disabilities,* 3rd ed., Copyright © 1991, p. 140. Reprinted by permission of Prentice Hall, Upper Saddle River, New Jersey.)

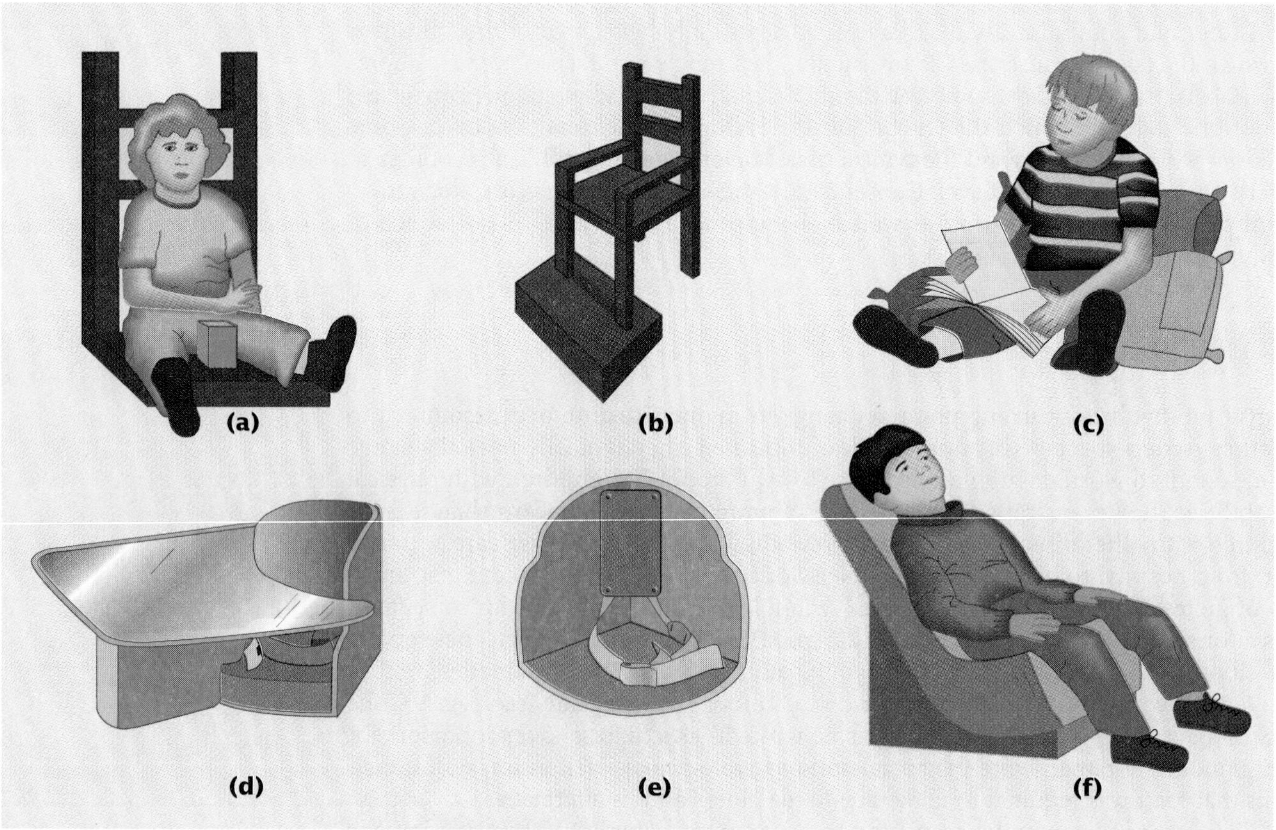

Children with physical disabilities need to engage in healthful, physical activities from an early age as much if not more than anyone else.

contemplating and experimenting with jobs, social relations, and sexuality in direct and serious ways. For the adolescent with a physical disability, these questions and trial behaviors are often especially perplexing, not just to themselves but to their families as well: Can I get and hold a satisfying job? Can I become independent? Will I have close and lasting friendships? Will anyone find me physically attractive? How can I gratify my sexual needs? Ordinary adolescents have a hard time coming to grips with these questions and the developmental tasks they imply; adolescents with physical disabilities often have an even harder time.

As we pointed out in discussing psychological characteristics, there is no formula for predicting the emotional or behavioral problems a person with a given physical disability will have. Much depends on the management and training the person has received. So it is particularly important to provide both career education and sociosexual education for students with physical disabilities.

Choosing a Career

For the adolescent or young adult with physical disabilities, career considerations are extremely important (Condeluci, 1994; Fonosch, Arany, Lee, & Loving, 1982). In working out an occupational goal, it is vital to realistically appraise the individual's specific abilities and disabilities and to assess motivation carefully. Postsecondary education must be considered in light of the individual's interests, strengths, demands, and accessibility (Norlund, 1994). Some disabilities clearly rule out certain occupational choices. With other disabilities, high motivation and full use of residual function may make it possible to achieve unusual professional status.

One of the greatest problems in dealing with adolescents who have physical disabilities is helping them attain a realistic employment outlook. Intelligence, emotional characteristics, motivation, and work habits must be assessed at least as carefully as physical limitations. Furthermore, the availability of jobs and the demands of certain occupations must be taken into account. The child who has moderate mental retardation and severe spastic quadriplegia, for instance, is highly unlikely to have a career as a lawyer, a laboratory technician, or a clerk-typist. But what of one who has severe

Cancer

Editor's Note: The following is a true story by a student at Albemarle High School.

Cancer! Brain tumor! Malignant! To most people, when these words are pronounced, they perceive it as a death sentence and immediately lose hope. Shock, disbelief, and denial are initial reactions. People believe, "It can't happen to me. I'm too young or I'm too healthy." Cancer and diseases are a part of our everyday life. Cancer can happen to anyone, me or you. In fact, it did happen to me.

Five years ago, I was diagnosed as having a brain tumor. My reaction was, I expect, typical. "Why me? Will I live or die? It can't be happening to me, of all people."

I was almost ten years old and I wasn't ready to give in to this major setback in my life. I guess that's why I'm alive today. I fought against the disease instead of quitting before the battle had begun. I had a positive attitude and knew I had a lot to offer. My whole life was ahead of me and there were goals I wanted to accomplish like going to college, getting married, and having a family.

Before I had a brain tumor, my lifestyle was far different from what it is now. I was popular and was one of the best athletes in my class. I played soccer, basketball, baseball, and was an excellent swimmer; all the while I had good grades also. My goal was to do the very best I could in everything. I thought I had the most perfect life a kid could want at that age. But one day, I started having excruciating headaches and nausea. I had just had a yearly check-up and the doctor said that everything was normal. Yet my headaches and sickness continued eventually becoming so severe that I was taken to UVA and Martha Jefferson hospitals, and the doctor's office for numerous tests, including bloodwork, an EEG, and neurological work-ups. The tests revealed nothing. Finally, my symptoms changed dramatically. My headaches became unbearable, I was combative, disoriented, and did not know anyone. The doctor ran a CAT scan and he found that I had an abnormal cell that was growing out of control in my brain and it was cancerous. He told my parents that I might not make it and that surgery as well as extensive follow-up therapy such as radiation would be necessary.

The illness put a lot of pressure on my parents and me. There were numerous trips to the hospital to see a number of doctors and huge medical bills. Because of a loss of my motor abilities there were things such as writing that I could no longer do which presented a problem with even the tiniest task I undertook. I lost my hair and to help relieve my double vision I had to wear an eye patch over one eye. I had to face my family, friends, and school knowing that I had cancer and that people couldn't help but think that I might die.

My parents and I were fortunate that we had a lot of friends that gave us not only moral support but they helped out with errands and chores so that my parents could spend as much time as possible with me. They were constantly fixing meals, running errands, and doing chores and especially praying for me and my family.

spastic quadriplegia and a bright mind? Such a person may well overcome both the physical limitation and the associated social stigma and be successful in a wide variety of fields in which the work is more mental than physical.

There are no simple conclusions regarding the occupational outlook for students with physical disabilities. Those with mild or transitory disabling conditions may not be affected at all in their occupational choices. Yet some with relatively mild physical disabilities may be unemployed or even unemployable because of inappropriate social and emotional behavior or poor work habits; they may need vocational rehabilitation training to function even in a vocation with limited demands. Some people with severe physical disabilities are able to use their intelligence, social skills, and residual physical abilities to the fullest and become competitive employees (or employers) in demanding occupations.

The outlook for employment of students with physical or multiple and severe disabilities has been improved dramatically by legislation and research and demonstration projects. As mentioned in Chapter 1, the Americans with Disabilities Act (ADA) of 1990 requires that reasonable accommodations be made to create equal employment opportunities for people with disabilities. More accessible transportation and buildings, increased skill in using technology to allow people to accomplish tasks at work, and greater commitment to preparing people with disabilities for work are resulting

It was a frightening and difficult time, but the funny thing was that I never thought that I was going to die. It may sound sort of weird, but I had faith— faith that I could overcome the odds and someday I would be as good as before I became ill.

I had to face many struggles. After I went through surgery, I realized that my head had been shaved so that the doctors could see the area more clearly. The surgery lasted five and one-half hours. I was in intensive care for less than a day, a shorter time period than the doctors had predicted. The doctor said that I had a little paralysis in my left eye causing double vision and my motor skills were impaired. I had to undergo radiation for thirty-one days, physical and occupational therapy for about two months. Physical and occupational therapy helped me to improve the motor skills that I had lost, such as writing, walking, balancing, etc. I had to have radiation so that the disease would not return and also to make sure that abnormal cells did not spread to other parts of my body. The radiation destroyed many of the good cells with the bad cells, but it did not make me sick.

The effects of the illness still aren't over. People, especially other kids, treat me differently since I've had cancer. They tease me about how I can't do things as well any more or that I look different because of my thinning hair or double vision. It's almost as if they're afraid of me.

I wish people realized that cancer is not contagious and that people who have cancer just want to be treated the same as everyone else. They still like to talk to their friends, play sports, have girlfriends and boyfriends, and goof-off. At times, having cancer made me feel like a handicapped person— lonely and that people just don't understand. I've seen that cancer causes children and young people to grow old before their time and I feel like I missed out on being a kid. Now life has a different meaning to me, because I almost lost it. I don't take things for granted and I live each day knowing that no one is promised a tomorrow.

Having cancer, I lost my popularity and good athletic abilities, and I thought I had lost everything that was ever important to me. It took a while, but then I realized that I was wrong. I had my new health, my new life, and my parents. That's a lot. I also gained a new perspective on life: caring for others. Now when I see people who are disabled or different from everyone else, I compare them to me and how my life would be in that situation.

To some people, cancer, a disease, or a handicap are reasons to give up, stop trying, but to a kid who's been there, I'm with W. Mitchell, a paralyzed millionaire who says, "All limitations are self-imposed. It's not what happens to you in life, it's what you do about it." For me, I've learned to live with life's limitations, even cancer, and I've learned that you can overcome those limitations if you put your mind to it.

Source: By Matt Radcliffe, *The Patriot,* 1/19/90, p. 11.

in more personal independence, economic self-sufficiency, and social acceptance—which benefit not only people with disabilities but the economy and society, as well.

We now recognize that "preparation for work begins in early childhood and continues well into adulthood" (Bigge, 1991, p. 484). Long before adolescence, children—including those with physical disabilities—need to be taught about and explore various careers. They need to be thinking about what they like to do, as well as what they are particularly good at, and the demands and rewards of various kinds of jobs. The objective should be to help students select training and enter a career that makes maximum use of their abilities in ways that they find personally gratifying.

Supported employment for people with severe disabilities is a relatively new concept that is being adopted widely. Recall from Chapter 4 that in this approach, a person with a severe disability works in a regular work setting. He or she becomes a regular employee, performs a valued function in the same workplace as nondisabled employees, and receives fair remuneration. Training and continued support are necessary, hence the term *supported employment.* Trach (1990) describes the distinguishing features of a supported employment program:

> Notably, these procedures include surveying the community for jobs, identifying and analyzing the requisite skills of potential employment sites, assessing the current skill

Investing in Technology-Assisted Employability

Accountant Steven's workday begins when the beep on his fax machine signals the arrival of the daily transactions from ten small businesses that employ him to manage their accounts. Steven enters each transaction into his computerized accounting program and efficiently summarizes the day's business activities. Turning to his fax machine once more, Steven sends each company a printout of their daily records and shuts off his machine with the satisfaction of a job well done. Unusual activity—no. Unusual circumstances—yes. It is three in the morning when Steven finishes his work, and he never leaves his home, in fact, Steven never leaves his bed. You see, Steven has no controlled movement below his neck and due to recent medical problems, he must remain in a special bed and constantly use respiratory support. The accounting work was accomplished through the use of a mouthstick and a home workstation arranged to allow him access to the equipment he needs to function successfully with relative independence.

When Steven was in school, little was done to prepare him for the world of work. His educational program had been based on his deficits rather than his strengths and no one assumed he would be able to compete successfully in the open marketplace. After graduation, Steven spent several years at home until he learned from a friend about a high-tech program at a local community college. This high-tech program was designed to ensure that college students with disabilities would have equal access to the available academic and training programs. Once enrolled, Steven's strengths were identified, he determined his career choice, and access to technology and to academic instruction was provided. He successfully completed a program in accounting and, with the help of the counselor in the placement office, found a job with a small accounting firm. When it became medically necessary for Steven to remain at home, with minimal expense, the accounting firm in conjunction with the Department of Rehabilitation, provided Steven with a home workstation.

Situations like this are well known to Carl Brown, Director of High Tech Center for the Disabled, California Community Colleges, who is dedicated to providing efficient, practical, and cost-effective adapted computer technology to people with disabilities in post-secondary educational settings. He and his staff have prepared extensive training guides for software and hardware adaptations, and develop intensive workshops and programs for post-secondary educators concerned with providing access to technology (Brown, Norris, & Crownover, 1987). Rather than focus on specialized mechanical devices, exotic software, or customized computer systems, Brown and staff have sought software-based solutions to the problem of access and have been very successful in finding programs that allow full and unencumbered access to the complete range of commercially available software.

Waiting until a student has reached the post-secondary level before providing academic and training access is an unacceptable educational practice. Students for whom technology offers independence and equal opportunity must be given access from the very beginning of their educational program with the integrated goals of getting an education and preparing for work.

Adequately preparing today's students for tomorrow's world of work would require a long look into a crystal ball. In lieu of access to this magic, educators must carefully examine the work skills curriculum and make instructional decisions based on concept mastery rather than specific skills mastery. This is particularly true in the area of technology because of the rapidly changing nature of the equipment and software programs used in business and industry. So, an appropriate educational objective would be to understand a technology-related process and to develop strategies for its implementation, regardless of the machine or the software program being used. For example, when a student's ability to type in information is slow and laborious, strategies for speeding up the process are critical.

Source: Bigge, June L., *Teaching individuals with physical and multiple disabilities,* 3rd ed., Copyright © 1991, pp. 480–481. Reprinted by permission of Prentice Hall, Upper Saddle River, New Jersey.

> levels of supported employees, matching jobs to prospective employees, providing systematic training in job-related skills, and providing follow-up training and maintenance of learned skills, satisfying employers, and coordinating related services. (p. 79)

New technologies, especially computing and other electronic devices, offer great promise for enabling students with physical disabilities to achieve personal independence, acquiring education and training that will make them employable and finding

Figure 10–11

A keyboard positioned for efficient use with a headstick.

(*Source:* Bigge, June L., *Teaching individuals with physical and multiple disabilities,* 3rd ed., Copyright © 1991, p. 486. Reprinted by permission of Prentice Hall, Upper Saddle River, New Jersey.)

employment. The box on page 440 illustrates how people with disabilities might use their abilities in successful employment as well as how schools can fail to provide appropriate education and training. In some cases, the technology is readily available and educators need only to become aware of the software (e.g., software that allows the function of keys to be altered), find ways in which keystrokes can be saved through subprogramming routines (e.g., macro or find-and-replace features in word processing), or provide substitutions for physical manipulation of materials (e.g., computer graphics programs as substitutes for paper paste-ups or model construction) (Bigge, 1991).

Sometimes, an individual's ability to use standard equipment is greatly enhanced by a simple modification, such as orientation or location. Figure 10–11 shows how simply placing a keyboard in a vertical position over a monitor may enhance the ability of someone who uses a headstick to use a computer. Teachers must always look for simple, virtually cost-free ways to facilitate the performance of students with disabilities—to prevent an environment designed for people without disabilities from handicapping those who must do things a different way. Overlooking the seemingly obvious is perhaps the way in which we most frequently handicap people with disabilities.

Sociosexuality

Until fairly recently, physical disabilities were assumed to cancel human sexuality (see Edmonson, 1988). People who were not normal physically, especially if they had limited mobility, were thought of as having no sex appeal for anyone and as having little or no ability or right to function sexually.

Fortunately, attitudes and experiences are changing. It is now recognized that people with disabilities have a right to family life education, including sex education, and to a full range of human relationships, including appropriate sexual expression (Duncan & Canty-Lemke, 1986; Edmonson, 1988). Sociosexual education for students with physical disabilities, as such education for all other children and youths, should begin early, continue through adulthood, and include information about the structure and functions of bodies, human relationships and responsibilities, and alternative modes of sexual gratification (Bigge, 1991).

Youths with physical disabilities need to experience close friendships and warm physical contact that is not sexually intimate. But it is neither realistic nor fair to expect people with physical disabilities to keep all their relationships platonic or to limit themselves to fantasy. Most physical disability, even if severe, does not in itself kill sexual desire or prevent sexual gratification; nor does it preclude marriage and children. The purpose of special education and rehabilitation is to make exceptional individuals' lives as full and complete as possible. In the case of youths with physical disabilities, this may involve teaching or providing alternative means of sexual stimulation and accepting sexual practices and relationships that are different from the norm. With sensitive education and rehabilitation, satisfying sociosexual expression can be achieved by all but a small minority (DeLoach & Greer, 1981; Edmonson, 1988).

Suggestions for Teaching
Students with Physical Disabilities in General Education Classrooms

By Peggy L. Tarpley

WHAT TO LOOK FOR IN SCHOOL

As you know from reading the chapter, children and adolescents attending school experience a wide range of health and physical problems. This range is increasing as medical, educational, and technological advancements make possible the integration of students with severe disabilities. Although many children with physical problems will be diagnosed before being mainstreamed, some may experience changes in their conditions or in their reactions to medication during the schoolyear; other students may develop illnesses or be involved in accidents after entering school; and still others may experience abuse or neglect. The following questions may help you identify potential problems (Dykes & Venn, 1983; Shore, 1986). Ask yourself if your students:

- seem as energetic as usual?
- initiate contact as usual?
- have normal skin tone?
- have any sores, rashes, cuts that you haven't seen before?
- are wearing clothing that seems to fit differently than usual?
- tire easily?
- indicate verbally or nonverbally that they are experiencing discomfort or pain?

HOW TO GATHER INFORMATION

Although as a teacher, you are not expected to be a medical diagnostician, you may have more opportunities than any other adult to observe your students. Therefore, you have an important responsibility to be aware of changes in your students' physical conditions and to notify the school nurse and parents or guardians about your observations so they can arrange for medical examination and treatment.

For those students in your class with diagnosed physical and health impairments, you will want to gather information that enables you to answer these questions (Berdine & Blackhurst, 1985, cited in Lewis & Doorlag, 1991):

Medical Concerns

1. Does the student take medication? How frequently? In what amounts? Is the school authorized to administer the medication during school hours?
2. What are the side effects of the medication?
3. What procedures should be followed in the event of a seizure, insulin shock, diabetic coma, or other problem?
4. Should the student's activities be restricted in any way?

Travel

1. How will the student be transported to school?
2. Will the student arrive and leave at the usual school times?
3. Will the student need special accommodations to travel within the school building or the classroom?

Communication

1. Can the student write? Type? How?
2. If the student does not communicate verbally, what type of communication will be used?
3. Is an electronic communication aid used? If so, are special instructions necessary for the student to use it or for me to understand and maintain it?
4. Can the student make his or her needs known to the teacher? How?
5. Are there other aids or devices that I should know about?

Self-Care

1. What types of self-care help, such as feeding and toileting, does the student need? Who is responsible for providing this care?
2. What equipment does the student need?

Positioning

1. What positioning aids or devices (braces, pillows, wedges) does the student use?
2. What particular positions are most useful for specific academic activities and for resting?
3. Are there other aids or devices that I should know about?

Reading your students' individualized educational programs (IEPs) and consulting other school personnel or outside agencies who work with them may provide answers to these questions. For additional medical information about specific diseases and disorders and practical suggestions for teachers, see *Physically handicapped children: A medical atlas for teachers* (Bleck & Nagel, 1982) and the chapters concerning physical disabilities and emergency medical procedures in the *Handbook of special education.* (Kauffman & Hallahan, 1981).

TEACHING TECHNIQUES TO TRY

The educational interventions required for students with physical disabilities vary greatly, depending on the type and severity of their conditions. Some students may require specialized assistance or training in areas such as mobility or communications. Others may need additional support to manage the sensory, learning, and behavioral disorders that can accompany some physical disabilities (see appropriate chapters for these interventions). Still others may require no modifications or only minimal adjustments. For example, teachers simply may need to increase the length of time students have to complete assignments when they are absent or fatigued by their illnesses or the treatment of their illnesses.

In fact, most students with physical and health impairments attend regular education classes for most of the schoolday and are expected to progress through the same curricular materials as nondisabled students (Reynolds & Birch, 1982). Many of these students, however, require some adaptation of instructional materials and activities in order to succeed in school and to maximize their independence.

Adapting Instructional Methods

Heller, Dangel, and Seatman (1995) provide teachers with a system for selecting appropriate physical and behavioral adaptations for students with muscular dystrophy and other physically degenerative conditions. It would seem that this system could be used for students with other physical disabilities, as well. First, the student's performance of a particular activity should be assessed. The assessment should include comparing the skills needed to complete the activity (task analysis) by a student *without* physical disabilities with the performance (of the same activity) of the student *with* physical disabilities. Given this information, the teacher can pinpoint the area of difficulty—physical, sensory, communication, learning, or behavioral (such as motivation)—for the student with physical impairment. Next, after having received input from parents and other appropriate school or medical personnel, the teacher selects and implements the necessary adaptations. The final step for the teacher, parents, and others involved in the student's education is to evaluate the adaptation and then make modifications or choose new adaptations.

Heller and her colleagues (1995) define three types of adaptations that might be used in the classroom:

1. adaptations that allow access to the task (e.g., the use of adapted devices, behavior management strategies, or personal aids; changes in the physical environment; or changes in how the student responds)
2. adaptations in how the teacher teaches the task (i.e., modified instruction)
3. adaptations in part or all of the tasks (i.e., alter the material, activity, or curriculum) (p. 258)

One of the most common adaptations teachers make for students with physical disabilities is of the first type: adapting access to the task, which includes modifying response patterns, using adaptive devices, and employing people as assistants or partners.

Adapting Response Patterns and Using Adaptive Devices

Written Responses

To complete written activities, some students need simple modifications, such as assistance in stabilizing and selecting appropriate materials. These adaptations include (Hale, 1979; Bigge, 1991):

Stabilization Techniques

- writing on a pad of paper, rather than on loose sheets
- using masking tape (two-inch width is strongest) or a clipboard to secure loose papers
- placing a rubber strip on the back of a ruler or using a magnetic ruler to prevent slipping when measuring or drawing lines
- using adhesive-backed Velcro to attach items to a desk or wheelchair laptray

Modifying/Selecting Appropriate Materials

- using pens (felt tip) and pencils (soft lead) that require less pressure
- twisting a rubber band around the shaft of the pen or pencil or slipping corrugated rubber, a form curler, or a golf practice ball over the writing instrument to make it easier to hold
- using an electronic typewriter, word processor, or computer
- using typing aids, such as a pointer stick attached to a head or mouthpiece to strike the keys; a keyboard guard that prevents striking two keys at once; and line spacers that hold written materials while typing
- audiotaping assignments, lectures, and other instructional activities that require extensive writing (Tape recorders can be modified so students can operate them with a single switch.)

For students who have limited strength, muscular control, or mobility, selecting and designing instructional materials that require no word formation may simplify their responding to written tasks. For example, numbering problems and coding possible answers with letters allow students to write single-letter responses (Bigge, 1991). Using worksheets and tests that direct students to put lines through the correct answers requires no letter formation. It is important, however, to provide enough space between the answer alternatives so that students can indicate their choices without marking other responses accidentally (Bigge, 1982).

Still other adaptations do not require students to hold pencils or pens. Bigge (1991) indicates that students can respond to matching, sorting, classifying, and sequencing tasks by manipulating objects. For example, they can move magnetic letters and numbers on a metal cookie sheet to indicate their responses or put wooden blocks on top of their answer choices. In addition, students may indicate their comprehension of content-area reading by matching a set of picture cards with a set of cards with sentences or paragraphs written on them by pushing the two correct card sets together. Students also can use this response method in practicing vocabulary, especially homonyms, synonyms, and antonyms. Similarly, they can indicate the sequence of historical events, plot episodes from literary works, and organize steps in scientific experiments by pushing cards in the correct order that have pictures or sentences describing each event.

In addition, special input devices for computers facilitate student responding. Computers, for example, can be equipped with a variety of switches that allow students to operate them with a single movement. Selection of the type of switch will depend on the type of movement the student can best perform. The Adaptive Firmware Card (AFC), available from Don Johnston Developmental Equipment, Inc., is a computer peripheral that permits students to use any commercial software program (Lewis & Doorlag, 1991). The AFC provides a line of letters and symbols called a *scanning array* on the computer screen that students select by pressing a switch. This array allows them to spell words, indicate numbers, and operate the computer. Alternate keyboards (e.g., Unicorn Expanded Keyboard) offer several features, such as providing a larger response area than standard keyboards and removing the need for simultaneous key pressing. Consequently, they offer another means by which students with limited muscular control can use computers. Touch-sensitive screens also enable students to respond to instructions and questions by touching specific areas of the screen. Still other input devices allow students to bypass keyboards completely by talking or by making consistent sounds into a microphone and by making muscular movements.

Oral Responses

Speech synthesizers voice the responses that students with severe speech impairments type on the computer and enable them to participate in class discussions and ask questions immediately. Less expensive communication boards (charts of pictures, symbols, numbers, or words) allow students to indicate their responses to specific items represented on the charts. To facilitate communication using these boards, Bigge (1982) recommends that listeners name the pictures or say the letters or words quickly, so the conversation moves along more rapidly. Teachers also have found less comprehensive response adaptations useful during oral activities. For example, they may give students color-coded objects (such as blocks of wood that are easy to handle and that do not slip) to indicate their response to polar questions, such as true/false; agree/disagree/don't know; same/different (Bigge, 1982).

Reading Tasks

In addition to response modifications, students with physical disabilities often require equipment that facilitates reading. These devices include book holders; reading stands that adjust to reclining, sitting, and standing positions; and page turners that range from pencil erasers to electric-powered devices that can be operated with minimal mobility (Hale, 1979). Furthermore, "talking" books enable students who cannot hold books to tape lectures and to enjoy a variety of recorded novels, textbooks, and magazines. Specialized talking books, called *compressed speech machines,* play at faster than usual speeds and may be helpful to students who must learn large amounts of information (Dykes & Venn, 1983). This equipment is available at no cost from the Library of Congress.

In addition to these devices, instructional materials can be adapted to facilitate student use during reading and thinking activities. For example, teachers can use photo albums that have sticky backings and plastic cover sheets and plastic photo cubes to hold instructional materials, such as pictures or words cards. This latter adaptation allows students to move the cubes to respond to a variety of tasks.

Using Personal Assistants

Some students with physical disabilities have personal assistants who work with them in their classrooms. In these cases, it is important that the assistant aids the student *only* when he or she is unable to perform the task without help. An assistant or peer can also assist with physical components of a task. Heller and colleagues (1995) suggest that a peer might help a student with limited head/arm use with the mechanics of dissecting a frog, while they verbally select and plan the sequence of steps together. Another scenario might be that a student with physical impairments might read the directions for a physical task to a peer who has difficulty with reading. These interactions may promote social interaction between students and foster positive attitudes between students with disabilities and those without.

HELPFUL RESOURCES

School Personnel

Because students with health impairments and physical disabilities often require the expertise of a variety of professionals, several individuals may provide services to your student. Understanding the role of each is important in coordinating instructional and medical interventions. The following list describes the functions professionals typically fulfill in the treatment of these students (Dykes & Venn, 1983, pp. 261–263):

- *Physicians* are licensed medical doctors who provide services that include diagnosing; prescribing medication; making referrals for physical therapy, occupational therapy, and orthopedic treatment; and recommending the extent and length of various activities and treatments. Specialized physicians include orthopedists (specialists in diagnosing and treating joint, bones, and muscles impairments), neurologists (specialists in diagnosing and treating impairments to the nervous system, such as cerebral palsy and muscular dystrophy), and radiologists (specialists in using X-rays and radioactive substances to diagnose and treat conditions such as cancer).
- *School nurses'* responsibilities vary, depending on the school system in which they are employed. Often, they administer

medications at school, treat medical emergencies, provide medical information to students and staff, and help identify community health agencies for families.

- *Occupational therapists* provide medically prescribed assistance to help individuals manage their disabilities. They may teach various self-help, daily living, prevocational, leisure time, and perceptual-motor skills. They may also provide instruction in the use of adaptive devices.
- *Rehabilitation counselors* perform a range of services related to vocational training and employment. For example, they may conduct vocational assessment and counseling and arrange for work training and experience. Typically, they are employed by the state vocational rehabilitation agency, rather than the school district.
- *Physical therapists* provide services designed to restore or improve physical functioning and engage in such activities as exercising to increase coordination, range of motion, and movement.

Instructional Methods and Materials

Bigge, J. L. (1989). *Curriculum-based instruction for special education students* (2nd ed.). Mountain View, CA: Mayfield.

Bigge, J. L. (1991). *Teaching individuals with physical and multiple disabilities* (3rd ed.). New York: Merrill/Macmillan.

Byron, E., & Katz, G. (Eds.). (1991). *HIV prevention and AIDS education: Resources for special educators.* Reston, VA: Council for Exceptional Children.

Campbell, P. H. (1989). Students with physical disabilities. In R. Gaylord-Ross (Ed.), *Integration strategies for students with handicaps.* Baltimore, MD: Brookes.

Collins, J. L., & Britton, P. O. (1990). *Training educators in HIV prevention: An inservice manual.* Santa Cruz, CA: Network Publications.

Eastman, M. K., & Safran, J. S. (1986). Activities to develop your students' motor skills. *Teaching Exceptional Children, 19,* 24–27.

Fithian, J. (Ed.). (1984). *Understanding the child with a chronic illness in the classroom.* Phoenix: Oryx Press.

Fraser, B. A., & Hensinger, R. N. (1983). *Managing physical handicaps.* Baltimore, MD: Brookes.

Fredrick, J., & Fletcher, D. (1985). Facilitating children's adjustment to orthotic and prosthetic appliances. *Teaching Exceptional Children, 17,* 228–230.

Lynch, E. W., Murphy, D. S., & Lewis, R. B. (1986). *Making things better for chronically ill children: A guide for school and families.* (Available through the Department of Special Education, c/o State Study of Chronically Ill Children, San Diego State University, San Diego, CA 92182.)

McGinnis, J. S., & Beukelman, D. R. (1989). Vocabulary requirements for writing activities for the academically mainstreamed student with disabilities. *Augmentative and Alternative Communication, 5,* 183–191.

Miller, S. E., & Schaumberg, K. (1988). Physical education activities for children with severe cerebral palsy. *Teaching Exceptional Children, 20,* 9–11.

Orelove, F. P., & Sobsey, D. (1987). *Educating children with multiple disabilities.* Baltimore, MD: Brookes.

Self, P. C. (1984). *Physical disability: An annotated literature guide.* New York: Marcel Dekker.

Smith, A. K., Thurston, S., Light, J., Parnes, P., & O'Keefe, B. (1989). The form and use of written communication produced by physically disabled individuals using microcomputers. *Augmentative and Alternative Communication, 5,* 115–124.

Umbreit, J. (Ed.). (1983). *Physical disabilities and health impairments: An introduction.* Columbus, OH: Merrill/Macmillan.

Curricular Materials

*Brown, S., Hemphill, N. J., & Voeltz, L. (1982). *The smallest minority: Adapted regular education social studies curricula for understanding and integrating severely disabled students. Lower elementary: Understanding self and others.* Honolulu: University of Manoa, Hawaii Integration Project.

*Hemphill, N. J., Zukas, D., & Brown, S. (1982). *The smallest minority: Adapted regular education social studies curricula for understanding and integrating severely disabled students. The secondary grades: Understanding alienation.* Honolulu: University of Hawaii/Manoa, Hawaii Integration Project.

Office for the Education of Children with Handicapping Conditions. (1982). *Motor impairment: Accepting individual differences.* Albany, NY: New York State Education Department.

Phi Delta Kappa. (1990). *Looking into AIDS.* Bloomington, IN: Phi Delta Kappa.

*Noonan, M. J., Hemphill, N. J., & Levy, G. (1983). *Social skills curricular strategy for students with severe disabilities.* Honolulu: University of Hawaii/Manoa, Hawaii Integration Project.

Teaching AIDS. (1990). Santa, Cruz, CA: ERT Associates.

*Voeltz, L., Hemphill, N. J., Brown, S., Kishi, G., Klein, R., Fruehling, R., Levy, G., Collie, J., & Kube, C. (1983). *The special friends program: A trainer's manual for integrated school settings.* Honolulu: University of Hawaii/Manoa, Hawaii Integration Project.

Wisconsin Department of Public Instruction. (1990). *Instruction about AIDS.* Madison, WI: Wisconsin Department of Public Instruction.

Literature about Individuals with Physical Disabilities

Elementary

Aiello, B., & Shulman, J. (1989). *A portrait of me.* Frederick, MD: Twenty-First Century Books. (Ages 9–12, diabetes) (Fiction = F, includes factual information about diabetes and its treatment)

Aiello, B., & Shulman, J. (1989). *Friends for life.* Frederick, MD: Twenty-First Century Books. (Ages 9–12, AIDS) (Nonfiction = NF)

Aiello, B., & Shulman, J. (1989). *Hometown hero.* Frederick, MD: Twenty-First Century Books. (Ages 9–12, asthma) (F, includes factual information about asthmatic episodes)

Aiello, B., & Shulman, J. (1989). *Trick or treat or trouble.* Frederick, MD: Twenty-First Century Books. (Ages 9–21, epilepsy) (F, includes factual information about responding to seizures)

Arnold, K. (1983) Anna joins in. New York: Abingdon. (Ages 5–8, cystic fibrosis) (F)

Auch, M. J. (1990). *Kidnapping Kevin Kolwalski.* New York: Holiday House. (Grades 3–6, brain injury) (F)

*Available from Media Productions and Distributions, University of Hawaii, Castle Memorial Hall, 1776 University Avenue, Honolulu, HI 96822.

Bergman, T. (1989). *On our own terms: Children living with physical handicaps.* Milwaukee, WI: Gareth Stevens. (Grades 3–5, spina bifida, cerebral palsy, and spinal injuries) (NF)

Bernstein, J. E., & Fireside, B. (1991). *Special parents, special children.* Chicago: Albert Whitman. (Grades 4–7, parents with physical disabilities) (NF)

Blair, M. (1989). *Kids want to know about AIDS.* Rockville, MD: National AIDS Information Clearinghouse. (Grades 4–7, AIDS) (NF)

Bunnett, R. (1993). *Friends in the park.* New York: Checkerboard. (Preschool–Grade 1, various disabilities including physical disabilities) (NF)

Butler, B. (1993). *Witch's fire.* New York: Dutton. (Grades 4–6, adjusting to a wheelchair) (F)

Carlson, N. (1990). *Arnie and the new kid.* New York: Viking. (K–Grade 2, wheelchair use) (F)

Caseley, J. (1991). *Harry and Willy and Carrothead.* New York: Greenwillow. Grades K–2, prosthetic hand) (F)

Cowen-Fletcher, J. (1993). *Mama zooms.* New York: Scholastic. (Preschool–Grade 2, mother in a wheelchair) (F)

Damrell, L. (1991). *With the wind.* New York: Orchard House. (Preschool–Grade 3, wheelchair) (F)

Dwight, L. (1992). *We can do it!* New York: Checkerboard. (Preschool–Grade 2, various disabilities) (NF)

Frevert, P. D. (1983). *Patty gets well.* Mankato, MN: Creative Education. (Grades 4–7, Leukemia) (NF)

Krementz, J. (1992). *How it feels to live with a physical disability.* New York: Simon & Schuster. (Grades 6–9, various disabilities including missing limbs and cerebral palsy) (NF)

Powers, M. E. (1986). *Our teacher's in a wheelchair.* Chicago: Albert Whitman. (Preschool–Grade 1, teacher with a physical disability) (NF)

Rabe, B. (1981). *The balancing girl.* New York: Dutton. (Grades K–3) (F)

Rabe, B. (1986). *Margaret's moves.* New York: Dutton. (Grades 4–6) (F)

Russo, M. (1992). *Alex is my friend.* New York: Greenwillow. (Preschool–Grade 2) (F)

Slepian, J. (1980). *The Alfred summer.* New York: Macmillan. (Grades 4–7, cerebral palsy) (F)

Thompson, M. (1992). *My brother Matthew.* Frederick, MD: Woodbine House. (Grades K–3) (F)

Secondary

Blos, J. W. (1985). *Brothers of the heart: A story of the old northwest, 1837–1839.* New York: Charles Scribner's. (Grades 4–9) (F)

Calvert, P. (1993). *Picking up the pieces.* New York: Charles Scribner's. (Grades 5–8, wheelchair) (F)

Crutcher, C. (1987). *The crazy horse electric game.* New York: Greenwillow. (Grades 8–12, brain injury) (F)

Ferguson, K. (1991). *Stephen Hawking: Quest for a theory of the universe.* New York: Watts. (Grades 7–12, Lou Gehrig's disease) (NF)

Haldane, S. (1991). *Helping hands: How monkeys assist people who are disabled.* New York: Dutton. (Grades 3–6) (NF)

Hall, L. (1990). *Halsey's pride.* New York: Charles Scribner's. (Grades 6–8, epilepsy) (F)

Kriegsman, K. H. (1992). *Taking charge: Teenagers talk about life and physical disabilities.* Frederick, MD: Woodbine House. (Grades 7–12, various disabilities) (NF)

Metzger, L. (1992). *Barry's sister.* New York: Atheneum. (Grades 6–9, cerebral palsy) (F)

Miklowitz, G. D. (1987). *Good-bye tomorrow.* New York: Delacorte Press. (Grades 8–12, AIDS) (F)

Radley, G. (1984). *CF in his corner.* Soquel, CA: Four Winds Press. (Grades 7–10, cystic fibrosis) (F)

Sirof, H. (1993). *Because she's my friend.* New York: Atheneum. (Grades 7–10) (F)

Thiele, C. (1990). *Jodie's journey.* New York: HarperCollins. (Grades 4–7, arthritis) (F)

Voight, C. (1986). *Izzy, Willy-Nilly.* New York: Atheneum. (Grades 7–10, amputation) (F)

Software

The following programs may be operated by adaptive switch or touch-sensitive screens:

Academics with scanning: Language arts, ACS Software, University of Washington, Department of Speech and Hearing Sciences JG–15, Seattle, WA 98195, (206) 543–7974. (Program includes phonics and word attack).

Academics with scanning: Math, ACS Software, University of Washington, Department of Speech and Hearing Sciences JG–15, Seattle, WA 98195, (206) 543–7974 (does not provide instruction, but allows students to use the computer as pencil/paper to complete math problems).

Adventures of Jimmy-Jumper, Exceptional Children's Software, P.O. Box 487, Hays, KS 67601, (913) 625–9281 (Prepositions; speech synthesizer required).

Counting Critters, MECC, 6160 Summit Drive N., Minneapolis, MN 55430–4003, (800) 685–6322.

Exploratory Plan, PEAL Software, 5000 North Parkway Calabasas, Ste. 105, Calabasas, CA 91302, (818) 883–7849 (Communication).

First Verbs, Laureate Learning Systems, 110 East Spring Street, Winooski, VT 05404, (800) 562–6801 (Speech synthesizer required).

First Words I and II, Laureate Learning Systems, 110 East Spring Street, Winooski, VT 05404, (800) 562–6801 (Speech synthesizer required).

Interaction Games, Don Johnston, Inc., 1000 North Rand Road, Building 115, P.O. Box 639, Wauconda, IL 60084, (800) 999–4660 (Row and column scanning).

Keyboarding for the Physically Handicapped, Gregg/McGraw-Hill, 1221 Avenue of the Americas, New York, NY 10020, (800) 262–4729.

Keyboarding with One Hand, Educational, computability Corporation, 40000 Grand River, Ste. 109, Novi, MI 48375, (313) 477–6720.

Keytalk, PEAL Software, 5000 North Parkway Calabasas, Ste. 105, Calabasas, CA 91302, (818) 325–2001 (Electronic communication aid).

My Words, Hartley Courseware, Inc., 3451 Dunkle Drive, Suite 200, Lansing, MI 48911–4216, (800) 247–1380 (Combines a language experience approach with a talking word-processing program).

Muppet Slate, Sunburst Communications, 101 Castleton Street, Pleasantville, NY 10570, (800) 628–8897.

Rabbit Scanner, Exceptional Children's Software, P.O. Box 487, Hays, KS 67601, (913) 625–9281 (Scanning trainer).

Representational Play, PEAL Software, 5000 North Parkway Calabasas, Ste. 105, Calabasas, CA 91302, (818) 883–7849 (Communication).

Single Switch Game Library, Arthur Schwartz, 1801 East Twelfth Street, #1119, Cleveland, OH 44114, (216) 371–3820.

Sunny Days, Don Johnston, Inc., 1000 North Rand Road, Building 115, P.O. Box 639, Wauconda, IL 60084, (800) 999–4660 (Word recognition, spelling, and reading skills).

Switchmaster, Expert Systems Software, Suite 316, Nashville, TN 37215, (615) 292–7667 (Operation of switches).

Touch and Match, Exceptional Children's Software, P.O. Box 487, Hays, KS 67601, (913) 625–9281.

Organizations

AIDS

National Association of People with AIDS, 2025 I Street N.W., Suite 415, Washington, DC 20006, (202) 429–2856.

Arthritis

American Juvenile Arthritis Organization, 1314 Spring Street N.W., Atlanta, GA 30309, (404) 872–7100, FAX (404) 872–0457.

Asthma

National Foundation for Asthma, P.O. Box 30069, Tucson, AZ 85751, (602) 323–6046.

Birth (Congenital) Defects

Association of Birth Defect Children, 5400 Diplomat Circle, Ste. 270, Orlando, FL 32812, (407) 629–1466.

March of Dimes Birth Defects Foundation, 1275 Marmaroneck Avenue, White Plains, NY 10605, (914) 428–7100.

Cancer

American Cancer Society, 1599 Clifton Road N.E., Atlanta, GA 30329, (404) 320–3333.

Cancer Information Service, Boy Scout Building, Room 340, Rockville Pike, Bethesda, MD 20892, (301) 496–8664.

Cerebral Palsy

United Cerebral Palsy Associations, 7 Penn Plaza, Ste. 804, New York, NY 10001, (212) 268–6655.

Child Abuse

American Association for Protecting Children, c/o American Humane Association, 63 Inverness Drive E., Englewood, CO 80112, (303) 792–9900.

CHILDHELP U.S.A., Inc., 6463 Independence Avenue, Woodland Hills, CA 91370, (818) 347–7280.

Diabetes

American Diabetes Association, National Service Center, P.O. Box 25757, 1660 Duke Street, Alexandria, VA 22313, (703) 549–1500.

Epilepsy

Epilepsy Foundation of America, 4351 Garden City Drive, Landover, MD 20785, (301) 459–3700.

Muscular Dystrophy

Muscular Dystrophy Association, 3300 E. Sunrise Drive, Tucson, AZ 85718, (602) 529–2000, FAX (602) 529–5300.

Multiple Sclerosis

National Multiple Sclerosis Society, 733 Third Avenue, New York, NY 10017, (212) 986–3240, FAX (212) 486–7981.

Spina Bifida

Spina Bifida Association of America, 209 Shiloh Drive, Madison, WI 53705.

Other

National Head Injury Foundation, 1776 Massachusetts Avenue N.W., Suite 100, Washington, DC 20036, (202) 296–6443, FAX (202) 296–8850.

National Spinal Cord Injury Association, 600 W. Cummings Park, Suite 2000, Woburn, MA 01801, (617) 935–2722, FAX (617) 932–8369.

BIBLIOGRAPHY FOR TEACHING SUGGESTIONS

Bigge, J. L. (1982). *Teaching individuals with physical and multiple disabilities* (2nd ed.). Columbus, OH: Merrill/Macmillan.

Bigge, J. L. (1991). *Teaching individuals with physical and multiple disabilities* (3rd ed.). New York: Merrill/Macmillan.

Bleck, E. E., & Nagel, D. A. (1982). *Physically handicapped children: A medical atlas for teachers* (2nd ed.). New York: Grune & Stratton.

Dykes, M. K., & Venn, J. (1983). Using health, physical, and medical data in the classroom. In J. Umbreit (Ed.), *Physical disabilities and health impairments: An introduction.* Columbus, OH: Merrill/Macmillan.

Hale, G. (1979). *The source book for the disabled.* Philadelphia: Saunders.

Heller, K. W., Dangel, H., & Sweatman, L. (1995). Systematic selection of adaptations for students with muscular dystrophy. *Journal of Developmental and Physical Disabilities, 7*(3), 253–265.

Kauffman, J. M., & Hallahan, D. P. (Eds.). (1981). *Handbook of special education.* Englewood Cliffs, N J: Prentice Hall.

Lewis, R. B. & Doorlag, D. H. (1991). *Teaching special students in the mainstream.* New York: Merrill.

Oettinger, L., & Coleman, J. (1981) Emergency medical procedures. In J. M. Kauffman & D. P. Hallahan (Eds.), *Handbook of special education.* Englewood Cliffs, NJ: Prentice Hall.

Reynolds, M. C., & Birch, J. W. (1982). *Teaching exceptional children in all America's schools.* Reston, VA: Council for Exceptional Children.

Shore, K. (1986). *The special education handbook: A comprehensive guide for parents and educators.* New York: Teachers College Press.

Tyler, J. S., & Colson, S. (1994). Common pediatric disabilities: Medical aspects and educational implications. *Focus on Exceptional Children, 27*(4), 1–16.

Verhaaren, P., & Connor, F. P. (1981). Physical disabilities. In J. M. Kauffman & D. P. Hallahan (Eds.). *Handbook of special education.* Englewood Cliffs, NJ: Prentice Hall.

SUMMARY

Children with physical disabilities have physical limitations or health problems that interfere with school attendance or learning to such an extent that special services, training, equipment, materials, or facilities are required. These children may also have other disabilities, such as mental retardation and emotional or behavioral disorders. Even so, the medical nature of the problem highlights the need for interdisciplinary cooperation in special education.

Less than 0.5 percent of the child population in the United States receives special education and related services for physical disabilities. Because of advances in medical technology, more children with severe disabilities are surviving and many more are living with disease or injury with mild impairments, such as hyperactivity and learning disabilities. The needs of children and youths with physical disabilities and chronic illnesses far outstrip the public programs and services for them.

An increasingly frequent cause of neurological impairment is traumatic brain injury (TBI), which may range from mild to profound. Medical and educational personnel must work together as a team to provide transition from the hospital or rehabilitation center to school. Frequent educational problems are focusing or sustaining attention, remembering, and learning new skills. Emotional, behavioral, and social problems may also be apparent. Traumatic brain injury became a separate category of disability under IDEA in 1990.

Children with neurological impairments have experienced damage to or deterioration of the central nervous system. Their behavioral symptoms include mental retardation, learning problems, perceptual-motor dysfunction, paralysis, seizures, and emotional or behavioral disorders. The causes of neurological impairments include infections, diseases, hypoxia, poisoning, congenital malformations, accidents, and child abuse.

Cerebral palsy (CP)—a condition characterized by paralysis, weakness, uncoordination, and/or other motor dysfunction—accounts for about half the children with physical impairments in the United States. It is nonprogressive brain damage that occurs before or during birth or in early childhood. Classification of CP is generally made according to the limbs involved and the type of motor disability. The educational problems associated with CP are varied because of the multiplicity of symptoms; a careful clinical appraisal must be made of each individual to determine the type of special education needed.

Seizures are caused by abnormal discharges of electrical energy in the brain. They may be generalized or partial. Recurrent seizures are referred to as *epilepsy*. Most people with seizure disorders are able to function normally, except when having seizures. Intelligence is not directly affected by a seizure disorder, so educational procedures consist chiefly of attaining knowledge of the disorder and how to manage seizures as well as a commitment to help dispel the ignorance and fear connected with seizures.

Spina bifida is a congenital midline defect, resulting from failure of the bony spinal column to close completely during fetal development. The resulting damage to the nerves generally causes paralysis and lack of sensation below the site of the defect. The cause of spina bifida is not known. Educational implications of spina bifida are determined by the extent of the paralysis and medical complications as well as the child's cognitive and behavioral characteristics. Intelligence and physical stamina are not directly affected by spina bifida, so most children with this condition attend regular classes.

A number of physical disabilities derive from musculoskeletal conditions, in which there are defects or diseases of the muscles or bones. Children with such disabilities have a range of difficulties in walking, standing, sitting, or using their hands. Muscular dystrophy is a degenerative disease causing a progressive weakening and wasting away of muscle tissues. Progressive physical immobility and the prospect of total disability or death make this condition especially difficult to manage. But intellectual capacity is not affected, and with proper motivation and educational procedures, most children with muscular dystrophy can benefit from regular or special education programs. Arthritis is a disease that causes acute inflammation around the joints; its symptoms vary from mild to profound, and it affects children as well as adults. These and other musculoskeletal conditions do not cause lowered intelligence, so educational considerations include overcoming the child's limited mobility so that he or she can continue learning in as normal a way as possible.

Congenital malformations may involve any organ system and may range from minor to fatal flaws in structure or function. Some malformations are genetic (caused by faulty chromosomes), but the causes of many remain unknown. Fetal alcohol syndrome (FAS), which is now one of the most common causes of malformation and mental retardation, is caused by the mother's abuse of alcohol during pregnancy.

Accidents that bring about neurological impairment, disfigurement, or amputation are an important cause of physical disabilities among children and youths. And, AIDS, a fatal viral infection, also involves neurological complications such as mental retardation, seizures, cerebral palsy, and emotional or behavioral disorders. As children and youths with AIDS live longer, due to improved medical treatments, there will be a greater need for special health and education services.

Besides alcohol, women may abuse other substances during pregnancy and give birth to children with disabilities. Use of cocaine and intravenous drugs by pregnant women is resulting in the birth of more babies with severe physiological, cognitive, and emotional problems.

Children who are medically fragile or dependent on ventilators are being returned home from hospitals in increasing numbers. Many of these children are returning to public schools. Careful consideration of the mainstreaming of these children is required.

Many physical disabilities—including those that result from accidents, substance use, and poisoning—are fully preventable. Preventing adolescent pregnancies also would reduce the number of children born with disabilities. Teenage mothers are more likely than older women to give birth to premature or low-birthweight babies, and the babies of teens remain at risk for developing a range of physical and psychological problems when they reach school age.

Abused and neglected children represent an alarming and large number of those with physical disabilities. Many thousands of children each year are damaged—emotionally and physically—by adults who neglect, burn, beat, sexually molest, starve, and otherwise brutalize them. Children who already have disabilities are more likely to be abused than those without disabilities. Teachers must be especially alert to signs of possible child abuse and neglect, and must be aware of reporting procedures in their states.

As a group, children with physical disabilities represent the total range of impairment, and their behavioral and psychological characteristics vary greatly. The necessity for hospitalization, bed rest, prosthetic devices, and so on means that their academic achievement depends on individual circumstances, motivation, and the caliber of care received both at home and at school. The two major effects of a physical disability, especially if it is severe or prolonged, are that a child may be deprived of educationally relevant experiences and that he or she may not be able to learn to manipulate educational materials and respond to educational tasks the way most children do.

There does not appear to be a certain personality type associated with any particular physical disability. The reactions of the public, family, peers, and educational personnel—as well as the child's own reactions to the disability—are all closely interwoven in the determination of his or her personality, motivation, and progress. Given ample opportunity to develop educationally, socially, and emotionally in as normal a fashion as possible, many children with physical disabilities are able to make healthy adjustments to their impairments.

Many individuals with physical disabilities use prosthetics, orthotics, and other adaptive devices to improve functioning. A *prosthesis* replaces a missing body part. An *orthosis* is a device that enhances the partial function of a body part. An *adaptive device* aids a person's daily activity. Important considerations in choosing prostheses, orthoses, and adaptive devices are simplicity, reliability, and the use of residual function.

Education for students with physical disabilities must focus on making the most of their assets. The student's individual characteristics (intellectual, sensory, physical, and emotional) must be considered when developing educational plans. Plans for young children must include services for the family.

Increasingly, students with physical disabilities are being placed in regular classrooms. The problem of educating students with physical disabilities is often a problem of educating students *without* disabilities about the needs of people with disabilities. Along with scholastic education, the child may need special assistance in daily living, mobility, and occupational skills. Consequently, many other disciplines may be involved. The major considerations are to help each child become as independent and self-sufficient in daily activities as possible, to provide basic academic skills, and to prepare him or her for advanced education and work.

Besides early identification and intervention to develop communication, handling and positioning are important considerations. Motor skills must be taught as part of daily lessons in self-help and communication.

Career choice and sociosexuality are two primary concerns of youths with physical disabilities. Career considerations must include careful evaluation of the young person's intellectual, emotional, and motivational characteristics as well as physical capabilities. Young people with physical disabilities have the right to the social relationships and modes of sexual expression afforded others in society.

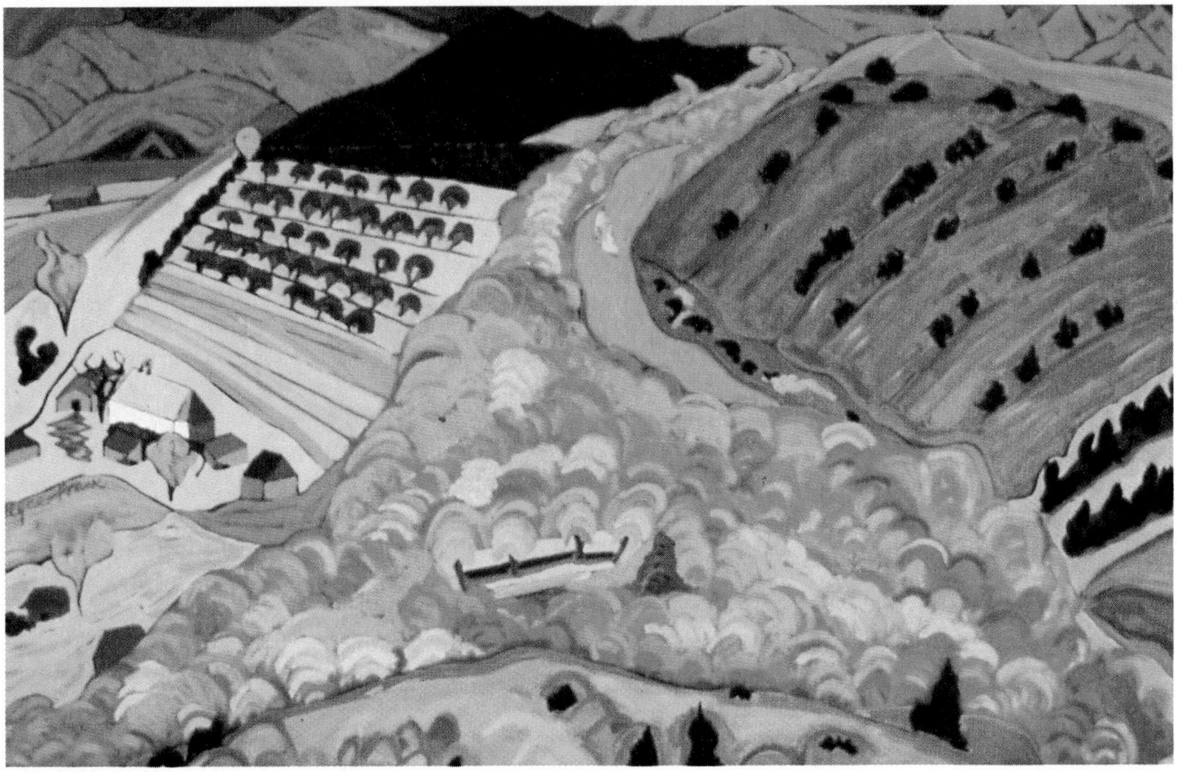

Alyce Frank

Alyce Frank attended the University of Chicago after her sophomore year of high school. Her interest in art developed from her experiences as an educational filmmaker after college and her move to New Mexico. Largely self-taught, she began painting in 1973, and over the years attended workshops with artists from the Southwest including Ray Vinella, Richard Deibenhorn, and Lee Mullican.

11

Giftedness

I think Jim Gillis was a much more remarkable person than his family and his intimates ever suspected. He had a bright and smart imagination and it was of the kind that turns out impromptu work and does it well, does it with easy facility and without previous preparation, just builds a story as it goes along, careless of whether it is proceeding, enjoying each fresh fancy as it flashes from the brain and caring not at all whether the story shall ever end brilliantly and satisfactorily or shan't end at all. Jim was born a humorist and a very competent one. When I remember how felicitous were his untrained efforts, I feel a conviction that he would have been a star performer if he had been discovered and had been subjected to a few years of training with a pen. A genius is not very likely to ever discover himself; neither is he very likely to be discovered by his intimates; they are so close to him that he is out of focus to them and they can't get at his proportions; they cannot perceive that there is any considerable difference between his bulk and their own. They can't get a perspective on him and it is only by a perspective that the difference between him and the rest of their limited circle can be perceived.

The Autobiography of Mark Twain

People who have special gifts or at least have the potential for gifted performance, can go through life unrecognized. As Mark Twain pointed out (see p. 451), they may seem unremarkable to their closest associates. Sometimes gifted children and youths are not discovered because their families and intimates simply place no particular value on their special abilities. And sometimes, they are not recognized because they are not given the necessary opportunities or training. Especially in the case of individuals who are poor or members of minority groups, gifted children may be deprived of chances to demonstrate and develop their potential (Howley, Howley, & Pendarris, 1995). How many more outstanding artists and scientists would we have if every talented child had the opportunity and the training necessary to develop his or her talents to the fullest possible extent? There is no way of knowing, but it is safe to say we would have more.

Unlike mental retardation and other disabling conditions, giftedness is something to be fostered deliberately. Yet giftedness is not something a child can show without risk of stigma and rejection. Many people have a low level of tolerance for those who eclipse the ordinary individual in some area of achievement. A child who achieves far beyond the level of his or her average peers may be subject to criticism or social isolation by other children or their parents. Had Jim Gillis been discovered, given a few years of training with a pen, and become a gifted writer, it is possible that some of his intimates would have found his giftedness hard to accept.

Some of the problems presented by giftedness parallel those presented by the disabling conditions discussed in the other chapters of this book. For instance, the definition and identification of children who are gifted involve the same sort of difficulties that exist in the case of children with mental retardation or emotional or behavioral disorders. But there is an underlying philosophical question regarding giftedness that makes us think differently about this exceptionality: Most of us feel a moral obligation to help those who are at some disadvantage compared to the average person, who have a difference that prevents them from achieving ordinary levels of competence, unless they are given special help. But in the case of a person who is gifted, we may wonder about our moral obligation to help someone who is already advantaged become even better, to distinguish himself or herself further by fulfilling the highest promise of his or her extraordinary resources. It is on this issue—the desirability or necessity of helping the most capable children become even better—that special education for students who are gifted is likely to founder (Gallagher, 1994; Howley et al., 1995).

DEFINITION

Children with special gifts excel in some way compared to other children of the same age. Beyond this almost meaningless statement, however, there is little agreement about how giftedness should be defined (Gallagher & Gallagher, 1994). In describing how giftedness has been treated in American culture, Resnick and Goodman (1994) noted that "as to 'giftedness' itself, there is no tight definition, no single agreed-on meaning. It is a flexible construct which is part of the debate over culture and policy" (p. 109).

We are indebted to Dr. Carolyn M. Callahan of the University of Virginia for her invaluable assistance in preparing this chapter.

Misconceptions about Persons Who Are Gifted

Myth People who are gifted are physically weak, socially inept, narrow in interests, and prone to emotional instability and early decline.	**Fact** There are wide individual variations, and most gifted individuals are healthy, well adjusted, socially attractive, and morally responsible.
Myth Gifted individuals are in a sense superhuman.	**Fact** Gifted people are not superhuman; rather, they are human beings with extraordinary gifts in particular areas. And like everyone else, they may have particular faults.
Myth Gifted children are usually bored with school and antagonistic toward those who are responsible for their education.	**Fact** Most gifted children like school and adjust well to their peers and teachers, although some do not like school and have social or emotional problems.
Myth People who are gifted tend to be mentally unstable.	**Fact** Those who are gifted are about as likely to be well-adjusted and emotionally healthy as those who are not gifted.
Myth We know that 3 to 5 percent of the population is gifted.	**Fact** The percentage of the population that is gifted depends on the definition of *giftedness* used. Some definitions include only 1 or 2 percent of the population; others, over 20 percent.
Myth Giftedness is a stable trait, always consistently evident in all periods of a person's life.	**Fact** Some of the remarkable talents and productivity of people who are gifted develop early and continue throughout life; in other cases, a person's gifts or talents are not noticed until adulthood. Occasionally, a child who shows outstanding ability becomes a nondescript adult.
Myth People who are gifted do everything well.	**Fact** Some people characterized as gifted have superior abilities of many kinds; others have clearly superior talents in only one area.
Myth A person is gifted if he or she scores above a certain level on intelligence tests.	**Fact** IQ is only one indication of one kind of giftedness. Creativity and high motivation are as important indications as general intelligence. Gifts or talents in some areas, such as the visual and performing arts, are not assessed by IQ tests.
Myth Students who are truly gifted will excel without special education. They need only the incentives and instruction that are appropriate for all students.	**Fact** Some gifted children will perform at a remarkably high level without special education of any kind, and some will make outstanding contributions even in the face of great obstacles to their achievement. But most will not come close to achieving at a level commensurate with their potential unless their talents are deliberately fostered by instruction that is appropriate for their advanced abilities.

The disagreements about definition are due primarily to differences of opinion regarding the following questions:

1. *In what ways do gifted children excel?* Do they excel in general intelligence, insight, creativity, special talents, and achievements in academic subjects or in a valued line of work, moral judgment, or some combination of such factors? Perhaps nearly everyone is gifted in some way or other. What kind of giftedness is most important? What kind of giftedness should be encouraged?
2. *How is giftedness measured?* Is it measured by standardized tests of aptitude and achievement, teacher judgments, past performance in school or everyday life, or by some other means? If it is measured in one particular way, some individuals will be overlooked. If past performance is the test, giftedness is being defined after the fact. What measurement techniques are valid and reliable? What measurements will identify which children have the potential to become gifted?
3. *To what degree must a child excel to be considered gifted?* Must the child do better than 50 percent, 80 percent, 90 percent, or 99 percent of the comparison group? The number of gifted individuals will vary depending on the criterion (or criteria) for giftedness. What percentage of the population should be considered gifted?
4. *Who should make up the comparison group?* Should it be every child of the same chronological age, the other children in the child's school, all children of the same ethnic or racial origin, or some other grouping? Almost everyone is the brightest or most capable in some group. What group should set the standard?
5. *Why should gifted students be identified?* What social or cultural good is expected to come from their identification? Is it important meet individual students' educational needs? Are national economic or security issues at stake? Does identifying these individuals maintain an elite group or social power? By providing special educational opportunities for these students, will others reap personal or social benefits? What criteria will be used to judge whether identifying gifted students pays off?

You may have concluded already that giftedness is whatever we choose to make it, just as mental retardation is whatever we choose to make it. Someone can be considered gifted (or retarded) one day and not the next, simply because an arbitrary definition has been changed. There is no inherent rightness or wrongness in the definitions professionals use. Some definitions may be more logical, more precise, or more useful than others, but we are still unable to say they are more correct in some absolute sense. We have to struggle with the concept of giftedness and the reasons for identifying individuals who are gifted before we can make any decisions about definition. Our definition of giftedness will be shaped, to a large extent, by what our culture believes is most useful or necessary for its survival. Giftedness is invented, not discovered (Howley et al., 1995; Sternberg & Davidson, 1986).

Even the terminology of giftedness can be rather confusing. Besides the word *gifted*, a variety of other terms have been used to describe individuals who are superior in some way: *talented*, *creative*, *insightful*, *genius*, and *precocious*, for example:

- **Precocity** refers to remarkable early development. Many highly gifted children show precocity in particular areas of development, such as language, music, or mathematical ability, and the rate of intellectual development of all gifted children exceeds that for nongifted children.

precocity. Remarkable early development.

- **Insight** may be defined as separating relevant from irrelevant information, finding novel and useful ways of combining relevant bits of information, or relating new and old information in a novel and productive way.
- **Genius** has sometimes been used to indicate a particular aptitude or capacity in any area. More often, it has been used to indicate extremely rare intellectual powers (extremely high IQ or creativity).
- **Creativity** refers to the ability to express novel and useful ideas, to sense and elucidate novel and important relationships, and to ask previously unthought of, but crucial, questions.
- **Talent** ordinarily has been used to indicate a special ability, aptitude, or accomplishment.
- **Giftedness,** as we use the term in this chapter, refers to cognitive (intellectual) superiority (not necessarily of genius caliber), creativity, and motivation in combination and of sufficient magnitude to set the child apart from the vast majority of agemates and make it possible for him or her to contribute something of particular value to society (Renzulli, Reis, & Smith, 1981).

Federal and State Definitions

Students who are gifted have special educational needs, but since giftedness is not a disability, in any usual sense, it is not defined in IDEA (the Individuals with Disabilities Education Act, passed in 1990). So no federal law requires special education for students who are gifted as it does for students with disabilities. Federal legislation does, however, encourage states to develop programs for gifted students and support research. *Gifted and talented students* are defined in federal law as children and youths who (1) give evidence of high performance capability in such areas as intellectual, creative, artistic, or leadership capacity or in specific academic fields and (2) require services or activities not ordinarily provided by the school in order to develop such capabilities fully (Gallagher & Gallagher, 1994).

In 1990, twenty-six states had mandatory programs for gifted students. Each state has its own definition of giftedness, however. The most common elements of state definitions in 1990 were (1) general intellectual ability, (2) specific academic aptitude, (3) creative thinking ability, (4) advanced ability in the fine arts and performing arts, and (5) leadership ability (Council of State Directors of Programs for the Gifted, 1991). The role of gifted education in educational reform is clearly affected primarily by state policies (Mitchell, 1994).

Changes in the Definition of *Giftedness*

Intelligence is far more complex than can be measured by the relatively narrow focus of standard intelligence tests.* Furthermore, giftedness seems to be characterized by qualitative differences in thinking and insightfulness, which may not be clearly reflected by performance on intelligence tests (see Reis, 1989; Sternberg & Davidson, 1983). The box on page 456 illustrates the type of insight that might be shown by a student who is gifted in mathematics. Insight of this kind may not be picked up by many tests.

*Recall that the limitations of IQ have become obvious also in the definition of mental retardation. An exceptionally low IQ by itself is no longer sufficient to define mental retardation but must be accompanied by deficits in adaptive behavior (see Chapter 4 and Zigler & Farber, 1985).

insight. The ability to separate and/or combine various pieces of information in new, creative, or useful ways.

genius. A word sometimes used to indicate a particular aptitude or capacity in any area; rare intellectual powers.

creativity. The ability to express novel and useful ideas, to sense and elucidate new and important relationships, and to ask previously unthought of but crucial questions.

talent. A special ability, aptitude, or accomplishment.

giftedness. Refers to cognitive (intellectual) superiority, creativity, and motivation of sufficient magnitude to set the child apart from the vast majority of agemates and make it possible for him or her to contribute something of particular value to society.

Insight: A Qualitative Difference in Thinking

The thinking of gifted children is qualitatively different from that of ordinary people. Many times I have, in classes of gifted children, written on the blackboard:

1 + 2 + 4 + 8 + and so on + 1024 = ?

and asked the children to find the sum. Very often, I have hardly stated the problem before someone shouts out "2047!" If I ask, "How did you get it so fast?," a typical answer might be "1 + 2 is 3, and 4 more is 7, and the sum is always one less than the next number."

When I teach the same topic to average college students, I must explain the concept of a geometrical progression, how to recognize this problem as such, how to derive a formula for the sum, and then show how to apply it to this special case. The gifted children have a capacity for insights which cannot be taught at any level. If this ability exists, it can be developed and stimulated.

Source: From P. C. Rosenbloom, "Programs for the gifted in mathematics," *Roeper Review, 8,* (1986), p. 243. Reprinted with permission.

Given the limitations of IQ tests, the meaning of *intelligence* is being reconceptualized. In fact, the whole notion of what giftedness is has gone through substantial change during the past decade. Today, giftedness is seen as a much more complicated phenomenon than was believed earlier. The field of special education is beginning to appreciate the many different ways in which giftedness can be expressed in various areas of human endeavor. Likewise, educators are starting to acknowledge the extent to which the meaning of giftedness is rooted in cultural values.

Reconceptualization of Intelligence. Whereas the usual tests of intelligence assess the ability to think deductively and arrive at a single answer that can be scored right or wrong, tests of creativity suggest many different potential answers. Recognizing the many facets of human intelligence led to dissatisfaction with previous conceptualizations of *general intelligence* or *primary mental abilities* (Maker, 1986). Today, many researchers conclude that "giftedness cannot possibly be captured by a single number" (Sternberg, 1991, p. 45).

For example, Sternberg (1991) describes a theory of intelligence that suggests three main kinds of giftedness: analytic, synthetic, and practical.

- *Analytic* giftedness involves being able to take a problem apart—to understand the parts of a problem and how they are interrelated, which is a skill typically measured by conventional intelligence tests.
- *Synthetic* giftedness involves insight, intuition, creativity, or adeptness at coping with novel situations, skills typically associated with high achievement in the arts and sciences.
- *Practical* giftedness involves applying analytic and synthetic abilities to the solution of everyday problems, the kinds of skills that characterize people who have successful careers.

Other researchers are finding evidence of multiple intelligences (Gardner & Hatch, 1989). Seven different kinds of intelligence, their end states (adult roles assumed by people high in that intelligence), and core components are shown in Table 11–1. Gardner and Hatch (1989) are convinced that these seven intelligences are highly independent and that nearly all children and adults show distinctive profiles of strengths and weaknesses in these different areas. Gardner and Hatch suggest that these intelligences cannot all be measured through the usual types of testing but must be assessed in the natural contexts in which they can be exhibited. Consequently,

Gardner and others are devising curriculum activities that allow children to develop and demonstrate their intelligences in common or typical contexts (Ramos-Ford & Gardner, 1991). For example, young children's intelligences may be assessed by using the kinds of materials and activities with which they have become familiar in their preschools.

Whether intelligence should be considered as a general characteristic or identified as having distinctive qualities is an ongoing debate with significant implications for defining giftedness (Bower, 1995; Reis, 1989). Regardless of how the debate is ultimately resolved, it is clear that we have come a long way since the invention of the IQ in conceptualizing human intelligence.

Reconceptualization of *Giftedness*. Old stereotypes of giftedness die hard. For example, many still hold the myth that people who are gifted are superior in every way, that they comprise a distinct category of human beings. This myth may account, in part, for the general public's fascination with particularly creative people and the tendency to fawn over those who distinguish themselves in glamorous lines of work.

For decades, however, experts in gifted education have recognized that individuals who are gifted are *not* a distinct or superior class. Not surprisingly, numerous studies of people who are gifted have found correlations among certain human characteristics—meaning that some individuals who are considered gifted share many characteristics

Table 11–1
The Seven Intelligences

Intelligence	*End States*	*Core Components*
Logical-mathematical	Scientist Mathematician	Sensitivity to and capacity to discern logical or numerical patterns; ability to handle long chains of reasoning
Linguistic	Poet Journalist	Sensitivity to the sounds, rhythms, and meanings of words; sensitivity to the different functions of language
Musical	Composer Violinist	Abilities to produce and appreciate rhythm, pitch, and timbre; appreciation of the forms of musical expressiveness
Spatial	Navigator Sculptor	Capacities to perceive the visual–spatial world accurately and to perform transformations on one's initial perceptions
Bodily-kinesthetic	Dancer Athlete	Abilities to control one's body movements and to handle objects skillfully
Interpersonal	Therapist Salesman	Capacities to discern and respond appropriately to the moods, temperaments, motivations, and desires of other people
Intrapersonal	Person with detailed, accurate self-knowledge	Access to one's own feelings and the ability to discriminate among them and draw on them to guide behavior; knowledge of one's own strengths, weaknesses, desires, and intelligences

Source: Adapted from "Multiple intelligences go to school: Educational implications of the theory of multiple intelligences," by H. Gardner & T. Hatch, 1989, *Educational Researcher, 18*(8) 6.

Giftedness and talent occur in many fields, in many cultures; these representatives are recognized around the world.

Aung San Suu Kyi, imprisoned in Burma for many years for her political views, is the eighth woman to have been awarded the Nobel Peace Prize.

Alice Walker is an essayist, poet, novelist and short story writer who has inspired a generation of writers.

Hakeem Olajuwon is the center for the National Basketball Association's Houston Rockets who were NBA champions in 1994 and 1995.

Robin Williams is a versatile comedic film actor/performer whose range of interpretation and ability to convey the human condition appears endless.

The Dalai Lama, spiritual leader of Tibet, now in exile, won the Nobel Peace Prize in 1989.

Nelson Mandela, who survived 26 years of imprisonment under apartheid in South Africa, was elected President of South Africa for which he won the Nobel Peace Prize in 1993.

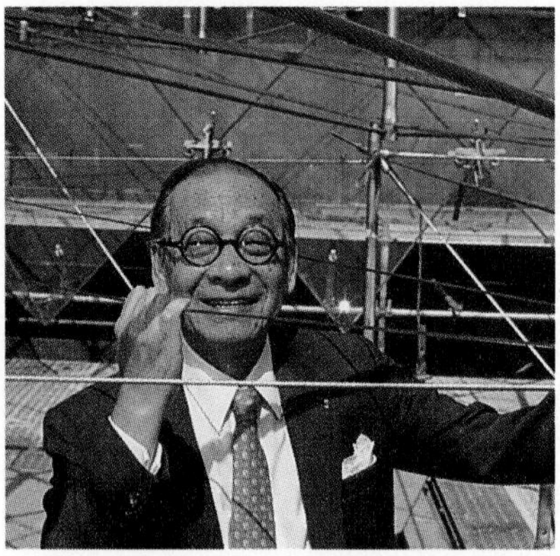

I.M. Pei is an architect whose buildings have revolutionized skylines in daring and habitable style from Boston to Beijing.

Twyla Tharp is a prize-winning choreographer and dancer whose innovative work is performed by dance troupes from many countries.

Elie Wiesel, the conscience of the Holocaust, is the author of numerous books, and won the Nobel Peace Prize in 1986.

believed to be desirable (as do some individuals who are not considered gifted). However, it is a serious leap in judgment to conclude that giftedness designates a superior class of people.

Today, most experts in gifted education suggest that *giftedness* refers to superior abilities in specific areas of performance, which may be exhibited under some circumstances but not others (cf. Gallagher & Gallagher, 1994). So even though giftedness is believed to be a remarkable ability to do something valued by society, it is not an inherent, immutable trait that a person necessarily carries for life. Moreover, being gifted at one thing does not mean that a person is good at every thing.

Another significant issue in reconceptualizing giftedness is recognizing that it, like beauty, is something defined by cultural consensus. Accordingly, Sternberg and Zhang (1995) propose five criteria for judging whether someone exhibits giftedness:

1. *excellence,* meaning that the individual must be superior to the peer group in one or more specific dimensions of performance
2. *rarity,* meaning that very few members of the peer group exhibit the characteristic or characteristics
3. *demonstrability,* meaning that the person must be able to actually exhibit the excellent and rare ability through some type of valid assessment (i.e., he or she cannot just claim to have it)
4. *productivity,* meaning that the person's performance must lead to or have the potential to lead to producing something
5. *value,* meaning that the person's performance is highly valued by society

Sternberg and Zhang also suggest that most people intuitively believe that each of these five criteria is necessary and all five together are sufficient to define giftedness. Similar intuitive, consensual definitions appear to have existed in all cultures throughout history (cf. Hunsaker, 1995; Tannenbaum, 1993).

Regardless of the consensual definition used, we may assume that a person may exhibit giftedness if the conditions are right for gifted performance—that is, if, besides possessing above-average ability and creativity, the person is given opportunities and incentives to perform at an extraordinarily high level. Given this perspective, perhaps we should speak of people who exhibit *gifted behavior,* rather than of *gifted people,* because people typically act gifted only under particular circumstances (Renzulli & Reis, 1991b).

A Suggested Definition

As mentioned earlier, an adequate definition of giftedness includes the requirement that a person show at least the *potential* for making a remarkable and valued contribution to the human condition. The problem, then, is one of predicting future performance. Given what is known about people whose achievements have been remarkable, we believe that, for purposes of education, *gifted children* should be defined (as suggested by Renzulli & Reis 1991b) as those who have demonstrated or shown potential for the following in a given domain or field:

1. *high ability,* including high intelligence
2. *high creativity,* the ability to formulate new ideas and apply them to the solution of problems
3. *high task commitment,* a high level of motivation and the ability to see a project through to its conclusion

Children who are gifted may have superior cognitive abilities that allow them to compete with adults of average intellect.

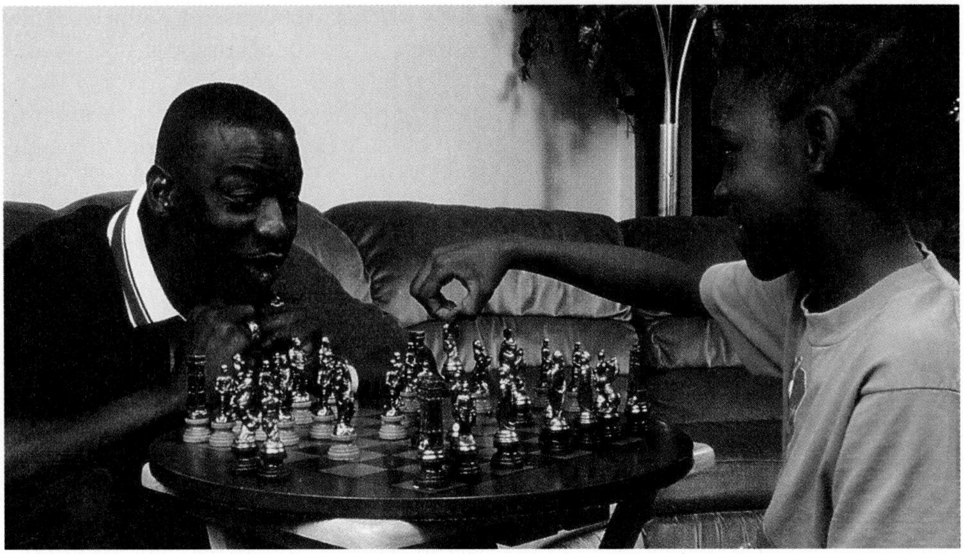

The reason for using the multiple-criterion definition is that all three characteristics—high ability, high creativity, and high task commitment—seem to be necessary for truly gifted performance in any field.

PREVALENCE

It has been assumed in federal reports and legislation that 3 to 5 percent of the U.S. school population could be considered gifted or talented. Obviously the prevalence of giftedness is a function of the definition chosen. If giftedness is defined as the top *x* percent on a given criterion, the question of prevalence has been answered. Of course, if *x* percent refers to a percentage of a national sample, the prevalence of gifted pupils in a given school or cultural group may vary from that of the comparison group regardless of the criteria used to measure performance. As we suggested earlier, giftedness—like all categories of disability—is whatever a given society or community says it is. That is, giftedness is a **social construct.** Thus, the prevalence of giftedness could be set at any level, depending on how it is defined.

Renzulli (1982) argues convincingly that the assumption that only 3 to 5 percent of the population is gifted is needlessly restrictive and may result in overlooking the contributions of many potentially gifted students. He notes that 15 to 25 percent of all children may have sufficient ability, motivation, and creativity to exhibit gifted behavior at some time during their school careers. Renzulli and Reiss (1991b) suggest identifying about 15 percent of students in most schools for a "talent pool," to serve as the major (but not the only) target group for supplementary services.

social construct. A concept created by a society to serve certain social purposes; an idea created by and commonly held in a society and used for making social judgments (e.g., *democracy, good, disability, giftedness*).

ORIGINS OF GIFTEDNESS

As defined today, giftedness is *not* something that sets people apart in every way from those who are average. Instead, it refers to specific, valued, and unusual talents that people may exhibit during some periods of their lives. Therefore, the main factors that contribute to giftedness are really much the same as those that foster any type of behavior, whether typical or exceptional:

1. genetic and other biological factors, such as neurological functioning and nutrition
2. social factors, such as family, school, the peer group, and community

We are are all combinations of the influences of our genetic inheritances and social and physical environments; to say otherwise is to deny reality. Having said this, we must decide what to make of these influences—what to emphasize and what to do about them. In a society such as that of the United States (or in any humane and democratic society), the social and physical environments that foster gifted performance must be emphasized without denying that genetics and neurological factors are involved in creating virtually every human characteristic.

Genetic and Other Biological Factors

The proposition that intelligence and highly valued abilities are inherited is not very popular in an egalitarian society such as that of the United States. This is understandable when we consider that this notion can be used as a springboard for arguments for selective reproduction of humans (with intelligence or other characteristics being the primary factors in selection of mates), as a reason to downplay the importance of improving environmental conditions for citizens already born or conceived, or to perpetuate the social and economic classes of ethnic groups, families, or individuals. For example, recent publication of *The Bell Curve* (Herrnstein & Murray, 1994)—which purported to show that intelligence is related to race and social class—was greeted by withering criticism (e.g., Gould, 1995; Lewis, 1994). Many people questioned the factual basis of the argument and denounced Herrnstein and Murray's efforts to link intelligence and other signs of giftedness to race and social class.

As one proponent of special education for gifted students suggested, attempts to assign racial or class superiority or inferiority are unacceptable and have no place in a society in which equal opportunity and justice are valued: "In an interdependent, pluralistic, complex and multifaceted world, we are all our brothers' keepers" (Roeper, 1994, p. 150). Although giftedness may be determined *in part* by one's genetic inheritance, whatever genetic combinations are involved are exceedingly complex and *not* distributed by race or social class. Genetic differences in abilities apply *within* various ethnic groups and social classes, not between them (cf. Plomin, 1989; Thompson & Plomin, 1993).

New conceptions of intelligence and giftedness might seem to allow us to sidestep the issue of genetic factors in giftedness. That is, if IQ is abandoned as the criterion for defining giftedness in favor of a variety of practical intelligences (see Table 11–1 on page 457), then giftedness might be seen as something that is less affected by genetics. Research in behavioral genetics, however, suggests that every type of behavioral development is affected significantly by genes:

> The first message of behavioral genetic research is that genetic influence on individual differences in behavioral development is usually significant and often substantial. Genetic influence is so ubiquitous and pervasive in behavior that a shift in emphasis is warranted: Ask not what is heritable, ask what is not heritable. (Plomin, 1989, p. 108)

Regardless of how it is defined, the fact that giftedness is partly inherited should not be misinterpreted as an indication that social factors are unimportant. Although genetic influences on the development of superior abilities cannot be denied, these biological influences are clearly no more important (and probably a lot less important) than the environments in which children are nurtured.

Biological factors that *are not* genetic may also contribute to the determination of intelligence. Nutritional and neurological factors, for example, may partially determine how intellectually competent a child becomes. In previous chapters, we pointed out that severe malnutrition in infancy or childhood, as well as neurological damage at any age, can result in mental retardation. But it does not follow that good nutrition and normal neurological status early in life will lead to or are necessary for giftedness. We do know that malnutrition or neurological damage *can prevent* giftedness from developing, however (Brown & Pollitt, 1996).

In summary, genetic and other biological factors clearly are involved to some extent in the determination of giftedness. Environmental influences alone cannot account for the fact that some individuals perform so far above the average. We emphasize, however, that an individual does not *inherit* an IQ or talent. What is inherited is a collection of genes that, along with experiences, determine the limits of intelligence and other abilities (Gallagher & Gallagher, 1994; Zigler & Farber, 1985). These limits are not bound by race or social class.

Social Factors

Families, schools, peer groups, and communities obviously have a profound influence on the development of giftedness (Tannenbaum, 1991). Stimulation, opportunities, expectations, demands, and rewards for performance all affect children's learning. For decades, researchers have found a correlation between socioeconomic level and IQ, undoubtedly in part because the performances measured by standard intelligence tests are based on what families, schools, and communities of the upper classes expect and teach. As definitions of intelligence and giftedness are broadened to include a wider range of skills and abilities that are not so specific to socioeconomic class, we will no doubt see changes in how environmental effects on giftedness are viewed.

Plomin (1989) suggests that we must recognize the important influence of genetics in behavioral development, but this is not his only message:

> The second message [of behavioral genetic research] is just as important: These same data provide the best available evidence of the importance of environment. The data . . . suggest pandemic genetic influence, but they also indicate that nongenetic factors are responsible for more than half of the variance in most complex behaviors. . . . The phrase "behavioral genetics" is in a sense a misnomer because it is as much the study of nurture as nature. (p. 108)

We must ask, therefore: How can families, schools, and the larger culture nurture children's giftedness?

Research has shown that parents differ greatly in their attitudes toward and management of their gifted children. Some parents view having a child who is gifted as positive, some as negative; fathers appear to see their children as gifted less often than mothers (Cornell, 1983; see also Silverman, 1991). A study of individuals who have been successful in a variety of fields has shown that the home and family, especially in the child's younger years, are extremely important (Bloom, 1982; Bloom & Sosniak, 1981). The following were found to occur in the families of highly successful persons:

- Someone in the family (usually one or both parents) had a personal interest in the child's talent and provided great support and encouragement for its development.
- Most of the parents were role models (at least at the start of their child's development of talent), especially in terms of lifestyle.

- There was specific parental encouragement of the child to explore, to participate in home activities related to the area of developing talent, and to join the family in related activities. Small signs of interest and capability by the child were rewarded.
- Parents took it for granted that their children would learn in the area of talent, just as they would learn language.
- Expected behaviors and values related to the talent were present in the family. Clear schedules and standards for performance appropriate for the child's stage of development were held.
- Teaching was informal and occurred in a variety of settings. Early learning was exploratory and much like play.
- The family interacted with a tutor/mentor and received information to guide the child's practice. Interaction included specific tasks to be accomplished, information or specific points to be emphasized or problems to be solved, a set time by which the child could be expected to achieve specific goals and objectives, and the amount of time to be devoted to practice.
- Parents observed practice, insisted that the child put in the required amount of practice time, provided instruction where necessary, and rewarded the child whenever something was done especially well or when a standard was met.
- Parents sought special instruction and special teachers for the child.
- Parents encouraged participation in events (recitals, concerts, contests, etc.) in which the child's capabilities were displayed in public.

In sum, children who realize most fully their potential for accomplishment have families that are stimulating, directive, supportive, and rewarding of their abilities. This appears to be true, regardless of the family's ethnic or cultural identification (Ford, 1994a; Hine, 1994; Robinson, 1993b). Robinson (1993b) described parenting young children who are gifted as "labor intensive," and the same could be said for parenting older gifted children, as well. Families in which gifted children thrive are not laissez-faire in their approach to child rearing. Research does not indicate much else about how families encourage gifted performance. Moreover, the stresses and needs of families of gifted children are poorly understood (Silverman, 1991).

Students from countries that outperform American students academically usually credit their high achievement to hard work, rather than native ability; American students, however, typically believe the opposite.

Different nations and cultural groups have different ways of structuring schooling and supporting children's learning that have implications for giftedness. In spite of severe socioeconomic disadvantages, some microcultural groups in the United States are able to foster high academic achievement in schools in which most other students perform very poorly (Caplan, Choy, & Whitmore, 1992). Overall, high-ability students in the United States do not compare favorably to high-ability students in most other industrialized countries of the world (Callahan, 1994). There are no simple answers to questions about why students in many other countries outperform American students. It appears, though, that one contributing factor may be the much smaller emphasis that American students' place on effort in explaining their achievement (Stevenson, Lee, Chen, Kato, & Londo, 1994). Students in the United States appear less likely to attribute extraordinary achievement to hard work and more likely to attribute it to native ability.

How schools may nurture children's giftedness has received too little attention. Yet the ways in which schools identify giftedness, group children for instruction, design curricula, and reward performance have a profound effect on what the most able students achieve. When schools facilitate the performance of all students who are able to achieve at a superior level in specific areas, giftedness is found among children of all cultural and socioeconomic groups (Feldhusen, 1989; Frazier, 1989; Mills, Stork, & Krug, 1992; Renzulli, 1994).

In summary, environmental influences have much to do with how a child's genetic endowment is expressed in performance. But neither environment nor genetics can be entirely responsible for the performance whether an individual is gifted or retarded. Genetic factors apparently determine the range within which a person will function, and environmental factors determine whether the individual will function in the lower or upper reaches of that range.

IDENTIFICATION OF GIFTEDNESS

Measurement of giftedness is a complicated matter. Some components cannot be assessed by traditional means; in addition, the particular definition of giftedness will determine how test scores are interpreted. But if it is indeed important to identify gifted children early so that they will achieve self-fulfillment and be aided in the development of their special potential to make a unique and valuable contribution to society, it is important that appropriate methods be used.

The most common methods of identification include IQ (based on group or individual tests), standardized achievement test scores, teacher nominations, parent nominations, peer nominations, self-nominations, and evaluations of students' work or performances. Typically, some combination of several of these methods is used. Identification practices have been extremely controversial, and best practices have frequently been ignored. Richert (1991) lists six rampant problems in identification practices:

1. elitist and distorted definitions of giftedness
2. confusion about the purpose of identification
3. violation of education equity
4. misuse and abuse of tests
5. cosmetic and distorting use of multiple criteria
6. exclusive program design (p. 81)

The concerns expressed by this list are that biased and unreliable criteria for identifying giftedness (e.g., overreliance on IQ and achievement tests) are sometimes used to provide special educational opportunities in exclusive programs that are discriminatory, even when school systems claim that they are using multiple and fair criteria (e.g., the criteria may all measure essentially the same thing). As Renzulli and Reis (1991b) put it, in some cases, "the multiple criteria game ends up being a smoke screen for the same old test-based approach" (p. 118). Yet it is possible to develop identification methods that are fair, reliable, and equitable, and that do not result in an exclusive or discriminatory program design (Renzulli & Reis, 1991b; Shore, Cornell, Robinson, & Ward, 1991).

In devising identification procedures that are fair to individuals from all cultural and ethnic groups and all social classes, educators must take into account the varied definitions of giftedness and recognize the effects of cultural variation on children's behavior (Ford, 1994b; Frasier & Passow, 1994; Hunsaker & Callahan, 1995; Patton & Baytops, 1995). In addressing multicultural differences, it is important to recognize the variations of socioeconomic status, language, and values that occur *within* various ethnic and cultural groups, not just between them. Hunsaker and Callahan (1995) propose eight general identification principles that will help ensure fairness:

1. Assessments go beyond a narrow conception of talent.
2. Separate and appropriate identification strategies are used to identify different aspects of giftedness.
3. Reliable and valid instruments and strategies are used to assess talent.
4. Appropriate instruments are employed for underserved populations.
5. Each child is viewed as an individual, recognizing the limits of a single score on any measure.
6. A multiple-measure/multiple-criteria approach is followed.
7. Appreciation is shown for the value of the individual case study and limitations of combinations of scores.
8. Identification and placement are based on individual students' needs and abilities rather than on the numbers who can be served.

Renzulli and Reis (1991b) describe a six-step identification system associated with their definition of giftedness (which, as mentioned earlier, consists of above-average ability, task commitment, and creativity). The six steps result in the nomination of students according to multiple criteria and the eventual identification of a talent pool of about 15 to 25 percent of the school enrollment (see Figure 11–1):

- Step one is nomination on the basis of *test scores*—any single test or subtest score or other performance indicator that would put the student in the top 8 percent according to local norms.
- Step two is *teacher nominations*. Teachers are informed of which students in their classes have been nominated by test scores and are asked to name any additional students who show particularly high levels of creativity, task commitment, interest, talent, performance, or potential.
- Step three allows for alternative pathways to identification—nomination by parents, peers, or self, tests of creativity, product evaluations, or any other pathway that can be reviewed by a screening committee or evaluated in a case study approach.
- In step four, a list of all nominated students is circulated to all teachers in the school and to past teachers who may know of students' abilities that have somehow gone unrecognized in steps one through three. The idea is to provide a "safety net" for recognition of students who might otherwise have been overlooked.
- Step five involves notification and orientation of parents. Parents and students are not told that gifted students have been identified; rather, the nature of the program for students in the talent pool this year is described.

Figure 11–1

Six steps to identification of a talent pool.

(*Source:* Based on "The schoolwide enrichment model: A comprehensive plan for the development of creative productivity," by J. S. Renzulli & S. M. Reis, 1991, in *Handbook of gifted education,* edited by N. Colangelo & G. A. Davis, Boston: Allyn and Bacon.)

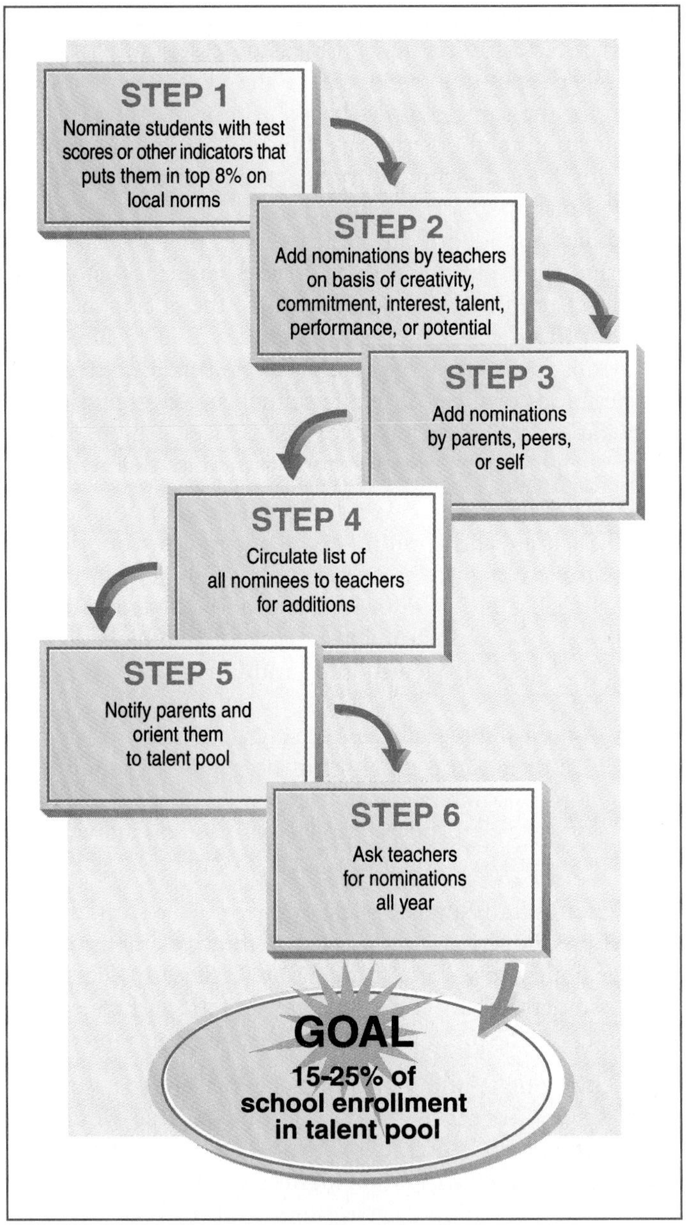

- Step six provides another procedural check by seeking nominations from teachers throughout the year when they notice a student's high interest in a particular topic, area of study, issue, idea, or event taking place in or outside of school.

Although no identification system is perfect, the procedures described by Renzulli and Reis (1991b) have widespread support and are consistent with recommended practices (Hunsaker & Callahan, 1995; Shore et al., 1991). The focus of identification methods should be on balancing concern for identifying only those students whose capabilities are markedly above average with concern for including all who show promise for gifted performance.

PHYSICAL, PSYCHOLOGICAL, AND BEHAVIORAL CHARACTERISTICS

Giftedness has been recognized in some form in every society throughout recorded history (Hunsaker, 1995; Morelock & Feldman, 1991). In many societies, individuals who are gifted have been stereotyped in one of two ways: (1) as physically weak, socially inept, narrow in interests, and prone to emotional instability and early decline or, in the opposite direction, (2) as superior in intelligence, physique, social attractiveness, achievement, emotional stability, and moral character and immune to ordinary human frailties and defects. Although it may be possible to find a few individuals, both gifted and nongifted, who seem to fit one stereotype or the other, the vast majority of people who are gifted fit neither.

Early studies in the United States reported that gifted children were physically superior (Terman & Oden, 1959). However, the basis for selection was solely on the children's IQ scores, and many came from economically privileged environments (Gallagher & Gallagher, 1994). The physical superiority of these children may have been ascribed by their teachers, who nominated them for testing. Although some children are gifted primarily in physical abilities and excel in sports and some with other remarkable abilities also are talented athletes, giftedness does not require and is often not accompanied by physical superiority. Given the possible permutations of genetic and environmental factors and their interactions, it is not surprising that some students exhibit superior abilities in a variety of areas.

Students who are gifted tend to be far ahead of their agemates in specific areas of academic performance. Most gifted children learn to read easily, often before entering school. They may be far advanced in one area, such as reading or math but not in another, such as writing or art (e.g., skills requiring manual dexterity). Contrary to

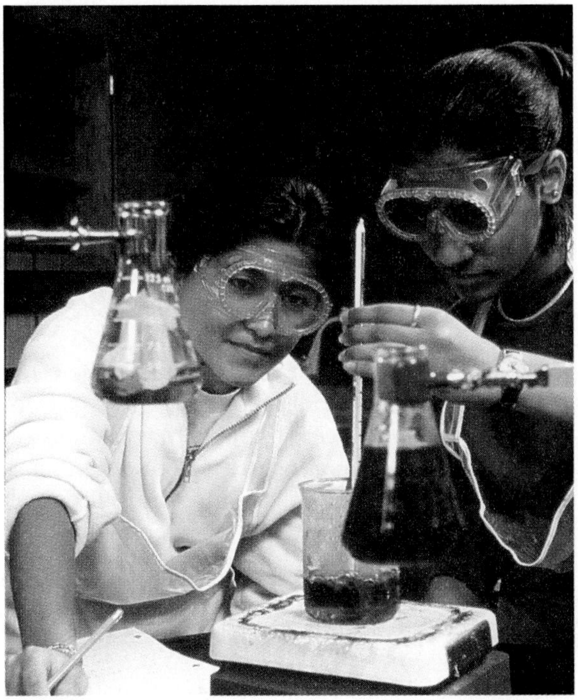

Contrary to myth, most students who are gifted are not constantly bored with and antagonistic toward school, if they are given work that is challenging.

The Eight Gripes of Gifted Kids

1. No one explains what being gifted is all about—it's kept a big secret.
2. The stuff we do in school is too easy and it's boring.
3. Parents, teachers and friends expect us to be perfect, to "do our best" all the time.
4. Kids often tease us about being smart.
5. Friends who really understand us are few and far between.
6. We feel too different and wish people would accept us for what we are.
7. We feel overwhelmed by the number of things we can do in life.
8. We worry a lot about world problems and feel helpless to do anything about them.

Source: From J. Galbraith, "The eight great gripes of gifted kids: Responding to special needs," *Roeper Review, 7*(1985), 16.

popular opinion, most gifted students are not constantly bored with and antagonistic toward school, if they are given work that is reasonably challenging for them (Gallagher & Gallagher, 1994). Some, however, become disinterested in school and perform poorly in the curriculum or drop out. Not surprisingly students who are gifted become upset and maladjusted when they are discriminated against and prevented from realizing their full potential. But such a reaction is not unique to any group of children, exceptional or average along any dimension.

When gifted students do complain, what are their concerns? The eight most frequent "gripes," found in a study by Galbraith (1985), are listed in the box above. Notice that most of these complaints are not exclusive to students identified as gifted. However, Galbraith's findings do suggest that gifted students need more than intellectual challenges to feel good about themselves and to use their special abilities to the fullest.

Perhaps it should not be surprising that the majority of students who show giftedness enter occupations that demand greater-than-average intellectual ability, creativity, and motivation. Most find their way into the ranks of professionals and managers, and many distinguish themselves among their peers in adulthood (Gallagher & Gallagher, 1994; Perrone, 1991). But not all gifted students enjoy occupational success in demanding jobs; some choose career paths that do not make use of their talents or otherwise fail to distinguish themselves.

The self-concepts, social relationships, and other psychological characteristics of students who are gifted have been matters of considerable interest. Many of these students are happy, well liked by their peers, emotionally stable, and self-sufficient. They may have wide and varied interests and perceive themselves in positive terms (Coleman & Fultz, 1985; Janos & Robinson, 1985). However, the links between many aspects of self-concept and giftedness are uncertain (Hoge & Renzulli, 1993). For example placing students in homogeneous classes, in which all students are selected because of their advanced abilities, appears to lower academic self-concept but not self-concept related to such things as appearance and peer relations (Marsh, Chessor, Craven, & Roche, 1995). Gifted students are often acutely sensitive to their own feelings and those of others and highly concerned about interpersonal relationships, intrapersonal states, and moral issues (Gruber, 1985; Piechowski, 1991; Silverman, 1994). Using their advanced cognitive abilities appears to help many gifted children develop at a young age the social and emotional adjustment strategies used by most adults (Sowa, McIntire, May, & Bland, 1994). In short many, but not all gifted students are self-aware, self-assured, and socially skilled.

It is important to realize that giftedness includes a wide variety of abilities and degrees of difference from average. Moreover, the nature and degree of an individual's giftedness may affect his or her social and emotional adjustment and educational and psychological needs. Consider, for example, that categorizing only people with IQs of 180 or higher as "gifted" is roughly like categorizing as "mentally retarded" only those individuals with IQs of 20 or less (Zigler & Farber, 1985). In fact, children who are exceptionally precocious or gifted—those whose talents are *extremely* rare—may constitute a group for which extraordinary adaptations of schooling are required (just as extraordinary adaptations are required for children with very severe mental retardation) (see Gross, 1992, 1993; Lovecky, 1994).

CULTURAL VALUES REGARDING GIFTED STUDENTS AND THEIR EDUCATION

In American culture, it is relatively easy to find sympathy for children with disabilities but more than a little difficult to turn that sympathy into public support for effective educational programs. However, for gifted children, it is difficult to elicit sympathy and next to impossible to arrange sustained public support for education that meets their needs (Reis, 1989).

This is not a peculiarly American problem, but there is something self-limiting, if not self-destructive, about a society that refuses to acknowledge and nourish the special talents of its most gifted children (cf. Tannenbaum, 1993). Hunsaker (1995) has examined the perception and treatment of giftedness in traditional West African, Egyptian, Greco-Roman, Semitic, Chinese, Meso-American, and European Renaissance cultures. He found that few of these cultures used the term *gifted;* however, as in contemporary American society, individuals with advanced abilities were viewed with ambivalence:

> They were considered exceptional because of the hopes people had that they would ensure the continued existence of their culture. Their ability was seen as a divine or inherited gift. Great efforts personally and societally were needed to develop their abilities, and special opportunities were generally not available to the socially disadvantaged. Finally, the exceptional were the objects of ambivalent feelings directed toward them as persons and toward their knowledge. Beliefs and feelings about individuals of exceptional ability have not changed a great deal from those we inherited from other cultures. (Hunsaker, 1995, pp. 265–266)

Gallagher (1986) describes American society's attitude toward students who are gifted and talented as a love-hate relationship. Our society loves the good things that gifted people produce, but it hates to acknowledge superior intellectual performance. Opponents of special education for gifted students argue that it is inhumane and un-American to segregate such students for instruction, and to allocate special resources for educating those who are already advantaged; also, there is the danger of leaving some children out, when only the ablest are selected for special programs (e.g., Margolin, 1994; Sapon-Shevin, 1994). It would seem, however, impossible to argue against special education for gifted and talented students without arguing against special education in general, for all special education involves recognizing individual differences and accommodating those differences in schooling.

Although it can be argued on the basis of sound logic, common sense, and anecdotal reports that special education *should* be provided for gifted children, few controlled research studies showing the effects of such education have been done. Callahan (1986) suggests that the wrong questions are often asked in evaluating programs. When the primary objective of a program is to provide education that is appropriate for the capabilities of the students, the major evaluation questions should involve the appropriateness of the education provided, not the outcome of producing more productive citizens (Callahan, 1993). In a study of over 1,000 elementary students, researchers found that students in gifted programs showed higher achievement and self-perception of scholastic ability than their gifted peers who were not in special programs (Delcourt, Loyd, Cornell, & Goldberg, 1994).

Legal arguments for education of students who are gifted are quite different from those for education of students with disabilities. Much of the litigation for educating children with disabilities is based on the fact that they are being excluded from school or from regular classes, leading to the argument that they are being denied equal protection of law. Gifted students are seldom denied an education or access to regular classes, so the legal basis for special provisions to meet their needs is less clear (Stronge, 1986).

In 1989, the Jacob K. Javits Gifted and Talented Students Education Act provided federal funding for a limited number of model educational projects and for the National Research Center on the Gifted and Talented. Similarly, most states increased their support of programs for gifted students in the 1980s. However, as Ford, Russo, and Harris (1995) point out, federal and state laws still fail to provide adequate safeguards for the educational rights of students who are gifted and talented. If exceptional children of *all categories* have the civil right to receive an education appropriate for their abilities, then the civil rights of gifted students have not yet been assured (Gallagher, 1995).

Special programs for students with special gifts and talents remain highly controversial. Even among gifted students there are differences of opinion (Delisle, 1987).

The Educational Reform Movement and Controversy Regarding the Education of Students Who Are Gifted and Talented

The educational reform movement of the 1990s holds both promise and danger for education of gifted students (Gallagher, 1991a; Renzulli & Reis, 1991a; Treffinger, 1991; VanTassel-Baska, 1991a). The promise and danger are perhaps most clearly evident when reformers emphasize both excellence and heterogeneous grouping for instruction. To the extent that the emphasis of school reform is on improving the quality of instruction and encouraging the highest performance of which students are capable, the movement holds promise for all students, including those who are gifted. To the extent that reformers reject the idea of grouping students for instruction in specific curriculum areas, based on their knowledge of and facility in the subject matter, however, the movement may mean disaster—not only for students who are gifted but also for those with special difficulties in learning. Table 11–2 presents a summary of the possible effects that five popular reforms of the 1990s might have on gifted students.

Ability grouping is one of the most controversial topics related to school reform, largely because it is seen by some as a way of perpetuating racial or ethnic inequalities in achievement and social class. Some researchers suggest that ability grouping of virtually any kind is discriminatory and ineffective and should be abolished (Oakes, 1985, 1992). Others find that ability grouping across grades and within classes has beneficial effects (Kulik & Kulik, 1992). Grouping students for instruction based on their level of interest and achievement in specific curriculum areas should not be confused with a rigid tracking system. Flexible grouping in which students are not locked into groups or tracks but have opportunities for learning in a variety of homogeneous and heterogeneous groups is seen as highly desirable by most advocates for gifted students (Fiedler, Lange, & Winebrenner, 1993; Tomlinson, 1994a; VanTassel-Baska, 1992).

Many school reformers have suggested that students of all ability levels learn best in heterogeneous groups, in which cooperative learning and peer tutoring are used as strategies for meeting individual needs. Cooperative learning, peer tutoring, and other arrangements for addressing individual differences in heterogeneous groups

Table 11–2
Educational Reform Devices and Impact on Gifted Students

Middle Schools	This strong movement to replace the junior high school stresses many similar goals to education of gifted students, such as stressing interdisciplinary curriculum, instruction in thinking strategies, emphasis on counseling, team teaching, and individualization. Many proponents also stress heterogeneous grouping, which threatens to exacerbate the lack of challenge that many of these students feel.
Site-Based Management	This drive to bring educational decision making back to the local school level is a reaction to excessive control of activities by a distant central administration or state department of education. How well gifted students will do will depend on who at the site knows about the special needs of gifted students. This is basis for some concern.
Cooperative Learning	This is an instructional strategy that has become quite popular. It stresses small-group activities around a central goal, with the team being evaluated by the performance of all of the members of the team. The stress on heterogeneous grouping in the small groups has caused some distress among teachers of the gifted, who admit to liking the approach if it is used with groups of gifted students.
Outcome-Based Learning	Outcome-based learning emphasizes products (demonstrated learning) as the basis for evaluating programs, as opposed to input measures (e.g., teachers employed) or process information (e.g., number of reports made). This movement could be of some stimulus for programs for gifted students if the expectations of performance are placed high enough to challenge this student group.
Accountability	All educators will be required to demonstrate how effective they have been in helping students to learn. Special programs, such as gifted education, would be required to demonstrate, with some tangible evidence, that the program achieves more than the regular program and justifies the additional expense and resources assigned to it.

Source: From J. Gallagher & S. A. Gallagher, *Teaching the gifted child* (4th ed.). Copyright © 1994 by Allyn and Bacon. Reprinted by permission.

may meet the needs of most students. However, students who are truly gifted in specific curriculum areas are very poorly served by these strategies. Advocates for the gifted argue that these students need instruction that is conceptually more complex and abstract than most learners of similar chronological ages can handle (Feldhusen & Moon, 1992; Renzulli & Reis, 1991b).

Creating a truly "gifted-friendly" classroom, in which there is a very great range of abilities among students, is actually quite difficult. Furthermore, some students who are gifted are not well served in regular classrooms (Kennedy, 1995a, 1995b). Tomlinson (1994b) describes the "easy lie" about giftedness and excellence: that it is possible to achieve excellence without challenging each individual to do his or her best. Maintaining the challenge for and demanding excellence of *all* students is an extraordinary challenge in extremely heterogeneous groups, and many teachers may find it overwhelming.

NEGLECTED GROUPS OF GIFTED STUDENTS

There has been recent concern for neglected groups of gifted children and youths—who are disadvantaged by economic needs, racial discrimination, disabilities, or gender bias—and it is not misplaced. Two facts cannot be ignored.

1. Gifted children from higher socioeconomic levels already have many of the advantages—such as more appropriate education, opportunities to pursue their interests in depth, and intellectual stimulation—that special educators recommend for those who are gifted.
2. There are far too many gifted individuals who are disadvantaged by life circumstances or disabilities and who have been overlooked and discriminated against, resulting in a tremendous waste of human potential (Howley et al., 1995; Whitmore, 1986).

Gifted Students Who Are Underachievers

Students may fail to achieve at a level consistent with their abilities for a variety of reasons. Many females achieve far less than they might because of social or cultural barriers to their selection or progress in certain careers. Students who are members of racial or ethnic minorities also are often underachievers because of bias in identification or programming for their abilities. Likewise, students with obvious disabilities are frequently overlooked or denied opportunities to achieve.

Still, underachievement cannot be explained simply by discrimination; many males, nonminority, and nondisabled students also are underachievers. Underachievement of children who are gifted and talented can result from any of the factors that lead to underachievement in any group, such as emotional conflicts or a chaotic, neglectful, or abusive home environment. A frequent cause is inappropriate school programs—schoolwork that is unchallenging and boring because gifted students have already mastered most of the material or because teachers have low expectations or mark students down for their misbehavior (Kolb & Jussim, 1994). A related problem is that gifted underachievers often develop negative self-images and negative attitudes toward school (Delisle, 1982; Gallagher & Gallagher, 1994). And when a student shows negative attitudes toward school and self, any special abilities he or she may have will likely be overlooked.

Whitmore (1986) suggests that lack of motivation to excel is usually a result of a mismatch between the student's motivational characteristics and opportunities provided in the classroom. Students are typically highly motivated when (1) the social climate of the classroom is nurturant, (2) the curriculum content is relevant to students' personal interests and challenging, and (3) the instructional process is appropriate to students' natural learning styles.

One way of preventing or responding to underachievement is allowing students to skip grades or subjects so school becomes more nurturing and provides greater interest and challenge. However, acceleration is not always appropriate nor is it typically sufficient by itself to address the problems of the underachieving gifted student (Jones & Southern, 1991; Rimm & Lovance, 1992). Counseling, individual and family therapy, and a variety of supportive or remedial strategies may be necessary alternatives or additions to acceleration (Gallagher, 1991b; VanTassel-Baska, 1990).

Underachievement must not be confused with nonproductivity (Delisle, 1981). A lapse in productivity does not necessarily indicate that the student is underachieving. The gifted student should not be expected to be constantly producing something remarkable. But this points up our difficulty in defining *giftedness:* How much time must elapse between episodes of creative productivity before we say that someone is no longer gifted or has become an underachiever? We noted earlier that giftedness is in the performance, not the person. Yet we know that the unrelenting demand for gifted performance is unrealistic and can be inhumane.

Gifted Students from Cultural- and Ethnic-Minority Groups

Three characteristics may be used to define gifted students with unique needs because of their cultural or minority status: cultural diversity, socioeconomic deprivation, and geographic isolation (Baldwin, 1985). These characteristics may occur singly or in combination. For example, Swanson (1995) describes the problems of serving gifted African-American students in rural areas, and Kitano and Espinosa (1995) discuss the complications of working with gifted students who are learning English as a second language. Each group has unique needs for different reasons. Children from minority cultural groups may be viewed negatively, or the strengths and special abilities valued in their cultures may conflict with those of the majority. Children reared in poverty may not have toys, reading materials, opportunities for travel and exploration, good nutrition and medical care, and many other advantages typically provided by more affluent families. Lack of basic necessities and opportunities for learning may mask intelligence and creativity. Children living in remote areas may not have access to many of the educational resources that are typically found in more populated regions.

Among the greatest challenges in the field today are identifying culturally diverse and disadvantaged gifted students and including and retaining these students in special programs. Some cultural and ethnic groups have been sorely neglected in programs for gifted students. For example, Patton and Baytops (1995) note that although African-American students comprise about 16 percent of public school enrollment, they make up only about 8 percent of those enrolled in programs for the gifted. Frasier (1991) observes that addressing the underrepresentation of cultural or ethnic groups is a task with many proposed solutions, none of which has yet been entirely successful.

The desegregation of public schooling following the landmark 1954 decision of the U.S. Supreme Court in *Brown v. Board of Education* has not yet resulted in racial balance in programs for students who are gifted (Ford & Webb, 1994). Bias in testing and referral practices—as well as a tendency of educators to focus on the deficits, rather than the strengths, of minority students—contribute to the underrepresentation

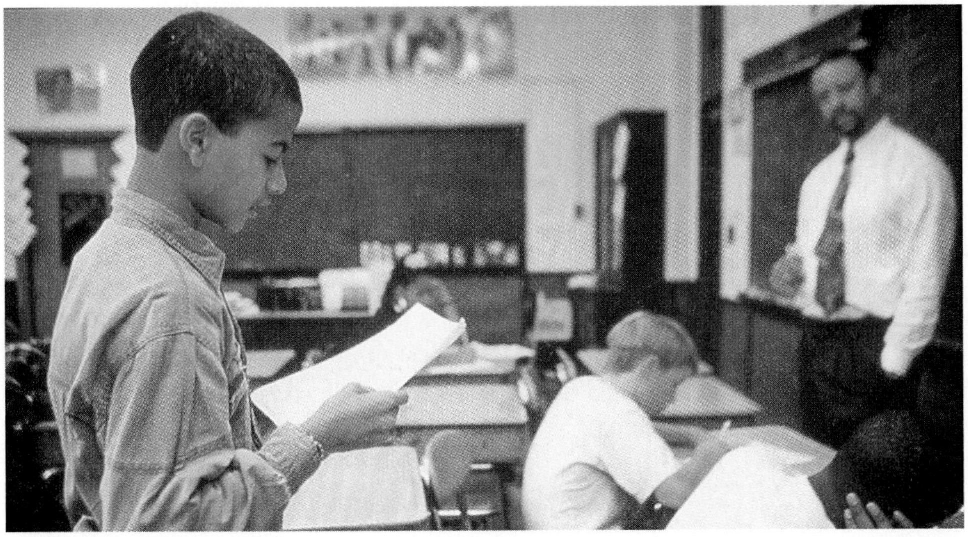

Many gifted individuals have been disadvantaged by life circumstances or other disabilities and thus overlooked and discriminated against, resulting in a tremendous waste of human potential.

of some ethnic groups in gifted programs (Frasier, Garcia, & Passow, 1995). Many gifted African-American students remain underachievers, even if they recognize the importance of achievement in American society (Ford, 1993). And some, perhaps many, gifted students of color feel misunderstood by peers, family, and teachers, who are not trained to respond competently to cultural differences in giftedness (cf. Ford, 1994b).

Appropriate identification and programming for students who are gifted will result in including approximately equal proportions of all ethnic groups. This proportionality will likely be achieved only if renewed efforts are made to:

- devise and adopt culturally sensitive identification criteria
- provide counseling to raise the educational and career aspirations of students in underrepresented groups
- make high-achieving models from all ethnic groups available
- retain underrepresented ethnic students in programs
- adopt a workable system to ensure the inclusion of underrepresented groups

Ultimately, the larger social-environmental issue of making families and communities safe, as well as intellectually stimulating, for children and youths of all cultural and ethnic backgrounds must be addressed. Equal opportunity for development outside the school environment would help address the underrepresentation of minority students in programs for the gifted.

Gifted Students with Disabilities

The education of students who are gifted and have disabilities is just emerging as a field (Whitmore & Maker, 1985). The major goals of the field are identification of gifted students with specific disabilities, research and development, preparation of professionals to work with gifted children and youths, improvement of interdisciplinary cooperation for the benefit of such children and youths, and preparation of students for adult living.

Whitmore and Maker (1985) note that our stereotypic expectations of people with disabilities frequently keep us from recognizing their abilities. For example, if a child lacks the ability to speak or to be physically active or presents the image associated with intellectual dullness (e.g., drooling, slumping, dull eyes staring), we tend to assume that he or she has mental retardation. The fact is, students with physical characteristics typically associated with severe mental retardation may be intellectually brilliant; unless this is acknowledged, however, the talents of students with cerebral palsy and other physical disabilities may be easily overlooked (Willard-Holt, 1994). Students who are gifted and have impaired hearing also may be overlooked if their communication skills are poorly developed, if their teachers are not looking for signs of talent, or if they are taught by teachers who have limited competence in communicating with people who are deaf (Rittenhouse & Blough, 1995). Some students with learning disabilities have extraordinarily high intellectual abilities, yet their talents will be missed if those abilities are not properly assessed (Hannah & Shore, 1995; Reis, Neu, & McGuire, 1995).

In fact, giftedness can occur in combination with disabilities of nearly every description, as depicted in cases described by Sacks (1995) and illustrated in the following:

"Alec (a pseudonym) reads. He reads all the time."

"What does he read?"

"*Scientific American, National Geographic, Omni, Air and Space,* Isaac Asimov."

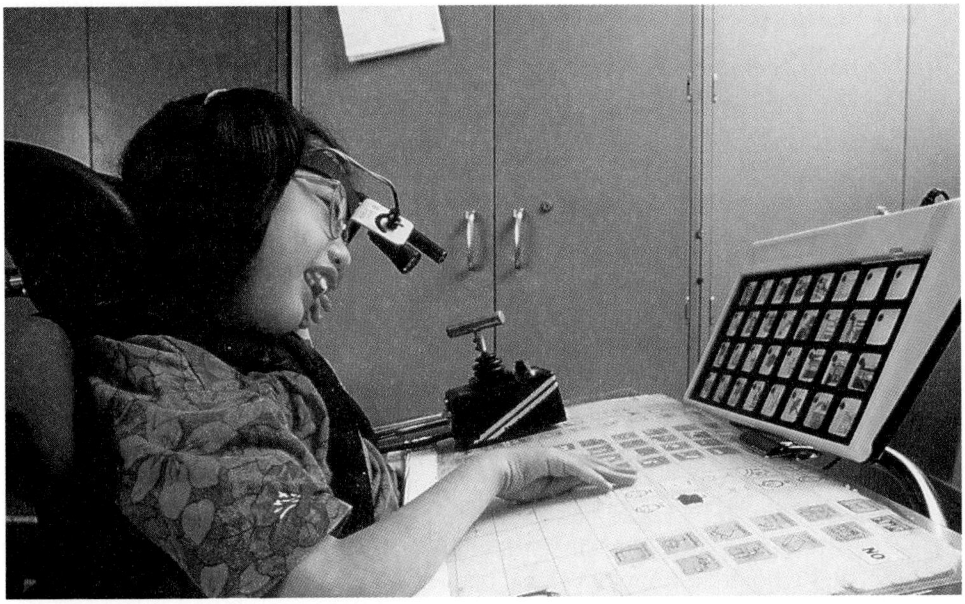

Students whose disabilities prevent them from speaking or physically expressing themselves may have potential that is not obvious through casual observation.

> Alec's mother paused briefly. "For hours at a time he just disappears into books and magazines. He comprehends well. His science vocabulary is incredible."
>
> "How old did you say he is?"
>
> "Eleven."
>
> "And he doesn't go to school?"
>
> "We've kept him home because of his health problems."
>
> As the case conference progressed, it became apparent that Alec was an extraordinary child. His disabilities included asthma, severe food and chemical sensitivities, poor motor skills, difficulties with perception and orientation, hyperactivity, and learning disabilities. In spite of all these problems, Alec was verbally gifted. (Moon & Dillon, 1995, p. 111)

We do not want to foster the myth that giftedness is found as often among students with disabilities as among those who do not have disabilities. But clearly, gifted students with disabilities have been a neglected population. Whitmore and Maker (1985) estimate that at least 2 percent of children with disabilities, excluding those with mental retardation, may be gifted. (Recall that 3 to 5 percent is the typical estimate for the general population.)

VanTassel-Baska (1991b) summarizes what is known about gifted students with disabilities:

> We know that these learners exist, many times hidden inside their specific disabling condition, and we know because of their discrepant pattern, they are difficult to find and identify. Moreover, we also know that these learners require more extensive services in order to develop their potential. (pp. 261–262)

The more extensive services to which VanTassel-Baska refers can seldom be provided by single teachers or schools. So a key factor in meeting these students' needs is the collaboration of a variety of disciplines and institutions to provide appropriate technology and training (Karnes & Johnson, 1991a).

Gifted Females

Clearly, females comprise the largest group of neglected gifted students. As Callahan (1991) and Kerr (1991) point out, *some* aspects of the way females are treated in U.S. society are undergoing rapid change. Gifted females today have many opportunities for education and choice of careers that were denied to females a generation ago. "Yet, there is certainly convincing data that suggest that this particular group of gifted students is facing inequities, they are still not achieving at the levels we would expect, and they are not choosing career options commensurate with their abilities" (Callahan, 1991, p. 284).

Cultural factors work against the development and recognition of females who are gifted (Eccles, 1985). Females simply have not been provided with equal opportunity and motivation to enter many academic disciplines or careers that have, by tradition, been dominated by males, such as chemistry, physics, medicine, and dentistry. When females have entered these fields, they have often been rewarded inappropriately (according to irrelevant criteria or with affection rather than promotion) for their performance. English literature has tended to portray females as wives, mothers, or "weaker" sisters, who are either dependent on males or sacrifice themselves for the sake of males who are dominant. These barriers to giftedness in females have only recently been brought forcefully to public attention.

Females lag behind males in many measures of achievement and aptitude (e.g., professional and career achievement, standardized test scores, grades) and tend not to pursue courses of study or careers involving science and math (Hedges & Nowell, 1995; Junge & Dretzke, 1995; Terwilliger & Titus, 1995). In short, they are underrepresented in many fields of advanced study and in professions and careers that carry high status, power, and pay. We can only presume to know the reasons for their underrepresentation (Callahan, 1991). Factors contributing to the situation may include lower parental expectations for females, overemphasis on and glamorization of gender differences, school and societal stereotypes of gender roles, and educational practices detrimental to achievement (e.g., less attention to high-achieving girls, expectations of less independence of girls).

Research reviewed by Callahan (1991) and Kerr (1991) suggests that the problems of neglect and underrepresentation of gifted females are much more complex than previously believed. Like underrepresentation of ethnic and cultural minorities, the problems involving females are closely tied to cultural, social, and political issues, and they do not have simple or easy solutions. Nevertheless, the education of females who are gifted might be improved by encouraging females to take risks by enrolling in challenging courses, to make career choices appropriate for their abilities, and to explore avenues that break stereotypical female roles.

EDUCATIONAL CONSIDERATIONS

Today, the consensus of leaders in the field is that special education for students who are gifted and talented should have three characteristics:

1. a curriculum designed to accommodate the students' advanced cognitive skills;
2. instructional strategies consistent with the learning styles of gifted students in the particular content areas of the curriculum; and
3. administrative arrangements facilitating appropriate grouping of students for instruction (cf. VanTassel-Baska, 1993).

States and localities have devised a wide variety of plans for educating gifted students. Generally, the plans can be described as providing **enrichment** (additional experiences provided to students without placing them in a higher grade) or **acceleration** (placing the students ahead of their agemates).

Many variations of enrichment and acceleration have been invented, however, ranging from regular classroom placement, with little or no assistance for the teacher, to special schools offering advanced curricula in special areas, such as science and mathematics or the arts. Between these extremes are consulting teacher programs, resource rooms, community mentor programs (in which gifted students work individually with professionals), independent study programs, special classes, and rapid advancement of students through the usual grades, including early admission to high school or college.

Not every community offers all possible options. In fact, there is great variation in the types of services offered within the school systems of given states and from state to state (Passow & Rudnitski, 1993). As one might expect, large metropolitan areas typically offer more program options than small towns or rural areas. New York City, for example, has a long history of special high schools for students who are gifted and talented.

Some of the educational options for gifted students are extremely controversial. For example, the extent to which these students should be served in general education classrooms is hotly debated in the literature (e.g., Maker, 1993). Some educators argue that when students who are gifted are pulled out of regular classes, there is a negative impact on the attitudes and perceptions of the students who are *not* pulled out (e.g., Sapon-Shevin, 1994); research findings contradict this assumption, however (Shields, 1995). Others have found that although offering a variety of program options for gifted students produces good outcomes, no single type of program option meets the needs of all such students (Delcourt et al., 1994).

Ideally, assessment, identification, and instruction are closely linked, whether students have disabilities or gifts and talents. Sternberg has proposed a model that uses the three kinds of intelligence he has identified—analytic, synthetic, and practical (see page 456)—as the basis for assessing, identifying, and teaching students who are gifted (Sternberg & Clinkenbeard, 1995). According to this model, students' ability to exhibit the three types of intelligence would be assessed, and those who showed extraordinary facility in using a particular form of intelligence in a given area of the curriculum then would be provided instruction that emphasized their unusual strengths. Although this three-dimensional model might be applicable to all program options and areas of the curriculum, its validity for program design has not yet been established.

The future holds particularly exciting possibilities for education of students who are gifted and talented. Note that advances in telecommunications, the presence of microcomputers in the home and classroom, and the call for excellence in American education are three developments with implications for educating the most able students. Telecommunications—including instructional television, telephone conferencing, and electronic mail—are technological means of facilitating the interaction of gifted students and their teachers over wide geographical areas. These communication systems are important for extending appropriate education to gifted students living in rural and remote areas. The possible uses of microcomputers for enhancing the education of gifted students are enormous. Using software tutorials, accessing data banks, playing or inventing computer games that are intellectually demanding, writing and editing in English and foreign languages, learning computer languages, and solving advanced problems in mathematics are only a few of the possibilities.

enrichment. An approach in which additional learning experiences are provided for gifted students while they remain in the grade levels appropriate for their chronological ages.

acceleration. An approach in which gifted students are placed in grade levels ahead of their peers in one or more academic subjects.

SUCCESS STORIES

Palo Alto, CA: **Noshua Watson** *is enrolled in the Ph.D. program in economics at Stanford University. Just eighteen years old, she recently completed high school and college through a residential acceleration program for gifted students. Along with her parents, Aremita and Rudy Watson, and program director Celeste Rhodes, Noshua is satisfied that, for her, this educational alternative makes sense.*

At age thirteen, Noshua Watson enrolled in the Program for the Exceptionally Gifted, known as PEG, which is an acceleration program at Mary Baldwin College in Virginia. "The intellectual challenges I had as a young teenager blew my mind. It was so exciting to realize what I could do!" she remembers. "It was the first time I felt part of a school community."

Noshua's parents saw her academically challenged beyond what was possible with the high school curriculum and in a supportive environment that encouraged her personal growth. Noshua thrived on the stimulation of campus activities, including lacrosse, theater, music, and the college's judicial review board. She assisted with institutional research and helped to teach an economics course during her senior year.

"Acceleration programs like PEG challenge our culture," says Celeste Rhodes, the program's director. "Parents and students must be courageous in their ability to accept uniqueness." Noshua's mother, Aremita Watson, explains, "My husband and I feel it's our responsibility to provide opportunities for our girls, and PEG was something Noshua really wanted to do. Most children don't get the chance to be their best because too often we teach them to be like others, instead of encouraging them to be motivated by a belief about life that can shape their dreams and aspirations."

Celeste describes this ten-year-old program as an alternative for the motivated student who may have teenage interests but demonstrates what she calls "a serious sense of purpose." "You see it in the interviews," she says. "There is an energy, a spark, a drive."

To Celeste, giftedness is not defined narrowly by IQ but includes multiple measures including consistent achievement over time. "We are accelerating students by four years. That requires a history of discipline, hard work, and high grades." Through a lengthy essay and interview process, an optimal match is sought between student and program. Explains Celeste, "Since we are residential, emotional stability is extremely important." Noshua agrees. "As PEG students, we were ready and eager for the academic rigors, but emotionally and physically we were not as mature. We were still teenagers with a lot of special needs."

In this acceleration program, Noshua was supported by an individualized, integrated curriculum that addressed her advanced cognitive skills. Small-group instruction with college students and PEG peers was combined with personal mentoring and alternatives such as independent study and accelerated pacing. According to Noshua, "I was intellectually challenged, but I could socially mature at my own rate, and for me, that was really key."

Acceleration

Acceleration involves moving a student ahead of her or his age peers in one or more areas of the curriculum. It may mean skipping one or more grades or attending classes with students in higher grades for one or a few specific subjects. Acceleration has not been used frequently, especially in rural areas (Jones & Southern, 1992). It has been used primarily with students who are extremely intellectually precocious (i.e., those scoring 160 or higher on individually administered intelligence tests). Radical acceleration of extremely precocious students, combined with enrichment at each stage of their school careers, appears to offer many of these students the best social experiences as well as academic progress commensurate with their abilities (Charlton, Marolf, & Stanley, 1994; Gross, 1992).

Special Educators at Work

For her first two years in the program, Noshua lived in a special dormitory for younger PEG students, along with residential coordinators sensitive to the needs of adolescents. Social activities were sponsored and friendships nurtured through residence life, and the coordinators also served as academic advisors to first-year students. Noshua was free to choose among the college's liberal arts offerings but was required to take two specific PEG-level courses: one in literature and one in mathematics. She also took several study skills workshops. Celeste explains, "Study skills is taught by older PEG students and directed toward how to organize for college-level learning. These tutors, or 'near peers,' help acculturate the younger students to life at the college." For her last two years, Noshua lived independently in a regular dorm, and her academic advisor was a faculty member in her chosen major of economics.

Selecting educational alternatives is a familiar practice for Noshua and her family. As a youngster, she attended a magnet school and was described as an avid learner who was strong willed and knew her own mind. Her first experience with gifted education came from a centralized public school program for third- through fifth-graders. Noshua remembers hoping that when the family moved, she would attend a similar school, but there were no separate programs in her new district. Enrichment classes were held before and after school, but her parents opted not to enroll her because of transportation problems.

Aremita Watson remembers that junior high was not a positive experience for her daughter, who has bad memories. "I was frustrated academically because my guidance counselor said if I wanted to take both French and Spanish, I also had to take an honors math course one level beyond my grade. Socially, I was frustrated because most kids at school just wanted to 'hang out.' My parents wouldn't allow me to do this, and it was hard for me to relate. I guess you could say I was sort of a geek!"

Through a talent search at a local university, Noshua discovered a residential camp for gifted students and happily attended for three summers. "I felt I could finally be myself," she says. In eighth grade, a national search service identified programs offering alternatives to conventional high schools. "That's where I heard about PEG, and so did a fellow camper. We graduated from college together last June."

Noshua is the recipient of a National Science Foundation Graduate Fellowship. As a doctoral student, she is part of a minority on several counts: At eighteen, she is younger than her peers and considered to be gifted. She is also female and African American. Undaunted, her voice is filled with energy when she says, "I just love being at Stanford! I have more in common with graduate students, since most people my age are just starting to live away from home for the first time. My life experience has been different, and I'm used to a lot more independence."

For Noshua, getting an early start on education and career has been satisfying. But as the oldest of three sisters, she believes that everyone has to make her own choices. Her sister Tenea is now a PEG student, and twelve-year-old Cambria will decide soon if she wants to take the same route. "My parents never pressure us to do things the same way," says Noshua. "They've done so much to provide us with unique experiences."

—By Jean Crockett

Opponents of acceleration fear that gifted children who are grouped with older students will suffer negative social and emotional consequences or that they will become contemptuous of their age peers. Proponents of acceleration argue that appropriate curriculums and instructional methods are available only in special schools or in regular classes for students who are older than the gifted child. Furthermore, proponents argue that by being grouped with other students who are their intellectual peers in classes in which they are not always first or correct, gifted students acquire more realistic self-concepts and learn tolerance for others whose abilities are not so great as their own.

Research on the effects of acceleration does not clearly indicate that it typically has negative effects, but neither does it clearly indicate benefits in all cases (Jones & Southern, 1991). Acceleration appears to be a plan that can work very well but demands careful attention to the individual case and to specific curriculum areas.

Models of Enrichment

Renzulli (1977) notes that many of the activities provided under the guise of "special education for the gifted and talented" cannot be justified. If children who are gifted or average spend their time playing games designed to foster creativity or problem-solving strategies, they are not being served well. Likewise, if the traditional content-oriented curriculum (which emphasizes pouring facts into students' heads) is replaced by an equally inane process-oriented curriculum (which emphasizes pouring cognitive processes into students' heads), no real progress will have been made. A defensible program for gifted pupils must state how education for them will be the same as and how it will be different from education for all students.

Renzulli and his colleagues have developed an enrichment model based on the notion that children exhibit gifted behaviors in relation to particular projects or activities to which they apply their above-average ability, creativity, and task commitment. Students selected into a "talent pool" through case study identification methods are engaged in enrichment activities that involve individual or small-group investigation of real-life problems; they become practicing pollsters, politicians, geologists, editors, and so on. The teacher (1) helps students translate and focus a general concern into a solvable problem, (2) provides them with the tools and methods necessary to solve the problem, and (3) assists them in communicating their findings to authentic audiences (i.e., consumers of information). Students may stay in the enrichment program as long as they have the ability, creativity, and motivation to pursue productive activities that go beyond the usual curriculum for students their age. The model has become known as the *schoolwide enrichment model* (Olenchak & Renzulli, 1989; Renzulli, 1994; Renzulli & Reis, 1985; 1991b). The major components of this model are shown in Table 11–3 on page 481.

The schoolwide model was designed to address the need to reduce the separateness of special and regular programs and to make certain that all students who can profit from enrichment activities are given opportunities to engage in them. The goals of *curriculum compacting* are to create a challenging learning environment, guarantee proficiency in the basic curriculum, and make time for enrichment and acceleration (Starko, 1986). All students' strengths are assessed, and information on their performance during general exploratory experiences (Type I enrichment) is used to plan group-training activities (Type II enrichment) and individual and small-group investigations of real problems (Type III enrichment).

Type II enrichment activities have four major objectives:

1. General skills in creative thinking and problem solving, critical thinking, and affective processes such as sensing, appreciating, and valuing
2. A variety of how-to-learn skills such as note-taking, interviewing, classifying, analyzing data, drawing conclusions
3. Skills in the appropriate use of advanced-level reference materials such as reader's guides, directories, abstracts
4. Written, oral, and visual communication skills that maximize the impact of students' products upon appropriate audiences (Renzulli & Reis, 1991b, p. 129)

All students selected for the talent pool engage in Type I and Type II activities, but Type III activities are self-selected and optional.

On the basis of an experimental study of the schoolwide enrichment model in elementary schools, Olenchak and Renzulli (1989) suggest that their approach can improve the learning environment for all students, improve attitudes of students and teachers toward education of the gifted, and make special programming for students

Table 11–3
Major Components of the Schoolwide Enrichment Model

Curriculum Compacting	Modifying or "streamlining" the regular curriculum in order to eliminate repetition of previously mastered material, upgrade the challenge level of the regular curriculum, and provide time for appropriate enrichment and/or acceleration activities while ensuring mastery of basic skills
Assessment of Student Strengths	A systematic procedure for gathering and recording information about student's abilities, interests, and learning styles
Type I Enrichment: General Exploratory Experiences	Experiences and activities that are designed to expose students to a wide variety of disciplines (fields of study), visual and performing arts, topics, issues, occupations, hobbies, persons, places, and events that are not ordinarily covered in the general curriculum
Type II Enrichment: Group Training Activities	Instructional methods and materials that are purposefully designed to promote the development of thinking and feeling processes
Type III Enrichment: Individual and Small Group Investigations of Real Problems	Investigative activities and artistic productions in which the learner assumes the role of a first-hand inquirer; the student thinking, feeling, and acting like a practicing professional

Source: From F. R. Olenchak & J. S. Renzulli, "The effectiveness of the schoolwide enrichment model on selected aspects of elementary school change," *Gifted Child Quarterly, 33*(1) (1989), 37. Reprinted with permission.

who are gifted a more integral part of general education. These outcomes are critical to sustained support for special programs for the most able students. "The gains that gifted education has made in instructional technology and the commitment that this field has made to serving our most potentially able youth will only have long term endurance when they are woven into the fabric of general education rather than perceived as dangling threads that can be snipped off at any time" (p. 46).

TEACHERS OF GIFTED STUDENTS

Teaching students who are gifted may at first thought seem easy. Who would not like to teach students who are particularly bright, creative, and motivated? In reality, teachers of gifted students, just like other special and general education teachers, are vulnerable to burnout (Dettmer, 1982). Gifted and talented students often challenge the system of school, and they can be verbally caustic. Their superior abilities and unusual or advanced interests demand teachers who are highly intelligent, creative, and motivated. Simply leading a productive discussion with a gifted student is a demanding task for even a master teacher (cf. Coleman, 1992). Teachers who are successful in fostering the creativity of students have developed their own creative competencies and are able to use creative teaching procedures with great skill (Esquivel, 1995).

collaboration

a key to success

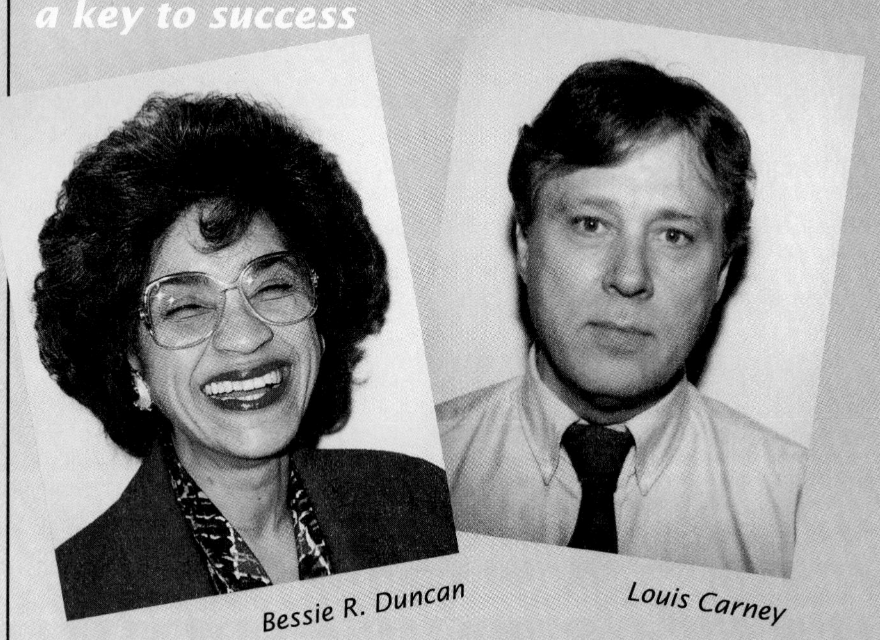

Bessie This is my eighth year as Supervisor of Gifted and Talented Education for the Detroit Public Schools. I'm responsible for planning and implementing programs for students with a variety of talents. Before 1985, we had no gifted and talented education department. Rather, everyone was responsible for identifying and nurturing bright students. I'm a very creative person. So, when the position was created, I convinced my supervisor to continue the tradition and allow me to make gifted education part of the fabric of the education of all children rather than a separate program. I wanted to avoid labeling students and creating a "we" and a "they." One part of our program identifies students who may have undiscovered special talent. Another part of our program provides direct services for the needs of identified children in a variety of areas—academic talents, visual and performing arts, and leadership. A part of our philosophy is that when programs are developed and implemented collaboratively with others we guard against these programs' demise because of their being person-dependent. When more people are involved, you have more champions for the program; they feel some personal ownership of the program and want to sustain it and see it grow. So the middle-school debate program first evolved in this context. Initially, I went to the supervisor of Communication Arts because, again, I don't develop programs in isolation; I always collaborate with another curriculum department. That's when I first met Lou. I had heard a lot about Lou—that he was a very fine fellow with lots of talent. So, I thought, he sounds just like the person we need—someone who cares a lot about kids, who is gentle and will help us get this program started.

Lou Bessie and Sterling Jones, the supervisor of Communication Arts, were really enthusiastic about the success of the high school debate program. They believed that the traditional cross-examination debate format could also be effective in the middle school. The intent of the program is to promote the intellectual development of middle school students by accelerating and differentiating the curriculum through debate. Debate becomes a vehicle for stimulating middle school students' learning and encouraging them to view the world in more global terms. Reaching the goal of this program depends on a collaborative learning philosophy. Success is linked to the middle school teachers' acceptance of ownership for all decisions and by-laws. We guide them in keeping the program enthusiastic and fair for all participants. We have developed four workshops for interested middle school teachers. The first centers on basic debate terminology. Teachers receive materials describing generative thinking strategies that they can share with their students. The second workshop focuses on defining the resolution, in which the teachers write in the roles of the team members. These plans are made in collaboration with the high school science and social studies teachers. In the third workshop, teachers work in debate squads. Their task is to write a brief based upon a partial brief with supporting literature supplied by me. The opposing squad is also furnished with research to counter the brief. The goal is to redefine what they know and share this with their students. The final workshop is a practice debate among the teachers to review the format. Teachers who are seasoned debate veterans are paired with the first-year debate coaches. Rules and procedures are finalized by the coaches. The first debate is a practice meet. Students are not judged in terms of winning or losing. Instead they are critiqued and walked through the format. They are given suggestions on strengthening their stance by high school debate students,

Bessie R. Duncan is a Supervisor, Gifted and Talented Education, Detroit Public Schools; B.S., Medical Technology and M.A., Special Education, Wayne State University. **Louis Carney** is an English teacher, Mackenzie High School, Detroit, Michigan; B.S., Speech and English and M.A., Education Administration, Eastern Michigan University; M.S, Mathematics Education, University of Detroit.

who serve as judges. All judges are given an informal inservice on format and suggestions on evaluating middle-school students.

Bessie I want to enlarge on what Lou just brought up—our high school debaters serving as judges. These students have to be released from their classes, and many times their coaches will come to sort of cheer them on. So, it's really a collaborative project that has many layers. The collaboration is among administrators, administrators and teachers, teachers and students, and among students. I think that's what makes for the richness of the program, and I think that explains why it's so celebrated by everybody. Problems do arise, but because everybody likes the program, they work around them—arranging transportation to the meet or covering classes for coaches, for example.

Lou I want to comment further on the high school debaters. When they debate, they often complain and are frustrated at times by judges. In competition, they sometimes don't feel that they deserve this or they should've received that. "I don't understand why the judge didn't vote for us," they say. So, now they're the judges for the middle school kids. All of a sudden they're wearing a different hat and they have to make those decisions on winning or losing and balloting for speaker points. They're required to justify their ballots and give the details in the synopsis of their decision. This changes their perspective. It gives them a comprehensive understanding of the debate process and makes their competitions more palatable. They understand that an issue might be interpreted a different way by a different listener. It seems to make them better debaters.

Bessie I'll look at it from the perspective of another group of students—the seventh- and eighth- graders who participate in this project. We have heard many success stories about students who chose to participate. As I said earlier, middle school debate is a collaborative project that's used to identify middle school students who have leadership abilities. It's certainly done that. For many of the students who have strong thinking and language skills that emerge in debate, teachers have observed that they have shown increased achievement, better attendance, and a change in their aspirations in terms of what they are going to do next. Many of the high schools who learn about these strong debate teams are courting the middle school students to come and be part of their high school debate teams or the students choose a high school based on the strength of its debate team. In our first year, we started with five or six schools. In the second year we had fourteen, and now we're up to eighteen schools with debate teams with three others watching and getting ready. That's out of a total of sixty middle schools. So, we predict that in the next three or four years we may have a pretty high ratio of our students participating. That's a reason for celebration for all of us. Living in an urban area, self-management skills are a key to students being successful in school as well as outside of school. For students involved in debate, another payoff is that even when they're upset they are able to choose, more often, appropriate responses to stress because of their thinking and language skills.

Lou Some middle school teachers are not comfortable with the win/lose outcome of debates. They accept the fact that in basketball games there are winners and losers; in chess games, too, there are winners and losers; and in academic games there are winners and losers. But when it comes to debate, there is concern about winning and losing. The majority of people involved in the program, though, believe that what we are doing is great. They see this activity as being designed to be low-risk and low in stress, and students share their stories with their peers in the school, including faculty and administrators. It seems that the enthusiasm generated by the debate program is developing and growing within the schools, and so as far as the little frustrations go I think the success of the program has outweighed them.

Bessie I certainly agree with that. We really don't have many major frustrations, and I know when I speak to people about Detroit they find it just unfathomable that we are in a district that is very friendly toward identifying and nurturing bright children. But we've done it for years even when there was no centralized leadership for gifted and talented. So, it's just part of the way we look at students, and I think that that willingness to accommodate and to do things that would help to develop talent makes everyone just very cooperative and willing to be flexible. It's had terrific benefits for students. The students have gotten involved in community service projects as a result of the topics that they've discussed and debated. For example, they gave a wonderful play on homelessness that really just mirrored all the things that they had learned.

> ***Self-management skills are a key to students being successful in school as well as outside school.***

Lou One last point is that this debate program has also extended the collaborative effort at my high school, and I receive a lot of support from my fellow English teacher, Ellen Harcourt. In addition, several teachers in science and social studies and English are collaborating on writing across the curriculum. A collaborative class is currently being initiated at our school using teachers from various disciplines, and this is supported by funds from Bessie's office. These students will be using their debate skills and legal terminology to write a bill and, we hope, introduce it in the state legislature. Again, this program has transcended the departmentalized atmosphere of a high school, and if it continues to nourish talent and flourish, we will be way ahead of the game.

Teachers of gifted students must be adept at assessing students' abilities, interests, and commitment to tasks and skilled at helping other teachers recognize the characteristics that indicate students could profit from special education. Frequent communication with regular teachers, observation, interpretation of test scores, and interviews with students, parents, and other professionals are required to identify students who are gifted. Only teachers with broad interests, extensive information, and abundant creative energy will be able to accomplish the identification, instruction, and guidance of gifted students.

In many ways, excellent teachers of gifted students are very similar to excellent teachers of all other types of students (Baldwin, 1993). In fact, *all* good teachers probably share certain core characteristics. Nevertheless, students who are gifted obviously pose a particular challenge for teachers in terms of the breadth and level of information and the degree of creativity they must bring to the classroom. Whitlock and DuCette (1989) suggest that the following characteristics distinguish outstanding teachers of gifted students:

- enthusiasm for and dedication to work with gifted students
- self-confidence in their ability to be effective
- facilitation of other people as resources and learners
- ability to apply knowledge of theory to practice
- strong achievement orientation

EARLY INTERVENTION

Giftedness in young children presents special problems of definition, identification, programming, and evaluation (Lewis & Louis, 1991). Karnes and Johnson (1991b) point out that although progress has been made in building model programs and providing better services for young gifted children, negative attitudes toward such efforts persist. Barriers inhibiting the development of better education for these children include lack of parental advocacy, lack of appropriate teacher training, an emphasis on older gifted students, financial constraints, and legal roadblocks, such as laws preventing the early admission of gifted children to school.

The barriers to early identification and programming for students who are gifted include school policies and ideologies that Robinson and Weimer (1991) refer to as "the tyranny of the calendar":

> Very few districts pay systematic heed to kindergartners who have already mastered the goals of the curriculum, leaving it up to their already burdened teachers to make provisions. Because many districts favor only enrichment programs, special planning for advanced students does not begin until late into the elementary school years, after basic skills have been mastered. Leaving these students locked into standard grade-level curriculum, which does not match their learning pace or interest level, means that children with advanced conceptual and academic skills, so eager at first to enter school, are in clear danger of becoming casualties of the system. (p. 30)

Many questions regarding the education of young children who are gifted remain unanswered. Relatively little is known about how advantageous it is to identify and program for gifted children before they are in third or fourth grade or how best to train parents and teachers to work with gifted preschoolers. Yet some statements can be made with a high degree of confidence, as Karnes and Johnson (1991b) point out:

1. We have not been committed to early identification and programming for the young gifted.
2. We have few advocates for young gifted children.
3. We do not have institutions of higher learning training personnel in gifted education to work with our young gifted children.
4. We are in need of financial resources to: conduct research with young gifted children and their families, develop more effective and efficient procedures and instruments for screening and assessing young gifted children, determine the most effective strategies for meeting their unique needs, including ways of differentiating instruction, and follow-up data that will give us insights into the effectiveness of our identification and programming.
5. We don't have the legislation we need to permit public schools to serve young gifted children below the age of five, nor to help public schools finance programming.
6. There is little awareness among educators and parents alike of the importance of early identification and programming for the gifted.
7. Procedures and instruments for identification of children who are handicapped and those who come from low income homes must compare children of like kind rather than expect children to demonstrate or score on instruments at the level of their more affluent or non-handicapped peers.
8. Identification of young gifted children must be an ongoing process. This is particularly true for children from low-income and minority groups as well as children with handicapping conditions because these children need time and the opportunity to display their special gifts and talents. (pp. 279-280)

Although not a panacea, early admission to school and acceleration through grades and subjects offer significant advantages for some young gifted students. What many young gifted children need most is the freedom to make full and appropriate use of school systems as they now exist. They need the freedom to study with older children in specific areas where their abilities are challenged. Gifted children need to be able to get around the usual eligibility rules so they can go through the ordinary

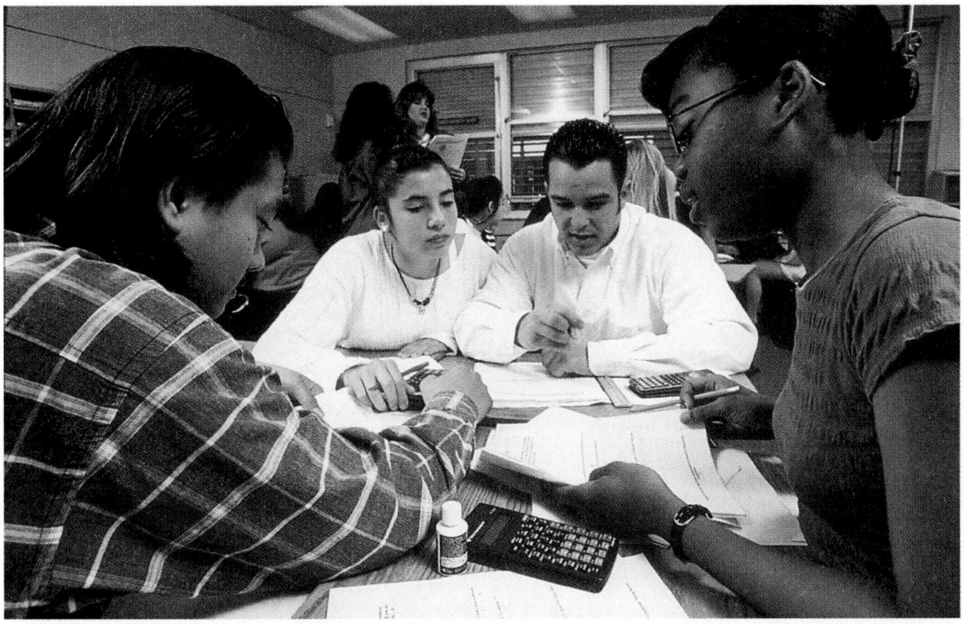

Accelerated educational programs, particularly in mathematics, have been evaluated favorably and may support early college entrance for some students who are gifted.

curriculum at an accelerated rate. Unfortunately, relatively few gifted preschoolers receive the kind of educational programming appropriate for their abilities. This is especially the case for young gifted children who are also from minority or poor families or have disabilities (Gallagher & Gallagher, 1994).

Preschoolers who are gifted may be intellectually superior and have above-average adaptive behavior and leadership skills, as well. Their advanced abilities in many areas, however, do not mean that their development will be above average across the board. Emotionally, they may develop at an average pace for their chronological age. Sometimes, their uneven development creates special problems of social isolation, and adults may have unrealistic expectations for their social and emotional skills because their cognitive and language skills are so advanced (see the box below). They may require special guidance by sensitive adults who not only provide appropriate educational environments for them but also discipline them appropriately and teach them the skills required for social competence (Baum, 1986; Roedell, 1985). They may need help, for example, in acquiring self-understanding, independence, assertiveness, sensitivity to others, friend-making skills, and social problem-solving skills (Robinson, 1993a).

The Gifted Preschooler: Chris and Jonathan

Chris came running into the house, bubbling over with excitement, "Mommy, mommy. I did it! I put the bird back together. Its bones were scattered all around. Look. I have a skeleton of a bird! I guess I am a paleontologist for real! Let's go to the library and find out what species it is."

Chris, only 4, resembles Stephen Gould, world renowned paleontologist whose interest also began at an early age. A visit to the dinosaur exhibit at the American Museum of Natural History inspired both to the world of paleontological inquiry. Will Chris eventually become a paleontologist? Chris has both advanced knowledge and an all-consuming interest in paleontology.

From this scenario we can attest readily to his superior levels in vocabulary development and comprehension skills. Intense interest, in-depth knowledge, and accelerated development in language provide positive evidence of giftedness. But more important, these characteristics strongly imply that Chris has educational needs different from most 4-year-olds.

Will these special needs be met within the school setting? Unfortunately there are a limited number of educational programs adequately equipped to address the unique requirements of children like Chris. Chris' parents, like most parents of bright preschoolers, voice their concern since many of these youngsters are already reading, composing original stories, and computing simple addition and subtraction problems on their own.

One would only have to listen and watch children like Chris to confirm the need for such services. These children frequently demonstrate advanced vocabularies and often an early ability to read. In addition, they seem to learn easily and spontaneously. Logic appears early in some bright youngsters, often to the embarrassment of adults.

For instance, Jonathan, at 3, requested a grilled cheese sandwich at a restaurant. The waitress explained that grilled cheese was not on the menu. Jonathan, determined to have his way, queried, "Do you have cheese and bread?" The waitress nodded, "We do. . . ." "Then," Jon blurted, "do you have a pan?" Jon got his sandwich. When the sandwich arrived, the waitress took beverage orders. Jonathan ordered a milkshake, but this time the waitress was one step ahead. "Jonathan, we have milk and ice cream, but I'm sorry we don't have any syrup." To which Jon asked, "Do you have a car?"

Other youngsters may show advanced abilities in number concepts, maps, telling time, and block building. Their skills in such activities far exceed that of their age-mates. Not only do these characteristics define gifted preschoolers but they also provide a rationale and structure for intervention.

Source: From S. Baum, "The gifted preschooler: An awesome delight," *Gifted Child Today, 9*(4), 42–43. Reprinted with permission.

TRANSITION

For gifted students who are achieving near their potential and are given opportunities to take on adult roles, the transitions from childhood to adolescence to adulthood and from high school to higher education or employment are typically not very problematic. In many ways, transitions for gifted youths tend to mirror the problems in transitions faced by adolescents and young adults with disabilities.

Consider the case of Raymond Kurzweil, inventor of the Kurzweil Reading Machine for blind persons (see Chapter 9).

> A summer job, at age 12, involved statistical computer programming. Could a kid comprehend IBM's daunting Fortran manual? He very well could. Soon, in fact, IBM would be coming to young Kurzweil for programming advice.
>
> By the time he was graduated from high school, the whiz kid had earned a national reputation, particularly for a unique computer program that could compose original music in the styles of Mozart and Beethoven, among others.
>
> After carefully weighing all his options, Kurzweil decided to enroll in the Massachusetts Institute of Technology so that he could mingle with the gurus of the then-emerging science of artificial intelligence. Kurzweil was in his element. He was also rather quickly in the chips. (Neuhaus, 1988, p. 66)

Today, at middle age, Kurzweil is a highly successful entrepreneur who is chairman of several high-tech corporations he founded. (See the box on p.488 for the story of another "whiz kid.")

Not all adolescents and young adults who are gifted take transitions in stride. Many need personal and career counseling and a networking system that links students to school and community resources (Clifford, Runions, & Smyth, 1986; Delisle, 1992). Some are well served by an eclectic approach that employs the best features of enrichment and acceleration (Feldhusen & Kolloff, 1986).

If there is a central issue in the education of gifted adolescents, it is that of acceleration versus enrichment. Proponents of enrichment feel that students who are gifted need continued social contact with their age peers. They argue that gifted students should follow the curriculum of their agemates and study topics in greater depth. Proponents of acceleration feel that the only way to provide challenging and appropriate education for those with special gifts and talents is to let them compete with older students. These educators argue that since the cognitive abilities of gifted students are advanced beyond their years, they should proceed through the curriculum at an accelerated pace.

Acceleration for adolescents who are gifted may mean early entrance to college or enrollment in college courses while attending high school. Acceleration programs, particularly in mathematics, have been evaluated very favorably (Brody & Stanley, 1991; Kolitch & Brody, 1992). In fact, early entrance to college on a full-time or part-time basis appears to work very well for the vast majority of gifted adolescents, as long as it is done with care and sensitivity to the needs of individual students (Brody & Stanley, 1991; Noble & Drummond, 1992). As Buescher (1991) points out, "Talented adolescents are *adolescents* first and foremost. They experience fully the regression, defensiveness, and relational fluctuations of normal adolescence" (p. 399). Thus, it is important to provide counseling and support services for students who enter college early to ensure that they have appropriate, rewarding social experiences that enhance their self-esteem, as well as academic challenges and successes in the courses they take.

The Gifted Adolescent: Richard

Richard P. Feynman grew up during the Depression, when most of his family probably did not know what to think about this unusually inquisitive boy. A Nobel Prize-winning physicist, Feynman traveled around the world and experienced firsthand many things as a painter, musician, safecracker, and gambler.

The following excerpt from his autobiography, *Surely You're Joking, Mr. Feynman,* describes the recollections of a former eleven-year-old electronics whiz.

> I enjoyed radios. I started with a crystal set that I bought at the store, and I used to listen to it at night in bed while I was going to sleep, through a pair of earphones. When my mother and father went out until late at night, they would come into my room and take the earphones off—and worry about what was going into my head while I was asleep.
>
> About that time I invented a burglar alarm, which was a very simple-minded thing: it was just a big battery and a bell connected with some wire. When the door to my room opened, it pushed the wire against the battery and closed the circuit, and the bell would go off.
>
> One night my mother and father came home from a night out and very, very quietly, so as not to disturb the child, opened the door to come into my room and take my earphones off. All of a sudden this tremendous bell went off with a helluva racket—BONG BONG BONG BONG BONG!!! I jumped out of bed yelling, "It worked! It worked!"

Source: From Richard P. Feynman, *Surely you're joking, Mr. Feynman* (New York: Bantam, 1989), pp. 3–4.

Beyond acceleration and enrichment, gifted adolescents need attention to social and personal development if they are to make successful and gratifying transitions to adulthood and careers. Like other groups of students with special characteristics and needs, they may benefit from opportunities to socialize and learn from other students who have similar characteristics and face similar challenges. They may be able to obtain particular benefit from reflecting on the nature and meaning of life and the directions they choose for themselves. Delisle (1992) discusses six realities that adults might use in guiding gifted adolescents in transition:

1. *Remember that the real basics go beyond reading, writing, and arithmetic.* (They include play and relaxation.) . . .
2. *You can be good at something you don't enjoy doing.* (Just because you're good at something doesn't mean you have to plan your life around doing it.) . . .
3. *You can be good at some things that are unpopular with your friends.* (It's a good idea to connect with others who share your preferences, beliefs, and experiences and to guard against stereotyping yourself or others.) . . .
4. *Life is not a race to see who can get to the end the fastest.* (Don't become preoccupied with performance, work, or success, and don't be afraid to try something at which you might not succeed.) . . .
5. *You have the ability to ask questions that should have answers but don't.* (Look and listen to the world around you, and become involved in making the world a better place.) . . .
6. *It's never too late to be what you might have been.* (Remember that you always have career options and pursue those goals that you want most.) (pp. 137–145)

Suggestions for Teaching
Students Who Are Gifted and Talented in General Education Classrooms

By Peggy L. Tarpley

WHAT TO LOOK FOR IN SCHOOL

As you know from reading the chapter, students who demonstrate gifted behavior are, in part, superior in some way and exhibit abilities and sensitivities that may allow them to express themselves in special ways, learn quickly, be self-sufficient, or understand their own and others' feelings, motivations, and strengths and weaknesses. Although this combination of characteristics, coupled with exceptional eagerness and curiosity, may make gifted students easy to recognize in your class, formally identifying students for gifted and talented programs may be more difficult.

HOW TO GATHER INFORMATION

Because there is no federal definition of *gifted and talented,* each state has established its own criteria for identifying these students and subsequently has developed programs based on these criteria. Consequently, programs differ from state to state. If you think any of your students may be gifted, ask your principal for the state guidelines to determine if the student might qualify for your district's specialized program. You may also contact the person in your building or in the central office who serves as coordinator for the gifted program and discuss the criteria your system has established. If you believe your student may meet these guidelines, collect samples of his or her work and record your observations of his or her productivity and creativity and share them with the gifted coordinator, who then may initiate a referral to the gifted and talented program.

TEACHING TECHNIQUES TO TRY

Just as school systems have different definitions and eligibility criteria, so they have different ways of meeting the educational needs of gifted students. In some schools, classroom teachers alone provide programming for their students who are gifted. Other schools offer resource classes taught by teachers trained in gifted education that students attend for specified periods of time each week. Still other school systems offer a variety of specialized programs, including honor classes, advanced placement courses, and special schools for students gifted in math or science or the arts. In all these arrangements (except special schools), classroom teachers assume the responsibility for providing educational experiences for their gifted students during most of the schoolday (Milgrim, 1989).

As educators of students who are gifted and talented continue to reflect on what teaching practices best encourage the potential of these students, they find that the content, process, product, and learning environment that comprise best practices for gifted and talented students are the same as those that comprise best practices for *all* students. It is important that all learners experience concepts at higher levels of thinking, interact with real-life problems, and generate products that require integrating skills and understanding. As is true of students with other exceptionalities, the assessment of learner needs and capabilities is what leads to identifying appropriate activities for individual learners.

Tomlinson (1995) illustrates the basic elements of effective practice and the variables that can be manipulated to produce the differentiation necessary to meet the needs of a variety of gifted students. She suggests that the learning environment should have an active orientation, in which flexible groupings take place based on the activity, the process, and the product desired. Both students and teachers should have escalating expectations about learning, and teachers should continually assess progress and adapt environments accordingly.

Given this learning environment:

- The *content* of learning will be rooted in basic principles such as high relevance, purposefulness, and transferability.
- The *process* of learning will balance critical and creative thought, be driven by concepts and generalizations, and promote cognition and metacognition.
- The *product* of learning will center on concepts and issues, use multiple modes of expression, and reflect real problems for which real audiences are interested in the solutions.

The differentiation for individual learner profiles comes in finding each student's balance on nine variables impacting content, process, and product. The variables refer to the individual ways in which learners act on or interact with information, ideas, materials, decision making, planning, and products/solutions. These variables span continua from foundational to transformational; from concrete to abstract; from simple to complex; from fewer facets to multifacets; from a smaller leap to a greater leap; from more structured to more open; from clearly defined to vaguely defined; from less independent to more independent; and from slower to faster.

What follows is a sampling of the ways you can differentiate for gifted learners in the areas of content, process, and product. Tomlinson (1995) lists many more and suggests that individual teachers—like you—will be able to add to the lists:

Content
Multiple texts
Compacting
Interest/learning centers

Process
Learning centers
Simulation
Tiered assignments
Graphic organizers
Problem-based learning
Multiple-intelligences assignments

Product
Tiered products assignments
Independent study
Negotiated criteria
Multiple-intelligences-based orientation

Through acceleration, enrichment, and independent learning, teachers strive to meet the unique needs of gifted learners. For these learners, as well as other exceptional learners, a "one-size-fits-all" approach is not recommended. Among the techniques from which teachers may select are curriculum compacting, mastery learning, problem-based learning, higher-level thinking, critical thinking, self-directed learning, learning centers, independent study, and contracts.

Remember, regardless of the techniques you choose, differentiation is the key to the best education for all students. As Tomlinson (1995) suggests:

> A given inquiry for advanced learners would be appropriate for them when it is at a level of transformation, abstractness, complexity, multifacetedness, mental leap, openness, and ambiguity that it causes those learners to stretch a moderate amount beyond their comfort zones in areas such as understanding, insight, skill, cognition, metacognition, production, and self-awareness. Pacing and independence required should be adjusted to the nature of the task and learner as well. By implication, these same learning experiences should not be too demanding for students less advanced in that particular area at that particular time. (pp. 18–19).

Curriculum Compacting

One means by which curricula are accelerated is by *curriculum compacting,* a procedure in which the teacher modifies the regular curriculum to provide additional time for students who are gifted to pursue alternate learning activities. To make these modifications, first identify the academic strengths of your gifted students, using a variety of information sources, such as school records, previous teacher recommendations, standardized and informal test results, and observation. Then decide what curricular area(s) is most appropriate for compacting, considering the following questions:

1. What does the student already know?
2. What does the student need to learn?
3. What activities will meet the student's learning needs?

Next, outline learning experiences, based on your student's strengths and interests. Finally, decide how to provide these alternative educational activities.

Mastery Learning

Teachers also use *mastery learning* to provide time for advanced study. In one application of mastery learning, students with high ability move sequentially through a body of knowledge at their own pace (Eby & Smutny, 1990). If these students demonstrate mastery of a new skill on a pretest, they progress immediately to the next skill in the sequence. Some schools extend the use of mastery learning from individual classrooms to a schoolwide system to eliminate students' being retaught mastered skills from year to year. Mastery learning may be managed in a variety of ways. Eby and Smutny (1990) report that in some schools, one classroom teacher has the responsibility for managing the schoolwide system and for teaching the nongraded material to all students. In other buildings, teachers from different grade levels team teach and students move from classroom to classroom. In order to implement either program, however, the schoolday must be scheduled so that certain subjects are taught to all students in the school at the same time of day. The key is to provide alternate learning experiences appropriate for gifted students once they have progressed through grade-level materials.

Problem-Based Learning

This approach uses an ill-structured or vague problem as the basis of student investigations. Teachers act as facilitators and tutors, rather than information givers. Students must employ planning, resource-gathering, and especially creative- and critical-thinking skills. This approach gives gifted students practice in attacking problems just as professionals in the field might do. In fact, this approach is currently used in a number of medical schools.

Higher-Level Thinking

This approach is based on Benjamin Bloom's *Taxonomy of educational objectives* (Bloom et al., 1956), which outlines six levels of thinking: the lower levels of knowledge and comprehension and the higher levels of application, analysis, synthesis, and evaluation. Teachers enrich gifted students' learning by providing educational experiences at the four higher levels of the taxonomy. For example:

> The primary social studies curriculum usually includes content on the topic of "communities." While textbooks . . . cover the basic knowledge and comprehension levels on this topic by providing students with definitions and main ideas, a gifted curriculum can be developed on the topic by writing educational objectives at the higher levels.
>
> At the application level, students can be asked to draw a map of their own community.
>
> At the analysis level, students can compare and contrast two or more communities.
>
> At the synthesis level, students can create a play about important people in the community.
>
> At the evaluation level, students can share their opinions about their own community's services. (Eby & Smutny, 1990, p. 171)

In general, developing higher-level thinking skills means that students spend time exploring ideas, testing the applicability of theories, synthesizing ideas into original solutions, and judging the quality of these solutions (Feldhusen 1989). Consult the gifted education specialist in your building or school system for assistance in developing higher-level thinking skills.

Critical Thinking

Although there are many types of thinking skills in addition to the cognitive skills represented in Bloom's taxonomy (e.g., creative thinking skills and metacognitive skills), "teaching children to think critically has been perhaps the most popular, fastest growing part of the thinking skills movement" (French & Rhoder, 1992, p. 183).

Ennis (1985) defines *critical thinking* as "reflective and reasonable thinking that is focused on deciding what to believe or do" (p. 45). It includes skills such as judging information and making decisions. Raths and his colleagues (1986) provide examples of the following critical-thinking skills:

Judging/Examining Assumptions

1. When we hear our class is getting a new student—a girl from Vietnam—what assumptions might we make?
2. When we fill a thermos with hot soup and seal the thermos, what assumptions are we making?

Making Decisions

1. Give students a flashlight. Ask them to design investigations to show what they can find out about light.
2. When Michael sees Sarah throwing trash from her lunch on the playground, what should Michael do? What are his responsibilities?

As Eby and Smutny (1990) point out, many educators do not advocate adding new critical-thinking programs but rather suggest that teachers remodel existing programs so that students apply critical-thinking strategies to the subject matter they study. In addition, Chaffee (1987, cited in Eby and Smutny) recommends that students apply problem-solving and critical-thinking strategies to real problems in their own lives, rather than to puzzles and simulated problems. Again, the specialist in gifted education in your building or district can provide assistance in the systematic development of critical-thinking skills.

Self-Directed Learning

One model of self-directed learning is Renzulli's *enrichment triad curriculum model* (Renzulli, 1977), which is designed to develop student interest in topics and higher-order thinking skills and to enable gifted students to conduct investigations in areas of interest. For more information on this model, see Renzulli and Reis's book *The triad reader* (1986).

Treffinger developed another independent study curriculum called *self-directed learning.* Treffinger and Barton (1988) believe the process of self-directed learning culminates in students being able to "initiate plans for their own learning, identify resources, gather data, and develop and evaluate their own products and projects" (p. 30). Teachers use a variety of techniques—such as learning centers, independent study, and contracting—to promote self-directed learning in regular education classes.

Learning Centers

Teachers often use *learning centers* to provide enrichment activities for their students. To promote self-directed learning, however, these centers must offer instructional opportunities in areas that are specifically designed and sequenced to encourage student independence.

Teachers in Richland County, Ohio, found they could offer activities in regular education classes that developed the productivity and creativity of their gifted students by designing interest development centers (IDCs)(Burns, 1985). Unlike traditional learning centers, which help students master basic curriculum skills, IDCs facilitate students' independent explorations of a wide range of topics not included in the regular curriculum. The teachers stocked their centers with manipulative, media, and print materials along with several suggestions for examining and experimenting in special interest areas. In keeping with the Renzulli model, they also included methodological resources that helped promote interest in long-term research. For example, one teacher developed a center about bicycling that contained materials on how to create a bike path and how to approach the city council for permission to build bike racks near businesses that students frequented. For additional information and specific independent learning center resources and ideas, see Burns (1985).

Independent Study

Sometimes, students will develop and/or maintain great interest in topics they have explored. When this happens, you may decide to help them conduct independent study on a topic. *Independent study* involves not only exploring a topic in depth but also producing an original product that is disseminated to an appropriate audience. Because directing an independent study project is time consuming and requires an understanding of the topic, teachers often solicit the help of the gifted resource teacher or another person who is knowledgeable about the subject and willing to participate in the project (Pendarvis, Howley, & Howley, 1990). The role of the teacher and resource person(s) is not to direct the study but rather to serve as assistants who help the student define and frame the problem, establish realistic goals and timelines, become aware of a variety of available usable resources, identify both the product that the study will produce and an audience for the product, and evaluate the study. In addition, the adults involved in the project must reinforce the student's work throughout the study and provide methodological help when necessary. To learn more about the process of guiding gifted students through independent study, see Reis and Cellerino (1983) .

Contracts

You also can facilitate self-directed learning by providing individualized exploration and instruction in the form of *student contracts.* Like business contracts, these documents are negotiated with the student and describe the area he or she will study and the procedures and resources he or she will use in the investigation. When contracts are used to guide independent study, they also can specify the intended audience, the means of dissemination, deadlines for stages or steps in the study, and dates and purposes of periodic meetings with the teacher (Tuttle & Becker, 1983).

HELPFUL RESOURCES

School Personnel

In the pursuit of ideas, information, and materials to use in self-directed learning activities, the school media specialist can be a valuable resource. He or she can orient students to the variety of materials that are available, including yearbooks, geographical, political, and economic atlases; career files; subject-related dictionaries; periodical indexes; bibliographic references and databases; and information available on microfilm and microfiche. Specialists also can help students learn how to evaluate resource materials by assessing such factors as the purpose of the work and its intended audience; the author's (or editor's) credentials; completeness of index and reference citations; and accuracy and completeness of charts, statistics, graphs, timelines, and other illustrative materials (Flack, 1986, p. 175).

For students involved in independent study, media specialists may be helpful resources in creating research products by instructing students in the use of such processes as videotaping, laminating, and making transparencies. Media specialists also may encourage and facilitate the dissemination of the products. For example, a second-grade student decided to write a children's talking book on Tchaikovsky that was intended for other elementary students and that would be housed permanently in his school's library (Reis & Cellerino, 1983).

Instructional Methods and Materials

Adams, D. M., & Hamm, M. E. (1989). *Media and literacy: Learning in an electronic age—Issues, ideas, and teaching strategies.* Springfield, IL: Charles C. Thomas.

Clark, B. (1992). *Growing up gifted: Developing the potential of children at home and at school* (4th ed.). New York: Merrill/Macmillan.

Cook, C., & Carlisle, J. (1985). *Challenges for children: Creative activities for gifted and talented primary students.* West Nyack, NY: The Center for Applied Research in Education.

Cox, J., Daniel, N., & Boston, B.O. (1985). *Educating able learners: Programs and promising practices.* Austin, TX: University of Texas Press.

Cushenbery, D. C. (1987). *Reading instruction for the gifted.* Springfield, IL: Charles C. Thomas.

Davis, G. A., & Rimm, S. B. (1989). *Education of the gifted and talented.* Englewood Cliffs, NJ: Prentice Hall.

Dirkes, M.A. (1988). Self-directed thinking in the curriculum. *Roeper Review, 11,* 92–94.

Feldhuser, J., Van Tassel-Baska, J., & Seeley, K. (1989). *Excellence in educating the gifted.* Denver: Love.

French, J. N., & Rhoder, C. (1992). *Teaching thinking skills: Theory and practice.* New York: Garland.

Gallagher, J. J. (1986). *Teaching the gifted child* (3rd. ed.). Boston: Allyn and Bacon.

Greenlaw, M. J., & McIntosh, M. E. (1988). *Educating the gifted.* Chicago: American Library Association.

Kondziolka, G., & Normandeau, P. (1986). Investigation: An interdisciplinary unit. *Gifted Child Today, 9,* 52–54.

Lewis, R. B., & Doorlag, D. H. (1991). *Teaching special students in the mainstream* (3rd ed.). New York: Merrill/Macmillan.

Lukasevich, A. (1983). Three dozen useful information sources on reading for the gifted. *Reading Teacher, 36,* 542–548.

Milgrim, R. M. (1989). *Teaching gifted and talented learners in regular classrooms.* Springfield, IL: Charles C. Thomas.

Parker, B. N. (1989). *Gifted students in regular classrooms.* Boston: Allyn and Bacon.

Parker, J. P. (1989). *Instructional strategies for teaching the gifted.* Boston: Allyn and Bacon.

Pendarvis, E. D., Howley, A. A., & Howley, C. B. (1990). *The abilities of gifted children.* Englewood Cliffs, NJ: Prentice Hall.

Romey, W. D., & Hibert, M. L. (1988). *Teaching the gifted and talented in the science classroom* (2nd ed.). Washington, DC: National Education Association.

Schlichter, C. L. (1988). Thinking skills instruction for all classrooms. *Gifted Child Today, 11,* 24–28.

Shore, B. M., Cornell, D. G., Robinson, A., & Ward, V. S. (1991). *Recommended practices in gifted education.* New York: Teachers College Press.

Sisk, D. (1987). *Creative teaching of the gifted.* New York: McGraw-Hill.

Curricular Models, Adaptations, and Materials

Beyer, B. K. (1991). *Teaching thinking skills: A handbook for secondary school teachers.* Boston: Allyn and Bacon.

Betts, G. T. (1985). *Autonomous learner model for the gifted and talented.* Greeley, CO: Autonomous Learning Publications and Specialists.

Bloom, B. J., et. al. (1956). *Taxonomy of educational objectives—Handbook I: Cognitive domain.* New York: McKay.

Clausen, R. E., & Clausen, D. R. (1990). *Gifted and talented students.* Milwaukee, WI: Department of Public Instruction.

Feldhusen, J. F. (1988). *Purdue creative thinking program.* West LaFayette, IN: Purdue University Media-Based Services.

Feldhusen, J. F., & Kolloff, M. B. (1988). A three-stage model for gifted education. *Gifted Child Today, 11,* 14–18.

Guilford, J. P. (1967). *The nature of human intelligence.* New York: McGraw-Hill.

Juntune, J. J. (1986). *Successful programs for the gifted and talented.* St. Paul, MN: National Association for Gifted Children.

Maker, C. J., & Nielson, A. B. (1995). *Teaching models in education of the gifted* (2nd ed.). Austin, TX: Pro-Ed.

Maker, C. J., & Orzechowski-Harland, D. (1993). *Critical issues in gifted education: Vol. III. Programs for the gifted in regular classrooms.* Austin, TX: Pro-Ed.

Renzulli, J. (1977). *The enrichment triad model.* Mansfield, CT: Creative Learning Press.

Renzulli, J. S. (Ed.). (1986). *Systems and models for developing programs for the gifted and talented.* Mansfield Center, CT: Creative Learning Press.

Renzulli, J. S., & Callahan, C. M. (1986). *New directions in creativity.* Mansfield Center, CT: Creative Learning Press.

Renzulli, J. S., & Reis, S. (1985). *The schoolwide enrichment model: A comprehensive plan for educational excellence.* Mansfield Center, CT: Creative Learning Press.

Robinson, A. (1986). Elementary language arts for the gifted: Assimilation and accommodation in the curriculum. *Gifted Child Quarterly, 30,* 178–181.

Treffinger, D. J. (1975). Teaching for self-directed learning: A priority for the gifted and talented. *Gifted Child Quarterly, 12,* 46–59.

Treffinger, D. J. (1978). Guidelines for encouraging independence and self-direction among gifted students. *Journal of Creative Behavior, 12,* 14–19.

Udall, A. J., & Daniels, M. A. (1991). *Creating the thoughtful classroom: Strategies to promote student thinking.* Tucson, AZ: Zephyr Press.

Van Tassel-Baska, J., Feldhusen, J., Seeley, K., Wheatley, G., Silverman, L., & Foster, W. (Eds.). *Comprehensive curriculum for gifted learners.* Boston: Allyn and Bacon.

Literature about Individuals Who Are Gifted and Talented

Elementary

Aliki. (1984). *Feelings.* New York: Greenwillow. (Nonfiction = NF)
Berger, G. (1980). *The gifted and talented.* New York: Franklin Watts. (NF)
Calvert, P. (1980). *The snowbird.* New York: Charles Scribner's Sons. (Fiction = F)
Cooney B. (1982). *Miss Rumphius.* New York: Viking. (F)
Fitzgerald, J. D. (1967). *The great brain.* New York: Dial Press. (F)
Fitzhugh, L. (1984). *Harriet the spy.* New York: Harper & Row. (F)
Greenwald, S. (1987). *Alvin Webster's surefire plan for success (and how it failed).* Boston: Little, Brown. (F)
Hassler, J. (1981). *Jemmy.* New York: Atheneum. (F)
Heide, F. (1985). *Tales for the perfect child.* New York: Lothrop, Lee, and Shepard. (F)
Manes, S. (1982). *Be a perfect person in just three days!* Boston: Houghton Mifflin. (F)
Oneal, Z. (1980). *The language of goldfish.* New York: Viking Press. (F)
Sobol, D. J. (1963). *Encyclopedia Brown: Boy detective.* New York: Thomas Nelson. (F)

Middle and High School

Evernden, M. (1985). *The dream keeper.* New York: Lothrop, Lee & Shepard Books. (F)
Pfeffer, S. B. (1989). *Dear dad, love Laurie.* New York: Scholastic. (F)
Voight, C. (1982). *Tell me if the lovers are losers.* New York: Atheneum. (F)
Voight, C. (1983). *Solitary blue.* New York: Atheneum. (F)
Zindel, P. (1989). *A begonia for Miss Applebaum.* New York: Harper and Row. (F)

Software

Adventure Master, CBS Software, One Fawcett Place, Greenwich, CT 06836.
Analogies, Hartley Courseware, Inc., 3451 Dunkle Drive, Suite 200, Lansing, MI 48911–4216, (800) 247–1380.
Animate, Brøderbund Software, Inc., 500 Redwood Blvd., P.O. Box 6121, Novato, CA 94948–6121, (800) 521–6263.
Appleworks, Claris, 440 Clyde Avenue, Mountain View, CA 94043, (415) 960–1500. (Word-processing).
Astronomy, The Voyager Company, 2139 Manning Avenue, Los Angeles, CA 90025.
Bank Street Music Writer, Mindscape, Inc., 344 Dundee Road, North Brook, IL 60062.
Bank Street School Filer Databases, Sunburst Communications, 101 Castleton Street, Pleasantville, NY 10570, (800) 628–8897.
Creativity Unlimited, Sunburst Communications, 101 Castleton Street, Pleasantville, NY 10570, (800) 628–8897.
Dazzle Draw, Brøderbund Software, Inc., 500 Redwood Blvd., P.O. Box 6121, Novato, CA 94948–6121, (800) 521–6263.
Dinosaurs, Advanced Ideas, Inc., 680 Hawthorne Dr., Tiburon, CA 94920, (415) 425–5086.
Electronic Encyclopedia, Grolier Electronic Publishing, Inc., Sherman Turnpike, Danbury, CT 06816, (800) 858–8858.
Fermi-Pico-Bagel Logo Game, Trillium Press, Box 921, Madison Square Station, New York, NY 10159, (212) 505–1440.
Gears, Sunburst Communications, 101 Castleton Street, Pleasantville, NY 10570, (800) 628–8897.
In Search of the Amazing Thing, Spinnaker, One Kendall Square, Cambridge, MA 02139, (617) 494–1200.
Incredible Laboratory, Sunburst Communications, 101 Castleton Street, Pleasantville, NY 10570, (800) 628–8897.
Mathware, Trillium Software, Box 921, Madison Square Station, New York, NY 10159.
Music Studies, Activision, Inc., 2350 Bayshore Frontage Road, Mountain View, CA 94043.
National Gallery of Art, The Voyager Company, 2139 Manning Avenue, Los Angeles, CA 90025, (213) 475–3524.
Newsroom, Springboard, 7807 Creekridge Creek, Minneapolis, MN 55435, (800) 655–6301.
Operation Fog, Scholastic, Inc., P.O. Box 7503, 2931 East McCarty, Jefferson City, MO 65102, (800) 654–6301.
Planetary Construction Set, Sunburst Communications, 101 Castleton Street, Pleasantville, NY 10570, (800) 628–8897.
Print Shop, Brøderbund Software, Inc., 500 Redwood Blvd., P.O. Box 6121, Novato, CA 94948–6121, (800) 521–6263.
Science Tool Kit, Brøderbund Software, Inc., 500 Redwood Blvd., P.O. Box 6121, Novato, CA 94948–6121, (800) 521–6263.
Slide Show, Videodiscovery, P.O. Box 85878, Seattle, WA 98145, (206) 547–7981.

Organizations

Association for the Gifted, the Council for Exceptional Children, 1920 Association Drive, Reston, VA 22091, (703) 620–3660.
Gifted Child Society, 190 Rock Road, Glen Rock, NJ 07452, (201) 444–6530.
National Association for Gifted Children, 1155 Fifteenth Street, N.W., No. 1002, Washington, DC 20005, (202) 785–4268.

BIBLIOGRAPHY FOR TEACHING SUGGESTIONS

Bloom, B. J., et al. (1956). *Taxonomy of educational objectives—Handbook I: Cognitive domain.* New York: McKay.
Burns, D. E. (1985). Land of opportunity. *Gifted Child Today, 37,* 41–45.
Clark, B. (1992). *Growing up gifted: Developing the potential of children at home and school* (4th ed.). New York: Merrill/Macmillan.
Eby, J. W., & Smutny, J. F. (1990). *A thoughtful overview of gifted education.* New York: Longman.
Ennis, R. H. (1985). A logical basis for measuring critical thinking skills. *Educational Leadership, 43,* 44–48.
Feldhusen, J., Van Tassel-Baska, J., & Seeley, K. (1989). *Excellence in educating the gifted.* Denver, CO: Love.

Flack, J. D. (1986). A new look at a valued partnership: The library media specialist and gifted students. *School Library Media Quarterly, 14,* 174–179.

French, J. N., & Rhoder, C. (1992). *Teaching thinking skills: Theory and practice.* New York: Garland.

Maker, C. J., & Nielson, A. B. (1995). *Teaching models in education of the gifted* (2nd ed.). Austin, TX: Pro-Ed.

Milgrim, R. M., (1989). *Teaching gifted and talented learners in regular classrooms.* Springfield, IL: Charles C. Thomas.

Pendarvis, E. D., Howley, A. A., & Howley, C. B. (1990). *The abilities of gifted children.* Englewood Cliffs, NJ: Prentice Hall.

Raths, L. E., Wassermann, S., Jonas, A., & Rothstein, A. (1986). *Teaching for thinking: Theory, strategies, and activities for the classroom* (2nd ed.). New York: Teachers College, Columbia University.

Reis, S. M., & Cellerino, M. (1983). Guiding gifted students through independent study. *Teaching Exceptional Children, 15,* 136–139.

Renzulli, J. S. (1977). *The enrichment triad model.* Mansfield Center, CT: Creative Learning Press.

Renzulli, J. S. (1981). *The revolving door identification model.* Mansfield Center, CT: Creative Learning Press.

Renzulli, J. S., & Reis, S. M. (Eds.). (1986). *The triad reader.* Mansfield Center, CT: Creative Learning Press.

Starko, A. (1986). Meeting the needs of the gifted throughout the school day: Techniques for curriculum compacting. *Roeper Review, 9,* 27–33.

Tomlinson, C. A. (1995). *Good teaching for one and all: Does gifted education have an instructional identity?* Unpublished manuscript, University of Virginia.

Treffinger, D. J., & Barton, B. L. (1988). Foster independent learning. *Gifted Child Today, 11,* 28–30.

Tuttle, F. B., & Becker, L. A. (1983). *Program design and development for gifted and talented students* (2nd ed.). Washington, DC: National Education Association.

SUMMARY

Disagreements about how to define *giftedness* center on the questions of exactly how gifted children excel; how this excellence is measured; the degree to which the individual must excel to be considered gifted; who should make up the comparison group; and why giftedness should be identified at all. Even the terms used can be confusing: *Precocity* indicates remarkable early development; *insight* involves separating relevant from irrelevant information and combining information in novel and productive ways; *genius* refers to rare intellectual powers; *creativity* has to do with the ability to express novel and useful ideas, to see novel relationships, to ask original and crucial questions; and *talent* indicates a special ability within a particular area.

The use of individually administered intelligence tests as the only basis for defining giftedness has met with increasing dissatisfaction. First, traditional intelligence tests are limited in what they measure. Second, intelligence is being reconceptualized. Whether intelligence should be considered a general characteristic or distinguished according to unique areas is an ongoing controversy. Third, children exhibit gifted performance in specific domains. For example, a child with a physical disability might be gifted in any area not impaired by his or her other specific disability.

A consistent myth is that individuals who are gifted are superior beings. Current thinking suggests that individuals may have extraordinary talents in specifics areas but ordinary talents in others. The concept of giftedness is now considered to be a social construct, as opposed to a fixed human characteristic. Moreover, giftedness may be present or not present at different times in an individual's life. Thus, prevalence figures are difficult to establish.

As with some other exceptionalities, the causes of gifted behavior are varied and most likely represent a combination of biological and environmental factors. Although genetic inheritance may be a factor, giftedness is not specific to any socioeconomic or cultural or ethnic minority group. Current research suggests that one's collection of genes sets limits of performance; but the actual performance within those limits is determined by environmental factors.

A culturally consensual definition of giftedness includes five criteria: excellence, rarity, demonstrability, productivity, and value. For the purposes of education this definition would be expanded to include high ability, high creativity, and high task commitment.

Identification and selection of students for special programs must be based on multiple criteria to avoid bias against neglected groups of gifted students. To ensure fairness, principles of identification must take into account the varied definitions of giftedness and recognize the effects of cultural variation—both among and within cultures—on children's behavior.

Giftedness has been recognized in every society throughout history, and gifted individuals have been stereotyped as either physically and socially inept or as superhuman. Most individuals who are gifted fit neither category. Identification of giftedness based on IQ scores has often been flawed or biased in favor of physically superior or economically privileged children. Gifted students tend to be far ahead of their agemates in specific areas of academic performance, and the majority of students who show giftedness enter occupations that demand greater than average intellectual ability, creativity, and motivation.

The link between giftedness and self-concept is uncertain. Many students who are gifted are self-aware, self-assured, and socially skilled. Exceptionally gifted or precocious children may constitute a group for which extraordinary adaptations of schooling are required.

American societal attitudes toward giftedness reflect a love–hate relationship: We love the good things giftedness can produce but hate to acknowledge superior intelligence. This is in contrast to some other cultures, in which advanced abilities are seen as a divine gift to be nurtured.

Educational reforms during the 1990s hold both promise and danger for the education of students who are gifted. One of the most controversial reform topics is that of ability grouping, which some believe to be discriminatory. Five popular reforms of the 1990s with potential impact of gifted students are middle schools, site-based management, cooperative learning, outcome-based learning, and teacher accountability.

Neglected groups of gifted students include underachievers—those who fail to achieve at a level consistent with their abilities, for whatever reason. Underachievement is often a problem of minority students and those with disabilities, whose special abilities tend to be overlooked because of biased expectations and/or the values of the majority. Students who display physical characteristics typically associated with severe mental retardation may be intellectually brilliant; unless this is acknowledged, however, the talents of students with cerebral palsy and other physical disabilities may be easily overlooked. Gifted females are the largest single group of neglected gifted students.

Education of students who are gifted and talented should be based on three characteristics: (1) curriculum designed to accommodate advanced cognitive skills, (2) instructional strategies consistent with learning styles in particular curriculum areas, and (3) administrative facilitation of grouping for instruction. Programs and practices in the education of gifted students are extremely varied and include special schools, acceleration, special classes, tutoring, and enrichment during the schoolyear or summer. Administrative plans for modifying the curriculum include enrichment in the classroom, use of consultant teachers, resource rooms, community mentors, independent study, special classes, and special schools.

Acceleration has not been a popular plan for educating gifted students, although considerable research supports it. Models of enrichment include a schoolwide plan in which students continue to engage in enrichment activities for as long as they are able to go beyond the usual curriculum of their agemates. This model is designed to improve the learning environment for all students.

Teachers of students who are gifted should exhibit characteristics that are desirable for all teachers. However, they also must be particularly intelligent, creative, energetic, enthusiastic, and committed to excellence.

Early intervention entails early identification of special abilities, providing stimulation to preschool children to foster giftedness, and special provisions such as acceleration to make education appropriate for the young child's advanced skills. Gifted young children appear to have particular skills much like those of older nongifted children. Special care is needed not to assume that a child's emotional and social development are advanced just because his or her language and cognitive skills are advanced.

Transitions to adolescence, adulthood, and higher education and employment are typically not the problems for high-achieving gifted children that they are for children with disabilities. Nevertheless, many do need personal and career counseling and help in making contacts with school and community resources. A major issue is acceleration versus enrichment. Programs of acceleration (especially in mathematics, in which students skip grades or complete college-level work early) have been evaluated very positively.

Joanne O'Connell
Joanne O'Connell was left with a number of disabilities, including a visual impairment after a near drowning accident that happened when she was 11. She is now 28 years old. She exhibits her painting widely in the East, and won a 1995 National Juried Art Competition through the Ebensburg (PA) Center. She is also a poet and actress.

12

Parents and Families

Sun shone that day long ago in Corcloon. Asleep in his blue bed Joseph looked the picture of pleasant childlike thimblework. Nora serenely simpered as she lifted him. He gazed his hurt gaze, lip protruding, eyes busy in conversation. He ordered her to look out the window at the sunshine. He looked hard at her ear ordering her to listen to the birds singing. Then jumping on her knees he again asked her to cock her ear and listen to the village children . . . He showed her his arms, his legs, his useless body. Looking at his mother he blamed her, he damned her, he mouthed his cantankerous why, why, why me? . . . she tried to distract him. Lifting him in her arms she brought him outside into the farmyard. "Come on till I show you the calves," she coaxed. His lonely tears rushed even faster. He knew why she tried to divert his boyish questioning. . . . "All right," she said, "we'll go back inside and talk." . . . she then sat down and faced her erstwhile boy, . . . Meanwhile he cried continuously, conning himself that he had beaten her to silence. "I never prayed for you to be born crippled," she said. "I wanted you to be full of life, able to run and jump and talk . . . Listen here Joseph, you can see, you can hear, you can think, you can understand everything you hear, you like your food, you like nice clothes, you are loved by me and Dad. We love you just as you are.". . . She got on with her work while he got on with his crying. The decision arrived at that day was burnt forever in his mind. He was only three years in age but he was now fanning the only spark he saw, his being alive and more immediate, his being wanted just as he was.

Christopher Nolan
Under the Eye of the Clock: The Life Story of Christopher Nolan

A fertile ground for conflict or harmony, the family—especially the family with a family member who has a disability—is the perfect locale for studying the interplay of human emotion and behavior. Think of your own family as you were growing up. Think of the dynamics of interaction among you and your siblings and parents. These interactions were no doubt carried out within the full range of human emotions. Now, add to this mixture of human interaction a dose of disability. Consider how much more complex living in your family would have been if you had had a brother like Joseph, with severe cerebral palsy (see p. 497).

In addition to underscoring the complexities of living with a family member with disabilities, the autobiographical account of Joseph and his mother also demonstrates how resilient some families can be in the face of extreme difficulties. A child with disabilities does not always threaten the well-being of a family. Reactions of family members to the individual with a disability can run the gamut from absolute rejection to absolute acceptance, from intense hate to intense love, from total neglect to total overprotection. In fact, some parents and siblings assert that having a family member with a disability has actually strengthened the family. As highlighted by the interaction between Joseph and his mother, however, coping with the stress of raising and living with a child who has a disability rarely comes easily.

In this chapter, we explore the dynamics of families with children who are disabled and discuss parental involvement in their treatment and education. Before proceeding further, however, it is instructive to consider the role of parents of children who are disabled from a historical perspective.

PROFESSIONALS' CHANGING VIEWS OF PARENTS

Today, knowledgeable professionals who work with exceptional learners are aware of the importance of the family. They now recognize that the family of the person with a disability, especially the parents, can help in their educational efforts. To ignore the family is shortsighted because it can lessen the effectiveness of teaching.

Even though today we recognize how crucial it is to consider the concerns of parents and families in treatment and educational programs for individuals who are disabled, this was not always the case. Professionals' views of the role of parents have changed dramatically. In the not too distant past, some professionals looked to the parents primarily as a cause of some of the child's problems or as a place to lay blame when practitioners' interventions were ineffective. According to one set of authorities, negative views of parents were in some ways a holdover from the **eugenics movement** of the late nineteenth and early-twentieth centuries (Turnbull & Turnbull, 1990). Professionals associated with the eugenics movement believed in the selective breeding of humans. For example, they proposed sterilization of people with mental retardation because they erroneously believed that virtually all cases of mental retardation were caused by heredity.

eugenics movement. A popular movement of the late-nineteenth and early-twentieth centuries that supported the selective breeding of humans; resulted in laws restricting the marriage of individuals with mental retardation and sterilization of some of them.

Although the eugenics movement had largely died out by the 1930s and few professionals any longer blamed disabilities primarily on heredity, the climate was ripe for some of them to blame a variety of disabilities, especially emotional problems, on the childrearing practices of parents. For example, until the 1970s and 1980s, when research demonstrated a biochemical basis for autism, it was quite popular to pin the blame for this condition on the parents, especially the mother. The leading proponent of this viewpoint, Bruno Bettelheim, asserted that mothers who were cold

Misconceptions about
Parents and Families of Persons with Disabilities

Myth	Fact
Myth Parents are to blame for many of the problems of their children with disabilities.	**Fact** Parents can influence their children's behavior, but so, too, can children affect how their parents behave. Research shows that some children with disabilities are born with difficult temperaments, which can affect parental behavior.
Myth Parents must experience a series of reactions—shock and disruption, denial, sadness, anxiety and fear, and anger—before adapting to the birth of a child with a disability.	**Fact** Parents do not go through emotional reactions in lockstep fashion. They may experience some, or all, of these emotions but not necessarily in any particular order.
Myth Many parents of infants with disabilities go from physician to physician, "shopping" for an optimistic diagnosis.	**Fact** Just the opposite is often true. Parents frequently suspect that something is wrong with their baby but are told by professionals not to worry—that the child will outgrow the problem. Then they seek another opinion.
Myth The father is unimportant in the development of the child with a disability.	**Fact** Although they are frequently ignored by researchers and generally do experience less stress than mothers, fathers can play a critical role in the dynamics of the family. The father's role has become more important, but research indicates that his role is still often indirect, that is, the father can influence the mother's reactions to the child.
Myth Siblings are usually unaffected by the addition of a child with a disability to the family.	**Fact** Siblings often experience the same emotional reactions as parents, and their lack of maturity can make coping with these emotions more difficult.
Myth The primary role of the early intervention professional should be to provide expertise for the family.	**Fact** Many authorities now agree that professionals should help parents become more involved in making decisions for the family.
Myth The typical family in the United States has two parents, is middle class, and has only the father working outside the home.	**Fact** Demographics are changing rapidly. There are now many more families with both parents working as well as more single-parent families and families living in poverty.
Myth Parents who elect not to be actively involved (e.g., attending and offering suggestions at IEP meetings or visiting the school frequently) in their child's education and treatment are neglectful.	**Fact** Although it is desirable for parents to be involved, it is sometimes very difficult for them to do so because of their commitments to other family functions (e.g., work and child care).
Myth Professionals are always in the best position to help families of people with disabilities.	**Fact** Informal sources of support, such as extended family and friends, are often more effective than formal sources of support, such as professionals and agencies, in helping families adapt to a family member with a disability.
Myth Teachers should respect the privacy of parents and communicate with them only when absolutely necessary—for example, when their child has exhibited serious behavior problems.	**Fact** Teachers should initiate some kind of contact with parents as soon as possible, so that if something like a serious behavior infraction does occur, some rapport with the parents will already have been established.

Federal law stipulates that schools must make a concerted effort to involve parents and families in the education of their children with disabilities.

and unresponsive toward their children—"refrigerator moms"—produced autism in their children (Bettelheim, 1950, 1967).

In the late 1970s and early 1980s, professionals became less likely to blame parents automatically for the problems of their children. There were at least two reasons for this more positive view:

1. Richard Bell forwarded the notion that the direction of causation between child and adult behavior is a two-way street (Bell & Harper, 1977). Sometimes, the parent changes the behavior of the child or infant; sometimes, the reverse is true. With specific regard to children who are disabled, some researchers point out that these children, even as infants, sometimes possess difficult temperaments, which influence how parents respond to them (Brooks-Gunn & Lewis, 1984; Mahoney & Robenalt, 1986). Some infants who are disabled, for example, are relatively unresponsive to stimulation from their parents, making it more difficult to interact with them. With an understanding of the reciprocal nature of parent–child interaction, we are thus more likely, for example, to sympathize with a mother's frustration in trying to cuddle an infant with severe retardation or a father's anger in attempting to deal with his teenager who has an emotional or behavior disorder.
2. Professionals began to recognize the potentially positive influence of the family in the educational process. Although at first many authorities tended to think that parents needed training to achieve a positive effect on their children, more and more now have recognized that parents often have as much, or more, to offer than professionals regarding suggestions for the treatment of their children. The prevailing philosophy now dictates that, whenever possible, professionals should seek the special insights that parents can offer by virtue of living with their children. Furthermore, authorities today are less likely to view the purpose of early intervention to be training parents to assume the role of quasi-therapist or quasi-teacher (Guralnick, 1991). Instead, many believe the goal should be to develop and preserve the natural parent–child relationship as much as possible. In sum, a healthy parent–child relationship is inherently beneficial.

Recognizing the importance of the family, Congress has passed several federal laws stipulating that schools make a concerted effort to involve parents and families in the education of their children with disabilities. One of the provisions of Public Law (PL 94–142), the Education for All Handicapped Children Act (EHA, 1975), was to mandate that schools attempt to include parents in crafting their children's individualized education programs (IEPs) (see Chapter 1). In the case of children under three years of age, PL 99-457 (which amended EHA in 1986) dictated that schools must involve parents in developing **individualized family service plans (IFSPs)**. The focus of the IFSP is not only on the individual child who has a disability but also on his or her family; it specifies what services the family needs to enhance the child's development. The Individuals with Disabilities Education Act (IDEA, PL 101–476), passed in 1990, confirmed the provisions of earlier legislation, among other things.

THE EFFECTS OF A CHILD WITH A DISABILITY ON THE FAMILY

The birth of any child can have a significant effect on the dynamics of the family. The parents and other children must undergo a variety of changes to adapt to the presence of a new member. The effects on the family of the birth of a child who has a disability can be even more profound.

The everyday routines that most families take for granted are frequently disrupted in families with children who are disabled (Gallimore, Weisner, Bernheimer, Guthrie, & Nihira, 1993). For example, the child with a disability may require alterations in housing (e.g., the family may decide to move closer to therapists), household maintenance schedules (e.g., chores may not be done as quickly because of lack of time), and even parents' career goals (e.g., a parent may pass up a promotion in order to spend more time with the child).

Moreover, the child with a disability can have an impact on both parents and siblings and in different ways. We discuss parental reactions first and then sibling reactions.

Parental Reactions

A Stage Theory Approach. Traditionally, researchers and clinicians have suggested that parents go through a series of stages after learning they have a child with a disability. Some of these stages parallel the proposed sequence of responses that accompany a person's reactions to the death of a loved one. Based on interviews of parents of infants with serious physical disabilities, a representative set of stages includes shock and disruption, denial, sadness, anxiety and fear, anger, and finally adaptation (Drotar, Baskiewicz, Irvin, Kennell, & Klaus, 1975).

Several authorities have questioned the wisdom of this stage approach in understanding parental reactions. It is clear that parents should not be thought of as marching through a series of stages in lockstep fashion. It would be counterproductive, for example, to think, "This mother is now in the anxiety and fear stage; we need to encourage her to go through the anger stage, so she can finally adapt."

One argument against a strict stage model comes from the fact that many parents report that they do *not* engage in denial. In fact, they are often the first to suspect a problem. It is largely a myth that parents of children who are disabled go from physician to physician, "shopping" for a more favorable diagnosis. In fact, all too frequently, they have to convince the doctor that there is something wrong with their child (Akerley, 1985).

individualized family service plan (IFSP). A plan for services for young children with disabilities (under three years of age) and their families drawn up by professionals and parents; similar to an IEP for older children; mandated by PL 99–457.

Although parents may not go through these reactions in a rigid fashion, some do experience some or all these emotions at one time or another. A commonly reported reaction is guilt.

The Role of Guilt. The parents of a child with a disability frequently wrestle with the terrifying feeling that they are in some way responsible for their child's condition. Even though in the vast majority of cases, there is absolutely no basis for such thoughts, guilt is one of the most commonly reported feelings of parents of exceptional children.

The high prevalence of guilt is probably due to the fact that the primary cause of so many disabilities is unknown. Uncertainty about the cause of the child's disability creates an atmosphere conducive to speculation by the parents that they themselves are to blame. Mothers are particularly vulnerable. As Featherstone (1980), the mother of a boy who is blind and has hydrocephaly, mental retardation, cerebral palsy, and seizures, relates:

> Our children are wondrous achievements. Their bodies grow inside ours. If their defects originated in utero, we blame our inadequate bodies or inadequate caution. If . . . we accept credit for our children's physical beauty (and most of us do, in our hearts), then inevitably we assume responsibility for their physical defects.
>
> The world makes much of the pregnant woman. People open doors for her, carry her heavy parcels, offer footstools and unsolicited advice. All this attention seems somehow posited on the idea that she is creating something miraculously fine. When the baby arrives imperfect, the mother feels she has failed not only herself and her husband, but the rest of the world as well.
>
> Soon this diffuse sense of inadequacy sharpens. Nearly every mother fastens on some aspect of her own behavior and blames the tragedy on that. (pp. 73-74)

Dealing with the Public. In addition to ambivalence concerning the cause of the child's disability, parents can feel vulnerable to criticism from others about how they deal with their child's problems. Parents sometimes sense, whether deservedly or not, that they are the focus of others' attention and that their decisions regarding treatment, educational placement, and so forth are being evaluated by others (Featherstone, 1980).

The public sometimes can be cruel in their reactions to people with disabilities. People with disabilities—especially those who have disabilities that are readily observable—are inevitably faced with inappropriate reactions from those around them. John Hockenberry (1995), an award-winning correspondent for National Public Radio, who has been in a wheelchair since he was nineteen due to an automobile accident, talks about how total strangers sometimes ask him inappropriate questions:*

> Once on a very hot day on the Washington, D.C., subway a woman sat looking at me for a long time. She was smiling. I suspected that she knew me from the radio, that she had some picture of me somewhere. I am rarely recognized in public, but it was the only plausible explanation for why she kept watching me with a look of some recognition. Eventually, she walked up to me when the train stopped, said hello, then proceeded in a very serious voice.
>
> "Your legs seem to be normal."
>
> "They are normal, I just can't move them."

*From *Moving violations: War zones, wheelchairs, and declarations of independence,* by J. Hockenberry, 1995, New York: Hyperion. Reprinted with permission.

In Defense of My Daughter

One of the most difficult things that parents of children with disabilities are likely to face is the inappropriate reactions of others to their children, which can range from stares to taunting. The following excerpt tells how one mother decided to respond to mocking from one of her daughter's peers. Certainly, not all parents would respond in this way under similar circumstances, but for this mother, it proved satisfying:

> Years ago we played with our fat baby and occasionally worried that the day would come when she would go out into the world, and the world would be cruel to her for no reason at all. . . .
>
> "I'll be understanding," I said. "If some kid is mean, I'll explain to him about Kelly. It's really just a matter of education. Kids need to learn. They're afraid of what they don't understand." . . .
>
> Now that baby is eight years old, a person of fine sensibilities and definite opinions. Although we know she gets teased, we seldom see it.
>
> But one day last year I saw it, on the playground of a church summer day care program for elementary school-aged kids. As we entered the yard one girl stage-whispered loudly to her two friends. "Look! There's that REE-tard. Ooooh, I hope she's not coming here!"
>
> My eyes flew to Kelly's face where I saw a mask of stony indifference and icy dignity instantly install itself across her delicate features. And I knew that this was not the first time Kelly had experienced being summed up in the word "REE-tard." . . .
>
> I hated myself for being tongue-tied. I hated Taylor, Texas. I hated the church. I hated the little girl. I hated her friends. I hated the day care worker and the director too.
>
> We came home and Kelly went to her room to play with Heather, the imaginary friend who never fails her. My husband, Jerry, came home, and I cried and raged. I resolved I would never allow a thing like that to happen to my child again in my presence. I stormed to the word processor and wrote a script for myself entitled *In Defense of My Daughter.* I committed it to memory.
>
> Yesterday, a year later, I recited it to a young boy at the town swimming pool. He was putting on a macho act for his little friends as Kelly played by herself in the water. He twisted his mouth around and hung his tongue out in a grotesque parody of our brothers and sisters and children who have mental retardation. . . . He pulled his hands up and bent them over at awkward angles and lurched around with his head contorted against his neck. . . .
>
> I strode confidently to the side of the pool and caught his eye. "Come over here," I said. He glanced around nervously, hoping I was talking to someone else. "You!" I said loudly—Ursala the Sea Witch appears at Taylor Pool! He approached the rim of the pool. I did not crouch down in a friendly manner. I drew myself up even taller.
>
> "You were making fun of my little girl," I said.
>
> "No ma'am," he said. "I wasn't really."
>
> "You were too," I said, "and I want you to stop it. My daughter has Down syndrome. That's the way she was born. God made her just as he made you. That's the way he made her, and he does not make mistakes. He is ashamed of you for the way you are acting, and I am ashamed of you, and you should be ashamed of yourself."
>
> "Yes, ma'am," he said to the Sea Witch whose voice had risen and now drew the attention of a major portion of the kiddie pool. His eyes were huge and full of fear, all bravado long since gone. . . .
>
> "Please tell me you will never do that again," I said, committing him to a lifetime of disability awareness and inclusive behavior.
>
> "Yes, ma'am," he said. "I mean, no ma'am, I won't."
>
> "Thank you," I said. "She is my daughter, and I love her just like your own mom loves you. I won't let anyone hurt her feelings, just like your mom won't let anyone hurt you"—I hoped this was true.
>
> "Yes, ma'am," he repeated, tentatively backing away. He may have been uncertain of God's intentions in this matter, but he made no mistakes about mine.
>
> He was thus demoted from tormentor to just another towheaded eight-year-old with big blue eyes. Likewise, I hoped that Ursala the Sea Witch had become just some kid's mom as I returned to my bench.
>
> Kelly had watched this exchange from a corner silently, a little alarmed that perhaps she had done something wrong. She stood transfixed in the water as the offender returned to his friends and began a game of chase.
>
> Then, she looked up at me and smiled. "Look at me, Mommy," she said. "I can stand on my hands." She dived down and stood on her hands, then surfaced, happily proclaiming, "I am a fish."
>
> And my heart was sad, and my heart was happy.

Source: From "In defense of my daughter," by J. Horton, 1994, *Exceptional Parent, 24*(3), 47–48. Reprinted with the expressed consent and approval of *Exceptional Parent,* a monthly magazine for parents and families of children with disabilities and special health care needs. Subscription cost is $24 per year for 12 issues; call 1–800–247–8080. Offices at 120 State Street, Hackensack, NJ 07601.

> "Right, I know that. I mean, I can see that you are paralyzed." I was beginning to wonder where she was going with this. "Why aren't you shriveled up more?" she asked, as though she was inquiring about the time of day. "I notice that your legs aren't shrunken and all shriveled up. Why is that?" I was wearing shorts. She looked at my legs as though she was pricing kebab at the market. "I mean, I thought paralyzed legs got all shriveled up after a while. Were you injured recently?"
>
> "Uh . . . twelve years ago."
>
> This was a line of questioning I was unprepared for. I continued to smile and listen. I wondered under what circumstances I would ever roll up to a perfect stranger and ask the question, "Why aren't you shriveled up more?" . . .
>
> Perhaps the correct answer to the woman . . . was to take a deep breath and calmly explain the details of my legs and muscles as I understood them. Yet to do so I would have had to admit that there was a category of shriveled-up people, and that I was not one of them. I would also have had to concede that it was perfectly permissible for her to walk up to me and say something outrageous when that was the last thing I believed. (Hockenberry, 1995, pp. 93–95)

Hockenberry, an adult, had a difficult time knowing how to handle interactions with insensitive people. So think about how much more difficult it would be for a child. Understandably, parents often assume the burden of responding to inappropriate or even cruel reactions from the public. The box on page 503 relates how one mother decided to handle taunting from her child's peers.

Dealing with the Child's Feelings. In addition to dealing with the public's reactions to their child's disability, parents are also faced with the delicate task of talking with their child about his or her disability. This can be a difficult responsibility because the parents need to address the topic without making the disability seem more important than it actually is. In other words, the parents do not want to alarm the child or make him or her more concerned about the disability than is necessary.

Nevertheless, the child with a disability usually has questions about it: How did he or she get it? Will it go away? Will it get worse? Will he or she be able to live independently as adults? If possible, the parents should wait for the child to ask specific questions to which they can respond, rather than lecturing about generalities. However, it is a good idea for the parents to talk with the child at as early an age as possible, especially before the teenage years, when so many parents and children have problems communicating. Finally, most authorities recommend that parents be honest in their responses. Here is advice from an adult with cerebral palsy:

> Some parents have a tendency to hold back information, wanting to spare their son's or daughter's feelings. What they fail to realize is that, in the long term, being given correct information at an early age is very good for healthy development. And, if kids are informed, they can answer questions themselves, rather than depending on Mom or Dad to speak up for them. (Pierro, 1995, p. 92).

The Role of the Father. The vast majority of research on parental reactions to children with disabilities has focused on mothers. Recently, however, researchers have begun to turn their attention to fathers. Thus far, studies comparing the reactions of mothers and fathers to having children with disabilities have found that fathers experience the same amount or perhaps less stress than mothers (Bailey, Blasco, & Simeonsson, 1992; Beckman, 1991; Krauss, 1993). The likely reason mothers may experience more stress is probably due to the fact that they often assume more caretaking responsibilities.

Today, fathers' roles in families with children with disabilities are acknowledged to be more significant than was traditionally thought.

Even so, it would be inaccurate to conclude that fathers are unaffected by their children with disabilities or that they do not play a critical role in how their families adapt overall to having a member with a disability. Some fathers experience a great deal of stress, especially pertaining to their relationships with their children (Krauss, 1993). Fathers can also influence the functioning of their families indirectly by the amount of support they provide the mothers and the rest of the family members (Bristol & Gallagher, 1986; Kazak & Marvin, 1984). In addition, the more fathers are willing to help care for their children with disabilities the greater the degree of marital harmony that results (Willoughby & Glidden, 1995).

Parental Adjustment. Evidence is abundant that parents of children with disabilities undergo more than the average amount of stress (Beckman, 1991; Dumas, Wolf, Fisman, & Culligan, 1991; Hanson, Ellis, & Deppe, 1989; Singer & Irvin, 1989). The stress usually is not the result of major catastrophic events but rather the consequence of daily responsibilities related to child care. A single event, such as a family member coming down with a serious illness, may precipitate a family crisis, but its effects will be even more devastating if the family was already under stress because of a multitude of "daily hassles."

There is no universal parental reaction to the added stress of raising a child with a disability. Much depends on the parents' prior psychological makeup, the severity of the child's disability, and the amount of support the parents receive from friends, relatives, professionals, and each other. Although there are exceptions, it is fair to say that parents who were well adjusted and happily married before the birth of the child have a better chance of coping with the situation than those who were already having psychological or marital problems. It is also evident that parents of children with more severe disabilities usually have a more difficult time than parents of children with mild disabilities because the child-care burdens are greater.

Evidence clearly documents that the parents of children with disabilities undergo more than the average amount of stress. The parents who are well adjusted and happily married before the birth of their disabled child stand the best chance of coping with the challenges they face.

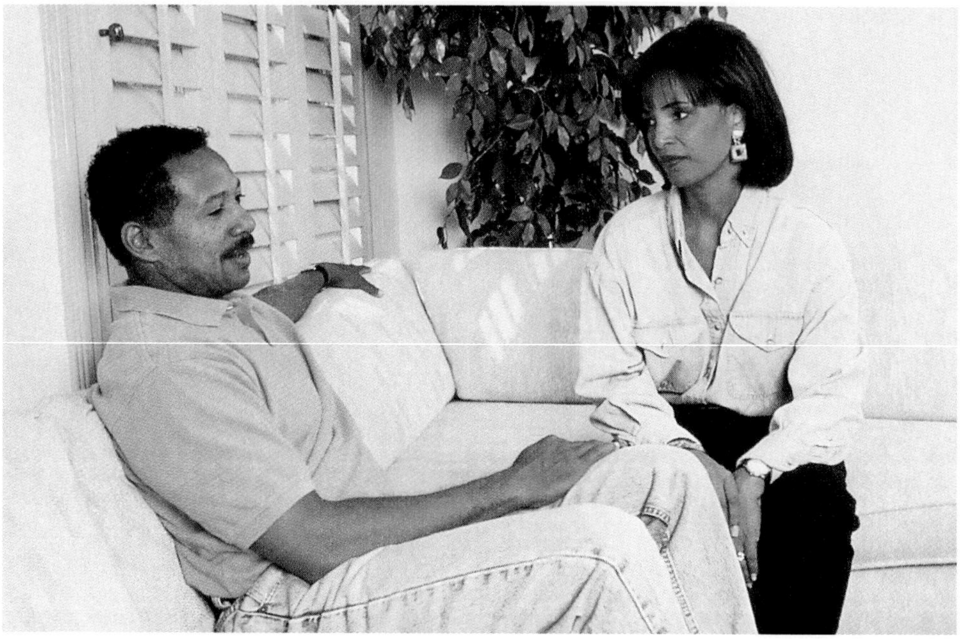

Again, however, there are exceptions. As Bronicki and Turnbull (1987) state:

> A more severe disability does not always produce greater stress. As one parent of a young adolescent commented:
>
> Don has been labeled profoundly retarded. He is not able to do anything to take care of himself, cannot walk, and has no language. Sure, he creates strains and stresses. But I remind myself that I never have to chase him around the house, he never talks back or sasses, he doesn't have to enter the rat race of teen-age years like my other sons, and he does not try to hurt himself. (p. 23)

It is important to keep in mind that the majority of parents of children with disabilities do not have major psychological problems. The types of problems some of them may be at risk to develop, however, would be characterized as relatively mild forms of depression (Carr, 1988; Singer & Irvin, 1989).

Some parents report that adding a child with a disability to the family actually has some unanticipated positive results. Some parents note, for example, that they have become more concerned about social issues and are more tolerant of differences in other people than they were before. Moreover, some parents claim that the birth of their child with a disability has brought the family closer together. This is not to minimize the fact that the added stress a child with a disability often brings can have a devastating impact on the stability of the family. It is dangerous to assume, though, that the birth of a child with a disability automatically spells doom for the psychological well-being of the parents or for the stability of their marriage.

Sibling Reactions

Although a relatively large body of literature pertains to parental reactions, there is much less information about siblings of persons with disabilities. What is available, however, indicates that siblings can and frequently do experience the same emotions—

fear, anger, guilt, and so forth—that parents do. In fact, in some ways, siblings may have an even more difficult time than their parents in coping with some of these feelings:

1. Being less mature, they may have trouble putting some of their negative sensations into proper perspective.
2. They may not have as broad a base of individuals with whom they can discuss their feelings (Featherstone, 1980).
3. They may be uncomfortable asking their parents the questions that bother them—for example, whether they will catch what their brother has, whether they were in some way responsible for their sister's disability, whether they will be called on to take care of their brother after their parents die.

Table 12–1 provides examples of sibling concerns.

Although some feelings about their siblings' disabilities may not appear for many years, a substantial number of accounts indicate that nondisabled siblings are aware at an amazingly early age that their brothers or sisters are different in some way. Jewell (1985), for example, recounts how her sister would make allowances for her cerebral palsy by playing a special version of "dolls" with her, a version in which all the dolls had disabilities. Even though young children may have a vague sense that their siblings with disabilities are different, they may still have misconceptions about the nature of their siblings' conditions, especially regarding what caused them.

Table 12–1
Examples of Sibling Concerns

Concerns about the Sibling with a Disability	▪ What caused the disability? ▪ Why does my brother behave so strangely? ▪ Will my sister ever live on her own?
Concerns about Parents	▪ Why do they let my brother get away with so much? ▪ Why must all their time be given to my sister? ▪ Why do they always ask me to babysit?
Concerns about Themselves	▪ Why do I have such mixed feelings about my sister? ▪ Will I catch the disability? ▪ Will we have a normal brother-sister relationship?
Concerns about Friends	▪ How can I tell my best friend about my brother? ▪ Will my friends tell everyone at school? ▪ What should I do when other kids make fun of people with disabilities?
Concerns about School and the Community	▪ What happens in special education classes? ▪ Will I be compared with my sister? ▪ What should I tell strangers?
Concerns about Adulthood	▪ Will I be responsible for my brother when my parents die? ▪ Do I need genetic counseling? ▪ Should I join a parents' and/or siblings' group?

Source: Adapted from *Brothers & sisters—a special part of exceptional families* (2nd ed.), by T. H. Powell & P. A. Gallagher, 1993, Baltimore, MD: Paul H. Brookes (P. O. Box 10624, Baltimore, MD 21285–0624).

As nondisabled siblings grow older, their concerns often become more focused on how society views them and their siblings who are disabled. Adolescence can be a particularly difficult period. As Featherstone (1980) notes, it is important for teenagers not to be considered different by their peers but at the same time to be considered special within the confines of their own families. Being the brother or sister of a child with a disability, however, often singles a person out as being different.

At the same time, the nondisabled sibling can feel slighted because his or her brother or sister with a disability receives so much attention from their parents. The following account, by the sister of a brother with cerebral palsy and mental retardation, is an example of the reactions of some siblings:*

> I cannot pinpoint exactly the time or the circumstance when I first became aware of Robin's handicaps. Several incidents come to mind, all of which occurred around the time I was eleven years old. One involved a trip to the shoe store where Robin was to be fitted for orthopedic shoes; another, a trip to the town near our country home for dinner at the YMCA. On both of these occasions, I can remember being acutely embarrassed by the ill-concealed stares our family received as we entered pushing Robin in his wheelchair. I was certain that everyone was looking at my brother with his obvious handicap and then wondering what was wrong with the rest of us. As a result of the feelings aroused in me by these occurrences, I began to refuse to go out to dinner or shopping with my family and took precautions to avoid being seen on the street or in the yard with Robin.
>
> These avoidance procedures on my part were not taken without an accompanying sense of guilt. I knew that it was wrong for me to be ashamed of my brother. I loved Robin dearly and realized that the opinions (real or imagined) of others should have no bearing on my relationship with him. . . .
>
> Following my period of avoidance, I entered a phase of false pretenses. I forced myself to appear in public with him—but only if I looked my very best (freshly washed hair, make-up, snazzy outfit, etc.). My specious reasoning was that if people were going to stare, they weren't going to find anything wrong with me. Also, though I am reluctant to admit such a selfish thought, I suppose I wanted to encourage people to think along the lines of "Oh, dear, look at that sweet young girl pushing her poor crippled brother around. What a wonderful child she must be." (Turnbull & Turnbull, 1985, pp. 94–95)

Siblings' Adjustment. Children, like parents, can adapt well or poorly to having family members with disabilities. Research indicates that some siblings have trouble adjusting, some have no trouble adjusting, and some actually appear to benefit from the experience (Seligman & Darling, 1989; Senapati & Hayes, 1988). Like parents, however, siblings of children with disabilities are at a greater risk than siblings of nondisabled children to have difficulties in adjustment.

Why some individuals respond negatively, whereas others do not, is not completely understood. Authorities point to three situations that can make it particularly difficult for a child to develop a positive attitude toward his or her sibling with a disability:

1. When the two siblings are close in age, there is more chance of conflict (Simeonsson & Bailey, 1986). Apparently, the similarity in age makes the differences in ability between the two siblings more obvious.

*From *Parents speak out: Then and now,* 2nd ed., edited by H. R. Turnbull & A. P. Turnbull, 1985, Columbus, OH. Merrill/Macmillan.

Siblings of children with disabilities often recount being aware at a very early age that something is different about their brothers or sisters. Siblings' attitudes change at different stages of their own lives; for example, adolescents become more concerned about public perceptions of themselves and their siblings with disabilities.

2. Siblings of the same sex are more likely to experience conflict (Simeonsson & Bailey, 1986).
3. A nondisabled girl who is older than her sibling, who has a disability, is likely to have a negative attitude when she reaches adolescence because she often has to shoulder child-care responsibilities (Stoneman, Brody Davis, & Crapps, 1988).

Teachers can sometimes play an important role in helping students adjust to having siblings with disabilities. Some strategies teachers can use are to talk with students about the materials and contents of programs for their siblings with disabilities, and to offer support, should students wish to talk about their fears or concerns (Powell & Gallagher, 1993).

FAMILY INVOLVEMENT IN TREATMENT AND EDUCATION

As noted earlier, today's professionals are more likely to recognize the positive influence parents can have on their exceptional children's development than was once the case. This more positive attitude toward parents is reflected in how parents are now involved in the treatment and education of their children.

At one time, most early intervention programs for families who had children with disabilities operated according to the philosophy that the *professionals* had the expertise and that the families needed that expertise to function. Most programs today, however, use a **family-centered model**, in which the professionals work *for* the family,

family-centered model. A type of early intervention program; consumer-driven in that professionals are viewed as working *for* families; views family members as the most important decision makers.

looking for ways to increase the decision-making power of the family and to encourage family members to obtain nonprofessional (e.g., family and friends) as well as formal sources of support. In this sense, family-centered models are consumer driven. These models are also designed with considerable flexibility to accommodate a diversity of family values and interaction styles and to respond to changes in priorities and concerns (Beckman, Robinson, Rosenberg, & Filer, 1994). The use of family-centered models reflects a change from viewing parents as passive recipients of professional advice to equal partners in the development of treatment and educational programs for their children.

The effort to build professional-parent partnerships is consistent with the thinking of child development theorists who stress the importance of the social context within which child development occurs. Urie Bronfenbrenner (1979), a renowned child development and family theorist, has been most influential in stressing that an individual's behavior cannot be understood without understanding the influence of the family on that behavior. Furthermore, the behavior of the family cannot be understood without considering the influence of other social systems (e.g., the extended family friends, and professionals) on the behavior of the family. The interaction between the family and the surrounding social system is critical to how the family functions. A supportive network of professionals (and especially friends) can be beneficial to the family with a child who has a disability.

Current approaches to involving families in treating and educating their children take into account how the family fits within the broader societal context. We now discuss two such approaches: (1) the family systems approach of the Turnbulls (Turnbull & Turnbull, 1990) and (2) the social support systems approach of Dunst and his colleagues (Dunst, Trivette, & Deal, 1988; Dunst, Trivette, Gordon, & Pletcher, 1989). These two approaches are very similar and overlap in many ways; they differ only with regard to emphasis. The family systems approach considers events that occur within the family as well as the broader social context. The social systems approach, although hardly ignoring the inner workings of the family unit, tends to focus more on the family's relationship with its social environment.

family characteristics. A component of the Turnbulls' family systems model; includes type and severity of the disability as well as such things as size, cultural background, and socioeconomic background of the family.

family interaction. A component of the Turnbulls' family systems model; refers to how cohesive and adaptable the family is.

family functions. A component of the Turnbulls' family systems model; includes such things as economic, daily care, social, medical, and educational needs.

family life cycle. A component of the Turnbulls' family systems model; consists of birth and early childhood (0–5 years), childhood (5–12 years), adolescence (12–21), and adulthood.

The Family Systems Approach

The philosophy behind the family systems approach is that all parts of the family are interrelated, so that events affecting any one family member also affect the others. It follows that the more treatment and educational programs take into account the relationships and interactions among family members, the more likely they will be successful. In other words, family systems theorists advocate that the family, rather than the individual, should be the focus of intervention efforts. The Turnbulls' model includes four interrelated components: **family characteristics, family interaction, family functions,** and **family life cycle** (Turnbull & Turnbull, 1990).

Family Characteristics. Family characteristics provide a description of basic information related to the family. They include characteristics of the exceptionality (e.g., the type and severity), characteristics of the family (e.g., size, cultural background, socioeconomic status, and geographic location), personal characteristics of each family member (e.g., health and coping styles), and special conditions (e.g., child or spousal abuse and poverty). Family characteristics help determine how family members interact with themselves and with others outside the family. To begin to understand how a family functions, we need to have a good picture of its characteristics. It will probably make a difference, for example, whether the child with a disability is mentally retarded or hearing impaired, whether he or she is an only child or has five siblings, whether the family is upper middle class or lives in poverty, and so forth.

Recent trends in U.S. society make it even more important for teachers and other professionals who work with families to take into account family characteristics. Demographic changes that have occurred over the past few decades make it imperative for professionals to be prepared to encounter a wide diversity of families. The middle-class nuclear family, with two parents and only the father working outside the home, is no longer the norm. There have been increases in the numbers of (1) families in which both parents work outside the home (Hofferth & Phillips, 1987), (2) single-parent families (Norton & Glick, 1986), and (3) families who are living in poverty (Baumeister, Kupstas, & Klindworth, 1990).

Coupled with these demographic changes—and to a certain extent influenced by them—families today live under a great deal more stress. For one thing, today's parents have less leisure time than ever before. Compared to parents in the late 1960s, for example, today's mothers and fathers between the ages of eighteen and thirty-nine put in 241 and 189 more annual hours of work, respectively (Leete-Guy & Schor, 1992).

The result of these demographic changes and more stressful living conditions may be that a reduced amount of support is available from parents for children with disabilities (Hallahan, 1992). Parents today are so consumed with meeting their own needs that they are unable to provide as much support to their children as was once the case. A counselor with over twenty years' experience in working with families with and without members who have disabilities has observed:

> It has only been recently that I have observed so much anger, insecurity, and despair among all families. . . . Families are experiencing a great deal of fatigue, and lack energy to advocate like they used to on behalf of their son or daughter, brother or sister. Both parents are working, they have no leisure time, and many are barely able to take care of their own responsibilities. (Stark, 1992, pp. 248–249)

These dramatic societal changes present formidable challenges for teachers and other professionals working with families of children with disabilities. As the configuration of families changes, professionals will need to alter their approaches. For example, the same approaches that are successful with middle-class, two-parent families may not be suitable for single mothers. Also, professionals need to understand that today's parent is living under more and more stress and may find it increasingly difficult to devote time and energy to working on behalf of his or her child.

Family Interaction. Family members can have a variety of functional and dysfunctional modes of interaction. Turnbull and colleagues note that the amount of family cohesion and adaptability will determine how individuals within families interact. In general, families are healthier if they have moderate degrees of cohesion and adaptability.

Cohesion. *Cohesion* refers to the degree to which an individual family member is free to act independent of other family members. An appropriate amount of family cohesion permits the individual to be his or her own person while at the same time allowing him or her to draw on other family members for support, as needed. Families with low cohesion may not offer the child with a disability the necessary support, whereas the overly cohesive family may overprotect the child and not allow him or her enough freedom.

When adults with disabilities live away from home, their parents are often concerned about providing enough support so that they do not become socially isolated.

It is frequently very difficult for otherwise healthy families to find the right balance of cohesion. They sometimes go overboard in wanting to help their children and, in so doing, limit their children's independence. A particularly stressful time can be adolescence, when the teenager strives to break some of the bonds that have tied him or her to the family. This need for independence is normal behavior. What makes the situation difficult for many families of children with disabilities is that the child, because of his or her disability, has often by necessity been more protected by parents. As one psychologist severely disabled by cerebral palsy recounts:*

> I remember the first time I wanted to travel alone, I had just turned sixteen. Some friends had invited me to stay with them in Baltimore. I sat down and discussed this with my parents. I said that I wanted to go by train, and that my friends would meet me in Baltimore at the train station. My parents were frightened and said so openly. They expressed their fears of my physical safety. . . . We talked and argued and cried for hours. The decision was that I was to go. . . . I'll never forget that day. My mother did not go to the train station with my father and me. She said she could give her permission for this to happen, but she couldn't watch it. My father settled me in a train seat and stood on the platform waving goodbye. I was trying not to cry and so was he. Blinking back tears, I waved goodbye to my father from the train window. He was vigorously waving goodbye with one hand—for his other was resting on the arm of my wheelchair. The train began pulling out of the station, and a panic gripped me. "My God! He still has my wheelchair. . . . Stop this train!" By this time we were a few blocks out of the station. What a ridiculous scene this must have appeared, this wriggly, little kid (I always looked young for my age) screaming at the top of my lungs to stop the train. . . . [The conductor] pulled the emergency cord and stopped the train. The words stuck in my throat as I looked up at this towering man. What a big question this little kid was about to ask, "Would you please back up the train so that I can get my wheelchair?" As the train backed up to the platform, there was my poor father still standing there waving goodbye with one hand and holding my wheelchair with the other, unaware of anything but his departing daughter. He was shocked out of his numb pose only when the conductor jumped off the train and wrenched the chair from his hand. (Diamond, 1981, pp. 41–42)

Even though children who are disabled ultimately need to gain as much independence from their families as possible, they also need to feel like they belong to them. Children with disabilities require responsible roles within their families such that other family members come to rely on them for what they contribute. Parents, for example, can consider assigning household chores. Certain adaptations might be necessary—such as taping a dish towel to the hands of a child with cerebral palsy so that it will not drop on the floor and allowing more time for him or her to complete the chore (Diamond, 1981). But the important thing is to provide the opportunity for the child to be a contributing member of the family.

Cohesion can also be an issue for adults with disabilities. For example, adults with mental retardation, especially those who live at home, often have special problems finding the right degree of independence from their families. Compared with those who live in the community, adults with mental retardation who live at home have a narrower range of social contacts outside their families but do experience more support from them, as well (Krauss, Seltzer, & Goodman, 1992).

*From "Growing up with parents of a handicapped child: A handicapped person's perspective," by S. Diamond, 1981, in *Understanding and working with parents of children with special needs,* edited by J. L. Paul, New York: Holt, Rinehart, & Winston. Reprinted with permission.

When adults with disabilities live away from home, their parents are often concerned about providing enough support so that their grown children do not become socially isolated. One mother who was interviewed about future living arrangements for her daughter, who is severely retarded, explained:

> I would like to see her live fairly close so that she can come over and visit when she wants to or if she needed help. She's going to have to have some support, I know that. There are lots of apartments close by that I think she can handle, . . . and I would like to see her close enough so that we always have the constant, not constant, [sic] but we will always be there if she needs us. And both Tim and I agree that that's something we will always do. We will be here. But, on the other hand, if we want to go away for a month, we'll know there are other people that can be called upon to give her the support she needs. (Lehmann & Baker, 1995, p. 30)

Current thinking dictates two principles that are sometimes difficult to coordinate (Blacher & Baker, 1992): (1) Adults with disabilities should live in the community, if at all possible; and (2) family support is critical across the lifespan. Achieving the right degree of independence from the family, while also encouraging family involvement, can be a difficult challenge.

Adaptability. *Adaptability* refers to the degree to which families are able to change their modes of interaction when they encounter unusual or stressful situations. Some families are so chaotic that it is difficult to predict what any one member will do in a given situation. In such an unstable environment, the needs of the family member who is disabled may be overlooked or neglected. At the other end of the continuum are families characterized by extreme rigidity. Each family member has his or her prescribed role in the family. Such rigidity makes it difficult for the family to adjust to the addition of a member with a disability. The addition of any child requires adjustment on the part of the family, but it is even more important if the child has special needs. For example, it may be that the mother's involvement in transporting the child with a disability from one therapy session to another will necessitate that the father be more involved than previously in household chores and taking care of the other children.

Family Functions. Family functions are the numerous tasks and activities in which families engage to meet their many and diverse needs. Economic, daily care, social, medical, and educational needs are just a few examples of the functions to which families need to attend.

An important point for teachers to consider is that *education* is only one of several functions in which families are immersed. And for some students, especially those with multiple disabilities, several professionals may be vying for the time of the parents. It is only natural, of course, that teachers should want to involve parents in the educational programming of their children as much as possible. Teachers know the positive benefits that can occur when parents are part of the treatment program. At the same time, however, teachers need to respect the fact that education is just one of the many functions to which families must attend. If the child has chronic medical problems, for example, the family may be consumed by decisions regarding medical treatment (Martin, Brady, & Kotarba, 1992).

Several authorities have reported that many families of students with disabilities prefer a passive, rather than active, degree of involvement in their children's education (Lynch & Stein, 1982; Vaughn, Bos, Harrell, & Lasky, 1988). Although some counselors are troubled by the fact that many parents are not more involved, others are less perplexed. They warn against automatically assuming, for example, that parents who do not contribute many suggestions at their child's IEP meeting are neglectful. Given the number and diversity of functions for which families are responsible and the configuration of some families noted earlier (e.g., single-parent families), some authorities are not surprised when families decide to delegate most of the educational decisions for their children to teachers (Benson & Turnbull, 1986). By so doing, they can concentrate on other needs of their children and families.

Respecting the parents' desire to play a relatively passive role in their child's education does not mean that teachers should discourage or discount parental involvement. Teachers should encourage involvement for those families who want to be involved. Also, it may be that parents who desire not to be involved at one time will want to take a more active role later.

Family Life Cycle. Several family theorists have noted that the impact of a child with a disability on the family changes over time (Beckman & Pokorni, 1988; Seligman & Darling, 1989; Turnbull & Turnbull, 1990). For this reason, some have pointed to the value of looking at families with children with a disability from a *life-cycle perspective.* Turnbull and Turnbull (1990), for example, have presented four major life-cycle stages that are representative of other family theorists:

1. early childhood (zero to five years)
2. childhood (five to twelve years)
3. adolescence (twelve to twenty-one years)
4. adulthood (twenty-one years and up)

Table 12–2 depicts some of the possible issues that parents and siblings of children with disabilities encounter during each of these four stages.

Transitions between stages in the life cycle are particularly stressful for families, especially families with children who are disabled. We have already mentioned the difficulties facing families at the transition point when their child, as an adult, moves into more independent work and living settings. Another particularly troublesome transition can be from the relatively intimate confines of an infant or preschool program to the larger context of a kindergarten setting. For the child, the transition often requires a sudden increase in independent functioning (Fowler, Schwartz, & Atwater, 1991). For the parents, it often means giving up a sense of security for their child. As one parent relates:

> As my daughter's third birthday approached, I lived in dread, not wishing to leave the familiar, comfortable environment of her infant program. The infant program had become home away from home for me. It was supportive and intimate. I had made some lifelong friendships, as well as having established a comfortable routine in our lives. I saw making the transition to a preschool program in the school district as an extremely traumatic experience, second only to learning of Amy's diagnosis.
>
> What were my fears? First, I was concerned that my husband and I, along with professionals, would be deciding the future of our child. How could we play God? Would our decisions be the right ones? Second, I feared loss of control, as I would be surrendering my child to strangers—first to the school district's intake assessment team and then to the preschool teacher. The feeling of being at the mercy of professionals was overwhelming. In addition, I had more information to absorb and a new system with which to become familiar. Finally, I feared the "label" that would be attached to my child and feared that this label would lower the world's expectations of her. (Hanline & Knowlton, 1988, p. 116)

Transitions between stages are difficult because of the uncertainty that each new phase presents to the family. One of the reasons for the uncertainty pertains to

Table 12–2
Possible Issues Encountered at Life-Cycle Stages

Life-Cycle Stage	*Parents*	*Siblings*
Early Childhood, Ages 0–5	▪ Obtaining an accurate diagnosis ▪ Informing siblings and relatives ▪ Locating services ▪ Seeking to find meaning in the exceptionality ▪ Clarifying a personal ideology to guide decisions ▪ Addressing issues of stigma ▪ Identifying positive contributions of exceptionality ▪ Setting great expectations	▪ Less parental time and energy for sibling needs ▪ Feelings of jealousy over less attention ▪ Fears associated with misunderstandings of exceptionality
School Age, Ages 5–12	▪ Establishing routines to carry out family functions ▪ Adjusting emotionally to educational implications ▪ Clarifying issues of mainstreaming v. special class placement ▪ Participating in IEP conferences ▪ Locating community resources ▪ Arranging for extracurricular activities	▪ Division of responsibility for any physical care needs ▪ Oldest female sibling may be at risk ▪ Limited family resources for recreation and leisure ▪ Informing friends and teachers ▪ Possible concern over surpassing younger sibling ▪ Issues of "mainstreaming" into same school ▪ Need for basic information on exceptionality
Adolescence, Ages 12–21	▪ Adjusting emotionally to possible chronicity of exceptionality ▪ Identifying issues of emerging sexuality ▪ Addressing possible peer isolation and rejection ▪ Planning for career/vocational development ▪ Arranging for leisure time activities ▪ Dealing with physical and emotional change of puberty ▪ Planning for postsecondary education	▪ Overidentification with sibling ▪ Greater understanding of differences in people ▪ Influence of exceptionality on career choice ▪ Dealing with possible stigma and embarrassment ▪ Participation in sibling training programs ▪ Opportunity for sibling support groups
Adulthood, Ages 21–	▪ Planning for possible need for guardianship ▪ Addressing the need for appropriate adult residence ▪ Adjusting emotionally to any adult implications of dependency ▪ Addressing the need for socialization opportunities outside the family for individuals with exceptionality ▪ Initiating career choice or vocational program	▪ Possible issues of responsibility for financial support ▪ Addressing concerns regarding genetic implications ▪ Introducing new in-laws to exceptionality ▪ Need for information on career/living options ▪ Clarify role of sibling advocacy ▪ Possible issues of guardianship

Source: From A. P. Turnbull & H. R. Turnbull, *Families, professionals, and exceptionality: A special partnership*, 2nd ed., © 1990, pp. 134–135. Adapted by permission of Prentice Hall, Upper Saddle River, New Jersey.

Getting to Know You

Parents of children with disabilities, especially those with multiple disabilities, must deal with a multitude and variety of professionals, some of whom may change from time to time. If the child is mainstreamed into general education, he or she may get a new teacher or set of teachers each year. A change from elementary to middle school or from middle to high school also brings additional changes in personnel.

These many changes make it difficult for parents to keep all of the many professionals informed about their child's particular needs. The mother of a child with cerebral palsy, mental retardation, severe hearing impairment, and lack of speech has come up with a strategy for familiarizing professionals with her child. She recommends that the family develop a "My Story" booklet pertaining to the child, which can be updated periodically (Comegys, 1989). Following are excerpts from her daughter's booklet written when she was in her early teens:

MY GOALS

1. I want to be as independent as I can possibly be.
2. I want to make friends with my nonhandicapped peers at the high school, and participate in all school activities which interest me, including afterschool activities.
3. I want to be included in community functions such as recreational and park activities, church, and social functions.
4. I plan on living and working in my home town after I graduate from high school.
5. I plan to work in the community (with support)—not in a sheltered workshop.
6. I want to learn to communicate with people better (eye contact, smile, and actions).
7. I want to learn to do things for people.
8. I want to learn to do more things for myself such as feed myself and participate more fully in dressing.
9. I want to develop my own sense of worth.
10. I want to be able to ride my bike by myself.
11. I am eager to operate the computer for my recreation now (Fire Organ, Sticky Bears, and Musicomp are some of the software used at home). Later, I hope to apply these skills to a real job. I enjoy working a Xerox machine now.
12. I want to make choices for: partners in activities; when to stop or start an activity, my clothes, leisure, food.
13. I want to be asked to go out by a friend spontaneously—not always preplanned.

MY INTERESTS

I enjoy lights, windows, the computer, photographs and slides of familiar activities and people, TV (nature, sports, comedy), and watching a fire in the fireplace.

I enjoy books, magazines, newspapers and catalogues, and maps. Geometric designs, too.

I like to swim, ride horseback, ride my bike around town.

I like to go places in a car. I like the school bus.

replacements of the professionals who work with the child who is disabled. In particular, parents of a child with multiple disabilities, who requires services from multiple professionals, can be anxious about the switches in therapists and teachers that occur many times throughout the child's life, especially at transition points. The box above describes one strategy for alleviating some of the problems resulting from changes in professionals.

A Social Support Systems Approach

Like a family systems approach, a social support systems approach focuses education and treatment efforts on the broader social context, rather than on individuals (Dunst et al., 1988). There are two important features of this approach:

1. It focuses on informal, rather than formal, sources of support. More and more authorities are pointing to informal sources of support, such as extended family, friends, church groups, neighbors, and social clubs, as more effective than professionals and agencies in helping families cope with the stress of having children with disabilities. Unfortunately, these informal supports, once so

I like warmth much better than cold—it helps my muscles—spring and summer, sunbathing, warm baths, warm feet and hands are important to me.

I like to be at the piano with people who can play it.

I like to be read to.

I like to be hugged—if you know me well enough. I also like to be tickled.

I like birds and fish, very much! I have a parakeet: Pete!

I have long enjoyed many family slides on the Ectagraphic which I can fully operate alone with a special switch.

I am very interested in cookies and good things to drink (frappes, tonics, etc.)!

I like lots of daily physical exercise—walking two city blocks is prescribed—it helps me sleep and helps my digestion.

I MAY NOT SPEAK—BUT I DO COMMUNICATE

I use total communication (visual, audiological, physical cues). I communicate in many ways: here are three—

- *Line Drawings.* I use both single and multiple line drawings (called "Commenting Boards") which are black and white or lightly colored. They enable me to both give and receive cues. If you show me a line drawing for car, I will know we are going out for a drive and I will start to move toward the door. I tap some line drawings to let you know what I want. I use many line drawings. A few of them appear in this booklet. [Not shown here.]
- *Signs.* I understand some of your signs. I am learning to make some signs. Some are my own gestures and others are formal signs. Here is a list: [Not shown here.]
- *Body Language and Sounds.* Please watch me closely and you will see that I:

1. point with my knuckles, or a finger, or a sweep of my arm.
2. nod my head "yes."
3. pull you when I want you to do something.
4. push an object away (I may or may not want it).
5. pull or push the bathroom door shut for privacy.
6. tilt my head up and back which can mean I want to get up.
7. rotate my head which can mean that it's time to get moving.

Please *listen* to my tone of voice. It changes constantly, and indicates pleasure, frustration, humming, questioning, loneliness, hunger. It helps when you pair these directions with a gesture, sign, or line drawing. For example, when it is time for me to get up from the chair and go somewhere, you might sign *stand* and show me the line drawing of car.

Please do not talk "around or through" me as though I am not in the room. It hurts my feelings. Include me by asking my opinion, questioning me, and showing me the appropriate line drawings and signs. It will make both of us much happier.

Source: By A.Comegys, "Integration strategies for parents of students with handicaps," in R. Gaylord-Ross (Ed.), *Integration Strategies for Students with Handicaps*, pp. 345–346. Copyright © 1989 by Paul H. Brookes Publishing Co. Reprinted with permission.

prevalent in U.S. society, are fast disappearing (Zigler & Black, 1989). Largely because of the demographic changes noted earlier (e.g., increases in single-parent families and poverty), families are less able today to rely on informal social networks for support.

2. A social support systems approach focuses on helping families help themselves. Because many families do not have their own informal sources of support, a social systems approach helps establish them. The goal is to enhance the self-esteem of the family by setting up a situation in which the helpseeker is less dependent on the helpgiver than is the case in more traditional approaches. Rather than focusing on the helpseeker as the cause of problems, the model encourages the family to accept responsibility for setting and achieving needed goals. The family, not the professional, assumes the primary decision-making role for the family's needs. The professional does not act so much on behalf of the helpseeker "but rather creates opportunities for the helpseeker to acquire competencies that permit him or her to mobilize sources of resources and support necessary to cope, adapt, and grow in response to life's many challenges" (Dunst et al., 1988, p. 44).

When professionals do not just provide direct services but encourage the family to help themselves and their children, the family takes more control over their own lives and avoids the dependency sometimes associated with typical professional-family relationships. Situations in which the family looks to professionals for all its help can result in family members becoming dependent on professionals and losing their feelings of competence and self-esteem.

Parental Support Groups. One of the most beneficial types of social support, especially for parents of recently diagnosed children, is parental support groups, which consist of parents of children with the same or similar disabilities. Such groups can be relatively unstructured, meeting infrequently with unspecified agendas, or they can be more structured. For example, some authorities recommend that parents of older children be paired with those of younger children, so the latter can learn from the former (Turnbull & Turnbull, 1990). In any case, parental groups provide a number of benefits, "including (1) alleviating loneliness and isolation, (2) providing information, (3) providing role models, and (4) providing a basis for comparison" (Seligman & Darling, 1989, p. 44).

Internet Resources for Parents. The Internet is rapidly turning into an excellent resource for parents of children with disabilities. Dozens of electronic mailing lists, newsgroups, and World Wide Web sites are now devoted to disability-related topics. Through mailing lists and newsgroups, parents of children with disabilities can communicate with each other, with people who have disabilities, and with professionals concerning practical as well as theoretical issues. Lists and newsgroups are available regarding specific disabilities (e.g, Down syndrome, attention deficit hyperactivity disorder, cerebral palsy, cystic fibrosis) as well as more general ones. The box on p. 519 describes such a list for parents of children with attention deficit disorders. (Maintenance of these lists can change rapidly, but as of this printing, to subscribe to this list, send a message to "majordomo@mv.mv.com" (no quotes) and, in the first line of text, type "subscribe add-parents".) An example of a more general list, which also has a mix of researchers, teachers, and parents, is "spedtalk," created and main-

Parent support groups provide help to many parents of children with disabilities.

Information for Parents on the Internet

ALDER CASTRANOLI
E-mail: "Alder@aol.com"

My four-year-old son, Christopher, was diagnosed with attention deficit disorder (ADD) early this year. At first, my wife and I were ashamed and worried to have a "hyperactive" child.

I had just received a new Macintosh computer for my birthday, so I thought I would use it to try to learn something about ADD. I joined America Online (AOL) and started to get involved in "chats" with other parents of children with ADD and other disabilities. During one of these chats, I learned about an Internet mailing list for parents of children with ADD. I found out that I could subscribe to this list through my e-mail address on AOL.

In a few short months since subscribing to the ADD-Parents mailing list, I have learned that my child is not a freak. I now know that Christopher has a medical condition that is treatable through medication and behavior modification techniques, many of which I have learned about through e-mail exchanges with other parents on the list.

The ADD-Parents list includes parents from all over the U.S. and Canada, so we can compare notes on special education laws and practices in various locations. When we have an especially trying day with our kids, we can share our frustrations by sending e-mail to the list; often, we will get rapid return e-mail with suggestions or, just as importantly, moral support. The particular computer service each individual member of the list uses is not important—we can receive e-mail from commercial services like CompuServe, America Online, Prodigy, GEnie or any other service that provides an Internet mailing address.

I have learned how to better be a father to my son. And thanks to the parents of older children on the mailing list, I also have learned about the challenges that lie ahead. I know about the potential pitfalls of elementary school and higher education, and I am ready to deal with problems as they arise.

Alder Castranoli lives in Key West, Florida.

Source: From "Cruising the Internet," by B. McGarry, 1994, *Exceptional Parent, 24* (6), 39–43. Reprinted with the expressed consent and approval of *Exceptional Parent,* a monthly magazine for parents and families of children with disabilities and special health care needs. Subscription cost is $24 per year for 12 issues; call 1–800–247–8080. Offices at 120 State Street, Hackensack, NJ 07601.

tained by Professor John Lloyd at the University of Virginia. (To subscribe, send a message to "majordomo@virginia.edu" and, in the first line of text, type "subscribe spedtalk".)

Via web sites, parents can access information on disabilities. A good example is The Office of Special Education, based at the University of Virginia. (The address for this site is "http://curry.edschool.Virginia.EDU/go/specialed".) This site provides information and links to other web sites on such topics as legislation, legal issues, documented teaching techniques, and upcoming articles in special education journals.

Communication between Parents and Professionals

Virtually all family theorists agree that, no matter what particular approach one uses to work with parents, the key to the success of a program is how well parents and professionals are able to work together. Even the most creative, well-conceived model is doomed to fail if professionals and parents are unable to communicate effectively.

Unfortunately, special education does not have a long tradition of excellent working relationships between parents and teachers (Michael, Arnold, Magliocca, & Miller, 1992). This is not too surprising, considering the ingredients of the situation. On the one hand, there are the parents, who may be trying to cope with the stresses of raising a child with a disability in a complex and changing society. On the other hand, there are the professionals—teachers, speech therapists, physicians, psychologists, physical therapists, and so forth—who may be frustrated because they do not have all the answers to the child's problems.

As the parent of a child with autism has stated:*

> We don't begin in anger. We start the way all parents of all children do: with respect, reverence really, for the professional and his skills. The pediatrician, the teacher, the writer of books and articles on child development, they are the sources of wisdom from which we must draw in order to be good parents. We believe, we consult, we do as we are told, and all goes well . . . unless one of our kids has a handicap.
>
> We parents are almost always the first to notice that something is amiss, and one of our early consolations is often our pediatrician's assurance that "it's nothing—he'll outgrow it." That, of course, is exactly what we want to hear because it corresponds perfectly to the dwindling hope in our hearts, so we defer to the expert and our child loses another year. Finally, the time does come when not even the most conservative professional can deny the existence of a problem. . . . With luck, our pediatrician refers us to an appropriate specialist. . . .
>
> We transfer our trust to the new god and wait expectantly for the oracle to speak. Instead of the strong authoritative voice of wisdom, we more often hear an evasive stammer: "Can't give you a definite diagnosis . . . uh. . . . virtually untestable . . . let's see him . . . cough, cough . . . again in a year." Ironically, when the oracle is loud and clear, it is often wrong: "Seriously emotionally disturbed; it's a severe withdrawal reaction to maternal ambivalence." The parents have just been treated to their first dose of professional puffery. . . .
>
> Its one potentially redeeming feature may be realized if the parents react with sufficient anger to take charge, to assert their right to be their child's "case manager." Unfortunately, this is not likely to happen at such an early stage; it takes more than one false god to make us give up religion entirely. And when (or if) we do manage to assert ourselves, our behavior is viewed by professionals as the final stage in our own pathology; and any of us who may still be practicing religion are immediately excommunicated. (Akerley, 1985, pp. 23-24)

Fortunately this parent's frustrating experiences are not the norm. There are enough other parents who echo the same sentiments, however, to indicate that professional-parent relationships are often far from perfect and that teachers are frequently the targets of parental frustrations.

One of the keys to avoiding professional-parent misunderstandings is *communication.* It is critical that teachers attempt to communicate with the parents of their students. There are advantages to receiving information from parents as well as imparting information to them. Given that the parents have spent considerably more time with the child and have more invested in the child emotionally, they can be an invaluable source of information regarding his or her characteristics and interests. And by keeping parents informed of what is going on in class, teachers can foster a relationship in which they can call on parents for support should the need arise. Even those parents mentioned earlier, who do not want to be actively involved in making decisions regarding their child's educational program, should receive periodic communication from their child's teacher.

One area, in particular, that requires the cooperation of parents is homework. For mainstreamed students who are disabled, homework is often a source of misunderstanding and conflict (Mims, Harper, Armstrong, & Savage, 1991; Salend & Gajria, 1995). To avoid this often requires that the regular educator stay in close communica-

*From "False gods and angry prophets," by M. S. Akerley, 1985, pp. 23–31, in *Parents speak out: Then and now,* 2nd ed., edited by H. R. Turnbull & A. P. Turnbull, Columbus, OH: Merrill/Macmillan. Copyright © 1985 by Merrill Publishing Company. Reprinted with permission of Merrill, an imprint of Macmillan Publishing Company.

Table 12–3
Suggested Responsibilities of General Education Teachers and Parents with Regard to Homework

Suggestions for General Educators	▪ Establish a method of recordkeeping. This can be accomplished by maintaining a homework notebook or chart. ▪ Ensure that all homework is at the child's academic functional level. ▪ Inform parents and students in advance when special materials or resources are required for homework completion (e.g., study guides, a calculator, or a stop watch). ▪ Make homework a review of skills that are currently being taught. ▪ Avoid homework that requires new knowledge or skills that have not been presented previously. ▪ Allow time for homework at the end of class when appropriate. If time is available for homework in class, the teacher can answer questions. ▪ Consider the attention span and functional level of the child when assigning homework. Lower-functioning children should not be required to complete the same amount of work as those who are higher functioning.
Suggestions for Parents	▪ Establish a scheduled time and place for homework to be completed. ▪ Decide who will supervise the homework. This does not mean that the person will always check every problem or every sentence. ▪ Provide an atmosphere conducive to learning. Make sure the area is well lighted and ample work space is provided. ▪ Monitor the noise level. ▪ Provide appropriate supplies. ▪ Provide a tutor for subject areas with which parents are unfamiliar.

Source: Adapted from A. Mims, C. Harper, S. W. Armstrong, & S. Savage, "Effective instruction in homework for students with disabilities," *Teaching Exceptional Children, 24*(1), 42–44. Copyright © 1991 by The Council for Exceptional Children. Reprinted with permission.

tion with the parents of the student with a disability. Table 12-3 lists recommendations for the respective roles of general education teachers and parents with regard to homework.

Most authorities agree that the communication between the teacher and parents should take place as soon as possible and that it should not be initiated only by negative behavior on the part of the student. Parents, especially those of students with behavior disorders, often complain that the only time they hear from school personnel is when their child has misbehaved (Kauffman, Mostert, Nuttycombe, Trent, & Hallahan, 1993). To establish a degree of rapport with parents, some teachers make a practice of sending home a brief form letter at the beginning of the schoolyear, outlining the goals for the year. Others send home periodic newsletters or make occasional phone calls to parents. Even if teachers do not choose to use some of these techniques, authorities recommend that they be open to the idea of communicating with parents as soon as possible in the schoolyear. By establishing a line of communication with parents early in the year, the teacher is in a better position to initiate more intensive and focused discussions should the need arise. Three such methods of communication are parent-teacher conferences, home-note programs, and traveling notebooks.

Parent-Teacher Conferences. Parent-teacher conferences can be an effective way for teachers to share information with parents. Likewise, they are an opportunity for teachers to learn from parents more about the students from the parents' perspec-

Table 12–4
Questions for Teachers to Ask Themselves Regarding Parent-Teacher Conferences

Preconference Preparation	**Notifying Families** ▪ Did I, or the school, provide parents with written notification of the conference? ▪ Did I provide a means of determining that the parents knew the date and time? **Preparing for the Conference** ▪ Did I review the student's cumulative records? ▪ Did I assess the student's behavior and pinpoint areas of concern? ▪ Did I make notes of the student's misbehavior to show to parents? ▪ Did I consult with other relevant professionals about the student's behavior? ▪ Did I mentally rehearse and review what I was going to say at the conference? **Preparing the Physical Environment** ▪ Did the setting provide enough privacy? ▪ Did the setting provide enough comfort?.
Conference for Activities	**Developing Rapport** ▪ Did I allow time to talk informally before the start of the meeting? ▪ Did I express appreciation for the parents' coming to the meeting? **Obtaining Information from Parents** ▪ Did I ask enough open-ended questions? ▪ Did my body language indicate interest in what parents were saying? (Did I maintain eye contact and look attentive?) ▪ Did I ask for clarification on points I didn't understand? **Providing Information to Parents** ▪ Did I speak as positively as possible about the student? ▪ Did I use jargon-free language? ▪ Did I use specific examples to clarify my points? **Summarizing and Follow-Up** ▪ Did I review the main points to determine next steps? ▪ Did I restate who was responsible for completing the next steps and by when? ▪ Did I end the meeting on a positive note? ▪ Did I thank the parents for their interest in attending?
Postconference Follow-Up	▪ Did I consider reviewing the meeting with the student? ▪ Did I share the results with the appropriate other professionals who work with the student? ▪ Did I make a record of the conference proceedings?

Source: From A. P. Turnbull & H. R. Turnbull, *Families, professionals, and exceptionality: A special partnership*, 2nd ed., © 1990, pp. 186–187. Adapted by permission of Prentice Hall, Upper Saddle River, New Jersey.

tive. In addition to regularly scheduled meetings open to all parents, teachers may want to hold individual conferences with the parents of particular students. Most authorities agree that a key to conducting successful parent-teacher conferences is planning (Turnbull & Turnbull, 1990). How the teacher initiates the meeting, for example, can be crucial. Some recommend that the first contact be a telephone call that proposes the need for the meeting, without going into great detail, followed by a letter reminding the parents of the time and place of the meeting (Kauffman et al.,

1993). Table 12–4 presents several questions that authorities recommend teachers ask themselves in planing for conferences and evaluating their performance after each conference is over (Turnbull & Turnbull, 1990).

If the focus of the meeting is the student's poor work or misbehavior, the teacher will need to be as diplomatic as possible. Most authorities recommend that the teacher find something positive to say about the student, while still providing an objective account of what the student is doing that is troubling. The teacher needs to achieve a delicate balance of providing an objective account of the student's transgressions or poor work while demonstrating advocacy for the student. Conveying only bad or good news can lose the parents' sense of trust:

> Conveying only good news skews their perspective . . . just as much as conveying only negative information. If a serious incident arises, they have no sense of background or warning. [This] may lead them to conclude that the teacher is withholding information and provoke a sense of mistrust. When telling parents unpleasant information, it helps not only to be as objective as possible, but also state the case in a way that clearly conveys your advocacy of the student. When it is obvious to the parents that the teacher is angry or upset with their child, parents become apprehensive about the treatment the child may receive. A common response to this sense of dread is a defensiveness which polarizes parent-teacher relationships. (Kauffman et al., 1993, pp. 123–124)

Home-Note Programs. Sometimes referred to as *home-contingency programs*, **home-note programs** are a way of communicating with parents and having them reinforce behavior that occurs at school (Kelley, 1990). By having parents dispense the reinforcement, the teacher takes advantage of the fact that parents usually have a greater number of reinforcers at their disposal than do teachers.

There are a number of different types of home-notes. A typical one consists of a simple form on which the teacher records "yes," "no," or "not applicable" to certain categories of behavior (e.g., social behavior, homework completed, homework accurate, in-class academic work completed, inclass academic work accurate). The form also may contain space for the teacher and the parents to write a few brief comments. The student takes the form home, has his or her parents sign it, and returns it the next day. The parents deliver reinforcement for the student's performance. The teacher often starts out sending a note home each day and gradually decreases the frequency until he or she is using a once-a-week note.

Traveling Notebooks. Less formal than home-notes and particularly appropriate for students who see multiple professionals are traveling notebooks. A **traveling notebook** goes back and forth, between school and home. The teacher and other professionals, such as the speech and physical therapists, can write brief messages to the parents and vice versa. In addition, a traveling notebook allows the different professionals to keep up with what each of them is doing with the student. See Figure 12–1 for excerpts from a traveling notebook of a two-year-old with cerebral palsy.

home-note program. A system of communication between the teacher and parents; the teacher evaluates the behavior of the student using a simple form, the student takes the form home, gets the parents' signatures, and returns the form the next day.

traveling notebook. A system of communication in which parents and professionals write messages to each other by way of a notebook or log that accompanies the child to and from school.

IN CONCLUSION

Today's knowledgeable educators recognize the tremendous impact a child with a disability can have on the dynamics of a family. They appreciate the negative as well as the positive influence such a child can exert. Today's knowledgeable educators also

The following short excerpts are taken at random from a notebook that accompanies two-year-old Lauren, who has cerebral palsy, back and forth to her special class for preschoolers. The notebook provides a convenient mode for an ongoing dialogue among her mother, Lyn; her teacher, Sara; her occupational therapist, Joan; and her speech therapist, Marti. As you can see from this representative sample, the communication is informal but very informative on a variety of items relating to Lauren.

Lyn, 9/7

Lauren did very well-We had several criers but-She played & worked very nicely. She responds so well to instruction -that's such a plus!

She fed herself crackers & juice & did a good job. She was very vocal & enjoyed the other children too. She communicated ō me very well for the 1st day. Am pleased ō her first day.

Sara

Sara. 9/15

Please note that towel, toothbrush / paste + clean clothes may be removed from bag today —WED. We witnessed an apparently significant moment in her oral communication: She'll try to say "all done" after a meal. The execution is imperfect, to say the least, but she gets an "A" for effort. Could you please reinforce this after snack? Just ask her, "What do you say after you finish your snack?"

Thanks,

Lyn

9/28

Lauren had an esp. good day! She was jabbering a lot! Being very expressive ō her vocalness & jabbering. I know she said "yes" or an approximate thereof, several times when asked if she wanted something. She was so cute ō the animal sounds esp. pig & horse-she was really trying to make the sounds. It was the first time we had seen such a response. Still cruising a lot! She walked ō me around the room & in the gym. She used those consonant & vowel sounds: dadada, mamama – her jabbering was just so different & definitely progressive. I am sending her work card ō stickers home tomorrow for good working.

Several notes:

① Susie (VI) came today & evaluated Lauren. She will compile a report & be in touch with you and me. She seemed very pleased ō Lauren's performance.

② Marti (speech) will see Lauren at 11 AM for evaluation She'll be in touch afterwards.

③ Susie informed me about the addition to the IEP meeting on Mon. Oct. 4 at 10 AM here at Woodbrook.

How are the tape & cards working at home? I know you both are pleased ō her jabbering. She seems so ready to say "something" – we are very, very pleased. See you tomorrow.

Sara

9/29

Lauren was a bit fussy during O.T. today - she stopped fussing during fine motor reaching activities (peg board, block building) but wasn't too pleased with being handled on the ball. She did a great job with the peg board & readily used her left hand.

I want to bring in some different spoons next week to see if she can become more independent in scooping with a large handle spoon or a spoon that is covered

Joan

Figure 12–1

A traveling notebook.

realize that the family of a child with a disability can be a bountiful reservoir of support for the child as well as an invaluable source of information for the teacher. Although tremendous advances have been made, we are just beginning to tap the potential that families have for contributing to the development of their children with disabilities. We are just beginning to enable families to provide supportive and enriching environments for their children. and we are just beginning to harness the expertise of families so we can provide the best possible programs for their children.

Joan — 10/1

Although Lauren would very much approve of your idea for making her more independent during feeding, we'd rather not initiate self-feeding with an adaptive spoon at this time. Here's why:

① When I feed Lauren or get her to grip a spoon and then guide her hand, I can slip the entire bowl of the spoon into her mouth and get her to close her lips on it. When Lauren uses a spoon without help, she turns it upside-down to lick it or inserts just the tip of it into her mouth and then sucks off the food...

② Lauren has always been encouraged to do things "normally". She never had a special cup or a "Tommy Tippee", for instance. Of course it took a year of practice before she could drink well from a cup, and she still dribbles a little occasionally; but she's doing well now. We really prefer to give Lauren practice in using a regular spoon so that she doesn't get dependent on an adaptive utensil. I'd like to assure you that we appreciate your communication about sessions with Lauren and ideas for her therapy. Coordinating her school, home and CRC programs is going to be a challenge, to say the least.

Lyn

2/26

☺! Lauren walked all the way from the room to Gym & back — She also walked up & down the full length of the gym!

Several other teachers saw her and were thrilled.

She fell maybe twice! But picked herself right up —

Sara

3/2

Lauren had a great speech session! We were playing with some toys and she said "I want help" as plain as day. Later she said "I want crackers" and at the end of the session, she imitated "Cindy, let's go." Super!

Marti

Figure 12–1 *continued*

A traveling notebook.

SUMMARY

At one time, the prevailing attitude toward parents of persons with disabilities was negative. Professionals viewed them as causes of their children's problems, at worst, or as roadblocks to educational efforts, at best. Two factors have contributed to a much more positive attitude toward parent: First, current theory dictates that children, even young infants, can cause changes in adults' behavior. Professionals now view adult-child interaction as a two-way street—sometimes adults affect children, and sometimes the reverse is true. Second, professionals began to see parents as a potential source of information about how to educate their children. Most authorities now believe that parents should not be viewed as quasi-therapists or quasi-teachers—the goal should be to preserve the natural parent-child relationship.

Many theorists believe that parents go through a series of stages after learning that they have a child with a disability. There are limitations to a stage approach, however, including the tendency to view all parents as going through all the stages in the same order. Nevertheless, many parents do have emotional reactions, for example, guilt.

While most research on parents of children with disabilities has focused on mothers, recent studies, however, have found that fathers experience the same amount or perhaps less stress than mothers (depending on caretaking responsibilities, most likely). Fathers can influence the functioning of their families by the amount of support they provide mothers and other family members.

Parents of children with a disability often undergo a great deal of stress. How parents cope with the stress varies. Although very few experience major psychological disturbances, they are at risk for mild forms of depression. In most cases, parents who are well adjusted and happily married before the birth of a child with a disability will have a better chance of coping than parents who were not.

Siblings of children with disabilities experience some of the same emotions that parents do. Because they are less mature, may not have a broad base of people with whom they can talk, and may be hesitant to talk over sensitive issues with their parents, siblings may have a difficult time coping with their emotions. Teachers can play a very important role in talking to children about their siblings, and providing support. As they grow older, children's feelings often become centered on how society views them and their family. Like their parents, most children are able to adjust to siblings with disabilities.

Current family practitioners advocate a family-focused or family-centered approach, in which professionals work for families, helping them obtain access to nonprofessional (e.g., family and friends) as well as formal sources of support. Families are encouraged to be active in decision making. Current theorists also stress the influence of the social context on child development. They note that the family, as a whole, affects individual family members and that society affects the family. Two educational approaches to families that consider the social context are the *family systems approach* and the *social support systems approach*.

The family systems model includes four components: family characteristics, family interaction, family functions, and family life cycle. *Family characteristics* comprise the type and severity of the disability as well as such things as the size, cultural background, and socioeconomic background of the family. *Family interaction* refers to how cohesive and adaptable the family is. *Family functions* include such things as economics, daily care, social, medical, and educational needs. It is important for teachers to keep in mind that education is just one of many needs to which the family must attend; some parents prefer more passive than active involvement in educational programming. The *family life cycle* is made up of birth and early childhood, childhood, adolescence, and adulthood. Transitions between stages, especially between preschool and school and between adolescence and adulthood, can be very difficult for families with children who are disabled. The model suggests that the impact on the family of a child with a disability as well as the impact of the family on the child are determined by the complex interactions within and between the four stages.

A social support systems approach stresses the importance of the broader societal influence on family functioning. It emphasizes the value of informal sources of social support, such as the extended family, friends, neighbors, and church groups. A particularly effective social support is that of parent support groups, made up of parents who have children with similar disabilities. The Internet has grown into an excellent resource for parents, as well. A social systems program is built on the assumption that it is better to enable families to help themselves than to provide only direct services to them.

Family theorists agree that the key to working with and involving parents is *communication*. The parent-teacher conference is one of the most common avenues, and preparation is the key to a successful conference. Teachers need to consider preconference, conference, and postconference planning. A home-note program, in which teachers send home brief checklists of students' behavior that they have filled out, can keep parents informed and involve them in reinforcing the students' behavior. A traveling notebook is a log that accompanies the child to and from school, in which the parent, teacher, and other professionals can write messages to one another concerning the child's progress.

Glossary

A

acceleration. Educating gifted students by placing them in grade levels ahead of their peers in one or more academic subjects.

acquired aphasia. Loss or impairment of the ability to understand or formulate language because of accident or illness.

Acquired immune deficiency syndrome (AIDS). A fatal virus-caused illness resulting in a breakdown of the immune system. Currently, no known cure exists.

adaptive devices. Special tools that are adaptations of common items to make accomplishing self-care, work, or recreation activities easier for someone who has a physical disability.

adaptive skills. Skills needed to adapt to one's living environment, e.g., communication, self-care, home living, social skills, community use, self-direction, health and safety, functional academics, leisure, and work; usually estimated by an adaptive behavior survey; one of two major components (the other is intellectual functioning) of the AAMR definition.

adventitiously deaf. Deafness that occurs through illness or accident in an individual who was born with normal hearing.

affective disorder. A disorder of mood or emotional tone characterized by depression or elation.

aggression. Behavior that intentionally causes others harm or that elicits escape or avoidance responses from others.

Americans with Disabilities Act (ADA). Civil rights legislation for persons with disabilities ensuring nondiscrimination in a broad range of activities.

amniocentesis. A medical procedure that allows examination of the amniotic fluid around the fetus; sometimes recommended to determine the presence of abnormality.

anoxia. Loss of oxygen; can cause brain injury.

anxiety disorder. A disorder characterized by anxiety, fearfulness, and avoidance of ordinary activities because of anxiety or fear.

applied behavior analysis. The application and evaluation of principles of learning theory applied to teaching situations; used with all types of students with disabilities, but particularly appropriate for persons with severe and profound disabilities. It consists of six steps: identifying overall goals, accumulating further information through baseline measurement, specifying learning objectives, implementing the intervention, monitoring student performance, and evaluating the intervention.

apraxia. The inability to move the muscles involved in speech or other voluntary acts.

aqueous humor. A watery substance between the cornea and the lens of the eye.

articulation. Refers to the movements the vocal tract makes during production of speech sounds; enunciation of words and vocal sounds.

astigmatism. Blurred vision caused by an irregular cornea or lens.

asymmetrical tonic neck reflex (ATNR). A normal reflex in babies up to about four months of age in which turning the head to one side results in extension of the arm and leg on the side toward which the head is turned and flexion of the opposite arm and leg. It is an abnormal reflex indicative of brain injury in infants older than about four months.

atonic. Characterized by lack of muscle tone; associated with atonic cerebral palsy.

attention deficit hyperactivity disorder (ADHD). A condition characterized by severe problems of inattention, hyperactivity, and/or impulsivity; often found in persons with learning disabilities.

audiologist. An individual trained in audiology, a science dealing with hearing impairments, their detection, and remediation.

audiometric zero. Lowest level at which normal people can hear.

auditory–verbal approach. Part of the oral approach to teaching students who are hearing impaired; stresses teaching the person to use his or her remaining hearing as much as possible; heavy emphasis on use of amplification.

augmentative communication. Alternative forms of communication that do not use the oral sounds of speech.

auricle. The visible part of the ear, composed of cartilage; collects the sounds and funnels them via the external auditory canal to the eardrum.

authentic assessment. A method that evaluates a student's critical-thinking and problem-solving ability in real-life situations in which he or she may work with or receive help from peers, teachers, parents, or supervisors.

autism. A disorder characterized by extreme withdrawal, self-stimulation, cognitive deficits, language disorders, and onset before the age of thirty months.

B

baseline. Used to assess the effects of an intervention. The therapist or teacher measures the client's or student's skill or behavior before instruction.

blindisms. Repetitive, stereotyped movements such as rocking or eye rubbing; also characteristic of some people who are blind, severely retarded, or psychotic; more appropriately referred to as stereotypic behaviors.

Braille bills. Legislation passed in several states making Braille more available to students with visual impairment. Specific provisions vary from state to state, but major advocates have lobbied for (a) making Braille available if parents want it, and for (b) ensuring that teachers of students with visual impairment are proficient in Braille.

Braille. A system in which raised dots are used to allow blind people to "read" with their fingertips; consists of a quadrangular cell containing from one to six dots whose arrangement denotes different letters and symbols.

Braille 'n Speak. A portable electronic Braille note taker with speech-synthesizing capabilities.

BrailleMate. A portable electronic Braille note taker with speech synthesizing capabilities.

C

cataracts. A condition caused by a clouding of the lens of the eye; affects color vision and distance vision.

catheterization. Insertion of a tube into the urethra to drain urine from the bladder.

cerebral palsy (CP). A condition characterized by paralysis, weakness, incoordination, and/or other motor dysfunction because of damage to the brain before it has matured.

choreoathetoid. Characterized by involuntary movements and difficulty with balance; associated with choreoathetoid cerebral palsy.

chorionic villus sampling (COS). A method of testing the unborn fetus for a variety of chromosomal abnormalities, such as Down syndrome; a small amount of tissue from the chorion (a membrane that eventually helps form the placenta) is extracted and tested; can be done earlier than amniocentesis but risk of miscarriage is slightly higher.

chromosome. A rod-shaped entity in the nucleus of the cell; contains genes, which convey hereditary characteristics.

chronological age. Refers to how old a person is; used in comparison with mental age to determine the IQ score of an individual:

$$IQ = \frac{MA}{CA} \times 100$$

cleft palate. Condition in which there is a rift or split in the upper part of the oral cavity or the upper lip (cleft lip).

cochlea. A snail-shaped organ that lies below the vestibular mechanism; its parts convert the sound coming from the middle ear into an electrical signal in the inner ear, which is transmitted to the brain.

cochlear implantation. A surgical procedure that allows people who are deaf to hear some environmental sounds; an external coil fitted on the skin by the ear picks up sound from a microphone worn by the person and transmits it to an internal coil implanted in the bone behind the ear, which carries it to an electrode implanted in the cochlea of the inner ear.

cognition. The ability to solve problems and use strategies; an area of difficulty for many persons with learning disabilities.

cognitive mapping. A nonsequential way of conceptualizing the spatial environment that allows a person who is visually impaired to know where several points in the environment are simultaneously; allows for better mobility than does a strictly sequential conceptualization of the environment.

cognitive training. Training procedures designed to change thoughts or thought patterns.

collaborative consultation. A special educator and a general educator collaborate to come up with teaching strategies for a student with disabilities. The relationship between the two professionals is based on the premises of shared responsibility and equal authority.

coloboma. A degenerative disease in which the central and/or peripheral areas of the retina are incompletely formed, resulting in impairment of the visual field and/or central visual acuity.

communication disorders. An impairment in the ability to use speech or language to communicate.

community residential facility (CRF). A place, usually a group home, in an urban or residential neighborhood where from about three to ten retarded adults live under supervision.

competitive employment. A workplace that provides employment at at least minimum wage and one in which most workers are nondisabled.

comprehension monitoring. The ability to keep track of one's own comprehension of reading material and to make adjustments to comprehend better while one is reading; often deficient in students with learning disabilities.

computerized axial tomographic (CAT) scans. A neuroimaging technique whereby X-rays of the brain are compiled by a computer to produce an overall picture of the brain.

conceptual intelligence. The traditional conceptualization of intelligence emphasizing problem solving related to academic material; what IQ tests primarily focus on assessing.

conduct disorder. A disorder characterized by overt, aggressive, disruptive behavior or covert antisocial acts such as stealing, lying, and fire setting; may include both overt and covert acts.

conductive hearing impairment. A hearing loss, usually mild, resulting from malfunctioning along the conductive pathway of the ear, i.e., the outer or middle ear.

congenital anomaly. An irregularity (anomaly) present at birth; may or not be due to genetic factors.

congenital cytomegalovirus (CMV). The most frequently occurring viral infection in newborns; can result in a variety of disabilities, especially hearing impairment.

congenitally deaf. Deafness that is present at birth; can be caused by genetic factors, by injuries during fetal development, or by injury incurred at birth.

contractures. Permanent shortening of muscles and connective tissues and consequent distortion of bones and/or posture because of neurological damage.

cooperative learning. A teaching approach in which the teacher places students with heterogeneous abilities (for example, some might have disabilities) together to work on assignments.

cooperative teaching. An approach in which regular class teachers and special educators teach together in the general classroom; it helps the special educator know the context of the regular classroom better.

cornea. A transparent cover in front of the iris and pupil in the eye; responsible for most of the refraction of the light rays in focusing on an object.

creativity. Ability to express novel and useful ideas, to sense and elucidate new and important relationships, and to ask previously unthought of but crucial questions.

criterion-referenced testing. A procedure used to determine a child's level of achievement; when this level is established, a criterion, or goal, is set to fix a level at which the child should be achieving.

cued speech. A method to aid speechreading in those with hearing impairment; the speaker uses hand shapes to represent sounds.

cultural-familial retardation. Today, a term used to refer to mild retardation due to an unstimulating environment and/or genetic factors.

curriculum-based assessment (CBA). This approach to assessment is a formative evaluation method designed to evaluate performance in the particular curriculum to which students are exposed. It usually involves giving students a small sample of items from the curriculum in use in their schools. Proponents of this assessment technique argue that it is preferable to comparing students with national norms or using tests that do not reflect the curriculum content learned by students.

D

decibels. Units of relative loudness of sounds; zero decibels (0 dB) designates the point at which people with normal hearing can just detect sound.

deinstitutionalization. A social movement of the 1960s and 1970s whereby large numbers of persons with mental retardation and/or mental illness were moved from large mental institutions into smaller community homes or into the homes of their families; recognized as a major catalyst for integrating persons with disabilities into society.

Descriptive Video Service. Provides audio narrative of key visual elements; available for several public television programs; for use of people with visual impairment.

detectable warnings. Rubberized strips with raised bumps; designed to help people who are blind detect railway and subway platform edges; mandated by ADA.

diabetic retinopathy. A condition resulting from interference of the blood supply to the retina; the fastest-growing cause of blindness.

diplegia. A condition in which the legs are paralyzed to a greater extent than the arms.

Direct Instruction. A method of teaching academics, especially reading and math. It emphasizes drill and practice and immediate feedback. The lessons are precisely sequenced, fast-paced, and well-rehearsed by the teacher.

disability rights movement. Patterned after the civil rights movement of the 1960s, this is a loosely organized effort to advocate for the rights of people with disabilities through lobbying legislators and other activities. Members view people with disabilities as an oppressed minority.

discourse. Conversation; skills used in conversation, such as turn-taking and staying on the topic.

Doppler effect. Term used to describe the phenomenon of the pitch of a sound rising as the listener moves toward the source of that sound.

Down syndrome. A condition resulting from a chromosomal abnormality; characterized by mental retardation and such physical signs as slanted-appearing eyes, flattened features, shortness, tendency toward obesity. The three major types of Down syndrome are trisomy 21, mosaicism, and translocation.

dysarthria. A condition in which brain damage causes impaired control of the muscles used in articulation.

E

early expressive language delay (EELD). A significant lag in the development of expressive language that is apparent by age 2.

echolalia. The meaningless repetition (echoing) of what has been heard.

electroencephalogram (EEG). A graphic recording of the brain's electrical impulses.

encephalitis. An inflammation of the brain; can affect the child's mental development adversely.

enrichment. Provision of additional learning experiences for gifted students while they remain in the grade level appropriate for their chronological age.

eugenics movement. A drive by some professionals to "better" the human race through selective breeding and sterilization of "unfit" parents such as people with mental retardation. This popular movement of the late nineteenth and early twentieth centuries resulted in laws restricting the marriage of individuals with mental retardation and sterilization of some of them.

evoked-response audiometry. A technique involving electroencephalograph measurement of changes in brain-wave activity in response to sounds.

external otitis. An infection of the skin of the external auditory canal.

externalizing. Acting-out behavior; aggressive or disruptive behavior that is observable as behavior directed toward others.

F

familiality studies. A method of determining the degree to which a given condition is inherited; looks at the prevalence of the condition in relatives of the person with the condition.

family characteristics. A component of the Turnbulls' family systems model; includes type and severity of the disability as well as such things as size, cultural background, and socioeconomic background of the family.

family functions. A component of the Turnbulls' family systems model; includes such things as economic, daily care, social, medical,. and educational needs.

family interaction. A component of the Turnbulls' family systems model; refers to how cohesive and adaptable the family is.

family life cycle. A component of the Turnbulls' family systems model; consists of birth and early childhood (0 to 5 years), childhood (5 to 12 years), adolescence (12 to 21), and adulthood.

family-centered model. Type of early intervention program; consumer-driven in that professionals are viewed as working for families; views family members as the most important decision makers.

fetal alcohol syndrome (FAS). Abnormalities associated with the mother's drinking alcohol during pregnancy. Defects range from mild to severe, including growth retardation, brain damage, mental retardation, hyperactivity, anomalies of the face, and heart failure.

fingerspelling. Spelling the English alphabet by various finger positions on one hand.

fluency. The flow with which oral language is produced.

formative evaluation methods. Measurement procedures used to monitor an individual student's progress. They are used to compare an individual to himself or herself, in contrast to standardized tests, which are primarily used to compare an individual to other students.

Fragile X syndrome. Condition in which the bottom of the X chromosome in the twenty-third pair of chromosomes is pinched off; can result in a number of physical anomalies as well as mental retardation; occurs more often in males than females; thought to be the most common hereditary cause of mental retardation.

full inclusion. All students with disabilities are placed in their neighborhood schools in general education classrooms for the entire day; general education teachers have the primary responsibility for students with disabilities.

functional academics. Practical skills rather than academic learning.

G

genius. A word sometimes used to indicate a particular aptitude or capacity in any area; rare intellectual powers.

genre. A plan or map for discourse; type of narrative discourse.

giftedness. Refers to cognitive (intellectual) superiority, creativity, and motivation of sufficient magnitude to set the child apart from the vast majority of age-mates and make it possible for him or her to contribute something of particular value to society.

glaucoma. A condition of excessive pressure in the eyeball; the cause is unknown but if untreated, blindness results.

Goals 2000: Educate America Act. Legislation passed in 1994 aimed at increasing the academic standards in U.S. schools; some educators fear that the focus on high standards may harm students with disabilities.

guide dog. A dog specially trained to help guide a person who is blind; not recommended for children and not used by very many adults who are blind because the user needs special training in how to use the dog properly; contrary to popular opinion, the dog does not "take" the person anywhere but serves primarily as a safeguard against walking into dangerous areas.

H

handicapism. A term used by activists who fault the unequal treatment of individuals with disabilities. This term is parallel to the term *racism,* coined by those who fault unequal treatment based on race.

Handicapped Children's Early Education Program (HCEEP). The first federal special education program aimed at young children with disabilities and their families. It has funded numerous demonstration and outreach projects.

hemiplegia. A condition in which one half (right or left side) of the body is paralyzed.

heritability studies. A method of determining the degree to which a condition is inherited; a comparison of the prevalence of a condition in identical (i.e., monozygotic, from the same egg) twins versus fraternal (i.e., dizygotic, from two eggs) twins.

herpes simplex. A type of veneral disease that can cause cold sores or fever blisters; if it affects the genitals and is contracted by the mother-to-be in the later stages of fetal development, it can cause mental subnormality in the child.

hertz (Hz). A measurement of the frequency of sound; refers to highness or lowness of a sound.

home-note program. A system of communication between teacher and parent; the teacher evaluates the behavior of the student using a simple form, the student takes the form home, gets the parents' signatures, and returns the form the next day.

homophenes. Sounds identical in terms of revealing movements (visible articulatory patterns).

hydrocephalus. A condition characterized by enlargement of the head because of excessive pressure of the cerebrospinal fluid.

hyperopia. Farsightedness; usually results when the eyeball is too short.

hypotonic. Low muscle tone; sometimes occurs as a result of cerebral palsy.

I

inclusive schools movement. A reform movement designed to restructure general education schools and classrooms so they better accommodate all students, including those with disabilities.

incus. Anvil-shaped bone in the ossicular chain of the middle ear.

individualized education program (IEP). IDEA requires an IEP to be drawn up by the educational team for each exceptional child; the IEP must include a statement of present educational performance, instructional goals, educational services to be provided, and criteria and procedures for determining that the instructional objectives are being met.

individualized family service plan (IFSP). A plan for services for young children with disabilities (under 3 years of age) and their families drawn up by professionals and parents; similar to an IEP for older children; mandated by PL 99–457.

Individuals with Disabilities Education Act (IDEA). The Individuals with Disabilities Education Act of 1990; replaced PL 94–142.

informal reading inventory (IRI). A method of assessing reading in which the teacher has the student read progressively more difficult series of passages or word lists; the teacher notes the difficulty level of the material read and the types of errors the student makes.

insight. Ability to separate and/or combine various pieces of information in new, creative, or useful ways.

intellectual functioning. The ability to solve problems related to academics; usually estimated by an IQ test; one of two major components (the other is adaptive skills) of the AAMR definition.

internalizing. Acting-in behavior; anxiety, fearfulness, withdrawal, and other indications of an individual's mood or internal state.

IQ-achievement discrepancy. Academic performance markedly lower than would be expected based on a student's intellectual ability.

iris. The colored portion of the eye; contracts or expands depending on the amount of light striking it.

itinerant teacher services. Services for students who are visually impaired, in which the special education teacher visits several different schools to work with students and their general education classroom teachers; the students attend their local schools and remain in general education classrooms.

J

job coach. A person who assists adult workers with disabilities (especially those with mental retardation), providing vocational assessment, instruction, overall planning, and interaction assistance with employers, family, and related government and service agencies.

juvenile rheumatoid arthritis. See "R".

K

Kurzweil Reading Machine. A computerized device that converts print into speech for persons with visual impairment. The user places the printed material over a scanner that then "reads" the material aloud by means of an electronic voice.

L

language. An arbitrary code or system of symbols to communicate meaning.

language disorders. A lag in the ability to understand and express ideas that puts linguistic skill behind an individual's development in other areas, such as motor, cognitive, or social development.

language learning disability. A learning disability in the specific area of language.

larynx. The structure in the throat containing the vocal apparatus (vocal cords); laryngitis is a temporary loss of voice caused by inflammation of the larynx.

learned helplessness. A motivational term referring to a condition wherein a person believes that no matter how hard he or she tries, failure will result.

least restrictive environment (LRE). A legal term referring to the fact that exceptional children must be educated in as "normal" an environment as possible.

legally blind. A person who has visual acuity of 20/200 or less in the better eye even with correction (e.g., eyeglasses) or has a field of vision so narrow that its widest diameter subtends an angular distance no greater than 20 degrees.

lens. A structure that refines and changes the focus of the light rays passing through the eye.

levels of support. The basis of the AAMR classification scheme; the amount of support needed for someone with mental retardation to function as competently as possible as: (1) intermittent, (2) limited, (3) extensive, or (4) pervasive.

locus of control. A motivational term referring to how people attribute their successes or failures; people with an internal locus of control believe that they themselves are the reason for success or failure, whereas people with an external locus of control believe outside forces (e.g., other people) influence how they perform.

long cane. A mobility aid used by individuals with visual impairment who sweep it in a wide arc in front of them; proper use requires considerable training. It is the mobility aid of choice for most travelers who are blind.

low vision. A term used by educators to refer to individuals whose visual impairment is not so severe that they are unable to read print of some kind. They may read large or regular print, and they may need some kind of magnification.

M

macroculture. A nation or other large social entity with a shared culture.

magnetic resonance imaging (MRI). A neuroimaging technique whereby radio waves are used to produce cross-sectional images of the brain.

mainstreaming. The placement of students with disabilities in general education classes for all or part of the day and for all or only a few classes; special education teachers maintain the primary responsibility for students with disabilities.

malleus. Hammer-shaped bone in the ossicular chain of the middle ear.

meningitis. A bacterial or viral infection of the linings of the brain or spinal cord.

mental age. Refers to the IQ test score that specifies the age level at which an individual is functioning.

metacognition. One's understanding of the strategies available for learning a task and the regulatory mechanisms to complete the task.

microcephalus. A condition causing development of a small head with a sloping forehead; proper development of the brain is prevented, resulting in mental retardation.

microculture. A smaller group existing within a larger cultural group and having unique values, style, language, dialect, ways of communicating nonverbally, awareness, frame of reference, and identification.

mild retardation. A classification used to specify an individual whose IQ test score is between 55 and 69.

milieu teaching. A naturalistic approach to language intervention in which the goal is to teach functional language skills in a natural environment.

minimal brain injury. A term used to describe a child who shows behavioral but not neurological signs of brain injury; the term is not as popular as it once was, primarily because of its lack of diagnostic utility—i.e., some children who learn normally show signs indicative of MBI.

mixed hearing impairment. A hearing loss resulting from a combination of conductive and sensorineural hearing impairment.

mnemonic keyword method. A cognitive training strategy used to help children with memory problems remember curriculum content. The teacher transforms abstract information into a concrete picture, which depicts the material in a more meaningful way.

mnemonics. Techniques that aid memory, such as using rhymes, songs, or visual images to remember information.

moderate retardation. A classification used to specify an individual whose IQ test score is between approximately 40 and 55.

morphology. The study within psycholinguistics of word formation; of how adding or deleting parts of words changes their meaning.

multicultural education. Reform of educational institutions and curricula to provide equal educational opportunity to students regardless of their cultural identities (e.g., gender, social class, race, ethnicity, disability, etc.).

muscular dystrophy. A hereditary disease characterized by progressive weakness caused by degeneration of muscle fibers.

myopia. Nearsightedness; usually results when the eyeball is too long.

N

narrative. Self-controlled, self-initiated discourse; description or storytelling.

native-language emphasis. An approach to teaching language-minority students in which the student's native language is used for most of the day, and English is taught as a separate subject.

neologism. A coined word that is meaningless to others; meaningless words used in the speech of a person with a mental disorder.

nonsupperative otitis media. Inflammation of the middle ear that occurs without an infection; often preceded by infectious otitis media.

normalization. A philosophical belief in special education that every individual, even the most disabled, should have an educational and living environment as close to normal as possible.

nystagmus. Condition in which there are rapid involuntary movements of the eyes; sometimes indicates a brain malfunction and/or inner ear problems.

O

obstacle sense. A skill possessed by some people who are blind whereby they can detect the presence of obstacles in their environment. Research has shown that it is not an indication of an extra sense, as popularly thought; it is the result of being able to detect subtle changes in the pitch of high frequency echoes.

Optacon. A device used to enable persons who are blind to "read"; consists of a camera that converts print into an image of letters, which are then produced by way of vibration onto the finger.

orthosis. A device designed to restore, partially or completely, a lost function of the body (e. g. , a brace or crutch).

ossicles. Three tiny bones (malleus, incus, and stapes) that together make possible an efficient transfer of sound waves from the eardrum to the oval window, which connects the middle ear to the inner ear.

otitis media. Inflammation of the middle ear.

oval window. Connects the middle and inner ear.

P

paraplegia. A condition in which both legs are paralyzed.

partial participation. Students with disabilities, while in the regular classroom, engage in the same activities as nondisabled students but on a reduced basis; teacher makes adaptations in the activity to allow student to participate as much as possible.

PC/Kurzweil Personal Reader. A version of the Kurzweil Reading Machine that can be used with an IBM or Apple computer.

pediatric AIDS. Acquired immune deficiency syndrome that occurs in infants or young children; can be contracted by unborn fetuses from the blood of the mother through the placenta or through blood transfusions; an incurable virus that can result in a variety of physical and mental disorders; thought to be the fastest growing infectious cause of mental retardation.

peer collaboration. A process in which two general educators engage in structured dialogue to generate ideas for working with a student having problems in the general education class, rather than referring him or her to special education; the student's classroom teacher proposes interventions and how to measure their success while the other teacher guides the process.

peer tutoring. A method that can be used to integrate students with disabilities in regular classrooms, based on the notion that students can effectively tutor one another. The role of learner or teacher may be assigned to either the student with a disability or the nondisabled student.

Perkins Brailler. A system making it possible to write in Braille; has six keys, one for each of the six dots of the cell, which leave an embossed print on paper.

pervasive developmental disorder. Severe disorder characterized by abnormal social relations, including bizarre mannerisms, inappropriate social behavior, and unusual or delayed speech and language.

phenylketonuria (PKU). A metabolic genetic disorder caused by the inability of the body to convert phenylalanine to tyrosine; an accumulation of phenylalanine results in abnormal brain development.

phonological skills. The ability to understand grapheme-phoneme correspondence, the rules by which sounds go with letters to make up words; generally thought to be the reason for the reading problems of many students with learning disabilities.

phonology. The study of how individual sounds make up words.

PL 90–538. Congressional legislation passed in 1968 that created the Handicapped Children's Early Education Program (HCEEP).

PL 94–142. The Education for All Handicapped Children Act, which contains a mandatory provision stating that to receive funds under the act, every school system in the nation must make provision for a free, appropriate public education for every child between the ages of three and eighteen (now extended to ages three to twenty-one) regardless of how, or how seriously, he or she may be disabled.

PL 99-457. Extended the requirements of PL 94-142 to children aged three to five, with special incentive to states for instituting programs for ages birth to three years.

PL 101–476. Enacted in 1990, stipulates that schools provide transition services from secondary school to adulthood for all children with disabilities; scope includes post-secondary education, vocational training, integrated employment, continuing and adult education, independent living, and community living; stipulates that a transition plan be included in the IEP no later than 16 years of age.

portfolios. A collection of samples of a student's work done over time; a type of authentic assessment.

positron emission tomography (PET) scans. A computerized method for measuring bloodflow in the brain; during a cognitive task, a low amount of radioactive dye is injected in the brain; the dye collects in active neuron, indicating which areas of the brain are active.

postlingual deafness. Deafness occurring after the development of speech and language.

practical intelligence. The ability to solve problems related to activities of daily living; an aspect of the adaptive skills component of the AAMR definition.

pragmatics. The study within psycholinguistics of how one uses language in social situations; emphasizes functional use of language rather than its mechanics.

preacademic skills. Behaviors that are needed before formal academic instruction can begin (e. g., ability to identify letters, numbers, shapes, and colors).

precocity. Remarkable early development.

prelingual deafness. Deafness that occurs before the development of spoken language, usually at birth.

prelinguistic communication. Communication through gestures and noises before the child has learned oral language.

prereferral teams (PRTs). Made up of a variety of professionals, especially regular and special educators. These teams work with regular class teachers to come up with strategies for teaching difficult-to-teach children. Designed to influence regular educators to take ownership of difficult-to-teach students and to minimize inappropriate referrals to special education.

profound retardation. A classification used to specify an individual whose IQ test score is below approximately 25.

prosthesis. A device designed to replace, partially or completely, a part of the body (e.g., artificial teeth or limbs).

pull-out programs. Special education programs in which students with disabilities leave the regular classroom for part or all of the school day, e. g., to go to special classes or resource rooms.

pupil. The contractile opening in the middle of the iris of the eye.

pure-tone audiometry. A system whereby tones of various intensities and frequencies are presented to determine a person's hearing loss.

Q

quadriplegia. A condition in which all four limbs are paralyzed.

R

readiness skills. Skills deemed necessary before academics can be learned (e. g. , attending skills, the ability to follow directions, knowledge of letter names).

reciprocal teaching. A teaching method in which students and teachers are involved in a dialogue to facilitate reading comprehension.

reflex audiometry. The testing of responses to sounds by observation of such reflex actions as the orienting response and the Moro reflex.

regular education initiative (REI). A philosophy that maintains that general education, rather than special education, should be primarily responsible for the education of students with disabilities.

relay service. A system whereby a person with a teletypewriter (TTY) can communicate with a non-TTY user through an operator; now required by federal law in all states.

resonance. Refers to the quality of the sound imparted by the size, shape, and texture of the organs in the vocal tract.

retina. The back portion of the eye, containing nerve fibers connected to the optic nerve.

retinitis pigmentosa. A hereditary condition resulting in degeneration of the retina; causes a narrowing of the field of vision.

retinopathy of prematurity (ROP). Formerly referred to as retrolental fibroplasia, a condition resulting from administration of an excessive concentration of oxygen at birth; causes scar tissue to form behind the lens of the eye.

juvenile rheumatoid arthritis. A systemic disease with major symptoms involving the muscles and joints.

rubella (German measles). A serious viral disease, which, if it occurs during the first trimester of pregnancy, is likely to cause a deformity in the fetus.

S

scaffolded instruction. A cognitive approach to instruction whereby the teacher provides temporary structure or support while students are learning a task; the support is gradually removed as the students are able to perform the task independently.

schizophrenia. A disorder characterized by psychotic behavior manifested by loss of contact with reality, distorted thought processes, and abnormal perceptions.

seizure (convulsion). A sudden alteration of consciousness, usually accompanied by motor activity and/or sensory phenomena; caused by an abnormal discharge of electrical energy in the brain.

self-instruction. A type of cognitive training technique that requires individuals to talk aloud and then to themselves as they solve problems.

self-monitoring. A type of cognitive behavior modification technique that requires individuals to keep track of their own behavior.

self-regulation. Referring generally to a person's ability to regulate his or her own behavior, e.g., to employ strategies to help in a problem-solving situation; an area of difficulty for persons who are mentally retarded.

semantics. The study of the meanings attached to words and sentences.

sensorineural hearing impairment. A hearing loss, usually severe, resulting from malfunctioning of the inner ear.

sequelae. Consequences or secondary results.

severe retardation. A classification used to specify an individual whose IQ test score is between approximately 25 and 40.

sheltered-English approach. A method in which language-minority students are taught all their subjects in English at a level that is modified constantly according to individuals' needs.

sheltered workshop. A facility that provides a structured environment for persons with disabilities in which they can learn skills; can be either a transitional placement or a permanent arrangement.

short-term memory. The ability to recall information after a short period of time.

sign language. A manual language, used by people who are deaf, to communicate a true language with its own grammar.

signing English systems. Used simultaneously with oral methods in the total communication approach to teaching students who are deaf; different from American Sign Language because it maintains the same word order as spoken English.

slate and stylus. A method of writing in Braille in which the paper is held in a slate while the stylus is pressed through openings to make indentations in the paper. With this method the Braille cells are written in reverse order, and thus it is more difficult to use than the Perkins Brailler. It is more portable than the Perkins Brailler, however.

Snellen chart. Used in determining visual competence; consists of rows of letters or *E*s arranged in different positions; each row corresponds to the distance at which a normally sighted person can discriminate the letters; does not predict how accurately a child will be able to read print.

social construct. A concept created by a society to serve certain social purposes; an idea created by and commonly held in a society and used for making social judgments (e.g., *democracy, good, disability, giftedness*)

social intelligence. The ability to understand social expectations and to cope in social situations; an aspect of the adaptive skills component of the AAMR definition.

sociopathic. Behavior characteristic of a sociopath; someone whose behavior is aggressively antisocial and who shows no remorse or guilt for misdeeds.

sonography. High-frequency sound waves are converted into a visual picture; used to detect major physical malformations in the unborn fetus.

spastic. A term describing a sudden, involuntary contraction of muscles that makes accurate, voluntary movement difficult; a type of cerebral palsy.

spasticity. Characterized by muscle stiffness and problems in voluntary movement; associated with spastic cerebral palsy.

specific language impairment (SLI). A language disorder with no identifiable cause; language disorder not attributable to hearing impairment, mental retardation, brain dysfunction, or other plausible cause; also called specific language disability.

speech. Forming and sequencing oral language sounds during communication.

speech audiometry. A technique that tests a person's detection and understanding of speech rather than using pure tones to detect hearing loss.

speech disorders. Oral communication that involves abnormal use of the vocal apparatus, is unintelligible, or so inferior that it draws attention to itself and causes anxiety, feelings of inadequacy, or inappropriate behavior in the speaker.

speech reception threshold (SRT). The decibel level at which a person can understand speech.

speechreading. A method that involves teaching children to use visual information from a number of sources to understand what is being said to them; more than just lipreading, which uses only visual clues arising from the movement of the mouth in speaking.

spina bifida. A congenital midline defect resulting from failure of the bony spinal column to close completely during fetal development.

stapes. Stirrup-shaped bone in the ossicular chain of the middle ear.

stereotypic behaviors. Any of a variety of repetitive behaviors (e.g., eye rubbing) that are sometimes found in individuals who are blind, severely retarded, or psychotic. Sometimes referred to as stereotypies or blindisms.

stimulus reduction. A concept largely forwarded by Cruickshank; an approach to teaching distractible and hyperactive children that emphasizes reducing extraneous (nonrelevant to learning) material.

strabismus. A condition in which the eyes are directed inward (crossed eyes) or outward.

structured program. A concept largely forwarded by Cruickshank; emphasizes a teacher-directed approach in which activities and environment are structured for children who are distractible and hyperactive.

stuttering. Speech characterized by abnormal hesitations, prolongations, and repetitions; may be accompanied by grimaces, gestures, or other bodily movements indicative of a struggle to speak, anxiety, blocking of speech, or avoidance of speech.

supported competitive employment. A workplace where adults who are disabled or retarded earn at least a minimum wage and receive ongoing assistance from a specialist or job coach, and where the majority of workers are nondisabled.

supported employment. A method of integrating people with disabilities who cannot work independently into competitive employment; includes use of an employment specialist, or job coach, who helps person with disability function on the job.

syntax. The way words are joined together to structure meaningful sentences.

syphilis. A venereal disease that can cause mental subnormality in a child, especially if it is contracted by the mother-to-be during the latter stages of fetal development.

T

talent. A special ability, aptitude, or accomplishment.

Tay-Sachs disease. An inherited condition that can appear when both mother and father are carriers; results in brain damage and eventual death; it can be detected before birth through amniocentesis.

teletypewriter (TTY). A device connected to a telephone by a special adapter; allows communication between persons who are hearing impaired and the hearing over the telephone.

temperament. Inborn behavioral style, including general level of activity, regularity or predictability, approach or withdrawal, adaptability, intensity of reaction, responsiveness, mood, distractibility, and persistence. The temperament is present at birth but may be modified by parental management.

total communication approach. An approach for teaching the hearing impaired that blends oral and manual techniques.

Tourette's syndrome. A neurological disorder beginning in childhood (about 3 times more prevalent in boys than in girls) in which stereotyped motor movements (tics) are accompanied by multiple vocal outbursts that may include grunting or barking noises or socially inappropriate words or statements.

transliteration. A method used by sign language interpreters in which the signs maintain the same word order as that of spoken English; although used by most interpreters, found through research not to be as effective as American Sign Language (ASL).

traumatic brain injury (TBI). Injury to the brain (not including conditions present at birth, birth trauma, or degenerative diseases or conditions), resulting in total or partial disability or psychosocial maladjustment that affects educational performance; may affect cognition, language, memory, attention, reasoning, abstract thinking, judgement, problem solving, sensory or perceptual and motor disabilities, psychosocial behavior, physical functions, information processing, or speech.

traveling notebook. A system of communication in which parents and professionals write "messages" to each other by way of a notebook, or log, that accompanies the child to and from school.

trisomy 21. A type of Down syndrome in which the twenty-first chromosome is a triplet, making forty-seven, rather than the normal forty-six, chromosomes in all.

tympanic membrane (eardrum). The anatomical boundary between the outer and middle ear; the sound gathered in the outer ear vibrates here.

V

vestibular mechanism. Located in the upper portion of the inner ear; consists of three soft, semicircular canals filled with a fluid that is sensitive to head movement, acceleration, and other movements related to balance.

visual efficiency. A term used to refer to how well one uses one's vision, including such things as control of eye movements, attention to visual detail, and discrimination of figure from background. It is believed by some to be more important than visual acuity alone in predicting a person's ability to function visually.

vitreous humor. A transparent gelatinous substance that fills the eyeball between the retina and the lens of the eye.

W

working memory. The ability to remember information while also performing other cognitive operations.

PHOTOGRAPH AND ART CREDITS continued:

Chapter Opening Art

Chapter 1: Gordon Sasaki, *Thru The Fence;* **Chapter 2:** Louise Bego, *Sweet 2020;* **Chapter 3:** Daniel Napier, *Last Trumpet;* **Chapter 4:** Rodney Sullivan, *WVSA;* **Chapter 5:** Robin Chappell, *Georgetown Saturday Night;* **Chapter 6:** Geraldine Mlynek, *Qua;* **Chapter 7:** John Andrew Haas, *A Jag Portrait;* **Chapter 8:** Mary Thornley, *Self Portrait;* **Chapter 9:** Fran Benson, *Vivaldi;* **Chapter 10:** Greg Depauw; *untitled;* **Chapter 11:** Alyce Frank, *#9;* **Chapter 12:** Joanne O'Connell, *Picnic.*

Interior Photos:

Spencer Grant/Gamma Liaison: p. 4; Lyrl Ahern: p. 26; North Wind Picture Archives: p. 27; Cynthia Johnson/Gamma: p. 49; Bob Krist/Black Star: p. 61; Courtesy of Toys R Us and Saturn Corporation: p. 63; Stan Godlewski/Gamma Liaison: p. 94; Alan S. Weiner/Gamma Liaison: p. 128; Cindy Karp/Black Star: p. 143; Jim Pickerell: p. 151; Photo Researchers: p. 171; John Coletti: p. 195; Dan Habib/Impact Visuals: p. 219; Monkmeyer/Grantpix: p. 288; James King Holmes/Science Source/Photo Researchers: p. 316; Courtesy of Susan Duane: p. 328; Lynn Johnson: p. 329; David Butow: p. 336; Courtesy of Jewish Guild for the Blind: p. 360; John Bunting/Impact Visuals: p. 370; Wyman/Monkmeyer: p. 376; Michael Newman: PhotoEdit: p. 377; Paul S. Howell/Gamma Liaison: p. 378; Paul S. Howell/Gamma Liaison: p. 379; Joe Polimoni/Gamma Liaison: p. 381; Glasheen Graphics/Picture Cube: p. 399; Susan Greenwood/Gamma Liaison: p. 411; David Young-Wolff/PhotoEdit: p. 413; Courtesy of James Koefler/Children's Orthopedic Surgery Foundation: p. 422 (top); Charles Gupton/Stock Boston: p. 423 (top); Bob Daemmrich/Stock Boston; p. 423 (bottom); Courtesy of Surf Chair: p. 425; Daniel Simon/Gamma Liaison: p. 458 (top left); Agostini/Gamma Liaison: p. 458 (top center); Michael Broddy/Reuters/Archive: p. 458 (top right); Steve Allen/Gamma Liaison: p. 458 (middle left); Jim Levitt/Impact Visuals: p. 458 (middle center); Paula Bronstein/Impact Visuals: p. 458 (middle right); Owen Franken/Gamma Liaison: p. 458 (bottom left); Don Perdue/Gamma Liaison: p. 458 (bottom center); Hemsey/Gamma Liaison: p. 458 (bottom right); John Nordell/Picture Cube: p. 463; Will & Deni McIntyre/Photo Researchers: p. 505; Michael Newman/Photo Researchers: p. 506; Richard Hutchings/Photo Researchers: p. 512; Will Faller: pp. 6, 15, 55, 70, 91, 92, 111, 113, 131, 148, 164, 173, 187, 193, 214, 223, 245, 271, 279, 295, 318, 334, 298, 422 (bottom), 437, 475; Will Hart: pp. 25, 51, 52, 65, 98, 103, 167, 217, 233, 270, 298, 312, 342, 369, 460, 476, 485; Brian Smith: pp. 24, 69, 106, 125, 175, 500; Stephen Marks: 32, 97, 181, 213, 228, 265, 282, 418; Robert Harbison: pp. 76, 178, 278, 338, 386, 425 (right), 473.

References

Chapter 1

Bateman, B. D. (1992). *Better IEPS (p. 19)*. Creswell, OR: OtterInk.

Clark, D. L., & Astuto, T. A. (1988). *Education policy after Reagan—What next?* Occasional paper No. 6, Policy Studies Center of the University Council for Educational Administration, University of Virginia, Charlottesville.

Cruickshank, W. M. (1977). Guest editorial. *Journal of Learning Disabilities, 10*, 193–194.

Fuchs, D., & Fuchs, L. S. (1994). Inclusive schools movement and the radicalization of special education reform. *Exceptional Children, 60*, 294–309.

Goodlad, J. I., & Lovitt, T. C. (Eds.) (1993). *Integrating general and special education*. Columbus, OH: Merrill/Macmillan.

Goodman, J. F., & Bond, L. (1993). The individualized education program: A retrospective critique. *Journal of Special Education, 26*, 408–422.

Hart, B., & Risley, T. R. (1995). *Meaningful differences in the everyday experience of young American children*. Baltimore: Paul H. Brookes.

Hendrick, I. G., & MacMillan, D. L. (1989). Selecting children for special education in New York City: William Maxwell, Elizabeth Farrell, and the development of ungraded classes, 1900–1920. *Journal of Special Education, 22*, 395–417.

Howe, K. R., & Miramontes, O. B. (1992). *The ethics of special education*. New York: Teachers College Press.

Huefner, D. S. (1994). The mainstreaming cases: Tensions and trends for school administrators. *Educational Administration Quarterly, 30*, 27–55.

Hungerford, R. (1950). On locusts. *American Journal of Mental Deficiency, 54*, 415–418.

Itard, J. M. G. (1962). *The wild boy of Averyron*. (Trans. George & Muriel Humphrey). Englewood Cliffs, NJ: Prentice Hall.

Kanner, L. (1964). *A history of the care and study of the mentally retarded*. Springfield, IL: Charles C. Thomas.

Kauffman, J. M. (1995). Why we must celebrate a diversity of restrictive environments. *Learning Disabilities Research and Practice, 10*, 225–232.

Kauffman, J. M., & Hallahan, D. P. (Eds.). (1995). *The illusion of full inclusion: A comprehensive critique of a current special educational bandwagon*. Austin, TX: Pro-Ed.

Lloyd, J. W., Singh, N. N., & Repp, A. C. (Eds.). (1991). *The regular education initiative: Alternative perspectives on concepts, issues, and models*. Sycamore, IL: Sycamore.

MacMillan, D. L., & Hendrick, I. G. (1993). Evolution and legacies. In J. I. Goodlad & T. C. Lovitt (Eds.), *Integrating general and special education*. Columbus, OH: Merrill/Macmillan.

Martin, E. W. (1995). Case studies of inclusion: Worst fears realized. *Journal of Special Education, 29*, 192–199.

Morse, W. C. (1984). Personal perspective. In B. Blatt & R. Morris (Eds.), *Perspectives in special education: Personal orientations*. Glenview, IL: Scott, Foresman.

Patterson, G. R., Reid, J. B., & Dishion, T. J. (1992). *Antisocial boys*. Eugene, OR: Castalia.

Rhode, G., Jenson, W. R., & Reavis, H. K. (1992). *The tough kid book: Practical classroom management strategies*. Longmont, CA: Sopris West.

Sarason, S. B. (1990). *The predictable failure of educational reform: Can we change course before it's too late?* San Francisco: Jossey-Bass.

Taylor, H. (1995, July 18). Louis Harris/N.O.D. survey finds employers overwhelmingly support the ADA—and jobs. *The Washington Post*, p. A10.

U.S. Department of Education. (1992). *Fourteenth annual report to Congress on implementation of the Individuals with Disabilities Education Act*. Washington, DC: Author.

U.S. Department of Education. (1995). *Seventeenth annual report to Congress on implementation of the Individuals with Disabilities Education Act*. Washington, DC: Author.

Verstegen, D. A., & Clark, D. L. (1988). The diminution of federal expenditures for education during the Reagan administration. *Phi Delta Kappan, 70*, 134–138.

Werner, E. E. (1986). The concept of risk from a developmental perspective. In B. K. Keogh (Ed.), *Advances in special education, Vol. 5. Developmental problems in infancy and the preschool years*. Greenwich, CT: JAI Press.

Winzer, M. A. (1986). Early developments in special education: Some aspects of Enlightenment thought. *Remedial and Special Education, 7*(5), 42–49.

Winzer, M. A. (1993). *The history of special education: From isolation to integration*. Washington, DC: Gallaudet University Press.

Yanok, J. (1986). Free appropriate public education for handicapped children: Congressional intent and judicial interpretation. *Remedial and Special Education*, *7*(2), 49–53.

Ysseldyke, J. E., Algozzine, B., & Thurlow, M. L. (1992). *Critical issues in special education* (2nd ed.). Boston: Houghton Mifflin.

Zelder, E. Y. (1953). Public opinion and public education for the exceptional child—Court decisions 1873–1950. *Exceptional Children*, *18*, 187–198.

Zigmond, N., & Baker, J. M. (1995). Concluding comments: Current and future practices in inclusive schooling. *Journal of Special Education, 29*, 245–250.

Chapter 2

Abt Associates. (1976–1977). *Education as experimentation: A planned variation model (Vol. 3A and 4)*. Cambridge, MA: Author.

Baker, J. M., & Zigmond, N. (1995). The meaning and practice of inclusion for students with learning disabilities: Themes and implications from the five cases. *Journal of Special Education, 29*, 163–180.

Bank-Mikkelsen, N. E. (1969). A metropolitan area in Denmark: Copenhagen. In R. B. Kugel & W. Wolfensberger (Eds.), *Changing patterns of residential services for the mentally retarded* (pp. 227–254). Washington, DC: President's Committee on Mental Retardation.

Baumeister, A. A., Kupstas, F., & Klindworth, L. M. (1990). New morbidity: Implications for prevention of children's disabilities. *Exceptionality, 1*(1), 1–16.

Blatt, B., & Kaplan, F. (1966). *Christmas in Purgatory: A photographic essay on mental retardation.* Boston: Allyn and Bacon.

Bogdan, R. (1986). The sociology of special education. In R. J. Morris & B. Blatt (Eds.), *Special education: Research and trends* (pp. 344–359). New York: Pergamon Press.

Bogdan, R., & Biklen, D. (1977). Handicapism. *Social Policy*, *7*(5), 14–19.

Brantlinger, E. A., & Guskin, S. L. (1987). Ethnocultural and social-psychological effects on learning characteristics of handicapped children. In M. C. Wang, M. C. Reynolds, & H. J. Walberg (Eds.), *Handbook of special education: Research and practice. Vol. 1. Learner characteristics and adaptive education* (pp. 7–34). New York: Pergamon Press.

Bricker, D. D. (1986). An analysis of early intervention programs: Attendant issues and future directions. In R. J. Morris & B. Blatt (Eds.), *Special education: Research and trends* (pp. 28–65). New York: Pergamon Press.

Carta, J. J. (1995). Developmentally appropriate practice: A critical analysis as applied to young children with disabilities. *Focus on Exceptional Children, 27*(8), 1–14.

Chadsey-Rusch, J., & Heal, L. W. (1995). Building consensus from transition experts on social integration outcomes and interventions. *Exceptional Children, 62,* 165–187.

Chalfant, J. C., Pysh, M. V., & Moultrie, R. (1979). Teacher assistance teams: A model for within-building problem solving. *Learning Disability Quarterly*, *2*, 85–96.

Children's Museum of Boston, with WGBH Boston. (1978). *What if you couldn't? An elementary school program about handicaps.* Weston, MA: Burt Harrison.

Cohen, S. (1977). *Accepting individual differences.* Allen, TX: Developmental Learning Materials.

Crissey, M. S., & Rosen, M. (Eds.). (1986). *Institutions for the mentally retarded: A changing role in changing times*. Austin, TX: Pro-Ed.

DeStefano, L., & Wermuth, T. R. (1992). IDEA (P.L. 101–476): Defining a second generation of transition services. In F. R. Rusch, L. DeStefano, J. Chadsey-Rusch, L. A. Phelps, & E. Szymanski (Eds.), *Transition from school to adult life* (pp. 537–549). Sycamore, IL: Sycamore Publishing.

Edgar, E. (1987). Secondary programs in special education: Are many of them justifiable? *Exceptional Children*, *53*(6), 555–561.

Eiserman, W. D., Weber, C., & McCoun, M. (1995). Parent and professional roles in early intervention: A longitudinal comparison of the effects of two intervention configurations. *Journal of Special Education, 29,* 20–44.

Fiedler, C. R., & Simpson, R. L. (1987). Modifying the attitudes of nonhandicapped high school students toward handicapped peers. *Exceptional Children*, *53*, 342–349.

Fowler, S. A., Schwartz, I., & Atwater, J. (1991). Perspectives on the transition from preschool to kindergarten for children with disabilities and their families. *Exceptional Children*, *58*(2), 136–145.

Fuchs, D., & Fuchs, L. S. (1991). Framing the REI debate: Abolitionists versus conservationists. In J. W. Lloyd, N. N. Singh, & A. C. Repp (Eds.), *The regular education initiative. Alternative perspectives on concepts, issues, and models* (pp. 241–255). Sycamore, IL: Sycamore Publishing.

Fuchs, D., & Fuchs, L. S. (1992). Limitations of a feel-good approach to consultation. *Journal of Educational and Psychological Consultation*, *3,* 93–97.

Gallagher, J. J. (1972). The special education contract for mildly handicapped children. *Exceptional Children*, *38*, 527–535.

Gallagher, J. J. (1992). The roles of values and facts in policy development for infants and toddlers with disabilities and their families. *Journal of Early Intervention*, *16*(1), 1–10.

Gartner, A., & Joe, T. (1986). Introduction. In A. Gartner & T. Joe (Eds.), *Images of the disabled/disabling images*. New York: Praeger.

Gerber, M. M., & Kauffman, J. M. (1981). Peer tutoring in academic settings. In P. S. Strain (Ed.), *The utilization of classroom peers as behavior change agents* (pp. 155–187). New York: Plenum Press.

Gerber, M. M., & Semmel, M. I. (1984). Teacher as imperfect test: Reconceptualizing the referral process. *Educational Psychologist*, *19*, 137–148.

Gerber, M. M., & Semmel, M. I. (1985). Microeconomics of referral and reintegration: A paradigm for evaluation of special education. *Studies in Educational Evaluation*, *11*(1), 13–29.

Giangreco, M. F., & Putnam, J. W. (1991). Supporting the education of students with severe disabilities in regular education environments. In L. H. Meyer, C. A. Peck, & L. Brown (Eds.), *Critical issues in the lives of people with severe disabilities* (pp. 245–270). Baltimore, MD: Paul H. Brookes.

Guralnick, M. J. (1991). The next decade of research on the effectiveness of early intervention. *Exceptional Children*, *58*(2), 174–183.

Guterman, B. R. (1995). The validity of categorical learning disabilities services: The consumer's view. *Exceptional Children, 62,* 111–124.

Halpern, A. S. (1985). Transition: A look at the foundations. *Exceptional Children, 51*(6), 479–486.

Halpern, A. S. (1992). Transition: Old wine in new bottles. *Exceptional Children, 58*(3), 202–211.

Halpern, A. S. (1993). Quality of life as a conceptual framework for evaluating transition outcomes. *Exceptional Children, 59,* 486–498.

Heal, L. W., & Rusch, F. R. (1995). Predicting employment status for students who leave special education high school programs. *Exceptional Children, 61,* 472–487.

Hebbeler, K. M., Smith, B. J., & Black, T. L. (1991). Federal early childhood special education policy: A model for the improvement of services for children with disabilities. *Exceptional Children, 58*(2), 104–112.

Hendrick, I. G., MacMillan, D. L., & Balow, I. H. (1989, April). *Early school leaving in America: A review of the literature.* Riverside: University of California, California Educational Research Cooperative.

Hershey, L. (1991, July/August). Pride. *The disability rag*, pp. 1, 4–5. Louisville, KY: Advocato Press.

ICD Survey III. (1989, June). *A report card on special education.* New York: Louis Harris and Associates. (Conducted for International Center for the Disabled in cooperation with National Council on Disability.)

Jenkins, J. R., & Jenkins, L. M. (1987). Making peer tutoring work. *Educational Leadership, 44*(6), 64–68.

Johnson, D. W., & Johnson, R. (1986). Mainstreaming and cooperative learning strategies. *Exceptional Children, 52,* 553–561.

Johnson, L. J., & Pugach, M. C. (1991). Peer collaboration: Accommodating students with mild learning and behavior problems. *Exceptional Children, 57,* 454–461.

Kauffman, J. M. (1989). The regular education initiative as a Reagan-Bush education policy: A trickle-down theory of education of the hard-to-teach. *Journal of Special Education, 23*(3), 256–278.

Kauffman, J. M., & Hallahan, D. P. (1992). Deinstitutionalization and mainstreaming exceptional children. In M. C. Alkin (Ed.), *Encyclopedia of educational research: Vol. 1* (6th ed.) (pp. 299–303). New York: Macmillan.

Kauffman, J. M., & Hallahan, D. P. (1993). Toward a comprehensive delivery system: The necessity of identity, focus, and authority for special education and other compensatory programs. In J. I. Goodlad & T. C. Lovitt (Eds.), *Integrating general and special education (pp. 73–102).* Columbus, OH: Merrill.

Klobas, L. (1985, January-February). TV's concept of people with disabilities: Here's lookin' at you. *The disability rag*, pp. 2–6. Louisville, KY: Advocado Press.

Landesman, S., & Butterfield, E. C. (1987). Normalization and deinstitutionalization of mentally retarded individuals: Controversy and facts. *American Psychologist, 42,* 809–816.

Laski, F. J. (1991). Achieving integration during the second revolution. In L. H. Meyer, C. A. Peck, & L. Brown (Eds.), *Critical issues in the lives of people with severe disabilities* (pp. 409–421). Baltimore, MD: Paul H. Brookes.

Lieberman, L. M. (1992). Preserving special education . . . for those who need it. In W. Stainback & S. Stainback (Eds.), *Controversial issues confronting special education: Divergent perspectives* (pp. 13–25). Boston: Allyn and Bacon.

Lloyd, J. W., Crowley, E. P., Kohler, F. W., & Strain, P. S. (1988). Redefining the applied research agenda: Cooperative learning, prereferral, teacher consultation, and peer-mediated interventions. *Journal of Learning Disabilities, 21,* 43–52.

Longmore, P. K. (1985). Screening stereotypes: Images of disabled people. *Social Policy, 16,* 31–37.

Lord, W. (1991, November). Parent point of view: What is the least restrictive environment for a deaf child? *Michigan Statewide Newsletter*, p. 4.

MacMillan, D. L., Widaman, K. F., Balow, I. H., Borthwick-Duffy, S., Hendrick, I. G., & Hemsley, R. E. (1992). Special education students exiting the educational system. *Journal of Special Education, 26*(1), 20–36.

McCann, S. K., Semmel, M. I., & Nevin, A. (1985). Reverse mainstreaming: Nonhandicapped students in special education classrooms. *Remedial and Special Education, 6*(1), 13–19.

McMurray, G. L. (1986). Easing everyday living: Technology for the physically disabled. In A. Gartner & T. Joe (Eds.), *Images of the disabled/disabling images.* New York: Praeger.

Nowacek, E. J. (1992). Professionals talk about teaching together: Interviews with five collaborating teachers. *Intervention in School and Clinic, 27*(5), 262–276.

Padden, C., & Humphries, T. (1988). *Deaf in America: Voices from a culture.* Cambridge, MA: Harvard University Press.

Position Statement of National Association for the Education of Young Children and National Association of Early Childhood Specialists in State Departments of Education. (1991). *Young Children, 46*(3), 21–38.

Pugach, M. C., & Johnson, L. J. (1995). Unlocking expertise among classroom teachers through structured dialogue: Extending research on peer collaboration. *Exceptional Children, 62,* 101–110.

Raynes, M., Snell, M., & Sailor, W. (1991). A fresh look at categorical programs for children with special needs. *Phi Delta Kappan, 73*(4), 326–331.

Reeve, P. T., & Hallahan, D. P. (1994). Practical questions about collaboration between general and special educators. *Focus on Exceptional Children, 26*(7), 1–10, 12.

Rusch, F. R., & Hughes, C. (1990). Historical overview of supported employment. In F. R. Rusch (Ed.), *Supported employment: Models, methods, and issues* (pp. 5–14). Sycamore, IL: Sycamore Publishing.

Rusch, F. R., Szymanski, E. M., & Chadsey-Rusch, J. (1992). The emerging field of transition services. In F. R. Rusch, L. DeStefano, J. Chadsey-Rusch, L. A. Phelps, & E. Szymanski (Eds.), *Transition from school to adult life* (pp. 5–15). Sycamore, IL: Sycamore Publishing.

Sailor, W. (1991). Special education in the restructured school. *Remedial and Special Education, 12*(6), 8–22.

Sale, P., & Carey, D. M. (1995). The sociometric status of students with disabilities in a full-inclusion school. *Exceptional Children, 62,* 6–19.

Sands, D. J., & Kozleski, E. B. (1994). Quality of life differences between adults with and without disabilities. *Education and Training in Mental Retardation and Developmental Disabilities, 29,* 90–101.

Schram, L., Semmel, M. I., Gerber, M. M., Bruce, M. M., Lopez-Reyna, N., & Allen, D. (1984). *Problem solving teams in California.* Unpublished manuscript, University of California at Santa Barbara.

Scruggs, T. E., & Richter, L. (1986). Tutoring learning disabled students: A critical review. *Learning Disability Quarterly*, *9*, 2–14.

Scruggs, T. E., & Mastropieri, M. A. (in press). Teacher perceptions of mainstreaming: A research synthesis. *Exceptional Children.*

Semmel, M. I., Abernathy, T. V., Butera, G., & Lesar, S. (1991). Teacher perceptions of the regular education initiative. *Exceptional Children*, *58*(1), 9–24.

Sitlington, P. L., Frank, A. R., & Carson, R. (1992). Adult adjustment among high school graduates with mild disabilities. *Exceptional Children, 59,* 221–233.

Slavin, R. E. (1988). Cooperative learning and student achievement. *Educational Leadership*, *46*(2), 31–33.

Slavin, R. E. (1991). Synthesis of research on cooperative learning. *Educational Leadership*, *48*(5), 71–82.

Slentz, K. L., & Bricker, D. (1992). Family-guided assessment for IFSP development: Jumping off the family assessment bandwagon. *Journal of Early Intervention*, *16*(1), 11–19.

Stainback, S., & Stainback, W. (1992). Schools as inclusive communities. In W. Stainback & S. Stainback (Eds.), *Controversial issues confronting special education: Divergent perspectives* (pp. 29–43). Boston: Allyn & Bacon.

Szymanski, E. M. (1994). Transition: Life-span and life-space considerations for empowerment. *Exceptional Children, 60,* 402–410.

Trent, S. C. (1992). *Collaboration between special education and regular education teachers: A cross-case analysis.* Doctoral dissertation, University of Virginia, Charlottesville, VA.

Turnbull, A. P., & Turnbull, H. R. (1990). *Families, professionals, and exceptionality: A special partnership* (2nd ed.). Columbus, OH: Merrill.

U.S. Department of Education. (1990). *National goals for education.* Washington, DC: U. S. Government Printing Office.

U.S. Senate-House. (1994, March 21). *Goals 2000: Educate America Act.* (Conference Report 103-446). Washington, DC: Author.

Walker, H. M., & Bullis, M. (1991). Behavior disorders and the social context of regular class integration: A conceptual dilemma? In J. W. Lloyd, N. N. Singh, & A. C. Repp (Eds.), *The regular education initiative: Alternative perspectives on concepts, issues, and models* (pp. 75–93). Sycamore IL: Sycamore Publishing.

Wesson, C., & Mandell, C. (1989). Simulations promote understanding of handicapping conditions. *Teaching Exceptional Children*, *22*(1), 32–35.

West, J. F., & Idol, L. (1990). Collaborative consultation in the education of mildly handicapped and at-risk students. *Remedial and Special Education*, *11*(1), 22–31.

Will, M. C. (1986). Educating children with learning problems: A shared responsibility. *Exceptional Children*, *52*, 411–415.

Wolf, B. (1974). *Don't feel sorry for Paul.* Philadelphia: Lippincott.

Wolfensberger, W. (1972). *The principle of normalization in human services.* Toronto: National Institute on Mental Retardation.

Wolman, C., Bruininks, R., & Thurlow, M. (1989). Dropouts and drop out programs: Implications for special education. *Remedial and Special Education*, *10*(5), 6–20, 50.

Zigler, E., Hodapp, R. M., & Edison, M. R. (1990). From theory to practice in the care and education of mentally retarded individuals. *American Journal on Mental Retardation*, *95*(1), 1–12.

Zigmond, N., & Miller, S. E. (1992). Improving high school programs for students with learning disabilities: A matter of substance as well as form. In F. R. Rusch, L. DeStefano, J. Chadsey-Rusch, L. A. Phelps, & E. Szymanski (Eds.), *Transition from school to adult life* (pp. 17–31). Sycamore IL: Sycamore Publishing.

Zigmond, N. (1995). An exploration of the meaning and practice of special education in the context of full inclusion of students with learning disabilities. *Journal of Special Education, 29,* 109–115.

Zigmond, N., & Baker, J. M. (1995). Concluding comments: Current and future practices in inclusive schooling. *Journal of Special Education, 29,* 245–250.

Zigmond, N., Jenkins, J., Fuchs, L. S., Deno, S., Fuchs, D., Baker, J. N., Jenkins, L., & Couthino, M. (1995). Special education in restructured schools: Findings from three multi-year studies. *Phi Delta Kappan, 76,* 531–540.

Chapter 3

Adger, C. T., Wolfram, W., & Detwyler, J. (1993). Language differences: A new approach for special educators. *Teaching Exceptional Children, 26*(1), 44–47.

Ascher, C. (1992). School programs for African-American males . . . and females. *Phi Delta Kappan, 73,* 777–782.

Banks, J. A. (1993). *Introduction to multicultural education.* Boston: Allyn and Bacon.

Banks, J. A. (1994). *Multiethnic education: Theory and practice* (3rd ed.). Boston: Allyn and Bacon.

Banks, J. A. (1995). The historical reconstruction of knowledge about race: Implications for transformative teaching. *Educational Researcher, 24*(2), 15–25.

Banks, J. A., & Banks, C. A. M. (Eds.). (1993). *Multicultural education: Issues and perspectives* (2nd ed.). Boston: Allyn and Bacon.

Bateman, B. D. (1994). Who, how, and where: Special education's issues in perpetuity. *Journal of Special Education, 27*, 509–520.

Bauer, G. B., Dubanoski, R., Yamauchi, L. A., & Honbo, K. M. (1990). Corporal punishment and the schools. *Education and Urban Society*, *22*, 285–299.

Bempechat, J., & Omori, M. (1990). Meeting the educational needs of Southeast Asian children. *Digest*. New York: ERIC Clearinghouse on Urban Education, Institute for Urban and Minority Education, Teachers College, Columbia University.

Bender, W. N. (1988). The other side of placement decisions: Assessment of the mainstream learning environment. *Remedial and Special Education*, *9*(5), 28–33.

Boutte, G. S. (1992). Frustrations of an African-American parent: A personal and professional account. *Phi Delta Kappan*, *73*, 786–788.

Caplan, N., Choy, M. H., & Whitmore, J. K. (1992, February). Indochinese refugee families and academic achievement. *Scientific American, 266*(2), 36–42.

Carnes, J. (1994). An uncommon language: The multicultural making of American English. *Teaching Tolerance, 3*(1), 56–63.

Chinn, P. C., & Hughes, S. (1987). Representation of minority students in special education classes. *Remedial and Special Education, 8*(4), 41–46.

Council for Children with Behavioral Disorders. (1989). White paper. Best assessment practices for students with behavioral disorders: Accommodation to cultural diversity and individual differences. *Behavioral Disorders, 14*, 263–278.

Davidson, F. H., & Davidson, M. M. (1994). *Changing childhood prejudice: The caring work of the schools*. Westport, CT: Bergin & Garvey.

Dean, A. V., Salend, S. J., & Taylor, L. (1993). Multicultural education: A challenge for special educators. *Teaching Exceptional Children, 26*(1), 40–43.

Delpit, L. D. (1988). The silenced dialogue: Power and pedagogy in educating other people's children. *Harvard Educational Review, 58*, 280–298.

Delpit, L. (1995). *Other people's children: Cultural conflict in the classroom.* New York: New Press.

Deno, S. L. (1985). Curriculum-based measurement: The emerging alternative. *Exceptional Children, 52*, 219–232.

Devore, W., & Schlesinger, E. G. (1987). *Ethnic-sensitive social work practice* (2nd ed.). Columbus, OH: Merrill/Macmillan.

Duke, D. L. (1990). *Teaching: An introduction*. New York: McGraw-Hill.

Edgar, E., & Siegel, S. (1995). Postsecondary scenarios for troubled and troubling youth. In J. M. Kauffman, J. W. Lloyd, D. P. Hallahan, & T. A. Astuto (Eds.), *Issues in educational placement: Students with emotional and behavioral disorders* (pp. 251–283). Hillsdale, NJ: Lawrence Erlbaum.

Farrington, D. P. (1986). The sociocultural context of childhood disorders. In H. C. Quay & J. S. Werry (Eds.), *Psychopathological disorders of childhood* (3rd ed.). New York: Wiley.

Ford, B. A., Obiakor, F. E., & Patton, J. M. (Eds.). (1995). *Effective education of African American exceptional learners: New perspectives*. Austin, TX: Pro-Ed.

Franklin, M. E. (1992). Culturally sensitive instructional practices for African-American learners with disabilities. *Exceptional Children, 59*, 115–122.

Garcia, R. (1978). *Fostering a pluralistic society through multi-ethnic education*. Bloomington, IN: Phi Delta Kappa.

Garcia, S. B., & Malkin, D. H. (1993). Toward defining programs and services for culturally and linguistically diverse learners in special education. *Teaching Exceptional Children, 26*(1), 52–58.

Gerber, P. J., Ginsberg, R., & Reiff, H. B. (1992). Identifying alterable patterns in employment success for highly successful adults with learning disabilities. *Journal of Learning Disabilities, 25*, 475–487.

Gersten, R., Brengelman, S., & Jimenez, R. (1994). Effective instruction for culturally and linguistically diverse students: A reconceptualization. *Focus on Exceptional Children, 27*(1), 1–16.

Gersten, R., & Woodward, J. (1994). The language-minority student and special education: Issues, trends, and paradoxes. *Exceptional Children, 60*, 310–322.

Gollnick, D., & Chinn, P. (Eds.). (1990). *Multicultural education in a pluralistic society* (3rd ed.). Columbus, OH: Merrill/Macmillan.

Gollnick, D. M., & Chinn, P. C. (1994). *Multicultural education in a pluralistic society* (4th ed.). New York: Macmillan.

Hallahan, D. P., & Kauffman, J. M. (1994). Toward a culture of disability in the aftermath of Deno and Dunn. *Journal of Special Education, 27*, 496–508.

Hanna, J. (1988). *Disruptive school behavior: Class, race and culture*. New York: Holmes & Meier.

Harrison-Ross, P., & Wyden, B. (1973). *The black child*. Berkeley, CA: Medallion.

Harry, B., Torguson, C., Katkavich, J., & Guerrero, M. (1993). Crossing social class and cultural barriers in working with families. *Teaching Exceptional Children, 26*(1), 48–51.

Harry, B. (1995). African American families. In B. A. Ford, F. E. Obiakor, & J. M. Patton (Eds.), *Effective education of African American exceptional learners: New perspectives* (pp. 211–233). Austin, TX: Pro-Ed.

Hilliard, A. G. (1989). Teachers and cultural styles in a pluralistic society. *NEA Today, 7*(6), 65–69.

Hilliard, A. G. (1992). The pitfalls and promises of special education practice. *Exceptional Children, 59*, 168–172.

Hirsch, E. D. (1987). *Cultural literacy: What every American needs to know*. Boston: Houghton Mifflin.

Horton, P., & Hunt, C. (1968). *Sociology* (2nd ed.). New York: McGraw-Hill.

Howell, K. W., & Morehead, M. K. (1987). *Curriculum-based evaluation for special and remedial education*. Columbus, OH: Merrill/Macmillan.

Hunter, J. D. (1991). *Culture wars: The struggle to define America*. New York: Basic Books.

Hyman, I. A. (1988). *Eliminating corporal punishment in schools: Moving from advocacy research to policy development*. Paper presented at the 96th annual convention of the American Psychological Association, Atlanta.

Jacob, E., & Jordan, C. (Eds.). (1987). Explaining the school performance of minority students. *Anthropology and Education Quarterly, 18*(4) [special issue].

Johnson, D. W., & Johnson, R. (1986). Mainstreaming and cooperative learning strategies. *Exceptional Children, 52*, 553–561.

Kauffman, J. M., Mostert, M. P., Nuttycombe, D. G., Trent, S. C., & Hallahan, D. P. (1993). *Managing classroom behavior: A reflective case-based approach*. Boston: Allyn and Bacon.

Kidder, J. T. (1989). *Among schoolchildren*. Boston: Houghton Mifflin.

Leake, D., & Leake, B. (1992). African-American immersion schools in Milwaukee: A view from inside. *Phi Delta Kappan, 73*, 783–785.

Lloyd, J. W., & Blandford, B. J. (1991). Assessment for instruction. In H. L. Swanson (Ed.), *Handbook on the assessment of learning disabilities* (pp. 45–58). Austin, TX: Pro-Ed.

Lynch, J., Modgil, C., & Modgil, S. (Eds.). (1992a). *Cultural diversity and the schools. Vol. 1. Education for cultural diversity: Convergence and divergence*. London: Falmer.

Lynch, J., Modgil, C., & Modgil, S. (Eds.). (1992b). *Cultural diversity and the schools. Vol. 2. Prejudice, polemic or progress?* London: Falmer.

Lynch, J., Modgil, C., & Modgil, S. (Eds.). (1992c). *Cultural diversity and the schools. Vol. 3. Equity or excellence? Education and cultural reproduction*. London: Falmer.

Lynch, J., Modgil, C., & Modgil, S. (Eds.). (1992d). *Cultural diversity and the schools. Vol. 4. Human rights, education and global responsibilities*. London: Falmer.

Martin, D. S. (1987). Reducing ethnocentrism. *Teaching Exceptional Children, 20*(1), 5–8.

McDowell, E., & Friedman, R. (1979). An analysis of editorial opinion regarding corporal punishment: Some dynamics of regional differences. In I. A. Hyman & J. H. Wise (Eds.), *Corporal punishment in American education* (pp. 384–393). Philadelphia, PA: Temple University Press.

McIntyre, T. (1987). Teacher awareness of child abuse and neglect. *Child Abuse and Neglect, 11*(1), 33–35.

McIntyre, T. (1992a). The "invisible culture" in our schools: Gay and lesbian youth. *Beyond Behavior, 3*(3), 6–12.

McIntyre, T. (1992b). The culturally sensitive disciplinarian. In R. B. Rutherford & S. R. Mathur (Eds.), *Monograph in behavioral disorders: Severe behavior disorders of children and youth, 15*, 107–115.

McIntyre, T. (1992c). A primer on cultural diversity for educators. *Multicultural Forum, 1*(1), 6–7, 12.

McIntyre, T., & Silva, P. (1992). Culturally diverse childrearing practices: Abusive or just different? *Beyond Behavior, 4*(1), 8–12.

McLoughlin, J. A., & Lewis, R. B. (1990). *Assessing special students*. Columbus, OH: Merrill/Macmillan.

McNergney, R. F. (1992). *Teaching and learning in multicultural settings: The case of Hans Christian Anderson School*. Video cassette. Boston: Allyn and Bacon.

Mehta, V. (1989). *The stolen light*. New York: W. W. Norton.

Miller, W. (1959). Implications of urban lower class culture for social work. *Social Service Review, 33*, 232–234.

Minow, M. (1985). Learning to live with the dilemma of difference: Bilingual and special education. In K. T. Bartlett & J. W. Wegner (Eds.), *Children with special needs* (pp. 375–429). New Brunswick, NJ: Transaction Books.

Ogbu, J. U. (1990). Understanding diversity: Summary comments. *Education and Urban Society, 22*, 425–429.

Ogbu, J. U. (1992). Understanding cultural diversity and learning. *Educational Researcher, 21*(8), 5–14.

Ortiz, A., Yates, J. R., & Garcia, S. B. (1990). Competencies associated with serving exceptional language minority students. *Bilingual Special Education Newsletter*, Vol. 9. Austin, TX: University of Texas, College of Education, Office of Bilingual Education.

Padden, C., & Humphries, T. (1988). *Deaf in America: Voices from a culture*. Cambridge, MA: Harvard University Press.

Patterson, O. (1993, Feb. 7). Black like all of us: Celebrating multiculturalism diminishes blacks' role in American culture. *The Washington Post*, p. C2.

Patton, J. M. (1992). Assessment and identification of African-American learners with gifts and talents. *Exceptional Children, 59*, 150–159.

Patton, J. M., & Baytops, J. L. (1995). Identifying and transforming the potential of young, gifted African Americans: A clarion call. In B. A. Ford, F. E. Obiakor, & J. M. Patton (Eds.), *Effective education of African American exceptional learners: New perspectives* (pp. 27–67). Austin, TX: Pro-Ed.

Persky, B. (1974). Urban health problems. In L. Golubchick & B. Persky (Eds.), *Urban, social, and educational issues*. Dubuque, IA: Kendall/Hunt.

Poteet, J. A., Choate, J. S., & Stewart, S. C. (1993). Performance assessment and special education: Practices and prospects. *Focus on Exceptional Children, 26*(1), 1–20.

Price, H. B. (1992). Multiculturalism: Myths and realities. *Phi Delta Kappan, 74*, 208–213.

Reschly, D. J. (1987). Learning characteristics of mildly handicapped students: Implications for classification, placement, and programming. In M. C. Wang, M. C. Reynolds, & H. J. Walberg (Eds.), *Handbook of special education: Research and practice. Vol. 1: Learner characteristics and adaptive education*. New York: Pergamon Press,

Rodriguez, R. (1982). *Hunger of memory: The education of Richard Rodriguez. An autobiography*. Boston: D. R. Godine.

Rodriguez, R. (1992). *Days of obligation: An argument with my Mexican father*. New York: Viking.

Rogoff, B., & Morelli, G. (1989). Culture and American children. *American Psychologist, 44*, 341–342.

Rosenfeld, G. (1971). *Shut those thick lips! A study of slum school failure*. New York: Holt, Rinehart, & Winston.

Russell, K. Y. (1992). *The color complex: The "last taboo" among African Americans*. San Diego, CA: Harcourt Brace Jovanovich.

Shor, I. (1986). *Culture wars: School and society in the conservative restoration, 1969–1984*. Boston: Routledge & K. Paul.

Siccone, F. (1995). *Celebrating diversity: Building self-esteem in today's multicultural classrooms*. Boston: Allyn and Bacon.

Silverstein, B., & Krate, R. (1975). *Children of the dark ghetto: A developmental psychology*. New York: Praeger.

Slavin, R. E. (1988). Cooperative learning and student achievement. *Educational Leadership, 46*(2), 31–33.

Sleeter, C. E., & Grant, C. A. (1994). *Making choices for multicultural education: Five approaches to race, class, and gender* (2nd ed.). New York: Macmillan.

Spinetta, J. J., & Rigler, D. (1972). The child-abusing parent: A psychological review. *Psychological Bulletin, 77*, 296–304.

Stack, C. (1974). *All our kin: Strategies for survival in a black community*. New York: Harper & Row.

Steele, C. M. (1992, April). Race and the schooling of black Americans. *Atlantic Monthly*, 68–78.

Spring, J. (1994). *Deculturalization and the struggle for equality: A brief history of education of dominated cultures in the United States*. New York: McGraw-Hill.

Swisher, K. (1990, January). Cooperative learning and the education of American Indian/Alaskan Native students: A review of the literature and suggestions for implementation. *Journal of American Indian Education*, 36–43.

Takaki, R. (1994). Interview: Reflections from a different mirror. *Teaching Tolerance, 3*(1), 11–15.

Uribe, V., & Harbeck, K. M. (1992). *Coming out of the classroom closet: Gay and lesbian students, teachers, and curricula*. Binghamton, NY: Hayworth Press.

U.S. Department of Education. (1992). *Fourteenth annual report to Congress on the implementation of the Individuals with Disabilities Education Act*. Washington, DC: Author.

Wallace, G., Larsen, S. C., & Elksnin, L. K. (1992). *Educational assessment of learning problems: Testing for teaching* (2nd ed.). Boston: Allyn and Bacon.

Williams, E. (1994). North meets South: Pen pals in Alabama and New York discover shared interests, dispel regional stereotypes. *Teaching Tolerance, 3*(1), 17–19.

Wortham, A. (1992, September). Afrocentrism isn't the answer for black students in American society. *Executive Educator, 14*, 23–25.

Ysseldyke, J. E., & Christenson, S. L. (1987). Evaluating students' instructional environments. *Remedial and Special Education, 8*(3), 17–24.

Ysseldyke, J. E., & Marston, D. (1988). Issues in the psychological evaluation of children. In V. B. Van Hasselt, P. S. Strain, & M. Hersen (Eds.), *Handbook of developmental and physical disabilities* (pp. 21–37). New York: Pergamon.

Chapter 4

AAMR Ad Hoc Committee on Terminology and Classification. (1992). *Mental retardation: Definition, classification, and systems of support* (9th ed.). Washington, DC: American Association on Mental Retardation.

Baker, L. (1982). An evaluation of the role of metacognitive deficits in learning disabilities. *Topics in Learning and Learning Disabilities, 2*(1), 27–35.

Bates, P., Renzaglia, A., & Wehman, P. (1981). Characteristics of an appropriate education for severely and profoundly handicapped students. *Education and Training of the Mentally Retarded, 16*, 142–149.

Batshaw, M. L., & Perret, Y. M. (1986). *Children with handicaps: A medical primer* (2nd ed.). Baltimore: Paul H. Brookes.

Baumeister, A. A., Kupstas, F., & Klindworth, L. M. (1990). New morbidity: Implications for prevention of children's disabilities. *Exceptionality, 1*(1), 1–16.

Berkell, D. (1988). Identifying programming goals for productive employment. In B. L. Ludlow, A. P. Turnbull, & R. Luckasson (Eds.), *Transitions to adult life for people with mental retardation: Principles and practices* (pp. 159–175). Baltimore: Paul H. Brookes.

Blacher, J., & Baker, B. L. (1992). Toward meaningful family involvement in out-of-home placement settings. *Mental Retardation, 30*(1), 35–41.

Blackman, J. A. (1984a). Down syndrome. In J. A. Blackman (Ed.), *Medical aspects of developmental disabilities in children birth to three* (Rev. 1st ed., pp. 92–95). Rockville, Md: Aspen Systems.

Blackman, J. A. (1984b). Low birth weight. In J. A. Blackman (Ed.), *Medical aspects of developmental disabilities in children birth to three* (Rev. 1st ed., pp. 143–146). Rockville, MD: Aspen Systems.

Brooks, P. H., & McCauley, C. (1984). Cognitive research in mental retardation. *American Journal of Mental Deficiency, 88*, 479–486.

Brown, L., Shiraga, B., Ford, A., Nisbet, J., Van Deventer, P., Sweet, M., York, J., & Loomis, R. (1986). Teaching severely handicapped students to perform meaningful work in nonsheltered vocational environments. In R. J. Morris & B. Blatt (Eds.), *Special education: Research and trends* (pp. 131–189). New York: Pergamon Press.

Butterworth, J., & Strauch, J. D. (1994). The relationship between social competence and success in the competitive work place for persons with mental retardation. *Education and Training in Mental Retardation and Developmental Disabilities, 29*, 118–133.

Campbell, F. A., & Ramey, C. T. (1994). Effects of early intervention on intellectual and academic achievement: A follow-up study of children from low-income families. *Child Development, 65*, 684–698.

Carr, J. (1994). Annotation: Long term outcome for people with Down's syndrome. *Journal of Child Psychology and Psychiatry, 35*, 425–439.

Chadsey-Rusch, J., Rusch, F. R., & O'Reilly, M. F. (1991). Transition from school to integrated communities. *Remedial and Special Education, 12*(6), 23–33.

Craik, F. I. M., & Lockhart, R. S. (1972). Levels of processing: A framework for memory research. *Journal of Verbal Learning and Verbal Behavior, 11*, 671–684.

Craik, F. I. M., & Tulving, E. (1975). Depth of processing and the retention of words in episodic memory. *Journal of Experimental Psychology: General, 104*, 268–294.

Cravioto, J., & DeLicardie, E. R. (1975). Environmental and nutritional deprivation in children with learning disabilities. In W. M. Cruickshank & D. P. Hallahan (Eds.), *Perceptual and learning disabilities in children. Vol. 2: Research and theory*. Syracuse, NY: Syracuse University Press.

Cunningham, P. J., & Mueller, C. D. (1991). Individuals with mental retardation in residential facilities: Findings from the 1987 national medical expenditure survey. *American Journal on Mental Retardation, 96*(2), 109–117.

Evenhuis, H. M. (1990). The natural history of dementia in Down's syndrome. *Archives of Neurology, 47*, 263–267.

Ferguson, B., McDonnell, J., & Drew, C. (1993). Type and frequency of social interaction among workers with and without mental retardation. *American Journal on Mental Retardation, 97*, 530–540.

Finucane, B. (1988). *Fragile X syndrome: A handbook for families and educators*. Elwyn, PA: Elwyn.

Fraser, J., & Mitchell, A. (1876). Kalmuc idiocy: Report of a case with autopsy, with notes on sixty-two cases. *Journal of Mental Science, 22*, 161–179.

Garber, H. L., Hodge, J. D., Rynders, J., Dever, R., & Velu, R. (1991). The Milwaukee Project: Setting the record straight. *American Journal on Mental Retardation, 95*(5), 493–525.

Greenspan, S., & Granfield, J. M. (1992). Reconsidering the construct of mental retardation: Implications of a model of social competence. *American Journal on Mental Retardation, 96*(4), 442–453.

Guralnick, M. J., Connor, R. T., & Hammond, M. (1995). Parent perspectives of peer relationships and friendships in integrated and specialized programs. *American Journal on Mental Retardation, 99,* 457–476.

Guthrie, R. (1984). Explorations in prevention. In B. Blatt & R. Morris (Eds.), *Perspectives in special education: Personal orientations* (pp. 157–172). Glenview, IL: Scott, Foresman.

Hallahan, D. P., & Cruickshank, W. M. (1973). *Psychoeducational foundations of learning disabilities.* Englewood Cliffs, NJ: Prentice Hall.

Hansen, H. (1970). Decline of Down's Syndrosme after abortion reform in New York State. *American Journal of Mental Deficiency, 83,* 185–188.

Hasazi, S. B., & Clark, G. M. (1988). Vocational preparation for high school students labeled mentally retarded: Employment as a graduation goal. *Mental Retardation, 26*(6), 343–349.

Hasazi, S. B., Collins, M., & Cobb, R. B. (1988). Implementing transition programs for productive employment. In B. L. Ludlow, A. P. Turnbull, & R. Luckasson (Eds.), *Transitions to adult life for people with mental retardation—Principles and practices* (pp. 177–195). Baltimore: Paul H. Brookes.

Hasazi, S. B., Gordon, L. R., Roe, C. A., Hull, M., Finck, K., & Salembier, G. (1985). A statewide follow-up on post-high school employment and residential status of students labeled "mentally retarded." *Education and Training of the Mentally Retarded, 20*(6), 222–234.

Heal, L. W., Gonzalez, P., Rusch, F. R., Copher, J. I., & DeStefano, L. (1990). A comparison of successful and unsuccessful placements of youths with mental handicaps into competitive employment. *Exceptionality, 1*(3), 181–195.

Heber, R. F. (1959). A manual on terminology and classification in mental retardation. *American Journal of Mental Deficiency Monograph.*

Hetherington, E. M., & Parke, R. D. (1986). *Child psychology: A contemporary viewpoint* (3rd ed.). New York: McGraw-Hill.

Hof, P. R., Bouras, C., Perl, D. P., Sparks, L., Mehta, N., & Morrison, J. H. (1995). Age-related distribution of neuropathologic changes in the cerebral cortex of patients with Down's syndrome. *Archives of Neurology, 52,* 379–391.

Kamphaus, R. W., & Reynolds, C. R. (1987). Clinical and research applications of the K-ABC. Circle Pines, MN: American Guidance.

Kaufman, A. S., & Kaufman, N. L. (1983). *Kaufman Assessment Battery for Children.* Circle Pines, MN: American Guidance Service.

Klein, T., Gilman, E., & Zigler, E. (1995). Special Olympics: An evaluation by professionals and parents. *Mental Retardation, 31,* 15–23.

Kopp, C. B., Baker, B. L., & Brown, K. W. (1992). Social skills and their correlates: Preschoolers with developmental delays. *American Journal on Mental Retardation, 96*(4), 357–366.

Krauss, M. W., Seltzer, M. M., & Goodman, S. J. (1992). Social support networks of adults with mental retardation who live at home. *American Journal on Mental Retardation, 96*(4), 432–441.

Lagomarcino, T. R., Hughes, C., & Rusch, F. R. (1989). Utilizing self-management to teach independence on the job. *Education and Training of the Mentally Retarded, 24*(2), 139–148.

Lambert, N., & Windmiller, M. (1981). *AAMD Adaptive Behavior Scale—School Edition.* Washington, DC: American Association of Mental Deficiency.

Levy, J. M., Jessop, D. J., Rimmerman, A., & Levy, P. H. (1992). Attitudes of Fortune 500 corporate executives toward the employability of persons with severe disabilities: A national study. *Mental Retardation, 30*(2), 67–75.

Luftig, R. L. (1988). Assessment of the perceived school loneliness and isolation of mentally retarded and nonretarded students. *American Journal of Mental Retardation, 92*(5), 472–475.

MacMillan, D. L. (1982). *Mental retardation in school and society* (2nd ed.). Boston: Little, Brown.

MacMillan, D. L., Gresham, F. M., & Siperstein, G. N. (1993). Conceptual and psychometric concerns about the 1992 AAMR definition of mental retardation. *American Journal of Mental Retardation, 98,* 325–335.

McCaughrin, W. B., Ellis, W. K., Rusch, F. R., & Heal, L. W. (1993). Cost-effectiveness of supported employment. *Mental Retardation, 31,* 41–48.

Martin, J. E., Rusch, F. R., Tines, J. J., Brulle, A. R., & White, D. M. (1985). *Mental Retardation, 23*(3), 142–147.

McCall, R. B., Appelbaum, M. I., & Hogarty, P. S. (1973). Developmental changes in mental performance. *Monographs of the Society for Research in Child Development, 38* (Ser. No. 150). Chicago: University of Chicago Press.

Mercer, J. R. (1973). *Labelling the mentally retarded.* Berkeley: University of California Press.

Mercer, J. R., & Lewis, J. F. (1977). *Adaptive behavior inventory for children, parent interview manual: System of multicultural pluralistic assessment.* New York: The Psychological Corporation.

Orelove, F., Wehman, P., & Wood, J. (1982). An evaluative review of Special Olympics: Implications for community integration. *Education and Training of the Mentally Retarded, 17,* 325–329.

Patton, J. R., Payne, J. S., & Beirne-Smith, M. (1990). *Mental retardation* (3rd ed.). Columbus OH: Merrill.

Pinel, P. J. (1993). *Biopsychology.* (2nd ed.). Boston: Allyn and Bacon.

Polloway, E., & Smith, J. (1978). Special Olympics: A second look. *Education and Training of the Mentally Retarded, 13,* 432–433.

Ramey, C. T., & Campbell, F. A. (1984). Preventive education for high-risk children: Cognitive consequences of the Carolina Abecedarian Project. *American Journal of Mental Deficiency, 88,* 515–523.

Ramey, C. T., & Campbell, F. A. (1987). The Carolina Abecedarian Project: An educational experiment concerning human malleability. In J. J. Gallagher & C. T. Ramey (Eds.), *The malleability of children* (pp. 127–139). Baltimore, MD: Paul H. Brookes.

Rasmussen, D. E., & Sobsey, D. (1994). Age, adaptive behavior, and Alzheimer disease in Down syndrome: Cross-sectional and longitudinal analyses. *American Journal of Mental Retardation, 99,* 151–165.

Revell, W. G., Wehman, P., Kregel, J., West, M., & Rayfield, R. (1994). Supported employment for persons with severe disabilities: Positive trends in wages, models, and funding. *Education and Training in Mental Retardation and Developmental Disabilities, 29,* 256–264.

Riggen, K., & Ulrich, D. (1993). The effects of sport participation on individuals with mental retardation. *Adapted Physical Activity Quarterly, 10,* 42–51.

Robinson, N. M., & Robinson, H. B. (1976). *The mentally retarded child: A psychological approach* (2nd ed.). New York: McGraw-Hill.

Roper, P. A. (1990). Special Olympics volunteers' perceptions of people with mental retardation. *Education and Training in Mental Retardation, 25,* 164–175.

Rubinstein, A. (1989). Background, epidemiology, and impact of HIV infection in children. *Mental Retardation, 27*(4), 209–211.

Rusch, F. R., & Hughes, C. (1988). Supported employment: Promoting employee independence. *Mental Retardation, 26*(6), 351–355.

Rusch, F. R., Martin, J. E., & White, D. M. (1985). Competitive employment: Teaching mentally retarded employees to maintain their work behavior. *Education and Training of the Mentally Retarded, 20*(3), 182–189.

Sailor, W., Halvorsen, A., Anderson, J., Goetz, L., Gee, K., Doering, K., & Hunt, P. (1986). Community intensive instruction. In R. H. Horner, L. H. Meyer, & H. D. Fredericks (Eds.), *Education of learners with severe handicaps: Exemplary service strategies* (pp. 251–288). Baltimore: Paul H. Brookes.

Salend, S. J., & Giek, K. A. (1988). Independent living arrangements for individuals with mental retardation: The landlords' perspective. *Mental Retardation, 26*(2), 89–92.

Salzberg, C. L., Lignugaris/Kraft, B., & McCuller, G. L. (1988). Reasons for job loss: A review of employment termination studies of mentally retarded workers. *Research in Developmental Disabilities, 9,* 153–170.

Schalock, R. L., & Harper, R. S. (1978). Replacement from community-based mental retardation programs: How well do clients do? *American Journal of Mental Deficiency, 83,* 240–247.

Schalock, R. L., Harper, R. S., & Carver, G. (1981). Independent living placement: Five years later. *American Journal of Mental Deficiency, 86,* 170–177.

Schalock, R. L., McGaughey, M. J., & Kiernan, W. E. (1989). Placement into nonsheltered employment: Findings from national employment surveys. *American Journal of Mental Retardation, 94*(1), 80–87.

Schalock, R. L., Stark, J. A., Snell, M. E., Coulter, D. L., Polloway, E. A., Luckasson, R., Reiss, S., & Spitalnik, D. M. (1994). The changing conception of mental retardation: Implications for the field. *Mental Retardation, 32,* 181–193.

Schultz, E. E., Jr. (1983). Depth of processing by mentally retarded and MA-matched nonretarded individuals. *American Journal of Mental Deficiency, 88,* 307–313.

Schultz, F. R. (1984). Fetal alcohol syndrome. In J. A. Blackman (Ed.), *Mental aspects of developmental disabilities in children birth to three* (Rev. 1st ed., pp. 109–110). Rockville, MD: Aspen Systems.

Schweinhart, L. J., & Weikart, D. P. (1993). Success by empowerment: The High/Scope Perry Preschool Study through age 27. *Young Children, 49,* 54–58.

Skeels, H. M. (1966). Adult status of children with contrasting early life experiences. *Monographs of the Society for Research in Child Development, 31* (Ser. No. 105). University of Chicago Press.

Skeels, H. M., & Dye, H. B. (1939). A study of the effects of differential stimulation on mentally retarded children. *Convention Proceedings, American Association on Mental Deficiency, 44,* 114–136.

Smith, J. D. (1994). The revised AAMR definition of mental retardation: The MRDD position. *Education and Training in Mental Retardation and Developmental Disabilities, 29,* 179–183.

Snell, M. E. (1988). Curriculum and methodology for individuals with severe disabilities. *Education and Training in Mental Retardation, 23*(4), 302–314.

Sparrow, S. S., Balla, D. A., & Cicchetti, D. V. (1984). *Vineland Adaptive Behavior Scales.* Circle Pines, MN: American Guidance Service.

Stodden, R. A., & Browder, P. M. (1986). Community-based competitive employment preparation of developmentally disabled persons: A program description and evaluation. *Education and Training of the Mentally Retarded, 21,* 43–53.

Streissguth, A. P., Barr, H. M., & Martin, D. C. (1983). Maternal alcohol use and neonatal habituation assessed with the Brazelton Scale. *Child Development, 54*(5), 1109–1118.

Thorndike, R. L., Hagen, E. P., & Sattler, J. M. (1986). *Technical manual, Stamford-Binet Intelligence Scale* (4th ed.). Chicago: Riverside.

U.S. Department of Education. (1989). *Eleventh annual report to Congress on The Implementation of the Education of the Handicapped Act.* Washington, DC: Government Printing Office.

Walker, H. M., McConnell, S., Holmes, D., Todis, B., Walker, J., & Golden, N. (1983). *The Accepts Program.* Austin, TX: Pro-Ed.

Warren, S. F., & Abbeduto, L. (1992). The relation of communication and language development to mental retardation. *American Journal of Mental Retardation, 97*(2), 125–130.

Wechsler, D. (1991). *Wechsler Intelligence Scale for Children* (3rd ed.). San Antonio, TX: Psychological Corporation.

Wehman, P., Moon, M. S., Everson, J. M., Wood, W., & Barcus, J. M. (1988). *Transition from school to work: New challenges for youth with severe disabilities.* Baltimore: Paul H. Brookes.

Wheeler, J. J., Bates, P., Marshall, K. J., & Miller, S. R. (1988). Teaching appropriate social behaviors to a young man with moderate mental retardation in a supported competitive employment setting. *Education and Training in Mental Retardation, 23*(2), 105–116.

Whitman, T. L. (1990). Self-regulation and mental retardation. *American Journal on Mental Retardation, 94*(4), 347–362.

Wisniewski, H. M., Silverman, W., & Wegiel, J. (1994). Aging, Alzheimer disease, and mental retardation. *Journal of Intellectual Disability Research, 38,* 233–239.

Wolery, M., Bailey, D. B., & Sugai, G. M. (1988). *Effective teaching: Principles and procedures of applied behavior analysis with exceptional students.* Boston: Allyn and Bacon.

Zeaman, D., & House, B. J. (1963). The role of attention in retardate discrimination learning. In N. R. Ellis (Ed.), *Handbook of mental deficiency.* New York: McGraw-Hill.

Zetlin, A. G., & Murtaugh, M. (1988). Friendship patterns of mildly handicapped and nonhandicapped high school students. *American Journal of Mental Retardation, 92*(5), 447–454.

Chapter 5

Adams, M. J., & Bruck, M. (1995). Resolving the "great debate." *American Educator, 19*(2), 7, 10–20.

American Psychiatric Association. (1994). *Diagnostic and statistical manual of mental disorders* (4th ed.). Washington, DC: Author.

Baker, L. (1982). An evaluation of the role of metacognitive deficits in learning disabilities. *Topics in Learning and Learning Disabilities*, 2(1), 27–35.

Ball, E. W., & Blachman, B. A. (1991). Does phoneme awareness training in kindergarten make a difference in early word recognition and developmental reading? *Reading Research Quarterly, 26*, 49–66.

Baumeister, A. A., Kupstas, F., & Klindworth, L. M. (1990). New morbidity: Implications for prevention of children's disabilities. *Exceptionality*, *1*(1), 1–16.

Baumgartner, D., Bryan, T., & Donahue, M., & Nelson, C. (1993). Thanks for asking: Parent comments about homework, tests, and grades. *Exceptionality, 4*, 177–185.

Beichtman, J. H., Hood, J., & Inglis, A. (1992). Familial transmission of speech and language impairment: A preliminary investigation. *Canadian Journal of Psychiatry, 37*, 151–156.

Borkowski, J. G. (1992). Metacognitive theory: A framework for teaching literacy, writing, and math skills. *Journal of Learning Disabilities*, *25*(4), 253–257.

Bos, C. S., & Filip, D. (1982). Comprehension monitoring skills in learning disabled and average students. *Topics in Learning and Learning Disabilities*, 2(1), 79–85.

Brinckerhoff, L. C., Shaw, S. F., & McGuire, J. M. (1992). Promoting access, accommodations, and independence for college students with learning disabilities. *Journal of Learning Disabilities, 25*, 417–429.

Brown, A. L., & Campione, J. C. (1984). Three faces of transfer: Implications for early competence, individual differences, and instruction. In M. E. Lamb, A. L. Brown, & B. Rogoff (Eds.), *Advances in developmental psychology* (Vol. 3, pp. 143–192). Hillsdale, NJ: Lawrence Erlbaum.

Bryan, T. H., & Bryan, J. H. (1986). *Understanding learning disabilities.* Palo Alto, CA: Mayfield.

Bryan, T. H., Donahue, M., Pearl, R., & Sturm, C. (1981). Learning disabled children's conversational skills—The "TV Talk Show." *Learning Disability Quarterly*, *4*(3), 250–260.

Bryan, T., & Donahue, M. (1994, April). *Homework: Perspectives of teachers, parents and students of different class settings.* Paper presented at the Council for Exceptional Children Convention, Denver, CO.

Case, L. P., Harris, K. R., & Graham, S. (1992). Improving the mathematical problem-solving skills of students with learning disabilities. *Journal of Special Education*, *26*(1), 1–19.

Cawley, J. F., & Parmar, R. S. (1992). Arithmetic programming for students with disabilities: An alternative. *Remedial and Special Education*, *13*(3), 6–18.

Ch.A.D.D. (1992). *Ch.A.D.D. educators manual: An in-depth look at attention deficit disorders from an educational perspective*. Plantation, FL: Ch.A.D.D.

Clarizio, H. F., & Phillips, S. E. (1986). Sex bias in the diagnosis of learning disabled students. *Psychology in the Schools, 23*, 44–52.

Cravioto, J., & DeLicardie, E. R. (1975). Environmental and nutritional deprivation in children with learning disabilities. In W. M. Cruickshank & D. P. Hallahan (Eds.), *Perceptual and learning disabilities in children. Vol. 2: Research and Theory*. Syracuse, NY: Syracuse University Press.

Cruickshank, W. M., Bentzen, F. A., Ratzeburg, F. H., & Tannhauser, M. T. (1961). *A teaching method for brain-injured and hyperactive children.* Syracuse, NY: Syracuse University Press.

DeFries, J. C., Gillis, J. J., & Wadsworth, S. J. (1993). Genes and genders: A twin study of reading disability. In A. M. Galaburda (Ed.), *Dyslexia and development: Neurological aspects of extraordinary brains* (pp. 187–294). Cambridge, MA: Harvard University Press.

Deno, S. L. (1985). Curriculum-based measurement: The emerging alternative. *Exceptional Children*, *52*(3), 219–232.

Deshler, D. D., & Schumaker, J. B. (1986). Learning strategies: An instructional alternative for low-achieving adolescents. *Exceptional Children*, *52*(6), 583–590.

DiGangi, S. A., Maag, J. W., & Rutherford, R. B. (1991). Self-graphing of on-task behavior: Enhancing the reactive effects of self-monitoring on on-task behavior and academic performance. *Learning Disability Quarterly*, *14*(3), 221–230.

Ellis, E. S., Deshler, D. D., & Schumaker, J. B. (1989). Teaching adolescents with learning disabilities to generate and use task-specific strategies. *Journal of Learning Disabilities*, 22(2), 108–119, 130.

Englemann, S. E. (1977). Sequencing cognitive and academic tasks. In R. D. Kneedler & S. G. Tarver (Eds.), *Changing perspectives in special education.* Columbus, OH: Merrill.

Engelmann, S., Carnine, L., Johnson, G., & Meyers, L. (1988). *Corrective reading: Decoding.* Chicago: Science Research Associates.

Engelmann, S., Carnine, L., Johnson, G., & Meyers, L. (1989). *Corrective reading: Comprehension.* Chicago: Science Research Associates.

Engelmann, S., Carnine, D., Engelmann, O., & Kelly, B. (1991). *Connecting math concepts.* Chicago: Science Research Associates.

Englert, C. S. (1992). Writing instruction from a sociocultural perspective: The holistic, dialogic, and social enterprise of writing. *Journal of Learning Disabilities*, *25*(3), 153–172.

Englert, C. S., Raphael, T. E., Anderson, L. M., Anthony, H. M., Fear, K. L., & Gregg, S. L. (1988). A case for writing intervention: Strategies for writing informational text. *Learning Disabilities Focus*, *3*(2), 98–113.

Englert, C. S., Raphael, T. E., Anderson, L. M., Anthony, H. M., & Stevens, D. D. (1991). Making strategies and self-talk visible: Writing instruction in regular and special education classrooms. *American Educational Research Journal*, *28*(2), 337–372.

Federal Register. (1977, December 29). *Procedures for evaluating specific learning disabilities*. Washington, DC: Department of Health, Education and Welfare.

Fletcher, J. M., Shaywitz, S. E., Shankweiler, D. P., Katz, L., Liberman, I. Y., Stuebing, K. K., Francis, D. J., Fowler, A. E., & Shaywitz, B. A. (1994). Cognitive profiles of reading disability: Comparisons of discrepancy and low achievement definitions. *Journal of Educational Psychology, 25*, 6–23.

Flowers, D. L. (1993). Brain basis for dyslexia: A summary of work in progress. *Journal of Learning Disabilities, 26*, 575–582.

Flowers, D. L., Wood, F. B., & Naylor, C. E. (1991). Regional cerebral blood flow correlates of language processes in reading disability. *Archives of Neurology, 48,* 637–643.

Foorman, B. R., & Liberman, D. (1989). Visual and phonological processing of words: A comparison of good and poor readers. *Journal of Learning Disabilities, 22*(6), 349–355.

Frostig, M., & Horne, D. (1964). *The Frostig program for the development of visual perception: Teacher's guide.* Chicago: Follett.

Fuchs, L. S. (1986). Monitoring progress among mildly handicapped pupils: Review of current practice and research. *Remedial and Special Education, 7*(5), 5–12.

Fuchs, L., Deno, S. L., & Mirkin, P. K. (1984). The effects of frequent curriculum-based measurement and evaluation of pedagogy, student achievement and student awareness of learning. *American Educational Research Journal, 24*(2), 449–460.

Fuchs, L. S., & Fuchs, D. (1986). Effects of systematic formative evaluation: A meta-analysis. *Exceptional Children, 53*(3), 199–208.

Fuchs, L. S., Fuchs, D., & Strecker, P. M. (1989). Effects of curriculum-based measurement on teachers' instructional planning. *Journal of Learning Disabilities, 22*(1), 51–59.

Gajar, A. H. (1989). A computer analysis of written language variables and a comparison of compositions written by university students with and without learning disabilities. *Journal of Learning Disabilities, 22*(2), 125–130.

Gerber, P. J., Ginsberg, R., & Reiff, H. B. (1992). Identifying alterable patterns in employment success for highly successful adults with learning disabilities. *Journal of Learning Disabilities, 25*(8), 475–487.

Gerber, P. J., & Reiff, H. B. (1991). *Speaking for themselves: Ethnographic interviews with adults with learning disabilities.* Ann Arbor, MI: University of Michigan Press.

Germann, G., & Tindal, G. (1985). An application of curriculum-based assessment: The use of direct and repeated measurement. *Exceptional Children, 52*(3), 244–265.

Gross-Glenn, K., Duara, R., Barker, W. W., Loewenstein, D., Chang, J., Yoshii, F., Apicella, A. M., Pascal, S., Boothe, T., Sevush, S., Jallad, B. J., Novoa, L., & Lubs, H. A. (1991). Positron emission tomographic studies during serial word-reading by normal and dyslexic adults. *Journal of Clinical and Experimental Neuropsychology, 13,* 531–544.

Hagman, J. O., Wood, F., Buchsbaum, M. S., Tallal, P., Flowers, L., & Katz, W. (1992). Cerebral metabolism in adult dyslexic subjects assessed with positron emission tomography during performance on an auditory task. *Archives of Neurology, 49,* 734–739.

Hall, R. V., Lund, D., & Jackson, D. (1968). Effects of teacher attention on study behavior. *Journal of Applied Behavior Analysis, 1*(1), 1–12.

Hallahan, D. P. (1975). Comparative research studies on the psychological characteristics of learning disabled children. In W. M. Cruickshank & D. P. Hallahan (Eds.), *Perceptual and learning disabilities in children. Vol. 1: Psychoeducational practices.* Syracuse, NY: Syracuse University Press.

Hallahan, D. P. (1992). Some thoughts on why the prevalence of learning disabilities has increased. *Journal of Learning Disabilities, 25*(8), 523–528.

Hallahan, D. P., & Bryan, T. H. (1981). Learning disabilities. In J. M. Kauffman & D. P. Hallahan (Eds.), *Handbook of special education.* Englewood Cliffs, NJ: Prentice Hall.

Hallahan, D. P., & Cruickshank, W. M. (1973). *Psychoeducational foundations of learning disabilities.* Englewood Cliffs, NJ: Prentice Hall.

Hallahan, D. P., Gajar, A. H., Cohen, S. B., & Tarver, S. G. (1978). Selective attention and locus of control in learning disabled and normal children. *Journal of Learning Disabilities, 4,* 47–52.

Hallahan, D. P., & Kauffman, J. M. (1977). Labels, categories, behaviors: ED, LD, and EMR reconsidered. *Journal of Special Education, 11,* 139–149.

Hallahan, D. P., Kauffman, J. M., & Ball, D. W. (1973). Selective attention and cognitive tempo of low achieving and high achieving sixth grade males. *Perceptual and Motor Skills, 36,* 579–583.

Hallahan, D. P., Kauffman, J. M., & Lloyd, J. W. (1996). *Introduction to learning disabilities.* Boston: Allyn and Bacon.

Hallahan, D. P., Kneedler, R. D., & Lloyd, J. W. (1983). Cognitive behavior modification techniques for learning disabled children: Self-instruction and self-monitoring. In J. D. McKinney & L. Feagans (Eds.), *Current topics in learning disabilities* (Vol. 1). Norwood, NJ: Ablex.

Hallahan, D. P., Lloyd, J., Kosiewicz, M. M., Kauffman, J. M., & Graves, A. W. (1979). Self-monitoring of attention as a treatment for a learning disabled boy's off-task behavior. *Learning Disability Quarterly, 2,* 24–32.

Hallahan, D. P., & Reeve, R. E. (1980). Selective attention and distractibility. In B. K. Keogh (Ed.), *Advances in special education. Vol. 1: Basic constructs and theoretical orientations.* Greenwich, CT: J.A.I. Press.

Hallgren, B. (1950). Specific dylexia (congenital word blindness: A clinical and genetic study). *Acta Psychiatrica er Neurologica, 65,* 1–279.

Hallowell, E. M., & Ratey, J. J. (1994). *Driven to distraction.* New York: Pantheon Books.

Hammill, D. D. (1990). On defining learning disabilities: An emerging consensus. *Journal of Learning Disabilities, 23,* 74–84.

Hammill, D. D., & Larsen, S. (1974). The effectiveness of psycholinguistic training. *Exceptional Children, 41,* 5–15.

Hammill, D. D., Leigh, J. E., McNutt, G., & Larsen, S. C. (1981). A new definition of learning disabilities. *Learning Disability Quarterly, 4,* 336–342.

Haring, K. A., Lovett, D. L., Haney, K. F., Algozzine, B., Smith, D. D., & Clarke, J. (1992). Labeling preschoolers as learning disabled: A cautionary position. *Topics in Early Childhood: Special Education, 12,* 151–173.

Haring, K. A., Lovett, D. L., & Smith, D. D. (1990). A follow-up of recent special education graduates of learning disabilities programs. *Journal of Learning Disabilities, 23,* 108–113.

Harris, K. R., Graham, S., Reid, R., McElroy, K., & Hamby, R. S. (1994). Self-monitoring of attention versus self-monitoring of performance: Replication and cross-task comparison studies. *Learning Disability Quarterly, 17,* 121–139.

Henker, B., & Whalen, C. K. (1989). Hyperactivity and attention deficits. *American Psychologist, 44*(2), 216–223.

Hoy, C., & Gregg, N. (1994). *Assessment: The special educator's role.* Pacific Grove, CA: Brooks/Cole.

Hynd, G. W., Marshall, R., & Gonzalez, J. (1991). Learning disabilities and presumed central nervous system dysfunction. *Learning Disability Quarterly, 14*(4), 283–296.

Kauffman, J. M., & Hallahan, D. P. (1979). Learning disability and hyperactivity (with comments on minimal brain dysfunction). In B. B. Lahey & A. E. Kazdin (Eds.), *Advances in clinical child psychology* (Vol. 2). New York: Plenum Press.

Kavale, K. A. (1988). The long-term consequences of learning disabilities. In M. C. Wang, M. C. Reynolds, & H. J. Walberg (Eds.), *Handbook of special education: Research and practice. Vol. 2: Mildly handicapped conditions*. New York: Pergamon Press.

Kavale, K. A. (1995). Setting the record straight on learning disability and low achievement: The tortuous path of ideology. *Learning Disabilities Research and Practice, 10,* 145–152.

Kavale, K. A., & Reese, J. H. (1992). The character of learning disabilities: An Iowa profile. *Learning Disabilities Quarterly, 15*(2), 74–94.

Keogh, B. K., & Glover, A. T. (1980, November). Research needs in the study of early identification of children with learning disabilities. *Thalamus* (Newsletter of the International Academy for Research in Learning Disabilities).

Kephart, N. C. (1971, 1975). *The slow learner in the classroom* (2nd ed.) Columbus, OH: Merrill.

Kirk, S. A., & Kirk, W. D. (1971). *Psycholinguistic learning disabilities: Diagnosis and remediation.* Urbana: University of Illinois Press.

Kneedler, R. D., & Hallahan, D. P. (1984). Self-monitoring as an attentional strategy for academic tasks with learning disabled children. In B. Gholson & T. Rosenthal (Eds.), *Applications of cognitive development theory*. New York: Academic Press.

Kosiewicz, M. M., Hallahan, D. P., Lloyd, J. W., & Graves, A.W. (1982). Effects of self-instruction and self-correction procedures on handwriting performance. *Learning Disability Quarterly, 5,* 71–78.

Kravets, M., & Wax, I. F. (1993). *The K & W guide to colleges for the learning disabled* (2nd ed.). New York: HarperCollins.

Learning Disabilities Association of America. (1993). Position paper on full inclusion of all students with learning disabilities in the regular education classroom. *LDA Newsbrief, 28*(2).

Leete-Guy, L., & Schor, J. B. (1992). *The great American time squeeze: Trends in work and leisure: 1969–1989*. (Briefing paper for the Economic Policy Institute, Washington, DC).

Leinhardt, G., Seewald, A., & Zigmond, N. (1982). Sex and race differences in learning disabilities classrooms. *Journal of Educational Psychology, 74,* 835–845.

Lewis, B. A. (1992). Pedigree analysis of children with phonology disorders. *Journal of Learning Disabilities, 25,* 586–597.

Lewis, B. A., & Thompson, L. A. (1992). A study of development of speech and language disorders in twins. *Journal of Speech and Hearing Research, 35,* 1086–1094.

Liberman, I. Y., & Shankweiler, D. (1991). Phonology and beginning reading: A tutorial. In L. Rieben & C. A. Perfetti (Eds.), *Learning to read: Basic research and its implications* (pp. 3–17). Hillsdale, NJ: Lawrence Erlbaum.

Lloyd, J. W. (1988). Direct academic interventions in learning disabilities. In M. C. Wang, M. C. Reynolds, & H. J. Walberg (Eds.), *Handbook of special education: Research and practice. Vol. 2: Mildly handicapped conditions*. New York: Pergamon Press.

Lloyd, J., Hallahan, D. P., Kosiewicz, M. M., & Kneedler, R. D. (1980). *Self-assessment versus self-recording: Two comparisons of reactive effects on attention to task and academic productivity.* (Technical Report No. 29). Charlottesville: University of Virginia Learning Disabilities Research Institute.

Lovitt, T. C. (1977). *In spite of my resistance . . . I've learned from children.* Columbus, OH: Merrill.

Lyon, G. R. (1989). IQ is irrelevant to the definition of learning disabilities: A position in search of logic and data. *Journal of Learning Disabilities, 22,* 504–506, 512.

Mann, V. A., Cowin, E., & Schoenheimer, J. (1989). Phonological processing, language comprehension, and reading ability. *Journal of Learning Disabilities, 22*(2), 76–89.

Marston, D., & Magnusson, D. (1985). Implementing curriculum-based measurement in special and regular education settings. *Exceptional Children, 52*(3), 266–276.

Mastropieri, M. A., & Scruggs, T. E. (1988). Increasing content area learning of learning disabled students: Research implementation. *Learning Disabilities Research, 4*(1), 17–25.

Mather, N., & Roberts, R. (1994). Learning disabilities: A field in danger of extinction? *Learning Disabilities Research and Practice, 9,* 49–58.

Mathinos, D. A. (1988). Communicative competence of children with learning disabilities. *Journal of Learning Disabilities, 21*(7), 437–443.

McGuire, J. M., & Shaw, S. F. (1987). A decision-making process for the college-bound student: Matching learner, institution, and support program. *Learning Disability Quarterly, 10,* 106–111.

McKinney, J. D. (1987a). Research on conceptually and empirically derived subtypes of specific learning disabilities. In M. C. Wang, M. C. Reynolds, & H. J. Walberg (Eds.), *Handbook of special education: Research and practice*. New York: Pergamon Press.

McKinney, J. D. (1987b). Research on the identification of LD children: Perspectives on changes in educational policy. In S. Vaughn & C. Bos, *Future directions and issues in research for the learning disabled.* San Diego, CA: College-Hill Press.

McKinney, J. D. (1989). Longitudinal research on the behavioral characteristics of children with learning disabilities. *Journal of Learning Disabilities, 22*(3), 141–150, 165.

McKinney, J. D., & Feagans, L. (1984). Academic and behavioral characteristics: Longitudinal studies of learning disabled children and average achievers. *Learning Disability Quarterly, 7,* 251–265.

McKinney, J. D., Short, E. J., & Feagans, L. (1985). Academic consequences of perceptual-linguistic subtypes of learning disabled children. *Learning Disabilities Research, 1*(1), 6–17.

McKinney, J. D., & Speece, D. L. (1986). Academic consequences and longitudinal stability of behavioral subtypes of learning disabled children. *Journal of Educational Psychology, 78*(5), 365–272.

Meichenbaum, D. H. (1975, June). *Cognitive factors as determinants of learning disabilities: A cognitive-functional approach.* Paper presented at the NATO Conference on The Neuropsychology of Learning Disorders: Theoretical Approaches, Korsor, Denmark.

Meichenbaum, D. H., & Goodman, J. (1971). Training impulsive children to talk to themselves: A means of developing self-control. *Journal of Abnormal Psychology*, *77*, 115–126.

Mercer, C. D., Algozzine, B., & Trifiletti, J. (1979). Early identification—An analysis of the research. *Learning Disability Quarterly*, *2*, 12–24.

Mercer, C. D., & Miller, S. P. (1992). Teaching students with learning problems in math to acquire, understand, and apply basic math facts. *Remedial and Special Education*, *13*(3), 19–35, 61.

Montague, M., & Bos, C. S. (1990). Cognitive and metacognitive characteristics of eighth grade students' mathematical problem solving. *Learning and Individual Differences*, *2*(3), 371–388.

Montague, M., & Graves, A. (1992). In M. Pressley, K. Harris, & J. T. Guthrie (Eds.), *Promoting academic competence and literacy in schools* (pp. 261–276). New York: Academic Press.

Montague, M., Graves, A., & Leavell, A. (1991). Planning, procedural facilitation, and narratvie composition of junior high students with learning disabilities. *Learning Disabilities Research & Practice*, *6*(4), 219–224.

Murphy, S. T. (1992). *On being L.D.: Perspectives and strategies of young adults*. New York: Teachers College Press.

National Joint Committee on Learning Disabilities. (1989, September 18). *Letter from NJCLD to member organizations. Topic: Modifications to the NJCLD definition of learning disabilities*. Washington, DC: Author.

Newcomer, P. L., & Barenbaum, E. M. (1991). The written composing ability of children with learning disabilities: A review of the literature from 1980 to 1990. *Journal of Learning Disabilities*, *24*(10), 578–593.

Olson, R., Wise, B., Conners, F., Rack, J., & Fulker, D. (1989). Specific deficits in component reading and language skills: Genetic and environmental influences. *Journal of Learning Disabilities*, *22*(6), 339–348.

Palincsar, A. S. (1986). Metacognitive strategy instruction. *Exceptional Children*, *53*(2), 118–124.

Pearl, R. (1992). Psychosocial characteristics of learning disabled students. In N. N. Singh & I. L. Beale (Eds.), *Current perspectives in learning disabilities: Nature, theory, and treatment* (pp. 96–125). New York: Springer-Verlag.

Pelham, W. E., & Murphy, H. A. (1986). Attention deficit and conduct disorders. In M. Hersen (Ed.), *Pharmacological and behavioral treatment: An integrative approach* (pp. 108–148). New York: John Wiley.

Pennington, B. F. (1990). Annotation: The genetics of dyslexia. *Journal of Child Psychology and Child Psychiatry, 31,* 193–201.

Pennington, B. F., Gilger, J. W., Olson, R. K., & DeFries, J. C. (1992). The external validity of age- versus IQ-discrepant definitions of reading disability: Lessons from a twin study. *Journal of Learning Disabilities, 25,* 562–573.

Polloway, E. A., Foley, R. M., & Epstein, M. H. (1992). A comparison of the homework problems of students with learning disabilities and nonhandicapped students. *Learning Disabilities Research and Practice*, *7*(4), 203–209.

Prater, M. A., Joy, R., Chilman, B., Temple, J., & Miller, S. R. (1991). Self-monitoring of on-task behavior by adolsescents with learning disabilities. *Learning Disability Quarterly*, *14*(3), 164–177.

Pressley, M., Symons, S., Snyder, B. L., & Cariglia-Bull, T. (1989). Strategy instruction comes of age. *Learning Disability Quarterly*, *12*(1), 16–30.

Reiff, H. B., & Gerber, P. J. (1992). Adults with learning disabilities. In N. N. Singh & D. L. Beale (Eds.), *Current perspectives in learning disabilities: Nature, theory, and treatment* (pp. 170–198). New York: Springer-Verlag.

Riccio, C. A., Gonzalez, J. J., & Hynd, G. W. (1994). Attention-deficit hyperactivity disorder (ADHD) and learning disabilities. *Learning Disability Quarterly, 17,* 311–322.

Robinson, F. P. (1946). *Effective study.* New York: Harper & Row.

Roffman, A. J., Herzog, J. E., & Wershba-Gershon, P. M. (1994). Helping young adults understand their learning disabilities. *Journal of Learning Disabilities, 27,* 413–419.

Schumaker, J. B., Deshler, D. D., Alley, G. R., Warner, M. M., & Denton, P. H. (1982). Multipass: A learning strategy for improving reading comprehension. *Learning Disability Quarterly*, *5*(3), 295–304.

Schunk, D. H. (1989). Self-efficacy and cognitive achievement: Implications for students with learning problems. *Journal of Learning Disabilities*, *22*(1), 14–22.

Scruggs, T. E., & Mastropieri, M. A. (1992). Classroom applications of mnemonic instruction: Acquisition, maintenance, and generalization. *Exceptional Children*, *58*(3), 219–229.

Seligman, M. E. (1992). *Helplessness: On depression, development and death.* San Francisco: W. H. Freeman.

Shaywitz, S. E., & Shaw, R. (1988). The admissions process: An approach to selecting learning disabled students at the most selective colleges. *Learning Disabilities Focus*, *3*(2), 81–86.

Shaywitz, S. E., & Shaywitz, B. A. (1987). *Attention deficit disorder: Current perspectives.* Paper presented at National Conference on Learning Disabilities, National Institutes of Child Health and Human Development (NIH), Bethesda, MD.

Shaywitz, S. E., Shaywitz, B. A., Fletcher, J. M., & Escobar, M. D. (1990). Prevalence of reading disability in boys and girls: Results of the Connecticut Longitudinal Study. *Journal of the American Medical Association, 264,* 998–1002.

Short, E. J., & Weissberg-Benchell, J. (1989). The triple alliance for learning: Cognition, metacognition, and motivation. In C. B. McCormick, G. E. Miller, & M. Pressley (Eds.), *Cognitive strategy research: From basic research to educational applications* (pp. 33–63). New York: Springer-Verlag.

Siegel, L. S. (1989). IQ is irrelevant to the definition of learning disabilities. *Journal of Learning Disabilities*, *22*(8), 468–478, 486.

Siperstein, G. N. (1988). Students with learning disabilities in college: The need for a programmatic approach to critical transitions. *Journal of Learning Disabilities*, *21*(7), 431–436.

Slovak, I. (Ed.). (1995). *BOSC directory: Facilities for people with learning disabilities.* Congers, NY: BOSC.

Speece, D. L., McKinney, J. D., & Applebaum, M. I. (1985). Classification and validation of behavioral subtypes of learning-disabled children. *Journal of Educational Psychology*, *77*(1), 67–77.

Spekman, N. J., Goldberg, R. J., & Herman, K. L. (1992). Learning disabled children grow up: A search for factors related to success

in the young adult years. *Learning Disabilities Research and Practice, 7*(3), 161–170.
Stanovich, K. E. (1991a). Conceptual and empirical problems with discrepancy definitions of reading disability. *Learning Disability Quarterly. 14*(4), 269–280.
Stanovich, K. E. (1991b). Reading disability: Assessment issues. In H. L. Swanson (Ed.), *Handbook of assessment of learning disabilities: Theory, research, and practice* (pp. 147–175). Austin, TX: Pro-Ed.
Stanovich, K. E., & Siegel, L. S. (1994). Phenotypic performance profile of children with reading disabilities: A regression-based test of the phonological-core variable-difference model. *Journal of Educational Psychology, 86,* 24–53.
Straughn, C. T. (Ed.). (1988). *Lovejoy's college guide for the learning disabled.* New York: Monarch Press.
Strauss, A. A., & Kephart, N. C. (1955). *Psychopathology and education of the brain-injured child. Vol. 2. Progress in theory and clinic.* New York: Grune & Stratton.
Strauss, A. A., & Lehtinen, L. E. (1947). *Psychopathology and education of the brain-injured child.* New York: Grune & Stratton.
Swanson, H. L. (Ed.). (1987). *Memory and learning disabilities: Advances in learning and behavioral disabilities.* Greenwich, CT: J.A.I. Press.
Swanson, H. L. (1994). Short-term memory and working memory: Do both contribute to our understanding of academic achievement in children and adults with learning disabilities? *Journal of Learning Disabilities, 27,* 34–50.
Thomas, C. C., Englert, C. S., & Gregg, S. (1987). An analysis of errors and strategies in the expository writing of learning-disabled students. *Remedial and Special Education, 8*(1), 21–30, 46.
Thomas, C. H., & Thomas, J. L. (Eds.). (1991). *Directory of college facilities and services for people with learning disabilities.* (3rd ed.). Phoenix, AZ: Oryx Press.
Torgesen, J. K. (1977). The role of nonspecific factors in the task performance of learning disabled children: A theoretical assessment. *Journal of Learning Disabilities, 10,* 27–34.
Torgesen, J. K. (1988). Studies of children with learning disabilities who perform poorly on memory span tasks. *Journal of Learning Disabilities, 21*(10), 605–612.
Torgesen, J. K., & Kail, R. V. (1980). Memory processes in exceptional children. In B. K. Keogh (Ed.), *Advances in special education. Vol. 1: Basic constructs and theoretical orientations.* Greenwich, CT: J.A.I. Press.
U.S. Department of Education. (1990, January 9). Reading and writing proficiency remains low. *Daily Education News,* 1–7.
U.S. Department of Education. (1992). *Fourteenth annual report to Congress on the implementation of the Individuals with Disabilities Education Act.* Washington, DC: Author.
Vellutino, F. R. (1987). Dyslexia. *Scientific American, 256*(3), 34–41.
Vogel, S. (1987). Issues and concerns in LD college programming. In D. Johnson & J. Blalock (Eds.), *Adults with learning disabilities* (pp. 239–275). New York: Grune & Stratton.
Weiss, G., & Hechtman, L. T. (1993). *Hyperactive children grown up: ADHD in children, adolescents, and adults* (2nd ed.). New York: Guilford Press.
Werner, H., & Strauss, A. A. (1941). Pathology of figure-background relation in the child. *Journal of Abnormal and Social Psychology, 36,* 236–248.
White, O., & Haring, N. (1980). *Exceptional teaching.* Columbus, OH: Merrill.
White, W. J. (1992). The postschool adjustment of persons with learning disabilities: Current status and future projections. *Journal of Learning Disabilities, 25,* 448–456.
Willis, W. G., Hooper, S. R., & Stone, B. H. (1992). Neurological theories of learning disabilities. In N. N. Singh & D. L. Beale (Eds.), *Current perspectives in learning disabilities: Nature, theory, and treatment* (pp. 201–245). New York: Springer-Verlag.
Zametkin, A. J., Nordahl, T. E., Gross, M., King, A. C., Semple, W. E., Rumsey, J., Hamburger, M. S., & Cohen, R. M. (1990). Cerebral glucose metabolism in adults with hyperactivity of childhood onset. *New England Journal of Medicine, 323,* 1361–1366.
Zigmond, N. (1990). Rethinking secondary programs for students with learning disabilities. *Focus on Exceptional Children, 23*(1), 1–22.

Chapter 6

Achenbach, T. M. (1985). *Assessment and taxonomy of child and adolescent psychopathology.* Newbury Park, CA: Sage.
Achenbach, T. M., Howell, C. T., Quay, H. C., & Conners, C. K. (1991). National survey of problems and competencies among four- to sixteen-year-olds: Parents' reports for normative and clinical samples. *Monographs of the Society for Research in Child Development, 56*(3), serial no. 225.
Alberto, P., & Troutman, A. (1995). *Applied behavior analysis for teachers* (4th ed.). Columbus, OH: Merrill/Macmillan.
Allison, M. (1993). Exploring the link between violence and brain injury. *Headlines, 4*(2), 12–17.
Anderson, J., & Werry, J. S. (1994). Emotional and behavioral problems. In I. B. Pless (Ed.), *The epidemiology of childhood disorders* (pp. 304–338). New York: Oxford University Press.
Asarnow, R. F., Asamen, J., Granholm, E., Sherman, T., Watkins, J. M., & Williams, M. E. (1994). Cognitive/neuropsychological studies of children with a schizophrenic disorder. *Schizophrenia Bulletin, 20,* 647–669.
Asarnow, J. R., Tompson, M. C., & Goldstein, M. J. (1994). Childhood-onset schizophrenia: A follow-up study. *Schizophrenia Bulletin, 20,* 599–617.
Bandura, A. (1973). *Aggression: A social learning analysis.* Englewood Cliffs, NJ: Prentice Hall.
Bandura, A. (1986). *Social foundations of thought and action: A social cognitive theory.* Englewood Cliffs, NJ: Prentice Hall.
Bateman, B. D., & Chard, D. J. (1995). Legal demands and constraints on placement decisions. In J. M. Kauffman, J. W. Lloyd, D. P. Hallahan, & T. A. Astuto (Eds.), *Issues in educational placement: Students with emotional and behavioral disorders* (pp. 285–316). Hillsdale, NJ: Lawrence Erlbaum.
Baumeister, A. A., Kupstas, F., & Klindworth, L. M. (1990). New morbidity: Implications for prevention of children's disabilities. *Exceptionality, 1,* 1–16.

Becker, W. C. (1964). Consequences of different kinds of parental discipline. In M. L. Hoffman & L. W. Hoffman (Eds.), *Review of child development research* (Vol. 1). New York: Russell Sage Foundation.

Bergland, M., & Hoffbauer, D. (1996). New opportunities for students with traumatic brain injuries. *Teaching Exceptional Children, 28*(2), 54–56.

Bettelheim, B. (1950). *Love is not enough*. New York: Macmillan.

Bettelheim, B. (1967). *The empty fortress*. New York: Free Press.

Bower, E. M. (1981). *Early identification of emotionally handicapped children in school* (3rd ed.). Springfield, IL: Charles C. Thomas.

Bower, E. M. (1982). Defining emotional disturbance: Public policy and research. *Psychology in the Schools, 19*, 55–60.

Brandenburg, N. A., Friedman, R. M., & Silver, S. E. (1990). The epidemiology of childhood psychiatric disorders: Prevalence findings from recent studies. *Journal of the American Academy of Child and Adolescent Psychiatry, 29*, 76–83.

Caplan, N., Choy, M. H., & Whitmore, J. K. (1992). Indochinese refugee families and academic achievement. *Scientific American, 266*(2), 36–42.

Carson, R. R., Sitlington, P. L., & Frank, A. R. (1995). Young adulthood for individuals with behavioral disorders: What does it hold? *Behavioral Disorders, 20*, 127–135.

Chesapeake Institute. (1994, September). *National agenda for achieving better results for children and youth with serious emotional disturbance*. Washington, DC: Author.

Cline, D. H. (1990). A legal analysis of policy initiatives to exclude handicapped/disruptive students from special education. *Behavioral Disorders, 15*, 159–173.

Deaton, A. V. (1994). Changing the behaviors of students with acquired brain injury. In R. C. Savage & G. F. Wolcott (Eds.), *Educational dimensions of acquired brain injury* (pp. 257–276). Austin, TX: Pro-Ed.

Deaton, A. V., & Waaland, P. (1994). Psychosocial effects of acquired brain injury. In R. C. Savage & G. F. Wolcott (Eds.), *Educational dimensions of acquired brain injury* (pp. 239–255). Austin, TX: Pro-Ed.

Delpit, L. D. (1986). Skills and other dilemmas of a progressive black educator. *Harvard Educational Review, 56*, 379–385.

Drabman, R. S., & Patterson, J. N. (1981). Disruptive behavior and the social standing of exceptional children. *Exceptional Education Quarterly, 1*(4), 45–55.

Duncan, B. B., Forness, S. R., & Hartsough, C. (1995). Students identified as seriously emotionally disturbed in school-based day treatment: Cognitive, psychiatric, and special education characteristics. *Behavioral Disorders, 20*, 238–252.

Dunlap, G., dePerczel, M., Clarke, S., Wilson, D., Wright, S., White, R., & Gomez, A. (1994). Choice making to promote adaptive behavior for students with emotional and behavioral challenges. *Journal of Applied Behavior Analysis, 27*, 505–518.

Edgar, E., & Siegel, S. (1995). Postsecondary scenarios for troubled and troubling youth. In J. M. Kauffman, J. W. Lloyd, D. P. Hallahan, & T. A. Astuto (Eds.), *Issues in educational placement: Students with emotional or behavioral disorders* (pp. 251–283). Hillsdale, NJ: Lawrence Erlbaum.

Feeney, T. J., & Urbanczyk, B. (1994). Behavior as communication. In R. C. Savage & G. F. Wolcott (Eds.), *Educational dimensions of acquired brain injury* (pp. 277–302). Austin, TX: Pro-Ed.

Forness, S. R. (1988). School characteristics of children and adolescents with depression. In R. B. Rutherford, C. M. Nelson, & S. R. Forness (Eds.), *Bases of severe behavioral disorders of children and youth*. Boston: Little, Brown.

Forness, S. R. (1992). Legalism versus professionalism in diagnosing SED in the public schools. *School Psychology Review, 21*, 29–34.

Forness, S. R., & Knitzer, J. (1992). A new proposed definition and terminology to replace "serious emotional disturbance" in Individuals with Disabilities Act. *School Psychology Review, 21*, 12–20.

Freedman, J. (1993). *From cradle to grave: The human face of poverty in America*. New York: Atheneum.

Fuchs, D., Fuchs, L. S., Fernstrom, P., & Hohn, M. (1991). Toward a responsible reintegration of behaviorally disordered students. *Behavioral Disorders, 16*, 133–147.

Garmezy, N. (1987). Stress, competence, and development: Continuities in the study of schizophrenic adults, children vulnerable to psychopathology, and the search for stress-resistant children. *American Journal of Orthopsychiatry, 57*, 159–174.

Goldstein, A. P. (1983). United States: Causes, controls, and alternatives to aggression. In A. P. Goldstein & M. H. Segall (Eds.), *Aggression in global perspective*. New York: Pergamon Press.

Gottesman, I. I. (1991). *Schizophrenia genesis: The origins of madness*. New York: W. H. Freeman.

Guetzloe, E. C. (1991). *Depression and suicide: Special education students at risk*. Reston, VA: Council for Exceptional Children.

Hallenbeck, B. A., & Kauffman, J. M. (1995). How does observational learning affect the behavior of students with emotional or behavioral disorders? A review of research. *Journal of Special Education, 29*, 45–71.

Harris, S. L. (1995). Autism. In M. Hersen & R. T. Ammerman (Eds.), *Advanced abnormal child psychology* (pp. 305–317). Hillsdale, NJ: Lawrence Erlbaum.

Henggeler, S. W. (1989). *Delinquency in adolescence*. Newbury Park, CA: Sage.

Hobbs, N. (1975). *The futures of children*. San Francisco: Jossey-Bass.

Hodgkinson, H . L. (1995). What should we call people? Race, class, and the census for 2000. *Phi Delta Kappan, 77*, 173–179.

James, M., & Long, N. (1992). Looking beyond behavior and seeing my needs: A red flag interview. *Journal of Emotional and Behavioral Problems, 1*(2), 35–38.

Jordan, D., Goldberg, P., & Goldberg, M. (1991). *A guidebook for parents of children with emotional or behavioral disorders*. Minneapolis: Pacer Center.

Kauffman, J. M. (1986). Educating children with behavior disorders. In R. J. Morris & B. Blatt (Eds.), *Special education: Research and trends* (pp. 249–271). New York: Pergamon Press.

Kauffman, J. M. (1997). *Characteristics of emotional and behavioral disorders of children and youths* (6th ed.). New York: Merrill/Macmillan.

Kauffman, J. M., & Hallenbeck, B. A. (Eds.). (in press). Why we need to preserve specialized placements for students with emotional or behavioral disorders. *Canadian Journal of Special Education* [special issue].

Kauffman, J. M., Lloyd, J. W., Baker, J., & Riedel, T. M. (1995). Inclusion of all students with emotional or behavioral disorders? Let's think again. *Phi Delta Kappan, 76,* 542–546.

Kauffman, J. M., Lloyd, J. W., Hallahan, D. P., & Astuto, T. A. (Eds.). (1995). *Issues in educational placement: Students with emotional and behavioral disorders.* Hillsdale, NJ: Lawrence Erlbaum.

Kauffman, J. M., Mostert, M. P., Nuttycombe, D. G., Trent, S. C., & Hallahan, D. P. (1993). *Managing classroom behavior: A reflective case-based approach.* Boston: Allyn and Bacon.

Kauffman, J. M., & Pullen, P. L. (1996). Eight myths about special education. *Focus on Exceptional Children, 28* (5), 1–16.

Kazdin, A. E. (1987). *Conduct disorders in childhood and adolescence.* Newbury Park, CA: Sage.

Kazdin, A. E. (1989). Developmental psychopathology: Current research, issues, and directions. *American Psychologist, 44,* 180–187.

Kazdin, A. E. (1992). Overt and covert antisocial behavior: Child and family characteristics among psychiatric inpatient children. *Journal of Child and Family Studies, 1,* 3–20.

Kerr, M. M., & Nelson, C. M. (1989). *Strategies for managing behavior problems in the classroom* (2nd ed.). Columbus, OH: Merrill/Macmillan.

Klass, E., & Koplewica, H. S. (Eds.). (1993). *Depression in children and adolescents.* New York: Harwood.

Knitzer, J., Steinberg, Z., & Fleisch, F. (1990). *At the schoolhouse door: An examination of programs and policies for children with behavioral and emotional problems.* New York: Bank Street College of Education.

Kozol, J. (1995, October 1). The kids that society forgot. *The Washington Post,* pp. C1, C4.

Leone, P. E. (Ed.). (1990). *Understanding troubled and troubling youth.* Newbury Park, CA: Sage.

Leone, P. E., Rutherford, R. B., & Nelson, C. M. (1991). *Special education in juvenile corrections.* Reston, VA: Council for Exceptional Children.

Loeber, R., Green S. M., Lahey, B. B., Christ, M. A. G., & Frick, P. J. (1992). Developmental sequences in age of onset of disruptive child behaviors. *Journal of Child and Family Studies, 1,* 21–41.

Lovaas, O. I. (1987). Behavioral treatment and normal educational and intellectual functioning in young autistic children. *Journal of Consulting and Clinical Psychology, 55,* 3–9.

Lovaas, O. I. (1993). The development of a treatment-research project for developmentally disabled and autistic children. *Journal of Applied Behavior Analysis, 26,* 617–630.

Lozoff, B. (1989). Nutrition and behavior. *American Psychologist, 44,* 231–236.

Martin, R. P. (1992). Child temperament effects on special education: Process and outcomes. *Exceptionality, 3,* 99–115.

McCracken, J. T., Cantwell, D. P., & Hanna, G. L. (1993). Conduct disorder and depression. In E. Klass & H. S. Koplewica (Eds.), *Depression in children and adolescents* (pp. 121–132). New York: Harwood.

McIntyre, T. (1993). Behaviorally disordered youth in correctional settings: Prevalence, programming, and teacher training. *Behavioral Disorders, 18,* 167–176.

Morganthau, T., Annin, P., Wingert, P., Foote, D., Manly, H., & King, P. (1992). It's not just New York . . . *Newsweek, 119*(10), 25–29.

Moynihan, D. P. (1995, September 21). "I cannot understand how this could be happening." *The Washington Post,* p. A31.

Nelson, C. M. (1992). Searching for meaning in the behavior of antisocial pupils, public school education, and lawmakers. *School Psychology Review, 21,* 35–38.

Nelson, C. M., & Kauffman, J. M. (1977). Educational programming for secondary school age delinquent and maladjusted pupils. *Behavioral Disorders, 2,* 102–113.

Nelson, C. M., & Pearson, C. A. (1991). *Integrating services for children and youth with emotional and behavioral disorders.* Reston, VA: Council for Exceptional Children.

Nelson, C. M., Rutherford, R. B., Center, D. B., & Walker, H. M. (1991). Do public schools have an obligation to serve troubled children and youth? *Exceptional Children, 57,* 406–415.

Nelson, C. M., Rutherford, R. B., & Wolford, B. I. (Eds.). (1987). *Special education in the criminal justice system.* Columbus, OH: Merrill/Macmillan.

Newcomb, M. D., & Bentler, P. M. (1989). Substance use and abuse among children and teenagers. *American Psychologist, 44,* 242–248.

Patterson, C. J., Kupersmidt, J. B., & Griesler, P. C. (1989). *Self-concepts of children in regular education and in special education classes.* Unpublished manuscript, Virginia Behavior Disorders Project, University of Virginia, Charlottesville, VA.

Patterson, G. R., DeBaryshe, B. D., & Ramsey, E. (1989). A developmental perspective on antisocial behavior. *American Psychologist, 44,* 329–335.

Patterson, G. R., Reid, J. B., & Dishion, T. J. (1992). *Antisocial boys.* Eugene, OR: Castalia.

Peacock Hill Working Group. (1991). Problems and promises in special education and related services for children and youth with emotional or behavioral disorders. *Behavioral Disorders, 16,* 299–313.

Plomin, R. (1989). Environment and genes: Determinants of behavior. *American Psychologist, 44,* 105–111.

Pollack, I. W. (1994). Reestablishing an acceptable sense of self. In R. C. Savage & G. F. Wolcott (Eds.), *Educational dimensions of acquired brain injury* (pp. 303–318). Austin, TX: Pro-Ed.

Prior, M., & Werry, J. S. (1986). Autism, schizophrenia, and allied disorders. In H. C. Quay & J. S. Werry (Eds.), *Psychopathological disorders of childhood* (3rd ed.). New York: John Wiley.

Quay, H. C. (1986). Classification. In H. C. Quay & J. S. Werry (Eds.), *Psychopathological disorders of childhood* (3rd ed.). New York: Wiley.

Quay, H. C., & Peterson, D. R. (1987). *Manual for the revised behavior problem checklist.* Coral Gables, FL: Author.

Rabian, B., & Silverman, W. K. (1995). Anxiety disorders. In M. Hersen & R. T. Ammerman (Eds.), *Advanced abnormal child psychology* (pp. 235–252). Hillsdale, NJ: Lawrence Erlbaum.

Reitman, D., & Gross, A. M. (1995). Familial determinants. In M. Hersen & R. T. Ammerman (Eds.), *Advanced abnormal child psychology* (pp. 87–104). Hillsdale, NJ: Lawrence Erlbaum.

Rhode, G., Jensen, W. R., & Reavis, H. K. (1992). *The tough kid book: Practical classroom management strategies*. Longmont, CO: Sopris West.

Richardson, G. A., McGauhey, P., & Day, N. L. (1995). Epidemiologic considerations. In M. Hersen & R. T. Ammerman (Eds.), *Advanced abnormal child psychology* (pp. 37–48). Hillsdale, NJ: Lawrence Erlbaum.

Rogoff, B., & Morelli, G. (1989). Perspectives on children's development from cultural psychology. *American Psychologist, 44*, 343–348.

Rutter, M. (1985). Family and school influences on behavioral development. *Journal of Child Psychology and Psychiatry, 26*, 349–368.

Rutter, M., & Schopler, E. (1987). Autism and pervasive developmental disorders: Concepts and diagnostic issues. *Journal of Autism and Developmental Disabilities, 17*, 159–186.

Sacks, O. (1995). *An anthropologist on Mars: Seven paradoxical tales.* New York: Knopf.

Schopler, E., & Mesibov, G. B. (Eds.). (1994). *Behavioral issues in autism*. New York: Plenum Press.

Schopler, E., & Mesibov, G. B. (Eds.). (1995). *Learning and cognition in autism*. New York: Plenum.

Sherburne, S., Utley, B., McConnell, S., & Gannon, J. (1988). Decreasing violent and aggressive theme play among preschool children with behavior disorders. *Exceptional Children, 55*, 166–172.

Siegel, L. J., & Senna, J. J. (1994). *Juvenile delinquency: Theory, practice, and law* (5th ed.). St. Paul, MN: West.

Silver, S. E., Duchnowski, A. J., Kutash, K., Friedman, R. M., Eisen, M., Prange, M. E., Brandenburg, N. A., & Greenbaum, P. E. (1992). A comparison of children with serious emotional disturbance served in residential and school settings. *Journal of Child and Family Studies, 1*, 43–59.

Skiba, R., & Grizzle, K. (1992). Qualifications v. logic and data: Excluding conduct disorders from the SED definition. *School Psychology Review, 21*, 23–28.

Slenkovich, J. E. (1992a). Can the language "social maladjustment" in the SED definition be ignored? *School Psychology Review, 21*, 21–22.

Slenkovich, J. E. (1992b). Can the language "social maladjustment" in the SED definition be ignored? The final words. *School Psychology Review, 21*, 43–44.

Smith, S., & Couthino, M. (Eds.). (in press). National agenda for achieving better results for children and youth with serious emotional disturbance. *Journal of Emotional and Behavioral Disorders* [special issue].

Stark, K. D., Ostrander, R., Kurowski, C. A., Swearer, S., & Bowen, B. (1995). Affective and mood disorders. In M. Hersen & R. T. Ammerman (Eds.), *Advanced abnormal child psychology* (pp. 253–282). Hillsdale, NJ: Lawrence Erlbaum.

Strain, P. S., McConnell, S. R., Carta, J. J., Fowler, S. A., Neisworth, J. T., & Wolery, M. (1992). Behaviorism in early intervention. *Topics in Early Childhood Special Education, 12*(1), 121–141.

Tankersley, M. (1992). *Classification and identification of internalizing behavioral subtypes*. Doctoral dissertation, University of Virginia.

Thomas, A., & Chess, S. (1984). Genesis and evolution of behavioral disorders: From infancy to early adult life. *American Journal of Psychiatry, 141*, 1–9.

Timm, M. A. (1993). The Regional Intervention Program: Family treatment by family members. *Behavioral Disorders, 19*, 34–43.

U.S. Department of Education. (1992). *Fourteenth annual report to Congress on the implementation of the Individuals with Disabilities Education Act*. Washington, DC: Author.

U.S. Department of Education. (1994). *Sixteenth annual report to Congress on implementation of the Individuals with Disabilities Education Act.* Washington, DC: Author.

U.S. Department of Education. (1995). *Seventeenth annual report to Congress on implementation of the Individuals with Disabilities Education Act.* Washington, DC: Author.

Walker, H. M., & Bullis, M. (1991). Behavior disorders and the social context of regular class integration: A conceptual dilemma? In J. W. Lloyd, N. N. Singh, & A. C. Repp (Eds.), *The regular education initiative: Alternative perspectives on concepts, issues, and models*. Sycamore, IL: Sycamore.

Walker, H. M., Colvin, G., & Ramsey, E. (1995). *Antisocial behavior in school: Strategies and best practices*. Pacific Grove, CA: Brooks/Cole.

Walker, H. M., & Severson, H. H. (1990). *Systematic screening for behavior disorders (SSBD): A multiple gating procedure*. Longmont, CO: Sopris West.

Walker, H. M., Severson, H. H., & Feil, E. G. (1994). *The early screening project: A proven child-find process*. Longmont, CO: Sopris West.

Walker, H. M., Stieber, S., & O'Neill, R. E. (1990). Middle school behavioral profiles of antisocial and at-risk control boys: Descriptive and predictive outcomes. *Exceptionality, 1*, 61–77.

Wehby, J. H., Dodge, K. A., & Valente, E. (1993). School behavior of first grade children identified as at-risk for development of conduct problems. *Behavioral Disorders, 19*, 67–78.

Wenar, C., Ruttenberg, B. A., Kalish-Weiss, B., & Wolf, E. G. (1986). The development of normal and autistic children: A comparative study. *Journal of Autism and Developmental Disorders, 16*, 317–333.

Werry, J. S., McClellan, J. M., Andrews, L. K., & Ham, M. (1994). Clinical features and outcome of child and adolescent schizophrenia. *Schizophrenia Bulletin, 20*, 619–630.

Wolf, M. M., Braukmann, C. J., & Ramp, K. A. (1987). Serious delinquent behavior as part of a significantly handicapping condition. *Journal of Applied Behavior Analysis, 20*, 347–359.

Wood, F. H. (Ed.). (1990). When we talk with children: The life space interview. *Behavioral Disorders* [Special section], *15*, 110–126.

Wood, M. M., & Long, N. J. (1991). *Life space intervention: Talking with children and youth in crisis.* Austin, TX: Pro-Ed.

Chapter 7

Alpert, C. L., & Kaiser, A. P. (1992). Training parents as milieu language teachers. *Journal of Early Intervention, 16*(1), 31–52.

American Speech-Language-Hearing Association (AHA). (1993). Definitions of communication disorders and variations. *Asha, 35* (Suppl. 10), 40–41.

Anderson, N. B., & Battle, D. E. (1993). Cultural diversity in the development of language. In D. E. Battle (Ed.), *Communication disorders in multicultural populations* (pp. 158–185). Boston: Andover Medical Publishers.

Baca, L., & Amato, C. (1989). Bilingual special education: Training issues. *Exceptional Children, 56*, 168–173.

Battle, D. E. (Ed.). (1993). *Communication disorders in multicultural populations*. Boston: Andover Medical Publishers.

Benson, B. (1995). *Knotted tongues: Stuttering in history and the quest for a cure.* New York: Simon & Schuster.

Bernstein, D. K., & Tiegerman, E. (1989). *Language and communication disorders in children* (2nd ed.). Columbus, OH: Merrill/Macmillan.

Beukelman, D. R. (1991). Magic and cost of communicative competence. *Augmentative and Alternative Communication, 7*, 2–10.

Biklen, D. (1990). Communication unbound: Autism and praxis. *Harvard Educational Review, 60*, 291–314.

Biklen, D. (1992a). Autism orthodoxy versus free speech: A reply to Cummins and Prior. *Harvard Educational Review, 62*, 242–256.

Biklen, D. (1992b). Typing to talk: Facilitated communication. *American Journal of Speech-Language Pathology, 1*(2), 15–17.

Biklen, D., & Schubert, A. (1991). New words: The communication of students with autism. *Remedial and Special Education, 12*(6), 46–57.

Blank, M., & White, S. J. (1986). Questions: A powerful form of classroom exchange. *Topics in Language Disorders, 6*(2), 1–12.

Bloodstein, O. (1993). *Stuttering: The search for a cause and cure.* Boston: Allyn and Bacon.

Bloom, L. (1991). *Language development from two to three.* New York: Cambridge University Press.

Blosser, J. L., & DePompei, R. (1989). The head-injured student returns to school: Recognizing and treating deficits. *Topics in Language Disorders, 9*(2), 67–77.

Bobrick, B. (1995). *Knotted tongues: Stuttering in history and the quest for a cure.* New York: Simon & Schuster.

Brown, J., & Prelock, P. A. (1995). The impact of regression on language development in autism. *Journal of Autism and Developmental Disorders, 25*, 305–309.

Buzolich, M. J., & Lunger, J. (1995). Empowering system users in peer training. *Augmentative and Alternative Communication, 11*, 37–45.

Calculator, S. N., & Jorgensen, C. M. (1991). Integrating AAC instruction into regular education settings: Expounding on best practices. *Augmentative and Alternative Communication, 7*, 204–212.

Campbell, S. L., Reich, A. R., Klockars, A. J., & McHenry, M. A. (1988). Factors associated with dysphonia in high school cheerleaders. *Journal of Speech and Hearing Disorders, 53*, 175–185.

Carrow-Woolfolk, E. (1988). *Theory, assessment and intervention in language disorders: An integrative approach.* Philadelphia, PA: Grune & Stratton.

Cheng, L. L. (1989). Service delivery to Asian/Pacific LEP children: A cross-cultural framework. *Topics in Language Disorders, 9*(3), 1–14.

Cirrin, F. M., & Penner, S. G. (1995). Classroom-based and consultative service delivery models for language intervention. In M. E. Fey, J. Windsor, & S. F. Warren (Eds.), *Language intervention: Preschool through the elementary years* (pp. 333–362). Baltimore: Paul H. Brookes.

Crais, E. R. (1991). Moving from "parent involvement" to family-centered services. *American Journal of Speech-Language Pathology, 1*(1), 5–8.

Crawford, J. (1992). *Hold your tongue: Bilingualism and the politics of "English only."* Reading, MA: Addison-Wesley.

Crews, W. D., Sanders, E. C., Hensley, L. G., Johnson, Y. M., Bonaventura, S., & Rhodes, R. D. (1995). An evaluation of facilitated communication in a group of nonverbal individuals with mental retardation. *Journal of Autism and Developmental Disorders, 25*, 205–213.

Culatta, R., & Goldberg, S. A. (1995). *Stuttering therapy: An integrated approach to theory and practice.* Boston: Allyn and Bacon.

Delpit, L. (1988). The silenced dialogue: Power and pedagogy in educating other people's children. *Harvard Educational Review, 58*, 280–298.

Delpit, L. (1995). *Other people's children: Cultural conflict in the classroom.* New York: New Press.

Duchan, J. F., Hewitt, L. E., & Sonnenmeier, R. M. (Eds.). (1994). *Pragmatics: From theory to practice.* Englewood Cliffs, NJ: Prentice Hall.

Falvey, M. A., McLean, D., & Rosenberg, R. L. (1988). Transition from school to adult life: Communication strategies. *Topics in Language Disorders, 9*(1), 82–86.

Feenick, J. J., & Judd, D. (1994). Physical interventions and accommodations. In R. C. Savage & G. F. Wolcott (Eds.), *Educational dimensions of acquired brain injury* (pp. 367–390). Austin, TX: Pro-Ed.

Felsenfeld, S., Broen, P. A., & McGue, M. (1992). A 28-year follow-up of adults with a history of moderate phonological disorder: Linguistic and personality results. *Journal of Speech and Hearing Research, 35*, 1114–1125.

Fey, M. E., Catts, H. W., & Larrivee, L. S. (1995). Preparing preschoolers for academic and social challenges of school. In M. E. Fey, J. Windsor, & S. F. Warren (Eds.), *Language intervention: Preschool through the elementary years* (pp. 3–37). Baltimore: Paul H. Brookes.

Foster, H. L. (1986). *Ribin', jivin', and playin' the dozens* (2nd ed.). Cambridge, MA: Ballinger.

Fradd, S. H., Figueroa, R. A., & Correa, V. I. (1989). Meeting the multicultural needs of Hispanic students in special education. *Exceptional Children, 56*, 102–103.

Franklin, K., & Beukelman, D. R. (1991). Augmentative communication: Directions for future research. In J. F. Miller (Ed.), *Research on child language disorders: A decade of progress* (pp. 321–337). Austin, TX: Pro-Ed.

Gersten, R., Brengelman, S., & Jimenez, R. (1994). Effective instruction for culturally and linguistically diverse students: A reconceptualization. *Focus on Exceptional Children, 27*(1), 1–16.

Gersten, R., & Woodward, J. (1994). The language-minority student and special education: Issues, trends, and paradoxes. *Exceptional Children, 60*, 310–322.

Goldstein, H., & Strain, P. S. (1989). Peers as communication intervention agents: Some new strategies and research findings. *Topics in Language Disorders, 9*(1), 44–57.

Hallahan, D. P., Kauffman, J. M., & Lloyd, J. W. (1996). *Introduction to learning disabilities* (3rd ed.). Boston: Allyn and Bacon.

Happe, F. G. E. (1994). An advanced test of theory of mind: Understanding of story characters' thoughts and feelings by able autistic, mentally handicapped, and normal children and adults. *Journal of Autism and Developmental Disorders, 24*, 129–154.

Happe, F. G. E., & Frith, U. (1995). Theory of mind in autism. In E. Schopler & G. B. Mesibov (Eds.), *Learning and cognition in autism* (pp. 177–197). New York: Plenum Press.

Hardy, J. C. (1994). Cerebral palsy. In G. H. Shames, E. H. Wiig, & W. A. Secord (Eds.), *Human communication disorders: An introduction* (4th ed.; pp. 563–604). New York: Merrill/Macmillan.

Harris, S. L. (1995). Educational strategies in autism. In E. Schopler & G. B. Mesibov (Eds.), *Learning and cognition in autism* (pp. 293–309). New York: Plenum Press.

Hart, B., & Risley, T. R. (1995). *Meaningful differences in the everyday experience of young American children*. Baltimore: Paul H. Brookes.

Huer, M. B. (1991). University students using augmentative and alternative communication in the USA: A demographic study. *Augmentative and Alternative Communication, 7*, 231–239.

Johnston, E. B., Weinrich, B. D., & Glaser, A. J. (1991). *A sourcebook of pragmatic activities: Theory and intervention for language therapy (PK–6)* (Rev.). Tucson, AZ: Communication Skill Builders.

Kaiser, A. P., Hemmeter, M. L., Ostrosky, M. M., Alpert, C. L., & Hancock, T. B. (1995). The effects of training and individual feedback on parent use of milieu teaching. *Journal of Childhood Communication Disorders, 16*, 39–48.

Koegel, R. L., O'Dell, M. C., & Koegel, L. C. (1987). A natural language teaching paradigm for nonverbal autistic children. *Journal of Autism and Developmental Disabilities, 17*, 187–200.

Koegel, L. K., & Koegel, R. L. (1995). Motivating communication in children with autism. In E. Schopler & G. B. Mesibov (Eds.), *Learning and cognition in autism* (pp. 73–87). New York: Plenum Press.

Koegel, R. L., Rincover, A., & Egel, A. L. (1982). *Educating and understanding autistic children*. San Diego: College-Hill Press.

LaPointe, L. L., & Katz, R. C. (1994). Neurogenic disorders of speech. In G. H. Shames, E. H. Wiig, & W. A. Secord (Eds.), *Human communication disorders: An introduction* (4th ed.; pp. 481–518). New York: Merrill/Macmillan.

Lee, A., Hobson, R. P., & Chiat, S. (1994). I, you, me, and autism: An experimental study. *Journal of Autism and Developmental Disorders, 24*, 155–176.

Lord, C. (1988). Enhancing communication in adolescents with autism. *Topics in Language Disorders, 9*(1), 72–81.

Lovaas, O. I. (1987). Behavioral treatment and normal educational and intellectual functioning in young autistic children. *Journal of Consulting and Clinical Psychology, 55*, 3–9.

Love, R. J. (1992). *Childhood motor speech disability*. New York: Macmillan.

Marvin, C. A., Beukelman, D. R., Brockhaus, J., & Kast, L. (1994). "What are you talking about?" Semantic analysis of preschool children's conversational topics in home and preschool settings. *Augmentative and Alternative Communication, 10*, 75–86.

Matthews, J., & Frattali, C. (1994). The professions of speech-language pathology and audiology. In G. H. Shames, E. H. Wiig, & W. A. Secord (Eds.), *Human communication disorders: An introduction* (4th ed.; pp. 2–33). New York: Merrill/Macmillan.

McKnight-Taylor, M. (1989). Stimulating speech and language development of infants and other young children. In P. J. Valletutti, M. McKnight-Taylor, & A. S. Hoffnung (Eds.), *Facilitating communication in young children with handicapping conditions: A guide for special educators*. Boston: Little, Brown.

Mesibov, G. B. (1995). Facilitated communication: A warning for pediatric psychologists. *Journal of Pediatric Psychology, 20*, 127–130.

Montee, B. B., Miltenberger, R. G., & Wittrock, D. (1995). An experimental analysis of facilitated communication. *Journal of Applied Behavior Analysis, 28*, 189–200.

Moore, G. P., & Hicks, D. M. (1994). Voice disorders. In G. H. Shames, E. H. Wiig, & W. A. Secord (Eds.), *Human communication disorders: An introduction* (4th ed.; pp. 292–335). New York: Merrill/Macmillan.

Nelson, N. W. (1993). *Childhood language disorders in context: Infancy through adolescence*. Columbus, OH: Merrill/Macmillan.

Ogletree, B. T., Wetherby, A. M., & Westling, D. L. (1992). Profile of the prelinguistic intentional communicative behaviors of children with profound mental retardation. *American Journal on Mental Retardation, 97*, 186–196.

Onslow, M. (1992). Choosing a treatment procedure for early stuttering: Issues and future directions. *Journal of Speech and Hearing Research, 35*, 983–993.

Ortiz, A., Yates, J. R., & Garcia, S. B. (1990). Competencies associated with serving exceptional language minority students. *Bilingual Special Education Newsletter* (Vol. 9). Austin, TX: University of Texas, College of Education, Office of Bilingual Education.

Owens, R. E. (1986). Communication, language, and speech. In G. H. Shames & E. H. Wiig (Eds.), *Human communication disorders* (2nd ed.; pp. 27–79). Columbus, OH: Merrill/Macmillan.

Owens, R. E. (1994). Development of communication, language, and speech. In G. H. Shames, E. H. Wiig, & W. A. Secord (Eds.), *Human communication disorders: An introduction* (4th ed.; pp. 35–81). New York: Merrill/Macmillan.

Owens, R. E. (1995). *Language disorders: A functional approach to assessment and intervention* (2nd ed.). Boston: Allyn and Bacon.

Roberts, J. E., Babinowitch, S., Bryant, D. M., Burchinal, M. R., Koch, M. A., & Ramey, C. T. (1989). Language skills of children with different preschool experiences. *Journal of Speech and Hearing Research, 32*, 773–786.

Ruscello, D. M., St. Louis, K. O., & Mason, N. (1991). School-aged children with phonologic disorders: Coexistence with other speech/language disorders. *Journal of Speech and Hearing Research, 34*, 236–242.

Schlosser, R. W., & Lloyd, L. L. (1991). Augmentative and alternative communication: An evolving field. *Augmentative and Alternative Communication, 7*, 154–160.

Schopler, E., Misibov, G. B., & Hearsey, K. (1995). Structured teaching in the TEACCH system. In E. Schopler & G. B. Mesibov (Eds.), *Learning and cognition in autism* (pp. 243–268). New York: Plenum Press.

Schwartz, R. G. (1994). Phonological disorders. In G. H. Shames, E. H. Wiig, & W. A. Secord (Eds.), *Human communication disorders: An introduction* (4th ed.; pp. 251–290). New York: Merrill/Macmillan.

Seymour, H. N., Champion, T., & Jackson, J. (1995). The language of African American learners: Effective assessment and instructional programming for children with special needs. In B. A. Ford, F. E. Obiakor, & J. M. Patton (Eds.), *Effective education of African American exceptional learners* (pp. 89–121). Austin, TX: Pro-Ed.

Shames, G. H., & Ramig, P. R. (1994). Stuttering and other disorders of fluency. In G. H. Shames, E. H. Wiig, & W. A. Secord (Eds.). *Human communication disorders: An introduction* (4th ed.; pp. 336–386). New York: Merrill/Macmillan.

Shames, G. H., & Wiig, E. H. (Eds.). (1986). *Human communication disorders* (2nd ed.). Columbus, OH: Merrill/Macmillan.

Shames, G. H., Wiig, E. H., & Secord, W. A. (Eds.). (1994). *Human communication disorders: An introduction* (4th ed.). New York: Merrill/Macmillan.

Shane, H. C. (Ed.). (1994). *Facilitated communication: The clinical and social phenomenon*. San Diego: Singular Publishing Group.

Siegel, B. (1995). Assessing allegations of sexual molestation made through facilitated communication. *Journal of Autism and Developmental Disorders, 25*, 319–326.

Sigafoos, J., Kerr, M., Roberts, D., & Couzens, D. (1994). Increasing opportunities for requesting in classrooms serving children with developmental disabilities. *Journal of Autism and Developmental Disorders, 24*, 631–645.

Sigman, M. (1994). What are the core deficits in autism? In S. H. Broman & J. Grafman (Eds.), *Atypical cognitive deficits in developmental disorders: Implication for brain function* (pp. 139–157). Hillsdale, NJ: Lawrence Erlbaum.

Simpson, R. L., & Myles, B. S. (1995). Effectiveness of facilitated communication with children and youth with autism. *Journal of Special Education, 28*, 424–439.

Slentz, K. L., & Bricker, D. (1992). Family-centered assessment for IFSP development: Jumping off the family assessment bandwagon. *Journal of Early Intervention, 16*(1), 11–19.

Stephens, M. I. (Ed.). (1985). Language impaired youth: The years between 10 and 18. *Topics in Language Disorders, 5*(3), [special issue].

Stoel-Gammon, C. (1991). Issues in phonological development and disorders. In J. F. Miller (Ed.), *Research on child language disorders: A decade of progress* (pp. 255–265). Austin, TX: Pro-Ed.

Swindell, C. S., Holland, A. L., & Reinmuth, O. M. (1994). Aphasia and related adult disorders. In G. H. Shames, E. H. Wiig, & W. A. Secord (Eds.), *Human communication disorders: An introduction* (4th ed.; pp. 521–560). New York: Merrill/Macmillan.

Szekeres, S. F., & Meserve, N. F. (1995). Collaborative intervention in schools after traumatic brain injury. *Topics in Language Disorders, 15*(1), 21–36.

U.S. Department of Education. (1994). *Sixteenth annual report to Congress on the implementation of the Individuals with Disabilities Education Act*. Washington, DC: Author.

U.S. Department of Education. (1995) *Seventeenth annual report to Congress on the implementation of the Individuals with Disabilities Education* Act. Washington, DC: Author.

Vanderheiden, G. C. (1984). High and low technology approaches in the development of communication systems for severely physically handicapped persons. *Exceptional Education Quarterly, 4*(4), 40–56.

Wallace, G., Larsen, S. C., & Elksnin, L. K. (1992). *Educational assessment of learning problems: Testing for teaching* (2nd ed.). Boston: Allyn and Bacon.

Wallach, G. P., & Butler, K. G. (Eds.). (1994). *Language learning disabilities in school-age children and adolescents: Some principles and applications*. New York: Merrill/Macmillan.

Warren, S. F., & Abbaduto, L. (1992). The relation of communication and language development to mental retardation. *American Journal on Mental Retardation, 97*, 125–130.

Warren, S. F., Yoder, P. J., Gazdag, G. E., Kim, K., & Jones, H. A. (1993). Facilitating prelinguistic communication skills in young children with developmental delay. *Journal of Speech and Hearing Research, 36*, 83–97.

Westby, C. E. (1994). The effects of culture and genre, structure, and style of oral and written texts. In G. P. Wallach, & K. G. Butler (Eds.), *Language learning disabilities in school-age children and adolescents: Some principles and applications* (pp. 180–218). New York: Merrill/Macmillan.

Westby, C. E., & Roman, R. (1995). Finding the balance: Learning to live in two worlds. *Topics in Language Disorders, 15*(4), 68–88.

Wilcox, M. J., Kouri, T. A., & Caswell, S. B. (1991). Early language intervention: A comparison of classroom and individual treatment. *American Journal of Speech-Language Pathology, 1*(1), 49–62.

Wong, B. Y. L., Wong, R., Darlington, D., & Jones, W. (1991). Interactive teaching: An effective way to teach revision skills to adolescents with learning disabilities. *Learning Disabilities Research and Practice, 6*, 117–127.

Yairi, E., & Ambrose, N. (1992). A longitudinal study of stuttering in children: A preliminary report. *Journal of Speech and Hearing Research, 35*, 755–760.

Ylvisaker, M., & Szekeres, S. F. (1989). Metacognitive and executive impairments in head-injured children and adults. *Topics in Language Disorders, 9*(2), 34–49.

Ylvisaker, M., Szekeres, S. F., Haarbauer-Krupa, J., Urbanczyk, B., & Feeney, T. J. (1994). Speech and language intervention. In R. C. Savage & G. F. Wolcott (Eds.), *Educational dimensions of acquired brain injury* (pp. 185–235). Austin, TX: Pro-Ed.

Yoder, P. J., Warren, S. F., Kim, K., & Gazdag, G. E. (1994). Facilitating prelinguistic communication skills in young children with developmental delay II: Systematic replication and extension. *Journal of Speech and Hearing Research, 37*, 841–851.

Zebrowski, P. M. (Issue Ed.). (1995). Language and stuttering in children: Perspectives on an interrelationship. *Topics in Language Disorders, 15*(3).

Chapter 8

Allen, T. E. (1986). Patterns of achievement among hearing-impaired students: 1974 and 1983. In A. N. Schildroth & M. A. Karchmer (Eds.), *Deaf children in America* (pp.161–206). San Diego, CA: College-Hill Press.

Andersson, Y. (1994). Comment on Turner. *Sign Language Studies, 83,* 127–131.

Bellugi, U., & Klima, E. (1991). What the hands reveal about the brain. In D. S. Martin (Ed.), *Advances in cognition, education, and deafness.* Washington, DC: Gallaudet University Press.

Bornstein, H., Hamilton, L., & Saulnier, K. (1983). *The comprehensive Signed English dictionary.* Washington, DC: Gallaudet University Press.

Braden, J. P. (1992). Intellectual assessment of deaf and hard-of-hearing people: A quantitative and qualitative research synthesis. *School Psychology Review, 21,* 82–94.

Brill, R. G., MacNeil, B., & Newman, L. R. (1986). Framework for appropriate programs for deaf children. *American Annals of the Deaf, 131*(2), 65–77.

Buchino, M. A. (1993). Perceptions of the oldest hearing child of deaf parents. *American Annals of the Deaf, 138,* 40–45.

Bull, B., & Bullis, M. (1991). A national profile of school-based transition programs for deaf adolescents. *American Annals of the Deaf, 136*(4), 339–343.

Bullis, M., Bull, B., Johnson, B., & Peters, D. (1995). The school-to-community transition experiences of hearing young adults and young adults who are deaf. *Journal of Special Education, 28,* 405–423.

Castiglia, P. T., Aquilina, S. S., & Kemsley, M. (1983). Focus: Nonsuppurative otitis media. *Pediatric Nursing, 9,* 427–431.

Charlson, E., Strong, M., & Gold, R. (1992). How successful deaf teenagers experience and cope with isolation. *American Annals of the Deaf, 137*(3), 261–270.

Crowson, K. (1994). Errors made by deaf children acquiring sign language. *Early Child Development and Care, 99,* 63–78.

Davis, H. (1978a). Abnormal hearing and deafness. In H. Davis & S. R. Silverman (Eds.), *Hearing and deafness* (4th ed.). New York: Holt, Rinehart & Winston.

Desselle, D. D. (1994). Self-esteem, family climate, and communication patterns in relation to deafness. *American Annals of the Deaf, 139,* 322–328.

Donner, C., Liesnard, C., Brancart, F., & Rodesch, F. (1994). Accuracy of amniotic fluid testing before 21 weeks' gestation in prenatal diagnosis of congenital cytomegalovirus infection. *Prenatal Diagnosis, 14,* 1055–1059.

Drasgow, E. (1993). Bilingual/bicultural deaf education: An overview. *Sign Language Studies, 80,* 243–266.

Fant, L. J. (1971). *Say it with hands.* Silver Spring, MD: National Association for the Deaf.

Fry, D. B. (1966). The development of a phonological system in the normal and the deaf child. In F. Smith & G. A. Miller (Eds.), *The genesis of language: A psycholinguistic approach.* Cambridge, MA: MIT Press.

Gaustad, M. G., & Kluwin, T. N. (1992). Patterns of communication among deaf and hearing adolescents. In T. N. Kluwin, D. F. Moores, & M. G. Gaustad (Eds.), *Toward effective public school programs for deaf students: Context, process, & outcomes* (pp. 107–128). New York: Teachers College Press.

Giebink, G. S. (1990). Medical issues in hearing impairment: The otitis media spectrum. In J. Davis (Ed.), *Our forgotten children: Hard-of-hearing pupils in the schools* (pp. 49–55). Bethesda, MD: Self Help for Hard of Hearing People.

Goldberg, D. M. (1993). Auditory-verbal philosophy: A tutorial. *Volta Review, 95,* 181–186.

Gustason, G., Pfetzing, D., & Zawolkow, E. (1972). *Signing Exact English.* Silver Spring, MD: National Association of the Deaf.

Hawkins, D. B. (1990). Amplification in the classroom. In J. Davis (Ed.), *Our forgotten children: Hard-of-hearing pupils in the schools* (pp. 39–47). Bethesda, MD: Self Help for Hard of Hearing People.

Higgins, P. C. (1992). Working at mainstreaming. In P. M. Ferguson, D. L. Ferguson, & S. J. Taylor (Eds.), *Interpreting disability* (pp. 103–123). New York: Teachers College Press.

Innes, J. J. (1994). Full inclusion and the deaf student: A deaf consumer's review of the issue. *American Annals of the Deaf, 139,* 152–156.

Janesick, V. J., & Moores, D. F. (1992). Ethnic and cultural considerations. In T. N. Kluwin, D. F. Moores, & M. G. Gaustad (Eds.), *Toward effective public school programs for deaf students: Context, process, & outcomes* (pp. 49–65). New York: Teachers College Press.

Jensma, C. J. (1994). Telecommunications for the deaf: Echoes of the past—a glimpse of the future. *American Annals of the Deaf, 193,* 22–27.

Johnston, T. (1994). Comment on Turner. *Sign Language Studies, 83,* 133–138.

Kampfe, C. M., & Turecheck, A. G. (1987). Reading achievement of prelingually deaf students and its relationship to parental method of communication: A review of the literature. *American Annals of the Deaf, 132*(1), 11–15.

Klima, E. S., & Bellugi, U. (1979). *The signs of language.* Cambridge, MA: Harvard University Press.

Kluwin, T. N. (1992). What does "local public school" mean? In T. N. Kluwin, D. F. Moores, & M. G. Gaustad (Eds.), *Toward effective public school programs for deaf students: Context, process, & outcomes* (pp. 30–48). New York: Teachers College Press.

Kluwin, T. N. (1993). Cumulative effects of mainstreaming on the achievement of deaf adolescents. *Exceptional Children, 60,* 73–81.

Kluwin, T. N., & Gaustad, M. G. (1994). The role of adaptability and communication in fostering cohesion in families of deaf adolescents. *American Annals of the Deaf, 139,* 329–335.

Koester, L. S., & Meadow-Orlans, K. P. (1990). Parenting a deaf child: Stress, strength, and support. In D. F. Moores & K. P. Meadow-Orlans (Eds.), *Educational and developmental aspects of deafness* (pp. 299–320). Washington, DC: Gallaudet University Press.

Lane, H. (1984). *When the mind hears: A history of the deaf.* New York: Random House.

Lane, H. (1987, July 17). Listen to the needs of deaf children. *New York Times.*

Lane, H. (1992). *The mask of benevolence: Disabling the Deaf community.* New York: Knopf.

Ling, D., & Ling, A. (1978). *Aural habilitation.* Washington, DC: Alexander Graham Bell Association for the Deaf.

Livingston, S., Singer, B., & Abrahamson, T. (1994). Effectiveness compared: ASL interpretation vs. transliteration. *Sign Language Studies, 82,* 1–54.

Loeb, R., & Sarigiani, P. (1986). The impact of hearing impairment on self-perceptions of children. *Volta Review, 88*(2), 89–100.

MacTurk, R. H., Meadow-Orlans, K. P., Koester, L. S., & Spencer, P. E. (1993). Social support, motivation, language, and interaction. *American Annals of the Deaf, 138,* 19–25.

Martin, F. N. (1986). *Introduction to audiology* (3rd ed.). Englewood Cliffs, NJ: Prentice Hall.

Meadow-Orlans, K. P. (1987). An analysis of the effectiveness of early intervention programs for hearing-impaired children. In M. J. Guralnick & F. C. Bennett (Eds.), *The effectiveness of early intervention for at-risk and handicapped children* (pp. 325–362). New York: Academic Press.

Meadow-Orlans, K. P. (1990). Research on developmental aspects of deafness. In D. F. Moores & K. P. Meadow-Orlans (Eds.), *Educational and developmental aspects of deafness* (pp. 283–298). Washington, DC: Gallaudet University Press.

Menchel, R. S. (1988). Personal experience with speechreading. *Volta Review, 90*(5), 3–15.

Moaven, L. D., Gilbert, G. L., Cunningham, A. L., & Rawlinson, W. D. (1995). Amniocentesis to diagnose congenital cytomegalovirus infection. *Medical Journal of Australia, 162,* 334–335.

Moog, J. S., & Geers, A. E. (1991). Educational management of children with cochlear implants. *American Annals of the Deaf, 136*(2), 69–76.

Moores, D. F., Cerney, B., & Garcia, M. (1990). School placement and least restrictive environment. In D. F. Moores & K. P. Meadow-Orlans (Eds.), *Educational and developmental aspects of deafness* (pp. 115–136). Washington, DC: Gallaudet University Press.

Moores, D. F., & Maestas y Moores, J. (1981). Special adaptations necessiated by hearing impairments. In J. M. Kauffman & D. P. Hallahan (Eds.), *Handbook of special education.* Englewood Cliffs, NJ: Prentice Hall.

Moseley, K. A., & Moseley, P. L. (1994). The TTY: A tool for inclusion. *Perspectives in Education and Deafness, 13,* 10–11, 18.

Padden, C., & Humphries, T. (1988). *Deaf in America: Voices from a culture.* Cambridge, MA: Harvard University Press.

Quigley, S., Jenne, W., & Phillips, S. (1968). *Deaf students in colleges and universities.* Washington, DC: Alexander Graham Bell Association for the Deaf.

Reagan, T. (1990). Cultural considerations in the education of deaf children. In D. F. Moores & K. P. Meadow-Orlans (Eds.), *Educational and developmental aspects of deafness* (pp. 73–84). Washington, DC: Gallaudet University Press.

Robinshaw, H. M. (1994). Deaf infants, early intervention and language acquisition. *Early Child Development and Care, 99,* 1–22.

Sacks, O. (1989). *Seeing voices: A journey into the world of the deaf.* Berkeley: University of California Press.

Saur, R., Coggiola, D., Long, G., & Simonson, J. (1986). Educational mainstreaming and the career development of hearing-impaired students: A longitudinal analysis. *Volta Review, 88*(2), 79–88.

Schildroth, A. N., & Hotto, S. (1992). Hearing impaired children under age 6: Data from the Annual Survey of Hearing Impaired Children and Youth. *American Annals of the Deaf, 137*(2), 168–175.

Schildroth, A. N., Rawlings, B. W., & Allen, T. E. (1989). Hearing-impaired children under age 6: A demographic analysis. *American Annals of the Deaf, 134*(2), 63–69.

Schow, R., & Nerbonne, M. (Eds.). (1980). *Introduction to aural rehabilitation.* Baltimore: University Park Press.

Singleton, J. L., Morford, J. P., & Goldin-Meadow, S. (1993). Once is not enough: Standards of well-formedness in manual communication created over three different timespans. *Language, 69,* 683–715.

Siple, L. (1993). Working with the sign language interpreter in your classroom. *College Teaching, 41,* 139–142.

Spencer, P. E., & Gutfreund, M. K. (1990). Directiveness in mother-infant interactions. In D. F. Moores & K. P. Meadow-Orlans (Eds.), *Educational and developmental aspects of deafness* (pp. 350–365). Washington, DC: Gallaudet University Press.

Spencer, P. E. (1993). The expressive communication of hearing mothers and deaf infants. *American Annals of the Deaf, 138,* 275–283.

Spradley, T. S., & Spradley, J. P. (1978). *Deaf like me.* Washington, DC: Gallaudet University Press.

Stinson, M. S., & Whitmire, K. (1992). Students' views of their social relationships. In T. N. Kluwin, D. F. Moores, & M. G. Gaustad (Eds.), *Toward effective public school programs for deaf students: Context, process, & outcomes* (pp. 149–174). New York: Teachers College Press.

Stoel-Gammon, C., & Otomo, K. (1986). Babbling development of hearing-impaired and normally hearing subjects. *Journal of Speech and Hearing Disorders, 51,* 33–41.

Stokoe, W. C. (1960). *Sign language structure.* Silver Spring, MD: Linstok Press.

Stokoe, W. C., Casterline, D. C., & Croneberg, C. G. (1976). *A dictionary of American Sign Language on linguistic principles* (2nd ed.). Silver Spring, MD: Linstok Press.

Stokoe, W. C. (1995). Deaf culture working. *Sign Language Studies, 86,* 81–94.

Street, B. (1994). Comment on Turner. *Sign Language Studies, 83,* 145–148.

Trybus, R. J., & Karchmer, M. A. (1977). School achievement scores of hearing impaired children. National data on achievement status and growth patterns. *American Annals of the Deaf, 122,* 62–69.

Turner, G. H. (1994). *How* is deaf culture? Another perspective on a fundamental concept. *Sign Language Studies, 83,* 103–125.

Viadero, D. (1992, August 5). E. D. revises policy favoring regular classes for the deaf. *Education Week*, p. 39.

Valdes, K., Williamson, C., & Wagner, M. (1990). *The national longitudinal transition study of special education students* (Vol. 1). Palo Alto, CA: SRI International.

Vygotsky, L. S. (1962). *Thought and language*. New York: John Wiley.

Walker, L. A. (1986). *A loss for words: The story of deafness in a family.* New York: Harper & Row.

Williamson, W. D., Demmler, G. J., Percy, A. K., & Catlin, F. I. (1992). Progressive hearing loss in infants with asymptomatic congenital cytomegalovirus infection. *Pediatrics, 90,* 862–866.

Withrow, F. B. (1994). Jericho: The walls come tumbling down! *American Annals of the Deaf, 139,* 18–21.

Wolk, S., & Allen, T. E. (1984). A five-year follow-up of reading comprehension achievment of hearing-impaired students in special education programs. *Journal of Special Education*, *18,* 161–176.

Wolk, S., & Schildroth, A. N. (1986). Deaf children and speech intelligibility: A national study. In A. N. Schildroth & M. A. Karchmer (Eds.), *Deaf children in America* (pp. 139–159). San Diego: College-Hill Press.

Wolkomir, R. (1992). American Sign Language: 'It's not mouth stuff—it's brain stuff.' *Smithsonian*, *23*(4), 30–38, 40–41.

Wood, D. (1991). Communication and cognition: How the communication styles of hearing adults may hinder—rather than help—deaf learners. *American Annals of the Deaf*, *136*(3), 247–251.

Chapter 9

Andersen, E. S., Dunlea, A., & Kekelis, L. S. (1984). Blind children's language: Resolving some differences. *Journal of Child Language*, *2*, 645–664.

Andrews, D. (1995, January). The other half of the equation: PC-based reading systems—a comparative review. *Braille Monitor,* pp. 27–39.

Bailey, B. R., & Head, D. N. (1993). Providing O&M services to children and youth with severe multiple disabilities. *RE:view, 25,* 57–66.

Bambring, M., & Troster, H. (1992). On the stability of stereotyped behaviors in blind infants and preschoolers. *Journal of Visual Impairment and Blindness, 86*(2), 105–110.

Barraga, N. C. (1983). *Visual handicaps and learning* (Rev. Ed.). Austin, TX: Exceptional Resources.

Barraga, N. C., & Collins, M. E. (1979). Development of efficiency in visual functioning: Rationale for a comprehensive program. *Journal of Visual Impairment and Blindness*, *73*, 121–126.

Baumeister, A. A. (1978). Origins and control of stereotyped movements. In C. E. Meyers (Ed.), *Quality of life in severely and profoundly retarded people: Research foundations for improvment* (pp. 353–384). Washington, DC: American Association on Mental Deficiency.

Berla, E. P. (1981). Tactile scanning and memory for a spatial display by blind students. *Journal of Special Education*, *15*, 341–350.

Bigelow, A. (1991). Spatial mapping of familiar locations in blind children. *Journal of Visual Impairment and Blindness*, *85*(3), 113–117.

Bischoff, R. W. (1979). Listening: A teachable skill for visually impaired persons. *Journal of Visual Impairment and Blindness*, *73*, 59–67.

Bishop, V. E. (1991). Preschool visually impaired children: A demographic study. *Journal of Visual Impairment and Blindness*, *85*(2), 69–74.

Bower, T. J. R. (1977). Blind babies see with their ears. *New Scientist*, *73*, 255–257.

Brody, H. (1989, July). The great equalizer: PCs empower the disabled. *PC Computing*, pp. 82–93.

Cheadle, B. (1991, October). Canes and preschoolers: The eight-year revolution. *Braille Monitor*, pp. 533–538.

Cheadle, B. A., & Boone, D. C. (1994, December). Linda gets a cane: Parents prevail in due process hearing. *Braille Monitor,* pp. 680–684.

Chong, C. (1994, January). Problems and challenges of the graphical user interface. *Braille Monitor,* 52–56.

Collins, M. E., & Barraga, N. C. (1980). Development of efficiency in visual functioning: An evaluation process. *Journal of Visual Impairment and Blindness*, *74*, 93–96.

Conant, S., & Budoff, M. (1982). The development of sighted people's understanding of blindness. *Journal of Visual Impairment and Blindness*, *76*, 86–90.

Cronin, P. J. (1992). A direct service program for mainstreamed students by a residential school. *Journal of Visual Impairment and Blindness*, *86*(2), 101–104.

Cronin, B. J., & King, S. R. (1990). The development of the Descriptive Video Service. *Journal of Visual Impairment and Blindness*, *84*(12), 503–506.

Davidson, P. W., Appelle, S., & Haber, R. N. (1992). Haptic scanning of Braille cells by low- and high-proficiency blind readers. *Research in Developmental Disabilities, 13,* 99–111.

Davidson, P. W., Dunn, G., Wiles-Kettenmann, M., & Appelle, S. (1981). Haptic conservation of amount in blind and sighted children: Exploratory movement effects. *Journal of Pediatric Psychology*, *6*, 191–200.

Dekker, R. Drenth, P. J. D., & Zaal, J. N. (1991). Results of the Intelligence Test for Visually Impaired Children (ITVIC). *Journal of Visual Impairment and Blindness*, *85*(6), 261–267.

Dekker, R., Drenth, P. J. D., Zaal, J. N., & Koole, F. D. (1990). An intelligence series for blind and low vision children. *Journal of Visual Impairment and Blindness*, *84*(2), 71–76.

Detectable warnings debate continues. (1993, December). *Braille Monitor,* pp. 1084–1093.

Dykes, J. (1992). Opinions of orientation and mobility instructors about using the long cane with preschool-age children. *RE:view, 24,* 85–92.

Erin, J. N. (1993). The road less traveled: New directions for schools for students with visual impairments. *Journal of Visual Impairment and Blindness, 87,* 219–223.

Erwin, E. J. (1991). Guidelines for integrating young children with visual impairments in general education settings. *Journal of Visual Impairment and Blindness*, *85*(6), 253–260.

Estevis, A. H., & Koenig, A. J. (1994). A cognitive approach to reducing stereotypic body rocking. *RE:view, 26,* 119–125.

Farmer, L. W. (1975). Travel in adverse weather using electronic mobility guidance devices. *New Outlook for the Blind, 69,* 433–451.

Farmer, L. W. (1980). Mobility devices. In R. L. Welsh & B. B. Blasch (Eds.), *Foundations of orientation and mobility.* New York: American Foundation for the Blind.

Ferrell, K. A., Trief, E., Dietz, S. J., Bonner, M. A., Cruz, D., Ford, E., Stratton, & J. M. (1990). Visually impaired infants research consortium (VIIRC): First year results. *Journal of Visual Impairment and Blindndess, 84*(10), 404–410.

Fichten, C. S., Judd, D., Tagalakis, V., Amsel, R., & Robillard, K. (1991). Communication cues used by people with and without visual impairments in daily conversations and dating. *Journal of Visual Impairment and Blindness, 85*(9), 371–378.

Foy, C. J., Von Scheden, M., & Waiculonis, J. (1992). The Connecticut pre-cane: Case study and curriculum. *Journal of Visual Impairment and Blindness, 86*(4), 178–181.

Fraiberg, S. (1977). *Insights from the blind.* New York: Basic Books.

Freeman, R. D., Goetz, E., Richards, D. P., & Groenveld, M. (1991). Defiers of negative prediction: A 14-year follow-up study of legally blind children. *Journal of Visual Impairment and Blindness, 85*(9), 365–370.

Gabias, P. (1992, July). Unique features of guide dogs: Backtracking and homing. *Braille Monitor,* pp. 392–399.

Gashel, J. (1995, April). The jig is up: Detectable warnings proven safety hoax. *Braille Monitor,* pp. 181–189.

Griffin, H. C., & Gerber, P. J. (1982). Tactual development and its implications for the education of blind children. *Education of the Visually Handicapped, 13,* 116–123.

Groenveld, M., & Jan, J. E. (1992). Intelligence profiles of low vision and blind children. *Journal of Visual Impairment and Blindness, 86*(1), 68–71.

Hanley-Maxwell, C., Griffin, S., Szymanski, E. M., & Godley, S. H. (1990). Supported and time-limited transitional employment services. *Journal of Visual Impairment and Blindness, 84*(4), 160–166.

Hanninen, K. A. (1975). *Teaching the visually handicapped.* Columbus, OH: Merrill.

Hatlen, P. H. (1993). A personal odyssey on schools for blind children. *Journal of Visual Impairment and Blindness, 87,* 171–174.

Hayes, S. P. (1942). Alternative scales for the mental measurement of the visually handicapped. *Outlook for the Blind and the Teachers Forum, 36,* 225–230.

Hayes, S. P. (1950). Measuring the intelligence of the blind. In P. A. Zahl (Ed.), *Blindness.* Princeton, NJ: Princeton University Press.

Herman, J. F., Chatman, S. P., & Roth, S. F. (1983). Cognitive mapping in blind people: Acquisition of spatial relationships in a large-scale environment. *Journal of Visual Impairment and Blindness, 77,* 161–166.

Holbrook, M. C., & Koenig, A. J. (1992). Teaching Braille reading to students with low vision. *Journal of Visual Impairment and Blindness, 86*(1), 44–48.

Hull, J. M. (1990). *Touching the rock.* New York: Pantheon Books.

Ianuzzi, J. W. (1992, May). Braille or print: Why the debate? *Braille Monitor,* pp. 229–233.

Jackson, J., Bogart, D., & Caton, H. (1993, December). The Unified Braille Code: Some myths and realities. *Braille Monitor,* pp. 1108–1110.

Jernigan, K. (1985, August–September). Blindness: The pattern of freedom. *Braille Monitor,* pp. 386–398.

Jernigan, K. (1991, January). Airline safety: What happens when you can see fire on the wing? *Braille Monitor,* pp. 51–54.

Jernigan, K. (1992, June). Equality, disability, and empowerment. *Braille Monitor,* pp. 292–298.

(The) Jewish Guild for the Blind, 15 West 65th Street, New York, New York 10023.

Kay, L. (1973). Sonic glasses for the blind: A progress report. *Research Bulletin: American Foundation for the Blind,* 25, 25–58.

Kirchner, C., & Peterson, R. (1989). Employment: Selected characteristics. In C. Kirchner (Ed.), *Blindness and visual impairment in the U.S.* New York: American Foundation for the Blind.

Leventhal, J. D., & Uslan, M. M. (1992). A comparison of the two leading electronic Braille notetakers. *Journal of Visual Impairment and Blindness, 86,* 258–260.

Maloney, P. L. (1981). *Practical guidance for parents of the visually handicapped preschooler.* Springfield, IL: Thomas.

Matsuda, M. M. (1984). Comparative analysis of blind and sighted children's communication skills. *Journal of Visual Impairment and Blindness, 78,* 1–5.

Maurer, M. (1991, May 20). All children should learn Braille: Here's why. Scripps Howard News Service.

Maurer, M. (1994, June). Who wants Braille on the money? *Braille Monitor,* pp. 345–348.

McAdam, D. B., O'Cleirigh, M., & Cuvo, A. J. (1993). Self-monitoring and verbal feedback to reduce stereotypic body rocking in a congenitally blind adult. *RE:view, 24,* 163–172.

McGinnis, A. R. (1981). Functional linguistic strategies of blind children. *Journal of Visual Impairment and Blindness, 75,* 210–214.

McLinden, D. J. (1988). Spatial task performance: A metaanalysis. *Journal of Visual Impairment and Blindness, 82,* 231–236.

Mehta, V. (1982). *Vedi.* New York: W. W. Norton.

Mehta, V. (1984). *The ledge between the streams.* New York: W. W. Norton.

Mehta, V. (1985). *Sound-shadows of the new world.* New York: W. W. Norton.

Mehta, V. (1989). *The stolen light: Continents of exile.* New York: W. W. Norton.

National Society for the Prevention of Blindness. (1964). Pub. V-7.

National Society for the Prevention of Blindness. (1972). *Teaching about vision.*

Newland, T. E. (1979). The Blind Learning Aptitude Test. *Journal of Visual Impairment and Blindness,* 73, 134–139.

Nicely, B. (1991, October). Guidelines for Braille literacy: A first step. *Braille Monitor,* pp. 551–556.

Nielsen, L. (1991). Spatial relations in congenitally blind infants. *Journal of Visual Impairment and Blindness, 85*(1), 11–16.

Ochaita, E., & Huertas, J. A. (1993). Spatial representation by persons who are blind: A study of the effects of learning and development. *Journal of Visual Impairment and Blindness, 87,* 37–41.

Palazesi, M. A. (1986). The need for motor development programs for visually impaired preschoolers. *Journal of Visual Impairment and Blindness, 80*, 573–576.

Pierce, B. (1991, August–September). APH figures show Braille is still declining. *Braille Monitor*, pp. 390–391.

Plain-Switzer, K. (1993). A model for touch technique and computation of adequate cane length. *International Journal of Rehabilitation Research, 16,* 66–71.

Pogrund, R. L., Fazzi, D. L., & Schreier, E. M. (1993). Development of a preschool "Kiddy Cane." *Journal of Visual Impairment and Blindness, 87,* 52–54.

Raeder, W. M. (1991, July–August). Overcoming roadblocks to literacy for blind children. *Braille Monitor*, pp. 363–365.

Rapp D. W., & Rapp, A. J. (1992). A survey of the current status of visually impaired students in secondary mathematics. *Journal of Visual Impairment and Blindness*, *86*(2), 115–117.

Rathgeber, A. J. (1981). Manitoba vision screening study. *Journal of Visual Impairment and Blindness*, *75*, 239–243.

Rickelman, B. L., & Blaylock, J. N. (1983). Behaviors of sighted individuals perceived by blind persons as hindrances to self-reliance in blind persons. *Journal of Visual Impairment and Blindness*, *77*, 8–11.

Rieser, J. J., Guth, D. A., & Hill, E. W. (1982). Mental processes mediating independent travel: Implications for orientation and mobility. *Journal of Visual Impairment and Blindness*, *76*, 213–218.

Ross, D. B., & Koening, A. J. (1991). A cognitive approach to reducing stereotypic head rocking. *Journal of Visual Impairment and Blindness*, *85*(1), 17–19.

Rovig, L. (1992, May). Ideas for increasing your chance of job success while still in college. *Braille Monitor*, pp. 238–244.

Sacks, S. Z., & Pruett, K. M. (1992). Summer transition training project for professionals who work with adolescents and young adults. *Journal of Visual Impairment and Blindness*, *86*(5), 211–214.

Scholl, G. T. (1993). Educational programs for blind children: A kaleidoscopic view. *Journal of Visual Impairment and Blindness, 87*, 177–180.

Schroeder, F. K. (1990, January). Literacy: The key to opportunity. *Braille Monitor*, pp. 33–41.

Schroeder, F. K. (1992, June). Braille bills: What are they and what do they mean? *Braille Monitor*, pp. 308–311.

Scott, E. P. (1982). *Your visually impaired student: A guide for teachers.* Baltimore, MD: University Park Press.

Scott, R. A. (1969). *The making of blind men.* New York: Russell Sage Foundation.

Skellenger, A. C., & Hill, E. W. (1991). Current practices and considerations regarding long cane instruction with preschool children. *Journal of Visual Impairment and Blindness*, *85*(3), 101–104.

Stephens, B., & Grube, C. (1982). Development of Piagetian reasoning in congenitally blind children. *Journal of Visual Impairment and Blindness*, *76*, 133–143.

Strelow, E. R., & Boys, J. T. (1979). The Canterbury Child's Aid: A binaural spatial sensor for research with blind children. *Journal of Visual Impairment and Blindness*, *73*, 179–184.

Suppes, P. (1974). A survey of cognition in handicapped children. *Review of Educational Research*, *44*, 145–175.

Swallow, R. M., & Conner, A. (1982). Aural reading. In S. S. Mangold (Ed.), *A teachers' guide to the special educational needs of blind and visually handicapped children.* New York: American Foundation for the Blind.

Thomas, C. L. (Ed.). (1985). *Taber's cyclopedic medical dictionary* (15th ed.). Philadelphia: F. A. Davis.

Thurrell, R. J., & Rice, D. G. (1970). Eye rubbing in blind children: Application of a sensory deprivation model. *Exceptional Children*, *36*, 325–330.

Ulrey, P. (1994). When you meet a guide dog. *RE:view, 26,* 143–144.

Van Reusen, A. K., & Head, D. N. (1994). Cognitive and metacognitive interventions: Important trends for teachers of students who are visually impaired. *RE:view, 25,* 153–162.

Walhof, R. (1993, September–October). Braille: A renaissance. *Braille Monitor,* pp. 971–977.

Warren, D. H. (1981). Visual Impairments. In J. M. Kauffman & D. P. Hallahan (Eds.), *Handbook of special education,* Englewood Cliffs, NJ. Prentice Hall.

Warren, D. H. (1984). *Blindness and early childhood development* (2nd ed.). New York: American Foundation for the Blind.

Warren, D. H., & Kocon, J. A. (1974). Factors in the successful mobility of the blind: A review. *Research Bulletin: American Foundation for the Blind 28,* 191–218.

Willis, D. H. (1976). *A study of the relationship between visual acuity, reading mode, and school systems for blind students—1976.* Louisville, KY: American Printing House for the Blind.

Wolffe, K. E., Roessler, R. T., & Schriner, K. F. (1992). Employment concerns of people with blindness or visual impairments. *Journal of Visual Impairment and Blindness*, *86*(4), 185–187.

Wunder, G. (1993, March). Mobility: Whose responsibility is it? *Braille Monitor,* pp. 567–572.

Chapter 10

Allison, M. (1992). The effects of neurologic injury on the maturing brain. *Headlines*, *3*(5), 2–10.

Batshaw, M. L., & Parret, Y. M. (1986). *Children with handicaps: A medical primer*. Baltimore: Paul H. Brookes.

Baumeister, A. A., Kupstas, F., & Klindworth, L. M. (1990). New morbidity: Implications for prevention of children's disabilities. *Exceptionality*, *1*, 1–16.

Begali, V. (1992). *Head injury in children and adolescents* (2nd ed.). Brandon, VT: Clinical Psychology Publishing.

Besag, F. M. C. (1995). Epilepsy, learning, and behavior in children. *Epilepsia, 36*, 58–63.

Bigge, J. L. (1991). *Teaching individuals with physical and multiple disabilities* (3rd ed.). Columbus, OH: Merrill/Macmillan.

Blackman, J. A. (Ed.). (1984). *Medical aspects of developmental disabilities in children birth to three* (Rev. Ed.). Rockville, MD: Aspen.

Blum, R. W. (1992). Chronic illness and disability in adolescence. *Journal of Adolescent Health*, *13*, 364–368.

Brown, R. T. (1993). An introduction to the special series: Pediatric chronic illness. *Journal of Learning Disabilities*, *26*, 4–6.

Chowder, K. (1992). How TB survived its own death to confront us again. *Smithsonian*, *23*(8), 180–194.

Condeluci, A. (1994). Transition to employment. In R. C. Savage & G. F. Wolcott (Eds.), *Educational dimensions of acquired brain injury* (pp. 519–542). Austin, TX: Pro-Ed.

Coulter, D. L. (1993). Epilepsy and mental retardation: An overview. *American Journal on Mental Retardation, 98*, 1–11.

Crosse, S. B., Kaye, E., & Ratnofsky, A. C. (no date). *A report on the maltreatment of children with disabilities*. Washington, DC: National Center on Child Abuse and Neglect.

Deden, S. (1993, September/October). Why your hospital needs a child abuse team. *Headlines*, 22.

DeLoach, C., & Greer, B. G. (1981). *Adjustment to severe physical disability: A metamorphosis*. New York: McGraw-Hill.

DuBose, R. F., & Deni, K. (1980). Easily constructed adaptive and assistive equipment. *Teaching Exceptional Children, 12*, 116–123.

Duncan, D., & Canty-Lemke, J. (1986). Learning appropriate social and sexual behavior: The role of society. *Exceptional Parent, 16*(5), 24–26.

Dyar, S. E. (1988). A step in the right direction. *Helix: The University of Virginia Health Sciences Quarterly, 6*(3), 5–11.

Edmonson, B. (1988). Disability and sexual adjustment. In V. B. Van Hasselt, P. S. Strain, & M. Hersen (Eds.), *Handbook of developmental and physical disabilities* (pp. 91–106). New York: Pergamon Press.

Engel, J. (1995). Concepts of epilepsy. *Epilepsia, 36*, 23–29.

Fonosch, G. G., Arany, J., Lee, A., & Loving, S. (1982). Providing career planning and placement services for college students with disabilities. *Exceptional Education Quarterly, 3*(3), 67–74.

Fraser, B. A., & Hensinger, R. N. (1983). *Managing physical handicaps: A practical guide for parents, care providers, and educators*. Baltimore: Paul H. Brookes.

Freeman, J. M., Jacobs, H., Vining, E., & Rabin, C. E. (1984). Epilepsy and the inner city schools: A school-based program that makes a difference. *Epilepsia, 25*, 438–442.

Gillberg, C. (Ed.). (1989). *Diagnosis and treatment of autism*. New York: Plenum Press.

Girvin, J. P. (1992). Is epilepsy a progressive disorder? *Journal of Epilepsy, 5*, 94–104.

Gover, A. M., & McIvor, J. (1992). Upper limb deficiencies in infants and young children. *Infants and Young Children, 5*(1), 58–72.

Gouvier, W. D., Brown, L. M., Prestholdt, P. H., Hayes, J. S., & Apostolas, G. (1995). A survey of common misconceptions about epilepsy. *Rehabilitation Psychology, 40*, 51–59.

Grandin, T. (1995). How people with autism think. In E. Schopler & G. B. Mesibov (Eds.), *Learning and cognition in autism* (pp. 137–156). New York: Plenum Press.

Grayson, J. (1992, Fall). Child abuse and developmental disabilities. *Virginia Child Protection Newsletter, 37* (1), 3–7, 10, 12–13, 16.

Gregorchik, L. A. (1992). The cocaine-exposed children are here. *Phi Delta Kappan, 73*, 709–711.

Hanson, M. J., & Harris, S. R. (1986). *Teaching the young child with motor delays*. Austin, TX: Pro-Ed.

Hoare, P. (1984). The development of psychiatric disorder among schoolchildren with epilepsy. *Developmental Medicine and Child Neurology, 26*, 3–13.

Huberty, T. J., Austin, J. K., Risinger, M. W., & McNelis, A. M. (1992). Relationship of selected seizure variables in children with epilepsy to performance on school-administered achievement tests. *Journal of Epilepsy, 5*, 10–16.

Indacochea, J. J., & Scott, G. B. (1992). HIV-1 infection and the acquired immunodeficiency syndrome in children. *Current Problems in Pediatrics, 22*, 166–204.

Katsiyannis, A. (1992). Policy issues in school attendance of children with AIDS: A national survey. *Journal of Special Education, 26*, 219–226.

Kerbeshian, J., & Burd, L. (1994). Tourette's syndrome: A developmental psychobiologic view. *Journal of Developmental and Physical Disabilities, 6*, 203–218.

Korabek, C. A., & Cuvo, A. J. (1986). Children with spina bifida: Educational implications of their medical characteristics. *Education and Treatment of Children, 9*, 142–152.

Larkin, M. (1992). New hospital-school liaisons: Ensuring success for the student with neurologic impairments. *Headlines, 3*(5), 12–17.

Martin, D. A. (1992). Children in peril: A mandate for change in health care policies for low-income children. *Family and Community Health, 15*(1), 75–90.

McCarthy, A. M., Richman, L. C., & Yarbrough, D. (1995). Memory, attention, and school problems in children with seizure disorders. *Developmental Neuropsychology, 11*, 71–86.

McCormick, M. C., Brooks-Gunn, J., Workman-Daniels, K., Turner, J., & Peckham, G. J. (1992). The health and developmental status of very low-birth-weight children at school age. *Journal of the American Medical Association, 267*, 2204–2208.

Mira, M. P., & Tyler, J. S. (1991). Students with traumatic brain injury: Making the transition from hospital to school. *Focus on Exceptional Children, 23*(5), 1–12.

Moore, J. (1985). Technology is not magic. *Exceptional Parent, 15*(7), 41–42.

Murphy, J. M., Jellinek, M., Quinn, D., Smith, G., Poitrast, F. G., & Goshko, M. (1991). Substance abuse and serious child mistreatment: Prevalence, risk, and outcome in a court sample. *Child Abuse and Neglect, 15*, 197–211.

National Head Injury Foundation. (1988). *An educator's manual: What educators need to know about students with traumatic brain injury*. Southborough, MA: Author.

Neisworth, J. T., & Fewell, R. R. (Eds.). (1989). Transition. *Topics in Early Childhood Special Education, 9*(4).

Norlund, M. R. (1994). Transition to postsecondary education. In R. C. Savage & G. F. Wolcott (Eds.), *Educational dimensions of acquired brain injury* (pp. 507–518). Austin, TX: Pro-Ed.

Parette, H. P., & VanBiervliet, A. (1991). Rehabilitation assistive technology issues for infants and young children with disabilities: A preliminary examination. *Journal of Rehabilitation, 57*(3), 27–36.

Pless, I. B. (Ed.). (1994). *The epidemiology of childhood disorders*. New York: Oxford University Press.

Reed, S. (1988). Children with AIDS: How schools are handling the crisis. *Phi Delta Kappan, 69*, K1–K12 [Kappan Special Report].

Rudigier, A. F., Crocker, A. C., & Cohen, H. J. (1990). The dilemmas of childhood: HIV infection. *Children Today, 19,* 26–29.

Sacks, O. (1995). *An anthropologist on Mars: Seven paradoxical tales.* New York: Knopf.

Sautter, R. C. (1992). Crack: Healing the children. *Phi Delta Kappan, 74,* K1–K12 [Kappan Special Report].

Savage, R. C. (1988). Introduction to educational issues for students who have suffered traumatic brain injury. *An educator's manual: What educators need to know about students with traumatic brain injury.* Southborough, MA: Author.

Savage, R. C., & Mishkin, L. (1994). A neuroeducational model for teaching students with acquired brain injuries. In R. C. Savage & G. F. Wolcott (Eds.), *Educational dimensions of acquired brain injury* (pp. 393–411). Austin, TX: Pro-Ed.

Savage, R. C., & Wolcott, G. F. (1994). (Eds.). *Educational dimensions of acquired brain injury.* Austin, TX: Pro-Ed.

Schopler, E., & Mesibov, G. B. (Eds.). (1994). *Behavioral issues in autism.* New York: Plenum Press.

Schopler, E., & Mesibov, G. B. (Eds.). (1995). *Learning and cognition in autism.* New York: Plenum Press.

Sillanpaa, M. (1992). Epilepsy in children: Prevalence, disability, and handicap. *Epilepsia, 33,* 444–449.

Snell, M. E., & Browder, D. M. (1986). Community-referenced instruction: Research and issues. *Journal of the Association for Severely Handicapped, 11,* 1–11.

Snow, J. H., & Hooper, S. R. (1994). *Pediatric traumatic brain injury.* Thousand Oaks, CA: Sage.

Stanley, F. J., & Blair, E. (1994). Cerebral palsy. In I. B. Pless, (Ed.), *The epidemiology of childhood disorders* (pp. 473–497). New York: Oxford University Press.

Trach, J. S. (1990). Supported employment program characteristics. In F. R. Rusch (Ed.), *Supported employment: Models, methods, and issues* (pp. 65–81). Sycamore, IL: Sycamore.

Tyler, J. S., & Colson, S. (1994). Common pediatric disabilities: Medical aspects and educational implications. *Focus on Exceptional Children, 27*(4), 1–16.

Tyler, J. S., & Mira, M. P. (1993). Educational modifications for students with head injuries. *Teaching Exceptional Children, 25*(3), 24–27.

U.S. Department of Education. (1994). *Sixteenth annual report to Congress on the implementation of the Individuals with Disabilities Education Act.* Washington, DC: Author.

Valentine, P. W. (1995, March 21). Every movement counts: Device gives quadriplegics a chance to grasp. *The Washington Post,* pp. A1, A8.

Van Dyke, D. C., & Fox, A. A. (1992). Fetal drug exposure and its possible implications for learning in the preschool and school-age population. *Journal of Learning Disabilities, 23,* 160–163.

Verhaaren, P., & Connor, F. (1981a). Physical disabilities. In J. M. Kauffman & D. P. Hallahan (Eds.), *Handbook of special education.* Englewood Cliffs, NJ: Prentice Hall.

Verhaaren, P., & Connor, F. (1981b). Special adaptations necessitated by physical disabilities. In J. M. Kauffman & D. P. Hallahan (Eds.), *Handbook of special education.* Englewood Cliffs, NJ: Prentice Hall.

Walker, B. (1995, June). African-American fathers: In raising a child with disabilities, believe only the best, demand only the best, give only the best. *Pacesetter,* 14–15.

Walker, C. (1993). Predicting outcome after cerebral insult. *Headlines,* 4–8, 11.

Westbook, L. E., Silver, E. J., Coupey, S. M., & Shinnar, S. (1991). Social characteristics of adolescents with ideopathic epilepsy: A comparison to chronically ill and nonchronically ill peers. *Journal of Epilepsy, 4,* 87–94.

Wolraich, M. L. (1984). Seizure disorders. In J. A. Blackman (Ed.), *Medical aspects of developmental disabilities in children birth to three* (Rev. 1st. Ed., pp. 215–221). Rockville, MD: Aspen.

Zadig, J. M. (1983). The education of the child with cerebral palsy. In G. H. Thompson, I. L. Rubin, & R. M. Bilenker (Eds.), *Comprehensive management of cerebral palsy.* New York: Grune & Stratton.

Chapter 11

Baldwin, A. Y. (1985). Programs for the gifted and talented: Issues concerning minority populations. In F. D. Horowitz & M. O'Brien (Eds.), *The gifted and talented: Developmental perspectives* (pp. 251–295). Washington, DC: American Psychological Association.

Baldwin, A. Y. (1993). Teachers of the gifted. In K. A. Heller, F. J. Monks, & A. H. Passow (Eds.), *International handbook of research and development of giftedness and talent* (pp. 621–629). New York: Pergamon Press.

Baum, S. (1986). The gifted preschooler: An awesome delight. *Gifted Child Today, 9*(4), 42–45.

Bloom, B. J., et al. (1956). *Taxonomy of educational objectives—Handbook I: Cognitive domain.* New York: McKay.

Bloom, B. S. (1982). The role of gifts and markers in the development of talent. *Exceptional Children, 48,* 510–522.

Bloom, B. S., & Sosniak, L. A. (1981). Talent development vs. schooling. *Educational Leadership, 39,* 86–94.

Bower, B. (1995). IQ's evolutionary breakdown: Intelligence may have more facets than testers realize. *Science News, 147,* 220–222.

Brody, L. E., & Stanley, J. C. (1991). Young college students: Assessing factors that contribute to success. In W. T. Southern & E. D. Jones (Eds.), *The academic acceleration of gifted children* (pp. 102–132). New York: Teachers College Press.

Brown, J. L., & Pollitt, E. (1996). Malnutrition, poverty and intellectual development. *Scientific American, 274*(2), 38–43.

Buescher, T. M. (1991). Gifted adolescents. In W. T. Southern & E. D. Jones (Eds.), *The academic acceleration of gifted children* (pp. 382–401). New York: Teachers College Press.

Callahan, C. M. (1986). Asking the right questions: The central issue in evaluating programs for the gifted and talented. *Gifted Child Quarterly, 30,* 38–42.

Callahan, C. M. (1991). An update on gifted females. *Journal for the Education of the Gifted, 14,* 284–311.

Callahan, C. M. (1993). Evaluation programs and procedures for gifted education: International problems and solutions. In K. A. Heller, F. J. Monks, & A. H. Passow (Eds.), *International handbook of research and development of giftedness and talent* (pp. 605–618). New York: Pergamon Press.

Callahan, C. M. (1994). The performance of high ability students in the United States on national and international tests. In P. O. Ross (Ed.), *National excellence: A case for developing America's talent. An anthology of readings* (pp. 5–26). Washington, DC: U.S. Department of Education, Office of Educational Research and Improvement.

Callahan, C. M., & McIntire, J. A. (1994). *Identifying outstanding talent in American Indian and Alaska native students*. Washington, DC: U.S. Department of Education, Office of Research and Improvement.

Caplan, N., Choy, M. H., & Whitmore, J. K. (1992, February). Indochinese refugee families and academic achievement. *Scientific American, 266*(2), 36–42.

Charlton, J. C., Marolf, D. M., & Stanley, J. C. (1994). Follow-up insights on rapid educational acceleration. *Roeper Review, 17*, 123–130.

Clifford, J. A., Runions, T., & Smyth, E. (1986). The Learning Enrichment Service (LES): A participatory model for gifted adolescents. In J. S. Renzulli (Ed.), *Systems and models for developing programs for the gifted and talented*. Mansfield, CT: Creative Learning Press.

Coleman, J. M., & Fultz, B. A. (1985). Special class placement, level of intelligence, and the self-concepts of gifted children: A social comparison perspective. *Remedial and Special Education, 6*(1), 7–12.

Cornell, D. G. (1983). Gifted children: The impact of positive labeling on the family system. *American Journal of Orthopsychiatry, 53*, 322–335.

Coleman, L. J. (1992). The cognitive map of a master teacher conducting discussions with gifted students. *Exceptionality, 3*, 1–16.

Council of State Directors of Programs for the Gifted. (1991). *The 1990 state of the states gifted and talented education report*. Washgton, DC: Author.

Delcourt, M. A. B., Loyd, B. H., Cornell, D. G., & Goldberg, M. D. (1994, October). *Evaluation of the effects of programming arrangements on student learning outcomes*. Storrs, CT: National Research Center on the Gifted and Talented, University of Connecticut.

Delisle, J. (1981). The non-productive gifted child: A contradiction. *Roeper Review, 3*, 20–22.

Delisle, J. (1982). The gifted underachiever: Learning to underachieve. *Roeper Review, 4*, 16–18.

Delisle, J. R. (1987). *Gifted kids speak out*. Minneapolis, MN: Free Spirit Publishing.

Delisle, J. R. (1992). *Guiding the social and emotional development of gifted youth: A practical guide for educators and counselors*. New York: Longman.

Dettmer, P. (1982, January–February). Preventing burnout in teachers of the gifted. *Gifted/Creative/Talented*, pp. 37–41.

Eccles, J. S. (1985). Why doesn't Jane run? Sex differences in educational and occupational patterns. In F. D. Horowitz & M. O'Brien (Eds.), *The gifted and talented: Developmental perspectives*. Washington, DC: American Psychological Association.

Esquivel, G. B. (1995). Teacher behaviors that foster creativity. *Educational Psychology Review, 7*, 185–202.

Feldhusen, J. F. (1989). Synthesis of research on gifted youth. *Educational Leadership, 46*(6), 6–11.

Feldhusen, J. F., & Kolloff, P. B. (1986). The Purdue secondary model for gifted and talented youth. In J. S. Renzulli (Ed.), *Systems and models for developing programs for the gifted and talented*. Mansfield, CT: Creative Learning Press.

Feldhusen, J. F., & Moon, S. M. (1992). Grouping students: Issues and concerns. *Gifted Child Quarterly, 36*, 63–67.

Fiedler, E. D., Lange, R. E., & Winebrenner, S. (1993). The concept of grouping in gifted education. *Roeper Review, 16*, 4–7.

Ford, D. Y. (1993). An investigation of the paradox of underachievement among gifted black students. *Roeper Review, 16*, 78–84.

Ford, D. Y. (1994a). Nurturing resilience in gifted black youth. *Roeper Review, 17*, 80–85.

Ford, D. Y. (1994b, September). *The recruitment and retention of African-American students in gifted education programs: Implications and recommendations*. Storrs, CT: National Research Center on the Gifted and Talented, University of Connecticut.

Ford, D. Y., Russo, C. J., & Harris, J. J., III. (1995). Meeting the educational needs of the gifted: A legal imperative. *Roeper Review, 17*, 224–231.

Ford, D. Y., & Webb, K. S. (1994). Desegregation of gifted educational programs: The impact of *Brown* on underachieving children of color. *Journal of Negro Education, 63*, 358–375.

Frasier, M. M. (1989). Poor and minority students can be gifted too! *Educational Leadership, 46*(6), 16–18.

Frasier, M. M. (1991). Disadvantaged and culturally diverse gifted students. *Journal for the Education of the Gifted, 14*, 234–245.

Frasier, M. M., Garcia, J. H., & Passow, A. H. (1995, February). *A review of assessment issues in gifted education and their implications for identifying gifted minority students*. Storrs, CT: National Research Center on the Gifted and Talented, University of Connecticut.

Frasier, M. M., & Passow, A. H. (1994, December). *Toward a new paradigm for identifying talent potential*. Storrs, CT: National Research Center on the Gifted and Talented, University of Connecticut.

Gailbraith, J. (1985). The eight great gripes of gifted kids: Responding to special needs. *Roeper Review, 7*, 15–18.

Gallagher, J. J. (1986). Our love-hate affair with gifted children. *Gifted Child Today, 9*(3), 47–49.

Gallagher, J. J. (1991a). Educational reform, values, and gifted students. *Gifted Child Quarterly, 35*, 12–19.

Gallagher, J. J. (1991b). Personal patterns of underachievement. *Journal of the Education of the Gifted, 14*, 221–233.

Gallagher, J. J. (1994). Current and historical thinking on education for gifted and talented students. In P. O. Ross (Ed.), *National excellence: A case for developing America's talent, An anthology of readings* (pp. 83–107). Washington, DC: U.S. Department of Education, Office of Educational Research and Improvement.

Gallagher, J. J. (1995). Education of gifted students. A civil rights issue? *Phi Delta Kappan, 76*, 408–410.

Gallagher, J. J., & Gallagher, S. A. (1994). *Teaching the gifted child* (4th ed.). Boston: Allyn and Bacon.

Gardner, H., & Hatch, T. (1989). Multiple intelligences go to school: Educational implications of the theory of multiple intelligences. *Educational Researcher, 18*(8), 4–9.

Gould, S. J. (1995). Ghosts of bell curves past. *Natural History, 104*, 12.

Gross, M. U. M. (1992). The use of radical acceleration in cases of extreme intellectual precocity. *Gifted Child Quarterly*, *36*, 91–99.

Gross, M. U. M. (1993). *Exceptionally gifted children*. London: Routledge.

Gruber, H. E. (1985). Giftedness and moral responsibility: Creative thinking and human survival. In F. D. Horowitz & M. O'Brien (Eds.), *The gifted and talented: Developmental perspectives* (pp. 301–330). Washington, DC: American Psychological Association.

Hannah, C. L., & Shore, B. M. (1995). Metacognition and high intellectual ability: Insights from the study of learning-disabled gifted students. *Gifted Child Quarterly, 39*, 95–109.

Hedges, L. V., & Nowell, A. (1995). Sex differences in mental test scores, variability, and numbers of high-scoring individuals. *Science, 269*, 41–45.

Herrnstein, R. J., & Murray, C. A. (1994). *The bell curve: Intelligence and class structure in American life*. New York: Free Press.

Hine, C. Y. (1994, August). *Helping your child find success at school: A guide for Hispanic parents*. Storrs, CT: National Research Center on the Gifted and Talented, University of Connecticut.

Hoge, R. D., & Renzulli, J. S. (1993). Exploring the link between giftedness and self-concept. *Review of Educational Research, 63*, 449–465.

Howley, C. B., Howley, A., & Pendarvis, E. D. (1995). *Out of our minds: Anti-intellectualism and talent development in American schooling*. New York: Teachers College Press.

Hunsaker, S. L. (1995). The gifted metaphor from the perspective of traditional civilizations. *Journal for the Education of the Gifted, 18*, 255–268.

Hunsaker, S. L., & Callahan, C. M. (1995). Creativity and giftedness: Published instrument uses and abuses. *Gifted Child Quarterly, 39*, 110–114.

Janos, P. M., & Robinson, N. M. (1985). Psychosocial development in intellectually gifted children. In F. D. Horowitz & M. O'Brien (Eds.), *The gifted and talented: Developmental perspectives* (pp. 149–195). Washington, DC: American Psychological Association.

Jones, E. D., & Southern, W. T. (1991). Conclusions about acceleration: Echoes of debate. In W. T. Southern & E. D. Jones (Eds.), *The academic acceleration of gifted children* (pp. 223–228). New York: Teachers College Press.

Jones, E. D., & Southern, W. T. (1992). Programming, grouping, and acceleration in rural school districts: A survey of attitudes and practices. *Gifted Child Quarterly*, *36*, 112–117.

Junge, M. E., & Dretzke, B. J. (1995). Mathematical self-efficacy gender differences in gifted/talented adolescents. *Gifted Child Quarterly, 39*, 22–28.

Karnes, M. B., & Johnson, L. J. (1991a). Gifted handicapped. In N. Colangelo & G. A. Davis (Eds.), *Handbook of gifted education* (pp. 428–437). Boston: Allyn and Bacon.

Karnes, M. B., & Johnson, L. J. (1991b). The preschool/primary gifted child. *Journal for the Education of the Gifted*, *14*, 267–283.

Kennedy, D. M. (1995a). Glimpses of a highly gifted child in a heterogeneous classroom. *Roeper Review, 17*, 164–168.

Kennedy, D. M. (1995b). Plain talk about creating a gifted-friendly classroom. *Roeper Review, 17*, 232–234.

Kerr, B. (1991). Educating gifted girls. In N. Colangelo & G. A. Davis (Eds.), *Handbook of gifted education* (pp. 402–415). Boston: Allyn and Bacon.

Kitano, M. K., & Espinosa, R. (1995). Language diversity and giftedness: Working with gifted English language learners. *Journal for the Education of the Gifted, 18*, 234–254.

Kolb, K. J., & Jussim, L. (1994). Teacher expectations and underachieving gifted children. *Roeper Review, 17*, 26–30.

Kolitch, E. R., & Brody, L. E. (1992). Mathematics acceleration of highly talented students: An evaluation. *Gifted Child Quarterly*, *36*, 78–86.

Kulik, J. A., & Kulik, C. C. (1992). Meta-analytic findings on grouping programs. *Gifted Child Quarterly*, *36*, 73–77.

Lewis, M., & Louis, B. (1991). Young gifted children. In N. Colangelo & G. A. Davis (Eds.), *Handbook of gifted education* (pp. 365–381). Boston: Allyn and Bacon.

Lewis, A. C. (1994). Hucksters we have always with us. *Phi Delta Kappan, 76*, 268–269.

Lovecky, D. V. (1994). Exceptionally gifted children: Different minds. *Roeper Review, 17*, 116–120.

Maker, C. J. (1986). Education of the gifted: Significant trends. In R. J. Morris & B. Blatt (Eds.), *Special education: Research and trends* (pp. 190–221). New York: Pergamon.

Maker, C. J. (Ed.). (1993). *Critical issues in gifted education: Programs for the gifted in regular classrooms*. Austin, TX: Pro-Ed.

Margolin, L. (1994). *Goodness personified: The emergence of gifted children*. New York: Aldine de Gruyter.

Marsh, H. W., Chessor, D., Craven, R., & Roche, L. (1995). The effects of gifted and talented programs on academic self-concept: The big fish strikes again. *American Educational Research Journal, 32*, 285–319.

Milgrim, R. M. (1989). *Teaching gifted and talented learners in regular classrooms*. Springfield, IL: Charles C. Thomas.

Mills, C. J., Stork, E. J., & Krug, D. (1992). Recognition and development of academic talent in educationally disadvantaged students. *Exceptionality*, *3*, 165–180.

Mitchell, P. B. (1994). State policy issues in the education of gifted and talented students. In P. O. Ross (Ed.), *National excellence: A case for developing America's talent, An anthology of readings* (pp. 61–82). Washington, DC: U.S. Department of Education, Office of Educational Research and Improvement.

Moon, S. M., & Dillon, D. R. (1995). Multiple exceptionalities: A case study. *Journal for the Education of the Gifted, 18*, 111–130.

Morelock, M. J., & Feldman, D. H. (1991). Extreme precocity. In N. Colangelo & G. A. Davis (Eds.), *Handbook of gifted education* (pp. 347–364). Boston: Allyn and Bacon.

Neuhaus, C. (1988). Genius at work. *US Air, 10*(2), 64–68.

Noble, K. D., & Drummond, J. E. (1992). But what about the prom? Students' perceptions of early college entrance. *Gifted Child Quarterly*, *36*, 106–111.

Oakes, J. (1985). *Keeping track: How schools structure inequality*. New Haven, CT: Yale University Press.

Oakes, J. (1992). Can tracking research inform practice? Technical, normative, and political considerations. *Educational Researchers*, *22*(4), 12–21.

Olenchak, F. R., & Renzulli, J. S. (1989). The effectiveness of the schoolwide enrichment model on selected aspects of elementary school change. *Gifted Child Quarterly*, *33*(1), 36–46.

Passow, A. H., & Rudnitski, R. A. (1993, October). *State policies regarding education of the gifted as reflected in legislation and regulation.* Storrs, CT: National Research Center on the Gifted and Talented, University of Connecticut.

Patton, J. M., & Baytops, J. L. (1995). Identifying and transforming the potential of young, gifted African Americans: A clarion call. In B. A. Ford, F. E. Obiakor, & J. M. Patton (Eds.), *Effective education of African American exceptional learners: New perspectives* (pp. 27–67). Austin, TX: Pro-Ed.

Perrone, P. A. (1991). Career development. In N. Colangelo & G. A. Davis (Eds.), *Handbook of gifted education* (pp. 321–327). Boston: Allyn and Bacon.

Piechowski, M. M. (1991). Emotional development and emotional giftedness. In N. Colangelo & G. A. Davis (Eds.), *Handbook of gifted education* (pp. 285–306). Boston: Allyn and Bacon.

Plomin, R. (1989). Environment and genes: Determinants of behavior. *American Psychologist*, *44*, 105–111.

Ramos-Ford, V., & Gardner, H. (1991). Giftedness from a multiple intelligences perspective. In N. Colangelo & G. A. Davis (Eds.), *Handbook of gifted education* (pp. 55–64). Boston: Allyn & Bacon.

Reis, S. M. (1989). Reflections on policy affecting the education of gifted and talented students: Past and future perspectives. *American Psychologist*, *44*, 399–408.

Reis, S. M., Neu, T. W., & McGuire, J. M. (1995, January). *Talents in two places: Case studies of high ability students with learning disabilities who have achieved.* Storrs, CT: National Research Center on the Gifted and Talented, University of Connecticut.

Renzulli, J. S. (1977). *The enrichment triad model.* Mansfield, CT: Creative Learning Press.

Renzulli, J. S. (1982). Dear Mr. and Mrs. Copernicus: We regret to inform you . . . *Gifted Child Quarterly*, *26*(1), 11–14.

Renzulli, J. S., & Reis, S. M. (1985). *The schoolwide enrichment model: A comprehensive plan for educational excellence.* Mansfield Center, CT: Creative Learning Press.

Renzulli, J. S., & Reis, S. M. (1991a). The reform movement and the quiet crisis in gifted education. *Gifted Child Quarterly*, *35*, 26–35.

Renzulli, J. S., & Reis, S. M. (1991b). The schoolwide enrichment model: A comprehensive plan for the development of creative productivity. In N. Colangelo & G. A. Davis (Eds.), *Handbook of gifted education* (pp. 111–141). Boston: Allyn and Bacon.

Renzulli, J. S., Reis, S. M., & Smith, L. H. (1981). *The revolving door identification model.* Mansfield Center, CT: Creative Learning Press.

Renzulli, J. S. (1994). *Schools for talent development: A practical plan for total school improvement.* Mansfield Center, CT: Creative Learning Press.

Resnick, D. P., & Goodman, M. (1994). American culture and the gifted. In P. O. Ross (Ed.), *National excellence: A case for developing America's talent. An anthology of readings* (pp. 109–121). Washington, DC: U.S. Department of Education, Office of Educational Research and Improvement.

Richert, E. S. (1991). Rampant problems and promising practices in identification. In N. Colangelo & G. A. Davis (Eds.), *Handbook of gifted education* (pp. 81–96). Boston: Allyn and Bacon.

Rimm, S. B., & Lovance, K. J. (1992). The use of subject and grade skipping for the prevention and reversal of underachievement. *Gifted Child Quarterly*, *36*, 100–105.

Rittenhouse, R. K., & Blough, L. K. (1995). Gifted students with hearing impairments: Suggestions for teachers. *Teaching Exceptional Children*, *27*(4), 51–53.

Robinson, N. M., & Weimer, L. J. (1991). Selection of candidates for early admission to kindergarten and first grade. In W. T. Southern & E. D. Jones (Eds.), *The academic acceleration of gifted children* (pp. 29–50). New York: Teachers College Press.

Robinson, N. M. (1993a). Identifying and nurturing gifted, very young children. In K. A. Heller, F. J. Monks, & A. H. Passow (Eds.), *International handbook of research and development of giftedness and talent* (pp. 507–524). New York: Pergamon Press.

Robinson, N. M. (1993b, November). *Parenting the very young, gifted child.* Storrs, CT: National Research Center on the Gifted and Talented, University of Connecticut.

Roedell, W. C. (1985). Developing social competence in gifted preschool children. *Remedial and Special Education*, *6*(4), 6–11.

Roeper, A. (1994). Gifted education must take a stand on *The Bell Curve*. *Roeper Review*, *17*, 150.

Sacks, O. (1995). *An antropologist on Mars: Seven paradoxical tales.* New York: Knopf.

Sapon-Shevin, M. (1984). The tug-of-war nobody wins: Allocation of educational resources for handicapped, gifted, and "typical" students. *Curriculum Inquiry*, *14*, 57–81.

Sapon-Shevin, M. (1994). *Playing favorites: Gifted education and the disruption of community.* Albany: State University of New York Press.

Shields, C. M. (1995). A comparison study of student attitudes and perceptions in homogeneous and heterogeneous classrooms. *Roeper Review*, *17*, 234–238.

Shore, B. M., Cornell, D. G., Robinson, A., & Ward, V. S. (1991). *Recommended practices in gifted education: A critical analysis.* New York: Teachers College Press.

Silverman, L. K. (1991). Family counseling. In N. Colangelo & G. A. Davis (Eds.), *Handbook of gifted education* (pp. 307–320). Boston: Allyn and Bacon.

Silverman, L, K. (1994). The moral sensitivity of gifted children and the evolution of society. *Roeper Review*, *17*, 110–116.

Sowa, C. J., McIntire, J., May, K. M., & Bland, L. (1994). Social and emotional adjustment themes across gifted children. *Roeper Review*, *17*, 95–98.

Starko, A. J. (1986). *It's about time: Inservice strategies for curriculum compacting.* Mansfield Center, CT: Creative Learning Press.

Sternberg, R. J. (1991). Giftedness according to the triarchic theory of human intelligence. In N. Colangelo & G. A. Davis (Eds.), *Handbook of gifted education* (pp. 45–54). Boston: Allyn and Bacon.

Sternberg, R. J., & Clinkenbeard, P. R. (1995). The triarchic model applied to identifying, teaching, and assessing gifted children. *Roeper Review*, *17*, 255–260.

Sternberg, R. J., & Davidson, J. E. (1983). Insight in the gifted. *Educational Psychologist, 18*, 51–57.

Sternberg, R. J., & Davidson, J. E. (Eds.) (1986). *Conceptions of giftedness*. New York: Cambridge University Press.

Sternberg, R. J., & Zhang, L. (1995). What do we mean by giftedness? A pentagonal implicit theory. *Gifted Child Quarterly, 39*, 88–94.

Stevenson, H. W., Lee, S., Chen, C., Kato, K., & Londo, W. (1994). Education of gifted and talented students in China, Taiwan, and Japan. In P. O. Ross (Ed.), *National excellence: A case for developing America's talent, An anthology of readings* (pp. 27–60). Washington, DC: U.S. Department of Education, Office of Educational Research and Improvement.

Stronge, J. H. (1986). Gifted education: Right or privilege? *Gifted Child Today, 9*(3), 52–54.

Swanson, J. D. (1995). Gifted African-American children in rural schools: Searching for the answers. *Roeper Review, 17*, 261–266.

Tannenbaum, A. J. (1991). The social psychology of giftedness. In N. Colangelo & G. A. Davis (Eds.), *Handbook of gifted education* (pp. 27–44). Boston: Allyn and Bacon.

Tannenbaum, A. J. (1993). History of giftedness and "gifted education" in world perspective. In K. A. Heller, F. J. Monks, & A. H. Passow (Eds.), *International handbook of research and development of giftedness and talent* (pp. 3–27). New York: Pergamon Press.

Terman, L. M., & Oden, M. H. (1959). *Genetic studies of genius, Vol. 5: The gifted group at midlife*. Palo Alto, CA: Stanford University Press.

Terwilliger, J. S., & Titus, J. C. (1995). Gender differences in attitudes and attitude changes among mathematically talented youth. *Gifted Child Quarterly, 39*, 29–35.

Thompson, L. A., & Plomin, R. (1993). Genetic influence on cognitive ability. In K. A. Heller, F. J. Monks, & A. H. Passow (Eds.), *International handbook of research and development of giftedness and talent* (pp. 103–113). New York: Pergamon Press.

Tomlinson, C. A. (1994a). Gifted learners: The boomerang kids of middle school? *Roeper Review, 16*, 177–182.

Tomlinson, C. A. (1994b). The easy lie and the role of gifted education in school excellence. *Roeper Review, 16*, 258–259.

Treffinger, D. J. (1991). School reform and gifted education—Opportunities and issues. *Gifted Child Quarterly, 35*, 6–11.

VanTassel-Baska, J. (Ed.). (1990). *A practical guide to counseling the gifted in a school setting* (2nd ed.). Reston, VA: Council for Exceptional Children.

VanTassel-Baska, J. (1991a). Gifted education in the balance: Building relationships with general education. *Gifted Child Quarterly, 35*, 20–25.

VanTassel-Baska, J. (1991b). Serving the disabled gifted through educational collaboration. *Journal for the Education of the Gifted, 14*, 246–266.

VanTassel-Baska, J. (1992). Educational decision making on acceleration and grouping. *Gifted Child Quarterly, 36*, 68–72.

VanTassel-Baska, J. (1993). Theory and research on curriculum development for the gifted. In K. A. Heller, F. J. Monks, & A. H. Passow (Eds.), *International handbook of research and development of giftedness and talent* (pp. 365–386). New York: Pergamon Press.

Whitlock, M. S., & DuCette, J. P. (1989). Outstanding and average teachers of the gifted: A comparative study. *Gifted Child Quarterly, 33*, 15–21.

Whitmore, J. (1987). Conceptualizing the issue of underserved populations of gifted students. *Journal for the Education of the Gifted, 10*, 141–153.

Whitmore, J. R. (1986). Understanding a lack of motivation to excel. *Gifted Child Quarterly, 30*, 66–69.

Whitmore, J. R., & Maker, C. J. (1985). *Intellectual giftedness in disabled persons*. Rockville, MD: Aspen.

Willard-Holt, C. (1994, September). *Recognizing talent: Cross-case study of two high potential students with cerebral palsy*. Storrs, CT: National Research Center on the Gifted and Talented, University of Connecticut.

Zigler, E., & Farber, E. A. (1985). Commonalities between the intellectual extremes: Giftedness and mental retardation. In F. D. Horowitz & M. O'Brien (Eds.), *The gifted and talented: Developmental perspectives* (pp. 378–408). Washington, DC: American Psychological Association.

Chapter 12

Akerley, M. S. (1985). False gods and angry prophets. In H. R. Turnbull & A. P. Turnbull (Eds.), *Parents speak out: Then and now* (2nd ed., pp. 23–31). Columbus, OH: Merrill.

Bailey, D. B., Blasco, P. M., & Simeonsson, R. J. (1992). Needs expressed by mothers and fathers of young children with disabilities. *American Journal on Mental Retardation, 97*, 1–10.

Baumeister, A., Kupstas, F., & Klindworth, L. M. (1990). New morbidity: Implications for prevention of children's disabilities. *Exceptionality, 1*(1), 1–16.

Beckman, P. J. (1991). Comparison of mothers' and fathers' perceptions of the effect of young children with and without disabilities. *American Journal on Mental Retardation, 95*(5), 585–595.

Beckman, P. J., & Pokorni, J. L. (1988). A longitudinal study of families of preterm infants: Changes in stress and support over the first two years. *Journal of Special Education, 22*(1), 55–65.

Beckman, P. J., Robinson, C. C., Rosenberg, S., & Filer, J. (1994). In L. J. Johnson, R. J. Gallagher, & M. J. LaMontagne (Eds.), *Meeting early intervention challenges: Issues from birth to three* (2nd. ed., pp. 13–31). Baltimore: Paul H. Brookes.

Bell, R. Q., & Harper, L. V. (1977). *Child effects on adults*. Hillsdale, NJ: Lawrence Erlbaum.

Benson, H. A., & Turnbull, A. P. (1986). Approaching families from an individualized perspective. In R. H. Horner, L. H. Meyer, & H. D. B. Fredericks (Eds.), *Education of learners with severe handicaps: Exemplary service strategies* (pp. 127–157), Baltimore: Paul H. Brookes.

Bettelheim, B. (1950). *Love is not enough*. New York: Macmillan.

Bettelheim, B. (1967). *The empty fortress*. New York: Free Press.

Blacher, J., & Baker, B. L. (1992). Toward meaningful family involvement in out-of-home placement settings. *Mental Retardation, 30*(1), 35–43.

Bristol, M. M., & Gallagher, J. J. (1986). In J. J. Gallagher & P. M. Vietze (Eds.), *Families of handicapped persons: Research, programs, and policy issues* (pp. 81–100). Baltimore: Paul H. Brookes.

Bronfenbrenner, U. (1979). *The ecology of human development: Experiments by nature and design*. Cambridge, MA: Harvard University Press.

Bronicki, G. J., & Turnbull, A. P. (1987). Family-professional interactions. In M. E. Snell (Ed.), *Systematic instruction of persons with severe handicaps* (pp. 9–35). Columbus, OH: Merrill.

Brooks-Gunn, J., & Lewis, M. (1984). Maternal responsivity in interactions with handicapped infants. *Child Development, 55*(3), 858–868.

Carr, J. (1988). Six weeks to twenty-one years old: A longitudinal study of children with Down's syndrome and their families. *Journal of Child Psychology and Psychiatry, 29*(4), 407–431.

Comegys, A. (1989). Integration strategies for parents of students with handicaps. In R. Gaylord-Ross (Ed.), *Integration strategies for students with handicaps* (pp. 339–350). Baltimore: Paul H. Brookes.

Diamond, S. (1981). Growing up with parents of a handicapped child: A handicapped person's perspective. In J. L. Paul (Ed.), *Understanding and working with parents of children with special needs*. New York: Holt, Rinehart & Winston.

Drotar, D., Baskiewicz, A., Irvin, N., Kennell, J., & Klaus, M. (1975). The adaptation of parents to the birth of an infant with a congenital malformation: A hypothetical model. *Pediatrics, 56*, 710–717.

Dumas, J. E., Wolf, L. C., Fisman, S. N., & Culligan, A. (1991). Parenting stress, child behavior problems, and dysphoria in parents of children with autism, Down syndrome, behavior disorders, and normal development. *Exceptionality, 2*(2), 97–110.

Dunst, C. J., Trivette, C. M., & Deal, A. (1988). *Enabling and empowering families*. Cambridge, MA: Brookline Books.

Dunst, C. J., Trivette, C. M., Gordon, N. J., & Pletcher, L. L. (1989). Building and mobilizing informal family support networks. In G. H. S. Singer & L. K. Irvin (Eds.), *Support for caregiving families: Enabling positive adaptation to disability* (pp. 121–141). Baltimore: Paul H. Brookes.

Featherstone, H. (1980). *A difference in the family: Life with a disabled child*. New York: Basic Books.

Fowler, S. A., Schwartz, I., & Atwater, J. (1991). Perspectives on the transition from preschool to kindergarten for children with disabilities and their families. *Exceptional Children, 58*(2), 136–145.

Gallimore, R., Weisner, T. S., Bernheimer, L. P., Guthrie, D., & Nihira, K. (1993). Family responses to young children with developmental delays: Accommodation activity in ecological and cultural context. *American Journal on Mental Retardation, 98*, 185–206.

Guralnick, M. J. (1991). The next decade of research on the effectiveness of early intervention. *Exceptional Children, 58*(2), 174–183.

Hallahan, D. P. (1992). Some thoughts on why the prevalence of learning disabilities has increased. *Journal of Learning Disabilities, 25*(8), 523–528.

Hanline, M. F., & Knowlton, A. (1988). A collaborative model for providing support to parents during their child's transition from infant intervention to preschool special education public school programs. *Journal of the Division for Early Childhood, 12*(2), 116–125.

Hanson, M. J., Ellis, L., & Deppe, J. (1989). Support for families during infancy. In G. H. S. Singer & L. K. Irvin (Eds.), *Support for caregiving families: Enabling positive adaptation to disability* (pp. 207–219). Baltimore: Paul H. Brookes.

Helsel Family, The. (1985). The Helsels' story of Robin. In H. R. Turnbull & A. P. Turnbull (Eds.), *Parents speak out: Then and now* (2nd ed., pp. 81–89). Columbus, OH: Merrill.

Hockenberry, J. (1995). *Moving violations: War zones, wheelchairs, and declarations of independence*. New York: Hyperion.

Hofferth, S. L., & Phillips, D. A. (1987). Child care in the United States, 1970 to 1995. *Journal of Marriage and the Family, 49*, 559–571.

Jewell, G. (1985). *Geri*. New York: Ballantine Books.

Kauffman, J., Mostert, M., Nuttycombe, D., Trent, S., & Hallahan, D. (1993). *Managing classroom behavior: A reflective case-based approach*. Boston, MA: Allyn and Bacon.

Kazak, A. E., & Marvin, R. S. (1984). Differences, difficulties, and adaptation: Stress and social networks in families with a handicapped child. *Family Relations, 33*, 67–77.

Kelley, M. L. (1990). *School-home notes: Promoting children's classroom success*. New York: Guilford Press.

Krauss, M. W., Seltzer, M. M., & Goodman, S. J. (1992). Social support networks of adults with mental retardation who live at home. *American Journal on Mental Retardation, 96*(4), 432–441.

Krauss, M. W. (1993). Child-related and parenting stress: Similarities and differences between mothers and fathers of children with disabilities. *American Journal on Mental Retardation, 97*, 393–404.

Leete-Guy, L., & Schor, J. B. (1992). *The great American time squeeze: Trends in work and leisure, 1969–1989*. Briefing paper, Economic Policy Institute, Washington, DC.

Lehmann, J. P., & Baker, C. (1995). Mothers' expectations for their adolescent children: A comparison between families with disabled adolescents and those with non-labeled adolescents. *Education and Training in Mental Retardation and Developmental Disabilities, 30*, 27–40.

Lynch, E. W., & Stein, R. (1982). Perspectives on parent participation in special education. *Exceptional Education Quarterly, 3*(2), 56–63.

McDonnell, A., & Hardman, M. (1988). A synthesis of "best practice" guidelines for early childhood services. *Journal of the Division for Early Childhood, 12*(2), 328–341.

McGarry, B. (1994). Cruising the Internet. *Exceptional Parent, 24*(6), 39–43.

Mahoney, G., & Robenalt, K. (1986). A comparison of conversational patterns between mothers and their Down syndrome and normal infants. *Journal of the Division for Early Childhood, 10*, 172–180.

Martin, S. S., Brady, M. P., & Kortarba, J. A. (1992). Families with chronically ill children: The unsinkable family.

Remedial and Special Education, 13(2), 6–15.

Michael, M. G., Arnold, K. D., Magliocca, L. A., & Miller, S. (1992). Influences on teachers' attitudes of the parents' role as collaborator. *Remedial and Special Education, 13*(2), 24–30, 39.

Mims, A., Harper, C., Armstong, S. W., & Savage, S. (1991). Effective instruction in homework for students with disabilities. *Teaching Exceptional Children, 24*(1), 42–47.

Nolan, C. (1987). *Under the eye of the clock: The life story of Christopher Nolan*. New York: St. Martin's Press.

Norton, A. J., & Glick, P. C. (1986). One parent families: A social and economic profile. *Family Relations, 35*(1), 9–17.

Pierro, C. (1995). Talking with your child about disabilities. *Exceptional Parent, 25*(6), 92.

Powell, T. H., & Gallagher, P. A. (1993). *Brothers & sisters—A special part of exceptional families*. (2nd ed.). Baltimore: Paul H. Brookes.

Salend, S. J., & Gajria, M. (1995). Increasing the homework completion rates of students with mild disabilities. *Remedial and Special Education, 16,* 271–278.

Seligman, M., & Darling, R. B. (1989). *Ordinary families, special children: A systems approach to childhood disability*. New York: Guilford Press.

Senapati, R., & Hayes, A. (1988). Sibling relationships of handicapped children: A review of conceptual and methodological issues. *International Journal of Behavioral Development, 11*(1), 89–115.

Simeonsson, R. J., & Bailey, D. B. (1986). Siblings of handicapped children. In J. J. Gallagher & P. M. Vietze (Eds.), *Families of handicapped persons: Research, programs, and policy issues* (pp. 67–77). Baltimore: Paul H. Brookes.

Singer, G. H. S., & Irvin, L. K. (1989). Family caregiving, stress, and support. In G. H. S. Singer & L. K. Irvin (Eds.), *Support for caregiving families: Enabling positive adaptation to disability* (pp. 3–25). Baltimore: Paul H. Brookes.

Stark, J. (1992). Presidential Address 1992: A professional and personal perspective on families. *Mental Retardation, 30*(5), 247–254.

Stoneman, Z., Brody, G. H., Davis, C. H., & Crapps, J. M. (1988). Childcare responsibilities, peer relations, and sibling conflict: Older siblings of mentally retarded children. *American Journal of Mental Retardation, 93*(2), 174–183.

Turnbull, A. P., & Turnbull, H. R. (1990). *Families, professionals, and exceptionality: A special partnership* (2nd ed.). Columbus, OH: Merrill.

Turnbull, H. R., & Turnbull, A. P. (1985). *Parents speak out: Then and now* (2nd ed.). Columbus, OH: Merrill/Macmillan.

Vaughn, S., Bos, C., Harrell, J., & Lasky, B. (1988). Parent participation in the initial placement/IEP conference 10 years after mandated involvement. *Journal of Learning Disabilities, 21*(2), 82–89.

Willoughby, J, C., & Glidden, L. M. (1995). Fathers helping out: Shared child care and marital satisfaction of parents with disabilities. *American Journal on Mental Retardation, 99,* 399–406.

Zigler, E., & Black, K. B. (1989). America's family support movement: Strengths and limitations. *American Journal of Orthopsychiatry, 59*(1), 6–19.

Name Index

Subject Index

Note: A bold-faced page number indicates the page on which the subject is defined in a marginal note.

F

G

M

T

u

v

W

Z